# Strategic Management
## Concepts and Cases

### Competitiveness and Globalization

# Henk W. Volberda
# Robert E. Morgan
# Patrick Reinmoeller
# Michael A. Hitt
# R. Duane Ireland
# Robert E. Hoskisson

SOUTH-WESTERN
CENGAGE Learning

Australia • Brazil • Japan • Korea • Mexico • Singapore • Spain • United Kingdom • United States

# SOUTH-WESTERN
## CENGAGE Learning™

**Strategic Management: Competitiveness and Globalization (Concepts and Cases)**

**Henk W. Volberda,**

**Robert E. Morgan,**

**Patrick Reinmoeller,**

**Michael A. Hitt,**

**R. Duane Ireland,**

**Robert E. Hoskisson**

Publishing Director: Linden Harris

Publisher: Brendan George

Development Editor: Jennifer Seth

Editorial Assistant: Charlotte Green

Production Editor: Alison Cooke

Production Controller: Tom Relf

Marketing Manager: Amanda Cheung

Typesetter: S4Carlisle Publishing Services

Cover design: Adam Renvoize

For product information and technology assistance,
contact **emea.info@cengage.com**.

For permission to use material from this text or product,
and for permission queries,
email **clsuk.permissions@cengage.com**.

This work is adapted from *Strategic Management: Competitiveness and Globalization, Concepts and Cases* 9th Edition by Michael A. Hitt, R. Duane Ireland, Robert E. Hoskisson published by South-Western Higher Education, a division of Cengage Learning, Inc. © 2010.

*British Library Cataloguing-in-Publication Data*
A catalogue record for this book is available from the British Library.

ISBN: 978-1-4080-1918-4

**Cengage Learning EMEA**
Cheriton House, North way, Andover, Hampshire, Sp10 5BE, United Kingdom

Cengage Learning products are represented in Canada by Nelson Education Ltd.

For your lifelong learning solutions, visit
**www.cengage.co.uk**

Purchase e-books or e-chapters at:
**www.cengagebrain.com**

Printed in Singapore
1 2 3 4 5 6 7 8 9 10–13 12 11

To our *wives and children:*

Anna, Lisa, Celine & Marrit (Henk W. Volberda)
Tracey, Cian & Ffin (Robert E. Morgan)
Kumiyo & Karna (Patrick Reinmoeller)
Frankie, Shawn & Angie (Michael A. Hitt)
Mary Ann, Rebecca & Scott (R. Duane Ireland)
Kathy, Robyn, Dale, Becky, Angela, Joseph & Matthew (Robert E. Hoskisson)

# BRIEF CONTENTS

# CONTENTS

**PART I**

## STRATEGIC MANAGEMENT INPUTS  1

PART II

# REFINING THE STRATEGIC ACTIONS   163

PART III

# IMPLEMENTATION OF STRATEGIC ACTIONS 397

# PART IV

# INTEGRATIVE CASES 599

# LIST OF FIGURES

# LIST OF TABLES

# LIST OF CASES

# PREFACE

LIST OF CASES

Strategic Focus Louis Vuitton Moet Hennessy

Strategic Focus IKEA... With all over the world

Closing Case Oticon's Spaghetti Organization

14 Strategic Entrepreneurship 721

Opening Case The continuing innovation revolution at Xerox the
new or organization

Our goal in writing this book is to present a new, up-to-date standard for explaining the strategic management process in a way that meets what the international student of strategy needs. In adapting the original North-American text to be truly international, we present you with an intellectually rich yet thoroughly practical analysis of strategic management, specifically tailored to the European, Middle-Eastern and African (EMEA) market.

In writing this book, we were challenged and invigorated by the goal of establishing a new standard for presenting strategic management knowledge in a readable style. To prepare for this EMEA edition, we carefully studied the most recent academic research to ensure that the strategic management content we present to you is highly current and relevant for organizations. Highly relevant case studies, most of which we have researched for this volume, illustrate how strategy works. In addition, we continuously read articles appearing in many different business publications (e.g., *Business Week, The Economist, Financial Times, Forbes, Fortune, Wall Street Journal,* to name just a few); scan leading business blogs; scour current and emerging ideas from business applications and management consulting websites; listen to podcasts of critical strategy influences and thought leaders; and, work with companies directly in the executive education classroom and on consulting assignments. We do this to identify valuable examples of how companies use the strategic management process.

Though many of the hundreds of companies we discuss in the book will be quite familiar to you, some companies will likely be new to you as well. One reason for this is that we use the "best practices" of companies from around the world to demonstrate how globalized business has become. Another reason is that we want to unleash the "next practices" of strategic management by selecting those companies that clearly use the strategic management process to achieve superior performance. To maximize your opportunities to learn as you read and think about how actual companies use strategic management tools, techniques and concepts (based on the most current research), we write in a lively and user-friendly style.

## Key Characteristics

Several characteristics of this book will enhance your learning opportunities:

- This book presents you with the most comprehensive and thorough coverage of strategic management that is available in the market. Various aspects of Strategy Analysis, Strategy Formulation and Strategy Implementation are discussed in this book. In particular, this EMEA version provides full coverage of implementation issues, such as leadership, structures and controls, corporate governance, strategic entrepreneurship and strategic renewal. Moreover, this EMEA edition contains several new themes in new and adapted chapters. For example, Chapter 4 addresses the important opportunity to tap and integrate external with internal resources and introduces new concepts such as open innovation. Chapter 12, which is devoted to Corporate Governance, shows how firms' ability to simultaneously satisfy their stakeholders' different interests is critical to firms' success and has become an essential part of the strategic management process. Chapter 15 discusses how implementation of strategic actions may help the firm to realize strategic renewal by revitalizing and transforming their core businesses, and seeking new avenues for growth. Other revised chapters show various other topics of the strategic management process examined in this book.

- The research that underpins this book is drawn from the "classics" as well as the most recent contributions to the strategic management literature, knowledge and practice. The historically significant "classic" research provides the foundation for much of what is known about strategic management; the most recent contributions reveal insights about how to effectively use strategic management in the complex, global business environment in which most firms operate while trying to outperform their competitors. Our book also presents you with many examples of how firms use the strategic management tools, techniques and concepts developed by leading researchers. Indeed this book is strongly application oriented and presents you, our readers, with a vast number of examples and applications of strategic management concept, techniques, and tools. Collectively, no other strategic management book offers the *combination* of useful and insightful *research* and *applications* in a wide variety of organizations as does this text. Company examples cover a wide international range of large firms including firms such as Apple, BMW, Google, Henkel, ING, IKEA, Muji, Nestlé, Nokia, Philips, Shell, Siemens and Tata. We also include examples of successful younger and newer firms such as Armani, Alessi, BehavioSec, Diesel, East-West Seed, Mamas & Papas, Ryanair, Suntech, and Virgin.

- By providing *cases* and *insights* that emerge from research in EMEA, we present the "global" standard and at the same time show how it is applied in "local" markets. We use the ideas of leading scholars from around the world to shape the discussion of *what* strategic management is (strategy content). We describe the practices of prominent executives and practitioners to help us describe *how* strategic management is used in many types of organizations (strategy process). On the basis of the numerous cases of various firms operating in diverse industries, we also demonstrate how *differences* in firms, industries and geographical locations affect the strategic management process (strategy context). Our cases challenge students to critically take into account the content, process and context dimensions of strategy.

- We carefully *integrate* two of the most popular and well-known theoretical concepts in the strategic management field: industrial-organization economics and the resource-based view of the firm. Other texts usually emphasize one of these two theories (at the cost of explaining the other one to describe strategic management). However, such an approach is incomplete. We argue that research and practical experience indicate that both theories play a major role in understanding the linkage between strategic management and organizational success. No other book integrates these two theoretical perspectives effectively to explain the strategic management process and its application across organization types.

- Focusing only on formulations of strategy is misguided. Strategy formulation is important yet nothing without strategy implementation. This is especially important in the current global economic climate and, with the dramatic changes that are unfolding, careful attention to feedback loops that enable companies to better adjust to the shifting context make the implementation and renewal of strategy paramount for long term success. Unlike many other textbooks, we devote five chapters to the implementation of strategy. No other book offers the formulation-development link and the renewal loop in such clarity as presented here.

■ We, the authors of this book, are also active scholars. We conduct research on a range of contemporary and challenging strategic management topics. Our passion for doing so is to contribute to the strategic management literature and to better understand how to effectively apply strategic management tools, techniques and concepts to create pay-offs in organizational performance. Thus, our own US- and European-based research is integrated in the appropriate chapters along with the research of numerous other scholars and thought leaders.

## Key Features

In addition to our book's characteristics, there are some specific features that we want to highlight for you. Understanding that a great textbook is not just text, we have composed more than that. Our composition allows you to experience the strategic management process through the key features listed below. Each feature enhances the learning experience and provides a rounded solution to your education in strategic management.

■ **Integrative Process Approach** In this EMEA version, the whole strategic management process is covered starting from strategy analysis, strategy formulation, strategy implementation and renewal – we see this process as iterative and dynamic not sequential, linear and static as many other textbooks do. This approach provides the pathway through which firms are able to achieve strategic competitiveness and earn above-average returns. Mastering this strategic management process will effectively serve you, our readers, and the organizations for which you will choose to work.

■ **An Exceptional Balance** We strike a fine balance between both current research and the state-of-the-art knowledge, and its application in contemporary organizations. The content has not only the best research documentation, but also the largest amount of effective real-world examples to help readers understand the different types of strategies that organizations use to achieve their vision and mission. We believe current research is a vital input to your knowledge while the applications serve as the platform for comprehending these sometimes challenging ideas.

■ **Lively, Concise Writing Style** All chapters are written in a style designed to hold readers' interest and attention in strategic management while also demonstrating the relevance of this subject to day-to-day company news and current business affairs.

■ **Opening Cases and Closing Cases** We provide a wealth of examples detailing how actual organizations use the strategic management process to outperform rivals and increase their performance. These Opening and Closing Cases of each chapter cover a wide range of industries in many different countries to help you get a better understanding of how strategy matters in a global marketplace. These relatively short case vignettes provide excellent support for individual reflection and class discussions.

- **Strategic Focus Boxes** Each chapter provides three in-depth contemporary examples that further support and broaden the strategic issues covered in the chapter. They provide short case descriptions, from mainly European companies, to illustrate the added value of the strategy concepts and tools discussed in the text.

- **Key Debate features** In addition to boosting the critical coverage throughout the main text, a new boxed feature highlighting a crucial debate in the literature is introduced. Each chapter contains a discussion of a thought-provoking and controversial topic to encourage students to think critically and analyze what they have read. Questions following each Debate allow students to monitor and test their understanding.

- **Summary and Margin Notes** Chapter summaries help you to recap and review the main points of the chapter. In the Margin Notes of each chapter you will find clear definitions of the strategy concepts used in the text.

- **Review and Discussion Questions** The review questions stimulate students to absorb the theory, reflect on the concepts and make new connections. The Discussion questions involve a mixture of active discussion, library assignments and web projects.

- **Experiential Exercises** These exercises place the reader in a variety of situations requiring application of some part of the strategic management process. Inviting you to engage with real businesses these exercises allow learners to lead their own progress and to enjoy discovery of new insights.

- **Video Cases** Following each chapter we seek to stimulate critical thinking and curiosity of the reader by introducing different perspectives through a link to an online video stream. These videos often introduce cases or issues that encourage creative and critical reflection.

- **Further Reading** Recommendations of relevant books and crucial articles are meant to broaden your horizon. On purpose we have selected books and articles to help you explore other voices often beyond management. We hope you enjoy these, as we think, productive *divertissements* or *divertimenti* create different and delightful tunes.

- **Full Four-color Format** This format and the visuals used enhance readability by attracting and maintaining readers' interest.

## STRUCTURE OF THE BOOK

This book covers the full spectrum of strategic management. We illustrate this with a simple framework (Figure 1) that provides a solid foundation to those students embarking upon strategic management education who seek to learn about how companies are led to success, as well as to more advanced students and practitioners wishing to understand holistically the integrative nature of this discipline. In line with our definition of strategic management, we seek to help explain and achieve above average returns (performance) by transforming the company through strategic actions for which the availability and awareness about strategic inputs are essential. In our book, we provide a logical step-by-step progression towards above average performance and feedback loops to further improve strategic fit in the long run.

The book has three parts that address the three key questions: 1. What do I need to achieve strategic competitiveness? 2. How do I articulate strategy? 3. How do I implement strategy? Each of the three respective parts – Inputs, Formulation, Implementation – helps the strategic leader to create, to strengthen and to renew competitive advantage.

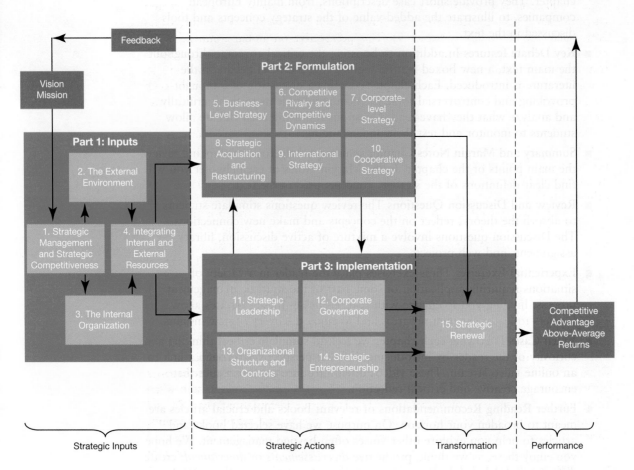

Part 1 – Inputs – consists of four chapters. Chapter 1 delivers what is needed to initiate strategic management and provides an overview, fundamental concepts and a holistic view of how core concepts relate to each other and to strategic competitiveness. Of special importance here is the dynamic nature of strategic competitiveness which is the outcome of a feedback process that provides the foundation to building effective strategic management. We then develop the mainstream approaches in strategy, focusing first on understanding the inputs related to the external environment and then the internal environment where we explain the outside-in and inside-out dichotomy in Chapter 2 and Chapter 3. Going beyond conventional textbook writing, we offer a new view on how to integrate internal and external inputs in Chapter 4.

With the strategic inputs necessary for Part 2 – Formulation – we present in six chapters how strategic leaders articulate new strategies in ways that are more competitive (Chapter 5–9) and more cooperative (Chapter 10). Carefully developing strategies requires heightened attention to the context of the new strategy. We focus on three main themes – business-level, corporate-level and international strategy. First, we address competition in product-market encounters at the business-unit level (Chapter 5) to understand how to develop business-level strategies. Competition is not limited to one competitive bout, which is why we devote Chapter 6 to competitive rivalry and competitive dynamics and the means that companies have to formulate strategies to win under the most challenging circumstances. Following this, we present chapters that explain how to develop corporate-level strategy (Chapter 7) and how to formulate strategies to develop corporations through strategic acquisition and restructuring (Chapter 8). Both business-level strategy and corporate-level strategy needs to be attenuated when the development of companies is pursued internationally (Chapter 9). This perspective on global competitiveness emphasizes the need for more cooperative strategies because the means of competition within the boundaries of a specific institutional setting reach their limits in a context where the same institutions cannot be taken for granted. Under such circumstances, being able to formulate cooperative strategy may be the only way to competitive advantage (Chapter 10).

Building on Part 1, Inputs and Part 2, Formulation, Part 3's five chapters are devoted to 'how to get it done'. The critical role of strategic leadership (Chapter 11) opens this part and explains the institutional setting in which strategic leaders operate. Chapter 12 examines corporate governance and illustrates the similarities and differences in customs, rules and regulations that support or afflict leaders in their quest to implement strategies by designing the organizational structure and establishing controls (Chapter 13). In order to innovate and increase the odds of long term viability of companies, strategic leaders have to find ways to start new corporate activities without disrupting the organization which is the basis of Chapter 14 on strategic entrepreneurship. The implementation of strategies against a backdrop of rapidly changing environments where dynamic competition alters the configurations of inputs, strategies and outcomes cannot be static. Strategic renewal (Chapter 15) is a key concept which shows how strategic leaders make choices to escape their legacy and to engage, over time, in a new and better fit between the organization and its environment. This chapter concludes Part 3 and explains how firms can sustain above-average returns. Feedback from the market and the broader environment then inform a company's strategic leaders' vision and mission often triggering a new analysis of inputs (Part 1), alternative formulations (Part 2) and differing means of implementation (Part 3). While this logical sequence of inputs, formulation and implementation is compelling, we acknowledge that the world of practice often fails to conform to such order and rational behaviour. Our attempt to reflect the interconnections between themes and topics in different chapters can be seen in the frequent links made across chapters. Seeking to reveal this complex reality with cross-references we also try to keep the structure of the ideas and themes crisp. In short, our quest for rigour and relevance in helping you succeed with strategic management is what you will find in this book.

## Currency

The authors employ the Citibank (North America) dollar/euro conversion rate as applicable on 13 May, 2010: 1 US dollar = 0.78746358 euros, and British pound/euro conversion rate as on 6th June, 2010: 1 British pound = 1.19660 euro.

# ABOUT THE AUTHORS

## Henk W. Volberda

**Henk W. Volberda** is Professor of Strategic Management and Business Policy and Director of Knowledge Transfer at the Rotterdam School of Management, Erasmus University (The Netherlands), where he previously served as Chair of the Department of Strategic Management and as Vice-Dean of the Business School. He is Director of the Erasmus Strategic Renewal Centre (ESRC) and Fellow of the Strategy Research Program of the Erasmus Research Institute of Management (ERIM). He is also Chairman of the Executive Board and Scientific Director of the top institute INSCOPE: Research for Innovation, and Board member of the Netherlands Institute for Social Innovation (NCSI). Moreover, he is Vice-President of the European Academy of Management (EURAM) and Chair of the Interest Group Strategic Management.

Henk Volberda has been a visiting scholar at the Wharton School at the University of Pennsylvania and Cass Business School, London. Professor Volberda obtained his Ph.D. cum laude in Business Administration of the University of Groningen. He teaches strategic management, strategic business planning and strategy process at all levels (undergraduate, masters, doctoral). Henk Volberda is also active in executive education and consulting and has worked with many large European corporations, including ABN Amro, Atos Origin, Air France KLM, BP, Cap Gemini, Coface, DSM, Ericsson, ING, KPN, NXP, Rabobank, Randstad, Philips, Schlumberger, Vopak and Shell.

His research on strategic flexibility and organizational renewal received many awards, including the NCD Award 1987, the ERASM Research Award 1994, the Erasmus University Research Award 1997, the Igor Ansoff Strategic Management Award 1993, the Dutch ROA Award for best consultancy paper, the Cap Gemini Ernst & Young Strategy Award 2003, the ERIM Impact Award 2003, 2005 and 2007, the ERIM Top Article Award 2007 and the SAP Strategy Award 2005. His work on strategic renewal, coevolution of firms and industries, knowledge flows, new organizational forms and innovation has been published in *Academy of Management Journal*, *Academy of Management Review*, *Business Strategy Review*, *Decision Support Systems*, *European Business Forum*, *European Management Journal*, *European Management Review*, *Group & Organization Management*, *International Journal of Disclosure and Governance*, *International Journal of Business Environment*, *International Studies of Management & Organization*, *Journal of Business Venturing*, *Journal of Management Studies*, *Journal of International Business Studies*, *Long Range Planning*, *Management Science*, *Omega*, *Organization Development Journal*, *Organization Studies*, *Organization Science* and *Schmalenbach Business Review*. He co-edited special issues of *Organization Science*, *Journal of International Business Studies*, *Journal of Management Studies*, *International Business Review* and *Technology Analysis and Strategic Management*.

He is serving as a member of the Editorial Review Board of *Journal of Management Studies, Journal of Strategy and Management, Global Journal of Flexible Systems Management, Long Range Planning, Management Executive, Organization Studies* and *Organization Science*. He was Senior Editor of *Long Range Planning* and *Journal of International Business Studies*. His monograph, *Building the Flexible Firm: How to Remain Competitive* (Oxford University Press, 2001) received wide acclaim and his book with Tom Elfring, *Rethinking Strategy* (Sage, 2001), was awarded with the ERIM Best Book Award.

## Robert E. Morgan

**Robert E. Morgan** holds the Sir Julian Hodge Professorship, and is both Department Chair and Professor of Marketing and Strategy at Cardiff Business School, Cardiff University (UK), where, until recently, he also served as Associate Dean. He has previously held industrial appointments in the international electronics sector and been Visiting Scholar at INSEAD, France, and Visiting Professor at the ALBA Graduate School of Business in Athens, Greece. His strategy teaching experience has ranged from strategic management principles and practice to advanced strategy masterclasses and workshops spanning undergraduate, postgraduate and post-experience levels. He is a Fellow of the Higher Education Academy, a Chartered Marketer and a Fellow of the Chartered Institute of Marketing and Academy of Marketing Science. His contributions to many other professional organizations include the Strategic Management Society, American Marketing Association, European Marketing Academy and British Academy of Management. He was a founding member of the Academy of Marketing Research Committee and has served as a Senator to the Chartered Institute of Marketing. Having published more than one hundred scholarly articles in marketing, his recent research focuses on mainstream strategy and the marketing and strategy interface. From this research, articles from his: capabilities-based projects have appeared in *Strategic Management Journal, Journal of Business Research, European Management Journal* and *Long Range Planning*; international entrepreneurship projects have appeared in *Journal of the Academy of Marketing Science, Journal of International Marketing* and *Omega*; and, organizational learning projects have appeared in *Journal of Management Studies, British Journal of Management, Group & Organization Management* and *Industrial Marketing Management*.

He has presented to academic, executive and student audiences in Argentina, Austria, Denmark, France, Germany, Greece, Iceland, Italy, Malaysia, Mexico, Norway, Spain, Turkey and the USA. He is the recipient of several distinctions for his executive white papers, management writing and teaching excellence awards with the most recent being a Best Paper Prize at the Strategic Management Society conference. He serves on the Editorial Review Boards of six international journals and was Co-Editor of *International Marketing Review*.

Rob Morgan has been engaged as a Special UK Government Advisor since 1997 drawing upon his research expertise in international entrepreneurship. He has conducted extensive government advisory work ranging from the carrying out of tailored primary research activities through to project impact, evaluation and assessment of policy initiatives. In addition, he has been engaged in applied research, consulting and executive education activities and has worked with the European Union and UK Government Departments (UK Department of Business, Innovation and Skills; Foreign and Commonwealth Office; Her Majesty's Treasury) as well as public bodies and private sector corporations such as British Trade International, Welsh Development Agency, The Environment Agency, BBC, S4C, PwC Management Consultants, RS Components Limited, Dell Corporation, Siemens plc, and, BT plc.

## Patrick Reinmoeller

**Patrick Reinmoeller** is Professor of Strategic Management and Director of the Breakthrough Strategic Thinking Program at Cranfield School of Management, Cranfield University (UK). He is Visiting Professor at Rotterdam School of Management and Core Member of the China Business Research Centre at Erasmus University (Netherlands). Recently, he has been appointed as Visiting Professor to the Gordon Institute of Business Science at the University of Pretoria (South Africa). Prior to joining Cranfield University he was a full time faculty member at Erasmus University and the Graduate School of Knowledge Science, Japan Advanced Institute of Science and Technology. He joined JAIST after completing his post-doc research at the Institute of Innovation Research and the Faculty of Commerce, Hitotsubashi University (Japan). Patrick Reinmoeller was educated in Italy, Japan and Germany. Professor Reinmoeller received his PhD (cum laude) in Business Administration at the University of Cologne (Germany).

Patrick Reinmoeller has been a visiting scholar at the Graduate School of International Corporate Strategy and the Institute for Innovation Research IIR at Hitotsubashi University (Japan), LIUC University Castellanza (Italy) and St. Gallen University (Switzerland). Patrick Reinmoeller's research interests include (a) innovation and knowledge creation, (b) management practices and concepts, (c) international strategy, in particular of Asian corporations and corporations in Asia. He teaches strategic management, strategic business planning and strategic innovation at all levels – undergraduate, masters (MBA) and doctoral. Dr. Patrick Reinmoeller develops and leads customized company modules and courses for executives, MBA modules on Strategy, International Strategy and Innovation. He won several best teaching awards.

He is active in executive education and consulting in the areas of strategy development, implementation, and innovation. He has worked with large international organizations such as ABN Amro, Atos Origin, BankSeta, Barr, Deutsche Telecom, Eisai, Grohe, GlaxoSmithKline Biologicals (GSK Bio), ING, International Atomic Energy Agency (IAEA), International Filmfestival Rotterdam (IFFR), KPN, UK Ministry of Defence, Unicef, Mori Building, Philips, Shell, Schlumberger and others.

His research on innovation, knowledge creation and strategy has been published in leading journals in Europe, Asia and the US. He is associated editor of the *International Journal of Business Environment* and a member of the editorial board of the *International Journal of Learning and Intellectual Capital*, *International Journal of Technology Intelligence and Planning*, *International Journal of Strategic Change Management*. He reviews for *Academy of Management Review*, *Organization*

*Science, Organization Studies, MIT Sloan Management, Journal of Management Studies,* and other leading journals, and he has won reviewer awards of the Business Policy Division and Organization and Management Theory (OMT) Divisions at the Academy of Management. He has been a member of the research committee of the OMT Division since 2008.

Patrick Reinmoeller's forthcoming book *The Ambidextrous Organization,* a monograph which addresses the ways to manage paradox today is scheduled to appear in Spring 2011. His most recent paper: "The Lost Decade: Rethinking Presence and Performance of Japanese Corporations in International Competition" appeared in autumn 2010 in the *Hitotsubashi Business Review,* the premier academic journal for executives in Japan. His paper "Embedding CSR" is forthcoming in the *International Journal of Business Ethics,* UIBE, Beijing.

Patrick enjoys Tai Chi, Kendo, Tennis, Squash and languages.

## Michael A. Hitt

**Michael A. Hitt** is a Distinguished Professor and holds the Joe B. Foster Chair in Business Leadership at Texas A&M University, USA. He received his Ph.D. from the University of Colorado. He has co-authored or co-edited 26 books and 150 journal articles.

Some of his books are *Downscoping: How to Tame the Diversified Firm* (Oxford University Press, 1994); *Mergers and Acquisitions: A Guide to Creating Value for Stakeholders* (Oxford University Press, 2001); *Competing for Advantage* 2nd edition (South-Western College Publishing, 2008); and *Understanding Business Strategy* (South-Western College Publishing, 2006). He is co-editor of several books including the following: *Managing Strategically in an Interconnected World* (1998); *New Managerial Mindsets: Organizational Transformation and Strategy Implementation* (1998); *Dynamic Strategic Resources: Development, Diffusion, and Integration* (1999); *Winning Strategies in a Deconstructing World* (John Wiley & Sons, 2000); *Handbook of Strategic Management* (2001); *Strategic Entrepreneurship: Creating a New Integrated Mindset* (2002); *Creating Value: Winners in the New Business Environment* (Blackwell Publishers, 2002); *Managing Knowledge for Sustained Competitive Advantage* (Jossey-Bass, 2003); *Great Minds in Management: The Process of Theory Development* (Oxford University Press, 2005), and *The Global Mindset* (Elsevier, 2007). He has served on the editorial review boards of multiple journals, including the *Academy of Management Journal, Academy of Management Executive, Journal of Applied Psychology, Journal of Management, Journal of World Business,* and *Journal of Applied Behavioral Sciences.* Furthermore, he has served as Consulting Editor and Editor of the *Academy of Management Journal.* He is currently a co-editor of the *Strategic Entrepreneurship Journal.* He is president of the Strategic Management Society and is a past president of the Academy of Management.

He is a Fellow in the Academy of Management and in the Strategic Management Society. He received an honorary doctorate from the Universidad Carlos III de Madrid and is an Honorary Professor and Honorary Dean at Xi'an Jiao Tong

University. He has been ackowledged with several awards for his scholarly research and he received the Irwin Outstanding Educator Award and the Distinguished Service Award from the Academy of Management. He has received best paper awards for articles published in the *Academy of Management Journal, Academy of Management Executive,* and *Journal of Management.*

## R. Duane Ireland

**R. Duane Ireland** holds the Foreman R. and Ruby S. Bennett Chair in Business from the Mays Business School, Texas A&M University, USA, where he previously served as head of the Management Department. He teaches strategic management courses at all levels (undergraduate, masters, doctoral, and executive). His research, which focuses on diversification, innovation, corporate entrepreneurship, and strategic entrepreneurship, has been published in a number of journals, including *Academy of Management Journal, Academy of Management Review, Academy of Management Executive, Administrative Science Quarterly, Strategic Management Journal, Journal of Management, Strategic Entrepreneurship Journal, Human Relations, Entrepreneurship Theory and Practice, Journal of Business Venturing,* and *Journal of Management Studies,* among others. His recently published books include *Understanding Business Strategy, Concepts and Cases* (South-Western College Publishing, 2006), *Entrepreneurship: Successfully Launching New Ventures* (Prentice-Hall, Second Edition, 2008), and *Competing for Advantage* (South-Western College Publishing, 2008). He is serving or has served as a member of the editorial review boards for a number of journals, including *Academy of Management Journal, Academy of Management Review, Academy of Management Executive, Journal of Management, Journal of Business Venturing, Entrepreneurship Theory and Practice, Journal of Business Strategy,* and *European Management Journal,* and more. He has completed terms as an associate editor for *Academy of Management Journal,* as an associate editor for *Academy of Management Executive,* and as a consulting editor for *Entrepreneurship Theory and Practice.* He is the current editor of *Academy of Management Journal.* He has co-edited special issues of *Academy of Management Review, Academy of Management Executive, Journal of Business Venturing, Strategic Management Journal, Journal of High Technology and Engineering Management,* and *Organizational Research Methods* (forthcoming). He received awards for the best article published in *Academy of Management Executive* (1999) and *Academy of Management Journal* (2000). In 2001, his co-authored article published in *Academy of Management Executive* won the Best Journal Article in Corporate Entrepreneurship Award from the U.S. Association for Small Business & Entrepreneurship (USASBE). He is a Fellow of the Academy of Management. He served a three-year term as a Representative-at-Large member of the Academy of Management's Board of Governors. He is a Research Fellow in the National Entrepreneurship Consortium. He received the 1999 Award for Outstanding Intellectual Contributions to Competitiveness Research from the American Society for Competitiveness and the USASBE Scholar in Corporate Entrepreneurship Award (2004) from USASBE.

# Robert E. Hoskisson

**Robert E. Hoskisson** is a Professor and W. P. Carey Chair in the Department of Management at Arizona State University, USA. He received his Ph.D. from the University of California-Irvine. Professor Hoskisson's research topics focus on corporate governance, acquisitions and divestitures, corporate and international diversification, corporate entrepreneurship, privatization, and cooperative strategy. He teaches courses in corporate and international strategic management, cooperative strategy, and strategy consulting, among others. Professor Hoskisson's research has appeared in over ninety publications, including the *Academy of Management Journal, Academy of Management Review, Strategic Management Journal, Organization Sci-*  *ence, Journal of Management, Journal of International Business Studies, Journal of Management Studies, Academy of Management Executive* and *California Management Review*. He is currently an Associate Editor of the *Strategic Management Journal* and a Consulting Editor for the *Journal of International Business Studies,* as well as serving on the Editorial Review board of the *Academy of Management Journal.* Professor Hoskisson has served on several editorial boards for such publications as the *Academy of Management Journal* (including Consulting Editor and Guest Editor of a special issue), *Journal of Management* (including Associate Editor), *Organization Science, Journal of International Business Studies* (Consulting Editor), *Journal of Management Studies* (Guest Editor of a special issue) and *Entrepreneurship Theory and Practice.* He has co-authored several books including *Understanding Business Strategy* (South-Western/Thomson), *Competing for Advantage,* 2nd edition (South-Western College Publishing, 2008), and *Downscoping: How to Tame the Diversified Firm* (Oxford University Press).

He has an appointment as a Special Professor at the University of Nottingham and as an Honorary Professor at Xi'an Jiao Tong University. He is a Fellow of the Academy of Management and a Charter Member of the Academy of Management Journals Hall of Fame. He is also a Fellow of the Strategic Management Society. In 1998, he received an award for Outstanding Academic Contributions to Competitiveness, American Society for Competitiveness. He also received the William G. Dyer Distinguished Alumni Award given at the Marriott School of Management, Brigham Young University. He completed three years of service as a representative at large on the Board of Governors of the Academy of Management and currently is on the Board of Directors of the Strategic Management Society.

# ACKNOWLEDGEMENTS

This textbook is the outcome of a great team effort. The renowned authors of the best-selling American version, currently in its 9th edition, have continued to support our efforts to develop a completely new 1st edition for EMEA. Thank you Mike, Duane and Bob for providing us with a great platform and for your support and helpful advice.

We have planned and tested with students parts of this textbook over several years. However, all of this would not have been possible without the hands-on help of our colleagues who have contributed greatly to many of the chapters. For this we thank especially:

- Ignacio Vaccaro, *BTS* for his work on Chapter 11;
- Pieter-Jan Bezemer, *Queensland University of Technology* for his work on Chapter 12;
- Ernst Verwaal, *Queen's University Belfast* for his work on Chapter 13;
- Sebastiaan van Doorn, *Rotterdam School of Management, Erasmus University* for his work on Chapter 14;
- Shiko M. Ben-Menahem and Mariano Heyden, *Rotterdam School of Management, Erasmus University* for their work on creating a completely new Chapter 15.

Moreover, an enthusiastic, diligent and energetic team of international assistant researchers provided additional insights to our ideas, cases, vignettes and themes reflecting truly the geographic and cultural richness and diversity that is the hallmark of the EMEA Region. George Ankomah, Martin Ahe, Muhammed Akbas, Haydn Gush, Saskia van Ommeren and Lisa Thomas have supported us in better understanding the different contexts and applications that influence the Inputs, Formulation and Implementation of Strategic Management.

The content of this book is enriched by the countless stimulating, challenging, though-provoking and always fun discussions we have had with current and former students in the Strategic Management Programmes of the Rotterdam School of Management, Cardiff Business School and Cranfield School of Management. These class discussions as well as the case presentations have helped us to fine-tune our line of reasoning and forced us to convey our strategy frameworks in meaningful and manageable packets of learning. In addition, the many interactions with managers participating in MBA executive and in-company programmes on strategy proved to be extremely useful in developing this book and further improving the strategic management process framework.

Of course, our colleagues also deserve recognition for their valuable suggestions, support and inspiration. We especially want to thank Shahzad Ansari, Justin Jansen, Nikos Kavadis, Tom Mom, Pepijn van Neerijnen, Ilan Oshri, Jatinder Sidhu, Marten Stienstra, Frans Van den Bosch, Vareska van de Vrande and Raymond van Wijk from the Rotterdam School of Management, Costas Andriopoulos, George Boyne, Yiannis Kouropalatis, Luigi de Luca, Bob McNabb, Kelly Page and Taman Powell from Cardiff Business School, and Cliff Bowman, Mark Jenkins, Joe Nellis and Alessandro Giudici from Cranfield School of Management.

Towers of strength in orchestrating our research integration efforts to deliver this textbook were the secretarial offices, particularly Miriam Stikkelorum, Carolien Heintjes and Patricia de Wilde-Mes from Rotterdam School of Management, Sally Daniels from Cardiff Business School and Rosemary Cockfield from Cranfield School of Management.

We also express our appreciation for the excellent support received from our editorial and production team at Cengage Learning EMEA. We especially wish to thank Charlotte Green, our Editorial Assistant; Alison Cooke, our Content Project Manager; Jennifer Seth and Hywel Evans, our Development Editors; Brendan George and Tom Rennie, our Publishers; and Amanda Cheung, our Marketing Manager. We are grateful for their dedication, commitment and outstanding contributions to the development and publication of this book and its package of support materials.

The scientific debates we had with peers in the field, as well as comments from reviewers on previous work, served as the engine for progress. In particular, we are highly indebted to the reviewers of this EMEA edition:

- Olivier Furrer, *Nijmegen School of Management, Radboud University Nijmegen*
- Paul Hughes, *Loughborough University Business School*
- Nicholas O'Reagan, *Bristol Business School, University of the West of England*
- Sajjad Jasimuddin, *School of Management and Business, Aberystwyth University*
- Hans-Erich Mueller, *FHW-Berlin School of Economics*
- Anders Drejer, *Aarhus School of Business*
- Andy Adcroft, *School of Management, University of Surrey*
- Frank Piller, *RWTH Aachen University*

Finally, we are grateful to our closest partners in this endeavour, our wives and children. Many days and evenings were spent on this book and too many weekends were sacrificed. This work would not have been accomplished without their unconditional support. We dedicate this joint work to them.

*Henk W. Volberda*
*Robert E. Morgan*
*Patrick Reinmoeller*

# WALK THROUGH TOUR

**Opening Case** feature at the start of each chapter to show how issues are tackled in real-life business situations.

**Strategic Focus** appear throughout the book to show how each chapter's main issues are applied in real-life business situations in a variety of international and national companies. Each case is accompanied by questions to help test your understanding of the issues.

**Key Debate** present a discussion of opposing perspectives on pivotal issues expanding on each chapter's content and examples.

**Closing Case** feature at the end of each chapter to illustrate how businesses react to different strategic issues.

**Margin terms** are highlighted in the margins throughout and explained in full in the glossary at the end of the book.

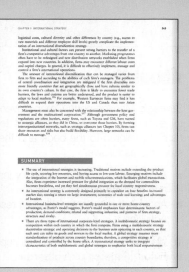

**Summary** Each chapter ends with a comprehensive summary that provides a thorough re-cap of the key issues, helping you to assess your understanding and revise core concepts.

**Review Questions** provided at the end of each chapter, to help reinforce and test your knowledge and understanding.

**Discussion Questions** at the end of each chapter involve a mixture of active discussion, library assignments and web projects.

**Further Reading** provide recommendations of relevant books and crucial articles, designed to help you explore other voices often beyond management.

**Experiential Exercises** place the reader in a variety of situations requiring application of some part of the strategic management process.

**Video Case** is designed to stimulate critical thinking and curiosity of the reader by introducing different perspectives through a link to an online video stream.

**Integrative Cases** Full length cases appear at the end of the book offering detailed discussion of strategic management concepts.

# About the website

*Strategic Management: Competitiveness and Globalization* is accompanied by a range of exciting digital support resources to support teaching and enhance the learning experience. Each resource is carefully tailored to the book and the needs of the reader. The website is structured for lecturers and students as follows:

■ A password protected area for instructors with resources such as a Testbank, PowerPoint Slides and an Instructor's Manual.
■ An area for students including resources such as Multiple Choice Questions and Internet Based Activities.

To discover the dedicated digital support resources accompanying this textbook please go to:
**www.cengage.co.uk/volberda**

## For students

■ Video Case Program
■ Multiple Choice Questions
■ Case Study Maps
■ Internet Based Activities

## For lecturers

■ Instructor's Manual
■ PowerPoint Slides
■ ExamView Test Bank
■ Instructor's Case Notes
■ Case Study Maps
■ Online Case bank

## CENGAGENOW™

Designed by lecturers for lecturers, CengageNOW™ for *Strategic Management: Competitiveness and Globalization* mirrors the natural teaching workflow with an easy-to-use online suite of services and resources, all in one program. With this system, lecturers can easily plan their courses, manage student assignments, automatically grade, teach with dynamic technology, and assess student progress. CengageNOW™ operates seamlessly with Blackboard/WebCT, Moodle and other virtual learning environments. Ask your Cengage Learning sales representative for a demonstration of what CengageNOW™ for *Strategic Management: Competitiveness and Globalization* can bring to your courses http:/edu.cengage.co.uk/contact_us.aspx).

## CourseMate

Cengage Learning's CourseMate brings course concepts to life with interactive learning, study and exam preparation tools that support the printed textbook. Watch student comprehension soar as your class works with the printed textbook and the textbook-specific website. CourseMate includes: an interactive eBook; interactive teaching and learning tools including videos, games, quizzes and flash-cards (resources are mapped to specific disciplines so the range of resources will vary with each text); Engagement Tracker, a first-of-its-kind tool that monitors student engagement in the course. For more information please contact your local Cengage Learning representative.

## The Business and Company Resource Center (BCRC)

Put a complete business library at your students' fingertips! This premier online business research tool allows you and your students to search thousands of periodicals, journals, references, financial data, industry reports, and more. This powerful research tool saves time for students—whether they are preparing for a presentation or writing an essay. You can use the BCRC to quickly and easily assign readings or research projects. Visit http://www.cengage.com/bcrc to learn more about this indispensable tool.

# STRATEGIC MANAGEMENT INPUTS

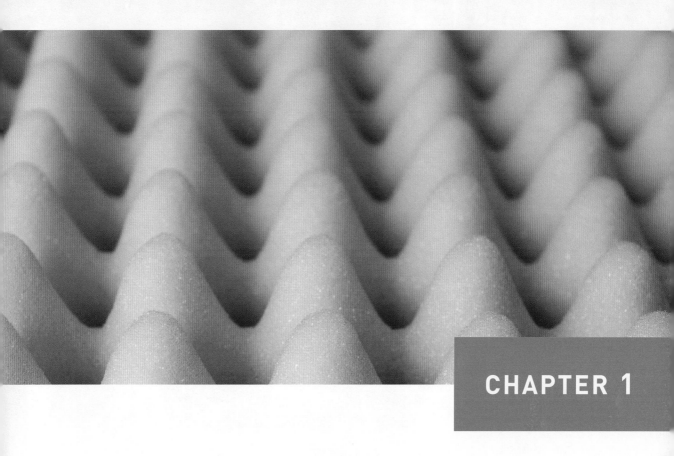

# CHAPTER 1

# STRATEGIC MANAGEMENT AND STRATEGIC COMPETITIVENESS

## LEARNING OBJECTIVES

Studying this chapter should provide you with the strategic management knowledge needed to:

1 Define strategic competitiveness, strategy, competitive advantage, above-average returns and the strategic management process.
2 Describe the competitive landscape and explain how globalization and technological changes shape it.
3 Use the industrial organization (I/O) model to explain how firms can earn above-average returns.
4 Use the resource-based model to explain how firms can earn above-average returns.
5 Describe vision and mission and discuss their usefulness.
6 Define stakeholders and describe their ability to influence organizations.
7 Describe the work of strategic leaders.
8 Explain the strategic management process.

## OPENING CASE

# Airbus and Boeing

Boeing has historically been a global leader in manufacturing commercial airplanes. However, in 2001, Airbus had more orders than Boeing for the first time in its competitive history. The battle for customer orders has been most visible in the super jumbo category with Airbus's A380 versus Boeing's 787.

In 1992, Boeing and Airbus's parent EADS, agreed to a joint study on prospects for a super jumbo aircraft. The impetus for the study was the growing traffic in China and India. However, Airbus and Boeing reached different conclusions concerning the market trends, and the joint effort was disbanded.

Both firms differ strongly in their strategies. (We define strategy in this chapter as an integrated and coordinated set of commitments and action designed to exploit core competencies and gain a competitive advantage.) Airbus's strategy emphasis is on economic long-haul flights with the A380 offering 550-plus seats, whereas Boeing's 787 Dreamliner design focused on long-range efficient flight, capable of transporting 250 passengers. In their diverging strategies, Airbus selected flying to larger airports that use the existing hub-and-spoke system, whereas Boeing concentrated more on a point-to-point system in which smaller airports are more abundant. In reality, the Airbus A380 aircraft, because of its size and weight, is currently able to land at approximately only 35 airports, however the airports able to accommodate planes of its size are projected to increase in the major growth markets, such as China and India. The Boeing aircraft, on the other hand, can currently land at many more airports around the world and the number is growing in emerging economies, such as throughout Eastern Europe where smaller airports desire international connections.

Airbus won the competitor battle that occurred between 2001 and 2005 because it focused on the midsized market as well, developing the A320 plane, which competes with Boeing's 737 and 757 aircraft. The A320 is more efficient than the aircraft used by Boeing, and Boeing did not respond to customer demands to create new, efficient aircraft. In fact, it had slowed its innovation process in regard to new models. Besides the lack of new models, the commercial aircraft business was sluggish; new orders significantly ebbed due to the complications of the terrorist attacks and the subsequent recession. It was a bleak time for Boeing relative to Airbus.

More recently, Boeing's strategic approach to overall design with the 787 Dreamliner appears advantageous, as far as the order battle goes. Airbus is behind in its schedule to produce the A380. The midsized A350, comparable to the Boeing 787, is also behind schedule because of redesign issues and Airbus has had to provide significant incentive discounts to increase future orders.

On-time delivery has for a long time been a problem in the industry. Airbus, a part of EADS, has an intricate manufacturing process that leverages competencies distributed across Europe but also needs to carefully balance the political sensitivities that often demand emphasizing one manufacturing location over another. Airbus has also been forced to produce more of its plane parts in European countries because governments have significant ownership and provide subsidies to Airbus. Accordingly, these governments, Spain, France, Germany and the United Kingdom, want to maintain employment levels in their countries, and thus Airbus must continue to produce primarily in European countries. While the manufacturing process has been improving, on-time delivery of products as complex as the revolutionary A380, which includes private bathrooms for first-class passengers, bars and lounges, remained elusive and Airbus had to postpone delivery several times. Airbus's postponements reduced its advantage in being to the market early, and in 2006, Boeing regained its lead with 1044 versus 790 orders for commercial aircraft. However Boeing had problems of its own.

Boeing has implemented a different strategy in regard to its established production process. Boeing has been able to plan for speeding up the process by creating an efficient global supply chain that involves many potential customers around the world, including Japan, China and others. "Boeing outsources 85 per cent of the work for its 787 Dreamliner aircraft. The corresponding figure for Airbus's A380 is 15 per cent." As a result of the design and development delays, Airbus's development costs for the A380 have risen to €11 billion versus the €6.2 billion invested by Boeing for the 787. Recently, however, Boeing discovered design problems and had difficulties realizing the efficiencies promised by a distributed supply chain.

In making its decision to move ahead with the 787 Dreamliner versus a more jumbo aircraft comparable to the A380, Boeing made a concerted effort in connecting and getting input from its airline customers, as well as the ultimate customers, the passengers. Overwhelmingly the passengers in particular, and thereby the airlines, preferred smaller aircraft which would enable them to get to smaller airports quickly, without as many transfers on a point-to point system. Additionally, Boeing followed up with the ultimate creditors, the leasing agents, and asked what they would prefer as far as risks in financing versus the large super jumbo A380. These business-level strategies may have created an obvious advantage in the near term for Boeing.

The ultimate battle will continue between these two firms. While currently Boeing seems to have extended its range of offerings, taking a longer-term perspective, some have pointed out that Boeing seems to have lost its supremacy in the market for commercial aircraft. Airbus has with the A380 created for the first time in its history of playing catch-up with Boeing, a new category on its own. This innovation has already attracted many orders, especially from airlines that strategically choose the hub-and-spoke system, such as Emirates and others. Finally, distributing manufacturing activities beyond the borders of a company or close alliance, and involving Japanese and Chinese manufacturers, may be the beginning of a rapid spillover of skills and knowledge needed for these to develop aircrafts on their own. These countries are likely to compete in the future within Boeing and Airbus's range and possibly innovate.

**Sources:** Robertson, D. "Airbus will lose €4.8bn because of A380 delays", *The Times Business News*, http://www.business.timesonline.co.uk/article/09077-2387999,00.html October 4, 2006; "Strong euro weighs on Airbus suppliers", *Wall Street Journal*, October 30, 2009, B3; "WTO to weigh in on EU subsidies for Airbus", *New York Times*, September 3, 2009; O'Connell, D. and Porter, A. "Trade war threatened over £379m subsidy for Airbus", *The Times*, http://www.timesonline.co.uk/article/0,,2095-1631948,00.html 29 May, 2005; "Boeing set for victory over Airbus in illegal subsidy case", *Wall Street Journal*, September 3, 2009, A1; "US refuses to disclose WTO ruling on Boeing-Airbus row", *EU Business*, http://www.eubusiness.com/news-eu/wto-trade-dispute-us.bq/ September 5, 2009; "Airbus, Boeing double orders on leasing demand as show opens", *Bloomberg Businessweek*, July 19, 2010; Mustoe, H. "Airbus, Boeing may force supplier mergers to reduce costs", July 22, 2010.

## Questions

**1** How does globalization shape the competitive landscape of Airbus and Boeing?

**2** What are the environmental conditions that Airbus needs to succeed? What are the environmental conditions Boeing needs to succeed?

**3** Use the industrial organization (I/O) model to explain how Airbus can earn above-average returns.

**4** What are the main resources and capabilities that determine the success of Airbus?

**5** What is the specific meaning of above-average returns in a market such as that of Airbus and Boeing?

As we can see from the Opening Case, Boeing has outperformed Airbus in some key projects for a long time. Boeing is a highly competitive company (something we call a condition of strategic competitiveness) as it earned *above-average returns*. All firms, including Boeing, use the strategic management process (see Figure 1.1) as the foundation for the commitments, decisions and actions they will take when pursuing strategic competitiveness and above-average returns.

**Strategic competitiveness**

Strategic competitiveness is achieved when a firm successfully formulates and implements a value-creating strategy.

**FIGURE 1.1** The strategic management process

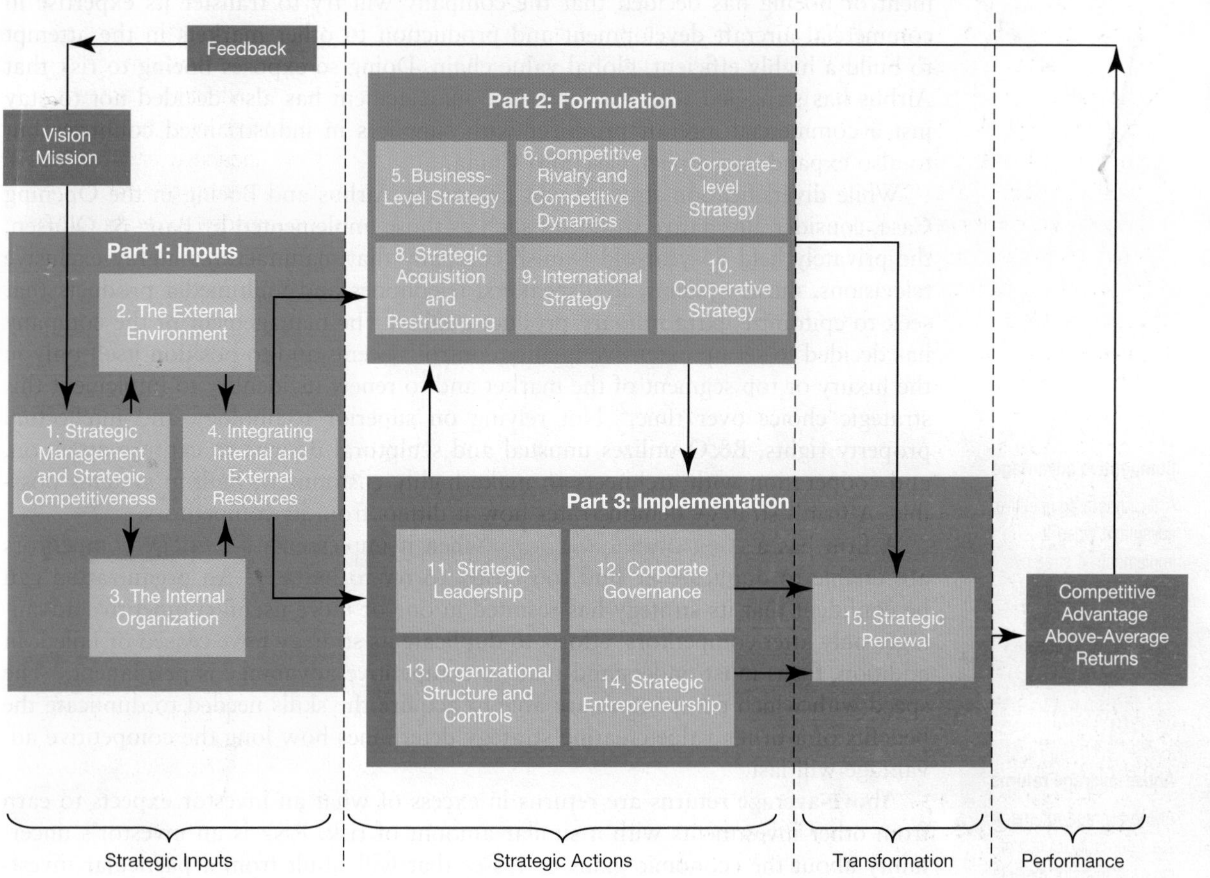

We introduce you to the strategic management process in the next few paragraphs and use the remaining chapters of this book to fully explain it.

Strategic competitiveness is achieved when a firm successfully formulates and implements a value-creating strategy. A **strategy** is an integrated and coordinated set of commitments and actions designed to develop and exploit core competencies and gain a competitive advantage. When choosing a strategy, firms make choices among competing alternatives as the pathway for deciding how they will pursue strategic competitiveness.[1] In this sense, the chosen strategy indicates what the firm will do as well as what the firm will not do.

As explained in the Opening Case Airbus and Boeing have decided to pursue a diversification strategy. Airbus has pioneered a new category in commercial aviation and seeks to beat Boeing in supersized planes and be the first to this market, with demand forecasted to boom. Integrating the product development process with the different people across sites within Airbus's complex organization, and formulating the strategy, is clearly a great accomplishment for Airbus. It manages internal complexity successfully. Boeing, on the other hand, is taking a very different approach and diversifying beyond commercial aviation. Boeing's revenues come not only from commercial aircraft sales but also from military and space satellite contracts. This strategy has enabled Boeing not only to hedge against volatility in these markets, but has also helped it to decrease development costs due to

**Strategy**

A strategy is an integrated and coordinated set of commitments and actions designed to exploit core competencies and gain a competitive advantage.

synergies among the divisions. Seeking to further increase synergies, the management of Boeing has decided that the company will try to transfer its expertise in commercial aircraft development and production to other markets in the attempt to build a highly efficient, global value chain. Doing so exposes Boeing to risk that Airbus has struggled with for long. The management has also decided not to stay just a commercial aircraft producer with suppliers in industrialized countries but to also expand its supplier base into China.

While diversification strategy was chosen by Airbus and Boeing in the Opening Case, consider alternative strategies such as those implemented by Bang & Olufsen, the privately held 85-year-old Danish company that manufactures highly exclusive televisions, music systems, loudspeakers, telephones and multimedia products that seek to epitomize extraordinary product quality. The management of the company has decided to set up extensive quality control systems and to position itself only in the luxury or top segment of the market and to renew its identity to implement this strategic choice over time.[2] Not relying on superior technology and intellectual property rights, B&O utilizes unusual and sculptural designs to capture attention, and cooperation with architects to make highly customized, built-in systems possible. A firm's strategy demonstrates how it differs from its competitors.

A firm has a **competitive advantage** when it implements a strategy competitors are unable to duplicate or find too costly to try to imitate.[3] An organization can be confident that its strategy has resulted in one or more useful competitive advantages only after competitors' efforts to duplicate its strategy have ceased or failed. In addition, firms must understand that no competitive advantage is permanent.[4] The speed with which competitors are able to acquire the skills needed to duplicate the benefits of a firm's value-creating strategy determines how long the competitive advantage will last.[5]

**Above-average returns** are returns in excess of what an investor expects to earn from other investments with a similar amount of risk. **Risk** is an investor's uncertainty about the economic gains or losses that will result from a particular investment.[6] The most successful companies learn how to effectively manage risk. Effectively managing risks reduces investors' uncertainty about the results of their investment in individual companies.[7] Returns are often measured in terms of accounting figures, such as return on assets, return on equity, or return on sales. Alternatively, returns can be measured on the basis of stock market returns, such as monthly returns (the end-of-the-period stock price minus the beginning stock price, divided by the beginning stock price, yielding a percentage return). In smaller, new venture firms, returns are sometimes measured in terms of the amount and speed of growth (e.g., in annual sales) rather than more traditional profitability measures.[8] The reason for this is that new ventures require time to earn acceptable returns (in the form of return on assets and so forth) on investors' investments.[9]

Understanding how to exploit a competitive advantage is important for firms seeking to earn above-average returns.[10] Firms without a competitive advantage or that are not competing in an attractive industry earn, at best, average returns. **Average returns** are returns equal to those an investor expects to earn from other investments with a similar amount of risk. In the long run, an inability to earn at least average returns results first in decline and then eventually, failure. Failure occurs because investors withdraw their investments from those firms earning less-than-average returns. When this happens, firms file for bankruptcy or sometimes liquidate their operations.

In the Strategic Focus below we demonstrate how first the failure to fight commoditization,[11] then the revival of Apple Inc. in 2001 has changed the music player industry, the electronics industry, the personal computer industry as well as the way

**Competitive advantage**

A firm has a competitive advantage when it implements a strategy competitors are unable to duplicate or find too costly to try to imitate.

**Above-average returns**

Above-average returns are returns in excess of what an investor expects to earn from other investments with a similar amount of risk.

**Risk**

Risk is an investor's uncertainty about the economic gains or losses that will result from a particular investment.

**Average returns**

Average returns are returns equal to those an investor expects to earn from other investments with a similar amount of risk.

people around the world shop for music. Many companies that used to be market leaders in these industries had to give up large pieces of their market share, revenues as well as profit margins, as they did not anticipate this change and could not keep up with the new competitor. Having suffered from the limitations of focusing on a small segment in the computer market, Apple evaluated its deteriorating performance and options. In need of cash flow to finance important strategic moves, Apple first launched and successfully sold the iMac, a colourful innovation in a commoditized market at that time. Then, in 2001, Apple linked electronics, intuitive operations and music in an innovative way that substantiated the turnaround.[12]

Interestingly, during the time of Apple's recent rise, another company that had written history in electronics, the Japanese electronics manufacturer Sony, had to face many difficulties. Sony had invented the Walkman, which in the 1980s married mobility and audio technology. Even better positioned after a long string of acquisitions, in the late 1990s Sony owned large units focusing on the music and movies as well as electronics and computing. Yet, the units did not innovate together but optimized within given product areas. Run as separate business units for years, it has been challenging for Howard Stringer, the British chief executive officer (CEO) of Sony, to increase cooperation between these units and facilitate joint innovation.

The strategic management process (see Figure 1.1) is the full set of commitments, decisions and actions required for a firm to achieve strategic competitiveness and earn above-average returns. Analysing its external environment and internal organization to determine its resources, capabilities, and core competencies—the sources of its "strategic inputs"—is the first step the firm takes in this process. With the results of these analyses at hand, the firm develops its vision and mission and formulates its strategy. To implement this strategy, the firm takes actions toward achieving strategic competitiveness and above-average returns. The effectiveness of the firm's implementation and formulation actions increases when those actions are effectively integrated. The strategic management process is dynamic in nature as ever-changing markets and competitive structures are coordinated with a firm's continuously-evolving strategic inputs.[13]

In the following chapters, we use the strategic management process to explain what firms do to achieve strategic competitiveness and earn above-average returns. These explanations demonstrate why some firms consistently achieve competitive success while others fail to do so.[14] As you will see, the reality of global competition is a critical part of the strategic management process and significantly influences firms' performances.[15] Indeed, learning how to successfully compete in the globalized world is one of the most significant challenges for firms competing in the current century.[16]

We discuss several topics in this chapter. First, we describe the current competitive landscape. This challenging landscape is being created primarily by the emergence of a global economy, globalization resulting from that economy, and rapid technological changes. Next, we examine two models firms use to gather the information and knowledge required to choose and then effectively implement their strategies. The insights gained from these models also serve as the foundation for forming the firm's vision and mission. The first model (the industrial organization or I/O model) suggests that the external environment is the primary determinant of a firm's strategic actions. Identifying and then competing successfully in an attractive (i.e., profitable) industry or segment of an industry is the key to successfully using this model.[17] The second model (resource-based) suggests that a firm's unique resources and capabilities are the critical link to strategic competitiveness.[18] Thus, the first model is concerned primarily with the firm's external environment, while

**Strategic management process**

The strategic management process is the full set of commitments, decisions and actions required for a firm to achieve strategic competitiveness and earn above-average returns.

STRATEGIC FOCUS

© Neil Fraser/Alamy

# Apple: using innovation to create technology trends and sustain competitive advantage

During the recession in 2008, Apple posted record sales. The firm's strong performance in poor economic times is largely accorded to its innovation capabilities. Apple has continued to upgrade its current products such as laptops with enhancements (e.g., MacBook and MacBook Pro). Analysts believe that these innovation additions will keep Apple's "hot streak" alive and well. Furthermore, projections suggest that smartphone sales will surge over the next few years. These projections include a 200 per cent increase in the sales of high-end mobile phones to 300 million units annually by 2013. The growing popularity of web 2.0 applications such as Facebook and Twitter is increasing the desire for these phones. And, such demand is very positive for the future of Black-Berry and Apple's iPhone. By 2013, analysts believe that approximately 23 per cent of all new mobile phone sales will be smartphones.

After the proliferation of the PC format with Microsoft products and Intel semiconductors as the standard configuration, Apple hit difficult times. A rapid succession of CEOs, limited scale, elevated prices and products that did not seem to offer value, Apple had lost its way. Only when Steve Jobs, its co-founder returned, was Apple able to capture positive attention by launching the iMac, a product that was pared down yet generated considerable excitement, not only among Apple enthusiasts. For what followed, Steve Jobs received the "CEO of the Decade" by *Fortune* magazine in autumn 2009.

Apple started its regeneration in 2001 with its unveiling of the iPod, a portable digital music device, and then followed up with its complementary iTunes online music store, a service for downloading songs and other digital music and video clips. With the launch of the iPhone, Apple entered a new category in a market, i.e. mobile phones, in which it had no experience. Not only has it done well in producing simply designed products, such as the iPod or the iPhone and its other recent devices, but it also excels in marketing its aesthetic or elegant designs, which seem to please the customer and create a "market buzz" for Apple products.

Apple has also continued to upgrade its innovative iPod with its second generation of iPod Touch. One analyst gave it a perfect score for the significant enhancements made. The iPod Touch provides similar functions as the iPhone, such as an Internet connection using the same touchscreen, and playing music and videos in the same way. An example of the continuous innovation is the four-gigabyte iPod Shuffle introduced in 2009. The new Shuffle can handle songs in 14 different languages and can store approximately 1000 songs, i.e. four times more than the first generation Shuffle, launched in 2005. Apple has repeatedly "set the standard" for design of personal computers since the mid-1990s. The innovations created since 1996 include a tool that created a quantum increase in the sale of digital music, made the mobile phone a flexible computer that is fun to use, and in customer service through a chain of unique and popular retail stores. Thus, most external observers argue that Apple is one of the most innovative companies. Because of its innovative products, Apple has become one of the fastest growing companies in the US.

In 2010, with more than 2 million brand new iPads sold in two months following its launch, Apple has created a new market and captured the largest share.

Although others are seeking to simply duplicate the complementary and innovative relationships between Apple's devices (e.g., iPod and iPhone) and iTunes, Apple continues to innovate with products such as the iPad and its ways of usage, e.g., opening a platform for Apps, the small applications customers can download for generally small fees. Apple's focus on innovation has helped it maintain a competitive advantage and marketing prowess over other industry players, who have historically been much stronger than Apple. Coupled with its innovation, Apple is an aggressive marketer. While most firms are paring back their costs and advertising during the recession, Apple has increased its marketing and advertising programmes. It is rated as the second most prolific technology advertiser, behind Microsoft.

Apple seeks to change the way people behave versus just competing in the marketplace for traditional products. In doing so, it has been able to establish first mover advantages through radical concepts using elegant design and excellent market timing to establish its advantage. Others seem to compete in commodity businesses with incremental innovations, while Apple influences what is on the consumer's mind.

**Sources:** Fackler, M. (2005) "Sony Plans 10000 Job Cuts", *New York Times*, September 23; Edwards, C. (2006) "Hitting the Right Notes at Sony", *BusinessWeek Online*, http://www.businessweek.com/print/technology/content/jan2006/tc20060109_265301; Stross, R. (2007) "Apple's lesson for Sony's stores: Just connect", *New York Times*, http://www.nytimes.com, May 27; "Apple's "magical" iPhone unveiled", BBC, http://www.bbc.co.uk, January 9 2007; Furchgott, R. (2006) "Cell phones for the music fan", *New York Times*, http://www.nytimes.com, December 28; Wildstrom, S. H. (2008) "Apple laptops: The hits keep coming", *BusinessWeek*, http://www.businessweek.com, November 4; Edwards, C. (2008) "Apple's superlative sequel: The latest iPod touch", *BusinessWeek*, http://www.businessweek.com, November 20; Waters, R. and Nutialin, C. (2009) "Apple moves to clear up uncertainty ahead of Jobs' absence", *Financial Times*, http://www.ft.com, January 16; Stone, B. (2009) "Can Apple fill the void?", *New York Times*, http://www.nytimes.com, January 16; "Apple bobbing", *Financial Times*, http://www.ft.com, January 22, 2009; Lomas, N. (2009) "Smartphones set to surge", *BusinessWeek*, http://www.businessweek.com, February 3; Stone, B. (2009) "In campaign wars, Apple still has Microsoft's number", *New York Times*, http://www.nytimes.com, February 4; Elmer-Dewitt, P. (2009) "Apple is 14th fastest-growing tech company", *Fortune*, http://www.fortune.cnn.com, February 6; "Apple launches smaller, 4-gigabyte iPod shuffle", *Houston Chronicle,* (2009), http://www.chron.com, March 11.

*Questions*

**1** Will Apple be able to continue innovating?

**2** What does success through innovation rely on?

**3** Over the years, Apple has grown from a small player to a dominant player. Will this change the perceived value of Apple products, and if so how?

the second model is concerned primarily with the firm's internal organization. After discussing vision and mission, direction-setting statements that influence the choice and use of strategies, we describe the stakeholders that organizations serve. The degree to which stakeholders' needs can be met directly increases when firms achieve strategic competitiveness and earn above-average returns. Closing the chapter are introductions to strategic leaders and the elements of the strategic management process.

# The competitive landscape

The fundamental nature of competition in many of the world's industries is changing. Reasons for this include the realities that financial capital is scarce and markets are increasingly volatile.[19] Because of this, the pace of change in the nature of competition is relentless and is increasing. Even determining the boundaries of an industry has become challenging. Consider, for example, how advances in interactive computer networks and telecommunications have blurred the boundaries of the entertainment industry. Today, cable companies and satellite networks compete for entertainment revenue from television; and telecommunication companies are moving into the entertainment business through significant improvements in fibre-optic lines.[20] Partnerships among firms in different segments of the entertainment industry further blur industry boundaries. For example, a listed UK subscription television service company, British Sky Broadcasting, which is also the largest pay-TV provider in the UK, is partly owned by the US-based NewsCorp and gets one-third of its customers through partnerships with Virgin Media, Tiscali TV and UPC. Similarly, partnerships across the boundaries of industries are essential for Apple. Bringing on board the hardware suppliers in Asia and elsewhere, the owners of content in the music and the movie business, and making thousands of entrepreneurial individuals enthusiastic about the opportunity to write a successful app for the iPhone or the iPad, illustrate how important partnerships, even across industry boundaries, are for Apple's competitiveness.

There are other examples of fundamental changes to competition in various industries. For instance, many firms are looking for the most profitable and interesting way to deliver video on demand (VOD) online besides cable and satellite companies. Raketu, a voice-over-the-Internet-protocol (VoIP) phone service in the United Kingdom, is seeking to provide a social experience while watching the same entertainment on a VOD using a chat feature on its phone service.[21] Raketu's vision is to "... bring together communications, information and entertainment into one service, to remove the complexities of how people communicate with one another, make a system that is contact centric, and to make it fun and easy to use."[22] More competitive possibilities and potentially the competitive challenges for more "traditional" communications companies are suggested by social networking sites such as Facebook, StudieVZ (Germany), Hyves (the Netherlands), Vkontakte (Russia) and others.[23]

Other characteristics of the current competitive landscape are noteworthy. Conventional sources of competitive advantage such as economies of scale and huge advertising budgets are not as effective as they once were. Moreover, the traditional managerial mindset is unlikely to lead a firm to strategic competitiveness. Managers must adopt a new mindset that values flexibility, speed, innovation, integration and the challenges that evolve from constantly changing conditions.[24] The conditions of the competitive landscape result in a perilous business world, one where the investments that are required to compete on a global scale are enormous and the consequences of failure are severe.[25] Increasingly, governments take a more active stance and have begun to interfere with markets where they perceive them to fail, as has happened in industries such as banking, IT and oil. This influence of governments is particularly important when firms are active in many countries. Facing the need to negotiate with politicians in different countries complicates the challenge of building competitive advantage. Effective use of the strategic management process reduces the likelihood of failure for firms as they encounter the conditions of today's competitive landscape.

*Hypercompetition* is a term often used to capture the realities of the competitive landscape. Under conditions of hypercompetition, assumptions of market stability are replaced by notions of inherent instability and change.[26] Hypercompetition results from the dynamics of strategic maneuvering among global and innovative combatants.[27] It is a condition of rapidly escalating competition based on price-quality positioning, competition to create new know-how and establish first-mover advantage, and competition to protect or invade established product or geographic markets.[28] In a hypercompetitive market, firms often aggressively challenge their competitors in the hopes of improving their competitive position and ultimately their performance.[29]

Several factors create hypercompetitive environments and influence the nature of the current competitive landscape. The emergence of a global economy and technology, specifically rapid technological change, are the two primary drivers of hypercompetitive environments and the nature of today's competitive landscape.

## The global economy

A global economy is one in which goods, services, people, skills and ideas move freely across geographic borders. Relatively unfettered by artificial constraints, such as tariffs, the global economy significantly expands and complicates a firm's competitive environment.[30]

Interesting opportunities and challenges are associated with the emergence of the global economy.[31] For example, Europe, instead of the United States, is today the world's largest single market, with 700 million potential customers. The European Union and the other Western European countries also have a gross domestic product that is more than 35 per cent higher than the GDP of the United States.[32] Tomorrow may look different. Especially, large emerging markets such as Brazil, China, India, Russia, Turkey, Indonesia, Malaysia, South Africa and others have growing populations and economies that outperform industrialized economies on growth. The gross domestic product (GDP) of Brazil, Russia, India and China (BRIC) is expected to be greater than that of the G6 countries by 2040.[33] Since the first estimates about how these countries will exert decisive influence on the global economy in the future have been disseminated, emerging markets have come to redefine the strategic context. "In the past, China was generally seen as a low-competition market and a low-cost land. Today, China is an extremely competitive market in which local market-seeking MNCs [multinational corporations] must fiercely compete against other MNCs and against those local companies that are more cost effective and faster in product development. While it is true that China has been viewed as a country from which to source low-cost goods, lately many MNCs are actually net exporters of local management talent; they have been dispatching more Chinese abroad than bringing foreign expatriates to China."[34] India, the world's largest democracy, has an economy that also is growing rapidly and now ranks as the fourth largest in the world.[35] Consider the opportunities not only within such countries but related to them. Hong Kong, Taiwan and Singapore have benefited through their cultural proximity to mainland China. Now the Gulf region, an emerging area of economic activity in its own right, has built the hubs that India lacks and the regions' airlines successfully exploit them. These hubs effectively link the East and West. Not exactly a copy of the ancient Silk Road that connected the rich East with the emerging West, but the analogy is intriguing. Many large multinational companies are also starting as significant global competitors from these emerging economies.[36] Consider how the Mexican cement manufacturer, Cemex, has flawlessly executed an internationalization strategy that was heavily leveraged, fueled by low interest rates, and turned itself into a top three global player before 2008. In the Closing Case (see page 36) we describe the rapid rise of Tata Group, a diversified Indian conglomerate.

The statistics detailing the nature of the global economy reflect the realities of a hypercompetitive business environment, and challenge individual firms to think seriously about the markets in which they will compete. Consider how Volkswagen AG spotted opportunities in the Chinese market as early as 1984.[37] Today 18 per cent of the sales of the whole Volkswagen group, which includes Volkswagen, Audi, Skoda, Bentley and Lamborghini, come from the Chinese market. Having set up a wholly-owned subsidiary, the group is still capitalizing on the soaring growth of the Chinese market and is planning to invest a further €4 billion in increasing its production capacity there. This is just one example of how companies

### Global economy

A global economy is one in which goods, services, people, skills and ideas move freely across geographic borders.

are making strategic decisions today, such as investing significantly in BRIC countries, Africa or other emerging markets, in order to improve their competitive position in what they believe are becoming vital sources of revenue and profitability.

## The march of globalization

**Globalization** is the increasing economic interdependence among countries and their organizations as reflected in the flow of goods and services, financial capital and knowledge across country borders.[38] Globalization is a product of a large number of firms competing against one another in an increasing number of global economies.

In globalized markets and industries, financial capital might be obtained in one national market and used to buy raw materials in another one. Manufacturing equipment bought from a third national market can then be used to produce products that are sold in yet a fourth market. Thus, globalization increases the range of opportunities for companies competing in the current competitive landscape.[39]

For instance, the German-based discount supermarket chain Aldi is growing internationally through replicating its low-cost business model throughout the world. By offering deeply discounted prices on about 1400 popular food items (a typical grocery store has 30000), Aldi buys cheap land mostly on city outskirts, builds cheap warehouses, employs a tiny staff and carries mostly private-label items, displaying them on pallets rather than shelves. Starting its international expansion in 1968 with Austria, the company has been growing on an evolutionary basis. For example, after Austria, most of Aldi's original international investments were in neighbouring Belgium, the Netherlands and Denmark because it was easier for the firm to apply its global practices in the countries that are geographically close to its home base. Because of the success it had in the proximate international markets, Aldi is now pursuing further retailing opportunities in countries such as USA, Australia and Ireland. A new store opens every week in Britain alone[40] and there are around 1000 Aldi stores in 30 US states. Firms experiencing and engaging in globalization to the degree Aldi is, must make culturally sensitive decisions when using the strategic management process. Additionally, highly globalized firms must anticipate ever-increasing complexity in their operations as goods, services and people move freely across geographic borders and throughout different economic markets.

Overall, it is also important for firms to understand that globalization has led to higher levels of performance standards in many competitive dimensions, including those of quality, cost, productivity, product introduction time and operational efficiency. In addition to firms competing in the global economy, these standards affect firms competing on a domestic-only basis. The reason is that customers will purchase from a global competitor rather than a domestic firm when the global company's good or service is superior. Because workers now flow rather freely among global economies, and because employees are a key source of competitive advantage, firms must understand that increasingly, "the best people will come from ... anywhere".[41] Thus, firms must understand that in the competitive landscape of the twenty-first century, only companies capable of meeting, if not exceeding global standards, typically have the capability to earn above-average returns.

Although globalization does offer potential benefits to firms, it is not without risks. However, managers in a given firm or country who decide not to benefit from all that globalization offers, may take the highest risk as the competitors that they are already know, and *de novo* competitors, will seize the opportunity and put the firm at a disadvantage. Research shows that firms in industries with open markets see the opportunities and the threats and are more likely to have both a higher

**Globalization**

Globalization is the increasing economic interdependence among countries and their organizations as reflected in the flow of goods and services, financial capital and knowledge across country borders.

degree and a greater scope of international diversification.[42] Collectively, the risks of participating outside a firm's domestic country in the global economy are labelled a "liability of foreignness".[43]

One risk of entering the global market is the amount of time typically required for firms to learn how to compete in markets that are new to them. A firm's performance can suffer until this knowledge is either developed locally or transferred from the home market to the newly established global location.[44] Additionally, a firm's performance may suffer with substantial amounts of globalization. In this instance, firms may overdiversify internationally beyond their ability to manage these extended operations.[45] The result of over diversification can have strong negative effects on a firm's overall performance.[46]

Thus, entry into international markets, even for firms with substantial experience in the global economy, requires effective use of the strategic management process. It is also important to note that even though global markets are an attractive strategic option for some companies, they are not the only source of strategic competitiveness. In fact, for most companies, even for those capable of competing successfully in global markets, it is critical to remain committed to and strategically competitive in both domestic and international markets by staying attuned to technological opportunities and potential competitive disruptions that result from innovations.[47]

# Technology and technological changes

Technology-related trends and conditions can be placed into two categories: technology diffusion and disruptive technologies, the information age and increasing knowledge intensity. Through these categories, technology is significantly altering the nature of competition and contributing to unstable competitive environments as a result of doing so.

## Technology diffusion and disruptive technologies

The rate of technology diffusion, which is the speed at which new technologies become available and are used, has increased substantially over the last 15 to 20 years. Consider the following rates of technology diffusion:

> It took the telephone 35 years to get into 25 per cent of all homes in the United States. It took TV 26 years. It took radio 22 years. It took PCs 16 years. It took the Internet 7 years.[48]

Perpetual innovation is a term used to describe how rapidly and consistently new information-intensive technologies replace older ones. The shorter product life cycles resulting from these rapid diffusions of new technologies place a competitive premium on being able to quickly introduce new, innovative goods and services into the marketplace.[49]

In fact, when products become somewhat indistinguishable because of the widespread and rapid diffusion of technologies, speed to market with innovative products may be the primary source of competitive advantage (see Chapter 5).[50] Indeed, some argue that increasingly the global economy is driven by or revolves around constant innovations. Not surprisingly, such innovations must be derived from an understanding of global standards and global expectations in terms of product functionality.[51]

Another indicator of rapid technology diffusion is that it now may take only 12 to 18 months for firms to gather information about their competitors' research and development and product decisions.[52] In the global economy, competitors can

**Technology diffusion**

Technology diffusion is the rate at which new technologies become available and are used.

**Perpetual innovation**

Perpetual innovation describes how rapidly and consistently new information-intensive technologies replace older ones.

sometimes imitate or circumvent a firm's successful competitive actions within a few days. In this sense, the rate of technological diffusion has reduced the competitive benefits of patents. Today, patents may be an effective way of protecting proprietary technology in a small number of industries such as pharmaceuticals. Indeed, many firms competing in the electronics industry often do not apply for patents to prevent competitors from gaining access to the technological knowledge included in the patent application.

Disruptive technologies – technologies that destroy the value of an existing technology and create new markets[53] – surface frequently in today's competitive markets. Disruptive technologies such as sequencing technologies in biotech or the battery powered car are examples beyond information technology. Think of the new markets created by the technologies underlying the development of products such as mobile phones, iPods, Wi-Fi and the browser. These types of products are thought by some to represent radical or breakthrough innovations.[54] (We talk more about radical innovations in Chapter 13.) A disruptive or radical technology can create what is essentially a new industry or can harm industry incumbents. Some incumbents, however, are able to adapt based on their superior resources, experience and ability to gain access to the new technology through multiple sources (e.g., alliances, acquisitions and ongoing internal research).[55]

**Disruptive technologies**

Disruptive technologies can destroy the value of an existing technology and create new markets.

## The information age

Dramatic changes in information technology have taken place in recent years. Personal computers, mobile phones, artificial intelligence, virtual reality, massive databases and multiple social networking sites are a few examples of how information is used differently as a result of technological developments. An important outcome of these changes is that the ability to effectively and efficiently access and use information has become an important source of competitive advantage in virtually all industries. Information technology advances have given small firms more flexibility in competing with large firms, if that technology can be used with efficiency.[56]

Both the pace of change in information technology and its diffusion will continue to increase. For instance, over two billion personal computers had been sold around the world by 2008, with developing countries occupying an ever-increasing share of this trend. The declining costs of information technologies and the increased accessibility to them are also evident in the current competitive landscape. The global proliferation of relatively inexpensive computing power, and its linkage on a global scale via computer networks, combine to increase the speed and diffusion of information technologies. Thus, the competitive potential of information technologies is now available to companies of all sizes that are located in countries throughout the world including those in emerging as well as developed economies.

The Internet is another technological innovation contributing to hypercompetition. Available to an increasing number of people throughout the world, the Internet provides an infrastructure that allows the delivery of information to computers in any location. Access to the Internet on smaller devices such as mobile phones is having an ever-growing impact on competition in a number of industries. Overall, however, possible changes to Internet Service Providers' (ISPs) pricing structures could affect the rate of growth of Internet-based applications. In mid-2009, ISPs such as Vodafone, Time Warner Cable and Verizon were "… trying to convince their customers that they should pay for their service based on how much data they download in a month".[57] Users downloading or streamlining high-definition movies, playing video games online and so forth would be affected the most if ISPs were to base their pricing structure around total usage.

## Increasing knowledge intensity

Knowledge (information, intelligence, and expertise) is the basis of technology and its application. In the competitive landscape of the twenty-first century, knowledge is a critical organizational resource and an increasingly valuable source of competitive advantage.[58] Indeed, starting in the 1980s, the basis of competition shifted from hard assets to intangible resources. For example, to gain detailed insight into customer buying behaviour, Avis Europe – the leading car rental provider in Europe, Africa, the Middle East and Asia – implemented a groundbreaking data warehouse which helps the company to more effectively collect the vital data necessary to target specific marketing campaigns and loyalty programmes. This helps the company to increase customer retention, provide insights into individual customer buying patterns and reduce query response times from hours to under a minute. Relationships with customers and suppliers are an example of an intangible resource.

Knowledge is gained through experience, observation and inference and is an intangible resource (we fully describe tangible and intangible resources in Chapter 3). The value of intangible resources, including knowledge, is growing as a proportion of total shareholder value in today's competitive landscape.[59] The probability of achieving strategic competitiveness is enhanced for the firm that realizes its survival depends on the ability to capture intelligence, transform it into usable knowledge, and diffuse it rapidly throughout the company.[60] Therefore, firms must develop (e.g., through training programmes) and acquire (e.g., by hiring educated and experienced employees) knowledge, integrate it into the organization to create capabilities, and then apply it to gain a competitive advantage. In addition, firms must build routines that facilitate the diffusion of local knowledge throughout the organization for use where it has value.[61] Firms are better able to do these things when they have strategic flexibility.

Strategic flexibility is a set of capabilities used to respond to various demands and opportunities existing in a dynamic and uncertain competitive environment (we fully describe tangible and intangible resources in Chapter 3). Thus, strategic flexibility involves coping with uncertainty and its accompanying risks.[62] Firms should try to develop strategic flexibility in all areas of their operations. However, those working within firms to develop strategic flexibility should understand that the task is not an easy one, largely because of inertia that can build up over time. A firm's focus and past core competencies may actually slow change and limit strategic flexibility.[63]

To be strategically flexible on a continuing basis and to gain the competitive benefits, a firm has to develop the capacity to learn. In the words of John Browne, former CEO of British Petroleum: "In order to generate extraordinary value for shareholders, a company has to learn better than its competitors and apply that knowledge throughout its businesses faster and more widely than they do."[64] Continuous learning provides the firm with new and up-to-date sets of skills, which allow it to adapt to its environment as it encounters changes.[65] Firms capable of rapidly and broadly applying what they have learned, exhibit the strategic flexibility and the capacity to change in ways that will increase the probability of successfully dealing with uncertain, hypercompetitive environments.

**Knowledge**

Knowledge (information, intelligence, and expertise) is gained through experience, observation and inference.

**Strategic flexibility**

Strategic flexibility is a set of capabilities used to respond to various demands and opportunities existing in a dynamic and uncertain competitive environment.

## The I/O model of above-average returns

From the 1960s through the 1980s, the external environment was thought to be the primary determinant of strategies that firms selected to be successful.[66] The I/O model of above-average returns explains the external environment's dominant influence on a firm's strategic actions. The model specifies that the industry or segment of an industry in which a company chooses to compete has a stronger influence on performance than do the choices managers make inside their organizations.[67] The firm's performance is believed to be determined primarily by a range of industry properties, including economies of scale, barriers to market entry, diversification, product differentiation and the degree of concentration of firms in the industry.[68] We examine these industry characteristics in Chapter 2.

Grounded in economics, the I/O model has four underlying assumptions. First, the external environment is assumed to impose pressures and constraints that determine the strategies that would result in above-average returns. Second, most firms competing within an industry or within a segment of that industry are assumed to control similar strategically relevant resources and to pursue similar strategies in light of those resources. Third, resources used to implement strategies are assumed to be highly mobile across firms, so any resource differences that might develop between firms will be short-lived. Fourth, organizational decision makers are assumed to be rational and committed to acting in the firm's best interests, as shown by their profit-maximizing behaviours.[69] The I/O model challenges firms to find the most attractive industry in which to compete and shape the structure of the industry to their advantage. Because most firms are assumed to have similar valuable resources that are mobile across companies, their performance generally can be increased only when they operate in the industry with the highest profit potential and learn how to use their resources to implement the strategy required by the industry's structural characteristics.[70]

Firms use an analytical tool called the five forces model of competition to help them find the industry that is the most attractive for them. The model (explained in Chapter 2) encompasses several variables and tries to capture the complexity of competition. The five forces model suggests that an industry's profitability (i.e., its rate of return on invested capital relative to its cost of capital) is a function of interactions among five forces: suppliers, buyers, competitive rivalry among firms currently in the industry, product substitutes and potential entrants to the industry.[71]

Firms use the five forces model to identify the attractiveness of an industry (as measured by its profitability potential) as well as the most advantageous position for the firm to take in that industry, given the industry's structural characteristics.[72] Typically, the model suggests that firms can earn above-average returns by producing either standardized goods or services at costs below those of competitors (a cost leadership strategy) or by producing differentiated goods or services for which customers are willing to pay a price premium (a differentiation strategy). We discuss the cost leadership and differentiation strategies in Chapter 4. The Opening Case has shown the clearly different strategies of Airbus and Boeing. Airbus focus lies on a selected set of airlines flying to selected large hubs, and on providing a highly differentiated interior accommodating the airline's desires to a much greater extent than previously customary in the industry. As we can see in the Strategic Focus on Apple, the company has used a clear differentiation strategy by creating computers and advancing new categories through design and hardware–software complementarity, so that consumers see more value in Apple's products and are willing to spend more. Some competing digital music players were cheaper, had more features and arguably better technical performance yet the perceived value of Apple's successful products including the iPod, iPhone and the iPad exceeds that of other offerings.

As shown in Figure 1.2, the I/O model suggests that above-average returns are earned by firms able to effectively study the external environment as the foundation for identifying an attractive industry, or an attractive part of an industry in which to locate, and then by implementing the strategy that is appropriate in light of the

FIGURE 1.2 The I/O model of above-average returns

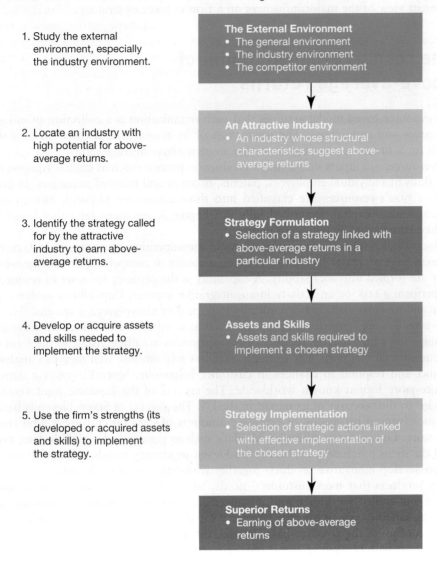

1. Study the external environment, especially the industry environment.

**The External Environment**
- The general environment
- The industry environment
- The competitor environment

2. Locate an industry with high potential for above-average returns.

**An Attractive Industry**
- An industry whose structural characteristics suggest above-average returns

3. Identify the strategy called for by the attractive industry to earn above-average returns.

**Strategy Formulation**
- Selection of a strategy linked with above-average returns in a particular industry

4. Develop or acquire assets and skills needed to implement the strategy.

**Assets and Skills**
- Assets and skills required to implement a chosen strategy

5. Use the firm's strengths (its developed or acquired assets and skills) to implement the strategy.

**Strategy Implementation**
- Selection of strategic actions linked with effective implementation of the chosen strategy

**Superior Returns**
- Earning of above-average returns

characteristics of the chosen industry. Companies that develop or acquire the internal skills needed to implement strategies required by the external environment are likely to succeed, while those that do not are likely to fail. Hence, this model suggests that returns are determined primarily by external characteristics rather than by the firm's unique internal resources and capabilities.

Research findings support the I/O model, in that approximately 20 per cent of a firm's profitability is explained by the industry in which it chooses to compete. However, this research also shows that 36 per cent of the variance in firm profitability is attributed to the firm's characteristics and actions.[73] These findings suggest that the external environment and a firm's resources, capabilities, core competencies and competitive advantages (see Chapter 3) all influence the company's ability to achieve strategic competitiveness and earn above-average returns.

As shown in Figure 1.2, the I/O model considers a firm's strategy to be a set of commitments and actions flowing from the characteristics of the industry in which the firm has decided to compete. The resource-based model, discussed next, takes a different view of the major influences on a firm's choice of strategy.

# The resource-based model of above-average returns

The resource-based model assumes that each organization is a collection of unique resources and capabilities. The *uniqueness* of its resources and capabilities is the basis for a firm's strategy and its ability to earn above-average returns.[74]

**Resources** are inputs into a firm's production process, such as capital equipment, the skills of individual employees, patents, finances and talented managers. In general, a firm's resources are classified into three categories: physical, human and organizational capital. Described fully in Chapter 3, resources are either tangible, or like knowledge, intangible in nature.

Individual resources alone may not yield a competitive advantage.[75] In fact, resources have a greater likelihood of being a source of competitive advantage when they are formed into a capability. A **capability** is the capacity for a set of resources to perform a task or an activity in an integrative manner. Capabilities evolve over time and must be managed dynamically in pursuit of above-average returns.[76] Core competencies are resources and capabilities that serve as a source of competitive advantage for a firm over its rivals. Core competencies are often visible in the form of organizational functions. For example, retailers rely on how well they can analyse, predict and respond to changes in customer behaviour. Seven-Eleven is a convenience store format known worldwide. The success of the Japanese joint venture has led to the takeover of its parent in the US. The success of Seven-Eleven is based on its advanced processing of extensive amounts of data on customers who enter the store. Linking basic demographic data such as gender and age with date, time and the items purchased, enables Seven-Eleven to identify trends and opportunities to co-develop innovative products together with partners or on its own as private-label products that meet customers' needs. Seven-Eleven relies on its highly dedicated and skilled workforce and advanced information technology equipment including satellite systems and the necessary capabilities to seize opportunities.

According to the resource-based model, differences in performances across time occur primarily because of firms' unique resources and capabilities rather than because of the industry's structural characteristics. This model also assumes that firms acquire different resources and develop unique capabilities based on how they combine and use the resources; that resources and certainly capabilities are not highly mobile across firms; and that the differences in resources and capabilities are the basis of competitive advantage.[77] Through continued use, capabilities become stronger and more difficult for competitors to understand and imitate. As a source of competitive advantage, a capability "should be neither so simple that it is highly imitable, nor so complex that it defies internal steering and control".[78]

The resource-based model of above-average returns is shown in Figure 1.3. This model suggests that the strategy the firm chooses should allow it to use its competitive advantages in an attractive industry (the I/O model is used to identify an attractive industry).

Not all of a firm's resources and capabilities have the potential to be the foundation for a competitive advantage. This potential is realized when resources and capabilities are valuable, rare, costly to imitate and nonsubstitutable.[79] Resources are *valuable* when they allow a firm to take advantage of opportunities or neutralize threats in its external environment. They are *rare* when possessed by few, if any,

**Resources**

Resources are inputs into a firm's production process, such as capital equipment, the skills of individual employees, patents, finances, and talented managers.

**Capability**

A capability is the capacity for a set of resources to perform a task or an activity in an integrative manner.

**Core competencies**

Core competencies are capabilities that serve as a source of competitive advantage for a firm over its rivals.

**FIGURE 1.3** The resource-based model of above-average returns

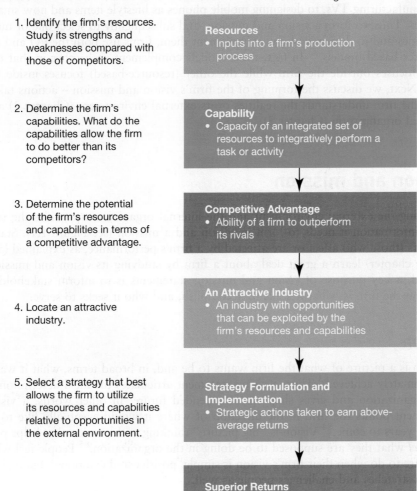

1. Identify the firm's resources. Study its strengths and weaknesses compared with those of competitors.

**Resources**
- Inputs into a firm's production process

2. Determine the firm's capabilities. What do the capabilities allow the firm to do better than its competitors?

**Capability**
- Capacity of an integrated set of resources to integratively perform a task or activity

3. Determine the potential of the firm's resources and capabilities in terms of a competitive advantage.

**Competitive Advantage**
- Ability of a firm to outperform its rivals

4. Locate an attractive industry.

**An Attractive Industry**
- An industry with opportunities that can be exploited by the firm's resources and capabilities

5. Select a strategy that best allows the firm to utilize its resources and capabilities relative to opportunities in the external environment.

**Strategy Formulation and Implementation**
- Strategic actions taken to earn above-average returns

**Superior Returns**
- Earning of above-average returns

current and potential competitors. Resources are *costly to imitate* when other firms either cannot obtain them or are at a cost disadvantage in obtaining them compared with the firm that already possesses them. And they are *nonsubstitutable* when they have no structural equivalents. Many resources can either be imitated or substituted over time. Therefore, it is difficult to achieve and sustain a competitive advantage based on resources alone.[80] When these four criteria are met, however, resources and capabilities become core competencies.

As noted previously, research shows that both the industry environment and a firm's internal assets affect that firm's performance over time.[81] How a firm formulates and implements its strategy depends also on its founding condition as well as on strategic leadership. The founding conditions can imprint elements of the vision, mission and ethical standards of firms and this can have long term significance for a firm. Consider how after more than one hundred years, the logo mark of General Electric (GE) is still reminiscent of the light bulb even though today GE stands for many other more profitable businesses. Founded by the inventor of the light bulb, it is still part of the company's identity. Strategic leadership can change organizational identity. Nokia is a good example of a company that shifted from producing pulp, to manufacturing TVs, to designing mobile phones as lifestyle items and now smart-phones. Thus, to form a vision and mission, and subsequently to select one or more strategies and to determine how to implement them, firms use both the I/O and the resource-based models.[82] In fact, these models complement each other in that one (I/O) focuses outside the firm while the other (resource-based) focuses inside the firm. Next, we discuss the forming of the firm's vision and mission – actions taken after the firm understands the realities of its external environment (Chapter 2) and internal organization (Chapter 3).

## Vision and mission

Studying the external environment and the internal organization provides the firm with information it needs to form its vision and a mission (see Figure 1.1). Stake-holders (those who affect or are affected by a firm's performance, as explained later in the chapter) learn a great deal about a firm by studying its vision and mission. Indeed, a key purpose of vision and mission statements is to inform stakeholders of what the firm is, what it seeks to accomplish, and who it seeks to serve.

### Vision

Vision is a picture of what the firm wants to be and, in broad terms, what it wants to ultimately achieve.[83] Thus, a vision statement articulates the ideal description of an organization and gives shape to its intended future. In other words, a vision statement points the firm in the direction of where it would eventually like to be in the years to come.[84] Vision is "big picture" thinking with passion that helps people *feel* what they are supposed to be doing in the organization.[85] People feel what they are to do when their firm's vision is simple, positive and emotional, but a good vision stretches and challenges people as well.

It is also important to note that vision statements reflect a firm's values and as-pirations and are intended to capture the heart and mind of each employee and, hopefully, many of its other stakeholders. A firm's vision tends to be enduring while its mission can change in light of changing environmental conditions. A vision state-ment tends to be relatively short and concise, making it easily remembered. Exam-ples of vision statements include the following:

> Our vision is to create a better everyday life for many people. (IKEA)

> Our vision is to be the world's best quick service restaurant. (McDonald's)

As a firm's most important and prominent strategic leader, the CEO is responsi-ble for working with others to form the firm's vision. Experience shows that the most effective vision statement results when the CEO involves a host of people (e.g., other top-level managers, employees working in different parts of the organi-zation, suppliers and customers) to develop it. In addition, to help the firm reach its desired future state, a vision statement should be clearly tied to the conditions in the firm's external environment and internal organization. Moreover, the decisions and actions of those involved with developing the vision, especially the CEO and the other top-level managers, must be consistent with that vision. At IKEA, for exam-ple, a failure to understand the common elements of everyday life across country borders would undermine IKEA's ability to maintain a low cost structure while im-proving lives through design, manufacturing and distribution internationally.

**Vision**

Vision is a picture of what the firm wants to be and, in broad terms, what it wants to ultimately achieve.

## Mission

The vision is the foundation for the firm's mission. A mission specifies the business or businesses in which the firm intends to compete and the customers it intends to serve.[86] The firm's mission is more concrete than its vision. However, like the vision, a mission should establish a firm's individuality and should be inspiring and relevant to all stakeholders.[87] Together, vision and mission provide the foundation the firm needs to choose and implement one or more strategies. The probability of forming an effective mission increases when employees have a strong sense of the ethical standards that will guide their behaviours as they work to help the firm reach its vision.[88] Thus, business ethics are a vital part of the firm's discussions to decide what it wants to become (its vision) as well as who it intends to serve and how it desires to serve those individuals and groups (its mission).[89]

Even though the final responsibility for forming the firm's mission rests with the CEO, the CEO and other top-level managers tend to involve a larger number of people in forming the mission. The main reason is that mission deals more directly with product markets and customers, and middle- and first-level managers and other employees have more direct contact with customers and the markets in which they are served. Examples of mission statements include the following:

> Carrefour is totally focused on meeting the expectations of its customers. Our mission is to be the benchmark in modern retailing in each of our markets. As a global retailer, Carrefour is committed to enabling as many people as possible to purchase consumer goods, in accordance with the principles of fair trade and sustainable development. (Carrefour)

> Be the best employer for our people in each community around the world and deliver operational excellence to our customers in each of our restaurants. (McDonald's)

Notice how the McDonald's mission statement flows from its vision of being the world's best quick-service restaurant. Carrefour's mission statement describes the business area (retail) in which the firm intends to compete and specifies ethical standards.

Some believe that vision statements and mission statements fail to create value for the firms forming them. Speaking about vision statements for example, one person observed that "Most vision statements are either too vague, too broad in scope, or riddled with superlatives".[90] If this is the case, we have to wonder why firms such as Carrefour, IKEA, McDonald's and so many others spend time developing a vision statement and a mission statement. As we explain in the following Strategic Focus, vision statements (and mission statements too) that are poorly developed do not provide the direction the firm requires to take appropriate strategic actions. As shown in Figure 1.1 however, the firm's vision and mission are critical aspects of the *strategic inputs* it requires to engage in *strategic actions* as the foundation for achieving strategic competitiveness and earning above-average returns. Thus, as we also discuss in the Strategic Focus, firms must accept the challenge of forming *effective* vision and mission statements.

## Stakeholders

Every organization involves a system of primary stakeholder groups with whom it establishes and manages relationships (see also Chapter 12 on Corporate Governance).[91] Stakeholders are the individuals and groups who can affect the firm's vision and mission, are affected by the strategic outcomes the firm achieves through its operations, and who have enforceable claims on the firm's

**Mission**

A mission specifies the business or businesses in which the firm intends to compete and the customers it intends to serve.

**Stakeholders**

Stakeholders are the individuals and groups who can affect the firm's vision and mission, are affected by the strategic outcomes the firm achieves through its operations, and who have enforceable claims on the firm's performance.

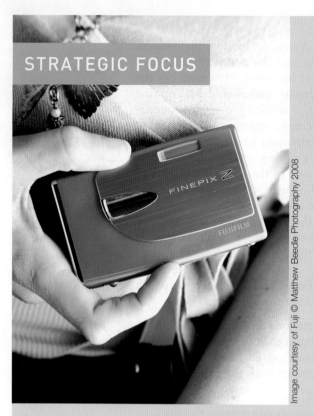

## STRATEGIC FOCUS

Image courtesy of Fuji © Matthew Beedle Photography 2008

# From Fuji Photo Film to Fujifilm: facing a turbulent competitive environment

In 2000, Fujifilm was in crisis. Digital photography was replacing film faster than executives had expected. This rapid shift toward digitalization has strongly reduced demand for films and photographic products. In 2001 Fuji produced a record two hundred million films in the Netherlands alone; this amount reduced by 50 per cent in the five years that followed, as consumers started to switch to digital photography. The CEO of Fujifilm, Komori, realized he needed to change its vision. For many years Fuji had emphasized film and printing of pictures taken—hence the name Fuji Photo Film. With the advent of digital technology, a disruptive technology for Fuji, the company had to reconsider what it wanted to be. Fuji chose to prioritize digital imaging and phase out film. Komori also mapped out a two-year, top-to-bottom reorganization costing nearly €1.57 billion. In short order, Komori cut 5000 jobs and streamlined the company's supply chain, shutting unprofitable film factories and transferring camera production in Japan to China. In doing so, flowing from Fuji's new vision, he formulated a fundamentally different strategy and took the necessary steps to implement by changing the organization and reconfiguring the value chain.

In order to stay competitive in this market Fuji changed its mission and expanded its product portfolio to serve its customers with digital cameras and colour film, as well as photofinishing equipment and services. Flat panel display materials, medical imaging, graphic arts and other businesses constitute its Information Solutions segment, and digital colour copiers and other office products and services comprise the Document Solutions segment. Through development and selective application of its advanced digital, network, image processing and other proprietary technologies, the Fujifilm Group expanded from its original field of silver-halide photographic films into diverse new business fields. Following its new vision, the company phased out the film-centric model and consequently dropped the word "photo" from the company name and changed it from Fuji Photo Film Co into Fujifilm Holdings.

Fujifilm Holdings Corporation is now the world's largest photographic and imaging company. It operates with 223 subsidiary companies for research, manufacture and distribution of products and manufacturing facilities in Asia, Europe and the US. Fujifilm makes a range of digital imaging products, medical imaging products, office automation systems, and industrial films and chemicals. In 2009 they reported an annual revenue of €3477.6 billion. Yet the decline in revenue from photography is ongoing. Enabled by its vision and its redefined mission, Fujifilm continues to seek new opportunities.

In 2008 Fujifilm had diversified out of its traditional base in photographic equipment to build on the established capabilities of its Medical Equipment/Life Sciences Business. Fujifilm wants to apply both its production expertise and nanotechnology techniques, originally developed for film production, to drug making. Before the global financial crisis, medical systems and life science products accounted for about €2.2 billion in revenues, a tenth of the company's total. In a decade, Komori wanted them to triple to more than €7.48 billion, to as much as a quarter of the overall figure. The division could become a key growth engine, offsetting declines in traditional photo film making, where sales have suffered from the double whammy of rising metal prices and a shift to digital photography. And though the company won't be immune to an economic slump, its medical business "should be relatively unaffected" because prices don't fluctuate much.

**Sources:** "Fujifilm, Konica Minolta and Eastman Kodak establish Everplay Standard. New standard encourages industry participation to develop compatible products and services for digital photos and motion images", ANP, February 22, 2006; "Fujifilm's statement regarding its photography business", January 16, 2006; ANP, August 25, 2006; Mansell, P. (2008) "Toyama acquisition shows Fujifilm's Pharma

ambitions", *In-Pharma,* March 25; Hall, K. (2008) "Fujifilm focuses on Pharma", *BusinessWeek,* March 17.

### Questions

**1** What happened to Fuji Photo Film when they first encountered digital photography?

**2** What are the most critical issues for established firms that face disruptive technologies?

**3** How did Fuji Photo Film start to turn around?

**4** How does Fujifilm seek new growth? Discuss.

performance.[92] (We describe stakeholders and their role in governance more fully in Chapter 14.) Claims on a firm's performance are enforced through the stakeholders' ability to withhold participation or contributions essential to the organization's survival, competitiveness and profitability.[93] Stakeholders continue to support an organization when its performance meets or exceeds their expectations.[94] When organizations do not meet stakeholders' expectations they may try to influence them to effectuate change. Also, research suggests that firms that manage stakeholder relationships effectively outperform those that do not. Stakeholder relationships can therefore be managed to be a source of competitive advantage.[95]

Although organizations have dependency relationships with their stakeholders, they are not equally dependent on all stakeholders at all times;[96] as a consequence, not every stakeholder has the same level of influence.[97] The more critical and valued a stakeholder's participation, the greater a firm's dependency on it. Greater dependence, in turn, gives the stakeholder more potential influence over a firm's commitments, decisions and actions. Managers must find ways to either accommodate or insulate the organization from the demands of stakeholders controlling critical resources.[98]

## Classifications of stakeholders

The parties involved with a firm's operations can be separated into three main groups.[99] As shown in Figure 1.4, these groups are the capital market stakeholders (shareholders and the major suppliers of a firm's capital), the product market stakeholders (the firm's primary customers, suppliers, host communities and unions representing the workforce), and the organizational stakeholders (all of a firm's employees, including both non-managerial and managerial personnel). In addition, societal stakeholders such as local or regional government, country level or international institutions as well as activists, can challenge organizations with demand but also foster them through their advocacy.

Each stakeholder group expects those making strategic decisions in a firm to provide the leadership through which its valued objectives will be reached.[100] The objectives of the various stakeholder groups often differ from one another, sometimes placing those involved with a firm's strategic management process in situations where trade-offs have to be made. Obvious stakeholders in firms are the owners. Owners of publicly listed organizations, are shareholders – individuals and groups who have invested capital in a firm in the expectation of earning a positive return on their investments. While the expectation to earn a positive return is common, shareholders can differ in their demands. In family-owned businesses, ownership is often tightly linked to the relationships within

FIGURE 1.4  The three stakeholder groups

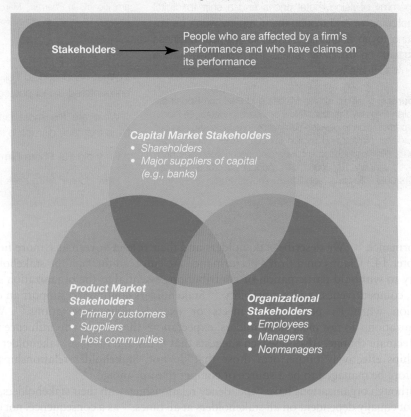

a family. Often, the families are more interested in long-term survival and continued ownership by the family, rather than in short-term results. In larger organizations, ownership tends to become less concentrated in few hands and more distributed amongst many, sometimes anonymous shareholders, sometimes more prominent. Since the financial crisis in 2008/9, in many countries governments have interfered within the financial services sector. The nationalization of Northern Rock in the UK was followed by the Dutch government's taking of major stakes in several Dutch banks. Certainly, the government is a very special shareholder, whose interest is often not the maximization of returns on investment. Consider how difficult outsourcing and offshoring decisions are. Acquisitions abroad were even difficult for the German Volkswagen Group which is partly owned by the state in which its headquarters is located. Sovereign investment funds have become important players, not only as passive shareholders in large Western multinationals, but also as drivers behind societal change through publicly traded organizations. Before the recession Dubai had become a new financial centre, a tourist destination and a hub in the region, partly due to the strong leadership of shareholders related to the government. Other obvious stakeholders include a firm's employees. Dependent on the legislative contexts, the rights of employees can be firmly grounded in laws governing business, rights and responsibilities linked to private property and private enterprise. Strong representation of the works council on the board of Europe's largest corporations is common. How demand for increasing societal influence on markets seems to be gaining ground even in the United States of America is illustrated with the aftermath of the global financial crisis in the following Strategic Focus.

The Strategic Focus below shows that the discussion of stakeholders vis-à-vis shareholders' rights is also alive in countries where free markets are taken for granted.

STRATEGIC FOCUS

# The strip in Manhattan: societal impact – a case for more regulation?

The astonishing performance of Goldman Sachs during the financial crisis (2008–2009) has shown the firm to be extraordinarily resilient to threatening environments. While many of their rivals in investment banking ceased to exist or were acquired, JP Morgan Chase and Goldman Sachs have not only escaped the world's most severe crisis in almost a century: they excelled. Both firms filed record profits in 2009 when other world financial institutions were reeling, political leaders scrambled to provide the largest bail-outs in recent history, and the world economy dramatically deteriorated with rapidly rising unemployment rates.

In his letter to shareholders of Berkshire Hathaway, Inc., Warren Buffet wrote in February 2008: "You may recall a 2003 Silicon Valley bumper sticker that implored, "Please, God, Just One More Bubble". Unfortunately, this wish was promptly granted, as just about all Americans came to believe that house prices would forever rise. That conviction made a borrower's income and cash equity seem unimportant to lenders, who shovelled out money, confident that HPA – house price appreciation – would cure all problems. Today, our country is experiencing widespread pain because of that erroneous belief. As house prices fall, a huge amount of financial folly is being exposed. You only learn who has been swimming naked when the tide goes out – and what we are witnessing at some of our largest financial institutions is an ugly sight" (Buffet, 2008, 2).

Shortly before the housing bubble popped, Goldman Sachs understood that frequently used but often incomprehensible mortgage-backed securities and financial instruments such as collateralized mortgage obligations, may hide enormous destructive risk and that the shrewdest move was to shorten the position. Consequently, Goldman Sachs radically reduced its exposure to high-risk investments, especially the US housing market's asset categories that are now known for their toxicity.

Goldman Sachs sold these assets to eager investors when demand for so-called subprime mortgage-based products was still high, which led to profitable sales. In addition, when Goldman Sachs started to invest, without much visibility, in other assets mainly unrelated to housing, it faced over-supply and was able to purchase at rock bottom prices. Once the bubble had started to deflate, its investment strategy paid off: (1) the firm had sold profitably what was soon to lose value; (2) it was not overexposed to assets with tumbling prices; and (3) the new investments were in high demand and appreciated strongly.

Goldman Sachs had performed an outstanding change of investment strategy, while other banks continued to believe in the fantasy of their own creation. Assessing the macro environment, analysing the most important developments, leveraging internal resources to swiftly develop strategic options, Goldman Sachs selected the best and implement it.

Notwithstanding its extraordinary performance during the crisis, Goldman Sachs gave up its status as investment bank as the crisis unfolded, and became a bank in part due to the severity of the crisis, the market's fears and distrust of investment banks on Wall Street. This change opens possibilities to broaden the product portfolio but it also increases the level of scrutiny by regulatory institutions. In order to avoid accepting more than $10 billion in financial support (and more intense supervision) from the new administration, Goldman Sachs sought to restore trust in its capabilities and secure its financial base.

The firm accepted a large investment by Warren Buffet, one of the world's richest philanthropists. Buffet's reputation in the financial markets and the track record of his company, Berkshire Hathaway, which is similar to an investment fund and picks, holds and sells investments, were useful for Goldman Sachs in a brief period of intense market scepticism. This investment underscored not only Goldman Sachs' standing but also Buffet's reputation as a shrewd investor. Warren Buffet received privileged shares that are served prior to others in case of bankruptcy and earn an annual interest on his investment of 10%. Goldman Sachs received liquidity for continued superior performance and (re)earned what is needed most in banking crises: trust.

In 2010, after the immediate crisis, the financial world (and beyond) started to reflect on what had gone wrong and on the costs. The taxpayers in the US had spent about 1 per cent of gross domestic product ($87 billion) on bail-outs. Beyond the recognition that loose monetary policy, inevitability of a bust following the boom, international developments especially of saving rates played an important role, the search for a (simple) explanation let several views on who brought Wall Street down emerge. The housing price inflation in the US received special attention for which some blamed the greed in general, some blamed Wall Street for bringing down Wall Street, some blamed the government (especially Wall Street experienced members), and others blamed the financial firms that had miraculously managed to stay profitable during the crisis, e.g. Goldman Sachs. Goldman Sachs had repaid its government loan in full, which relieved it from regulations that restricted it from raising compensation and performance-related bonus payments, shortly before announcing its record results. In the eyes of the general public this did not appear a fortuitous coincidence.

During the Goldman Sachs' executives hearings by a Senate subcommittee, the need for regulation and governance in banking and financial services was widely discussed, and Manhattan's financial centre was compared to a casino, similar to those on Las Vegas' Strip.

The practice of (re)selling financial products with very limited economic value to clients was questioned by the Securities and Exchange Commission (SEC), which suggested that selling complex products of little value was akin to defrauding clients. Goldman Sachs was also accused of withholding information from potential investors about a third party, also a client with Goldman Sachs, who was making investment decisions based on the assumption that the same complex products would lose value. Commenting on this practice, Carl Levin, the committee chair said: "They're buying something from you – and you are betting against it. And you want people to trust you.

I wouldn't trust you." In an editorial, the *New York Times* wrote:

> Banks like Goldman turned the financial system into a casino. Like gambling, the transactions mostly just shifted money around. Unlike gambling, they packed an enormous capacity for economic destruction – hobbling banks that made bad bets, freezing credit and economic activity. Society – not the bankers – bore the cost …

David Viniar, Goldman Sachs' chief financial officer, expressed the view that "we share responsibility" for the financial crisis, while the SEC suggests more, basing its accusations on emails, e.g. by Fabrice Tourre, an executive director at Goldman Sachs, London, who wrote in January 2007: "The whole building is about to collapse anytime now … all these complex, highly leveraged, exotic trades … created without necessarily understanding all of the implications of those monstrosities!!!"

The Goldman Sachs hearings triggered much discussion in the media, which reflected the extraordinary financial performance of Goldman Sachs, in stark contrast to the dire straits of the US and world economy between 2007 and 2010. Many seemed surprised to find that financial firms are not always agents of good (e.g. creating an abundant supply of houses without dwellers and shopping malls without shoppers) and that they can cause risk to increase and concentrate (e.g. Lehman Brothers). Operating in a similar way to drug dealers serving addicts, Goldman achieved, as Paul Krugman, the Nobel prize-winning economist summarizes in his *Times* column, record profitability at the expense of taxpayers.

Under intense criticism, Goldman Sachs' executives stood their ground suggesting that buying from suppliers and selling financial products to consenting buyers, often other leading financial institutions, is legal, common and ethical in financial markets.

**Sources:** Adams, R. (2010) "Richard Adams' Blog: Goldman Sachs Senate hearing: As it happened", *The Guardian*, Tuesday April 28, http://www.guardian.co.uk; Bowley, G. (2009) "Two giants emerge from Wall Street ruins", *New York Times*, http://www.nytimes.com, July 16; Buffet, W. E. (2008) "To the shareholders of Berkshire Hathaway, Inc.", 1–22; Editorial (2010) "Wall Street Casino", *New York Times*, April 28, online edition; Shenn, J. and M. J. Moore (2010) "Goldman Sachs executives grilled in Senate Hearing", *Bloomberg Business Week*, April 27, online edition; Krugman, P. (2009) "The joy of Sachs", *New York Times*, July 17, online edition; Sloan, A. (2007) *Fortune*, online; Stein, B. (2007) "The long and short of it at Goldman Sachs",

*New York Times*, http://www.nytimes.com, December 2; Taylor, J. B. (2009) "The financial crisis and the policy responses: An empirical analysis of what went wrong", NBER Working Paper Series, Working paper 14631, http://www.nber.org/papers/w14631.

## Questions

1 Who is to be blamed?

2 Who are the stakeholders in firms in the financial services sector?

3 Are there stakeholders who deserve special protection?

4 "If a financial firm buys a financial product and sells it at the same time it is engaging in risk management." Do you agree? If so, why? If not, why not?

5 Do informed buyers need trust?

6 Can regulation help? If so, how?

In contrast to shareholders, another group of stakeholders – the firm's customers – may have other preferences than investors, e.g., regarding safety standards of products and responsibility and liability issues in case safety standards were not met. This is a fundamental concern raised with Goldman Sachs in the Strategic Focus above, where Goldman Sachs allegedly has acted against the interests of selected clients and favoured others.

In general, customers can have their interests maximized when the quality and reliability of a firm's products are improved, but without, or only limited, price increases. High returns to customers might come at the expense of lower returns negotiated with capital market shareholders or with lower wages for employees. However, good management can help by recognizing that higher productivity provides more value to customers, better places of work to employees and higher returns to shareholders. While this may be hard to achieve, the strategic management process can help to realize such successes as in the case of Apple or Nokia as mentioned above.

Because of potential conflicts, each firm is challenged to manage its stakeholders. First, a firm must carefully identify all the important stakeholders specifically. Second, it must prioritize them, in case it cannot satisfy all of them. Power is the most critical criterion in prioritizing stakeholders. Other criteria might include the urgency of satisfying each particular stakeholder group and the degree of importance of each to the firm.[101]

When earning above-average returns, the firm's challenge of effectively managing stakeholder relationships is lessened substantially. With the capability and flexibility above-average returns provide, a firm can more easily satisfy multiple stakeholders simultaneously. When the firm earns only average returns, it is unable to maximize the interests of all stakeholders. The objective then becomes one of at least minimally satisfying each stakeholder. Trade-off decisions are made in light of how important the support of each stakeholder group is to the firm. For example, environmental groups may be very important to firms in the energy industry but less important to professional service firms.[102] A firm earning below-average returns does not have the capacity to minimally satisfy all stakeholders. The managerial challenge in this case is to make trade-offs that minimize the amount of support lost from stakeholders. Societal values also influence the general weightings allocated among the three stakeholder groups shown in Figure 1.4. Although all three groups are served by firms in the major industrialized nations, the priorities in their service vary because of cultural differences in legal systems. The next section provides additional details about each of the three major stakeholder groups.

## Capital market stakeholders

Shareholders and lenders both expect a firm to preserve and enhance the wealth they have entrusted to it. The returns they expect are commensurate with the degree of risk accepted with those investments (i.e., lower returns are expected with low-risk investments while higher returns are expected with high-risk investments). Dissatisfied lenders may impose stricter covenants on subsequent borrowing of capital. Dissatisfied shareholders may reflect their concerns through several means, including selling their stock.

When a firm is aware of potential or actual dissatisfactions among capital market stakeholders, it may respond to their concerns. The firm's response to stakeholders who are dissatisfied is affected by the nature of its dependency relationship with them (which, as noted earlier, is also influenced by a society's values). The greater and more significant the dependency relationship is, the more direct and significant the firm's response becomes. For example, in the Airbus and Boeing Opening Case, both companies face pressures from numerous stakeholders. These include airlines, workers' unions, governments and politicians, regulatory organizations, safety organizations, environmentalist groups and many more. However, the pressures of some stakeholders (like the Federal Aviation Administration) have direct impact on the standards to which airplanes must adhere and thus have a very strong impact on the business. The interests of other stakeholders can have lesser impact, either because of the stakeholder's low power or because of the weak relationship between the stakeholder and the business or lack of attention.

## Product market stakeholders

Some might think that product market stakeholders (customers, suppliers, host communities and unions) share few common interests. However, all four groups can benefit as firms engage in competitive battles. For example, depending on product and industry characteristics, marketplace competition may result in higher quality and/or lower product prices being charged to a firm's customers, and higher prices being paid to its suppliers (the firm might be willing to pay higher supplier prices to ensure delivery of the types of goods and services that are linked with its competitive success).[103]

Customers, as stakeholders, demand reliable products at the lowest possible prices. Suppliers seek loyal customers who are willing to pay the highest sustainable prices for the goods and services they receive. Host communities want companies willing to be long-term employers and providers of tax revenue without placing excessive demands on public support services. Union officials are interested in secure jobs, under highly desirable working conditions, for the employees they represent. Thus, product market stakeholders are generally satisfied when a firm's profit margin reflects at least a balance between the returns to capital market stakeholders (i.e., the returns lenders and shareholders will accept and still retain their interests in the firm), and the returns in which they share.

## Organizational stakeholders

Employees – the firm's organizational stakeholders – expect the firm to provide a dynamic, stimulating and rewarding work environment. As employees, we are usually satisfied working for a company that is growing and actively developing our skills, especially those skills required to be effective team members and to meet or exceed global work standards. Workers who learn how to use new knowledge productively are critical to organizational success. In a collective sense, the education and skills of a firm's workforce are competitive weapons affecting strategy implementation and firm performance.[104] As suggested by the following statement, strategic leaders are ultimately responsible for serving the needs of organizational stakeholders on a day-to-day basis: "[T]he job of [strategic] leadership is to fully utilize human potential, to create organizations in which people can grow and learn while still achieving a common objective, to nurture the human spirit."[105] Interestingly, research suggests that outside directors are more likely to propose layoffs compared to inside strategic leaders, while such insiders are likely to use preventative cost-cutting measures and seek to protect incumbent employees.[106]

# Strategic leaders

Strategic leaders are people located in different parts of the firm using the strategic management process to help the firm reach its vision and mission. (For a more detailed discussion, we refer to Chapter 11). Regardless of their location in the firm, successful strategic leaders are decisive, committed to nurturing those around them,[107] and committed to helping the firm create value for all stakeholder groups.[108] In this vein, research evidence suggests that employees who perceive that their CEO emphasizes the need for the firm to operate in ways that are consistent with the values of all stakeholder groups, rather than focusing only on maximizing profits for shareholders, identify that CEO as a visionary leader. In turn, visionary leadership has been found to be related to extra effort by employees, with employee effort leading to enhanced firm performance. These intriguing findings suggest that decision-making values "... that are oriented toward a range of stakeholders may yield more favourable outcomes for leaders than values that focus primarily on economic-based issues".[109] These findings are consistent with the argument that "To regain society's trust ... business leaders must embrace a way of looking at their role that goes beyond their responsibility to the shareholder, to include a civic and personal commitment to their duty as institutional custodians."[110]

When identifying strategic leaders, most of us tend to think of chief executive officers and other top-level managers. Clearly, these people are strategic leaders. And, in the final analysis, CEOs are responsible for making certain their firm effectively uses the strategic management process. Indeed, the pressure on CEOs to manage strategically is stronger than ever.[111] However, many other people in today's organizations help choose a firm's strategy and then determine the actions for successfully implementing them.[112] The main reason is that the realities of twenty-first-century competition that we discussed earlier in this chapter (e.g., the global economy, globalization, rapid technological change, and the increasing importance of knowledge and people as sources of competitive advantage) are creating a need for those "closest to the action" to be the ones making decisions and determining the actions to be taken.[113] In fact, the most effective CEOs and top-level managers understand how to delegate strategic responsibilities to people throughout the firm who influence the use of organizational resources.[114]

Organizational culture also affects strategic leaders and their work. In turn, strategic leaders' decisions and actions shape a firm's culture. Organizational culture refers to the complex set of ideologies, symbols and core values that are shared throughout the firm and that influence how the firm conducts business. It is the social energy that drives – or fails to drive – the organization.[115] For example, Virgin Atlantic is known for having a unique and valuable culture. Part of Richard Branson's network of entrepreneurial ventures linked by the Virgin brand and an irreverent "can do" culture, encourages employees to work hard but also to have fun while doing so. Moreover, Virgin Atlantic's culture entails respect for others – employees and customers alike. The firm also places a premium on customer orientation, as suggested by the many commitments Richard Branson has made. The most successful ventures are those that identify a need in the market, and are often related to providing better value by servicing customer needs.

**Strategic leaders**

Strategic leaders are people located in different parts of the firm using the strategic management process to help the firm reach its vision and mission.

**Organizational culture**

Organizational culture refers to the complex set of ideologies, symbols and core values that are shared throughout the firm and that influence how the firm conducts business.

Some organizational cultures are a source of disadvantage. It is important for strategic leaders to understand, however, that whether the firm's culture is functional or dysfunctional, their work takes place within the context of that culture. The relationship between organizational culture and strategic leaders' work is reciprocal in that the culture shapes how they work while their work helps shape an ever-evolving organizational culture.

## The work of effective strategic leaders

Perhaps not surprisingly, hard work, thorough analyses, a willingness to be brutally honest, a penchant for wanting the firm and its people to accomplish more and tenacity, are prerequisites to an individual's success as a strategic leader.[116] In addition, strategic leaders must be able to "think seriously and deeply … about the purposes of the organizations they head or functions they perform, about the strategies, tactics, technologies, systems and people necessary to attain these purposes, and about the important questions that always need to be asked".[117] Effective strategic leaders work to set an ethical tone in their firms. In the Closing Case of this chapter, the rise of the Tata Group with emphasis on Tata Motors is described. The conglomerate is highly diversified because the founder envisioned to provide Indians with what they need, hence seeking to be useful to society in a variety of ways, leading to a wide portfolio of businesses.

Similarly, Carlos Ghosn, Renault-Nissan's CEO suggests, "It is important to balance the growth of the *business* and the effectiveness of *business in society*."[118] Strategic leaders, regardless of their location in the organization, often work long hours; and, their work is filled with ambiguous decision situations.[119] However, the opportunities afforded by this work are appealing and offer exciting chances to dream and to act.[120] The following words, given as advice to the late Time Warner chair and co-CEO, Steven J. Ross, by his father, describe the opportunities in a strategic leader's work:

> There are three categories of people – the person who goes into the office, puts his feet up on his desk, and dreams for 12 hours; the person who arrives at 5 a.m. and works for 16 hours, never once stopping to dream; and the person who puts his feet up, dreams for one hour, then does something about those dreams.[121]

The organizational term used for a dream that challenges and energizes a company is *vision*. Strategic leaders have opportunities to dream and to act, and the most effective ones provide a vision as the foundation for the firm's mission and subsequent choice and use of one or more strategies.

## Predicting outcomes of strategic decisions: profit pools

Strategic leaders attempt to predict the outcomes of their decisions before taking efforts to implement them, which is difficult to do. Many decisions that are a part of the strategic management process are concerned with an uncertain future and the firm's place in that future.[122]

Mapping an industry's profit pool is something strategic leaders can do to anticipate the possible outcomes of different decisions and to focus on growth in profits rather than strictly growth in revenues. A profit pool entails the total profits earned in an industry at all points along the value chain.[123] (We explain the value chain in Chapter 3 and discuss it further in Chapter 4.) Analysing the profit pool in the industry may help a firm see something others are unable to see by helping it understand the primary

**Profit pool**

A profit pool entails the total profits earned in an industry at all points along the value chain.

sources of profits in an industry. There are four steps to identifying profit pools: (1) define the pool's boundaries, (2) estimate the pool's overall size, (3) estimate the size of the value-chain activity in the pool, and (4) reconcile the calculations.[124]

Let's think about how Airbus might map the airplane manufacturing industry's profit pools. First, Airbus would need to define the industry's boundaries and, second, estimate its size. As discussed in the Opening Case, these boundaries would include markets across the globe. As noted, the largest increase in the market size comes from the developing countries. The net result of this is that Airbus is trying to increase its market share by taking share away from its competitor – Boeing, when making aircrafts that appeal to these markets. Armed with information about its industry, Airbus would then be prepared to estimate the amount of profit potential in each part of the value chain (step 3). In the airplane manufacturing industry, R&D, operations management and supply chain management are probably more important sources of potential profits than marketing campaigns and customer service (see Chapter 3). With an understanding of where the greatest amount of profits are likely to be earned, Airbus would then be ready to select the strategy to use to be successful where the largest profit pools are located in the value chain.[125] This brief discussion shows how firms can use the profit pools' tool to identify the strategy to use and the actions to take to implement that strategy. Proper use of this tool can help the firm seeking strategic competitiveness and above-average returns.

## The strategic management process

As suggested by Figure 1.1, the strategic management process is a rational approach firms use to achieve strategic competitiveness and earn above-average returns. Figure 1.1 also features the topics we examine in this book to present the strategic management process to you.

This book is divided into three parts. In Part 1, we describe what firms do to analyse their external environment (Chapter 2) and internal organization (Chapter 3). These analyses are completed to identify marketplace opportunities and threats in the external environment (Chapter 2) and to decide how to use the resources, capabilities, core competencies and competitive advantages in the firm's internal organization to pursue opportunities and overcome threats (Chapter 3). With knowledge about its external environment and internal organization, the firm forms its vision and mission and decides how to integrate external and internal resources (Chapter 4).

The firm's strategic inputs (see Figure 1.1) provide the foundation for choosing one or more strategies and deciding how to implement them. As suggested in Figure 1.1 by the vertical arrow linking the two types of strategic actions, formulation and implementation must be simultaneously integrated if the firm is to successfully use the strategic management process. Integration happens as decision makers think about implementation issues when choosing strategies and as they think about possible changes to the firm's strategies while implementing a currently chosen strategy.

In Part 2, we discuss the different strategies firms may choose to use. First, we examine business-level strategies (Chapter 5). A business-level strategy describes the actions a firm decides to take in order to exploit its competitive advantage over rivals. We note in Chapter 5 that a company competing in a single product market (e.g., a locally owned grocery store operating in only one location) has but one business-level strategy, whereas a diversified firm competing in multiple product markets (e.g., Siemens), forms a business-level strategy for each of its businesses. In Chapter 6,

# KEY DEBATE

© sebastian-julian

# Influence of internal and external factors of strategic management success

Strategic management helps firms to develop and implement strategies successfully. Two key debates emerge from this statement.

Assuming a decisive influence of strategic decision makers, strong agency is characteristic for the field of strategic management. Inherently there may be a strong bias towards agency, which is seen to shape a firm's success. In other words, strategic management matters for a firm's success. While research has found much support for this general view, there is another perspective that has equally been supported. If success were purely based on mechanisms similar to those of natural selection of the fittest firms in a given environment, decision-making and strategies may not matter much. All that mattered would be the environmental context.

This describes the range of positions in the key debate. There is evidence for the environment being key to above-average performance and there is evidence for decision making to be key. This debate on the relative influence of internal and external factors is foundational for strategic management, hence the importance of strengths and weaknesses (internal) and opportunities and threats (external).

## Questions

**1** Agency or context – which matters more?

**2** On what does the answer depend? Under which circumstances does context influence strongly? Under which does agency seem to matter more?

**3** Can you see combinations of environmental circumstances and resources that are more likely to influence success? Try to develop a small map or matrix.

**4** Compare your map or matrix with that of one of the growth matrices by e.g. Ansoff, BCG or McKinsey. Discuss similarities and differences.

The second debate that emerges from the statement "strategic management helps firms to succeed" is related to causal directionality. The purpose of strategic management is to first explain, and then predict success. Yet, often, after success has been achieved, the temptation to label any plausible explanation strategy may be too big to resist. The debate thus is on whether strategy is an ex-post rationalization or the way that leads to success.

## Questions

**1** Science is about explaining and predicting what happens. Can we say the same about strategic management?

**2** Recipe for success or rationalization of outcome – what is needed to establish causality?

**3** What is needed to predict success in the social sciences?

**4** What happens if a strategy is successful? What can happen to the value of this successful strategy over time? Will it continue to be successful?

we describe the actions and reactions that occur among firms while using their strategies in marketplace competitions. As we will see, competitors respond to and try to anticipate each other's actions. The dynamics of competition affect the strategies firms choose to use as well as how they try to implement the chosen strategies.[126]

For the diversified firm, corporate-level strategy (Chapter 7) is concerned with determining the businesses in which the company intends to compete, as well as how to manage its different businesses. Other topics vital to strategy formulation, particularly in the diversified corporation, include acquiring other companies and, as appropriate, restructuring the firm's portfolio of businesses (Chapter 8) and selecting an international strategy (Chapter 9). With cooperative strategies (Chapter 10), firms form a partnership to share their resources and capabilities in order to develop a competitive advantage. Cooperative strategies are becoming increasingly important as firms seek ways to compete in the global economy's array of different markets.[127]

To examine actions taken to implement strategies, we consider several levers of strategy implementation in Part 3. Strategic leadership (Chapter 11) facilitates the development of appropriate strategic actions and determines how to implement them. Strategic leaders can make a major difference how a firm performs. Also corporate governance (Chapter 12) is critical to firms' success and has become an increasingly important part of the strategic management process. It is the set of mechanisms used to manage the relationship between stakeholders and to determine and control the strategic direction and performance of organizations. With demands for improved corporate governance being voiced today by many stakeholders, organizations are challenged to learn how to simultaneously satisfy their stakeholders' different interests.[128] In addition to strategic leadership and corporate governance, we examine how the firm's structure and controls can be properly matched with the firm's strategy (Chapter 13). The match or degree of fit between strategy and structure influences the firm's attempt to earn above-average returns. We discuss separate structures and controls that are required to successfully implement different strategies. Besides adequate structures and controls, firm survival and success depend on a firm's ability to continuously find new opportunities and quickly produce innovations to pursue them. Firms engaging in strategic entrepreneurship (Chapter 14) integrate their actions to find opportunities and to successfully innovate as a primary means of pursuing them. In the end, these levers of strategy implementation may help the firm to realize strategic renewal by revitalizing and transforming their core businesses, and seeking new avenues for growth (Chapter 15). Strategic renewal refers to the choices and actions a firm undertakes to alter its legacy and path dependence in order to maintain a dynamic fit with changing environments over time. This dynamic strategic management process of searching for consistency and fit between analyzing the strategic inputs, formulating and implementing strategic actions, and transforming the firm will help the firm to realize competitive advantages and above-average returns. Increased performance will stimulate the firm to further tighten its strategic fit by strengthening its vision and mission and further improving the consistencies between strategic inputs, strategic actions and firm transformation. On the other hand, when performance decreases over time due to changes in the industry environment or firm's internal resources base, this negative performance feedback loop may be the start of new strategic management cycle for reconsidering the vision and mission of the firm, analyzing changes in the strategic inputs, reformulating and re-implementing the strategic actions, and fundamentally transforming the firm.

Before closing this introductory chapter, it is important to emphasize that primarily because they are related to how a firm interacts with its stakeholders, almost all strategic management process decisions have ethical dimensions.[129] Organizational ethics are revealed by an organization's culture; that is to say, a firm's decisions are a product of the core values that are shared by most or all of a company's managers and employees. Especially in the turbulent and often ambiguous competitive landscape of the twenty-first century, those making decisions that are part of the strategic management process are challenged to recognize that their decisions affect capital market, product market, and organizational stakeholders differently and to evaluate the ethical implications of their decisions on a daily basis.[130] Decision makers failing to recognize these realities accept the risk of putting their firm at a competitive disadvantage when it comes to consistently engaging in ethical business practices.[131]

As you will discover, the strategic management process we examine in this book calls for firms to use disciplined approaches as the foundation for developing one or more competitive advantages. These approaches provide the pathway through which firms will be able to achieve strategic competitiveness and earn above-average returns. Mastery of this strategic management process will effectively serve you, our readers, and the organizations for which you will choose to work.

## CLOSING CASE

# The Nano within Tata Group: Tata Motors' rise and a revolution in the global automotive industry

The launch of the Tata Nano has captured the world's attention. Dismissed by some as a poor man's car and admired by others for this revolutionary step in automotive history, Tata Motors has put another Indian firm at the centre of attention. Yet, Tata Motor's sucess is only a part of a larger group that has become a leading multinational, the Tata Group, based in India.

Tata Group has significant international operations and operates in seven business sectors: communications and information technology, engineering, materials, services, energy, consumer products and chemicals. The total revenue of Tata companies, taken together, was €49.2 billion in 2007–2008, with 61 per cent of this coming from business outside India. Approx 350000 people are employed worldwide. Founded in the 1860s by Jamsetji Tata, the Tata Group is one of India's oldest and largest diversified conglomerates. From its early strength in textiles, the group has become a pioneer of modern industry in India, responsible for the country's first private-sector

steel mill, power utility, luxury hotel chain, international airline and software venture. Traditionally, the bulk of the group's sales lay in heavy industry, raw materials, energy and chemicals. During the 1990s, however, the Tata Group's business grew and changed, concentrating less on heavy industry and more on new technology and services. The group also became more consumer-focused, with brand-driven segments of the business accounting for 48 per cent of profits in 2002–2003, up from 41 per cent 10 years earlier. By the 2000s, the group claimed a major global presence as both a brand name and an owner of other brands.

In recent years, Tata has made several high profile acquisitions abroad. In June 2005, Tata Coffee bought US-based Eight O'Clock Coffee Co. for €173.2 million from Gryphon Investors. In August 2006 Tata Tea bought 30 per cent of US enhanced water firm Energy Brands Inc for €533 million. It sold the stake less than a year later to Coca-Cola for €0.94 billion. In January 2007 Tata Steel acquired Anglo-Dutch steelmaker Corus Group for €10.23 billion, India's largest overseas takeover yet. In March 2007 Tata Power bought stakes in Indonesian PT Bumi Resources Tbk's two coal mines for €1.02 billion.

Among the recent takeovers by Tata Motors is the acquisition of the British luxury icons, Jaguar and Land Rover for $1.8 billion in cash. It signed a deal to buy the commercial vehicle unit of South Korea's Daewoo Group for €80.3 million. Tata Motors is India's largest automobile company, with revenues of €6.9 billion in 2007–08. With over 4 million vehicles being used in India, Tata Motors is the local leader in commercial vehicles and among the top three in passenger vehicles. Tata cars, buses and trucks are being marketed in several countries with high growth rates in parts of Europe, Africa, the Middle East, South Asia, South East Asia and South America. Besides selling abroad, Tata Motors has operations through subsidiaries and associate companies in South Korea, Thailand and Spain.

Tata used acquisitions to enter international markets and provide the businesses with growth, but also to add new products to their portfolio. While the business climate in the early 2000s was encouraging leveraged strategies, the global financial crisis has changed the way firms grow and finance their growth. The downside of all those acquisitions is that Tata has accumulated considerable debt. Several of the acquisitions have required special financing efforts. The acquisitions of Corus and Jaguar Land Rover, for instance, required significant capital infusions from the Tata Group. In May 2009, Tata Steel renegotiated €4.2 billion in acquisition-related debt. Tata Motors executives said in the same month that the company had spent 78.1 billion rupees (€1.3 billion) to fund the acquisition and was now working to reduce its debt.

Sources: Deshpande, R. (2005) "Tata Consultancy Services", Harvard Business School; Pandit, R. V. (2005) "What's next for Tata Group: An Interview with its Chairman", *McKinsey Quarterly*, 4: 61–69; Engardio, P. (2007) "The last Rajah", *BusinessWeek*, August 13; "British union regrets Ford's Jaguar exit, welcomes Tata takeover" (2008) *Economic Times*; "Tata's acquisition of Jaguar and Land Rover: A collector's item or a business deal?" (2008) *Economic Times*; http://www.tata.com, visited on 04-05-2009; Kinetz, E. (2009) "India's Tata Steel downgraded amid burden of foreign acquisitions" http://www.btstrips.com/blog/2009/06/09/indias-tata-steel-downgraded-amid-burden-of-foreign-acquisitions/; Tellis, R. (2009) "Tata Nano: Poor man's car or radical innovation", March 30, http://ssrn.com/abstract=1537473.

*Questions*

1 What are the main differences between the positioning of the Tata Nano and a car of your choice?

2 Describe the competitive landscape of Tata Motors. How does globalization change this landscape?

3 Following an analysis of the industrial organization (I/O) model, how can Tata Motors earn above-average returns?

4 Use the resource-based model to compare Tata Motors' ability to earn above-average returns with a competitor. Which resources explain the Tata Nano's success?

## SUMMARY

- Firms use the strategic management process to achieve strategic competitiveness and earn above-average returns. A firm achieves strategic competitiveness by developing and learning how to implement a value-creating strategy. Above-average returns (in excess of what investors expect to earn from other investments with similar levels of risk) are the foundation a firm needs to simultaneously satisfy all of its stakeholders.

- The fundamental nature of competition is different in the current competitive landscape. As a result, those making strategic decisions must adopt a different mindset, one that allows them to learn how to compete in highly turbulent and chaotic environments that are producing disorder and a great deal of uncertainty. The globalization of industries and their markets and rapid and significant technological changes are the two primary factors contributing to the turbulence of the competitive landscape.

- Firms use two major models to help them form their vision and mission and then choose one or more strategies to pursue strategic competitiveness and above-average returns. The core assumption of the I/O model is that the firm's external environment should have more influence on the choice of strategies than do the firm's internal resources, capabilities and core competencies. Thus, the I/O model is used to understand the effects an industry's characteristics can have on a firm when deciding what strategy or strategies to use to compete against rivals. The logic supporting the I/O model suggests that above-average returns are earned when the firm locates an attractive industry or part of an industry and successfully implements the strategy dictated by its characteristics. The core assumption of the resource-based model is that the firm's unique resources, capabilities and core competencies should have more of an influence on selecting and using strategies than does the firm's external environment. Above-average returns are earned when the firm uses its valuable, rare, costly-to-imitate, and nonsubstitutable resources and capabilities to compete against its rivals in one or more industries. Evidence indicates that both models yield insights that are linked to successfully selecting and using strategies. Thus, firms want to use their unique resources, capabilities and core competencies as the foundation for one or more strategies that will allow them to compete in industries they understand.

- Vision and mission are formed in light of the information and insights gained from studying a firm's internal and external environments. Vision is a picture of what the firm wants to be and, in broad terms, what it wants to ultimately achieve. Flowing from the vision, the mission specifies the business or businesses in which the firm intends to compete and the customers it intends to serve. Vision and mission provide direction to the firm and signal important descriptive information to stakeholders.

- Stakeholders are those who can affect, and are affected by, a firm's strategic outcomes. Because a firm is dependent on the continuing support of stakeholders (shareholders, customers, suppliers, employees, host communities, etc.), they have enforceable claims on the company's performance. When earning above-average returns, a firm has the resources it needs to at minimum simultaneously satisfy the interests of all stakeholders. However, when earning only average returns, the firm must carefully manage its stakeholders in order to retain their support. A firm earning below-average returns must minimize the amount of support it loses from unsatisfied stakeholders.

- Strategic leaders are people located in different parts of the firm using the strategic management process to help the firm reach its vision and mission. In the final analysis however, CEOs are responsible for making certain that their firms properly use the strategic management process. Grounding the strategic management process in ethical intentions and behaviours increases its effectiveness. The strategic leader's work demands decision trade-offs, often among attractive alternatives. It is important for all strategic leaders and especially the CEO and other members of the top-management team, to (1) work hard, (2) thoroughly analyse situations facing the firm, (3) be brutally and consistently honest, and (4) ask the right questions of the right people at the right time.

- Strategic leaders predict the potential outcomes of their strategic decisions. To do this, they first calculate profit pools in their industry that are linked to value chain activities. Predicting the potential outcomes of their strategic decisions reduces the likelihood of the firm formulating and implementing ineffective strategies.

## REVIEW QUESTIONS

1 What are strategic competitiveness, strategy, competitive advantage, above-average returns and the strategic management process?

2 What are the characteristics of the current competitive landscape? What two factors are the primary drivers of this landscape?

3 According to the I/O model, what should a firm do to earn above-average returns?

4 What does the resource-based model suggest a firm should do to earn above-average returns?

5 What are vision and mission? What is their value for the strategic management process?

6 What are stakeholders? How do the three primary stakeholder groups influence organizations?

7 How would you describe the work of strategic leaders?

8 What are the elements of the strategic management process? How are they interrelated?

## DISCUSSION QUESTIONS

1 The strategic management process is a sequence of steps. In times of increasing competition, speed of change and pressures to perform beyond expectations, time is a scarce resource. Where do you see temptations to shorten, postpone or skip steps all together? What are the consequences for firms?

2 Compare specific characteristics of the competitive landscape in Africa, the Middle East and new member states of the EU with the situation in your country. Identify primary drivers and discuss the differences and their consequences for managing strategically.

3 Firms' influence in changing the structure of competition is limited. A classic example is the success of the OPEC countries in the oil industry in the 1970s. Where do you see opportunities for a firm of your choice to promote changes in the oil industry today?

4 Compare the resource-based model's suggestions to earn above-average returns with what a firm could do that is severely resource constrained.

5 What are possible risks related to vision and missions? How can firms mitigate these risks?

6 Among the stakeholders of firms, advocacy or pressure groups have a special role. Discuss how

strategic leaders in the pharmaceutical industry should face the challenge of radical groups opposing all kinds of experiments using animals.

7  Some suggest that strategic leaders need to develop strategies to win in the marketplace and strategies to ensure political support. Should they develop two different kinds of strategies or one approach? How would you describe this challenge for strategic leaders?

## FURTHER READING

There are two big picture readings that illustrate in a fascinating way what is at the core of strategic management and competitiveness, i.e., winning and risk.

Malcolm Gladwell's *Outliers* (2009; Penguin) provides fascinating stories that put extraordinary success in context. Explaining how the Beatles or Bill Gates and many other exceptional successes came about, Gladwell illustrates how outliers cannot be understood without proper understanding of the context and capabilities.

Nassim Taleb's *Black Swan* (2007; Allen Lane) has become a must-read for people interested in the financial crisis but more importantly it has lessons to be learned for those involved in strategic management. Asking to prepare for the unlikely events that have large impacts, Taleb pinpoints a dilemma that managers are facing. Preparing for cataclysmic but highly unlikely events is hard to justify before they happen – after they have happened it might be too late.

For a discussion on existing and new perspectives and paradigms in strategic management, we refer to Henk Volberda and Tom Elfring's book on *Rethinking Strategy* (2001; Sage) and Henry Mintzberg, Joe Lampel and Bruce Ahlstrand's *Strategy Safari: A guided tour through the wilds of strategic management* (1998; Free Press).

## EXPERIENTIAL EXERCISES

### Exercise 1: Business and blogs

One element of industry structure analysis is the leverage that buyers can exert on firms. Is technology changing the balance of power between customers and companies? If so, how should business respond?

Blogs offer a mechanism for consumers to share their experiences – good or bad – regarding different companies. Bloggers first emerged in the late 1990s, and today the Technorati search engine currently monitors roughly 100 million blogs. With the wealth of this "citizen media" available, what are the implications for consumer power? One of the most famous cases of a blogger drawing attention to a company was Jeff Jarvis of the website http://www.buzzmachine.com. Jarvis, who writes on media topics, was having problems with his Dell computer, and shared his experiences on the Web. Literally thousands of other people recounted similar experiences, and the phenomena became known as "Dell hell". Eventually, Dell created its own corporate blog in an effort to deflect this wave of consumer criticism. What are the implications of the rapid growth in blogs? Work in a group on the following exercise.

#### Part One

Visit a corporate blog. Only a small percentage of large firms maintain a blog presence on the Internet. *Hint:* Multiple wikis online provide lists of such companies. A Web search using the term *fortune global 500 blogs* will turn up several options. Review the content of the firm's blog. Was it updated regularly or not? Multiple contributors or just one? What was the writing style? Did it read like a marketing brochure, or something more informal? Did the blog allow viewer comments, or post replies to consumer questions?

#### Part Two

Based on the information you collected in the blog review, answer the following questions:

- Have you ever used blogs to help make decisions about something that you are considering purchasing? If so, how did the blog material affect your decision? What factors would make you more (or less) likely to rely on a blog in making your decision?

- How did the content of the corporate blog affect your perception of that company and its good and services? Did it make you more or less likely to view the company favourably, or have no effect at all?

- Why do so few large companies maintain blogs?

### Exercise 2: Creating a shared vision

Drawing on an analysis of internal and external constraints, firms create a mission and vision as a cornerstone of their strategy. This exercise will look at some of the challenges associated with creating a shared direction for the firm.

### Part One

The instructor will divide the class into a set of small teams. Half of the teams will be given an "A" designation, and the other half assigned a "B". Each individual team will need to plan a time outside class to complete Part 2; the exercise should take about half an hour.

Teams given the A designation will meet in a face-to-face setting. Each team member will need paper and a pen or pencil. Your meeting location should be free from distraction. The location should have enough space so that no person can see another's notepad.

Teams given the B designation will meet electronically. You may choose to meet through text messaging or instant messaging (IM). Be sure to confirm everyone's contact information and meeting time beforehand.

### Part Two

Each team member prepares a drawing of a real structure. It can be a famous building, a monument, museum, or even your bedroom. Do not tell other team members what you have drawn.

## VIDEO CASE

### Honda output hit by China strikes
www.cengage.co.uk/volberda/students/video_cases

China has come to be widely regarded as the world's shop floor. Millions of migrant workers have for decades provided labour for factories in the coastal areas, where they worked hard for low wages and often under conditions that are not acceptable when compared to international standards. In summer 2010 strikes erupted after several suicides at Foxconn, an electronics supplier to Apple and many other leading firms. Successful Japanese car manufacturers, such as Honda became targets of unprecedented strikes in China.

This news clip reports on the situation on the ground. Before you watch the video consider the following concepts from the text, search online to understand what the relative labour cost difference between China and your country is and be prepared to address the following questions:

### Concepts

- Competitive advantage
- Above-average returns
- Global economy
- Resources

Randomly select one team member. The goal is for everyone else to prepare a drawing as similar to the selected team member as possible. That person is not allowed to show his or her drawing to the rest of the team. The rest of the group can ask questions about the drawing, but only ones that can be answered "yes" or "no".

After ten minutes, have everyone compare their drawings. If you are meeting electronically, describe your drawings, and save them for the next time your team meets face to face.

Next, select a second team member and repeat this process again.

### Part Three

In class, discuss the following questions:

- How easy (or hard) was it for you to work out the "vision" of your team members?
- Did you learn anything in the first iteration that made the second drawing more successful?
- What similarities might you find between this exercise and the challenge of sharing a vision among company employees?
- How did the communication structure affect your process and outcomes?

- Stakeholders
- Vision and mission
- Organizational culture
- Profit pool

### Questions

1   How does the low cost of labour in China manifest itself in your everyday life?

2   Most leading automobile manufacturers produce cars in China. How do low labour costs in China influence the competitiveness of Honda? How do low labour costs in China influence the relative competitiveness of automobile firms?

3   What is the difference, or is there a difference, between a company's objectives and those of its employees?

4   Which are the stakeholder groups that are most affected by the strikes (and rising wages) in China?

5   How can unionization change the organizational culture and the relationships between stakeholders?

6   Which context factors need to taken into account when Japanese firms, or other foreign firms, operate in China and face public criticism?

## NOTES

1. J. McGregor, 2009, "Smart management for tough times", *BusinessWeek*, http://www.businessweek.com, March 12.
2. D. Ravasi and M. Schultz, 2006, "Responding to organizational identity threats: Exploring the role of organizational culture", *Academy of Management*, 49(3): 1–30.
3. H. R. Greve, 2009, "Bigger and safer: The diffusion of competitive advantage", *Strategic Management Journal*, 30: 1–23; D. G. Sirmon, M. A. Hitt and R. D. Ireland, 2007, "Managing firm resources in dynamic environments to create value: Looking inside the black box", *Academy of Management Review*, 32: 273–292.
4. R. D. Ireland and J. W. Webb, 2009, "Crossing the great divide of strategic entrepreneurship: Transitioning between exploration and exploitation", *Business Horizons*, 52: 469–479; D. Lei and J. W. Slocum, 2005, "Strategic and organizational requirements for competitive advantage", *Academy of Management Executive*, 19(1): 31–45.
5. J. A. Lamberg, H. Tikkanen, T. Nokelainen and H. Suur-Inkeroinen, 2009, "Competitive dynamics, strategic consistency and organizational survival", *Strategic Management Journal*, 30: 45–60; G. Pacheco-de-Almeida and P. Zemsky, 2007, "The timing of resource development and sustainable competitive advantage", *Management Science*, 53: 651–666.
6. K. D. Miller, 2007, "Risk and rationality in entrepreneurial processes", *Strategic Entrepreneurship Journal*, 1: 57–74.
7. R. M. Stulz, 2009, "6 ways companies mismanage risk", *Harvard Business Review*, 87(3): 86–94.
8. P. Steffens, P. Davidsson and J. Fitzsimmons, 2009, "Performance configurations over time: Implications for growth- and profit-oriented strategies", *Entrepreneurship Theory and Practice*, 33: 125–148.
9. T. Bates, 2005, "Analysis of young, small firms that have closed: Delineating successful from unsuccessful closures", *Journal of Business Venturing*, 20: 343–358.
10. K. D. Miller, F. Fabian and S. J. Lin, 2009, "Strategies for online communities", *Strategic Management Journal*, 30: 305–322; A. M. McGahan and M. E. Porter, 2003, "The emergence and sustainability of abnormal profits", *Strategic Organization*, 1: 79–108.
11. Richard D'Aveni, 2010, *The Commodity Trap*, Boston, MA: Harvard Business School Press.
12. P. Reinmoeller and S. Yonekura, 2007, "Corporate resilience by design: Managing design innovation", *Hitotsubashi Business Review*, Autumn, 6–24.
13. T. R. Crook, D. J. Ketchen, Jr., J. G. Combs and S. Y. Todd, 2008, "Strategic resources and performance: A meta-analysis", *Strategic Management Journal*, 29: 1141–1154; J. T. Mahoney and A. M. McGahan, 2007, "The field of strategic management within the evolving science of strategic organization", *Strategic Organization*, 5: 79–99;

H. W. Volberda and T. Elfring, 2001, *Rethinking Strategy*, London: Sage; H.W. Volberda, 2004, "Crisis in strategy: Fragmentation, integration or synthesis", *European Management Review*, Special Issue: The Millennium Nexus: Strategic Management at the cross-roads, 1(1): 35–42; H. W. Volberda, 2005, "Rethinking the strategy process: A co-evolutionary approach", in: S. W. Floyd, J. Roos, C. D. Jacobs and F. W. Kellermans (eds.), *Innovating Strategy Process*, Oxford: Blackwell, 81–87.
14. J. Barthelemy, 2008, "Opportunism, knowledge and the performance of franchise chains", *Strategic Management Journal*, 29: 1451–1463.
15. J. Li, 2008, "Asymmetric interactions between foreign and domestic banks: Effects on market entry", *Strategic Management Journal*, 29: 873–893.
16. P. Ghemawat and T. Hout, 2008, "Tomorrow's global giants", *Harvard Business Review*, 86(11): 80–88.
17. A. Nair and S. Kotha, 2001, "Does group membership matter? Evidence from the Japanese steel industry", *Strategic Management Journal*, 22: 221–235; A. M. McGahan and M. E. Porter, 1997, "How much does industry matter, really?", *Strategic Management Journal*, 18 (Special Issue): 15–30.
18. T. R. Holcomb, R. M. Holmes, Jr. and B. L. Connelly, 2009, "Making the most of what you have: Managerial ability as a source of resource value creation", *Strategic Management Journal*, 30: 457–485; J. Acedo, C. Barroso and J. L. Galan, 2006, "The resource-based theory: Dissemination and main trends", *Strategic Management Journal,* 27: 621–636.
19. E. Thornton, 2009, "The new rules", *BusinessWeek*, January 19, 30–34; T. Friedman, 2005, *The World Is Flat: A Brief History of the 21st Century*, New York, NY: Farrar, Strauss and Giroux; H. W. Volberda, 1998, *Building the flexible firm: How to remain competitive*, Oxford: Oxford University Press.
20. D. Searcey, 2006, "Beyond cable. Beyond DSL", *Wall Street Journal*, July 24, R9.
21. P. Taylor, 2007, "Tools to bridge the divide: Raketu aims to outperform Skype in Internet telephony while throwing in a range of information and entertainment services", *Financial Times*, May 11, 16.
22. 2009, "Be entertained", http://www.raketu.com, April 22.
23. 2009, "Social networking websites review", http://www.social-networking-websites-review.toptenreivews.com, April 22.
24. D. F. Kuratko and D. B. Audretsch, 2009, "Strategic entrepreneurship: Exploring different perspectives of an emerging concept", *Entrepreneurship Theory and Practice*, 33: 1–17; H. W. Volberda, 1996, "Towards the flexible form: How to remain vital in hypercompetitive environments", *Organization Science*, 7(4): 359–387.

25. J. Hagel, III, J. S. Brown and L. Davison, 2008, "Shaping strategy in a world of constant disruption", *Harvard Business Review*, 86(10): 81–89; G. Probst and S. Raisch, 2005, "Organizational crisis: The logic of failure", *Academy of Management Executive*, 19(1): 90–105.

26. J. W. Selsky, J. Goes and O. N. Babüroglu, 2007, "Contrasting perspectives of strategy making: Applications in "Hyper" environments", *Organization Studies*, 28(1): 71–94; G. McNamara, P. M. Vaaler and C. Devers, 2003, "Same as it ever was: The search for evidence of increasing hypercompetition", *Strategic Management Journal*, 24: 261–278; H. W. Volberda, 2003, "Strategic flexibility: Creating dynamic competitive advantages", Ch. 32 in: D. Faulkner and A. Campbell (eds.), *The Oxford Handbook of Strategy,* Oxford: Oxford University Press, 939–998.

27. A. V. Izosimov, 2008, "Managing hypergrowth", *Harvard Business Review*, 86(4): 121–127.

28. R. A. D'Aveni, 1995, "Coping with hypercompetition: Utilizing the new 7S's framework", *Academy of Management Executive*, 9(3): 45–60.

29. D. J. Bryce and J. H. Dyer, 2007, "Strategies to crack well-guarded markets", *Harvard Business Review* 85(5): 84–92; R. A. D'Aveni, 2004, "Corporate spheres of influence", *MIT Sloan Management Review*, 45(4): 38–46; W. J. Ferrier, 2001, "Navigating the competitive landscape: The drivers and consequences of competitive aggressiveness", *Academy of Management Journal*, 44: 858–877.

30. S. H. Lee and M. Makhija, 2009, "Flexibility in internationalization: Is it valuable during an economic crisis?" *Strategic Management Journal*, 30: 537–555; S. J. Chang and S. Park, 2005, "Types of firms generating network externalities and MNCs' co-location decisions", *Strategic Management Journal*, 26: 595–615.

31. S. E. Feinberg and A. K. Gupta, 2009, "MNC subsidiaries and country risk: Internalization as a safeguard against weak external institutions", *Academy of Management Journal*, 52: 381–399; R. Belderbos and L. Sleuwaegen, 2005, "Competitive drivers and international plant configuration strategies: A product-level test", *Strategic Management Journal*, 26: 577–593.

32. 2005, "Organisation for Economic Cooperation and Development, OECD Statistical Profile of the United States – 2005", http://www.oecd.org; S. Koudsi and L. A. Costa, 1998, "America vs. the new Europe: By the numbers", *Fortune*, December 21, 149–156.

33. D. Wilson, R. Purushothaman, 2003, "Dreaming with BRICs: The path to 2050", Goldman Sachs, Global Economics Paper Number 99, October 1, http://www.gs.com; A. Y. Lewin and C. Peeters, 2006, "Offshoring work: Business hype or the asset of fundamental transformation?", *Long Range Planning*, 39(3): 221–239.

34. Y. Luo, 2007, "From foreign investors to strategic insiders: Shifting parameters, prescriptions and paradigms for MNCs in China", *Journal of World Business*, 42(1): 14–34.

35. M. A. Hitt and X. He, 2008, "Firm strategies in a changing global competitive landscape", *Business Horizons,* 51: 363–369; A. Ratanpal, 2008, "Indian economy and Indian private equity", *Thunderbird International Business Review*, 50: 353–358.

36. Y. Gorodnichenko, J. Svejnar and K. Terrell, 2008, "Globalization and innovation in emerging markets", NBER Working Paper No. w14481. Available at SSRN: http://ssrn.com/abstract=1301929; A. Y. Lewin, S. Massini, and C. Peeters, 2009, "Why companies are offshoring innovation? The emerging global race for talent", *Journal of International Business Studies*, 40(6): 901–925.

37. C. Rauwald, 2009, "Volkswagen to boost production in China", *Wall Street Journal Online*, http://www.wsj.com/, September 14, 14.

38. C. H. Oh, 2009, "The international scale and scope of European multinationals", *European Management Journal*, 27(5): 336–343; G. D. Bruton, G. G. Dess and J. J. Janney, 2007, "Knowledge management in technology-focused firms in emerging economies: Caveats on capabilities, networks and real options", *Asia Pacific Journal of Management*, 24(2): 115–130.

39. A. Ciarione, P. Piselli and G. Trebeschi, 2009, "Emerging markets' spreads and global financial conditions", *Journal of International Financial Markets, Institutions and Money*, 19: 222–239.

40. Harry Wallop, 2008, "Aldi pledges to open new store every week", *Telegraph,* June 30, 15.

41. M. A. Prospero, 2005, "The march of war", *Fast Company,* May: 14.

42. M. F. Wiersema and H. P. Bowen, 2007, "Corporate diversification: The impact of foreign competition, industry globalization and product diversification", *Strategic Management Journal*, 29: 115–132.

43. B. Elango, 2009, "Minimizing effects of 'liability of foreignness': Response strategies of foreign firms in the United States", *Journal of World Business*, 44: 51–62.

44. D. J. McCarthy and S. M. Puffer, 2008, "Interpreting the ethicality of corporate governance decisions in Russia: Utilizing integrative social contracts theory to evaluate the relevance of agency theory norms", *Academy of Management Review*, 33: 11–31.

45. M. A. Hitt, R. E. Hoskisson and H. Kim, 1997, "International diversification: Effects on innovation and firm performance in product-diversified firms", *Academy of Management Journal,* 40: 767–798.

46. Richard D'Aveni, 1995, "Coping with hypercompetition", *The Academy of Management Executive*, Aug, 9(3): 45–60.

47. R. D. Ireland and J. W. Webb, 2007, "Strategic entrepreneurship: Creating competitive advantage through streams of innovation", *Business Horizons,* 50(1): 49–59; G. Hamel, 2001, "Revolution vs. evolution: You need both", *Harvard Business Review*, 79(5): 150–156.

48. K. H. Hammonds, 2001, "What is the state of the new economy?", *Fast Company,* September, 101–104.

49. B. Peters, 2009, "Persistence of innovation: Stylised facts and panel data evidence", *The Journal of Technology Transfer*, 34: 226–243.

50. J. L. Boyd and R. K. F. Bresser, 2008, "Performance implications of delayed competitive responses: Evidence from the US retail industry", *Strategic Management Journal*, 29:

1077–1096; T. Talaulicar, J. Grundeil and A. V. Werder, 2005, "Strategic decision making in startups: The effect of top management team organization and processes on speed and comprehensiveness", *Journal of Business Venturing,* 20: 519–541; J. H. Burgers, F. A. J. van den Bosch and H. W. Volberda, 2008, "Why new business development projects fail: Coping with the differences of technological versus market knowledge", *Long Range Planning,* 41(1): 55–73.

51. J. Kao, 2009, "Tapping the world's innovation hot spots", *Harvard Business Review,* 87(3): 109–117.

52. C. W. L. Hill, 1997, "Establishing a standard: Competitive strategy and technological standards in winner-take-all industries", *Academy of Management Executive,* 11(2): 7–25.

53. J. L. Funk, 2008, "Components, systems and technological discontinuities: Lessons from the IT sector", *Long Range Planning,* 41: 555–573; C. M. Christensen, 1997, *The Innovator's Dilemma,* Boston, MA: Harvard Business School Press.

54. C. M. Christensen, 2006, "The ongoing process of building a theory of disruption", *Journal of Product Innovation Management,* 23(1): 39–55; R. Adner, 2002, "When are technologies disruptive? A demand-based view of the emergence of competition", *Strategic Management Journal,* 23: 667–688; G. Ahuja and C. M. Lampert, 2001, "Entrepreneurship in the large corporation: A longitudinal study of how established firms create breakthrough inventions", *Strategic Management Journal,* 22 (Special Issue): 521–543.

55. C. L. Nichols-Nixon and C. Y. Woo, 2003, "Technology sourcing and output of established firms in a regime of encompassing technological change", *Strategic Management Journal,* 24: 651–666; C. W. L. Hill and F. T. Rothaermel, 2003, "The performance of incumbent firms in the face of radical technological innovation", *Academy of Management Review,* 28: 257–274.

56. K. Celuch, G. B. Murphy and S. K. Callaway, 2007, "More bang for your buck: Small firms and the importance of aligned information technology capabilities and strategic flexibility", *Journal of High Technology Management Research,* 17: 187–197.

57. V. Godinez, 2009, "Broadband ISPs test download caps, face resistance from more data-heavy users", *The Dallas Morning News,* http://www.dallasnews.com, April 26.

58. C. F. Fey and P. Furu, 2008, "Top management incentive compensation and knowledge sharing in multinational corporations", *Strategic Management Journal,* 29: 1301–1323.

59. L. F. Mesquita, J. Anand and T. H. Brush 2008, "Comparing the resource-based and relational views: Knowledge transfer and spillover in vertical alliances", *Strategic Management Journal,* 29: 913–941; K. G. Smith, C. J. Collins and K. D. Clark, 2005, "Existing knowledge, knowledge creation capability and the rate of new product introduction in high-technology firms", *Academy of Management Journal,* 48: 346–357.

60. A. Capaldo, 2007, "Network structure and innovation: The leveraging of a dual network as a distinctive relational capability", *Strategic Management Journal,* 28: 585–608; S. K. Ethirau, P. Kale, M. S. Krishnan and J. V. Singh, 2005, "Where do capabilities come from and how do they matter?", *Strategic Management Journal,* 26: 25–45; H. W. Volberda, N. J. Foss, and M. A. Lyles, 2010, "Absorbing the concept of absorptive capacity: How to realize its potential in the organization field", *Organization Science,* 21(4): 931–951.

61. A. C. Inkpen, 2008, "Knowledge transfer and international joint ventures: The case of NUMMI and General Motors", *Strategic Management Journal,* 29: 447–453; P. L. Robertson and P. R. Patel, 2007, "New wine in old bottles: Technological diffusion in developed economies", *Research Policy,* 36(5): 708–721; K. Asakawa and M. Lehrer, 2003, "Managing local knowledge assets globally: The role of regional innovation relays", *Journal of World Business,* 38: 31–42; F. A. J van den Bosch, H. W. Volberda and M. de Boer, 1999, "Co-evolution of firm absorptive capacity and knowledge environment: Organizational forms and combinative capabilities", *Organization Science,* 10(5): 551–568; R. van Wijk, J. J. P. Jansen and M. A. Lyles, 2008, "Inter- and intra-organizational knowledge transfer: A meta-analytical review and assessment of its antecedents and consequences", *Journal of Management Studies,* 45(4): 830–853; F. A. J. van den Bosch, R. van Wijk and H. W. Volberda, 2003, "Absorptive capacity: Antecedents, models, and outcomes", Ch. 14 in: M. Easterby-Smith and M. A. Lyles, (eds.), *Handbook of Organizational Learning and Knowledge Management,* Oxford: Blackwell, 278–301.

62. R. E. Hoskisson, M. A. Hitt and R. D. Ireland, 2008, *Competing for Advantage,* 2nd edn, Cincinnati: Thomson South-Western; K. R. Harrigan, 2001, "Strategic flexibility in old and new economies", in M. A. Hitt, R. E. Freeman and J. S. Harrison (eds.), *Handbook of Strategic Management,* Oxford, UK: Blackwell Publishers, 97–123; H. W. Volberda, 1996, "Towards the flexible form: How to remain vital in hypercompetitive environments", *Organization Science,* 7(4): 359–387.

63. S. Nadkarni and V. K. Narayanan, 2007, "Strategic schemas, strategic flexibility and firm performance: The moderating role of industry clockspeed", *Strategic Management Journal,* 28: 243–270; H. W. Volberda, 2003, "Strategic flexibility: Creating dynamic competitive advantages", Ch. 32 in: D. Faulkner and A. Campbell (eds.), *The Oxford Handbook of Strategy,* Oxford: Oxford University Press, 939–998.

64. L. Gratton and S. Ghoshal, 2005, "Beyond best practice", *MIT Sloan Management Review,* 46(3): 49–55.

65. A. C. Edmondson, 2008, "The competitive imperative of learning", *Harvard Business Review,* 86(7/8): 60–67; K. Shimizu and M. A. Hitt, 2004, "Strategic flexibility: Organizational preparedness to reverse ineffective strategic decisions", *Academy of Management Executive,* 18(4): 44–59; K. Uhlenbruck, K. E. Meyer and M. A. Hitt, 2003, "Organizational transformation in transition economies: Resource-based and organizational learning perspectives", *Journal of Management Studies,* 40: 257–282.

66. R. E. Hoskisson, M. A. Hitt, W. P. Wan and D. Yiu, 1999, "Swings of a pendulum: Theory and research in strategic management", *Journal of Management,* 25: 417–456.

67. E. H. Bowman and C. E. Helfat, 2001, "Does corporate strategy matter?", *Strategic Management Journal,* 22: 1–23; F. A. J. van den Bosch and A. P. de Man (eds.), *Perspectives on Strategy: Contributions of Michael E. Porter,* Boston: Kluwer Academic.

68. M. A. Delmas and M. W. Toffel, 2008, "Organizational responses to environmental demands: Opening the black box," *Strategic Management Journal,* 29: 1027–1055; J. Shamsie, 2003, "The context of dominance: An industry-driven framework for exploiting reputation", *Strategic Management Journal,* 24: 199–215.

69. J. Galbreath and P. Galvin, 2008, "Firm factors, industry structure and performance variation: New empirical evidence to a classic debate", *Journal of Business Research,* 61: 109–117.

70. M. B. Lieberman and S. Asaba, 2006, "Why do firms imitate each other?", *Academy of Management Journal,* 31: 366–385; L. F. Feldman, C. G. Brush and T. Manolova, 2005, "Co-alignment in the resource-performance relationship: Strategy as mediator", *Journal of Business Venturing,* 20: 359–383.

71. M. E. Porter, 1985, *Competitive Advantage,* New York: Free Press; M. E. Porter, 1980, *Competitive Strategy,* New York: Free Press.

72. J. C. Short, D. J. Ketchen, Jr., T. B. Palmer and G. T. M. Hult, 2007, "Firm, strategic group and industry influences on performance", *Strategic Management Journal,* 28: 147–167.

73. A. M. McGahan, 1999, "Competition, strategy and business performance", *California Management Review,* 41(3): 74–101; A. M. McGahan and M. E. Porter, 1997, "How much does industry matter, really?" , *Strategic Management Journal,* Summer Special Issue, 18: 15–30.

74. S. L. Newbert, 2008, "Value, rareness, competitive advantage and performance: A conceptual-level empirical investigation of the resource-based view of the firm", *Strategic Management Journal,* 29: 745–768; F. J. Acedo, C. Barroso and J. L. Galan, 2006, "The resource-based theory: Dissemination and main trends", *Strategic Management Journal,* 27: 621–636.

75. E. Verwaal, H. Commandeur and W. Verbeke, 2009, "Value creation and value claiming in strategic outsourcing decisions: A resource contingency perspective", *Journal of Management,* 35: 420–444; B. S. Teng and J. L. Cummings, 2002, "Trade-offs in managing resources and capabilities", *Academy of Management Executive,* 16(2): 81–91.

76. S. Kaplan, 2008, "Cognition, capabilities and incentives: Assessing firm response to the fiber-optic revolution", *Academy of Management Journal,* 51: 672–694; S. A. Zahra, H. Sapienza and P. Davidsson, 2006, "Entrepreneurship and dynamic capabilities: A review, model and research agenda", *Journal of Management Studies,* 43(4): 927–955; M. Blyler and R. W. Coff, 2003, "Dynamic capabilities, social capital and rent appropriation: Ties that split pies", *Strategic Management Journal,* 24: 677–686.

77. S. L. Newbert, 2007, "Empirical research on the resource-based view of the firm: An assessment and suggestions for future research", *Strategic Management Journal,* 28: 121–146; P. Bansal, 2005, "Evolving sustainability: A longitudinal study of corporate sustainable development", *Strategic Management Journal,* 26: 197–218.

78. P. J. H. Schoemaker and R. Amit, 1994, "Investment in strategic assets: Industry and firm-level perspectives", in: P. Shrivastava, A. Huff and J. Dutton (eds.), *Advances in Strategic Management,* Greenwich, CT: JAI Press, 3–33.

79. A. A. Lado, N. G. Boyd, P. Wright and M. Kroll, 2006, "Paradox and theorizing within the resource-based view", *Academy of Management Review,* 31: 115–131; D. M. DeCarolis, 2003, "Competencies and imitability in the pharmaceutical industry: An analysis of their relationship with firm performance", *Journal of Management,* 29: 27–50.

80. C. Zott, 2003, "Dynamic capabilities and the emergence of intra-industry differential firm performance: Insights from a simulation study", *Strategic Management Journal,* 24: 97–125.

81. E. Levitas and H. A. Ndofor, 2006, "What to do with the resource-based view: A few suggestions for what ails the RBV that supporters and opponents might accept", *Journal of Management Inquiry,* 15(2): 135–144; G. Hawawini, V. Subramanian and P. Verdin, 2003, "Is performance driven by industry- or firm-specific factors? A new look at the evidence", *Strategic Management Journal,* 24: 1–16.

82. M. Makhija, 2003, "Comparing the resource-based and market-based views of the firm: Empirical evidence from Czech privatization", *Strategic Management Journal,* 24: 433–451; T. J. Douglas and J. A. Ryman, 2003, "Understanding competitive advantage in the general hospital industry: Evaluating strategic competencies", *Strategic Management Journal,* 24: 333–347.

83. R. D. Ireland, R. E. Hoskisson and M. A. Hitt. 2009, *Understanding Business Strategy,* 2nd edn, Cincinnati: South-Western Cengage Learning.

84. S. Ward, 2009, "Vision statement", *About.com,* http://www.sbinfocanada.about.com, April 22; R. Zolli, 2006, "Recognizing tomorrow's hot ideas today", *BusinessWeek,* September 25: 12.

85. P. Kaihla, 2005, "The CEO's secret handbook", *Business 2.0,* July, 69–76.

86. S. Kemp and L. Dwyer, 2003, "Mission statements of international airlines: A content analysis", *Tourism Management,* 24: 635–653; R. D. Ireland and M. A. Hitt, 1992, "Mission statements: Importance, challenge and recommendations for development", *Business Horizons,* 35(3): 34–42; J. S. Sidhu, 2000, *Organization Mission, Business Domain Orientation, and Performance: A Conceptual and Empirical Inquiry,* Rotterdam: Tinbergen Institute Research Series; J. S. Sidhu, H. W. Volberda and H. Commandeur, 2004, "Exploring exploration orientation and its determinants: Some empirical evidence", *Journal of Management Studies,* 41(6): 913–932; J. S. Sidhu, 2004, "Business-domain

definition and performance: An empirical study", *SAM Advanced Management Journal*, 69(4): 40–45.

87. J. I. Siciliano, 2008, "A comparison of CEO and director perceptions of board involvement in strategy", *Nonprofit and Voluntary Sector Quarterly*, 27: 152–162; W. J. Duncan, 1999, *Management: Ideas and Actions*, New York: Oxford University Press, 122–125.

88. J. H. Davis, J. A. Ruhe, M. Lee and U. Rajadhyaksha, 2007, "Mission possible: Do school mission statements work?", *Journal of Business Ethics*, 70: 99–110.

89. L. W. Fry and J. W. Slocum, Jr., 2008, "Maximizing the triple bottom line through spiritual leadership", *Organizational Dynamics*, 37: 86–96; A. J. Ward, M. J. Lankau, A. C. Amason, J. A. Sonnenfeld and B. A. Agle, 2007, "Improving the performance of top management teams", *MIT Sloan Management Review*, 48(3): 85–90.

90. M. Rahman, 2009, "Why strategic vision statements *won't* measure up", *Strategic Direction*, 25: 3–4.

91. K. Basu and G. Palazzo, 2008, "Corporate social responsibility: A process model of sensemaking", *Academy of Management Review*, 33: 122–136.

92. D. A. Bosse, R. A. Phillips and J. S. Harrison, 2009, "Stakeholders, reciprocity and firm performance", *Strategic Management Journal*, 30: 447–456; J. P. Walsh and W. R. Nord, 2005, "Taking stock of stakeholder management", *Academy of Management Review*, 30: 426–438; T. M. Jones and A. C. Wicks, 1999, "Convergent stakeholder theory", *Academy of Management Review*, 24: 206–221.

93. G. Donaldson and J. W. Lorsch, 1983, *Decision Making at the Top: The Shaping of Strategic Direction*, New York: Basic Books, 37–40.

94. S. Sharma and I. Henriques, 2005, "Stakeholder influences on sustainability practices in the Canadian Forest products industry", *Strategic Management Journal*, 26: 159–180.

95. A. Mackey, T. B. Mackey and J. B. Barney, 2007, "Corporate social responsibility and firm performance: Investor preferences and corporate strategies", *Academy of Management Review*, 32: 817–835; A. J. Hillman and G. D. Keim, 2001, "Shareholder value, stakeholder management and social issues: What's the bottom line?", *Strategic Management Journal*, 22: 125–139.

96. G. Van der Laan, H. Van E. and A. Van Witteloostuijn, 2008, "Corporate social and financial performance: An extended stakeholder theory and empirical test with accounting measures", *Journal of Business Ethics*, 79: 299–310; J. M. Stevens, H. K. Steensma, D. A. Harrison and P. L. Cochran, 2005, "Symbolic or substantive document? The influence of ethics codes on financial executives' decisions", *Strategic Management Journal*, 26: 181–195.

97. M. L. Barnett and R. M. Salomon, 2006, "Beyond dichotomy: The curvilinear relationship between social responsibility and financial performance", *Strategic Management Journal*, 27: 1101–1122.

98. T. Kuhn, 2008, "A communicative theory of the firm: Developing an alternative perspective on intra-organizational power and stakeholder relationships", *Organization Studies*, 29: 1227–1254; L. Vilanova, 2007, "Neither shareholder nor stakeholder management: What happens when firms are run for their short-term salient stakeholder?", *European Management Journal*, 25(2): 146–162.

99. J. L. Murrillo-Luna, C. Garces-Ayerbe and P. Rivera-Torres, 2008, "Why do patterns of environmental response differ? A stakeholders' pressure approach", *Strategic Management Journal*, 29: 1225–1240; R. E. Freeman and J. McVea, 2001, "A stakeholder approach to strategic management", in M. A. Hitt, R. E. Freeman and J. S. Harrison (eds.), *Handbook of Strategic Management*, Oxford, UK: Blackwell Publishers, 189–207.

100. R. Boutilier, 2009, *Stakeholder Politics: Social Capital, Sustainable Development and the Corporation*, Sheffield, UK: Greenleaf Publishing; C. Caldwell and R. Karri, 2005, "Organizational governance and ethical systems: A conventional approach to building trust", *Journal of Business Ethics*, 58: 249–267; A. Pugliese, P. Bezemer, A. Zattoni, M. Huse, F. A. J. Van den Bosch and H. W. Volberda, 2009, "Boards of directors' contribution to strategy: A literature review and research agenda", *Corporate Governance*, 17(3): 292–306; P. J. Bezemer, G. F. Maassen, F. A. J. Van den Bosch and H. W. Volberda, 2007, "Investigating the development of the internal and external service tasks of non-executive directors: The case of the Netherlands (1997–2005)", *Corporate Governance*, 15(6): 1119–1129.

101. F. G. A. de Bakker and F. den Hond, 2008, "Introducing the politics of stakeholder influence", *Business and Society*, 47: 8–20; C. Hardy, T. B. Lawrence and D. Grant, 2005, "Discourse and collaboration: The role of conversations and collective identity", *Academy of Management Review*, 30: 58–77.

102. S. Maitlis, 2005, "The social process of organizational sensemaking", *Academy of Management Journal*, 48: 21–49.

103. B. A. Neville and B. Menguc, 2006, "Stakeholder multiplicity: Toward an understanding of the interactions between stakeholders", *Journal of Business Ethics*, 66: 377–391.

104. D. A. Ready, L. A. Hill and J. A. Conger, 2008, "Winning the race for talent in emerging markets", *Harvard Business Review*, 86(11): 62–70; A. M. Grant, J. E. Dutton and B. D. Rosso, 2008, "Giving commitment: Employee support programs and the prosocial sensemaking process", *Academy of Management Journal*, 51: 898–918; T. M. Gardner, 2005, "Interfirm competition for human resources: Evidence from the software industry", *Academy of Management Journal*, 48: 237–256.

105. J. A. Byrne, 2005, "Working for the boss from hell", *Fast Company*, July, 14.

106. N. Abe and S. Shimizutani, 2007, "Employment policy and corporate governance — An empirical comparison of the stakeholder and the profit-maximization model", *Journal of Comparative Economics*, 35: 346–368.

107. J. Welch and S. Welch, 2009, "An employee bill of rights", *BusinessWeek*, March 16, 72.

108. J. P. Jansen, D. Vera and M. Crossan, 2008, "Strategic leadership for exploration and exploitation: The moderating role of environmental dynamism", *The Leadership*

*Quarterly,* 20: 5–18; E. T. Prince, 2005, "The fiscal behaviour of CEOs", *MIT Sloan Management Review,* 46(3): 23–26.

109. M. S. de Luque, N. T. Washburn, D. A. Waldman and R. J. House, 2008, "Unrequited profit: How stakeholder and economic values related to subordinates' perceptions of leadership and firm performance", *Administrative Science Quarterly,* 53: 626–654.

110. R. Khurana and N. Nohria, 2008, "It's time to make management a true profession", *Harvard Business Review,* 86 (10): 70–77.

111. N. Byrnes, 2009, "Executives on a tightrope", *Business-Week,* January 19, 43; D. C. Hambrick, 2007, "Upper echelons theory: An update", *Academy of Management Review,* 32: 334–339.

112. A. Priestland and T. R. Hanig, 2005, "Developing first-level managers", *Harvard Business Review,* 83(6): 113–120.

113. R. T. Pascale and J. Sternin, 2005, "Your company's secret change agent", *Harvard Business Review,* 83(5): 72–81.

114. Y. L. Doz and M. Kosonen, 2007, "The new deal at the top", *Harvard Business Review,* 85(6): 98–104; H. W. Volberda, Ch. Baden-Fuller and F. A. J. Van den Bosch, 2001, "Mastering strategic renewal: Mobilizing renewal journeys in multi-unit firms", *Long Range Planning,* 34(2): 159–178.

115. B. Stevens, 2008, "Corporate ethical codes: Effective instruments for influencing behaviour," *Journal of Business Ethics,* 78: 601–609; D. Lavie, 2006, "The competitive advantage of interconnected firms: An extension of the resource-based view", *Academy of Management Review,* 31: 638–658.

116. H. Ibarra and O. Obodru, 2009, "Women and the vision thing", *Harvard Business Review,* 87(1): 62–70; M. Crossan, D. Vera and L. Nanjad, 2008, "Transcendent leadership: Strategic leadership in dynamic environments", *The Leadership Quarterly,* 19: 569–581.

117. T. Leavitt, 1991, *Thinking about Management,* New York: Free Press, 9.

118. A. Schultz, 2007, "100 Best corporate citizens for 2007", *CRO Magazine,* http://www.thecro.com, June 19; "Nissan Sustainability Report 2005", CEO Statement, http://www.nissan-global.com/EN/COMPANY/CSR/CEO/index.html.

119. C. A. Montgomery, 2008, "Putting leadership back into strategy", *Harvard Business Review,* 86(1): 54–60; D. C. Hambrick, S. Finkelstein and A. C. Mooney, 2005, "Executive job demands: New insights for explaining strategic decisions and leader behaviours", *Academy of Management Review,* 30: 472–491; J. Brett and L. K. Stroh, 2003, "Working 61 plus hours a week: Why do managers do it?", *Journal of Applied Psychology,* 88: 67–78.

120. J. A. Byrne, 2005, "Great work if you can get it", *Fast Company,* April, 14.

121. M. Loeb, 1993, "Steven J. Ross, 1927–1992", *Fortune,* January 25, 4.

122. K. M. Green, J. G. Covin and D. P. Slevin, 2008, "Exploring the relationship between strategic reactiveness and entrepreneurial orientation: The role of structure-style fit", *Journal of Business Venturing,* 23: 356–383; H. W. Volberda and T. Elfring, 2001, *Rethinking Strategy,* London: Sage

123. O. Gadiesh and J. L. Gilbert, 1998, "Profit pools: A fresh look at strategy", *Harvard Business Review,* 76(3): 139–147.

124. O. Gadiesh and J. L. Gilbert, 1998, "How to map your industry's profit pool", *Harvard Business Review,* 76(3): 149–162.

125. C. Zook, 2007, "Finding your next CORE business", *Harvard Business Review,* 85(4): 66–75; M. J. Epstein and R. A. Westbrook, 2001, "Linking actions to profits in strategic decision making", *Sloan Management Review,* 42(3): 39–49.

126. T. Yu, M. Subramaniam and A. A. Cannella, Jr., 2009, "Rivalry deterrence in international markets: Contingencies governing the mutual forbearance hypothesis", *Academy of Management Journal,* 52: 127–147; D. J. Ketchen, C. C. Snow and V. L. Street, 2004, "Improving firm performance by matching strategic decision-making processes to competitive dynamics", *Academy of Management Executive,* 18(4): 29–43.

127. P. Ozcan and K. M. Eisenhardt, 2009, "Origin of alliance portfolios: Entrepreneurs, network strategies and firm performance", *Academy of Management Journal,* 52: 246–279.

128. C. Eesley and M. J. Lenox, 2006, "Firm responses to secondary stakeholder action", *Strategic Management Journal,* 27: 765–781; G. F. Maassen, F. A. J. Van den Bosch and H.W. Volberda, 2004, "The importance of disclosure in corporate governance self-regulation across Europe: A review of the Winter Report and the EU Action Plan", *International Journal of Disclosure and Governance,* 1(2): 146–159.

129. Y. Luo, 2008, "Procedural fairness and interfirm cooperation in strategic alliances", *Strategic Management Journal,* 29: 27–46; S. J. Reynolds, F. C. Schultz and D. R. Hekman, 2006, "Stakeholder theory and managerial decision-making: Constraints and implications of balancing stakeholder interests", *Journal of Business Ethics,* 64: 285–301; L. K. Trevino and G. R. Weaver, 2003, *Managing Ethics in Business Organizations,* Stanford, CA: Stanford University Press.

130. D. Pastoriza, M. A. Arino and J. E. Ricart, 2008, "Ethical managerial behaviour as an antecedent of organizational social capital", *Journal of Business Ethics,* 78: 329–341.

131. B. W. Heineman Jr., 2007, "Avoiding integrity land minds", *Harvard Business Review,* 85(4): 100–108.

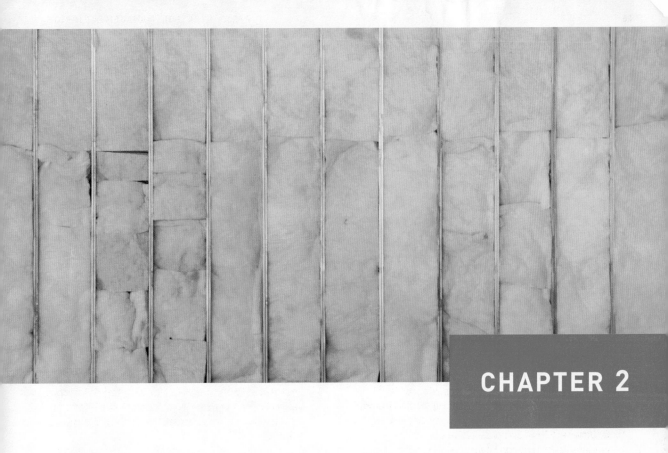

# THE EXTERNAL ENVIRONMENT: OPPORTUNITIES, THREATS, INDUSTRY COMPETITION AND COMPETITOR ANALYSIS

## LEARNING OBJECTIVES

Studying this chapter should provide you with the strategic management knowledge needed to:

1  Explain the importance of analysing and understanding the firm's external environment.
2  Define and describe the general environment and the industry environment.
3  Discuss the four activities of the external environmental analysis process.
4  Name and describe the general environment's seven segments.
5  Identify the five competitive forces and explain how they determine an industry's profit potential.
6  Define strategic groups and describe their influence on the firm.
7  Describe what firms need to know about their competitors and different methods (including ethical standards) used to collect intelligence about them.

## OPENING CASE

© Tor Lindqvist/iStock

# Indian Oil Corporation

Indian Oil Corporation Ltd (Indian Oil) is India's largest state-owned enterprise, with a sales turnover of Rs 2,47,479 core (€48.58 billion) for the year 2007–08. In 2009, Indian Oil ranked 105th on the *Fortune* Global 500 listing, the highest-ranked Indian company in the prestigious listing. It is also the eighteenth largest petroleum company in the world.

As the flagship national oil company in India, Indian Oil provides petroleum products to millions of people every day through a countrywide network of about 35 000 sales points. The Indian Oil Group of companies owns and operates 10 of India's 19 refineries with a combined refining capacity of 60.2 million metric tons per year. They are backed for supplies by 166 bulk storage terminals and depots, 101 aviation fuel stations and 89 Indane (LPGas) bottling plants.

But despite those figures Indian Oil is far from raking in the profits, as it is struggling to save the company from bankruptcy. Indian Oil was running losses of €59.84 million a day, and had been projected to run through its line of credit of €16.85 billion by July 2008. We would expect a company of this size, situated in one of the world's most promising markets in terms of growth, to perform at least on par with the average in one of the world's most profitable industries. What are the factors that hold Indian Oil back?

As usual, there is not just one factor. However, the influence of the government seems important. It has insisted that all the petrol, diesel and cooking oil sold by India Oil should be subsidized. Subsidies are so high that prices are a third cheaper at the pump in India than they are in the US, and the price per gallon in the US is close to what a litre costs in the EU. By not allowing Indian Oil to price according to market standards, the government impedes profit seeking at Indian Oil. Since the crude oil it purchases abroad is more expensive than what it sells for at home, Indian Oil appears to lose money every time it makes a sale. Indian Oil is not alone. The two other state-controlled oil companies, Bharat Petroleum and Hindustan Petroleum are suffering from the same problems.

The dilemma of these Indian firms reflects one of the distortions in the global energy industry today: the widespread influence the state exerts on the industry has many different shades. Regarding reserves, the National Oil Companies (NOC) in oil-producing countries actually own the vast majority of the world's known oil reserves. Regulations regarding refinement and standards of production are numerous. The final products are levied with high taxes in many countries, particularly in Europe. The use of state subsidies, as in India, to soften the blow for consumers, is also known in countries like Venezuela, China and Taiwan. Regulations that are part of the political/legal segment of Indian Oil's general environment affect how Indian Oil conducts its business. Indian Oil must be aware of how the regulations might change in its main market and those it may desire to serve in the future, and it must prepare to deal with these changes.

The high costs of subsidies are burdening the Indian national budget as they do in other emerging markets. The Indian market has suffered not only from the expenses for the subsidies but also from unexpected consequences. Private players like Essar Oil and Reliance Petroleum had begun a major roll-out of filling stations. But as oil prices began to soar, their higher, unsubsidized prices proved uncompetitive with the subsidized prices of such state-owned players as Indian Oil and Bharat. Unable to compete, Reliance Petroleum has shut down all 1400 of its new filling stations, while Essar Oil has shut half its 1250 pumps.

Change, however, can come quickly. When Indonesia's budget problems spiralled, the government drastically reduced its subsidies. Malaysia did the same. Following the financial crisis that put a burden on many governments, in June 2010 the Indian government finally announced the intention to lift subsidies, leaving more room for companies to charge market prices and offering competitive firms the chance to outperform others. Will lifting subsidies favour the established players such as Indian Oil or will smaller players such as Reliance Petroleum seize the opportunity?

**Sources:** Indian Oil (Mauritius) Ltd, October 8, 2007; The Curious Case of India's Oil Policy, Sushma Ramachandran, August 24, 2008; Indian Oil Conferred BML Munjal Award 2009 for Excellence in Learning & Development, February 14, 2009; Manjeet Kripalani, India: Soaked by Oil Subsidies; Its state-controlled companies are losing a lot of money, and private rivals can't compete; Vivek Nair, Oil subsidy revamp on way, Mumbai, Aug. 30; BBC June 28.

*Questions*

1 Focus on the case, specify the general environment's seven segments and describe. Which segment exerts the (least) strongest influence?

2 Discuss how the industry may change after the subsidies are no longer provided.

3 Analyse how the five competitive forces influence the industry's profit potential. Which forces are primarily responsible for the current levels of profitability?

4 Can you define strategic groups and describe their influence on the firm?

5 Advise on competitive intelligence, describe what firms need to know about their competitors and which methods they should employ to collect intelligence about them (and which not).

As described in the Opening Case and suggested by research, the external environment affects a firm's strategic actions.[1] As we explain in this chapter, a firm's external environment creates both opportunities (e.g. automobile manufacturers in India benefited from subsidized prices as the cost of driving remained low and made their products cheaper to operate), and threats (e.g. the subsidies and regulations made it impossible for private oil companies in India to absorb external shocks such as oil price increases). Collectively, opportunities and threats affect a firm's strategic actions.[2]

Regardless of the industry in which they compete, the external environment influences firms as they seek strategic competitiveness and the earning of above-average returns. This chapter focuses on how firms analyse their external environment. The understanding of conditions in its external environment that the firm gains by analysing that environment, is matched with knowledge about its internal environment (discussed in the next chapter) as the foundation for forming the firm's vision, developing its mission, and identifying and implementing strategic actions (see Figure 1.1).

As noted in Chapter 1, the environmental conditions in the current global economy differ from historical conditions. For example, technological changes and the continuing growth of information gathering and processing capabilities, increase the need for firms to develop effective competitive actions on a timely basis.[3] (To put it another way, firms have little time to correct errors when implementing their competitive actions.) The rapid sociological changes occurring in many countries affect labour practices and the nature of products demanded by increasingly diverse consumers. Governmental policies and laws affect where and how firms choose to compete.[4] Cultural factors also play an important role in firms' choice of markets and products. Evidently this is the case in food related product categories, but also decisions related to services are strongly related to culture. Consider the rising importance of Islamic banking practice, even within firms that are more familiar with traditional banking practice in the West. Additionally, changes to nations' financial

**FIGURE 2.1** The external environment

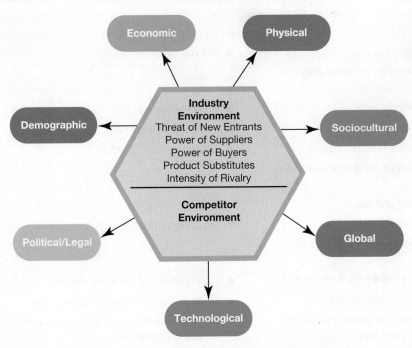

regulatory systems that were being enacted in 2009 and beyond are expected to increase the complexity of organizations' financial transactions.[5]

Viewed in their totality, the conditions we are describing that affect firms today indicate that for most organizations, their external environment is filled with uncertainty.[6] To successfully deal with this uncertainty and to achieve strategic competitiveness and thrive as a result of doing so, firms must be aware of and fully understand the different segments of the external environment.

Firms understand the external environment by acquiring information about competitors, customers and other stakeholders to build their own base of knowledge and capabilities.[7] On the basis of the new information, firms take actions, such as building new capabilities and core competencies, in hopes of buffering themselves from any negative environmental effects and to pursue opportunities as the basis for better serving their stakeholders' needs.[8] A firm's strategic actions are influenced by the conditions in the three parts (the general, industry and competitor) of its external environment (see Figure 2.1).

# The general, industry and competitor environments

The general environment is composed of dimensions in the broader society that influence an industry and the firms within it.[9] We group these dimensions into seven environmental *segments:* demographic, economic, political/legal, sociocultural, technological, physical and global. The global dimension is the most complex. Examples of *elements* analysed in each of these segments are shown in Table 2.1.

Firms cannot directly control the general environment's segments. For example, dairy farmers in Europe face a great deal of financial uncertainty due to the monetary policies of the European Union. Clearly, dairy farmers may experience financial difficulties due to overproduction. The price a farmer receives for one litre of

**General environment**

The general environment is composed of dimensions in the broader society that influence an industry and the firms within it.

**Table 2.1**　The general environment: segments and elements

| Demographic Segment | • Population size<br>• Age structure<br>• Geographic distribution | • Ethnic mix<br>• Income distribution |
|---|---|---|
| Economic Segment | • Inflation rates<br>• Interest rates<br>• Trade deficits or surpluses<br>• Budget deficits or surpluses | • Personal savings rate<br>• Business savings rates<br>• Gross domestic product |
| Political/Legal Segment | • Antitrust laws<br>• Taxation laws<br>• Deregulation philosophies | • Labour training laws<br>• Educational philosophies and policies |
| Sociocultural Segment | • Women in the workforce<br>• Workforce diversity<br>• Attitudes about the quality of work life | • Concerns about the environment<br>• Shifts in work and career preferences<br>• Shifts in preferences regarding product and service characteristics |
| Technological Segment | • Product innovations<br>• Applications of knowledge | • Focus of private and government-supported R&D expenditures<br>• New communication technologies |
| Global Segment | • Important political events<br>• Critical global markets | • Newly industrialized countries<br>• Different cultural and institutional attributes |
| Physical Environment Segment | • Natural resources (finite supply)<br>• Sustainable technologies<br>• Advocacy groups | • Increasing demand (conflicts of interests)<br>• Waste reduction<br>• Environmental risk management |

**Industry environment**

The industry environment is the set of factors that directly influences a firm and its competitive actions and competitive responses: the threat of new entrants, the power of suppliers, the power of buyers, the threat of product substitutes and the intensity of rivalry among competitors.

milk recently dropped from 42 euro-cents to 25 euro-cents in a year. Farmers insist that the European Union should restrict milk production. In setting or not setting production limits, the European Union, as a segment of external environment, influences the profitability of dairy farmers.[10]

The aborted takeover attempt of General Motors' European brands, including Opel in Germany, by Fiat SpA is closely related to the fact that the firms involved could not directly control various parts of their external environment, including the economic and political/legal segments; however, these segments, in particular the negotiations with governments, influenced the actions Fiat took, i.e., its merger with Chrysler.[11] Because firms cannot directly control the segments of their external environment, successful ones learn how to gather the information needed to understand all segments and their implications for selecting and implementing the firm's strategies.

The industry environment is the set of factors that directly influences a firm and its competitive actions and competitive responses:[12] the threat of new entrants, the power of suppliers, the power of buyers, the threat of product substitutes, and the intensity of rivalry among competitors. In total, the interactions among these five factors determine an industry's profit potential. In turn, the industry's profit potential influences the choices each firm makes about its strategic actions. The challenge for a firm is to locate a position within an industry where it can favourably influence the five factors or where it can successfully defend against their influence. While the focus on how to succeed in open markets has received most attention in the last decades, more recently managers and researchers have come to focus more on strategies on how to change the macro context.[13] The need for political strategies[14] to manage their general environment in the realms of what is possible, legal and ethical, has become more important with globalization and the increasing percentage of sales abroad and foreign direct investment. In particular, the challenging contexts of environments with weak institutions such as the rule of law, often to be found in emerging markets, make diplomatic capabilities essential for successfully executing political strategies.[15] The greater a firm's capacity to favourably influence its industry environment, the greater the likelihood will be that the firm will earn above-average returns. Hence, lobbying and cooperation with legislators to influence the development of legal frameworks on unduly strong market power, on intellectual property rights, basic conditions for foreign direct investments or other important issues seem as critical in Beijing as in Brussels.

How companies gather and interpret information about their competitors is called *competitor analysis* or competitive intelligence. Understanding the firm's competitor environment complements the insights provided by studying the general and industry environments.[16] This means, for example, that Philips Electronics wants to learn as much as it can about its major competitors, such as Sony and General Electric Company, and vice versa, while also learning about its general and industry environments.[17]

Analysis of the general environment is focused on environmental trends; analysis of the industry environment is focused on the factors and conditions influencing an industry's profitability potential; and, analysis of competitors is focused on predicting competitors' actions, responses and intentions. In combination, the results of these three analyses influence, and are influenced by, the firm's vision, mission and strategic actions. Although we discuss each analysis separately, performance improves when the firm integrates the insights provided by analyses of the general environment, the industry environment and the competitor environment.

## External environmental analysis

Most firms face external environments that are highly turbulent, complex and global – conditions that make interpreting those environments difficult.[18] To cope with often ambiguous and incomplete environmental data and to increase understanding of the general environment, firms engage in external environmental analysis. This analysis has four parts: scanning, monitoring, forecasting, and assessing (see Table 2.2). Analysing the external environment is a difficult, yet significant, activity.[19]

Identifying opportunities and threats is an important objective of studying the general environment. An opportunity is a condition in the general environment that, if exploited effectively, helps a company achieve strategic competitiveness. For example, in 2001 Albert Heijn, a Dutch retailer, introduced in collaboration with other speciality retailers such as Etos and Gall & Gall a delivery service for consumers, called "Albert". As shopping takes a lot of time, many consumers desire to save time. Additionally, shopping is a tiring activity for older consumers. Albert addresses such needs. By introducing Albert, Albert Heijn anticipated these increasingly important market developments.[20]

**Opportunity**

An opportunity is a condition in the general environment that, if exploited, helps a company achieve strategic competitiveness.

**Table 2.2** Components of the external environment analysis

| | |
|---|---|
| Scanning | • Identifying early signals of environmental changes and trends |
| Monitoring | • Detecting meaning through ongoing observations of environmental changes and trends |
| Forecasting | • Developing projections of anticipated outcomes based on monitored changes and trends |
| Assessing | • Determining the timing and importance of environmental changes and trends for firms' strategies and their management |

**Threat**

A threat is a condition in the general environment that may hinder a company's efforts to achieve strategic competitiveness.

A **threat** is a condition in the general environment that may hinder a company's efforts to achieve strategic competitiveness.[21] For example, a popular example concerns the bookstores in the Netherlands. The dominant bookseller store, De Slegte, with a history of starting out as a second-hand bookstore, did not adapt its strategy to advancements in information technology. More specifically, while leading booksellers like Bol.com and Selexyz embraced e-commerce as part of their distribution channel, De Slegte remained with its "traditional selling" strategy. However, after some time, many second-hand booksellers started to provide their services via the Internet. As a consequence, De Slegte suffered a strong blow to its position in the market.

Firms use several sources to analyse the general environment, including a wide variety of printed materials (such as trade publications, newspapers, business publications, and the results of academic research and public polls), trade shows and suppliers, customers, and employees of public-sector organizations. People in *boundary-spanning* positions can obtain a great deal of this type of information. Salespersons, purchasing managers, public relations directors and customer service representatives, each of whom interacts with external constituents, are examples of boundary-spanning positions.

## Scanning

*Scanning* entails the study of all segments in the general environment. Through scanning, firms identify early signals of potential changes in the general environment and detect changes that are already under way.[22] Scanning often reveals ambiguous, incomplete or unconnected data and information. Thus, environmental scanning is challenging but critically important for firms, especially those competing in highly volatile environments.[23] In addition, scanning activities must be aligned with the organizational context; a scanning system designed for a volatile environment is inappropriate for a firm in a stable environment.[24]

Many firms use specialist software to help them identify events that are taking place in the environment and that are announced in public sources. News event detection, which uses information-based systems to categorize text and reduce the trade-off between an important missed event and false alarm rates, is an example of this type of software.[25] The Internet provides significant opportunities for scanning. Amazon.com, for example, records significant information about individuals visiting its website, particularly if a purchase is made. Amazon then welcomes these customers by name when they visit the website again. The firm sends messages to customers new products similar to those they purchased previously. A number of other companies such as Netflix also collect demographic data about their customers with the interest of identifying their unique preferences (demographics is one of the segments in the general environment). Facebook is expert in analyzing the changing preferences of its 500 million users.

Pricing of airline tickets is strongly dependent on levies and changes to regulations, and airline companies such as KLM and Air France continuously scan the political environment for changes to taxes and legal charges. For example, the eruption of a volcano on Iceland in 2010, threw the European airline industry into crisis. Many planes were grounded, airports were closed and passengers were stranded across Europe. Airlines' support to such passengers differed widely, giving rise to complaints. These complaints convinced regulators that their doubts about practices in the industry were justified and that their case was strong enough to introduce new legislation. While the doubts had been there, they were not open and obvious. Careful scanning may have given early warnings on what followed. Eventually, an EU ruling specified the services that airlines have to provide to stranded passengers included refunds. This has raised the costs for many airlines at the same time.

## Monitoring

When *monitoring*, analysts observe environmental changes to see if an important trend is emerging from among those spotted through scanning.[26] Critical to successful monitoring is the firm's ability to detect meaning in different environmental events and trends. For example, it is expected that the culture of immigrants from Asia and Africa will be more and more integrated in Europe. Monitoring this development is especially important for grocers and food producers. For example, as a result of monitoring, Knorr, a popular food and beverage producer in Europe, introduced world meals such as Mexican Tacos and Turkish Dürüm in order to adapt its business to this development.[27] The world's financial crisis that started in 2008 found companies carefully monitoring the emerging trend of customers deciding to "go back to basics" when purchasing products. A reduction in brand loyalty may be an outcome of this trend. Companies selling carefully-branded products should monitor this trend to determine its meaning – both in the short- and long-term.[28]

Effective monitoring requires the firm to identify important stakeholders as the foundation for serving their unique needs.[29] (Stakeholders' unique needs are described in Chapter 1.) Scanning and monitoring are particularly important when a firm competes in an industry with a high rate of change and technological or legal uncertainty.[30] Scanning and monitoring can provide the firm with information and provide knowledge about markets and about how to successfully commercialize new technologies the firm has developed.[31]

## Forecasting

Scanning and monitoring are concerned with events and trends in the general environment at a point in time. When *forecasting*, analysts develop feasible projections of what might happen, and how quickly, as a result of the changes and trends detected through scanning and monitoring.[32] For example, analysts might forecast the time that will be required for a new technology to reach the marketplace, the length of time before different corporate training procedures are required to deal with anticipated changes in the composition of the workforce, or how much time will elapse before changes in governmental taxation policies affect consumers' purchasing patterns.

© Christine Osborne/Corbis

**STRATEGIC FOCUS**

# Philip Morris International: effects of its external environment

Employing over 75000 people, Philip Morris International (PMI) is the leading international tobacco company in terms of market share. The firm's product line features seven of the world's top 15 brands, including Marlboro, which is the top-selling cigarette brand on a worldwide basis. PMI sells products in over 160 countries, holds about a 16 per cent share of the total international cigarette market outside the United States, and has the largest market share in 11 of the top 30 cigarette markets, excluding the US market. PMI continues to develop its brand portfolio to serve different needs of different customers and as a means of stimulating sales of its products.

As is true for all firms, the strategic actions (see Figure 1.1) PMI is taking today, and will take in the future, are influenced by conditions in its external environment. The challenge for a firm's strategic leaders (including those at PMI) is to understand what the external environment's effects are on the firm today and

to predict (with as high a degree of accuracy as possible) what those effects will be on the firm's strategic actions in the future.

The regulations that are a part of the *political/legal segment* of PMI's general environment (the general environment and all of its segments are discussed in this chapter), affect how PMI conducts its business in its current markets. In general, the regulations regarding the selling of tobacco products are less restrictive in emerging markets compared to the more established markets in industrialized markets. Nonetheless, PMI must be aware of how the regulations might change in the markets it does serve, as well as those it may desire to serve in the future, and must prepare to deal with the conditions created by any changes that take place. Aware of the possible effects of the political/legal environment on its operations in the future, PMI has made the following public pronouncement: "We are proactively working with governments and other stakeholders to advocate for a comprehensive, consistent and cohesive regulatory framework that applies to all tobacco products and is based on the principle of harm reduction." Encouraging all companies competing in the tobacco industry to develop products with the potential to reduce the risk of tobacco-related diseases is part of the harm reduction principle.

PMI predicts cigarette consumption will not continue in its markets. In this respect, PMI anticipates that changes will occur in the *socio-cultural segment* of the general environment and that fewer people will be willing to risk disease by consuming tobacco products. Anticipating this possibility, PMI recently formed a joint venture with Swedish Match AB, the world's largest seller of smokeless tobacco, to market smokeless tobacco worldwide. Leveraging PMI's marketing prowess and its strong global presence across multiple markets, this approach seeks to kindle long-term growth based on less dangerous smokeless tobacco. As a measure of the effects of the *physical environment segment* of the external environment, PMI states that it is strongly committed to the "promotion of sustainable tobacco farming, the efficient use of natural resources, the reduction of waste in (its) manufacturing processes, eliminating child labour and giving back to the communities in which (it) operates".

The *global segment* of the general environment also affects PMI's strategic actions. To pursue what it believes are opportunities to sell additional quantities of its products, PMI recently acquired companies in Colombia, Indonesia and Serbia to establish a stronger foothold in emerging markets. Such countries offer opportunities in demographic and economic development as well as a relatively high socio-cultural acceptance of smoking. The fact that taxes on tobacco products are lower in many emerging markets compared to developed markets, and that the consumption of tobacco products is increasing in these markets, are conditions in the external environment influencing the choices PMI makes as it pursues growth and profitability.

**Sources:** 2009, Altria Group Inc., *Standard & Poor's Stock Report*, http://standardandpoors.com, April 25; 2009, Philip Morris International Home Page, http://www.philipinternational.com, May 15; Byrnes, N. and Balfour, F. "Philip Morris' global race", *BusinessWeek Online*, http://www.businessweek.com, April 23; Helliker, K. (2009) "Smokeless tobacco to get push by venture overseas", *Wall Street Journal Online*,

http://www.wsj.com, February 4; Pressman, A. (2009), "Philip Morris unbound", *BusinessWeek*, May 4, 66; Wilson, D. (2009) "Senate votes to allow FDA to regulate tobacco", *Wall Street Journal Online*, http://www.wsj.com, June 12.

## Questions

**1** What are the main factors in PMI's general environment that influence its performance?

**2** Scanning, monitoring and forecasting these factors how do you assess PMI's future?

**3** To what extend is PMI able to exert influence on its environment?

**4** How can PMI's strategy be summarized?

**5** Discuss other industries in which firms have followed similar approaches.

Forecasting events and outcomes accurately is challenging. The current trend for firms to outsource call centre work and logistics activities to specialist companies appeared to accelerate as a result of the recent global crisis. Companies dependent on understanding changes in consumer behaviour, such as Nokia, are forecasting trends in fields such as digital entertainment. Conducting careful analysis, Nokia expects that entertainment will be more "collaborative, democratic, emotional and customized".[33] Building on such forecasts Nokia is developing hardware and software solutions to enable individual users to connect in ways they prefer.

## Assessing

The objective of *assessing* is to determine the timing and significance of the effects of environmental changes and trends that have been identified.[34] Through scanning, monitoring, and forecasting, analysts are able to understand the general environment. Going a step further, the intent of assessment is to specify the implications of that understanding. Without assessment, the firm is left with data that may be interesting but are of unknown competitive relevance. Even if formal assessment is inadequate, the appropriate interpretation of that information is important: "Research found that how accurate senior executives are about their competitive environments is indeed less important for strategy and corresponding organizational changes than the way in which they interpret information about their environments."[35] Thus, although gathering and organizing information is important, appropriately interpreting that intelligence to determine if an identified trend in the external environment is an opportunity or threat is equally important.

Firms with well-known brands have also detected a trend among consumers to receive more "value" when purchasing branded products. Having forecasted that this trend towards "wanting more value" may last beyond the current global recession, many of these firms are taking actions in response to their assessment of the significance of what may be a long-lasting trend towards value purchases. In the Strategic Focus, we describe actions some firms with well-known brands are taking in response to an assessment that this trend may have significant effects on their operations, at least in the short run if not the longer term as well.

# Segments of the general environment

The general environment is composed of segments that are external to the firm (see Table 2.1). Although the degree of impact varies, these environmental segments affect all industries and the firms competing in them. The challenge to each firm is to scan, monitor, forecast and assess the elements in each segment to determine their effects on the firm. Effective scanning, monitoring, forecasting and assessing are foundational to the firm's efforts to recognize and evaluate opportunities and threats.

## *The demographic segment*

The demographic segment is concerned with a population's size, age structure, geographic distribution, ethnic mix and income distribution.[36] Demographic segments are commonly analysed on a global basis because of their potential effects across countries' borders and because many firms compete in global markets.

**Demographic segment**

The demographic segment is concerned with a population's size, age structure, geographic distribution, ethnic mix and income distribution.

**Population size**  The world's population doubled (from 3 billion to 6 billion people) in the roughly 40-year period between 1959 and 1999. Current projects suggest that population growth will continue in the twenty-first century, but at a slower pace. Demonstrating this expectation is the US Census Bureau's projection that the world's population will be 9 billion by 2040.[37] By 2050, India is expected to be the most populous nation in the world (with over 1.8 billion people). China, the United States, Indonesia and Pakistan are predicted to be the next four largest nations by population count in 2050; others are shrinking. Firms seeking to find growing markets in which to sell their goods and services want to recognize the market potential that may exist for them in these five nations.

**Age structure**  While observing the population of different nations and regions of the world, firms also want to study changes occurring within different populations to assess their strategic implications. Ageing populations are a significant problem for countries such as Japan, Italy and Germany because of the need for workers and the burden of funding pension and health care programmes. In Japan and other countries, employees are urged to work longer to overcome these problems. Interestingly, while the United States has a higher birthrate and significant immigration, placing it in a better position than Japan and other European nations, it is Japan that may become the laboratory for a future of senescence. Firms seeking to experiment with novel solutions to meet the emergent societal needs find opportunities to prepare for the future in Japan, where already in 2006, 20 per cent of Japan's citizens were 65 or older, while the United States and China will not reach this level until 2036.[38]

Ageing populations also influence economies in many ways. In North America and Europe, millions of baby boomers (those born between 1946 and 1965) are approaching retirement. However, even in developing countries with large numbers of people under the age of 35, birth rates have been declining sharply. In China, for example, the successful one-child policy of Chinese administrations, intended to limit the growth of China's population, is likely to lead to unintended consequences including the rapid ageing of China. By 2040 there will be more than 400 million people in China over the age of 60. These changes will affect societies, economies and companies not only in Asia but around the world. Some have questioned whether China will grow rich quick enough before it grows old.

The 90-plus million baby boomers in North America may postpone retirement given the recent financial crisis. In fact, data now suggest that baby boomers are struggling to meet their retirement goals and are uncertain if they will actually be

© Chris Willson/Alamy

STRATEGIC FOCUS

# Serving seniors smartly: collaborative strategy for Japan's ageing population

Seven-Eleven Japan (SEJ) sells and Yamato Transport Takkyubin (YTT) delivers goods and both created a venture to offer these complementary services in retail and logistics as Seven Meal Service (7Meal) a new subsidiary of SEJ in Japan. In 2000 when 7Meal started operations SEJ operated about only 8000 stores in Japan. In 2009 it operates around 12 000 in Japan and 32 500 worldwide. Selling a wide variety of meals and sub-meals through catalogues, websites and the chain of Seven-Eleven convenience stores, 7Meal offers home delivery of the pre-ordered meals primarily to the growing number of seniors in Japan. As discussed earlier, forecasts suggest that by 2050 about 40 per cent of Japan's population will be over 65 years. SEJ's skills and experience with fresh food sold in its stores was instrumental in developing 7Meal practices. This first-hand retail experience helped to gain an early understanding of what kind of meals

may be needed at which price levels. Allying with YTT helped to solve the issue of affordable yet high quality transport.

YTT has revolutionized what haulage means in Japan. The YTT delivery comprises haulage of parcels, packages, suitcases for travellers and also golf bags, clubs and skis. Originally, haulage had been a packages service for mainly corporate customers. After years of striving to become a company that would transport any quantity to anywhere in Japan, Masao Ogura, a former president, radically changed the business model. YTT started to offer only focused services (mainly limiting size), which helped a quick return to profitability and reputation. Starting the home-to-home services with a distribution network similar to the hub-and-spoke system of airlines, YTT chose Seven-Eleven's convenience stores as agents for drop-off and pick-up, thus starting the cooperation between the two companies. YTT's service innovation was so successful that 150 million parcels were delivered in 1984, exceeding that of the Japanese postal system. YTT has developed an excellent reputation for customer service and quality of delivery, despite the time pressure on delivery staff. In 1988 it increased its appeal further by the introduction of haulage of chilled cargoes.

SEJ and YTT together venture to exploit the new opportunities and develop new capabilities to increase the value added by their service innovation, i.e., for-profit, large scale meal delivery service that includes the silver market (over 60s) as a key target segment. The alliance between SEJ and YTT had so far been centred on the SEJ stores serving as pick-up and drop-off points and complementing YTT's haulage system.

In August 2000 SEJ established Seven Meal Service, a subsidiary focusing on home delivery of food and meals, which started pilot services in September 2000 in the Tokyo metropolitan area. Since starting the service, 7Meal has been expanding the area it covers and in 2007 the Northern Island of Hokkaido was included in the coverage area, effectively completing full coverage of Japan. 7Meal successfully addressed three main obstacles that made rapid extension of coverage difficult; variety, freshness and price.

Successful meal services need to offer enough variety to guarantee that heavy users will be satisfied. Freshness of meals requires efficient production and delivery suited to the nature of the meals. Allying itself with YTT, 7Meal is able to reduce transport costs for each 7Meal delivery to about €1.5, charged additionally to the cost of the products, which range from approximately €4 to €15. 7Meal offers its customers the choice between front-door deliveries by YTT or pick up at a designated Seven-Eleven convenience store. SEJ's Seven Meal Services has currently about 200 000 users with one-half being older than 60 years.

**Sources:** Kon, K. (1997) Yamato Takkyubin. In TTUMS Group (ed.), Cases ni manabu keieigaku, Tokyo: Yuhikaku Books, 79–94; Ogura, M. (2001) Watakushino rirekisho. *Nippon Keizan Shimbun*; Reinmoeller, P. (2010) "Service innovation: Towards designing new business models for aging societies", in: Kohlbacher and Herstatt (eds.), The Silver Market Phenomenon, Springer.

*Questions*

1 What is the opportunity that SEJ and YTT have identified?

2 What are the main factors in PMI's general environment that influence its performance?

3 How do both companies work together to exploit this opportunity?

4 What are the basic assumptions underlying their strategy and its implementation?

5 Can you identify other opportunities for similar services in your country? Why does the opportunity not exist in your country?

6 Discuss the implications of the successfully implemented strategy for future business extension.

able to retire as originally expected, partly because of declines in the value of their homes as well as declines in their other retirement investments.[39] The fact that a number of baby boomers experienced at least a 20 per cent decline in their retirement assets between 2007 and 2008 is also influencing their retirement decisions. The possibility of future declines is creating uncertainty about how to invest for baby boomers, and when they might be able to retire.[40] On the other hand, delayed retirements by baby boomers with value-creating skills may facilitate firms' efforts to successfully implement their strategies. Moreover, delayed retirements may allow companies to think of creative ways for skilled, long-time employees to impart their accumulated knowledge to younger employees as they work a little longer than originally anticipated.

**Geographic distribution**  Geographic distribution patterns are not identical throughout the world. Roughly separating countries into those with dense and growing populations and those with sparse and stagnant populations, it is evident that many emerging countries fall into the second category. In fact, Asia, Africa and America are growing, whereas population growth in Europe is very limited, e.g., to countries such as the Netherlands. Similarly, the distribution patterns within countries differ while similarities are striking. Population density is extreme in large cities, wherever they are located. Megacities such as Tokyo, Shanghai, Mexico City, Mumbai, London or Paris attract talent. In general, urban areas house half of the world's people, and continue to grow in both rich and poor countries.[41]

For example, in China, 60 per cent of the Chinese population lives in rural areas; however, the growth is in urban communities such as Shanghai (with a current population in excess of 13 million) and Beijing (over 12.2 million). These data suggest that firms seeking to sell their products in China should recognize the growth in metropolitan areas rather than in rural areas.[42]

Changes in the distribution patterns will strongly influence firms' strategies in the future. For decades Western Europe has attracted immigrants from other European countries, Turkey and Nord-African and some Asian countries. Particularly during times of economic boom, immigrants from North-African and Asian countries came as foreign workers to Western European countries such as the

Netherlands, Germany and the UK. The immigration to Western Europe began from countries such as Italy and Spain, followed by countries including Morocco and Turkey. Parallel to the different waves of immigrants arriving, despite some remaining issues with adaptation and acceptance, many naturalized and rose to occupy positions at all levels in their new home countries. Besides the importance of having a sufficient labour force where production takes place, the different growth rates of markets are significant for firms that seek to internationally diversify. The idea of selling profitably and thereby improving the lives of many consumers at the bottom end of emerging markets addresses the current potential of emerging markets today, and not only in the future.[43]

**Ethnic mix**  The ethnic mix of countries' populations continues to change. For example, the ethnic mix in Europe has considerably changed in the last 40 years. As discussed earlier, many immigrants came to Western Europe after the Second World War, bringing cultural changes with them: an example is how Chicken Tikka is now considered a British dish in the UK. A large number of workers from South European countries such as Italy and Spain returned to their country after some years. However, immigrants from countries such as Algeria, Morocco and Turkey did not return and continued to stay in France, the Netherlands and Germany. Additionally, family reunification took place. As a result, nowadays millions of people with a non-European background live in Western Europe.[44]

Changes in the ethnic mix also affect a workforce's composition and cooperation.[45] In Western Europe, for example, the population and labour force will continue to diversify, as immigration accounts for a sizeable part of population growth. In 2004, when many East-European countries joined the EU, thousands of people from countries such as Bulgaria and Romania migrated to West European countries. In 2008, for example, 110 000 people from East European countries worked in the Netherlands.[46] In the UK more than 640000 workers from Eastern Europe have sought work since May 2004. Most work in factories, warehouses and in the construction sector. Many East European workers have started to return to their home country, the main reason being the higher economic growth rates in their countries of origin. In Slovakia for example, the average wage rose 7.2 per cent in 2007 as the economy grew by 11.6 per cent,[47] outperforming West European countries by far.

**Income distribution**  Understanding how income is distributed within and across populations informs firms of different groups' purchasing power and discretionary income. Studies of income distributions suggest that although living standards have improved over time, variations exist within and between nations.[48] Of interest to firms are the average incomes of households and individuals. For instance, the increase in dual-career couples has had a notable effect on average incomes. Although real income has been generally declining in some nations, the household income of dual-career couples has increased, particularly in the United States. These figures yield strategically relevant information for firms. For instance, research indicates that where an employee is part of a dual-career couple, this can strongly influence their willingness to accept an international assignment.[49]

The assessment by some that in 2005 about 55 per cent of the world's population could be defined as "middle class" generates interesting possibilities for many firms. (For the purpose of this survey, middle class was defined as people with one-third of their income left for discretionary spending after providing for basic food and shelter.) The size of this market may have "… immense implications for companies selling their products and services on a global scale".[50] Of course, the recent global financial crisis may affect the size of the world's "middle class".

## The economic segment

The economic environment refers to the nature and direction of the economy in which a firm competes or may compete.[51] In general, firms seek to compete in relatively stable economies with strong growth potential. Because nations are interconnected as a result of the global economy, firms must scan, monitor, forecast and assess the health of their host nation and the health of the economies outside their host nation.

As firms prepare to compete during the second decade of the twenty-first century, the world's economic environment seemed quite uncertain. Some business people were even beginning to question the ability of economists to provide valid and reliable predictions about trends to anticipate in the world's economic environment.[52] The lack of confidence in predictions from those specializing in providing such predictions complicates firms' efforts to understand the conditions they might face during future competitive battles.

In terms of specific economic environments, companies competing in Japan or desiring to do so might carefully evaluate the meaning of the position recently taken by some that this nation's economy has ingrained flaws such as "... unwieldy corporate structures, dogged loyalty to increasingly commoditized business lines and a history of punting problems into the future".[53] Because of its acknowledged growth potential, a number of companies are evaluating the possibility of entering Russia to compete or for those already competing in that nation, to expand the scope of their operations. However, statements by analysts in mid-2009 that "the banking crisis in Russia is at its very beginning"[54] could indicate a trend warranting careful analysis. If this prediction were to become true, the concern would be the possible destabilization in the Russian economy that a longer-term banking crisis might create. In contrast, Vietnam's economy was expanding during late 2009 and being recognized as one in which opportunities might exist for companies from across the globe to pursue.[55]

## The political/legal segment

The political/legal segment is the arena in which organizations and interest groups compete for attention, resources and a voice in overseeing the body of laws and regulations guiding interactions among nations as well as between firms and various local governmental agencies.[56] Essentially, this segment represents how organizations try to influence governments and how they try to understand the influences (current and projected) of those governments on their strategic actions.

When regulations are formed in response to new legislation, they often influence a firm's strategic actions. For example, less restrictive regulations on firms' actions are a product of the recent global trend toward privatization of government-owned or government-regulated firms. Some believe that the transformation from state-owned to private firms taking place in multiple nations has substantial implications for the competitive landscapes in a number of countries and across multiple industries.[57] In the United States, the 2009 allocation by the federal government of €10.23 billion to high-speed train travel is expected to provide a critical boost to the nation's efforts to reduce traffic congestion and cut pollution.[58] For global firms manufacturing high-speed rail equipment, this political support in the United States of systems requiring their products is a trend to forecast and assess. Already, leading technology firms with their own high-speed rail products from France, Germany and Japan have started making advances. Interestingly, China raised eyebrows when it signed preliminary cooperation agreements with the State of California and General Electric to help build such lines. It offers the latest technologies at most competitive prices.[59]

Firms must carefully analyse a new political administration's business-related policies and philosophies. Antitrust laws, taxation laws, industries chosen for deregulation, labour training laws and the degree of commitment to educational institutions are areas in which an administration's policies can affect the operations and profitability of industries and individual firms across the globe. For example, in July 2000 the Dutch government decided to introduce a new tax, the so-called "flight tax". This new tax made airline tickets €11.25 more expensive and had considerable consequences for the aviation industry in the Netherlands. Many airline companies such as EasyJet decided to reduce the number of flights or even to stop operating in the Netherlands.[60] Another step taken by some airline companies was to shift operations to airports in neighbouring countries. Passengers reacted as well. As a consequence the airport at Düsseldorf, a German city close to the Dutch border, recorded 62 per cent more Dutch passengers. For Brussels airport, also in easy reach for Dutch travellers, this percentage was as high as 74 per cent.[61]

To deal with issues such as these, firms develop a political strategy to influence governmental policies that might affect them. As mentioned earlier, some argue that developing an effective political strategy is essential to the newly-formed General Motors' efforts to achieve strategic competitiveness.[62] Additionally, the effects of global governmental policies (e.g., those related to firms in India that are engaging in IT outsourcing work) on a firm's competitive position increase the need for firms to have an effective political strategy.[63]

Firms competing in the global economy encounter an interesting array of political/legal questions and issues. For example, in 2010, leaders from South Korea and the European Union signed a free trade agreement.[64] The two parties had worked for about three years to develop an agreement that many thought would benefit both sides by creating a host of opportunities for firms to sell their goods and services in what would be a new market for them. The key political challenge affecting the parties' efforts was the European Union's decision not to permit "...refunds South Korea pays to local companies who import parts from third countries before exporting finished goods".[65] Both South Korea and European Union firms are monitoring the progress of these talks in order to be able to forecast the effects of a possible trade agreement on their strategic actions.

## The socio-cultural segment

The socio-cultural segment is concerned with a society's attitudes and cultural values. Because attitudes and values form the cornerstone of a society, they often drive demographic, economic, political/legal and technological conditions and changes.

Societies' attitudes and cultural values are undergoing change at the start of the second decade of the twenty-first century. Looking at economic production, the modern economic landscape has three important kinds of places. First, the few cities like San Francisco, London, Amsterdam or Tokyo that have the capacity to attract global talent and create new products and innovate. Second, places that have a strong manufacturing base or provide services support the innovation activities in the cities. If they are not growing into innovative cities like Seoul, they may decline because their rising labour costs may erode their only competitive edge.[66]

Third, in the Middle East, the participation of women in the workforce has been an issue for decades. Women usually stayed at home instead of joining the workforce. However, there has been a change in the attitude of women towards business and participation in the labour market, and between 1960 and 2000 the participation of women has increased by 47 per cent in the Middle East and North Africa. There are considerable differences between Arab countries. For example, between

**Socio-cultural segment**

The sociocultural segment is concerned with a society's attitudes and cultural values.

1960 and 2000 women's participation increased by 668 per cent and by 486 per cent in Kuwait, but in Yemen this percentage is equal to just 15 per cent.[67] The growing gender, ethnic and cultural diversity in the workforce creates challenges and opportunities, including combining the best of both men's and women's traditional leadership styles. Although diversity in the workforce has the potential to add improved performance, research indicates that important conditions require management of diversity initiatives in order to reap these organizational benefits. Human resource practitioners are trained to successfully manage diversity issues to enhance positive outcomes.[68]

Attitudes and values about health care are changing worldwide. In the United States, one of the largest and most attractive markets for pharmaceutical companies, rethinking and change may be under way. For example, while the United States "... has the highest overall health care expenditure as well as the highest expenditure per capital of any country in the world",[69] millions of the nation's citizens lacked health insurance. Some feel that effective health care reform in the United States requires securing coverage for all citizens and lowering the cost of services.[70] The recent changes to the nature of health care policies and their delivery in the United States are likely to affect business firms, meaning that they must carefully monitor the changes and future trends regarding health care in order to anticipate the effects on their operations.

Another manifestation of changing attitudes towards work is the continuing growth of contingency workers (part-time, temporary, and contract employees) throughout the global economy. This trend is significant in many parts of the world, including Canada, Japan, Latin America, Western Europe and the United States. In the US, the fastest growing group of contingency workers is those with 15–20 years of work experience. Since the burst of its financial bubble in the early 1990s, Japan has seen a strong increase in part-time work. The Netherlands is among the countries with the highest level of part-time work and female participation in the workforce. The layoffs resulting from the recent global crisis and the loss of retirement income of many experienced members of the workforce – many of whom feel they must work longer to recover losses to their retirement portfolios – are a key reason for this. Companies interested in hiring on a temporary basis, however, may benefit by gaining access to the long-term work experience of these newly-available workers.[71]

Although the lifestyle and workforce changes reflect the values of the US population, each country and culture has unique values and trends. As suggested earlier, national cultural values affect behaviour in organizations and thus also influence organizational outcomes.[72] For example, the importance of collectivism and social relations in Chinese and Russian cultures may lead to the open sharing of information and knowledge among members of an organization.[73] Knowledge sharing is important for defusing new knowledge in organizations and increasing the speed in implementing innovations. Personal relationships are especially important in China as *guanxi* (personal connections) has become a way of doing business within the country and for individuals to advance their careers in what is becoming a more open market society.[74] Understanding the importance of *guanxi* is critical for foreign firms doing business in China.

## The technological segment

Pervasive and diversified in scope, technological changes affect many parts of societies. These effects occur primarily through new products, processes and materials. The technological segment includes the institutions and activities involved with creating new knowledge and translating that knowledge into new outputs, products, processes and materials.

**Technological segment**

The technological segment includes the institutions and activities involved with creating new knowledge and translating that knowledge into new outputs, products, processes, and materials.

Given the rapid pace of technological change, it is vital for firms to thoroughly study the technological segment.[75] The importance of these efforts is suggested by the finding that early adopters of new technology often achieve higher market shares and earn higher returns. Thus, both large and small firms should continuously scan the external environment to identify potential substitutes for technologies that are in current use, as well as to identify newly emerging technologies from which their firm could derive competitive advantage.[76]

As a significant technological development, the Internet has a remarkable capability to provide information easily, quickly and effectively to an increasing percentage of the world's population. Companies continue studying the Internet's capabilities to anticipate how it may allow them to create more value for customers and to anticipate future trends with this technological tool.

In spite of the Internet's far-reaching effects, wireless communication technology is predicted to be the next significant technological opportunity for companies to apply when pursuing strategic competitiveness. Handheld devices and other wireless communications equipment are used to access a variety of network-based services. The use of handheld computers with wireless network connectivity, Web-enabled mobile phone handsets, and other emerging platforms (e.g., consumer Internet-access devices) are expected to increase substantially, soon becoming the dominant form of communication and commerce.[77]

Amazon.com's Kindle is an emerging wireless technology with capabilities firms should evaluate. Customers can download an increasing variety of products to the Kindle in addition to books, the most obvious item. In mid-2009, over 275 000 of Amazon's books were available through the Kindle. Magazines and newspapers are available for purchase and use on the Kindle as well. The ease of reading daily newspapers on the Kindle instead of waiting for hard copy to be delivered to one's home or office is threatening the very existence of a host of newspapers. The Kindle can also be used to surf the Web and send e-mail messages.[78] Although Kindle was the first in this field, other brands have entered the market for digital reading. It was Sony that developed the e-reader as an alternative to the Kindle. The Sony Reader was introduced in November 2006 in the US and in 2008 to the European market, the UK being first. Both devices have similar features such as digital reading of books, listening to audio and so on.[79] Currently in their next generations, there is no doubt that Amazon and Sony will continue developing more advanced versions of the Kindle and the Sony Reader with each version having additional functionalities.[80] As a service, the Kindle and similar products may create opportunities for those wanting to distribute knowledge electronically but poses a threat for companies whose strategies call for the distribution of physical, "hard copies" of written words. In particular, the recent launch of the iPad has again changed the competitive dynamics (see Strategic Focus in Chapter 1). While some newspapers see light at the end of a long decline in revenue, because the iPad enables them to generate healthy returns, the Kindle and the Sony Reader are now being sold at discounts.

## The global segment

The global segment includes relevant new global markets, existing markets that are changing, important international political events, and critical cultural and institutional characteristics of global markets.[81] There is little doubt that markets are becoming more global and that consumers as well as companies throughout the world accept this fact. The manufacturing industries are as an example of this. Specifically, the global auto industry is one in which an increasing number of people believe that because "we live in a global community," consumers in multiple nations are willing to buy cars and trucks "from whatever area of the world".[82]

**Global segment**

The global segment includes relevant new global markets, existing markets that are changing, important international political events, and critical cultural and institutional characteristics of global markets.

When studying the global segment, firms (including automobile manufacturers) should recognize that globalization of business markets may create *opportunities* to enter new markets as well as *threats* that new competitors from other economies may enter their market. Consider the possibility of a simultaneous opportunity and threat for the world's automobile manufacturers. The core issue here is that worldwide production capacity is now a potential threat to all of these global companies, while entering another market to sell their own products appears to be an opportunity. In terms of overcapacity, evidence indicated that in mid-2009, this global industry had "… the capacity to make an astounding 94 million vehicles each year (which is roughly) 34 million too many, based on current sales".[83] This prediction of excess capacity suggests that most, if not all, automobile manufacturers may decide to enter markets that are new to them in order to try to sell more of the units they are producing.

Some countries with strong export orientation such as China, Germany, Japan and South Korea are home to many firms that primarily serve international markets. Consequently, many firms in such countries, e.g. Haier, Siemens, Fujitsu and Samsung which have high foreign sales, also have considerable foreign assets. The markets from which firms generate sales and income are one indication of the degree to which they are participating in the global economy. Since its foundation in 1985, the Italian fashion brand Dolce & Gabbana has turned into one of the leading groups in the fashion textile and luxury goods market. Operating from Italy as a hub in a global network Dolce & Gabbana is offering its goods in sophisticated retail outlets in more than one hundred countries worldwide. Food giant H.J. Heinz earns over 60 per cent of its revenue outside the United States.[84] Consumer products giant Procter & Gamble, with operations in over 180 countries, recently generated over 56 per cent of its sales revenue in markets outside the United States.[85] In 2008 for example, 53 per cent of McDonald's operating income was accounted for by its international operations.[86] By mid-2009 McDonald's was operating roughly 32 000 restaurants in 118 countries. Thus, for these companies and so many others, understanding the conditions of today's global segment and being able to predict conditions in this segment to expect in the future is critical to their success.

As our discussion shows, the global segment presents firms with both opportunities and threats or risks. Because of the threats and risks, some firms choose to take a more cautious approach to competing in international markets. These firms participate in what some refer to as *global focusing*. Global focusing is often used by firms with moderate levels of international operations who increase their internationalization by focusing on global niche markets.[87] In this way, they build on and use their special competencies and resources while limiting their risks with the niche market. Another way in which firms limit their risks in international markets is to focus their operations and sales in one region of the world.[88] In this way, they can build stronger relationships in and knowledge of their markets. As they build these strengths, rivals find it more difficult to enter their markets and compete successfully.

In all instances, firms competing in global markets should recognize the different socio-cultural and institutional attributes of global markets. While the US Korea free trade agreement, KORUS, is still stalled in the US Congress although negotiations about this agreement started long before the EU's. The last European hurdle for the EU-South Korea Free trade agreement to pass is the European Parliament's approval which seems likely to occur by the end of 2010. The trade deal will take effect from July 2011 with a combined trade in goods worth about 53 billion euros in 2009. EU producers hope that the agreement creates the estimated 19 billion euros ($24 billion) of new exports for them. To seize such opportunities, European Union companies (as well as those from other regions of the world as well) who choose to compete in South Korea must understand the value placed on hierarchical order, formality, and self-control as well as on duty rather than rights.

Furthermore, Korean ideology emphasizes communitarianism, a characteristic of many Asian countries. Korea's approach differs from that of Japan and China, however, in that it focuses on *inhwa*, or harmony. *Inhwa* is based on a respect of hierarchical relationships and obedience to authority. Alternatively, the approach in China stresses *guanxi* – personal relationships or good connections – while in Japan, the focus is on *wa*, or group harmony and social cohesion.[89] The institutional context of China suggests a major emphasis on centralized planning by the government. The Chinese government provides incentives to firms to develop alliances with foreign firms that have sophisticated technology, in hopes of building knowledge and introducing new technologies to the Chinese markets over time.[90]

## The physical environment segment

The physical environment segment refers to potential and actual changes in the physical environment and business practices that are intended to positively respond to and deal with those changes.[91] Concerned with trends oriented to sustaining the world's physical environment, firms recognize that ecological, social and economic systems interactively influence what happens in this particular segment.[92]

There are many parts or attributes of the physical environment that firms should consider as they try to identify trends in this segment. Some argue that global warming is a trend firms and nations should carefully examine in efforts to predict any potential effects on the global society as well as on their business operations.[93] Energy consumption is another part of the physical environment that concerns both organizations and nations. Spain, for example, has the largest renewable energy operator in the world, Iberdola.[94] Although it was Germany that had been the leader of wind energy capacity, this place has now been taken by the US and China[95] and a competitive race in the field of wind energy is under way that sees small economies competing with large ones, e.g. Denmark and China, as well as export-oriented firms competing with more domestically-oriented firms.

Because of the increasing concern about sustaining the quality of the physical environment, a number of companies are developing environmentally friendly policies. Nokia, for example, the leading producer of mobile phones wants to be the leader in sustainability. In the company's words, "The growth of mobile communications means it's important for Nokia as a market leader, to lead the way also in sustainability and demonstrate best practices. As part of our responsibility, we provide in-depth information on how we aim to be a leading company in terms of environmental performance." [96] While the corporations are confronted with demands to "reduce their environmental footprint" and to be good stewards of the physical environment as a result of doing so, how this can be done most productively and profitably is widely discussed.

As our discussion of the general environment shows, identifying anticipated changes and trends among external elements is a key objective of analysing the firm's general environment. With a focus on the future, the analysis of the general environment allows firms to identify opportunities and threats. It is necessary to have a top management team with the experience, knowledge, and sensitivity required to effectively analyse this segment of the environment.[97] Also critical to a firm's choices of strategic actions to take is an understanding of its industry environment and its competitors; we consider these issues next.

# Industry environment analysis

An industry is a group of firms producing products that are close substitutes. In the course of competition, these firms influence one another. Typically, industries

**Physical environment segment**

The physical environment segment refers to potential and actual changes in the physical environment and business practices that are intended to positively respond to and deal with those changes.

**Industry**

An industry is a group of firms producing products that are close substitutes.

**FIGURE 2.2** The five forces of competition model

include a rich mixture of competitive strategies that companies use in pursuing above-average returns. In part, these strategies are chosen because of the influence of an industry's characteristics.[98]

Compared with the general environment, the industry environment has a more direct effect on the firm's strategic competitiveness and ability to earn above-average returns.[99] An industry's profit potential is a function of five forces of competition: the threats posed by new entrants, the power of suppliers, the power of buyers, product substitutes and the intensity of rivalry among competitors (see Figure 2.2).

The five forces model of competition expands the arena for competitive analysis. Historically, when studying the competitive environment, firms concentrated on companies with which they directly competed. However, firms must search more broadly to recognize current and potential competitors by identifying potential customers as well as the firms serving them. For example, the communications industry is now broadly defined as encompassing media companies, telecoms, entertainment companies and companies producing devices such as phones and iPods. In such an environment, firms must study many other adjacent industries to identify firms with capabilities (especially technology-based capabilities) that might be the foundation for producing a good or a service that can compete against what they are producing.[100] Using this perspective finds firms focusing on customers and their needs rather than on specific industry boundaries to define markets.

When studying the industry environment, firms must also recognize that suppliers can become a firm's competitors (by integrating forward) as can buyers (by integrating backward). For example, several firms have integrated forward in the pharmaceutical industry by acquiring distributors or wholesalers. In addition, firms choosing to enter a new market and those producing products that are adequate substitutes for existing products can become a company's competitors. Next, we examine the five forces the firm analyses to understand the profitability potential within the industry (or a segment of an industry) in which it competes or may choose to compete.

## Threat of new entrants

Identifying new entrants is important because they can threaten the market share of existing competitors.[101] One reason new entrants pose such a threat is that they bring additional production capacity. Unless the demand for a good or service is increasing, additional capacity holds consumers' costs down, resulting in less revenue and lower returns for competing firms. Often, new entrants have a keen interest in gaining a large market share. As a result, new competitors may force existing firms to be more efficient and to learn how to compete on new dimensions (e.g., using an Internet-based distribution channel).

The likelihood that firms will enter an industry is a function of two factors: barriers to entry and the retaliation expected from current industry participants. Entry barriers make it difficult for new firms to enter an industry and often place them at a competitive disadvantage even when they are able to enter. As such, high entry barriers tend to increase the returns for existing firms in the industry and may allow some firms to dominate the industry.[102] Thus, firms competing successfully in an industry want to maintain high entry barriers in order to discourage potential competitors from deciding to enter the industry.

**Barriers to entry**   Firms competing in an industry (and especially those earning above-average returns) seek to develop entry barriers to thwart potential competitors. For example, the server market is hypercompetitive and dominated by IBM, Hewlett-Packard and Dell. Historically, the scale economies these firms have developed by operating efficiently and effectively have created significant entry barriers, causing potential competitors to think very carefully about entering the server market to compete against them. Recently, however, Oracle paid €5.82 billion to acquire Sun Microsystems, which is primarily a computer hardware company. Early evidence suggests that Oracle intends to "... focus Sun's server business on a small but promising segment of the market: computer appliances preloaded with Oracle software".[103] The degree of success Oracle will achieve as a result of its decision to enter the server market via an acquisition remains uncertain.

Several kinds of potentially significant entry barriers may discourage competitors from entering a market.

**Economies of scale**   Economies of scale are derived from incremental efficiency improvements through experience as a firm grows larger. Therefore, the cost of producing each unit declines as the quantity of a product produced during a given period increases. This is the case for IBM, Hewlett-Packard and Dell in the server market, as described above.

Economies of scale can be developed in most business functions, such as marketing, manufacturing, research and development, and purchasing.[104] Increasing economies of scale enhances a firm's flexibility. For example, a firm may choose to reduce its price and capture a greater share of the market. Alternatively, it may keep its price constant to increase profits. In so doing, it likely will increase its free cash flow, which is very helpful in times of recession.

New entrants face a dilemma when confronting current competitors' scale economies. Small-scale entry places them at a cost disadvantage. Given Sun Microsystems' size relative to the three major competitors in the server market, Oracle may be at least initially be at a disadvantage in competing against the well-established firms in this particular market. Alternatively, large-scale entry, in which the new entrant manufactures large volumes of a product to gain economies of scale, risks strong competitive retaliation.

Some competitive conditions reduce the ability of economies of scale to create an entry barrier. Many companies now customize their products for large numbers of small customer groups. Customized products are not manufactured in the volumes necessary to achieve economies of scale. Customization is made possible by new flexible manufacturing systems (this point is discussed further in Chapter 4). In fact, the new manufacturing technology facilitated by advanced information systems has allowed the development of mass customization in an increasing number of industries. Although it is not appropriate for all products and while implementing can be challenging, mass customization has become increasingly common in manufacturing products.[105] In fact, online ordering has enhanced the ability of customers to obtain customized products. They are often referred to as "markets of one".[106] Companies manufacturing customized products learn how to respond quickly to customers' needs in lieu of developing scale economies.

**Product differentiation**  Over time, customers may come to believe that a firm's product is unique. This belief can result from the firm's service to the customer, effective advertising campaigns, or being the first to market a good or service. Pret A Manger, a popular sandwich retailer in the UK, tries to differentiate itself from other sandwich retailers by using natural ingredients only, preparing the sandwiches in the kitchen of each location and by donating sandwiches which are left at the end of the day instead of keeping them overnight.[107] Pret A Manger reinforces its positioning by emphasizing the freshness of ingredients in an engaging way through product display and point of sale advertising. It eschews mass marketing closely associated with different fast food retailers such as McDonald's and relies on building reputation and loyalty with its patrons.

Companies such as Unilever and its competitor Procter and Gamble (P&G) spend a great deal of money on advertising and product development to convince potential customers of their products' distinctiveness and the value buying their brands provides.[108] Customers valuing a product's uniqueness tend to become loyal to both the product and the company producing it. In turn, customer loyalty is an entry barrier for firms thinking of entering an industry and competing against the likes of P&G and Unilever. To compete against firms offering differentiated products to individuals who have become loyal customers, new entrants often allocate many resources over time to overcome existing customer loyalties. To combat the perception of uniqueness, new entrants frequently offer products at lower prices. This decision, however, may result in lower profits or even losses.

**Capital requirements**  Competing in a new industry requires a firm to have resources to invest. In addition to physical facilities, capital is needed for inventories, marketing activities, and other critical business functions. Even when a new industry is attractive, the capital required for successful market entry may not be available to pursue the market opportunity. For example, defence industries are difficult to enter because of the substantial resource investments required to be competitive. In addition, because of the high knowledge requirements of the defence industry, a firm might enter this industry through the acquisition of an existing firm. But it must have access to the capital necessary to do it. Obviously, in the recent acquisition Oracle had the capital required to acquire Sun Microsystems as a foundation for entering the server market.

**Switching costs**  Switching costs are the one-time costs customers incur when they buy from a different supplier. The costs of buying new ancillary equipment and of retraining employees, and even the psychic costs of ending a relationship, may be incurred in switching to a new supplier. In some cases, switching costs are low, such as when the consumer switches to a different soft drink or when a smoker switches from a Philip Morris International cigarette to one produced by competitor Japan Tobacco International. Switching costs can vary as a function of time. For example, in terms of credit hours toward graduation, the cost to a student to transfer from one university to another as a freshman is much lower than it is when the student is entering the senior year. Occasionally, a decision made by manufacturers to produce a new, innovative product creates high switching costs for the final consumer. Customer loyalty programmes, such as airlines' frequent flyer miles, are intended to increase the customer's switching costs.

If switching costs are high, a new entrant must offer either a substantially lower price or a much better product to attract buyers. Usually, the more established the relationships between parties, the greater are switching costs.

**Access to distribution channels**   Over time, industry participants typically develop effective means of distributing products. Once a relationship with its distributors has been built, a firm will nurture it, thus creating switching costs for the distributors. Access to distribution channels can be a strong entry barrier for new entrants, particularly in consumer non-durable goods industries (e.g., in grocery stores where shelf space is limited) and in international markets. New entrants have to persuade distributors to carry their products, either in addition to or in place of those currently distributed. Price breaks and cooperative advertising allowances may be used for this purpose; however, these practices reduce the new entrant's profit potential.

**Cost disadvantages independent of scale**   Sometimes established competitors have cost advantages that new entrants cannot duplicate. Proprietary product technology, favourable access to raw materials, desirable locations and government subsidies are examples. Successful competition requires new entrants to reduce the strategic relevance of these factors. Delivering purchases directly to the buyer can counter the advantage of a desirable location; new food establishments in an undesirable location often follow this practice.

**Government policy**   Through licensing and permit requirements, governments can also control entry into an industry. Liquor retailing, radio and TV broadcasting, banking, and trucking are examples of industries in which government decisions and actions affect entry possibilities. Also, governments often restrict entry into some industries because of the need to provide quality service or the need to protect jobs. Alternatively, deregulation of industries, exemplified by the airline industry and utilities in the United States, allows more firms to enter.[109] However, some of the most publicized government actions are those involving antitrust. In 2009, for example, the European Commission announced a fine of €1.1 billion, the largest ever assessed, against Intel, the world's largest computer-chip maker. The fine was for "… breaking European antitrust rules".[110] In the main, the commission's conclusion was that Intel's competitive actions were having the net effect of blocking effective access by competitors to European markets. In response to the announcement, Intel indicated that it would appeal the fine, as well as the ruling that the firm would have to change its business practices in the European Union.[111] This ruling caused other dominant firms such as Microsoft and Google to wonder about potential governmental rulings that the Commission might assess against them in the future.

**Expected retaliation**   Firms seeking to enter an industry also anticipate the reactions of firms in the industry. An expectation of swift and vigorous competitive responses reduces the likelihood of entry. Vigorous retaliation can be expected when the existing firm has a major stake in the industry (e.g., it has fixed assets with few, if any, alternative uses), when it has substantial resources and when industry growth is slow or constrained. For example, any firm attempting to enter the airline industry at the current time can expect significant retaliation from existing competitors due to overcapacity.

Locating market niches not being served by incumbents allows the new entrant to avoid entry barriers. Small entrepreneurial firms are generally best suited for identifying and serving neglected market segments. When Honda first entered the US motorcycle market, it concentrated on small-engine motorcycles, a market that firms such as Harley-Davidson ignored. By targeting this neglected niche, Honda avoided competition. After consolidating its position, Honda used its strength to attack rivals by introducing larger motorcycles and competing in the broader market. Similarly, Toyota's Lexus was first launched in the US, a large and important market with the added advantage of not being home to leading competitors in the luxury space. After succeeding there through a high service strategy, Toyota eventually entered the European market.[112] Competitive actions and competitive responses between firms such as Honda and Harley-Davidson, or Lexus and Daimler are discussed more fully in Chapter 5.

## Bargaining power of suppliers

Increasing prices and reducing the quality of their products are potential means used by suppliers to exert power over firms competing within an industry. If a firm is unable to recover cost increases by its suppliers through its own pricing structure, its profitability is reduced by its suppliers' actions. A supplier group is powerful when:

- It is dominated by a few large companies and is more concentrated than the industry to which it sells.
- Satisfactory substitute products are not available to industry firms.
- Industry firms are not a significant customer for the supplier group.
- Suppliers' goods are critical to buyers' marketplace success.
- The effectiveness of suppliers' products has created high switching costs for industry firms.
- It poses a credible threat to integrate forward into the buyers' industry. Credibility is enhanced when suppliers have substantial resources and provide a highly differentiated product.

The airline industry is one in which suppliers' bargaining power is changing. As mentioned in the Opening Case of Chapter 1, the number of suppliers is low and the demand for major aircraft is also relatively low. Expecting future competition from Canada's Bombardier, Brazil's Embraer, or firms from China, Boeing and Airbus strongly compete for orders of major aircraft, creating more power for buyers in the process. In mid-2009, United Airlines announced that it might place a "significant" order for wide-body airliners with either Airbus or Boeing in that year's fourth quarter if the firm could earn an acceptable return on its investment. United's expectation that the winning bid from either Airbus or Boeing would include a financing arrangement that would strengthen its "... balance sheet over the long term and not impact (the firm's) cash flow position"[113] suggests that the buyer's power in this instance exceeds the supplier's power.

## Bargaining power of buyers

Firms seek to maximize the return on their invested capital. Alternatively, buyers (customers of an industry or a firm) want to buy products at the lowest possible price – the point at which the industry earns the lowest acceptable rate of return on its invested capital. To reduce their costs, buyers bargain for higher quality, greater levels of service, and lower prices. These outcomes are achieved by encouraging competitive battles among the industry's firms. Customers (buyer groups) are powerful when:

- They purchase a large portion of an industry's total output.
- The sales of the product being purchased account for a significant portion of the seller's annual revenues.
- They could switch to another product at little, if any, cost.
- The industry's products are undifferentiated or standardized, and the buyers pose a credible threat if they were to integrate backward into the sellers' industry.

Greater amounts of information about the manufacturer's costs and the power of the Internet as a shopping and distribution alternative have increased consumers' bargaining power in many industries. One reason for this shift is that individual buyers incur virtually zero switching costs when they decide to purchase from one manufacturer rather than another or from one dealer as opposed to a second or third one.

## Threat of substitute products

Substitute products are goods or services from outside a given industry that perform similar or the same functions as a product that the industry produces. For example, as a substitute for high school or university education, many firms such as LOI and NTI in the Netherlands and Globis in Japan provide distance education.[114] These firms provide the required tools and materials for students who are not able to join a "regular" education. Other product substitutes include e-mail and fax machines instead of overnight deliveries, plastic containers rather than glass jars, and tea instead of coffee. Newspaper firms have experienced significant circulation declines over the past 10-plus years. The declines are due to substitute outlets for news including Internet sources, cable television news channels, e-mail and mobile phone alerts. These products are increasingly popular, especially among younger people, and as product substitutes they have significant potential to continue to reduce overall newspaper circulation sales.

In general, product substitutes present a strong threat to a firm when customers face few, if any, switching costs and when the substitute product's price is lower or its quality and performance capabilities are equal to or greater than those of the competing product. Differentiating a product along dimensions that customers value (such as price, quality, service after the sale and location) reduces a substitute's attractiveness.

## Intensity of rivalry among competitors

Because an industry's firms are mutually dependent, actions taken by one company usually invite competitive responses. In many industries, firms actively compete against one another. Competitive rivalry intensifies when a firm is challenged by a competitor's actions or when a company recognizes an opportunity to improve its market position.

Firms within industries are rarely homogeneous; they differ in resources and capabilities and seek to differentiate themselves from competitors.[115] Typically, firms seek to differentiate their products from competitors' offerings in ways that customers value and in which the firms have a competitive advantage. Common dimensions on which rivalry is based include price, service after the sale, and innovation.

Next, we discuss the most prominent factors that experience shows affect the intensity of firms' rivalries.

### Numerous or equally balanced competitors

Intense rivalries are common in industries with many companies. With multiple competitors, it is common for a few firms to believe they can act without eliciting a response. However, evidence suggests that other firms generally are aware of competitors' actions, often choosing to respond to them. At the other extreme, industries with only a few firms of equivalent size and power also tend to have strong rivalries. The large and often similar-sized resource bases of these firms permit vigorous actions and responses. The competitive battles between Airbus and Boeing tend to be intense and almost certainly will be so as the companies bid for the order to produce wide-body planes for United Airlines or other potential clients in the world's fastest growing markets for air travel such as China, India or Brazil.

### Slow industry growth

When a market is growing, firms try to effectively use resources to serve an expanding customer base. Growing markets reduce the pressure to take customers from competitors. However, rivalry in no-growth or slow-growth markets (slow change) becomes more intense as firms battle to increase their market shares by attracting competitors' customers.[116]

Typically, battles to protect market share are fierce. Certainly, this has been the case in the airline industry and the fast-food industry as McDonald's, Wendy's and Burger King try to win each other's customers. The rivalry between the razor divisions of Philips in the Netherlands and Braun in Germany, now owned by Gillette is legendary for its differences in technology and design strategy. The instability in the market that results from these competitive engagements may reduce the profitability for all firms engaging in such competitive battles.

### High fixed costs or high storage costs

When fixed costs account for a large part of total costs, companies try to maximize the use of their productive capacity. Doing so allows the firm to spread costs across a larger volume of output. However, when many firms attempt to maximize their productive capacity, excess capacity is created on an industry-wide basis. To then reduce inventories, individual companies typically cut the price of their product and offer rebates and other special discounts to customers. However, these practices, common in the automobile manufacturing industry in the recent past, often intensify competition. The pattern of excess capacity at the industry level followed by intense rivalry at the firm level is observed frequently in industries with high storage costs. Perishable products, for example, lose their value rapidly with the passage of time. As their inventories grow, producers of perishable goods often use pricing strategies to sell products quickly.

### Lack of differentiation or low switching costs

When buyers find a differentiated product that satisfies their needs, they frequently purchase the product loyally over time. Industries with many companies that have successfully differentiated their products have less rivalry, resulting in lower competition for individual firms. Firms that develop and sustain a differentiated product that cannot be easily imitated by competitors often earn higher returns. However, when buyers view products as commodities (i.e., as products with few differentiated features or capabilities), rivalry intensifies. In these instances, buyers' purchasing decisions are based primarily on price and, to a lesser degree, service. Personal computers are a commodity product. Thus, the rivalry among Dell, Hewlett-Packard (HP), and other computer manufacturers is strong, although these companies are now finding ways to differentiate their offerings. Interestingly, both companies have tried to use product design as a source of differentiation. Even more extreme is the competition between BP and Shell selling mainly undifferentiated products, i.e. petrol to consumers. Seeking to differentiate different product categories (e.g. super vs regular) they attempt to create preferences through branding and their service stations where they engage in rivalry close to that of retailers.

**High strategic stakes** Competitive rivalry is likely to be high when it is important for several of the competitors to perform well in the market. For example, although it is diversified and is a market leader in other businesses, Samsung has targeted market leadership in the consumer electronics market and is doing quite well. This market is important to Sony and other major competitors, such as GE, LG Hitachi, Panasonic formerly know as Matsushita, Mitsubishi and Philips, suggesting that rivalry among these competitors will remain strong.

High strategic stakes can also exist in terms of geographic locations. For example, European and Asian automobile manufacturers are committed to a significant presence in the US marketplace because it is still the world's most lucrative single market for automobiles and trucks. Because of the stakes involved in this country for European, Asian and US manufacturers, rivalry among firms in the US and the global automobile industry is intense. With the excess capacity in this industry we mentioned earlier, there is every reason to believe that the rivalry among global automobile manufacturers will become even more intense, certainly in the foreseeable future. Paying more attention to the large and growing Chinese market and other emerging markets, manufacturers such as Ford, GM, Honda, Hyundai, Renault, Toyota or Volkswagen are unlikely to reduce overall capacity but in a display of commitment they may well raise the stakes.

**High exit barriers** Sometimes companies continue competing in an industry even though the returns on their invested capital are low or negative. Firms making this choice likely face high exit barriers, which include economic, strategic and emotional factors causing them to remain in an industry when the profitability of doing so is questionable. This appears to be the case for airline companies. Although earning even average returns is difficult for these firms, they face substantial exit barriers such as their ownership of specialized assets (e.g., large aircraft).[117] Common exit barriers firms may face include the following:

- Specialized assets (assets with values linked to a particular business or location).
- Fixed costs of exit (such as labour agreements).
- Strategic interrelationships (relationships of mutual dependence, such as those between one business and other parts of a company's operations, including shared facilities and access to financial markets).
- Emotional barriers (aversion to economically justified business decisions because of fear for one's own career, loyalty to employees, and so forth).
- Government and social restrictions (often based on government concerns for job losses and regional economic effects).

# Interpreting industry analyses

Effective industry analyses are products of careful study and interpretation of data and information from multiple sources. A wealth of industry-specific data is available for firms to analyse. Because of globalization, international markets and rivalries must be included in the firm's analyses. In fact, research shows that in some industries, international variables are more important than domestic ones as determinants of strategic competitiveness. Furthermore, because of the development of global markets, a country's borders no longer restrict industry structures. In fact, movement into international markets enhances the chances of success for new ventures as well as more established firms.[118]

Analysis of the five forces in the industry allows the firm to determine the industry's attractiveness in terms of the potential to earn adequate or superior returns. In general, the stronger competitive forces are, the lower the profit potential for an industry's firms. An unattractive industry has low entry barriers, suppliers and buyers with strong bargaining positions, strong competitive threats from product substitutes, and intense rivalry among competitors. These industry characteristics make it difficult for firms to achieve strategic competitiveness and earn above-average returns. Alternatively, an attractive industry has high entry barriers, suppliers and buyers with little bargaining power, few competitive threats from product substitutes, and relatively moderate rivalry.[119] Next, we explain strategic groups as an aspect of industry competition.

## Strategic groups

A set of firms that emphasize similar strategic dimensions and use a similar strategy is called a **strategic group**.[120] The competition between firms within a strategic group is greater than the competition between a member of a strategic group and companies outside that strategic group. Therefore, intra-strategic group competition is more intense than is inter-strategic group competition. In fact, more heterogeneity is evident in the performance of firms within strategic groups than across the groups. The performance leaders within groups are able to follow strategies similar to those of other firms in the group and yet maintain strategic distinctiveness to gain and sustain a competitive advantage.[121]

The extent of technological leadership, product quality, pricing policies, distribution channels and customer service are examples of strategic dimensions that firms in a strategic group may treat similarly. Thus, membership in a particular strategic group defines the essential characteristics of the firm's strategy.[122]

The notion of strategic groups can be useful for analysing an industry's competitive structure. Such analyses can be helpful in diagnosing competition, positioning and the profitability of firms within an industry.[123] High mobility barriers, high rivalry and low resources among the firms within an industry, limit the formation of strategic groups.[124] However, research suggests that after strategic groups are formed, their membership remains relatively stable over time, making analysis easier and more useful.[125] Using strategic groups to understand an industry's competitive structure requires the firm to plot companies' competitive actions and competitive responses along strategic dimensions such as pricing decisions, product quality, distribution channels and so forth. This type of analysis shows the firm how certain companies are competing similarly in terms of how they use similar strategic dimensions.

Strategic groups have several implications. First, because firms within a group offer similar products to the same customers, the competitive rivalry between them can be intense. The more intense the rivalry, the greater the threat to each firm's profitability. Second, the strengths of the five industry forces differ across strategic

**Strategic group**

A strategic group is a set of firms emphasizing similar strategic dimensions to use a similar strategy.

groups. Third, the closer the strategic groups are in terms of their strategies, the greater is the likelihood of rivalry between the groups.

## Competitor analysis

The competitor environment is the final part of the external environment requiring study. Competitor analysis focuses on each company against which a firm directly competes. For example, supermarket chains Lidl and Aldi, television channels Al Jazeera and Al Arabiya, Kraft and Nestlé, Financial Times and Wall Street Journal, Starbucks and Costa and Boeing and Airbus are keenly interested in understanding each other's objectives, strategies, assumptions and capabilities. Indeed, intense rivalry such as exists between the pairs of competitors mentioned creates a strong need to understand competitors.[126] In a competitor analysis, the firm seeks to understand the following:

■ What drives the competitor, as shown by its *future objectives*.

■ What the competitor is doing and can do, as revealed by its *current strategy*.

■ What the competitor believes about the industry, as shown by its *assumptions*.

■ What the competitor's capabilities are, as shown by its *strengths* and *weaknesses*.[127]

Information about these four dimensions helps the firm prepare an anticipated response profile for each competitor (see Figure 2.3). The results of an effective

**FIGURE 2.3** Competitor analysis components

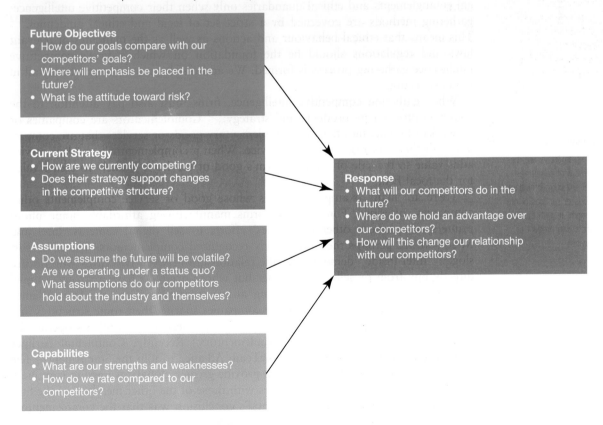

competitor analysis help a firm understand, interpret and predict its competitors' actions and responses. Understanding the actions of competitors clearly contributes to the firm's ability to compete successfully within the industry.[128] Interestingly, research suggests that executives often fail to analyse competitors' possible reactions to competitive actions their firm takes,[129] placing their firm at a potential competitive disadvantage as a result.

The following Strategic Focus illustrates how IBM is employing competitive intelligence to its advantage.

Critical to an effective competitor analysis is gathering data and information that can help the firm understand its competitors' intentions and the strategic implications resulting from them.[130] Useful data and information combine to form competitor intelligence: the set of data and information the firm gathers to better understand and better anticipate competitors' objectives, strategies, assumptions and capabilities. In competitor analysis, the firm gathers intelligence not only about its competitors, but also regarding public policies in countries around the world. Such intelligence facilitates an understanding of the strategic posture of foreign competitors. Through effective competitive and public policy intelligence, the firm gains the insights needed to make effective strategic decisions about how to compete against its rivals.

When asked to describe competitive intelligence, it seems that a number of people respond with phrases such as "competitive spying" and "corporate espionage". These phrases denote the fact that competitive intelligence is an activity that appears to involve trade-offs.[131] According to some, the reason for this is that "what is ethical in one country is different from what is ethical in other countries". This position implies that the rules of engagement to follow when gathering competitive intelligence change in different contexts. However, firms avoid the possibility of legal entanglements and ethical quandaries only when their competitive intelligence-gathering methods are governed by a strict set of legal and ethical guidelines.[132] This means that ethical behaviour and actions as well as the mandates of relevant laws and regulations should be the foundation on which a firm's competitive intelligence-gathering process is formed. We address this matter in greater detail in the next section.

When gathering competitive intelligence, firms must also pay attention to the complementors of its products and strategy.[133] Complementors are companies or networks of companies that sell complementary goods or services that are compatible with the focal firm's good or service. When a complementor's good or service adds value to the sale of the focal firm's good or service it is likely to create value for the focal firm.

There are many examples of firms whose good or service complements other companies' offerings. For example, firms manufacturing affordable home photo printers complement other companies' efforts to sell digital cameras. Intel and Microsoft are perhaps the most widely recognized complementors. The Microsoft slogan "Intel Inside" demonstrates the relationship between two firms who do not directly buy from or sell to each other but whose products have a strong complementary relationship. Alliances among airline operations (e.g., the Star Alliance and the SkyTeam Alliance) find these companies sharing their route structures and customer loyalty programmes as means of complementing each other's operations. (Each alliance is a network of complementors.) Recently, Continental Airlines announced that it was leaving the SkyTeam Alliance to join the Star Alliance. The primary reason for this change was to provide greater global coverage to Continental's customers by combining its routes with those of the other members of the Star Alliance.[134] In essence then, Continental's conclusion was that the complementors

**Competitor intelligence**

Competitor intelligence is the set of data and information the firm gathers to better understand and better anticipate competitors' objectives, strategies, assumptions, and capabilities.

**Complementors**

Complementors are the network of companies that sell complementary goods or services or are compatible with the focal firm's own product or service.

## STRATEGIC FOCUS

# IBM closely watches its competitors to stay at the top of its game

It is critical for companies to study their major rivals to help them shape and implement their strategies to counter competitors' strengths and to exploit their weaknesses. Armed with effective analyses of competitors, companies can enhance their market position and increase returns on their investments. International Business Machines (IBM) is the world's top provider of computer products and services. IBM makes mainframes and servers, storage systems and peripherals, but also has the largest computer service unit in the world; it accounts for more than half of IBM's total revenue. To remain competitive in its various markets, IBM established a competitive analysis team with the sole purpose of observing and analysing competitors such as Hewlett-Packard (HP) and Sun Microsystems. IBM uses the data from these analyses to adjust its strategies and business plans accordingly, to ensure that the firm effectively competes with its major rivals.

IBM's competitive analysis team found that Sun's direct sales team focuses on the top 1500 accounts in its installed base, and that its remaining customers are being serviced by business partners. The IBM team also found that Sun's sales reps primarily emphasize selling hardware instead of solutions, a definitive weakness that provided opportunities for IBM to take away customers from Sun. In addition, IBM's team carefully analysed a large number of HP announcements for its e-business weak points in its high availability campaign. IBM said that the 5Minutes campaign is only a vision that has little business value for its customers, but the campaign has strong marketing value for HP. The analysis showed that HP has low software and services revenues and thus is primarily a hardware company. HP lost approximately 15 per cent of its potential customers because it lacked its own support and consulting services and is too reliant on EDS, Accenture, Cisco, HP resellers and EDS (which HP has recently acquired).

IBM was a pioneer of the multinational business model. It created mini-IBMs in each country, each with its own administration, manufacturing and service operations. Based on the analyses of rival Indian technology companies, IBM identified that a flatter structure and leaner organization was needed to compete effectively. Likewise the competitor analyses discovered that Chinese competitors provided high-quality goods and services for a much lower price. These competitor analyses led IBM to develop global integrated operations. IBM's global shift makes it possible to use lower-cost talent in India to manage machines and software in data centres. In addition, the data centres are interchangeable, so if India has problems, IBM can reroute computing jobs and calls to other locations. Eventually, international competitors will build global delivery hubs, but they will be unlikely to compete with IBM's scientific research capabilities. IBM's integrated global services and research organizations enable it to design innovative services. The cost savings achieved through its global integration efforts led to a higher earnings growth. The overall goal of this global integration plan is to lower costs while simultaneously providing superior services to customers. In doing so, IBM can enhance its competitiveness, increase its market share, and drive revenue and profit growth.

Based on the information obtained from recent competitor analyses, IBM decided only a few adjustments were needed. For example, IBM decided to emphasize its higher margin business consulting services, which help companies change the way they operate, and to focus less on technology integration. IBM also changed the strategy of its software division. Because software is the fastest growing and most profitable segment of the company, IBM has made several acquisitions of software companies, including FileNet, MRO Software, and Webify Solutions. These acquisitions fill holes in IBM's product portfolio and increase its ability to compete effectively with Sun Microsystems and similar rivals.

IBM's strategic actions are creating positive results. Total revenues for the first quarter of 2007 reached €17.3 billion, an increase of 7 per cent from the first quarter of 2006. First quarter 2007 income increased 8 per cent over 2006 to €1.4 billion. And its first quarter 2007 earnings of €0.95 per share represented an increase of 12 per cent over the first quarter of 2006.

**Sources:** Hamm, S. (2006) "Big blue shift", *BusinessWeek*, http://www.businessweek.com, June 6; Morgan, T. P. (1999) "IBM's competitive analysis on Sun, HP", *Computer-*

*gram International*, http://www.findarticles.com, Oct. 4; Lex: IBM (2005) *Financial Times*, http://www.ft.com, May 5; Hamm, S. (2006) "IBM's revved-up software engine", *BusinessWeek*, http://www.businessweek.com, Aug. 15; Krippel, J. (2007) "International Business Machines Corporation", Hoovers, http://www.hoovers.com; 2007, http://www.ibm.com/news, May 5.

### Questions

**1** How does IBM benefit from competitive intelligence?

**2** Discuss whether competitor analysis makes is useful for all firms.

**3** What are the conditions for it to be most effective?

**4** What conditions make competitor analysis less effective?

**5** Can competitor analysis be detrimental to company performance? Explain and discuss.

KEY DEBATE

© sebastian-julian

# Environmental analysis – how much?

The analysis of the external environment is comprehensive. It includes scrutiny of the changes in the general environment, the developments in the industry and the actions and intentions of rivals. Engaging in comprehensive analysis certainly has benefits, it enables firms to better understand, anticipate and implement the right strategies at the right time. However, exhaustive analysis also has some downsides. Such comprehensive analysis is costly as it takes skill and time to be done well. It focuses attention on the outside to an extent that does not seem justified by the degree to which firms can change their external environment. This chapter made the case that firms

should engage in analysing what cannot easily (or only under great difficulty) be influenced.

Advocates who point out the immediate and irrevocable costs of environmental analysis and its uncertain returns may counter this position. Rather than focusing on what cannot be changed firms need to understand how they can best act to improve their situation. In the extreme, some suggest to avoid (excessive) analysis in favour of engaging with reality. While exhaustive analysis and direct engagement may be two extreme positions, they illustrate the range of positions taken in the ongoing debate on the questions:

### Questions

**1** How much environmental analysis is good and how much is excessive?

**2** How useful is it to know about what cannot be influenced?

**3** Is environmental analysis like an insurance in the sense that if you conduct more environmental analysis you will be safer and not fall victim to negative turns of events?

of the Star Alliance created more value for its customers than did its complementors in the SkyTeam Alliance.

As our discussion shows, complementors expand the set of competitors firms must evaluate when completing a competitor analysis. For example, when Delta Airlines wants to study Continental Airlines, it must examine Continental's strategic actions as an independent company as well as its actions as a member of the Star Alliance. And, the same is true in reverse – Continental must study Delta's actions as an independent firm as well as its actions as a member of the SkyTeam Alliance. Similarly, Intel and Microsoft analyse each other's actions in that those actions might either help each firm gain a competitive advantage or damage each firm's ability to exploit a competitive advantage.

## Ethical considerations

As noted above, firms must follow relevant laws and regulations as well as carefully articulated ethical guidelines when gathering competitor intelligence. Industry associations often develop lists of these practices that firms can adopt. Practices considered both legal and ethical include (1) obtaining publicly available information (e.g., court records, competitors' help-wanted advertisements, annual reports, financial reports of publicly held corporations, and Uniform Commercial Code filings), and (2) attending trade fairs and shows to obtain competitors' brochures, view their exhibits and listen to discussions about their products. In contrast, certain practices (including blackmail, trespassing, eavesdropping, and stealing drawings, samples or documents) are widely viewed as unethical and often are illegal.

Some competitor intelligence practices may be legal, but a firm must decide whether they are also ethical, given the image it desires as a corporate citizen. Especially with electronic transmissions, the line between legal and ethical practices can be difficult to determine. For example, a firm may develop website addresses that are similar to those of its competitors and thus occasionally receive e-mail transmissions that were intended for those competitors. The practice is an example of the challenges companies face in deciding how to gather intelligence about competitors while simultaneously determining how to prevent competitors from learning too much about them. Again, establishing principles and taking actions that are consistent with them is what firms should do to deal with these types of challenges. ING, a global financial company offering banking, investments, life insurance and retirement services, expresses the principles guiding its actions as follows: "ING conducts business on the basis of clearly defined business principles. In all our activities, we carefully weigh the interests of our various stakeholders: customers, employees, communities and shareholders. ING strives to be a good corporate citizen."[135]

Open discussions of intelligence-gathering techniques can help a firm ensure that employees, customers, suppliers and even potential competitors understand its convictions to follow ethical practices for gathering competitor intelligence. An appropriate guideline for competitor intelligence practices is to respect the principles of common morality and the right of competitors not to reveal certain information about their products, operations and strategic intentions.[136]

© Allstar Picture Library/Alamy

**CLOSING CASE**

## Does Google have the market power to ignore external pressures?

Google's continued growth and expansion of its services is astonishing. Currently, after only ten years, Google is the most widely used Internet search engine and as such, it dominates online advertising. In 2004 Google was worth €18.11 billion. By mid-2007, the firm's market capitalization hit €133.07 billion, making Google worth more than IBM, a symbol of US enterprise.

Google is known for its loose corporate culture with informal principles and appears to have the goodwill of its customers. But as Google continues to extend its reach, it is also experiencing more pressures from the external environment. Google's strategy of bringing to the market "search with content" by acquiring You-Tube, upset the global media industry. The industry felt, a search engine that shows films and other copyrighted content for free is committing piracy. Viacom filed a 1 billion euro lawsuit against Google and YouTube alleging that they were airing clips of its hit programmes without permission. The lawsuit cited

"massive intentional copyright infringement". Viacom accused YouTube of violating copyright law. In February 2007, Viacom demanded that YouTube remove more than 100 000 clips, and YouTube agreed. Viacom stated that more than 160 000 clips available on YouTube are being used without Viacom's permission.

In addition, Google became involved in other lawsuits focused around copyright violations and trademark infringements. In 2006, a Belgium court ruled that Google should refrain from posting news articles from French and German language newspapers on the Google News services. In the United States, the Authors Guild and some additional publishers, supported by the Association of American Publishers, sued Google for making digital copies of copyrighted books from libraries. Microsoft has also accused Google of "systematically violating copyright" by scanning millions of books and journals from libraries around the world and making them available online. Google disputes these accusations, suggesting that all of their products comply with copyright law. Google argues that because only a small extract of a copyrighted work is shown in its search process, it is not in violation of the copyright law. For books that have been digitized in US libraries and under copyright, Google only reports that the book exists. Google reached a settlement in the case.

Google's acquisition of DoubleClick represents another critical building block in its strategy. But this move is being scrutinized by companies such as Microsoft and AT&T, because Google, as they suspect, is violating antitrust laws. Basically they argued that Google's share of the search advertisements placed on third-party websites, combined with the recent purchase of DoubleClick an online advertising company, will create a dominant position in the overall online advertising business. Central to this complaint is the question of whether the search and display advertising businesses, until now separate, should be treated as a single market for regulatory purposes. According to AT&T, this acquisition would make any Web company that depends on online advertising dependent on a single supplier and, in effect, Google would be able to influence the revenue lifeline of other rival Internet companies. In this case settlement has been achieved.

A combination of these external pressures has affected Google's standing on Wall Street since 2007. Google is no longer considered as the hot company. In fact, its stock price has underperformed the broader market index because investors fear that re-taliation from competitors could limit the company's growth. As a result, Google's stock price has fallen. But after the financial crisis, share prices have been climbing again in 2009. Google reported revenues of €4.68 billion for the quarter ended September 30, 2009. Eric Schmidt, CEO of Google stated: "Google had a strong quarter; we saw 7 per cent year-over-year revenue growth despite the tough economic conditions. "While there is a lot of uncertainty about the pace of economic recovery, we believe the worst of the recession is behind us and now feel confident about investing heavily in our future."

In a recent setback for Google, in April 2010 ten privacy and data-protection commissioners wrote a public letter to Eric Schmidt, demanding changes to Google Buzz, a social-networking service that was transparently using Gmail accounts to find "followers" for users. The European data protection agencies also demanded independent proof from Google, Microsoft and Yahoo! on their progress with making the prom-ised changes to protect the privacy of users' search history. Google was asked to store data for only six months instead of nine. European regulators protect data privacy as a fundamental right of the individual and see the need for the individuals to remain in con-trol of how the data is used. This contrasts with the more casual understanding prevalent in the United States of America, where individuals are expected to sue if their privacy has been violated, and companies are trusted to regulate themselves.

Most embarrassingly, "Wi-Figate" exemplifies Google's difficulties. Capturing visual information of streets and houses for its mapping project, which in itself proved to be very controversial in some countries while unproblematic in others, Google gathered data from unsecured Wi-Fi networks in people's homes. While Google insisted that the data had been taken without intent, several regulators launched investigations. Google is now being formally investi-gated in Austria, France, Germany and Spain and suf-fers bad press in other countries. However, data deletion was requested also in Britain, Denmark and Ireland while not yet in France, Germany and Spain.

**Sources:** 2009 "Google announces third quarter 2009 re-sults", *Financial Release*, 15 October; Waters, R. (2007) "All eyes on Google advertising", *Financial Times*, http://www.ft.com, April 16; Wachman, R. (2007) "Google's expansion is coming at a price: It's losing its popularity", *The Observer*, http://www.observer.co.uk, March 25; Hof, R. (2006), "Ganging up on Google", *BusinessWeek*, http://www.businessweek.com, April 24; Devichand, M. (2007) "Is Google really flouting copyright law?" BBC Law in Action, http://www.news.bbc.co.uk, March 9; 2007 "Viacom sues Google and YouTube", *International Herald Tribune*, http://www.IHT.com, March 13; Helft, M. (2009) "Lawsuit says Google was unfair to rival site", *New York Times*, February 18, http://www.nyt.com; Elhauge, E. (2009) "Framing the Antitrust Issues in the Google Settlement", *Competition Policy International*, October, Release 2; Helft, M. (2009) "Google Offers Users a Peek at Stored Data", *New York Times*, November 5; http://www.nyt.com; 2010 "The clash of data civilizations: Legal confusion on internet privacy", *The Economist*, June 19.

*Questions*

1 Discuss the general environment's seven segments.

2 How should Google conduct environmental analysis?

3 What are the main challenges to Google arising from its international, external environment?

4 Identify the five competitive forces and explain how they determine the profit potential.

5 How is Google positioned? What are the main threats?

## SUMMARY

- The firm's external environment is challenging and complex. Because of the external environment's effect on performance, the firm must develop the skills required to identify opportunities and threats existing in that environment.

- The external environment has three major parts: (1) the general environment (elements in the broader society that affect industries and their firms); (2) the industry environment (factors that influence a firm, its competitive actions and responses, and the industry's profit potential); and (3) the competitor environment (in which the firm analyses each major competitor's future objectives, current strategies, assumptions, and capabilities).

- The external environmental analysis process has four steps: scanning, monitoring, forecasting and assessing. Through environmental analyses, the firm identifies opportunities and threats.

- The general environment has seven segments: demographic, economic, political/legal, socio-cultural, technological, global and physical. For each segment, the firm wants to determine the strategic relevance of environmental changes and trends.

- Compared with the general environment, the industry environment has a more direct effect on the firm's strategic actions. The five forces model of competition includes the threat of entry, the power of suppliers, the power of buyers, product substitutes, and the intensity of rivalry among competitors. By studying these forces, the firm finds a position in an industry where it can influence the forces in its favour or where it can buffer itself from the power of the forces in order to achieve strategic competitiveness and earn above-average returns.

- Industries are populated with different strategic groups. A strategic group is a collection of firms following similar strategies along similar dimensions. Competitive rivalry is greater within a strategic group than between strategic groups.

- Competitor analysis informs the firm about the future objectives, current strategies, assumptions and capabilities of the companies with which it directly competes. A thorough analysis examines complementors that sustain a competitor's strategy and major networks or alliances in which competitors participate. When analysing competitors, the firm should also identify and carefully monitor major actions taken by firms with performance below the industry norm.

- Different techniques are used to create competitor intelligence: the set of data, information and knowledge that allows the firm to better understand its competitors and thereby predict their likely strategic and tactical actions. Firms should use only legal and ethical practices to gather intelligence. The Internet enhances firms' capabilities to gather insights about competitors and their strategic intentions.

## REVIEW QUESTIONS

1   Why is it important for a firm to study and understand the external environment?

2   What are the differences between the general environment and the industry environment? Why are these differences important?

3   What is the external environmental analysis process (four steps)? What does the firm want to learn when using this process?

4   What are the seven segments of the general environment? Explain the differences between them.

5   How do the five forces of competition in an industry affect its profit potential? Explain.

6   What is a strategic group? Of what value is knowledge of the firm's strategic group in formulating that firm's strategy?

7   What is the importance of collecting and interpreting data and information about competitors? What practices should a firm use to gather competitor intelligence and why?

## DISCUSSION QUESTIONS

1   Studying and understanding the external environment is important. How far does a firm need to understand its environment? Where are there boundaries between the relevant and irrelevant environment, if they exist?

2   Industries are no longer clear cut. Think of how mobile devices bring together multiple industries such as telephony, music, movie, television,

communication and organization. How can firms deal with such industry convergence?

3   The four-step process of environmental analysis provides important information after careful analysis. However, the environment is changing rapidly. How should firms deal with the problem of keeping up with the changes?

4   The seven segments of the general environment are rarely equally important. Frequently the importance of one or more of these segments changes. How can a firm focus on the key segments when needed?

5   The five forces model has been discussed frequently and candidates for a sixth or seventh force have been suggested. Which additions would you consider and why they should or should not be included?

6   Discuss the practice of gathering competitor intelligence. For which strategies is competitor intelligence more important?

## FURTHER READING

Much of the discourse on strategic management is rational and analytical. It is important to point to the emotional and irrational side of human cognition, which can provide great insights when tacit knowledge can be enriched. Nonaka and Takeuchi's classic, *The Knowledge Creating Company* (Oxford University Press) from 1995 is still foundational for putting tacit knowledge to use by corporations. For the readers interested in exploring the emotional basis of rational decision making, Damasio's *Descartes Error* (Harper Perennial, 1995) is a deep and rewarding read.

Finally, Tom Davenport has been at the forefront of many a management fashion (e.g. re-engineering, knowledge management). His work, *Competing on Analytics* (Harvard Business School Press, 2007) is a timely introduction into how quantitative analysis enables businesses, like Google, Carrefour, or Bol.com to mine data and make money doing so.

## EXPERIENTIAL EXERCISES

### Exercise 1: Airline competitor analysis

The International Air Transport Association (IATA) reports statistics on the number of passengers carried each year by major airlines. Passenger data for 2007 is reported for the top ten fliers in three categories:

- Domestic flights
- International flights
- Combined traffic, domestic and international flights

The table below lists both passenger data and rankings for each category.

For this exercise, you will develop competitor profiles of selected air carriers.

### Part One

Working in groups select one airline from the table. The pool of selected airlines should contain a roughly even balance of three regions: North America, Europe/Middle East and Asia. Answer the following questions:

1   What drives this competitor (i.e., what are their objectives)?

2   What is their current strategy?

3   What does this competitor believe about their industry?

4   What are their strengths and weaknesses?

5   Does this airline belong to an airline alliance (e.g. Oneworld, Star, SkyTeam)

When researching your companies, you should use multiple resources. The company's website is a good starting point. Public firms headquartered in the US will also have annual reports and 10-K reports filed with the Securities and Exchange Commission.

### Part Two

As a group, summarize the results of each competitor profile into a single table under the columns of objectives, current strategy, beliefs, strengths, weaknesses and alliance partner. Then discuss the following topics:

1   Which airlines had the most similar strategies? The most different? Would you consider any of the firms you studied to be in the same strategic group – i.e., a group of firms that follow similar strategies along similar dimensions?

2   Create a composite five forces model based on the firms you reviewed. How might these elements of industry structure (e.g., substitutes, or bargaining power of buyers) differ from the perspective of individual airlines?

| Airline | Intl Rank | Intl Passengers | Domestic Rank | Domestic Passengers | Combined Rank | Combined Passengers |
|---|---|---|---|---|---|---|
| Air France | 3 | 31 549 | | | 8 | 50 465 |
| All Nippon Airways | | | 6 | 44 792 | | |
| American Airlines | 7 | 21 479 | 2 | 76 687 | 2 | 98 166 |
| British Airways | 5 | 28 302 | | | | |
| Cathay Pacific | 10 | 17 695 | | | | |
| China Southern Airlines | | | 5 | 52 505 | 5 | 56 522 |
| Continental Airlines | | | 9 | 37 175 | 9 | 49 059 |
| Delta Air Lines | | | 3 | 61 651 | 3 | 73 086 |
| Easyjet | 4 | 30 173 | | | | |
| Emirates | 8 | 20 448 | | | | |
| Japan Airlines International | | | 10 | 35 583 | | |
| KLM | 6 | 23 165 | | | | |
| Lufthansa | 2 | 41 322 | | | 7 | 54 165 |
| Northwest Airlines | | | 7 | 44 337 | 6 | 54 696 |
| Ryanair | 1 | 49 030 | | | 10 | 49 030 |
| Singapore Airlines | 9 | 18 957 | | | | |
| Southwest Airlines | | | 1 | 101 911 | 1 | 101 911 |
| United Airlines | | | 4 | 58 162 | 4 | 68 363 |
| US Airways Inc. | | | 8 | 37 560 | | |

3   Which airlines appear best positioned to succeed in the future? Why?

### Exercise 2: what does the future look like?

A critical ingredient to studying the general environment is identifying opportunities and threats. An opportunity is a condition in the environment that, if exploited, helps a company achieve strategic competitiveness. In order to identify opportunities one must be aware of trends that affect the world around us now or those that are projected to do so in the future.

Thomas Fry, senior futurist at the DaVinci Institute, says that the chaotic nature of interconnecting trends and the vast array of possibilities that arise from these is somewhat akin to watching a spinning compass needle. From the way we use phones, email, or recruit new workers to organizations, the climate for business is changing and shifting dramatically and at rapidly increasing rates. Sorting these out and making sense of them provides the basis for opportunity decision making. Which ones will dominate and which will fade? Understanding this is crucial for business success.

Your challenge (either individually or as a group) is to identify a trend, technology, entertainment, or design that is likely to alter the way in which business is conducted in the future. Once you have identified this be prepared to discuss:

- Which of the six dimensions of the general environment will this affect? (There may be more than one.)

- Describe the impact.

- List some business opportunities that will come from this.

- Identify some existing organizations that stand to benefit

- What, if any, are the ethical implications?

You should consult a wide variety of sources. For example, the Gartner Group and McKinsey & Company both produce market research and forecasts for business. There are also a host of web forecasting tools and addresses such as TED (technology, entertainment, design where you can find videos of their discussions) which hosts an annual conference for path-breaking new ideas. Similarly, the DaVinci Institute for Global Futures and a wide host of others take their own unique vision for tomorrow's environment.

## VIDEO CASE

### Indy labels and major music labels in the digital landscape

www.cengage.co.uk/volberda/students/video_cases

Music is big business. Major companies dominate the music business, while independent record labels seek niches in which they can break free from the majors' influence. Digital technology has proven to be highly disruptive in the camera industry, disk drive industry and others. The two clips provide a survey of views of Indies and their competition with majors in the era of digital technology.

The interviewees, representing Indies, talk about how digital technology influences their industry and the rivalry therein. Before you watch the video reflect on what kind of music, Indy or Majors, you and your friends purchase, consider the following concepts from the text and be prepared to address the following questions:

### Concepts

- Competition
- Opportunity

- Threat
- Industry environment—5 forces
- Competitor analysis

### Questions

1   Compare the strengths and weaknesses of Indies and Majors.

2   How do they make use of digital technologies?

3   Who are the players in the music industry?

4   Digital technologies can be seen as threatening to Indies and Majors. Why?

5   Are Indies and Majors competitors or are they strategic groups?

6   What is the difference, or is there a difference, between a musician's objectives and those of Indies and Majors?

## NOTES

1.   D. A. Bosse, R. A. Phillips and J. S. Harrison, 2009, "Stakeholders, reciprocity, and firm performance", *Strategic Management Journal*, 30: 447–456.

2.   P. Berrone and L. R. Gomez-Mejia, 2009, "Environmental performance and executive compensation: An integrated agency-institutional perspective", *Academy of Management Journal*, 52: 103–126; P. Chattopadhyay, W. H. Glick and G. P. Huber, 2001, "Organizational actions in response to threats and opportunities", *Academy of Management Journal*, 44: 937–955.

3.   C. Weigelt and M. B. Sarkar, 2009, "Learning from supply-side agents: The impact of technology solution providers' experiential diversity on clients' innovation adoption", *Academy of Management Journal*, 52: 37–60; D. G. Sirmon, S. Gove and M. A. Hitt, 2008, "Resource management in dyadic competitive rivalry: The effects of resource bundling and deployment", *Academy of Management Journal*, 51: 919–935.

4.   J. P. Bonardi, G. I. F. Holburn and R. G. Vanden Bergh, 2006, "Nonmarket strategy performance: Evidence from

US electric utilities", *Academy of Management Journal,* 49: 1209–1228.

5.  S. Labaton, 2009, "Obama plans fast action to tighten financial rules", *New York Times Online,* http://www.nytimes.com, January 25.

6.  J. Welch and S. Welch, 2009, "The economy: A little clarity", *BusinessWeek,* May 4, 80; H. W. Volberda, N. J. Foss, and M. A. Lyles, 2010, "Absorbing the concept of absorptive capacity: How to realize its potential in the organization field", *Organization Science,* 21(4): 931–951; J. S. Sidhu, H. R. Commandeur and H. W. Volberda, 2007, "The multifaced nature of exploration and exploitation: Value of supply, demand, and spatial search for innovation", *Organization Science,* 18 (1): 20–38; J. J. P. Jansen, F. A. J Van den Bosch and H. W. Volberda, 2005, "Managing potential and realized absorptive capacity: How do organizational antecedents matter", *Academy of Management Journal,* 48 (6): 999–1015.

7.  J. Uotila, M. Maula, T. Keil and S. A. Zahra, 2009, "Exploration, exploitation, and financial performance: Analysis of S&P 500 corporations", *Strategic Management Journal,* 30: 221–231; J. L. Murillo-Luna, C. Garces-Ayerbe and P. Rivera-Torres, 2008, "Why do patterns of environmental response differ? A stakeholders' pressure approach", *Strategic Management Journal,* 29: 1225–1240.

8.  A. Kacperczyk, 2009, "With greater power comes greater responsibility? Takeover protection and corporate attention to stakeholders", *Strategic Management Journal,* 30: 261–285; C. Eesley and M. J. Lenox, 2006, "Firm responses to secondary stakeholder action", *Strategic Management Journal,* 27: 765–781.

9.  L. Fahey, 1999, *Competitors,* New York: John Wiley & Sons; B. A. Walters and R. L. Priem, 1999, "Business strategy and CEO intelligence acquisition", *Competitive Intelligence Review,* 10(2): 15–22.

10. http://online.wsj.com/article/SB125473606240264063. html; http://news.bbc.co.uk/2/hi/8289976.stm; http://www.nrc.nl/economie/article2228550.ece/ Melkboeren_protesteren_tegen_de_lage_melkprijs

11. A. Taylor, III, 2010, "Chrysler's speed merchant", *Fortune,* 162(4): 77–82.

12. J. C. Short, D. J. Ketchen, Jr., T. B. Palmer and G. T. Hult, 2007, "Firm, strategic group, and industry influences on performance", *Strategic Management Journal,* 28: 147–167.

13. A. Humphreys, 2010, "Megamarketing: The Creation of Markets as a Social Process", *Journal of Marketing,* 74 (March), 1–19; M. C. Suchman, 1995, "Managing Legitimacy: Strategic and Institutional Approaches," *Academy of Management Review,* 20(3): 571–611; M. A. Cusumano, Y. Mylonadis and R. S. Rosenbloom, 1992, "Strategic Maneuvering and Mass-Market Dynamics: The Triumph of VHS over Beta," *Business History Review,* 66(1): 51–95.

14. J. P. Bonardi and G. D. Klein, 2005, "Corporate political strategies for widely salient issues", *Academy of Management Review,* 30: 555–576; J. G. Frynas, K. Mellahi and G. A. Pigman, 2006, "First mover advantages in international business and firm-specific political resources", *Strategic Management Journal,* 27: 321–345. Lawton, T. and S. McGuire, 2005, "Adjusting to Liberalization: tracing the impact of the WTO on the European textiles and chemicals industries", *Business and Politics,* 7(2):1–25.

15. X. Zhang, P. Reinmoeller and B. Krug, 2010, "Political strategies: Understanding how foreign MNCs survive in China" (with Krug and Zhang), in: T. Goydke (ed.) *Corporate Culture in China and Japan: Culture and Management in East Asia,* MV-Wissenschaft, 179–195.

16. K. P. Coyne and J. Horn, 2009, "Predicting your competitor's reaction", *Harvard Business Review,* 87(4): 90–97.

17. http://www.wikinvest.com/stock/Koninklijke_Philips_ Electronics_(PHG)

18. D. Sull, 2009, "How to thrive in turbulent markets", *Harvard Business Review,* 87(2): 78–88; J. Hagel, III, J. S. Brown and L. Davison, 2008, "Shaping strategy in a world of constant disruption", *Harvard Business Review* 86(10): 80–89; H. W. Volberda, 2004, "Crisis in strategy: Fragmentation, integration or synthesis", *European Management Review,* Special Issue: The Millennium Nexus: Strategic Management at the cross-roads, 1(1): 35–42; H. W. Volberda, 1998, *Building the flexible firm: How to remain competitive,* Oxford: Oxford University Press.

19. J. A. Lamberg, H. Tikkanen, T. Nokelainen and H. Suur-Inkeroinen, 2009, "Competitive dynamics, strategic consistency, and organizational survival", *Strategic Management Journal,* 30: 45–60.

20. http://nl.wikipedia.org/wiki/Albert_Heijn_(supermarkt)# Albert.nl; http://economie.nieuws.nl/174248

21. W. B. Gartner, K. G. Shaver and J. Liao, 2008, "Opportunities as attributions: Categorizing strategic issues from an attributional perspective", *Strategic Entrepreneurship Journal,* 2: 301–315.

22. W. H. Stewart, R. C. May and A. Kalla, 2008, "Environmental perceptions and scanning in the United States and India: Convergence in entrepreneurial information seeking?", *Entrepreneurship Theory and Practice,* 32: 83–106; K. M. Patton and T. M. McKenna, 2005, "Scanning for competitive intelligence", *Competitive Intelligence Magazine,* 8(2): 24–26; A. J. Verdu, J. M. Gomez-Gras and H. W. Volberda, 2006, "Managers' environmental perceptions: an institutional perspective", *International Journal of Business Environment,* 1(1): 5–23.

23. J. O. Schwarz, 2008, "Assessing the future of futures studies in management", *Futures,* 40: 237–246; K. M. Eisenhardt, 2002, "Has strategy changed?", *MIT Sloan Management Review,* 43(2): 88–91.

24. J. R. Hough and M. A. White, 2004, "Scanning actions and environmental dynamism: Gathering information for strategic decision making", *Management Decision,* 42: 781–793; V. K. Garg, B. A. Walters and R. L. Priem, 2003, "Chief executive scanning emphases, environmental dynamism, and manufacturing firm performance", *Strategic Management Journal,* 24: 725–744; H. W. Volberda, 1998, *Building the flexible firm: How to remain competitive,* Oxford: Oxford University Press.

25. C. P. Wei and Y. H. Lee, 2004, "Event detection from online news documents for supporting environmental scanning", *Decision Support Systems,* 36: 385–401.

26. L. Fahey, 1999, *Competitors: Outwitting, Outmaneuvering and Outperforming*, Wiley, 71–73.

27. http://www.knorr.nl/site/producten/543226/groep

28. S. M. Kalita, 2009, "Companies world-wide rethink strategies", *Wall Street Journal Online*, http://www.wsj.com, April.

29. T. M. Jones, W. Felps and G. A. Bigley, 2007, "Ethical theory and stakeholder-related decisions: The role of stakeholder culture", *Academy of Management Review*, 32: 137–155.

30. M. J. Leiblein and T. L. Madsen, 2009, "Unbundling competitive heterogeneity: Incentive structures and capability influences on technological innovation", *Strategic Management Journal*, 30: 711–735; S. B. Rodrigues and J. Child, 2008, *Corporate Co-evolution*, Chichester: Wiley.

31. D. Matten and J. Moon, 2008, "Implicit and explicit CSR: A conceptual framework for a comparative understanding of corporate social responsibility", *Academy of Management Review*, 33: 404–424; F. Sanna-Randaccio and R. Veugelers, 2007, "Multinational knowledge spillovers with decentralized R&D: A game theoretic approach", *Journal of International Business Studies,* 38: 47–63.

32. L. Fahey, 1999, *Competitors: Outwitting, Outmaneuvering and Outperforming*, Wiley.

33. http://www.nokia.com/NOKIA_COM_1/Press_Center/Bulletin_board/pdf/NOKIA%20INTRO%20POSTCARDS.pdf

34. P. E. Bierly, III, F. Damanpour and M. D. Santoro, 2009, "The application of external knowledge: Organizational conditions for exploration and exploitation", *Journal of Management Studies*, 46: 481–509; L. Fahey, 1999, *Competitors: Outwitting, Outmaneuvering and Outperforming*, Wiley, 75–77.

35. K. M. Sutcliffe and K. Weber, 2003, "The high cost of accurate knowledge", *Harvard Business Review,* 81(5): 74–82.

36. E. K. Foedermayr and A. Diamantopoulos, 2008, "Market segmentation in practice: Review of empirical studies, methodological assessment, and agenda for future research", *Journal of Strategic Marketing*, 16: 223–265; L. Fahey and V. K. Narayanan, 1986, *Macroenvironmental Analysis for Strategic Management,* St. Paul, MN: West Publishing Company, 58.

37. US Census Bureau, 2009, International data base, http://www.census.gov/pic/www/idb/worldpopgraph.html, May 24.

38. S. Moffett, 2005, "Fast-aging Japan keeps its elders on the job longer", *Wall Street Journal,* June 15, A1, A8.

39. S. Armour, 2009, "Mortgage crisis robbing seniors of golden years" *USA Today*, June 5–7, A1 & A2.

40. J. M. Nittoli, 2009, "Now is no time to skimp on retirement plans", *Wall Street Journal*, http://www.wsj.com, June 5.

41. R. Florida, 2005, "The world is spiky", *The Atlantic Monthly*, October, 50–51.

42. 2009, CultureGrams World Edition, http://www.culturegrams.com, June 5.

43. C. Prahalad, 2002. "Strategies for the bottom of the economic pyramid", *Reflections*, 3(4): 617; C. Prahalad and A. Hammond, 2002, "Serving the world's poor, profitably", *Harvard Business Review*, September, 4–11; C. Prahalad, 2006, *The Fortune at the Bottom of the Pyramid: Eradicating Poverty Through Profits*, Upper Saddle River, NJ: Wharton School Publishing.

44. http://www.oecdobserver.org/news/fullstory.php/aid/337/

45. J. A. Chatman and S. E. Spataro, 2005, "Using self-categorization theory to understand relational demography-based variations in people's responsiveness to organizational culture", *Academy of Management Journal,* 48: 321–331.

46. http://www.cbs.nl/NR/rdonlyres/321B3C72-39D6-48A9-B3EC-975C5B79F56B/0/2009k1v4p19art.pdf

47. http://www.expatica.com/nl/employment/employment_information/Are-eastern-Europe_s-migrant-workers-heading-home_-_12004.html?ppager=2

48. A. K. Fosu, 2008, "Inequality and the growth-poverty nexus: Specification empirics using African data", *Applied Economics Letters*, 15: 563–566; A. McKeown, 2007, "Periodizing globalization", *History Workshop Journal*, 63(1): 218–230.

49. O. Sullivan, 2008, "Busyness, status distinction and consumption strategies of the income rich, time poor", *Time & Society*, 17: 5–26.

50. 2009, "Half the world is middle class?", http:///www.edwardsglobal.com, May 10.

51. D. Vrontis and P. Pavlou, 2008, *Journal for International Business and Entrepreneurship Development*, 3: 289–307; A. Jones and N. Ennis, 2007, "Bringing the environment into economic development", *Local Economy*, 22(1): 1–5; L. Fahey and V. K. Narayanan, 1986, *Macroenvironmental Analysis*, West Publishing company, 105.

52. P. Coy, 2009, "What good are economists anyway?", *BusinessWeek*, April 27, 26–31.

53. J. Simms, 2009, "Losses at Japan's electronics companies are no shock", *Wall Street Journal Online*, http://www.wsj.com, February 4.

54. J. Bush, 2009, "The worries facing Russia's banks", *Wall Street Journal Online*, http://www.wsj.com, April 13.

55. A. Peaple and N. P. Muoi, 2009, "Vietnam's market – the fizz is deliberate", *Wall Street Journal Online*, http://www.wsj.com, June 11.

56. R. H. Lester, A. Hillman, A. Zardkoohi and A. A. Cannella, Jr., 2008, "Former government officials as outside directors: The role of human and social capital", *Academy of Management Journal*, 51: 999–1013; C. Oliver and I. Holzinger, 2008, "The effectiveness of strategic political management: A dynamic capabilities framework", *Academy of Management Review*, 33: 496–520.

57. J. W. Spencer, 2008, "The impact of multinational enterprise strategy on indigenous enterprises: Horizontal spillovers and crowding out in developing countries",

*Academy of Management Review*, 33: 341–361; W. Chen, 2007, "Does the colour of the cat matter? The red hat strategy in China's private enterprises", *Management and Organizational Review*, 3: 55–80.

58. P. Engardio, 2009, "Clearing the track for high-speed rail", *BusinessWeek*, May 4, 29.

59. K. Bradsher, 2010, "China Offers High-Speed Rail to California", *New York Times*, April 7.

60. http://www.z24.nl/bedrijven/transport_vervoer/arti-kel_3452.z24/EasyJet_verhuist_om_vliegtax.html

61. http://www.nu.nl/economie/1764426/nederlanders-ontwijken-vliegtaks.html

62. H. W. Jenkins, Jr., 2009, "GM needs a political strategy", *Wall Street Journal Online*, http://www.wsj.com, June 10.

63. G. L. F. Holburn and R. G. Vanden Bergh, 2008, "The effectiveness of strategic political management: A dynamic capabilities framework", *Academy of Management Review*, 33: 521–540; M. A. Hitt, L. Bierman, K. Uhlenbruck and K. Shimizu, 2006, "The importance of resources in the internationalization of professional service firms: The good, the bad, and the ugly", *Academy of Management Journal*, 49: 1137–1157; Lawton, T. and T. Rajwani "Designing Lobbying Capabilities: managerial choices in unpredictable environments", *European Business Review*, 23(2), 2011 (forthcoming); V. Ambrosini and C. Bowman, 2009, "What are dynamic capabilities and are they a useful construct in strategic management?", *International Journal of Management Reviews*, 11(1): 29–49; C. Salvato, 2009, "Capabilities unveiled: The role of ordinary activities in the evolution of product development processes", *Organization Science*, 20(2): 384–409.

64. J. Parello-Plesner, 2010, "Europe, Asia and the South Korea Free Trade agreement", *Govmonitor – Public Sector News & Information*, http://www.thegovmonitor.com/world_news/europe/europe-asia-and-the-south-korea-free-trade-agreement-2-40192.html, October 10, 2010)

65. K. Olsen, 2009, "South Korea, EU call for early conclusion of trade pact", *Houston Chronicle Online*, http://www.chron.com, May 23.

66. R. Florida, 2005, "The world is spiky", *The Atlantic Monthly*, October, 50–51.

67. http://proquest.umi.com/pqdlink?Ver=1&Exp=11-29-2014&FMT=7&DID=1581385591&RQT=309&cfc=1

68. E. S. W. Ng, 2008, "Why organizations choose to manage diversity: Toward a leadership-based theoretical framework", *Human Resource Development Review*, 7: 58–78.

69. L. Manchikanti, 2008, "Health care reform in the United States: Radical surgery needed now more than ever", *Pain Physician*, 11: 13–42.

70. S. A. Burd, 2009, "How Safeway is cutting health-care costs", *Wall Street Journal Online*, http://www.wsj.com, June 12.

71. A. McConnon, 2009, "For a temp giant, a boom in boomers", *BusinessWeek*, June 1, 54.

72. F. Moore and C. Rees, 2008, "Culture against cohesion: Global corporate strategy and employee diversity in the UK plant of a German MNC", *Employee Relations*, 30: 176–189; B. L. Kirkman, K. B. Lowe and C. B. Gibson, 2006, "A quarter of a century of culture's consequences: A review of empirical research incorporating Hofstede's cultural values framework", *Journal of International Business Studies*, 37: 285–320.

73. S. Michailova and K. Hutchings, 2006, "National cultural influences on knowledge sharing: A comparison of China and Russia", *Journal of Management Studies*, 43: 384–405.

74. J. B. Knight and L. Yueh, 2008, "The role of social capital in the labour market in China", *Economics of Transition*, 16: 389–414; P. J. Buckley, J. Clegg and H. Tan, 2006, "Cultural awareness in knowledge transfer to China – The role of guanxi and mianzi", *Journal of World Business*, 41: 275–288; B. Krug, and H. Hendrischke, 2007, *The Chinese Economy in the 21st Century: Enterprise and Business Behaviour*, Edgar Elgar: Cheltenham.

75. R. K. Sinha and C. H. Noble, 2008, "The adoption of radical manufacturing technologies and firm survival", *Strategic Management Journal*, 29: 943–962.

76. K. H. Tsai and J. C. Wang, 2008, "External technology acquisition and firm performance: A longitudinal study", *Journal of Business Venturing*, 23: 91–112; D. Lavie, 2006, "Capability reconfiguration: An analysis of incumbent responses to technological change", *Academy of Management Review*, 31: 153–174.

77. S. A. Brown, 2008, "Household technology adoption, use, and impacts: Past, present, and future", *Information Systems Frontiers*, 10: 397–402.

78. W. S. Mossberg, 2009, "The latest Kindle: Bigger, not better, that its sibling", *Wall Street Journal Online*, http://www.wsj.com, June 11.

79. http://www.forbes.com/2008/01/29/disruptometer-amazon-sony-lead-clayton-in_sa_0129claytonchristensen_inl.html

80. http://www.foxnews.com/story/0,2933,537072,00.html

81. L. F. Mesquita and S. G. Lazzarini, 2008, "Horizontal and vertical relationships in developing economies: Implications for SMEs' access to global markets", *Academy of Management Journal*, 51: 359–380; W. P. Wan, 2005, "Country resource environments, firm capabilities, and corporate diversification strategies", *Journal of Management Studies*, 42: 161–182.

82. J. R. Healey, 2009, "Penske-Saturn deal could change how cars are sold", *USA Today*, June 8, B2.

83. D. Welch, 2009, "A hundred factories too many", *BusinessWeek*, January 12, 42–43.

84. G. Marcial, 2009, "Heinz: The time may be ripe", *BusinessWeek*, May 11, 67.

85. 2009, Procter & Gamble Co, *Standard & Poor's Stock Report*, http://www.standardandpoors.com, May 16.

86. 2009, McDonald's Corp, *Standard & Poor's Stock Report*, http://www.standardandpoors.com, May 16.

87. K. E. Meyer, 2009, "Uncommon common sense", *Business Strategy Review*, 20: 38–43; K. E. Meyer, 2006, "Globalfocusing: From domestic conglomerates to global

specialists", *Journal of Management Studies, 43:* 1110–1144.

88. C. H. Oh and A.M. Rugman, 2007, "Regional multinationals and the Korean cosmetics industry", *Asia Pacific Journal of Management,* 24: 27–42.

89. P. K. Ong and Y. Kathawala, 2009, "Competitive advantage through good Guanxi in the marine industry", *International Journal of Chinese Culture and Management,* 2: 28–55; X. P. Chen and S. Peng, 2008, "Guanxi dynamics: Shifts in the closeness of ties between Chinese coworkers", *Management and Organizational Review,* 4: 63–80; M. A. Hitt, M. T. Dacin, B. B. Tyler and D. Park, 1997, "Understanding the differences in Korean and US executives' strategic orientations", *Strategic Management Journal,* 18: 159–167.

90. M. A. Hitt, D. Ahlstrom, M. T. Dacin, E. Levitas and L. Svobodina, 2004, "The institutional effects on strategic alliance partner selection: China versus Russia", *Organization Science,* 15: 173–185.

91. L. Berchicci and A. King, 2008, "Postcards from the edge: A review of the business and environment literature", in: J. P. Walsh and A. P. Brief (eds.) *Academy of Management Annals,* New York: Lawrence Erlbaum Associates, 513–547.

92. M. J. Hutchins and J. W. Sutherland, 2008, "An exploration of measures of social sustainability and their application to supply chain decisions", *Journal of Cleaner Production,* 16: 1688–1698.

93. P. K. Dutta and R. Radner, 2009, "A strategic analysis of global warming: Theory and some numbers", *Journal of Economic Behaviour & Organization,* 71(2): 187–209.

94. http://www.forbes.com/feeds/afx/2008/05/25/ afx5046256.html

95. http://www.nawindpower.com/naw/e107_plugins/content/ content_lt.php?content.3459

96. http://www.nokia.com/environment/our-responsibility

97. C. A. Bartlett and S. Ghoshal, 2003, "What is a global manager?", *Harvard Business Review,* 81(8): 101–108; M. A. Carpenter and J. W. Fredrickson, 2001, "Top management teams, global strategic posture and the moderating role of uncertainty", *Academy of Management Journal,* 44: 533–545.

98. J. Galbreath and P. Galvin, 2008, "Firm factors, industry structure and performance variation: New empirical evidence to a classic debate", *Journal of Business Research,* 61: 109–117; B. R. Koka and J. E. Prescott, 2008, "Designing alliance networks: The influence of network position, environmental change, and strategy on firm performance", *Strategic Management Journal,* 29: 639–661.

99. V. F. Misangyi, H. Elms, T. Greckhamer and J. A. Lepine, 2006, "A new perspective on a fundamental debate: A multilevel approach to industry, corporate, and business unit effects", *Strategic Management Journal,* 27: 571–590; G. Hawawini, V. Subramanian and P. Verdin, 2003, "Is performance driven by industry or firm-specific factors? A new look at the evidence", *Strategic Management Journal,* 24: 1–16.

100. D. Bonnet and G. S. Yip, 2009, "Strategy convergence", *Business Strategy Review,* 20: 50–55; E. Nelson, R. van den Dam and H. Kline, 2008, "A future in content(ion): Can telecom providers win a share of the digital content market?", *Journal of Telecommunications Management,* 1: 125–138.

101. K. E. Kushida and J. Zysman, 2009, "The services transformation and network policy: The new logic of value creation", *Review of Policy Research,* 26: 173–194; E. D. Jaffe, I. D. Nebenzahl and I. Schorr, 2005, "Strategic options of home country firms faced with MNC entry", *Long Range Planning,* 38: 183–196.

102. M. R. Peneder, 2008, "Firm entry and turnover: The nexus with profitability and growth", *Small Business Economics,* 30: 327–344; A. V. Mainkar, M. Lubatkin and W. S. Schulze, 2006, "Toward a product-proliferation theory of entry barriers", *Academy of Management Review,* 31: 1062–1075; J. Shamsie, 2003, "The context of dominance: An industry-driven framework for exploiting reputation", *Strategic Management Journal,* 24: 199–215.

103. S. Hamm, 2009, "Oracle faces its toughest deal yet", *BusinessWeek,* May 4, 24.

104. S. K. Ethiraj and D. H. Zhu, 2008, "Performance effects of imitative entry", *Strategic Management Journal,* 29: 797–817; R. Makadok, 1999, "Interfirm differences in scale economies and the evolution of market shares", *Strategic Management Journal,* 20: 935–952.

105. M. J. Rungtusanatham and F. Salvador, 2008, "From mass production to mass customization: Hindrance factors, structural inertia, and transition hazard", *Production and Operations Management,* 17: 385–396; F. Salvador and C. Forza, 2007, "Principles for efficient and effective sales configuration design", *International Journal of Mass Customisation,* 2(1,2): 114–127; F. T. Piller, K. M. Moslein and C. M. Stotko, 2004, "Does mass customisation pay? An economic approach to evaluate customer integration", *International Journal of Production Planning and Control,* 15(4): 435–444.

106. F. Keenan, S. Holmes, J. Greene and R. O. Crockett, 2002, "A mass market of one", *BusinessWeek,* December 2, 68–72.

107. http://www.pret.com/about/

108. E. Byron, 2009, "P&G, Colgate hit by consumer thrift", *Wall Street Journal Online,* http://www.wsj.com, May 1.

109. M. A. Hitt, R. M. Holmes, T. Miller and M. P. Salmador, 2006, "Modeling country institutional profiles: The dimensions and dynamics of institutional environments", paper presented at the Strategic Management Society Conference, October.

110. P. Kiviniem, 2009, "Intel to get EU antitrust fine," *Wall Street Journal Online,* http://www.wsj.com, May 14.

111. C. Forelle and D. Clark, 2009, "Intel fine jolts tech sector", *Wall Street Journal Online,* http://www.wsj.com, May 14.

112. Takeuchi, H., E. Osono and N. Shimizu, "The Contradictions That Drive Toyota's Success, " *Harvard Business Review,* June 2008 96–104.

113. L. Ranson, 2009, "United confirms aircraft order talks with Airbus and Boeing", *FlightGlobal*, http://www.flightglobal.com, April 6.

114. K. Mangu-Ward, 2010, Traditional schools aren't working. Let's move learning online, *The Washington Post*, March 28, B01 (http://www.washingtonpost.com/wpdyn/content/article/2010/03/26/AR2010032602224.html); http://www.nti.nl/; http://confluence.sakaiproject.org/display/EUROSAKAI/Leidse+Onderwijsinstellingen+(LOI); http://imba.globis.ac.jp/j/index.html.

115. D. G. Sirmon, S. Gove and M. H. Hitt, 2008, "Resource management in dyadic competitive rivalry: The effects of resource bundling and deployment", *Academy of Management Journal*, 51: 919–935.

116. S. Nadkarni and V. K. Narayanan, 2007, "Strategic schemas, strategic flexibility, and firm performance: The moderating role of industry clockspeed", *Strategic Management Journal*, 28: 243–270.

117. P. Prada and M. Esterl, 2009, "Airlines predict more trouble, broaden cut's", *Wall Street Journal Online*, 'http://www.wsj.com, June 12.

118. S. E. Feinberg and A. K. Gupta, 2009, "MNC subsidiaries and country risk: Internalization as a safeguard against weak external institutions", *Academy of Management Journal*, 52: 381–399.

119. M. E. Porter, 1980, *Competitive Strategy,* New York: Free Press.

120. B. Kabanoff and S. Brown, 2008, "Knowledge structures of prospectors, analyzers, and defenders: Content, structure, stability, and performance", *Strategic Management Journal*, 29: 149–171; M. S. Hunt, 1972, "Competition in the major home appliance industry, 1960–1970", doctoral dissertation, Harvard University; Porter, *Competitive Strategy*, 129.

121. G. McNamara, D. L. Deephouse and R. A. Luce, 2003, "Competitive positioning within and across a strategic group structure: The performance of core, secondary, and solitary firms", *Strategic Management Journal*, 24: 161–181.

122. F. Zen and C. Baldan, 2008, "The strategic paths and performance of Italian mutual banks: A nonparametric analysis", *International Journal of Banking, Accounting and Finance*, 1: 189–214; M. W. Peng, J. Tan and T. W. Tong, 2004, "Ownership types and strategic groups in an emerging economy", *Journal of Management Studies,* 41: 1105–1129.

123. W. S. DeSarbo and R. Grewal, 2008, "Hybrid strategic groups", *Strategic Management Journal*, 29: 293–317; M. Peteraf and M. Shanley, 1997, "Getting to know you: A theory of strategic group identity", *Strategic Management Journal,* 18(Special Issue): 165–186.

124. J. Lee, K. Lee and S. Rho, 2002, "An evolutionary perspective on strategic group emergence: A genetic algorithm-based model", *Strategic Management Journal,* 23: 727–746.

125. J. A. Zuniga-Vicente, J. M. de la Fuente Sabate and I. S. Gonzalez, 2004, "Dynamics of the strategic group membership-performance linkage in rapidly changing environments", *Journal of Business Research,* 57: 1378–1390.

126. T. Yu, M. Subramaniam and A. A. Cannella, Jr., 2009, "Rivalry deterrence in international markets: Contingencies governing the mutual forbearance hypothesis", *Academy of Management Journal*, 52: 127–147.

127. M. E. Porter, 1998, *Competitive Strategy*, New York: Free Press, 49.

128. L. Capron and O. Chatain, 2008, "Competitors resource-oriented strategies: Acting on competitors' resources through interventions in factor markets and political markets", *Academy of Management Review*, 33: 97–121; M. B. Lieberman and S. Asaba, 2006, "Why do firms imitate each other?", *Academy of Management Journal*, 31: 366–385.

129. D. B. Montgomery, M. C. Moore and J. E. Urbany, 2005, "Reasoning about competitive reactions: Evidence from executives", *Marketing Science,* 24: 138–149.

130. S. Jain, 2008, "Digital piracy: A competitive analysis", *Marketing Science*, 27: 610–626.

131. J. G. York, 2009, "Pragmatic sustainability: Translating environmental ethics into competitive advantage", *Journal of Business Ethics*, 85: 97–109.

132. K. A. Sawka, 2008, "The ethics of competitive intelligence", *Kiplinger Business Resource Center Online*, http://www.kiplinger.com, March.

133. T. Mazzarol and S. Reboud, 2008, "The role of complementary actors in the development of innovation in small firms", *International Journal of Innovation Management*, 12: 223–253; A; Brandenburger and B. Nalebuff, 1996, *Co-opetition,* New York: Currency Doubleday.

134. 2009, "Continental to join Star alliance", *Continental Airlines Homepage*, http://www.continental.com, June 12.

135. 2009, ING Profile and fast facts, http://www.ing.com, June 12.

136. C. S. Fleisher and S. Wright, 2009, "Examining differences in competitive intelligence practice: China, Japan, and the West", *Thunderbird International Business Review*, 51: 249–261; A. Crane, 2005, "In the company of spies: When competitive intelligence gathering becomes industrial espionage", *Business Horizons*, 48(3): 233–240.

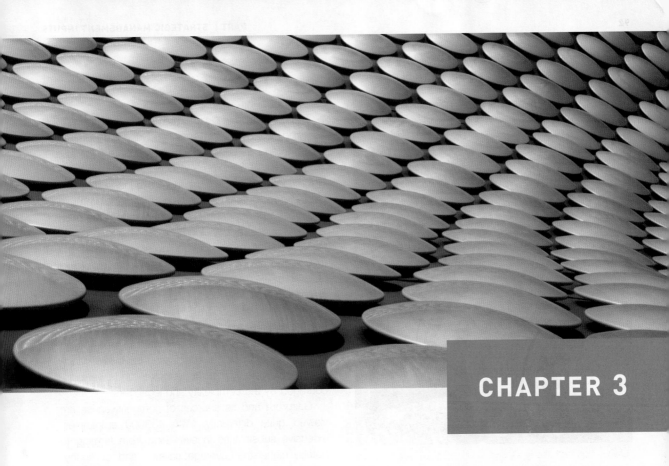

## CHAPTER 3

# THE INTERNAL ORGANIZATION: RESOURCES, CAPABILITIES, CORE COMPETENCIES AND COMPETITIVE ADVANTAGES

### LEARNING OBJECTIVES

Studying this chapter should provide you with the strategic management knowledge needed to:

1 Explain why firms need to study and understand their internal organization.
2 Define value and discuss its importance.
3 Describe the differences between tangible and intangible resources.
4 Define capabilities and discuss their development.
5 Describe four criteria used to determine whether resources and capabilities are core competencies.
6 Explain how value chain analysis is used to identify and evaluate resources and capabilities.
7 Define outsourcing and discuss reasons for its use.
8 Discuss the importance of identifying internal strengths and weaknesses.

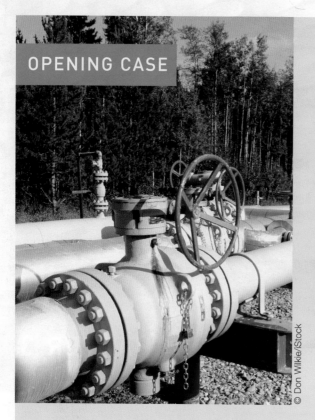

OPENING CASE

© Don Wilkie/iStock

## Gazprom: strong pipelines

Russia's Gazprom is the world's largest gas company with €70 billion in revenue in 2007 and taking a €14 billion profit. With about 17 per cent of the world's proven gas reserves, and over 60 per cent of Russia's reserves, Gazprom owns more natural resources than any other gas company in the world. When the credit crisis in 2008 depressed oil prices, Gazprom's market capitalization also decreased from €350 billion in 2008 to €90 billion in 2009, despite considerable improvements in organizational management and professionalization. Its strong position in the marketplace for gas deliveries to Europe promises long-term benefits, yet increasing competition in this market, stable gas prices, and technologies pioneered by US competitors to extract shale gas do not bode well.

Restrictions, also called the "ring fence", imposed by the Russian government in 1997 prevented foreigners from buying Gazprom shares traded on Russian exchanges. With the Russian state owning a 51 per cent controlling stake in Gazprom, in theory, minority shareholders in government-run companies would not face the risk that their assets would be nationalized.

The only way that Gazprom shares could be legally acquired was by buying American Depositary Shares (ADS) traded in London, which accounted for just 3.5 per cent of Gazprom's equity. The resulting scarcity meant that ADSs were more expensive than the locally traded shares, at one time trading at a premium of almost 100 per cent. Their absence from the main US exchanges also helped to scare off American investors. But many foreign investors evaded the restrictions through so-called "grey schemes" tolerated by the Russian authorities. For example, a Russian entity would buy local Gazprom shares and then give foreigners an opportunity to gain indirect access by selling shares in itself. As a result, some 15–20 per cent of Gazprom stock was estimated to be in foreign hands, mainly investors speculating in Russia. Mainstream investors such as large mutual funds were discouraged by the complexity and legal risks.

Gazprom and its sources of competitiveness are viewed quite differently. With 436000 employees, extensive subsidiaries in everything from farming to hotels, higher-than-average salaries and company-sponsored housing and resorts on the Black Sea, some critics hold that Gazprom perpetuates the Soviet paternalistic economy well into the capitalist era. Others see Gazprom's advances to trounce competition threatening its new monopoly on gas deliveries to Europe as a sinister plot. Seeking to curtail the German energy giant RWE's support for Gazprom's competition, it is viewed with suspicion that one of Gazprom's officials, Gerhard Schroeder, a former German federal chancellor, maintains a close friendship with RWE CEO, Juergen Grossmann. Again others see Gazprom which had evolved from the former Soviet ministry of gas and investors as the model for energy investing at a time of resource nationalism, when governments in oil-rich regions were wrenching their resources from Western majors.

**Sources:** www.gazprom.com, accessed 15.07.2009; Elder, M. (2009) "Gazprom, Russia's largest company, Acts more like a company", *The Huffington Post*; Kramer, A. E. (2008) "Gazprom, Once Mighty, Is Reeling", *New York Times*; Blau, J. (2010) "Gazprom courts RWE on controversial pipeline", Deutsche Welle, DW-World.de, accessed 12.07.2010.

## Questions

1 Why does Gazprom need to study and understand its internal organization?

**2** What are the tangible and intangible resources that Gazprom relies on?

**3** Are these resources core competencies? Check the four criteria and report.

**4** Discuss the importance of identifying internal strengths and weaknesses. What is Gazprom's mitigation strategy to overcome its weaknesses?

As discussed in the first two chapters, several factors in the global economy, including the rapid development of the Internet, technological capabilities[1] and globalization in general, have made it increasingly difficult for firms to find ways to develop a competitive advantage that can be sustained for any period of time.[2] As is suggested in the Opening Case, legal changes can quickly end competitiveness as access to and ownership of resources can be redefined e.g., by governments. Correspondingly, innovation may be a vital path to develop sustainable competitive advantages.[3] When Shell anticipated the oil crisis in the 1970s it put much effort into diversifying its portfolio of supplies and to exploring fresh fields, i.e., innovating. Sometimes, product innovation serves simultaneously as the foundation on which a firm is started as well as the source of its competitive advantages. At other times such foundation is more than the capacity to innovate the extant network and ties to important players such as the government, as in the case of Gazprom. Its strong linkages to the government help Gazprom to internalize what more commonly is part of the context of organizations. In combination with the wealth of reserves, Gazprom's political clout helps to exploit its resources and capture the value.

Competitive advantages and the differences they create in firm performance are often strongly related to the resources firms hold and how they are managed.[4] "Resources are the foundation for strategy, and unique bundles of resources generate competitive advantages that lead to wealth creation."[5] As Gazprom's case shows, resources must be managed to simultaneously allow production efficiency and an ability to form competitive advantages such as the consistent exploitation of proprietary resources.

To identify and successfully use resources over time, leading firms need to think constantly about how to manage them to increase the value for customers who "are arbiters of benefit"[6] as they compare firms' goods and services against each other before making a purchase decision. As this chapter shows, firms achieve strategic competitiveness and earn above-average returns when their unique core competencies are effectively acquired, bundled, and leveraged to take advantage of opportunities in the external environment in ways that create value for customers.[7]

People are an especially critical resource for helping organizations learn how to continuously innovate as a means of achieving successful growth.[8] In other words, "smart growth" happens when the firm manages its need to grow with its ability to successfully manage growth.[9]

Employees are a critical resource to efforts to grow successfully at Vanderlande Industries, a provider of automated material handling systems mainly for airports. Vanderlande attaches high value to its employees; it gives employees enough space to develop their own ideas.[10] While such practices are often associated with large multinationals such as 3M and more recently Google, Vanderlande is a case in point that illustrates how similar approaches are chosen by smaller players with similar effect. People at Vanderlande, as well as virtually all other firms who know how to effectively manage resources to help organizations learn how to continuously innovate, are themselves a source of competitive advantage.[11] In fact, a global labour market now exists as firms seek talented individuals to add to their fold.

As Richard Florida argues, "[W]herever talent goes, innovation, creativity and economic growth are sure to follow".[12]

The fact that over time the benefits of any firm's value-creating strategy can be duplicated by its competitors is a key reason for having employees who know how to manage resources. These employees are critical to firms' efforts to perform well. Because all competitive advantages have a limited life,[13] the question of duplication is not "if" it will happen, but "when". In general, the sustainability of a competitive advantage is a function of three factors: (1) the rate of core competence obsolescence because of environmental changes; (2) the availability of substitutes for the core competence; and (3) the imitability of the core competence.[14] The challenge for all firms, then, is to effectively manage current core competencies while simultaneously developing new ones.[15] Only when firms develop a continuous stream of capabilities that contribute to competitive advantages do they achieve strategic competitiveness, earn above-average returns, and remain ahead of competitors (see Chapter 5).

In Chapter 2 we examined general, industry and competitor environments. Armed with this knowledge about the realities and conditions of their external environment, firms have a better understanding of marketplace opportunities and the characteristics of the competitive environment in which those opportunities exist. In this chapter we focus on the firm itself. By analysing its internal organization, a firm determines what it can do. Matching what a firm can do (a function of its resources, capabilities, core competencies and competitive advantages) with what it might do (a function of opportunities and threats in the external environment) allows the firm to develop vision, pursue its mission and select and implement its strategies.

We begin this chapter by briefly discussing conditions associated with analysing the firm's internal organization. We then discuss the roles of resources and capabilities in developing core competencies, which are the sources of the firm's competitive advantages. Included in this discussion are the techniques firms use to identify and evaluate resources and capabilities and the criteria for selecting core competencies from among them. Resources and capabilities are not inherently valuable, but they create value when the firm can use them to perform certain activities that result in a competitive advantage. Accordingly, we also discuss the value chain concept and examine four criteria to evaluate core competencies that establish competitive advantage.[16] The chapter closes with cautionary comments about the need for firms to prevent their core competencies from becoming core rigidities. The existence of core rigidities indicates that the firm is too anchored to its past, which prevents it from continuously developing new competitive advantages.

# Analysing the internal organization

## The context of internal analysis

In the global economy, traditional factors such as labour costs, access to financial resources and raw materials, and protected or regulated markets remain sources of competitive advantage, but to a lesser degree.[17] One important reason is that over time competitors can apply their resources to successfully use an international strategy (discussed in Chapter 8) as a means of overcoming the advantages created by these more traditional sources. For example, Volkswagen began establishing production facilities in Slovakia "shortly after the Russians moved out" as part of its international strategy. Volkswagen is thought to have a competitive advantage over rivals such as France's Peugeot Citroën and South Korea's Kia Motors, firms that are now investing in Slovakia in an effort to duplicate the competitive advantage that has accrued to Volkswagen. In 2008, a total of 770000 autos were manufactured in Slovakia and saturation has set in.[18]

Increasingly, those who analyse their firm's internal organization should use a global mindset to do so. A global mindset is the ability to analyse, understand and manage (if in a managerial position) an internal organization in ways that are not dependent on the assumptions of a single country, culture, or context.[19] Because they are able to span artificial boundaries,[20] those with a global mindset recognize that their firms must possess resources and capabilities that allow understanding of, and appropriate responses to, competitive situations that are influenced by country-specific factors and unique societal cultures. Firms populated with people having a global mindset have a "key source of long-term competitive advantage in the global marketplace".[21]

Finally, analysis of the firm's internal organization requires that evaluators examine the firm's portfolio of resources and the bundles of heterogeneous resources and capabilities managers have created.[22] This perspective suggests that individual firms possess at least some resources and capabilities that other companies do not—at least not in the same combination. Resources are the source of capabilities, some of which lead to the development of a firm's core competencies or its competitive advantages.[23] Understanding how to leverage the firm's unique bundle of resources and capabilities is a key outcome decision makers seek when analysing the internal organization.[24] Figure 3.1 illustrates the relationships between resources, capabilities and core competencies, and shows how firms use them to create strategic competitiveness. Before examining these topics in depth, we describe value and its creation.

**Global mindset**

A global mindset is the ability to analyse, understand and manage (if in a managerial position) an internal organization in ways that are not dependent on the assumptions of a single country, culture or context.

**FIGURE 3.1** Components of internal analysis leading to competitive advantage and strategic competitiveness

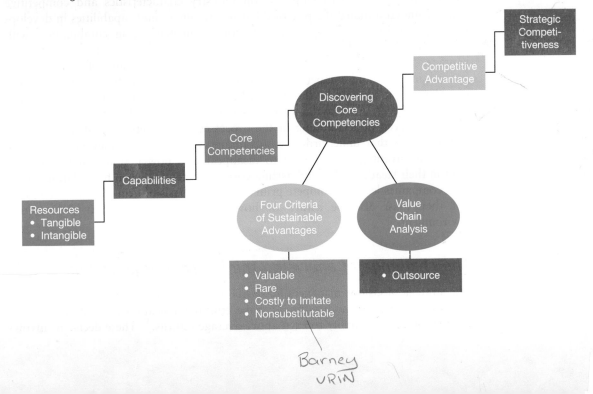

## Creating value

**Value**

Value is measured by a product's performance characteristics and by its attributes for which customers are willing to pay.

By exploiting their core competencies to meet if not exceed the standards of global competition, firms create value for customers.[25] Value is measured by a product's performance characteristics and by its attributes for which customers are willing to pay. Tata Technologies, for example, creates value for its customers by combining state-of-the-art technologies with a real-world understanding of engineering and manufacturing processes, thus bringing down costs and reducing time to market.

Firms with a competitive advantage offer value to customers that is superior to the value competitors provide.[26] Firms create value by innovatively bundling and leveraging their resources and capabilities.[27] Firms unable to perform in ways that create value for customers suffer performance declines. Sometimes, it seems that these declines may happen because firms fail to understand what customers value. For example, after learning that General Motors (GM) intended to focus on visual design to create value for buyers, one former GM customer said that in his view, people buying cars and trucks valued durability, reliability, good fuel economy and a low cost of operation more than visual design. In fact, GM should heed advice to co-create the automobile with customers to ensure that they receive the desired value.[28]

Ultimately, creating value for customers is the source of above-average returns. What the firm intends regarding value creation affects its choice of business-level strategy (see Chapter 5) and its organizational structure (see Chapter 11).[29] In the discussion of business-level strategies (see Chapter 4), we note that value is created by a product's low cost, by its highly differentiated features, or by a combination of low cost and high differentiation, compared with competitors' offerings. A business-level strategy is effective only when it is grounded in exploiting the firm's core competencies and competitive advantages. Thus, successful firms continuously examine the effectiveness of current and future core competencies and advantages.[30]

At one time, the strategic management process was concerned largely with understanding the characteristics of the industry in which the firm competed and, in light of those characteristics, determining how the firm should be positioned relative to competitors. This emphasis on industry characteristics and competitive strategy underestimated the role of the firm's resources and capabilities in developing a competitive advantage. In fact, core competencies, in combination with product-market positions, are the firm's most important sources of competitive advantage.[31] The core competencies of a firm, in addition to results of analyses of its general, industry and competitor environments, should drive its selection of strategies. The resources held by the firm and their context are important when formulating strategy.[32] As Clayton Christensen noted, "Successful strategists need to cultivate a deep understanding of the processes of competition and progress and of the factors that undergird each advantage. Only thus will they be able to see when old advantages are poised to disappear and how new advantages can be built in their stead."[33] By emphasizing core competencies when formulating strategies, companies learn to compete primarily on the basis of firm-specific differences, but they must also be aware of how things are changing in the external environment.[34]

## The challenge of analysing the internal organization

The strategic decisions managers make about the components of their firms' internal organization are non-routine,[35] have ethical implications,[36] and significantly influence the firm's ability to earn above-average returns.[37] These decisions involve choices about the assets the firm needs to collect and how to best use those assets. "Managers make choices precisely because they believe these contribute substantially to the performance and survival of their organizations."[38]

Making decisions involving the firm's assets – identifying, developing, deploying, and protecting resources, capabilities and core competencies – may appear to be relatively easy. However, this task is as challenging and difficult as any other with which managers are involved; moreover, it is increasingly internationalized.[39] Some believe that the pressure on managers to pursue only decisions that help the firm meet the quarterly earnings expected by market analysts makes it difficult to accurately examine the firm's internal organization.[40]

The challenge and difficulty of making effective decisions are implied by preliminary evidence suggesting that one-half of organizational decisions fail.[41] Sometimes, mistakes are made as the firm analyses conditions in its internal organization.[42] Managers might, for example, identify capabilities as core competencies that do not create a competitive advantage. This misidentification may have been the case at Polaroid Corporation as decision makers continued to believe that the skills it used to build its instant film cameras were highly relevant at the time its competitors were developing and using the skills required to introduce digital cameras.[43] When a mistake occurs, such as occurred at Polaroid, decision makers must have the confidence to admit it and take corrective actions.[44] A firm can still grow through well-intended errors; the learning generated by making and correcting mistakes can be important to the creation of new competitive advantages.[45] Moreover, firms and those managing them can learn from the failure resulting from a mistake– that is, what not to do when seeking competitive advantage.[46] Thus, difficult managerial decisions concerning resources, capabilities and core competencies are characterized by three conditions: uncertainty, complexity and intraorganizational conflicts (see Figure 3.2).[47]

Managers face uncertainty in terms of new proprietary technologies, rapidly changing economic and political trends, transformations in societal values, and shifts in customer demands.[48] Environmental uncertainty increases the complexity and range of issues to examine when studying the internal environment.[49] Consider the complexity associated with the decisions Gregory H. Boyce is encountering as

**FIGURE 3.2** Conditions affecting managerial decisions about resources, capabilities and core competencies

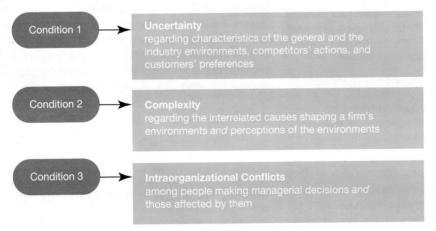

| Condition 1 | → | **Uncertainty** regarding characteristics of the general and the industry environments, competitors' actions, and customers' preferences |
| Condition 2 | → | **Complexity** regarding the interrelated causes shaping a firm's environments *and* perceptions of the environments |
| Condition 3 | → | **Intraorganizational Conflicts** among people making managerial decisions *and* those affected by them |

Source: Adapted from R. Amit and P. J. H. Schoemaker, 1993, "Strategic assets and organizational rent", *Strategic Management Journal*, 14: 33.

Image courtesy of General Electric

**STRATEGIC FOCUS**

# GE builds management capabilities and shares them with others

For many years, GE was considered one of the best organizations for management talent in the world. For the period, 1993–2002, GE was ranked first or second in market value added among the Stern Stewart 1000 firms. In fact, GE was one of the top producers of shareholder value throughout more than 20 years of Jack Welsh's tenure as CEO. Most analysts attribute this phenomenal record to GE's exceptional leadership development programme.

Approximately 9000 managers participated in programmes annually at GE's Leadership Center in Crotonville, New York. Managers received extensive leadership and team-based training and they even provided internal consulting by working on major GE projects in these programmes, such as evaluating joint venture partners and analysing opportunities for the use of artificial intelligence. Its world-class management development programmes provide GE with an inventory of successors for almost any management

position in the company as it becomes vacant. In fact, many analysts believe that the management development programmes help GE achieve a competitive advantage. Some argue that the management development process has the characteristics of a core competence; it is valuable, rare, difficult to imitate and non-substitutable.

Jack Welsh has often been quoted as saying that people are first and strategy second. He actively participated in the management development programme, sharing his expertise with other GE managers. Welsh's successor, Jeff Immelt, does the same. Immelt believes that effective leaders learn constantly and also help others in the firm to learn as well. GE's leadership development programme is so good that many companies look for talent among GE's management team. And GE's programme produces more leaders than it can usefully absorb. Thus, there are many company CEOs who are ex-GE managers. Several scholars at the University of Western Ontario's Ivey School studied a large set of CEOs who were ex-GE managers, comparing them to groups of CEOs with no prior connection to GE. They found that the ex-GE CEO firms outperformed the non-GE CEOs by a significant margin. One author put it this way, "When a company needs a loan, it goes to a bank. When a company needs a CEO, it goes to GE" (Lehmberg, Rowe, White and Phillips, 2009).

GE experienced problems in the economic malaise of 2008–2009. This was partly because of problems in its major financial services business (similar to the whole financial services industry). But it was also partly due to the current CEO's emphasis on innovation for the future of the company. To innovate effectively requires that the firm invest now for returns several years later. And, it must take risks. As such, shorter-term returns are likely to suffer with high costs and lower returns awaiting the major longer-term payoffs of important innovations. Only time will tell if these investments to create innovations with long-term payoffs (as opposed to short-term returns) will work.

**Sources:** Spotts, G. (2006) "GE's Immelt may have 'ecomagination', but he needs project managers for jumbo-sized ideas", *FastCompany*. http://www.fastcompany.com. June 11, 2007; "Things leaders do", *FastCompany*. http://www.fastcompany.com. December 19; Hamm, S. (2008) "Tech innovations for tough times", ADNetAsia. http://www.zdnetasia.com. December 26; Smith, E. (2009) "At GE, management development is a continuous process", Aprendia Corp. http://www.aprendiacorp.com. February 15; Rowe, G.,

White, R. E., Lehmbert, D. and Phillips, J. R. (2009) "General Electric: An outlier in CEO talent development", *IVEY Business Journal*. http://www.iveybusinessjournal.com/article. January/February; Eavis P. and Denning. L. (2009) "GE needs a circuit breaker", *Wall Street Journal*. http://www.wsj.com. March 5; Eaves, P. (2009) "GE paper cut is greeted with relief", *Wall Street Journal*. http://www.wsj.com. March 13; Lehmberg, D., Rowe, W. G., White, R. E. and Phillips, R. R. (2009) "The GE paradox: Competitive advantage through tangible non-firm-specific investment", *Journal of Management*, Vol 35, issue 5, 1129–1153.

## Questions

1 Why is it important for GE to put people first and strategy second?

2 How is the creation of competitive advantage related to the internal nurture of top management talent?

3 Why does GE prefer internal development over hiring of external talent? What are the disadvantages of GE's approach?

4 What enables GE to create management capabilities?

5 Analysing the four criteria, discuss whether GE's talent development is a core competence.

6 Could talent development be outsourced? If possible, why and how? If not, why not?

---

CEO of Peabody Energy Corp. Peabody is the world's largest coal company. But coal is thought of as a "dirty fuel", meaning that some think its future prospects are gloomy in light of global warming issues.

Boyce is building a new "clean" coal-fired plant to produce energy and is a proponent of strong emissions standards. The firm argues for more use of "clean coal". Obviously, the complexity of these decisions is quite significant.[50] Biases about how to cope with uncertainty affect decisions about the resources and capabilities that will become the foundation of the firm's competitive advantage.[51] For example, Boyce strongly believes in coal's future, suggesting that automobiles capable of burning coal should be built. Finally, intraorganizational conflict surfaces when decisions are made about the core competencies to nurture as well as how to nurture them.

In making decisions affected by these three conditions, judgement is required. Judgement is the capability of making successful decisions when no obviously correct model or rule is available or when relevant data are unreliable or incomplete. In this type of situation, decision makers must be aware of possible cognitive biases. Overconfidence, for example, can often lower value when a correct decision is not obvious, such as making a judgement as to whether an internal resource is a strength or a weakness.[52]

When exercising judgement, decision makers often take intelligent risks. In the current competitive landscape, executive judgement can be a particularly important source of competitive advantage. One reason is that, over time, effective judgement allows a firm to build a strong reputation and retain the loyalty of stakeholders whose support is linked to above-average returns.[53]

As explained in the Strategic Focus, GE's managers build their capabilities in its executive leadership programme. Recognized as one of the best in the world, GE's managers develop capabilities to deal with uncertainty, complexity and intraorganizational conflict. As such, they learn to use their judgement to make decisions helps GE navigate effectively in an uncertain and complex competitive landscape. The effectiveness of GE's managers to exercise good judgement in making strategic decisions is evident in at least two ways. First, GE created more value for its shareholders over time than almost all other companies. Second, many former GE managers have been selected to become CEOs of other major companies, primarily because of the capabilities that they developed at GE.

**Judgement**

Judgement is the capability of making successful decisions when no obviously correct model or rule is available or when relevant data are unreliable or incomplete.

In the next section, we discuss how resources (such as young professionals and low-level managers) are developed and bundled to create capabilities.

## Resources, capabilities and core competences

Resources, capabilities and core competencies are the foundation of competitive advantage. Resources are bundled to create organizational capabilities. In turn, capabilities are the source of a firm's core competencies, which are the basis of competitive advantages.[54] Figure 3.1 (see page 98), depicts these relationships. Here, we define and provide examples of these building blocks of competitive advantage.

### Resources

Broad in scope, resources cover a spectrum of individual, social and organizational phenomena.[55] Typically, resources alone do not yield a competitive advantage.[56] In fact, a competitive advantage is generally based on the unique bundling of several resources.[57] For example, www.Ocado.com combined service and distribution resources to develop its competitive advantages. The firm started as an online retailer, directly shipping orders from the product range of Waitrose, a leading UK retailer to customers. It quickly grew and established a distribution network through which it could deliver groceries to customers' doorsteps. With its 2010 initial public offer (IPO) to employees, managers and customers who spent more than £300, Ocado has opened retail furthermore to the internet. Lacking Ocado's combination of resources, traditional bricks-and-mortar retailers initially found it difficult to establish an effective online presence. These difficulties led some of them to experimenting and to developing partnerships with Ocado. Through these arrangements, Ocado now handles the online presence and shipping of goods for several firms, including Waitrose – which can now focus on sales in its stores. These types of arrangements are useful to the bricks-and-mortar companies because they have little experience in shipping large amounts of diverse merchandise directly to individuals.

Some of a firm's resources (defined in Chapter 1 as inputs to the firm's production process) are tangible, while others are intangible. Tangible resources are assets that can be observed and quantified. Production equipment, manufacturing facilities, distribution centres and formal reporting structures are examples of tangible resources. Intangible resources are assets that are rooted deeply in the firm's history and have accumulated over time. Because they are embedded in unique patterns of routines, intangible resources are relatively difficult for competitors to analyse and imitate. Knowledge, trust between managers and employees, managerial capabilities, organizational routines (the unique ways people work together), scientific capabilities, the capacity for innovation, brand name, and the firm's reputation for its goods or services and how it interacts with people (such as employees, customers, and suppliers) are intangible resources.[58]

The four types of tangible resources are financial, organizational, physical and technological (see Table 3.1). The three types of intangible resources are human, innovation and reputational (see Table 3.2).

**Tangible resources**  As tangible resources, a firm's borrowing capacity and the status of its physical facilities are visible. The value of many tangible resources can be established through financial statements; but these statements do not account for the value of all the firm's assets, because they disregard some intangible resources.[59] The value of tangible resources is also constrained because they are difficult to leverage–it is difficult to derive additional business or value from a tangible resource. For example, an airplane is a tangible resource, but "You can't use the

**Tangible resources**

Tangible resources are assets that can be observed and quantified.

**Intangible resources**

Intangible resources include assets that are rooted deeply in the firm's history, accumulating over time, and are relatively difficult for competitors to analyse and imitate.

## Table 3.1  Tangible resources

| Financial Resources | • The firm's borrowing capacity<br>• The firm's ability to generate internal funds |
| --- | --- |
| Organizational Resources | • The firm's formal reporting structure and its formal planning, controlling, and coordinating systems |
| Physical Resources | • Sophistication and location of a firm's plant and equipment<br>• Access to raw materials |
| Technological Resources | • Stock of technology, such as patents, trademarks, copyrights, and trade secrets |

Sources: Adapted from J. B. Barney, 1991, "Firm resources and sustained competitive advantage", *Journal of Management*, 17: 101; R. M. Grant, 1991, *Contemporary Strategy Analysis*, Cambridge, UK: Blackwell Business, 100–102.

## Table 3.2  Intangible resources

| Human Resources | • Knowledge<br>• Trust<br>• Managerial capabilities<br>• Organizational routines |
| --- | --- |
| Innovation Resources | • Ideas<br>• Scientific capabilities<br>• Capacity to innovate |
| Reputational Resources | • Reputation with customers<br>• Brand name<br>• Perceptions of product quality, durability and reliability<br>• Reputation with suppliers<br>• For efficient, effective, supportive, and mutually beneficial interactions and relationships |

Sources: Adapted from R. Hall, 1992, "The strategic analysis of intangible resources", *Strategic Management Journal*, 13: 136–139; R. M. Grant, 1991, *Contemporary Strategy Analysis*, Cambridge, UK: Blackwell Business, 101–104.

same airplane on five different routes at the same time. You can't put the same crew on five different routes at the same time. And the same goes for the financial investment you've made in the airplane."[60]

Although production assets are tangible, many of the processes necessary to use these assets are intangible. Thus, the learning and potential proprietary processes associated with a tangible resource, such as manufacturing facilities, can have unique intangible attributes, e.g., quality control processes, unique manufacturing processes and technology that develop over time and create competitive advantage.[61]

**Intangible resources**   Compared to tangible resources, intangible resources are a superior source of core competencies.[62] In fact, in the global economy, "the success of a corporation lies more in its intellectual and systems capabilities than in its physical assets. Moreover, the capacity to manage human intellect – and to convert it into useful products and services – is fast becoming the critical executive skill of the age."[63]

Because intangible resources are less visible and more difficult for competitors to understand, purchase, imitate or substitute for, firms prefer to rely on them rather than on tangible resources as the foundation for their capabilities and core competencies. In fact, the less a resource can be observed (i.e., intangible), the more sustainable will be the competitive advantage that is based on it.[64] Another benefit of intangible resources is that, unlike most tangible resources, their use can be leveraged. For instance, sharing knowledge among employees does not diminish its value for any other person. To the contrary, two people sharing their individualized knowledge sets often can be leveraged to create additional knowledge that, although new to each of them, contributes to performance improvements for the firm. This is especially true when members of the top management team share knowledge with each other to make more effective decisions. The new knowledge created is then often shared with managers and employees in each of the units managed by executives in the top management team.[65] With intangible resources, the larger the network of users, the greater the benefit to each party.

As shown in Table 3.2, the intangible resource of reputation is an important source of competitive advantage. Indeed, some argue that "a firm's reputation is widely considered to be a valuable resource associated with sustained competitive advantage".[66] Earned through the firm's actions as well as its words, a value-creating reputation is a product of years of superior marketplace competence as perceived by stakeholders.[67] A reputation indicates the level of awareness a firm has been able to develop among stakeholders and the degree to which they hold the firm in high esteem.[68]

A well-known and highly valued brand name is an example of reputation as a source of competitive advantage.[69] A continuing commitment to innovation and aggressive advertising facilitate firms' efforts to take advantage of the reputation associated with their brands.[70] Because of the desirability of its products and its reputation, Hermes, the French fashion house's brand name, for example, has such status that not only limited editions are very sought after but also the number of counterfeit products is large. Even established firms need to build their reputations in new markets. For example, Ford hired a well respected Indian actor, Suneil Shetty, to serve as the brand ambassador for the Ford Endeavour launched in India. The Endeavour had the highest sales of SUVs in 2008.[71] Similarly, Studio Ghibli, the Japanese animation company that has produced films including *Princess Mononoke* and *Ponyo* has successfully exploited blockbusters, especially after forming an alliance with Pixar and Walt Disney to distribute Ghibli products.

## Capabilities

Capabilities exist when resources have been purposely integrated to achieve a specific task or set of tasks. These tasks range from human resource selection to product marketing and research and development activities.[72] Critical to the building of competitive advantages, capabilities are often based on developing, carrying and ex-changing information and knowledge through the firm's human capital.[73] Client-specific capabilities often develop from repeated interactions with clients and learn-ing about their needs. As a result, capabilities often evolve and develop over time.[74] The foundation of many capabilities lies in the unique skills and knowledge of a firm's employees and, often, their functional expertise. Hence, the value of human capital in developing and using capabilities and, ultimately, core competencies can-not be overstated.[75]

While global business leaders increasingly support the view that the knowledge possessed by human capital is among the most significant of an organization's capabilities and may ultimately be at the root of all competitive advantages,[76] firms must also be able to utilize the knowledge they have and transfer it among their business units.[77] Given this reality, the firm's challenge is to create an environment that allows people to integrate their individual knowledge with that held by others in the firm so that, collectively, the firm has significant organizational knowledge.[78] As noted in the earlier Strategic Focus, GE has been effective in developing its hu-man capital and in promoting the transfer of their knowledge throughout the com-pany. Building important capabilities is critical to achieving high firm performance.[79]

As illustrated in Table 3.3, capabilities are often developed in specific functional areas (such as manufacturing, R&D, and marketing) or in a part of a functional area (e.g., advertising). Table 3.3 shows a grouping of organizational functions and the capabilities that some companies are thought to possess in terms of all or parts of those functions.

## Core competencies

Defined in Chapter 1, core competencies are capabilities that serve as a source of competitive advantage for a firm over its rivals. Core competencies distinguish a company competitively and reflect its personality. Core competencies emerge over time through an organizational process of accumulating and learning how to de-ploy different resources and capabilities.[80] As the capacity to take action, core com-petencies are the "crown jewels": the activities the company performs especially well when compared with competitors, and through which the firm adds unique value to its goods or services over a long period of time.[81]

How many core competencies are required for the firm to have a sustained com-petitive advantage? Responses to this question vary. McKinsey & Co. recommends that its clients identify no more than three or four competencies around which their strategic actions can be framed. Supporting and nurturing more than four core competencies may prevent a firm from developing the focus it needs to fully exploit its competencies in the marketplace.

## Building core competencies

Two tools help firms identify and build their core competencies. The first consists of four specific criteria of sustainable competitive advantage that firms can use to de-termine those capabilities that are core competencies. Because the capabilities shown in Table 3.3 have satisfied these four criteria, they are core competencies. The second tool is the value chain analysis. Firms use this tool to select the value-creating competencies that should be maintained, upgraded or developed and those that should be outsourced.

**Table 3.3** Examples of firms' capabilities

| Functional Areas | Capabilities | Examples of Firms |
|---|---|---|
| Distribution | Effective use of logistics management techniques | Kuehne & Nagel |
| Human Resources | Motivating, empowering, and retaining employees | Microsoft |
| Management Information Systems | Effective and efficient control of inventories through point-of-purchase data collection methods | Tesco |
| Marketing | Effective promotion of brand-name products | Unilever |
| | | ING Direct |
| | | Innocent |
| | | Polo Ralph Lauren Corp. |
| | | McKinsey & Co. |
| | Effective customer service | Nordstrom Inc. |
| | | Norrell Corporation |
| | Innovative merchandising | Crate & Barrel |
| Management | Ability to envision the future of clothing | Hugo Boss |
| | Effective organizational structure | PepsiCo |
| | Adaptation to change | Stihl |
| Manufacturing | Development and production skills yielding reliable products | Komatsu |
| | Product quality | Porsche |
| | | Volkswagen |
| | Miniaturization of components and products | Sony |
| | Exploitation of platform | |
| Research & development | Innovative technology | Siemens |
| | Development of sophisticated elevator solutions | Kone |
| | Rapid transformation of technology into new products and processes | Chaparral Steel |
| | | Thomson Consumer Electronics |
| Design | Digital technology | SAP |
| | Usage innovation | Bang & Olufsen |
| | Emotional differentiation | Alessi |
| | Aesthetic attachment | Marimekko |

## Four criteria of sustainable competitive advantage

As shown in Table 3.4, capabilities that are valuable, rare, costly to imitate and non-substitutable are core competencies. In turn, core competencies are sources of competitive advantage for the firm over its rivals. Capabilities failing to satisfy the four criteria of sustainable competitive advantage are not core competencies, meaning that although every core competence is a capability, not every capability is a core competence. To put it a different way, for a capability to be a core competence, it must be valuable and unique from a customer's point of view. For a competitive advantage to be sustainable, the core competence must be inimitable and non-substitutable by competitors.[82]

**Table 3.4** The four criteria of sustainable competitive advantage

| Valuable Capabilities | • Help a firm neutralize threats or exploit opportunities |
|---|---|
| Rare Capabilities | • Are not possessed by many others |
| Costly-to-Imitate Capabilities | • Historical: A unique and a valuable organizational culture or brand name |
| | • Ambiguous cause: The causes and uses of a competence are unclear |
| | • Social complexity: Interpersonal relationships, trust, and friendship among managers, suppliers, and customers |
| Nonsubstitutable Capabilities | • No strategic equivalent |

A sustained competitive advantage is achieved only when competitors cannot duplicate the benefits of a firm's strategy or when they lack the resources to attempt imitation. For some period of time, the firm may earn a competitive advantage by using capabilities that are valuable and rare, but imitable. For example, some firms are trying to gain an advantage by out-greening their competitors. Sainsbury's, one of the largest supermarket chains in the UK, has attempted to out-green Tesco in the fields of healthy food and environment. Moreover, Sainsbury's decided to double the number of products that carry the traffic light food labelling system and remove all hydrogenated fat from its own-brand products. Tesco, on the other hand, decided to introduce a 10-point "community plan" based around the environment and healthy eating.[83]

Another sector in which companies try to out-green each other is the automobile industry. In Europe Audi and Peugeot have attempted to "out green" each other by introducing cars which emit less $CO_2$. For example, in July 2009, Audi launched the A3 Sportback TDI which emits only 109 grams of $CO_2$ per kilometre. Peugeot responded by introducing its 207 Economique model which emits 99 grams of $CO_2$ per kilometre.[84] The length of time a firm can expect to retain its competitive advantage is a function of how quickly competitors can successfully imitate a good, service, or process. Sustainable competitive advantage results only when all four criteria are satisfied.

**Valuable**   Valuable capabilities allow the firm to exploit opportunities or neutralize threats in its external environment. By effectively using capabilities to exploit opportunities, a firm creates value for customers. Under former CEO Jack Welch's leadership, GE built a valuable competence in financial services. It built this powerful competence largely through acquisitions and its core competence in integrating newly acquired businesses. In addition, making such competencies as financial services highly successful required placing the right people in the right jobs. As noted in the Strategic Focus, Welch emphasized human capital because it is important in creating value for customers. And that emphasis has continued following Welch's retirement.

**Rare**   Rare capabilities are capabilities that few, if any, competitors possess. A key question to be answered when evaluating this criterion is, "How many rival firms possess these valuable capabilities?" Capabilities possessed by many rivals are unlikely to be sources of competitive advantage for any one of them. Instead, valuable but common (i.e., not rare) resources and capabilities are sources of competitive parity.[85]

**Valuable capabilities**

Valuable capabilities allow the firm to exploit opportunities or neutralize threats in its external environment.

**Rare capabilities**

Rare capabilities are capabilities that few, if any, competitors possess.

Competitive advantage results only when firms develop and exploit valuable capabilities that differ from those shared with competitors.

### Costly to imitate
Costly-to-imitate capabilities are capabilities that other firms cannot easily develop. Capabilities that are costly to imitate are created because of one reason or a combination of three reasons (see Table 3.4). First, a firm sometimes is able to develop capabilities because of unique historical conditions. As firms evolve, they often acquire or develop capabilities that are unique to them.[86]

A firm with a unique and valuable organizational culture that emerged in the early stages of the company's history "may have an imperfectly imitable advantage over firms founded in another historical period",[87] one in which less valuable or less competitively useful values and beliefs strongly influenced the development of the firm's culture. Briefly discussed in Chapter 1, organizational culture is a set of values shared by members in the organization, as we explain in Chapter 15. An organizational culture is a source of advantage when employees are held together tightly by their belief in it.[88] The BBC and Al Jazeera's cultural distinctiveness vis-à-vis its US rivals help them stand out in the TV 24-hour-news competition.

A second condition of being costly to imitate occurs when the link between the firm's capabilities and its competitive advantage is causally ambiguous.[89] In these instances, competitors can't clearly understand how a firm uses its capabilities as the foundation for competitive advantage. As a result, firms are uncertain about the capabilities they should develop to duplicate the benefits of a competitor's value-creating strategy. For years, firms tried to imitate Southwest Airlines' low-cost strategy but most have been unable to do so, primarily because they can't duplicate Southwest's unique culture. Of all Southwest's imitators, Ryanair, an Irish airline headquartered in Dublin, is the most successful. However, Ryanair is also a controversial company, praised by some, criticized by others as described in the following Strategic Focus. Ryanair's core competence is its capability to keep its costs excessively low and to generate alternative sources of revenue.

Social complexity is the third reason that capabilities can be costly to imitate. Social complexity means that at least some, and frequently many, of the firm's capabilities are the product of complex social phenomena. Interpersonal relationships, trust, friendships among managers and between managers and employees, and a firm's reputation with suppliers and customers are examples of socially complex capabilities. Ryanair is careful to hire people that fit with its culture to avoid diluting its focus. This complex interrelationship between the culture and human capital adds value in ways that other airlines cannot, such as jokes on flights by the flight attendants or the cooperation between gate personnel and pilots.

### Nonsubstitutable
Nonsubstitutable capabilities do not have strategic equivalents. This final criterion for a capability to be a source of competitive advantage "is that there must be no strategically equivalent valuable resources that are themselves either not rare or imitable. Two valuable firm resources (or two bundles of firm resources) are strategically equivalent when they each can be separately exploited to implement the same strategies."[90] In general, the strategic value of capabilities increases as they become more difficult to substitute. The more invisible capabilities are, the more difficult it is for firms to find substitutes and the greater the challenge for competitors trying to imitate a firm's value-creating strategy. Firm-specific knowledge and trust-based working relationships between managers and non-managerial personnel, such as existed for years at Southwest Airlines, are examples of capabilities that are difficult to identify and for which finding a substitute is challenging. However, causal ambiguity may make it difficult for the firm to

---

**Costly-to-imitate capabilities**

Costly-to-imitate capabilities are capabilities that other firms cannot easily develop.

**Nonsubstitutable capabilities**

Nonsubstitutable capabilities are capabilities that do not have strategic equivalents.

## STRATEGIC FOCUS

© Steven May/Alamy

# Ryanair: the passionate cost cutter that is both loved and hated

Ryanair is the leading low-cost airline in Europe. It has achieved a high market share by relentlessly holding down costs and thereby offering the lowest prices on its routes. To attract new customers, it once offered flights for one penny to selected destinations. It sold almost half a million tickets with the promotion. While Michael O'Leary, Ryanair's CEO, is known to be extremely cost-conscious (he will not provide employees with pens; he recommends that they get them from hotels where they stay overnight), the primary reason for Ryanair's lowest cost status is that it has the fastest turnarounds in the industry (resembling a race car pit crew operation). O'Leary is also constantly identifying new revenue streams such as charges for use of airport check-in facilities, charging for each piece of luggage, offering rental cars at the destination, charging to use the toilet on the plane, etc.

To obtain free publicity, O'Leary or his executives often make outrageous statements and roundly criticize their competitors to get Ryanair's name in the news. The firm uses multiple marketing gimmicks such as advertising that directly criticizes competitors

on specific routes, excessively low fares and even some provovative advertising slogans. The firm's core competence is the capability to maintain the lowest costs in the industry and to generate alternative revenues. Because of its very low fares, its passenger load grew at an annual rate of approximately 25 per cent until the economic crisis in 2008. The company even made profits in 2008, a very difficult year financially.

All of this said, Ryanair receives a significant amount of criticism. In 2006, for example, it was voted as the least favourite airline (despite its popularity evidenced in passenger numbers). It receives a large amount of criticism for its lack of customer service, with special focus on an unfriendly uncaring staff and hidden charges.

Yet, O'Leary believes that Ryanair may be one of the few airlines in Europe left standing after the latest severe economic recession. He is planning growth (although the airline announced some small reductions in service and staff in 2009) and is negotiating with Boeing and Airbus to buy as many as 400 new aircraft. The airline already is one of the largest in the world in terms of number of passengers served annually. With its decided strengths and also acknowledged weaknesses, the future of Ryanair will be interesting.

**Sources:** 2005 "Ryanair exercises options on five Boeing 737s", Wikinews, http://en.wikinews.org. June 13; Scott, M. (2007) "Ryanair flying high", *BusinessWeek*. http://www.businessweek.com. July 31; Davidson, A. (2008) "Michael O'Leary: Ryanair's rebel with a cause", *The Sunday Times*. http://business.timesonline.co.uk. December 7; Done, K. (2009) "Ryanair in talks to buy 400 aircraft", *Financial Times*. http://www.ft.com. February 2; Done, K. (2009) "Virgin and Ryanair to cut jobs", *Financial Times*. http://www.ft.com. February 12; 2009 "Ryanair Hldgs PLC", Answers.com. http://www.answers.com. March 13; 2009 "Ryanair", Wikipedia. http://www.widipedia.org, March 13.

## Questions

1 What is Ryanair's strategy?

2 Explain why Ryanair needs to continuously study and understand its internal organization.

3 Define Ryanair's value and discuss its importance for strategy development and implementation.

4 Describe the differences between Ryanair's tangible and intangible resources.

5 Use the value chain analysis to identify and evaluate Ryanair's resources and capabilities.

6 Define outsourcing and discuss reasons for its possible use by Ryanair.

**Table 3.5** Outcomes from combinations of the criteria for sustainable competitive advantage

| Is the Resource or Capability Valuable? | Is the Resource or Capability Rare? | Is the Resource or Capability Costly to Imitate? | Is the Resource or Capability Nonsubstitutable? | Competitive Consequences | Performance Implications |
|---|---|---|---|---|---|
| No | No | No | No | Competitive disadvantage | Below-average returns |
| Yes | No | No | Yes/no | Competitive parity | Average returns |
| Yes | Yes | No | Yes/no | Temporary competitive advantage | Average returns to above-average returns |
| Yes | Yes | Yes | Yes/no | Sustainable competitive advantage | Above-average returns |

learn as well and may stifle progress, because the firm may not know how to improve processes that are not easily codified and thus are ambiguous.[91]

In summary, only using valuable, rare, costly-to-imitate, and nonsubstitutable capabilities creates sustainable competitive advantage. Table 3.5 shows the competitive consequences and performance implications resulting from combinations of the four criteria of sustainability. The analysis suggested by the table helps managers determine the strategic value of a firm's capabilities. The firm should not emphasize capabilities that fit the criteria described in the first row in the table (i.e., resources and capabilities that are neither valuable nor rare and that are imitable and for which strategic substitutes exist). Capabilities yielding competitive parity and either temporary or sustainable competitive advantage, however, will be supported. Some competitors such as Danone or Nestlé may have capabilities that may result in competitive parity. In such cases, the firms will nurture these capabilities while simultaneously trying to develop capabilities that can yield either a temporary or sustainable competitive advantage.

## Value chain analysis

Value chain analysis allows the firm to understand the parts of its operations that create value and those that do not.[92] Such understanding is important because the firm earns above-average returns only when the value it creates is greater than the costs incurred to create that value.[93]

The value chain is a template that firms use to analyse their cost position and to identify the multiple means that can be used to facilitate implementation of a chosen business-level strategy.[94] Today's competitive landscape demands that firms examine their value chains in a global, rather than a domestic-only context.[95] In particular, activities associated with supply chains should be studied within a global context.[96]

As shown in Figure 3.3, a firm's value chain is segmented into primary and support activities. Primary activities are involved with a product's physical creation, its

**Primary activities**

Primary activities are involved with a product's physical creation, its sale and distribution to buyers and its service after the sale.

**FIGURE 3.3** The basic value chain

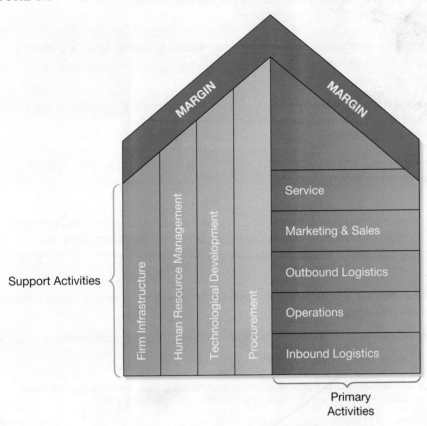

sale and distribution to buyers, and its service after the sale. Support activities provide the assistance necessary for the primary activities to take place.

The value chain shows how a product moves from the raw-material stage to the final customer. For individual firms, the essential idea of the value chain is to create additional value without incurring significant costs while doing so, and to capture the value that has been created. In a globally competitive economy, the most valuable links on the chain are people who have knowledge about customers. This locus of value-creating possibilities applies just as strongly to retail and service firms as to manufacturers. Moreover, for organizations in all sectors, the effects of e-commerce make it increasingly necessary for companies to develop value-adding knowledge processes to compensate for the value and margin that the Internet strips from physical processes.[97]

Table 3.6 lists the items that can be evaluated to determine the value-creating potential of primary activities. In Table 3.7, the items for evaluating support activities are shown. All items in both tables should be evaluated relative to competitors' capabilities. To be a source of competitive advantage, a resource or capability must allow the firm (1) to perform an activity in a manner that provides value superior to that provided by competitors; or (2) to perform a value-creating activity that competitors cannot perform. Only under these conditions does a firm create value for customers and have opportunities to capture that value.

Creating value through value chain activities often requires building effective alliances with suppliers (and sometimes others to which the firm outsources activities as discussed in the next section) and developing strong positive relationships with customers. When firms have such strong positive relationships with suppliers and

**Support activities**

Support activities provide the assistance necessary for the primary activities to take place.

**Table 3.6** Examining the value-creating potential of primary activities

**Inbound Logistics**

Activities, such as materials handling, warehousing, and inventory control, used to receive, store, and disseminate inputs to a product.

**Operations**

Activities necessary to convert the inputs provided by inbound logistics into final product form. Machining, packaging, assembly, and equipment maintenance are examples of operations activities.

**Outbound Logistics**

Activities involved with collecting, storing, and physically distributing the final product to customers. Examples of these activities include finished-goods warehousing, materials handling, and order processing.

**Marketing and Sales**

Activities completed to provide means through which customers can purchase products and to induce them to do so. To effectively market and sell products, firms develop advertising and promotional campaigns, select appropriate distribution channels, and select, develop, and support their sales force.

**Service**

Activities designed to enhance or maintain a product's value. Firms engage in a range of service-related activities, including installation, repair, training, and adjustment.

Each activity should be examined relative to competitors' abilities. Accordingly, firms rate each activity as *superior*, *equivalent*, or *inferior*.

Source: Adapted with the permission of The Free Press, an imprint of Simon & Schuster Adult Publishing Group, from *Competitive Advantage: Creating and Sustaining Superior Performance*, by Michael E. Porter, 39–40, Copyright © 1985, 1998 by Michael E. Porter.

**Table 3.7** Examining the value-creating potential of support activities

**Procurement**

Activities completed to purchase the inputs needed to produce a firm's products. Purchased inputs include items fully consumed during the manufacture of products (e.g., raw materials and supplies, as well as fixed assets – machinery, laboratory equipment, office equipment, and buildings).

**Technological Development**

Activities completed to improve a firm's product and the processes used to manufacture it. Technological development takes many forms, such as process equipment, basic research and product design, and servicing procedures.

**Human Resource Management**

Activities involved with recruiting, hiring, training, developing, and compensating all personnel.

**Firm Infrastructure**

Firm infrastructure includes activities such as general management, planning, finance, accounting, legal support, and governmental relations that are required to support the work of the entire value chain. Through its infrastructure, the firm strives to effectively and consistently identify external opportunities and threats, identify resources and capabilities, and support core competencies.

Each activity should be examined relative to competitors' abilities. Accordingly, firms rate each activity as *superior*, *equivalent*, or *inferior*.

Source: Adapted with the permission of The Free Press, an imprint of Simon & Schuster Adult Publishing Group, from *Competitive Advantage: Creating and Sustaining Superior Performance*, by Michael E. Porter, 40–43, Copyright © 1985, 1998 by Michael E. Porter.

customers, they are said to have "social capital".[98] The relationships themselves have value because they produce knowledge transfer and access to resources that a firm may not hold internally.[99] To build social capital whereby resources such as knowledge are transferred across organizations requires trust between the parties. The partners must trust each other in order to allow their resources to be used in such a way that both parties will benefit over time and neither party will take advantage of the other.[100] Trust and social capital usually evolve over time with repeated interactions but firms can also establish special means to jointly manage alliances that promote greater trust with the outcome of enhanced benefits for both partners.[101] An example for such a network of allies can be found in logistics. Maersk, a Danish transport and energy company, creates value by executing the shipping activities of companies.

Sometimes start-up firms create value by uniquely reconfiguring or recombining parts of the value chain. As shown in Figure 3.4, the Internet has changed many

**FIGURE 3.4** Prominent applications of the Internet in the value chain

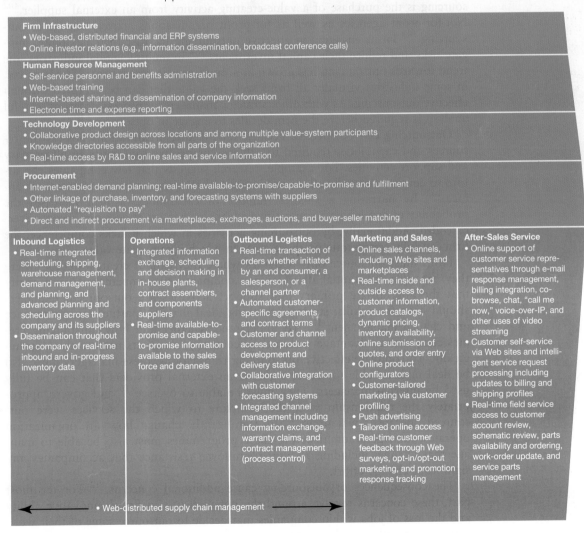

aspects of the value chain for a broad range of firms. A key reason is because the Internet affects how people communicate, locate information, and buy goods and services.

Evaluating a firm's capability to execute its primary and support activities is challenging. Earlier in the chapter, we noted that identifying and assessing the value of a firm's resources and capabilities requires judgement. Judgement is equally necessary when using value chain analysis, because no obviously correct model or rule is universally available to help in the process.

What should a firm do about primary and support activities in which its resources and capabilities are not a source of core competence and, hence, of competitive advantage? Outsourcing is an alternative chosen by an increasing number of companies in recent years.

## Outsourcing

**Outsourcing**

Outsourcing is the purchase of a value-creating activity from an external supplier.

Concerned with how components, finished goods or services will be obtained, outsourcing is the purchase of a value-creating activity from an external supplier.[102] Not-for-profit agencies as well as for-profit organizations actively engage in outsourcing.[103] Firms engaging in effective outsourcing increase their flexibility, mitigate risks and reduce their capital investments.[104] In multiple global industries, the trend towards outsourcing has grown at a rapid pace in recent years.[105] Moreover, in some industries virtually all firms seek the value that can be captured through effective outsourcing. As with other strategic management process decisions, careful analysis is required before the firm decides to engage in outsourcing.[106]

Outsourcing can be effective because few, if any, organizations possess the resources and capabilities required to achieve competitive superiority in all primary and support activities. For example, research suggests that few companies can afford to develop internally all the technologies that might lead to competitive advantage.[107] By nurturing a smaller number of capabilities, a firm increases the probability of developing a competitive advantage because it does not become overextended. Additionally, by outsourcing activities in which it lacks competence, the firm can fully concentrate on those areas in which it can create value.

Firms must outsource only activities where they cannot create value or where they are at a substantial disadvantage compared to competitors.[108] To verify that the appropriate primary and support activities are outsourced, managers should have four skills: strategic thinking, deal making, partnership governance and change management.[109] To understand whether and how outsourcing creates competitive advantage within their company, managers need to think strategically. To complete effective outsourcing transactions, these managers must also be deal makers, able to secure rights from external providers that can be fully used by internal managers. They must be able to oversee[110] and govern appropriately the relationship with the company to which the services were outsourced. Because outsourcing can significantly change how an organization operates, managers administering these programmes must also be able to manage that change, including resolving employee resistance that accompanies any significant change effort.[111]

The consequences of outsourcing cause additional concerns.[112] For the most part, these concerns revolve around the potential loss in firms' innovative ability and the loss of jobs within companies that decide to outsource some of their work activities to others. Thus, innovation and technological uncertainty are two

© Ryan Klos/iStock

## STRATEGIC FOCUS

# From e-retailing to e-books: changing the context changes the capabilities needed

E-commerce has changed our lives and industries. Online retailing, especially of travel arrangements, cars, brokerage, groceries and books, have all become commonplace, yet through e-commerce these industries have changed dramatically in the last 20 years. While the number of travel agencies that employed more than 100 people grew by 60 per cent (from 109 to 174) between 1994 and 2003, the number of small ones declined from 18 186 to 12 865. Only the smallest book shops (one to four employees) focusing on niche markets, such as children's books or cookbooks, seem able to develop capabilities that help withstand the pressure.

The Internet has reduced costs of gathering and analysing information about products and prices. For consumers this results in increased transparency of offerings in the market, and it creates more pressure on retailers to price competitively. Reducing the variation of prices the Internet drives the prices towards what consumers perceive to be a "fair" price, which is often closer to the lower prices. In book retailing, sales of books or other categories on Amazom.com are more often used as a point of reference because it has a comprehensive list of products for sale, and the price that Amazon charges has become a reference point for book retailers, especially for bestsellers. With online sales, retailers needed to develop new capabilities for the online world which was not easy. For instance, they did not master the skill of increasing customer loyalty without meeting the customer in person, were neither comprehensive nor specialized enough, and they focused on the logistics to their stores – not on the logistics to the customer's door. Similarly, initially they did not exploit the synergies between online and offline retail. Over time, some adjusted (e.g. Barnes & Nobles) and developed new capabilities, some allied with online retailers, such as Borders cooperation with Amazon, and many went out of business.

After changing retailing, the Internet is now facilitating the next wave of change in the bookselling market. In July 2010 Amazon announced it had reached a new milestone by selling more e-books than hardbacks in the period April–June. For every 100 hardcover books sold, the company sold 180 Kindle books. Kindle customers can download books and other products to the Kindle, read them or listen to them or surf the Web and send e-mail messages. Rivalry related to e-books is fierce. Introduced as an alternative to the Kindle in November 2006 in the US, and in 2008 in the UK and European market, the Sony Reader has similar features such as digital reading of books, listening audio, and so on. Barnes & Noble, a bookseller with a traditional book retailing background, launched the Nook e-reader and promotes it aggressively. On June 21, 2010, Barnes & Noble, a direct competitor to Amazon's bookselling business in the US, reduced the price of its Nook e-reader to $199 in the US. Amazon followed within hours with a price cut of its Kindle product to $189 – reduced from $259. Amazon's CEO, Jeff Bezos, claimed leadership in the e-book market and stated that since the price reduction, sales of Kindle have tripled. Similarly, Sony has stated that sales of its reader have tripled since 2009. The iPhone and many other devices also facilitate book reading, yet with the recent launch of Apple's iPad, yet another successful device featuring book and magazine reading functionalities has entered the market. This flurry of new market entrants creates price pressure but it also raises the attention paid to e-books and may ultimately benefit market development.

How e-books are changing the way books and other kind of content are read, sold and made, is not yet known. While some newspapers hope that such devices enable them to charge for their product, and some publishers are delighted about the new opportunities, others are wary, pointing out the increasing influence of booksellers and publishers' growing dependence on them. Currently, it is also unclear how e-books relate to traditional books. Amazon and Barnes & Noble suggest that the increasing growth rates of e-books does not cannibalize traditional books. Amazon states that book and e-book sales are both growing, but data may not be sufficient to show the connection between traditional and e-books today. Apple and Sony may not be at all concerned about a possible cannibalization of books by e-books. In June, Steve Jobs, CEO of Apple, claimed that the Apple iBookstore, since its launch in April, had taken 20 per cent of the growing e-book market.

In view of these uncertainties, the contenders have to develop the right capabilities that will allow them to create competitive advantage in a growing market.

**Sources:** Anonymous, "E-commerce favours large companies but only because that is what people want", *The Economist*, July 3, 2010, 69; Goldmanis, M., Horacsu, A., Syverson, C. and Emre, O. (2010), "E-commerce and the market structure of retail industries", *Economist Journal*, June; "Borders teamed with amazon.com", http://www.amazon.com, July 7, 2007; Fowler, G. A. and Trachtenberg, J. A. (2010) "E-books elbowing hardbacks aside", *Wall Street Journal*, July 20, B1; Mossberg, W. S. (2009) "The latest Kindle: Bigger, not better, than its sibling", *Wall Street Journal online*, http://www.wsj.com, June 11; http://www.forbes.com/2008/01/29/disruptometer-amazon-sony-lead-clayton-in_sa_0129claytonchristensen_inl.html.

## Questions

**1** How did traditional booksellers compete before e-commerce? What capabilities were important?

**2** How do online booksellers compete? What capabilities became relatively important?

**3** With e-books sales increasing and the market gaining in importance, the future of the rivals depends much on developing the right capabilities. Which capabilities do you think will become more important in the future?

**4** Discuss the consequences for the market players, i.e. Amazon, Apple, Barnes & Noble, Sony, the publishers, the authors.

important issues to consider in making outsourcing decisions. Nevertheless, firms can also learn from outsource suppliers so that they can increase their own innovation capabilities.[113] Companies must be aware of these issues and be prepared to fully consider the concerns about opportunities from outsourcing suggested by different stakeholders (e.g., employees). The opportunities and concerns may be especially great when firms outsource activities or functions to a foreign supply source (often referred to as offshoring).[114] Bangalore and Belfast are the newest hot spots for technology outsourcing, competing with other major operations in China and India.[115]

As is true with all strategic management tools and techniques, criteria should be established to guide outsourcing decisions. Outsourcing is big business, but not every outsourcing decision is successful. For example, amid delays and cost overruns, Electronic Data Systems abandoned a €1 billion opportunity to run Dow Chemical Co.'s phone-and-computer networks. Lloyds TSB, a commercial bank in the UK, decided in July 2009 to stop offshoring activities to India.[116] Less-than-desirable outcomes indicate that firms should carefully study outsourcing opportunities to verify that they will indeed create value in excess of the cost incurred.

## KEY DEBATE

© sebastian-julian

# Resources and temporary advantage

The Resource-based View (RBV) of strategy has become main stream because of its powerful approach to explain persistent performance differences of firms with the underlying resource equipment that are unique to firms. Barney (1991) provided a practical way to assess resources by considering their value, uniqueness and the likelihood of them being substituted and imitated. Long lasting advantage is more likely when imitation and substitution are unlikely. This suggests that firms need tools that help them enhance and exploit value and uniqueness. However, in a recent special issue of the Strategic Management Journal, D'Aveni, Dagnino and Smith (2010) ask whether strategic management has entered "The Age of Temporary Advantage?" Many causes of temporary advantage have been mentioned, including numerous developments such as technological change, globalization, convergence of industries and aggressive competitive behavior, deregulation and privatization, reemergence of China and other emerging markets, patient capital financing ventures, political conflicts and terrorism. If under such circumstances resources lose their value or their uniqueness vanishes more quickly than in the past, as research on disruptive and fast-paced environments suggests, then resources alone may not provide sustained competitive advantage. Managing temporary advantage and anticipating the consequences may come at a premium. In fact, what to do with core competences *and* weaknesses may need to be revisited. Should companies give up on their strengths or cannibalize their own strengths in anticipation of their loosing value? Should companies invest in improving their weaknesses at all, or just wait for changing times? Do resources still matter in unprecedented times? Should they be conservative when it comes to resources or should they be bold and aggressive?

**Sources:** Barney, J. B. (1991) "Firm resources and sustained competitive advantage", *Journal of Management*, 17(1): 99–120; Volberda, H. W. (1996) "Toward the flexible form: How to remain vital in hypercompetitive environments", *Organization Science*, 7(4): 359–374; Brown, S. and K. M. Eisenhardt (1998) *Competing on the Edge*, Harvard Business School Press: Boston, MA; Danneels, E. (2011) "Trying to become a different type of company: Dynamic capability at Smith Corona", *Strategic Management Journal*, 32(1), 1–31; D'Aveni, R. A. (1995) *Hypercompetition: Managing the Dynamics of Strategic Manouvering*, Free Press: New York; R. D'Aveni, G. B. Dagnino and K. G. Smith (2010) "The age of temporary advantage?", *Strategic Management Journal*, Special Issue, 31(13): 1371–1548; Schreyögg, G. and M. Kliesch-Eberl (2007) "How dynamic can organizational capabilities be? Towards a dual-process model of capability dynamization", *Strategic Management Journal*, 28(9): 913–933.

## Questions

1 Before consulting the special issue of the Strategic Management Journal on Temporary Advantage, ask yourself which strategies make more sense. Relying on current strengths or developing new strengths? Overcoming current weaknesses or leaving current weaknesses as they are?

2 After reading the special issue, discuss the different contexts that are closely linked with temporary advantages. What are the resources and capabilities that are most important to succeed in disruptive and fast-paced environments?

3 Schreyögg, G. and M. Kliesch-Eberl (2007) and Danneels (2011) point out that organizations often do not understand the sources of their success and failure. How much does this matter in stable environments and how much in contexts characterized by high uncertainty.?

# Competencies, strengths, weaknesses and strategic decisions

At the conclusion of the internal analysis, firms must identify their strengths and weaknesses in resources, capabilities and core competencies. For example, if they have weak capabilities or do not have core competencies in areas required to achieve a competitive advantage, they must acquire those resources and build the capabilities and competencies needed. Alternatively, they could decide to outsource a function or activity where they are weak in order to improve the value that they provide to customers.[117]

Therefore, firms need to have the appropriate resources and capabilities to develop the desired strategy and create value for customers and other stakeholders such as shareholders.[118] Having a significant quantity of resources does not suggest that they have the "right" resources. Moreover, decision makers sometimes become more focused and productive when their organization's resources are constrained.[119] Managers must help the firm obtain and use resources, capabilities and core competencies in ways that generate value-creating competitive advantages.

Tools such as outsourcing help the firm focus on its core competencies as the source of its competitive advantages. However, evidence shows that the value-creating ability of core competencies should never be taken for granted. Moreover, the ability of a core competence to be a permanent competitive advantage can't be assumed. The reason for these cautions is that all core competencies have the potential to become core rigidities. A core competence is the source of competitive advantage. If emphasized when it is no longer competitively relevant, it can become a weakness, a seed of organizational inertia.

Inertia has been the main cause of the challenges Alitalia faces. Following years without restructuring and instead sticking with an outdated business concept, Alitalia faces bankruptcy. The company failed to modernize its processes and airplanes and became more and more unprofitable. For example, most of the company's airplanes are McDonnell Douglas 80s, which are less fuel-efficient than new aircraft, take longer to service and need more regular checks. As Alitalia was not able to restructure itself, many other airline companies such as easyJet won market share from Alitalia.[120]

Events occurring in the firm's external environment create conditions through which core competencies can become core rigidities, generate inertia and stifle innovation. "Often the flip side, the dark side, of core capabilities is revealed due to external events when new competitors figure out a better way to serve the firm's customers, when new technologies emerge, or when political or social events shift the ground underneath."[121] However, changes in the external environment do not cause core competencies to become core rigidities; rather, strategic myopia and inflexibility on the part of managers are the cause.

After studying its external environment to determine what it might choose to do (as explained in Chapter 2) and its internal organization to understand what it can do (as explained in this chapter), the firm needs to consider how to link internal with external resources (chapter 4) and to select a business-level strategy that will help it reach its vision and mission. We describe different ways to combine internal and external sources of advantage in the next chapter.

## CLOSING CASE

© PSL Images/Alamy

# RIM at the edge: privacy, protection, policy and company performance

In the late 1990s the first commercial spam email triggered much discussion about the Internet. Many users regarded the Internet as a tool for personal and intellectual communication that would bypass the state, liberating and still safeguarding privacy. Today, Google with its popular email service keeps many secrets private. For specific and legitimate requests, e.g. FBI agents in Washington who need deep insight into suspects' emails, it can allow access. The increasing importance of digitization and the related possibilities of personalization of services led to many opportunities to create value and improve services. However, often personalization and privacy seem to involve a trade-off. The erosion of privacy and the spectre of surveillance gather more attention as an increasing number of cases of personal identity theft and of detailed personal profiling and data mining are reported. In 1999, Scott McNealy, former CEO of Sun Microsystem, summarized: "You have zero privacy. Get over it."

Responding to such concerns, the Canadian BlackBerry maker, Research in Motion (RIM) based in Waterloo, Ontario, started as a small manufacturer selling secure mobile email devices in the US, Canada and Britain. Its primary customer groups were big companies and government agencies. The exceptionally strong encryption of the BlackBerry system was an important advantage because it provided security even from surveillance by powerful national security agencies. Unlike other smart phone makers, RIM relies on peer-to-peer encryption technology and it routes the data through its own server networks, the biggest of which is in Canada, which keeps its customers' communications private.

RIM's rise began in the early 2000s when 2900 companies used BlackBerrys. In 2001 RIM launched BlackBerry in Europe and developed partnerships with Hutchison Telecom in Hong Kong and Telstra in Australia. In 2004 BlackBerry reached the milestone of one million subscribers. When the smartphone market took off after 2005, RIM's sales outside North America began to grow rapidly. By 2006, 25 per cent of subscribers were based outside North America. Today, RIM sells its highly secure BlackBerrys in 175 countries offering its service through 550 mobile network operators to more than 46 million subscribers (June 2010). Sales outside North America accounted for less than 25 per cent five years ago; today it is 40 per cent of RIM's annual revenues (€11.3bn). Now a controversy threatens to undermine RIM's competitive advantage and derail its global ambitions.

RIM's rapid growth and internationalization has lead RIM into markets where governments are concerned about opposition, crime, drug traffickers and terrorism. Governments abroad cannot read messages exchanged through RIM they may want to intercept which are exchanged within their borders. Nor can they monitor communications sent and received by BlackBerry users and have no access to secure data handled by the devices. RIM has been locked into negotiations with several governments for extended periods to address such concerns. Since 2008, when the Indian government discovered that the Mumbai terror attackers used BlackBerry to orchestrate the siege, it has been negotiating with RIM to force the company to comply with domestic regulation. After talks to persuade the Canadian company to comply with local regulations and enable authorities to access BlackBerry data broke down after three years, the United Arab Emirates (UAE) threatened to ban the service from October 11, 2010. After discussing with RIM the possibility of getting access to data in cases of pressing national security concerns, the Saudi Arabia government threatened to ban the service for the 700 000 customers in the kingdom until the country's three mobile phone operators fulfilled some regulatory requirements. Saudi Telecom Co. stopped BlackBerry services for four hours on August 6, 2010. Algeria and Lebanon also insisted on easier access to RIM's network.

RIM has long promoted its services claiming that interested third parties cannot access encrypted emails and messages that are routed through the Canadian servers. RIM declared it does not have access to the encrypted data from corporate users, even if routed over its network, because the design of its system and the peer-to-peer technology prohibit RIM from holding the encryption codes needed to unlock the data.

RIM said it complies with lawful requests from authorities to intercept communications but it does not give any government preferential treatment. In the past, RIM has been able to satisfy the demands of nations including Russia and China that seem to have overcome the encryption problem. China for instance requires all Internet and telecom companies to monitor, report on and even censor their customers' communications. In these nations technological ingenuity and intelligence resources may have enabled governments to intercept communications. In 2008 the US national counter-intelligence executive expressed concern with BlackBerry security in a warning about possible tagging, monitoring and exploitation of US nationals on arrival in China. Blackberry's launch in China had to be delayed by almost a year until the government's demands were satisfied.

The governments in Canada and the US defend RIM's encryption practices as part of the free flow of information that is foundational to an innovative economy, and the US state department is seeking a solution that reconciles the need for freedom with the security needs of other countries. One likely solution discussed in the past relates to the possibility of placing BlackBerry servers inside the country, which would undermine an important strength of RIM's value proposition for its BlackBerry devices. Are there other solutions?

**Sources:** Glenny, M. (2010) "BlackBerry is but a skirmish in the battle for the web", *Financial Times*, August 7/August 8, 7; Said, S. and Dvorak, P. (2010) "BlackBerry in crosshairs", *Wall Street Journal*, August 7–8, B5; Research in Motion websites; Taylor, P. (2010) "BlackBerry faces wrath of Mid-east spy masters", *Financial Times*, August 7–8, 2; USA Today website.

## Questions

1 Is RIM's ability to safeguard privacy a tangible and or an intangible asset?

2 How valuable, rare, costly to imitate and non-substitutable are RIM's capabilities to safeguard privacy?

3 What threatens to undermine RIM's value provided to customers?

4 Discuss possible options for RIM to reconcile the value it provides with local legislations.

5 Which of the options has what kind of effects on the value provided?

## SUMMARY

- In the global business environment, traditional factors (e.g., labour costs and superior access to financial resources and raw materials) can still create a competitive advantage. However, these factors are less often a source of competitive advantage in the current competitive landscape. The resources, capabilities and core competencies in the firm's internal organization are likely to have a stronger influence on its performance than are conditions in the external environment. The most effective organizations recognize that strategic competitiveness and above-average returns result only when core competencies (identified by studying the firm's internal organization) are matched with opportunities (determined by studying the firm's external environment).

- No competitive advantage lasts for ever. Over time, rivals use their own unique resources, capabilities and core competencies to form different value-creating propositions that duplicate the value-creating ability of the firm's competitive advantages. In general, the Internet's capabilities are reducing the sustainability of many competitive advantages. Because competitive advantages are not permanently sustainable, firms must exploit their current advantages while simultaneously using their resources and capabilities to form new advantages that can lead to future competitive success.

- Effectively managing core competencies requires careful analysis of the firm's resources (inputs to the production process) and capabilities (resources that have been purposely integrated to achieve a specific task or set of tasks). The knowledge possessed by human capital is among the most significant of an organization's capabilities and ultimately provides the base for most competitive advantages. The firm must create an environment that allows people to integrate their individual knowledge with that held by others so that, collectively, the firm has significant organizational knowledge.

- Individual resources are usually not a source of competitive advantage. Capabilities are a more likely source of competitive advantages, especially more sustainable ones. The firm's nurturing and support of core competencies is based on capabilities that are less visible to rivals and, therefore more difficult to understand and imitate.

- Only when a capability is valuable, rare, costly to imitate and nonsubstitutable is it a core competence and a source of competitive advantage. Over time, core competencies must be supported, but they cannot be allowed to become core rigidities. Core competencies are a source of competitive advantage only when they allow the firm to create value by exploiting opportunities in its external environment. When this is no longer possible, the company shifts its attention to selecting or forming other capabilities that satisfy the four criteria for a sustainable competitive advantage.

- Value chain analysis is used to identify and evaluate the competitive potential of resources and capabilities. By studying their skills relative to those associated with primary and support activities, firms can understand their cost structure and identify the activities through which they can create value.

- When the firm cannot create value in either an internal primary or support activity, outsourcing is considered. Commonly used in the global economy, outsourcing is the purchase of a value-creating activity from an external supplier. The firm should outsource only to companies possessing a competitive advantage in terms of the particular primary or support activity under consideration. In addition, the firm must continuously verify that it is not outsourcing activities from which it could create value.

## REVIEW QUESTIONS

1 Why is it important for a firm to study and understand its internal organization?

2 What is value? Why is it critical for the firm to create value? How does it do so?

3 What are the differences between tangible and intangible resources? Why is it important for decision makers to understand these differences? Are tangible resources linked more closely to the creation of competitive advantages than are intangible resources, or is the reverse true? Why?

4 What are capabilities? How do firms create capabilities?

5 What are the four criteria used to determine which of a firm's capabilities are core competencies? Why is it important for firms to use these criteria in developing capabilities?

6 What is value chain analysis? What does the firm gain when it successfully uses this tool?

7 What is outsourcing? Why do firms outsource? Will outsourcing's importance grow as we progress in the twenty-first century? Why or why not?

8 How do firms identify internal strengths and weaknesses? Why is it vital that managers have a clear understanding of their firm's strengths and weaknesses?

## DISCUSSION QUESTIONS

1  Understanding the internal organization of firms often focuses on the formal relationships (i.e. reporting lines) between units and between individuals. Informal relationships are all too often left out. What are possible consequences for strategy development and implementation?

2  Making resources that individuals possess accessible to the organization is important for strategic management. What are the differences between resources that are organizational and those that are individual? Discuss possible reasons why individuals may resist attempts to make their individual knowledge organizational.

3  How do firms create capabilities under time pressure? What are the consequences?

4  Are there other criteria that you would like to add to the four that are used to determine which of a firm's capabilities are core competencies? Develop a shortlist and discuss how they could help firms in developing capabilities.

5  Should a firm have one core competence or several? What are possible logics that suggest one or the other?

6  If outsourcing's importance grows as we progress in the twenty-first century, which will be one of the most important core competencies?

7  Often the leaders lose touch with the rest of their organizations. What can strategic leaders do to become aware of their organization's weaknesses in a timely fashion? Discuss advantages and disadvantages of these approaches.

## FURTHER READING

Understanding what is essential to succeed is not easy. How difficult it is to develop capabilities that help to increase competitiveness is shown in Michael Mol and Julian Birkinshaw's accessible book, *Giant Steps in* *Management* (FT/Prentice Hall, 2007) where they review the great leaps companies have made in improving the way they organize people and processes and the new methods they developed to do so effectively.

## EXPERIENTIAL EXERCISES

### Exercise 1: Dot.com boom and bust

The focus of this chapter has been on understanding how resources and capabilities serve as the cornerstone for competencies, and, ultimately, a competitive advantage. Strategists have long understood the importance of internal analysis: For example, Porter's value chain model was introduced in 1985, more than 20 years ago. How, then, can a large number of prominent firms create strategies while apparently disregarding the importance of internal analysis?

The late 1990s saw the launch of thousands of Internet start-ups, often supported by venture capital. These new businesses were heralded as part of the "new economy" and were characterized as having a superior business model compared to the models being used by traditional bricks-and-mortar firms. The collapse of the dot.com bubble had global economic ramifications. Some of the more prominent e-business failures included:

Webvan.com

Kosmo.com

Cyberrebate.com

Go.com

Boo.com

Kibu.com

Pets.com

Zap.com

Flooz.com

Digiscents.com

eToys.com

Yadayada.com

Working as a group, select a failed dot.com business. You may choose one of the companies from the preceding list, or another dot.com that you identify on your own. Using library and Internet resources, prepare a brief PowerPoint presentation that covers these questions:

- How did the company describe its value proposition (i.e., how did the firm plan to create value for its customers)?

- Describe the resources, capabilities and competencies that supported this value proposition.

- Why do you think the firm failed? Was it a poor concept, or a sound concept that was not well executed? Apply the concepts of value, rarity, imitation and sustainability when preparing your answer.

- Are any other firms presently using a similar approach to create value for their customers? If so, what makes them different from the failed company that you studied?

## Exercise 2: Competitive advantage and pro sports

What makes one team successful while another team struggles? At first glance, a National Football League franchise or a women's National Basketball Association team may not appear to be a typical business. However, professional sports have been around for a long time: Pro hockey in the United States emerged around the First World War, and pro basketball shortly after the Second World War; both could be considered newcomers relative to the founding of baseball leagues. Other pro sports are big business as well, as evidenced by David Beckham's 2007 multimillion-dollar contract with Major League Soccer.

With this exercise, you should use tools and concepts from the chapter to analyse factors underlying the success or failure of different sports teams. Working as a group, select two teams that play in the same league. For each team, address the following questions:

- How successful are the two teams you selected? How stable has their performance been over time?

- Develop an inventory of the characteristics of the two teams. Characteristics you might choose to identify include reputation, coaching, fan base, playing style and tactics, individual players, and so on. For each characteristic you describe:

  - Decide whether it is best characterized as a tangible or intangible resource or capability.

  - Apply the concepts of value, rarity, imitation and sustainability to analyse its value-creating ability.

- Does any evidence show bundling in this situation (i.e., the combination of different resources to create special capabilities)?

- What would be required for these two teams to substantially change their competitive position over time? For example, if a team is a leader, what types of changes in resources and capabilities might affect it negatively? If a team is below average, what changes would you recommend to its portfolio of resources and capabilities?

## VIDEO CASE

### Social intelligence, leadership and teamwork

www.cengage.co.uk/volberda/students/video_cases

Intelligence is multi-faceted. In recent years, emotional and social intelligence have received considerable attention. These facets of intelligence become more important as companies, even in the high tech domain, cannot rely only on explicit knowledge but need to emphasize soft skills as important cornerstones of what is needed to succeed in teams, organizations and societies.

In the first clip the best-selling author Daniel Goleman is interviewed on how emotional and social intelligence can help to improve organizational performance. The second clip shows an interview with John T. Chambers, Chairman and CEO of Cisco, who explains how collaboration and teamwork helped Cisco to innovate and do well even in tough times. Before you watch the video consider the following concepts from the text and be prepared to address the following questions:

Concepts

- A global mindset
- Intangible resources
- Valuable capabilities
- Rare capabilities
- Costly-to-imitate capabilities
- Nonsubstitutable capabilities
- Outsourcing

## Questions

1   How do emotional and social intelligence matter at work? How have emotional and social intelligence (or the lack of them) affected you recently in your everyday life?

2   A global mindset requires emotional and social intelligence across country boundaries. What are the main challenges? How can a global mindset be developed?

3   Does a global mindset including emotional and social intelligence provide sustainable competitive advantage? Provide an example.

4   Outsourcing of business activities to low labour cost locations can reduce costs. What are the risks related to emotional and social intelligence?

5   What is essential for outstanding teamwork? If it is intuition and highly personal skill can these soft skills be taught?

6   Emotional and social intelligence are often portrayed as forces for good. Discuss the dark side of emotional and social intelligence in the context of teamwork. How can you avoid falling victim?

## NOTES

1.   M. E. Mangelsdorf, 2007, "Beyond enterprise 2.0", MIT *Sloan Management Review*, 48(3): 50–55.

2.   J. G. Covin and M. P. Miles, 2007, "Strategic use of corporate venturing", *Entrepreneurship Theory and Practice*, 31: 183–207; R. R. Wiggins and T. W. Ruefli, 2002, "Sustained competitive advantage: Temporal dynamics and the incidence of persistence of superior economic performance", *Organization Science*, 13: 82–105; J. H. Burgers, F. A. J. Van den Bosch and H. W. Volberda, 2008, "The Impact of corporate venturing on a firm's competence modes", in: R. Martens, A. Heene and R. Sanchez (eds.), Competence-Building and Leveraging in Inter-organizational Relations, *Advances in Applied Business Strategy*, Oxford: Elsevier, 11: 117–140; H. W. Volberda, 2003, "Strategic flexibility: Creating dynamic competitive advantages", Ch. 32 in: D. Faulkner and A. Campbell (eds.), *The Oxford Handbook of Strategy,* Oxford: Oxford University Press, 939–998.

3.   W. M. Becker and V. M. Freeman, 2006, "Going from global trends to corporate strategy", *McKinsey Quarterly*, 3:17–27; S. K. McEvily, K. M. Eisenhardt and J. E. Prescott, 2004, "The global acquisition, leverage, and protection of technological competencies", *Strategic Management Journal*, 25: 713–722.

4.   R. T. Crook, D. J. Ketchen, J. G. Combs and S. Y. Todd, 2008, "Strategic resources and performance: A meta-Analysis", *Strategic Management Journal,* 29: 1141–1154; N. T. Sheehan and N. J. Foss, 2007, "Enhancing the prescriptiveness of the resource-based view through Porterian activity analysis", *Management Decision*, 45: 450–461; S. Dutta, M. J. Zbaracki and M. Bergen. 2003, "Pricing process as a capability: A resource-based perspective", *Strategic Management Journal*, 24: 615–630.

5.   C. G. Brush, P. G. Greene and M. M. Hart, 2001, "From initial idea to unique advantage: The entrepreneurial challenge of constructing a resource base", *Academy of Management Executive*, 15(1): 64–78.

6.   R. L. Priem, 2007, "A consumer perspective on value creation", *Academy of Management Review*, 32: 219–235.

7.   D. G. Sirmon, M. A. Hitt and R. D. Ireland, 2007, "Managing firm resources in dynamic markets to create value: Looking inside the black box", *Academy of Management Review*, 32: 273–292.

8.   A. Leiponen, 2008, "Control of intellectual assets in client relationships: Implications for innovation", *Strategic Management Journal*, 29: 1371–1394; S. C. Kang, S. S. Morris and S. A. Snell, 2007, "Relational archetypes, organizational learning, and value creation: Extending the human resource architecture", *Academy of Management Review*, 32: 236–256.

9.   S. Raisch and G. von Krogh, 2007, "Navigating a path to smart growth", MIT *Sloan Management Review*, 48(3): 65–72.

10.  http://www.vanderlande.nl/web/Carriere.htm

11.  C. D. Zatzick and R. D. Iverson, 2007, "High-involvement management and work force reduction: Competitive advantage or disadvantage?", *Academy of Management Journal*, 49: 999–1015.

12.  R. Florida, 2005, *The Flight of the Creative Class*, New York: HarperBusiness.

13.  A. W. King, 2007, "Disentangling interfirm and intrafirm causal ambiguity: A conceptual model of causal ambiguity and sustainable competitive advantage", *Academy of Management Review*, 32:156–178; J. Shamsie, 2003, "The context of dominance: An industry-driven framework for exploiting reputation", *Strategic Management Journal*, 24: 199–215.

14.  U. Ljungquist, 2007, "Core competency beyond identification: Presentation of a model", *Management Decision*, 45: 393–402; M. Makhija, 2003, "Comparing the resource-based and market-based view of the firm: Empirical evidence from Czech privatization", *Strategic Management Journal*, 24: 433–451.

15.  R. D. Ireland and J. W. Webb, 2007, "Strategic entrepreneurship: Creating competitive advantage through

streams of innovation", *Business Horizons*, 50: 49–59; J. J. P. Jansen, F. A. J. Van den Bosch and H. W. Volberda, 2006, "Exploratory innovation, exploitative innovation, and performance: Effects of organizational antecedents and environmental moderators", *Management Science*, 52 (11): 1661–1674; J. S. Sidhu, H. R. Commandeur and H. W. Volberda, 2007, "The multifaced nature of exploration and exploitation: Value of supply, demand, and spatial search for innovation", *Organization Science*, 18 (1): 20–38; T. J. M. Mom, F. A. J. Van den Bosch and H. W. Volberda, 2005, "Managing the tension between competence building and competence leveraging by influencing managerial and organizational determinants of horizontal knowledge exchange", in: *Research in Competence-Based Management*, 2: 165–191, R. Sanchez and A. Heene (eds.), *A Focused Issue on Managing Knowledge Assets and Organizational Learning*, Oxford: Elsevier.

16. M. A. Peteraf and J. B. Barney, 2003, "Unraveling the resource-based tangle", *Managerial and Decision Economics*, 24: 309–323; J. B. Barney, 2001, "Is the resource-based 'view' a useful perspective for strategic management research? Yes", *Academy of Management Review*, 26: 41–56.

17. D. P. Lepak, K. G. Smith and M. Susan Taylor, 2007, "Value creation and value capture: A multilevel perspective", *Academy of Management Review*, 32: 180–194.

18. T. Papot, 2009, "Slovakia's headache as car sales fall", Radio Netherlands Worldwide, http//:www.radionetherlands.nl, March 5; Z. Vilikovska, 2008, "Slovak factories manufactured around 770 000 cars in 2008", Flash News, http//:www.spector.sk; G. Katz. 2007, "Assembling a future", *Houston Chronicle*, July 5, DI, D4.

19. M. Javidan, R. M. Steers and M. A. Hitt (eds.), 2007, *The Global Mindset,* Amsterdam: Elsevier Ltd; T. M. Begley and D. P. Boyd, 2003, "The need for a corporate global mindset", MIT *Sloan Management Review*, 44(2): 25–32.

20. L. Gratton, 2007, "Handling hot spots", *Business Strategy Review*, 18(2): 9–14.

21. O. Levy, S. Beechler, S. Taylor and N. A. Boyacigiller, 2007, "What we talk about when we talk about 'global mindset': Managerial cognition in multinational corporations", *Journal of International Business Studies*, 38: 231–258.

22. D. G. Simon, M. A. Hitt and R. D. Ireland, 2007, "Managing firm resources in dynamic environments to create value: looking inside the black box", *Academy of Management Review*, 32(1): 273–292.

23. E. Danneels, 2008, "Organizational antecedents of second-order competences", *Strategic Management Journal*, 29: 519–543; J. B. Barney, 2001, "Is the resource-based 'view' a useful perspective for strategic management research? Yes", *Academy of Management Review*, 26: 41–56; M. W. Huygens, Ch. Baden-Fuller, F. A. J. Van den Bosch and H. W. Volberda, 2001, "Coevolution of Firm Capabilities and Industry Competition: Investigating the Music Industry 1877–1997", *Organization Studies,* 22 (6): 971–1011; Ch. Baden-Fuller and H. W. Volberda, 1997, "Strategic renewal in large complex organizations: A competence based view", in: A. Heene and R. Sanchez (eds.), *Competence-Based Strategic Management*, Chichester: Wiley, 89–110; H. W. Volberda and Ch. Baden-Fuller, 1999, "Strategic Renewal and competence building: Four dynamic mechanisms", in: G. Hamel, C. K. Prahalad, H. Thomas and D. O'Neal (eds.), *Strategic Flexibility: Managing in a Turbulent Economy*, Chichester, 371–389.

24. S. Kaplan, 2008, "Cognition, capabilities, and incentives: Assessing firm response to the fiber-optic revolution", *Academy of Management Journal*, 51: 672–695; K. J. Mayer and R. M. Salomon, 2006, "Capabilities, contractual hazards, and governance: Integrating resource-based and transaction cost perspectives", *Academy of Management Journal*, 49: 942–959.

25. S. K. McEvily and B. Chakravarthy, 2002, "The persistence of knowledge-based advantage: An empirical test for product performance and technological knowledge", *Strategic Management Journal*, 23: 285–305; M. G. Baaij, F. A. J. Van den Bosch and H. W. Volberda, 2005, "The Impact of management consulting firms on building and leveraging clients' competences", in: R. Sancez and A. Heene (eds.), *Advances in Applied Business Strategy*, 8: 27–44, *Competence Perspectives on Managing Interfirm Interactions*, Oxford: Elsevier; R. Van Wijk, F. A. J. Van den Bosch and H. W. Volberda, 2006, "Knowledge and networks", Ch. 22 in: M. Easterby-Smith and M. A. Lyles (eds.), *Handbook of Organizational Learning and Knowledge Management*, Oxford, Blackwell: 428–453 (paperback edition); M. W. Wielemaker, H. W. Volberda, T. Elfring and Ch. Baden-Fuller, 2003, "The conditioning and knowledge-creating view: Managing strategic initiatives in large firms", Ch. 8 in: B. Chakravarthy, G. Mueller-Stewens, P. Lorange and C. Lechner (eds.), *Strategy Process: Shaping the Contours of the Field*, Oxford: Blackwell, 164–190; R. Van Wijk, F. A. J. Van den Bosch, H. W. Volberda and S. M. Heinhuis, 2005, "Knowledge reciprocity as a managerial competence: The determinants of reciprocity of knowledge flows in internal network forms of organizing", in: R. Sanchez and A. Heene (eds.), *Research in Competence-Based Management*, 2: 117–140, *A Focused Issue on Managing Knowledge Assets And Organizational Learning*, Oxford: Elsevier; M. De Boer, F. A. J. Van den Bosch and H. W. Volberda, 1999, "Managing organizational knowledge integration in the emerging multimedia complex", *Journal of Management Studies*, 36 (3): 379–398.

26. J. Barthelemy, 2008, "Opportunism, knowledge, and the performance of franchise chains", *Strategic Management Journal*, 29: 1451–1463; J. L. Morrow, Jr., D. G. Sirmon, M. A. Hitt and T. R. Holcomb, 2007, "Creating value in the face of declining performance: Firm strategies and organizational recovery", *Strategic Management Journal*, 28: 271–283.

27. D. G. Sirmon, S. Gove and M. A. Hitt, 2008, "Resource management in dyadic competitive rivalry: The effects of resource bundling and deployment", *Academy of*

*Management Journal*, 51: 919–935; E. Danneels, 2007, "The process of technological competence leveraging", *Strategic Management Journal*, 28: 511–533; T. J. M. Mom, F. A. J. Van den Bosch and H. W. Volberda, 2005, "Managing the tension between competence building and competence leveraging by influencing managerial and organizational determinants of horizontal knowledge exchange", in: *Research in Competence-Based Management*, 2: 165–191, R. Sanchez and A. Heene (eds.), *A Focused Issue on Managing Knowledge Assets and Organizational Learning*, Oxford: Elsevier; B. Flier, F. A. J. Van den Bosch, H. W. Volberda and Ch. Baden-Fuller, 2005, "Strategic renewal in the Dutch financial services sector: Renewal trajectories from a competence-based perspective", in: *Advances in Applied Business Strategy*, 9: 237–274, R. Sanchez and A. Heene (eds.), *Competence Perspectives on Resources, Stakeholders and Renewal*, Oxford: Elsevier; Ch. Baden-Fuller and H. W. Volberda, 2003, "Dormant capabilities, complex organizations, and renewal", in: R. Sanchez (ed.), *Knowledge Management and Organizational Competence* (paperback edition), Oxford: Oxford University Press, 114–136.

28. "Putting co-creation to work for you: Build more value by co-creating with your customers", 2009, *Internetviz*, http//: www.internetviz-newsletters.com; J. J. Neff, 2007, "What drives consumers not to buy cars", *BusinessWeek*, July 9, 16.

29. K. Chaharbaghi, 2007, "The problematic of strategy: A way of seeing is also a way of not seeing", *Management Decision*, 45: 327–339.

30. V. Shankar and B. L. Bayus, 2003, "Network effects and competition: An empirical analysis of the home video game industry", *Strategic Management Journal*, 24: 375–384.

31. J. L. Morrow, D. G. Sirmon, M. A. Hitt and T. R. Holcomb, 2007, "Creating value in the face of declining performance"; G. Hawawini, V. Subramanian and P. Verdin, 2003, "Is performance driven by industry- or firm-specific factors? A new look at the evidence", *Strategic Management Journal*, 24: 1–16.

32. J. Woiceshyn and L. Falkenberg, 2008, "Value creation in knowledge-based firms: Aligning problems and resources", *Academy of Management Perspectives*, 22 (2): 85–99; M. R. Haas and M. T. Hansen, 2005, "When using knowledge can hurt performance: The value of organizational capabilities in a management consulting company", *Strategic Management Journal*, 26: 1–24; F. A. J. Van den Bosch, M. G. Baaij and H. W. Volberda, 2005, "How knowledge accumulation has changed strategy consulting: strategic options for established strategy consulting firms", *Strategic Change*, 14 (1): 25–34.

33. C. M. Christensen, 2001, "The past and future of competitive advantage", *Sloan Management Review*, 42(2): 105–109.

34. O. Gottschalg and M. Zollo, 2007, "Interest alignment and competitive advantage", *Academy of Management Review*. 32: 418–437.

35. D. P. Forbes, 2007, "Reconsidering the strategic implications of decision comprehensiveness", *Academy of Management Review*, 32: 361–376; J. R. Hough and M. A. White, 2003, "Environmental dynamism and strategic decision-making rationality: An examination at the decision level", *Strategic Management Journal*, 24: 481–489; H. W. Volberda, 1997, "Building flexible organizations for fast-moving markets", *Long Range Planning*, 30 (2): 169–183.

36. T. M. Jones, W. Felps and G. A. Bigley, 2007, "Ethical theory and stakeholder-related decisions: The role of stakeholder culture", *Academy of Management Review*, 32: 137–155; D. C. Kayes, D. Stirling and T. M. Nielsen, 2007, "Building organizational integrity", *Business Horizons*, 50: 61–70.

37. Y. Deutsch, T. Keil and T. Laamanen, 2007, "Decision making in acquisitions: The effect of outside directors" compensation on acquisition patterns', *Journal of Management*, 33: 30–56.

38. M. De Rond and R. A. Thietart, 2007, "Choice, chance, and inevitability in strategy", *Strategic Management Journal*, 28: 535–551.

39. A. Phene and P. Almieda, 2008, "Innovation in multinational subsidiaries: The role of knowledge assimilation and subsidiary capabilities", *Journal of International Business Studies*, 39: 901–919; C. C. Miller and R. D. Ireland, 2005, "Intuition in strategic decision making: Friend or foe in the fast-paced 21st century?", *Academy of Management Executive*, 19(1): 19–30; M. G. Baaij, F. A. J. Van den Bosch and H. W. Volberda, 2004, "The international relocation of corporate centres: Are corporate centres sticky?", *European Management Journal*, 22(2): 141–149; T. Hutzschenreuter, T. Pedersen and H. W. Volberda, 2007, "The role of path dependency and managerial intentionality: A perspective on international business research", *Journal of International Business Studies*, 38(7): 1055–1068; J. S. Sidhu and H. W. Volberda, "Knowledge management across onshore and offshore teams: The role of organizational politics", *International Business Review*, forthcoming.

40. L. M. Lodish and C. F. Mela, 2007, "If brands are built over years, why are they managed over quarters?", *Harvard Business Review*, 85(7/8): 104–112; H. J. Smith, 2003, "The shareholders vs stakeholders debate", MIT *Sloan Management Review*, 44(4): 85–90; A. Pugliese, P. Bezemer, A. Zattoni, M. Huse, F. A. J. Van den Bosch and H. W. Volberda, 2009, "Boards of directors' contribution to strategy: A literature review and research agenda", *Corporate Governance*, 17 (3): 292–306.

41. P. C. Nut, 2002, *Why Decisions Fail*, San Francisco: Berrett-Koehler Publishers.

42. R. Martin, 2007, "How successful leaders think", *Harvard Business Review*, 85(6): 61–67.

43. Polaroid Corporation, 2007. Wikipedia, http://en.wikipedia. org/wiki/Polaroid_Corporation, July 5.

44. J. M. Mezias and W. H. Starbuck, 2003, "What do managers know, anyway?", *Harvard Business Review*. 81(5): 16–17.

45. I. Mitroff, 2008, "Knowing: How we know is as important as what we know", *Journal of Business Strategy*, 29 (3):

13–22; P. G. Audia, E. Locke and K. G. Smith, 2000, "The paradox of success: An archival and a laboratory study of strategic persistence following radical environmental change", *Academy of Management Journal*, 43: 837–853.

46. C. O. Longenecker, M. J. Neubert and L. S. Fink, 2007, "Causes and consequences of managerial failure in rapidly changing organizations", *Business Horizons*, 50: 145–155; G. P. West III and J. DeCastro, 2001, "'The Achilles' heel of firm strategy: Resource weaknesses and distinctive inadequacies", *Journal of Management Studies*, 38: 417–442; G. Gavetti and D. Levinthal, 2000, "Looking forward and looking backward: Cognitive and experimental search", *Administrative Science Quarterly*, 45: 113–137.

47. R. Arnit and P. J. H. Schoemaker, 1993, "Strategic assets and organizational rent", *Strategic Management Journal*, 14: 33–46.

48. S. J. Carson, A. Madhok and T. Wu, 2006, "Uncertainty, opportunism, and governance: The effects of volatility and ambiguity on formal and relational contracting", *Academy of Management Journal*, 49: 1058–1077; R. E. Hoskisson and L. W. Busenitz, 2001, "Market uncertainty and learning distance in corporate entrepreneurship entry mode choice", in M. A. Hitt, R. D. Ireland, S. M. Camp and D. L. Sexton (eds.), *Strategic Entrepreneurship: Creating a New Integrated Mindset*, Oxford, UK: Blackwell Publishers, 151–172.

49. C. M. Fiol and E. J. O'Connor, 2003, "Waking up! Mindfulness in the face of bandwagons", *Academy of Management Review*, 28: 54–70.

50. P. Davidson, "Coal king Peabody cleans up", *USA Today*, http//:www.usatoday.com, August 18; J. Pasternak, 2008, "Global warming has a new battleground: Coal plants", *Chicago Tribune*, http//:www.chicagotribune.com, April 14.

51. G. P. West, III, 2007, "Collective cognition: When entrepreneurial teams, not individuals, make decisions", *Entrepreneurship Theory and Practice*, 31: 77–102.

52. N. J. Hiller and D. C. Hambrick, 2005, "Conceptualizing executive hubris: The role of (hyper-) core self-evaluations in strategic decision making", *Strategic Management Journal*, 26: 297–319.

53. C. Stadler, 2007, "The four principles of enduring success", *Harvard Business Review*, 85(7/8): 62–72; Z. Kwee, F. A. J. Van den Bosch and H. W. Volberda, 2008, "Coevolutionary competence in the realm of corporate longevity: How long-lived firms strategically renew themselves", in: *Research in Competence-Based Management*, R. Sanchez (ed.), A Focused Issue on Fundamental Issues in Competence Theory Development, Bingley: Emerald, 4: 281–313; Z. Kwee, F. A. J. Van den Bosch and H. W. Volberda, 2011, "The Influence of top management team's corporate governance orientation on strategic renewal trajectories: A longitudinal analysis of Royal Dutch Shell plc, 1907–2004", *Journal of Management Studies*, forthcoming.

54. J. K. Mayer and R. M. Salomon, 2006, "Capabilities. contractual hazards, and governance"; D. M. De Carolis, 2003,

"Competencies and imitability in the pharmaceutical industry: An analysis of their relationship with firm performance", *Journal of Management*, 29: 27–50.

55. R. H. Lester, A. Hillman, A. Zardkoohi and A. A. Cannella, 2008, "Former government officials as outside directors: The role of human and social capital", *Academy of Management Journal*, 51: 999–1013; G. Ahuja and R. Katila, 2004, "Where do resources come from? The role of idiosyncratic situations", *Strategic Management Journal*, 25: 887–907.

56. K. Meyer, S. Estrin, S. K. Bhaumik and M. W. Peng, 2009, "Institutions, resources, and entry strategies in emerging economies", *Strategic Management Journal*, 30: 61–80; J. McGee and H. Thomas, 2007, "Knowledge as a lens on the jigsaw puzzle of strategy", *Management Decision*, 45: 539–563.

57. D. G. Sirmon, M. A. Hitt and R. D. Ireland, "Managing firm resources in dynamic environments to create value: Looking inside the black box", *Academy of Management Review*, 32(1): 273–292; S. Berman, J. Down and C. Hill, 2002, "Tacit knowledge as a source of competitive advantage in the National Basketball Association", *Academy of Management Journal*, 45: 13–31.

58. K. G. Smith, C. J. Collins and K. D. Clark, 2005, "Existing knowledge, knowledge creation capability, and the rate of new product introduction in high-technology firms", *Academy of Management Journal*, 48: 346–357; S. G. Winter, 2005, "Developing evolutionary theory for economics and management", in: K. G. Smith and M. A. Hitt (eds.) *Great Minds in Management: The Process of Theory Development*, Oxford, UK: Oxford University Press, 509–546.

59. J. A. Dubin, 2007, "Valuing intangible assets with a nested logit market share model", *Journal of Econometrics*, 139: 285–302.

60. A. M. Webber, 2000, "New math for a new economy", *Fast Company*, January/February, 214–224.

61. F. T. Rothaermel and W. Boeker, 2008, "Old technology meets new technology: Complementarities, similarities, and alliance formation", *Strategic Management Journal*, 29: 47–77; M. Song, C. Droge, S. Hanvanich and R. Calantone, 2005, "Marketing and technology resource complementarity: An analysis of their interaction effect in two environmental contexts", *Strategic Management Journal*, 26: 259–276.

62. M. A. Hitt and R. D. Ireland, 2002, "The essence of strategic leadership: Managing human and social capital", *Journal of Leadership and Organization Studies*, 9(1): 3–14; J. J. P. Jansen, G. George, F. A. J. Van den Bosch and H. W. Volberda, 2008, "Senior team attributes and organizational ambidexterity: The moderating role of transformational leadership", *Journal of Management Studies*, 45(5): 982–1007.

63. I. Nonaka, 1991, "The knowledge creating company", *Harvard Business Review*, Nov–Dec 96–104; J. B. Quinn, P. Anderson and S. Finkelstein, 1996, "Making the most of the best", *Harvard Business Review*, 74(2): 71–80.

64. N. Stieglitz and K. Heine, 2007, "Innovations and the role of complementarities in a strategic theory of the firm", *Strategic Management Journal*, 28: 1–15.

65. S. A. Fernhaber, B. A. Gilbert and P. P. McDougal, 2008, "International entrepreneurship and geographic location: An empirical examination of new venture internationalization", *Journal of International Business Studies*, 39: 267–290; R. D. Ireland, M. A. Hitt and D. Vaidyanath, 2002, "Managing strategic alliances to achieve a competitive advantage", *Journal of Management*, 28: 416–446.

66. E. Fischer and R. Reuber, 2007, "The good, the bad, and the unfamiliar: The challenges of reputation formation facing new firms", *Entrepreneurship Theory and Practice*, 31: 53–75.

67. D. L. Deephouse, 2000, "Media reputation as a strategic resource: An integration of mass communication and resource-based theories", *Journal of Management* 26: 1091–1112.

68. P. Engardio and M. Arndt, 2007, "What price reputation?", *BusinessWeek*, July 9, 70–79.

69. P. Berthon, M. B. Holbrook and J. M. Hulbert, 2003, "Understanding and managing the brand space", MIT *Sloan Management Review*, 44(2): 49–54; D. B. Holt, 2003, "What becomes an icon most?", *Harvard Business Review*, 81 (3): 43–49.

70. J. Song and J. Shin, 2008, "The paradox of technological capabilities: A study of knowledge sourcing from host countries of overseas R&D operations", *Journal of International Business Studies*, 39: 291–303; J. Blasberg and V. Vishwanath, 2003, "Making cool brands hot", *Harvard Business Review*, 81(6): 20–22.

71. S. Kalepu, 2009, "Ford names Suneil Shetty as its brand ambassador", *CartradeIndia*, http//:www.cartradeindia. com, January 22.

72. T. Isobe, S. Makino and D. B. Montgomery, 2008, "Technological capabilities and firm performance: The case of small manufacturing firms in Japan", *Asia Pacific Journal of Management*, 25: 413–425; S. Dutta, O. Narasimhan and S. Rajiv, 2005, "Conceptualizing and measuring capabilities: Methodology and empirical application", *Strategic Management Journal*, 26: 277–285.

73. M. Kroll, B. A. Walters and P. Wright, 2008, "Board vigilance, director experience and corporate outcomes", *Strategic Management Journal*, 29: 363–382; J. Bitar and T. Hafsi, 2007, "Strategizing through the capability lens: Sources and outcomes of integration", *Management Decision*, 45: 403–419.

74. S. K. Ethiraj, P. Kale, M. S. Krishnan and J. V. Singh, 2005, "Where do capabilities come from and do they matter? A study in the software services industry", *Strategic Management Journal*, 26: 25–45; M. G. Jacobides and S. G. Winter, 2005, "The co-evolution of capabilities and transaction costs: Explaining the institutional structure of production", *Strategic Management Journal*, 26: 395–413.

75. T. A. Stewart and A. P. Raman, 2007, "Lessons from Toyota's long drive", *Harvard Business Review*, 85(7/8): 74–83.

76. Y. Uu, J. G. Combs, D. J. Ketchen, Jr and R. D. Ireland, 2007, "The value of human resource management for organizational performance", *Business Horizons*, 50: 503–511.

77. B. Connelly, M. A. Hitt, A. S. DeNisi and R. D. Ireland, 2007, "Expatriates and corporate-level international strategy: Governing with the knowledge contract", *Management Decision*, 45: 564–581.

78. M. J. Tippins and R. S. Sohi, 2003, "IT competency and firm performance: Is organizational learning a missing link?", *Strategic Management Journal*, 24: 745–761.

79. M. B. Neeley and R. Jacobson, 2008, "The recency of technological inputs and financial performance", *Strategic Management Journal*, 29: 723–744.

80. K. E. Meyer, S. Estrin, S. K. Bhaumik and M. W. Peng, 2009, "Institutions, resources, and entry strategies in emerging economies, *Strategic Management Journal*, 30 (1): 61–80.

81. H. R. Greve, 2009, "Bigger and safer: The diffusion of competitive advantage", *Strategic Management Journal*, 30: 1–23; C. K. Prahalad and G. Hamel, 1990, "The core competence of the corporation", *Harvard Business Review*, 68(3): 79–93.

82. S. Newbert, 2008, "Value, rareness, competitive advantage, and performance: A conceptual-level empirical investigation of the resource-based view of the firm", *Strategic Management Journal*, 29: 745–768.

83. http://www.telegraph.co.uk/finance/2947470/Sainsbury-plots-to-outgreen-Tesco.html

84. http://blogs.mirror.co.uk/cars-motorbikes/2009/07/frugal-cars-retain-value-best.html

85. S. A. Zahra, 2008, "The virtuous cycle of discovery and creation of entrepreneurial opportunities", *Strategic Entrepreneurship Journal*, 2: 243–257; J. B. Barney, 1995, "Looking inside for competitive advantage", *Academy of Management Executive*, 9(4): 49–60; H. W. Volberda and H. B. Cheah, 1993, "A new perspective on entrepreneurship: A dialectic process of transformation within the entrepreneurial mode, type of flexibility and organizational form", in: H. Klandt (ed.), *Entrepreneurship and Business Development*, Aldershot: Avebury, 261–286.

86. G. Pacheco-de-Almeida, J. E. Henderson and K. O. Cool, 2008, "Resolving the commitment versus flexibility trade-off: The role of resource accumulation lags", *Academy of Management Journal*, 51: 517–536; Z. Kwee, F. A. J. Van den Bosch and H. W. Volberda, 2008, "Coevolutionary competence in the realm of corporate longevity: How long-lived firms strategically renew themselves", in: *Research in Competence-Based Management*, R. Sanchez (ed.), A Focused Issue on Fundamental Issues in Competence Theory Development, Bingley: Emerald, 4: 281–313; J. P. Murmann, 2003, *Knowledge and Competitive Advantage: The Coevolution of Firms, Technology, and National Institutions*, Cambridge: Cambridge University Press; H. W. Volberda, 2005, "Book review of 'Knowledge and Competitive Advantage: The Coevolution of Firms, Technology, and National Institutions' by Johann Peter Murmann, Cambridge:

Cambridge University Press, 2003", *Academy of Management Review*, 30(2): 446–448.

87. J. B. Barney, 1991, "Firm resources and sustained competitive advantage", *Journal of Management*, 17: 99–120.

88. L. E. Tetrick and N. Da Silva, 2003, "Assessing the culture and climate for organizational learning", in S. E. Jackson, M. A. Hitt and A. S. DeNisi (eds.), *Managing Knowledge for Sustained Competitive Advantage*, San Francisco: Jossey-Bass, 333–359.

89. A. W. King and C. P. Zeithaml, 2001, "Competencies and firm performance: Examining the causal ambiguity paradox", *Strategic Management Journal*, 22: 75–99.

90. Barney, J. B., 1991, "Firm resources and sustained competitiveness advantage", 111.

91. A. K. Chatterij, 2009, "Spawned with a silver spoon? Entrepreneurial performance and innovation in the medical device industry", *Strategic Management Journal*, 30: 185–206; S. K. McEvily, S. Das and K. McCabe, 2000, "Avoiding competence substitution through knowledge sharing", *Academy of Management Review*, 25: 294–311.

92. D. J. Ketchen, Jr and G. T. M. Hult, 2007, "Bridging organization theory and supply chain management: The case of best value supply chains", *Journal of Operations Management*, 25: 573–580.

93. M. E. Porter, 1985, *Competitive Advantage*, New York: Free Press, 33–61.

94. J. Alcacer, 2006, "Location choices across the value chain: How activity and capability influence co-location", *Management Science*, 52: 1457–1471.

95. H. U. Lee and J. H. Park, 2008, "The influence of top management team international exposure on international alliance formation", *Journal of Management Studies,* 45: 961–981; Anonymous, 2007, "Riding the global value chain", *Chief Executive Online*, January/February, http://www.chiefexecutive.net; J. A. J. Draulans, A. P. De Man and H. W. Volberda, 2003, "Building alliance capability: Management techniques for superior alliance performance", *Long Range Planning*, 36 (2): 151–166.

96. R. Locke and M. Romis, 2007, "Global supply chain", *MIT Sloan Management Review*, 48(2): 54–62.

97. R. Amit and C. Zott, 2001, "Value creation in e-business", *Strategic Management Journal*, 22 (Special Issue): 493–520; M. E. Porter, 2001, "Strategy and the Internet", *Harvard Business Review*, 79(3): 62–78; A. P. De Man, M. Stienstra and H. W. Volberda, 2002, "E-Partnering: Moving bricks and mortar online", *European Management Journal*, 20 (4): 329–339; M. Hensmans, F. A. J. Van den Bosch and H. W. Volberda, 2001, "Clicks versus bricks in the emerging online financial services industry", *Long Range Planning,* 34(2): 231–247.

98. C. L. Luk, O. H. M. Yau, L. Y. M. Sin, A. C. B. Tse, R. P. M. Chow and J. S. Y. Lee, 2008, "The effects of social capital and organizational innovativeness in different institutional contexts", *Journal of International Business Studies,* 39: 589–612; M. Tempelaar, J. J. P. Jansen, F. A. J. Van den Bosch and H. W. Volberda, 2010, "Embeddedness and organizational ambidexterity: The combined effect of

internal and external social capital", research paper presented at Academy of Management Chicago.

99. L. F. Mesquita, J. Anand and T. H. Brush, 2008, "Comparing the resource-based and relational views: Knowledge transfer and spillover in vertical alliances", *Strategic Management Journal*, 29: 913–941; A. Azadegan, K. J. Dooley, P. L. Carter and J. R. Carter, 2008, "Supplier innovativeness and the role of interorganizational learning in enhancing manufacturer capabilities", *Journal of Supply Chain Management,* 44 (4): 14–35; P. W. L. Vlaar, F. A. J. Van den Bosch and H. W. Volberda, 2006, "Coping with problems of understanding in interorganizational relationships: Using formalization as a means to make sense", *Organization Studies*, Special Issue on "Making Sense of Organizing: in Honor of Karl Weick", 27(11): 1617–1638; P. W. L. Vlaar, F. A. J. Van den Bosch and H. W. Volberda, 2005, "On the relation between information technology and interorganizational competitive advantage: A competence perspective", in: *Advances in Applied Business Strategy*, 8: 45–68, R. Sanchez and A. Heene (eds.), *Competence Perspectives on Managing Interfirm Interactions*, Oxford: Elsevier.

100. A. A. Lado, R. R. Dant and A. G. Tekleab, 2008, "Trust-opportunism paradox, relationalism, and performance in interfirm relationships: Evidence from the retail industry", *Strategic Management Journal*, 29: 401–423; S. N. Wasti and S. A. Wasti, 2008, "Trust in buyer–supplier relations: The case of the Turkish automotive industry", *Journal of International Business Studies,* 39: 118–131; P. W. L. Vlaar, F. A. J. Van den Bosch and H. W. Volberda, 2007, "On the evolution of trust, distrust, and formal coordination and control in interorganizational relationships: Toward an integrative framework", *Group & Organization Management*, Special Issue Trust and Control Interrelations: New Perspectives on the Trust-Control Nexus, 32 (4): 407–429; P. W. L. Vlaar, F. A. J. Van den Bosch and H. W. Volberda, 2007, "Towards a dialectic perspective on formalization in interorganizational relationships: How alliance managers capitalize on the duality inherent in contracts, rules, and procedures", *Organization Studies*, 28 (4): 437–466.

101. D. Faems, M. Janssens, A. Madhok and B. Van Looy, 2008, "Toward an integrative perspective on alliance governance: Connecting contract design, trust dynamics and contract application", *Academy of Management Journal,* 51: 1053–1078; P. W. L. Vlaar, F. A. J. Van den Bosch and H. W. Volberda, 2006, "Interorganizational governance trajectories: Towards a better understanding of the connections between partner selection, negotiation and contracting", Ch. 10 in: A. Arino and J. J. Reuer (eds.), *Strategic Alliances: Governance and Contracts*, Houndmills: Palgrave, 98–110.

102. M. J. Power, K. C. DeSouze and C. Bonifazi, 2006, *The Outsourcing Handbook: How to Implement a Successful Outsourcing Process*, Philadelphia: Kogan Page.

103. P. W. Tam, 2007, "Business technology: Outsourcing finds new niche", *Wall Street Journal*, April 17, B5.

104. S. Nambisan and M. Sawhney, 2007, "A buyer's guide to the innovation bazaar", *Harvard Business Review*, 85(6): 109–118.

105. Y. Shi, 2007, "Today's solution and tomorrow's problem: The business process outsourcing risk management puzzle", *California Management Review*, 49(3): 27–44; I. Oshri, J. Kotlarsky and L. P. Willcocks, 2009, "The Handbook of Global Outsourcing and Offshoring", Macmillan, London.

106. C. C. De Fontenay and J. S. Gans, 2008, "A bargaining perspective on strategic outsourcing and supply competition", *Strategic Management Journal*, 29: 819–839; A. Tiwana and M. Keil, 2007, "Does peripheral knowledge complement control? An empirical test in technology outsourcing alliances", *Strategic Management Journal*, 28: 623–634.

107. A. Tiwana, 2008, "Does interfirm modularity complement ignorance? A field study of software outsourcing alliances", *Strategic Management Journal*, 29: 1241–1252; J. C. Linder, S. Jarvenpaa and T. H. Davenport, 2003, "Toward an innovation sourcing strategy", MIT *Sloan Management Review*, 44(4): 43–49.

108. S. Lohr, 2007, "At IBM, a smarter way to outsource", *New York Times Online*, July 5, http://www.nytimes.com.

109. C. Horng and W. Chen, 2008, "From contract manufacturing to own brand management: The role of learning and cultural heritage identity", *Management and Organization Review,* 4: 109–133; M. Useem and J. Harder, 2000, "Leading laterally in company outsourcing", *Sloan Management Review*, 41(2): 25–36.

110. R. C. Insinga and M. J. Werle, 2000, "Linking outsourcing to business strategy", *Academy of Management Executive*, 14(4): 58–70; S. M. Ansari, J. S. Sidhu, H. W. Volberda and I. Oshri, 2010, "Managing globally disaggregated teams: The role of organizational politics", in: F. J. Contractor et al. (eds.), *Global Outsourcing and Offshoring: An integrated approach to Theory and Corporate Strategy*, Cambridge: Cambridge University Press; I. Oshri, 2011, *Offshoring Strategies: Evolving Captive Center Models*, Boston, MA: MIT Press.

111. B. Arrunada and X. H. Vazquez, 2006, "When your contract manufacturer becomes your competitor", *Harvard Business Review*, 84(9): 135–144.

112. C. S. Katsikeas, D. Skarmeas and D. C. Bello, 2009, "Developing successful trust-based international exchange relationships", *Journal of International Business Studies,* 40: 132–155; E. Perez and J. Karp, 2007, "U.S. to probe outsourcing after ITT case", *Wall Street Journal* (Eastern Edition). March 28, A3, A6.

113. C. Weigelt and M. B. Sarkar, 2009, "Learning from supply-side agents: The impact of technology solution providers' experiential diversity on clients' innovation adoption", *Academy of Management Journal (AMJ)* 52: 37–60; M. J. Mol, P. Pauwels, P. Matthyssens and L. Quintens, 2004, "A technological contingency perspective on the depth and scope of international outsourcing", *Journal of International Management*, 10: 287–305.

114. K. Couke and L. Sleuwaegen, 2008, "Offshoring as a survival strategy: Evidence from manufacturing firms in Belgium", *Journal of International Business Studies,* 39: 1261–1277; A. Y. Lewin and C. Peeters, 2006, "Offshoring work: Business hype or the asset of fundamental transformation?", *Long Range Planning*, 39(3): 221–239; A. Y. Lewin, S. Massini, and C. Peeters, 2009, "Why companies are offshoring innovation? The emerging global race for talent", *Journal of International Business Studies*, 40(6): 901–925.

115. N. Heath, 2009, "Outsourcing: The new hot spots", *BusinessWeek*, http//:www.businessweek.com, February 20.

116. http://www.computerweekly.com/Articles/2009/07/01/236724/lloyds-cuts-thousands-more-jobs-but-halts-offshoring.htm

117. M. H. Safizadeh, J. M. Field and L. P. Ritzman, 2008, "Sourcing practices and boundaries of the firm in the financial services industry", *Strategic Management Journal*, 29: 79–91; M. A. Hitt, D. Ahlstrom, M. T. Dacin, E. Levitas and L. Svobodina, 2004, "The institutional effects on strategic alliance partner selection in transition economies: China versus Russia", *Organization Science,* 15: 173–185.

118. T. Felin and W. S. Hesterly, 2007, "The knowledge-based view, nested heterogeneity, and new value creation: Philosophical considerations on the locus of knowledge", *Academy of Management Review,* 32: 195–218; Y. Mishina, T. G. Pollock and J. F. Porac, 2004, "Are more resources always better for growth? Resource stickiness in market and product expansion", *Strategic Management Journal*, 25: 1179–1197.

119. M. Gibbert, M. Hoegl and L. Valikangas, 2007, "In praise of resource constraints", MIT *Sloan Management Review*, 48(3): 15–17; D. S. Elenkov and I. M. Manev, 2005, "Top management leadership and influence in innovation: The role of sociocultural context", *Journal of Management*, 31: 381–402.

120. http://news.bbc.co.uk/2/hi/business/7328319.stm

121. D. Leonard-Barton, 1995, *Wellsprings of Knowledge: Building and sustaining the sources of innovation*, Boston, MA: Harvard Business School Press, 30–31.

# CHAPTER 4

# INTEGRATING INTERNAL AND EXTERNAL RESOURCES: OPEN INNOVATION, ABSORPTIVE CAPACITY AND INTEGRATION APPROACHES

## LEARNING OBJECTIVES

Studying this chapter should provide you with the strategic management knowledge needed to:

1  Explain why firms need to bring the internal organization to bear on the environment.
2  Compare different ways of how firms may bring important aspects of the environment inside the organization.
3  Describe the differences between closed and open innovation.
4  Weigh benefits and costs of open innovation.
5  Explain different approaches to integration.
6  Link how firms can increase their absorptive capacity to open innovation.
7  Define outsourcing and discuss reasons for its use.
8  Discuss the importance and practicality of internalizing external resources.

## OPENING CASE

# Muji: designing with markets

Its products are being sold in the Museum of Modern Art in New York and it operates dozens of stores in Europe, Asia and the US, yet Muji is not widely recognized abroad. In Japan, Muji is a household name for a variety of consumer commodities, including apparel, household goods and food. The company positions its products, which bear the message "no brand, quality goods", at prices 20 per cent to 30 per cent lower than other brands in Japan. Different to other generic brands, Muji's post-industrial designs tap into the less-is-more aesthetic visible in Japan's temple gardens and *haiku* and growing brand fatigue. Muji-brand products feature simple, functional and timeless designs and are known for their reasonable pricing in Japan, yet abroad the products are 15–30 per cent more expensive due to taxation and transport costs.

Muji is the retail brand name of Ryohin Keikaku Co. Ltd of Tokyo. The naming of both goes back to Ikko Tanaka, a famous Japanese designer who early on took charge of Muji's branding. Once a part of the Seiyu department store chain, Muji is now independently listed on the Tokyo Stock Exchange with annual sales in excess of €1 billion. Muji has expanded globally, with more than 150 stores in Japan and 20 abroad. Larger Muji outlets in Japan carry more than 8000 products that range from €4 striped socks up to a €1200 front-loading washer-dryer combo. In Japan there is even a line of prefab houses that start at €120 000.

Muji is cost-conscious. It controls manufacturing of 80 per cent of its apparel, its largest product category in Japan, and 50 per cent of its household goods. Muji has also cut costs by using natural materials in a few monochrome colours, minimal packaging and focuses on apparel, which has the highest profit margin of its product lines. This has created a somewhat spartan, futuristic brand image that is positioned "beyond fashion" and has gained popularity with Japanese and people in their 20s and 30s all over the world.

Although Muji is famous for its internal design capability, many of its most successful products have been the result of its move towards co-designing with customers. All of the 3800 product lines are designed in Japan, often in response to customer feedback from the company's Internet service. Led by an external team of designers, Muji manages a process of extramural idea generation and collection, selection and even product introductions that lean on Muji's most loyal customers. Approximately 500 000 members submit and pre-evaluate new designs, some representing radical concepts. For the highest ranked ideas, Muji's internal design team together with its external design consultants create professional design specs and estimate the expected costs of the first production batch, approximating a minimum number of orders. With this information, Muji can determine the possible sales price of the item. After some feasibility checks, the refined design is published and customers are asked to place pre-orders. Once the minimum order quantity is obtained, Muji proceeds with manufacturing and distribution. If a design fails to garner the necessary number of pre-orders, however, it is discarded.

At Muji, for example, product developers use their tacit knowledge about technical constraints and market reception to interpret customer evaluations. In this process, Muji has discarded some ideas that customers had scored highly because the concepts were regarded as just novelties that would be unable to sustain sales. Other new designs have been dismissed because their manufacturing costs were prohibitive. The results have been impressive. Muji's customers have co-designed a number of products that have generated sales far beyond comparable items developed with conventional methods. The most successful of these is a type of beanbag sofa with a special filling that combines stability with comfort and takes up less space than a traditional sofa. Other successful user-developed items include a stylish portable lamp and the "freedom shelf" — a bookshelf with an innovative hanging mechanism that doesn't damage the wall and enables the shelf to be set up in different arrangements. The freedom shelf received 300 orders (the required minimum amount) in just one day, prompting Muji to commercialize the product – at once.

**Sources**: Harney, A. (1998) "Japanese retailer blooms in a recessionary wilderness: Muji has found that its no-frills approach has won it a loyal consumer base", *Financial Times*, London, Oct. 1, 33; Reinmoeller, P. (2002) "Dynamic contexts for innovation strategy: Utilizing customer knowledge", *Design Management Journal* 2(1): 37–50; Hall, K. and Woyke, E. (2007) "Zen and the art of selling minimalism: Muji, Japan's unbranded Ikea-cum-target, is planning its first outlet in America", *BusinessWeek*, Apr. 09, 45; Ogawa, S. and Piller, F. T. (2006) "Reducing the risks of new product development", MIT *Sloan Management Review*, Winter, 65–70; Heathcote, E. (2007) "Discovery of pleasure in anonymity", http://www.ft.com. Feb. 22; Oki, H. (2010) Managing Director, Muji Europe, Personal Communication, July.

## Questions

1 Why does Muji involve external resources?

2 How does Muji bring external resources to bear on its internal resources?

3 Which different external resources does Muji utilize to develop and market its products?

4 How does Muji become aware of new possibilities? How are the best ideas selected and how does it exploit the external resources it has access to?

5 What are the benefits of its internal resources and what are the benefits of its external resources?

The first three chapters have shown how several factors in the global economy, including the rapid development of technologies and of globalization in general, erode firms' competitive advantages and force strategists to find new ways to sustain these advantages.[1] One of the oldest and most frequently used tools in strategic management, the SWOT analysis,[2] suggests that threats are posed by external changes. Strengths (S) and weaknesses (W) are defined as internal factors and opportunities (O) and threats (T) as external factors. While entrepreneurial strategy emphasizes the importance of opportunity recognition, in much research on external environment's influence, environmental change is portrayed as threatening. Threats are external changes that undermine a company's strength. As is suggested in the Opening Case, changes in customer preferences or fashions can quickly make capabilities redundant and end competitiveness, as what customers valued and what firms focused on may become obsolete.

Sometimes macro level changes such as political instability, global economic downturns or shifts in economic influence are used to substantiate how threatening external changes are. Consider how China, which used less than 50 per cent of the energy consumed in the US at the beginning of 2000, rose to consume more energy than the US in 2010 and how its workforce became more outspoken and demanding. In 2010 Foxconn, Honda and other companies experienced strikes related to demands for better pay and working conditions. Such changes are clearly threatening for firms that manufacture most of their products in China, such as Muji in the Opening Case, because they rely on low costs of energy and labour in China. Threats are often perceived to lie in the context of a company's external environment. However, when Muji found a way to position itself above the fray of changing fashions and customer tastes by avoiding associations with fashionable and unfashionable, it became somewhat immune to such external threats.

This illustrates the theme of this chapter: when firms are able to use external resources to support their strategy they are able to create strategic advantages.

Similarly, competitive advantages and the differences they create in firm performance are often strongly related to internal factors, most prominently the resources of firms and management.[3] Internal resources, such as the patents that pharmaceutical companies own, allow them to exploit legal protection from competition for an extended period and benefit particularly from so-called blockbusters, pharmaceutical products with large sales volumes. Other internal resources include routines and practices that are deeply embedded in a firm and distinguish it from competition. Take for example, Swarovski an Austrian manufacturer of eponymous synthetic crystals. Having developed the method to grow crystals, the company has grown based on this core competence. Seeking direct contact with consumers, Swarovski recently sought to extend this core by opening retail outlets and its online shop.

Consider another example of internal resources, Berlitz, a globally operating language school under Japanese ownership. Responding to the urgent need for language instructors, the company founder, Berlitz, hired French language teachers who were not able to communicate as well in English as would have been expected. Surprisingly, the results of these teachers' students were superior to those of other students learning French with teachers who would use English as the language of instruction in class. Based on this observation, Berlitz developed the Berlitz Method, which emphasizes full immersion of students to accelerate and improve the quality of language learning. The success with this approach has turned Berlitz into one of the few, globally recognized, leading brands in language education.

Consistent with such cases, resources are often perceived to be the internally embedded strengths of firms. However, as the Muji Opening Case shows, seminal insights can come from loyal customers and its new product development is led by associated but independent designers. Customers provide particularly critical insights which help organizations learn how to continuously improve and innovate. In other words, bringing intrinsically motivated customers inside allows firms to capture emergent needs and opportunities to successfully manage growth.[4] Such creative and motivated individuals or communities of users who experiment to invent, improve and develop existing products further are also called lead users; they can be a very important source of innovation for organizations as they do not insist on rights related to their innovations.[5] Such free revealing has been found to be important for the innovation of physical goods similar to those in the Opening Case and recently also for the innovation of (open) software and services, where a large number of granular and diverse tasks increases the potential pool of participants.[6]

In these cases, strategic resources are external. Some of Muji's key resources are external and threats emerge as much from the environment as from the firm itself. A company's ability to form competitive advantage depends on its capability to exploit resources that is does not own and avoid seeing external change as threatening. Summarizing, typically threats are associated with the external environment (see Chapter 2) and resources are associated with the internal environment (see Chapter 3). This chapter shows how to overcome the inherent rigidities and to use resources wherever they reside.

To identify and successfully use internal and external resources over time, leading firms need to think constantly about how to manage them and at the same time seek to understand how to overcome not only external but internal threats. As this chapter shows, firms achieve strategic competitiveness and earn above-average returns when they manage to integrate internal with external resources effectively and efficiently to overcome threats in the external environment and take advantage of opportunities in ways that create value for customers.[7]

**External resources**

External resources are assets, knowledge and skills that lie outside the boundary of corporations and are often owned by other market players.

**Lead users**

Lead users are often intrinsically motivated individuals or communities, who experiment to invent, improve and adapt existing products.

Sensing and understanding customers' latent needs is a critical capability that takes effort to grow successfully.[8] Access to customers and making sense of their unaltered, authentic behaviour is often a fundamental way to gain insight. Consumer ethnography and fieldwork is a management practice that is gathering more attention.[9] Best practices in generating novel ideas for new product development, such as the Deep Dive of IDEO, use fieldwork to tap into what matters for different relevant groups, e.g., consumers or retailers. The systematic way in which IDEO makes use of external insights is exemplary yet it does not really bring the users inside. In contrast, Muji in Japan has developed a loyal customer following that not only engages in repeat purchases but also spends holidays at Muji summer camps where they enjoy existing Muji products and experience prototypes. For providing such customers with peeks of new products, Muji is compensated with feedback from its most important customer group. Similarly, Ocado, the British online retailer with home delivery service, made its initial public offering to restricted groups, including loyal customers, to align them with the interests of the company.[10]

Over time the benefits of any firm's internal resources erode because of competitive rivalry but also internal change. This is a key reason for exploring the external environment in search of resources that could replace, complement or upgrade internal resources. All competitive advantages will eventually erode.[11] The question of how competitive advantage can be sustained is inexorably linked to weaning firms from their reliance on internal resources and their focus on threats. Appreciating that (1) the external environment is resource rich, especially when it comes to knowledge,[12] and (2) understanding that change is not always threatening, are basics that companies need to master. The challenge for all firms, then, is to effectively manage current internal resources while simultaneously developing and exploiting external resources.[13] Only when firms tap internal and external knowledge and synthesize capabilities that contribute to competitive advantages can they earn above-average returns.

With knowledge about their external environment, firms gain a better understanding of fundamental changes, the characteristics of their competitive environment and opportunities in the marketplace (see Chapter 2). In Chapter 3, we focused on the firm and its internal environment. By analysing its internal organization, determining what it can do, and matching its resources, capabilities, core competencies, and competitive advantages[14] with the external environment, the firm can develop, select and implement its strategies. In this chapter, we show how the apparent paradox between focus on external threats and internal resources can be overcome by integration. By developing four main approaches to integration a firm can (1) identify critical external resources; (2) internalize them and develop synergies with internal resources; (3) increase performance by exploiting these complementary assets; and (4) institutionalize the integration of external and internal resources and analysis of risks pertaining to internal and external factors.

We begin by briefly discussing unintended consequences associated with focusing on the firm's internal resources and external threats only (core rigidities). Core rigidities indicate that a firm is too reliant on its internal resources, which change more slowly than the external environment. This prevents the firm from integrating internal and external resources to gain competitive advantages. We then discuss the roles of external resources and capabilities in developing a firm's competitive advantages. Included in this discussion are the techniques firms use to identify and evaluate external resources and capabilities. Internal resources and capabilities become more valuable when the firm can use them together with external resources to perform certain activities that result in a competitive advantage. Accordingly, we discuss inclusion as bringing external resources in, cooperative models of additive integration and spiral models of iterative integration of resources.

# The context of resource integration

In the current economic environment, with unprecedented rivalry and powerful competitors from emerging markets, knowledge and capabilities are important sources of competitive advantage. The economies of Brazil, Russia, India and China are developing rapidly, and the demand for primary resources by these so-called BRIC countries, and other high-growth countries such as Turkey and many parts of Eastern Europe, has multiplied. We mentioned earlier how China, which used less than 50 per cent of the energy consumed in the US at the beginning of 2000, rose to consume more energy than the US in 2010. In recent years in particular, China's efforts to secure rights to natural resources in other countries e.g., Australia or Africa, illustrate the importance of external resources on the macro level. Traditional factors such as raw materials, labour at low costs, and access to financial resources and regulated markets remain important sources of competitive advantage, or barriers to success for other firms. When emerging markets are discussed as possible destinations for market entry or as the arena for competitive activities such as a new product launch, the topic of intellectual property rights often becomes a key issue. While stronger protection of intellectual property is desirable for firms that own strategic assets such as patents, excessive emphasis on property rights may lead to missed opportunities in a rapidly growing market that is still developing stable institutions such as a legal system or enforcement. Consider how companies such as LVMH, the French luxury corporation, approach emerging markets by seeking a balance between enforcing their intellectual property rights (IPR) and searching to overcome the threat of imitation through internal mechanisms. Similarly, the large numbers of highly-educated university graduates offers firms great opportunities to tap into rich resources in China and other high growth markets such as India, not only in labour-intensive industries but also in knowledge-intensive industries.

Technological development, most significantly the rapid improvements and diffusion of information technology and the Internet have lowered barriers to integrating external resources. Today being connected with a call centre abroad, say in the Philippines or India, to make a reservation in the US or the UK is not a big surprise. Lower communication costs and speed of information processing allow for large communities to interact online and to exchange explicit knowledge, and increasingly also tacit knowledge. Facilitated by these developments of technology, programmers who share passion for the project, their profession and take pride in their skills, have created open source software such as Linux without tangible compensation. Muji, the company in the Opening Case, channelled information exchanges with loyal customers initially through regular mail and phone calls. Today the Internet is Muji's most important medium to generate insights and co-create ideas with customers.[15] On the company level, one of the most important phenomena related to resource integration is internationalization. Since 1950, world trade, i.e., import and export activities or in other words the use of resources in other contexts, has increased strongly and the percentage of world GDP generated in Asia is rising rapidly.[16] An analysis of the Fortune Global 500, a list of the world's largest companies by revenue from 1950 to 2006, shows the number of US companies being the largest, followed by Japanese firms. In recent years, the dominance of the US and Japan is decreasing; with more and more large multinational firms from different countries joining their ranks.[17] In particular, the internationalization successes of South Korean, Chinese, Indian and Brazilian firms are remarkable.

One important factor that explains successful internationalization is the skill with which companies integrate home country resources with host country

**Resource integration**

Resource integration is the mutually beneficial combination of external and internal resources.

STRATEGIC FOCUS

# Alessi – growing with a network of partners

A case in point is Alessi, the Italian company that is mainly known for manufacturing kitchenware and household goods. Between 1995 and 2002 Alessi has been able to achieve an average return on investment of about 20 per cent and return on equity of about 40 per cent. The North Italian family-owned business has become a best practice in new product development for business worldwide and McKinsey, a leading management consultancy, showed much interest in the practices of Alberto Alessi and the company he leads in Crusinallo, a small town to the north of Milan.

Alessi began with production facilities in Italy, focusing on stainless steel products. Emerging in the Cusio industrial district — a cluster which is famous worldwide for its production of metal household objects like cutlery, coffee makers, trays and pots — Alessi has extended its product portfolio to include other materials including wood and plastics, and multiple production technologies.

Alessi now develops products in a very different way compared to 30 years ago. Since then Alessi has shifted away from new product development and

in-house design and became more open to co-develop with external partners. Over time, Alessi has gathered experience in co-developing product lines such as kitchen appliances with many individual designers but also larger firms such as Philips. Today the firm has relationships with some 200 external designers, many of whom are famous architects such as Frank Gehry and Zaha Hadid, who designed a tea kettle and a vase respectively. Alessi's partners are enthusiastic about the level of engagement with the company and the support the external designers enjoy during the process of cooperation.

After several hundred projects Alessi has formalized its approach to selecting promising projects. Its "formula for success" includes four criteria with equal weight: (1) function, (2) sensory, memory, imagination, emotion, (3) aesthetics and (4) price. These criteria allow the company to gauge potential sales of advanced prototypes.

Alessi has been able to leverage its core competence in developing attractive items together with talented and famous designers from around the world, whose ideas have driven Alessi to expand into new materials such as plastics because these were better able to give form to the more exciting ideas. Developing manufacturing capacity in China, Alessi brings together design with low labour cost advantages available locally. In doing so it seems poised to benefit early from the growing middle class in China, which promises highly profitable business.

In recent years, Alessi has not only been engaged in developing its network with creative talents but also with companies. For example, Alessi's entry into the realm of bathroom products quickly went beyond accessories for the bathroom to include taps, basins and tubs. Mastering this new product range required expertise Alessi did not possess. Partnering with leading European players in the bathroom industry (Laufen, one of the largest producers of baked clay components for bathrooms; Oras, a Scandinavian company producing taps; Inda, an Italian firm specializing in design and production of high quality accessories for bathrooms), Alessi developed the strategy and managed design and communication, while the three partners focused on product development and production. This approach to partnering enabled Alessi to quickly establish itself as a strong niche player in the market through its distinctive design. Other partnerships relate to different products including wallpaper with Tapetenfabrik, a German wallpaper manufacturer, watches with SII Marketing International, which is better known for its Fossil brand, and phones with Siemens.

**Sources:** Alessi; Bryony, G. (2002) "Kitchen-sink comedies: From classic kettle to Philippe Starck lemon squeezer, an Alessi Gadget is a style icon", *The Daily Telegraph*, April 20; Salvato, C. (2009) "Capabilities unveiled: The role of ordinary activities in the evolution of product development processes", *Organization Science*, 20(2): 384–409; Capozzi, M. M. and Simpson, J. (2009) "Cultivating innovation: An interview with the CEO of a leading Italian design firm", *McKinsey Quarterly*, February.

*Questions*

1 What is characteristic of Alessi's approach to integrating external resources?

2 What are the advantages for a firm like Alessi? Are there disadvantages? If so what are they?

3 The web that Alessi casts is complex; Alessi is linked to many designers and firms. Do the advantages and downsides differ for the creative partners and the company partners?

4 How does Alessi find new ideas, select and exploit them?

resources (discussed in Chapter 8). For example, the successful multinationals in the global automobile industry have achieved growth by tapping into local resources for design, engineering, manufacturing and sales. Consider the case of Renault and how this leading European car manufacturer has been able to achieve a turnaround of Nissan in Japan by bringing in experienced top management, Carlos Ghosn,[18] who refocused the organization and mobilized Nissan's employees. Bringing together the strengths of Nissan's brand in Japan but also in the US, Japanese design, process technology and more efficient modular manufacturing of a limited number of models, Renault leveraged the combined strength of both firms while refraining from completely absorbing Nissan. This integration without absorption has enabled Renault and Nissan to increase their emphasis on the high growth market in India and introduce "no frills" cars to India's rising middle class.

Internationalization promises higher returns because it allows firms to broaden the pool of resources they can exploit. This is not only relevant for the world's largest corporations listed in the Fortune Global 500 but also for small and medium size enterprises. When we consider the strength of many a European economy (see World Economic Forum ranking, www.weforum.org) and the number of large multinationals, we understand that not only large firms contribute to countries' strong performance. Export oriented countries such as Germany, Italy, Japan and South Korea are strong performers because their small and medium sized firms often capture large market shares in small but highly profitable global markets. Often these "hidden champions"[19] find successful ways to leverage local and foreign resources.

As the Strategic Focus illustrates, the assets most needed to leverage internal resources are often possessed by other organizations and firms. Competing only with the assets within a single organization may be desirable (potential for value extraction may be higher), but it is becoming a more and more unlikely scenario. Capabilities to gain access[20] to and integrate complementary assets enable successful strategy development and implementation.

In Chapter 3 we introduced the notion of a global mindset, as managers' ability to analyse, understand and manage (if in a managerial position) in ways that are not dependent on the assumptions of a single context. It is particularly important to avoid being trapped by thinking in silos within the boundaries of a single firm. Only by spanning boundaries[21] are firms fully able to recognize what resources and capabilities they possess and which they need.

**Design**

Design is the pursuit of emotional, symbolic and functional performance of products.

**Turnaround**

Turnaround is the rare managerial accomplishment of organizational change that may follow dramatic performance decline.

Finally, understanding the internal resources, capabilities and the combinations that provide lasting advantages is not enough because the context of resource integration requires analysis also of possible bundles of heterogeneous resources and capabilities that lie outside the organizational boundaries. Such resources are the source of capabilities that in turn can lead to the development of core competencies.[22] Understanding how to leverage unique bundles of resources and capabilities available in the internal and external environment is the key to competitive advantage.[23]

# Benefits of integration and its costs

Creating value for customers by exploiting internal resources[24] can provide competitive advantage, however it does not always maximize the value that could be created. As mentioned in Chapter 3, value is measured by customers' willingness to pay for a product's attributes and performance characteristics. Firms cannot always increase the willingness to pay without utilizing external resources. Consider the recent success of the new Mini's market introduction. Prior to the acquisition by BMW the Mini was a mythical vehicle with limitations when it came to state-of-the art engineering, service and maintenance network. With the acquisition by BMW the original design and the myth were reconnected to the operational system of a leading manufacturer with sufficient scale and scope to establish the Mini as a high-end product. Weaving the UK myth into the network of a leading car manufacturer has led to one of the most successful product relaunches in recent automobile history.

The success of the Mini is exceptional, yet many of the most stunning successes in business have come about because firms cooperated to increase and exploit their pool of resources. The example of how Intel and Microsoft's new product developments have created demand for each other's product, is sometimes summarized with the label "Wintel". Increasing processing capacity of integrated circuits allowed for larger and more sophisticated software; software with higher memory and processing requirements stimulated the development of more powerful IC chips in turn. Sony's success with its first Playstation platform, PS1, was driven by Sony's decision to provide a favourable environment for external game developers that allowed them to create games that could be played on the platform. This notion of value creating cooperation between parties that have highly complementary products, or even compete when it comes to value capturing, is also called coopetition.[25]

The examples above show how firms with a competitive advantage were able to offer more value to customers than their competitors could.[26] More importantly, they were able to increase the willingness to pay beyond what they alone could have achieved by developing cooperation with other companies to jointly exploit shared resources. Firms create value by innovatively bundling and leveraging resources and capabilities they are able to recruit.[27] Firms unable to access, creatively bundle and leverage their own resources and capabilities and those available in the environment in ways that create value for customers, suffer performance declines. Using internal and external resources to create value for customers is the source of above-average returns for a firm. A major benefit in the firm's value creation processes and the source of above-average returns for a firm.

There are, however, costs attached to being open and integrating external resources. The strategic management process was first concerned largely with

**Coopetition**

Coopetition is the value creating constellation in which market players cooperate or develop complementary products and simultaneously compete, e.g. when it comes to value capture.

understanding the immediate competitive environment in which the firm competed (i.e. industry) and with positioning the firm relative to its competitors. The costs of this approach lay in underestimating the role of the firm's resources and capabilities in developing a competitive advantage.[28] Then core competencies of a firm were strongly emphasized.[29] The costs of emphasizing core competencies lies in companies' tendencies to compete primarily on the basis of firm-specific factors (competence trap).[30] Focusing on the environment or focusing on core competences leads to lock-in effects that prevent firms from seeing and using highly complementary assets (core rigidities). Integrating internal and external resources offers a way to avoid these limitations. Getting higher returns on managing internal and external resources at the same time requires specific management capabilities.[31]

## Resource integration: open innovation, absorptive capacity and organizational change

The diminishing returns of research and development that remain limited to the resources available within organizations are widely accepted. The main factors include the increasing rate of (technological) change, shortening product life cycles, globalization of technologies and competition but also the obsolescence of the principles with which organizations managed their innovation process, i.e. internally focused innovation also called closed innovation[32] (see Figure 4.1).

The summary concept of alternative models, open innovation or inclusive innovation, suggests that companies must enhance their value creating potential to survive the new competition, also hypercompetition,[33] by using their absorptive capacity[34] and tapping external resources, (see Figure 4.2).

Table 4.1 summarizes idealizations of the closed and open innovation models.

**Open innovation**

Contrary to closed innovation, which relies primarily on internal resources, open innovation involves commercializing external ideas by deploying outside (as well as in-house) pathways to the market.

**FIGURE 4.1** The current paradigm: a closed innovation system

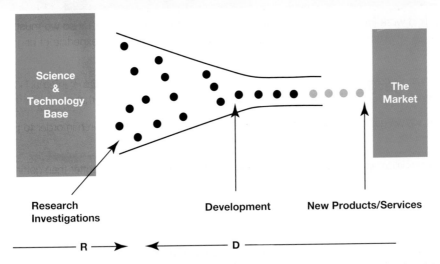

Source: J. West, W. Vanhaverbeke and H. Chesbrough, 2006, "Open innovation: A research agenda", in *Open Innovation: Researching a New Paradigm*, H. Chesbrough, W. Vanhaverbeke and J. West (eds.), 285–307. Oxford: Oxford University Press. Adapted with permission.

**FIGURE 4.2** The open innovation paradigm

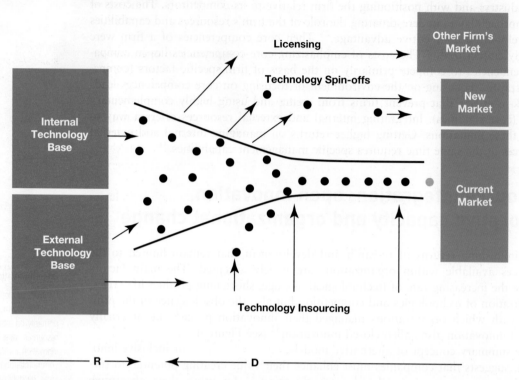

**Table 4.1** Contrasting "closed innovation" principles and "open innovation" principles

| Closed innovation principles | Open innovation principles |
|---|---|
| i  The smart people in our field work for us. | Not all of the smart people work for us so we must find and tap into the knowledge and expertise of bright individuals outside our company. |
| ii  To profit from R&D, we must discover, develop, produce and ship it ourselves. | External R&D can create significant value; internal R&D is needed to claim some portion of that value. |
| iii  If we discover it ourselves, we will get it to market first. | We don't have to originate the research in order to profit from it. |
| iv  If we are the first to commercialize an innovation, we will win. | Building a better business model is better than getting to market first. |
| v  If we create the most and best ideas in the industry, we will win. | If we make the best use of internal and external ideas, we will win. |
| vi  We should control our intellectual property (IP) so that our competitors do not profit from our ideas. | We should profit from others' use of our IP, and we should buy others' IP whenever it advances our own business model. |

While the important concept of open innovation is widely used, it has not remained without criticism[35]. Yet it builds on seminal work and seeks to integrates concepts such as lead users, network model of innovation, the importance of information and knowledge processes.

The emphasis on technology is generally strong in organizations so open innovation processes focus on developing and/or sourcing strategic technology where it may be available. While this emphasis on technology is understandable, especially in technology intensive industries, it may lead to underestimating the importance of new ways of managing and organizing. This kind of non-technological innovation, also management innovation, is particularly important for the competitiveness of companies.[36] Consider how important the conveyor belt was for Ford Motor Company's success with its Model T, reflect on how important the development of brand management has been for P&G to emerge as a leader in fast-moving consumer goods, or on how Toyota has seized leadership in the automobile industry exploiting its innovative Toyota Production System. Seven-Eleven has developed a business system that seeks to draw in external knowledge to optimize processes such as product development, distribution and display.

All these examples show that openness does not relate only to technology and R&D but also to management and renewal of companies. Often it is easier to acquire a new technology than to change the established way of doing things. Cases in point are the US automobile manufacturers who failed to change their ways to overcome the threat of Japanese and Korean competitors because they found it difficult to acknowledge the existence of external best practices and transfer them. Comparing the company from the Opening Case, Muji, with Seven-Eleven, illustrates that open innovation only partly relies on technology and to a large extent on a new way of managing including new leadership, processes, people and relationships. The similarities related to customer orientation and approaches to innovation as well as the overall consistency of each strategy are discussed.

Overall, open innovation or inclusive innovation helps us understand how organizations today seek to gain competitive advantage through innovation. The three main challenges are addressed below: organizations need to be open and closed, select and absorb knowledge and change and retain organizational routines.

**Knowledge processes**

Knowledge processes are the ways organizations create, absorb, transfer and transform knowledge.

**Seizing**

Seizing leads firms to act upon promising weak signals, opportunities or new knowledge.

# The challenge of being open and closed: identifying critical external resources

The strategic decisions managers make concerning the external environment often significantly influence the firm's ability to earn above-average returns.[37] These decisions involve choices about which assets the firm needs, how to gain access and how to best use those assets. The challenging task of making decisions on how to identify, develop, deploy and protect resources, capabilities and core competencies, is becoming more attractive but also more complex because external resources can today be found around the world.

Often companies that are not open enough have the most difficulty finding resources outside. They may not be aware of the resources that promise highest productivity, because they do not analyse the environment thoroughly enough to find the required resources. Consider a problem that all companies face: CEO succession.[38] In the searches related to succession of higher management positions external candidates are often excluded. This leaves internal search as the only option, which frequently results in less than optimal appointments. While the cultural fit of internal candidates is a given, the much larger number of possible external candidates is not taken into consideration. Similarly, managers might, for example, search for low labour costs in selected countries such as Vietnam, but overlook the difficulties associated with the prevailing business system. The identification of low labour costs for simple service tasks as the primary driver to internationalize and bring (for example) Indian resources to bear, may be misguided as it overlooks the possibility to engage highly educated graduates from excellent local universities for high level engineering jobs. In addition, there is a higher risk of identifying external resources and capabilities as complementary assets that then turn out to be lemons.

Managerial decisions concerning external resources, capabilities and core competencies are characterized by three conditions: uncertainty, complexity and interorganizational dynamics. Managers face uncertainty in terms of rapidly changing economic and political trends, transformations in societal values, and shifts in customer demands, the likelihood of success of technology seeds, and intellectual property rights, legislative changes and enforcement of rights.[39] Environmental uncertainty increases the complexity and range of issues to analyse when searching for external resources.[40]

As seen in the Strategic Focus, openness can include the willingness to acquire strategic resources even offshore, instead of developing knowledge and skills internally and possibly reinventing the wheel. Openness to external insight is thus crucial for competitiveness. In trying to answer how far openness should go, peripheral attention can help. Paying attention to the insights at the periphery is important but also paradoxical.[41] Wasting too much time and energy on the periphery in explorative search is one extreme that lacks focus on what the company's assets, knowledge and competences are. Focusing only on the current core locks companies in because they continue to focus on their past learning (competency trap).

**Peripheral vision**

Peripheral vision allows people to become aware of e.g. movement without visually focusing on what moves.

Peripheral vision allows people to become aware of e.g., movement, without focusing their eyes on what moves. Maintaining focus and becoming aware of weak signals is difficult for managers and the companies they lead. Sensing and adjusting to minor changes in the environment is particularly difficult if managers focus on current customers and seek to satisfy them by exploiting the dominant technologies. In doing so they may have made a good management decision in the short run, but if emergent technologies turn disruptive they will find that they missed the opportunity to avoid failure.[42] The dilemma of paying attention to what may seem insignificant is often framed as a threatening scenario; however recognizing what may constitute a resource essential to future growth is no less important. Consider how different the story of 3M might look if its managers had ultimately dismissed the "glue that does not stick". Not the most promising proposition for the development of a successful product, yet the case of how Post-it Notes were developed has entered management history.

**Clusters**

Clusters are regionally defined agglomerations of competing and cooperating firms and those with complementary products in the same or related industries.

Identifying unique resources is difficult; it involves making trade-offs. When scanning the globe for unique resources and knowledge,[43] some indicators help identify what is possibly valuable. Clusters of firms in specific locations for instance may indicate the presence of complementary resources. Silicon Valley is known worldwide as an agglomeration of many leading firms in the highly competitive information technology market space. In recent years, Web 1.0 and Web 2.0 have been driven by firms located in the cluster who benefit from the excellent labour supply within the Valley and the outstanding infrastructure and support including venture capitalists, consultants, contract manufacturers and consultants. In other words, clusters clearly indicate the presence of important assets.

## STRATEGIC FOCUS

© kkgas/iStock

# East-West Seed Company: picking the best of both worlds

East-West Seed Company, established in 1982 in the Philippines, has been leading hybrid seed technology in Thailand for the last 25 years. The company is the country's leading producer of hybrid seeds of squash, ampalaya, onion, pepper, tomato, eggplant and other tropical vegetables. The company's successes in breeding with bitter gourds, super-hot chilli peppers and sticky-rice corn, which requires high levels of science and skill, has made it a leader in its market space. With the high technology content of its products, East-West Seed Company sees itself as an outlier in the food industry. Occupying and exploiting a highly profitable market the company is now seeking new opportunities for growth.

In line with its growth ambitions, East-West Seed has recently started operations in China and India to further extend its access to ideas and insights from farmers through a network of field representatives that could strengthen its plant breeding technology and seed quality. Seeking to repeat the company's success in other geographical areas with new technologies,

East-West Seed recently took a stake in Dutch biotech company, Genetwister Technologies BV. This investment is expected to stimulate the development of innovative technologies and new applications for the benefit of East-West Seed's breeding programmes.

However, the social and political unrest that has gripped Thailand in recent years erupted in 2010 resulting in weeks of blockades and fights between demonstrators and Thai security forces and in the process shattering the reputation of Thailand as a politically stable location for foreign direct investment. With its weak government and an ageing monarch, Thailand may no longer be the location to best facilitate the integration of technology and local biodiversity.

Similarly, in the Netherlands, the ageing monarch of Thailand, King Bhumibol Adulyadej, had to wait to meet the prime minister in 2010 after the Dutch election resulted in a hung parliament and weeks of difficult negotiations to form a coalition government, which has to make budget decisions (e.g. taxation) that will influence the economy. Evaluating the mid to long-term scenarios of this specific multi-country context of East-West Seed Company, i.e. Philippines, Thailand and the Netherlands, is challenging for the firm's leadership. While analysing the developments in their current context, managers need to scan the periphery and pay attention[44] to possible alternatives or better resources elsewhere.

**Sources:** http://www.eastwestseed.com/; "East-West Seeds: Better seeds for better yields", *The Scientist*, 24(13): 8 (accessed online July 31, 2010); http://www.the-scientist.com/templates/trackable/display/supplementarticle.jsp?name=thailand&id=57301); "East-West Seed launches new flowering ornamentals", *Agriculture Business Week*, January 30 (accessed online July 31, 2010); http://www.agribusinessweek.com/east-west-seed-launches-new-flowering-ornamentals/); "De Rol van Bedrijfsnetwerken bij Successvolle Herstructureringstransacties", ABN-AMRO, 2010.

## Questions

1 Identifying external resources is a critical starting point for creating competitive advantage. What are East-West Seeds strengths?

2 Why is internationalization important for the company?

3 How do you see the internationalization in this case, which is unusual in that a firm from an emerging market seeks acquisition targets or investments in companies in advanced markets?

4 How do external factors influence East-West Seeds' search for new opportunities abroad?

This makes identification of crucial resources easier but with high visibility of these assets demand is strong. Many companies will compete for the same or similar resources because their value is clearly visible. In contrast, the absence of demand forces the company to identify resources alone but allows it to appropriate the benefits with limited competition. However, identifying what exactly is most valuable can be a challenge. In Formula 1 motor sport as well as in the music industry, shifts in competitive advantage are closely related to the complementary knowledge and dynamic exchange between the firm and cluster level.[45]

To summarize, realizing open innovation requires making an important trade-off between visibility and appropriability. Identifying organizational resources, understanding their potential to create value and anticipating related developments is challenging. Uncertainty, complexity and dynamics are even more challenging when it comes to identifying, understanding externally embedded resources and anticipating related changes. Managers need to make clear choices about the degree of openness and focus to best enhance, protect and exploit internal resources.

## The challenge of selecting and absorbing knowledge: internalizing critical external resources

After setting the organizational conditions for open innovation, companies need to develop ways to internalize or utilize the external resources that can help developing competitive advantage. In other words, the company's absorptive capacity influences the company's performance, innovativeness and flexibility.[46] A firm's success depends to a large extent on its prior knowledge and access to technology, and whether such resources lie within or outside the firm boundaries. The ability to learn – that is, to absorb external knowledge – depends to a great extent on the ability to value the new external knowledge, i.e., prior knowledge and experience.

The selection of resources is usually based on the size of the opportunities in terms of market potential and the technological positioning. However, recognizing such value is particularly difficult when the knowledge is radically new. Organizations frequently select new knowledge using the existing frame of references. Such fitting of new knowledge in the existing frame of reference is also called assimilation. For assimilation into the internal context to be successful, flexibility and energy, and also limited novelty are required. Assimilation will work only if the current ways of seeing the world are good enough to make sense of what is new. Radically new knowledge may be difficult to assimilate, as the distance between the old frame of reference and the new insight are too large. Consider how difficult it was for companies in the business of making money with prints from analog photography, e.g. Kodak and Fuji Photo Film, to change to digital technology. Such disruptive innovations are cases in which transforming the frame of reference is necessary. While this amounts to considerable organizational change (see part III), some cases show how successful transformation can be. Nokia, for instance, developed from manufacturing first paper pulp then TVs, to mobile phones and now smart phones.

After careful selection, the external resources need be brought to bear on extant resources and exploited. Owning technology may often be preferred but access through networks may be sufficient to gain competitive advantage. The different approaches to grow the organizational research pool include alliances and

---

**Ability to learn**

Ability to learn depends on the ability to value the new external knowledge, i.e. prior knowledge and experience.

**Assimilation**

Assimilation means placing new knowledge within the existing frame of reference.

**Transforming**

Disruptive innovations make transforming the frame of reference, i.e. fundamental organizational change necessary.

**Organizational change**

Strategy implementation is the necessary link between strategy formulation and performance that requires organizational change, which includes adapting structures, processes and methods, and cognition.

**Alliances**

Alliances are agreements between two or more parties to undertake activities to pursue shared goals or protect common interests.

acquisitions, but also focus on specific stakeholder groups, especially lead users. Alliances, joint ventures and M&A are different approaches with a common core: expanding an organization's pool of resources by gaining access to external resources. Absorptive capacity, or the ability to learn, underpins the successful implementation of practical alternatives to integrating knowledge such as alliances, M&A, lead users, ventures etc.

Securing access to superior technology, skills and knowledge motivates many alliances and acquisitions. Seven-Eleven Japan and Yamato Yubin's alliance (see Chapter 2) allows both firms to successfully develop, produce and deliver meals for the rapidly growing market of older people. Alliances, such as those that Alessi (see Strategic Focus on page 145), is pursuing now have their own difficulties. Differences in intent, organizational routines and culture, among others, make managing alliances challenging. *Alliances* are agreements between two or more parties to undertake activities to pursue shared goals or protect common interests. Based on contracts that stipulate equitable sharing of risks and opportunities for all partners, alliances are widely used in business. Well-known examples are code-sharing alliances of major airlines such as SkyTeam. SkyTeam includes Delta Airlines, Air-France, and KLM as core members and since 2009 its management team is based in the World Trade Centre, Schiphol Airport.

As well as alliances, acquisitions can play a key role in helping companies to access resources. *Acquisition* (also referred to as takeover or buyout) is another option to foster growth internationally by expanding the corporation's reach in foreign markets. Acquisitions are instances of corporate development where one corporate entity internalizes another entity, which subsequently ceases to exist independently. Offering the possibility to fast growth and returns out of the ordinary, this approach can carry higher risks. SAB Miller for instance acquired Grolsch in 2007 ending Grolsch's independence.

Consider how one of Spain's leading food and agribusiness groups was formed. In 2000 two Spanish firms, Ebro and Puleva, merged to create Ebro Puleva. Due to competitive pressures, Ebro Puleva decided to grow through a rapid series of acquisitions in the rice and pasta sector with a strong focus on technology. For example, in 2005 Ebro Puleva acquired Panzani, a leading French pasta maker. Then, in 2006, the company acquired Minute Rice from Kraft Food for €220 million and New World Pasta, a leading branded pasta company in the US and Canada, for €285 million. The key drivers of Ebro Pulevo's fast growth strategy were the unique windows of opportunity to build an international platform of expertise, technology, experience and innovation in the pasta and rice sectors. In particular, the opportunity to integrate the distribution channels and expertise in many countries was very important to fully exploit the strong logistics capabilities to their full potential. Similarly, Ebro Puleva integrated six R&D centres worldwide. Each R&D centre was engaged in developing new product innovations or innovations in packaging and food production technology. Integrating these centres allowed Ebro Puleva to globally develop and locally test the newest developments. This strengthened its technological capabilities but also increased its return on R&D investments. As a result, in 2009 Ebro Puleva became the world leader in rice production with nearly €900 million of turnover and achieved the second position worldwide as a pasta producer with nearly €1 billion turnover. In 2009, the Group garnered a record net profit of €135 million and an average growth in share price of nearly 40 per cent during the year.

**Acquisitions**

Acquisitions are instances of corporate development where one corporate entity internalizes another entity, which subsequently ceases to exist independently.

## New ways of integrating external resources

Alliances and acquisitions are frequently used to expand an organization's resource pool. However, they are not the only processes used. In the Opening Case, Muji illustrates how firms can integrate the tacit knowledge and undiscovered needs of customers into the new product development process. Through summer camps, regular and online submissions, Muji seeks to unobtrusively absorb knowledge of their customers whenever possible. In the Strategic Focus it became clear that what makes Alessi highly competitive is its ability to attract talented designers and weave them into the intensive process of developing new products in teams with internal and external experts. Other companies have developed different approaches to tap into the community of inventors, scientists and creatives and institutionalize integrating external resources.[47]

As shown in the following Strategic Focus, P&G has found a new, inclusive model for its innovation process. Bringing external resources into the internal processes has become a very important way of developing a stronger innovation pipeline. P&G leverages internal capabilities through its Connect & Develop programme by linking internal strengths to external resources. Recognized as one of the best in the world, P&G's managers have developed and implemented a new model of innovating that helps P&G to reduce the cost of R&D and expands its reach into the periphery and what might be useful. As such, P&G learns to attract and select the most promising of the ideas submitted. Effectively making P&G a marketplace for ideas increases the company's competitiveness in at least two ways. First, P&G's Connect & Develop programme generates higher innovation returns on R&D investments because of the beneficial effects of complementary external insight. Second, turning P&G into a marketplace for the most advanced ideas in the markets for fast mover consumer goods, limits rivals' opportunities to benefit from new ideas and insights.

In the next sections we discuss different models of how external resources can be linked effectively to internal resources by changing organizational routines.

## The challenge of developing routines for open innovation: why doing what is good is difficult

Implementing a more inclusive or open approach to exploring and exploiting external resources is difficult. As shown above innovation was the task of R&D groups within organizations that followed the closed model of innovation. Going beyond this by involving all organizational members in the innovation – incremental or radical – is a big leap. The confrontation with Japanese automobile manufacturers has presented competitors from Europe and the US with a more open approach. Expertly implemented by mainly Toyota with its Toyota Production System, which relies heavily on the creativity and alertness of all employees and the ingenuity of suppliers and sales partners to generate new ideas, it has proven to be resilient to the different setbacks it had to endure. Such setbacks include external crises such as sudden changes in currency exchange rates and volatility in energy prices, but also self-inflicted crises such as the sticky pedal crisis in 2010. This approach is different from the organizational model that separates white-collar workers from blue-collar workers and from the not invented here, or NIH syndrome, that holds back many large, successful industrial organizations.[48] Since the emergence of Toyota, its production system has been scrutinized and made largely transparent, yet Japanese, other Asian and Western competitors have so far not succeeded in emulating the Toyota Production System.

**Not invented here**

Not invented here (NIH) refers to the closedness of organizations, or within organizations, to external ideas.

STRATEGIC FOCUS

© Bloomberg/Contributor/Getty Images

## Procter & Gamble: capturing a world of ideas

Procter & Gamble is a consumer product giant with a long and proud tradition of powerful in-house science behind its many leading brands. By 2000 Procter & Gamble (P&G) had to acknowledge it was facing a problem that most mature companies need to address. Creating organic growth of e.g. 5 per cent annually had become too difficult. That often is equivalent to building a multi-billion Euro business each year. Relying on internal R&D to achieve such growth targets had been the standard in many industries. P&G historically had created most of its growth by building and leveraging global research facilities, hiring the best talent in the world and generating innovations in its labs. Increasing competition, new technologies and the burden of generating organic growth sufficient to influence the sales volume of a large firm, required more than the innovation budget could provide. Facing unprecedented levels of rivalry with stagnating R&D productivity and a 35 per cent rate of innovation success rate, i.e. the percentage of new products that met financial objectives, led to decreasing financial performance and a steep decline in market valuation.

P&G was working with an innovation model from the 1980s, a globally networked internal model which seemed no longer adequate to meet the targets, and the costs to maintain this model were increasing rapidly. Spending more on R&D was not an option. At the same time, it became clear that important innovations were increasingly carried out by entrepreneurial companies, small start-ups or even by individuals, and some leading firms started to engage in open innovation. In 2000, P&G realized it could not meet its growth objectives by spending more and more on R&D.

At the time, the newly appointed CEO, A. G. Lafley, challenged his staff to reinvent the company's way of innovating. Most of P&G's best innovations had come from connecting ideas across internal businesses. And after studying the performance of a small number of products that were acquired externally, P&G realized that external connections could produce highly profitable innovations. In what followed, P&G created a best practice in open innovation that ties into strong internal resources. P&G changed its approach to innovation, extending its internal R&D to the outside world through the slogan "Connect & Develop".[49] "As a result, we have access to more internal technologies than any other consumer products company. We multiply this internal innovation capability by reaching outside P&G to a global network of nearly two million researchers in technology areas connected to P&G businesses. This "connect and develop" collaboration results in a bigger and stronger innovation pipeline" (Annual report, 2006, 5). The company has created the position of Director of External Innovation and has set a goal of sourcing 50 per cent of its innovations from outside the company within five years. The percentage of new products introduced that were based on external input increased from less than 20 per cent in the early 2000s to more than 50 per cent by the end of the decade. One example of P&G's success with open innovation[50] is the SpinBrush, the best-selling, battery-powered toothbrush in the United States which sells for about €4. The idea for the product came not from P&G's labs but from four entrepreneurs in Cleveland. P&G also tries to move its own innovations outside, see Figure 4.3.

Recently, the company instituted a policy stating that any idea that originates in its labs will be offered to outside firms, even direct competitors, if an internal business does not use the idea within three years. The goal is to prevent promising projects from losing momentum and becoming stuck inside the organization. Throughout much of Lafley's tenure as CEO, P&G was able to increase customers' willingness to pay, mainly by adding value through innovation and design. However, by the end of 2009, P&G resorted to aggressive price

**FIGURE 4.3**   The Osaka Connection

In the connect-and-develop world, chance favors the prepared mind. When one of P&G's technology entrepreneurs discovered a stain-removing sponge in a market in Osaka, Japan, he sent it to the company for evaluation. The resulting product, the Mr. Clean Magic Eraser, is now in third-generation development and has achieved double its projected revenues.

| | German chemical company **BASF** manufactures a melamine resin foam called Basotect for soundproofing and insulation in the construction and automotive industries. | **LEC,** a Tokyo-based consumer-products company, markets Basotect foam in Japan as a household sponge called Cleenpro. | |
|---|---|---|---|
| **2001 DISCOVER** | Japan-based technology entrepreneur with **P&G** discovers the product in an Osaka grocery store. | The entrepreneur evaluates its market performance in Japan and establishes its fit with the **P&G** home-care product development and marketing criteria. | |
| **2002 EVALUATE** | The technology entrepreneur sends samples to R&D product researchers in Cincinnati for performance evaluation. | The technology entrepreneur posts a product description and evaluation of market potential on **P&G's** internal "eureka catalog" network. | Market research confirms enthusiasm for the product. Product is moved into portfolio for development, **P&G** negotiates purchase of Basotect from BASF and terms for further collaboration. |
| **2003 LAUNCH** | Basotect is packaged as-is and launched nationally as Mr. Clean Magic Eraser. | Mr. Clean Magic Eraser is launched in Europe. | BASF and P&G researchers collaborate in shared labs to improve Basotect's cleaning properties, durability, and versatility. |
| **2004 COCREATE** | The first cocreated Basotect product, the Magic Eraser Duo, is launched nationally in the United States. | The cocreated Magic Eraser Wheel & Tire is launched nationally in the United States. | BASF and P&G collaborate on next generation Magic Eraser products. |

Source: Adapted from L. Huston and N. Sakkab, 2006, "Connect and develop: Inside Procter & Gamble's new model for innovation", *Harvard Business Review*. March. 65.

reductions to stem declining sales, mainly due to the downturn in the economy, and CEO Lafley retired.

**Sources**: Sakkab, N. (2002) "Connect & Develop Complements Research & Develop at P&G," *Research Technology Management*, 45, 2, (March–April): 38–45; P&G Annual Report 2006; Huston, L. and Sakkab, N. (2006) Connect and Develop: Inside Procter & Gamble's new model for innovation, *Harvard Business Review*, March, 58–66; H. Chesbrough, (2003) Open Innovation: The New Imperative for Creating and Profiting from Technology, Boston, MA: Harvard Business School Press.

## Questions

1 Does Procter & Gamble follow the Principles of Open Innovation?

2 How does Procter & Gamble identify promising ideas?

3 Is Procter & Gamble's approach proactive or reactive?

4 Will inventors and creatives continue to fuel open innovation at commercial enterprises?

Reluctance motivated by behavioural reasons (e.g. habits) or (lack of) incentives (e.g. political games) can lead to adaptive resistance (e.g. humour, anticipation) and maladaption (e.g. dissociation, denial, obstruction).[51] Several examples for resistance to change are outlined below.

Broadening what was the task of one function and making it a responsibility of all functions curtails the unique position of the R&D department, which may lead to resistance. At the same time, other functions may feel burdened with yet another task that they do not see fits with their main focus. In technology-oriented firms, the fact that management innovation can be extremely effective often meets resistance, as organizations that have grown by focusing on technology are not reflective enough to understand the power of their size and the need to manage properly. Technology start-ups frequently fail when they are unable to switch from entrepreneurial attitudes to professional management.

Exploiting external resources internally may remain difficult even after they are internalized (assimilated/transformed). In particular, highly complex tasks that require tacit knowledge can be difficult to understand and replicate. Even copying a model exactly can prove extremely difficult although it may be the only foolproof way to avoid introducing mistakes.[52]

Focusing on exploitation of new resource combinations is only possible if other resources are released through e.g. spin-offs, licensing or selling. Letting go of what has been developed internally is difficult for the individuals involved and for the organizations that have invested into projects which are earmarked as spin-offs. Without appropriate processes to evaluate and release what is no longer needed, organizations will find it difficult to make good decisions on how to define core competencies and elaborate them.

Finally, changing organizational routines towards more integration of external resources implies finding a balance between incremental and revolutionary change. In what follows, several models of integration are outlined.

## Basic models of integration

Resources, internal and external, are the foundation of competitive advantage. Opening to include strategic resources from external sources while maintaining internal strengths is an important organizational capability. Sensing which resources matter, absorbing them and utilizing them appropriately,[53] or in other words, exploring and exploiting[54] resources unimpeded by their origin is an organizational design issue. Addressing this issue helps companies to increase their performance and stay resilient. Here we define and provide examples of models that seek a balance, i.e. stable integration, modular integration and dynamic integration.

*Stable integration* is visible when companies select and internalize resources without changing the new combination. Seeking synergies by bringing together different departments in the pharmaceutical industry e.g. Eisai's R&D groups are now focussing on oncology and Alzheimer's disease. Restructuring and reducing headcounts following acquisitions often results in combining resources in novel ways and can establish a new view of the world. Consider the series of acquisitions in the pharmaceutical industry. Recently also leading manufacturers of generics such as Israel's Teva, headquartered in Amsterdam, have started to integrate traditional pharmaceutical companies such as Baxter International to internalize their manufacturing base, the sales network and research capabilities.

*Modular integration* is the purposeful selection of resources that are better sourced externally. In the Opening Case and the Strategic Focus (see page 133 and 138), Muji and Alessi have integrated source-specific elements of their value chains from the outside. P&G taps into the community of scientists, researchers and

**Adaptive resistance**

Adaptive resistance (e.g. humour, anticipation) is related to habitual reluctance or the lack of incentives (e.g. political games), and it is constructive when compared to maladaptive (e.g. dissociation, denial, obstruction).

**Models of integration**

Basic models of integration describe broad, alternative approaches to integrate internal and external knowledge.

**Stable integration**

For stable integration companies select and internalize resources without trying to change the new combination.

**Modular integration**

Modular integration is the purposeful selection of resources that are better sourced externally to substitute specific elements of the original value chain.

**Dynamic integration**

Compared to stable and modular integration that result in more structural solutions, dynamic integration resembles a process.

## KEY DEBATE

# Market efficiency

Markets are highly efficient coordinating mechanisms that bring supply and demand together. The interactions between buyers and suppliers are regulated by customs, rules and most importantly, contracts that are enforceable. The market efficiency concept suggests that most economic interactions preferably utilize markets or coordination mechanisms that are closed to markets. This notion implies integration of external with internal resources based on contracts is most efficient (without much need for firms). This chapter suggests that internal resources need to be integrated with external resources to achieve the highest levels of competitiveness. Relating this to the market efficiency idea would suggest integrating primarily by using markets and shrinking the firm to maximize efficiency by exploiting market mechanisms.

Economists Coase and Williamson received Nobel prizes for developing and elaborating transaction cost theory, which explains the existence of firms by suggesting that organizations exist because transaction within firms can have lower costs than in external markets. In relation to this chapter, their findings would suggest that internalizing resources for integration incurs lower transaction costs than contracting externally. Hence, their view could be interpreted as a call for large organizations and smaller roles for markets.

While efficient organizations and efficient markets may be two extreme views on how to organize resource integration, they illustrate extreme positions taken in the ongoing debate on the question: Where should the boundaries of organizations lie? When should organizations internalize the resources they need or should they seek integration through market mechanisms?

## Questions

1 Where are the boundaries of organizations?

2 Where should these boundaries lie?

3 How can organizations find their best boundaries?

4 When should organizations internalize the resources they need?

---

inventors worldwide to accelerate the flow of ideas, yet it relies fully on internal strengths in marketing, logistics and sales. Modular integration is easier to revise and change than stable integration. Often modules that source ideas from outside, for instance, compete with other sources from inside that fit the same purpose. Muji, Alessi and P&G all continue to employ people in research, development and design jobs to develop ideas internally – they choose modular integration as an additional approach.

Compared to stable and modular integration that result in more structural solutions, *dynamic integration* resembles a process. Self-organized programmers and engineers motivated to contribute code and time worked on the earliest open source projects, such as Linux, without relation to the business world. By the mid-1990s, companies such as IBM embraced the concept because of the unrivalled quality and increased productivity. Today accessing external resources is often close to the idea of continued knowledge exchange with the environment. In the examples presented in this chapter, multiple ways including sophisticated social network analyses are employed to facilitate knowledge sharing between organizational members and external people. Expanding the number of alliances, partnerships and collaborations at any point in time, this approach is based on the temporary nature of the relationships. Loyal customers within Muji's pool of collaborators change, the designers working with Alessi do not always work with Alessi, and P&G's portfolio of alliances is dynamically evolving to optimize access to external resources over time, i.e. dynamic integration benefits from internalizing different resources over time with the intention to continuously refresh.

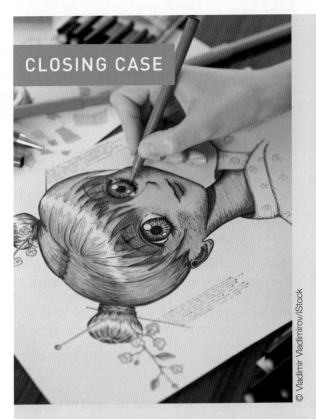

CLOSING CASE

© Vladimir Vladimirov/iStock

# Japanese Manga: publishers and innovation models

A weekly circulation of more than six million hard copies of a magazine is something the publishing industry in 2010 can only dream about. In Japan's publishing industry, Manga emerged as a main source of profits because dynamic integration of external resources (judgement, creativity and skill) have boosted sales of Manga since the 1970s.

The emergence of the Japanese Manga industry can be traced back to Osamu Tezuka and his comic book debut in 1947. The story was called *New Treasure Island*, and was published as a cheap comic book without much editorial oversight and control, in a small niche industry, providing children with what they could afford in early postwar Japan. *New Treasure Island* sold an unprecedented 400000 copies. Tezuka's timely innovations such as the use of 'cinematic techniques' for theme-driven 'story Manga' broadened the Manga market and raising its profitability. Publishers responded immediately and found young artists eager

to imitate Tezuka's revolutionary style and to also become stars in the publishing world. In 1956, Japan's first weekly magazine appeared, starting a boom in weeklies. In 1959 the first children's weeklies followed and Manga quickly came to occupy more than half of the total market share with emphasis shifting from education to exciting entertainment. In the late 1950s and 1960s new genres of more serious so-called theatrical picture, Manga and a new category of Manga magazine, known as youth Manga began to appear. The best among the Manga artists widely recognized as stars started to work for the new youth magazines, which quickly gained market share.

Shueisha Publishing's *Weekly Shônen Jump* founded in 1968, focused on pre-teen readers and became market leader in the early 1970s. *Jump*'s greatest handicap in its first few years – its inability to engage the best-known artists from the established magazines – turned out to be its greatest advantage. While leading magazines employed star artists who demanded freedom, *Jump* could manage unknown artists to produce Manga that met readers' demands. Exhaustive reader surveys conducted on a weekly and ongoing basis linked the magazine's avid readers with the production process. While the readership was growing and changing *Jump* kept a close watch on the changing needs and moods—and its weekly cycle allowed it to swiftly react to changes. Over the years, Manga competitions for readers became a mechanism for self-selection of aspiring Manga artists to present themselves to expert juries and begin their careers. The readers were also asked to evaluate preselected amateurs' work and propose award winners. This dynamic way of integrating young talent, readers and publishers together in a positive, reinforcing spiral helped to energize and grow the market for many years. *Jump* produced blockbuster hits one after the other, such as the long-running Dragonball, by Akira Toriyama, and Slam Dunk, by Takehiko Inoue. By 1980, *Jump*'s announced circulation was three million, reaching four million in 1985, five million in 1988, and 6 200 000 in 1994 – about 1.5 times and 5 times greater than their closest competitors. After the first run in a series format, the most successful series are then sold again in different formats such as booklets, TV animations, even TV series mostly with merchandising.

The success of changing the way Manga is produced and consumed has strongly influenced many

generations of readers. While in recent years the cir-
culations have plunged due to the Internet and other
factors, the former Japanese prime minister Taro Aso,
a self-declared Manga fan, announced the establishment of a 'Nobel prize' for foreign Manga comic artists, the 'International MANGA Award'. Aso first
suggested the idea in a policy speech he gave in
Tokyo's Akihabara district, the Mecca of Japan's
'otaku' or nerd subculture that cherishes Manga and
'anime' animation movies.

**Sources**: Sabin, R. (2001) *Comics, Comix & Graphic Novels:
A History of Comic Art*, London: Phaidon; Reinmoeller, P.
(1999) "Internationalization of Japanese Contents: Marketing
of 'Akira', A Global Manga Classic" in *The Age of Marketing
Innovation: Product Development Innovation*, Shimaguchi,
M., Takeuchi, H., Katahira, H. and Ishi, J. (eds.), Tokyo: Yu-
hikaku, 388–414 (in Japanese); Schodt, F. L. (1986) *Manga!
Manga!: The World of Japanese Comics*, Tokyo: Kodansha;
Schodt, F. L. (1996) *Dreamland Japan: Writings on Modern
Manga*, Berkeley: Stonebridge Press.

## Questions

**1** Two models of creating Manga are mentioned in the
closing case. One relies on well-known artists, the
other does not? Which is more successful? Why?

**2** Which external resources helped *Jump* to produce
blockbuster Manga?

**3** How does *Jump* identify strategic resources? How
does *Jump* tie these resources into its production process? How does *Jump* exploit blockbusters?

**4** Which internal resources are combined with external
resources? What are the benefits of the internal and
external resources?

**5** In the US comic artists are employees of comic publishers and their products are owned by the companies. In Japan the copyright lies with the artist. What
are the consequences of these differences? What is
necessary for dynamic integration to emerge in the
international arena?

After studying the external and internal environment (see Chapters 2 and 3) and the need to integrate
external resources (as explained in this chapter), the firm has the knowledge required to select corporate-
level strategies and organizational form to realize its goals. We describe different corporate-level and organizational form strategies in the next chapter.

## SUMMARY

- In the global business environment, internal resources can create a competitive advantage. However,
  internal resources are less often a source of sustainable competitive advantage in hypercompetition.
  In the current landscape, the resources, capabilities and core competencies in the firm's internal
  organization are likely to have a positive influence on its performance when they are combined with
  complementary resources in the external environment.

- Focusing on core competencies or the environment leads to lock-in effects that prevent firms from
  seeing and using highly complementary assets. Integrating internal and external resources offers a
  way to avoid these limitations. The cost is the difficulty of managing internal and external resources
  at the same time.

- The organizations that have build strategic competitiveness and enjoy above-average returns rely on internal
  as well as external resources, i.e. they have abandoned rigid adherence to the closed innovation model.

- Open innovation increases the range of resources of different origins that can be successfully
  employed for organizational value creation. At the same time this openness shifts companies'
  attention to options (e.g. licensing, spin-off) to capture value from ideas and technologies they
  cannot or do not want to pursue themselves.

- An important source of external resources is (loyal) customers who provide critical insights on how
  to improve the product. Connecting to (intrinsically) motivated customers promises the capture of
  emergent opportunities to successfully manage growth.

- Creative individuals or communities of users who experiment to improve and develop existing
  products further (also called lead users) can be a very important source of innovation. With large

numbers of limited and diverse tasks the potential pool of participants in open source projects increases and can contribute much to the innovation of goods, software and services.

■ Competitive advantage can be sustained by understanding that the external environment is resource rich, change need not be threatening and strategic bundles of heterogeneous resources and capabilities lie outside the organizational boundaries.

■ The most needed strategic assets to leverage internal resources are often possessed by other organizations and firms. Capabilities to gain access to and integrate complementary assets enable successful strategy development and implementation.

■ Firms create value by innovatively bundling and leveraging resources and capabilities, and recruiting external resources. In doing so, they are able to increase the willingness to pay beyond what they alone could have achieved by developing cooperation with other companies to jointly exploit shared resources. In particular, the skill with which companies integrate home country resources with host country resources influences the success of their internationalization efforts.

■ Under the umbrella of open innovation, technology is generally emphasized. While technology is important, such emphasis leads to underestimating the importance of new ways of managing and organizing. This kind of non-technological innovation, and also management innovation, is particularly important for the competitiveness of companies.

■ Paying attention to the insights at the periphery is important but also paradoxical. Firms need to distribute their attention optimally between core competencies and the periphery. Managers need to make clear choices about the degree of openness and focus to best enhance, protect and exploit internal resources.

■ After setting the organizational conditions for open innovation, companies need to develop absorptive capacity to influence the company's performance, innovativeness and flexibility. Sensing which resources matter, absorbing them and utilizing (or exploring and exploiting resources) is an issue of strategy implementation. The ability to learn and create knowledge depends to a great extent on the ability to value the new external knowledge, i.e. prior knowledge and experience.

■ Alliances, joint ventures and M&A are traditional approaches with a common core: expanding an organization's pool of resources by gaining access to external resources. Absorptive capacity, or the ability to learn, underpins the successful implementation of practical alternatives to integrating knowledge such as alliances, M&A, lead users, ventures etc.

■ Other models that seek a balance between exploring and exploiting include stable integration, modular integration and dynamic integration.

■ Habits or the lack of the right incentives can lead to adaptive resistance to change and maladaptation (e.g. obstruction).

## REVIEW QUESTIONS

1   Why is it important for a firm to study and understand how internal resources relate to external resources?

2   What are benefits and costs related to using internal and external resources?

3   Explain the difference between open innovation and closed innovation.

4   What are the traditional ways of integrating external resources?

5   What are their advantages? What are their disadvantages?

6   Discuss additional advantages and disadvantages of stable integration, modular integration and dynamic integration?

7   What are the steps companies have to make to benefit most from external resources, i.e. absorb external resources?

8   Discuss which departments or groups in organizations contribute to a company's absorptive capacity. Taking new insight into an organization and utilizing it requires organizational change. Describe the consequences of internalizing radically new knowledge.

9   Can you give examples for stable integration, modular integration and dynamic integration that have failed? What can we learn from them?

## DISCUSSION QUESTIONS

1   Is it possible to understand external resources? What is needed to understand what is external?

2   Using internal and external resources may require different skills. How can outsourcing help and how does it hinder integration?

3   What are the benefits of boundaries? Give examples of boundaries that can be open and closed at the same time.

4   The war for talent is a phenomenon that describes the increasing competition for employees. How does the war for talent create new boundaries and how does it tear down existing boundaries?

5   A key question for strategic management is how to achieve ambidexterity, the simultaneous pursuit of innovation and efficiency, which is discussed later in the book. How does open innovation relate to innovation and efficiency?

6   *America's Got Talent, Britain's Got Talent* and we believe the country you call home has talent. It may even have similar TV shows in which amateurs volunteer to participate in contests. Often, the more successful contestants are the winners and have the opportunity to start a new career. Is this form of television contest an open innovation approach to generate new content? Is reality TV open innovation? Discuss.

7   YouTube and similar websites have millions of short video clips mostly uploaded by amateurs. The number of new uploads is increasingly difficult to scan. How can media firms leverage on the availability of such clips utilizing an open innovation approach?

## FURTHER READING

There is much discussion on what makes character. Recently, Steven Pinker in the *Blank Slate* (2003, Penguin) analyses lucidly to what extent people are influenced by their genetic make-up and to what extend they are shaped by the external environment and resources they are able to exploit during their growth.

Google is a company with a unique business model. Reading *The Google Story* (2005, Thomas Arnold Publishing) by David A. Vise, updated for Google's 10th anniversary, provides a fascinating view on a company that turned external resources, i.e. the agglomeration of searches by users into a source of profitable growth. Facebook is also a wonderful illustration of a dynamic model of how to integrate external resources.

For viewing, Steve Jobs' commencement speech at Stanford University is available on youtube.com. It is a moving speech in which he explains his personal journey to success by showing how "connecting the dots", i.e. how internal and external resources, came together for him over time.

# EXPERIENTIAL EXERCISES

## Exercise 1: Customizing products and co-creating services

The focus of this chapter is on understanding how integrating external resources and capabilities create competitive advantage. The importance of market orientation e.g., for new product development is widely recognized. Developing open organizations is less common. Where are the boundaries between focusing on customers in developing products and developing organizations that co-create services with customers? This exercise explores the differences between customization and opening the organization for a specific target customer group. Many European countries' populations are ageing rapidly. Similar to Japan, Italy and Germany have growing numbers of people in the age group 65+ who are active and affluent. Even the Chinese population pyramid is structured in ways that makes the ageing population an important mid-term issue that companies need to address. Many product categories are part of our daily lives and of the senior members of our societies, e.g., durables such as cars, furniture, white goods, and fast moving consumer goods such as detergent, shampoo, chocolate bars, ice cream, or services such as delivery, maintenance, or health care.

As a group, select a specific product or service. You may choose durable, fast moving consumer goods, or services that you identify on your own. Using library and Internet resources, prepare a brief PowerPoint presentation that covers the following questions and your proposed solutions:

- How can the company providing the product/ service customize its offering for typical 65 years and older seniors? How would the product/service need to change?

- Are any firms presently using a similar approach to target senior customers? If so, how does their approach differ from your proposals?

## Exercise 2: Resource dependence role play

Resource dependence is a conceptual framework first proposed by Jeffrey Pfeffer (Stanford University) that explains the success of an organization with its ability to secure access to external resources. External resources may be more or less important in different industries.

With this exercise, you should use ideas, tools and concepts from the chapter on how firms in different industries manage their resource dependency. Working as a group, select two companies one each from the following groups of industries (A: extraction, forestry, fishing; B: energy generation (fossil fuels), manufacturing, pharmaceuticals). As a group, select one specific company active in the industries that belong to group A and one from group B.

1   Using library and Internet resources, prepare a brief PowerPoint presentation that covers the following questions and your proposed solutions. What changes would you recommend to its portfolio of resources and capabilities?

- What are the external resources the companies need to operate? What are the external resources the companies need to compete successfully? What do the companies of your choice do to secure access? What could they do to improve long-term access?

- What do the firms do to maintain access to the resources they need to operate? What do the firms do to maintain access to the resources they need to compete successfully? What do the companies of your choice do to secure success? What could they do to improve long-term performance?

- Compare your findings between the firms.

2   During the first part of this exercise you may have had some doubts or even discussions about whether some of the ways firms act to manage their resource dependency are ethical or legal. Each team picks the practice or proposal that generated most doubt and each team splits into two subgroups. Subgroup One prepares for 10 minuntes to develop a proposal in support of more investment into the practice/proposal. Subgroup Two prepares for 10 minutes to develop a proposal to terminate all investments into the practice/proposal. The two subgroups engage in the role play arguing for and against the practice/proposal in question. Discuss within each group what investment you would recommend. If time allows, each team reports back to the plenary about chosen practice, the discussion and outcome.

## VIDEO CASE

### Wikipedia founder Jimmy Wales in 2005 and 2009

www.cengage.co.uk/volberda/students/video_cases

Jimmy Wales has created Wikipedia and changed our lives. In the first clip he explains how he created it in 2005. In the second clip, four years later, he reflects on Wikipedia, the rapid increase of Wikipedia's importance, and the promise and challenges.

Jimmy Wales talks about competition and his drive to succeed. Before you watch the video consider the following concepts from the text and be prepared to address the following questions:

### Concepts

- External resources
- Modular integration
- Intrinsic motivation
- Open innovation
- Resource integration

- Boundary spanners
- Knowledge processes

### Questions

1  What is Wikipedia's vision and mission?

2  What is its strategic goal?

3  How does Wikipedia internationalize?

4  Describe the open innovation model of Wikipedia.

5  How does Wikipedia integrate external knowledge?

6  How can firms use Wikipedia (and its model) to achieve their goals?

7  How does Wikipedia manage to stay open and maintain control of its core competence? What is the core?

8  How do the perspectives of the "inclusionists" and "deletionists" relate to open innovation?

## NOTES

1. J. G. Covin and M. P. Miles, 2007, "Strategic use of corporate venturing", *Entrepreneurship Theory and Practice*, 31: 183–207; R. R. Wiggins and T. W. Ruefli, 2002, "Sustained competitive advantage: Temporal dynamics and the incidence of persistence of superior economic performance", *Organization Science*, 13: 82–105; M. Baaij, P. Reinmoeller, N. Niepce, 2007, "Sustained superior performance in changing environments: Towards a synthesis and a research agenda", *Strategic Change* 16: 87–95; H. W. Volberda, 1996, "Toward the flexible form: How to remain vital in hypercompetitive environments", *Organization Science*, 7(4): 359–387.

2. P. Ghemawat, 2002, "Competition and business strategy in historical perspective", *Business History Review*, Spring 76(1): 37–74.

3. R. T. Crook, D. J. Ketchen, J. G. Combs and S. Y. Todd, 2008, "Strategic resources and performance: A meta-analysis", *Strategic Management Journal*, 29: 1141–1154; N. T. Sheehan and N. J. Foss, 2007, "Enhancing the prescriptiveness of the resource-based view through Porterian activity analysis", *Management Decision*, 45: 450–461; S. Dutta, M. J. Zbaracki and M. Bergen, 2003, "Pricing process as a capability: A resource-based perspective", *Strategic Management Journal*, 24: 615–630.

4. M. Osterloh and B. Frey, 2000, "Motivation, knowledge transfer, and organizational forms", *Organization Science*, 11(5): 238–250.

5. E. von Hippel, 2001, "Innovating by user communities: Learning from open-source software", MIT *Sloan Management Review*, Summer, 82–86; E. von Hippel and G. von Krogh, 2006, "Free revealing and the private-collective model for innovation incentives", *R&D Management*, 36(3): 295–306.

6. C. Baldwin and K. Clark, 2006, "The architecture of participation: Does code architecture mitigate free riding in the open source", *Management Science*, 52(7): 1116–1127; K. R. Kakhani and J. Panetta, 2007, "The principles of distributed innovation", Berkman Center for Internet and Society, Harvard Law School, Research Publication No. 2007–1.

7. D. G. Sirmon, M. A. Hitt and R. D. Ireland, 2007, "Managing firm resources in dynamic markets to create value: Looking inside the black box", *Academy of Management Review*, 32: 273–292.

8. D. Teece, 2007, "Explicating dynamic capabilities", *Strategic Management Journal*, 28: 1319–1350.

9. D. Rigby and B. Bilodeau, 2009, *Management Tools and Trends*, Bain & Company.

10. Ocado website http://www.ocado.com.

11. A. W. King, 2007, "Disentangling interfirm and intrafirm causal ambiguity: A conceptual model of causal ambiguity and sustainable competitive advantage", *Academy of Management Review*, 32: 156–178; J. Shamsie, 2003, "The context of dominance: An industry-driven framework for exploiting reputation", *Strategic Management Journal*, 24: 199–215; H. W. Volberda, 2003, "Strategic flexibility: Creating dynamic competitive advantages", Ch. 32 in: D. Faulkner and A. Campbell (eds.), *The Oxford Handbook of Strategy*, Oxford: Oxford University Press, 939–998.

12. U. Ljungquist, 2007, "Core competency beyond identification: Presentation of a model", *Management Decision*, 45: 393–402; M. Makhija, 2003, "Comparing the resource-based and market-based view of the firm: Empirical evidence from Czech privatization", *Strategic Management Journal*, 24: 433–451; F. A. J. van den Bosch, H. W. Volberda and M. de Boer, 1999, "Co-evolution of firm absorptive capacity and knowledge environment: Organizational forms and combinative capabilities", *Organization Science*, 10(5): 551–568.

13. R. D. Ireland and J. W. Webb, 2007, "Strategic entrepreneurship: Creating competitive advantage through streams of innovation", *Business Horizons*, 50: 49–59; P. Reinmoeller and N. van Baardwijk, 2005, "The link between innovation and resilience", MIT *Sloan Management Review*, Summer, 46(4): 61–65; J. H. Burgers, F. A. J. Van den Bosch and H. W. Volberda, 2008, "The Impact of corporate venturing on a firm's competence modes", in: R. Mertens, A. Heene, and R. Sanchez (eds.), Competence-Building and Leveraging in Inter organizational Relations, *Advances in Applied Business Strategy*, Oxford, Elsevier, 11: 117–140; T. J. M. Mom, F. A. J. Van den Bosch and H. W. Volberda, 2005, "Managing the tension between competence building and competence leveraging by influencing managerial and organizational determinants of horizontal knowledge exchange", in: *Research in Competence-Based Management*, 2: 165–191, R. Sanchez and A. Heene (eds.), *A Focused Issue on Managing Knowledge Assets and Organizational Learning*, Oxford: Elsevier; J. S. Sidhu, H. R. Commandeur and H. W. Volberda, 2007, "The multifaced nature of exploration and exploitation: Value of supply, demand, and spatial search for innovation", *Organization Science*, 18(1): 20–38.

14. M. A. Peteraf and J. B. Barney, 2003, "Unraveling the resource-based tangle", *Managerial and Decision Economics*, 24: 309–323; J. B. Barney, 2001, "Is the resource-based 'view' a useful perspective for strategic management research? Yes", *Academy of Management Review*, 26: 41–56.

15. C. K. Prahalad and V. Ramaswamy, 2004, *The Future of Competition: Co-creating Unique Value with Customers*, Boston, MA: Harvard Business School Press.

16. P. Ghemawat, 2007, *Global Strategy in a World of Differences*, Boston, MA: Harvard Business School Press.

17. P. Reinmoeller and M. Baaij, 2010, "The lost decade: Rethinking the presence and performance of Japanese firms in the Fortune Global 500", *Hitotsubashi Business Review*, Autumn, 58(2): 44–56.

18. B. Witcher, V. S. Chau and P. Harding, 2008, "Dynamic capabilities: Top executive audits and hoshin kanri at Nissan South Africa", *International Journal of Operations & Production Management*, 28(6): 540–561; A. Taylor, 2002, "Nissan's turnaround artists", *Fortune*, February, 18: 47–51; T. Burt and D. Ibison, 2001, "Interview: Carlos Ghosn", *Financial Times*, http://www.ft.com, October 25; N. Shirouzu, J. B. White and T. Zaun, 2000, "A revival at Nissan shows there's hope for Japan Inc.", *Asian Wall Street Journal*, November, 17(1).

19. H. Simon, 2009, *Hidden Champions of the 21st Century: Success Strategies of Unknown World Market Leaders*, New York: Springer.

20. D. Teece, 2007, "Explicating dynamic capabilities", *Strategic Management Journal* 28: 1319–1350; P. W. L. Vlaar, F. A. J. Van den Bosch and H. W. Volberda, 2005, "On the relation between information technology and interorganizational competitive advantage: A competence perspective", in: *Advances in Applied Business Strategy*, 8: 45–68, R. Sanchez and A. Heene (eds.), *Competence Perspectives on Managing Interfirm Interactions*, Oxford: Elsevier.

21. D. Ancona, P, Goodman, B. Lawrence and M. Tushman, 2001, "Time: A New Research Lens", *The Academy of Management Review*, 26(4): 645–663.

22. E. Danneels, 2008, "Organizational antecedents of second-order competences", *Strategic Management Journal*, 29: 519–543; J. B. Barney, 2001, "Is the resource-based 'view' a useful perspective for strategic management research? Yes", *Academy of Management Review*, 26: 41–56; D. Teece, 2007, "Explicating Dynamic Capabilities", *Strategic Management Journal*, 28: 1319–1350; K. M. Eisenhardt and J. Martin, 2000, "Dynamic Capabilities: What are they?", *Strategic Management Journal*, 21(10–11): 1105–1121; L. Välikangas, 2010, *The Resilient Organization: How Adaptive Cultures Thrive Even When Strategy Fails*, New York: McGraw Hill.

23. S. Kaplan, 2008, "Cognition, capabilities, and incentives: Assessing firm response to the fiber-optic revolution", *Academy of Management Journal*, 51: 672–695; K. J. Mayer and R. M. Salomon, 2006, "Capabilities, contractual hazards, and governance: Integrating resource-based and transaction cost perspective", *Academy of Management Journal*, 49: 942–959.

24. S. K. McEvily and B. Chakravarthy, 2002, "The persistence of knowledge-based advantage: An empirical test for product performance and technological knowledge", *Strategic Management Journal*, 23: 285–305.

25. A. M. Brandenburger and B. Nalebuff, 1996, *Co-opetition: A Revolution Mindset that Combines Competition and Co-operation … The Game Theory Strategy That's Changing the Game of Business*, New York: Currency Doubleday.

26. J. Barthelemy, 2008, "Opportunism, knowledge, and the performance of franchise chains", *Strategic Management Journal*, 29: 1451–1463; J. L. Morrow, Jr., D. G. Sirmon,

M. A. Hitt and T. R. Holcomb, 2007, "Creating value in the face of declining performance: Firm strategies and organizational recovery," *Strategic Management Journal*, 28: 271–283.

27. E. Danneels, 2007, "The process of technological competence leveraging", *Strategic Management Journal*, 28: 511–533; Z. Kwee, F. A. J. Van den Bosch and H. W. Volberda, 2008, "Coevolutionary competence in the realm of corporate longevity: How long-lived firms strategically renew themselves", in: *Research in Competence-Based Management*, R. Sanchez (ed.), A Focused Issue on Fundamental Issues in Competence Theory Development, Bingley: Emerald, 4: 281–313; H. W. Volberda and Ch. Baden-Fuller, 1999, "Strategic Renewal and competence building: Four dynamic mechanisms", in: G. Hamel, C. K. Prahalad, H. Thomas and D. O'Neal (eds.), *Strategic Flexibility: Managing in a Turbulent Economy*, Chichester, 371–389; M. G. Baaij, F. A. J Van den Bosch and H. W. Volberda, 2005, "The Impact of management consulting firms on building and leveraging clients' competences", in: *Advances in Applied Business Strategy*, 8: 27–44, R. Sanchez and A. Heene (eds.), *Competence Perspectives on Managing Interfirm Interactions*, Oxford: Elsevier.

28. J. L. Morrow, D. G. Sirmon, M. A. Hitt and T. R. Holcomb 2007, "Creating value in the face of declining performance: Firm strategies and organizational recovery", *Strategic Management Journal*, 28(3): 271–283; G. Hawawini, V. Subramanian and P. Verdin, 2003, "Is performance driven by industry- or firm-specific factors? A new look at the evidence", *Strategic Management Journal*, 24: 1–16.

29. J. Woiceshyn and L. Falkenberg, 2008, "Value creation in knowledge-based firms: Aligning problems and resources", *Academy of Management Perspectives*, 22(2): 85–99; M. R. Haas and M. T. Hansen, 2005, "When using knowledge can hurt performance: The value of organizational capabilities in a management consulting company", *Strategic Management Journal*, 26: 1–24.

30. O. Gottschalg and M. Zollo, 2007, "Interest alignment and competitive advantage", *Academy of Management Review*, 32: 418–437.

31. T. J. M. Mom, F. A. J. Van Den Bosch and H. W. Volberda, 2009, "Understanding variation in manager's ambidexterity: Investigating direct and interaction effects of formal structural and personal coordination mechanisms", *Organization Science*, 20(4), 812–828; C. O'Reilly and M. Tushman, 2008, "Ambidexterity as a Dynamic Capability: Resolving the Innovator's Dilemma." *Research in Organizational Behaviour* 28: 185–206; P. Reinmoeller, 2011, *The Ambidextrous Organization*, Routledge.

32. H. Chesbrough, 2003, *Open Innovation: The New Imperative for Creating and Profiting from Technology*, Boston, MA: Harvard Business School Press; E. Enkel, O. Gassman and H. Chesbrough, 2009, "Open R&D and open innovation: exploring the phenomenon", *R&D Management*, 39(4): 311–316; K. Laursen and A. Salter, 2006, "Open for Innovation: The Role of Openness in Explaining Innovation Performance among U.K. Manufacturing Firms", *Strategic Management Journal*,

27: 131–150; U. Lichtenthaler, 2009, "Outbound open innovation and its effect on firm performance: examining environmental influences", *R&D Management*, 39(4): 317–330; P. Seybold, 2006, *Outside Innovation: How Your Customers Will Co-design Your Company's Future*, New York: HarperCollins; J. West, W. Vanhaverbeke and H. Chesbrough, 2006, "Open innovation: A research agenda", in *Open Innovation: Researching a New Paradigm*, H. Chesbrough, W. Vanhaverbeke and J. West (eds.), 285–307, Oxford: Oxford University Press; F. T. Piller and D. Walcher, 2006, "Toolkits for idea competitions: A novel method to integrate users in new product development", *R&D Management*, 36(3): 307–318.

33. R. A. D'Aveni, 1994, *Hypercompetition: Managing the Dynamics of Strategic Maneuvering*, New York: The Free Press; J. H. Burgers, F. A. J. Van den Bosch and H. W. Volberda, 2008, "The Impact of corporate venturing on a firm's competence modes", in: Competence-Building and Leveraging in Inter organizational Relations, R. Martens, A. Heene and R. Sanchez (eds.) *Advances in Applied Business Strategy*, Oxford, Elsevier, 11: 117–140.

34. M. W. Cohen and D. A. Levinthal, 1990, "Absorptive capacity:A new perspective on learning and innovation", *Administrative Science Quarterly*, 35: 128–152; S. A. Zahra and G. George, 2002, "Absorptive capacity: A review, reconceptualization, and extension", *Academy of Management Review*, 27: 185–203; H.W. Volberda, N. Foss and M. Lyles, 2010, "Absorbing the concept of absorptive capacity: How to realize its potential in the organization field", *Organization Science*, 21(4): 931–951.

35. P. Trott and D. Hartman, 2009, "Why open innovation is old wine in new bottles", *International Journal of Innovation Management*, 13(4): 715–736; E. von Hippel, 2007, *Democratizing Innovation*, Cambridge, MA: MIT Press; http://www.mit.edu/evhippel/www/democ.htm; J. Tidd,1993, "Development of novel products through intraorganizational and interorganizational networks", *Journal of Product Innovation Management*, 12: 307–322; T. J. Allen and W. M. Cohen, 1969, "Information flow in research and development laboratories", *Administrative Science Quarterly*, 14(1): 12–19; W. M. Cohen and D. A. Levinthal, 1990, "A new perspective on learning and innovation", *Administrative Science Quarterly*, 35(1): 128–152; H. W. Volberda and F. A. J. Van den Bosch, 2005, "Why management matters most", *European Business Forum*, 22: 36–41; I. G. Vaccaro, J. J. P. Jansen, F. A. J. Van den Bosch and H. W. Volberda, "Management innovation and leadership: The moderating role of organizational size", *Journal of Management Studies*, forthcoming.

36. J. Birkinshaw, M. Mol and G. Hamel, 2008, "Management innovation", *Academy of Management Journal*, 33(4): 825–845; I. G. Vaccaro, J. J. P. Jansen, F. A. J. Van den Bosch and H. W. Volberda, "Management innovation and leadership: The moderating role of organizational size", *Journal of Management Studies*, forthcoming.

37. Y. Deutsch, T. Keil and T. Laamanen, 2007, "Decision making in acquisitions: The effect of outside directors"

compensation on acquisition patterns', *Journal of Management*, 33: 30–56.

38. P. O. Karlsson and G. L. Neilson, 2009, "CEO succession 2008: Stability in the storm", *strategy+business*, Summer, reprint, 55: 2–12.

39. S. J. Carson, A. Madhok and T. Wu, 2006, "Uncertainty, opportunism, and governance: The effects of volatility and ambiguity on formal and relational contracting", *Academy of Management Journal*, 49: 1058–1077; R. E. Hoskisson and L. W. Busenitz, 2001, "Market uncertainty and learning distance in corporate entrepreneurship entry mode choice", in: M. A. Hitt, R. D. Ireland, S. M. Camp and D. L. Sexton (eds.), *Strategic Entrepreneurship: Creating a New Integrated Mindset*, Oxford, UK: Blackwell Publishers, 151–172.

40. C. M. Fiol and E. J. O'Connor, 2003, "Waking up! Mindfulness in the face of bandwagons", *Academy of Management Review*. 28: 54–70:

41. Y. Doz, J. Santos and P. Williamson, 2001, *From Global to Metanational: How Companies Win in the Knowledge Economy*, Harvard Business School Press.

42. P. J. H. Schoemaker and G. S. Day, 2009, "How to Make Sense of Weak Signals", *MIT Sloan Management Review*, 50(3): 81–89; S. G. Winter, 2004, "Specialized perception, selection, and strategic surprise: Learning from the moths and bees", *Long Range Planning*, 37, 163–169.

43. G. S. Day and P. H. Schoemaker, 2006, *Peripheral Vision: Detecting the Weak Signals That Will Make or Break Your Company*, Harvard Business School Press.

44. Y. Doz, J. Santos and P. Williamson, 2001, *From Global to Metanational: How Companies Win in the Knowledge Economy*, Boston, MA: Harvard Business School Press; F. A. J van den Bosch, H. W. Volberda and M. de Boer, 1999, "Co-evolution of firm absorptive capacity and knowledge environment: Organizational forms and combinative capabilities", *Organization Science*, 10 (5): 551–568.

45. M. Jenkins, 2010, "Technological discontinuities and competitive advantage: A historical perspective on Formula One motor racing", *Journal of Management Studies*, 47(5): 884–910; S. Tallman, M. Jenkins, N. Henry and S. Pinch, 2004, "Knowledge, clusters and competitive advantage", *Academy of Management Review*, 29: 258–271; F. A. J. van den Bosch, R. van Wijk and H. W. Volberda, 2003, "Absorptive capacity: Antecedents, models, and outcomes", Ch. 14 in: M. Easterby-Smith and M. A. Lyles, (eds.), *Handbook of Organizational Learning and Knowledge Management,* Oxford: Blackwell, 278–301; J. J. P. Jansen, F. A. J Van den Bosch and H. W. Volberda, 2005, "Managing potential and realized absorptive capacity: How do organizational antecedents matter?", *Academy of Management Journal,* 48 (6): 999–1015; M. W. Huygens, C. Baden-Fuller, F. A. J. Van den Bosch and H. W. Volberda, 2001, "Coevolution of firm capabilities and industry competition: Investigating the Music Industry 1877–1997", *Organization Studies*, 22(6): 971–1011.

46. See reference number 34 above. G. Todorova and B. Durisin, 2007, "Absorptive capacity: Valuing a reconceptualization", *Academy of Management Review*, 22(3): 774–796; H. W. Volberda, N. Foss and M. Lyles, 2010, "Absorbing the concept of absorptive capacity: How to realize its potential in the organization field", *Organization Science*, 21(4): 931–951; F. A. J. Van den Bosch, H. W. Volberda and M. De Boer, 1999, "Coevolution of firm absorptive capacity and knowledge environment: Organizational forms and combinative capabilities", *Organization Science*, 10(5): 551–568.

47. O. Gassmann, P. Sandmeier and C. H. Wecht, 2006, "Extreme customer innovation in the frontend: Learning from a new software paradigm", *International Journal of Technology Management*, 33(1): 46–66.

48. I. Nonaka and P. Reinmoeller, 2002, "Knowledge creation and utilization: Promoting dynamic systems of creative routines" in: *Creating Value: Winners in the New Business Environment*, M. A. Hitt, R. Amit, C. E. Lucier and R. D. Nixon (eds.), 104–127.

49. N. Sakkab, 2002, "Connect & Develop complements Research & Develop at P&G", *Research Technology Management,* March–April, 45(2): 38–45; P&G Annual Report, 2006; L. Huston and N. Sakkab, 2006, "Connect and Develop: Inside Procter & Gamble's new model for innovation", *Harvard Business Review*, March, 58–66; I. G. Vaccaro, 2010, *Management Innovation: Studies on the role of internal change agents*, Rotterdam: ERIM PhD Series in Management.

50. H. Chesbrough, 2003, *Open Innovation: The New Imperative for Creating and Profiting from Technology*, Boston, MA: Harvard Business School Press.

51. W. H. Bovey and A. Hede, 2000, "Resistance to organizational change: The role of defence mechanisms", *Journal of Managerial Psychology*, 16(7): 543–548.

52. S. Winter and G. Szulanski, 2001, "Replication as strategy", *Organization Science*, 12(6): 730–743; M. De Boer, F. A. J. Van den Bosch and H. W. Volberda, 1999, "Managing organizational knowledge integration in the emerging multimedia complex", *Journal of Management Studies*, 36(3): 379–398.

53. D. Teece, 2007, "Explicating dynamic capabilities", *Strategic Management Journal*, 28: 1319–1350; K. Eisenhardt and J. Martin, 2000, "Dynamic capabilities: What are they?", *Strategic Management Journal*, 21(10–11): 1105–1121; J. S. Sidhu, H. R. Commandeur and H. W. Volberda, 2007, "The multifaced nature of exploration and exploitation: Value of supply, demand, and spatial search for innovation", *Organization Science*, 18 (1): 20–38; J. J. P. Jansen, F. A. J. Van den Bosch and H. W. Volberda, 2006, "Exploratory innovation, exploitative innovation, and performance: Effects of organizational antecedents and environmental moderators", *Management Science*, 52(11): 1661–1674; J. J. P. Jansen, M. P. Tempelaar, F. A. J. Van den Bosch and H. W. Volberda, 2009, "Structural differentiation and ambidexterity: The mediating role of integration mechanisms", *Organization Science,* 20(4): 797–811.

54. J. G. March, 1991, "Exploration and exploitation in organizational learning", *Organization Science*, 2(1), 71–87; M. L. Tushman and C. A. O'Reilly, 1996, "Ambidextrous organizations: Managing evolutionary and revolutionary change", *California Management Review*, 38(4): 8–30; C. A. O'Reilly and M. L. Tushman, 2004, "The ambidextrous organiza-

tion", *Harvard Business Review*, 82(4): 74–81; M. L. Tushman, W. K. Smith, R. C. Wood, G. Westerman and C. A. O'Reilly III, "Organizational designs and innovation streams", *Industrial and Corporate Change*, 19(5): 1331–1366; P. Reinmoeller, 2011, *The Ambidextrous Organization*, Routledge.

# REFINING THE
# STRATEGIC ACTIONS

© Klaas Lingbeek-van Kranen/iStock

**PART II**

# CHAPTER 5

# BUSINESS-LEVEL STRATEGY

## LEARNING OBJECTIVES

Studying this chapter should provide you with the strategic management knowledge needed to:

1  Define business-level strategy.
2  Discuss the relationship between customers and business-level strategies in terms of *who*, *what*, and *how*.
3  Explain the differences between business-level strategies.
4  Use the five forces of competition model to explain how above-average returns can be earned through business-level strategy.
5  Describe the risks of using each of the business-level strategies.

**OPENING CASE**

# Acer Group: using a "bare bones" cost structure to succeed in global PC markets

Established in 1976, Acer Group uses four PC brands – Acer, Gateway, Packard Bell and eMachines – as the foundation for its multi-brand global strategy. Recent data indicate that Acer is the second largest PC seller in the world (with 13.4 per cent market share), behind only Hewlett-Packard (19.9 per cent market share) and having recently pipped Dell (12.9 per cent market share) to this position. These are followed by Lenovo and Toshiba at 8.7 per cent and 5 per cent market share respectively. Acer has over 7000 employees and revenue for 2009 was in excess of €14 billion. Prior to this, Acer's operating profit rose 38 per cent from 2007 to 2008 to roughly €326 million, indicating that Acer was competing very successfully during the global recession.

There is little question as to the business-level strategy Acer uses. Noting that running a business with lower costs is good when markets are growing but that doing so is even better when markets are not growing (which was the case during the global recession), Acer's CEO Gianfranco Lanci remains strongly committed to the cost leadership strategy (this strategy is discussed later in the chapter) as the path to strategic competitiveness and above-average returns for the firm he leads.

According to Lanci, a focus on controlling costs is part of Acer's culture. In his words: "We have always operated on the assumption that costs need to be kept under control. It's a kind of overall culture we have in the company. If you are used to it, you can run low costs without running into trouble." A decision to sell only through retailers and other outlets and to outsource all manufacturing and assembly operations are other actions Acer takes to reduce its costs as it uses the cost leadership strategy. Combined, the distribution channels Acer uses and its outsourcing of operations help to cut overhead costs – research and development and marketing and general and administrative expenses – to 8 per cent of sales, well below HP's 15 per cent and Dell's 14 per cent. Lanci describes the cost savings in the following manner: "We focus 100 per cent on indirect sales, while today most of the people are running direct and indirect at the same time. If you run direct and indirect, you need different setups; by definition, you add costs. We also focus only on consumers and small and midsize businesses. We never said we wanted to address the enterprise segment. This is another big difference."

Because of its lower overhead cost structure, Acer is able to price its products such as netbooks below those of competitors. Relatively new to the PC market, netbooks are relatively small and inexpensive PCs with functionalities below those offered by laptops and desktops. However, their popularity continues to grow. Unlike Dell, HP and Lenovo, Acer quickly entered the netbook market and sold 32 per cent of all netbooks shipped worldwide at the end of 2008.

Acer uses its "bare bones" cost structure as the foundation for pricing its laptops very aggressively. The firm's new ultrathin laptop was expected to have a starting price of just over €500. For products with similar capabilities, the price for the HP product was around €1400 and about €1570 for the Dell product. After observing these prices, an analyst said that Acer was changing "… customers' perception of what you should pay for a computer".

**Sources**: 2009, Acer Group, http://www.acer.com, June 15; Chao, L. (2009) "Acer expects low-cost laptops to lift shipments", *Wall Street Journal Online*, http://www.wsj.com, April 9; Einhorn, B. (2009) "Acer closes in on Dell's No. 2 PC ranking", *BusinessWeek Online*, http://www.businessweek.com, January 15; Einhorn, B. (2009), "How Acer is burning its PC rivals", *BusinessWeek Online*, http://www.businessweek.com, April 7; Einhorn, B. (2009) "Acer boss Lanci takes aim at Dell and HP", *BusinessWeek Online*, http://www.businessweek.com, April 13; Einhorn, B. (2009) "Acer's game-changing PC offensive", *Business-Week*, April 20, 65; Williams, S. (2009) "Essentially cool: Acer's timeline notebooks", *New York Times Online*, http://www.nytimes.com, April 10; 2010, Acer Group, http://www.acer.com, August 9; Kwong, R. (2010) "Acer in push for bigger China share", *Financial Times*, http://www.ft.com, April 29; Wilkins, M. (2009) "Acer takes no. 2 PC rank in Q3 – market returns to annual growth", iSuppli, http://www.isuppli.com, December 3.

## Questions

**1** What are the advantages of the indirect sales approach that Acer employs?

**2** In terms of business strategy, how does this indirect model compare with the historically direct model of Dell?

Increasingly important to a firm's success,[1] strategy is concerned with making choices among two or more alternatives.[2] As we noted in Chapter 1, when choosing a strategy, the firm decides to pursue one course of action instead of others. The choices are influenced by opportunities and threats in the firm's external environment[3] (see Chapter 3) as well as the nature and quality of the resources, capabilities and core competencies in its internal organization[4] (see Chapter 4). As we see in the Opening Case, Acer Group tries to drive its costs lower and lower as the foundation for how it competes in the global PC market. Recently, Acer's success has caused some of its competitors to renew their effort to reduce their costs. Dell Inc. for example, recently announced that it was committed to trimming over €3 billion from its cost structure to improve ability to compete against competitors such as Acer.[5]

The fundamental objective of using any type of strategy (see Figure 1.1) is to gain strategic competitiveness and earn above-average returns.[6] Strategies are purposeful, precede the taking of actions to which they apply, and demonstrate a shared understanding of the firm's vision and mission.[7] Acer's decisions to acquire Gateway and Packard Bell were quite purposeful. Acquiring Packard Bell helped it establish a stronger footprint in Europe while acquiring Gateway helped the firm establish a better foothold in the US market.

An effectively formulated strategy marshals, integrates and allocates the firm's resources, capabilities and competencies so that it will be properly aligned with its external environment.[8] A properly developed strategy also rationalizes the firm's vision and mission along with the actions taken to achieve them.[9] Information about a host of variables including markets, customers, technology, worldwide finance and the changing world economy must be collected and analysed to properly form and use strategies. In the final analysis, sound strategic choices that reduce uncertainty regarding outcomes[10] are the foundation for building successful strategies.[11]

**Business-level strategy**

A business-level strategy is an integrated and coordinated set of commitments and actions the firm uses to gain a competitive advantage by exploiting core competencies in specific product markets.

Business-level strategy, this chapter's focus, is an integrated and coordinated set of commitments and actions the firm uses to gain a competitive advantage by exploiting core competencies in specific product markets.[12] Business-level strategy indicates the choices the firm has made about how it intends to compete in individual product markets. The choices are important because long-term performance is linked to a firm's strategies.[13] Given the complexity of successfully competing in the global economy, the choices about how the firm will compete can be difficult.[14] For example, MySpace, a social networking site, recently reduced its workforce by almost one-third in order to "… rein in costs and contend with fast-growing rival Facebook Inc".[15] Competitive challenges in MySpace's international operations contributed to the difficult decision to reduce the firm's workforce, partly with the purpose of operating more efficiently.[16] At the same time, competitor Facebook's recently announced strong move into additional international markets such as India, challenged MySpace to further adjust or fine tune its strategy as it engages its major competitor in various competitive battles.[17]

Every firm must form and use a business-level strategy. However, every firm may not use all the strategies – corporate-level, acquisition and restructuring, international, and cooperative – that we examine in Chapters 7 to 10. A firm competing in a single-product market area in a single geographic location does not need a corporate-level strategy to deal with product diversity or an international strategy to deal with geographic diversity. In contrast, a diversified firm will use one of the corporate-level strategies as well as a separate business-level strategy for each product market area in which it competes. Every firm – from the local dry cleaner to the multinational corporation – chooses at least one business-level strategy. Thus, business-level strategy is the *core* strategy – the strategy that the firm forms to describe how it intends to compete in a product market.[18]

We discuss several topics to examine business-level strategies. Because customers are the foundation of successful business-level strategies and should never be taken for granted,[19] we present information about customers that is relevant to business-level strategies. In terms of customers, when selecting a business-level strategy the firm determines (1) *who* will be served, (2) *what* needs those target customers have that it will satisfy, and (3) *how* those needs will be satisfied. Selecting customers and deciding which of their needs the firm will try to satisfy, as well as how it will do so, are challenging tasks. Global competition has created many attractive options for customers, thus making it difficult to determine the strategy to best serve them. Effective global competitors have become adept at identifying the needs of customers in different cultures and geographic regions as well as learning how to quickly and successfully adapt the functionality of a firm's good or service to meet those needs.

Descriptions of the purpose of business-level strategies – and of the five business-level strategies – follow the discussion of customers. The five strategies we examine are called generic strategies because they can be used in any organization competing in any industry.[20] Our analysis describes how effective use of each strategy allows the firm to favourably position itself relative to the five competitive forces in the industry (see Chapter 2). In addition, we use the value chain (see Chapter 3) to show examples of the primary and support activities necessary to implement specific business-level strategies. Because no strategy is risk-free,[21] we also describe the different risks the firm may encounter when using these strategies. In Chapter 13, we explain the organizational structures and controls linked with the successful use of each business-level strategy.

> **Generic strategy**
>
> Generic strategy is a strategy that can be used by any organization competing in any industry.

## Customers: their relationship with business-level strategies

Strategic competitiveness results only when the firm satisfies a group of customers by using its competitive advantages as the basis for competing in individual product markets.[22] A key reason firms must satisfy customers with their business-level strategy is that returns earned from relationships with customers are the lifeblood of all organizations.[23]

The most successful companies try to find new ways to satisfy current customers and/or to meet the needs of new customers.[24] Being able to do this can be even more challenging when firms and consumers face challenging economic conditions such as in the recent past. During such times, firms may decide to reduce their workforce to control costs. As mentioned above, MySpace has done this. At issue though is that fewer employees make it harder for companies to meet individual customers" needs and expectations. In these instances, some suggest that firms should follow several courses of action including "babying their best customers" by paying extra attention to them and developing a flexible workforce by cross-training employees so they can fill a variety of responsibilities on their jobs. Amazon.com and Lexus were recently identified as "customer service champs" in that they devote extra care and attention to customer service during challenging economic times.[25]

## Effectively managing relationships with customers

The firm's relationships with its customers are strengthened when it delivers superior value to them. Strong interactive relationships with customers often provide the foundation for the firm's efforts to profitably serve customers' unique needs.

As the following statement shows, Harrah's Entertainment (the world's largest provider of branded casino entertainment) is committed to providing superior value to customers: "Harrah's Entertainment is focused on building loyalty and value with its customers through a unique combination of great service, excellent products, unsurpassed distribution, operational excellence and technology leadership."[26] Importantly, as Harrah's appears to anticipate, delivering superior value often results in increased customer loyalty. In turn, customer loyalty has a positive relationship with profitability. However, more choices and easily accessible information about the functionality of firms' products are creating increasingly sophisticated and knowledgeable customers, making it difficult to earn their loyalty.[27]

A number of companies have become skilled at the art of *managing* all aspects of their relationship with their customers.[28] For example, Amazon.com is widely recognized for the quality of information it maintains about its customers, the services it provides, and its ability to anticipate customers' needs. Using the information it has, Amazon tries to serve what it believes are the unique needs of each customer; and it has a strong reputation for being able to successfully do this.[29]

As we discuss next, firms' relationships with customers are characterized by three dimensions. Companies such as Acer and Amazon.com understand these dimensions and manage their relationships with customers in light of them.

## Reach, richness and affiliation

**Reach**

The reach dimension of relationships with customers is concerned with the firm's access and connection to customers.

The reach dimension of relationships with customers is concerned with the firm's access and connection to customers. In general, firms seek to extend their reach, adding customers in the process of doing so.

Reach is an especially critical dimension for social networking sites such as Facebook and MySpace in that the value these firms create for users is to connect them with others. Research conducted in February 2010 demonstrated that 10.6 per cent of UK Internet traffic was shared between social networks and blog sites. The most popular social network site in the UK is Facebook, which in February 2010 were found to have a share of 51 per cent of the social network and blog traffic; approximately 5 per cent of the wider UK Internet traffic in February 2010 was directed towards Facebook. The closest rivals in the study were YouTube (17 per cent of social network traffic) and Twitter (2 per cent).[30] In May 2010, MySpace attracted 113 million monthly active global users[31] while Facebook's global audience is now 400 million active users with more than 70 translations available on the website.[32] Reach is also important to Netflix – the world's largest subscription service for streaming movies and television episodes over the Internet and DVDs by mail. Fortunately for this firm, recent results indicate that its reach continues to expand: "Netflix ended the first quarter of 2010 with approximately 14 million total subscribers, representing a 36 per cent year-on-year growth from 10.3 million total subscribers at the end of the first quarter of 2009 and a 14 per cent sequential growth from 12.2 million subscribers at the end of the fourth quarter of 2009."[33]

Richness, the second dimension of firms' relationships with customers, is concerned with the depth and detail of the two-way flow of information between the firm and the customer. The potential of the richness dimension to help the firm establish a competitive advantage in its relationship with customers causes many firms to offer online services in order to better manage information exchanges with them. Broader and deeper information-based exchanges allow firms to better understand their customers and their needs. Such exchanges also enable customers to become more knowledgeable about how the firm can satisfy them. Internet technology and e-commerce transactions have substantially reduced the costs of meaningful information exchanges with current and potential customers. As we have noted, Amazon.com is a leader, if not the leader, in using the Internet to build relationships with customers. In fact, it bills itself as the most "customer-centric company" on earth.[34] The firm's decision in June 2009 to launch "Your Amazon Ad Contest" demonstrated its belief in and focus on its customers. This contest asked Amazon customers to submit their vision of an Amazon television commercial to the firm. The winning entry received over €15,000 in Amazon.com gift cards.[35]

Affiliation, the third dimension, is concerned with facilitating useful interactions with customers. Viewing the world through the customer's eyes and constantly seeking ways to create more value for the customer have positive effects in terms of affiliation.

Internet navigators such as Microsoft's MSN Autos helps online clients find and sort information. MSN Autos provides data and software to prospective car buyers that enable them to compare car models along multiple objective specifications. A prospective buyer who has selected a specific car based on comparisons of different models can then be linked to dealers that meet the customer's needs and purchasing requirements. Information about other relevant issues such as financing and insurance and even local traffic patterns is also available at the site. Because its revenues come not from the final customer or end user but from other sources (such as advertisements on its website, hyperlinks, and associated products and services), MSN Autos represents the customer's interests, a service that fosters affiliation.[36]

As we discuss next, effectively managing customer relationships (along the dimensions of reach, richness, and affiliation) helps the firm answer questions related to the issues of *who, what* and *how*.

## Who: determining the customers to serve

It is important to decide *who* the target customer is that the firm intends to serve with its business-level strategy.[37] Companies divide customers into groups based on differences in the customers' needs (needs are discussed further in the next section) to make this decision. Dividing customers into groups based on their needs is called market segmentation, which is a process that clusters people with similar needs into individual and identifiable groups.[38] In the animal food products business, for example, the needs for food products of owners of companion pets (e.g., dogs and cats) differ from the needs for food and health-related products of those owning production animals (e.g., livestock). A subsidiary of Colgate-Palmolive, Hill's Pet Nutrition sells food products for pets. In fact, the company's mission is "to help enrich and lengthen the special relationship between people and their pets".[39] Schering-Plough, on the other hand, sells medicines, healthcare products and services which focus on a wide range of conditions from antibiotics and fertility treatments to vaccines for livestock.[40] Thus, Hill's and Schering-Plough target the needs of different segments of customers with the food products they sell for animals.

---

**Richness**

Richness, of firms' relationships with customers, is concerned with the depth and detail of the two-way flow of information between the firm and the customer.

**Affiliation**

Affiliation, of firms' relationships with customers, is concerned with facilitating useful interactions with customers.

**Market segmentation**

Market segmentation is a process used to cluster people with similar needs into individual and identifiable groups.

**Table 5.1** Basis for customer segmentation

| Consumer Markets |
| --- |
| 1. Demographic factors (age, income, sex, etc.) |
| 2. Socioeconomic factors (social class, stage in the family life cycle) |
| 3. Geographic factors (cultural, regional, and national differences) |
| 4. Psychological factors (lifestyle, personality traits) |
| 5. Consumption patterns (heavy, moderate, and light users) |
| 6. Perceptual factors (benefit segmentation, perceptual mapping) |

| Industrial Markets |
| --- |
| 1. End-use segments (identified by Standard Industrial Classification code) |
| 2. Product segments (based on technological differences or production economics) |
| 3. Geographic segments (defined by boundaries between countries or by regional differences within them) |
| 4. Common buying factor segments (cut across product market and geographic segments) |
| 5. Customer size segments |

Source: Adapted from S. C. Jain, 2010, *Marketing Planning and Strategy*, Cincinnati: South-Western College Publishing.

Almost any identifiable human or organizational characteristic can be used to subdivide a market into segments that differ from one another on a given characteristic. Common characteristics on which customers' needs vary are illustrated in Table 5.1.

In light of what it learned about its customers, Gap Inc. used *shopping experience* as a characteristic to subdivide its customers into different segments as a basis for serving their unique needs. Specifically, Gap learned from market research that its female and male customers want different shopping experiences. In a company official's words, "Research showed that men want to come and go easily, while women want an exploration".[41] In light of these research results, women's sections in Gap stores are organized by occasion (e.g., work, entertainment) with accessories for those occasions scattered throughout the section to facilitate browsing. The men's sections of Gap stores are more straightforward, with signs directing male customers to clothing items that are commonly stacked by size.

## What: determining which customer needs to satisfy

After the firm decides *who* it will serve, it must identify the targeted customer group's needs that its goods or services can satisfy. In a general sense, *needs* (*what*) are related to a product's benefits and features.[42] Successful firms learn how to deliver to customers what they want and when they want it.[43] Having close and frequent interactions with both current and potential customers helps the firm identify those individuals' and groups' current and future needs.[44]

From a strategic perspective, a basic need of all customers is to buy products that create value for them. The generalized forms of value that goods or services provide are either low cost with acceptable features or highly differentiated features with acceptable cost. In the recent global financial crisis, companies across industries recognized customers' need to feel as secure as possible when making purchases. Allowing customers to return their cars if they lose their job within 12 months of the purchase is how Hyundai Motors decided to address this consumer need, creating value in the form of security in the process of doing so.[45]

The most effective firms continuously strive to anticipate changes in customers' needs. The firm that fails to anticipate and certainly to recognize changes in its customers' needs may lose its customers to competitors whose products can provide more value to the focal firm's customers. Recently for example, Ford Motor concluded that customers' needs across the global automobile market were becoming more similar. In response, the firm decided to build the Fiesta as a world car. While the car will be tailored somewhat to the needs of different customers in different markets, analysts believe that the firm "... is betting that it has figured out what has bedevilled mass-market automakers for decades, which is hitting a home run in every market with the same car".[46] Thus, Ford believes that changes have occurred resulting in more similarity in customers' needs for automotive transportation across multiple markets. If this assessment is correct, the firm may take customers away from automobile manufacturers failing to see the trend toward similarity rather than differences in customers' needs within multiple market segments.

In spite of the discussion about Ford Motor's Fiesta world car, consumers' needs within individual market segments often vary a great deal.[47] Paul Bakery and Patisserie seeks to satisfy the need some consumers have for high-quality, fresh breads, cakes, salads and sandwiches with its menu items. In contrast, many large fast-food companies satisfy customer needs for lower-cost food items with acceptable quality that are delivered quickly. Diversified food and soft-drink producer PepsiCo believes that "any one consumer has different needs at different times of the day". Through its soft drinks (Pepsi products), snacks (Walkers), juices (Tropicana), and cereals (Quaker), PepsiCo is developing new products from breakfast bars to healthier potato chips "to make certain that it covers all those needs".[48]

## How: determining core competencies necessary to satisfy customer needs

After deciding *who* the firm will serve and the specific *needs* of those customers, the firm is prepared to determine how to use its capabilities and competencies to develop products that can satisfy the needs of its target customers. *Core competencies* are resources and capabilities that serve as a source of competitive advantage for the firm over its rivals (see Chapters 3 and 4). Firms use core competencies (*how*) to implement value-creating strategies and thereby satisfy customers' needs. Only those firms with the capacity to continuously improve, innovate and upgrade their competencies can expect to meet and hopefully exceed customers' expectations across time.[49]

Companies draw from a wide range of core competencies to produce goods or services that can satisfy customers' needs. ProEnergy Services is an integrated service company operating seven business units in the energy industry. Superior client satisfaction is a core competence the firm relies on in competition with its competitors.[50] SAS Institute is the world's largest privately-owned software company and is the leader in business intelligence and analytics. Customers use SAS's programs for data warehousing, data mining, and decision support purposes. Allocating approximately 22 per cent of revenues to research and development (R&D), a percentage that exceeds percentages allocated by its competitors, SAS relies on its core competence in R&D to satisfy the data-related needs of its customers (from HSBC to the UK's National Health Service Blood and Transplant service).[51] Kraft Foods relies on the capabilities of its sales force to create value for its customers[52] while Tesco uses its competence to understand customers' unique needs to create its successful private-label sub-brands such as Finest and Value.[53]

Sometimes, firms may find it necessary to use their core competencies as the foundation for producing new goods or services for new customers. For example, Cirque du Soleil base their strategy around being a non-traditional circus, with no star performers or animals involved in shows. The value of going to see the show is in the innovation used to put it together, with state of the art stages and equipment giving the show a more sophisticated feel. The company is continually innovating which is core to its values. It does not seek consensus but rather encourages innovation across all its activities. By conducting thorough research into their audiences, Cirque targets more sophisticated audiences and have ensured that every development made to the offering is tailored for this audience.[54]

Our discussion about customers shows that all organizations must use their capabilities and core competencies (the *how*) to satisfy the needs (the *what*) of the target group of customers (the *who*) the firm has chosen to serve. Next, we describe the different business-level strategies that are available to firms to use to satisfy customers as the foundation for earning above-average returns.

## The purpose of a business-level strategy

The purpose of a business-level strategy is to create differences between the firm's position in an industry and those of its competitors.[55] To position itself differently from competitors, a firm must decide whether it intends to *perform activities differently* or to *perform different activities*. In fact, "choosing to perform activities differently or to perform different activities than rivals" is the essence of business-level strategy.[56] Thus, the firm's business-level strategy is a deliberate choice about how it will perform the value chain's primary and support activities to create unique value. Indeed, in the complex twenty-first century competitive landscape, successful use of a business-level strategy results only when the firm learns how to integrate the activities it performs in ways that create superior value for customers.

Firms develop an activity map to show how they integrate the activities they perform. The manner in which Ryanair has integrated its activities is the foundation for the successful use of its cost leadership strategy (this strategy is discussed later in the chapter). The tight integration among Ryanair's activities is a key source of the firm's ability to at least historically operate more profitably than its competitors. Ryanair has configured the activities it performs into key strategic themes—limited passenger service; frequent, reliable departures; lean, highly productive ground and gate crews; high aircraft utilization; very low ticket prices; and short-haul, point-to-point routes between mid-sized cities and secondary airports. Individual clusters of tightly linked activities make it possible for the outcome of a strategic theme to be achieved. For example, no meals, no seat assignments, and no baggage transfers form a cluster of individual activities that support the strategic theme of limited passenger service.

Ryanair's tightly integrated activities make it difficult for competitors to imitate the firm's cost leadership strategy.[57] Low cost competitors including easyJet and

BmiBaby have all failed to some degree in attempts to imitate Ryanair's strategy. Hindsight shows that these competitors offered low prices to customers, but were not able to operate at costs as low as those of Ryanair or to provide customers with any notable sources of differentiation, such as a unique experience while in the air. The key to Ryanair's success has been its ability to continuously reduce its costs while providing customers with acceptable levels of differentiation such as an engaging culture. Firms using the cost leadership strategy must understand that in terms of sources of differentiation that accompany the cost leader's product, the customer defines acceptable.

Activity fit is a key to the sustainability of competitive advantage for all firms, including Ryanair. As Michael Porter comments: "Strategic fit among many activities is fundamental not only to competitive advantage but also to the sustainability of that advantage. It is harder for a rival to match an array of interlocked activities than it is merely to imitate a particular sales-force approach, match a process technology, or replicate a set of product features. Positions built on systems of activities are far more sustainable than those built on individual activities."[58]

## Types of business-level strategies

Firms choose from among five business-level strategies to establish and defend their desired strategic position against competitors: *cost leadership, differentiation, focused cost leadership, focused differentiation* and *integrated cost leadership/differentiation* (see Figure 5.1). Each business-level strategy helps the firm to establish and exploit a particular *competitive advantage* within a particular *competitive*

**FIGURE 5.1**  Five business-level strategies

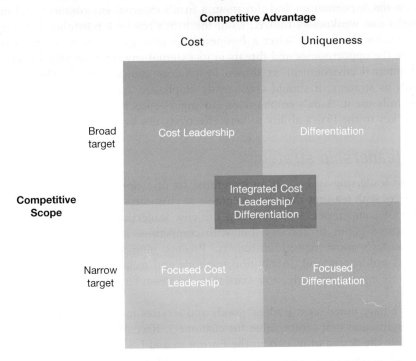

Source: Adapted with the permission of The Free Press, an imprint of Simon & Schuster Adult Publishing Group, from *Competitive Advantage: Creating and Sustaining Superior Performance*, by Michael E. Porter, 12. Copyright © 1985, 1998 by Michael E. Porter.

*scope*. How firms integrate the activities they perform within each different business-level strategy demonstrates how they differ from one another.[59] The Ryanair operation differs from those of competitors British Airways, Virgin, Thomson, and so forth. Superior integration of activities increases the likelihood of being able to gain an advantage over competitors and to earn above-average returns.

When selecting a business-level strategy, firms evaluate two types of potential competitive advantage: "lower cost than rivals, or the ability to differentiate and command a premium price that exceeds the extra cost of doing so".[60] Having lower cost derives from the firm's ability to perform activities differently to rivals; being able to differentiate indicates the firm's capacity to perform different (and value creating) activities.[61] Thus, based on the nature and quality of its internal resources, capabilities and core competencies, a firm seeks to form either a cost competitive advantage or a uniqueness competitive advantage as the basis for implementing its business-level strategy.

Two types of competitive scope are broad target and narrow target (see Figure 5.1). Firms serving a broad target market seek to use their competitive advantage on an industry-wide basis. A narrow competitive scope means that the firm intends to serve the needs of a narrow target customer group. With focus strategies, the firm "selects a segment or group of segments in the industry and tailors its strategy to serving them to the exclusion of others".[62] Buyers with special needs and buyers located in specific geographic regions are examples of narrow target customer groups.[63] As shown in Figure 5.1, a firm could also strive to develop a combined cost/uniqueness competitive advantage as the foundation for serving a target customer group that is larger than a narrow segment but not as comprehensive as a broad (or industry-wide) customer group. In this instance, the firm uses the integrated cost leadership/differentiation strategy.

None of the five business-level strategies shown in Figure 5.1 is inherently or universally superior to the others.[64] The effectiveness of each strategy is contingent both on the opportunities and threats in a firm's external environment and on the strengths and weaknesses derived from the firm's resource portfolio. It is critical, therefore, for the firm to select a business-level strategy that is based on a match between the opportunities and threats in its external environment and the strengths of its internal environment as shown by its core competencies.[65] Once the firm chooses its strategy, it should consistently emphasize actions that are required to successfully use it. Asda's emphasis on driving its costs lower and lower is thought to be a key to the firm's ability to very effectively use its cost leadership strategy.[66]

## Cost leadership strategy

The cost leadership strategy is an integrated set of actions taken to produce goods or services with features that are acceptable to customers at the lowest cost, relative to that of competitors.[67] Firms using the cost leadership strategy commonly sell standardized goods or services (but with competitive levels of differentiation) to the industry's most typical customers. Process innovations, which are newly-designed production and distribution methods and techniques that allow the firm to operate more efficiently, are critical to successful use of the cost leadership strategy.[68]

As we have noted, cost leaders' goods and services must have competitive levels of differentiation that create value for customers. Recently, Kia Motors decided to emphasize the design of its cars in the European and US markets as a source of differentiation while implementing its cost leadership strategy. Called "cheap chic," some analysts had a positive view of this decision, saying that "When they're done, Kia's cars will still be low-end (in price), but they won't necessarily look like

**Competitive scope**

A narrow (broad) competitive scope means that the firm intends to serve the needs of a narrow (broad) target customer group.

**Cost leadership strategy**

The cost leadership strategy is an integrated set of actions taken to produce goods or services with features that are acceptable to customers at the lowest cost, relative to that of competitors.

it".[69] It is important for firms using the cost leadership strategy such as Kia to do this in that at the extreme, concentrating only on reducing costs could result in the firm efficiently producing products that no customer wants to purchase. In fact, such extremes could lead to limited potential for all-important process innovations, employment of lower-skilled workers, poor conditions on the production line, accidents, and a poor quality of work-life for employees.[70]

As shown in Figure 5.1, the firm using the cost leadership strategy targets a broad customer segment or group. Cost leaders concentrate on finding ways to lower their costs relative to competitors by constantly rethinking how to complete their primary and support activities to reduce costs still further while maintaining competitive levels of differentiation.[71]

Cost leader FirstGroup PLC generated €7.3 billion in revenue in 2009 and one of their key divisions, the UK bus service, continuously seeks ways to reduce the costs it incurs to provide bus service while offering customers an acceptable level of differentiation. FirstGroup PLC have learned a great deal strategically from their operations in UK buses and rail, as well as in North America where they own the Greyhound business connecting 3800 destinations by bus, as well as contract business where First maintains a fleet of 60000 yellow school buses in the US and Canada.[72] First UK Bus offer new services to customers as a way of improving the quality of the experience customers have when paying the firm's low prices for its services. Changes in the economic segment of the general environment (see Chapter 2) in Europe are creating an opportunity for First to do this.[73] Specifically, the recent recessionary times found more people seeking to travel by bus instead of by planes and trains. However, these new customers demand certain amenities and they're offered, on certain services, Wi-Fi, extra legroom with reclining seats, toilets, free newspaper, power sockets, CCTV. First UK Bus enjoys economies of scale by being the largest UK bus operator. Maintaining a fleet of 8500 buses and enjoying a market share of approximately 23 per cent which equates to transporting approximately 3 million passengers a day. These scale economies allow the firm to keep its costs low while offering some of the differentiated services today's customers seek from the company.

As primary activities, inbound logistics (e.g., materials handling, warehousing and inventory control) and outbound logistics (e.g., collecting, storing and distributing products to customers) often account for significant portions of the total cost to produce some goods and services. Research suggests that having a competitive advantage in terms of logistics creates more value when using the cost leadership strategy than when using the differentiation strategy.[74] Thus, cost leaders seeking competitively valuable ways to reduce costs may want to concentrate on the primary activities of inbound logistics and outbound logistics. In so doing many firms choose to outsource their manufacturing operations to low-cost firms with low-wage employees (e.g., China).[75]

Cost leaders also carefully examine all support activities to find additional sources of potential cost reductions. Developing new systems for finding the optimal combination of low cost and acceptable levels of differentiation in the raw materials required to produce the firm's goods or services, is an example of how the procurement support activity can facilitate successful use of the cost leadership strategy.

TK Maxx employs the cost leadership strategy. With its vision of being "Europe's first and only major off-price retailer of apparel and home fashions", having introduced the off-price concept to the UK, TK Maxx is now the seventh largest fashion retailer in the United Kingdom and remains the only major off-price retailer in Europe, with stores in Germany and Poland supplementing their UK trade since 2007 and 2009 respectively. For TK Maxx, "off-price goods" "are the same first-quality, brand-name products found at other retailers, but at substantially lower

**Primary activities**

Primary activities include inbound logistics, operations, outbound logistics, marketing, sales and services.

prices". The firm relies on a disciplined merchandise cost and inventory management system to continuously drive its costs lower. The firm's stores sell name-brand products at prices that are up to 60 per cent below those of traditional retailers. TK Maxx's buyers search for manufacturer overruns and discontinued styles to find goods priced well below wholesale prices. In addition, the firm buys from overseas suppliers. TK Maxx satisfies the customers' need to access the differentiated features of brand-name products, but at a fraction of their cost. Tightly integrating its purchasing and inventory management activities across its stores is the main core competence TK Maxx uses to satisfy its customers' needs.[76]

As described in Chapter 3, firms use value-chain analysis to identify the parts of the company's operations that create value and those that do not. Figure 5.2 demonstrates the primary and support activities that allow a firm to create value through the cost leadership strategy. Companies unable to link the activities shown in this figure through the activity map they form typically lack the core competencies needed to successfully use the cost leadership strategy.

Effective use of the cost leadership strategy allows a firm to earn above-average returns in spite of the presence of strong competitive forces (see Chapter 2). The next sections (one for each of the five forces) explain how firms implement a cost leadership strategy.

### Rivalry with existing competitors

Having the low-cost position is valuable to deal with rivals. Because of the cost leader's advantageous position, rivals hesitate to compete on the basis of price, especially before evaluating the potential outcomes of such competition.[77] Lidl is known for its ability to continuously reduce its costs, creating value for customers in the process of doing so. In light of this ability, rivals such as Morrisons and Sainsbury's hesitate to compete against Lidl strictly on the basis of costs and subsequently, prices to consumers. Recently, Lidl decided to expand its offerings introducing its FairGlobe range and its organic range. Because it controls the costs associated with producing its private-label products, the firm is able to drive its costs lower when manufacturing and distributing its own products.

### Bargaining power of buyers (customers)

Powerful customers can force a cost leader to reduce its prices, but not below the level at which the cost leader's next-most-efficient industry competitor can earn average returns. Although powerful customers might be able to force the cost leader to reduce prices even below this level, they probably would not choose to do so. Prices that are low enough to prevent the next-most-efficient competitor from earning average returns would force that firm to exit the market, leaving the cost leader with less competition and in an even stronger position. Customers would thus lose their power and pay higher prices if they were forced to purchase from a single firm operating in an industry without rivals.

### Bargaining power of suppliers

The cost leader operates with margins greater than those of competitors. Cost leaders seek to constantly increase their margins as a result of driving their costs lower. Among other benefits, higher gross margins relative to those of competitors make it possible for the cost leader to absorb its suppliers' price increases. When an industry faces substantial increases in the cost of its supplies, only the cost leader may be able to pay the higher prices and continue to earn either average or above-average returns. Alternatively, a powerful cost leader may be able to force its suppliers to hold down their prices, which would reduce the suppliers' margins in the process.

The discount supermarket chain Aldi has approximately 7000 stores worldwide and is able "to provide our customers with the products they buy regularly and

**FIGURE 5.2** Examples of value-creating activities associated with the cost leadership strategy

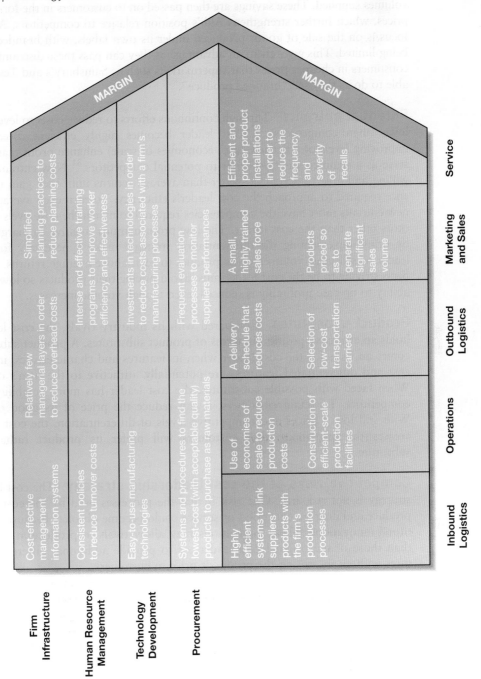

ensure that those products are of the highest possible quality at guaranteed low prices".[78] In the year ending 2008, Aldi's UK turnover was approximately €2.4 billion with a pre-tax profit of approximately €110 million. The Aldi, as well as that of Lidl, business model changed the retail industry model and allowed them to sell products cheaply as they stock only limited product lines based around items which staple consumers purchase regularly but at low costs as they buy in large volumes.[79] Consequently, they're able to extract lower prices from suppliers because of the high volumes supplied. These savings are then passed on to customers in the form of lower prices, which further strengthens Aldi's position relative to competitors. Also, Aldi's focus is on the sale of goods produced under its own labels, with branded products being limited. This gives them an advantage as they can pass these discounts onto the consumers in cheaper prices that supermarkets such as Sainsbury's and Tesco are not able to do as they sell "branded produce".[80]

**Potential entrants**   Through continuous efforts to reduce costs to levels that are lower than competitors', a cost leader becomes highly efficient. Because ever-improving levels of efficiency (e.g., economies of scale) enhance profit margins, they serve as a significant entry barrier to potential competitors.[81] New entrants must be willing and able to accept no-better-than-average returns until they gain the experience required to approach the cost leader's efficiency. To earn even average returns, new entrants must have the competencies required to match the cost levels of competitors other than the cost leader. The low profit margins (relative to margins earned by firms implementing the differentiation strategy) make it necessary for the cost leader to sell large volumes of its product to earn above-average returns. However, firms striving to be the cost leader must avoid pricing their products so low that their ability to operate profitably is reduced, even though volume increases.

**Product substitutes**   Compared with its industry rivals, the cost leader also holds an attractive position in terms of product substitutes. A product substitute becomes an issue for the cost leader when its features and characteristics, in terms of cost and differentiated features, are potentially attractive to the firm's customers. When faced with possible substitutes, the cost leader has more flexibility than its competitors. To retain customers, it can reduce the price of its good or service. With still lower prices and competitive levels of differentiation, the cost leader increases the probability that customers will prefer its product rather than a substitute.

**Competitive risks of the cost leadership strategy**   The cost leadership strategy is not risk free. One risk is that the processes used by the cost leader to produce and distribute its good or service could become obsolete because of competitors' innovations. These innovations may allow rivals to produce at costs lower than those of the original cost leader, or to provide additional differentiated features without increasing the product's price to customers.

A second risk is that too much focus by the cost leader on cost reductions may occur at the expense of trying to understand customers' perceptions of "competitive levels of differentiation". Aldi, for example, has been criticized for having too few sales people available to help customers and too few individuals at the checkouts. These complaints suggest that there might be a discrepancy between how Aldi's customers define minimal levels of service and the firm's attempts to drive its costs lower and lower.

Imitation is a final risk of the cost leadership strategy. Using their own core competencies, competitors sometimes learn how to successfully imitate the cost leader's strategy. When this happens, the cost leader must increase the value its good or service provides to customers. Commonly, value is increased by selling the current product at an even lower price or by adding differentiated features that create value for customers while maintaining price.

Lovefilm, a leading European DVD rental firm, may be encountering this risk from firms such as LidlMovies, which claims to be 15 per cent cheaper. Also, it claims to be cheaper than Blockbuster, Tesco and others in this space. Operating as a DVD rental service, LidlMovies' operations are run by OutNow Entertainment Limited and seeks to offer comparable service levels to competitors but at cheaper price points. In the United States, this market has evolved one point further where Netflix may be encountering this same risk, but with a difference, from Redbox, which is the largest operator of DVD rental kiosks in the US. Using vending machines that Redbox has established in supermarkets and discount stores, customers pay €0.79 per day for DVDs. In contrast, Netflix's cheapest plan is €3.94 per month (the customer receives two DVDs by mail per month with this plan). An analyst used the following words to describe this situation: "Netflix CEO Reed Hastings has something to worry about: an even cheaper DVD rental service run by one of his former lieutenants."[82] However, in 2010 this same Netflix CEO has responded by delivering television and movies over the Internet which will move it away from its core €1.5 billion DVD-by-mail business to new heights. The response has been remarkable with him winning the 2010 Fortune Business Person of the Year Award.

## Differentiation strategy

The differentiation strategy is an integrated set of actions taken to produce goods or services (at an acceptable cost) that customers perceive as being different in ways that are important to them.[83] While cost leaders serve a typical customer in an industry, differentiators target customers for whom value is created by the manner in which the firm's products differ from those produced and marketed by competitors. Product innovation, which is "the result of bringing to life a new way to solve the customer's problem – through a new product or service development – that benefits both the customer and the sponsoring company"[84] – is critical to successful use of the differentiation strategy.[85]

Firms must be able to produce differentiated products at competitive costs to reduce upward pressure on the price that customers pay. When a product's differentiated features are produced at non-competitive costs, the price for the product can exceed what the firm's target customers are willing to pay. When the firm has a thorough understanding of what its target customers value, the relative importance they attach to the satisfaction of different needs, and for what they are willing to pay a premium, the differentiation strategy can be successful.

Through the differentiation strategy, the firm produces non-standardized (that is, unique) products for customers who value differentiated features more than they value low cost. For example, superior product reliability and durability and high-performance sound systems are among the differentiated features of Toyota Motor Corporation's Lexus products. The Lexus promotional statement – "We pursue perfection, so you can pursue living" – suggests a strong commitment to overall product quality as a source of differentiation. However, Lexus offers its vehicles to customers at a competitive purchase price. As with Lexus products, a good's or service's unique attributes, rather than its purchase price, provide the value for which customers are willing to pay.

Continuous success with the differentiation strategy results when the firm consistently upgrades differentiated features that customers value and/or creates new ones (innovates) without significant cost increases.[86] This approach requires firms to constantly change their product lines.[87] These firms may also offer a portfolio of products that complement each other, thereby enriching the differentiation for the customer and perhaps satisfying a portfolio of consumer needs.[88] Because a differentiated product satisfies customers' unique needs, firms following the differentiation strategy are able to charge premium prices. However, customers are willing to pay a premium price for a product only when a "firm (is) truly unique at something or be perceived as unique".[89]

> **Differentiation strategy**
>
> The differentiation strategy is an integrated set of actions taken to produce goods or services (at an acceptable cost) that customers perceive as being different in ways that are important to them.

The ability to sell a good or service at a price that substantially exceeds the cost of creating its differentiated features, allows the firm to outperform rivals and earn above-average returns. For example, shirt and neckwear manufacturer Robert Talbott follows stringent standards of craftsmanship and pays meticulous attention to every detail of production. The firm imports exclusive fabrics from the world's finest mills to make men's dress shirts and neck-wear. Single-needle tailoring is used, and precise collar cuts are made to produce shirts. According to the company, customers purchasing one of its products can be assured that they are being provided with the finest fabrics available.[90] Thus, Robert Talbott's success rests on the firm's ability to produce and sell its differentiated products at a price exceeding the costs of imported fabrics and its unique manufacturing processes.

Rather than costs, a firm using the differentiation strategy always concentrates on investing in and developing features that differentiate a product in ways that create value for customers. Robert Talbott, for example, uses the finest silks from Europe and Asia to produce its "Best of Class" collection of ties. Overall, a firm using the differentiation strategy seeks to be different from its competitors on as many dimensions as possible. The less similarity between a firm's goods or services and those of competitors, the more buffered it is from rivals' actions. Commonly recognized differentiated goods include Toyota's Lexus, Ralph Lauren's wide array of product lines and Caterpillar's heavy-duty earth-moving equipment. McKinsey & Co. is a well-known example of a firm that offers differentiated services.

A good or service can be differentiated in many ways. Unusual features, responsive customer service, rapid product innovations and technological leadership, perceived prestige and status, different tastes, and engineering design and performance are examples of approaches to differentiation.[91] While the number of ways to reduce costs may be finite, virtually anything a firm can do to create real or perceived value is a basis for differentiation. Consider product design as a case in point. Because it can create a positive experience for customers, design is becoming an increasingly important source of differentiation (even for cost leaders seeking to find ways to add functionalities to their low cost products as a way of differentiating their products from competitors') and hopefully for firms emphasizing it, of competitive advantage.[92] As we noted above, design is a way Kia Motors is now trying to create some uniqueness for its products that are manufactured and sold as part of the firm's cost leadership strategy. Apple is often cited as the firm that sets the standard in design, with the iPod, iPhone and iPad, for example, demonstrating Apple's product design capabilities.[93]

The value chain can be analysed to determine if a firm is able to link the activities required to create value by using the differentiation strategy. Examples of primary and support activities that are commonly used to differentiate a good or service are shown in Figure 5.3. Companies without the skills needed to link these activities cannot expect to successfully use the differentiation strategy. Next, we explain how firms using the differentiation strategy can successfully position themselves in terms of the five forces of competition (see Chapter 2) to earn above-average returns.

**Rivalry with existing competitors** Customers tend to be loyal purchasers of products differentiated in ways that are meaningful to them. As their loyalty to a brand increases, customers' sensitivity to price increases is reduced. The relationship between brand loyalty and price sensitivity insulates a firm from competitive rivalry. Thus, Cartier is insulated from competition, even on the basis of price, as long as the company continues to satisfy the differentiated needs of its target customer group with the distinctive qualities of this brand. Likewise, Bose is insulated from intense rivalry as long as customers continue to perceive that its stereo equipment offers superior sound quality at a competitive purchase price. Both Cartier

**FIGURE 5.3** Examples of value-creating activities associated with the differentiation strategy

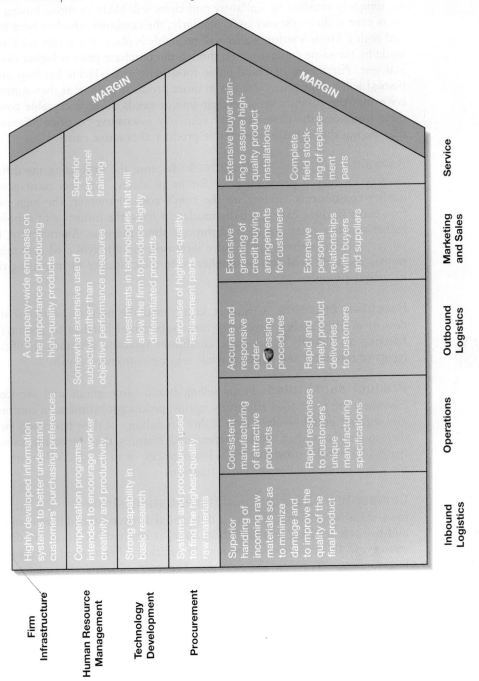

Source: Adapted with the permission of The Free Press, an imprint of Simon & Schuster Adult Publishing Group, from *Competitive Advantage: Creating and Sustaining Superior Performance*, by Michael E. Porter, 47. Copyright © 1985, 1998 by Michael E. Porter.

and Bose have strong positive reputations for the high quality and unique products that they provide. Thus, reputations can sustain the competitive advantage of firms following a differentiation strategy.[94]

**Bargaining power of buyers (customers)** The uniqueness of differentiated goods or services reduces customers' sensitivity to price increases. Customers are willing to accept a price increase when a product still satisfies their perceived unique needs better than does a competitor's offering. Thus, the golfer whose needs are uniquely satisfied by Callaway golf clubs will likely continue buying those products even if their cost increases. Similarly, the customer who has been highly satisfied with a Louis Vuitton wallet will probably replace that wallet with another one made by the same company even though the purchase price is higher than the original one. Purchasers of brand-name food items (e.g., Heinz ketchup and Kleenex tissues) will accept price increases in those products as long as they continue to perceive that the product satisfies their unique needs at an acceptable cost. In all of these instances, the customers are relatively insensitive to price increases because they do not think that an acceptable product alternative exists.

**Bargaining power of suppliers**  Because the firm using the differentiation strategy charges a premium price for its products, suppliers must provide high-quality components, driving up the firm's costs. However, the high margins the firm earns in these cases partially insulate it from the influence of suppliers in that higher supplier costs can be paid through these margins. Alternatively, because of buyers' relative insensitivity to price increases, the differentiated firm might choose to pass the additional cost of supplies on to the customer by increasing the price of its unique product.

**Potential entrants**  Customer loyalty and the need to overcome the uniqueness of a differentiated product present substantial barriers to potential entrants. Entering an industry under these conditions typically demands significant investments of resources and patience while seeking customers' loyalty.

**Product substitutes**  Firms selling brand-name goods and services to loyal customers are positioned effectively against product substitutes. In contrast, companies without brand loyalty face a higher probability of their customers switching either to products that offer differentiated features that serve the same function (particularly if the substitute has a lower price), or to products that offer more features and perform more attractive functions.

**Competitive risks of the differentiation strategy**  The fact that customers might decide that the price differential between the differentiator's product and the cost leader's product is too large, is one risk of using the differentiation strategy. In this instance, a firm may be offering differentiated features that exceed target customers' needs. The firm then becomes vulnerable to competitors that are able to offer customers a combination of features and price that is more consistent with their needs.

This risk seemed to be generalized across a number of companies producing different types of products during the recent global economic crisis – a time when forecasters suggested that "Sales of luxury goods, everything from apparel, to jewellery and leather goods, could plunge globally by 10 per cent ..."[95] in 2009. A decision made during this time by Coach Inc., a maker of high-quality, luxurious accessories and gifts for women and men, demonstrates one firm's reaction to the predicted decline in the sales of luxury goods. With an interest of providing products to increasingly cost conscious customers without "cheapening" the firm's image, Coach chose to introduce a new line of its products. Called Poppy, the average price of items in this line is approximately 20 per cent lower compared to the average price of Coach's typical products.[96]

Another risk of the differentiation strategy is that a firm's means of differentiation may cease to provide value for which customers are willing to pay.

## STRATEGIC FOCUS

© ERIC GAILLARD/Reuters/Corbis

# Declaring war against counterfeiters to protect product integrity and profitability

Many of us have seen them and some of us may own one or two of them – products that are intended to look like well-known branded items. Burberry goods, Louis Vuitton handbags and Rolex watches are but a few of the items for which counterfeit versions of the products are sold throughout the world. And, counterfeiting is big business! Having studied the issue, a consultant concluded that "Counterfeiting is one of the most significant threats to the free market". Potentially supporting the consultant's assertion is the fact that according to the International Chamber of Commerce, counterfeit goods accounted for about €470 billion in sales in 2007, which is roughly 6 per cent of global trade.

Producing and selling counterfeit products negatively affects societies and individual firms. Jobs are lost in companies making the "legitimate" versions of products that are sold by firms using the differentiation strategy. In turn, lost jobs mean lost tax revenues for local and national taxing agencies. While some work is created for those manufacturing the counterfeit goods, the jobs tend to be lower paying and the companies and their employees typically pay few if any taxes on what becomes unreported sales at the firm level and unreported income at the individual employee level.

The selling of counterfeit ink demonstrates the problems individual firms encounter. Analysts estimate that Hewlett-Packard's (HP) imaging and printing group lost over €780 million in revenue to counterfeit ink cartridges in 2008 alone. In addition to losing sales revenue, HP is concerned that counterfeit cartridges lack product quality and integrity which hurts the firm's reputation.

In light of the problems counterfeiting creates, HP has gone to war against counterfeiters. The firm employs teams of people to roam the globe looking for counterfeit versions of its products. Often, customers contact these teams if they suspect that a shipment of cartridges they purchased from a wholesaler is counterfeit. If HP's detectives discover that products are indeed counterfeit, "They take their findings to law enforcement to help nab big distributors of counterfeit ink supplies". HP views taking these actions as critical to the firm's efforts to earn revenues and profits from its products.

**Sources**: Edwards, C. (2009) "HP declares war on counterfeiters", *BusinessWeek*, June 8, 44–45; Chaudhry, P. E., Zimmerman, A., Peters, J. R. and Cordell, V. V. (2009) "Preserving intellectual property rights: Managerial insight into the escalating counterfeit market quandary", *Business Horizons*, 52: 57–66; Phau, I. and Teah, M. (2009) "Devil wears (counterfeit) Prada: A study of antecedents and outcomes of attitudes towards counterfeits of luxury brands", *Journal of Consumer Marketing*, 26: 15–27; Abelson, J. (2008) "Grim competition with counterfeiters", *Boston Globe Online*, http://www.boston.com, August 21.

## Questions

**1** What are the competitive reasons that underlie the market for counterfeit goods?

**2** How can corporate victims of counterfeiting respond to this endemic problem?

A differentiated product becomes less valuable if imitation by rivals causes customers to perceive that competitors offer essentially the same good or service, but at a lower price.[97] A third risk of the differentiation strategy is that experience can narrow customers' perceptions of the value of a product's differentiated features. For example, customers having positive experiences with generic tissues may decide that the differentiated features of the Kleenex product are not worth the extra cost. Similarly, while a customer may be impressed with the quality of a Cartier purse, positive experiences with a less expensive purse may lead to a conclusion that the price of the Cartier brand exceeds the benefit. To counter this risk, firms must continue to meaningfully differentiate their product for customers at a price they are willing to pay.

Counterfeiting is the differentiation strategy's fourth risk. "Counterfeits are those products bearing a trademark that is identical to or indistinguishable from a trademark registered to another party, thus infringing the rights of the owner of the trademark."[98] The Strategic Focus describes actions that firms such as Hewlett-Packard take to deal with the problems counterfeit goods create for firms whose rights are infringed.

## Focus strategies

**Focus strategy**

The focus strategy is an integrated set of actions taken to produce goods or services that serve the needs of a particular competitive segment.

The focus strategy is an integrated set of actions taken to produce goods or services that serve the needs of a particular competitive segment. Thus, firms use a focus strategy when they utilize their core competencies to serve the needs of a particular industry segment or niche to the exclusion of others. Examples of specific market segments that can be targeted by a focus strategy include (1) a particular buyer group (e.g., youths or senior citizens); (2) a different segment of a product line (e.g., products for professional painters or the do-it-yourself group); or (3) a different geographic market (e.g., Northern Italy and Southern Italy).[99]

There are many specific customer needs firms can serve by using a focus strategy. For example, Los Angeles-based investment banking firm Greif & Company positions itself as "The Entrepreneur's Investment Bank". Greif & Company is a leader in providing merger and acquisition advice to medium-sized businesses located in the western United States.[100] Goya Foods is the largest US-based Hispanic-owned food company in the United States. Segmenting the Hispanic market into unique groups, Goya offers more than 1500 products to consumers. The firm seeks "to be the be-all for the Latin community".[101] Electronics retailer Conn's Inc., operating stores in Texas, Louisiana and Oklahoma, uses a commissioned sales staff, which is "trained to explain increasingly complex televisions and washing machines", and its own financing business to help local citizens who dislike receiving what they perceive to be "impersonal" service from large national chains.[102] By successfully using a focus strategy, firms such as Greif & Company, Goya Foods and Conn's Inc. gain a competitive advantage in specific market niches or segments, even though they do not possess an industry-wide competitive advantage.

Although the breadth of a target is clearly a matter of degree, the essence of the focus strategy "is the exploitation of a narrow target's differences from the balance of the industry".[103] Firms using the focus strategy intend to serve a particular segment of an industry more effectively than can industry-wide competitors. They succeed when they effectively serve a segment whose unique needs are so specialized that broad-based competitors choose not to serve that segment or when they satisfy the needs of a segment being served poorly by industry-wide competitors.[104]

Firms can create value for customers in specific and unique market segments by using the focused cost leadership strategy or the focused differentiation strategy.

**Focused cost leadership strategy** Based in Sweden, IKEA, a global household retailer achieved turnover in 2009 of €22.7 billion from over 660 million customer visits in over 300 stores operating across 35 countries.[105] Customer demand and turnover have continued to rise for several years. The reason: customers are aware of the distinctive positioning of IKEA and are familiar with its strategy of well-designed household products at low prices using focused cost leadership strategy. Young buyers desiring style at a low cost are IKEA's target customers.[106] For these customers, the firm offers home furnishings that combine good design, function and acceptable quality with low prices. According to the firm, "Low cost is always in focus. This applies to every phase of our activities."[107]

IKEA emphasizes several activities to keep its costs low. For example, instead of relying primarily on third-party manufacturers, the firm's engineers design low-cost, modular furniture ready for assembly by customers. To eliminate the need for sales associates or decorators, IKEA positions the products in its stores so that customers can view different living combinations (complete with sofas, chairs, tables, etc.) in a single room-like setting, which helps the customer imagine how a grouping of furniture will look in the home. A third practice that helps keep IKEA's costs low is requiring customers to transport their own purchases rather than providing delivery service.

Although it is a cost leader, IKEA also offers some differentiated features that appeal to its target customers, including its unique furniture designs, in-store playrooms for children, wheelchairs for customer use and extended hours. IKEA believes that these services and products "Are uniquely aligned with the needs of [its] customers, who are young, are not wealthy, are likely to have children (but no nanny), and, because they work, have a need to shop at odd hours."[108] Thus, IKEA's focused cost leadership strategy also includes some differentiated features with its low-cost products.

**Focused differentiation strategy** Other firms implement the focused differentiation strategy. As noted earlier, there are many dimensions on which firms can differentiate their good or service. For example, New Look Laser Tattoo Removal, located in Houston, Texas, specializes in removing tattoos that customers no longer desire. According to the firm, some of its customers want to remove tattoos prior to interviewing for jobs while others believe that removing them can benefit their careers. As one of the firm's customers said, "Tattoos make you look a little rougher. I don't want to worry about what people are thinking about me."[109]

The new generation of lunch trucks populating US and European cities also use the focused differentiation strategy. Serving "high-end fare such as grass-fed hamburgers, escargots and crème brulee", highly-trained chefs and well-known restaurateurs own and operate many of these trucks. In fact, "the new breed of lunch truck is aggressively gourmet, tech-savvy and politically correct". Selling sustainably harvested fish tacos in a vehicle that is fuelled by vegetable oil, The Green Truck, located in Los Angeles, demonstrates these characteristics. Moreover, the owners of these trucks tend to use Twitter and Facebook to inform customers of their locations as they move from point to point in their focal city.[110]

Giorgio Armani S.p.A. uses the focused differentiation strategy to create value for design aware customers by delivering all aspects of superior design and creativity to its brands. By developing a repertoire of businesses, it has maintained a focused differentiation strategy across all areas of its activity.

With a focus strategy, firms such as Giorgio Armani S.p.A. must be able to complete various primary and support activities in a competitively superior manner

© Francis Dean/Alamy

## STRATEGIC FOCUS

# Giorgio Armani – brand extension

Giorgio Armani S.p.A. engages in the design, manufacture, distribution and retail of fashion and lifestyle products worldwide. The company was founded in 1975 and is still based in Milan, Italy, today. Not only has Giorgio Armani become one of the most respected and known brand names in the fashion industry, it is also one of the most highly valued fashion companies in the world and generated consolidated revenues of €1.51 billion in 2009.

In the beginning Giorgio Armani was particularly popular among the elite of the society and the fashion-literate segment. To extend their market they searched for different product lines, different segments, and even different markets. Today the Armani umbrella brand encompasses one corporate brand and five sub-brands, each catering to different sets of target customers and at different price levels. The *signature Giorgio Armani line* is the more traditional collection, consisting of signature Armani suits, Oscar gowns and so on. This collection is at the top end of the Armani price range and is essentially targeting

consumers in the 35–50-year-old age group. The *Armani Collezioni* is Armani's venture into a slightly lower market segment. This range caters to the segment of people who aspire to wear Armani apparel but cannot afford the ultimate signature line. *Emporio Armani* is targeted especially at the young professional segment in the 25–35-year-old age group. The *Emporio Armani* brand provides contemporary designs that are relevant to the target customers. *Armani Jeans* is the lowest range of Armani portfolio in terms of price. Catering to the young adults in the 18–30-year-old age group, the Armani Jeans collection provides a trendy yet fashionable and luxurious line of apparel. *A/X Armani Exchange* is the licensed brand of chain retail outlets of Armani fashion house.

With its many sub-brands designed under the umbrella parent brand, Armani anticipated the specific needs of different market segments. But this is not all. Not only does Armani straddle many segments of the same product category, they also possess many different product categories. Giorgio Armani has ventured into other related categories such as eye wear, watches and cosmetics. These are made available in each of the brand categories to ensure that it is available to the different segments of the market. Usually it is argued that eye wear, perfumes, watches and cosmetics are strongly related to fashion and luxury and thus it is natural for fashion houses to extend their brands to these categories. Giorgio Armani is a clear example of these initiatives. By leveraging its expert knowledge of the fashion and luxury industry, Armani has been able to come up with winning concepts in these other product lines.

But Armani has not restricted itself to these product categories: Armani has extended the brand into multiple other categories such as Armani Casa (up-market furniture), Armani-branded Dolci (confectionery) and Armani-branded Fiori (Flowers). In addition, expanding this wide portfolio of brands, Armani struck a deal with a Dubai-based property group, Emaar, to develop a chain of 14 Armani-branded hotels and resorts by 2011.

Companies active in a variety of different segments, like Armani, are in danger of over-extending their brand. One of the main factors that make fashion houses and their products premium are their exclusivity. By franchising their brand names to so many new markets, these brands are at risk of losing a significant portion of their strong brand equity. Robert Triefus, Armani's executive vice-president of worldwide communications, explains the thinking behind such diverse branding initiatives: "The Armani brand and its values have become understood globally. When you talk about Armani to someone on the street, they immediately have perception of what the name means. It has almost become generic, you can talk about the "Armani look: Italian, timeless, elegant, sophisticated but understated.""

Unlike the Gucci and LVMH groups, which have expanded by acquiring existing brands, Armani has created its own sub-brands and diversified into new product categories, creating a coherent brand. For example when the company moves into a new market, it always opens a Giorgio Armani boutique first, to set the standard, before any of the other brands follow. Robert Triefus stated, "Only if you go behind the logic of the brand, will over-extension be a threat."

**Sources:** Roll, M. (2010) Giorgio Armani the Ultimate fashion brand, Venture Republic, http://www.venturerepublic.com/resources/giorgio_armani_-_the_ultimate_fashion_brand.asp; Moore, M., Fernie, J. and Burt, S. (2000) "Brands without boundaries: The internationalization of the designer retailer's brand", *European Journal of Marketing*, 34(8): 919–937; Tungate, M. (2005) *Fashion Brands: Branding Style from Armani to Zara*, London: Kogan Page; 2010, Giorgio Armani S.p.A., http://www.businessweek.com/research/stocks/private/, August 9; 2010, Home, http://www.armanihotels.com, August 9.

### Questions

1 What do customers "buy" when they purchase Armani?

2 How does a leading focused differentiator such as Giorgio Armani S.p.A. protect its identity and maintain its luxury image?

to develop and sustain a competitive advantage and earn above-average returns. The activities required to use the focused cost leadership strategy are virtually identical to those of the industry-wide cost leadership strategy (Figure 5.2), and activities required to use the focused differentiation strategy are largely identical to those of the industry-wide differentiation strategy (Figure 5.3). Similarly, the manner in which each of the two focus strategies allows a firm to successfully deal with the five competitive forces, parallels those of the two broad strategies. The only difference is in the firm's competitive scope: the firm focuses on a narrow industry segment. Thus, Figures 5.2 and 5.3 and the text regarding the five competitive forces also describe the relationship between each of the two focus strategies and competitive advantage.

**Competitive risks of focus strategies**  With either focus strategy, the firm faces the same general risks as does the company using the cost leadership or the differentiation strategy, respectively, on an industry-wide basis. However, focus strategies have three additional risks.

First, a competitor may be able to focus on a more narrowly defined competitive segment and "outfocus" the focuser. This would happen to IKEA if another firm found a way to offer IKEA's customers (young buyers interested in stylish furniture at a low cost) additional sources of differentiation while charging the same price, or to provide the same service with the same sources of differentiation at a lower price. Second, a company competing on an industry-wide basis may decide that the market segment served by the firm using a focus strategy is attractive and worthy of competitive pursuit. For example, women's clothiers such as Chico's, Ann Taylor and Liz Claiborne might conclude that the profit potential in the narrow segment being served by Anne Fontaine is attractive and accordingly might decide to design and sell competitively similar clothing items. Initially, Anne Fontaine designed and sold only white shirts for women. Quite differentiated on the basis of their design, craftsmanship and high quality of raw materials, one customer describes her reaction to wearing an Anne Fontaine shirt in this manner: "Once you put on a Fontaine design, you'll find that not one other white shirt can compare as far as design and quality craftsmanship are concerned."[111]

The third risk involved with a focus strategy is that the needs of customers within a narrow competitive segment may become more similar to those of industry-wide customers as a whole, over time. As a result, the advantages of a focus strategy are either reduced or eliminated. At some point, for example, the needs of Anne Fontaine's customers for high-quality, uniquely designed white shirts may dissipate. If this were to happen, Anne Fontaine's customers might choose to buy white shirts from chains such as Liz Claiborne that sell clothing items with some differentiation, but at a lower cost.

## Integrated cost leadership/differentiation strategy

**Integrated cost leadership/ differentiation strategy**

The integrated cost leadership/ differentiation strategy involves engaging in primary and support activities that allow a firm to simultaneously pursue low cost and differentiation.

Most consumers have high expectations when purchasing a good or service. In general, it seems that most consumers want to pay a low price for products with somewhat highly differentiated features. Because of these customer expectations, a number of firms engage in primary and support activities that allow them to simultaneously pursue low cost and differentiation. Firm seeking to do this use the integrated cost leadership/differentiation strategy. The objective of using this strategy is to efficiently produce products with some differentiated features. Efficient production is the source of maintaining low costs while differentiation is the source of creating unique value. Firms that successfully use the integrated cost leadership/ differentiation strategy usually adapt quickly to new technologies and rapid changes in their external environments. Simultaneously concentrating on developing two sources of competitive advantage (cost and differentiation) increases the number of primary and support activities in which the firm must become competent. Such firms often have strong networks with external parties that perform some of the primary and support activities.[112] In turn, having skills in a larger number of activities makes a firm more flexible.

Screwfix, part of home improvement group Kingfisher PLC which also owns B&Q, Castorama, Brico Dépôt, Hornbach and Koçtas, is one the UK's leading suppliers of repair, maintenance and home improvement products. It uses an integrated cost leadership/differentiation strategy as shown by its "Where the Trade Buys" brand promise by combining low cost with high levels of service and availability. Screwfix supplies, via a multi-channel distribution model, a range of 18 000 products which include screws, fixings, hand tools, power tools, plumbing and electrical supplies. Screwfix combines trade prices whilst offering high levels of service which includes multiple ordering channels, technical advice and guidelines, fast and reliable service that can be accessed seven days a week, excellent distribution and each item is supplied with a 30-day money-back guarantee with free returns. Knowing how its target market is both price and service conscious it combines effectively these seemingly inconsistent competitive attributes.[113]

European-based Zara, which pioneered "cheap chic" in clothing apparel, is another firm using the integrated cost leadership/differentiation strategy. Zara offers current and desirable fashions goods at relatively low prices. To implement this strategy effectively requires sophisticated designers and effective means of managing costs, which fits well with Zara's capabilities. Zara can design and begin manufacturing a new fashion in three weeks, which suggests a highly flexible organization that can adapt easily to changes in the market or with competitors.[114]

Flexibility is required for firms to complete primary and support activities in ways that allow them to use the integrated cost leadership/differentiation strategy in order to produce somewhat differentiated products at relatively low costs. Flexible manufacturing systems, information networks, and total quality management systems are three sources of flexibility that are particularly useful for firms trying

STRATEGIC FOCUS

© Francis Dean/Alamy

# Zara – integrating both sides of the coin

Zara is one of seven chains owned by Europe's largest speciality clothing company, Inditex SA of Spain, which received the Global Retailer of the Year award from the World Retail Congress in 2007. Founded in 1975, Zara moved overseas for the first time in the early 1990s. By 2009 the company had grown to operate more than 1300 stores located in 72 countries worldwide, including China and Russia.

Zara sells what has been referred to as "fast" or "disposable" fashion, fashion "on demand" and "fashion that you wear 10 times". Its strategy is to copy catwalk fashions and produce similar looking but lower quality goods and sell them at affordable prices for the less affluent customer base. The prices Zara offer are market based. Zara determines the existing market price for a product, and then establishes a price below the lowest competitor's price for a similar product. Zara is vertically integrated and controls its products from the design decision to the point of sale. This level of control allows Zara to keep the costs low.

In-house designers closely monitor popular fashions, including styles that celebrities are seen wearing, throughout the year. As a new style is discovered Zara's teams work to develop products matching that style within a short time. A just-in-time manufacturing system is implemented, giving Zara the ability to develop and begin manufacturing a new product line in three weeks, compared to an industry average of nine months. Approximately 10 000 separate items are produced annually, all shipped directly from a central distribution centre in Spain. Even so, Zara's system allows them to get new merchandise to stores across Europe within 24 hours and, by flying goods via commercial airliners, to stores in the Americas and Asia in 48 hours or less. As a result of this just-in-time system, no warehouses are needed in Zara's distribution system as inventories are minimal. This lack of inventory leads to reduced costs of production, a benefit Zara uses as a competitive advantage by offering lower prices to their customers. Only a limited number of products are shipped to stores, to maintain the perception of scarcity. The most fashionable items are considered riskier and are produced in smaller quantities. Rapid product turnover at Zara increases this perception and also serves as a selling point with constant new designs drawing customers frequently back to the stores.

Zara locates in major shopping districts and designs attractive storefronts to bring customers in. The interiors of stores are designed with the comfort of customers in mind. An emphasis on an attractive decor motivates customers to return frequently. Salespeople frequently change the location of items in the stores, which also contributes to the perception of scarcity. Information downloaded on a daily basis from each store enables designers to better monitor customers' preferences. Zara spends a relatively small amount on advertising, usually only for its end-of-season sales, compared to its major competitors such as Benetton, Gap, and H&M of Sweden, relying more on word-of-mouth and brand reputation for generating custom and on generating return custom through good quality customer service.

**Sources**: 2009, Zara, http://www.zara.com, July 30; 2009, Inditex, http://www.inditex.com, July 30; 2008, "Zara thrives by breaking all the rules", *BusinessWeek*, October 9; 2006,

Inditex SA: "Net climbs 22 per cent amid cuts in costs, store openings", *Wall Street Journal*, December 14, B10; Rohwedder, C. (2006) "Can Inditex stock stay as hip as its "fast fashion" clothes?", *Wall Street Journal*, September 21, C14; Yaeger, L. (2003) "Fete accompli", *Village Voice*, December 17, 12; 2003, "Zara creates a ready to wear business: Leading fashion label designs its whole operation to fit the customer", *Strategic Direction*, November/December, 19(11): 24; Yaeger, L. (2002) "Spring breaks", *Village Voice*, April 23, 14; Jones, B. (2001) Madrid: Zara pioneers fashion on demand, Europe, September, 43; 2001, "Business: Floating on air", *Economist*, May 19, 56; Vitzthum, C. (2001) "Just-in-time fashion, Spanish retailer Zara makes low-cost lines in weeks by running its own show", *Wall Street Journal*, May 18, B1.

### Questions

1 What are the vulnerabilities of the Zara strategy?

2 Based on its distinctive positioning, with whom does Zara compete?

to balance the objectives of continuous cost reductions and continuous enhancements to sources of differentiation as called for by the integrated strategy.

**Flexible manufacturing systems**  A flexible manufacturing system (FMS) increases the "flexibilities of human, physical and information resources"[115] that the firm integrates to create relatively differentiated products at relatively low costs. A significant technological advance, FMS is a computer-controlled process used to produce a variety of products in moderate, flexible quantities with a minimum of manual intervention.[116] Often the flexibility is derived from modularization of the manufacturing process (and sometimes other value chain activities as well).[117]

The goal of an FMS is to eliminate the "low cost versus product variety" trade-off that is inherent in traditional manufacturing technologies. Firms use an FMS to change quickly and easily from making one product to making another. Used properly, an FMS allows the firm to respond more effectively to changes in its customers' needs, while retaining low-cost advantages and consistent product quality.[118] Because an FMS also enables the firm to reduce the lot size needed to manufacture a product efficiently, the firm's capacity to serve the unique needs of a narrow competitive scope is higher. In industries of all types, effective mixes of the firm's tangible assets (e.g., machines) and intangible assets (e.g., people's skills) facilitate implementation of complex competitive strategies, especially the integrated cost leadership/differentiation strategy.[119]

**Information networks**  By linking companies with their suppliers, distributors and customers, information networks provide another source of flexibility. These networks, when used effectively, help the firm to satisfy customer expectations in terms of product quality and delivery speed.[120]

Earlier, we discussed the importance of managing the firm's relationships with its customers in order to understand their needs. Customer relationship management (CRM) is one form of an information-based network process that firms use for this purpose.[121] An effective CRM system provides a 360-degree view of the company's relationship with customers, encompassing all contact points, business processes, and communication media and sales channels.[122] The firm can then use this information to determine the trade-offs its customers are willing to make between differentiated features and low cost – an assessment that is vital for companies using the integrated cost leadership/differentiation strategy.

To make comprehensive strategic decisions with effective knowledge of the organization's context, good information flow is essential. Better quality managerial decisions require accurate information on the firm's environment.[123]

**Total quality management systems** Total quality management (TQM) is a "managerial innovation that emphasizes an organization's total commitment to the customer and to continuous improvement of every process through the use of data-driven, problem-solving approaches based on empowerment of employee groups and teams".[128] Firms develop and use TQM systems in order to (1) increase customer satisfaction, (2) cut costs, and (3) reduce the amount of time required to introduce innovative products to the marketplace.[129]

Firms able to simultaneously reduce costs while enhancing their ability to develop innovative products increase their flexibility, an outcome that is particularly helpful to firms implementing the integrated cost leadership/differentiation strategy. Exceeding customers' expectations regarding quality is a differentiating feature, and eliminating process inefficiencies to cut costs allows the firm to offer that quality to customers at a relatively low price. Thus, an effective TQM system helps the firm develop the flexibility needed to spot opportunities to simultaneously increase differentiation and reduce costs. TQM systems are available to all competitors so they may help firms maintain competitive parity, but rarely alone will they lead to a competitive advantage.[130]

**Competitive risks of the integrated cost leadership/differentiation strategy** The potential to earn above-average returns by successfully using the integrated cost leadership/differentiation strategy is appealing. However, it is a risky strategy, because firms find it difficult to perform primary and support activities in ways that allow them to produce relatively inexpensive products with levels of differentiation that create value for the target customer. Moreover, to properly use this strategy across time, firms must be able to simultaneously reduce costs incurred to produce products (as required by the cost leadership strategy) while increasing products' differentiation (as required by the differentiation strategy).

Firms that fail to perform the primary and support activities in an optimum manner become stuck in the middle.[131] Being stuck in the middle means that the firm's cost structure is not low enough to allow it to attractively price its products and that its products are not sufficiently differentiated to create value for the target customer. These firms will not earn above-average returns and will earn average returns only when the structure of the industry in which it competes is highly favourable.[132] Thus, companies implementing the integrated cost leadership/differentiation strategy must be able to perform the primary and support activities in ways that allow them to produce products that offer the target customer some differentiated features at a relatively low cost/price.

Firms can also become stuck in the middle when they fail to successfully implement *either* the cost leadership *or* the differentiation strategy. In other words, industry-wide competitors can also become stuck in the middle. Trying to use the integrated strategy is costly in that firms must pursue both low costs and differentiation. Firms may need to form alliances with other firms to achieve differentiation, yet alliance partners may extract prices for the use of their resources that make it difficult to be a cost leader.[133] Firms may be motivated to make acquisitions to maintain their differentiation through innovation or to add products not offered by competitors to their portfolio.[134] Recent research suggests that firms using "pure strategies", either cost leadership or differentiation, often outperform firms attempting to use a "hybrid strategy" (i.e., integrated cost leadership/differentiation strategy). This research suggests the risky nature of using an integrated strategy (see also Chapter 15 for a more detailed discussion on organizational ambidexterity for realizing these hybrid strategies).[135] However, the integrated strategy is becoming more common and perhaps necessary in many industries due to technological advances and global competition.

**Total quality management (TQM)**

Total quality management (TQM) is a managerial innovation that emphasizes an organization's total commitment to the customer and to continuous improvement of every process through the use of data-driven, problem-solving approaches based on empowerment of employee groups and teams.

**Stuck in the middle**

Stuck in the middle means that the firm's cost structure is not low enough to allow it to attractively price its products and that its products are not sufficiently differentiated to create value for the target customer.

# KEY DEBATE

## Pure strategy or hybrid strategy

Since Porter first proposed his bases of competitive advantage,[124] there has been much debate about the nature and composition of business-level strategy. Porter initially argued that there are two different decisions that firms are confronted with: how to compete (based on either cost leadership or differentiation advantage) and where to compete (based on market scope being even narrow or broad). See Figure 5.1 "Five business-level strategies". Much of the business-level strategy debate that followed has focused on two polar views: (1) the mutual exclusivity argument and (2) the combinative argument.

The mutual exclusivity argument considers that the firm's business-level strategy can be captured by either cost leadership or differentiation forms of advantage (so-called "pure" strategy).[125] This argument follows Porter's view that because each strategy type requires different combinations of resources, capabilities, systems and organizational factors, then the simultaneous pursuit of both cost leadership and differentiation is not possible and the risks of being "stuck in the middle" can arise for the firm – where no decision is made about how to compete in the market and the firm can, at best, aspire to mediocrity in cost leadership and differentiation. When a firm seeks to invest in greater differentiation then it follows that this will invariably increase costs. For example, Marks & Spencer is one of the UK's leading retailers of clothing, food, home products and financial services whose vision is, quite simply, "to be the standard against which all others are measured".[126] This form of differentiation requires key values which Marks & Spencer imbue throughout the firm – quality, value, service, innovation and trust. Maintaining and investing in these values is costly and when Marks & Spencer

differentiate, for example, their food halls from their competitors, this often demands greater costs in sourcing superior products, providing high levels of customer service, innovating in product development and ensuring exceptional quality throughout. The demands for increased differentiation therefore become incompatible with pursuing cost leadership.

On the other hand, the combinative argument considers the extent to which the business-level strategies can be combined to form the integrated cost leadership/differentiation strategy (so-called "hybrid" strategy). A number of studies have shown that combining cost leadership and differentiation types of strategy can work well together and create above-average returns for the firm.[127] For instance, if a firm secures a dominant market position by following differentiation strategy, it is possible that corresponding cost advantages can be gained from the economies of scale effects. The reverse can also apply too in that a firm that has been a successful cost leader in a market can reinvest in differentiation attributes such as product quality, service delivery, branding and marketing efforts in a bid to integrate cost leadership/differentiation, thus pursuing a hybrid strategy.

Which of these strategic approaches is preferable can vary. The risks of pursuing a pure strategy include: (1) competitor imitation; (2) strategy specialization leading to a narrow view of market needs leading to important gaps in customer offerings; (3) being locked in to one strategic approach leading to inflexibility in responding to market developments and competitor innovations. Given these limitations of the pure strategy approach this might suggest that the hybrid strategy is more favourable. However, hybrid strategy typically exposes the firm to being stuck-in-the-middle seeking to reconcile two different and incompatible strategies.

### Questions

1 With examples, identify and describe the conditions under which a firm can achieve above-average returns by adopting a: (a) pure strategy; and (b) a hybrid strategy.

2 How do these conditions vary?

## CLOSING CASE

© Paul Rapson/Alamy

# BMW differentiates with Mini

BMW Group is a leading global provider of premium products and services for individual mobility. Revenues are generated through three business divisions: automobiles, financial services and motorcycles. BMW focuses on the premium segments of the global passenger car and motorcycle market. The automobiles division develops, manufactures, assembles and sells passenger cars and off-road vehicles under the brands BMW, Mini and Rolls-Royce. BMW acquired the Mini brand in 2001. Since this acquisition sales grew from 25000 units in 2001 to over 232000 units in 2008. The Mini, which is sold in more than 70 countries, is even a hit in countries that have strong local auto industries. The top five markets are Britain, with around 45000 cars sold in 2008; the United States with 41000; Germany 29000; Italy 22 000; and Japan 13000.

BMW has consistently positioned its Mini line as more than just a car. Instead it is marketed as a lifestyle brand, with a range of driver accessories and other miscellaneous branded items such as key fobs and clothing lines giving the brand more meaning to customers than being simply a car. In addition Mini has its own online social network, or "urban initiative", called Mini Space. A host of other marketing initiatives, both on and offline, are all designed to play on the car's perky appeal.

Mini buyers have a broad and in-depth choice for their car's specification, with 372 interior configurations, including a wide choice of options for seat cover materials and steering wheel covers, and 319 exterior options, with choices on factors from the type of engine in the car to whether to have racing stripes running over the top of the car. Combined, these options result in 15 trillion possible variations, making the Mini the closest thing to a customized car in its size and price range.

The BMW brand has traditionally been associated with larger and premium priced cars, therefore for BMW the ownership of the Mini brand provided the company with the opportunity to enter a very different segment of the automobile market whilst reducing the risk of affecting perceptions of their existing brand. In terms of strategic development for BMW, the purchase of the "Mini" brand provided the firm with a significant growth opportunity that involved both new product development and brand development. This was to be achieved by entering the very competitive small hatchback market with a premium product, competing against models such as the VW Golf, Ford Fiesta and Audi A3.

With their authentic and absolutely unique brands, BMW, Mini, and Rolls-Royce, BMW occupies a position as a major market shareholder in all of their markets, ranging from small cars to those of a more luxurious class. This makes BMW the only multi-brand manufacturer in the world not operating in the mass market.

**Sources**: Maynard, M. (2006) "Can the Mini stay up to speed?" *International Herald Tribune,* October 6; http://www.bmw.nl; http://www.wikipedia.nl; Statement by Prof. Dr. Ing Joachim Milberg, chairman of the board of management of BMW AG, and Dr Burkhard Göschel, member of the board of management of BMW AG, on the occasion of the Mini Press Conference Paris, 28 September 2000, 12.3; Highlights, http://www.mini.co.uk.

## Questions

1 What is the basis of the Mini's differentiation?

2 Given the pressure toward commoditization in many markets, how homogenized do you consider the small hatchback market will become in Europe?

## SUMMARY

- A business-level strategy is an integrated and coordinated set of commitments and actions the firm uses to gain a competitive advantage by exploiting core competencies in specific product markets. Five business-level strategies (cost leadership, differentiation, focused cost leadership, focused differentiation and integrated cost leadership/differentiation) are examined in the chapter.

- Customers are the foundation of successful business-level strategies. When considering customers, a firm simultaneously examines three issues: *who, what,* and *how.* These issues, respectively, refer to the customer groups to be served, the needs those customers have that the firm seeks to satisfy, and the core competencies the firm will use to satisfy customers' needs. Increasing segmentation of markets throughout the global economy creates opportunities for firms to identify more unique customer needs they can serve with one of the business-level strategies.

- Firms seeking competitive advantage through the cost leadership strategy produce no-frills, standardized products for an industry's typical customer. However, these low-cost products must be offered with competitive levels of differentiation. Above-average returns are earned when firms continuously emphasize efficiency such that their costs are lower than those of their competitors, while providing customers with products that have acceptable levels of differentiated features.

- Competitive risks associated with the cost leadership strategy include (1) a loss of competitive advantage to newer technologies; (2) a failure to detect changes in customers' needs; and (3) the ability of competitors to imitate the cost leader's competitive advantage through their own unique strategic actions.

- Through the differentiation strategy, firms provide customers with products that have different (and valued) features. Differentiated products must be sold at a cost that customers believe is competitive relative to the product's features, as compared to the cost/feature combinations available from competitors' goods. Because of their uniqueness, differentiated goods or services are sold at a premium price. Products can be differentiated along any dimension that a customer group values. Firms using this strategy seek to differentiate their products from competitors' goods or services along as many dimensions as possible. The less similarity to competitors' products, the more buffered a firm is from competition with its rivals.

- Risks associated with the differentiation strategy include (1) a customer group's decision that the differences between the differentiated product and the cost leader's goods or services are no longer worth a premium price; (2) the inability of a differentiated product to create the type of value for which customers are willing to pay a premium price; (3) the ability of competitors to provide customers with products that have features similar to those of the differentiated product, but at a lower cost; and (4) the threat of counterfeiting, whereby firms produce a cheap "knockoff" of a differentiated good or service.

- Through the cost leadership and the differentiated focus strategies, firms serve the needs of a narrow competitive segment (e.g., a buyer group, product segment or geographic area). This strategy is successful when firms have the core competencies required to provide value to a specialized market segment that exceeds the value available from firms serving customers on an industry-wide basis.

- The competitive risks of focus strategies include (1) a competitor's ability to use its core competencies to "outfocus" the focuser by serving an even more narrowly defined market segment; (2) decisions by industry-wide competitors to focus on a customer group's specialized needs; and (3) a reduction in differences of the needs between customers in a narrow market segment and the industry-wide market.

- Firms using the integrated cost leadership/differentiation strategy strive to provide customers with relatively low-cost products that also have valued differentiated features. Flexibility is required for the firm to learn how to use primary and support activities in ways that allow them to produce differentiated products at relatively low costs. The primary risk of this strategy is that a firm might produce products that do not offer sufficient value in terms of either low cost or differentiation. In such cases, the company is "stuck in the middle". Firms stuck in the middle compete at a disadvantage and are unable to earn more than average returns.

## REVIEW QUESTIONS

1   What is a business-level strategy?

2   What do *reach, richness* and *affiliation* refer to?

3   What are the differences between cost leadership, differentiation, focused cost leadership, focused differentiation and integrated cost leadership/differentiation business-level strategies?

4   How can each one of the business-level strategies be used to position the firm relative to the five forces of competition in a way that helps the firm earn above-average returns?

5   What are the specific risks associated with using each business-level strategy?

## DISCUSSION QUESTIONS

1   What is the relationship between a firm's customers and its business-level strategy in terms of *who, what, and how*? Why is this relationship important?

2   There is considerable evidence to suggest that strategic archetypes remain consistent over time. Discuss why, in dynamic and competitive marketplaces, firms' business-level strategies tend to follow similar patterns over time.

3   A coherent business-level strategy is only as effective as the tactics that action it. Discuss.

4   In what ways do policies and business-level strategies differ?

5   Identify similarities and differences in business-level strategy between: (1) a medium-sized information technology consultancy; (2) a municipal department in a local government organization; and, (3) a premium distilled water supplier.

## FURTHER READING

Some contend that business-level strategy is the core of what strategy is about: competing and prevailing over rivals. How to articulate a winning strategy and communicate it is capturing the attention of researchers and practitioners. Rich insight is provided by articles that address these issues (e.g. D. J. Collis and M. G. Rukstad (2008) "Can you say what your strategy is?", *Harvard Business Review*, 86(4): 82–90; M. Baghai, S. Smit and P. Viguerie (2009) "Is your growth strategy flying blind?", *Harvard Business Review*, 87(5): 86–96; D. Lei and J. W. Slocum (2009) "The tipping points of business strategy: The rise and decline of competitiveness", *Organizational Dynamics*, 38: 131–147). Of particular interest is the discussion related to Michael E. Porter's generic strategies and the possibility of hybrids (e.g. E. Pertusa-Ortega,

J. F. Molina-Azorín and E. Claver-Cortés (2009) "Competitive strategies and firm performance: A comparative analysis of pure, hybrid and stuck-in-the-middle strategies in Spanish firms", *British Journal of Management*, 20: 508–523) and specific capabilities to distance rivals (e.g. D. W. Vorhies, R. E. Morgan and C. W. Autry (2009) "Product-market strategy and the marketing capabilities of the firm: impact on market effectiveness and cash flow performance", *Strategic Management Journal*, 30: 1310–1334). It is in this context of seeking the right position in the market that framing, as S. Kaplan (2008) points out clearly ("Framing contests: Strategy making under uncertainty", *Organization Science*, 19: 729–752), becomes important in achieving above-average returns.

# EXPERIENTIAL EXERCISES

## Exercise 1: Customer needs and stock trading

Nearly 100 million Americans have investments in the stock market through shares of individual companies or positions in mutual funds. At its peak volume, the New York Stock Exchange has traded more than 3.5 billion shares in a single day. Stock brokerage firms are the conduit to help individuals plan their portfolios and manage transactions. Given the scope of this industry, there is no single definition of what customers consider as "superior value" from a brokerage operation.

### Part One

After forming small teams, the instructor will ask the teams to count off by threes. The teams will study three different brokerage firms, with team 1 examining TD Ameritrade (ticker: AMTD), team 2 E*;Trade (ticker: ETFC), and team 3, Charles Schwab (ticker: SCHW).

### Part Two

Each team should research its target company to answer the following questions:

- Describe the "*who*, *what*, and *how*" for your firm. How stable is this focus? How much have these elements changed in the last five years?
- Describe your firm's strategy.
- How does your firm's strategy offer protection against each of the five forces?

### Part Three

In class, the instructor will summarize the results for each team.

Then the whole class will discuss which firm is most effective at meeting the needs of its customer base.

## Exercise 2: Create a business-level strategy

This assignment brings together elements from the previous chapters. You and your team will create a business-level strategy for a firm of your own creation. The instructor will be assigning you an industry from which you will create a strategy for entering that industry using one of the five potential business-level strategies.

Each team is assigned one of the BLSs described in the chapter:

- Cost leadership
- Differentiation
- Focused cost leadership
- Focused differentiation
- Integrated cost leadership/differentiation

### Part One

Research your industry and describe the general environment and the industry. Using the dimensions of the general environment, identify some factors for each dimension that is influential for your industry. Next describe the industry environment using Porter's 5 Force model. Database services like Mint Global, Datamonitor or IBIS World can be helpful in this regard. If these are not available to you consult your local librarian for assistance. At the end of the exercise you should be able to clearly articulate the opportunities and the threats that exist.

### Part Two

In this section you are to create on a poster the business-level strategy assigned to your team. Be prepared to describe the following:

- Mission statement.
- Description of your target customer.
- Picture of your business. Where is it located (town centre, suburb, rural, etc).
- Describe trends that provide opportunities and threats for your intended strategy.
- List the resources, both tangible and intangible, required to compete successfully in this market.
- How will you go about creating a sustainable competitive advantage?

# VIDEO CASE

### The counter-intuitive strategy

**William Johnson, Chairman, president and chief executive officer, H. J. Heinz Company**
www.cengage.co.uk/volberda/students/video_cases

William Johnson, Chairman, president and chief executive officer, H. J. Heinz Company discusses the rationalization of business segments that the company found itself holding in 2002.

Be prepared to discuss the following concepts and questions in class:

## Concepts

- Customers
- Strategy
- Focusing on capabilities
- Portfolio of businesses
- Business-level strategy

## Questions

1 Research H. J. Heinz Company. Describe its portfolio of businesses and it business-level strategy.

2 Do you think the goal of any company should be to grow and get bigger? Particularly a publicly traded one like Heinz?

3 In any corporation, should underperforming business segments be sold off?

## NOTES

1. D. J. Collis and M. G. Rukstad, 2008, "Can you say what your strategy is?", *Harvard Business Review*, 86(4): 82–90.

2. H. Greve, 2009, "Bigger and safer: The diffusion of competitive advantage", *Strategic Management Journal*, 30: 1–23.

3. M. A. Delmas and M. W. Toffel, 2008, "Organisational responses to environmental demands: Opening the black box", *Strategic Management Journal*, 29: 1027–1055; S. Elbanna and J. Child, 2007, "The influence of decision, environmental and firm characteristics on the rationality of strategic decision-making", *Journal of Management Studies*, 44: 561–591; T. Yu and A. A. Cannella, Jr., 2007, "Rivalry between multinational enterprises: An event history approach", *Academy of Management Journal*, 50: 665–686.

4. S. L. Newbert, 2008, "Value, rareness, competitive advantage, and performance: A conceptual-level empirical investigation of the resource-based view of the firm", *Strategic Management Journal*, 29: 745–768.

5. M. V. Copeland, 2009, "Dell's bread-and-butter puts it in a jam", *CNNMoney.com*, http://www.cnnmoney.com, February 27.

6. N. A. Morgan and L. L. Rego, 2009, "Brand portfolio strategy and firm performance", *Journal of Marketing*, 73: 59–74; C. Zott and R. Amit, 2008, "The fit between product market strategy and business model: Implications for firm performance", *Strategic Management Journal*, 29: 1–26.

7. S. Kaplan, 2008, "Framing contests: Strategy making under uncertainty", *Organization Science*, 19: 729–752.

8. S. Maxfield, 2008, "Reconciling corporate citizenship and competitive strategy: Insights from economic theory", *Journal of Business Ethics*, 80: 367–377; K. Shimizu and M. A. Hitt, 2004, "Strategic flexibility: Organisational preparedness to reverse ineffective strategic decisions", *Academy of Management Executive*, 18(4): 44–59; H. W. Volberda, 1996, "Toward the flexible form: How to remain vital in hypercompetitive environments", *Organization Science*, 7(4): 359–387; H. W. Volberda, 2003, "Strategic flexibility: Creating dynamic competitive advantages", Ch. 32 in: D. Faulkner and A. Campbell (eds.), *The Oxford*

*Handbook of Strategy,* Oxford: Oxford University Press, 939–998; H. W. Volberda and T. Elfring, 2001, *Rethinking Strategy*, London: Sage.

9. B. Chakravarthy and P. Lorange, 2008, "Driving renewal: The entrepreneur-manager", *Journal of Business Strategy*, 29: 14–21.

10. R. Oriani and M. Sobrero, 2008, "Uncertainty and the market valuation of R&D within a real options logic", *Strategic Management Journal*, 29: 343–361.

11. J. A. Lamberg, H. Tikkanen, T. Nokelainen and H. Suur-Inkeroinen, 2009, "Competitive dynamics, strategic consistency, and organisational survival", *Strategic Management Journal*, 30: 45–60; R. D. Ireland and C. C. Miller, 2005, "Decision-making and firm success", *Academy of Management Executive*, 18(4): 8–12.

12. I. Goll, N. B. Johnson and A. A. Rasheed, 2008, "Top management team demographic characteristics, business strategy, and firm performance in the US airline industry: The role of managerial discretion", *Management Decision*, 46: 201–222; J. R. Hough, 2006, "Business segment performance redux: A multilevel approach", *Strategic Management Journal*, 27: 45–61.

13. P. Ozcan and K. M. Eisenhardt, 2009, "Origin of alliance portfolios: Entrepreneurs, network strategies, and firm performance", *Academy of Management Journal*, 52: 246–279; B. Choi, S. K. Poon and J. G. Davis, 2008, "Effects of knowledge management strategy on organisational performance: A complementarity theory-based approach", *Omega*, 36: 235–251.

14. J. W. Spencer, 2008, "The impact of multinational enterprise strategy on indigenous enterprises: Horizontal spillovers and crowding out in developing countries", *Academy of Management Review*, 33: 341–361.

15. E. Steel, 2009, "MySpace slashes jobs as growth slows down", *Wall Street Journal Online*, http://www.wsj.com, June 17.

16. R. Grover, 2009, "Van Natta cuts jobs at MySpace", *Wall Street Journal Online*, http://www.wsj.com, June 16; M. Garrahan, 2010, "MySpace plans phased revamp", *Financial Times Online*, http://www.ft.com, March 9.

17. B. Einhorn and M. Srivastava, 2009, "Social networking: Facebook looks to India", *Wall Street Journal Online*, http://www.wsj.com, June 15.

18. D. Lei and J. W. Slocum, 2009, "The tipping points of business strategy: The rise and decline of competitiveness", *Organizational Dynamics*, 38: 131–147.

19. R. J. Harrington and A. K. Tjan, 2008, "Transforming strategy one customer at a time", *Harvard Business Review*, 86(3): 62–72; R. Priem, 2007, "A consumer perspective on value creation", *Academy of Management Review*, 32: 219–235.

20. M. E. Porter, 1980, *Competitive Strategy*, New York: Free Press.

21. M. Baghai, S. Smit and P. Viguerie, 2009, "Is your growth strategy flying blind?", *Harvard Business Review*, 87(5): 86–96.

22. D. G. Sirmon, S. Gove and M. A. Hitt, 2008, "Resource management in dyadic competitive rivalry: The effects of resource bundling and deployment", *Academy of Management Journal*, 51: 919–935; D. G. Sirmon, M. A. Hitt and R. D. Ireland, 2007, "Managing firm resources in dynamic environments to create value: Inside the black box", *Academy of Management Review*, 32: 273–292.

23. D. W. Vorhies, R. E. Morgan and C. W. Autry, 2009, "Product-market strategy and the marketing capabilities of the firm: Impact on market effectiveness and cash flow performance", *Strategic Management Journal*, 30: 1310–1334; A. Wetergins and R. Boschma, 2009, "Does spatial proximity to customers matter for innovative performance? Evidence from the Dutch software sector", *Research Policy*, 38: 746–755.

24. R. E. Morgan and Pierre Berthon, 2008, "Organisational learning, innovation and business performance: interrelationships in bioscience firms", *Journal of Management Studies*, 45: 1329–1353,

25. J. McGregor, 2009, "When service means survival", *BusinessWeek*, March 2, 26–33.

26. 2010, Company information, http://www.harrahs.com, May 15.

27. Y. Liu and R. Yang, 2009, "Competing loyalty programs: Impact of market saturation, market share, and category expandability", *Journal of Marketing*, 73: 93–108; P. R. Berthon, L. F. Pitt, I. McCarthy and S. M. Kates, 2007, "When customers get clever: Managerial approaches to dealing with creative customers", *Business Horizons*, 50(1): 39–47.

28. P. E. Frown and A. F. Payne, 2009, "Customer relationship management: A strategic perspective", *Journal of Business Market Management*, 3: 7–27.

29. H. Green, 2009, "How Amazon aims to keep you clicking", *BusinessWeek*, March 2, 34–35.

30. S. Gadsby, 2010, Social media statistics, www.clicky media.co.uk, February.

31. 2010, Press Room – Factsheet, http://www.myspace.com, May 20.

32. 2010, Statistics, http://www.facebook.com, May 19.

33. 2009, Netflix announces Q1 2009 financial results, http://www.netflix.com, April 23.

34. J. Bezos, J. Kirby and T. A. Stewart, 2009, "The institutional yes", *Harvard Business Review*, 85(10): 74–82.

35. 2009, Amazon turns to customers for new TV advertising campaign, http://www.amazon.com, June 8.

36. 2010, http://cars.uk.msn.com/, June 17.

37. I. C. MacMillan and L. Selden, 2008, "The incumbent's advantage", *Harvard Business Review*, 86(10): 111–121; G. Dowell, 2006, "Product-line strategies of new entrants in an established industry: Evidence from the U.S. bicycle industry", *Strategic Management Journal*, 27: 959–979.

38. J. Zhang and M. Wedel, 2009, "The effectiveness of customised promotions in online and offline stores", *Journal of Marketing Research*, 46: 190–206; C. W. Lamb Jr., J. F. Hair Jr. and C. McDaniel, 2006, *Marketing* (8th edn), Mason, OH: Thomson South-Western, 224.

39. 2010, About Hill's pet nutrition, http://www.hillspet.com.uk, May 20.

40. 2010, http://www.schering-plough.co.uk/index.aspx, May 20.

41. S. Hamner, 2005, "Filling the Gap", *Business 2.0*, July, 30.

42. S. French, 2009, "Re-framing strategic thinking: The research – aims and outcomes", *Journal of Management Development*, 28: 205–224.

43. R. J. Brodie, J. R. M. Whittome and G. J. Brush, 2009, "Investigating the service brand: A customer value perspective", *Journal of Business Research*, 62: 345–355; P. D. Ellis, 2006, "Market orientation and performance: A meta-analysis and cross-national comparisons", *Journal of Management Studies*, 43: 1089–1107.

44. L. A. Bettencourt and A. W. Ulwick, 2008, "The customer-centered innovation map", *Harvard Business Review*, 86 (5): 109–114.

45. A. Feldman, 2009, "Wooing the worried", *BusinessWeek*, April 27, 24.

46. D. Kiley, 2009, "One Ford for the whole wide world", *BusinessWeek*, June 15, 58–59.

47. E. A. Borg, 2009, "The marketing of innovations in high-technology companies: A network approach", *European Journal of Marketing*, 43: 364–370.

48. D. Foust, F. F. Jespersen, F. Katzenberg, A. Barrett and R. O. Crockett, 2003, "The best performers", *BusinessWeek Online*, http://www.businessweek.com, March 24.

49. T. Y. Eng and J. G. Spickett-Jones, 2009, "An investigation of marketing capabilities and upgrading performance of manufacturers in Mainland China and Hong Kong", *Journal of World Business*, 44(4): 463–475; M. B. Heeley and R. Jacobson, 2008, "The recency of technological inputs and financial performance", *Strategic Management Journal*, 29: 723–744.

50. 2009, Experience our energy, http://www.proenergy services.com, June 17.

51. 2010, http://www.sas.com, May 20.

52. 2010, Strategies, http://www.kraft.com, May 20.

53. M. Mullick-Kanwar, 2010, "The evolution of private label branding", http://www.brandchannel.com, May 20.

54. D. Lamarre, 2010, "Talking management", http://www.podcasts.mcgill.ca/businessandleadership/, Karl Moore interviews D. Lamarre, CEO of Cirque du Soleil, McGill Business and Leadership podcast series, May 6.

55. M. E. Porter, 1985, *Competitive Advantage*, New York: Free Press, 26.

56. M. E. Porter, 1996, "What is strategy?", *Harvard Business Review*, 74(6): 61–78.

57. S. D. Barrett, 2004, "The sustainability of the Ryanair model", *International Journal of Transport Management*, 2(2): 89–98.

58. M. E. Porter, 1996, "What is strategy?", *Harvard Business Review*, 74(6): 61–78.

59. M. Reitzig and P. Puranam, 2009, "Value appropriation as an organisational capability: The case of IP protection through patents", *Strategic Management Journal*, 30: 765–789; C. Zott, 2003, "Dynamic capabilities and the emergence of intraindustry differential firm performance: Insights from a simulation study", *Strategic Management Journal*, 24: 97–125.

60. M. E. Porter, 1994, "Toward a dynamic theory of strategy", in: R. P. Rumelt, D. E. Schendel and D. J. Teece (eds.), *Fundamental Issues in Strategy*, Boston, MA: Harvard Business School Press, 423–461.

61. M. E. Porter, "What is strategy?", *Harvard Business Review*, 74(6): 62.

62. M. Porter, *Competitive Advantage*, New York: Free Press, 15.

63. S. Sun, 2009, "An analysis on the conditions and methods of market segmentation", *International Journal of Business and Management*, 4: 63–70.

64. J. Gonzales-Benito and I. Suarez-Gonzalez, 2011, "A study of the role played by manufacturing strategic objectives and capabilities in understanding the relationship between Porter's generic strategies and business performance", *British Journal of Management*, 21(4): 1027–1043.

65. G. B. Voss, D. Sirdeshmukh and Z. G. Voss, 2008, "The effects of slack resources and environmental threat on product exploration and exploitation", *Academy of Management Journal*, 51: 147–158.

66. J. Birchall and E. Rigby, 2010, "Walmart sets out goals for Asda", http://www.ft.com, April 15.

67. M. E. Porter, *Competitive Strategy*, 1980, New York: Free Press, 35–40.

68. M. J. Gehlhar, A. Regmi, S. E. Stefanou and B. L. Zoumas, 2009, "Brand leadership and product innovation as firm strategies in global food markets", *Journal of Product and Brand Management*, 18: 115–126.

69. M. Ihlwan, 2009, Kia Motors: "Still cheap, now chic", *BusinessWeek*, June 1, 58.

70. D. Mehri, 2006, "The dark side of lean: An insider's perspective on the realities of the Toyota production system", *Academy of Management Perspectives*, 20(2): 21–42.

71. N. T. Sheehan and G. Vaidyanathan, 2009, "Using a value creation compass to discover 'Blue Oceans'", *Strategy and Leadership*, 37: 13–20; D. F. Spulber, 2004, *Management Strategy*, New York: McGraw Hill/Irwin, 175.

72. 2010, Company Factsheet, www.firstgroup.com, August 11.

73. AGM Statement and Interim Management Statement, 2010, http://www.firstgroup.com, August 11.

74. M. Kotabe and R. Mudambi, 2009, "Global sourcing and value creation: Opportunities and challenges", *Journal of International Management*, 15: 121–125; D. F. Lynch, S. B. Keller and J. Ozment, 2000, "The effects of logistics capabilities and strategy on firm performance", *Journal of Business Logistics*, 21(2): 47–68.

75. J. Hatonen and T. Erikson, 2009, "30+ years of research and practice of outsourcing – Exploring the past and anticipating the future", *Journal of International Management*, 15: 142–155; P. Edwards and M. Ram, 2006, "Surviving on the margins of the economy: Working relationships in small, low-wage firms", *Journal of Management Studies*, 43: 895–916.

76. 2010, *About TK Maxx*, http://www.tkmaxx, August 11.

77. J. Morehouse, B. O'Mera, C. Hagen and T. Huseby, 2008, "Hitting back: Strategic responses to low-cost rivals", *Strategy & Leadership*, 36: 4–13; L. K. Johnson, 2003, "Dueling pricing strategies", *The McKinsey Quarterly*, 44(3): 10–11.

78. 2010, About us, http://www.aldi.co.uk, August 11.

79. E. Rigby, 2010, "Aldi UK sales soar by 25%", *Financial Times*, http://www.ft.com, January 13, 20.

80. J. B. Steenkamp and N. Kumar, 2009, "Don't be undersold!", *Harvard Business Review*, 87(12): 90–95.

81. O. Ormanidhi and O. Stringa, 2008, "Porter's model of generic competitive strategie", *Business Economics*, 43: 55–64; J. Bercovitz and W. Mitchell, 2007, "When is more better? The impact of business scale and scope on long-term business survival, while controlling for profitability", *Strategic Management Journal*, 28: 61–79.

82. J. Mintz, 2009, "Redbox's kiosks take on Netflix's red envelopes", *The Eagle*, June 21, A14.

83. M. E. Porter, *Competitive Strategy*, 1980, New York: Free Press, 35–40.

84. 2009, Product innovation, http://www.1000ventures.com, June 19.

85. R. Cowan and N. Jonard, 2009, "Knowledge portfolios and the organisation of innovation networks", *Academy of Management Review*, 34: 320–342.

86. D. Ashmos Plowman, L. T. Baker, T. E. Beck, M. Kulkarni, S. Thomas-Solansky and D. V. Travis, 2007, "Radical change accidentally: The emergence and amplification of small change", *Academy of Management Journal*, 50: 515–543; A. Wadhwa and S. Kotha, 2006, "Knowledge creation through external venturing: Evidence from the telecommunications equipment manufacturing industry", *Academy of Management Journal*, 49: 819–835.

87. D. W. Baack and D. J. Boggs, 2008, "The difficulties in using a cost leadership strategy in emerging markets", *International Journal of Emerging Markets*, 3: 125–139; M. J. Benner, 2007, "The incumbent discount: Stock

market categories and response to radical technological change", *Academy of Management Review*, 32: 703–720.

88. F. T. Rothaermel, M. A. Hitt and L. A. Jobe, 2006, "Balancing vertical integration and strategic outsourcing: Effects on product portfolio, product success and firm performance", *Strategic Management Journal*, 27: 1033–1056; A. V. Mainkar, M. Lubatkin and W. S. Schulze, 2006, "Toward a product-proliferation theory of entry barriers", *Academy of Management Review*, 31: 1062–1075.

89. M. E. Porter, *Competitive Advantage*, 1985, New York: Free Press, 14.

90. 2009, History, http://www.roberttalbott.com, June 19.

91. L. A. Bettencourt and A. W. Ulwick, 2008, "The customer-centered innovation map", *Harvard Business Review*, 86 (5): 109–114; W. C. Bogner and P. Bansal, 2007, "Knowledge management as a basis for sustained high performance", *Journal of Management Studies*, 44:165–188; M. Semadeni, 2006, "Minding your distance: How management consulting firms use service marks to position competitively", *Strategic Management Journal*, 27: 169–187.

92. M. Abbott, R. Holland, J. Giacomin and J. Shackleton, 2009, "Changing affective content in brand and product attributes", *Journal of Product & Brand Management*, 18: 17–26; J. A. Byrne, 2005, "The power of great design", *Fast Company*, June, 14.

93. B. Charny and J. A. Dicolo, 2009, "Apple debuts new iPhones to long lines", *Wall Street Journal Online*, http://www.wsj.com, June 19.

94. M. Jensen and A. Roy, 2008, "Staging exchange partner choices: When do status and reputation matter?", *Academy of Management Journal*, 51: 495–516; V. P. Rindova, T. G. Pollock and M. A. Hayward, 2006, "Celebrity firms: The social construction of market popularity", *Academy of Management Review*, 31: 50–71.

95. V. O'Connell, 2009, "Sales of luxury goods seen falling by 10%", *Wall Street Journal Online*, http://www.wsj.com, April 11.

96. S. Berfield, 2009, "Coach's Poppy line is luxury for recessionary times", *BusinessWeek Online*, http://www.wsj.com, June 18.

97. D. G. Sirmon, J. L. Arregle, M. A. Hitt and J. W. Webb, 2008, "The role of family influence in firms' strategic responses to threat of imitation", *Entrepreneurship Theory and Practice*, 32: 979–998; F. K. Pil and S. K. Cohen, 2006, "Modularity: Implications for imitation, innovation, and sustained advantage", *Academy of Management Review*, 31: 995–1011.

98. X. Bian and L. Moutinho, 2009, "An investigation of determinants of counterfeit purchase consideration", *Journal of Business Research*, 62: 368–378.

99. M. E. Porter, 1980, *Competitive Strategy*, New York: Free Press, 98.

100. 2009, Greif & Co., http://www.greifco.com, June 19.

101. 2009, About Goya foods, http://www.goyafoods.com, June 20.

102. M. Bustillo, 2009, "Small electronics chains thrive in downturn", *Wall Street Journal Online*, http://www.wsj.com, May 27.

103. M. E. Porter, 1985, *Competitive Advantage*, New York: Free Press, 15.

104. M. E. Porter, 1985, *Competitive Advantage*, New York: Free Press, 15–16.

105. 2010, Inter IKEA Sytems B.V., http://franchisor.ikea.com/, May 14.

106. K. Kling and I. Goteman, 2003, "IKEA CEO Andres Dahlvig on international growth and IKEA's unique corporate culture and brand identity", *Academy of Management Executive*, 17(1): 31–37.

107. 2009, About IKEA, http://www.ikea.com, June 21.

108. G. Evans, 2003, "Why some stores strike me as special", *Furniture Today*, 27(24): 91; M. E. Porter, 1996, "What is strategy?", *Harvard Business Review*, 74(6): 65.

109. J. Latson, 2009, "Tattoo removal makes mark in slow economy", *Houston Chronicle Online*, http://www.chron.com, April 25.

110. K. McLaughlin, 2009, "Food truck nation", *Wall Street Journal Online*, http://www.wsj.com, June 5.

111. 2009, "Woman of style: CEO Anne Fontaine", http://www.factio-magazine.com, June 20.

112. O. Furrer, D. Sudharshan, H. Thomas and M. T. Zlexandre, 2008, "Resource configurations, generic strategies, and firm performance: Exploring the parallels between resource-based and competitive strategy theories in a new industry", *Journal of Strategy and Management*, 1: 15–40; J. H. Dyer and N. W. Hatch, 2006, "Relation-specific capabilities and barriers to knowledge transfers: Creating advantage through network relationships", *Strategic Management Journal*, 27: 701–719.

113. 2010, Press Office, www.screwfix.com, August 11.

114. K. Capell, 2008, "Zara thrives by breaking all the rules", *BusinessWeek*, October 20, 66.

115. R. Sanchez, 1995, "Strategic flexibility in product competition", *Strategic Management Journal*, 16 (Special Issue): 140; H. W. Volberda, 1996, "Toward the flexible form: How to remain vital in hypercompetitive environments", *Organization Science*, 7(4): 359–387.

116. M. I. M. Wahab, D. Wu, and C. G. Lee, 2008, "A generic approach to measuring the machine flexibility of manufacturing systems", *European Journal of Operational Research*, 186: 137–149; H. W. Volberda, 1998, *Building the flexible firm: How to remain competitive*, Oxford: Oxford University Press; H. W. Volberda, 1996, "Flexible configuration strategies within Philips Semiconductors: A process of entrepreneurial revitalization", Ch. 11: in R. Sanchez, A. Heene and H. Thomas (eds.), *Dynamics of Competence-Based Competition: Theory and Practice in the New Strategic Management*, Oxford: Pergamon, 229–278.

117. M. Kotabe, R. Parente and J. Y. Murray, 2007, "Antecedents and outcomes of modular production in the Brazilian automobile industry: A grounded theory approach", *Journal of International Business Studies*, 38: 84–106.

118. T. Raj, R. Shankar and M. Sunhaib, 2009, "An ISM approach to analyse interaction between barriers of transition to flexible manufacturing systems", *International Journal of Manufacturing Technology and Management*, 16: 417–438; E. K. Bish, A. Muriel and S. Biller, 2005, "Managing flexible capacity in a make-to-order environment", *Management Science*, 51: 167–180.

119. S. M. Iravani, M. P. van Oyen and K. T. Sims, 2005, "Structural flexibility: A new perspective on the design of manufacturing and service operations", *Management Science*, 51: 151–166; H. W. Volberda, 1997, "Building flexible organizations for fast-moving markets", *Long Range Planning*, 30(2): 169–183; H. W. Volberda, 1998, *Building the flexible firm: How to remain competitive*, Oxford: Oxford University Press.

120. P. Theodorou and G. Florou, 2008, "Manufacturing strategies and financial performance – the effect of advanced information technology: CAD/CAM systems", *Omega*, 36: 107–121.

121. N. A. Morgan and L. L. Rego, 2009, "Brand portfolio strategy and firm performance", *Journal of Marketing*, 73: 59–74.

122. D. Elmuti, H. Jia and D. Gray, 2009, "Customer relationship management strategic application and organisational effectiveness: An empirical investigation", *Journal of Strategic Marketing*, 17: 75–96.

123. D. P. Forbes, 2007, "Reconsidering the strategic implications of decision comprehensiveness", *Academy of Management Review*, 32: 361–376.

124. M. E. Porter, 1980, *Competitive Strategy*, New York: Free Press.

125. S. Thornhill and R. E. White, 2007, "Strategic purity: A multi-industry evaluation of pure vs hybrid business strategies", *Strategic Management Journal*, 28: 553–561.

126. 2010, Our Stores, http://www2.marksandspencer.com/thecompany/our_stores/world.shtml, May 14.

127. E. Pertusa-Ortega, J. F. Molina-Azorín and E. Claver-Cortés, 2009, "Competitive strategies and firm performance: A comparative analysis of pure, hybrid and stuck-in-the-middle strategies in Spanish firms", *British Journal of Management*, 20: 508–523.

128. J. D. Westphal, R. Gulati and S. M. Shortell, 1997, "Customisation or conformity: An institutional and network perspective on the content and consequences of TQM adoption", *Administrative Science Quarterly*, 42: 366–394.

129. S. Modell, 2009, "Bundling management control innovations: A field study of organisational experimenting with total quality management and the balanced scorecard", *Accounting, Auditing & Accountability Journal*, 22: 59–90.

130. A. Keramati and A. Albadvi, 2009, "Exploring the relationship between use of information technology in total quality management and SMEs performance using canonical correlation analysis: A survey on Swedish car part supplier sector", *International Journal of Information Technology and Management*, 8: 442–462; R. J. David and S. Strang, 2006, "When fashion is fleeting: Transitory collective beliefs and the dynamics of TQM consulting", *Academy of Management Journal*, 49: 215–233; P. A. M. Vermeulen, F. A. J. Van den Bosch and H. W. Volberda, 2007, "Complex incremental product innovation in established service firms: A micro institutional perspective", *Organization Studies*, 28 (10): 1523–1546.

131. M. E. Porter, *Competitive Advantage*, 1985, New York: Free Press, 16.

132. B. Einhorn and M. Srivastava, 2009, "Social networking: Facebook looks to India", *Wall Street Journal Online*, http://www.wsj.com, June 15.

133. M. A. Hitt, L. Bierman, K. Uhlenbruck and K. Shimizu, 2006, "The importance of resources in the internationalisation of professional service firms: The good, the bad, and the ugly", *Academy of Management Journal*, 49: 1137–1157.

134. P. Puranam, H. Singh and M. Zollo, 2006, "Organizing for innovation: Managing the coordination-autonomy dilemma in technology acquisitions", *Academy of Management Journal*, 49: 263–280; N. O'Regan, A. Ghobadian and M. Sims, 2006, "Fasttracking innovation in manufacturing SMEs, *Technovation*, 25(2): 251–261.

135. S. Thornhill and R. E. White, 2007, "Strategic purity: A multi-industry evaluation of pure vs hybrid business strategies", *Strategic Management Journal*, 28: 553–561.

## CHAPTER 6

# COMPETITIVE RIVALRY AND COMPETITIVE DYNAMICS

### LEARNING OBJECTIVES

Studying this chapter should provide you with the strategic management knowledge needed to:

1 Define competitors, competitive rivalry, competitive behaviour and competitive dynamics.
2 Describe market commonality and resource similarity as the building blocks of a competitor analysis.
3 Explain awareness, motivation and ability as drivers of competitive behaviours.
4 Discuss factors affecting the likelihood a competitor will take competitive actions.
5 Describe factors affecting the likelihood a competitor will respond to actions taken against it.
6 Explain the competitive dynamics in each of slow-cycle, fast-cycle and standard-cycle markets.

## OPENING CASE

© ScottyH/Alamy

# Vodafone Group PLC and competition in the UK mobile phone network market – a hypercompetitive environment

Hypercompetition in a market or industry can be defined as a state when technologies or offerings are so new or quickly developed that standards and rules are in flux. As a result, the competitive advantages generated in an industry in which hypercompetition exists tend to be short term and hard to sustain. As a result of these market conditions, companies involved in a hypercompetitive market must constantly compete on price or quality, or innovate in supply chain management, new value creation, or have enough financial capital to outlast other competitors.

The industry for mobile telephone network provision in the UK over the last ten years exemplifies this; with approximately 20 network operators including Vodafone, Orange/T-Mobile, 3 and Tesco Mobile all competing for a share of a market in an industry with a consumer base of over 50 million people. The average revenue per user with the three largest networks of Orange, Vodafone and O2 was approximately €60 per month in 2009, making the UK mobile network market potentially lucrative for all incumbents.

When asked what factor influenced them in terms of choosing a mobile network, UK consumers responded by demonstrating that they are most interested in quality of customer service (33 per cent) and price (30 per cent). This has, until recently, been the main mantra upon which most of the companies operating in the market have tried to differentiate themselves from one another, due to the variety of financial deals available. However, the last five years has seen the introduction of value added extras which come at little or no extra cost to the consumer for being affiliated with a network. A successful example of this has been Orange's "Orange Wednesday" offer, under which subscribers can get a "2 for 1" price on cinema tickets on a Wednesday. This, in addition to a merger with German network provider T-Mobile, has helped move Orange into the position of being the largest UK mobile network in terms of number of subscribers in 2010, and shows the influence different offerings can have on a consumer's choice of network.

Vodafone is, in respect of revenue and profit, the largest mobile network/applications company, with revenue of €53 billion and a profit of over €10 billion from global operations in the 2009–10 financial year. Throughout the 1990s and early 2000s Vodafone was the leading UK network provider, both in financial terms and number of subscribers. However, by the end of 2009 Vodafone was the third biggest of the UK network providers behind O2 and Orange/T-Mobile. This was largely due to Vodafone tending to position itself based on the level of quality in terms of their network coverage and customer service and continually developing new products and services which utilize the latest technological advances.

This position resulted in premium prices on services for this quality. Vodafone stood out from the rest of the market in this regard, with many of their competitors offering lower prices in order to generate custom. This limited the number of consumers Vodafone was able to access against the competition, but did result in Vodafone generating the highest average turnover per user per month of all of the networks in the same year at €67, nearly €5 more per month on average than their closest competitor at the time, O2. This level of revenue has aided Vodafone in retaining its position as the world's leading mobile communications company.

Research conducted in 2009 shows that total mobile retail revenues fell by an estimated €720 million in 2009. This had a knock-on effect on Vodafone, who blamed the drop in their revenue on the global and UK economic downturns forcing them to drop prices in order to remain competitive with rivals who had a low cost and price strategy.

A significant development in the UK mobile phone network industry between 2007 and 2009 was the introduction of Apple's iPhone to the UK handset market in November 2007. The iPhone was seen to be a premium handset, and the network with the rights to provide it on a contract for consumers would be able to charge premium prices on such a contract. This handset would have fitted in very well with Vodafone's positioning strategy; "at the forefront of mobile innovation". However, O2 eventually won the sole right to supply the iPhone to the UK market due to their larger consumer base at the time. By the start of 2010 this deal ended and the iPhone was made available to more UK networks, including Vodafone. However, the two years in which O2 had been able to operate as sole distributor had helped it close down Vodafone in terms of customer's perceptions of the quality of customer offerings the two competitors could provide in the mobile phone market.

These factors saw Vodafone revenues drop seven per cent in the 2009–10 financial year. Vodafone had made moves to begin recovery in the UK in early 2010, with a new advertising campaign putting forward their slogan; "People depend on our network". The campaign is designed to demonstrate the importance of having a high quality and dependable mobile phone network on your phone, with important calls being made using Vodafone handsets. Now Vodafone

has the rights to distribute arguably the most advanced and popular handset in the UK, they are once again targeting a customer base who are willing to pay more for their network deal for a better quality service, as suggested by Vodafone's CEO Vittorio Colao: "We are creating a stronger Vodafone, which is positioned to return to revenue growth during the 2011 financial year, as economic recovery should benefit our key markets."

Due to the number of competitors involved and the market value, the UK mobile network market is highly competitive. Companies such as Vodafone must find a position in this market in which they stand out from their competitors in the eyes of subscribers. They have always taken the position of being high quality at a premium price. This has been punishing during an economic downturn, as subscribers have become more price sensitive.

**Sources:** Brownsell, A. (2010) "Vodafone profit doubles despite slump in UK business", *Marketing Magazine Online*, http://www.marketingmagazine.co.uk/news, May 18; Mintel (2010) "Mobile phones and networks: Re-igniting the replacement cycle – UK", *Mintel Online Reports*, http://www.academic.mintel.com, January; Mintel (2009) "Telecoms – UK", *Mintel Online Reports*, http://www.academic.mintel.com, April; Mintel (2010) "Vodafone reviews brand strategy", *Mintel Online Reports*, http://www.academic.mintel.com/, May; Oates, J. (2009) "Vodafone UK revenue down in Q1", *The Register*, http://www.theregister.co.uk, July 24; Times 100, Business case studies; Vodafone, *Times 100 Online*, http://www.thetimes100.co.uk; Wray, R. (2009) "Vodafone deepens cuts as profits halve", *Guardian Online*, http://www.guardian.co.uk, May 19; Computer Weekly (2009) "T-*Mobile* and Orange: the winners and losers", *Computer Weekly*, September 15, 8; Vodafone Annual Report (2010) http://www.vodafone.com, March 22; Vodafone (2010) We will be the communications leader in an increasingly connected world, http://www.vodafone.com, March 22.

## Questions

**1** On what basis does Vodafone compete in the UK mobile communications sector? What are the vulnerabilities of this business strategy?

**2** Profile three customer segments in mobile communications sector and describe how each is different, indicating how they respond to tactics that the mobile telecommunications firms employ.

Firms operating in the same market, offering similar products and targeting similar customers are competitors.[1] Vodafone, Orange/T-Mobile, and 3 are competitors in the mobile telecommunications market, while British Airways, Air France-KLM and Lufthansa are competitors in the airline industry, as are PepsiCo and Coca-Cola Company in the soft drinks sector.

While the bottled water industry suffered a little during the recent recession (sales decreased by 2 per cent in 2008), Coca-Cola, PepsiCo and Nestlé, three major bottled water distributors, are battling for enhanced market shares introducing lower-cost versions, flavoured-water varieties and even vitamin enhanced versions.[2] In addition, they must deal with the environmental concerns of the plastic bottles in which they are distributed. Interestingly, the economic decline has increased the number and type of competitors with which Coke, Pepsi and Nestlé must contend. For example, water filter manufacturers and distributors have experienced a growing demand for their products (replacing purchases of bottled water with filtered tap water). Clean drinking water is an increasing global concern causing companies such as IBM to enter the market with new "water-management services". IBM projects the water-management services market to reach nearly €16 billion by 2014.[3] In addition, major firms such as GE, Siemens and Veolia Environment are developing significant plans to help provide clean water in different parts of the world. PepsiCo and Coca-Cola are currently engaging in a heated competitive battle in the market for bottled water with sales slipping and the two companies trying to maintain or even increase their market share.[4]

Firms such as Vodafone interact with their competitors as part of the broad context within which they operate while attempting to earn above-average returns.[5] The decisions firms make about their interactions with their competitors significantly affect their ability to earn above-average returns.[6] Because 80 to 90 per cent of new firms fail, learning how to select the markets in which to compete and how to best compete within them is highly important.[7]

Competitive rivalry is the ongoing set of competitive actions and competitive responses that occur among firms as they manoeuvre for an advantageous market position.[8] Particularly in highly competitive industries, firms constantly jockey for advantage as they launch strategic actions and respond or react to rivals' moves.[9] It is important for those leading organizations to understand competitive rivalry, in that "the central, brute empirical fact in strategy is that some firms outperform others",[10] meaning that competitive rivalry influences an individual firm's ability to gain and sustain competitive advantages.[11]

A sequence of firm-level moves, rivalry results from firms initiating their own competitive actions and then responding to actions taken by competitors.[12] Competitive behaviour is the set of competitive actions and competitive responses the firm takes to build or defend its competitive advantages and to improve its market position.[13] Through competitive behaviour, the firm tries to successfully position itself relative to the five forces of competition (see Chapter 2) and to defend current competitive advantages while building advantages for the future (see Chapter 3). Increasingly, competitors engage in competitive actions and responses in more than one market.[14] Firms competing against each other in several product or geographic markets are engaged in multimarket competition.[15] All competitive behaviour – that is, the total set of actions and responses taken by all firms competing within a market—is called competitive dynamics. The relationships among these key concepts are shown in Figure 6.1.

This chapter focuses on competitive rivalry and competitive dynamics. A firm's strategies are dynamic in nature because actions taken by one firm elicit responses from competitors that, in turn, typically result in responses from the firm that took

**FIGURE 6.1** From competitors to competitive dynamics

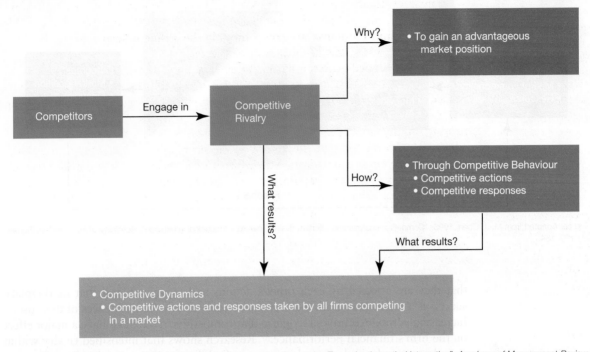

Source: Adapted from M. J. Chen, 1996, "Competitor analysis and interfirm rivalry: Toward a theoretical integration", *Academy of Management Review*, 21: 100–134.

the initial action.[16] As explained above, Coca-Cola and PepsiCo are changing how they compete because of the recession, of concerns for the environment and in response to each other and Nestlé, another major competitor. Also, Vodafone has found that with the economic downturn, its premium position based on quality and network coverage has been challenged by customers.

A strategy's success is determined not only by the firm's initial competitive actions but also by how well it anticipates competitors' responses to them *and* by how well the firm anticipates and responds to its competitors' initial actions (also called attacks).[17] Although competitive rivalry affects all types of strategies (e.g., corporate-level, acquisition, and international), its dominant influence is on the firm's business-level strategy or strategies. Indeed, firms' actions and responses to those of their rivals are the basic building blocks of business-level strategies.[18] Business-level strategy is concerned with what the firm does to successfully use its competitive advantages in specific product markets (see Chapter 5). In the global economy, competitive rivalry is intensifying,[19] meaning that the significance of its effect on firms' business-level strategies is increasing. However, firms that develop and use effective business-level strategies tend to outperform competitors in individual product markets, even when experiencing intense competitive rivalry that price cuts bring about.[20]

## A model of competitive rivalry

Competitive rivalry evolves from the pattern of actions and responses as one firm's competitive actions have noticeable effects on competitors, eliciting competitive responses from them.[21] This pattern suggests that firms are mutually interdependent,

**FIGURE 6.2** A model of competitive rivalry

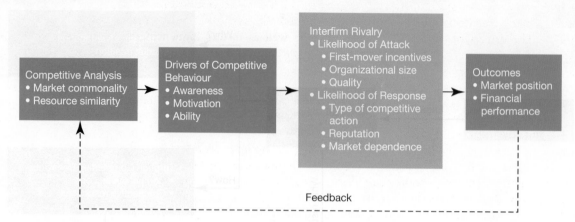

Source: Adapted from M. J. Chen, 1996, "Competitor analysis and interfirm rivalry: Toward a theoretical integration", *Academy of Management Review*, 21: 100–134.

that they are affected by each other's actions and responses, and that marketplace success is a function of both individual strategies and the consequences of their use.[22] Increasingly, too, executives recognize that competitive rivalry can have a major effect on the firm's financial performance.[23] Research shows that intensified rivalry within an industry results in decreased average profitability for the competing firms.[24]

Figure 6.2 presents a straightforward model of competitive rivalry at the firm level; this type of rivalry is usually dynamic and complex.[25] The competitive actions and responses the firm takes are the foundation for successfully building and using its capabilities and core competencies to gain an advantageous market position.[26] The model in Figure 6.2 presents the sequence of activities commonly involved in competition between a particular firm and each of its competitors. Companies can use the model to understand how to be able to predict competitors' behaviour (actions and responses) and reduce the uncertainty associated with competitors' actions.[27] Being able to predict competitors' actions and responses has a positive effect on the firm's market position and its subsequent financial performance.[28] The sum of all the individual rivalries modelled in Figure 6.2 that occur in a particular market reflects the competitive dynamics in that market.

The remainder of the chapter explains components of the model shown in Figure 6.2. We first describe market commonality and resource similarity as the building blocks of a competitor analysis. Next, we discuss the effects of three organizational characteristics – awareness, motivation and ability – on the firm's competitive behaviour. We then examine competitive rivalry between firms, or interfirm rivalry, in detail by describing the factors that affect the likelihood a firm will take a competitive action and the factors that affect the likelihood a firm will respond to a competitor's action. In the chapter's final section, we turn our attention to competitive dynamics to describe how market characteristics affect competitive rivalry in slow-cycle, fast-cycle and standard-cycle markets.

## Competitor analysis

As previously noted, a competitor analysis is the first step the firm takes to be able to predict the extent and nature of its rivalry with each competitor. The number of markets in which firms compete against each other (called market commonality) and the similarity in their resources (called resource similarity) determine the extent to which the firms are competitors. Firms with high market commonality and highly similar resources are "clearly direct and mutually acknowledged competitors".[29] The drivers of competitive behaviour – as well as factors influencing the likelihood that a competitor will initiate competitive actions and will respond to its competitor's actions – influence the intensity of rivalry, even for direct competitors.[30]

In Chapter 2, we discussed competitor analysis as a technique firms use to understand their competitive environment. Together, the general, industry and competitive environments comprise the firm's external environment. We also described how competitor analysis is used to help the firm *understand* its competitors. This understanding results from studying competitors' future objectives, current strategies, assumptions and capabilities (see Figure 3.3). In this chapter, the discussion of competitor analysis is extended to describe what firms study to be able to *predict* competitors' behaviour in the form of their competitive actions and responses. The discussions of competitor analysis in Chapter 2 and in this chapter are complementary in that firms must first *understand* competitors (Chapter 2) before their competitive actions and competitive responses can be *predicted* (this chapter). These analyses are highly important because they help managers to avoid "competitive blind-spots", in which managers are unaware of specific competitors or their capabilities. If managers have competitive blind-spots, they may be surprised by a competitor's actions allowing the competitor to increase its market share at the expense of the manager's firm.[31] Competitor analyses are especially important when a firm enters a foreign market. Managers need to understand the local competition and foreign competitors currently operating in the market.[32] Without such analyses, they are less likely to be successful.

## Market commonality

Each industry is composed of various markets. The financial services industry has markets for insurance, brokerage services, banks and so forth. To concentrate on the needs of different, unique customer groups, markets can be further subdivided. The insurance market, for example, could be broken into market segments (such as commercial and consumer), product segments (such as health insurance and life insurance), and geographic markets (such as Western Europe and South East Asia). In general, the capabilities the Internet's technologies generate help to shape the nature of industries' markets along with the competition among firms operating in them.[33] For example, widely available electronic news sources affect how traditional print news distributors, such as newspapers, conduct their business. Competitors tend to agree about the different characteristics of individual markets that form an industry.[34]

Firms sometimes compete against each other in several markets that are in different industries. As such these competitors interact with each other several times, a condition called market commonality. More formally, market commonality is concerned with the number of markets with which the firm and a competitor are jointly involved and the degree of importance of the individual markets to each.[35] And, when firms produce similar products and compete for the same customers, the competitive rivalry is likely to be high.[36] Additionally, firms competing against one another in several or many markets engage in multimarket competition.[37] Coca-Cola and PepsiCo compete across a number of product (e.g., soft drinks, bottled water) and geographic markets. Even smaller firms, such the authentic Italian food and restaurant chain Carluccio's operating in 45 UK cities, are likely to compete

**Market commonality**

Market commonality is concerned with the number of markets with which the firm and a competitor are jointly involved and the degree of importance of the individual markets to each.

with some competitors in several geographic markets as they enter new cities. Airlines, chemicals, pharmaceuticals and consumer foods are examples of other industries in which firms often simultaneously compete against each other in multiple markets.

Firms competing in several markets have the potential to respond to a competitor's actions not only within the market in which the actions are taken, but also in other markets where they compete with the rival. This potential creates a complicated competitive mosaic in which "the moves an organization makes in one market are designed to achieve goals in another market in ways that are not immediately apparent to its rivals".[38] This potential complicates the rivalry between competitors. In fact, research suggests that "a firm with greater multimarket contact is less likely to initiate an attack, but more likely to move (respond) aggressively when attacked".[39] Thus, in general, multimarket competition reduces competitive rivalry. Yet some firms will still compete when the potential rewards (e.g., potential market share gain) are high.[40]

## Resource similarity

Resource similarity is the extent to which the firm's tangible and intangible resources are comparable to a competitor's in terms of both type and amount.[41] Firms with similar types and amounts of resources are likely to have similar strengths and weaknesses and use similar strategies.[42] The competition between FedEx and United Parcel Service (UPS) in using information technology to improve the efficiency of their operations and to reduce costs, demonstrates these expectations. Pursuing similar strategies that are supported by similar resource profiles, personnel in these firms work at a feverish pace to receive, sort and ship packages. At a UPS hub, for example, "workers have less than four hours (on a peak night) to process more than a million packages from at least 100 planes and probably 160 lorries".[43] FedEx and UPS are both spending more than €800 million annually on research and development (R&D) to find ways to improve efficiency and reduce costs. Rival DHL Express is trying to compete with the two global giants supported by the privatized German postal service, Deutsche Post World Net, which acquired DHL in 2002. While DHL has made significant gains in recent years (e.g., increasing its brand awareness and building impressive operations), it still struggles to compete against its stronger rivals, each of which has similar resources. To survive, it has negotiated a partnership agreement with UPS in which UPS will handle DHL's air shipments. Such arrangements are often referred to as Coopetition (cooperation between competitors).[44]

When performing a competitor analysis, a firm analyses each of its competitors in terms of market commonality and resource similarity. The results of these analyses can be mapped for visual comparisons. In Figure 6.3, we show different hypothetical intersections between the firm and individual competitors in terms of market commonality and resource similarity. These intersections indicate the extent to which the firm and those with which it is compared are competitors. For example, the firm and its competitor displayed in quadrant I of Figure 6.3 have similar types and amounts of resources (i.e., the two firms have a similar portfolio of resources). The firm and its competitor in quadrant I would use their similar resource portfolios to compete against each other in many markets that are important to each. These conditions lead to the conclusion that the firms modelled in quadrant I are direct and mutually acknowledged competitors (e.g., FedEx and UPS). In contrast, the firm and its competitor shown in quadrant III share few markets and have little similarity in their resources, indicating that they are not direct and mutually

**FIGURE 6.3** A framework of competitor analysis

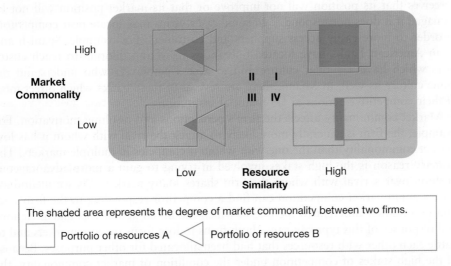

The shaded area represents the degree of market commonality between two firms.

▢ Portfolio of resources A ◁ Portfolio of resources B

Source: Adapted from M. J. Chen, 1996, "Competitor analysis and interfirm rivalry: Toward a theoretical integration", *Academy of Management Review*, 21: 100–134.

acknowledged competitors. Thus, a small local, family-owned Italian restaurant does not compete directly against Pizza Express nor does it have resources that are similar to those of Gondola Holdings (the owners of Pizza Express). The firm's mapping of its competitive relationship with rivals is fluid as firms enter and exit markets and as companies' resources change in type and amount. Thus, the companies with which the firm is a direct competitor change across time.

## Drivers of competitive actions and responses

As shown in Figure 6.3 market commonality and resource similarity influence the drivers (awareness, motivation and ability) of competitive behaviour. In turn, the drivers influence the firm's competitive behaviour, as shown by the actions and responses it takes while engaged in competitive rivalry.[45]

Awareness, which is a prerequisite to any competitive action or response taken by a firm, refers to the extent to which competitors recognize the degree of their mutual interdependence that results from market commonality and resource similarity.[46] Awareness tends to be greatest when firms have highly similar resources (in terms of types and amounts) to use while competing against each other in multiple markets. Komatsu Ltd, Japan's top construction machinery maker and US-based Caterpillar Inc. have similar resources and are certainly aware of each other's actions.[47] The same is true for the US's Wal-Mart and France's Carrefour, the two largest supermarket groups in the world – whose joint awareness has increased as they use similar resources to compete against each other for dominant positions in multiple European and South American markets.[48] Awareness affects the extent to which the firm understands the consequences of its competitive actions and responses. A lack of awareness can lead to excessive competition, resulting in a negative effect on all competitors' performance.[49]

Motivation, which concerns the firm's incentive to take action or to respond to a competitor's attack, relates to perceived gains and losses. Thus, a firm may be

**Awareness**

Awareness is a prerequisite to any competitive action or response taken by a firm and refers to the extent to which competitors recognize the degree of their mutual interdependence that results from market commonality and competitive rivalry.

**Motivation**

Motivation, which concerns the firm's incentive to take action or to respond to a competitor's attack, relates to perceived gains and losses.

aware of competitors but may not be motivated to engage in rivalry with them if it perceives that its position will not improve or that its market position will not be damaged if it does not respond.[50] In some cases, firms may locate near competitors in order to more easily access suppliers and customers. For example, Spanish and Latin American banks have located operations in Miami, Florida to reach customers which have a similar culture and to access employees who understand the home culture as well. In Miami, there are several of these banks which direct most of their competitive actions at US financial institutions.[51]

Market commonality affects the firm's perceptions and resulting motivation. For example, the firm is generally more likely to attack the rival with whom it has low market commonality than the one with whom it competes in multiple markets. The primary reason is the high stakes involved in trying to gain a more advantageous position over a rival with whom the firm shares many markets. As we mentioned earlier, multimarket competition can find a competitor responding to the firm's action in a market different to the one in which the initial action was taken. Actions and responses of this type can cause both firms to lose focus on core markets and to battle each other with resources that had been allocated for other purposes. Because of the high stakes of competition under the condition of market commonality, the probability is high that the attacked firm will respond to its competitor's action in an effort to protect its position in one or more markets.[52]

In some instances, the firm may be aware of the markets it shares with a competitor and may be motivated to respond to an attack by that competitor, but it lacks the ability to do so. Ability relates to each firm's resources and the flexibility they provide. Without available resources (such as financial capital and people), the firm lacks the ability to attack a competitor or respond to its actions. For example, smaller and newer firms tend to be more innovative but generally have fewer resources to attack larger and established competitors. Similarly, foreign firms are often at a disadvantage to local firms because of the local firm's social capital (relationships) with consumers, suppliers and government officials in local markets.[53] However, similar resources suggest similar abilities to attack and respond. When a firm faces a competitor with similar resources, careful study of a possible attack before initiating it is essential because the similarly resourced competitor is likely to respond to that action.[54]

Resource *dissimilarity* also influences competitive actions and responses between firms, in that "the greater the resource imbalance between the acting firm and competitors or potential responders, the greater will be the delay in response"[55] by the firm with a resource disadvantage. For example, Tesco initially used a focused cost leadership strategy to compete. Using sophisticated logistics systems and extremely efficient purchasing practices, among others, to gain competitive advantages, Tesco created a new type of value (primarily in the form of wide selections of products, in convenient locations at competitive prices) for customers. Across the Tesco stores, which range from its largest Extra stores to its Homeplus, Superstores, Metros, Express and OneStop formats, local competitors have been threatened and often lack the ability to marshal needed resources at the pace required to respond quickly and effectively. However, even when facing competitors with greater resources (greater ability) or more attractive market positions, firms should eventually respond, no matter how daunting the task seems.[56] Choosing not to respond can ultimately result in failure, as happened with at least some local retailers who failed to respond to Tesco's competitive actions. Of course, the actions taken by Tesco were only the beginning. Tesco has become the largest retailer in the UK and feared by all competitors, large and small.[57]

**Ability**

Ability relates to each firm's resources and the flexibility they provide in choosing to attack a competitor or to respond to an attack.

# Competitive rivalry

The ongoing competitive action/response sequence between a firm and a competitor affects the performance of both firms;[58] thus it is important for companies to carefully analyse and understand the competitive rivalry present in the markets they serve to select and implement successful strategies.[59] Understanding a competitor's awareness, motivation, and ability helps the firm to predict the likelihood of an attack by that competitor and the probability that a competitor will respond to actions taken against it.

As we described earlier, the predictions drawn from studying competitors in terms of awareness, motivation and ability are grounded in market commonality and resource similarity. These predictions are fairly general. The value of the final set of predictions the firm develops about each of its competitors' competitive actions and responses, is enhanced by studying the "Likelihood of Attack" factors (such as first-mover incentives and organizational size) and the "Likelihood of Response" factors (such as the actor's reputation) that are shown in Figure 6.2. Evaluating and understanding these factors allows the firm to refine the predictions it makes about its competitors' actions and responses.

## Strategic and tactical actions

Firms use both strategic and tactical actions when forming their competitive actions and competitive responses in the course of engaging in competitive rivalry.[60] A competitive action is a strategic or tactical action the firm takes to build or defend its competitive advantages or improve its market position. A competitive response is a strategic or tactical action the firm takes to counter the effects of a competitor's competitive action. Both strategic actions and strategic responses are market-based moves that involve a significant commitment of organizational resources and are difficult to implement and reverse. Alternatively, tactical actions and tactical responses are market-based moves that are taken to fine-tune a strategy; they involve fewer resources and are relatively easy to implement and reverse.

An example of a strategic response is shown by Guess Inc., known for its "European style, aristocratic image and collections full of charm".[61] Guess was losing market share,[62] so it was a natural choice of newly-installed leaders at Guess to take their firm's brand of denim jeans and related products upscale rather than dilute the brand more by lowering prices. And Europe's Airbus' decision to commit the resources required to build the A380 aircraft, described as its "Twenty-first century flagship which has made its name as the world's largest, greenest passenger aircraft, and has captured the imagination of air passengers everywhere"[63] demonstrates a strategic action. Changes in airfares are somewhat frequently announced by airlines. As tactical actions that are easily reversed, pricing decisions are often taken by these firms to increase demand in certain markets during certain periods.

Within European supermarket retailing, Lidl price aggressively as a means of increasing revenues and gaining market share at the expense of competitors. But discounted prices with higher expenses (as implemented by Asda for example) weigh on margins and slow profit growth (or possibly even produce losses). Although pricing aggressively is at the core of what Lidl is and how it competes, can the tactical action of aggressive pricing continue to lead to the competitive success the firm has enjoyed historically? Is Lidl achieving the type of balance between strategic and tactical competitive actions and competitive responses that is a foundation for all firms' success in marketplace competitions?

**Competitive action**

A competitive action is a strategic or tactical action the firm takes to build or defend its competitive advantages or improve its market position.

**Competitive response**

A competitive response is a strategic or tactical action the firm takes to counter the effects of a competitor's competitive action.

**Strategic actions and strategic responses**

A strategic action or a strategic response is a market-based move that involves a significant commitment of organizational resources and is difficult to implement and reverse.

**Tactical actions and tactical responses**

A tactical action or a tactical response is a market-based move that is taken to fine-tune a strategy; it involves fewer resources and is relatively easy to implement and reverse.

## STRATEGIC FOCUS

© Kevin Maskell/Alamy

# Turkish Airlines: responding to competitive rivalry

Turkish Airlines, the oldest and largest airline firm in Turkey, is experiencing continually increasing competition following deregulation of the Turkish aviation market, with several new airline firms entering the market in the last few years. In order to stay strong and competitive Turkish Airlines decided to set up a new brand – Anadolu Jet.

Anadolu Jet was founded on 23 April 2008 as an independent brand of Turkish Airlines. Turkish Airlines itself maintains the full service concept, which stands for offering travellers the full repertoire of services at high price points. In contrast, Anadolu Jet with its low cost concept, represents low fares for fewer services. This strategy aims to attract new customers for Turkish Airlines as a parent company, both from competing airlines and other forms of public transport.

Before Anadolu Jet was founded, many other low cost airline firms were already operating in the Turkish aviation sector. The largest low cost airline firm in the region is Pegasus Airlines. As flying became a more standardized mode of transport in Turkey, leading to more low cost airlines entering the market, full service carriers, such as Turkish Airlines, experienced challenges to its core market. Turkish Airlines was forced to respond in order to maintain its leading position both in international and domestic flights. This resulted in the decision to establish a new sub-brand –

Anadolu Jet – so as to strengthen its domestic position. By doing so, Turkish Airlines both maintained its own traditional full service business concept, which is especially important for international flights, and anticipated the need for low cost business.

Although destinations within Turkey are large (1600 km from the west border to east border), the most common mode of transport was bus. However, with the increased diffusion of air travel within Turkey, especially following deregulation which triggered the introduction of many low cost airlines to the region, new competitors appeared and new markets were formed. This sector has seen year on year growth of 200 per cent in domestic traffic since 2003. The Director General of Civil Aviation Institution (aligned to the Ministry of Transport and Communication) has launched regional aviation projects with the aim of "emplane every Turkish citizen at least once in his life".

Temel Kotil, general manager of Turkish Airlines, acknowledges the apparent incompatibility of launching low cost domestic operations when the overall strategy is to focus on a full-service offering and leave the low cost market to others, but explains, "In the Ankara operation we are exercising how we can lower the operational cost. We want to learn from that because it is a very similar operation compared to the whole business. We are trying to see as a full-service carrier how we can lower the cost. This is an exercise." He adds that Anadolu Jet is also part of a plan to create a second hub at Ankara, where Turkish Airlines plans to later add full-service international flights. "In order to cultivate the market from Ankara we needed to lower the ticket price but we don't want to lose money of course. Our rule is to make money from every route. We don't want to subsidize."

Whereas the main hub of Turkish Airlines is Istanbul, Anadolu Jet's main hub is Ankara, from where it flies to more than 25 destinations, all in Turkey. What Anadolu Jet does differently to the other low cost airline companies is that it is the only one which is exclusively dedicated to the Turkish domestic market. The advantage of Anadolu Jet is that it can make use of the widespread infrastructure of Turkish Airlines. The most important competitors of Anadolu Jet are Pegasus Airlines, Atlas Jet Airlines and IzAir. Interestingly, Pegasus Airlines became a co-owner of IzAir, which makes it more difficult for Anadolu Jet to maintain its market share in the low cost domestic flight market in Turkey. Instead of modifying its own business model which is the full ser-vice concept, Turkish Airlines chose to create Anadolu Jet to stay competitive. Since, its introduction in 2008, the utilization rate of Anadolu Jet increased from 64 per cent to 85 per cent in four months. Anadolu Jet aims to carry at least two million passengers per year and in 2008 the market share of Turkish Airlines and Anadolu Jet was 60 per cent for the domestic market. With Anadolu Jet, Turkish Airlines aims to maintain and improve this position.

*Sources: Anadolu Jet Online,* http://www.anadolujet.com; Yollari, H. (2008) "2 yeni noktaya daha sefer başlatıyor", *Ula-simonline,* http://www.ulasimonline.com, 3 Sept; Sobie, B.

(2008) "Temel Kotil: Turkish Airlines unphased by credit crunch", *Flight Global Online,* http://www.flightglobal.com/; Polat, K. (2008) "Anadolu Jet'in hedefi 2 milyon yolcu", online, http://www.hurarsiv.hurriyet.com.tr, July 8.

### Questions

**1** What are the risks that Anadolu Jet will cannibalize Turkish Airlines?

**2** Identify and profile another firm that has developed a sub-brand so as to protect core markets but pursue new and emerging customer segments, like those of Anadolu Jet.

When engaging rivals in competition, firms must recognize the differences between strategic and tactical actions and responses and should develop an effective balance between the two types of competitive actions and responses. Airbus, the US Boeing's major competitor, is aware that Boeing is strongly committed to taking actions it believes are necessary to successfully counter the launch the A380 aircraft, because deciding to design, build and launch the A380 is a major strategic action. In fact, many analysts believe that Boeing's development of their recent 787 aircraft was a strategic response to the launch of Airbus' A380.

## Likelihood of attack

In addition to market commonality, resource similarity and the drivers of aware-ness, motivation and ability, other factors affect the likelihood a competitor will use strategic actions and tactical actions to attack its competitors. Three of these factors – first-mover incentives, organizational size and quality – are discussed next.

### *First-mover incentives*

A first mover is a firm that takes an initial competitive action in order to build or defend its competitive advantages or to improve its market position. The first-mover concept has been influenced by the work of the famous economist Joseph Schumpeter, who argued that firms achieve competitive advantage by taking inno-vative actions[64] (innovation was defined and described in detail in Chapter 1). In general, first movers "allocate funds for product innovation and development, aggressive advertising, and advanced research and development".[65]

The benefits of being a successful first mover can be substantial.[66] Especially in fast-cycle markets (discussed later), where changes occur rapidly and where it is vir-tually impossible to sustain a competitive advantage for any length of time, a first mover can experience many times the valuation and revenue of a second mover.[67] This evidence suggests that although first-mover benefits are never absolute, they are often critical to a firm's success in industries experiencing rapid technological developments and relatively short product life cycles.[68] In addition to earning above-average returns until its competitors respond to its successful competitive

**First mover**

A first mover is a firm that takes an initial competitive action in order to build or defend its competitive advantages or to improve its market position.

action, the first mover can gain (1) the loyalty of customers who may become committed to the goods or services of the firm that first made them available; and (2) market share that can be difficult for competitors to take during future competitive rivalry.[69] The general evidence that first movers have greater survival rates than later market entrants[70] is perhaps the culmination of first-mover benefits.

The firm trying to predict its competitors' competitive actions might conclude that they will take aggressive strategic actions to gain first-movers' benefits. However, even though a firm's competitors might be motivated to be first movers, they may lack the ability to do so. First movers tend to be aggressive and willing to experiment with innovation and take higher, yet reasonable, levels of risk.[71] To be a first mover, the firm must have readily available the resources to significantly invest in R&D, as well as to rapidly and successfully produce and market a stream of innovative products.[72]

Organizational slack makes it possible for firms to have the ability (as measured by available resources) to be first movers. *Slack* is the buffer or cushion provided by actual or obtainable resources that are not currently in use and are in excess of the minimum resources needed to produce a given level of organizational output.[73] As a liquid resource, slack can quickly be allocated to support competitive actions, such as R&D investments and aggressive marketing campaigns that lead to first-mover advantages. This relationship between slack and the ability to be a first mover allows the firm to predict that a first mover competitor is likely to have available slack and will probably take aggressive competitive actions to continuously introduce innovative products. Furthermore, the firm can predict that as a first mover, a competitor will try to rapidly gain market share and customer loyalty in order to earn above-average returns until its competitors are able to effectively respond to its first move.

Firms evaluating their competitors should realize that being a first mover carries risk. For example, it is difficult to accurately estimate the returns that will be earned from introducing product innovations to the marketplace.[74] Additionally, the first mover's cost to develop a product innovation can be substantial, reducing the slack available to support further innovation. Thus, the firm should carefully study the results a competitor achieves as a first mover. Continuous success by the competitor suggests additional product innovations, while lack of product acceptance over the course of the competitor's innovations may indicate less willingness in the future to accept the risks of being a first mover.[75]

A second mover is a firm that responds to the first mover's competitive action, typically through imitation. More cautious than the first mover, the second mover studies customers' reactions to product innovations. In the course of doing so, the second mover also tries to find any mistakes the first mover made so that it can avoid them and the problems they created. Often, successful imitation of the first mover's innovations allows the second mover to avoid the mistakes and the major investments required of the pioneers [first movers].[76]

Second movers also have the time to develop processes and technologies that are more efficient than those used by the first mover or that create additional value for consumers.[77] The most successful second movers rarely act too fast (so they can fully analyse the first mover's actions), nor too slow so they do not give the first mover time to correct its mistakes and "lock-in" customer loyalty.[78] Overall, the outcomes of the first mover's competitive actions may provide an effective blueprint for second and even late movers as they determine the nature and timing of their competitive responses.[79] Determining whether a competitor is an effective second mover (based on its past actions) allows a first-mover firm to predict that the competitor will respond quickly to successful, innovation-based market entries. The first mover can expect a successful second-mover

**Second mover**

A second mover is a firm that responds to the first mover's competitive action, typically through imitation.

competitor to study its market entries and to respond with a new entry into the market within a short time period. As a second mover, the competitor will try to respond with a product that provides greater customer value than does the first mover's product. The most successful second movers are able to rapidly and meaningfully interpret market feedback to respond quickly, yet successfully, to the first mover's successful innovations.

A late mover is a firm that responds to a competitive action a significant amount of time after the first mover's action and the second mover's response. Typically, a late response is better than no response at all, although any success achieved from the late competitive response tends to be considerably less than that achieved by first and second movers. However, on occasion, late movers can be successful if they develop a unique way to enter the market and compete.[80]

The firm competing against a late mover can predict that the competitor will probably enter a particular market only after both the first and second movers have achieved success in that market. Moreover, on a relative basis, the firm can predict that the late mover's competitive action will allow it to earn average returns only after the considerable time required for it to understand how to create at least as much customer value as that offered by the first and second movers' products.

## Organizational size

An organization's size affects the likelihood it will take competitive actions as well as the types and timing of those actions.[81] In general, small firms are more likely than large companies to launch competitive actions and tend to do it more quickly. Smaller firms are thus perceived as nimble and flexible competitors who rely on speed and surprise to defend their competitive advantages or develop new ones while engaged in competitive rivalry, especially with large companies, to gain an advantageous market position.[82] Small firms' flexibility and nimbleness allow them to develop variety in their competitive actions; large firms tend to limit the types of competitive actions used.[83]

Large firms, however, are likely to initiate more competitive actions along with more strategic actions during a given period.[84] Thus, when studying its competitors in terms of organizational size, the firm should use a measurement such as total sales revenue or total number of employees. The competitive actions likely to be encountered from competitors larger than itself will be different from the competitive actions it will encounter from smaller competitors.

The organizational size factor adds another layer of complexity. When engaging in competitive rivalry, the firm often prefers a large number of unique competitive actions. Ideally, the organization has the amount of slack resources held by a large firm to launch a greater *number* of competitive actions, and a small firm's flexibility to launch a greater *variety* of competitive actions. Herb Kelleher, the cofounder and former CEO of the enormously successful Southwest Airlines in the US commented: "Think and act big and we'll get smaller. Think and act small and we'll get bigger."[85]

In the context of competitive rivalry, Kelleher's statement can be interpreted to mean that relying on a limited number or types of competitive actions (which is the large firm's tendency) can lead to reduced competitive success across time, partly because competitors learn how to effectively respond to the predictable. In contrast, remaining flexible and nimble (which is the small firm's tendency) in order to develop and use a wide variety of competitive actions, contributes to success against rivals.

HSBC Holdings is one of Europe's largest firms. With a market capitalization in excess of €95 billion,[86] HSBC is a huge firm and generates enormous sales revenue leading to vast profits even following a global financial crisis.[87] Partly because of its size,

**Late mover**

A late mover is a firm that responds to a competitive action a significant amount of time after the first mover's action and the second mover's response.

HSBC has the flexibility required to take many types of competitive actions. Its scale and many resources provide the flexibility few if any of its competitors can achieve.

## Quality

Quality has many definitions, including well-established ones relating to the production of goods or services with zero defects[88] and as a cycle of continuous improvement.[89] From a strategic perspective, we consider quality to be the outcome of how a firm completes primary and support activities (see Chapter 3). Thus, quality exists when the firm's goods or services meet or exceed customers' expectations. Some evidence suggests that quality may be the most critical component in satisfying the firm's customers.[90]

In the eyes of customers, quality is about doing the right things relative to performance measures that are important to them.[91] Customers may be interested in measuring the quality of a firm's goods and services against a broad range of dimensions. Sample quality dimensions in which customers commonly express an interest are shown in Table 6.1. Quality is possible only when top-level managers support it and when its importance is institutionalized throughout the entire organization and its value chain.[92] When quality is institutionalized and valued by all,

### Table 6.1  Quality dimensions of goods and services

| Product Quality Dimensions |
| --- |
| **1** *Performance* – Operating Characteristics |
| **2** *Features* – Important special characteristics |
| **3** *Flexibility* – Meeting operating specifications over some period of time |
| **4** *Durability* – Amount of use before performance deteriorates |
| **5** *Conformance* – Match with preestablished standards |
| **6** *Serviceability* – Ease and speed of repair |
| **7** *Aesthetics* – How a product looks and feels |
| **8** *Perceived quality* – Subjective assessment of characteristics (product image) |

| Service Quality Dimensions |
| --- |
| **1** *Timeliness* – Performed in the promised period of time |
| **2** *Courtesy* – Performed cheerfully |
| **3** *Consistency* – Giving all customers similar experiences each time |
| **4** *Convenience* – Accessibility to customers |
| **5** *Completeness* – Fully serviced, as required |
| **6** *Accuracy* – Performed correctly each time |

Source: Adapted from S. C. Jain, 2010, *Marketing Planning and Strategy*, Cincinnati: South-Western College Publishing. South-Western, a part of Cengage Learning, Inc. Reproduced by permission. www.cengage.com/permissions.

employees and managers alike become vigilant about continuously finding ways to improve quality.[93]

Quality is a universal theme in the global economy and is a necessary but not sufficient condition for competitive success.[94] Without quality, a firm's products lack credibility, meaning that customers do not think of them as viable options. Indeed, customers will not consider buying a product until they believe that it can satisfy at least their base-level expectations in terms of quality dimensions that are important to them. Boeing's new 787 aircraft may have problems in the marketplace because of quality concerns. For example, Chi Zhou, Chairman of Shanghai Airlines suggested that the 787 does not "fully meet the quality that Boeing touted earlier". As such Zhou stated that his airline may cancel or postpone delivery of its order for nine aircraft.[95]

Quality affects competitive rivalry. The firm evaluating a competitor whose products suffer from poor quality can predict declines in the competitor's sales revenue until the quality issues are resolved. In addition, the firm can predict that the competitor will probably not be aggressive in its competitive actions until the quality problems are corrected in order to gain credibility with customers. However, after the problems are corrected, that competitor is likely to take more aggressive competitive actions.

# Likelihood of response

The success of a firm's competitive action is affected by the likelihood that a competitor will also respond to it by the type (strategic or tactical) and effectiveness of that response. As noted earlier, a competitive response is a strategic or tactical action the firm takes to counter the effects of a competitor's competitive action. In general, a firm is likely to respond to a competitor's action when (1) the action leads to better use of the competitor's capabilities to gain or produce stronger competitive advantages or an improvement in its market position; (2) the action damages the firm's ability to use its capabilities to create or maintain an advantage; or (3) the firm's market position becomes less defensible.[96]

In addition to market commonality and resource similarity and awareness, motivation and ability, firms evaluate three other factors—type of competitive action, reputation and market dependence—to predict how a competitor is likely to respond to competitive actions (see Figure 6.2).

## Type of competitive action

Competitive responses to strategic actions differ from responses to tactical actions. These differences allow the firm to predict a competitor's likely response to a competitive action that has been launched against it. Strategic actions commonly receive strategic responses and tactical actions receive tactical responses. In general, strategic actions elicit fewer total competitive responses because strategic responses, such as market-based moves, involve a significant commitment of resources and are difficult to implement and reverse.[97]

Another reason that strategic actions elicit fewer responses than do tactical actions is that the time needed to implement a strategic action and to assess its effectiveness can delay the competitor's response to that action.[98] In contrast, a competitor will probably respond quickly to a tactical action, such as when an airline company almost immediately matches a competitor's tactical action of reducing prices in certain markets. Either strategic actions or tactical actions that target a large number of a rival's customers are likely to elicit strong responses.[99] In fact, if the effects of a competitor's strategic action on the focal firm are significant (e.g., loss of market share, loss of major resources such as critical employees), a response is likely to be swift and strong.[100]

## Actor's reputation

In the context of competitive rivalry, an *actor* is the firm taking an action or a response, while *reputation* is "the positive or negative attribute ascribed by one rival to another based on past competitive behaviour".[101] A positive reputation may be a source of above-average returns, especially for consumer goods producers.[102] Thus, a positive corporate reputation is of strategic value[103] and affects competitive rivalry. To predict the likelihood of a competitor's response to a current or planned action, firms evaluate the responses that the competitor has taken previously when attacked – past behaviour is assumed to be a predictor of future behaviour.

Competitors are more likely to respond to strategic or tactical actions when they are taken by a market leader.[104] In particular, evidence suggests that commonly successful actions, especially strategic actions, will be quickly imitated. For example, although a second mover, IBM committed significant resources to enter the PC market. When IBM was immediately successful in this endeavour, competitors such as Dell, Compaq, HP and Gateway responded with strategic actions to enter the market. IBM's reputation as well as its successful strategic action strongly influenced entry by these competitors. However, the competitive landscape has changed dramatically over time. For example, Lenovo, a Chinese PC firm, paid €1.37 billion in 2005 to buy IBM's PC division.

In contrast to a firm with a strong reputation such as IBM, competitors are less likely to take responses against a company with a reputation for competitive behaviour that is risky, complex, and unpredictable. The firm with a reputation as a price predator (an actor that frequently reduces prices to gain or maintain market share) generates few responses to its pricing tactical actions because price predators, which typically increase prices once their market share objective is reached, lack credibility with their competitors.[105] Yet, occasionally, a firm with a minor reputation can sneak up on larger more resourceful competitors and take market share from them. In recent years, for example, firms from emerging markets have taken market share from major competitors based in developed markets.[106]

## Dependence on the market

*Market dependence* denotes the extent to which a firm's revenues or profits are derived from a particular market.[107] In general, competitors with high market dependence are likely to respond strongly to attacks threatening their market position.[108] Interestingly, the threatened firm in these instances may not always respond quickly, even though an effective response to an attack on the firm's position in a critical market is important.

Hotel Chocolat is a UK-based upmarket confectioner. With sales approaching €63 million it has been profitable every year except one since its establishment 20 years ago. Everything it does is based around chocolate – from its cocoa estate in St Lucia to its Cambridgeshire production facilities, to its vast online sales and current 42 retail outlets with aggressive ambitions to expand production and nearly double its retail outlets over the next few years.[109] Hotel Chocolat's business is therefore founded on a passion for chocolate. Because Hotel Chocolat's business operations revolve strictly around confectionery products, it is totally dependent on the market for this. As such, any competitor that chooses to attack Hotel Chocolat and its market positions can anticipate a strong response to its competitive actions.

## STRATEGIC FOCUS

© franz pfluegl/iStock

## McKinsey – company reputation as a competitive advantage

An example of a company which is followed in this way is McKinsey, the management consulting firm. For an example of how successful and strong the company and its reputation is, McKinsey was ranked as the top consulting firm by Vault.com for six consecutive years up to and including 2009. The company has been regarded as one of the most influential and powerful consultancy firms in the world for a long time and is currently the largest consultancy firm globally, with an estimated revenue of €4.7 billion in 2008. The company can also claim to have developed the 7S Framework in the 1980s, a framework still used heavily in strategy development today. The company

is even used to help advise in the world of politics, having been brought in to consult on the restructuring of the British Cabinet in 2005. In addition to all of this, McKinsey runs a highly reputable business journal, *McKinsey Quarterly*, adding an extra arm to the company's product portfolio over those of its competitors.

This reputation brings with it a significant competitive advantage in the management consultancy market, with McKinsey often the first choice for consultancy on significant strategic decision making for most major businesses globally. This allows McKinsey not only to win more work from businesses ahead of competition, but to leverage higher fees for the work they conduct. While this is the case, McKinsey is the benchmark for all other consultancy firms to measure themselves against. Generally speaking this will result in any new practice McKinsey develop being imitated by competitors in a way lesser consultancy firms in the market would not experience.

In addition, due to the way the reputation McKinsey currently has in place was formed, it is unlikely that this will disappear quickly, meaning McKinsey is likely to remain at the top of the consultancy market for a long time, providing they remain a market leader in the quality and innovation of their products and services.

**Sources:** http://www.vault.com; "Commercial services and supplies: McKinsey & Company, Inc.", *BusinessWeek Online*, 2010 http://www.investing.businessweek.com/; Huey, J. (1993) "How McKinsey does it: The world's most powerful consulting firm commands unrivaled respect – and prices – but is being buffeted by a host of new challenges. Here's the inside story", *Fortune*, November 1; (2009) "America's Largest Private Companies", *Forbes Online*, October 28; "The McKinsey 7S Framework: Ensuring that all parts of your organization work in harmony", 2010 http://www.mindtools.com; Newman, C. (2005) "Blair faces storm over report by McKinsey", *Financial Times*, November 25; http://www.mckinsey.com; *McKinsey Quarterly Online*, http://www.mckinseyquarterly.com.

### Questions

**1** Why is an actor's reputation relevant in competitive dynamics?

**2** What characteristics qualify McKinsey as an exemplar of a valuable reputation?

## Competitive dynamics

Whereas competitive rivalry concerns the ongoing actions and responses between a firm and its direct competitors for an advantageous market position, competitive dynamics concern the ongoing actions and responses among *all* firms competing within a market for advantageous positions. Building and sustaining competitive advantages are at the core of competitive rivalry, in that advantages are the key to creating value for shareholders.[110]

To understand competitive dynamics, we explore the effects of varying rates of competitive speed in different markets (called slow-cycle, fast-cycle and standard-cycle markets) on the behaviour (actions and responses) of all competitors within a given market. Competitive behaviours as well as the reasons for taking them are similar within each market type, but differ across types of markets.[111] Thus, competitive dynamics differ in slow-cycle, fast-cycle and standard-cycle markets. The sustainability of the firm's competitive advantages differs across the three market types.

As noted in Chapter 1, firms want to sustain their competitive advantages for as long as possible, although no advantage is permanently sustainable. The degree of sustainability is affected by how quickly competitive advantages can be imitated and how costly it is to do so.

## Slow-cycle markets

Slow-cycle markets are those in which the firm's competitive advantages are shielded from imitation, commonly for long periods of time and where imitation is costly.[112] Thus, competitive advantages are sustainable over longer periods of time in slow-cycle markets.

Building a unique and proprietary capability produces a competitive advantage and success in a slow-cycle market. This type of advantage is difficult for competitors to understand. As discussed in Chapter 3, a difficult-to-understand and costly-to-imitate resource or capability usually results from unique historical conditions, causal ambiguity and/or social complexity. Copyrights, geography, patents and ownership of an information resource are examples of resources.[113] After a proprietary advantage is developed, the firm's competitive behaviour in a slow-cycle market is oriented to protecting, maintaining and extending that advantage. Thus, the competitive dynamics in slow-cycle markets usually concentrate on competitive actions and responses that enable firms to protect, maintain and extend their competitive advantage. Major strategic actions in these markets, such as acquisitions, usually carry less risk than in faster-cycle markets.[114]

Walt Disney Co. continues to extend its proprietary characters, such as Mickey Mouse, Minnie Mouse and Goofy. These characters have a unique historical development as a result of Walt and Roy Disney's creativity and vision for entertaining people. Products based on the characters seen in Disney's animated films are sold through Disney's theme park shops as well as freestanding retail outlets called Disney Stores. Because copyrights shield it, the proprietary nature of Disney's advantage in terms of animated character trademarks protects the firm from imitation by competitors.

Consistent with another attribute of competition in a slow-cycle market, Disney protects its exclusive rights to its characters and their use. As with all firms competing in slow-cycle markets, Disney's competitive actions (such as building theme parks in France, Japan and China) and responses (such as lawsuits to protect its right to fully control use of its animated characters) maintain and extend its proprietary competitive advantage while protecting it.

Patent laws and regulatory requirements such as those in Europe requiring European Medicines Evaluation Agency approval to launch new products, shield pharmaceutical companies' positions. Competitors in this market try to extend patents on their drugs to maintain advantageous positions that the patents provide.

**FIGURE 6.4** Gradual erosion of a sustained competitive advantage

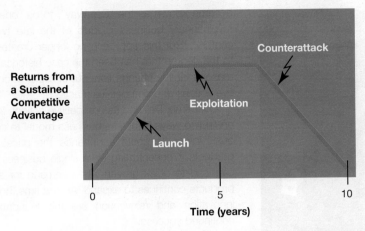

Source: Adapted from I. C. MacMillan, 1988, Controlling competitive dynamics by taking strategic initiative, *Academy of Management Executive*, II(2), 111–118.

However, after a patent expires, the firm is no longer shielded from competition, allowing generic imitations and usually leading to a loss of sales.

The competitive dynamics generated by firms competing in slow-cycle markets are shown in Figure 6.4. In slow-cycle markets, firms launch a product (e.g., a new drug) that has been developed through a proprietary advantage (e.g., R&D) and then exploit it for as long as possible while the product is shielded from competition. Eventually, competitors respond to the action with a counterattack. In markets for drugs, this counterattack commonly occurs as patents expire or are broken through legal means, creating the need for another product launch by the firm seeking a protected market position.

## Fast-cycle markets

Fast-cycle markets are markets in which the firm's capabilities that contribute to competitive advantages are not shielded from imitation and where imitation is often rapid and inexpensive. Thus, competitive advantages are not sustainable in fast-cycle markets. Firms competing in fast-cycle markets recognize the importance of speed; these companies appreciate that "time is as precious a business resource as money or head count – and that the costs of hesitation and delay are just as steep as going over budget or missing a financial forecast".[115] Such high-velocity environments place considerable pressures on top managers to quickly make strategic decisions that are also effective.[116] The often substantial competition and technology-based strategic focus make the strategic decision complex, increasing the need for a comprehensive approach integrated with decision speed, two often-conflicting characteristics of the strategic decision process.[117]

Reverse engineering and the rate of technology diffusion in fast-cycle markets facilitate rapid imitation. A competitor uses reverse engineering to quickly gain the knowledge required to imitate or improve the firm's products. Technology is diffused rapidly in fast-cycle markets, making it available to competitors in a short period. The technology often used by fast-cycle competitors isn't proprietary, nor is it protected by patents as is the technology used by firms competing in slow-cycle markets. For example, only a few hundred parts, which are readily available on the open market, are required to build a PC. Patents protect only a few of these parts, such as microprocessor chips.[118]

**Fast-cycle markets**

Fast-cycle markets are markets in which the firm's capabilities that contribute to competitive advantages aren't shielded from imitation and where imitation is often rapid and inexpensive.

## STRATEGIC FOCUS

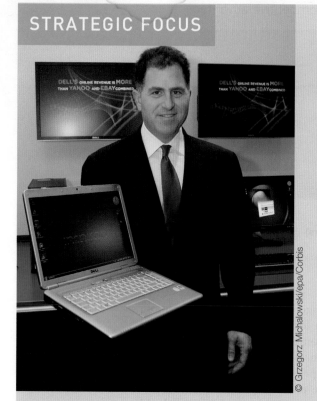

© Grzegorz Michalowski/epa/Corbis

# Competition between Hewlett-Packard and Dell: fast cycle market

"I'm going to be the CEO for the next several years. We're going to fix this business." Michael Dell's words suggest that Dell Inc.'s founder and newly reinstalled CEO intends to do everything he can to correct the problems that led to the business losing its position of market leader in respect of global sales of personal computers (PCs). At the close of 2009, Hewlett-Packard (HP) commanded 19.9 per cent of the global PC market while Dell's share had slipped to 12.9 per cent. The market share loss seemingly contributed to the 32 per cent total decline in the value of Dell Inc.'s stock during recent years (HP's stock doubled in value over the same time period).

The performance declines were a new experience for Dell, which grew from an initial €800 investment in 1984 to a nearly €50 billion business in 2009. Dell's growth was founded on an original production and product delivery strategy which bypassed the intermediary, selling custom-built computers direct to the customer. Some analysts consider this approach, which

became known as the "Dell Way". to be "one of the revolutionary business models of the late twentieth century". But this approach no longer creates value to the degree that has been the case historically. The reasons for the change flow out of a tale of competitive actions and competitive reactions.

Over time, Dell and its competitive actions focused on finding ways to use its business model to continuously lower its costs and hence the prices of its products. Concentrating on a single business model can lead to quick growth when demand for a firm's products continues to expand. Across time, however, innovation and reinvention are the foundation for continued success.

Over the past several years, HP found ways to innovate and reinvent itself. After examining its business model, Todd Bradely, the executive who now heads HP's PC operations, concluded that "HP was fighting on the wrong battlefield. HP was concentrating its resources to fight Dell where Dell was strong, in direct sales over the Internet and the phone. Instead (Bradely) decided, HP should focus on its strength, retail stores, where Dell had no presence at all." To successfully change its focus, HP developed close relationships with retailers, even trying to "personalize" PCs. Consistent with "The computer is personal again" campaign, HP features celebrities (e.g., fashion designer Vera Wang and hip-hop artist Jay-Z) in its advertisements and is producing unique products for different retailers.

Dell's decision to venture into retail selling is a competitive reaction to HP's actions. Dell partnered with a Japanese retailer (Bic Camera Inc.) to sell notebooks and desktops throughout Japan. Dell is also committing additional monies to research and development (to find product innovations) and is restructuring some of its advertising campaigns "to remind consumers of the benefits of customizing computers".

Both companies decided to diversify in their products and services in order to stay competitive. An important decision taken by HP concerns acquisitions; HP decided to get involved in services and networking products. HP decided to acquire 3Com, a computer networking company, in November 2009, having acquired EDS, a business and technology service company, in May of the same year. These new business avenues led to a 14 per cent increase in earnings in the fourth quarter of 2009 for the HP family. In September 2009, Dell bought Perot Systems, an information technology service provider in order to get involved in the service sector. It seems that both companies are convinced that diversification is inevitable in order to stay competitive.

**Sources:** Bartiromo, M. (2007) "Will Dell be a comeback kid?", *BusinessWeek*, February 26, 128; Byrnes N. and Burrows, P. (2007) "Where Dell went wrong", *BusinessWeek*, February 19, 62–66; Lawton, C. (2007) "How HP reclaimed its PC lead over Dell", *Wall Street Journal Online*, http://www.online.wsj.com, June 5; Lee L. and Burrows, P. (2007) "Is Dell too big for Michael Dell?", *BusinessWeek*, February 12, 33; Mullins, R. (2007) "Dell goes retail in Japan", *PCWorld*, http://www.pcworld.com, July 28; Einhorn B. and Culpan, T. (2010) "Acer: Past Dell and chasing HP", *Business Week Online*, http://www.businessweek.com, February 25.

## Questions

1 What are the advantages of the Dell and HP business models in the PC market?

2 What are the risks and disadvantages associated with the Dell and HP business models in the PC market?

Fast-cycle markets are more volatile than slow-cycle and standard-cycle markets. Indeed, the pace of competition in fast-cycle markets is almost frenzied, as companies rely on innovations as the engines of their growth. Because prices often decline rapidly in these markets, companies need to profit quickly from their product innovations. Imitation of many fast-cycle products is relatively easy, as demonstrated by Dell and HP and other PC vendors that have partly or largely imitated the original PC design to create their products. Continuous reductions in the costs of parts, as well as the fact that the information required to assemble a PC is not especially complicated and is readily available, make it possible for additional competitors to enter this market without significant difficulty.[119]

The fast-cycle market characteristics just described make it virtually impossible for companies in this type of market to develop sustainable competitive advantages. Recognizing this reality, firms avoid "loyalty" to any of their products, preferring to cannibalize their own before competitors learn how to do so through successful imitation. This emphasis creates competitive dynamics that differ substantially from those found in slow-cycle markets. Instead of concentrating on protecting, maintaining and extending competitive advantages, as in slow-cycle markets, companies competing in fast-cycle markets focus on learning how to rapidly and continuously develop new competitive advantages that are superior to those they replace. Commonly, they search for fast and effective means of developing new products. For example, it is common in some industries for firms to use strategic alliances to gain access to new technologies and thereby develop and introduce more new products into the market.[120] And, in recent years, many of these alliances have been offshore (with partners in foreign countries) in order to access appropriate skills while maintaining lower costs to compete.[121]

The competitive behaviour of firms competing in fast-cycle markets is shown in Figure 6.5. As suggested by this figure, competitive dynamics in this market type entail actions and responses oriented to rapid and continuous product introductions and the development of a stream of ever-changing competitive advantages. The firm launches a product to achieve a competitive advantage and then exploits the advantage for as long as possible. However, the firm also tries to develop another temporary competitive advantage before competitors can respond to the first one (see Figure 6.5). Thus, competitive dynamics in fast-cycle markets often result in rapid product upgrades as well as quick product innovations.[122]

As our discussion suggests, innovation plays a critical role in the competitive dynamics in fast-cycle markets. For individual firms, then, innovation is a key source of competitive advantage. Through innovation, the firm can cannibalize its own products before competitors successfully imitate them.

**FIGURE 6.5**  Developing temporary advantages to create sustained advantage

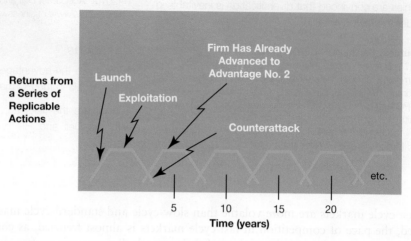

Source: Adapted from I. C. MacMillan, 1988, "Controlling competitive dynamics by taking strategic initiative", *Academy of Management Executive*, II(2), 111–118.

## Standard-cycle markets

Standard-cycle markets are markets in which the firm's competitive advantages are partially shielded from imitation and imitation is moderately costly. Competitive advantages are sustainable to a point in standard-cycle markets, but only when the firm is able to continuously upgrade the quality of its capabilities to stay ahead of competitors. The competitive actions and responses in standard-cycle markets are designed to seek large market shares, to gain customer loyalty through brand names, and to carefully control a firm's operations in order to consistently provide the same positive experience for customers.[123]

Standard-cycle companies serve many customers in competitive markets. Because the capabilities and core competencies on which their competitive advantages are based are less specialized, imitation is faster and less costly for standard-cycle firms than for those competing in slow-cycle markets. However, imitation is slower and more expensive in these markets than in fast-cycle markets. Thus, competitive dynamics in standard-cycle markets rest midway between the characteristics of dynamics in slow-cycle and fast-cycle markets. Imitation comes less quickly and is more expensive for standard-cycle competitors when a firm is able to develop economies of scale by combining coordinated and integrated design and manufacturing processes with a large sales volume for its products.

Because of large volumes, the size of mass markets, and the need to develop scale economies, the competition for market share is intense in standard-cycle markets. This form of competition is readily evident in the battles among consumer foods' producers. Hotel Chocolat competes in different market segments with Mars, Cadbury and Nestlé. In addition, similar to other consumer food manufacturers, some confectionery manufacturers have kept prices constant but downsized packages. Package design and ease of availability are the competitive dimensions on which these firms sometimes compete to outperform their rivals in this market.

Innovation can also drive competitive actions and responses in standard-cycle markets, especially when rivalry is intense. Some innovations in standard-cycle markets are incremental rather than radical in nature (incremental and radical innovations are discussed in Chapter 15). For example, consumer foods' producers are innovating in terms of healthy products. Overall, many firms are relying on innovation as a means of competing in standard-cycle markets and to earn above-average returns.

Overall, innovation has a substantial influence on competitive dynamics as it affects the actions and responses of all companies competing within a slow-cycle, fast-cycle or standard-cycle market. We have emphasized the importance of innovation to the firm's strategic competitiveness in earlier chapters. These discussions highlight the importance of innovation in most types of markets.

## KEY DEBATE

© sebastian-julian

# Confronting the inevitable commodity trap

Many firms, as they follow their growth strategies, find themselves in the position where they confront a commodity trap – this can be described as a situation in which a product or service cannot be distinguished by customers from its competitor offerings. The firm confronting the commodity trap has no basis for product or service differentiation and therefore its competitive position becomes undermined because the premium price it used to charge is no longer sustainable. Consequently, the firm's offering is valued no more highly than its competitor offerings. This situation recently confronted Starbucks. With increased demand at peak times came customer frustration with Starbucks whose wait times were increasing and several other challenges confronted the firm leading to it falling victim to commoditization: they were becoming simply a high-priced commodity beverage vendor. Howard Schultz, their CEO, identified that the relationship between the barista and the customer had become blurred and this formed the refocus of many activities at Starbucks. Following the increased focus on customer benefits and the Starbucks offering, their recent turnaround has been a success.

Commoditization affects many industries and most incumbents at some point in time. Richard D'Aveni suggests that a commodity trap can destroy markets, disrupt entire industries and push successful firms to the wall. Based on his analysis of more than 30 industries, D'Aveni maps commoditization along two paths – the benefits or features of a product and the price (margin) that the firm can command. He finds three determinants of the commodity trap. The first is *deterioration* where competition is based exclusively on low-cost and consumer value is nothing other than

the lowest priced within the market. Under these circumstances it is a battle of spiraling cost and price reduction in which the industry, the competitors and, ultimately, the customers lose out. The second is *proliferation* where the market repeatedly witnesses new competitor offerings with different customer benefit bundles set at different prices, each serving specific target customer segments. In a proliferating market the wide array of offerings leads to excessive choice without any one competitor being able to create a market space in which they have a truly differentiated offering with a distinctive value statement that warrants a price premium. The third is *escalation* whereby competitive behaviours mean that innovations are repeatedly introduced to the market which drives up the value of competitor offerings whilst preventing a corresponding increase in price premium. With numerous iterations of innovations come significantly improved benefits in competitor offerings but without being able to attract significantly higher margins. These factors independently can create a situation where firms fall victim to commoditization.

John Quelch argues, in contrast, that a firm can differentiate literally anything: "Even when a raw material has no value added and quality standards are set by law or the industry, there is still plenty of opportunity for differentiation around availability, delivery, shipment quantities, payment terms and all the other services that accompany the core product. Marketers must use their imagination. As the saying goes: *There are no mature products, only mature managers*." See the Jacques article in the sources material for this debate.

A key factor to appreciate is that the product life cycle dictates that with product maturity comes the inevitable forces of commoditization. The issue that firms face is that the cycle of product launch to maturity is exceptionally fast and becoming increasingly more so. Quelch argues that firms are confronted with three choices to fight commoditization: to innovate (develop a new product or adapt existing one to improve the fit with customer needs); to bundle (combining with a commoditized product a differentiated service for which a price premium can be secured); and, to segment (by sub-dividing further into multiple smaller segments thereby providing higher value for customer segments that are less price sensitive).

**Sources:** D'Aveni, R. A. (2010) *Beating the Commodity Trap: How to Maximize Your Competitive Position and Increase Your Pricing Power*, Cambridge, MA: Harvard Business School Press; Dickson, P. R. (1992) "Toward a general theory of competitive rationality", *Journal of Marketing*, 56(1): 69–83; Dryburgh, A. (2009) "Don't you believe it … costs are the best basis for pricing", *Management Today*, November: 18; Jacques, F. (2007) "Even commodities have customers", *Harvard Business Review*, 85(5): 110–119; Quelch, J. (2007) "How to avoid the commodity trap", http://www.blogs.hbr.org, December 13; Schultz, H. (2010) "Howard Schultz on Star-

bucks' Turnaround", http://www.blogs.hbr.org/ideacast, June 22; Stern, S. (2009) "Get your strategy right now before the dust settles", *Financial Times*, July 21: 14.

## Questions

**1** Identify and describe the competitive rivalry within three industries that characterize each of D'Aveni's three determinants of commoditization – deterioration, proliferation and escalation.

**2** In seeking to combat D'Aveni's commodity trap, to what extent do you agree with Quelch's notion that you can differentiate anything?

## CLOSING CASE

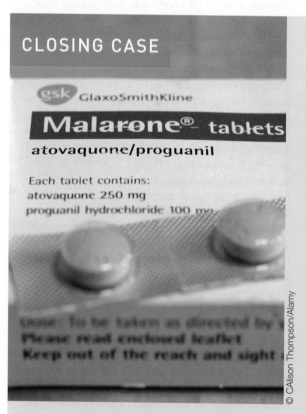

© CAlison Thompson/Alamy

# GlaxoSmithKline: finding a balance between GSK's strategic change with tactical implications

GlaxoSmithKline plc (GSK), the world's second largest pharmaceutical, biological and healthcare company, has experienced many difficulties with regard to its pricing policy down the years. As a

company leading research in the field of medicines and vaccines against various diseases such as AIDS and malaria, GSK is far from a regular profit-driven company. Especially when we consider that nowadays millions of people (particularly in developing countries) are dependent on these vaccines and medicines, it is perhaps not surprising that GSK has been criticized for its pricing and patent policy.

The main issue with GSK's price policy has always been the question of whether it is fair and reasonable to maintain a uniform price for its drugs in both the developed and developing worlds. The opposite of uniform pricing is differential pricing, which means that the same product is priced differently in different markets/regions depending on the conditions in that market/region. On one hand, GSK is a profit-driven company but at the other hand they recognize that with regular drug prices it is almost impossible to serve patients in Africa. Until 2000, GSK received heavy criticism from nongovernmental organizations such as Oxfam. However, the former CEO of GSK, Jan-Pierre Garnier, realized that the status quo could not be maintained and decided to make developing countries one of the main foci for the firm's future strategy: "The pharmaceutical industry today sells 80 per cent of its products to 20 per cent of the world's population. I don't want to be the CEO of the company that only caters to the rich … I want those medicines in the hands of many more people who need them." However, a more moderated pricing strategy could not be realized on its own.

In 1999, an umbrella organization, named Global Alliance for Vaccines and Immunizations (GAVI), was founded which consists of bilateral aid agencies of national governments, the Bill and Melinda Gates

Foundation, The Rockefeller Foundation, UNICEF, the World Bank, the World Health Organization and the international vaccine industry. In 2001 GSK delivered Tritanrix HB, a vaccine providing protection against diseases such as diphtheria, tetanus, pertussis and hepatitis B. Before GAVI, GSK introduced this vaccine to the developing world but despite "low" prices, it was not a success. However, as a result of the collaboration with GAVI and funding of many NGO's such as the Bill and Melinda Gates foundation, GSK was able to deliver this vaccine with a price tag which was 90 per cent lower than normal private market prices. In an important project aimed at developing an effective malaria vaccine, the Bill and Melinda Foundation granted €84 million to support the collaboration between the Malaria Vaccine Initiative and GSK, aiding GSK in offering this pricing.

According to Prahalad and Hammond (2002) there are four billion people living on less than €1500 each year, and who are poorly served by multinational companies. Serving this part of the world population could result in a win–win situation. In the case of GSK, this serves the population and can increase its revenues, and the African population will be helped in the fight against diseases. At first instance GSK does not make any profit with selling these vaccines and medicines for such a low price. However, with the funding of NGOs, GSK will be able to earn profits as a result of economies of scale.

Andrew Witty, the new Chief Executive at GSK, has formulated a new strategy which consists of cutting prices in the 50 least developed countries, putting property rights in a "patent pool" in order to make it possible for other researchers to continue with exploration, reinvesting 20 per cent of profits from developing countries and inviting scientists from outside to join the search for tropical disease treatments. These steps demonstrate that GSK is determined to move from a profit-maximizing perspective to a welfare-maximizing perspective.

**Sources:** Vachani, S. and Smith, N. C. (2004), "Socially responsible pricing: lessons from pricing of AIDS drugs in developing countries", *Centre for Marketing London Business School*; Boseley, S. (2009) "Drug giant GlaxoSmithKline pledges cheap medicine for world's poor", *The Guardian Online*, http://www.guardian.co.uk, 13 February; PR Newswire, 2005, "New Gates funding will enable MVI and GlaxoSmithKline biologicals to complete development of world's most advanced malaria vaccine candidate", *PR Newswire Online*, http://www.proquest.umi.com, 30 October; PR Newswire, 2001, "GAVI and GlaxoSmithKline deliver first vaccines to Africa in new vaccine initiative for the developing world", *PR Newswire Online*, http://www.proquest.umi.com, 6 April; Prahalad, C. K. and Hammond, A. (2002) "Serving the world's poor, profitably", *Harvard Business Review*, 80(9): 48–58; Smith, N. C. and Duncan, A. (2003) "GlaxoSmithKline and access to essential medicines", *London Business School case study*, January.

## Questions

1 What factors underlie GSK's position on differential pricing?

2 What are the potential longer-term implications for GSK's business and that of its competitors following this strategic change with tactical implications?

# SUMMARY

- Competitors are firms competing in the same market, offering similar products and targeting similar customers. Competitive rivalry is the ongoing set of competitive actions and competitive responses occurring between competitors as they compete against each other for an advantageous market position. The outcomes of competitive rivalry influence the firm's ability to sustain its competitive advantages as well as the level (average, below average or above average) of its financial returns.

- The set of competitive actions and responses that an individual firm takes while engaged in competitive rivalry is called competitive behaviour. Competitive dynamics is the set of actions and responses taken by all firms that are competitors within a particular market.

- Firms study competitive rivalry in order to predict the competitive actions and responses that each of their competitors are likely to take. Competitive actions are either strategic or tactical in nature. The firm takes competitive actions to defend or build its competitive advantages or to improve its market position. Competitive responses are taken to counter the effects of a competitor's competitive action. A strategic action or a strategic response requires a significant commitment of organizational resources, is difficult to successfully implement, and is difficult to reverse. In contrast, a tactical action or a tactical response requires fewer organizational resources and is easier to implement and reverse. An airline company, entering major new markets is an example of a strategic action or a strategic response; changing its prices in a particular market is an example of a tactical action or a tactical response.

■ A competitor analysis is the first step the firm takes to be able to predict its competitors' actions and responses. In Chapter 2, we discussed what firms do to *understand* competitors. This discussion was extended in this chapter describing what the firm does to *predict* competitors' market-based actions. Thus, understanding precedes prediction. Market commonality (the number of markets with which competitors are jointly involved and their importance to each) and resource similarity (how comparable competitors' resources are in terms of type and amount) are studied to complete a competitor analysis. In general, the greater the market commonality and resource similarity, the more firms acknowledge that they are direct competitors.

■ Market commonality and resource similarity shape the firm's awareness (the degree to which it and its competitors understand their mutual interdependence), motivation (the firm's incentive to attack or respond), and ability (the quality of the resources available to the firm to attack and respond). Having knowledge of these characteristics of a competitor increases the quality of the firm's predictions about that competitor's actions and responses.

■ In addition to market commonality and resource similarity and awareness, motivation, and ability, three more specific factors affect the likelihood a competitor will take competitive actions. The first of these concerns first-mover incentives. First movers, those taking an initial competitive action, often gain loyal customers and earn above-average returns until competitors can successfully respond to their action. Not all firms can be first movers in that they may lack the awareness, motivation, or ability required to engage in this type of competitive behaviour. Moreover, some firms prefer to be a second mover (the firm responding to the first mover's action). One reason for this is that second movers, especially those acting quickly, can successfully compete against the first mover. By evaluating the first mover's product, customers' reactions to it and the responses of other competitors to the first mover, the second mover can avoid the early entrant's mistakes and find ways to improve upon the value created for customers by the first mover's good or service. Late movers (those that respond a long time after the original action was taken) commonly are lower performers and are much less competitive.

■ Organizational size, the second factor, tends to reduce the variety of competitive actions that large firms launch while it increases the variety of actions undertaken by smaller competitors. Ideally, the firm would prefer to initiate a large number of diverse actions when engaged in competitive rivalry. The third factor, quality, is a base denominator to competing successfully in the global economy. It is a necessary prerequisite to achieve competitive parity. It is a necessary but insufficient condition for gaining an advantage.

■ The type of action (strategic or tactical) the firm took, the competitor's reputation for the nature of its competitor behaviour, and that competitor's dependence on the market in which the action was taken are studied to predict a competitor's response to the firm's action. In general, the number of tactical responses taken exceeds the number of strategic responses. Competitors respond more frequently to the actions taken by the firm with a reputation for predictable and understandable competitive behaviour, especially if that firm is a market leader. In general, the firm can predict that when its competitor is highly dependent for its revenue and profitability in the market in which the firm took a competitive action, that competitor is likely to launch a strong response. However, firms that are more diversified across markets are less likely to respond to a particular action that affects only one of the markets in which they compete.

■ In slow-cycle markets, where competitive advantages can be sustained for a period of time, the competitive dynamics commonly involve firms taking actions and responses intended to protect, maintain and extend their proprietary advantages. In fast-cycle markets, competition is substantial as firms concentrate on developing a series of temporary competitive advantages. This emphasis is necessary because firms' advantages in fast-cycle markets aren't proprietary and, as such, are subject to rapid and relatively inexpensive imitation. Standard-cycle markets have a level competition between that in slow-cycle and fast-cycle markets; firms are partially shielded from competition in these markets as they use capabilities that produce competitive advantages that are moderately sustainable. Competitors in standard-cycle markets serve mass markets and try to develop economies of scale to enhance their profitability. Innovation is vital to competitive success in each of the three types of markets. Companies should recognize that the set of competitive actions and responses taken by all firms differs by type of market.

## REVIEW QUESTIONS

1   Who are competitors? How are competitive rivalry, competitive behaviour and competitive dynamics defined in the chapter?

2   What is market commonality? What is resource similarity? What does it mean to say that these concepts are the building blocks for a competitor analysis?

3   How do awareness, motivation and ability affect the firm's competitive behaviour?

4   What factors affect the likelihood a firm will take a competitive action?

5   What factors affect the likelihood a firm will initiate a competitive response to the action taken by a competitor?

6   What competitive dynamics can be expected among firms competing in slow-cycle markets? In fast-cycle markets? In standard-cycle markets?

## DISCUSSION QUESTIONS

1   In the automobile market, does Range Rover compete with Seat? If not, why not?

2   Do competitive markets experience more or less innovation than less competitive markets? Why?

3   What are the characteristics of both a first mover and a second mover? What types of competitive situations favour each?

4   Illustrate, with examples, firms that compete in slow-cycle, fast-cycle and standard-cycle markets.

5   Distinguish between strategic and tactical actions. List the range of tactical responses a firm might consider in reply to a competitor's action.

## FURTHER READING

A selection of excellent scholarly material is provided here for further reading. The increasing dynamics and complexity of international competition seem closely linked to uncertainty and firms' efforts to succeed against the odds. Taken together these efforts of raising competitiveness collectively result in specific dynamics of rivalry in which what made a difference initially is in the process widely adopted, i.e. the red queen effect (P. J. Derfus, P. G. Maggitti, C. M. Grimm and K. G. Smith (2008) "The red queen effect: Competitive actions and firm performance", *Academy of Management Journal*, 51: 61–80; H. R. Greve (2009) "Bigger and safer: The diffusion of competitive advantage", *Strategic Management Journal*, 30: 1–23; W. T. Robinson and S. Min (2002) "Is the first to market the first to fail? Empirical evidence for industrial goods businesses', *Journal of Marketing Research*, 39: 120–128). In this context, understanding blinds spots and predicting competitors' moves can provide what is needed to leap ahead (e.g. K. P. Coyne and J. Horn (2009) "Predicting your competitor's reaction", *Harvard Business*

*Review*, 87(4): 90–97; D. Ng, R. Westgren and S. Sonka (2009) "Competitive blind spots in an institutional field", *Strategic Management Journal*, 30: 349–369).

Richard D'Aveni, who coined the term "hypercompetition", illustrates with much detail how firms can escape

the commodity trap (R. A. D'Aveni (2010) *Beating the Commodity Trap: How to Maximize Your Competitive Position and Increase Your Pricing Power*, Cambridge, MA: Harvard Business School Press).

# EXPERIENTIAL EXERCISES

## Exercise 1: Win–Win, Win–Lose, or Lose–Lose?

A key aspect of company strategy concerns the interactions between two or more firms. When a new market segment emerges, should a firm strive for a first-mover advantage, or wait to see how the market takes shape? Diversified firms compete against one another in multiple market segments and must often consider how actions in one market might be subject to retaliation by a competitor in another segment. Similarly, when a competitor initiates a price war, a firm must decide whether it should respond in kind.

Game theory is helpful for understanding the strategic interaction between firms. Game theory uses assumptions about the behaviour of rivals to help a company choose a specific strategy that maximizes its return. In this exercise, you will use game theory to help analyse business decisions.

### Individual

One of the classic illustrations of game theory can be found in the prisoner's dilemma. Two criminals have been apprehended by the police for suspicion of a robbery. The police separate the thieves and offer them the same deal: Inform on your peer and receive a lesser sentence. Let your peer inform on you and receive a harsher sentence. What should you tell the police?

Visit http://www.gametheory.net where you can play the prisoner's dilemma against a computer. Play the dilemma using different parameters, and make notes of your experience.

### Groups

Many examples of game theory can be found in popular culture, from the reality show *Survivor* to episodes of *The Simpsons*. Revisit http://www.gametheory.net and select either a TV or movie illustration. Discuss the applications of game theory with your team.

As a group, prepare a one-page summary of how game theory can be applied to competitive interactions between firms.

## Exercise 2: Strategy as warfare

It is common to see military analogies and phrasing used to describe strategy topics, particularly with regard to competitive dynamics and interfirm rivalry. For example, executives often speak about guerrilla marketing, launching pre-emptive strikes on rivals, or battles for market share. Al Dunlap, a former CEO of Sunbeam, was once known as "Rambo in pinstripes" and even posed for a business magazine photo shoot wearing machine guns.

Military texts are often used to help understand how firms should act in relation to their competitors. Von Clauswitz's book *On War* draws on his experience in the Napoleonic Wars. Sun Tzu's *Art of War* is a much earlier – circa 500 BCE – and more influential text, however. Sun Tzu was a Chinese general who, according to legend, was hired by the king after a demonstration of training using the king's concubines.

### Part One

Break into teams of 4–6 persons. Each member should select a different chapter of *Art of War* (which has 13 chapters in total). Numerous sources on the Internet offer free downloads of the book, including an audiobook version at Project Gutenberg (http://www.gutenberg.org). After reading your chapter, prepare a bullet-point summary for your team members on the chapter's relevance to corporate strategy.

### Part Two

Have the team meet and ask each member to explain her/his summary of what was read. Then, answer the following questions:

- Which of Sun Tzu's ideas offered the most insightful analogies for interfirm rivalry?

- Which of Sun Tzu's ideas seemed to be the *least* relevant for understanding competitive dynamics among firms?

- What ideas from *Art of War* can you apply to an example used earlier in this chapter?

## VIDEO CASE

### The birth of NetJets

### Richard Santulli, Chairman and CEO, NetJets

www.cengage.co.uk/volberda/students/video_cases

In 1986, NetJets founder Richard Santulli created the fractional airline ownership business model. Today his airline flies over 390 000 flights annually to more than 173 different countries. With 800 planes under its management, NetJets is the second largest airline in the world.

Be prepared to discuss the following concepts and questions in class:

### Concepts

- First mover
- Reputation
- Segmentation

- Industry competitive dynamics
- Standard-cycle markets

### Questions

1 Think about the airline industry in terms of standard-cycle markets. What does being in this type of industry mean for most aviation transportation competitors?

2 Think through the benefits to being a first mover. Why is this not always a sustainable advantage?

3 Why do you think Continental Airlines or American Airlines did not invent the concept of fractional ownership?

## NOTES

1. D. F. Spulber, 2004, *Management Strategy*, Boston, MA: McGraw-Hill/Irwin, 87–88; M. J. Chen, 1996, "Competitor analysis and interfirm rivalry: Toward a theoretical integration", *Academy of Management Review*, 21: 100–134.

2. 2008 "Keeping the water pure is suddenly in demand", *The New York Times*, http://www.nytimes.com, June 19.

3. J. Robertson, 2009, "IBM launches water-management services operation", *BusinessWeek*. http://www.businessweek.com, March 13.

4. C. Palmer and N. Byrnes, 2009, "Coke and Pepsi try reinventing water", *Business Week*, http://www.businessweek.com, February 19.

5. M. Schrage, 2007, "The myth of commoditization", *MIT Sloan Management Review*, 48(2): 10–14; T. Galvin, 2002, "Examining institutional change: Evidence from the founding dynamics of UA health care interest associations", *Academy of Management Journal*, 45: 673–696.

6. R. D. Ireland and J. W. Webb, 2007, "Strategic entrepreneurship: Creating competitive advantage through streams of innovation", *Business Horizons*, 50: 49–59.

7. B. R. Barringer and R. D. Ireland, 2008, *Entrepreneurship: Successfully Launching New Ventures*, 2nd edn, Upper Saddle River, NJ: Prentice Hall; A. M. Knott and H. E. Posen, 2005, "Is failure good?", *Strategic Management Journal*, 26: 617–641.

8. P. J. Derfus, P. G. Maggitti, C. M. Grimm and K. G. Smith, 2008, "The red queen effect: Competitive actions and firm performance", *Academy of Management Journal*, 51: 61–80; C. M. Grimm, H. Lee and K. G. Smith, 2006, *Strategy as Action: Competitive Dynamics and Competitive Advantage*, New York: Oxford University Press; C. Bowman, 1998, *Strategy in Practice*, Harlow, UK: Prentice Hall; H. W. Volberda, 2003, "Strategic flexibility: Creating dynamic competitive advantages", Ch. 32 in: D. Faulkner and A. Campbell (eds.), *The Oxford Handbook of Strategy,* Oxford: Oxford University Press, 939–998; H. W. Volberda and A. Y. Lewin, 2003, "Co-evolutionary dynamics within and between firms: From evolution to co-evolution", *Journal of Management Studies*, 40(8): 2111–2136; A. Y. Lewin and H. W. Volberda, 1999, "Prolegomena on coevolution: A framework for research on strategy and new organizational forms", *Organization Science*, 10(5): 519–534.

9. J. W. Selsky, J. Goes and O. N. Baburoglu, 2007, "Contrasting perspectives of strategy making: Applications in 'hyper' environments", *Organization Studies*, 28(1): 71–94; A. Nair and L. Filer, 2003, "Cointegration of firm strategies within groups: A long-run analysis of firm behaviour in the Japanese steel industry", *Strategic Management Journal*, 24: 145–159; H. W. Volberda, 1996, "Toward the flexible

form: How to remain vital in hypercompetitive environments", *Organization Science*, 7(4): 359–387.

10. T. C. Powell, 2003, "Varieties of competitive parity", *Strategic Management Journal*, 24: 61–86.

11. D. G. Sirmon, S. Gove and M. A. Hitt, 2008, "Resource management in dyadic competitive rivalry: The effects of resource bundling and deployment", *Academy of Management Journal*, 51: 919–935; J. Rodriguez-Pinto, J. Gutierrez-Cillan and A. I. Rodriguez-Escudero, 2007, "Order and scale market entry, firm resources, and performance", *European Journal of Marketing*, 41: 590–607.

12. S. K. Ethitaj and D. H. Zhu, 2008, "Performance effects of imitative entry", *Strategic Management Journal*, 29: 797–817.

13. C. M. Grimm, H. Lee and K. G. Smith, *Strategy as Action* Industry Rivalry and Coordination, Cincinnati: South-Western Publishing Co.; G. Young, K. G. Smith, C. M. Grimm and D. Simon, 2000, "Multimarket contact and resource dissimilarity: A competitive dynamics perspective", *Journal of Management*, 26: 1217–1236.

14. E. I. Rose and K. Ito, 2008, "Competitive interactions: The international investment patterns of Japanese automobile manufacturers", *Journal of International Business Studies*, 39: 864–879; T. L. Sorenson, 2007, "Credible collusion in multimarket oligopoly", *Managerial and Decision Economics*, 28(2): 115–128.

15. T. Yu, M. Subramaniam and A. A. Cannella, 2009, "Rivalry deterrence in international markets: Contingencies governing the mutual forbearance hypothesis", *Academy of Management Journal*, 52: 127–147; K. G. Smith, W. J. Ferrier and H. Ndofor, 2001, "Competitive dynamics research: Critique and future directions", in: M. A. Hitt, R. E. Freeman and J. S. Harrison (eds.), *Handbook of Strategic Management*, Oxford, UK: Blackwell Publishers, 326.

16. G. Young, K. G. Smith and C. M. Grimm, 1996, "'Austrian' and industrial organization perspectives on firm-level competitive activity and performance", *Organization Science*, 73: 243–254; H. W. Volberda and H. B. Cheah, 1993, "A new perspective on entrepreneurship: A dialectic process of transformation within the entrepreneurial mode, type of flexibility and organizational form", in: H. Klandt (eds.), *Entrepreneurship and Business Development*, Aldershot: Avebury, 261–286.

17. H. D. Hopkins, 2003, "The response strategies of dominant US firms to Japanese challengers", *Journal of Management*, 29: 5–25; G. S. Day and D. J. Reibstein, 1997, "The dynamic challenges for theory and practice", in: G. S. Day and D. J. Reibstein (eds.), *Wharton on Competitive Strategy*, New York: John Wiley & Sons, 2.

18. J. J. Li, K. Z. Zhou and A. T. Shao, 2009, "Competitive position, managerial ties and profitability of foreign firms in China: An interactive perspective", *Journal of International Business Studies*, 40: 339–352; M. J. Chen and D. C. Hambrick, 1995, "Speed, stealth and selective attack: How small firms differ from large firms in competitive behaviour", *Academy of Management Journal*, 38: 453–482.

19. T. Dewett and S. David, 2007, "Innovators and imitators in novelty-intensive markets: A research agenda", *Creativity and Innovation Management*, 16(1): 80–92.

20. A. Sahay, 2007, "How to reap higher profits with dynamic pricing", *MIT Sloan Management Review*, 48(4): 53–60; T. J. Douglas and J. A. Ryman, 2003, "Understanding competitive advantage in the general hospital industry: Evaluating strategic competencies", *Strategic Management Journal*, 24: 333–347.

21. T. Yu and A. A. Cannella, Jr., 2007, "Rivalry between multinational enterprises: An event history approach", *Academy of Management Journal*, 50: 665–686; W. J. Ferrier, 2001, "Navigating the competitive landscape: The drivers and consequences of competitive aggressiveness", *Academy of Management Journal*, 44: 858–877.

22. K. G. Smith, W. J. Ferrier and H. Ndofor, 2001, "Competitive dynamics research: Critique and future directions", in: M. A. Hitt, R. E. Freeman and J. S. Harrison (eds.), *Handbook of Strategic Management*, Oxford, UK: Blackwell Publishers, 326.

23. E. G. Olson and D. Sharma, 2008, "Beating the commoditization trend: A framework from the electronics industry", *Journal of Business Strategy*, 29(4): 22–28; J. Shamsie, 2003, "The context of dominance: An industry-driven framework for exploiting reputation", *Strategic Management Journal*, 24: 199–215.

24. J. Li, 2008, "Asymmetric interactions between foreign and domestic banks: Effects on market entry", *Strategic Management Journal*, 29: 873–893; K. Cool, L. H. Roller and B. Leleux, 1999, "The relative impact of actual and potential rivalry on firm profitability in the pharmaceutical industry", *Strategic Management Journal*, 20: 1–14.

25. G. Leask and D. Parker, 2007, "Strategic groups, competitive groups and performance within the UK pharmaceutical industry: Improving our understanding of the competitive process", *Strategic Management Journal*, 28: 723–745; D. R. Gnyawali and R. Madhavan, 2001, "Cooperative networks and competitive dynamics: A structural embeddedness perspective", *Academy of Management Review*, 26: 431–445; H. W. Volberda, 1998, *Building the flexible firm: How to remain competitive*, Oxford: Oxford University Press.

26. V. La, P. Patterson and C. Styls, 2009, "Client-perceived performance and value in professional B2B services: An international perspective", *Journal of International Business Studies*, 40: 274–300; Y. Y. Kor and J. T. Mahoney, 2005, "How dynamics, management, and governance of resource deployments influence firm-level performance", *Strategic Management Journal*, 26: 489–496.

27. R. L. Priem, L. G. Love and M. A. Shaffer, 2002, "Executives' perceptions of uncertainty scores: A numerical taxonomy and underlying dimensions", *Journal of Management*, 28: 725–746.

28. J. C. Bou and A. Satorra, 2007, "The persistence of abnormal returns at industry and firm levels: Evidence from Spain", *Strategic Management Journal*, 28: 707–722.

29. M. J. Chen, 1996, "Competitor analysis and interfirm rivalry: Toward a theoretical integration", *Academy of Management Review*, 21: 100–134.

30. M. J. Chen, 1996, "Competitor analysis and interfirm rivalry: Toward a theoretical integration", *Academy of Management Review*, 21: 100–134.

31. D. Ng, R. Westgren and S. Sonka, 2009, "Competitive blind spots in an institutional field", *Strategic Management Journal*, 30: 349–369.

32. S. J. Chang and D. Xu, 2008, "Spillovers and competition among foreign and local firms in China", *Strategic Management Journal*, 29: 495–518.

33. K. Uhlenbruck, M. A. Hitt and M. Semadeni, 2006, "Market value effects of acquisitions of Internet firms: A resource-based analysis", *Strategic Management Journal*, 27(10): 899–913; A. Afuah, 2003, "Redefining firm boundaries in the face of the Internet: Are firms really shrinking?", *Academy of Management Review*, 28: 34–53.

34. H. Gebauer, 2007, "Entering low-end markets: A new strategy for Swiss companies", *Journal of Business Strategy*, 27(5): 23–31.

35. M. J. Chen, 1996, "Competitor analysis and interfirm rivalry: Toward a theoretical integration", *Academy of Management Review,* 21: 100–134.

36. A. Kachra and R. E. White, 2008, "Know-how transfer: The role of social, economic/competitive, and firm boundary factors", *Strategic Management Journal*, 29: 425–445.

37. M. J. Chen, K. H. Su and W. Tsai, 2007, "Competitive tension: The awareness-motivation-capability perspective", *Academy of Management Journal*, 50: 101–118; J. Gimeno and C. Y. Woo, 1999, "Multimarket contact, economies of scope, and firm performance", *Academy of Management Journal*, 42: 239–259.

38. I. C. MacMillan, A. B. van Putten and R. S. McGrath, 2003, "Global gamesmanship, *Harvard Business Review*", 81(5): 62–71.

39. G. Young, K. G. Smith, C. M. Grimm and D. Simon, 2000, "Multimarket contact and resource dissimilarity: A competitive dynamics perspective", *Journal of Management*, 26: 1217–1236.

40. H. R. Greve, 2008, "Multimarket contact and sales growth: Evidence from insurance", *Strategic Management Journal*, 29: 229–249; J. Gimeno, 1999, "Reciprocal threats in multimarket rivalry: Staking out 'spheres of influence' in the US airline industry", *Strategic Management Journal*, 20: 101–128.

41. S. Jayachandran, J. Gimeno and P. R. Varadarajan, "Theory of multimarket competition", *Journal of Marketing*, 63: 59; M. J. Chen, 1996, "Competitor analysis and interfirm rivalry: Toward a theoretical integration", *Academy of Management Review*, 21: 100–134.

42. H. Schiele, 2008, "Location, location: The geography of industry clusters", *Journal of Business Strategy*, 29(3): 29–36; J. Gimeno and C. Y. Woo, 1996, "Hypercompetition in a multimarket environment: The role of strategic similarity and multimarket contact on competitive de-escalation", *Organization Science*, 7: 322–341.

43. C. H. Deutsch, 2007, "UPS embraces high-tech delivery methods", *New York Times Online*, http://www.nytimes.com, July 12.

44. S. MacMillan, 2008, "The issue: DHL turns to rival UPS", *BusinessWeek*, http://www.businessweek.com, June.

45. M. J. Chen, 1996, "Competitor analysis and interfirm rivalry: Toward a theoretical integration", *Academy of Management Review*, 21: 100–134.

46. M. J. Chen, 1996, "Competitor analysis and interfirm rivalry: Toward a theoretical integration", *Academy of Management Review*, 21: 100–134; W. Ocasio, 1997, "Towards an attention-based view of the firm", *Strategic Management Journal*, 18 (Special Issue): 187–206; K. G. Smith, W. J. Ferrier and H. Ndofor, 2001, "Competitive dynamics research: Critique and future direction's", in: M. A. Hitt, R. E. Freeman and J. S. Harrison (eds.), *Handbook of Strategic Management*, Oxford, UK: Blackwell Publishers, 326.

47. 2007, "Komatsu lifts outlook, outdoes rival Caterpillar", *New York Times Online*, http://www.nytimes.com, July 30.

48. M. Neal, 2009, "Carrefour's no Wal-Mart", *Wall Street Journal*, http://www.wsj.com, March 12; 2007, "Carrefour battles Wal-Mart in South America", Elsevier Food International, http://www.foodinternational.net, July 31.

49. S. Tallman, M. Jenkins, N. Henry and S. Pinch, 2004, "Knowledge, clusters and competitive advantage", *Academy of Management Review*, 29: 258–271; J. F. Porac and H. Thomas, 1994, "Cognitive categorization and subjective rivalry among retailers in a small city", *Journal of Applied Psychology*, 79: 54–66.

50. S. H. Park and D. Zhou, 2005, "Firm heterogeneity and competitive dynamics in alliance formation", *Academy of Management Review*, 30: 531–554.

51. S. R. Miller, D. E. Thomas, L. Eden and M. A. Hitt, 2008, "Knee deep in the big muddy: The survival of emerging market firms in developed markets", *Management International Review*, 48: 645–666.

52. M. J. Chen, 1996, "Competitor analysis and interfirm rivalry: Toward a theoretical integration", *Academy of Management Review*, 21: 100–134.

53. M. Leiblein and T. Madsen, 2009, "Unbundling competitive heterogeneity: Incentive structures and capability influences on technological innovation", *Strategic Management Journal*, 30(7): 711–735; J. J. Li, L. Poppo and K. Z. Zhou, 2008, "Do managerial ties in China always produce value? Competition, uncertainty and domestic vs. foreign competition", *Strategic Management Journal*, 29: 383–400.

54. R. Belderbos and L. Sleuwaegen, 2005, "Competitive drivers and international plant configuration strategies: A product-level test", *Strategic Management Journal*, 26: 577–593.

55. C. M. Grimm and K. G. Smith, 1997, *Strategy as Action: Industry Rivalry and Coordination*, Cincinnati: South-Western Publishing Co., 125.

56. 2010, "Ways for a small business to beat Tesco", http://www.businessopportunitiesandideas.com, May 27.

57. 2010, "The Tesco Takeover", http://www.foe.co.uk/resource/index.shtml, May 27.

58. B. Webber, 2007, "Volatile markets", *Business Strategy Review*, 18(2): 60–67; K. G. Smith, W. J. Ferrier and C. M. Grimm, 2001, "King of the hill: Dethroning the industry leader", *Academy of Management Executive*, 15(2): 59–70.

59. S. E. Jackson, 2008, "Grow your business without leaving your competitive stronghold", *Journal of Business Strategy*, 29(4): 60–62.

60. W. J. Ferrier and H. Lee, 2003, "Strategic aggressiveness, variation, and surprise: How the sequential pattern of competitive rivalry influences stock market returns", *Journal of Managerial Issues*, 14: 162–180.

61. 2010, "About Guess", http://www.guess.eu, May 27.

62. C. Palmeri, 2007, "How Guess got its groove back", *BusinessWeek*, July 23, 126.

63. 2010, "A380 Family", http://www.airbus.com, May 27.

64. J. Schumpeter, 1934, *The Theory of Economic Development*, Cambridge, MA: Harvard University Press.

65. J. L. C. Cheng and I. F. Kesner, 1997, "Organizational slack and response to environmental shifts: The impact of resource allocation patterns", *Journal of Management*, 23: 1–18.

66. F. F. Suarez and G. Lanzolla, 2007, "The role of environmental dynamics in building a first mover advantage theory", *Academy of Management Review*, 32: 377–392.

67. G. M. McNamara, J. Haleblian and B. J. Dykes, 2008, "The performance implications of participating in an acquisition wave: Early mover advantages, bandwagon effects, and the moderating influence of industry characteristics and acquirer tactics", *Academy of Management Journal*, 51, 113–130; F. Wang, 2000, "Too appealing to overlook", *America's Network*, December, 10–12.

68. R. K. Sinha and C. H. Noble, 2008, "The adoption of radical manufacturing technologies and firm survival", *Strategic Management Journal*, 29: 943–962; D. P. Forbes, 2005, "Managerial determinants of decision speed in new ventures", *Strategic Management Journal*, 26: 355–366.

69. H. R. Greve, 2009, "Bigger and safer: The diffusion of competitive advantage", *Strategic Management Journal*, 30: 1–23; W. T. Robinson and S. Min, 2002, "Is the first to market the first to fail? Empirical evidence for industrial goods businesses", *Journal of Marketing Research*, 39: 120–128.

70. T. Cottrell and B. R. Nault, 2004, "Product variety and firm survival in the microcomputer software industry", *Strategic Management Journal*, 25: 1005–1025; R. Agarwal, M. B. Sarkar and R. Echambadi, 2002, "The conditioning effect of time on firm survival: An industry life cycle approach", *Academy of Management Journal*, 45: 971–994.

71. A. Srivastava and H. Lee, 2005, "Predicting order and timing of new product moves: The role of top management in corporate entrepreneurship", *Journal of Business Venturing*, 20: 459–481.

72. M. S. Giarratana and A. Fosfuri, 2007, "Product strategies and survival in Schumpeterian environments: Evidence from the US security software industry", *Organization Studies*, 28(6): 909–929; J. W. Spencer and T. P. Murtha, 2005, "How do governments matter to new industry creation?", *Academy of Management Review*, 30: 321–337.

73. Z. Simsek, J. F. Veiga and M. H. Lubatkin, 2007, "The impact of managerial environmental perceptions on corporate entrepreneurship: Toward understanding discretionary slack's pivotal role", *Journal of Management Studies*, 44: 1398–1424. S. W. Geiger and L. H. Cashen, 2002, "A multidimensional examination of slack and its impact on innovation", *Journal of Managerial Issues*, 14: 68–84.

74. B. S. Teng, 2007, "Corporate entrepreneurship activities through strategic alliances: A resource-based approach toward competitive advantage", *Journal of Management Studies*, 44: 119–142; M. B. Lieberman and D. B. Montgomery, 1988, "First-mover advantages", *Strategic Management Journal*, 9: 41–58.

75. D. Lange, S. Boivie and A. D. Henderson, 2009, "The parenting paradox: How multibusiness diversifiers endorse disruptive technologies while their corporate children struggle", *Academy of Management Journal*, 52: 179–198.

76. S. Jonsson and P. Regner, 2009: "Normative barriers to imitation: Social complexity of core competences in a mutual fund industry", *Strategic Management Journal*, 30: 517–536; 2001, "Older, wiser, webbier", *The Economist*, June 30, 10; P. A. M. Vermeulen, F. A. J. Van den Bosch and H. W. Volberda, 2007, "Complex incremental product innovation in established service firms: A micro institutional perspective", *Organization Studies*, 28(10): 1523–1546; H. W. Volberda, F. A. J. Van den Bosch, B. Flier and E. R. Gedajlovic, 2001, "Following the herd or not? Patterns of renewal in the Netherlands and the UK", *Long Range Planning*, Special Theme: Mastering Strategic Renewal: Lessons from Financial Services, 34(2): 209–229.

77. M. Shank, 2002, "Executive strategy report, IBM business strategy consulting", http://www.ibm.com, March 14; W. Boulding and M. Christen, 2001, "First-mover disadvantage" *Harvard Business Review*, 79(9): 20–21.

78. J. L. Boyd and R. K. F. Bresser, 2008, "Performance implications of delayed competitive responses: Evidence from the US retail industry", *Strategic Management Journal*, 29: 1077–1096.

79. J. Gimeno, R. E. Hoskisson, B. B. Beal and W. P. Wan, 2005, "Explaining the clustering of international expansion moves: A critical test in the US telecommunications industry", *Academy of Management Journal*, 48: 297–319; K. G. Smith, C. M. Grimm and M. J. Gannon, 1992, *Dynamics of Competitive Strategy*, Newbury Park, CA.: Sage Publications.

80. J. Li and R. K. Koxhikode, 2008, "Knowledge management and innovation strategy: The challenge for latecomers in emerging economies", *Asia Pacific Journal of Management*, 25: 429–450; M. Stienstra, M. G. Baaij, F. A. J. Van den Bosch and H. W. Volberda, 2004, "Strategic renewal of Europe's largest telecom operators (1999–2001): From herd behaviour towards strategic choice?", *European*

*Management Journal*, 22 (3): 273–280; B. Flier, F. A. J. Van den Bosch and H. W. Volberda, 2003, "Coevolution in the strategic renewal behaviour of British, Dutch and French financial incumbents: interaction of environmental selection, institutional effects and managerial intentionality", *Journal of Management Studies*, 40(8): 2163–2188; M. Hensmans, F. A. J. Van den Bosch and H. W. Volberda, 2001, "Clicks versus bricks in the emerging online financial services industry", *Long Range Planning* 34(2): 231–247.

81. S. D. Dobrev and G. R. Carroll, 2003, "Size (and competition) among organizations: Modeling scale-based selection among automobile producers in four major countries, 1885–1981", *Strategic Management Journal*, 24: 541–558.

82. L. F. Mesquita and S. G. Lazzarini, 2008, "Horizontal and vertical relationships in developing economies: Implications for SMEs access to global markets", *Academy of Management Journal*, 51: 359–380; F. K. Pil and M. Hoiweg, 2003, "Exploring scale: The advantage of thinking small", *The McKinsey Quarterly*, 44(2): 33–39.

83. M. A. Hitt, L. Bierman and J. D. Collins, 2007, "The strategic evolution of US law firms", *Business Horizons*, 50: 17–28; D. Miller and M. J. Chen, 1996, "The simplicity of competitive repertoires: An empirical analysis", *Strategic Management Journal*, 17: 419–440.

84. G. Young, K. G. Smith and C. M. Grimm, 1996, "'Austrian' and industrial organization perspectives", *Organization Science*, 7(3): 243–254.

85. B. A. Melcher, 1993, "How Goliaths can act like Davids", *BusinessWeek*, Special Issue, 193.

86. Databank, 2010, *The Sunday Times*, May 23, Section 3: 13.

87. 2010, 2009, Final results highlights, http://www.hsbc.com, May 27.

88. P. B. Crosby, 1980, *Quality Is Free*, New York: Penguin.

89. W. E. Deming, 1986, *Out of the Crisis*, Cambridge, MA: MIT Press.

90. D. A. Mollenkopf, E. Rabinovich, T. M. Laseter and K. K. Boyer, 2007, "Managing Internet product returns: A focus on effective service operations", *Decision Sciences*, 38: 215–250; L. B. Crosby, R. DeVito and J. M. Pearson, 2003, "Manage your customers' perception of quality", *Review of Business*, 24(1): 18–24.

91. K. Watanabe, 2007, "Lessons from Toyota's long drive", *Harvard Business Review*, 85(7/8): 74–83; R. S. Kaplan and D. P. Norton, 2001, *The Strategy-Focused Organization*, Boston, MA: Harvard Business School Press. H. Takeuchi, E. Ohsono and N. Shimizu, 2009, "The Contradictions that drive Toyota's success", *Harvard Business Review*, June, 96–104.

92. A. Azadegan, K. J. Dooley, P. L. Carter and J. R. Carter, 2008, "Supplier innovativeness and the role of interorganizational learning in enhancing manufacturing capabilities", *Journal of Supply Chain Management*, 44 (4): 14–35; O. Bayazit and B. Karpak, 2007, "An analytical network process-based framework for successful total quality management (TQM): An assessment of Turkish manufacturing industry readiness", *International Journal of Production Economics*, 105(1): 79–96.

93. K. E. Weick and K. M. Sutcliffe, 2001, *Managing the Unexpected*, San Francisco, CA: Jossey-Bass, 81–82.

94. G. Macintosh, 2007, "Customer orientation, relationship quality and relational benefits to the firm", *Journal of Services Marketing*, 21(3): 150–159; G. Yeung and V. Mok, 2005, "What are the impacts of implementing ISOs on the competitiveness of manufacturing industry in China", *Journal of World Business*, 40: 139–157.

95. J Wallace, 2009, "Boeing at risk of losing more 787 orders", *Seattle-Post-Intelligence*, http//:www.seattlepi. nwsource.com, March 13.

96. T. R. Cook, D. J. Ketchen, J. G. Combs and S. Y. Todd, 2008, "Strategic resources and performance: A meta-analysis", *Strategic Management Journal*, 29: 1141–1154; K. G. Smith, W. J. Ferrier and H. Ndofor, 2001, "Competitive dynamics research: Critique and future directions", in: M. A. Hitt, R. E. Freeman and J. S. Harrison (eds.), *Handbook of Strategic Management*, Oxford, UK: Blackwell Publishers, 326.

97. M. J. Chen and I. C. MacMillan, 1992, "Nonresponse and delayed response to competitive moves", *Academy of Management Journal*, 35: 539–570; K .G. Smith, W. J. Ferrier and H. Ndofor, 2001, "Competitive dynamics research: Critique and future directions", in: M. A. Hitt, R. E. Freeman and J. S. Harrison (eds.), *Handbook of Strategic Management*, Oxford, UK: Blackwell Publishers, 326.

98. M. J. Chen, K. G. Smith and C. M. Grimm, 1992, "Action characteristics as predictors of competitive responses", *Management Science*, 38: 439–455.

99. M. J. Chen and D. Miller, 1994, "Competitive attack, retaliation and performance: An expectancy-valence framework", *Strategic Management Journal*, 15: 85–102.

100. T. Gardner, 2005, "Interfirm competition for human resources: Evidence from the software industry", *Academy of Management Journal*, 48: 237–258; N. Huyghebaert and L. M. van de Gucht, 2004, "Incumbent strategic behaviour in financial markets and the exit of entrepreneurial start-ups", *Strategic Management Journal*, 25: 669–688.

101. K. G. Smith, W. J. Ferrier and H. Ndofor, 2001, "Competitive dynamics research: Critique and future directions", in: M. A. Hitt, R. E. Freeman and J. S. Harrison (eds.), *Handbook of Strategic Management*, Oxford, UK: Blackwell Publishers, 326.

102. V. P. Rindova, A. P. Petkova and S. Kotha, 2007, "Standing out: How firms in emerging markets build reputation", *Strategic Organization*, 5: 31–70; J. Shamsie, 2003, "The context of dominance: An industry-driven framework for exploiting reputation", *Strategic Management Journal*, 24: 199–215.

103. A. D. Smith, 2007, "Making the case for the competitive advantage of corporate social responsibility", *Business Strategy Series*, 8(3): 186–195; P. W. Roberts and G. R. Dowling, 2003, "Corporate reputation and sustained superior financial performance", *Strategic Management Journal*, 24: 1077–1093.

104. W. J. Ferrier, K. G. Smith and C. M. Grimm, 1999, "The role of competitive actions in market share erosion and industry dethronement: A study of industry leaders and challengers", *Academy of Management Journal*, 42: 372–388.

105. K. G. Smith, C. M. Grimm and M. J. Gannon, 1992, *Dynamics of Competitive Strategy*, Newberry Park, CA.: Sage Publications.

106. L. Li, L. Zhang and B. Arys, 2008, "The turtle–hare story revisited: Social capital and resource accumulation for firms from emerging economies", *Asia Pacific Journal of Management*, 25: 251–275.

107. A. Karnani and B. Wernerfelt, 1985, "Multiple point competition", *Strategic Management Journal*, 6: 87–97.

108. K. G. Smith, W. J. Ferrier and H. Ndofor, 2001, "Competitive dynamics research: Critique and future directions", in: M. A. Hitt, R. E. Freeman and J. S. Harrison (eds.), *Handbook of Strategic Management,* Oxford, UK: Blackwell Publishers, 326.

109. 2010, "Bond pays interest in chocolate", *The Sunday Times*, May 23, Section 3: 1.

110. S. L. Newbert, 2007, "Empirical research on the resource-based view of the firm: An assessment and suggestions for future research", *Strategic Management Journal*, 28: 121–146; G. McNamara, P. M. Vaaler and C. Devers, 2003, "Same as it ever was: The search for evidence of increasing hypercompetition", *Strategic Management Journal*, 24: 261–278.

111. M. F. Wiersema and H. P. Bowen, 2008, "Corporate diversification: The impact of foreign competition, industry globalization and product diversification", *Strategic Management Journal*, 29: 115–132; A. Kalnins and W. Chung, 2004, "Resource-seeking agglomeration: A study of market entry in the lodging industry", *Strategic Management Journal*, 25: 689–699.

112. J. R. Williams, 1992, "How sustainable is your competitive advantage?", *California Management Review*, 34(3): 29–51.

113. J. A. Lamberg, H. Tikkanen and T. Nokelainen, 2009, "Competitive dynamics, strategic consistency and organizational survival", *Strategic Management Journal*, 30: 45–60; D. A. Chmielewski and A. Paladino, 2007, "Driving a resource orientation: Reviewing the role of resources and capability characteristics", *Management Decision*, 45: 462–483.

114. N. Pangarkar and J. R. Lie, 2004, "The impact of market cycle on the performance of Singapore acquirers", *Strategic Management Journal*, 25: 1209–1216.

115. 2003, "How fast is your company?", *Fast Company*, June, 18; H. W. Volberda, 1997, "Building flexible organizations for fast-moving markets", *Long Range Planning*, 30(2): 169–183.

116. D. P. Forbes, 2007, "Reconsidering the strategic implications of decision comprehensiveness", *Academy of Management Review*, 32: 361–376; T. Talaulicar, J. Grundei and A. V. Werder, 2005, "Strategic decision making in startups: The effect of top management team organization and processes on speed and comprehensiveness", *Journal of Business Venturing*, 20: 519–541.

117. A. H. Ang, 2008, "Competitive intensity and collaboration: Impact on firm growth across technological environments", *Strategic Management Journal*, 29: 1057–1075; M. Song, C. Droge, S. Hanvanich and R. Calantone, 2005, "Marketing and technology resource complementarity: An analysis of their interaction effect in two environmental contexts", *Strategic Management Journal*, 26: 259–276.

118. R. Williams, 1999, *Renewable Advantage: Crafting Strategy Through Economic Time*, New York: Free Press, 8.

119. R. Williams, 1999, *Renewable Advantage: Crafting Strategy Through Economic Time*, New York: Free Press, 8.

120. D. Li, L. E. Eden, M. A. Hitt and R. D. Ireland, 2008, "Friends, acquaintances or strangers? Partner selection in R&D alliances", *Academy of Management Journal*, 51: 315–334; D. Gerwin, 2004, "Coordinating new product development in strategic alliances", *Academy of Management Review*, 29: 241–257.

121. K. Coucke and L. Sleuwaegen, 2008, "Offshoring as a survival strategy: Evidence from manufacturing firms in Belgium", *Journal of International Business Studies*, 39: 1261–1277.

122. P. Carbonell and A. I. Rodriguez, 2006, "The impact of market characteristics and innovation speed on perceptions of positional advantage and new product performance", *International Journal of Research in Marketing*, 23(1): 1–12; R. Sanchez, 1995, "Strategic flexibility in production competition", *Strategic Management Journal*, 16(Special Issue): 9–26.

123. R. Adner and D. Levinthal, 2008, "Doing versus seeing: Acts of exploitation and perceptions of exploration", *Strategic Entrepreneurship Journal*, 2: 43–52; J. R. Williams, *Renewable Advantage: crafting strategy through economic time*, New York, NY: Free Press.

CHAPTER 7

# CORPORATE-LEVEL STRATEGY

## LEARNING OBJECTIVES

Studying this chapter should provide you with the strategic management knowledge needed to:

1 Define corporate-level strategy and discuss its purpose.
2 Describe different levels of diversification with different corporate-level strategies.
3 Explain three primary reasons why firms diversify.
4 Describe how firms can create value by using a related diversification strategy.
5 Explain the two ways value can be created with an unrelated diversification strategy.
6 Discuss the incentives and resources that encourage diversification.
7 Describe motives that can encourage managers to over-diversify a firm.

© Markus Leiminger/iStock

© WILL BURGESS/Reuters/Corbis

**OPENING CASE**

## Fosters' Group diversification into the wine business

"Fosters is Australian for beer" given that it produces some of Australia's top beers, including Fosters Lager, Asahi, Corona and Stella Artois. However, in 2008, wine contributed 76 per cent of the company's sale earnings. Although Fosters was traditionally a brewer and distributor of beer products, it foresaw more growth prospects with the sales of wine than beer. It also perceived an opportunity to co-mingle the marketing and distribution of these two spirit products to create economies of scope (a concept defined later in the chapter). In 2001, Fosters bought Beringer Wine Estates, a leading California winery with nearly €1 billion in sales. Then in 2005, Fosters acquired another premium wine maker, Southcorp; the combination of these companies made Fosters one of the world's biggest global wine companies with names such as Lindemans, Wolf Blass, Penfolds, Rosemount and Wynns Coonawarrra Estate.

In order to create the synergy between the beer and wine assets, Fosters used one sales force that was focused on the mass-marketing of beer and cheap spirits, and high-priced wine to specialized restaurants and off-licence stores that sell to wine connoisseurs with more sophisticated tastes. The sharing of these activities between businesses that focus on low-cost mass marketing and focused differentiation (premium wines) turned out to be a significant mistake. Furthermore, the assets, especially Southcorp, were purchased at a distinct premium. Although the higher growth rate potential for wine sales seemed like the perfect strategic fit with the low growth rate of beer sales, the potential fit between these two businesses was apparently not realized. Furthermore, one analyst said "they [Fosters] paid too much and they bought at the wrong time in the cycle".

To correct the problem Fosters has recently been separating these businesses and creating a new marketing group for the wine business while maintaining its current expertise in the brewing and distribution of beer. Because the separation of these businesses is crucial for Fosters to remain profitable, it may be willing to divest one of these businesses, most likely the wine segment, because its basic expertise among the key leaders and other personnel is in the beer business.

This is an example of related constrained diversification poorly executed. Interestingly, a new CEO was appointed after the strategic mistakes noted above. Related constrained diversification, as defined later in the chapter, focuses on managing different businesses which are highly related in regard to the manufacturing, sales and distribution activities among the firm's related business portfolio. Unfortunately, what Fosters focused on was the growth cycle differences and not on the detailed implementation differences related to the sharing of actual activities between beer and premium wine, which was not as great a fit as earlier suspected.

Interestingly, Fosters have recently announced the spin-off of their brewing unit from their struggling wine operations. In the media, this structural overhaul is thought to precipitate takeover interest from other international brewers, something investors and industry analysts have been encouraging for some time, given the poor returns of the wine business.

**Sources:** Koons, C. (2009) "Earnings: Fosters to retain, revamp struggling wine business", *Wall Street Journal*, February 18, B6; 2009, Fosters Company Limited, 2009 *Hoovers Company Records*, http://www.hoovers.com, March 15, 42414; Ellis, E. (2008) "What'll you have Mate?", *Barron's*, October

27, 34–36; Murdoch, S. (2008) "Corporate news: Fosters Group names Johnston to be CEO", *Wall Street Journal*, September 27, D6; Charles, G. 2007, "Fosters Group plans global wine brands relaunch", *Marketing*, November 29, 3; Smith, P. (2010) "Fosters to spin-off loss-making wine unit", *Financial Times*, http://www.ft.com, May 26.

## Questions

**1** There appeared *prima facie* to be evidence of a synergistic relationship between the wine and core business. What reasons can you provide for the apparent poor performance?

**2** In comparison, how can Diageo (which competes primarily in beer, wine and spirits sectors), a competitor to Fosters, compete so successfully given their diversified portfolio within the drinks and beverage business?

Our discussions of business-level strategies (Chapter 5) and the competitive rivalry and competitive dynamics associated with them (Chapter 6) concentrate on firms competing in a single industry or product market.[1] In this chapter, we introduce you to corporate-level strategies, which are strategies firms use to *diversify* their operations from a single business competing in a single market, into several product markets and, most commonly, into several businesses. Thus, a corporate-level strategy specifies actions a firm takes to gain a competitive advantage by selecting and managing a group of different businesses competing in different product markets. Corporate-level strategies help companies select new strategic positions – positions that are expected to increase the firm's value.[2] As explained in the Opening Case, Fosters Group Limited, an Australian drinks company, competes in several different beverage segments, dominated by beer and wine brands.

Another example is Interpublic Group, a marketing and advertising firm. It is taking advantage of the economic downturn to acquire companies at a decreased price and increase its portfolio of businesses. It is currently seeking to acquire firms in the digital and mobile sector to grow its Media Brands operations to help achieve its goal of being one of the top three players in its respective market by the year 2011.[3]

As is the case with Fosters, firms use corporate-level strategies as a means to grow revenues and profits. But there can be different strategic intents beside growth. Firms can pursue defensive or offensive strategies which realize growth but have different strategic intents. Firms can also pursue market development by moving into different geographic markets (this approach is discussed in Chapter 9). Firms can acquire competitors (horizontal integration) or buy a supplier or customer (vertical integration). These strategies are discussed in Chapter 8. The basic corporate strategy, the topic of this chapter, focuses on diversification.

The decision to take actions to pursue growth is never a risk-free choice. Indeed, as the Opening Case illustrated, Fosters Group experienced difficulty in integrating the beer and wine marketing and sales operations to share these activities. Also, Luxottica Group, a leader in the fashion sunglasses industry, has faced risks associated with its acquisition of Oakley, a firm focused on producing sporty sunglasses. Can a luxury goods manufacturer successfully integrate a sports goods manufacturing company?[4] Effective firms carefully evaluate their growth options (including the different corporate-level strategies) before committing firm resources to any of them.[5]

Given that the diversified firm operates in several different and unique product markets and probably in several businesses, it forms two types of strategies: corporate level (or company-wide) and business level (or competitive).[6] Corporate-level strategy is concerned with two key issues: in what product markets and businesses the firm should compete and how corporate headquarters should manage those businesses.[7] For the diversified corporation, a business-level strategy (see

**Corporate-level strategy**

A corporate-level strategy specifies actions a firm takes to gain a competitive advantage by selecting and managing a group of different businesses competing in different product markets.

Chapter 5) must be selected for each of the businesses in which the firm has decided to compete. In this regard, each of Fosters product divisions uses different business-level strategies; while both focus on differentiation, the beer business is focused more on differentiation by a mass market approach while the wine business targets unique customers based on individual tastes.

As is the case with a business-level strategy, a corporate-level strategy is expected to help the firm earn above-average returns by creating value.[8] Some suggest that few corporate-level strategies actually create value.[9] As the Opening Case indicates, realizing value through a corporate strategy can be difficult to achieve. In fact, the degree to which corporate-level strategies create value beyond the sum of the value created by all of a firm's business units, remains an important research question.[10]

Evidence suggests that a corporate-level strategy's value is ultimately determined by the degree to which "the businesses in the portfolio are worth more under the management of the company than they would be under any other ownership".[11] Thus, an effective corporate-level strategy creates, across all of a firm's businesses, aggregate returns that exceed what those returns would be without the strategy[12] and contributes to the firm's strategic competitiveness and its ability to earn above-average returns.[13]

Product diversification, a primary form of corporate-level strategies, concerns the scope of the markets and industries in which the firm competes as well as "how managers buy, create and sell different businesses to match skills and strengths with opportunities presented to the firm".[14] Successful diversification is expected to reduce variability in the firm's profitability as earnings are generated from different businesses.[15] Because firms incur development and monitoring costs when diversifying, the ideal portfolio of businesses balances diversification's costs and benefits. CEOs and their top-management teams are responsible for determining the ideal portfolio for their company.[16]

We begin this chapter by examining different levels of diversification (from low to high). After describing the different reasons firms diversify their operations, we focus on two types of related diversification (related diversification signifies a moderate to a high level of diversification for the firm). When properly used, these strategies help create value in the diversified firm, either through the sharing of resources (the related constrained strategy) or the transferring of core competencies across the firm's different businesses (the related linked strategy). We then discuss unrelated diversification, which is another corporate-level strategy that may create value. The chapter then shifts to the topic of incentives and resources that may stimulate diversification which is value neutral. However, managerial motives to diversify, the final topic in the chapter, can actually destroy some of the firm's value.

## Levels of diversification

Diversified firms vary according to their level of diversification and the connections between and among their businesses. Figure 7.1 lists and defines five categories of businesses according to increasing levels of diversification. The single- and dominant-business categories denote relatively low levels of diversification; more fully diversified firms are classified into related and unrelated categories. A firm is related through its diversification when its businesses share several links; for example, businesses may share products (goods or services), technologies, or distribution channels. The more links among businesses, the more "constrained" is the relatedness of diversification. Unrelatedness refers to the absence of direct links between businesses.

## FIGURE 7.1 Levels and types of diversification

**Low Levels of Diversification**

Single business: 95% or more of revenue comes from a single business.

Dominant business: Between 70% and 95% of revenue comes from a single business.

**Moderate to High Levels of Diversification**

Related constrained: Less than 70% of revenue comes from the dominant business, and all businesses share product, technological, and distribution linkages.

Related linked (mixed related and unrelated): Less than 70% of revenue comes from the dominant business, and there are only limited links between businesses.

**Very High Levels of Diversification**

Unrelated: Less than 70% of revenue comes from the dominant business, and there are no common links between businesses.

Source: Adapted from R. P. Rumelt, 1974, *Strategy, Structure and Economic Performance*, Boston: Harvard Business School.

## Low levels of diversification

A firm pursuing a low level of diversification uses either a single- or a dominant-business, corporate-level diversification strategy. A *single-business diversification strategy* is a corporate-level strategy wherein the firm generates 95 per cent or more of its sales revenue from its core business area.[17] For example, Wm Wrigley Jr Company, the world's largest producer of chewing and bubble gums, historically used a single-business strategy while operating in relatively few product markets. Wrigley's trademark chewing gum brands include Spearmint, Doublemint and Juicy Fruit, although the firm produces other products as well such as Sugar-free Extra, introduced in 1984.

In 2005 Wrigley shifted from its traditional focused strategy when it acquired the confectionery assets of Kraft Foods Inc. As Wrigley expanded, it may have intended to use the dominant business strategy with the diversification of its product lines beyond gum; however, Wrigley was acquired in 2008 by Mars, a privately held global confectionery company (the maker of Snickers and M&Ms).[18]

With the *dominant-business diversification strategy*, the firm generates between 70 and 95 per cent of its total revenue within a single business area. United Parcel Service (UPS) uses this strategy. Recently, UPS generated 56 per cent of its revenue from its US package delivery business and 28 per cent from its non-US package business, with the remaining 17 per cent coming from the firm's non-package business such as logistic services.[19] Although the US package delivery business currently generates the largest percentage of UPS's sales revenue, the firm anticipates that in the future its other two businesses will account for the majority of revenue growth. This expectation suggests that UPS may become more diversified, both in terms of its goods and services and in the number of countries in which those goods and services are offered.

## *Moderate and high levels of diversification*

A firm generating more than 30 per cent of its revenue outside a dominant business and whose businesses are related to each other in some manner uses a related diversification corporate-level strategy. When the links between the diversified firm's businesses are rather direct, a *related constrained diversification strategy* is being used. Campbell Soup, Procter & Gamble and Merck & Company all use a related constrained strategy, as do some large cable companies. With a related constrained strategy, a firm shares resources and activities between its businesses.

The diversified company with a portfolio of businesses that have only a few links between them is called a mixed related and unrelated firm and is using the *related linked diversification strategy* (see Figure 7.1). General Electric (GE) use this corporate-level diversification strategy. Compared with related constrained firms, related linked firms share fewer resources and assets between their businesses, concentrating instead on transferring knowledge and core competencies between the businesses. As with firms using each type of diversification strategy, companies implementing the related linked strategy constantly adjust the mix in their portfolio of businesses as well as make decisions about how to manage these businesses.

A highly diversified firm that has no relationships between its businesses follows an *unrelated diversification strategy*. United Technologies, Textron, Samsung and Hutchison Whampoa Limited (HWL) are examples of firms using this type of corporate-level strategy. Commonly, firms using this strategy are called *conglomerates*.

HWL is a leading international corporation committed to innovation and technology with businesses spanning the globe.[20] Ports and related services, telecommunications, property and hotels, retail and manufacturing, and energy and infrastructure are HWL's five core businesses. These businesses are not related to each other, and the firm makes no efforts to share activities or to transfer core competencies between or among them. Each of these five businesses is quite large; for example, the retailing arm of the retail and manufacturing business has more than 6200 stores in 31 countries. Groceries, cosmetics, electronics, wine and airline tickets are some of the product categories featured in these stores. This firm's size and diversity suggest the challenge of successfully managing the unrelated diversification strategy. However, Hutchison's CEO Li Ka-shing, has been successful at not only making smart acquisitions, but also at divesting businesses with good timing.[21]

# Reasons for diversification

A firm uses a corporate-level diversification strategy for a variety of reasons (see Table 7.1). Typically, a diversification strategy is used to increase the firm's value by improving its overall performance. Value is created either through related diversification or through unrelated diversification when the strategy allows a company's businesses to increase revenues or reduce costs while implementing their business-level strategies.

Other reasons for using a diversification strategy may have nothing to do with increasing the firm's value; in fact, diversification can have neutral effects or even reduce a firm's value. Value-neutral reasons for diversification include those of a desire to match and thereby neutralize a competitor's market power (such as to neutralize another firm's advantage by acquiring a similar distribution outlet). Decisions to expand a firm's portfolio of businesses to reduce managerial risk can have a negative effect on the firm's value. Greater amounts of diversification reduce managerial risk in that if one of the businesses in a diversified firm fails, the top

**Table 7.1** Reasons for diversification

**Value-Creating Diversification**

- Economies of scope (related diversification)
  - Sharing activities
  - Transferring core competencies
- Market power (related diversification)
  - Blocking competitors through multipoint competition
  - Vertical integration
- Financial economies (unrelated diversification)
  - Efficient internal capital allocation
  - Business restructuring

**Value-Neutral Diversification**

- Antitrust regulation
- Tax laws
- Low performance
- Uncertain future cash flows
- Risk reduction for firm
- Tangible resources
- Intangible resources

**Value-Reducing Diversification**

- Diversifying managerial employment risk
- Increasing managerial compensation

executive of that business does not risk total failure by the corporation. As such, this reduces the top executives' employment risk. In addition, because diversification can increase a firm's size and thus managerial compensation, managers have motives to diversify a firm to a level that reduces its value.[22] Diversification rationales that may have a neutral or negative effect on the firm's value are discussed later in the chapter.

Operational relatedness and corporate relatedness are two ways diversification strategies can create value (see Figure 7.2). Studies of these independent relatedness dimensions show the importance of resources and key competencies.[23] The figure's vertical dimension depicts opportunities to share operational activities between businesses (operational relatedness), while the horizontal dimension suggests opportunities for transferring corporate-level core competencies (corporate relatedness). The firm with a strong capability in managing operational synergy, especially in sharing assets between its businesses, falls in the upper left quadrant, which also represents vertical sharing of assets through vertical integration. The lower right quadrant represents a highly developed corporate capability for transferring one or more core competencies across businesses. This capability is located primarily in the

**FIGURE 7.2** Value-creating diversification strategies: operations and corporate relatedness

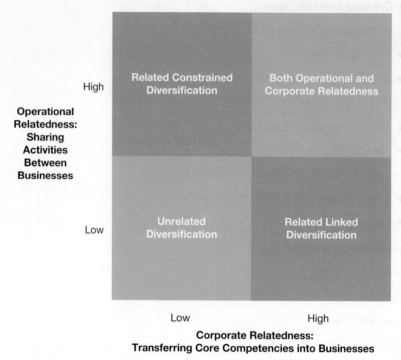

corporate headquarters office. Unrelated diversification is also illustrated in Figure 7.2 in the lower left quadrant. Financial economies (discussed later), rather than either operational or corporate relatedness, are the source of value creation for firms using the unrelated diversification strategy.

## Value-creating diversification: related constrained and related linked diversification

With the related diversification corporate-level strategy, the firm builds upon or extends its resources and capabilities to create value.[24] The company using the related diversification strategy wants to develop and exploit economies of scope between its businesses.[25] Available to companies operating in multiple product markets or industries,[26] economies of scope are cost savings that the firm creates by successfully sharing some of its resources and capabilities or transferring one or more corporate-level core competencies that were developed in one of its businesses to another of its businesses.

As illustrated in Figure 7.2, firms seek to create value from economies of scope through two basic kinds of operational economies: sharing activities (operational relatedness) and transferring corporate-level core competencies (corporate relatedness). The difference between sharing activities and transferring competencies is based on how separate resources are jointly used to create economies of scope. To create economies of scope tangible resources, such as plant and equipment or other business-unit physical assets, often must be shared. Less tangible resources, such as manufacturing know-how can also be shared. However, know-how transferred

**Economies of scope**

Economies of scope are cost savings that the firm creates by successfully sharing some of its resources and capabilities or transferring one or more corporate-level core competencies that were developed in one of its businesses to another of its businesses.

between separate activities with no physical or tangible resource involved is a transfer of a corporate-level core competence, not an operational sharing of activities.[27]

## Operational relatedness: sharing activities

Firms can create operational relatedness by sharing either a primary activity (such as inventory delivery systems) or a support activity (such as purchasing practices) – see discussion of the value chain in Chapter 3. Firms using the related constrained diversification strategy share activities in order to create value. Procter & Gamble (P&G) uses this corporate-level strategy. P&G's paper towel business and baby nappy business both use paper products as a primary input to the manufacturing process. The firm's paper production plant produces inputs for both businesses and is an example of a shared activity. In addition, because they both produce consumer products, these two businesses are likely to share distribution channels and sales networks.

As noted in the Opening Case, Fosters Group sought to create operational relatedness between the beer and wine business. Firms expect activity sharing among units to result in increased strategic competitiveness and improved financial returns. Through its shared product approach, Fosters Group was unable to improve its market share position, especially in the wine business. As previously mentioned, pursuing operational relatedness is not easy, and often synergies are not realized as planned.

Activity sharing is also risky because ties among a firm's businesses create links between outcomes. For instance, if demand for one business's product is reduced, it may not generate sufficient revenues to cover the fixed costs required to operate the shared facilities. These types of organizational difficulties can reduce activity-sharing success. This problem occurred in the Fosters Group in the Opening Case because there were problems in the sharing of activities between the beer and wine businesses, especially in marketing and distribution.

Although activity sharing across businesses is not risk-free, research shows that it can create value. For example, studies of acquisitions of firms in the same industry (horizontal acquisitions), such as the banking industry and software (see the Oracle Strategic Focus), found that sharing resources and activities and thereby creating economies of scope contributed to post-acquisition increases in performance and higher returns to shareholders.[28] Additionally, firms that sold off related units in which resource sharing was a possible source of economies of scope have been found to produce lower returns than those that sold off businesses unrelated to the firm's core business.[29] Still other research discovered that firms with closely related businesses have lower risk.[30] These results suggest that gaining economies of scope by sharing activities across a firm's businesses may be important in reducing risk and in creating value. Further, more attractive results are obtained through activity sharing when a strong corporate headquarters office facilitates it.[31]

The strategic focus on Oracle's acquisition strategy of other software firms illustrates an attempt to implement a related constrained strategy. However, as the example indicates it still remains to be seen how successful the strategy will be.

## Corporate relatedness: transferring of core competencies

Over time, the firm's intangible resources, such as its know-how, become the foundation of core competencies. Corporate-level core competencies are complex sets of resources and capabilities that link different businesses, primarily through

**Corporate-level core competencies**

Corporate-level core competencies are complex sets of resources and capabilities that link different businesses, primarily through managerial and technological knowledge, experience and expertise.

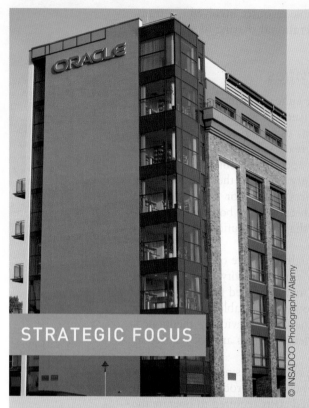

© INSADCO Photography/Alamy

STRATEGIC FOCUS

## Oracle's related constrained diversification strategy

Oracle has been diversifying its software business in a related way through a significant acquisition programme. In 2008 alone, it made 10 acquisitions of smaller software producers and companies that develop software production tools. Oracle, although hurt by the current economic downturn, retained over €10 billion in cash by the end of 2008 allowing it to pursue its acquisition strategy.

Historically, Oracle has been the largest player by market share in the "database" management software industry. Nonetheless, in 2003, it started buying large software makers including PeopleSoft (this was a hostile takeover bid which did not close until January 2005). It also bought Siebel Systems, Hyperion Solutions, and in early 2008 acquired BEA Systems for approximately €7 billion. Collectively, the company has spent near €20 billion on acquisitions between the years 2004 and 2008. Oracle's positioning has changed and it now derives more from Enterprise Resource Planning (ERP) software (its largest

acquisitions – for example, PeopleSoft, Siebel Systems and BEA Systems), and less from database management as it seeks to combine the whole company and its different segments to position itself as a strong competitor against SAP – the largest player in ERP. Additionally, Oracle's maintenance contracts have helped offset some of its lower sales in basic software in the down cycle. However, over time, the customers might protest the large margins associated with these maintenance contracts and seek to cut back on them during the recession.

The pursuit of acquisitions has created a challenge due to the extra complexity of the various systems and different cultures associated with the acquired firms. In order to manage its strategy and to compete in a more focused way, Oracle has targeted specific industries to allow it to compete more effectively with such competitors as SAP. These industries include financial services, insurance, retail and telecommunications. It set a goal to be the number one or number two software supplier in each of these industry segments.

The difficulty, however, is to organize and coordinate these acquisitions into a cohesive set of businesses by which Oracle can create economies of scope through more efficient management techniques. This is somewhat hindered by the differences in cultures and structures of it acquisitions as mentioned previously. The benefit has been that the assets have been purchased at a lower price because the private equity investors' (i.e., venture capitalists) funding has decreased 80 per cent and thus Oracle's funding has been the means for these firms to obtain funding. Thus, corporate venture capital has been a mainstay for firms in the Silicon Valley in the US in which Oracle has done much acquisition activity.

In summary, the organizational integration aspects have prevented much of the possible sharing of activities that this strategy requires to be successful. Oracle's continued success will be determined by how far its share price falls relative to its costs of acquisition of these new businesses and its ability to integrate these acquisitions into a cohesive structure that will allow the sharing of activities to take place more efficiently. It is important that central headquarters implement controls to foster the sharing of activities between related divisions for success to occur.

**Sources:** Worthen, B. (2009) "Cash-rich Oracle scoops up bargains in recession spree", *Wall Street Journal*, February 17, A1, A12; Hodgson, J. (2009) "Rethinking software support: Recession puts new focus on Oracle maintenance contracts", *Wall Street Journal*, March 12, B8; 2009, Oracle Corporation, *Hoovers Company Records*, March 15, 14337; Copeland, M. V. (2008) "Big tech goes bargain hunting", *Fortune*, November 10, 43; Vara, B. and Worthen, B. (2007) "As software firms merge, synergy is elusive: Shareholders may prosper from trend, but customers see scant benefits so far", *Wall Street Journal*, November 20, B1.

## Questions

**1** What are the primary reasons integration fails in the diversified corporation?

**2** Identify and describe the key criteria against which Oracle should consider future acquisitions.

managerial and technological knowledge, experience, and expertise.[32] Firms seeking to create value through corporate relatedness use the related linked diversification strategy.

In at least two ways, the related linked diversification strategy helps firms to create value.[33] First, because the expense of developing a core competence has been incurred in one of the firm's businesses, transferring it to a second business eliminates the need for that second business to allocate resources to develop it. Such is the case at Hewlett-Packard (HP), where the firm transferred its competence in ink printers to high-end copiers. Rather than the standard laser printing technology in most high-end copiers, HP is using ink-based technology. One manager liked the product because, as he noted, "We are able to do a lot better quality at less price".[34] This capability will also give HP the opportunity to sell more ink products, which is how it has been able to create higher profit margins.

Resource intangibility is a second source of value creation through corporate relatedness. Intangible resources are difficult for competitors to understand and imitate. Because of this difficulty, the unit receiving a transferred corporate-level competence often gains an immediate competitive advantage over its rivals.[35]

A number of firms have successfully transferred one or more corporate-level core competencies across their businesses. Virgin Group Limited transfers its marketing core competence across airlines, cosmetics, music, drinks, mobile phones, health clubs and a number of other businesses.[36] Honda has developed and transferred its competence in engine design and manufacturing to its businesses making products such as motorcycles, lawnmowers, and cars and trucks. With respect to smaller engines, for example, the transfers of the corporate-level competence in terms of engine design and manufacturing have been successful; company officials indicate that "Honda is the world's largest manufacturer of engines and has earned its reputation for unsurpassed quality, performance and reliability".[37]

One way managers facilitate the transfer of corporate-level core competencies is by moving key people into new management positions.[38] However, the manager of an older business may be reluctant to transfer key people who have accumulated knowledge and experience critical to the business's success. Thus, managers with the ability to facilitate the transfer of a core competence may come at a premium, or the key people involved may not want to transfer. Additionally, the top-level managers from the transferring business may not want the competencies transferred to a new business to fulfil the firm's diversification objectives. Research also suggests too much dependence on outsourcing can lower the usefulness of core competencies and thereby reduce their useful transferability to other business units in the diversified firm.[39]

## Market power

Firms using a related diversification strategy may gain market power when successfully using their related constrained or related linked strategy. Market power exists

**Market power**

Market power exists when a firm is able to sell its products above the existing competitive level or to reduce the costs of its primary and support activities below the competitive level, or both.

when a firm is able to sell its products above the existing competitive level or to reduce the costs of its primary and support activities below the competitive level, or both.[40] Mars' acquisition of the Wrigley assets was part of its related constrained diversification strategy and added market share to the Mars/Wrigley integrated firm as it realized 14.4 per cent of the market share. This catapulted Mars/Wrigley above Cadbury (now part of the Kraft Foods Company) and Nestlé with 10.1 and 7.7 per cent respectively.[41]

In addition to efforts to gain scale as a means of increasing market power, as Mars acquired Wrigley, firms can create market power through multipoint competition and vertical integration. **Multipoint competition** exists when two or more diversified firms simultaneously compete in the same product areas or geographic markets.[42] The actions taken by United Parcel Service (UPS) and FedEx in two markets, overnight delivery and ground shipping, illustrate multipoint competition. UPS has moved into overnight delivery, FedEx's stronghold; FedEx has been buying haulage and ground shipping assets to move into ground shipping, UPS's stronghold. Moreover, geographic competition for markets increases. The strongest shipping company in Europe is DHL. All three competitors (UPS, FedEx and DHL) are trying to move into large foreign markets to either gain a stake in a market or to expand their existing share of a market. For instance, because South China close to Hong Kong is becoming a top destination for shipping throughout Asia, competition is raging among these three international shippers.[43] If one of these firms successfully gains strong positions in several markets while competing against its rivals, its market power may increase. Interestingly, DHL had to exit the US market because it was too difficult to compete against UPS and FedEx that are entrenched in the market.

Some firms using a related diversification strategy engage in vertical integration to gain market power. **Vertical integration** exists when a company produces its own inputs (backward integration) or owns its own source of output distribution (forward integration). In some instances, firms partially integrate their operations, producing and selling their products by using company businesses as well as outside sources.[44]

Vertical integration is commonly used in the firm's core business to gain market power over rivals. Market power is gained as the firm develops the ability to save on its operations, avoid market costs, improve product quality, and, possibly, protect its technology from imitation by rivals.[45] Market power is also created when firms have strong ties between their assets for which no market prices exist. Establishing a market price would result in high search and transaction costs, so firms seek to vertically integrate rather than remain separate businesses.[46]

Vertical integration has its limitations. For example, an outside supplier may produce the product at a lower cost. As a result, internal transactions from vertical integration may be expensive and reduce profitability relative to competitors.[47] Also, bureaucratic costs may occur with vertical integration. And, because vertical integration can require substantial investments in specific technologies, it may reduce the firm's flexibility, especially when technology changes quickly. Finally, changes in demand create capacity balance and coordination problems. If one business is building a part for another internal business, but achieving economies of scale requires the first division to manufacture quantities that are beyond the capacity of the internal buyer to absorb, it would be necessary to sell the parts outside the firm as well as to the internal business. Thus, although vertical integration can create value, especially through market power over competitors, it is not without risks and costs.[48]

Many manufacturing firms have been reducing vertical integration as a means of gaining market power.[49] In fact, deintegration is the focus of most manufacturing firms, such as Intel and Dell, and even some large automobile companies, such as Ford and General Motors, as they develop independent supplier networks.[50] Flextronics, an electronics contract manufacturer, represents a new breed of large

**Multipoint competition**

Multipoint competition exists when two or more diversified firms simultaneously compete in the same product areas or geographical markets.

**Vertical integration**

Vertical integration exists when a company produces its own inputs (backward integration) or owns its own source of output distribution (forward integration).

contract manufacturers that is helping to foster this revolution in supply-chain management.[51] Such firms often manage their customers' entire product lines and offer services ranging from inventory management to delivery and after-sales service. Conducting business through e-commerce also allows vertical integration to be changed into "virtual integration".[52] Thus, closer relationships are possible with suppliers and customers through virtual integration or electronic means of integration, allowing firms to reduce the costs of processing transactions while improving their supply-chain management skills and tightening the control of their inventories. This evidence suggests that *virtual integration* rather than *vertical integration* may be a more common source of market power gains for today's firms.

## Simultaneous operational relatedness and corporate relatedness

As Figure 7.2 suggests (see 242), some firms simultaneously seek operational and corporate relatedness to create economies of scope.[53] The ability to simultaneously create economies of scope by sharing activities (operational relatedness) and transferring core competencies (corporate relatedness) is difficult for competitors to understand and learn how to imitate. However, firms that fail in their efforts to simultaneously obtain operational and corporate relatedness may create the opposite of what they seek – namely, diseconomies of scope instead of economies of scope.[54] If the cost of realizing both types of relatedness is not offset by the benefits created then the result is diseconomies of scope because the cost of organization and incentive structure is very expensive.[55]

As the Strategic Focus on Johnson & Johnson suggests, this company uses a strategy that combines operational and corporate relatedness with some success. Likewise, Walt Disney Co. uses a related diversification strategy to simultaneously create economies of scope through operational and corporate relatedness. Within the firm's Studio Entertainment business, for example, Disney can gain economies of scope by sharing activities among its different movie distribution companies such as Touchstone Pictures, Hollywood Pictures, and Dimension Films. Broad and deep knowledge about its customers is a capability on which Disney relies to develop corporate-level core competencies in terms of advertising and marketing. With these competencies, Disney is able to create economies of scope through corporate relatedness as it cross-sells products that are highlighted in its movies through the distribution channels that are part of its Parks and Resorts and Consumer Products businesses. Thus, characters created in movies (think of those in *The Lion King*) become figures that are marketed through Disney's retail stores (which are part of the Consumer Products business). In addition, themes established in movies become the source of new rides in the firm's theme parks, which are part of the Parks and Resorts business and provide themes for clothing and other retail business products.[56]

As we described, Johnson & Johnson and Walt Disney Co. have been able to successfully use related diversification as a corporate-level strategy through which they create economies of scope by sharing some activities and by transferring core competencies. However, it can be difficult for investors to actually observe the value created by a firm (such as Walt Disney Co.) as it shares activities and transfers core competencies. For this reason, the value of the assets of a firm using a diversification strategy to create economies of scope in this manner tends to be discounted by investors. For example, analysts have complained that both Citibank and UBS, two large, global, multiplatform banks, have underperformed their more focused counterparts in regard to stock market appreciation. In fact, both banks have heard calls for breaking up their separate businesses in insurance, hedge funds, consumer

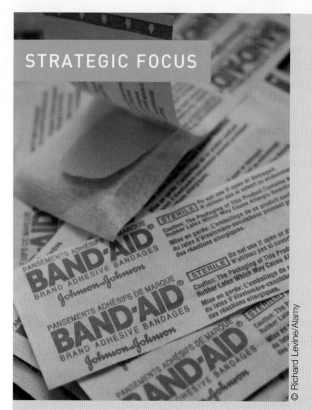

## STRATEGIC FOCUS

© Richard Levine/Alamy

# Johnson & Johnson uses both operational and corporate relatedness

Johnson & Johnson (J&J) is a widely diversified business. It is the world's seventh largest pharmaceutical company, fourth largest biologics company, the premier consumer health products company, and the largest medical devices and diagnostics company. These businesses are combined into three main groups: consumer health care, medical devices and diagnostics, and pharmaceuticals. The consumer health care business has hair, skin, teeth and baby products. The medical devices and diagnostics business develops stents (a stent is a small tube often made of a mesh material that is inserted within narrowed or weakened arteries) and many other products focused on cardiovascular care and equipment for surgical settings. The pharmaceutical business is focused on the central nervous system and internal medicines for helping with such disorders as schizophrenia, epilepsy, diabetes, and cardiovascular and infectious diseases. Within the pharmaceutical business, another unit focuses on biotechnology to treat

autoimmune disorders such as rheumatoid arthritis, psoriasis and Crohn's disease. Yet another unit, the neurology unit, focuses on developing drugs for HIV/AIDS, hepatitis C, and tuberculosis. Traditionally these businesses were managed with mixed related and unrelated strategy. Associated with this strategy was a definite approach focused on decentralization.

More recently however, J&J may have been seeking to not only have relatedness within the major businesses, but also to have corporate relatedness across all of its business units. The CEO, William Bolden, has sought to propel growth by getting autonomous divisions to work more closely together. The move suggests the desire to increase interaction to squeeze more value from areas where they overlap. The integrated approach is seeking to harness expertise from various units to assist its diagnostics testing equipment in diagnosing disease earlier than other products on the market. It is also seeking to harness expertise to better assist its glucose monitoring arm to more effectively monitor diabetes for its diabetic patients.

Other drug companies have been focused on either pharmaceuticals or consumer products and have been reducing the products' overlap. J&J has taken advantage of both positions and as a result has been more profitable during the current economic downturn than the more focused pharmaceutical or principle products companies. One major innovation between the pharmaceuticals and the device business was the drug coated stent which was originally created by Cordis, a division of its medical equipment business. This spurred much competition in the industry from other stent makers including the Abbott Laboratories. J&J also increased the competition with its new device, Nevo, a totally redesigned product in the stent business.

Besides innovation where the expertise of previously decentralized businesses is combined, J&J is seeking to pursue corporate relatedness in regard to marketing by completing a massive consolidation of its contracted media and advertising agencies. It has settled on a large involvement of several companies such as WPP and Interpublic Group. It is therefore pursuing a single brand according to market and channels and is forcing a consolidation across its businesses. The aim of this strategic change is to create a more unified brand and decrease the high costs that were associated with each business unit handling its own media and advertising concepts.

In summary, J&J moved from a related linked strategy to a strategy that is focused more on pursuing both operational relatedness (with its separate businesses sharing operation activities) and corporate relatedness across its business units. It has strived to achieve greater innovation and management of the regulatory process as well as much better coordination across its businesses in marketing. There are other areas where it is trying to develop more efficiencies, such as the production processes. As such, it is pursuing both operational and corporate relatedness.

**Sources:** Arnold, M. (2009) "J&J shows the way", *Medical Marketing and Media*, January, 39, 41, 43; 2008, "J&J perks up", *Financial Times*, http://www.ft.com, December 1; Bennett, J. (2008), "J&J: A balm for your portfolio", *Barron's*, October 27, 39; Bowe, C. (2008) "Cautious chief with an impulse for innovation", *Financial Times*, http://www.ft.com,

January 14, 14; Loftus, P. and Wang, S. (2008) "Earnings digest – pharmaceuticals: Diversified strategy buoys J&J's results", *Wall Street Journal*, July 16, B4; Wang, S. (2008) "Corporate news: J&J acquires wellness firm, widening scope", *Wall Street Journal*, October 28, B3; Johnson, A. (2007) "J&J realigns managers, revamps units; move calls for divisions to integrate their work", *Wall Street Journal*, November 16, A10.

### Questions

**1** Why is operational relatedness so critical within a diversification strategy?

**2** What problems do you anticipate a firm will encounter in moving from a related linked diversification to a both operational and corporate relatedness diversification?

lending, and investment banking.[57] One analyst speaking of Citigroup suggested that "creating real synergy between its divisions has been hard", implying that Citigroup's related diversification strategy suffered from some possible diseconomies of scale.[58] Due to its diseconomies and other losses related to the economic downturn, Citigroup has recently considered selling some of its foreign divisions, such as its Japanese investment bank and brokerage.[59] UBS is changing its strategy, the bank's three divisions, private banking, investment banking and asset management, will be reorganized into a more centralized unit to reduce costs. Previously each segment was given more autonomy over its operations; this model proved too costly and the new CEO, Oswald Grubel, is seeking to reduce possible diseconomies of scale through the centralization, especially of information technology.[60]

## Unrelated diversification

Firms do not seek either operational relatedness or corporate relatedness when using the unrelated diversification corporate-level strategy. An unrelated diversification strategy (see Figure 7.2) can create value through two types of financial economies. Financial economies are cost savings realized through improved allocations of financial resources based on investments inside or outside the firm.[61]

Efficient internal capital allocations can lead to financial economies. Efficient internal capital allocations reduce risk among the firm's businesses – for example, by leading to the development of a portfolio of businesses with different risk profiles. The second type of financial economy concerns the restructuring of acquired assets. Here, the diversified firm buys another company, restructures that company's assets in ways that allow it to operate more profitably, and then sells the company for a profit in the external market.[62] Next, we discuss the two types of financial economies in greater detail.

**Financial economies**

Financial economies are cost savings realized through improved allocations of financial resources based on investments inside or outside the firm.

### Efficient internal capital market allocation

In a market economy, capital markets are thought to efficiently allocate capital. Efficiency results as investors take equity positions (ownership) with high expected future cash-flow values. Capital is also allocated through debt as shareholders and debt holders try to improve the value of their investments by taking stakes in businesses with high growth and profitability prospects.

In large diversified firms, the corporate headquarters office distributes capital to its businesses to create value for the overall corporation. The nature of these distributions may generate gains from internal capital market allocations that exceed the gains that would accrue to shareholders as a result of capital being allocated by the external capital market.[63] Because those in a firm's corporate headquarters generally have access to detailed and accurate information regarding the actual and prospective performance of the company's portfolio of businesses, they have the best information to make capital distribution decisions.

Compared with corporate office personnel, external investors have relatively limited access to internal information and can only estimate the performances of individual businesses as well as their future prospects. Moreover, although businesses seeking capital must provide information to potential suppliers (such as banks or insurance companies), firms with internal capital markets may have at least two informational advantages. First, information provided to capital markets through annual reports and other sources may not include negative information, instead emphasizing positive prospects and outcomes. External sources of capital have limited ability to understand the operational dynamics of large organizations. Even external shareholders who have access to information have no guarantee of full and complete disclosure.[64] Second, although a firm must disseminate information, that information also becomes simultaneously available to the firm's current and potential competitors. With insights gained by studying such information, competitors might attempt to duplicate a firm's value-creating strategy. Thus, an ability to efficiently allocate capital through an internal market may help the firm protect the competitive advantages it develops while using its corporate-level strategy as well as its various business-unit level strategies.

If intervention from outside the firm is required to make corrections to capital allocations, only significant changes are possible, such as forcing the firm into bankruptcy or changing the top management team. Alternatively, in an internal capital market, the corporate headquarters office can fine-tune its corrections, such as choosing to adjust managerial incentives or suggesting strategic changes in one of the firm's businesses. Thus, capital can be allocated according to more specific criteria than is possible with external market allocations. Given that it has less accurate information, the external capital market may fail to allocate resources adequately to high-potential investments. The corporate headquarters office of a diversified company can more effectively perform such tasks as disciplining underperforming management teams through resource allocations.[65]

Large highly diversified businesses often face what is known as the "conglomerate discount". This discount results from analysts not knowing how to value a vast array of large businesses with complex financial reports. For instance, one analyst suggested in regard to understanding GE's financial results in its quarterly report, "A Rubik's cube may in fact be easier to figure out".[66] To overcome this discount many unrelated diversified or industrial conglomerates have sought to establish a brand for the parent company. For instance, recent advertisements by GE moved its focus from customer comfort and convenience ("We Bring Good Things to Life") to a more future-oriented mantra ("Imagination at Work") that promises creative and innovative products.[67] More recently United Technologies initiated a brand development approach with the slogan "United Technologies. You can see everything from here". United Technologies suggested that its earnings multiple (PE ratio) compared to its stock price is only average even though its performance has been better than other conglomerates. It is hoping that the "umbrella" brand advertisement will raise its PE to a level comparable with its competitors.[68]

In spite of the challenges associated with it, a number of corporations continue to use the unrelated diversification strategy, particularly throughout Europe and the Eastern European emerging markets. Siemens, for example, has a highly diversified approach. The former CEO argued that, "When you are in an up-cycle and the capital markets have plenty of opportunities to invest in single-industry companies ... investors savour those opportunities. But when things change pure plays go down faster than you can look."[69] In the recent downturn, diversification is helping some companies improve future performance,[70] as the Oracle Strategic Focus illustrates.

The Achilles' heel for firms using the unrelated diversification strategy in a developed economy is that competitors can imitate financial economies more easily than they can replicate the value gained from the economies of scope developed through operational relatedness and corporate relatedness. This issue is less of a problem in emerging economies, where the absence of a "soft infrastructure" (including effective financial intermediaries, sound regulations and contract laws) supports and encourages use of the unrelated diversification strategy.[71] In fact, in emerging economies such as those in Korea, India and Chile, research has shown that diversification increases the performance of firms affiliated with large diversified business groups.[72]

## Restructuring of assets

Financial economies can also be created when firms learn how to create value by buying, restructuring and then selling the restructured companies' assets in the external market.[73] As in the property business, buying assets at low prices, restructuring them and selling them at a price that exceeds their cost generates a positive return on the firm's invested capital.

Companies who pursue unrelated diversified strategy often recognize that creating financial economies by acquiring and restructuring other companies' assets requires an understanding of significant trade-offs. Success usually calls for a focus on mature, manufacturing businesses because of the uncertainty of demand for high-technology products. In high-technology businesses, resource allocation decisions become too complex, creating information-processing overload on the small corporate headquarters offices that are common in unrelated diversified firms. High-technology businesses are often human-resource dependent; these people can leave or demand higher pay and thus appropriate or deplete the value of an acquired firm.[74]

Buying and then restructuring service-based assets so they can be profitably sold in the external market is also difficult. Here, sales often are a product of close personal relationships between a client and the representative of the firm being restructured. Thus, for both high-technology firms and service-based companies, relatively few tangible assets can be restructured to create value and sell profitably. It is difficult to restructure intangible assets such as human capital and effective relationships that have evolved over time between buyers (customers) and sellers (firm personnel). Care must be taken in a downturn to restructure and buy and sell at appropriate times. The downturn can also present opportunities as the Oracle Strategic Focus notes. Ideally, executives will follow a strategy of buying businesses when prices are low such as in the bond of a recession and selling them at late stages in an expansion.[75]

# Value-neutral diversification: incentives and resources

The objectives firms seek when using related diversification and unrelated diversification strategies all have the potential to help the firm create value by using a corporate-level strategy. However, these strategies, as well as single- and dominant-business diversification strategies, are sometimes used with value-neutral rather than value-creating objectives in mind. As we discuss next, different incentives to diversify sometimes exist and the quality of the firm's resources may permit only diversification that is value neutral rather than value creating.

## Incentives to diversify

Incentives to diversify come from both the external environment and a firm's internal environment. External incentives include antitrust regulations and tax laws. Internal incentives include low performance, uncertain future cash flows, and the pursuit of synergy and reduction of risk for the firm.

### Anti-competition regulation and tax laws

Throughout the world, governments and trading blocs take seriously the issue of regulation. In the UK, for example, anti-competition regulation tends to be managed by The Competition Commission (CC) and the Office of Fair Trading (OFT). The former is a public body which is responsible for holding investigations into merger, market and other potentially related inquiries that concern the enforcement of competition law. In practice, the CC investigate situations where a merger may lead to the combined firm gaining more than 25 per cent market share or where the post-merger firm can contribute to a substantial decrease in competitive behaviour within one of more markets. They also investigate in market situations where it can be argued that competition is in some ways being prevented, distorted or restricted. The OFT, on the other hand, is a UK government department which is responsible for enforcing consumer protection and competition law.

Government anticompetitive policies and tax laws provided incentives for firms to diversify in the 1960s and 1970s.[76] Antitrust laws prohibiting mergers that created increased power (via either vertical or horizontal integration) were stringently enforced during that period.[77] Merger activity that produced conglomerate diversification was encouraged whilst horizontal and vertical mergers were discouraged. As a result, many of the mergers during the 1960s and 1970s were "conglomerate" in character, involving companies pursuing different lines of business. Between 1973 and 1977, 79.1 per cent of all mergers were conglomerate.[78]

During the 1980s, anti-competition enforcement lessened, resulting in more and larger horizontal mergers (acquisitions of target firms in the same line of business, such as a merger between two oil companies).[79] In addition, investment bankers became more open to the kinds of mergers facilitated by regulation changes; as a consequence, takeovers increased to unprecedented numbers.[80] The conglomerates, or highly diversified firms, of the 1960s and 1970s became more "focused" in the 1980s and early 1990s as merger constraints were relaxed and restructuring was implemented.[81]

In the late 1990s and early 2000s, anti-competition concerns emerged again with the large volume of mergers and acquisitions (see Chapter 8).[82] Mergers are now receiving more scrutiny than they did in the 1980s and through the early 1990s.[83] For example, in the merger between P&G and Gillette, regulators required that each firm divest certain businesses before they were allowed to secure the deal.

The tax effects of diversification stem not only from corporate tax changes, but also from individual tax rates. Some companies (especially mature ones) generate more cash from their operations than they can reinvest profitably. Some argue that *free cash flows* (liquid financial assets for which investments in current businesses are no longer economically viable) should be redistributed to shareholders as dividends.[84] However, in the 1960s and 1970s, dividends were taxed more heavily than were capital gains. As a result, before 1980, shareholders preferred that firms use free cash flows to buy and build companies in high-performance industries. If the firm's stock value appreciated over the long term, shareholders might receive a better return on those funds than if the funds had been redistributed as dividends, because returns from stock sales would be taxed more lightly than dividends would.

Although regulations were loosened somewhat in the 1980s and then retightened in the late 1990s, a number of industries experienced increased merger activity due to industry-specific deregulation activity, including banking, telecommunications, oil and gas, and electric utilities. Thus, regulatory changes create incentives or disincentives for diversification. Interestingly, anti-competition laws in Europe compared to the US have been historically stricter regarding horizontal mergers, but more recently have been more comparable.[85]

**Low performance**  Some research shows that low returns are related to greater levels of diversification.[86] If "high performance eliminates the need for greater diversification,"[87] then low performance may provide an incentive for diversification. eBay acquired Skype in 2005 for €2.4 billion in hopes that it would create synergies and improve communication between buyers and sellers. However, in 2008 eBay announced that it would sell Skype if the opportunity presents itself because it has failed to increase cash flow for its core business, ecommerce and the synergies have not been realized. Some critics have even urged eBay to rid itself of PayPal in order to boost its share price.[88]

Research evidence and the experience of a number of firms suggest that an overall curvilinear relationship, as illustrated in Figure 7.3, may exist between diversification and performance.[89] Although low performance can be an incentive to diversify, firms that are more broadly diversified compared to their competitors may have overall lower performance. Additionally, broadly based banks, such as Royal Bank of Scotland Group plc (RBS), have been under pressure to "break up" because they seem to underperform compared to their peer banks. In the case of RBS, recent announcements indicate that they intend to reduce their presence in the UK banking sector by divesting branches in England and Wales and their

**FIGURE 7.3**  The curvilinear relationship between diversification and performance

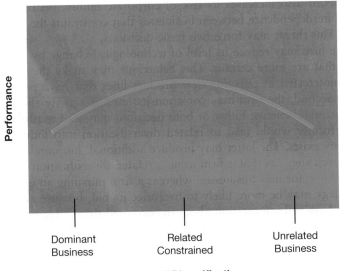

Level of Diversification

NatWest branches in Scotland, in combination with their direct small- and medium-sized business customers throughout the UK. Indications also suggest that by 2013 they plan to divest RBS Insurance, which includes brands such as Direct Line and Churchill businesses, as well as Global Merchant Services – their card payments acquiring business and RBS Sempra Commodities – a leading global commodities trader.[90] Similarly, before being acquired by Barclays in 2009, in 2008 Lehman Brothers divested much of its asset management and commercial mortgage businesses to improve the company's cash flow.[91]

### Uncertain future cash flows

As a firm's product line matures or is threatened, diversification may be taken as an important defensive strategy.[92] Small firms and companies in mature or maturing industries sometimes find it necessary to diversify for long-term survival.[93] For example, uncertainty was one of the dominant reasons for diversification among utilities providers during the 1970s and 1980s. BT Group plc diversified primarily because of deregulation affecting its monopoly position within the UK to now be one of the world's leading communications solutions and services provider with operations in over 170 countries and activities ranging from networked information technology services, local, national and international telecommunications services, and higher value broadband and Internet products and services.[94]

Diversifying into other product markets or into other businesses can reduce the uncertainty about a firm's future cash flows. Merck looked to expand into the biosimilars business (production of drugs which are similar to approved drugs) in hopes of stimulating its prescription drug business due to lower expected results as many of its drug patents expire.[95] For example, it purchased Insmed's portfolio of follow-on biologics in 2009 for €102 million. It will carry out the development of biologics that prevent infections in cancer patients receiving chemotherapy. INS-19 is in late-stage trials while INS-20 is in early-stage development.[96]

### Synergy and firm risk reduction

Diversified firms pursuing economies of scope often have investments that are too inflexible to realize synergy between business units. As a result, a number of problems may arise. Synergy exists when the value created by business units working together exceeds the value that those same units create working independently. But as a firm increases its relatedness between business units, it also increases its risk of corporate failure, because synergy produces joint interdependence between businesses that constrains the firm's flexibility to respond. This threat may force two basic decisions.

First, the firm may reduce its level of technological change by operating in environments that are more certain. This behaviour may make the firm risk averse and thus uninterested in pursuing new product lines that have potential, but are not proven. Second, the firm may constrain its level of activity sharing and forgo synergy's potential benefits. Either or both decisions may lead to further diversification.[97] The former would lead to related diversification into industries in which more certainty exists. The latter may produce additional, but unrelated, diversification.[98] Research suggests that a firm using a related diversification strategy is more careful in bidding for new businesses, whereas a firm pursuing an unrelated diversification strategy may be more likely to overprice its bid, because an unrelated bidder may not have full information about the acquired firm.[99] However, firms using either a related or an unrelated diversification strategy must understand the consequences of paying large premiums.[100] Meg Whitman, eBay former President and CEO, received much criticism for paying such a high price for Skype, especially when the firm has not realized the synergies it was seeking.

**Synergy**

Synergy exists when the value created by business units working together exceeds the value that those same units create working independently.

## STRATEGIC FOCUS

© David Kilpatrick/Alamy

# Samsung diversifies on the flash memory market

Korea's Samsung Electronics is a global leader in semiconductor, telecommunication, digital media and digital convergence technologies with consolidated sales of €119 billion in 2009. Samsung employs approximately 150 000 people in 62 countries. Recognized as one of the fastest growing global brands, Samsung is a leading producer of digital televisions, memory chips and mobile phones.

Samsung Electronics has invested billions in new facilities and technologies. In 2006 they started to invest particularly in so-called NAND flash memory. These chips can store vast amounts of data—a card containing 16GB NAND flash memory can store an entire music and personal video library on a small portable device. The production of those chips involved huge investments. Eight per cent of the investments made by Samsung was spent on memory chips. This brought great risks, especially because Samsung made the investments from retained earnings, instead of bringing in a partner to share the costs and risks. Samsung believed that there would be enormous demand for memory – replacing hard disks with flash, and that these new markets would open up rapidly if prices made the devices attractive enough to customers. "In rolling out the densest NAND flash in the world, we are throwing open the gates to a much wider playing field for flash-driven consumer electronics", said Jim Elliott, director flash marketing. With support technology in place, the demand for 16GB NAND flash memory is expected to grow rapidly.

In 2009, NAND was the most widely used memory for multi-feature mobile applications. NAND chips are a vital component in new digital devices such as mobile phones, MP3 players and cameras. The flash memory market has grown at an exponential rate. Much of this is due to the use of flash memory in Apple iPod portable media players, but also to the growth of the mobile phone market, where 2009 calculations were for 1.2 billion handsets sold worldwide in 2009, as well as other electronic devices. It is anticipated that the next wave of portable gadgets will be reliant upon NAND and will be a market worth €15 billion a year in 2010. In 1999 the NAND flash memory chip market was worth €850 million a year, but had grown to over €8 billion by 2007 with this growth being primary attributable to the Apple iPod.

The diversification of Samsung to flash memory appears to have generated significant value—Samsung is now the No. 1 producer of NAND flash memory, producing more than 40 per cent of the world's supply, having surpassed Texas Instruments, STMicroelectronics and Toshiba.

**Sources:** Hasseldahl, A. (2005) "A Memorable Deal for Apple and Samsung?", *BusinessWeek*, August 26; 2008, "Samsung withdraws proposal to acquire Sandisk", http://www.samsung.com, 23 October; Ranganathan, S. (2009) "Growing flash memory market", *The Hindu*, 8 March; Peters, M. (2007) "Samsung 16Gb NAND Flash Memory", http://www.letsgodigital.org, May 1; Samsung (2010) "About us", http://www.samsung.com, June 4.

### Questions

1 How did Samsung achieve economies of scope in developing their NAND flash memory technology?

2 How might the rest of the industry respond to the dominant position Samsung now holds in NAND flash memory technology?

## Resources and diversification

As already discussed, firms may have several value-neutral incentives as well as value-creating incentives (such as the ability to create economies of scope) to diversify. However, even when incentives to diversify exist, a firm must have the types and levels of resources and capabilities needed to successfully use a corporate-level diversification strategy.[101] Although both tangible and intangible resources facilitate diversification, they vary in their ability to create value. Indeed, the degree to which resources are valuable, rare, difficult to imitate and non-substitutable (see Chapter 4) influence a firm's ability to create value through diversification. For instance, free cash flows are a tangible, financial resource that may be used to diversify the firm. However, compared with diversification that is grounded in intangible resources, diversification based on financial resources only is more visible to competitors and thus more imitable and less likely to create value on a long-term basis.[102]

Tangible resources usually include the plant and equipment necessary to produce a product and tend to be less flexible assets. Any excess capacity often can be used only for closely related products, especially those requiring highly similar manufacturing technologies. For example, Acer Inc. hopes to benefit in the downturn and build market share through a related diversification move. Acer believes that the large computer makers such as Dell and Hewlett Packard have underestimated the demand for mini-notebook or "netbook" computers. Acer diversified into these compact machines and now has about 30 per cent of the market share. These smaller and less expensive machines are expected to become 15 to 20 per cent of the overall PC market. They are also expanding into smart phones and at the same time created seamless integration between such phones and PCs for data transfer from one product to the other. There are obvious manufacturing and sales integration opportunities between their basic tangible assets and these related diversification moves.[103]

Excess capacity of other tangible resources, such as a sales force, can be used to diversify more easily. Again, excess capacity in a sales force is more effective with related diversification, because it may be utilized to sell similar products. The sales force would be more knowledgeable about related-product characteristics, customers, and distribution channels.[104] Tangible resources may create resource interrelationships in production, marketing, procurement, and technology, defined earlier as activity sharing. Intangible resources are more flexible than tangible physical assets in facilitating diversification. Although the sharing of tangible resources may induce diversification, intangible resources such as tacit knowledge could encourage even more diversification.[105]

Sometimes, however, the benefits expected from using resources to diversify the firm for either value-creating or value-neutral reasons are not gained.[106] For example, as noted in the Opening Case, implementing operational relatedness has been difficult for the Fosters Group in integrating the wine and beer businesses; the joint marketing operation was a failure. Also, Sara Lee executives, with their wide range of brands from Ambi Pur and Douwe Egberts, to Kiwi, Sanex and Senseo,[107] found that they could not realize synergy between their diversified portfolio and subsequently shed businesses accounting for 40 per cent of revenues to focus on food and food-related products to more readily achieve synergy. However, the downturn has caused them to continue this process to more sharply focus possible synergies between businesses.[108]

# Value-reducing diversification: managerial motives to diversify

Managerial motives to diversify can exist independently of value-neutral reasons (i.e., incentives and resources) and value-creating reasons (e.g., economies of scope).

## KEY DEBATE

# The diversification dilemma

The extent and type of diversification presents a firm with as many opportunities as it does challenges. For a diversified corporation like Diageo who describe themselves as the "world's leading premium drinks business with an outstanding collection of international brands across spirits, wine and beer", diversification often tends to mean new related businesses and so they represent an examplar of related constrained diversification within their portfolio. In contrast, Amazon has plans to market computing power in the same way that a utility firm markets electricity. Equally, Google has developed and is progressing rapidly towards the expansion of their range of productivity software programs that are seeking to challenge Microsoft. These forms of related linked diversification offer distinctly different opportunity profiles for these firms in comparison with Diageo. Therefore, despite diversification appearing to embody a distinctive strategic manoeuvre it is rather a label that captures a *range* of activities beyond the firm's core and focal activities.

By diversifying into new business markets, firms seek to gain economies of scope. One of the measures of success in gaining economies of scope is coordination. Nonetheless, there are a series of coordination costs that need to be managed in diversification. Following diversification, the resources that were employed by the firm are likely to change, potentially significantly, in the post-diversification environment. Therefore, the coordination costs which are characterized as those that arise from managing the task interdependencies within the firm, become particularly apparent. That is, new coordination arrangements need to be determined so as to modify the various contractual structures and routines within the firm. Furthermore, given that change creates its own friction, the concept of organizational rigidity can further compound the costs of coordination in the post-diversification environment. These circumstances can create a series of challenges that need to be managed but equally can create a series of unanticipated consequences that the firm has difficulty in coordinating.

Most diversification theory has tended to focus on the efficiency at the corporate headquarters of the diversified firm or the secondary question as to whether diversification actually destroys value for the firm. However, it is only recently that the notion of coordination costs has been specifically addressed.

**Sources:** Diageo (2010) About Us, http://www.diageo.com, June 4; Villalonga, B. (2004) "Diversification discount or premium? New evidence from the business information tracking series", *Journal of Finance*, 59(2): 479–506; Rawley, E. (2010) "Diversification, coordination costs, and organizational rigidity: evidence from microdata", *Strategic Management Journal*, 31(8): 873–891; Knowledge@wharton (2010) "To diversify, or not to diversify: what's at stake for online giants in growth mode", Knowledge@wharton, http://www.wharton.edu, June 1; Kaplan S. and Henderson, R. (2005) "Inertia and incentives: Bridging organizational economics and organizational theory", *Organization Science*, 16(5): 509–521.

## Questions

1 Given that the extent of these coordination costs can be significant and organizational rigidity is in some ways inevitable, to what extent do these coordination costs vary across the different value-creating strategies depicted in Figure 7.2?

2 Compare and contrast two firms (one for whom the operational and corporate relatedness is high and the other which follows an unrelated diversification strategy; Figure 7.2) and identify the coordination costs and organizational rigidity problems that may have been encountered and how they have been addressed.

The desire for increased compensation and reduced managerial risk are two motives for top-level executives to diversify their firm beyond value-creating and value-neutral levels.[109] In slightly different words, top-level executives may diversify a firm in order to diversify their own employment risk, as long as profitability does not suffer excessively.[110]

Diversification provides additional benefits to top-level managers that shareholders do not enjoy. Research evidence shows that diversification and firm size are highly correlated, and as firm size increases, so does executive compensation.[111] Because large firms are complex, difficult-to-manage organizations, top-level managers commonly receive substantial levels of compensation to lead them.[112] Greater levels of diversification can increase a firm's complexity, resulting in still more compensation for executives to lead an increasingly diversified organization. Governance mechanisms, such as the board of directors, monitoring by owners, executive compensation practices and the market for corporate control, may limit managerial tendencies to over-diversify. These mechanisms are discussed in more detail in Chapter 12.

In some instances a firm's governance mechanisms may not be strong, resulting in a situation in which executives may diversify the firm to the point that it fails to earn even average returns.[113] The loss of adequate internal governance may result in poor relative performance, thereby triggering a threat of takeover. Although takeovers may improve efficiency by replacing ineffective managerial teams, managers may avoid takeovers through defensive tactics, such as "poison pills," or may reduce their own exposure with "golden parachute" agreements.[114] Therefore, an external governance threat, although restraining managers, does not flawlessly control managerial motives for diversification.[115]

Most large publicly-held firms are profitable because the managers leading them are positive stewards of firm resources, and many of their strategic actions, including those related to selecting a corporate-level diversification strategy, contribute to the firm's success.[116] As mentioned, governance mechanisms should be designed to deal with exceptions to the managerial norms of making decisions and taking actions that will increase the firm's ability to earn above-average returns. Thus, it is overly pessimistic to assume that managers usually act in their own self-interest as opposed to their firm's interest.[117]

Top-level executives' diversification decisions may also be held in check by concerns for their reputation. If a positive reputation facilitates development and use of managerial power, a poor reputation may reduce it. Likewise, a strong external market for managerial talent may deter managers from pursuing inappropriate diversification.[118] In addition, a diversified firm may police other firms by acquiring those that are poorly managed in order to restructure its own asset base. Knowing that their firms could be acquired if they are not managed successfully encourages executives to use value-creating, diversification strategies.

As shown in Figure 7.4, the level of diversification that can be expected to have the greatest positive effect on performance is based partly on how the interaction of resources, managerial motives and incentives affects the adoption of particular diversification strategies. As indicated earlier, the greater the incentives and the more flexible the resources, the higher the level of expected diversification. Financial resources (the most flexible) should have a stronger relationship to the extent of diversification than either tangible or intangible resources. Tangible resources (the most inflexible) are useful primarily for related diversification.

As discussed in this chapter, firms can create more value by effectively using diversification strategies. However, diversification must be kept in check by corporate governance (see Chapter 12). Appropriate strategy implementation tools, such as organisational structures, are also important (see Chapter 13).

We have described corporate-level strategies in this chapter. In Chapter 8, we discuss mergers and acquisitions as prominent means for firms to diversify and to grow profitably while doing so. These trends toward more diversification through acquisitions, which have been partially reversed due to restructuring (see Chapter 8),

**FIGURE 7.4** Summary model of the relationship between diversification and firm performance

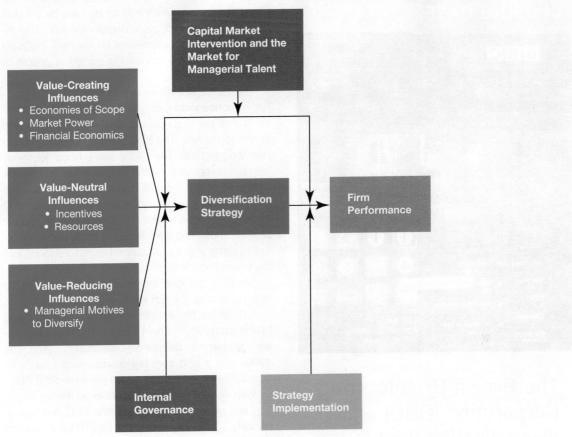

Source: Adapted from R. E. Hoskisson and M. A. Hitt, 1990, "Antecedents and performance outcomes of diversification: A review and critique of theoretical perspectives", *Journal of Management,* 16: 498.

indicate that learning has taken place regarding corporate-level diversification strategies.[119]

Accordingly, firms that diversify should do so cautiously, choosing to focus on relatively few, rather than many, businesses. In fact, research suggests that although unrelated diversification has decreased, related diversification has increased, possibly due to the restructuring that continued into the 1990s and early twenty-first century. This sequence of diversification followed by restructuring is now taking place throughout Europe and the US as well as elsewhere, notably in Korea.[120] Firms can improve their strategic competitiveness when they pursue a level of diversification that is appropriate for their resources (especially financial resources) and core competencies and the opportunities and threats in their country's institutional and competitive environments.[121]

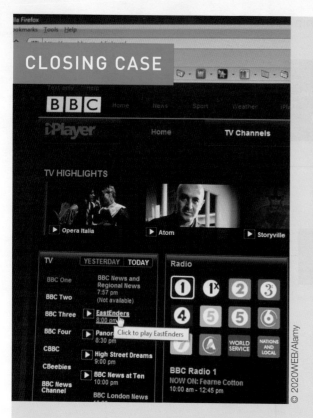

CLOSING CASE

© 2020WEB/Alamy

# The British Broadcasting Corporation (BBC) and diversification limits

The BBC has undergone many transitions since it began life in 1922. It has developed into the largest broadcasting organization in the world and is considered a national institution in the UK. The BBC has followed a related linked diversification strategy as many business units are related to each other in corporate terms. This contrasts with one of its competitors, News Corporation, which is more diversified and arguably pursuing related constrained diversification. While the BBC seeks to "enrich people's lives with programmes and services that inform, educate and entertain", News Corporation claim to "create and distribute top-quality news, sports and entertainment around the world". Although there is little to distinguish between the two media empires, their origins do have important implications on their current behaviours and future strategic ambitions.

The BBC was established by Royal Charter in 1922 as a public service broadcaster and originally consisted of the UK's six major radio manufacturers.

In order to fund this, the government created a Post Office licence fee which had to be paid by any UK household owning a wireless radio receiver. This income would be supplemented by royalties made on radio sales and the licence fee started at a cost of 10 shillings.

The 1930s saw an enormous increase in the number of households tuning in to listen to the different items that the BBC offered, ranging from news and sports to the arts. The BBC Television Service began operating in 1936. The 1950s saw a boost for television but competition for the BBC was just around the corner. In 1964 the BBC added another television channel to its portfolio in the form of BBC2. In 1967 the BBC launched Radio 1 in response to market analysis and noting the success of pirate pop stations. In this same year it re-organised its radio stations into the brands now known as Radios 2, 3 and 4.

The BBC has, over the years, been criticized for the high bureaucracy which exists within the organization and it was felt that if it did not adjust to the changing broadcasting environment it might not survive the digital age (see Key Debate on coordination costs). The 1990s saw a shift from high bureaucracy to an anti-bureaucratic organization, which reinvented the BBC.

With advancements in technology, market evolution and government pressure, the BBC has had to diversify significantly and in the late 1990s it invested in BBC Online and prepared for the start of its digital television channels. With the continual need to invest in new technological advances in the broadcasting sector the BBC now comprises eight national TV channels (BBC1, BBC2, BBC3, BBC4, CBBC, CBeebies, BBC News and BBC Parliament); ten national radio stations (Radio 1, 1Xtra, Radio 2, Radio 3, Radio 4, Radio 5 Live, 5 Live Sports Extra, 6 Music, Radio 7, BBC Asian Network) and both radio and television operated national services for Wales, Scotland and Northern Ireland. There are 40 local radio stations in England. BBC HD, BBC Interactive TV service and their company website, BBC Online, including BBC iPlayer, BBC Mobile and the BBC Channel broadcast through YouTube are also part of the public sector broadcasting business structure. All these services are supported by the income generated from licence fees which as of 1 April 2010 cost just over €170.

The BBC also operates a BBC World Service which broadcasts to the world via radio, TV and online. This service, however, is not funded through the income generated by licence fees but by the UK

Foreign and Commonwealth Office. This service achieves its objective to bring the UK to the world and broadcasts the news in 32 different languages. BBC's "Community Channel (TV)" is funded through a partnership agreement.

The BBC not only has its principal public sector services but also has various commercial activities within its organizational framework; BBC Worldwide, BBC Studios and Post Production and BBC World News. BBC Worldwide sales in 2009 were up by 9.5 per cent to over €1 billion, but profits were down by 12.8 per cent to approximately €154 million, with "digital media" and "global brand" subunits making losses of €27 million and €11.4 million respectively. The overall profits generated are re-invested back into the organization.

As part of the diversification process, the human resources department had to cut over €23 million from its costs during 2000–2003 by merging services together, such as centralizing and reducing the number of staff within its recruitment section. The BBC underwent further changes in 2005 with a great deal of restructuring, which saw thousands of job cuts. Its business model is highly regulated with limited funds and at the time was seen as unable to deliver what the stakeholders wanted and, above all, expected. In order to remain sustainable, the business model needs to be reflexive and one that is regulation centred. In 2005 the BBC began to put a strategy in place from which to launch its services through mobile phones over the next five years. With advancements in social media, the BBC began to expand its social media strategy in 2009 in order to keep in line with changes in the environment.

A report published in 2009 highlighted that the BBC generated €9.1 billion of economic value, therefore every euro generated from the licence fees means that two euros is generated in economic value. This is then re-invested to ensure the creation of quality programming but also to invest in local and regional economies.

The BBC is now focusing its strategy on "putting quality first". It is also making sure that it plans ahead for the next wave of technology. The BBC's 2010 "Strategy Review" states that in order to increase efficiency it is going to re-shape the structural layout by simplifying its operations and structure, further

improving the coordination costs that arise following diversification strategy. New proposals in 2009 stated that gradually over the next few years the BBC is planning to reduce the cost of managing the corporation in order to save on expenditures. It argues this can be achieved by cutting the salaries of senior management by 25 per cent and reducing the numbers of senior managers by 18 per cent.

As the BBC expands as a global player, John Smith, the CEO of BBC Worldwide claims that, "BBC worldwide adds significant new value to every licence fee every year by making the best possible return on selling BBC programmes and products across the world. To grow turnover by nearly 10 per cent in difficult trading conditions demonstrate that our diversification strategy is paying off." The future of the BBC's current charter runs out in 2016 and the government could then take away its public subsidy and allow it to operate as a private firm. The year 2012 sees the UK switch exclusively to digital, so could the BBC join the likes of Sky and become financed by subscription, as more questions are raised over the organization being publicly funded?

**Sources:** 2000 "100 face axe in BBC restructure", *Marketing Week*, 23(21): 12; 2007 "The *future* of the *BBC*; Public-service broadcasting", *The Economist*, 382(8510): 23; Anon (2005) "Changes to schedule at the BBC", *Strategic Direction*, 21(8): 12–14; Froud, J., Johal, S., Leaver, A., Phillips R. and Williams, K. (2009) "Stressed by choice: a business model analysis of the BBC", *British Journal of Management*, 20: 252–264; Harris, M. and Wegg-Prosser, V. (2007) "Post bureaucracy and the politics of forgetting; The management of change at the BBC, 1991-2002", *Journal of Organizational Change Management*, 20(3): 290–303; Wegg-Prosser, V. (2001) "Thirty years of managerial change at the BBC", *Public Money and Management*, January–March: 9–14; Deloitte. 2009, *The Economic Impact of the BBC: 2008/09*, London: Deloitte LLP; BBC Worldwide (2010) *The BBC Annual Report and Accounts 2008/09*, 23 March; BBC Trust (2010) *BBC Strategy Review*, http://www.bbc.co.uk, 23 March; BBC Worldwide ( 2010) *Annual Review 2008/09*, http://www.bbc. co.uk, 23 March.

## Questions

1 What further diversification opportunities exist for the BBC?

2 To what extent are the regulatory conditions imposed upon the BBC a constraint or an opportunity?

## SUMMARY

- The primary reason a firm uses a corporate-level strategy to become more diversified is to create additional value. Using a single- or dominant-business corporate-level strategy may be preferable to seeking a more diversified strategy, unless a corporation can develop economies of scope or financial economies between businesses, or unless it can obtain market power through additional levels of diversification. Economies of scope and market power are the main sources of value creation when the firm diversifies by using a corporate-level strategy with moderate to high levels of diversification.

- The corporate-level strategy of related diversification helps the firm to create value by sharing activities or transferring competencies between different businesses in the company's portfolio.

- Sharing activities usually involves sharing tangible resources between businesses. Transferring core competencies involves transferring core competencies developed in one business to another business. It also may involve transferring competencies between the corporate headquarters' office and a business unit.

- Sharing activities is usually associated with the related constrained diversification corporate-level strategy. Activity sharing is costly to implement and coordinate, may create unequal benefits for the divisions involved in the sharing, and may lead to fewer managerial risk-taking behaviours.

- Transferring core competencies is often associated with related linked (or mixed related and unrelated) diversification, although firms pursuing both sharing activities and transferring core competencies can also use the related linked strategy.

- Efficiently allocating resources or restructuring a target firm's assets and placing them under rigorous financial controls are two ways to accomplish successful unrelated diversification. Firms using the unrelated diversification strategy focus on creating financial economies to generate value.

- Diversification is sometimes pursued for value-neutral reasons. Incentives from tax and antitrust government policies, performance disappointments, or uncertainties about future cash flow, are examples of value-neutral reasons that firms may choose to become more diversified.

- Managerial motives to diversify (including to increase compensation) can lead to over-diversification and a subsequent reduction in a firm's ability to create value. Evidence suggests, however, that the majority of top-level executives seek to be good stewards of the firm's assets and to avoid diversifying the firm in ways that destroy value.

- Managers need to pay attention to their firm's internal organization and its external environment when making decisions about the optimum level of diversification for their company. Internal resources are important determinants of the direction that diversification should take. However, conditions in the firm's external environment may facilitate additional levels of diversification, as might unexpected threats from competitors.

## REVIEW QUESTIONS

1 What is corporate-level strategy and why is it important?

2 What are the different levels of diversification firms can pursue by using different corporate-level strategies?

3 What are three reasons firms choose to diversify their operations?

4 How do firms create value when using a related diversification strategy?

5 What are the two ways to obtain financial economies when using an unrelated diversification strategy?

6 What incentives and resources encourage diversification?

7 What motives might encourage managers to over-diversify their firm?

## DISCUSSION QUESTIONS

1   Comment on the nature and extent of diversification in various industries. Consider what factors underlie the diversification moves in two sectors and identify any patterns that are common.

2   To what extent do you believe that all diversification is highly risky because it moves away from the core business focused around core competency?

3   Can it be argued that diversification is highly inappropriate for a small- to medium-sized firm?

4   What are the primary and secondary conditions that managers should consider in screening the feasibility of diversification moves?

5   For a conglomerate pursuing unrelated diversification, how would its shareholder expectations differ from a corporation that exhibits both operational and corporate relatedness in its portfolio of businesses?

## FURTHER READING

Corporate strategy – high risks and high returns. (Re)kindling growth often leads to acquisition, if not series of acquisitions. The readings mentioned here stimulate to critically reflect on three risks and on how to mitigate them. Related country or company culture, cultural issues whether they are need to be managed with utmost care in the acquisition and integration process (e.g. M. Y. Brannen and M. F. Peterson (2009), "Merging without alienating: Interventions promoting cross-cultural organizational integration and their limitations," *Journal of International Business Studies*, 40(3): 468–489; A. O'Connell (2009) "Lego CEO Jørgen Vig Knudstorp on leading through survival and growth", *Harvard Business Review*, 87(1): 1–2). When acquisitions succeed they may trigger subsequent acquisitions. However these increase the complexity of developing and implementing the right strategy (E. N. K. Lim, S. S. Das and A. Das (2009) "Diversification strategy, capital structure, and the Asian financial crisis (1997–1998): Evidence from Singapore firms", *Strategic Management Journal*, 30(6): 577–594; J. M. Shaver and J. M. Mezias (2009) "Diseconomies of managing in acquisitions: Evidence from civil lawsuits", *Organization Science*, 20(1): 206–222).

At times the financial press illustrates how acquisitions and corporate diversification seem to come in waves. This points to a third risk: acquiring under the influence. It may be not entirely clear how much of the decision for corporate action is influenced by what other corporations do (e.g. T. Hutzschenreuter and F. Gröne (2009) "Changing vertical integration strategies under pressure from foreign competition: The case of US and German multinationals", *Journal of Management Studies*, 46(2): 269–307; P. Dastidar (2009) "International corporate diversification and performance: Does firm self-selection matter?" *Journal of International Business Studies*, 40(1): 71–86).

## EXPERIENTIAL EXERCISES

### Exercise 1: Comparison of diversification strategies

The use of diversification varies both across and within industries. In some industries, most firms may follow a single- or dominant-product approach. Other industries are characterized by a mix of both single-product and heavily diversified firms. The purpose of this exercise is to learn how the use of diversification varies across firms in an industry, and the implications of such use.

#### Part One

Working in small teams of 4–7 persons, select an industry to research. You will then select two firms in that industry for further analysis. Many resources can aid in your iden-

tification of specific firms in an industry for analysis. One option is to visit the website of the New York Stock Exchange (http://www.nyse.com), which has an option to screen firms by industry group. A second option is http://www.hoovers.com, which offers similar listings. Identify two public firms based in the United States. (Note that Hoovers includes some private firms, and the NYSE includes some foreign firms. Data for the exercise are often unavailable for foreign or private companies.)

Once you have identified your target firms, you will need to collect business segment data for each company. Segment data break down the company's revenues and net income by major lines of business. These data are reported in the firm's SEC 10-K filing, and may also be reported in the annual report. Both the annual report and 10-K are usually found on the company's website; both the Hoovers and NYSE listings include company homepage information. For the most recent three-year period available, calculate the following:

- Percentage growth in segment sales
- Net profit margin by segment
- Bonus item: Compare profitability to industry averages (*Industry Norms and Key Business Ratios* publishes profit norms by major industry segment).

Next, based on your reading of the company filings and these statistics, determine whether the firm is best classified as:

- Single product
- Dominant product
- Related diversified
- Unrelated diversified

### Part Two

Prepare a brief PowerPoint presentation for use in class discussion. Address the following in your presentation:

- Describe the extent and nature of diversification used at each firm.
- Can you provide a motive for their diversification strategy, given the rationales for diversification stated in the chapter?

- Which firm's diversification strategy appears to be more effective? Try to justify your answer by explaining why you think one firm's strategy is more effective than the other.

### Exercise 2: How does the firm's portfolio stack up?

The BCG (Boston Consulting Group) product portfolio matrix has been around for decades and was introduced by the BCG as a way for firms to understand the priorities that should be given to the various segments within their mix of businesses. It is based on a matrix with two vertices: firm market share and projected market growth rate, as shown below:

Each firm therefore can categorize its business units as follows:

- Stars: High growth and high market share. These business units generate large amounts of cash but also use large amounts of cash. These are often the focus of the firm's priorities as these segments have a potentially bright future.
- Cash cows: Low market growth coupled with high market share. Profits and cash generated are high; the need for new cash is low. Provides a foundation for the firm from which it can launch new initiatives.
- Dogs: Low market growth and low market share. This is usually a situation firms seek to avoid and is quite often the target of a turnaround plan or liquidation effort.

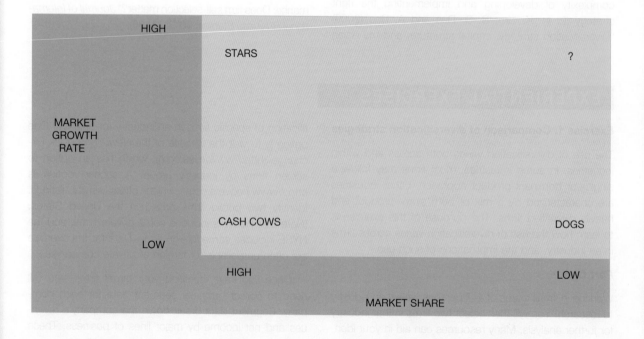

- Question marks: High market growth but low market share. Creates a need to move strategically because of high demands on cash due to market needs yet low cash returns because of the low firm market share.

This way of analysing a firm's corporate level strategy or the way in which it rewards and prioritizes its business units has come under some criticism. First, market share is not the only way in which a firm should view success or potential success; second, market growth is not the only indicator for the attractiveness of a market;

and third, sometimes "dogs" can earn as much cash as "cows."

**Part One**

Pick a publicly traded firm that has a diversified corporate-level strategy. The more unrelated the segments the better.

**Part Two**

Analyse the firm using the BCG matrix. In order to do this you will need to develop market share ratings for each operating unit and assess the overall market attractiveness for that segment.

## VIDEO CASE

### The risks of diversification

### Sir Mark Weinberg, President, St. James's Place Capital

www.cengage.co.uk/volberda/students/video_cases

Sir Mark Weinberg discusses the wisdom, or lack thereof, in firms that diversify their portfolio of businesses. Having been a director of a firm, British American Tobacco (BAT), that implemented an unrelated diversification strategy to reduce risk in the company's core business units, Sir Weinberg has keen insights into the wisdom of this strategy.

Before you watch the video consider the following concepts and questions and be prepared to discuss them in class:

### Concepts

- Executive hubris
- Diversification
- Risk
- Unrelated acquisition
- Core competency

### Questions

1 Think about firms that implement an unrelated diversification strategy. Why are some firms able to implement this corporate level strategy effectively while others struggle?

2 Read the history of British American Tobacco since 1969 from the company's website. What impressions do you take away from this?

3 British American Tobacco utilized the concept of risk minimization as a reason for diversification away from its core business. Do you consider this to be a valid rationale for implementing an unrelated diversification strategy?

4 How do public equity markets value unrelated diversification strategies and why do you think they do so?

## NOTES

1. M. E. Porter, 1980, *Competitive Strategy*, New York: The Free Press, xvi.
2. M. D. R. Chari, S. Devaraj and P. David, 2008, "The impact of information technology investments and diversification strategies on firm performance", *Management Science*, 54: 224–234; A. Pehrsson, 2006, "Business relatedness and performance: A study of managerial perceptions", *Strategic Management Journal*, 27: 265–282.
3. A. Hargrave-Silk, 2008, "Media brands moves to diversify", *Media 3*, November, http://www.britannica.com/bps/additionalcontent/18/35618620/Media-Brands-moves-to-diversify.
4. S. Walters and R. Stone, 2007, "The trouble with rose-colored glasses", *Barron's*, June 25. M10.
5. A. O'Connell, 2009, "Lego CEO Jørgen Vig Knudstorp on leading through survival and growth", *Harvard Business Review*, 87(1): 1–2.
6. M. E. Porter, 1987, "From competitive advantage to corporate strategy", *Harvard Business Review*, 65(3): 43–59; F. A. J. van den Bosch and A. P. de Man (eds.),

*Perspectives on Strategy: Contributions of Michael E. Porter*, Boston: Kluwer Academic.

7.  M. E. Porter, 1987, "From competitive advantage to corporate strategy", *Harvard Business Review*, 65(3): 43–59; F. A. J. van den Bosch and A. P. de Man (eds.), *Perspectives on Strategy: Contributions of Michael E. Porter*, Boston: Kluwer Academic; M. E. Raynor, 2007, "What is corporate strategy, really?", *Ivey Business Journal*, 71(8): 1–3.

8.  A. A. Calart and J. E. Ricart, 2007, "Corporate strategy: An agent-based approach", *European Management Review*, 4: 107–120; M. Kwak, 2002, Maximizing value through diversification, *MIT Sloan Management Review*, 43(2): 10.

9.  M. Ammann and M. Verhofen, 2006, "The conglomerate discount: A new explanation based on credit risk", *International Journal of Theoretical & Applied Finance*, 9(8): 1201–1214; S. A. Mansi and D. M. Reeb, 2002, "Corporate diversification: What gets discounted?", *Journal of Finance*, 57: 2167–2183; C. C. Markides and P. J. Williamson, 1996, "Corporate diversification and organisational structure: A resource-based view", *Academy of Management Journal*, 39: 340–367.

10. N. M. Schmid and I. Walter, 2009, "Do financial conglomerates create or destroy economic value?", *Journal of Financial Intermediation*, 18(2): 193–216; C. E. Helfat and K. M. Eisenhardt, 2004, "Intertemporal economies of scope, organisational modularity, and the dynamics of diversification", *Strategic Management Journal*, 25: 1217–1232.

11. A. Campbell, M. Goold and M. Alexander, 1995, "Corporate strategy: The question for parenting advantage", *Harvard Business Review*, 73(2): 120–132; S. Cartwright and R. Schoenberg, 2006, "30 Years of Mergers and Acquisitions Research: Recent advances and future opportunities", *British Journal of Management*, 17, S1, S1–S5.

12. D. Collis, D. Young and M. Goold, 2007, "The size, structure, and performance of corporate headquarters", *Strategic Management Journal*, 28: 283–405; M. Goold and A. Campbell, 2002, "Parenting in complex structures", *Long Range Planning*, 35(3): 219–243; T. H. Brush, P. Bromiley and M. Hendrickx, 1999, "The relative influence of industry and corporation on business segment performance: An alternative estimate", *Strategic Management Journal*, 20: 519–547; M. G. Baaij, F. A. J. Van den Bosch and H. W. Volberda, 2004, "The international relocation of corporate centres: Are corporate centres sticky?", *European Management Journal*, 22(2): 141–149; M. Baaij, D. Van den Berghe, F. Van den Bosch and H. Volberda, 2005, "Rotterdam or Anywhere: Relocating Corporate HQ", *Business Strategy Review*, 16(2): 45–48.

13. H. Chesbrough, 2007, "The market for innovation: Implications for corporate strategy", *California Management Review*, 49(3): 45–66; D. Miller, 2006, "Technological diversity, related diversification, and firm performance", *Strategic Management Journal*, 27: 601–619; D. J. Miller, 2004, "Firms' technological

resources and the performance effects of diversification: A longitudinal study", *Strategic Management Journal*, 25: 1097–1119.

14. D. D. Bergh, 2001, "Diversification strategy research at a crossroads: Established, emerging and anticipated paths", in: M. A. Hitt, R. E. Freeman and J. S. Harrison (eds.), *Handbook of Strategic Management*, Oxford, UK: Blackwell Publishers, 363–383.

15. H. C. Wang and J. B. Barney, 2006, "Employee incentives to make firm-specific investments: Implications for resource-based theories of corporate diversification", *Academy of Management Journal*, 31: 466–476.

16. J. J. Marcel, 2009, "Why top management team characteristics matter when employing a chief operating officer: A strategic contingency perspective", *Strategic Management Journal*, 30(6): 647–658; A. J. Ward, M. J. Lankau, A. C. Amason, J. A. Sonnenfeld and B. R. Agle, 2007, "Improving the performance of top management teams", *MIT Sloan Management Review*, 48(3): 85–90.

17. R. P. Rumelt, 1974, *Strategy, Structure, and Economic Performance*, Boston, MA: Harvard Business School; L. Wrigley, 1970, *Divisional Autonomy and Diversification* (Ph.D. dissertation), Boston, MA: Harvard Business School.

18. P. Gogoi, N. Arndt and J. Crown, 2008, "A bitter sweet deal for Wrigley: Selling the family business wasn't William Wrigley Jr's plan, but the Mars offer was too good to refuse", *BusinessWeek*, May 12, 34.

19. 2009, United Parcel Service, Inc., http://www.hoovers.com, March 15.

20. 2009, Hutchison Whampoa Limited, http://www.hoovers.com, March 15; J. Spencer, 2007, "Hutchison's Li Looks to make well-timed exit; Indian wireless assets may yield a windfall; a bigger risk to buyers", *Wall Street Journal*, January 29, B4.

21. M. Lee, 2008, Hutch Telecom to pay special dividend; shares surge (update2), http://www.Bloomberg.com, November 12; 2007, "What has Superman got up his sleeve?", *Euroweek*, February 23, 1.

22. M. A. Williams, T. B. Michael and E. R. Waller, 2008, "Managerial incentives and acquisitions: A survey of the literature", *Managerial Finance*, 34(5): 328–341; S. W. Geiger and L. H. Cashen, 2007, "Organisational size and CEO compensation: The moderating effect of diversification in downscoping organisations", *Journal of Managerial Issues*, 9(2): 233–252; R. K. Aggarwal and A. A. Samwick, 2003, "Why do managers diversify their firms? Agency reconsidered", *Journal of Finance*, 58: 71–118.

23. D. J. Miller, M. J. Fern and L. B. Cardinal, 2007, "The use of knowledge for technological innovation within diversified firms", *Academy of Management Journal*, 50: 308–326.

24. H. Tanriverdi and C. H. Lee, 2008, "Within-industry diversification and firm performance in the presence of network externalities: Evidence from the software industry", *Academy of Management Journal*, 51(2): 381–397; H. Tanriverdi and N. Venkatraman, 2005, "Knowledge relatedness and the performance of multibusiness firms", *Strategic Management Journal*, 26: 97–119.

25. M. D. R. Chari, S. Devaraj and Parthiban David, 2008, "The impact of information technology investments and diversification strategies on firm performance", *Management Science*, 54(1): 224–234; H. Tanriverdi, 2006, "Performance effects of information technology synergies in multibusiness firms", *MIS Quarterly*, 30(1): 57–78.

26. M. E. Porter, 1985, *Competitive Advantage*, New York: The Free Press, 328.

27. N. Shin, 2009, "Information technology and diversification: How their relationship affects firm performance", *International Journal of E-Collaboration*, 5(1): 69–83; D. Miller, 2006, "Technological diversity, related diversification, and firm performance", *Strategic Management Journal*, 27: 601–619; Ch. Baden-Fuller and H. W. Volberda, 2003, "Dormant capabilities, complex organizations, and renewal", in: R. Sanchez (ed.), *Knowledge Management and Organizational Competence* (paperback edition), Oxford: Oxford University Press, 114–136.

28. H. Tanriverdi and C. H. Lee, 2008, "Within-industry diversification and firm performance in the presence of network externalities: Evidence from the software industry", *Academy of Management Journal*, 51: 381–397; P. Puranam and K. Srikanth, 2007, "What they know vs what they do: How acquirers leverage technology acquisitions", *Strategic Management Journal*, 28: 805–825; C. Park, 2003, "Prior performance characteristics of related and unrelated acquirers", *Strategic Management Journal*, 24: 471–480; G. Delong, 2001, "Stockholder gains from focusing versus diversifying bank mergers", *Journal of Financial Economics*, 2: 221–252; T. H. Brush, 1996, "Predicted change in operational synergy and post-acquisition performance of acquired businesses", *Strategic Management Journal*, 17: 1–24.

29. D. D. Bergh, 1995, "Size and relatedness of units sold: An agency theory and resource-based perspective", *Strategic Management Journal*, 16: 221–239.

30. M. Lubatkin and S. Chatterjee, 1994, "Extending modern portfolio theory into the domain of corporate diversification: Does it apply?", *Academy of Management Journal*, 37: 109–136.

31. E. Dooms and A. A. Van Oijen, 2008, "The balance between tailoring and standardizing control", *European Management Review*, 5(4): 245–252; T. Kono, 1999, "A strong head office makes a strong company", *Long Range Planning*, 32(2): 225.

32. I. C. Hsu and Y. S. Wang, 2008, "A model of intraorganisational knowledge sharing: Development and initial test", *Journal of Global Information Management*, 16(3): 45–73; P. Puranam and K. Srikanth, 2007, "What they know vs what they do", *Strategic Management Journal*, 28: 805–825; F. T. Rothaermel, M. A. Hitt and L. A. Jobe, 2006, "Balancing vertical integration and strategic outsourcing: Effects on product portfolio, product success, and firm performance", *Strategic Management Journal*, 27: 1033–1056; S. Chatterjee and B. Wernerfelt, 1991, "The link between resources and type of diversification: Theory and evidence", *Strategic Management Journal*, 12: 33–48; R. J. Meyer and H. W. Volberda, 1997, "Porter on Corporate Strategy", in: F. A. J. van den Bosch and A. P. de Man (eds.), *Perspectives on Strategy: Contributions of Michael E. Porter*, Boston: Kluwer Academic, 25–33; F. A. Maljers, 1997, "Corporate Strategy from a Unilever perspective", in: F. A. J. van den Bosch and A. P. de Man (eds.), *Perspectives on Strategy: Contributions of Michael E. Porter*, Boston: Kluwer Academic.

33. A. Rodríguez-Duarte, F. D. Sandulli, B. Minguela-Rata and J. I. López-Sánchez, 2007, "The endogenous relationship between innovation and diversification, and the impact of technological resources on the form of diversification", *Research Policy*, 36: 652–664; L. Capron and N. Pistre, 2002, "When do acquirers earn abnormal returns?", *Strategic Management Journal*, 23: 781–794.

34. C. Lawton, 2007, H-P begins push into high-end copiers, *Wall Street Journal*, April 24, B3.

35. D. Miller, M. J. Fern and L. B. Cardinal, "The use of knowledge for technological innovation within diversified firms", *Academy of Management Journal*, 50: 308–326; J. W. Spencer, 2003, "Firms' knowledge-sharing strategies in the global innovation system: Empirical evidence from the flat panel display industry", *Strategic Management Journal*, 24: 217–233.

36. J. Thottam, 2008, "Branson's flight plan", *Time*, April 28, 40.

37. 2009, Honda engines, Honda Motor Company Home Page, http://www.honda.com, March 30.

38. L. C. Thang, C. Rowley, T. Quang and M. Warner, 2007, "To what extent can management practices be transferred between countries?: The case of human resource management in Vietnam", *Journal of World Business*, 42(1): 113–127; G. Stalk Jr, 2005, "Rotate the core", *Harvard Business Review*, 83(3): 18–19.

39. S. Gupta, A. Woodside, C. Dubelaar and D. Bradmore, 2009, "Diffusing knowledge-based core competencies for leveraging innovation strategies: Modeling outsourcing to knowledge process organisations (KPOs) in pharmaceutical networks", *Industrial Marketing Management*, 38(2): 219–227.

40. S. Chatterjee and J. Singh, 1999, "Are trade-offs inherent in diversification moves? A simultaneous model for type of diversification and mode of expansion decisions", *Management Science*, 45: 25–41.

41. J. Wiggins, 2008, "Mars' move for Wrigley leaves rivals trailing", *Financial Times*, April 29, 24.

42. L. Fuentelsaz and J. Gomez, 2006, "Multi-point competition, strategic similarity and entry into geographic markets", *Strategic Management Journal*, 27: 477–499; J. Gimeno and C. Y. Woo, 1999, "Multimarket contact, economies of scope, and firm performance", *Academy of Management Journal*, 42: 239–259.

43. B. P. Biederman, 2008, "Preparing for take-off", *Journal of Commerce*, July 28; R. Kwong, 2007, "Big four hope expansion will deliver the goods", *Financial Times*, May 23, 15.

44. T. A. Shervani, G. Frazier and G. Challagalla, 2007, "The moderating influence of firm market power on the transaction cost economics model: An empirical test in a forward channel integration context", *Strategic Management Journal*, 28: 635–652; R. Gulati, P. R. Lawrence and P. Puranam, 2005, "Adaptation in vertical relationships: Beyond incentive conflict", *Strategic Management Journal*, 26: 415–440.

45. P. Broedner, S. Kinkel and G. Lay, 2009, "Productivity effects of outsourcing: New evidence on the strategic importance of vertical integration decisions", *International Journal of Operations & Production Management*, 29(2): 127–150; D. A. Griffin, A. Chandra and T. Fealey, 2005, "Strategically employing natural channels in an emerging market", *Thunderbird International Business Review*, 47(3): 287–311.

46. R. Carter and G. M. Hodgson, 2006, "The impact of empirical tests of transaction cost economics on the debate on the nature of the firm", *Strategic Management Journal*, 27: 461–476; O. E. Williamson, 1996, "Economics and organisation: A primer", *California Management Review*, 38(2): 131–146.

47. S. Novak and S. Stern, 2008, "How does outsourcing affect performance dynamics? Evidence from the automobile industry", *Management Science*, 54(12): 1963–1979.

48. C. Wolter and F. M. Veloso, 2008, "The effects of innovation on vertical structure: Perspectives on transaction costs and competences", *Academy of Management Review*, 33(3): 586–605; M. G. Jacobides, 2005, "Industry change through vertical disintegration: How and why markets emerged in mortgage banking", *Academy of Management Journal*, 48: 465–498.

49. L. R. Kopczak and M. E. Johnson, 2003, "The supply-chain management effect", *MIT Sloan Management Review*, 3: 27–34; K. R. Harrigan, 2001, "Strategic flexibility in the old and new economies", in: M. A. Hitt, R. E. Freeman and J. S. Harrison (eds.), *Handbook of Strategic Management*, Oxford, UK: Blackwell Publishers, 97–123.

50. T. Hutzschenreuter and F. Gröne, 2009, "Changing vertical integration strategies under pressure from foreign competition: The case of US and German multinationals", *Journal of Management Studies*, 46(2): 269–307.

51. 2010, Flextronics International Ltd., http://www.flextronics.com, June 1.

52. P. Kothandaraman and D. T. Wilson, 2001, "The future of competition: Value-creating networks", *Industrial Marketing Management*, 30: 379–389.

53. K. M. Eisenhardt and D. C. Galunic, 2000, "Coevolving: At last, a way to make synergies work", *Harvard Business Review*, 78(1): 91–111.

54. J. M. Shaver and J. M. Mezias, 2009, "Diseconomies of managing in acquisitions: Evidence from civil lawsuits", *Organization Science*, 20(1): 206–222.

55. J. A. Nickerson and T. R. Zenger, 2008, "Envy, comparison costs, and the economic theory of the firm", *Strategic Management Journal*, (13): 1429–1449.

56. L. Greene, 2009, "Adult nostalgia for childhood brands", *Financial Times*. http://www.ft.com, February 14; M. Marr, 2007, "The magic kingdom looks to hit the road", *Wall Street Journal*, http://www.wsj.com, February 8.

57. E. Taylor and J. Singer, 2007, "New UBS chief keeps strategy intact", *Wall Street Journal*, July 7, A3.

58. 2009, "Breaking up the Citi", *Wall Street Journal*, January 14, A12; 2007, Breakingviews.com: "Citi to world: Drop 'group'", *Wall Street Journal*, January 17, C16.

59. 2009, Citigroup may sell Japanese units to raise cash, *Business 24-7*, http://www.business24-7.ae, February 26.

60. K Bart, 2009, "International finance: He cut costs at Credit Suisse; now he'll do it at UBS", *Wall Street Journal*, April 2, C2.

61. D.W. Ng, 2007, "A modern resource based approach to unrelated diversification", *Journal of Management Studies*, 44(8): 1481–1502; D. D. Bergh, 1997, "Predicting divestiture of unrelated acquisitions: An integrative model of ex ante conditions", *Strategic Management Journal*, 18: 715–731; C. W. L. Hill, 1994, "Diversification and economic performance: Bringing structure and corporate management back into the picture", in: R. P. Rumelt, D. E. Schendel and D. J. Teece (eds.), *Fundamental Issues in Strategy*, Boston, MA: Harvard Business School Press, 297–321.

62. M. E. Porter, 1985, *Competitive Advantage*, New York: The Free Press.

63. S. Lee, K. Park and H. H. Shin, 2009, "Disappearing internal capital markets: Evidence from diversified business groups in Korea", *Journal of Banking & Finance*, 33(2): 326–334; D. Collis, D. Young and M. Goold, 2007, "The size, structure, and performance of corporate headquarters", *Strategic Management Journal*, 28: 283–405; O. E. Williamson, 1975, *Markets and Hierarchies: Analysis and Antitrust Implications*, New York: Macmillan Free Press.

64. R. Aggarwal and N. A. Kyaw, 2009, "International variations in transparency and capital structure: evidence from European firms", *Journal of International Financial Management & Accounting*, 20(1): 1–34; R. J. Indjejikian, 2007, "Discussion of accounting information, disclosure, and the cost of capital", *Journal of Accounting Research*, 45(2): 421–426.

65. A. Mackey, 2008, "The effect of CEOs on firm performance", *Strategic Management Journal*, 29(12): 1357–1367; E. Dooms and A. A. C. J. van Oijen, 2008, "The balance between tailoring and standardizing control", *European Management Review*, 5, 245–252; D. Miller, R. Eisenstat and N. Foote, 2002, "Strategy from the inside out: Building capability-creating organisations", *California Management Review*, 44(3): 37–54; M. E. Raynor and J. L. Bower, 2001, "Lead from the center: How to manage divisions dynamically", *Harvard Business Review*, 79(5): 92–100.

66. K. Kranhold, 2007, "GE report raises doubts", *Wall Street Journal*, January 20–21, A3.

67. R. Ettenson and J. Knowles, 2008, "Don't confuse reputation with brand", *MIT Sloan Management Review*, 49(2): 21.

68. P. Engardio and M. Arndt, 2007, "What price reputation: Many savvy companies are starting to realise that a good name can be their most important asset – and actually boost the stock price", *BusinessWeek*, July 8, 70–79; J. Lunsford and B. Steinberg, 2006, "Conglomerates' conundrum", *Wall Street Journal*, B1, B7.

69. F. Guerrera, 2007, "Siemens chief makes the case for conglomerates", *Financial Times*, http://www.ft.com, February 5.

70. B. Quint, 2009, "Companies deal with tough times through diversification", *Information Today*, 26(3): 7–8.

71. A. Delios, D. Xu and P. W. Beamish, 2008, "Within-country product diversification and foreign subsidiary performance", *Journal of International Business Studies*, 39(4): 706–724; M. W. Peng and A. Delios, 2006, "What determines the scope of the firm over time and around the world? An Asia Pacific perspective", *Asia Pacific Journal of Management*, 23: 385–405; T. Khanna, K. G. Palepu and J. Sinha, 2005, "Strategies that fit emerging markets", *Harvard Business Review*, 83(6): 63–76.

72. S. Lee, K. Park, H. H. Shin, 2009, "Disappearing internal capital markets: Evidence from diversified business groups in Korea", *Journal of Banking & Finance*, 33: 326–334; A. Chakrabarti, K. Singh and I. Mahmood, 2006, "Diversification and performance: Evidence from East Asian firms", *Strategic Management Journal*, 28: 101–120; T. Khanna and K. Palepu, 2000, "Is group affiliation profitable in emerging markets? An analysis of diversified Indian business groups", *Journal of Finance*, 55: 867–892; T. Khanna and K. Palepu, 2000, "The future of business groups in emerging markets: Long-run evidence from Chile", *Academy of Management Journal*, 43: 268–285.

73. D. D. Bergh, R. A. Johnson and R. L. Dewitt, 2008, "Restructuring through spin-off or sell-off: Transforming information asymmetries into financial gain", *Strategic Management Journal*, 29(2): 133–148; C. Decker and M. Mellewigt, 2007, "Thirty years after Michael E. Porter: What do we know about business exit?", *Academy of Management Perspectives*, 2: 41–55; S. J. Chang and H. Singh, 1999, "The impact of entry and resource fit on modes of exit by multibusiness firms", *Strategic Management Journal*, 20: 1019–1035.

74. R. Coff, 2003, "Bidding wars over R&D-intensive firms: Knowledge, opportunism, and the market for corporate control", *Academy of Management Journal*, 46: 74–85.

75. P. Navarro, 2009, "Recession-proofing your organisation", *MIT Sloan Management Review*, 50(3): 45–51.

76. M. Lubatkin, H. Merchant and M. Srinivasan, 1997, "Merger strategies and shareholder value during times of relaxed antitrust enforcement: The case of large mergers during the 1980s", *Journal of Management*, 23: 61–81.

77. D. P. Champlin and J. T. Knoedler, 1999, "Restructuring by design? Government's complicity in corporate restructuring", *Journal of Economic Issues*, 33(1): 41–57.

78. R. M. Scherer and D. Ross, 1990, *Industrial Market Structure and Economic Performance*, Boston, MA: Houghton Mifflin.

79. A. Shleifer and R. W. Vishny, 1994, "Takeovers in the 1960s and 1980s: Evidence and implications", in: R. P. Rumelt, D. E. Schendel and D. J. Teece (eds.), *Fundamental Issues in Strategy*, Boston, MA: Harvard Business School Press, 403–422.

80. S. Chatterjee, J. S. Harrison and D. D. Bergh, 2003, "Failed takeover attempts, corporate governance and refocusing", *Strategic Management Journal*, 24: 87–96; M. Lubatkin, H. Merchant and M. Srinivasan, 1997, "Merger strategies and shareholder value during times of relaxed antitrust enforcement: The case of large mergers during the 1980s", *Journal of Management*, 23: 61–81; D. J. Ravenscraft and R. M. Scherer, 1987, *Mergers, Sell-Offs and Economic Efficiency*, Washington, DC: Brookings Institution, 22.

81. D. A. Zalewski, 2001, "Corporate takeovers, fairness, and public policy", *Journal of Economic Issues*, 35: 431–437; P. L. Zweig, J. P. Kline, S. A. Forest and K. Gudridge, 1995, "The case against mergers", *BusinessWeek*, October 30, 122–130; J. R. Williams, B. L. Paez and L. Sanders, 1988, "Conglomerates revisited", *Strategic Management Journal*, 9: 403–414.

82. E. J. Lopez, 2001, "New anti-merger theories: A critique", *Cato Journal*, 20: 359–378; 1998, The trustbusters' new tools, *The Economist*, May 2, 62–64.

83. R. Croyle and P. Kager, 2002, "Giving mergers a head start", *Harvard Business Review*, 80(10): 20–21.

84. M. C. Jensen, 1986, "Agency costs of free cash flow, corporate finance, and takeovers", *American Economic Review*, 76: 323–329.

85. M. T. Brouwer, 2008, "Horizontal mergers and efficiencies; theory and anti trust practice", *European Journal of Law and Economics*, 26(1): 11–26.

86. T. Afza, C. Slahudin and M. S. Nazir, 2008, "Diversification and corporate performance: An evaluation of Pakistani firms", *South Asian Journal of Management*, 15(3): 7–18; J. M. Shaver, 2006, "A paradox of synergy: Contagion and capacity effects in mergers and acquisitions", *Academy of Management Journal*, 31: 962–976; C. Park, 2002, "The effects of prior performance on the choice between related and unrelated acquisitions: Implications for the performance consequences of diversification strategy", *Journal of Management Studies*, 39: 1003–1019.

87. R. P. Rumelt, 1974, *Strategy, Structure, and Economic Performance*, Boston: Harvard Business School.

88. R. Waters, 2008, "eBay ready to sell Skype if strong synergies prove elusive", *Financial Times*, April 18, 17; A. Lashinsky, 2008, "Is Skype on sale at eBay?", *Fortune*, October 27, 158(8): 48.

89. L. E. Palich, L. B. Cardinal and C. C. Miller, 2000, "Curvilinearity in the diversification-performance linkage: An examination of over three decades of research", *Strategic Management Journal*, 21: 155–174.

90. 2010, General Meeting Statement, released 15 December, 2009, http://www.investors.rbs.com, June 1.

91. P. Eavis, 2008, "Lehman faces dilemma; signs of weakness abound with talk of Neuberger sale", *Wall Street Journal*, August 19, C14.

92.  D. G. Sirmon, M. A. Hitt and R. D. Ireland, 2007, "Managing firm resources in dynamic environments to create value: Looking inside the black box", *Academy of Management Review*, 32: 273–292; A. E. Bernardo and B. Chowdhry, 2002, "Resources, real options, and corporate strategy", *Journal of Financial Economics*, 63: 211–234.

93.  W. H. Tsai, Y. C. Kuo and J. H. Hung, 2009, "Corporate diversification and CEO turnover in family businesses: Self-entrenchment or risk reduction?", *Small Business Economics*, 32(1): 57–76; N. W. C. Harper and S. P. Viguerie, 2002, "Are you too focused?", *McKinsey Quarterly*, Mid-Summer, 29–38; J. C. Sandvig and L. Coakley, 1998, "Best practices in small firm diversification", *Business Horizons*, 41(3): 33–40.

94.  2010, Our Company, http://www.btplc.com, June 1.

95.  L. Jarvis, 2008, "Pharma strategies: Merck launches into the biosimilars business", *Chemical and Engineering News*, December, 86(50): 7.

96.  J. Carroll, 2009, "Merck acquires biosimilars in $130M pact", *Fierce Biotech*, http://www.fiercebiotech.com, February 12.

97.  T. B. Folta and J. P. O'Brien, 2008, "Determinants of firm-specific thresholds in acquisition decisions", *Managerial and Decision Economics*, 29(2/3): 209–225.

98.  N. M. Kay and A. Diamantopoulos, 1987, "Uncertainty and synergy: Towards a formal model of corporate strategy", *Managerial and Decision Economics*, 8: 121–130.

99.  R. W. Coff, 1999, "How buyers cope with uncertainty when acquiring firms in knowledge-intensive industries: Caveat emptor", *Organization Science*, 10: 144–161.

100.  P. B. Carroll and C. Muim 2008, "7 Ways to Fail Big", *Harvard Business Review*, 86(9): 82–91.

101.  D. G. Sirmon, S. Gove and M. A. Hitt, 2008, "Resource management in dyadic competitive rivalry: The effects of resource bundling and deployment", *Academy of Management Journal*, 51(5): 919–935; S. J. Chatterjee and B. Wernerfelt, 1991, "The link between resources and type of diversification: Theory and evidence", *Strategic Management Journal*, 12: 33–48.

102.  E. N. K. Lim, S. S. Das and A. Das, 2009, "Diversification strategy, capital structure, and the Asian financial crisis (1997–1998): Evidence from Singapore firms", *Strategic Management Journal*, 30(6): 577–594; W. Heuslein, 2003, "The Ebitda folly", *Forbes*, March 17, 165–167.

103.  T. I. Tsai and I. Johnson, 2009, "Acer hopes to thrive in downturn", *Wall Street Journal*, February 17, B7.

104.  L. Capron and J. Hulland, 1999, "Redeployment of brands, sales forces, and general marketing management expertise following horizontal acquisitions: A resource-based view", *Journal of Marketing*, 63(2): 41–54.

105.  M. V. S. Kumar, 2009, "The relationship between product and international diversification: The effects of short-run constraints and endogeneity", *Strategic Management Journal*, 30(1): 99–116; C. B. Malone and L. C. Rose, 2006, "Intangible assets and firm diversification", *International Journal of Managerial Finance*, 2(2): 136–153; A. M. Knott, D. J. Bryce and H. E. Posen, 2003, "On the

strategic accumulation of intangible assets", *Organization Science*, 14: 192–207.

106.  D. D. Bergh, R. A. Johnson and R. L. Dewitt, 2008, "Restructuring through spin-off or sell-off: Transforming information asymmetries into financial gain", *Strategic Management Journal*, 29(2): 133–148; K. Shimizu and M. A. Hitt, 2005, "What constrains or facilitates divestitures of formerly acquired firms? The effects of organisational inertia", *Journal of Management*, 31: 50–72.

107.  2010, Our brands, http://www.saralee.com, June 2.

108.  D. Cimilluca and J. Jargon, 2009, "Corporate news: Sara Lee weighs sale of European business", *Wall Street Journal*, March 13, B3; J. Jargon and J. Vuocolo, 2007, "Sara Lee CEO challenged on antitakeover defenses", *Wall Street Journal*, May 11, B4.

109.  M. A. Williams, T. B. Michael and E. R. Waller, 2008, "Managerial incentives and acquisitions: a survey of the literature", *Managerial Finance*, 34(5): 328–341; J. G. Combs and M. S. Skill, 2003, "Managerialist and human capital explanation for key executive pay premiums: A contingency perspective", *Academy of Management Journal*, 46: 63–73; M. A. Geletkanycz, B. K. Boyd and S. Finkelstein, 2001, "The strategic value of CEO external directorate networks: Implications for CEO compensation", *Strategic Management Journal*, 9: 889–898; W. Grossman and R. E. Hoskisson, 1998, "CEO pay at the crossroads of Wall Street and Main: Toward the strategic design of executive compensation", *Academy of Management Executive*, 12(1): 43–57.

110.  R. E. Hoskisson, M. W. Castleton and M. C. Withers, 2009, "Complementarity in monitoring and bonding: More intense monitoring leads to higher executive compensation", *Academy of Management Perspectives*, 23: 57–74; S. N. Kaplan, 2008a, "Are CEOs overpaid?", *Academy of Management Perspectives*, 22(2): 5–20.

111.  S. W. Geiger and L. H. Cashen, 2007, "Organisational size and CEO compensation: The moderating effect of diversification in downscoping organisations", *Journal of Managerial Issues*, 9(2): 233–252; J. J. Cordeiro and R. Veliyath, 2003, "Beyond pay for performance: A panel study of the determinants of CEO compensation", *American Business Review*, 21(1): 56–66; P. Wright, M. Kroll and D. Elenkov, 2002, "Acquisition returns, increase in firm size, and chief executive officer compensation", *Academy of Management Journal*, 45: 599–608; S. R. Gray and A. A. Cannella Jr, 1997, "The role of risk in executive compensation", *Journal of Management*, 23: 517–540.

112.  S. N. Kaplan, 2008, "Are CEOs overpaid?", *Academy of Management Perspectives*, 22(2): 5–20; R. Bliss and R. Rosen, 2001, "CEO compensation and bank mergers", *Journal of Financial Economics*, 1: 107–138; W. G. Sanders and M. A. Carpenter, 1998, "Internationalisation and firm governance: The roles of CEO compensation, top team composition, and board structure", *Academy of Management Journal*, 41: 158–178.

113.  J. Bogle, 2008, "Reflections on CEO compensation", *Academy of Management Perspectives*, 22(2): 21–25; J. J. Janney, 2002, "Eat or get eaten? How equity ownership

and diversification shape CEO risk-taking", *Academy of Management Executive*, 14(4): 157–158; J. W. Lorsch, A. S. Zelleke and K. Pick, 2001, "Unbalanced boards", *Harvard Business Review*, 79(2): 28–30; R. E. Hoskisson and T. Turk, 1990, "Corporate restructuring: Governance and control limits of the internal market", *Academy of Management Review*, 15: 459–477.

114. M. Kahan and E. B. Rock, 2002, "How I learned to stop worrying and love the pill: Adaptive responses to takeover law", *University of Chicago Law Review*, 69(3): 871–915.

115. R. C. Anderson, T. W. Bates, J. M. Bizjak and M. L. Lemmon, 2000, "Corporate governance and firm diversification", *Financial Management*, 29(1): 5–22; J. D. Westphal, 1998, "Board games: How CEOs adapt to increases in structural board independence from management", *Administrative Science Quarterly*, 43: 511–537; J. K. Seward and J. P. Walsh, 1996, "The governance and control of voluntary corporate spin offs", *Strategic Management Journal*, 17: 25–39; J. P. Walsh and J. K. Seward, 1990, "On the efficiency of internal and external corporate control mechanisms", *Academy of Management Review*, 15: 421–458.

116. S. M. Campbell, A. J. Ward, J. A. Sonnenfeld and B. R. Agle, 2008, "Relational ties that bind: Leader-follower relationship dimensions and charismatic attribution", *Leadership Quarterly*, 19(5): 556–568; M. Wiersema, 2002, "Holes at the top: Why CEO firings backfire", *Harvard Business Review*, 80(12): 70–77.

117. J. M. Bizjak, M. L. Lemmon and L. Naveen, 2008, "Does the use of peer groups contribute to higher pay and less efficient compensation?", *Journal of Financial Economics*, 90(2): 152–168; N. Wasserman, 2006, "Stewards, agents, and the founder discount: Executive compensation in new ventures", *Academy of Management Journal*, 49: 960–976; V. Kisfalvi and P. Pitcher, 2003, "Doing what feels right: The influence of CEO character and emotions on top management team dynamics", *Journal of Management Inquiry*, 12(10): 42–66; W. G. Rowe, 2001, "Creating wealth in organisations: The role of strategic leadership", *Academy of Management Executive*, 15(1): 81–94.

118. E. F. Fama, 1980, "Agency problems and the theory of the firm", *Journal of Political Economy*, 88: 288–307.

119. M. Y. Brannen and M. F. Peterson, 2009, "Merging without alienating: Interventions promoting cross-cultural organisational integration and their limitations", *Journal of International Business Studies*, 40(3): 468–489; M. L. A. Hayward, 2002, "When do firms learn from their acquisition experience? Evidence from 1990–1995", *Strategic Management Journal*, 23: 21–39; L. Capron, W. Mitchell and A. Swaminathan, 2001, "Asset divestiture following horizontal acquisitions: A dynamic view", *Strategic Management Journal*, 22: 817–844.

120. R. E. Hoskisson, R. A. Johnson, L. Tihanyi and R. E. White, 2005, "Diversified business groups and corporate refocusing in emerging economies", *Journal of Management*, 31: 941–965.

121. C. N. Chung and X. Luo, 2008, "Institutional logics or agency costs: The influence of corporate governance models on business group restructuring in emerging economies", *Organization Science*, 19(5): 766–784; A. Chakrabarti, K. Singh and I. Mahmood, 2006, "Diversification and performance: Evidence from East Asian firms", *Strategic Management Journal*, 28: 101–120; W. P. Wan and R. E. Hoskisson, 2003, "Home country environments, corporate diversification strategies, and firm performance", *Academy of Management Journal*, 46: 27–45.

# CHAPTER 8

# STRATEGIC ACQUISITION AND RESTRUCTURING

## LEARNING OBJECTIVES

Studying this chapter should provide you with the strategic management knowledge needed to:

1 Explain the popularity of merger and acquisition strategies in firms competing in the global economy.
2 Discuss reasons why firms use an acquisition strategy to achieve strategic competitiveness.
3 Describe seven problems that work against achieving success when using an acquisition strategy.
4 Name and describe the attributes of effective acquisitions.
5 Define the restructuring strategy and distinguish among its common forms.
6 Explain the short- and long-term outcomes of the different types of restructuring strategies.

© ICP/Alamy

## OPENING CASE

# Cross-border acquisitions: trends and patterns

Mergers and acquisitions (M&A) are a primary means of firm growth. We define these terms and discuss a number of reasons firms use merger and acquisition strategies in this chapter. Cross-border M&A activity (activity involving firms headquartered in different nations) increased during the 1990s and into the early part of the twenty-first century, largely because of the continuing globalization of the world's markets. A key advantage for firms is that they can grow rapidly both in domestic and international markets through mergers and acquisitions. For societies, mergers and acquisitions can be beneficial in that they "… are a critical tool for eliminating weaker players and wringing out excess capacity".

Merger and acquisition activity tends to be cyclical in nature, flowing and ebbing in light of the opportunities and threats associated with a firm's external environment at points in time. The economic downturn has inevitably affected recent M&A activity. In 2009, a general decline in overall M&A activity continued which

generated, within Europe, Middle East and Africa (EMEA) region, 3555 deals which were valued at €328.7bn, a decrease of 54 per cent in value and 35 per cent in number of deals compared with 2008. The UK accounted for 30 per cent and 19 per cent of this activity respectively. The recent M&A world has altered significantly from the boom of a few years ago. The reasons for this vary, but include limited access to funds from banks and the growing divergence of price expectations between buyers and sellers.

The number of cross-border acquisitions illustrates the increasingly globalized nature of conducting business affairs in globally competitive markets. The increase is particularly apparent as one looks at the number of foreign acquisitions in large, developed markets such as in the US and the UK. Indeed, the value of cross-border M&A activity declined by 77 per cent in the first quarter of 2009 compared to the same quarter a year earlier. In the first half of 2009, Pfizer's €53.5 billion acquisition of Wyeth was the largest transaction (see Strategic Focus later in this chapter).

In spite of the recent declines in M&A activity both globally and domestically, merger and acquisition strategies are still a very viable source of firm growth; as a result, they remain popular with many of the world's corporations. In the foreseeable future, M&A opportunities seem strong in several sectors such as energy and health care. In response to pushes toward greener, renewable energy sources, for example, major oil companies "… are eyeing players in alternative energy …" Fuel refiner Valero's purchase of ethanol producer VeraSun is an example of M&A activity taking place in this sector. However, as is true for all strategies, firms in these two sectors and all other companies must carefully evaluate the "deal" (either a merger or an acquisition) they are contemplating to verify that completing the transaction will facilitate the firm's efforts to achieve strategic competitiveness and create value for stakeholders as a result of doing so.

The United Kingdom has also benefited enormously from having open borders and open markets that allow foreign capital to purchase domestic UK assets, and from the foreign managerial talent associated with managing such acquired assets. However, concerns have surfaced about whether or not foreign acquisitions will make it much harder for British employees to become top-level managers. Furthermore, some industry watchers wonder if foreign takeovers will reduce intellectual property, such that foreign firms will reduce the long-term viability of British industry firms with foreign firms spending their R&D investment in their home countries. The takeover boom affected even significant icons such as Manchester United, which was purchased by Malcolm Glazer, a US sports tycoon.

Other European firms such as those from Spain have been purchasing a significant number of foreign firms. Spanish firms gained experience through an international push in Latin America decades ago. In particular, Telefonica, a large telecommunications firm, purchased a number of telecommunications companies that had been privatized in Latin America. Similarly, Spanish banks grew in Latin America through a number of purchases. This experience has now been transferred across Europe not only in the merging of telecommunications firms and banks, but also in merging train and airport management services, and infrastructure management services. For instance, Ferrobial sought to buy BAA, the largest train and airport manager in the UK, which was recently privatized. Banco Santander purchased Abbey National and Alliance & Leicester in the UK, as well as a number of other banks. Recently, Abertis sought to take over Autostrade SpA, which will provide the Spanish firm control over the train routes in Italy and other countries in Europe.

Japanese firms have also become active in large overseas takeovers after being somewhat inactive for a number of years. For example, Japan Tobacco Inc. recently acquired Gallaher Group plc for €11.5 billion. The acquisition of this British tobacco firm will greatly increase Japan Tobacco's overseas revenues. Interestingly, much of the acquisition activity by European and Japanese firms has been driven by currency valuations, especially relative to the US, because the dollar is much lower in value than either the euro or the Japanese yen currencies compared to the 1990s.

Emerging economies, for example from India, have become quite aggressive in overseas transactions as well. India's Tata Group won the bid for British steel maker Corus Group plc for €10.4 billion. Similarly, Hindalco Industries Ltd purchased Novelis Inc., an aluminium producer that manufactures products such as beer cans and rolled automobile aluminium, for €4.5 billion. Novelis was spun off from Alcan, the second largest (in size) aluminium producer next to Alcoa, and is incorporated in Canada but headquartered in Atlanta. Although pursuing smaller acquisitions, Infosys Technologies Ltd, another India-based company which provides software services, increased its growth 9 per cent a year by acquiring small software providers.

Similarly, many Latin American firms have been buying US firms. In fact, the largest producers of cement in the US are all owned by international firms, including France's Lafarge SA, Switzerland's Holcim Ltd and Mexico's Cemex SA. Besides these large global players, a number of medium-sized producers such as Brazil's Botoratin Cinentos SA and Colombia's Cementos Argos SA have been buying North American assets and fleets of mixing trucks to deliver the concrete. Similarly, a regional Mexican producer, Grupo Cementos de Chihuahua SA, made additional acquisitions in Colorado and Oklahoma following purchases in Minnesota and South Dakota. Many of these purchases were driven by the high consumption rate for cement during the building boom when cement was in a seller's market. With a slowdown in housing, it is likely this acquisition activity will slow down as well.

In summary the number of cross-border deals continues to increase, leading many emerging-country firms to pursue acquisitions in developed countries, especially in the United States, the United Kingdom and other European countries. These developed economies have more open policies that allow the emerging-country economies to make inroads, especially in mature globalizing businesses such as steel, aluminium and cement, or basic services such as managing toll roads.

**Sources**: Mergermarket (2010) "Deal drivers: The comprehensive review of mergers and acquisitions in the EMEA region", http://www.mergermarket.com, July 8; Hannon, P. (2009) "Foreign investing decreased by half earlier this year", *Wall Street Journal Online*, http://www.wsj.com, June 25; Jung-a, S. (2009) "Mergers & acquisitions: Ambitious companies with war-chests look for value", *Financial Times Online*, http://www.ft.com, May 20; Saigol, L. and Thomas, H. (2010) "Volatility dulls appetite for big M&A activity", *Financial Times Online*, http://www.ft.com, June 30; Silver-Greenberg, J. (2009) "Dealmakers test the waters" *BusinessWeek*, March 2, 18–20; 2008 "Global M&A falls in 2008", *New York Times Online*, http://www.nytimes.com, December 22; Saigol, L. (2008) "Record number of M&A deals cancelled in 2008", *Financial Times Online*, http://www.ft.com, December 22; 2007 "Marauding Maharajahs: India's acquisitive companies" *Economist*, March, 86; Berman, D. K. (2007) "Mergers hit record, with few stop signs", *Wall Street Journal*, C11; Daneshkhu, S. (2007) "FDI flow into richest countries set to rise 20% this year", *Financial Times*, June 22, 7; McCary, J. (2007) "Foreign investments rise", *Wall Street Journal*, June 6, A5; Saigol, J., "The return of global dealmaking", *Financial Times*, September 30, www.ftcom; McNeil, L. R. (2007) "Foreign direct investment in the United States: New investment in 2006", *Survey of Current Business*, 87(5): 44–48; Singer, J., Johnson, K. and O'Connell, V. (2007) "Tobacco consolidation speeds" *Wall Street Journal*,

March 16, A3; Thompson, A. (2007) "Foreign acquisitions: Success at home has bred victory abroad", *Financial Times*, May 9, 6; Wonacott, P. and Glader, P. (2007) "Hindalco pact to buy Novelis underlines India's push overseas" *Wall Street Journal*, February 12, A11; Galloni, A. (2006) "European acquisition creates toll-road giant", *Wall Street Journal*, April 24, A3; Johnson, K. (2006) "Spain emerges as M&A powerhouse", *Wall Street Journal*, September 26, A6; Millman, J. (2006) "Cement demand paves path to takeovers" *Wall Street Journal*, May 23, A8; Engardio, P., Arndt, M. and Smith, G. (2006) Emerging giants, *BusinessWeek*, July 31, 40.

*Questions*

1 Given the market volatility in recent years, it has become increasingly difficult for a buyer and seller to determine the value and premium for an M&A deal. What consequences arise from this difficulty?

2 Twenty-five per cent of global M&A deals last year were cross-border. Do you anticipate this percentage increasing or decreasing over the next few years? Why?

We examined corporate-level strategy in Chapter 7, focusing on types and levels of product diversification strategies that firms derive from their core competencies to create competitive advantages. As noted in that chapter, diversification allows a firm to create value by productively using excess resources.[1] In this chapter, we explore merger and acquisition strategies. Firms throughout the world use these strategies, often in concert with diversification strategies to help firms become more diversified. As noted in the Opening Case, even though the amount of merger and acquisition activity completed in 2008 and through mid-2009 fell short of such activity in previous years, merger and acquisition strategies remain popular as a source of firm growth and hopefully, of above-average returns.

Most corporations are very familiar with merger and acquisition strategies. For example, the latter half of the twentieth century found major companies using these strategies to grow and to deal with the competitive challenges in their domestic markets as well as those emerging from global competitors. Today, smaller firms also use merger and acquisition strategies to grow in their existing markets and to enter new markets.[2]

Not unexpectedly, some mergers and acquisitions fail to realize their promise.[3] Accordingly, explaining how firms can successfully use merger and acquisition strategies to create stakeholder value[4] is a key purpose of this chapter. To do this we first explain the continuing popularity of merger and acquisition strategies as a choice firms evaluate when seeking growth and strategic competitiveness. As part of this explanation, we describe the differences between a merger, an acquisition and a takeover. We next discuss specific reasons firms choose to use acquisition strategies and some of the problems organizations may encounter when implementing them. We then describe the characteristics associated with effective acquisitions before closing the chapter with a discussion of different types of restructuring strategies. Restructuring strategies are commonly used to correct or deal with the results of ineffective mergers and acquisitions.

# The popularity of merger and acquisition strategies

As noted previously, merger and acquisition strategies have been popular among US firms for many years. Opinion suggests that these strategies played a central role in the restructuring of US businesses during the 1980s and 1990s and that they continue generating these types of benefits in the twenty-first century.[5]

Although popular and appropriately so as a means of growth with the potential to lead to strategic competitiveness, it is important to emphasize that changing conditions in the external environment influence the type of M&A activity firms pursue. During the recent financial crisis for example, tightening credit markets made it more difficult for firms to complete "megadeals" (those costing €7.8 billion or more). As a result, "… many acquirers are focusing on smaller targets with a niche focus that complements their existing business".[6] Additionally, the relatively weak US dollar increased the interest of firms from other nations to acquire US companies. For example, speculation surfaced in mid-2009 that Singapore's sovereign wealth fund, Temasek Holdings, was considering acquiring the aircraft-leasing unit of insurer AIG.

In the final analysis, firms use merger and acquisition strategies to improve their ability to create more value for all stakeholders, including shareholders. As suggested by Figure 1.1 (see 7), this reasoning applies equally to all of the other strategies (e.g., business-level, corporate-level, international and cooperative) a firm may formulate and then implement.

However, evidence suggests that using merger and acquisition strategies in ways that consistently create value is challenging. This is particularly true for acquiring firms in that some research results indicate that shareholders of acquired firms often earn above-average returns from acquisitions while shareholders of acquiring firms typically earn returns that are close to zero.[7] Moreover, in approximately two-thirds of all acquisitions, the acquiring firm's stock price falls immediately after the intended transaction is announced. This negative response is an indication of investors' scepticism about the likelihood that the acquirer will be able to achieve the synergies required to justify the premium.[8] Premiums can sometimes be excessive as appeared to be the case with NetApp's proposed acquisition of Data Domain in mid-2009: "On straightforward valuation measures, the (acquisition) price already looks in the stratosphere. At €26.36, the offer is 419 times Data Domain's consensus 2009 earnings, including the enormous cost of employee stock options."[9] Obviously, creating the amount of value required to account for this type of premium would be extremely difficult. Overall then, those leading firms that are using merger and acquisition strategies must recognize that creating more value for their stakeholders by doing so is indeed difficult.[10]

## Mergers, acquisitions and takeovers: what are the differences?

A merger is a strategy through which two firms agree to integrate their operations on a relatively coequal basis. Recently, Towers Perrin Forster & Crosby Inc. and Watson Wyatt Worldwide Inc., two large human-resources consulting firms, formed a merger. Shareholders of each firm will own 50 per cent of the newly-formed company, which will be "… the world's biggest employee-benefits consultancy …"[11].

Even though the transaction between Towers Perrin and Watson Wyatt appears to be a merger, the reality is that few true mergers actually take place. The main reason for this is that one party to the transaction is usually dominant in regard to various characteristics such as market share, size or value of assets. The transaction proposed between Xstrata and Anglo American appears to be an example of this.

In 2009, Swiss-based Xstrata (a global diversified mining group) proposed a friendly merger with London-based Anglo American (a diversified mining and natural resource group). While some analysts thought the proposed merger of equals "should create some value", they also concluded that the "… friendly merger with Anglo American (was) a pretty aggressive bear hug" given the terms Xstrata was seeking and its potential inability to pay the premium Anglo's shareholders

**Merger**

A merger is a strategy through which two firms agree to integrate their operations on a relatively coequal basis.

expected. In this case too some felt that Anglo's assets were of higher quality, reducing the likelihood that the transaction was actually one of "equals".[12]

An acquisition is a strategy through which one firm buys a controlling or a 100 per cent interest in another firm with the intent of making the acquired firm a subsidiary business within its portfolio. After completing the transaction, the management of the acquired firm reports to the management of the acquiring firm.

In spite of the situation we described dealing with Xstrata and Anglo American, most of the mergers that are completed are friendly in nature. However, acquisitions can be friendly or unfriendly. A takeover is a special type of acquisition wherein the target firm does not solicit the acquiring firm's bid; thus, takeovers are unfriendly acquisitions. Research evidence showing "... that hostile acquirers deliver significantly higher shareholder value than friendly acquirers for the acquiring firm"[13] is a reason some firms are willing to pursue buying another company even when that firm is not interested in being bought. Often, determining the price the acquiring firm is willing to pay to "take over" the target firm is the core issue in these transactions. In mid-July 2009 for example, Exelon raised its hostile bid for rival power producer NRG Energy to nearly €5.9 billion in stock, marking the latest twist in the months-long takeover feud. At issue was NRG's position that Exelon's bids were inadequate. At the same time however, NRG "... said that it remained open to a deal at a fair price".[14]

On a comparative basis, acquisitions are more common than mergers. Accordingly, we focus the remainder of this chapter's discussion on acquisitions.

## Reasons for acquisitions

In this section, we discuss reasons why firms decide to acquire another company. Although each reason can provide a legitimate rationale, acquisitions are not always as successful as the involved parties want to be the case. Later in the chapter we examine problems firms may encounter when seeking growth and strategic competitiveness through acquisitions.

### Increased market power

Achieving greater market power is a primary reason for acquisitions.[15] Defined in Chapter 7, market power exists when a firm is able to sell its goods or services above competitive levels, or when the costs of its primary or support activities are lower than those of its competitors. Market power usually is derived from the size of the firm and its resources and capabilities to compete in the marketplace;[16] it is also affected by the firm's share of the market. Therefore, most acquisitions that are designed to achieve greater market power entail buying a competitor, a supplier, a distributor or a business in a highly related industry to allow the exercise of a core competence and to gain competitive advantage in the acquiring firm's primary market.

One goal firms seek in achieving market power is to become a market leader. For example, having already acquired Gateway and Packard Bell, Acer is contemplating acquiring other firms (perhaps Asustek of Taiwan or Lenovo of China) as a means of getting closer to its goal of being the leading seller of personal computers.[17] Vertu, already the ninth-largest motor retailer in the United Kingdom, recently acquired some of the businesses and assets of Brooklyn Motor, a Ford and Mazda dealership. The transaction provided Vertu with its first Mazda franchise and facilitated the firm's intention of increasing share of its core market in the Worcestershire area.[18]

**Acquisition**

An acquisition is a strategy through which one firm buys a controlling, or 100 per cent, interest in another firm with the intention of making the acquired firm a subsidiary business within its portfolio.

**Takeover**

A takeover is a special type of acquisition strategy wherein the target firm does not solicit the acquiring firm's bid.

Firms use different types of acquisitions to increase their market power. Next, we discuss horizontal, vertical and related as three types of acquisitions firms use to increase their market power.

### Horizontal acquisitions

The acquisition of a company competing in the same industry as the acquiring firm is a horizontal acquisition. Horizontal acquisitions increase a firm's market power by exploiting cost-based and revenue-based synergies.[19] For example, National Australia Bank Ltd recently acquired the wealth-management assets from Aviva plc's Australian business. A company spokesman said that the acquisition would enhance National Australia's "… offering in key wealth-management segments including insurance and investment platforms, adding scale, efficiency and new capabilities to our operations".[20] Toys "Я" Us Inc.'s acquisition of specialty toy retailer FAO Schwarz is another example of a horizontal acquisition. Toys "Я" Us officials indicated that they intended to use their firm's "… buying clout to offer a slightly broader appeal to FAO's toy offerings …"[21] and to reduce the price FAO was paying to buy products for its stores.

Research suggests that horizontal acquisitions result in higher performance when the firms have similar characteristics[22] such as strategy, managerial styles and resource allocation patterns. Similarities in these characteristics support efforts to integrate the acquiring and the acquired firm. The similarity in the strategies they use should facilitate the integration of National Australia's and Aviva's wealth-management assets. Toys "Я" Us and FAO Schwarz share similar product lines and allocate their resources similarly to buy and sell their products. Horizontal acquisitions are often most effective when the acquiring firm integrates the acquired firm's assets with its own assets, but only after evaluating and divesting excess capacity and assets that do not complement the newly combined firm's core competencies.[23]

### Vertical acquisitions

A vertical acquisition refers to a firm acquiring a supplier or distributor of one or more of its goods or services.[24] Through a vertical acquisition, the newly-formed firm controls additional parts of the value chain (see Chapters 3 and 7),[25] which is how vertical acquisitions lead to increased market power.

CVS/Caremark, a firm that was formed as a result of a transaction completed in 2007, is a product of a vertical acquisition. In 2007, CVS Corporation (a retail pharmacy) acquired Caremark Rx, Inc. (a PBM or pharmacy benefits manager) to create CVS/Caremark, which is the largest integrated pharmacy services provider in the United States. In the firm's words: "Payers and patients count on CVS/Caremark for a broad range of services, from managing pharmacy benefits to filling prescriptions by mail or offering clinical expertise."[26] CVS/Caremark controls multiple parts of the value chain allowing it to use the size of its purchases to gain price concessions from those selling medicines and related products to it.

### Related acquisitions

Acquiring a firm in a highly related industry is called a related acquisition. Through a related acquisition, firms seek to create value through the synergy that can be generated by integrating some of their resources and capabilities. For example, Boeing recently acquired eXMeritus Inc., a company providing hardware and software to federal government and law enforcement agencies. eXMeritus's products are intended to help agencies securely share information across classified and unclassified networks and systems. eXMeritus is operating as part of Boeing's Integrated Defence Systems' Network and Space Systems business unit. This related acquisition facilitates Boeing's intention of expanding its presence in the cyber and intelligence markets – markets that are related to other aspects of the firm's Integrated Defence Systems operations.[27]

STRATEGIC FOCUS

CVS pharmacy

OPEN 24 HOURS

DRIVE-THRU PHARMACY

1HourPhoto

PNC BANK

# Oracle makes a series of horizontal acquisitions while CVS makes a vertical acquisition

Oracle, SAP and Microsoft compete in the database management software area. Currently SAP is leading at approximately 22 per cent market share, while Oracle and Microsoft have 10 per cent and 5 per cent, respectively. Rivalry between these firms has heated up as they compete for customer firms that have not yet integrated their firm's business units using database software. Once a database software configuration is in place, significant switching costs to move to another software platform exist. This point has led Oracle to pursue growth through horizontal acquisition strategy. Oracle's acquisition strategy facilitates growth because each new firm acquired has existing customers that will likely be retained, a sales force that can be integrated into Oracle's existing sales force to pursue new sales and new software applications that can be applied in industries where Oracle may not yet be involved, but with which the target firm will already have a clientele.

In 2004 Oracle acquired PeopleSoft for €8.1 billion through a hostile takeover. This acquisition also gave it the rights to J. D. Edwards, another industry rival that PeopleSoft had previously acquired. Oracle's acquisition strategy began when Larry Ellison decided that the corporate software industry had matured and needed consolidation. Since then Oracle has spent €18.9 billion to buy a number of companies, including the recent €2.6 billion takeover of Hyperion Solutions. This series of acquisitions led to Oracle's revenue increase of 50 per cent to €13.9 billion in the fiscal year ending May 2007. The acquisitions also enabled Oracle to develop a refined set of industry focui with applications in retail, financial services, utilities, communications and government service.

As an example, Oracle acquired Retek Inc. as well as ProfitLogic and 360Commerce to put together a set of retail software applications. These acquisitions allowed Oracle to win 30 new retail customers in 2006 and 2007 such as Wal-Mart, Nordstrom and Perry Ellis International. Perry Ellis's Chief Information Officer indicated that the company expects to save more than €15.7 million a year in improved just-in-time inventory controls, improved merchandising efficiency and software that helps to adapt its pricing by store and region efficiently through the application of the newly integrated Oracle software applications.

Comparatively, SAP is ahead in specific industry applications. It has applications in 26 industries compared to Oracle's five. Also, beyond large corporations in specific industries, both companies are pursuing growth in small- to medium-sized enterprises. The equalizer for Oracle has been its acquisition strategy. However, facilitating alignment and integrating the operations of these firms with Oracle is no easy task, but Oracle's increasing acquisition experience has made for improved acquisition integration processes.

In a vertical merger, CVS Corporation, a retail pharmacy chain, purchased pharmacy-benefits manager (PBM) Caremark RX, Inc., for €16.5 billion in 2007. The combined company has €59 billion in annual sales, far higher than any other competitor in North America. In this vertical acquisition CVS purchased a powerful customer that negotiates on behalf of large companies and their health insurance providers. One of the incentives for this vertical merger is that PBMs have put pressure on pharmacy stores by negotiating prices on behalf of their clients and forcing firms into mail-order plans for prescription drugs. The merger will help CVS obtain large deals with big companies by offering significant discounts to employees for CVS private-label products.

**Sources**: Hamm, S. (2007) "Oracle; Larry Ellison engineered a string of acquisitions that have given boost to the software giant's revenues" *BusinessWeek*, March 26, 64–65; Marcial, G. (2007) "Hall to CVS/Caremark, 2007", *Business-Week*, April 9, 99; Ricadela, A. (2007) "Oracle vs SAP: Sound or fiery?", *BusinessWeek*, April 9, 38; Vara, V. (2007) "Oracle adds business-intelligence from Hyperion", *Wall Street Journal*, March 2, B3; Vara, V. (2007) "CVS/Caremark directors win election", *Wall Street Journal*, May 10, B6; Armstrong, D. and Martinez, B. (2006) "CVS, Caremark deal to create drug-sale giant", *Wall Street Journal*, November 2, B1, B2; Ber-

man, D. K., Bulkeley, W. M. and Hensley, S. (2006) "Higher bid lifts Caremark, for now," *Wall Street Journal*, December 19, A2; Pritchard, S. (2006) "How Oracle and SAP are moving down 'The Tail'", *Financial Times*, October 18, 5.

## Questions

**1** Identify and describe an industry sector where: (i) horizontal acquisitions and (ii) vertical acquisitions are common.

**2** What are the wider competitive implications of acquisitions in an industry sector for which this form of consolidation is common?

Sometimes, firms fail to create value through a related acquisition. This is the case for FAO Schwarz's recent acquisition of Best Co., a fashion-oriented children's clothing company. The economic downturn that started in 2007 made it extremely difficult for FAO Schwarz to generate the type of operational synergies it expected to accrue through this related acquisition. Indeed, acquiring Best Co. weakened FAO, making it a target for Toys "Я" Us as a horizontal acquisition.

Horizontal, vertical and related acquisitions that firms complete to increase their market power are subject to regulatory review as well as to analysis by financial markets.[28] For example, Procter & Gamble (P&G) completed a horizontal acquisition of Gillette Co. in 2006. In announcing the transaction, P&G noted that integrating Gillette into P&G's operations would result in between €790 million and €940 million in annual cost synergies and a 1 per cent incremental annual sales growth from revenue synergies for the first three years following the acquisition. However, before being finalized, this acquisition was subjected to a significant amount of government scrutiny as well as close examination by financial analysts. Ultimately, P&G had to sell off several businesses to gain the Federal Trade Commission's approval to acquire Gillette.[29] Thus, firms seeking growth and market power through acquisitions must understand the political/legal segment of the general environment (see Chapter 2) to successfully use an acquisition strategy.

## Overcoming entry barriers

*Barriers to entry* (introduced in Chapter 2) are factors associated with a market or with the firms currently operating in it that increase the expense and difficulty new firms encounter when trying to enter that particular market. For example, well-established competitors may have economies of scale in the manufacture or service of their products. In addition, enduring relationships with customers often create product loyalties that are difficult for new entrants to overcome. When facing differentiated products, new entrants typically must spend considerable resources to advertise their products and may find it necessary to sell at prices below competitors' to entice new customers.

Facing the entry barriers that economies of scale and differentiated products create, a new entrant may find acquiring an established company to be more effective than entering the market as a competitor offering a product that is unfamiliar to current buyers. In fact, the higher are entry barriers, the greater is the probability that a firm will acquire an existing firm to overcome them.

As this discussion suggests, a key advantage of using an acquisition strategy to overcome entry barriers is that the acquiring firm gains immediate access to a market. This advantage can be particularly attractive for firms seeking to overcome entry barriers associated with entering international markets.[30] Large multinational corporations from developed economies seek to enter emerging economies such as Brazil, Russia, India and China (BRIC) because they are among the fastest-growing economies in the current competitive landscape.[31] As we discuss next, completing a cross-border acquisition of a local target allows a firm to quickly enter fast-growing economies such as the BRIC economies.

**Cross-border acquisitions** Acquisitions made between companies with headquarters in different countries are called cross-border acquisitions.[32] The purchase of UK carmakers Jaguar and Land Rover by India's Tata Motors is an example of a cross-border acquisition. We discuss this acquisition further later in this chapter.

We noted in the Opening Case that global M&A activity declined in the recent global financial crisis. The declines continued throughout the first half of 2009 largely because "... shrinking economies, volatile markets and scarce debt hammered corporate confidence".[33] This decline was in stark contrast to the significant increase in cross-border M&A activity that occurred during the 1990s. Nonetheless, as explained in the Opening Case, cross-border acquisitions remain popular as a viable path to firm growth and strategic competitiveness.

There are other interesting changes taking place in terms of cross-border acquisition activity. Historically, North American and European companies were the most active acquirers of companies outside their domestic market. However, the current global competitive landscape is one in which firms from other nations may use an acquisition strategy more frequently than do their counterparts in North America and Europe. In this regard, some believe that "... the next wave of cross-border M&A may be led out of Asia. Chinese companies, in particular, are well-positioned for cross-border acquisitions. Relative to their overseas peers, Chinese corporates are well-capitalized with strong balance sheets and cash reserves."[34] In the Strategic Focus, we describe recent cross-border acquisitions some Chinese companies have completed or are evaluating. As you will see, the acquisitions we discuss involve natural resource companies and many are horizontal acquisitions through which the acquiring companies seek to increase their market power.

Firms headquartered in India are also completing more cross-border acquisitions than has been the case historically. The weakening US dollar and more favourable government policies toward cross-border acquisitions are supporting Indian companies' desire to rapidly become "global powerhouses".[35] In addition to rapid market entry, Indian companies typically seek access to product innovation capabilities and new brands and distribution channels when acquiring firms outside their domestic market.

Firms using an acquisition strategy to complete cross-border acquisitions should understand that these transactions are not risk free. For example, firms seeking to acquire companies in China must recognize that "... China remains a challenging environment for foreign investors. Cultural, regulatory, due diligence and legal obstacles make acquisitions in China risky and difficult."[36] Thus, firms must carefully study the risks as well as the potential benefits when contemplating cross-border acquisitions.

> **Cross-border acquisitions**
>
> Acquisitions made between companies with headquarters in different countries are called cross-border acquisitions.

## Cost of new product development and increased speed to market

Developing new products internally and successfully introducing them into the marketplace often requires significant investment of a firm's resources, including time,

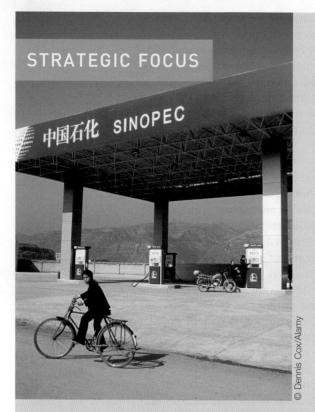

STRATEGIC FOCUS

中国石化 SINOPEC

© Dennis Cox/Alamy

# The increasing use of acquisition strategies by Chinese firms as a means of gaining market power in a particular industry

Taking advantage of depressed prices primarily for oil and gas assets and through the access to credit in their home country, recent activity suggests that Chinese stated-owned firms are using acquisitions as the path to securing "the resources needed to power China's growing economy" and to secure access to energy in future years. The belief that the recent global financial crisis has created an "unmatched buying opportunity" is also driving the Chinese firms' decision to acquire companies to gain access to their assets and to increase their market power as a result of doing so.

The pace of the Chinese firms' cross-border acquisitions was quickening as of mid-2009. By the end of June 2009, Chinese companies had completed 10 transactions in the oil and gas space. In contrast, these firms completed only 14 transactions in this space in 2008. Moreover, if outstanding bids were

accepted by target companies, the amount Chinese firms were spending on acquisitions would be 80 per cent greater than the amount spent previously on a year-to-year basis. Thomson Reuters data also indicate that in May 2010, Chinese overseas acquisitions have reached over €22 billion for the year, €4.5 billion higher than in the same period the year before; this is now the highest Chinese acquisition level since the data were first released.

Completed in mid-2009, state-owned Sinopec Group's acquisition of oil-exploration company Addax Petroleum Corp. for approximately €6.7 billion was at the time the largest cross-border acquisition by a Chinese company. Calling the acquisition a "transformational transaction" that would accelerate its international growth, Sinopec paid a 16 per cent premium for Addax. Based in Switzerland and listed in London and Toronto, Addax is one of the world's largest independent oil producers in West Africa and the Middle East on the basis of volume. Around the same time, CNOCC, China's top offshore oil and gas producer hired Goldman Sachs to advise it on bidding to acquire a stake in Kosmos Energy, an Africa-focused oil and gas exploration company. CNOCC hired an investment advisory firm in anticipation of a bidding war breaking out for Kosmos, largely because of the attractiveness of the firm's assets.

Analysts studying these acquisitions and others that are likely to be completed conclude that Chinese energy companies are becoming more confident in their ability to create value and gain market power through acquisitions. Business writers describe this confidence as follows: "... deals like the Addax acquisition show (that) they are gradually growing into international oil companies, capable of striking high-profile, cross-border deals. They are even expanding into countries, such as Syria, deemed too risky by Western oil companies."

But not all of the cross-border acquisitions attempted by Chinese companies have been successful. For example, Anglo-American mining giant Rio Tinto Ltd rejected Aluminium Corp. of China's (Chinalco) €15.4 billion bid to buy 18 per cent of the company. Rio was attractive to Chinalco in that at the time, it was the world's third largest miner and owner of rich iron-ore and copper mines in locations throughout the world, including major facilities in Australia. This acquisition would have given Cinalco a direct stake in mining assets – assets that are important to China's growth. In particular, iron ore is a crucial ingredient for China's steelmaking operations. Although disappointing, the rejection by Rio Tinto was not expected to slow China's commitment to allow its state-owned companies to pursue cross-border acquisitions as a means of improving their competitiveness in the global economy and as a means of gaining ownership of natural resources the nation believes are vital to its long-term growth.

**Sources**: 2009 "Is China Inc. overpaying in its merger deals?" *Wall Street Journal Online*, http://www.wsj.com, June 25; Carew, R. (2009) "Chinalco acts to preserve its stake in Rio Tinto", *Wall Street Journal Online*, http://www.wsj.com, July 1; Chazan, G. and Oster, S. (2009) "Sinopec pact for Addax boosts China's buying binge", *Wall Street Journal Online*, http://www.wsj.com, June 25; Fry, E. (2009) "Chinalco buys $1.5bn Rio Tinto shares" *Financial Times Online*, http://www.ft.com, July 2; Maxwell, K. (2009) "Shinsei and Aozora still talking", *Wall Street Journal Online*, http://www.wsj.com, June 26; Tucker, S. (2009) "CNOOC considers Kosmos stake bid", *Financial Times Online*, http://www.ft.com, June 20; 2010 "Chinese acquisitions may reach record high", http://www.english.peopledaily.com.cn, May 26.

### Questions

1 It has been argued that as new industrialized countries acquire firms overseas, they in turn need to learn a great deal about international product quality and product variety. For example: "Although China has been the largest producer of crude steel since 1996, China's steel firms have produced an overabundance of low-quality steel while domestic purchasers of steel have increasingly demanded higher quality steel products. Many have argued that for Chinese steel firms to improve product quality they must adopt more advanced technologies."[37] Based against these phenomena, describe the motives that Chinese firms have in acquiring overseas firms.

2 Perform some independent research of newspaper articles to determine how successful Chinese firms have been in managing their newly acquired overseas firms.

making it difficult to quickly earn a profitable return.[38] Because an estimated 88 per cent of innovations fail to achieve adequate returns, firm managers are also concerned with achieving adequate returns from the capital invested to develop and commercialize new products. Potentially contributing to these less-than-desirable rates of return is the successful imitation of approximately 60 per cent of innovations within four years after the patents are obtained. These types of outcomes may lead managers to perceive internal product development as a high-risk activity.[39]

Acquisitions are another means a firm can use to gain access to new products and to current products that are new to the firm. Compared with internal product development processes acquisitions provide more predictable returns as well as faster market entry. Returns are more predictable because the performance of the acquired firm's products can be assessed prior to completing the acquisition.[40]

Recently, AOL acquired two online media companies, Patch Media Corp. and Going Inc. AOL acquired these firms to move more rapidly into the relatively fast-growing local online and advertising market. Patch operates websites to help local communities publish news and information while Going makes it possible for users to share information about local events. Access to these new products and services supports AOL's other products in the local online and advertising market space such as MapQuest and social networking site Bebo.[41]

Because of the cost of new product development, a number of pharmaceutical firms use an acquisition strategy to enter markets quickly, and to increase the predictability of returns on their investments. To expand on these points, we discuss Pfizer's recently announced horizontal acquisition of Wyeth in the Strategic Focus.

## Lower risk compared to developing new products

Because the outcomes of an acquisition can be estimated more easily and accurately than the outcomes of an internal product development process, managers may view

© Adrian brockwell

## STRATEGIC FOCUS

# Pfizer's acquisition of Wyeth: will this acquisition be successful?

Pharmaceutical companies allocate significant amounts of money to research and development (R&D) in efforts to successfully develop new drugs. Pfizer Inc. for example, spends 15 per cent of its sales revenue on R&D. As is the case for most, if not all, of its major competitors, Pfizer is committed to upholding the highest ethical standards when engaging in R&D. According to Pfizer, the firm is "… committed to the safety of patients who take part in our trials and upholds the highest ethical standards in all of (its) research initiatives".

An issue associated with R&D allocations is that the outcomes from these expenditures are anything other than certain. In the words of a scholar who studies innovation: "R&D dollars by definition lead to uncertain outcome". Because of the high levels of uncertainty associated with efforts to develop products internally, a number of pharmaceutical companies use acquisitions to gain access to new products and to a target firm's capabilities. And, in the current

time period, some believe that the acquisitions taking place among these firms are "… reconfiguring the entire pharmaceutical sector".

Announced in early 2009, Pfizer's horizontal acquisition of Wyeth for roughly €53.5 billion was the largest transaction in the pharmaceutical industry in almost a decade. The purchase price meant that Pfizer would pay a premium of approximately 29 per cent to acquire Wyeth. As a horizontal acquisition, this price suggested that Pfizer felt that the transaction would result in cost and revenue synergies that at least equalled the amount of the premium it was willing to pay.

Why did Pfizer conclude that this acquisition was in the best of interests for its stakeholders including its shareholders? A key reason was that Wyeth had been investing heavily in biotechnology and vaccines for about three decades. In fact, Wyeth had become the third largest biotechnology company behind Amgen Inc. and Genentech Inc. Pfizer wanted to gain access to the new products that might flow from Wyeth's biotechnology-oriented R&D investments. Equally important is the contribution Wyeth would make to Pfizer's sales revenue – revenue that was expected to decline significantly after November 2011 when its hugely successful Lipitor drug (a drug for patients to control high cholesterol) is scheduled to come off patent. The impact of generic drugs being produced to compete against Lipitor was potentially huge for Pfizer in that this drug alone generates about 25 per cent of the firm's total revenue.

Analysts' reaction to this acquisition was mixed to negative. Some said that the core problem is that although Wyeth's sales revenue would help Pfizer replace the revenue it will lose after Lipitor goes off patent, it does not deal with the fact that Pfizer is struggling to develop new products in-house. One analyst said that "Pfizer is spending €5.9 billion a year in research and producing almost nothing and now it has to buy Wyeth. If its pipeline were producing it wouldn't need to buy Wyeth."

Evidence suggests that acquisitions in the pharmaceutical industry do tend to generate cost savings through operational synergies. Accordingly, Pfizer's acquisition of Wyeth may achieve one of the benefits of a horizontal acquisition. Simultaneously though, Pfizer seeks to rely on Wyeth's capabilities in the biotechnology space to develop new products that the newly-formed firm can quickly introduce to the market. With the acquisition completed on 15 October 2009 time will tell whether these goals will be realized.

**Sources**: 2009 "Pfizer's acquisition of Wyeth bring scale but will fail to deliver sustainable growth", *Trading Markets.com*, http://www.tradingmarkets.com, January 28; Arnst, C. (2009) "The drug mergers' harsh side effects" *BusinessWeek Online*, http://www.businessweek.com, March 12; Jana, R. (2009) "Do ideas cost too much?", *BusinessWeek*, April 20, 46–58; Jannarone, J. (2009) "Pfizer treatment is no cure", *Wall Street Journal Online*, http://www.wsj.com, January 24; Pettyprice, S., Randall, T. and Mider, Z. (2009) "Pfizer's $68 billion Wyeth deal eases Lipitor loss" *Bloomberg.com*, http://www.bloomberg.com, January 26; 2010 "Wyeth transaction", http://www.pfizer.com/investors, July 27.

*Questions*

**1** Explain the Pfizer's R&D rationale for this acquisition. To what extent will this rationale be realized longer term?

**2** What external influences do you believe will affect the success of Pfizer's acquisition of Wyeth?

acquisitions as being less risky.[42] However, firms should exercise caution when using acquisitions to reduce their risks relative to the risks the firm incurs when developing new products internally. Indeed, even though research suggests acquisition strategies are a common means of avoiding risky internal ventures (and therefore risky R&D investments) acquisitions may also become a substitute for innovation. Accordingly, acquisitions should always be strategic rather than defensive in nature. Thus, Pfizer's acquisition of Wyeth should be driven by strategic factors (e.g., cost and revenue synergies) instead of by defensive reasons (e.g., to gain sales revenue in the short term that will compensate for the revenue that will be lost when Lipitor goes off patent). Moreover, Pfizer should not reduce its emphasis on increasing the productivity from its R&D expenditures as a result of acquiring Wyeth.

## Increased diversification

Acquisitions are also used to diversify firms. Based on experience and the insights resulting from it, firms typically find it easier to develop and introduce new products in markets they are currently serving. In contrast, it is difficult for companies to develop products that differ from their current lines for markets in which they lack experience.[43] Thus, it is relatively uncommon for a firm to develop new products internally to diversify its product lines.[44]

Cisco Systems is an example of a firm that uses acquisitions to become more diversified. Historically, these acquisitions have helped the firm build its network components business that is focused on producing hardware. More recently however, Cisco purchased IronPort Systems Inc., a company focused on producing security software for networks. This acquisition will help Cisco diversify its operations beyond its original expertise in network hardware and basic software. Cisco previously acquired technology in the security area through its purchase of Riverhead Networks Inc., Protego Networks Inc. and Perfigo Inc. However, the IronPort deal provides software service in networks that can help guard against spam and viruses that travel through e-mail and Web-based traffic.[45] In 2009, Cisco IronPort announced its "... new managed, hosted and hybrid hosted e-mail security systems that provide the industry's most versatile set of e-mail protection offerings".[46] Thus, the IronPort acquisition seems to be successful in terms of helping Cisco diversify its operations in ways that create value.

Acquisition strategies can be used to support use of both unrelated diversification and related diversification strategies (see Chapter 7).[47] For example, United Technologies Corp. (UTC) uses acquisitions as the foundation for implementing its unrelated diversification strategy. Since the mid-1970s it has been building a portfolio of stable and noncyclical businesses including Otis (elevators and escalators and moving walkways) and Carrier (heating and air conditioning systems) in order to reduce its dependence on the volatile aerospace industry. Pratt & Whitney (aircraft engines), Hamilton Sundstrand (aerospace and industrial systems), Sikorsky (helicopters), UTC Fire & Security (fire safety and security products and services) and UTC Power (fuel cells and power systems) are the other businesses in which UTC competes as a result of using its acquisition strategy. While each business UTC acquires manufactures industrial and/or commercial products, many have a relatively low focus on technology (e.g., elevators, air conditioners and security systems).[48] In contrast to UTC, Procter & Gamble (P&G) uses acquisitions to implement its related diversification strategy. Beauty, Health & Well-Being and Household Care are P&G's core business segments. Gillette's products are included in the Beauty segment where they are related to other products in this segment such as cosmetics, hair care and skin care. As noted earlier in the chapter, P&G completed a horizontal acquisition of Gillette in 2006.

Firms using acquisition strategies should be aware that in general, the more related the acquired firm is to the acquiring firm, the greater is the probability the acquisition will be successful.[49] Thus, horizontal acquisitions and related acquisitions tend to contribute more to the firm's strategic competitiveness than do acquisitions of companies operating in product markets that are quite different from those in which the acquiring firm competes.[50]

## Reshaping the firm's competitive scope

In Chapter 2 we noted that the intensity of competitive rivalry is an industry characteristic that affects the firm's profitability.[51] To reduce the negative effect of an intense rivalry on their financial performance, firms may use an acquisition strategy to lessen their dependence on one or more products or markets. Reducing a company's dependence on specific markets shapes the firm's competitive scope.

Each time UTC enters a new business (such as UTC Power, the firm's latest business segment) for example, the corporation reshapes its competitive scope. In a more subtle manner, P&G's acquisition of Gillette reshaped its competitive scope by giving P&G a stronger presence in some products for whom men are the target market. By merging their operations, Towers Perrin and Watson Wyatt reshaped the scope of their formerly independent firms' operations in that Towers was stronger in healthcare consulting while Watson Wyatt was stronger in pension consulting. Using an acquisition strategy reshaped the competitive scope of each of these firms.

## Learning and developing new capabilities

Firms sometimes complete acquisitions to gain access to capabilities they lack. For example, acquisitions may be used to acquire a special technological capability. Supporting the decision to use acquisitions for this purpose are research results suggesting that gaining access to new capabilities helps a firm broaden its knowledge base as a means of remaining flexible in ways that allow it to effectively deal with rapidly changing situations.[52] For example, research suggests that firms increase the potential of their capabilities when they acquire diverse talent through cross-border acquisitions.[53] Firms are better able to learn these capabilities if they share some similar properties with the firm's current capabilities. Thus, firms should seek to acquire companies with different but related and complementary capabilities in order to build their own knowledge base.[54]

A number of large pharmaceutical firms are acquiring the ability to create "large molecule" drugs, also known as biological drugs, by buying bio-technology firms. These firms are seeking access to both the pipeline of possible drugs and the capabilities that these firms have to produce them. Such capabilities are important for

## KEY DEBATE

# To ally or acquire?

The decision whether or not to ally with another company, or consider it as a target for acquisition, are two alternative strategies. Historically, the waves of alliances and acquisitions appear not to be simultaneous activities. As firms consider their expansion options, invariably alliances and acquisitions become a key vehicle to achieve their growth ambitions. Against this backdrop are the all-too-familiar failure rates of both alliances and acquisitions. Typically, for acquisitions, they either destroy value or do not create the anticipated shareholder value, while alliances commonly create very little return for shareholders. Despite the wealth of knowledge that has been generated on managing alliances and acquisitions, these insights do not appear to have mapped on to the performance outcomes of the strategies for firms. Both are considered largely synonymous by executives, consultants and analysts but it remains that these are distinct avenues for growth. Each presents the firm with unique challenges and opportunities and managing a coherent strategy for alliances or acquisition is critical. Research evidence exists to identify many alliances that should probably have been acquisition targets while apparently successful acquisitions would have achieved far better outcomes on an alliance foundation.

The fundamental distinction between alliances and acquisitions is that the latter typically tends to be based on an aggressive competitive position, is founded on the market price and often tends to be extremely risky. For the former, alliances are significantly different and tend to be more open and collaborative in form where cooperation and negotiation are key to their functioning, and risk is often managed appropriately between the partners. It has been suggested by Dyer, Kale and Singh (2004) that there are three premises upon which to determine whether a firm should ally or acquire potential partners and targets respectively. The first concerns the resources and synergies available. There are three types of synergies that can be created when two firms work together and these are: (1) modular synergies; (2) sequential synergies; and, (3) reciprocal synergies.

Modular synergies are the most basic form and they combine the sum of the independent parts to create a combined pool of resources which can lead to greater opportunities. Sequential synergies occur when one firm delivers its tasks and responsibilities and then passes these on so that the partner can add further value and so the synergy is created following a sequential chain of activities. Reciprocal synergies arise when activities are iterative in type and so this forms the basis of multiple sequences which work back and forth between partners. Depending upon the resources available to firms and the types of synergies they seek to create, options ranging from acquisitions through to equity alliances or contractual alliances may be desirable.

The second issue that distinguishes between whether alliances or acquisitions are desirable is the marketplace in which firms compete. Primarily, uncertainty is a key factor here and is said to exist when it is not possible for firms to evaluate or judge future payoffs. Therefore, in order to determine the extent to which an alliance or acquisition is desirable, relevant frameworks need to be established to judge the nature of uncertainty and its sources. In addition, the forces of competition need to be evaluated closely so as to understand the dynamics at play at one point in time as well as their underlying drivers. The final consideration in determining whether an alliance or acquisition strategy is desirable is to evaluate the potential capabilities that underpin a firm's ability to develop and sustain an alliance or evaluate and execute an acquisition. Often firms stick to what they know and future behaviours tend to become programmed based on past behaviours. However, this does not always lead to successful outcomes despite the allure of remaining consistent. In many cases, each alliance or acquisition should be considered independently and the corresponding resources, capabilities and skillsets should be evaluated specific to each strategy.

The decision on whether to buy another company or build an alliance remains a key dilemma for firms. Finding the right strategic pathway towards these expansion opportunities is fraught with problems and challenges at every stage of the process. Recent research by Capron and Mitchell (2010) suggests that a wide portfolio of options should be pursued as firms develop their expansion strategies. Whichever option firms choose, be it internal organic development, mergers and acquisitions, or alliances, firms need to consider the mode of growth which is specific to their point of development. They develop a series of questions to consider in seeking to evaluate which of these three growth options is best as a means to acquiring new resources to develop the business further.

**Sources:** Dyer, J. H., Kale, P. and Singh, H. (2004) "When to ally and when to acquire", *Harvard Business Review*, 82 (7/8): 109–115; Capron, L. and Mitchell, W. (2010) "Finding the right path", *Harvard Business Review*, 88 (7/8): 103–107; Nollop, B. (2007), "Rules to acquire by", *Harvard Business Review*, 85 (9): 129–139.

### Questions

**1** What specific advantages and disadvantages can a firm anticipate from pursuing either an alliance strategy or an acquisition strategy?

**2** What advice would you offer a firm in seeking to make trade-offs between alliances and acquisitions and what main recommendations or frameworks would you offer to assist in making this strategic decision?

large pharmaceutical firms because these biological drugs are more difficult to duplicate by chemistry alone (the historical basis on which most pharmaceutical firms have expertise). These capabilities will allow generic drug makers to be more successful after chemistry-based drug patents expire. To illustrate the difference between these types of drugs, David Brennen, CEO of British drug maker AstraZeneca, suggested, "Some of these [biological-based drugs] have demonstrated that they're not just symptomatic treatments but that they actually alter the course of the disease."[55] Furthermore, biological drugs must clear more regulatory barriers or hurdles which, when accomplished, add more to the advantage the acquiring firm develops through successful acquisitions.

## Problems in achieving acquisition success

Acquisition strategies based on the reasons we have discussed have the potential to facilitate a firm's efforts to achieve strategic competitiveness and earn above-average returns. However, even when pursued for value-creating reasons, acquisition strategies are not problem-free. We show both the reasons for using an acquisition strategy and potential problems associated with using such a strategy in Figure 8.1.

Research suggests that perhaps 20 per cent of all mergers and acquisitions are successful, approximately 60 per cent produce disappointing results and the remaining 20 per cent are clear failures.[56] In general though, companies appear to be increasing their ability to effectively use acquisition strategies. An investment banker representing acquisition clients describes this improvement in the following manner: "I've been doing this work for 20-odd years and I can tell you that the sophistication of companies going through transactions has increased exponentially."[57] Greater acquisition success accrues to firms able to (1) select the "right" target, (2) avoid paying too high a premium (doing appropriate due diligence) and (3) effectively integrate the operations of the acquiring and target firms.[58] Additionally, retaining the target firm's human capital is foundational to efforts by employees of the acquiring firm to fully understand the target firm's operations and the capabilities on which those operations are based.[59] Next, we discuss the problems (see Figure 8.1) that may affect acquisition success.

### Integration difficulties

The importance of a successful integration should not be underestimated.[60] As suggested by a researcher studying the process, "Managerial practice and academic

**FIGURE 8.1** Reasons for acquisitions and problems in achieving success

Reasons for Acquisitions

- Increased market power
- Overcoming entry barriers
- Cost of new product development and increased speed to market
- Lower risk compared to developing new products
- Increased diversification
- Reshaping the firm's competitive scope
- Learning and developing new capabilities

Problems in Achieving Success

- Integration difficulties
- Inadequate evaluation of target
- Large or extraordinary debt
- Inability to achieve synergy
- Too much diversification
- Managers overly focused on acquisitions
- Too large

writings show that the post-acquisition integration phase is probably the single most important determinant of shareholder value creation (and equally of value destruction) in mergers and acquisitions."[61]

Although critical to acquisition success, firms should recognize that integrating two companies following an acquisition can be quite difficult. Melding two corporate cultures with differences, linking different financial and control systems, building effective working relationships (particularly when management styles differ), and resolving problems regarding the status of the newly acquired firm's executives are examples of integration challenges firms often face.[62]

Integration is complex and involves a large number of activities, which if overlooked can lead to significant difficulties. For example, when United Parcel Service

(UPS) acquired Mail Boxes Etc., a large retail shipping chain, it appeared to be a complementary merger that would provide benefits to both firms. The problem is that most of the Mail Boxes Etc. outlets were owned by franchisees. Once the merger took place the franchisees lost the ability to deal with other shipping companies such as FedEx, which reduced their competitiveness. Furthermore, franchisees complained that UPS often built company-owned shipping stores close by franchisee outlets of Mail Boxes Etc. Additionally, a culture clash evolved between the free-wheeling entrepreneurs who owned the franchises of Mail Boxes Etc. and the efficiency-oriented corporate approach of the UPS operation, which focused on managing a large fleet of trucks and an information system to efficiently pick up and deliver packages. Also, Mail Boxes Etc. was focused on retail traffic, whereas UPS was focused more on the logistics of wholesale pickup and delivery. Although 87 per cent of Mail Boxes Etc. franchisees decided to rebrand under the UPS name, many formed an owner's group and even filed suit against UPS in regard to the unfavourable nature of the franchisee contract.[63]

## Inadequate evaluation of target

**Due diligence** is a process through which a potential acquirer evaluates a target firm for acquisition. In an effective due-diligence process, hundreds of items are examined in areas as diverse as the financing for the intended transaction, differences in cultures between the acquiring and target firm, tax consequences of the transaction and actions that would be necessary to successfully meld the two workforces. Due diligence is commonly performed by investment bankers such as Deutsche Bank, Goldman Sachs and Morgan Stanley, accountants, lawyers and management consultants specializing in that activity, although firms actively pursuing acquisitions may form their own internal due-diligence team.[64]

Failing to complete an effective due-diligence process may easily result in the acquiring firm paying an excessive premium for the target company. Interestingly, research shows that in times of high or increasing stock prices due diligence is relaxed; firms often overpay during these periods and long-term performance of the newly-formed firm suffers.[65] Research also shows that without due diligence, "the purchase price is driven by the pricing of other 'comparable' acquisitions rather than by a rigorous assessment of where, when and how management can drive real performance gains. [In these cases], the price paid may have little to do with achievable value."[66] Additionally, firms sometimes allow themselves to enter a "bidding war" for a target, even though they realize that their current bids exceed the parameters identified through due diligence. Earlier, we mentioned NetApp's bid for Data Domain that represents a 419 per cent premium. Commenting about this, an analyst said that "... NetApp wouldn't be the first company to stay in a bidding war even when discretion was the better part of valour."[67] Rather than enter a bidding war, firms should extend only bids that are consistent with the results of their due diligence process.

## Large or extraordinary debt

To finance a number of acquisitions completed during the 1980s and 1990s, some companies significantly increased their levels of debt. A financial innovation called junk bonds helped make this possible. *Junk bonds* are a financing option through which risky acquisitions are financed with money (debt) that provides a large potential return to lenders (bondholders). Because junk bonds are unsecured obligations that are not tied to specific assets for collateral, interest rates for these high-risk debt instruments sometimes reached between 18 and 20 per cent during

---

**Due diligence**

Due diligence is a process through which a potential acquirer evaluates a target firm for acquisition.

the 1980s.[68] Some prominent financial economists viewed debt as a means to discipline managers, causing them to act in the shareholders' best interests.[69] Managers holding this view are less concerned about the amount of debt their firm assumes when acquiring other companies.

Junk bonds are now used less frequently to finance acquisitions, and the conviction that debt disciplines managers is less strong. Nonetheless, firms sometimes still take on what turns out to be too much debt when acquiring companies. This may be the case for Tata Motors. Some analysts describe Tata's problems with debt this way: "Tata Motors' troubles began last year when it paid €1.8 billion for Jaguar and Land Rover and borrowed €2.4 billion to finance the transaction and provide additional working capital."[70] Because of this, some felt that the firm was becoming less capable of providing the capital its various units required to remain competitive.

High debt can have several negative effects on the firm. For example, because high debt increases the likelihood of bankruptcy, it can lead to a downgrade in the firm's credit rating by agencies such as Moody's and Standard & Poor's.[71] In other instances, a firm may have to divest some assets to relieve its debt burden. South Korea's Kimho Asiana Group's decision to divest its Daewoo Engineering & Construction Co. may be an example of this in that the firm's liquidity was being questioned after acquiring both Daewoo and Korea Express within a short time period.[72] Firms using an acquisition strategy must be certain that their purchases do not create a debt load that overpowers the company's ability to remain solvent.

## Inability to achieve synergy

Derived from *synergos*, a Greek word that means "working together," *synergy* exists when the value created by units working together exceeds the value those units could create working independently (see Chapter 7). That is, synergy exists when assets are worth more when used in conjunction with each other than when they are used separately. For shareholders, synergy generates gains in their wealth that they could not duplicate or exceed through their own portfolio diversification decisions.[73] Synergy is created by the efficiencies derived from economies of scale and economies of scope and by sharing resources (e.g., human capital and knowledge) across the businesses in the merged firm.[74]

A firm develops a competitive advantage through an acquisition strategy only when a transaction generates private synergy. *Private synergy* is created when combining and integrating the acquiring and acquired firms' assets yields capabilities and core competencies that could not be developed by combining and integrating either firm's assets with another company. Private synergy is possible when firms' assets are complementary in unique ways; that is, the unique type of asset complementarity is not possible by combining either company's assets with another firm's assets.[75] Because of its uniqueness, private synergy is difficult for competitors to understand and imitate. However, private synergy is difficult to create.

A firm's ability to account for costs that are necessary to create anticipated revenue- and cost-based synergies affects its efforts to create private synergy. Firms experience several expenses when trying to create private synergy through acquisitions. Called transaction costs, these expenses are incurred when firms use acquisition strategies to create synergy.[76] Transaction costs may be direct or indirect. Direct costs include legal fees and charges from investment bankers who complete due diligence for the acquiring firm. Indirect costs include managerial time to evaluate target firms and then to complete negotiations, as well as the loss of key managers and employees following an acquisition.[77] Firms tend to underestimate the sum of indirect costs when the value of the synergy that may be created by combining and integrating the acquired firm's assets with the acquiring firm's assets is calculated.

## Too much diversification

As explained in Chapter 7, diversification strategies can lead to strategic competitiveness and above-average returns. In general, firms using related diversification strategies outperform those employing unrelated diversification strategies. However, conglomerates formed by using an unrelated diversification strategy also can be successful, as demonstrated by United Technologies Corp.

At some point, however, firms can become over-diversified. The level at which over-diversification occurs varies across companies because each firm has different capabilities to manage diversification. Recall from Chapter 7 that related diversification requires more information processing than does unrelated diversification. Because of this additional information processing, related diversified firms become over-diversified with a smaller number of business units than do firms using an unrelated diversification strategy.[78] Regardless of the type of diversification strategy implemented, however, over-diversification leads to a decline in performance, after which business units are often divested.[79] Commonly, such divestments, which tend to reshape a firm's competitive scope, are part of a firm's restructuring strategy. (We discuss the strategy in greater detail later in the chapter.)

Even when a firm is not over-diversified, a high level of diversification which may have been created partly by acquisitions can have a negative effect on its long-term performance. For example, the scope created by additional amounts of diversification often causes managers to rely on financial rather than strategic controls to evaluate business units' performance. Top-level executives often rely on financial controls to assess the performance of business units when they do not have a rich understanding of business units' objectives and strategies. Use of financial controls, such as return on investment (ROI), causes individual business-unit managers to focus on short-term outcomes at the expense of long-term investments. When long-term investments are reduced to increase short-term profits, a firm's overall strategic competitiveness may be harmed.[80]

Another problem resulting from too much diversification is the tendency for acquisitions to become substitutes for innovation. As we noted earlier, pharmaceutical firms such as Pfizer must be aware of this tendency as they acquire other firms to gain access to their products and capabilities. Typically, managers have no interest in acquisitions substituting for internal R&D efforts and the innovative outcomes that they can produce. However, a reinforcing cycle evolves. Costs associated with acquisitions may result in fewer allocations to activities, such as R&D, that are linked to innovation. Without adequate support, a firm's innovation skills begin to atrophy. Without internal innovation skills, the only option available to a firm to gain access to innovation is to complete still more acquisitions. Evidence suggests that a firm using acquisitions as a substitute for internal innovations eventually encounters performance problems.[81]

## Managers overly focused on acquisitions

Typically, a considerable amount of managerial time and energy is required for acquisitions strategies to be used successfully. Activities with which managers become involved include (1) searching for viable acquisition candidates, (2) completing effective due-diligence processes, (3) preparing for negotiations and (4) managing the integration process after completing the acquisition.

Top-level managers do not personally gather all of the data and information required to make acquisitions. However, these executives do make critical decisions on the firms to be targeted, the nature of the negotiations and so forth. Company experiences show that participating in and overseeing the activities required for making acquisitions can divert managerial attention from other matters that are necessary for long-term competitive success, such as identifying and taking advantage of other opportunities and interacting with important external stakeholders.[82]

Both theory and research suggest that managers can become overly involved in the process of making acquisitions.[83] One observer suggested, "Some executives can become preoccupied with making deals – and the thrill of selecting, chasing and seizing a target."[84] The over-involvement can be surmounted by learning from mistakes and by not having too much agreement in the board room. Dissent is helpful to make sure that all sides of a question are considered (see Chapter 11).[85] When failure does occur, leaders may be tempted to blame the failure on others and on unforeseen circumstances rather than on their excessive involvement in the acquisition process.

Actions taken at Liz Claiborne Inc. demonstrate the problem of being overly focused on acquisitions. Over time, Claiborne acquired a number of firms in sportswear apparel, growing from 16 to 36 brands in the process of doing so. However, while its managers were focused on making acquisitions, changes were taking place in the firm's external environment, including industry consolidation. Specifically, while most Claiborne sales were focused on traditional department stores, consolidations through acquisitions in this sector left less room for as many brands, given the purchasing habits of the large department stores. Additionally, competitors were gaining favour with customers leaving fewer sales for Claiborne's products. In response to these problems, CEO William McComb announced in July 2007 a "... framework of a new organizational structure that was a crucial step in making Liz Claiborne Inc. into a more brand-focused and cost-effective business that (could) successfully navigate a rapidly changing retail environment." As a result of these actions, Claiborne is less diversified in terms of brands and less focused on acquisitions. Today, the firm has three distinct brand segments – domestic-based direct brands, international-based direct brands and partnered brands.[86]

## Too large

Most acquisitions create a larger firm, which should help increase its economies of scale. These economies can then lead to more efficient operations – for example, two sales organizations can be integrated using fewer sales representatives because such sales personnel can sell the products of both firms (particularly if the products of the acquiring and target firms are highly related).[87]

Many firms seek increases in size because of the potential economies of scale and enhanced market power discussed earlier. At some level, the additional costs required to manage the larger firm will exceed the benefits of the economies of scale and additional market power. The complexities generated by the larger size often lead managers to implement more bureaucratic controls to manage the combined firm's operations. *Bureaucratic controls* are formalized supervisory and behavioural rules and policies designed to ensure consistency of decisions and actions across a firm's different units. However, through time, formalized controls often lead to relatively rigid and standardized managerial behaviour. Certainly, in the long run, the diminished flexibility that accompanies rigid and standardized managerial behaviour may produce less innovation. Because of innovation's importance to competitive success, the bureaucratic controls resulting from a large organization (i.e., built by acquisitions) can have a detrimental effect on performance. As one analyst noted, "Striving for size per se is not necessarily going to make a company more successful. In fact, a strategy in which acquisitions are undertaken as a substitute for organic growth has a bad track record in terms of adding value."[88]

## Effective acquisitions

Earlier in the chapter, we noted that acquisition strategies do not always create above-average returns for the acquiring firm's shareholders.[89] Nonetheless, some companies are able to create value when using an acquisition strategy.[90] The probability of success increases when the firm's actions are consistent with the "attributes of successful acquisitions' shown in Table 8.1.

Cisco Systems is an example of a firm that appears to pay close attention to Table 8.1's attributes when using its acquisition strategy. In fact, Cisco is admired for its ability to complete successful acquisitions. A number of other network companies pursued acquisitions to build up their ability to sell into the network equipment binge, but only Cisco retained much of its value in the post-bubble era. Many firms, such as Lucent, Nortel and Ericsson, teetered on the edge of bankruptcy after the dot.com bubble burst. When it makes an acquisition, "Cisco has gone much further in its thinking about integration. Not only is retention important, but Cisco also works to minimize the distractions caused by an acquisition. This is important, because the speed of change is so great, that even if the target firm's product development teams are distracted, they will be slowed, contributing to acquisition failure. So, integration must be rapid and reassuring."[91] Creating a link on its website called "Connection for Acquired Employees' is an example of what Cisco does to facilitate the transition for acquired employees to their new organizational home. The following words introduce readers to this material: "This website has been specifically designed for newly acquired employees and will provide up-to-date materials tailored to the specific integrations."[92]

Results from a research study shed light on the differences between unsuccessful and successful acquisition strategies and suggest that a pattern of actions improves

**Table 8.1** Attributes of successful acquisitions

| Attributes | Results |
|---|---|
| 1. Acquired firm has assets or resources that are complementary to the acquiring firm's core business | 1. High probability of synergy and competitive advantage by maintaining strengths |
| 2. Acquisition is friendly | 2. Faster and more effective integration and possibly lower premiums |
| 3. Acquiring firm conducts effective due diligence to select target firms and evaluate the target firm's health (financial, cultural, and human resources) | 3. Firms with strongest complementarities are acquired and overpayment is avoided |
| 4. Acquiring firm has financial slack (cash or a favourable debt position) | 4. Financing (debt or equity) is easier and less costly to obtain |
| 5. Merged firm maintains low to moderate debt position | 5. Lower financing cost, lower risk (e.g., of bankruptcy), and avoidance of trade-offs that are associated with high debt |
| 6. Acquiring firm has sustained and consistent emphasis on R&D and innovation | 6. Maintain long-term competitive advantage in markets |
| 7. Acquiring firm manages change well and is flexible and adaptable | 7. Faster and more effective integration facilitates achievement of synergy |

the probability of acquisition success.[93] The study shows that when the target firm's assets are complementary to the acquired firm's assets, an acquisition is more successful. With complementary assets, the integration of two firms' operations has a higher probability of creating synergy. In fact, integrating two firms with complementary assets frequently produces unique capabilities and core competencies. With complementary assets, the acquiring firm can maintain its focus on core businesses and leverage the complementary assets and capabilities from the acquired firm. In effective acquisitions, targets are often selected and "groomed" by establishing a working relationship prior to the acquisition.[94] As discussed in Chapter 10, strategic alliances are sometimes used to test the feasibility of a future merger or acquisition between the involved firms.[95]

The study's results also show that friendly acquisitions facilitate integration of the firms involved in an acquisition. Through friendly acquisitions, firms work together to find ways to integrate their operations to create synergy.[96] In hostile takeovers, animosity often results between the two top-management teams, a condition that in turn affects working relationships in the newly created firm. As a result, more key personnel in the acquired firm may be lost, and those who remain may resist the changes necessary to integrate the two firms.[97] With effort, cultural clashes can be overcome and fewer key managers and employees will become discouraged and leave.[98]

Additionally, effective due-diligence processes involving the deliberate and careful selection of target firms and an evaluation of the relative health of those firms (financial health, cultural fit and the value of human resources) contribute to successful acquisitions.[99] Financial slack in the form of debt equity or cash, in both the acquiring and acquired firms, also frequently contributes to acquisition success. Even though financial slack provides access to financing for the acquisition, it is still important to maintain a low or moderate level of debt after the acquisition to keep debt costs low. When substantial debt is used to finance the acquisition, companies with successful acquisitions reduce the debt quickly, partly by selling off assets from the acquired firm, especially non-complementary or poorly performing assets. For these firms, debt costs do not prevent long-term investments such as R&D and managerial discretion in the use of cash flow is relatively flexible.

Emphasizing innovation, as demonstrated by continuing allocations to R&D, is another attribute of successful acquisition. Significant R&D investments show a strong managerial commitment to innovation, a characteristic that is increasingly important to overall competitiveness in the global economy as well as to acquisition success.

Flexibility and adaptability are the final two attributes of successful acquisitions. When executives of both the acquiring and the target firms have experience in managing change and learning from acquisitions, they will be more skilled at adapting their capabilities to new environments.[100] As a result, they will be more adept at integrating the two organizations, which is particularly important when firms have different organizational cultures.

Firms use an acquisition strategy to grow and achieve strategic competitiveness, but sometimes the actual results of an acquisition strategy fall short of the projected results. When this happens, firms consider using restructuring strategies; we discuss these strategies next.

# Restructuring

Restructuring is a strategy through which a firm changes its set of businesses or its financial structure.[101] From the 1970s into the 2000s, divesting businesses from company portfolios and downsizing accounted for a large percentage of firms' restructuring strategies. Restructuring is a global phenomenon.[102] Commonly, firms

**Restructuring**
Restructuring is a strategy through which a firm changes its set of businesses or its financial structure.

focus on a reduced number of products and markets following restructuring. The words of an executive describe this typical outcome: "Focus on your core business, but don't be distracted, let other people buy assets that aren't right for you."[103]

Although restructuring strategies are generally used to deal with acquisitions that are not reaching expectations, firms sometimes use these strategies because of changes they have detected in their external environment. For example, opportunities sometimes surface in a firm's external environment that a diversified firm can pursue because of the capabilities it has formed by integrating firms' operations. In such cases, restructuring may be appropriate to position the firm to create more value for stakeholders, given the environmental changes.[104]

As discussed next, firms use three types of restructuring strategies: downsizing, downscoping and leveraged buyouts.

## Downsizing

**Downsizing** is a reduction in the number of a firm's employees and sometimes in the number of its operating units, but it may or may not change the composition of businesses in the company's portfolio. Thus, downsizing is an intentional proactive management strategy whereas "decline is an environmental or organizational phenomenon that occurs involuntarily and results in erosion of an organization's resource base".[105] Downsizing is often a part of acquisitions that fail to create the value anticipated when the transaction was completed; and, downsizing is almost certainly to be used when the acquiring firm paid too high of a premium to acquire the target firm.[106] Once thought to be an indicator of organizational decline, downsizing is now recognized as a legitimate restructuring strategy.

Reducing the number of employees and/or the firm's scope in terms of products produced and markets served occurs in firms to enhance the value being created as a result of completing an acquisition. When integrating the operations of the acquired firm and the acquiring firm, managers may not at first appropriately downsize. This is understandable in that "no one likes to lay people off or close facilities".[107] But, downsizing may be necessary in that acquisitions typically create a situation in which the newly-formed firm has duplicate organizational functions such as sales, manufacturing, distribution, human resource management and so forth. Failing to downsize appropriately may prevent the new firm from realizing the cost synergies it anticipated generating as a result of completing a horizontal acquisition, for example. In slightly different words, if too many employees are involved with duplicative work and work processes, the newly-formed firm will fail to create the full value that might be available as a result of cost and revenue synergies that were expected as part of completing the acquisition. Managers should remember that as a strategy, downsizing will be far more effective when they consistently use human resource practices that ensure procedural justice and fairness characterizes the firm's downsizing decisions.[108]

## Downscoping

**Downscoping** refers to divestiture, spin-off, or some other means of eliminating businesses that are unrelated to a firm's core businesses. Downscoping has a more positive effect on firm performance than does downsizing.[109] A key reason for this is that firms commonly find that downscoping causes them to refocus on their core business.[110] By refocusing on its core businesses, the firm can be managed more effectively by the top management team. Managerial effectiveness increases because the firm has become less diversified, allowing the top management team to better understand and manage the remaining businesses.[111]

**Downsizing**

Downsizing is a reduction in the number of a firm's employees and sometimes in the number of its operating units.

**Downscoping**

Downscoping refers to divestiture, spin-off, or some other means of eliminating businesses that are unrelated to a firm's core businesses.

Motorola Inc. is a firm that has struggled recently. With an interest of refocusing on "technologies that can grow its business' as one path to reversing the firm's fortunes, Motorola is divesting assets that are not related to its core businesses. The recent sale of its fibre-to-the-node product line to Communications Test Design Inc., an engineering, repair and logistics company, is an example of Motorola's use of a downscoping strategy.[112] In mid-2009, the McGraw-Hill Companies indicated that it was seeking a buyer for *Business Week* magazine. This magazine was one of the products in McGraw's Information and Media business unit (the firm has two other business units). As was the case with many other magazines during the global financial crisis, *Business Week* was being hurt by defections of readers and advertisers to the Internet as well as by the oversupply of business magazine titles.[113] Divesting *Business Week* would allow those leading McGraw's Information & Media unit to refocus on its other businesses such as J. D. Power and Associates and the Aviation Week Group. Previous to the announcement, McGraw had already divested most of its periodicals.[114]

Firms often use the downscoping and the downsizing strategies simultaneously. However, when doing this, firms avoid layoffs of key employees, in that such layoffs might lead to a loss of one or more core competencies. Instead, a firm that is simultaneously downscoping and downsizing becomes smaller by reducing the diversity of businesses in its portfolio.[115]

In general, US firms use downscoping as a restructuring strategy more frequently than do European companies; in fact, the trend in Europe, Latin America and Asia has been to build conglomerates. In Latin America, these conglomerates are called *grupos*. Many Asian and Latin American conglomerates are beginning to adopt Western corporate strategies in recent years and have been refocusing on their core businesses. This downscoping has occurred simultaneously with increasing globalization and with more open markets that have greatly enhanced competition. By downscoping, these firms have been able to focus on their core businesses and improve their competitiveness.[116]

## Leveraged buyouts

A *leveraged buyout* (LBO) is a restructuring strategy whereby a party (typically a private equity firm) buys all of a firm's assets in order to take the firm private. Once the transaction is completed, the company's stock is no longer traded publicly. Traditionally, leveraged buyouts were used as a restructuring strategy to correct for managerial mistakes or because the firm's managers were making decisions that primarily served their own interests rather than those of shareholders.[117] However, some firms use buyouts to build firm resources and expand rather than simply restructure distressed assets.[118]

Significant amounts of debt are commonly incurred to finance a buyout; hence, the term *leveraged* buyout. To support debt payments and to downscope the company to concentrate on the firm's core businesses, the new owners may immediately sell a number of assets.[119] It is not uncommon for those buying a firm through an LBO to restructure the firm to the point that it can be sold at a profit within a five- to eight-year period.

Management buyouts (MBOs), employee buyouts (EBOs) and whole-firm buyouts, in which one company or partnership purchases an entire company instead of a part of it, are the three types of LBOs. In part because of managerial incentives, MBOs, more so than EBOs and whole-firm buyouts, have been found to lead to downscoping, increased strategic focus and improved performance.[120] Research also shows that management buyouts can lead to greater entrepreneurial activity and growth.[121] As such, buyouts can represent a form of firm rebirth to facilitate entrepreneurial efforts and stimulate strategic growth.[122]

## Restructuring outcomes

The short- and long-term outcomes associated with the three restructuring strategies are shown in Figure 8.2. As indicated, downsizing typically does not lead to higher firm performance.[123] In fact, some research results show that downsizing contributes to lower returns for both US and Japanese firms. The stock markets in the firms' respective nations evaluated downsizing negatively, believing that it would have long-term negative effects on the firm's efforts to achieve strategic competitiveness. Investors also appear to conclude that downsizing occurs as a consequence of other problems in a company.[124] This assumption may be caused by a firm's diminished corporate reputation when a major downsizing is announced.[125]

The loss of human capital is another potential problem of downsizing (see Figure 8.2). Losing employees with many years of experience with the firm represents a major loss of knowledge. As noted in Chapter 3, knowledge is vital to competitive success in the global economy. Thus, research evidence and corporate experience suggest that downsizing may be of more tactical (or short-term) value than strategic (or long-term) value,[126] meaning that firms should exercise caution when restructuring through downsizing.

Downscoping generally leads to more positive outcomes in both the short- and the long-term than does downsizing or a leveraged buyout. Downscoping's desirable long-term outcome of higher performance is a product of reduced debt costs and the emphasis on strategic controls derived from concentrating on the firm's core businesses. In so doing, the refocused firm should be able to increase its ability to compete.[127]

Although whole-firm LBOs have been hailed as a significant innovation in the financial restructuring of firms, they can involve negative trade-offs.[128] First, the resulting large debt increases the financial risk of the firm, as is evidenced by the

**FIGURE 8.2** Restructuring outcomes

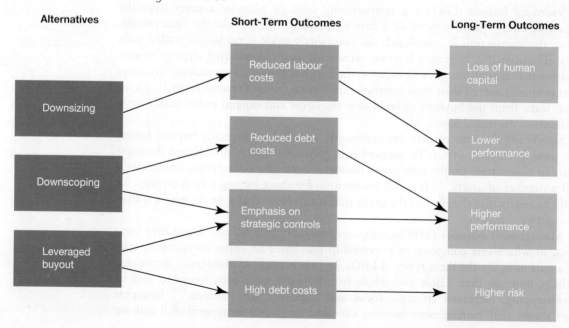

number of companies that filed for bankruptcy in the 1990s after executing a whole-firm LBO. Sometimes, the intent of the owners to increase the efficiency of the bought-out firm and then sell it within five to eight years creates a short-term and risk-averse managerial focus.[129]As a result, these firms may fail to invest adequately in R&D or take other major actions designed to maintain or improve the company's core competence.[130] Research also suggests that in firms with an entrepreneurial mindset, buyouts can lead to greater innovation, especially if the debt load is not too great.[131] However, because buyouts more often result in significant debt, most LBOs have been completed in mature industries where stable cash flows are possible.

## CLOSING CASE

© Caro/Alamy

## DaimlerChrysler is now Daimler AG – the failed merger with Chrysler Corporation

Daimler Benz acquired Chrysler in 1998 for €28.3 billion. In May 2007 DaimlerChrysler, the merged firm, sold the Chrysler business to a consortium of private equity investors led by Cerberus Capital Management LP for €5.8 billion. Through this deal, DaimlerChrysler changed its name to Daimler AG and retained only 20 per cent of the ownership of Chrysler

assets. Of the €5.8 billion provided by the private equity firm, €3.9 billion was put into the operations of Chrysler and approximately €790 million into Chrysler Financial Services with the rest going to pay miscellaneous expenses. Interestingly, DaimlerChrysler received only €1 billion, but Daimler was expected to pay Chrysler €1.3 billion before the deal closed to subsidize its negative cash flow. The bottom line is that Daimler did not get much out of its original €28.3 billion investment other than to unload €14 billion in pension and health care liabilities from its books. Many of the problems with the merger are derived from the labour and health care legacy cost differences, which have been estimated to be as high as €1180 per vehicle on average, compared to an estimated €197 per vehicle for foreign firms such as Toyota.

This deal failure is reminiscent of the failed acquisition of Rover by BMW. BMW ultimately sold the Rover assets for little in return except that BMW was able to unload debt off its books. The Rover assets were similarly acquired by private equity firms with additional investment from a Chinese firm, Nanjing Automobile, which wished to gain entry into more developed markets such as those in Europe and the United States.

The former Daimler CEO, Jurgen Scrempp, the mastermind behind the acquisition of Chrysler had likewise made acquisitions in Asia by acquiring a controlling interest in Japan's Mitsubishi Motors Corp. and with Korea's Hyundai Motors Corp. These investments also had problems, and Daimler divested the Mitsubishi assets in 2004 and likewise in the same year sold its 10 per cent stake in Hyundai because of significant losses after the recession of 2000.

In many private equity deals, such as the Chrysler deal in recent years, private equity firms buy up a large array of businesses across a wide variety of industries in automobiles, steel, natural resources and even electronics. (Philips Electronics recently sold pieces of its firm to private equity operations.)

The finance industry is able to facilitate the restructuring of these industrial assets due to the availability of debt, which is substituted for equity in publicly-traded firms.

The hope in Detroit among the other auto firms is that the financial experts associated with private equity firms will help the Big Three auto firms in the United States (GM, Ford and Chrysler), deal with their excessive cost structure associated with union pensions and health care costs, which make up the bulk of the cost differences between US and foreign firms. If they are not able to restructure the cost situation, the next step will be bankruptcy, the method used by many other firms in the airline and steel industries to restructure these costs. Private equity firms were also involved with these deals, especially after they came out of bankruptcy.

One potential opportunity for Chrysler is the area of financing auto and other purchases. Previous to the Chrysler deal, Cerberus purchased 51 per cent in the GMAC assets from General Motors Corporation. GMAC is the financing arm of General Motors. Similar to the Chrysler deal, Cerberus gains control of the Chrysler finance operation. In combination with the GMAC assets, once the financial unit activities are extracted from the operations of Chrysler, Cerberus hopes to develop a strong financing business, not only in financing automobiles but also potentially in financing opportunities such as mortgages. This move may lead them to a broader set of business-level financial offerings similar to the operation of GE Capital. The combined operations have nearly €11.3 billion of book value, whereas GE Capital has a book value at €42.6 billion. Compared to the automobile operations, the financing arms are already profitable even with the

problems that GMAC is having with its subprime home lending unit, Residential Capital Corp.

The Chrysler example represents many important aspects found throughout this chapter: the riskiness of acquisitions, the difficulty of integration, as well as what happens with failed acquisitions leading to divestiture and how private equity firms are involved in the process. Chrysler illustrates the potential for success as well as the risk of failure and how firms deal with exit when an acquisition strategy fails.

**Sources**: Fox, J. (2007) "Buying a used Chrysler", *Time*, May 28, 46; Gordon, J. S. (2007) "Back to the future, Detroit-style", *Barron's*, June 25, 45; Power, S. (2007) "After pact to shed Chrysler, Daimler turns focus to other challenges" *Wall Street Journal*, May 15, A14; Reed, J. (2007) "Nanjing Automobile begins UK production of MG cars" *Financial Times*, May 30, 20; Simon, B. (2007) "'New' Chrysler ready to party", *Financial Times*, July 5, 26; Taylor A., III, (2007) "America's best car company", *Fortune*, March 19, 98; Welch, D., Byrnes, N. and Bianco, A. (2007) "A deal that could save Detroit: A Chrysler sale to Cerberus may spark plan to eliminate most of the health care liabilities crushing carmakers" *BusinessWeek*, May 28, 30; White, B. (2007) "Chrysler's coy guardian: The Cerberus head has an onerous task turning round the carmaker", *Financial Times*, May 19, 9; Zuckerman, G., Ng, S. and Cimilluca, D. (2007) "Cerberus finds luster in Detroit", *Wall Street Journal*, May 15, C1-C2; Sloan, A. (2006) "A tough race for GM against Toyota", *Newsweek*, http://www.msnbc.msn.com, March 6.

## Questions

1 What were the core problems with the Daimler-Chrysler deal?

2 Could these problems have been anticipated and how might they have been overcome?

# SUMMARY

- Although the number of mergers and acquisitions completed in 2008 and early 2009 declined, largely because of the recent global financial crisis, merger and acquisition strategies remain popular as a path to firm growth and the earning of strategic competitiveness. Globalization and deregulation of multiple industries in many economies are two of the factors making mergers and acquisitions attractive to large corporations and small firms.

- Firms use acquisition strategies to (1) increase market power; (2) overcome entry barriers to new markets or regions; (3) avoid the costs of developing new products and increase the speed of new market entries; (4) reduce the risk of entering a new business; (5) become more diversified; (6) reshape their competitive scope by developing a different portfolio of businesses; and (7) enhance their learning as the foundation for developing new capabilities.

- Among the problems associated with using an acquisition strategy are (1) the difficulty of effectively integrating the firms involved; (2) incorrectly evaluating the target firm's value; (3) creating debt loads that preclude adequate long-term investments (e.g., R&D); (4) overestimating the potential for synergy; (5) creating a firm that is too diversified; (6) creating an internal environment in which managers devote increasing amounts of their time and energy to analysing and completing the acquisition; and (7) developing a combined firm that is too large, necessitating extensive use of bureaucratic, rather than strategic, controls.

- Effective acquisitions have the following characteristics: (1) the acquiring and target firms have complementary resources that are the foundation for developing new capabilities; (2) the acquisition is friendly, thereby facilitating integration of the firms' resources; (3) the target firm is selected and purchased based on thorough due diligence; (4) the acquiring and target firms have considerable slack in the form of cash or debt capacity; (5) the newly-formed firm maintains a low or moderate level of debt by selling off portions of the acquired firm or some of the acquiring firm's poorly performing units; (6) the acquiring and acquired firms have experience in terms of adapting to change; and (7) R&D and innovation are emphasized in the new firm.

- Restructuring is used to improve a firm's performance by correcting for problems created by ineffective management. Restructuring by downsizing involves reducing the number of employees and hierarchical levels in the firm. Although it can lead to short-term cost reductions, they may be realized at the expense of long-term success, because of the loss of valuable human resources (and knowledge) and overall corporate reputation.

- The goal of restructuring through downscoping is to reduce the firm's level of diversification. Often, the firm divests unrelated businesses to achieve this goal. Eliminating unrelated businesses makes it easier for the firm and its top-level managers to refocus on the core businesses.

- Through an LBO, a firm is purchased so that it can become a private entity. LBOs usually are financed largely through debt. The three types of LBOs are management buyouts (MBOs), employee buyouts (EBOs) and whole-firm LBOs. Because they provide clear managerial incentives, MBOs have been the most successful of the three. Often, the intent of a buyout is to improve efficiency and performance to the point where the firm can be sold successfully within five to eight years.

- Commonly, restructuring's primary goal is gaining or re-establishing effective strategic control of the firm. Of the three restructuring strategies, downscoping is aligned most closely with establishing and using strategic controls and usually improves performance more on a comparative basis.

## REVIEW QUESTIONS

1 Why are merger and acquisition strategies popular in many firms competing in the global economy?

2 What reasons account for firms' decisions to use acquisition strategies as a means to achieving strategic competitiveness?

3 What are the seven primary problems that affect a firm's efforts to successfully use an acquisition strategy?

4 What are the attributes associated with a successful acquisition strategy?

5 What is the restructuring strategy and what are its common forms?

6 What are the short- and long-term outcomes associated with the different restructuring strategies?

## DISCUSSION QUESTIONS

1   In what way is the industry life cycle associated with acquisition activities within a sector?

2   Cemex is the world's third largest cement manufacturer. It is currently considering an entry into the Indian market and has identified as a possible target the privately held firm, Penna Cement.[132] It has no knowledge of the Indian market. What advice would you offer Cemex as it considers further this acquisition?

3   Where do cost-cutting opportunities lie following an acquisition and what are both the strategic and operational implications of this?

4   Given the increasingly global nature of acquisition activity, what regulatory and security challenges confront national governments as a result?

5   There are numerous theories that explain acquisition activity. Identify three theories that describe acquisition strategy. For example, monopoly theory suggests that firms acquire others so as to gain market power. Efficiency theory finds that firms acquire so as to create synergies that would not otherwise exist.

## FURTHER READING

Synergies and combining resources is often an important goal of acquisitions (e.g. E. Devos, P. R. Kadapakkam and S. Krishnamurthy (2009) "How do mergers create value? A comparison of taxes, market power and efficiency improvements as explanations for synergies", *Review of Financial Studies*, 22: 1179–1211; J. Wiklund and D. A. Shepherd (2009) "The effectiveness of alliances and acquisitions: The role of resource combination activities", *Entrepreneurship Theory and Practice*, 33: 193–212) but the realized results depend on external and internal factors and can differ widely (e.g. G. M. McNamara, J. Haleblian and B. J. Dykes (2008) "The performance

implications of participating in an acquisition wave: Early mover advantages, bandwagon effects and the moderating influence of industry characteristics and acquirer tactics", *Academy of Management Journal*, 51: 113–130; R. Chakrabarti, N. Jayaraman and S. Mukherjee (2009) "Mars-Venus marriages: culture and cross-border M&A", *Journal of International Business Studies*, 40: 216–237; J. Y. Kim and S. Finkelstein (2009) "The effects of strategic and market complementarity on acquisition performance: Evidence form the US commercial banking industry, 1989–2001", *Strategic Management Journal*, 30(6): 617–646).

## EXPERIENTIAL EXERCISES

### Exercise 1: How did the deal work out?

The text argues that mergers and acquisitions are a popular strategy for businesses within countries and regions, and also globally. However, returns for acquiring firms do not always live up to expectations. This exercise seeks to address this notion by analysing, pre and post hoc, the results of actual acquisitions. By looking at the notifications of a deal beforehand, categorizing that deal and then following it for a year you will be able to learn about actual deals and their implications for strategists.

Work in teams and identify a merger or acquisition deal that has been completed in the last few years. This

may be a cross-border acquisition or a European centred one. Several sources for this are the Financial Times In-depth M&A section, Reuters online M&A section or Yahoo Finance in their Mergers and Acquisitions Calendar. Each team must get their M&A choice approved in advance so as to avoid duplicates.

To complete this assignment you should be prepared to answer the following questions:

1   Describe the environment for this deal at the time it was completed. Focus on management's representation to shareholders, industry environment and the overall rationale for the deal. Use concepts studied to date.

2 Did the acquirer pay a premium for the firm? If so, how much? Additionally, search for investor comments regarding the wisdom of this deal. Attempt to identify how the market reacted at the announcement of the deal (Lexis Nexus typically provides an article that will address this issue).

3 Describe the deal going forward. Use the concepts from the text such as, but not limited to:

a The reason for the deal, i.e. market power, overcoming entry barriers etc.

b Were there problems in achieving acquisition success?

c Categorize this deal as successful as of the time of your research. Why did you label it as such?

Plan on presenting your findings to the class in a 10–15 minute presentation. Organize the presentation as if you were updating the shareholders of the newly combined firm.

### Exercise 2: Cadbury Schweppes

Cadbury and Schweppes are two prominent and long-established companies. For present purposes, do not consider Kraft Foods Inc. acquisition of Cadbury. Cadbury was founded in 1824 and is the world's largest confectionery company. The bulk of Cadbury's sales come from Europe with a substantially smaller presence in the Americas.

Schweppes was founded in 1783, when Jacob Schweppes invented a system to carb[...] eral water. Its brands include 7-Up, Dr Pepper, [...] Snapple, Schweppes and Motts Juice. Cadbury and Schweppes merged in 1969. In 2008 the combined firm posted approximately €25 billion in revenue and a €6.9 billion loss. The firm also employed 160 000 employees at this time. In what is termed a demerger, in 2008 the firm spun off its North American beverage unit (Dr Pepper Snapple Group) and changed its name from Cadbury Schweppes to just Cadbury.

Working in teams, prepare a brief PowerPoint presentation to address the following questions. You will need to consult separate websites for each company: http://www.drpeppersnapplegroup.com and http://www.cadbury.com (this is now an archive site with activity since 2010 located at http://www.kraftfoodscompany.com) as well as news articles published about this event. Lexis Nexus is a good resource for news on topics such as this.

1 Why did Cadbury decide to divest itself of the beverage business?

2 What does it mean that Cadbury listed the separation as a demerger?

3 What factors hindered the success of a combined Cadbury Schweppes?

4 Do you feel that both the beverage and confectionery businesses are better, or worse off, separated?

## VIDEO CASE

### Focus on why a deal is done, not how

### Stuart Grief, vice president strategy and development, Textron

www.cengage.co.uk/volberda/students/video_cases

Stuart Grief, vice president of strategy and development at Textron talks about the art of the deal and how the company he represents goes through the deal making analysis. As you prepare for the video consider the concepts of negotiation and deal making, important ingredients of any M&A activity.

Be prepared to discuss the following concepts and questions in class:

### Concepts

- M&A strategies
- Reasons for acquisition
- Problems in achieving success

### Questions

1 Think through a deal you have made recently (e.g. purchased a car, bought a new computer, leased an apartment, taken out a loan). Describe the deal process and why you arrived at the conclusion ultimately. This could also be a deal you decided to walk away from.

2 How would you characterize Textron's corporate level strategy? Visit the firm's website to see the various business units under management. Describe what you think are their criteria for acquisition. Does it appear they are willing to acquire any type of firm in any industry?

3 Overall, in your opinion, how should a company plan and undertake its merger and acquisition strategic initiatives?

# NOTES

1. M. L. McDonald, J. D. Westphal and M. E. Graebner, 2008, "What do they know? The effects of outside director acquisition experience on firm acquisition performance", *Strategic Management Journal*, 29: 1155–1177; K. Uhlenbruck, M. A. Hitt and M. Semadeni, 2006, "Market value effects of acquisitions involving Internet firms: A resource-based analysis" *Strategic Management Journal*, 27: 899–913.

2. J. Wiklund and D. A. Shepherd, 2009, "The effectiveness of alliances and acquisitions: The role of resource combination activities" *Entrepreneurship Theory and Practice*, 33: 193–212; C. C. Lu, 2006, "Growth strategies and merger patterns among small and medium sized enterprises: An empirical study", *International Journal of Management*, 23: 529–547.

3. M. A. Hitt, D. King, H. Krishnan, M. Makri, M. Schijven, K. Shimizu and H. Zhu, 2009, "Mergers and acquisitions: Overcoming pitfalls, building synergy and creating value", *Business Horizons*, 52: 523–529.

4. G. M. McNamara, J. Haleblian and B. J. Dykes, 2008, "The performance implications of participating in an acquisition wave: Early mover advantages, bandwagon effects and the moderating influence of industry characteristics and acquirer tactics", *Academy of Management Journal*, 51: 113–130; J. Haleblian, J. Y. Kim and N. Rajagopalan, 2006, "The influence of acquisition experience and performance on acquisition behaviour: Evidence from the US commercial banking industry", *Academy of Management Journal*, 49: 357–370; M. A. Hitt, J. S. Harrison and R. D. Ireland, 2001, *Mergers and Acquisitions: A Guide to Creating Value for Stakeholders*, New York: Oxford University Press.

5. R. Dobbs and V. Tortorici, 2007, "Cool heads will bring in the best deals; Boardroom discipline is vital if the M&A boom is to benefit shareholders", *Financial Times*, February 28, 6.

6. J. Silver-Greenberg, 2009, "Dealmakers test the waters" *BusinessWeek*, March 2, 18–20.

7. J. Y. Kim and S. Finkelstein, 2009, "The effects of strategic and market complementarity on acquisition performance: Evidence from the US commercial banking industry, 1989–2001", *Strategic Management Journal*, 30: 617–646; J. J. Reuer, 2005, "Avoiding lemons in M&A deals" *MIT Sloan Management Review*, 46(3) 15–17.

8. M. Baker, X. Pan and J. Wurgler, 2009, "The psychology of pricing in mergers and acquisitions" Working paper: http://www.papers.ssrn.com/so13/papers.cfm?abstract_id=1364152; K. Cool and M. Van de Laar, 2006, "The performance of acquisitive companies in the US" in: L. Renneboog, (ed.), *Advances in Corporate Finance and Asset Pricing*, Amsterdam, Netherlands: Elsevier Science, 77–105.

9. M. Peers, 2009, "NetApp should end Data Domain chase", *Wall Street Journal Online*, http://www.wsj.com, July 6.

10. K. J. Martijn Cremers, V. B. Nair and K. John, 2009, "Takeovers and the cross-section of returns", *Review of Financial Studies*, 22: 1409–1445; C. Tuch and N. O'Sullivan, 2007, "The impact of acquisitions on firm performance: A review of the evidence", *International Journal of Management Review*, 9(2): 141–170.

11. J. McCracken and J. S. Lublin, 2009, "Towers Perrin and Watson Wyatt to merge", *Wall Street Journal Online*, http://www.wsj.com, June 29.

12. M. Curtin, 2009, "Xstrata's well-timed bear hug", *Wall Street Journal Online*, http://www.wsj.com, June 22.

13. S. Sudarsanam and A. A. Mahate, 2006, "Are friendly acquisitions too bad for shareholders and managers? Long-term value creation and top management turnover in hostile and friendly acquirers", *British Journal of Management: Supplement*, 17(1): S7–S30.

14. A. R. Sorkin, 2009, "Exelon raises hostile bid for NRG", *New York Times Online*, http://www.nytimes.com, July 2.

15. E. Akdogu, 2009, "Gaining a competitive edge through acquisitions: Evidence from the telecommunications industry", *Journal of Corporate Finance*, 15: 99–112; E. Devos, P. R. Kadapakkam and S. Krishnamurthy, 2009, "How do mergers create value? A comparison of taxes, market power and efficiency improvements as explanations for synergies", *Review of Financial Studies*, 22: 1179–1211.

16. J. Haleblian, C. E. Devers, G. McNamara, M. A. Carpenter and R. B. Davison, 2009, "Taking stock of what we know about mergers and acquisitions: A review and research agenda", *Journal of Management*, 35: 469–502; P. Wright, M. Kroll and D. Elenkov, 2002, "Acquisition returns, increase in firm size and chief executive officer compensation: The moderating role of monitoring", *Academy of Management Journal*, 45: 599–608.

17. A. Vance, 2009, "Acer's chief urges more consolidation of the PC industry", *New York Times Online*, http://www.nytimes.com, July 7.

18. C. Tighe, 2009, "Vertu buys up Brooklyn assets" *Financial Times Online*, http://www.ft.com, June 27.

19. K. E. Meyer, S. Estrin, S. K. Bhaumik and M. W. Peng, 2009, "Institutions, resources and entry strategies in emerging economies", *Strategic Management Journal*, 30: 61–80; D. K. Oler, J. S. Harrison and M. R. Allen, 2008, "The danger of misinterpreting short-window event study findings in strategic management research: An empirical illustration using horizontal acquisitions" *Strategic Organisation*, 6: 151–184.

20. A. Harrison, 2009, "NAB buys Aviva assets" *Wall Street Journal Online*, http://www.wsj.com, June 23.

21. N. Casey, 2009, "Toys 'Я' Us is purchasing retailer FAO Schwarz", *Wall Street Journal Online*, http://www.wsj.com, May 28.

22. C. E. Fee and S. Thomas, 2004, "Sources of gains in horizontal mergers: Evidence from customer, supplier and rival firms", *Journal of Financial Economics*, 74: 423–460.

23. T. Ushijima, 2009, "R&D intensity and acquisition and divestiture of corporate assets: Evidence from Japan", *Journal of Economics and Business*, 61: 415–433; L. Capron, W. Mitchell and A. Swaminathan, 2001, "Asset divestiture following horizontal acquisitions: A dynamic view", *Strategic Management Journal*, 22: 817–844.

24. B. Gulbrandsen, K. Sandvik and S. A. Haugland, 2009, "Antecedents of vertical integration: Transaction cost economics and resource-based explanations", *Journal of Purchasing and Supply Management*, 15: 89–102; F. T. Rothaermel, M. A. Hitt and L. A. Jobe, 2006, "Balancing vertical integration and strategic outsourcing: Effects on product portfolio, product success and firm performance", *Strategic Management Journal*, 27: 1033–1056.

25. A. Parmigiani, 2007, "Why do firms both make and buy? An investigation of concurrent sourcing", *Strategic Management Journal*, 28: 285–311.

26. 2009, Our businesses, http://www.info.cvscaremark.com, July 7.

27. 2009, Boeing completes acquisition of eXMeritus Inc., http://www.boeing.mediaroom.com, June 22.

28. J. W. Brock and N. P. Obst, 2009, "Market concentration, economic welfare and antitrust policy", *Journal of Industry, Competition and Trade*, 9: 65–75; M. T. Brouwer, 2008, "Horizontal mergers and efficiencies: Theory and antitrust practice", *European Journal of Law and Economics*, 26: 11–26.

29. 2008, Procter & Gamble Annual Report, http://www.pg.com, July.

30. K. E. Meyer, M. Wright and S. Pruthi, 2009, "Managing knowledge in foreign entry strategies: A resource-based analysis" *Strategic Management Journal*, 30: 557–574; S. F. S. Chen and M. Zeng, 2004, "Japanese investors' choice of acquisitions vs startups in the US: The role of reputation barriers and advertising outlays" *International Journal of Research in Marketing*, 21(2): 123–136.

31. C. Y. Tseng, 2009, "Technological innovation in the BRIC economies" *Research-Technology Management*, 52: 29–35; S. McGee, 2007, "Seeking value in BRIC's, *Barron's*, July 9, L10–L11.

32. R. Chakrabarti, N. Jayaraman and S. Mukherjee, 2009, "Mars-Venus marriages: culture and cross-border M&A", *Journal of International Business Studies*, 40: 216–237.

33. S. Jessop, 2009, "'Brave' post-Lehman M&A rewarded by market – Study", *New York Times Online*, http://www.nytimes.com, July 5.

34. E. Zabinski, D. Freeman and X. Jian, 2009, "Navigating the challenges of cross-border M&A", *The Deal Magazine*, http://www.thedeal.com, May 29.

35. N. Kumar, 2009, *The Economic Times*, http://www.economictimes.indiatimes.com, March 27.

36. J. Chapman and W. Xu, 2008, "Ten strategies for successful cross-border acquisitions in China", Nixon Peabody LLP Special Report, Mergers & Acquisitions, September, 30–35.

37. K. Fisher-Vanden and R. Rebecca Terry, 2009, "Is technology acquisition enough to improve China's product quality? Evidence from firm-level panel data", *Economics of Innovation and New Technology*, 18(1): 21–38.

38. M. Makri, M. A. Hitt and P. J. Lane, 2010, "Complementary technologies, knowledge relatedness and invention outcomes in high technology M&As" *Strategic Management Journal*, 31: 601–628; C. Homburg and M. Bucerius, 2006, "Is speed of integration really a success factor of mergers and acquisitions? An analysis of the role of internal and external relatedness", *Strategic Management Journal*, 27: 347–367.

39. H. K. Ellonen, P. Wilstrom and A. Jantunen, 2009, "Linking dynamic-capability portfolios and innovation outcomes" *Technovation*, 29: 753–762; M. Song and C. A. De Benedetto, 2008, "Supplier's involvement and success of radical new product development in new ventures", *Journal of Operations Management*, 26: 1–22; S. Karim, 2006, "Modularity in organisational structure: The reconfiguration of internally developed and acquired business units", *Strategic Management Journal*, 27: 799–823; J. H. Burgers, F. A. J. van den Bosch and H. W. Volberda, 2008, "Why New Business Development Projects Fail: Coping with the Differences of Technological versus Market Knowledge", *Long Range Planning*, 41(1): 55–73; J. H. Burgers, F. A. J. Van den Bosch and H. W. Volberda, 2008, "The Impact of corporate venturing on a firm's competence modes", in: Competence-Building and Leveraging in Inter-organizational Relations, R. Martens, A. Heene and R. Sanchez (eds.), *Advances in Applied Business Strategy*, Oxford: Elsevier, 11: 117–140; J. H. Burgers, J. J. P. Jansen, F. A. J. Van den Bosch and H. W. Volberda, 2009, "Structural differentiation and corporate venturing: The moderating role of formal and informal integration mechanisms", *Journal of Business Venturing*, 24: 206–220.

40. R. E. Hoskisson and L. W. Busenitz, 2002, "Market uncertainty and learning distance in corporate entrepreneurship entry mode choice", in: M. A. Hitt, R. D. Ireland, S. M. Camp and D. L. Sexton (eds.), *Strategic Entrepreneurship: Creating a New Mindset*, Oxford, UK: Blackwell Publishers, 151–172; M. A. Hitt, R. E. Hoskisson, R. A. Johnson and D. D. Moesel, 1996, "The market for corporate control and firm innovation", *Academy of Management Journal*, 39: 1084–1119.

41. E. Steel, 2009, "AOL buys two companies specializing in local online media", *Wall Street Journal Online*, http://www.wsj.com, June 11.

42. W. P. Wan and D. W Yiu, 2009, "From crisis to opportunity: Environmental jolt, corporate acquisitions and firm performance", *Strategic Management Journal*, 30: 791–801; L. F. Hsieh and Y. T. Tsai, 2005, "Technology investment mode of innovative technological corporations: M&A strategy intended to facilitate innovation", *Journal of American Academy of Business*, 6(1): 185–194; G. Ahuja and R. Katila, 2001, "Technological acquisitions and the innovation performance of acquiring firms: A longitudinal study", *Strategic Management Journal*, 22: 197–220.

43. F. Damanpour, R. M. Walker and C. N. Avellaneda, 2009, "Combinative effects of innovation types and organisational

performance: A longitudinal study of service organisations", *Journal of Management Studies*, 46: 650–675.

44. F. Vermeulen, 2005, "How acquisitions can revitalise companies", *MIT Sloan Management Review*, 46(4): 45–51; M. A. Hitt, R. E. Hoskisson, R. D. Ireland and J. S. Harrison, 1991, "Effects of acquisitions on R&D inputs and outputs", *Academy of Management Journal*, 34: 693–706.

45. B. White, 2007, "Cisco to buy IronPort, a network-security firm", *Wall Street Journal*, January 4, A10.

46. Cisco, 2009, "Cisco breaks new ground in e-mail security", Press release, http://www.cisco.com, March 3.

47. H. Prechel, T. Morris, T. Woods and R. Walden, 2008, "Corporate diversification revisited: The political-legal environment, the multilayer-subsidiary form and mergers and acquisitions", *The Sociological Quarterly*, 49: 849–878; C. E. Helfat and K. M. Eisenhardt, 2004, "Inter-temporal economies of scope, organisational modularity and the dynamics of diversification", *Strategic Management Journal*, 25: 1217–1232.

48. J. L. Lunsford, 2007, "Boss talk: Transformer in transition; He turned UTC into giant; now, CEO George David carefully prepares successor", *Wall Street Journal*, May 17, B1.

49. T. Laamanen and T. Keil, 2008, "Performance of serial acquirers: Toward an acquisition program perspective", *Strategic Management Journal*, 29: 663–672; D. J. Miller, M. J. Fern and L. B. Cardinal, 2007, "The use of knowledge for technological innovation within diversified firms", *Academy of Management Journal*, 50: 308–326.

50. J. Anand and H. Singh, 1997, "Asset redeployment, acquisitions and corporate strategy in declining industries", *Strategic Management Journal*, 18 (Special Issue): 99–118.

51. T. Yu, M. Subramaniam and A. A. Cannella, Jr, 2009, "Rivalry deterrence in international markets: Contingencies governing the mutual forbearance hypothesis", *Academy of Management Journal*, 52: 127–147; D. G. Sirmon, S. Gove and M. A. Hitt, 2008, "Resource management in dyadic competitive rivalry: The effects of resource bundling and deployment", *Academy of Management Journal*, 51: 919–935.

52. H. Rui and G. S. Yip, 2008, "Foreign acquisitions by Chinese firms: A strategic intent perspective", *Journal of World Business*, 43: 213–226; P. Puranam and K. Srikanth, 2007, "What they know vs what they do: How acquirers leverage technology acquisitions", *Strategic Management Journal*, 28: 805–825; H. W. Volberda, 1996, "Toward the flexible form: How to remain vital in hypercompetitive environments", *Organization Science*, 7(4): 359–387.

53. S. A. Zahra and J. C. Hayton, 2008, "The effect of international venturing on firm performance: The moderating influence of absorptive capacity", *Journal of Business Venturing*, 23: 195–220.

54. J. S. Harrison, M. A. Hitt, R. E. Hoskisson and R. D. Ireland, 2001, "Resource complementarity in business combinations: Extending the logic to organisational alliances", *Journal of Management*, 27: 679–690.

55. J. Whalen, 2007, "AstraZeneca thinks bigger; new chief increases commitment to "large molecule" biological drugs", *Wall Street Journal*, May 22, A7.

56. J. A. Schmidt, 2002, "Business perspective on mergers and acquisitions" in: J. A. Schmidt (ed.), *Making Mergers Work*, Alexandria, VA: Society for Human Resource Management, 23–46.

57. S. Jessop, 2009, "Brave" post-Lehman M&A rewarded by market – Study", *New York Times Online*, http://www.nytimes.com, July 5.

58. M. Cording, P. Christmann, D. R. King, 2008, "Reducing causal ambiguity in acquisition integration: Intermediate goals as mediators of integration decisions and acquisition performance", *Academy of Management Journal*, 51: 744–767; M. Zollo and H. Singh, 2004, "Deliberate learning in corporate acquisitions: Post-acquisition strategies and integration capability in US bank mergers", *Strategic Management Journal*, 25: 1233–1256; S. Spedale, F. A. J. Van den Bosch and H. W. Volberda, 2007, "Preservation and dissolution of the target firm's embedded ties in acquisitions", *Organization Studies*, 28(8): 1169–1196.

59. N. Kumar, 2009, "How emerging giants are rewriting the rules of M&A", *Harvard Business Review*, 87(5): 115–121; M. C. Sturman, 2008, "The value of human capital specificity versus transferability", *Journal of Management*, 34: 290–316.

60. K. M. Ellis, T. H. Reus and B. T. Lamont, 2009, "The effects of procedural and informational justice in the integration of related acquisitions", *Strategic Management Journal*, 30: 137–161; F. Vermeulen, 2007, "Business insight (a special report); bad deals: Eight warning signs that an acquisition may not pay off", *Wall Street Journal*, April 28, R10.

61. M. Zollo, 1999, "M&A – The challenge of learning to integrate", Mastering Strategy (Part Eleven), *Financial Times*, December 6, 14–15.

62. H. G. Barkema and M. Schijven, 2008, "Toward unlocking the full potential of acquisitions: The role of organisational restructuring", *Academy of Management Journal*, 51: 696–722; J. Harrison, 2007, "Why integration success eludes many buyers", *Mergers and Acquisitions*, 42(3): 18–20.

63. R. Gibson, 2006, "Package deal; UPS's purchase of Mail Boxes Etc. looked great on paper. Then came the culture clash", *Wall Street Journal*, May 8, R13.

64. Z. Kouwe, 2009, "Deals on ice in first half, with 40% drop in M.&A", *New York Times Online*, http://www.nytimes.com, July 1.

65. T. B. Folta and J. P. O'Brien, 2008, "Determinants of firm-specific thresholds in acquisition decisions", *Managerial and Decision Economics*, 29: 209–225; R. J. Rosen, 2006, "Merger momentum and investor sentiment: The stock market reaction to merger announcements", *Journal of Business*, 79: 987–1017.

66. A. L. Rappaport and M. L. Sirower, 1999, "Stock or cash? The trade-offs for buyers and sellers in mergers and acquisitions", *Harvard Business Review*, 77(6): 147–158.

67. M. Peers, 2009, "Magazine business suffers shakeout", *Wall Street Journal Online*, http://www.wsj.com, July 13.

68. G. Yago, 1991, *Junk Bonds: How High Yield Securities Restructured Corporate America*, New York: Oxford University Press, 146–148.

69. M. C. Jensen, 1986, "Agency costs of free cash flow, corporate finance and takeovers", *American Economic Review*, 76: 323–329.

70. J. Leahy and J. Reed, 2009, "Tata strained by UK acquisitions" *Financial Times Online*, http://www.ft.com, May 21.

71. T. H. Noe and M. J. Rebello, 2006, "The role of debt purchases in takeovers: A tale of two retailers", *Journal of Economics & Management Strategy*, 15(3): 609–648; M. A. Hitt and D. L. Smart, 1994, "Debt: A disciplining force for managers or a debilitating force for organisations?", *Journal of Management Inquiry*, 3: 144–152.

72. C. Jong-Woo, 2009, "Kumho Asiana to sell Daewoo Engineering", *Fidelity.com*, http://www.fidelity.com, June 28.

73. S. W. Bauguess, S. B. Moeller, F. P. Schlingemann and C. J. Zutter, 2009, "Ownership structure and target returns", *Journal of Corporate Finance*, 15: 48–65; H. Donker and S. Zahir, 2008, "Takeovers, corporate control and return to target shareholders", *International Journal of Corporate Governance*, 1: 106–134.

74. A. B. Sorescu, R. K. Chandy and J. C. Prabhu, 2007, "Why some acquisitions do better than others: Product capital as a driver of long-term stock returns", *Journal of Marketing Research*, 44(1): 57–72; T. Saxton and M. Dollinger, 2004, "Target reputation and appropriability: Picking and deploying resources in acquisitions", *Journal of Management*, 30: 123–147.

75. J. S. Harrison, M. A. Hitt, R. E. Hoskisson and R. D. Ireland, 2001, "Resource complementarity in business combinations: Extending the logic to organisational alliances", *Journal of Management*, 27: 679–690; J. B. Barney, 1988, "Returns to bidding firms in mergers and acquisitions: Reconsidering the relatedness hypothesis", *Strategic Management Journal*, 9 (Special Issue): 71–78.

76. O. E. Williamson, 1999, "Strategy research: Governance and competence perspectives", *Strategic Management Journal*, 20: 1087–1108.

77. S. Chatterjee, 2007, "Why is synergy so difficult in mergers of related businesses?", *Strategy & Leadership*, 35(2): 46–52.

78. J. Santalo and M. Becerra, 2009, "Competition from specialised firms and the diversification-performance linkage", *Journal of Finance*, 63: 851–883; C. W. L. Hill and R. E. Hoskisson, 1987, "Strategy and structure in the multiproduct firm", *Academy of Management Review*, 12: 331–341.

79. M. L. A. Hayward and K. Shimizu, 2006, "De-commitment to losing strategic action: Evidence from the divestiture of poorly performing acquisitions", *Strategic Management Journal*, 27: 541–557; R. A. Johnson, R. E. Hoskisson and M. A. Hitt, 1993, "Board of director involvement in restructuring: The effects of board versus managerial controls and characteristics", *Strategic Management Journal*, 14 (Special Issue): 33–50; C. C. Markides, 1992, "Consequences of corporate refocusing: Ex ante evidence", *Academy of Management Journal*, 35: 398–412.

80. D. Marginso and L. Mcaulay, 2008, "Exploring the debate on short-termism: A theoretical and empirical analysis", *Strategic Management Journal*, 29: 273–292;

R. E. Hoskisson and R. A. Johnson, 1992, "Corporate restructuring and strategic change: The effect on diversification strategy and R&D intensity", *Strategic Management Journal*, 13: 625–634.

81. T. Keil, M. V. J. Maula, H. Schildt and S. A. Zahra, 2008, "The effect of governance modes and relatedness of external business development activities in innovative performance", *Strategic Management Journal*, 29: 895–907; K. H. Tsai and J. C. Wang, 2008, "External technology acquisition and firm performance: A longitudinal study", *Journal of Business Venturing*, 23: 91–112.

82. A. Kacperczyk, 2009, "With greater power comes greater responsibility? Takeover protection and corporate attention to stakeholders", *Strategic Management Journal*, 30: 261–285; L. H. Lin, 2009, "Mergers and acquisitions, alliances and technology development: An empirical study of the global auto industry", *International Journal of Technology Management*, 48: 295–307; M. L. Barnett, 2008, "An attention-based view of real options reasoning", *Academy of Management Review*, 33: 606–628.

83. M. L. A. Hayward and D. C. Hambrick, 1997, "Explaining the premiums paid for large acquisitions: Evidence of CEO hubris", *Administrative Science Quarterly* 42: 103–127; R. Roll, 1986, "The hubris hypothesis of corporate takeovers", *Journal of Business*, 59: 197–216.

84. F. Vermeulen, 2007, "Business insight (a special report); bad deals: Eight warning signs that an acquisition may not pay off", *Wall Street Journal*, April 28, R10.

85. L. A. Nemanich and D. Vera, 2009, "Transformational leadership and ambidexterity in the context of an acquisition", *The Leadership Quarterly*, 20: 19–33.

86. 2009, Our company, http://www.lizclaiborne.com, July 12; R. Dobbs, 2007, "Claiborne seeks to shed 16 apparel brands", *Wall Street Journal*, July 11, B1, B2.

87. V. Swaminathan, F. Murshed and J. Hulland, 2008, "Value creation following merger and acquisition announcements: The role of strategic emphasis alignment", *Journal of Marketing Research*, 45: 33–47.

88. F. Vermeulen, 2007, "Business insight (a special report); bad deals: Eight warning signs that an acquisition may not pay off", *Wall Street Journal*, April 28, R10.

89. H. G. Barkema and M. Schijven, 2008, "How do firms learn to make acquisitions? A review of past research and an agenda for the future", *Journal of Management*, 34: 594–634.

90. S. Chatterjee, 2009, "The keys to successful acquisition programmes", *Long Range Planning*, 42: 137–163; C. M. Sanchez and S. R. Goldberg, 2009, "Strategic M&As: Stronger in tough times?", *Journal of Corporate Accounting & Finance*, 20: 3–7; C. Duncan and M. Mtar, 2006, "Determinants of international acquisition success: Lessons from FirstGroup in North America", *European Management Journal*, 24: 396–441.

91. D. Mayer and M. Kenney, 2004, "Economic action does not take place in a vacuum: Understanding Cisco's acquisition and development strategy", *Industry and Innovation*, 11(4): 299–325.

92. 2009, Connection for acquired employees, http://www.cisco.com, July 12.

93. M. A. Hitt, R. D. Ireland, J. S. Harrison and A. Best, 1998, "Attributes of successful and unsuccessful acquisitions of US firms", *British Journal of Management*, 9: 91–114.

94. K. Uhlenbruck, M. A. Hitt and M. Semadeni, 2006, "Market value effects of acquisitions involving Internet firms: A resource-based analysis", *Strategic Management Journal*, 27: 899–913; J. Hagedoorn and G. Dysters, 2002, "External sources of innovative capabilities: The preference for strategic alliances or mergers and acquisitions", *Journal of Management Studies*, 39: 167–188.

95. J. J. Reuer and R. Ragozzino, 2006, "Agency hazards and alliance portfolios", *Strategic Management Journal*, 27: 27–43; P. Porrini, 2004, "Can a previous alliance between an acquirer and a target affect acquisition performance?", *Journal of Management*, 30: 545–562.

96. D. J. Kisgen, J. Qian and W. Song, 2009, "Are fairness opinions fair? The case of mergers and acquisitions", *Journal of Financial Economics*, 91: 179–207; R. J. Aiello and M. D. Watkins, 2000, "The fine art of friendly acquisition", *Harvard Business Review*, 78(6): 100–107.

97. S. Chatterjee, 2009, "Does increased equity ownership lead to more strategically involved boards?", *Journal of Business Ethics*, 87: 267–277; D. D. Bergh, 2001, "Executive retention and acquisition outcomes: A test of opposing views on the influence of organisational tenure", *Journal of Management*, 27: 603–622; J. P. Walsh, 1989, "Doing a deal: Merger and acquisition negotiations and their impact upon target company top management turnover", *Strategic Management Journal*, 10: 307–322.

98. D. A. Waldman and M. Javidan, 2009, "Alternative forms of charismatic leadership in the integration of mergers and acquisitions", *The Leadership Quarterly*, 20: 130–142; F. J. Froese, Y. S. Pak and L. C. Chong, 2008, "Managing the human side of cross-border acquisitions in South Korea", *Journal of World Business*, 43: 97–108.

99. M. E. Graebner, 2009, "Caveat Venditor: Trust asymmetries in acquisitions of entrepreneurial firms", *Academy of Management Journal*, 52: 435–472; N. J. Morrison, G. Kinley and K. L. Ficery, 2008, "Merger deal breakers: When operational due diligence exposes risk", *Journal of Business Strategy*, 29: 23–28.

100. J. M. Shaver and J. M. Mezias, 2009, "Diseconomies of managing in acquisitions: Evidence from civil lawsuits", *Organization Science*, 20: 206–222; M. L. McDonald, J. D. Westphal and M. E. Graebner, 2008, "What do they know? The effects of outside director acquisition experience on firm acquisition performance", *Strategic Management Journal*, 29: 1155–1177.

101. D. D. Bergh and E. N. K. Lim, 2008, "Learning how to restructure: Absorptive capacity and improvisational views of restructuring actions and performance", *Strategic Management Journal*, 29: 593–616; J. K. Kang, J. M. Kim, W. L. Liu and S. Yi, 2006, "Post-takeover restructuring and the sources of gains in foreign takeovers: Evidence from US targets", *Journal of Business*, 79(5): 2503–2537.

102. Y. G. Suh and E. Howard, 2009, "Restructuring retailing in Korea: The case of Samsung-Tesco", *Asia Pacific Business Review*, 15: 29–40; Z. Wu and A. Delios, 2009, "The emergence of portfolio restructuring in Japan", *Management International Review*, 49: 313–335; R. E. Hoskisson, A. A. Cannella, L. Tihanyi and R. Faraci, 2004. "Asset restructuring and business group affiliation in French civil law countries", *Strategic Management Journal*, 25: 525–539.

103. S. Thurm, 2008, "Who are the best CEOs of 2008", *Wall Street Journal Online*, http://www.wsj.com, December 15.

104. J. L. Morrow Jr, D. G. Sirmon, M. A. Hitt and T. R. Holcomb, 2007, "Creating value in the face of declining performance: Firm strategies and organisational recovery", *Strategic Management Journal*, 28: 271–283; J. L. Morrow Jr., R. A. Johnson and L. W. Busenitz, 2004, "The effects of cost and asset retrenchment on firm performance: The overlooked role of a firm's competitive environment", *Journal of Management*, 30: 189–208.

105. G. J. Castrogiovanni and G. D. Bruton, 2000, "Business turnaround processes following acquisitions: Reconsidering the role of retrenchment", *Journal of Business Research*, 48: 25–34; W. McKinley, J. Zhao and K. G. Rust, 2000, "A sociocognitive interpretation of organisational downsizing", *Academy of Management Review*, 25: 227–243.

106. J. D. Evans and F. Hefner, 2009, "Business ethics and the decision to adopt golden parachute contracts: Empirical evidence of concern for all stakeholders", *Journal of Business Ethics*, 86: 65–79; H. A. Krishnan, M. A. Hitt and D. Park, 2007, "Acquisition premiums, subsequent workforce reductions and post-acquisition performance", *Journal of Management*, 44: 709–732.

107. K. McFarland, 2008, "Four mistakes leaders make when downsizing", *BusinessWeek Online*, http://www.businessweek.com, October 24.

108. C. O. Trevor and A. J. Nyberg, 2008, "Keeping your headcount when all about you are losing theirs: Downsizing, voluntary turnover rates and the moderating role of HR practices", *Academy of Management Journal*, 51: 259–276.

109. D. D. Bergh and E. N. K. Lim, 2008, "Learning how to restructure: Absorptive capacity and improvisational views of restructuring actions and performance", *Strategic Management Journal*, 29: 593–616; R. E. Hoskisson and M. A. Hitt, 1994, *Downscoping: How to Tame the Diversified Firm*, New York: Oxford University Press.

110. T. Ushijima, 2009, "R&D intensity and acquisition and divestiture of corporate assets: Evidence from Japan", *Journal of Economics and Business*, 61: 415–433; G. Benou, J. Madura and T. Ngo, 2008, "Wealth creation from high-tech divestitures", *The Quarterly Review of Economics and Finance*, 48: 505–519; L. Dranikoff, T. Koller and A. Schneider, 2002, "Divestiture: Strategy's missing link", *Harvard Business Review*, 80(5): 74–83.

111. R. E. Hoskisson and M. A. Hitt, 1990, "Antecedents and performance outcomes of diversification: A review and critique of theoretical perspectives", *Journal of Management*, 16: 461–509.

112. 2009, "Motorola sells fiber-to-the-node product line", *New York Times Online*, http://www.nytimes.com, July 7.

113. M Peers, 2009, "Magazine business suffers shakeout", *Wall Street Journal Online*, http://www.wsj.com, July 13.

114. R. Perez-Pena, 2009, "McGraw-Hill is said to be seeking a buyer for *BusinessWeek*", *New York Times Online*, http://www.nytimes.com, July 14.

115. A. Kambil, 2008, "What is your recession playbook?", *Journal of Business Strategy*, 29: 50–52; M. Rajand and M. Forsyth, 2002, "Hostile bidders, long-term performance and restructuring methods: Evidence from the UK", *American Business Review*, 20: 71–81.

116. D. Hillier, P. McColgan and S. Werema, 2008, "Asset sales and firm strategy: An analysis of divestitures by UK companies", *The European Journal of Finance*, 15: 71–87; R. E. Hoskisson, R. A. Johnson, L. Tihanyi and R. E. White, 2005, "Diversified business groups and corporate refocusing in emerging economies", *Journal of Management*, 31: 941–965.

117. S. N. Kaplan and P. Stromberg, 2009, "Leveraged buyouts and private equity", *Journal of Economic Perspectives*, 23: 121–146; C. Moschieri and J. Mair, 2008, "Research on corporate divestures: A synthesis", *Journal of Management & Organisation*, 14: 399–422.

118. J. Mair and C. Moschieri, 2006, "Unbundling frees business for take off", *Financial Times*, October 19, 2.

119. K. H. Wruck, 2009, "Private equity, corporate governance and the reinvention of the market for corporate control", *Journal of Applied Corporate Finance*, 20: 8–21; M. F. Wiersema and J. P. Liebeskind, 1995, "The effects of leveraged buyouts on corporate growth and diversification in large firms", *Strategic Management Journal*, 16: 447–460.

120. R. Harris, D. S. Siegel and M. Wright, 2005, "Assessing the impact of management buyouts on economic efficiency: Plant-level evidence from the United Kingdom", *Review of Economics and Statistics*, 87: 148–153; A. Seth and J. Easterwood, 1995, "Strategic redirection in large management buyouts: The evidence from post-buyout restructuring activity", *Strategic Management Journal*, 14: 251–274; P. H. Phan and C. W. L. Hill, 1995, "Organisational restructuring and economic performance in leveraged buyouts: An ex-post study", *Academy of Management Journal*, 38: 704–739.

121. M. Meuleman, K. Amess, M. Wright and L. Scholes, 2009, "Agency, strategic entrepreneurship and the performance of private equity-backed buyouts", *Entrepreneurship Theory and Practice*, 33: 213–239; C. M. Daily, P. P. McDougall, J. G. Covin and D. R. Dalton, 2002, "Governance and strategic leadership in entrepreneurial firms", *Journal of Management*, 3: 387–412.

122. W. Kiechel III, 2007, "Private equity's long view", *Harvard Business Review*, 85(8): 18–20; M. Wright, R. E. Hoskisson and L. W. Busenitz, 2001, "Firm rebirth: Buyouts as facilitators of strategic growth and entrepreneurship", *Academy of Management Executive*, 15(1): 111–125.

123. E. G. Love and M. Kraatz, 2009, "Character, conformity, or the bottom line? How and why downsizing affected corporate reputation", *Academy of Management Journal*, 52: 314–335; J. P. Guthrie and D. K. Datta, 2008, "Dumb and dumber: The impact of downsizing on firm performance as moderated by industry conditions", *Organization Science*, 19: 108–123.

124. H. A. Krishnan and D. Park, 2002, "The impact of work force reduction on subsequent performance in major mergers and acquisitions: An exploratory study", *Journal of Business Research*, 55(4): 285–292; P. M. Lee, 1997, "A comparative analysis of layoff announcements and stock price reactions in the United States and Japan", *Strategic Management Journal*, 18: 879–894.

125. D. J. Flanagan and K. C. O'shaughnessy, 2005, "The effect of layoffs on firm reputation", *Journal of Management*, 31: 445–463.

126. D. S. DeRue, J. R. Hollenbeck, M. D. Johnson, D. R. Ilgen and D. K. Jundt, 2008, "How different team downsizing approaches influence team-level adaptation and performance", *Academy of Management Journal*, 51: 182–196; C. D. Zatzick and R. D. Iverson, 2006, "High-involvement management and workforce reduction: Competitive advantage or disadvantage?", *Academy of Management Journal*, 49: 999–1015; N. Mirabal and R. DeYoung, 2005, "Downsizing as a strategic intervention", *Journal of American Academy of Business*, 6(1): 39–45.

127. K. Shimizu and M. A. Hitt, 2005, "What constrains or facilitates divestitures of formerly acquired firms? The effects of organisational inertia", *Journal of Management*, 31: 50–72.

128. D. T. Brown, C. E. Fee and S. E. Thomas, 2009, "Financial leverage and bargaining power with suppliers: Evidence from leveraged buyouts", *Journal of Corporate Finance*, 15: 196–211; S. Toms and M. Wright, 2005, "Divergence and convergence within Anglo-American corporate governance systems: Evidence from the US and UK, 1950–2000", *Business History*, 47(2): 267–295.

129. G. Wood and M. Wright, 2009, "Private equity: A review and synthesis", *International Journal of Management Reviews*, 11: 361–380; A. L. Le Nadant and F. Perdreau, 2006, "Financial profile of leveraged buy-out targets: Some French evidence", *Review of Accounting and Finance*, (4): 370–392.

130. G. D. Bruton, J. K. Keels and E. L. Scifres, 2002, "Corporate restructuring and performance: An agency perspective on the complete buyout cycle", *Journal of Business Research*, 55: 709–724; W. F. Long and D. J. Ravenscraft, 1993, "LBOs, debt and R&D intensity", *Strategic Management Journal*, 14 (Special Issue): 119–135.

131. M. Wright, R. E. Hoskisson, L. W. Busenitz and J. Dial, 2000, "Entrepreneurial growth through privatization" *Academy of Management Review*, 25: 591–601; S. A. Zahra, 1995, "Corporate entrepreneurship and financial performance: The case of management leveraged buyouts", *Journal of Business Venturing*, 10: 225–248.

132. R. Chandramouli and S. Bharadwaj-Chand, 2010, "Cemex eyes Penna acquisition", *The Times of India*, www.timesofindia.indiatimes.com, April 28.

# CHAPTER 9

# INTERNATIONAL STRATEGY

## LEARNING OBJECTIVES

Studying this chapter should provide you with the strategic management knowledge needed to:

1. Explain traditional and emerging motives for firms to pursue international diversification.
2. Identify the four major benefits of an international strategy.
3. Explore the four factors that provide a basis for international business-level strategies.
4. Describe the three international corporate-level strategies: multidomestic, global and transnational.
5. Discuss the environmental trends affecting international strategy, especially liability of foreignness and regionalization.
6. Name and describe the five alternative modes for entering international markets.
7. Explain the effects of international diversification on firm returns and innovation.
8. Name and describe two major risks of international diversification.

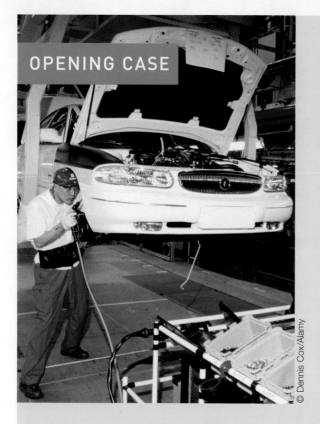

## OPENING CASE

© Dennis Cox/Alamy

# Entry into China by foreign firms and Chinese firms reaching for global markets

Many foreign firms choose to operate in the Chinese market because it is so large and important. This is certainly the case for automobile firms that have used China as a base to both produce cars more cheaply and expand their market by selling in China. In particular General Motors (GM), through its partnership with Shanghai Automotive Industry Corporation (SAIC), has created successful joint ventures. SAIC also has a joint venture with Volkswagen. More recently SAIC has sought to introduce its own automobiles domestically and plans to participate in global markets when possible. Similarly, another GM partner in China, Liuzhou Wuling Motors Co., is planning to develop its own vehicles rather than through a GM brand such as Opel or Vauxhall.

Porsche AG now owns 50.76 per cent of Volkswagen and considers China to be so important that it launched the first exposure of its new model, the Panamera, in a Shanghai automobile show in April 2009. Although the US market still counts as the most important sale zone for Porsche, China was thought to have the largest automobile market by sales volume in 2009. Because the US automobile market and other automobile markets elsewhere in the world are experiencing substantially lower sales, the Chinese market is becoming more important.

The Chinese market is not only important for manufacturing such as the automobile industry, but for services as well. For example, Google recently launched a music service supported by the world's four largest music labels: Warner Music Group Corp., Vivendi SA's Universal Music, EMI Group Ltd, and Sony Corporation's Music Entertainment. Google and its partners hope to draw users away from Google's main Chinese competitors, especially Baidu Inc. Baidu is the dominant market shareholder with approximately 62 per cent of the search market for Web downloads in China. Google increased its search engine market to 28 per cent from 23 per cent in 2007 in China, but Baidu retained its dominance with 62 per cent share, up from 59 per cent in 2007. Google launched this service because a music service is seen as one way to build more market share.

Interestingly, some Chinese firms are more successful abroad than they are in their own home market. Huawei Technologies Co. Ltd is making inroads all over the world. Huawei, a Chinese telecommunications equipment supplier, recently won a contract with Cox Communication, a television cable provider. Huawei is also in the running for a potentially bigger contract with Clearwire Corp. Clearwire is in the process of helping to build a wireless broadband network that would serve 120 million people in North America by 2010. Other finalists for the contract include many other global firms including Motorola Inc., Samsung Electronics Co., and Nokia Siemens Networks. Other competitors include Alcatel-Lucent and Telefon AB L.M. Ericsson. Another Chinese company, ZTE, also competes with these firms. Although Huwaei and ZTE have had more success in developing regions of the world, Huawei has become a major vendor in Europe where it has won numerous contracts with significant telecommunications providers such as Vodafone Group plc and France Telecom SA's Orange. Huawei also has a foothold in Canada where it is building a third generation (3G) network for BCE Inc.'s partners Bell Canada and Telus Corp.

Additionally, Huawei and ZTE were laggards in selling telephone equipment in their home market against Telephon AB L.M. Ericsson, Alcatel-Lucent and Nokia Siemens Networks, mainly because they were an unknown company when the first wireless networks were developed in China. However, thanks to government support for new wireless technology and an aggressive strategy of deeply undercutting competitors' prices, these two firms are beating the rivals previously noted for an estimated €46 billion of spending over the next three years for new 3G wireless networks. China has approximately 659 million mobile subscribers and the rollout of 3G is making sales growth for these markets even more important. It is expected that Huawei and ZTE will double their combined market share for 3G revenue with current wireless network growth. Although Ericsson's market share is remaining stable, Alcatel-Lucent and Nokia Siemens, a joint venture of Nokia Corp. and Siemens AG, market shares are expected to decline in China. Historically, Ericsson won the lion's share because Huawei and ZTE, as noted, were small when the existing network was built in the 1990s. Both companies have access to large credit lines from China's state-owned banks and other perks such as low cost land. This has allowed them to have more flexibility in pricing and to operate with lower margins without shareholder pressure. It will be interesting to see what happens when the fourth-generation (4G) networks are rolled out in a few years.

**Sources:** Back, A. and Chao, L. (2009) "Google begins China music service; Partnership with record labels gives users free access to licensed tracks", *Wall Street Journal*, March 30, B3; Chao, L. (2009) "China's telecom-gear makers, once laggards at home pass foreign rivals", *Wall Street Journal*, April 10, B1; Hille, K. and Parker, A. (2009) "Upwardly mobile-Huawei", *Financial Times*, http://www.ft.com, March 20; Li, K. (2009) "Google launches China service", *Financial Times*, March 31, 20; Rauwald, C. (2009) "Porsche chooses the China road; four-door Panamera's Shanghai debut signals focus on emerging markets", *Wall Street Journal*, April 20, B2; Sharma, A. and Silver, S. (2009) "Huawei tries to crack US market; Chinese telecom supplier wins Cox contract, is finalist for Clear Wire deal", *Wall Street Journal*, March 26, B2; Stoll, J. D. (2009) "Corporate news: GM pushes the throttle in China – affiliate's plan to expand into cars is seen as a key to growth in Asia", *Wall Street Journal*, April 27, B3; Teagarden, M. B. and Cai, D. H. (2009) "Learning from dragons who are learning from us; developmental lessons from China's global companies", *Organizational Dynamics*, 38(1): 73; Tschang, C. C. (2009) "Search engine squeeze?", *BusinessWeek*, January 12, 21; Woyke, E. (2009) "ZTE's smart phone ambitions", *Forbes,* http://www.forbes.com, March 16; Einhorn, B. (2008) "Huawei", *BusinessWeek*, December 22, 51; Tucker, S. (2008) "Case study: Huawei of China takes stock after frustrating year", *Financial Times*, http://www.ft.com, November 25.

## Questions

**1** Globalization means that Chinese firms will expand overseas, as will the Chinese market open to overseas firms. To what extent and how might the global business world alter in ten years time because of these phenomena?

**2** Many firms are now asking themselves, "is it too late to enter China?"[1] To what extent do you agree with this statement?

---

As the Opening Case indicates, firms are entering China because of the significance of the large market, but China's firms are building their competitive capabilities and also seeking to enter foreign markets. China's entrance into the World Trade Organization (WTO) brought change not only to China and its trading partners but also to industries and firms throughout the world. Despite its developing market and institutional environment, Chinese firms such as Huawei are taking advantage of the growing size of the Chinese market; they had previously learned new technologies and managerial capabilities from foreign partners and are now competing more strongly in the domestic markets as well as in foreign markets.[2]

Many firms choose direct investment in assets in foreign countries (e.g., establishing new subsidiaries, making acquisitions or building joint ventures) over indirect investment because it provides better protection for their assets[3]. As indicated in the Opening Case, Chinese firms are developing their manufacturing capabilities and building their own branded products (e.g., Huawei Technologies Co. and ZTE Corp.). As such, the potential global market power of Chinese firms is astounding.[4]

As foreign firms enter China and as Chinese firms enter into other foreign markets, both opportunities and threats for firms competing in global markets are exemplified. This chapter examines opportunities facing firms as they seek to develop and exploit core competencies by diversifying into global markets. In addition, we discuss different problems, complexities and threats that might accompany a firm's international strategy.[5] Although national boundaries, cultural differences, and geographical distances all pose barriers to entry into many markets, significant opportunities motivate businesses to enter international markets. A business that plans to operate globally must formulate a successful strategy to take advantage of these global opportunities.[6] Furthermore, to mould their firms into truly global companies, managers must develop global mindsets.[7] As firms move into international markets, they develop relationships with suppliers, customers and partners, and learn from these relationships. For example, as the opening case illustrates SAIC learned new capabilities from its partnerships with General Motors and Volkswagen.

As illustrated in Figure 9.1, we discuss the importance of international strategy as a source of strategic competitiveness and above-average returns. The chapter focuses on the incentives to internationalize. After a firm decides to compete internationally, it must select its strategy and choose a mode of entry into international markets. It may enter international markets by exporting from domestic-based operations, licensing some of its products or services, forming joint ventures with international partners, acquiring a foreign-based firm, or establishing a new subsidiary. Such international diversification can extend product life cycles, provide incentives for more innovation, and produce above-average returns. These benefits are tempered by political and economic risks and the problems of managing a complex international firm with operations in multiple countries.

Figure 9.1 provides an overview of the various choices and outcomes of strategic competitiveness. The relationships among international opportunities, the resources and capabilities that result in strategies, and the modes of entry that are based on core competencies are explored in this chapter.

**FIGURE 9.1** Opportunities and outcomes of international strategy

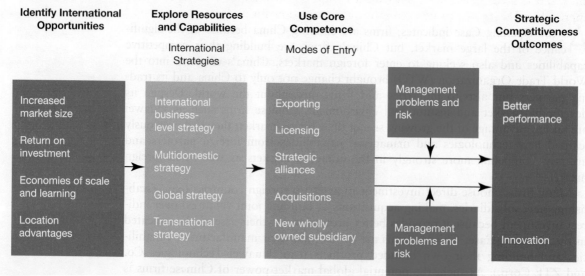

# Identifying international opportunities: incentives to use an international strategy

An international strategy is a strategy through which the firm sells its goods or services outside its domestic market.[8] One of the primary reasons for implementing an international strategy (as opposed to a strategy focused on the domestic market) is that international markets yield potential new opportunities.[9]

Raymond Vernon captured the classic rationale for international diversification.[10] He suggested that typically a firm discovers an innovation in its home-country market, especially in advanced economies such as those of Western Europe. Often demand for the product then develops in other countries, and exports are provided by domestic operations. Increased demand in foreign countries justifies making investments in foreign operations, especially to fend off foreign competitors. Vernon, therefore, observed that one reason why firms pursue international diversification is to extend a product's life cycle.

Another traditional motive for firms to become multinational is to secure needed resources. Key supplies of raw material – especially minerals and energy – are important in some industries. Other industries, such as clothing, electronics and watch making have moved portions of their operations to foreign locations in pursuit of lower production costs. Clearly one of the reasons for Chinese firms' international expansion is to gain access to important resources.[11]

Although these traditional motives persist, other emerging motivations also drive international expansion (see Chapter 1). For instance, pressure has increased for a global integration of operations, mostly driven by more universal product demand. As nations industrialize, the demand for some products and commodities appears to become similar. This borderless demand for globally branded products may be due to similarities in lifestyle in developed nations. Increases in global communication media also facilitate the ability of people in different countries to visualize and model lifestyles in different cultures.[12] IKEA, for example, has become a global brand by selling furniture in 35 countries through over 300 stores that it owns and operates through franchisees. All of its furniture is sold in components that can be packaged in flat packs and assembled by the consumer after purchase. This arrangement has allowed for easier shipping and handling than fully assembled units and has facilitated the development of the global brand. Given its low cost approach, sales are increasing even in the economic downturn.[13]

In some industries, technology drives globalization because the economies of scale necessary to reduce costs to the lowest level often require an investment greater than that needed to meet domestic market demand. Companies also experience pressure for cost reductions, achieved by purchasing from the lowest-cost global suppliers. For instance, research and development expertise for an emerging business start-up may not exist in the domestic market, but as foreign firms locate in the domestic market, learning spillovers occur for domestic firms.[14]

New large-scale, emerging markets, such as China and India, provide a strong internationalization incentive based on their high potential demand for consumer products and services.[15] Currency fluctuations mean firms may also choose to distribute their operations across many countries, including emerging ones, in order to reduce the risk of devaluation in one country.[16] However, the uniqueness of emerging markets presents both opportunities and challenges.[17] Although India, for example, differs from Western countries in many respects, including culture, politics and the precepts of its economic system, it also offers a huge potential market and its government is becoming more supportive of foreign direct investment.[18] However, the differences between China and India and Western countries pose

**International strategy**

An international strategy is a strategy through which the firm sells its goods or services outside its domestic market.

serious challenges to Western competitive paradigms that emphasize the skills needed to manage financial, economic and political risks.[19]

Employment contracts and labour forces differ significantly in international markets. For example, it is more difficult to lay-off employees in Europe than in the US because of employment contract differences. In many cases, host governments demand joint ownership with a local company in order to invest in local operations, and this allows the foreign firm to avoid tariffs. Also, host governments frequently require a high percentage of procurements, manufacturing and R&D to use local sources.[20] These issues increase the need for local investment and responsiveness as opposed to seeking global economies of scale.

We have discussed incentives that influence firms to use international strategies. When these strategies are successful, firms can derive four basic benefits: (1) increased market size; (2) greater returns on major capital investments or on investments in new products and processes; (3) greater economies of scale, scope or learning; and (4) a competitive advantage through location (e.g., access to low-cost labour, critical resources, or customers). We examine these benefits in terms of both their costs (such as higher coordination expenses and limited access to knowledge about host country political influences)[21] and their managerial challenges.

## Increased market size

Firms can expand the size of their potential market – sometimes dramatically – by moving into international markets. Pharmaceutical firms have been doing significant foreign direct investment into both developed and emerging markets due to the opportunity to increase the size of the market of potential drugs. For example, Japanese pharmaceutical firms have been making acquisitions of international rivals since 2008. One analyst noted: "One factor [driving the trend for outbound M&A] is that there are limited domestic growth opportunities … [these Japanese] companies are cash-rich and are in a good position to conduct acquisitions."[22] Indeed, Japan's large pharmaceutical firms collectively paid more than €16 billion recently to buy overseas firms.

Although changing consumer tastes and practices linked to cultural values or traditions is not simple, following an international strategy is a particularly attractive option to firms competing in domestic markets that have limited growth opportunities. For example, firms in the domestic soft drink industry have been searching for growth in foreign markets for some time now. Major competitors, Pepsi and Coca-Cola, have had relatively stable market shares in the US for several years. Most of their sales growth has come from foreign markets. Coca-Cola, for instance, has used a strategy of buying overseas bottlers or expanding into other beverages such as fruit juice. However, a recent acquisition attempt in China of China's largest fruit juice producer, China Huiyuan Juice Group Ltd, was turned down by Beijing regulators claiming that it would crowd out smaller players and increase consumer prices. China is Coca-Cola's fourth largest market by volume after the US, Mexico and Brazil. Like other emerging markets it is growing faster than their home market.[23]

The size of an international market also affects a firm's willingness to invest in R&D to build competitive advantages in that market. Larger markets usually offer higher potential returns and thus pose less risk for a firm's investments. The strength of the science base of the country in question can also affect a firm's foreign R&D investments.[24] Most firms prefer to invest more heavily in those countries with the scientific knowledge and talent to produce value-creating products and processes from their R&D activities.[25]

## *Return on investment*

Large markets may be crucial for earning a return on significant investments, such as plant and capital equipment or R&D. Therefore, most R&D-intensive industries such as electronics are international. In addition to the need for a large market to recoup heavy investment in R&D, the development pace for new technology is increasing. New products become obsolete more rapidly, and therefore investments need to be recouped more quickly. Moreover, firms' abilities to develop new technologies are expanding, and because of different patent laws across country borders, imitation by competitors is more likely. Through reverse engineering, competitors are able to disassemble a product, learn the new technology and develop a similar product. Because competitors can imitate new technologies relatively quickly, firms need to recoup new product development costs even more rapidly. Consequently, the larger markets provided by international expansion are particularly attractive in many industries such as pharmaceuticals, because they expand the opportunity for the firm to recoup significant capital investments and large-scale R&D expenditures.[26]

Regardless of other motives, however, the primary reason for investing in international markets is to generate above-average returns on investments. However, firms from different countries have different expectations and use different criteria, such as industry conditions and the potential for knowledge transfer, to decide whether to invest in international markets.[27]

## *Economies of scale and learning*

By expanding their markets, firms may be able to enjoy economies of scale, particularly in their manufacturing operations. To the extent that a firm can standardize its products across country borders and use the same or similar production facilities, thereby coordinating critical resource functions, it is more likely to achieve optimal economies of scale.[28]

Economies of scale are critical in the global automobile industry. China's decision to join the World Trade Organization has allowed lower tariffs to be charged (in the past, Chinese carmakers have had an advantage over foreign carmakers due to tariffs) and foreign automakers to enter the country. Ford, Honda, General Motors and Volkswagen are each producing an economy car to compete with the existing cars in China. Because of global economies of scale (allowing them to price their products competitively) and local investments in China, all of these companies are likely to obtain significant market share in China. Alternatively, SAIC is developing its branded vehicles to compete with the foreign automakers. SAIC's joint ventures with both GM and Volkswagen have been highly successful (as explained in the Opening Case). However, as also explained in the Opening Case, Porsche is seeking to market its vehicles in China to extend its scale economies, while Chinese firm are seek to begin exporting vehicles overseas and perhaps enter foreign markets in other ways such as through acquisitions.[29]

Firms may also be able to exploit core competencies in international markets through resource- and knowledge-sharing between units and network partners across country borders.[30] This sharing generates synergy, which helps the firm produce higher-quality goods or services at lower cost. In addition, working across international markets provides the firm with new learning opportunities.[31] Multinational firms have substantial occasions to learn from the different practices they encounter in separate international markets. However, research finds that to take advantage of the international R&D investments, firms need to already have a strong R&D system in place to absorb the knowledge.[32]

## Location advantages

Firms may locate facilities in other countries to lower the basic costs of the goods or services they provide. These facilities may provide easier access to lower-cost labour, energy, and other natural resources. Other location advantages include access to critical supplies and to customers. Once positioned favourably with an attractive location, firms must manage their facilities effectively to gain the full benefit of a location advantage.[33]

Such location advantages can be influenced by costs of production and transportation requirements as well as by the needs of the intended customers.[34] Cultural influences may also affect location advantages and disadvantages. If there is a strong match between the cultures in which international transactions are carried out, the liability of foreignness is lower than if there is high cultural distance.[35] Research also suggests that regulation distances influence the ownership positions of multinational firms as well as their strategies for managing local and expatriate human resources.[36]

As suggested in the Opening Case, General Motors (GM) entered international markets to expand its market size. It is also earning positive returns on its international investments, primarily in Asia. In fact, GM's recent return to profitability is due to its Asian operations, specifically in China. While GM has lost its position as the world's largest automaker after 76 years, it has major expansion plans for its China ventures. However, GM faces a number of challenges from domestic Chinese competitors, such as its partners, SAIC and Liuzhou Wuling Motors Co., and from foreign competitors, such as Toyota and Volkswagen. It will have to formulate and implement a successful strategy for the Chinese market to maintain its current competitive advantage there. As has been claimed recently: "China is expected to become the world's No. 1 vehicle producer this year [2009], surpassing Japan. Mr. Young [chief financial officer of GM] said he is starting to think China could outmuscle the United States this year as the No. 1 market for vehicle sales. GM had been predicting China would surpass the United States in 2015, but Chinese sales leapfrogged those in the United States in the first quarter [2009]."[37]

# International strategies

Firms choose to use one or both of two basic types of international strategies: business-level international strategy and corporate-level international strategy. At the business level, firms follow generic strategies: cost leadership, differentiation, focused cost leadership, focused differentiation, or integrated cost leadership/ differentiation. The three corporate-level international strategies are multidomestic, global, or transnational (a combination of multidomestic and global). To create competitive advantage, each strategy must utilize a core competence based on difficult-to-imitate resources and capabilities.[38] As discussed in Chapters 5 and 7, firms expect to create value through the implementation of a business-level strategy and a corporate-level strategy.

## International business-level strategy

Each business must develop a competitive strategy focused on its own domestic market. We discussed business-level strategies in Chapter 5 and competitive rivalry and competitive dynamics in Chapter 6. International business-level strategies have some unique features. In an international business-level strategy, the home country of operation is often the most important source of competitive advantage.[39] The resources and capabilities established in the home country frequently allow the firm to pursue the strategy into markets located in other countries.[40] However, research indicates that as a firm continues its growth into multiple international locations, the country of origin is less important for competitive advantage.[41]

Michael Porter's model, illustrated in Figure 9.2, describes the factors contributing to the advantage of firms in a dominant global industry and associated with a specific home country or regional environment.[42] The first dimension in Porter's model is the factors of production. This dimension refers to the inputs necessary to compete in any industry – labour, land, natural resources, capital and infrastructure (such as transportation, postal and communication systems). There are basic factors (for example, natural and labour resources) and advanced factors (such as digital communication systems and a highly educated workforce). Other production factors are generalized (highway systems and the supply of debt capital) and specialized (skilled personnel in a specific industry, such as the workers in a port that specialize in handling bulk chemicals). If a country has both advanced and specialized production factors, it is likely to serve an industry well by spawning strong home-country competitors that can also be successful global competitors.

Ironically, countries often develop advanced and specialized factors because they lack critical basic resources. For example, some Asian countries, such as South Korea, lack abundant natural resources but offer a strong work ethic, a large number of engineers and systems of large firms to create an expertise in manufacturing. Similarly, Germany developed a strong chemical industry, partially because Hoechst and BASF spent years creating a synthetic indigo dye to reduce their dependence on imports, unlike the UK, whose colonies provided large supplies of natural indigo.[43]

The second dimension in Porter's model, demand conditions, is characterized by the nature and size of buyers' needs in the home market for the industry's goods or services. A large market segment can produce the demand necessary to create scale-efficient facilities.

Chinese manufacturing companies have spent years focused on building their businesses in China, but are now beginning to look at markets beyond their

**FIGURE 9.2** Determinants of national strategy

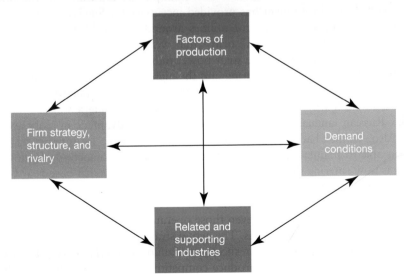

borders, as described in the Opening Case about SAIC. As mentioned, SAIC (along with other Chinese firms) has begun the challenging process of building its brand equity in China but especially in other countries. In doing so, most Chinese firms begin in the Far East with the intention of moving into Western markets when ready. Companies such as SAIC have been helped by China's entry to the World Trade Organization. Of course, companies such as SAIC are interested in entering international markets to increase their market share and profits.

Related and supporting industries are the third dimension in Porter's model. Italy has become the leader in the shoe industry because of related and supporting industries; a well-established leather-processing industry provides the leather needed to construct shoes and related products. Also, many people travel to Italy to purchase leather goods, providing support in distribution. Supporting industries in leather-working machinery and design services also contribute to the success of the shoe industry. In fact, the design services industry supports its own related industries, such as ski boots, fashion apparel and furniture. In Japan, cameras and copiers are related industries. Similarly, it is argued that the creative resources associated with popular cartoons such as Manga, and the animation sector along with technological knowledge from the consumer electronics industry, facilitated the emergence of a successful video game industry in Japan.[44] (see Chapter 4, closing case).

Firm strategy, structure and rivalry make up the final country dimension and also foster the growth of certain industries. The types of strategy, structure and rivalry among firms vary greatly from nation to nation. The excellent technical training system in Germany fosters a strong emphasis on continuous product and process improvements. In Japan, unusual cooperative and competitive systems have facilitated the cross-functional management of complex assembly operations. In Italy, the national pride of the country's designers has spawned strong industries in sports cars, fashion apparel and furniture. In the US, competition among computer manufacturers and software producers has contributed to the development of these industries.

The four basic dimensions of the "diamond" model in Figure 9.2 emphasize the environmental or structural attributes of a national economy that contribute to national advantage. Government policy also clearly contributes to the success and failure of many firms and industries. For example, as illustrated in the Strategic Focus, the Chinese government has provided incentives for SunTech, a Chinese firm focused on creating solar power for utilities around the world, particularly in Europe.[45] Sun Tech is a "born global" firm[46] that went directly into international markets that were emerging within the solar power industry. It has been successful so far because of the low-cost manufacturing and the high levels of engineering talent available in China. Likewise, Yandex in Russia (see the Strategic Focus) was successful because it found a way to meet the complexities of developing a search tool for the complex Russian language, which turned out to be an advantage in global competition.[47] Also, Yandex had strong demand conditions in Russia for Internet service and has been able to maintain its market share against strong competition from Google. Yandex is now entering the US market and establishing a research base near Google's headquarters to advance its knowledge base even further.

Although each firm must create its own success, not all firms will survive to become global competitors – not even those operating with the same country factors that spawned other successful firms. The actual strategic choices managers make may be the most compelling reason for success or failure. Accordingly, the factors illustrated in Figure 9.2 are likely to produce competitive advantages only when the firm develops and implements an appropriate strategy that takes advantage of distinct country factors. Thus, these distinct country factors must be given thorough consideration when making a decision regarding the business-level strategy to use (i.e., cost

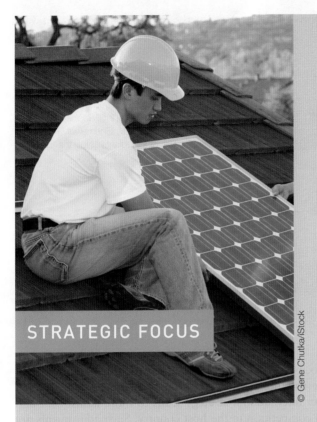

## STRATEGIC FOCUS

© Gene Chutka/iStock

# Country conditions spawn successful high technology firms in emerging markets

Few firms from large emerging economies have been more successful than SunTech Power Holdings which manufactures solar panels in China for the global electric utilities industry. It was a "born global" firm founded in China and was competing right away with large firms that dominated the industry such as Sharpe, Siemens and BP Solar. It was initiated by Shi Zhengrong and he is still the CEO of SunTech. He was allocated nearly €5 million start-up money from the government of Wuxi in China's Jiangsu province. Shi was trained in Australia at the University of New South Wales in Sydney where he gained his Ph.D.

SunTech's biggest markets for solar panels and modules are in Europe with German companies providing its largest amount of revenue. There was overcapacity in the industry in 2009, partly because SunTech spawned lots of imitators. iSuppli, a research company which provides analytical data for the solar industry, suggests that there were 11.1 gigawatts of

panels produced in 2009, up 62 per cent from 7.7 gigawatts in 2008. SunTech itself produces one gigawatt and hoped to produce 1.4 gigawatts by the end of 2009 and two gigawatts by 2010. However, SunTech's expansion plans are currently on hold until the financial crisis is over and the markets improve; in fact, SunTech laid-off of 800 employees in 2008.

The big advantage that SunTech has is its low-cost production system in China. It hopes to have "grid parity" which means that the cost of producing solar energy is at the point where there is no difference between competing fossil fuels like coal and natural gas relative to that produced by solar panels. Currently, SunTech is producing at a cost of €0.28 per kilowatt hour whereas the grid parity cost is near €0.11. Although this suggests that the firm has a long way to go to realize grid parity, Shi believes that it can be realized in several years given its low cost of production and improvements in technological efficiency. The company has improved the collective power of the solar panel primarily through advancements in silicon technology.

Russia's largest online search company, Yandex, is equivalent to Google in many other markets. Interestingly, Yandex started in the 1980s, long before Google's founders Sergey Brin and Larry Page had envisioned Google. Yandex arguably has superior search technology because of the peculiarities of the Russian language. Russian words often have 20 different endings that indicate their relationship one to another and make the language much more precise, but at the same time it makes searching words much more difficult than in English. However, Yandex found a way to catch all of this phraseology and as such it controls 56 per cent of the search engine market share in Russia, compared to Google's 23 per cent. More impressively it has two-thirds of all of the revenue from the search ads and draws three billion hits a month. Due to this, Firefox has dropped Google as its default search engine in Russia in favour of Yandex.

Yandex realizes that it must continue to innovate. For instance, it has an image search engine that eliminates repeated images and filters out faces, thus providing better search capabilities for imaging. In addition, as mentioned in the chapter, Yandex has opened labs not far from Google's headquarters in California, with a staff of 20 or more engineers that index pages for a Russian audience but also keep abreast of technology developments that surface near Silicon Valley. According to Arkady Volozh, CEO of Yandex, Yahoo, Microsoft and Google have made repeated buyout offers for Yandex. Such offers suggest that Google and other companies would be interested in increasing their market share in Russia. One reason for this interest is that Russia has the fastest growing Internet population in Europe. Google has increased its market share from 6 per cent in 2001 to 23 per cent in 2009, most likely because it hired engineers that understand the Russian language. One analyst indicated that due to the high demand for Internet service "Russia is a pivotal country for Google".

Yandex is one of the few high tech companies that was home grown in Russia and is successful. The Russians are proud of this fact. The company hopes to continue to be successful and possibly even compete for market share in Google's prime markets.

**Sources:** Ioffe, J. (2009) "The Russians are coming", *Fortune*, February 16, 36–38; Powell, B. (2009) "China's new king of

solar", *Fortune*, February 16, 94–97; White, G. L. (2009) "Russia web firm negotiates autonomy", *Wall Street Journal*, April 22, A10; 2008, "China-based Suntech plans to triple US sales through acquisitions, residential sales", *FinancialWire*, http://www.financialwire.net, October 2; Bush, J. (2008) "Where Google isn't Goliath: Russia's Yandex – set to go public on Nasdaq – is innovating in a hurry to hold off the US giant", *BusinessWeek*, http://www.businessweek.com, June 26; Ghemawat, P. and Hout, T. (2008) "Tomorrow's global giants: Not the usual suspects", *Harvard Business Review*, 86(11): 80–88.

## Questions

1 What are "born global" firms and what characteristics do they exhibit that enable them to become such high growth firms?

2 To what extent does Yandex pose an opposition to Google?

leadership, differentiation, focused cost leadership, focused differentiation and integrated cost leadership/differentiation, discussed in Chapter 5) in an international context. However, pursuing an international strategy leads to more adjustment and learning as the firm adjusts to competition in the host country. Such adjustments are continuous as illustrated by SunTech's operations, given the steep decline in demand for solar facilities in the economic downturn. It must adapt to the increasing competition from other start-ups, and its major competitors in global markets.

## International corporate-level strategy

The international business-level strategies are based at least partially on the type of international corporate-level strategy the firm has chosen. Some corporate strategies give individual country units the authority to develop their own business-level strategies; other corporate strategies dictate the business-level strategies in order to standardize the firm's products and sharing of resources across countries.[48] International corporate-level strategy focuses on the scope of a firm's operations through both product and geographic diversification.[49] International corporate-level strategy is required when the firm operates in multiple industries and multiple countries or regions.[50] The headquarters unit guides the strategy, although business- or country-level managers can have substantial strategic input, depending on the type of international corporate-level strategy followed. The three international corporate-level strategies are multidomestic, global and transnational, as shown in Figure 9.3.

### Multidomestic strategy

**Multidomestic strategy**

A multidomestic strategy is an international strategy in which strategic and operating decisions are decentralized to the strategic business unit in each country so as to allow that unit to tailor products to the local market.

A multidomestic strategy is an international strategy in which strategic and operating decisions are decentralized to the strategic business unit in each country so as to allow that unit to tailor products to the local market.[51] A multidomestic strategy focuses on competition within each country. It assumes that the markets differ and therefore are segmented by country boundaries. The multidomestic strategy uses a highly decentralized approach, allowing each division to focus on a geographic area, region, or country.[52] In other words, consumer needs and desires, industry conditions (e.g., the number and type of competitors),

**FIGURE 9.3** International corporate-level strategies

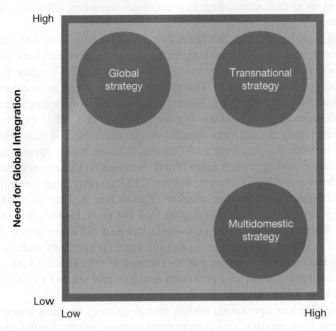

political and legal structures and social norms vary by country. With multidomestic strategies, the country managers have the autonomy to customize the firm's products as necessary to meet the specific needs and preferences of local customers. Therefore, these strategies should maximize a firm's competitive response to the idiosyncratic requirements of each market.[53]

The use of multidomestic strategies usually expands the firm's local market share because the firm can pay attention to the needs of the local clientele.[54] However, the use of these strategies results in less knowledge sharing for the corporation as a whole because of the differences across markets, decentralization and the different strategies employed by local country units.[55] Moreover, multidomestic strategies do not allow the development of economies of scale and thus can be more costly. As a result, firms employing a multidomestic strategy decentralize their strategic and operating decisions to the business units operating in each country. Historically, Unilever, an Anglo-Dutch consumer products firm, has had a highly decentralized approach to managing its international operations. This approach allows regional managers considerable autonomy to adapt the product offerings to fit the market needs. However, more recently it has sought better coordination between its independent country subsidiaries and to develop a strong global brand presence.[56]

**Global strategy** In contrast to a multidomestic strategy, a global strategy assumes more standardization of products across country markets.[57] As a result, a global strategy is centralized and controlled by the home office. The strategic business units operating in each country are assumed to be interdependent, and the home office attempts to achieve integration across these businesses.[58] The firm uses a global strategy to offer standardized products across country markets, with competitive strategy being dictated by the home office. Thus, a global strategy emphasizes economies of scale and offers greater opportunities to take innovations

**Global strategy**

A global strategy is an international strategy through which the firm offers standardized products across country markets, with competitive strategy being dictated by the home office.

developed at the corporate level in one country and utilize them in other markets.[59] Improvements in global accounting and financial reporting standards are facilitating this strategy.[60]

Although a global strategy produces lower risk, it may cause the firm to forego growth opportunities in local markets, either because those markets are less likely to be identified as opportunities or because the opportunities require that products be adapted to the local market.[61] The global strategy is not as responsive to local markets and is difficult to manage because of the need to coordinate strategies and operating decisions across country borders. Yahoo and eBay experienced these challenges when they moved into specific Asian markets. For example, eBay was unsuccessful in both the Japanese and Chinese markets when attempting to export its business model and approach from North America to these two countries. It has re-entered China but Meg Whitman, former CEO of eBay, suggested that she had no plans to re-enter the Japanese market. Yahoo has had rough times in China, going through several CEOs and trying to find the right formula to compete effectively in the Chinese market.[62] Also, Google has had difficulty penetrating foreign markets such as China and competing against local competitors such as Baidu, notwithstanding that fact that Google has threatened to retreat from China because of government interventions in its operations and has and started to channel searches through its Hong Kong servers.

Achieving efficient operations with a global strategy requires sharing resources and facilitating coordination and cooperation across country boundaries, which in turn require centralization and headquarters control. Furthermore, research suggests that the performance of the global strategy is enhanced if it deploys in areas where regional integration among countries is occurring, such as the European Union.[63] Many Japanese firms have successfully used the global strategy.[64]

CEMEX is the third largest cement company in the world, behind France's Lafarge and Switzerland's Holcim, and is the largest producer of ready mix, a prepackaged product that contains all the ingredients needed to make localized cement products. CEMEX has strong market power throughout Europe and the Americas. CEMEX serves customers in more than 50 countries with more than 50 000 employees globally. On the basis that CEMEX pursues an effective global strategy, its centralization process has facilitated the integration of several businesses it acquired in Europe, Asia and the US. To integrate its businesses globally, CEMEX uses the Internet to improve logistics and manage an extensive supply network thereby increasing revenue and reducing costs. Connectivity between the operations in different countries and universal standards dominates its approach. However, because of its recent acquisition of Ringer, a large Australian cement producer, it took on too much debt during the downturn and has had a very difficult time meeting its debt obligations.[65] Because of increasing global competition and the need to be cost efficient while simultaneously provide high-quality differentiated products, a number of firms have begun to pursue the transnational strategy, which is described next.

## Transnational strategy

**Transnational strategy**

A transnational strategy is an international strategy through which the firm seeks to achieve both global efficiency and local responsiveness.

A transnational strategy is an international strategy through which the firm seeks to achieve both global efficiency and local responsiveness. Realizing these goals is difficult: One requires close global coordination while the other requires local flexibility. "Flexible coordination" – building a shared vision and individual commitment through an integrated network – is required to implement the transnational strategy. Such integrated networks allow a firm to manage its connections with customers, suppliers, partners, and other parties more efficiently rather than using arm's-length transactions.[66] The transnational strategy is difficult to use because of its conflicting goals. On the positive side, the effective implementation of a transnational strategy often produces higher performance than does the implementation of either the multidomestic or global international corporate-level strategies, although it is difficult to accomplish.[67]

Transnational strategies are challenging to implement but are becoming increasingly necessary to compete in international markets. The growing number of global competitors heightens the requirement to hold costs down. However, the increasing sophistication of markets with greater information flow (e.g., based on the diffusion of the Internet) and the desire for specialized products to meet consumers' needs, pressures firms to differentiate and even customize their products in local markets. Differences in culture and institutional environments also require firms to adapt their products and approaches to local environments. However, some argue that most multinationals pursue more regional strategies and as such transnational strategies and structures may not be as necessary as once thought.[68]

# Environmental trends

Although the transnational strategy is difficult to implement, emphasis on global efficiency is increasing as more industries begin to experience global competition. To add to the problem, an increased emphasis on local requirements means that global goods and services often demand some customization to meet government regulations within particular countries or to fit customer tastes and preferences. In addition, most multinational firms desire coordination and sharing of resources across country markets to hold down costs, as illustrated by the CEMEX example.[69] Furthermore, some products and industries may be more suited than others for standardization across country borders.

As a result, some large multinational firms with diverse products employ a multidomestic strategy with certain product lines and a global strategy with others. Many multinational firms may require this type of flexibility if they are to be strategically competitive, in part due to trends that change over time. Two important trends are the liability of foreignness and regionalization.

## Liability of foreignness

The dramatic success of Japanese firms such as Toyota and Sony in international markets in the 1980s was a powerful jolt to European managers and awakened them to the importance of international competition in markets that were rapidly becoming global markets. In the twenty-first century, Brazil, Russia, India and China (the so-called BRIC countries) represent major international market opportunities for firms from many countries, including Japan, Korea, the European Union and the US.[70] However, there are legitimate concerns about the relative attractiveness of global strategies, due to the extra costs incurred to pursue internationalization, or the liability of foreignness relative to domestic competitors in a host country.[71] This is illustrated by the experience of Walt Disney Company in opening overseas theme parks. For example, Disney suffered "lawsuits in France, at Disneyland Paris, because of the lack of fit between its transferred personnel policies and the French employees charged to enact them".[72] Disney executives learned from this experience when building the firm's newest theme park in Hong Kong.

Research shows that global strategies are not as prevalent as they once were and are still difficult to implement, even when using Internet-based strategies.[73] In addition, the amount of competition vying for a limited amount of resources and customers can limit firms' focus to regional rather than global markets. A regional focus allows firms to marshal their resources to compete effectively in regional markets rather than spreading their limited resources across many international markets.[74]

As such, firms may focus less on truly global markets and more on regional adaptation. Although parallel developments in the Internet and mobile telecommunication facilitate communications across the globe, as noted earlier, the implementation of Web-based strategies also requires local adaptation. The globalization of businesses with local strategies is demonstrated by the strategy that Google is using (see the Opening Case) by developing an online music download business in China.

## Regionalization

Regionalization is a second trend that has become more common in global markets. A firm's location can affect its strategic competitiveness[75] and consequently it must decide whether to compete in all or many global markets, or to focus on a particular region or regions. Competing in all markets provides economies that can be achieved because of the combined market size. Research suggests that firms that compete in risky emerging markets can also have higher performance.[76]

However, a firm that competes in industries where the international markets differ greatly (in which it must employ a multidomestic strategy) may wish to narrow its focus to a particular region of the world. In so doing, it can better understand the cultures, legal and social norms, and other factors that are important for effective competition in those markets. For example, a firm may focus on Far East markets only rather than competing simultaneously in the Middle East, Europe and the Far East. Or the firm may choose a region of the world where the markets are more similar and some coordination and sharing of resources would be possible. In this way, the firm may be able not only to better understand the markets in which it competes, but also to achieve some economies, even though it may have to employ a multidomestic strategy. For instance, research suggests that most large retailers are better at focusing on a particular region rather than being truly global.[77] Firms commonly focus much of their international market entries into countries adjacent to their home country, which might be referred to as their home region.[78]

Countries that develop trade agreements to increase the economic power of their regions may promote regional strategies. The European Union (EU) and South America's Organization of American States (OAS) are country associations that developed trade agreements to promote the flow of trade across country boundaries within their respective regions.[79] Many European firms acquire and integrate their businesses in Europe to better coordinate pan-European brands as the EU creates more unity in European markets. With this process likely to continue as new countries are added to the agreement, some international firms may prefer to pursue regional strategies versus global strategies because the size of the market is increasing.[80]

The North American Free Trade Agreement (NAFTA), signed by the US, Canada, and Mexico, facilitates free trade across country borders in North America. NAFTA loosens restrictions on international strategies within this region and provides greater opportunity for regional international strategies.[81] NAFTA does not exist for the sole purpose of US businesses moving across its borders. In fact, Mexico is the number two trading partner of the United States, and NAFTA greatly increased Mexico's exports to the United States. Research suggests that managers of small and medium-sized firms are influenced by the strategy they implement (those with a differentiation strategy are more positively disposed to the agreement than are those pursuing a cost leadership strategy) and by their experience and rivalry with exporting firms.[82]

Most firms enter regional markets sequentially, beginning in markets with which they are more familiar. They also introduce their largest and strongest lines of business into these markets first, followed by their other lines of business once the first lines achieve success. They also usually invest in the same area as their original investment location.[83] However, research also suggests that the size of the market and industry characteristics can influence this decision.[84]

After the firm selects its international strategies and decides whether to employ them in regional or world markets, it must choose a market entry mode.[85]

# Choice of international entry mode

International expansion is accomplished by exporting products, participating in licensing arrangements, forming strategic alliances, making acquisitions and establishing new wholly owned subsidiaries. These means of entering international markets and their characteristics are shown in Table 9.1. Each means of market entry has its advantages and disadvantages. Thus, choosing the appropriate mode or path to enter international markets affects the firm's performance in those markets.

## Exporting

Many industrial firms begin their international expansion by exporting goods or services to other countries.[86] Exporting does not require the expense of establishing operations in the host countries, but exporters must establish some means of marketing and distributing their products. Usually, exporting firms develop contractual arrangements with host-country firms.

The disadvantages of exporting include the often high costs of transportation and tariffs placed on some incoming goods. Furthermore, the exporter has less control over the marketing and distribution of its products in the host country and

**Exporting**

Exporting describes the international trade of goods or services shipped from an exporting company in one country to an importing company in another country or countries.

**Table 9.1** Global market entry

| Entry mode | Characteristics |
| --- | --- |
| Exporting | High cost, low control |
| Licensing | Low cost, low risk, little control, low returns |
| Strategic alliances | Shared costs, shared resources, shared risks, problems of integration (e.g., two corporate cultures) |
| Acquisition | Quick access to new market, high cost, complex negotiations, problems of merging with domestic operations |
| New wholly owned subsidiary | Complex, often costly, time consuming, high risk, maximum control, potential above-average returns |

must either pay the distributor or allow the distributor to add to the price to recoup its costs and earn a profit.

As a result, it may be difficult to market a competitive product through exporting or to provide a product that is customized to each international market.[87] However, evidence suggests that cost leadership strategies enhance the performance of exports in developed countries, whereas larger scale differentiation strategies are more successful in emerging economies.[88]

Firms export mostly to countries that are closest to their facilities because of the lower transportation costs and the usually greater similarity between geographic neighbours. This is why export trade within the European Union is among the greatest in the world. The Internet has also made exporting easier.[89] Even small firms can access critical information about foreign markets, examine a target market, research the competition, and find lists of potential customers.[90] Governments also use the Internet to facilitate applications for trade licences.

Small businesses are most likely to use the exporting mode of international entry because of its limited risk and high potential. Currency exchange rates are one of the most significant problems small businesses face. The euro's strength in recent years has meant exports are more expensive for overseas consumers but corresponding imports are relatively cheaper. Despite this, considering Europe as one large domestic market, European business still accounts for 39 per cent of international trade.[91] The Euro currency crisis related to Greece and Ireland in 2010 has the potential to trigger much change.

## Licensing

**Licensing**

A licensing arrangement allows a foreign company to purchase the right to manufacture and sell the firm's products within a host country or set of countries.

Licensing is an increasingly common form of organizational network, particularly among smaller firms.[92] A licensing arrangement allows a foreign company to purchase the right to manufacture and sell the firm's products within a host country or set of countries.[93] The licensor is normally paid a royalty on each unit produced and sold. The licensee takes the risks and makes the monetary investments in facilities for manufacturing, marketing and distributing the goods or services. As a result, licensing is possibly the least costly form of international expansion.

China is a large and growing market for cigarettes, whereas the Western European market is shrinking due to health concerns. Nonetheless, European and US cigarette manufacturers have had trouble entering the Chinese market because state-owned tobacco firms have lobbied against such entry. Consequently, cigarette company Philip Morris International (PMI), which was separated from its former parent company Altria, had an incentive to form a deal with these state-owned firms. Such an agreement provides the state-owned firms access to the most famous brand in the world, Marlboro. Accordingly, both the Chinese firms and PMI have formed a licensing agreement to take advantage of the opportunity as China opens its markets more fully.[94] Because it is a licensing agreement rather than a foreign direct investment by PMI, China maintains control of the distribution. But the Chinese state-owned tobacco monopoly, as part of the agreement, also has PMI's help to distribute its own brands in select foreign markets. "The question is whether it can pluck three cigarette brands – RGD, Harmony and Dubliss – from relative obscurity and elevate them to an international, or at least regional, presence."[95]

Licensing is also a way to expand returns based on prior innovations.[96] Even if product life cycles are short, licensing may be a useful tool. For instance, because the toy industry faces relentless change and an unpredictable buying public, licensing is used and contracts are often completed in foreign markets where labour may be less expensive.[97] Google, as the Opening Case illustrates, facilitated licence agreements with the top four music producers in support of its strategy to gain more market share from Baidu in China.

Licensing also has disadvantages. For example, it gives the firm little control over the manufacture and marketing of its products in other countries. Thus, licence deals must be properly structured.[98] In addition, licensing provides the least potential returns, because returns must be shared between the licensor and the licensee. Additionally, the international firm may learn the technology and produce and sell a similar competitive product after the licence expires. Komatsu, for example, first licensed much of its technology from International Harvester, Bucyrus-Erie and Cummins Engine Co. to compete against Caterpillar in the earthmoving equipment business. Komatsu then dropped these licences and developed its own products using the technology it had gained from other companies.[99] Like most global hotel chains Starwood Hotels & Resorts Worldwide Inc. (the name behind Sheraton, Le Meridien and Westin Hotel brands among others) uses a franchise licensing arrangement and does not own most of its hotels. While focusing on other brands it has let its Sheraton brand slip in quality. Given the recent economic downturn, it is going to be difficult to get the owners to invest in needed design improvements and upgrades, especially given the owner differences in varying geographic markets.[100] Thus licensing can also lead to inflexibilities and as such it is important that a firm think ahead and consider the consequences of each entry, especially in international markets.[101] However, international expansion via franchising, even in the midst of an economic downturn, can be beneficial to the owners of a franchise as has been the experience of Mamas & Papas Ltd over the last four years. As the following Strategic Focus indicates, this is a firm that started to import on a small scale for wholesale distribution purposes, and has grown to become a leading international nursery brand.

## Strategic alliances

In recent years, strategic alliances have become a popular means of international expansion.[102] Strategic alliances allow firms to share the risks and the resources required to enter international markets.[103] Moreover, strategic alliances can facilitate the development of new core competencies that contribute to the firm's future strategic competitiveness.[104]

As explained in the Opening Case, GM formed a joint venture with SAIC and this venture produced Buick and Cadillac autos for the Chinese market. The alliance has been highly successful for both firms. Similar to this example, most international strategic alliances are formed with a host-country firm that knows and understands the competitive conditions, legal and social norms, and cultural idiosyncrasies of the country, which helps the expanding firm manufacture and market a competitive product. Often, firms in emerging economies want to form international alliances and ventures to gain access to sophisticated technologies that are new to them. Gaining access to new technologies and markets is one of ZTE's goals in seeking alliances with mobile telephone firms, Vodafone and Ericsson for example. ZTE, as introduced in the Opening Case, is a telecommunications network gear producer, but it also produces mobile phones. It is now working on agreements with firms to produce "smart phones" for 3G and 4G systems to advance its product portfolio.[105] This type of arrangement can benefit the non-emerging economy firm as well, in that it gains access to a new market and does not have to pay tariffs to do so (because it is

# STRATEGIC FOCUS

# Mamas & Papas

The group finance director of Mamas & Papas Ltd, Jason Greenwood, stated that "2009 was another strong year for Mamas & Papas, driven by the opening of new stores, diversification in our award-winning product ranges and the announcement of further global expansion". Established in 1981, Mamas and Papas is a privately-owned firm based in the UK which supplies high quality baby care products. The idea to set up the company was the result of identifying a gap in the market when David and Luisa Scacchetti began to shop for baby items in preparation for their own first child and wanted "beautiful things" to surround their newly born child. They were unsuccessful in finding anything that suited their tastes in the UK market and so began to import high quality baby items for wholesale. The success of this led to the opening of their first store in 1998 in Northampton, when they began retailing under their own brand name having found a need to provide the UK market with baby products with a designer edge.

Mamas & Papas offers over 2500 products from a range that includes prams, car seats, baby carriers,

nursery furnishings (including furniture and interiors), toys, monitors, baby wear and also maternity clothing. Following an expansion programme in response to a boost in sales in 2009 there are currently more than 40 stores in the UK and Ireland alone, and they also distribute their items through 250 national and independent retailers. Mamas & Papas opened a flagship store on Regent Street in London in 2006.

Mamas & Papas now operate within the US and Hong Kong but are also increasing their number of franchises in the Middle East. In 2007, they began their international franchising strategy in the Middle East following a franchise agreement with the Al Taver Group based in Dubai and signed in 2006. (Al Taver Group represent some of the world's most well-known brands.) This includes the opening of stores in the United Arab Emirates, Kuwait, Qatar, Bahrain and Oman. In order to gather invaluable information about the franchise markets within the Middle East, the firm worked with their local UK Trade and Investment advisors, critical for a company without previous experience within the Middle East market; 2007 saw the first outlet in the UAE opening in Abu Dhabi followed closely by Qatar and Kuwait. As a result of the success of the first batch of franchise stores opened in the Middle East, a further seven retail stores in the region has since opened. The first in the expansion programme was a flagship store opened in Dubai Mall in 2009. There are now more than ten stores within the Middle East.

The Mamas & Papas mission is to become the world's favourite nursery brand and so has undertaken an extensive expansion strategy. As a result of their phenomenal success internationally they won the Global Retail & Leisure International Awards 2008 "Rising Star of the Year Award". At the time of the award, Mamas & Papas had opened eight international stores in as many months. At the end of 2008, the firm also signed agreements with a Russian company FD Lab Group who would open an estimated 30 stores around Russia over a five-year period.

The Mamas & Papas brand has grown enormously in the worldwide arena since the opening of its flagship store and is becoming the fastest growing UK-based brand worldwide in the luxury goods sector. They have seen a high number of enquiries relating to their international franchises. They believe, however, that the "key to this global expansion is choosing the right partner who shares the same vision and synergies as

Mamas & Papas" (Richard Faulkner, Deputy CEO). Although there are extensive plans for international growth the firm believes that it should not be rushed. In 2010, the firm secured a new funding package from HSBC to support its expansion overseas which included Europe, the Middle East, Russia and Japan. Partners of the company must understand the brand fully and take as much pride in the brand as the family members who run the firm. The company remains a family business and Mamas and Papas currently has 1200 employees worldwide.

**Sources:** AMEInfo (2007) "Mamas & Papas – UK's leading nursery and maternity retailer launches in the UAE", http://www.ameinfo.com, February 8; AMEInfo Website (2009) "Mamas & Papas celebrates major expansion into the Middle East through partnership with Al Tayer Group", http://www.ameinfo.com/180899.html, January 12; Billings, S. (2006) "Mamas & Papas conceives international expansion plans", *Design Week Magazine*, June 1: 4; Bridge, E. (2007) "Prams importer turned her baby into £100m firm", *Times Online*, http://www.business.timesonline.co.uk, August 26 ; Corporate Information (2010) Mamas & Papas, http://www.mamasandpapas.com, June 10; Franchiseek Limited Website (2010) "Mamas and Papas aiming to become the world's favourite nursery brand" http://www.franchiseek.com, June 18; Instore Magazine (2008) "Russia expecting Mamas & Papas stores", October: 15; Griffiths, J. (2008) "Market Assessment – Baby Products" (Fourth Edition), Key Note Report, November; King, I. (2010) "Mamas & Papas secures funds for global expansion", *Times Online*, http://www.business.timesonline.co.uk, January 11.

## Questions

**1** What are the strategic and marketing reasons for Mamas & Papas success internationally?

**2** What international strategy challenges do you anticipate confront Mamas & Papas over the next five to ten years?

partnering with a local company). In return, the host-country firm may find its new access to the expanding firm's technology and innovative products attractive.

Each partner in an alliance brings knowledge or resources to the partnership. Indeed, partners often enter an alliance with the purpose of learning new capabilities.[106] Common among those desired capabilities are technological skills. However, for technological knowledge to be transferred in an alliance usually requires trust between the partners.[107] Managing these expectations can facilitate improved performance.

The alliance between GM and SAIC has been successful over the years because of the way it is managed. In fact, both firms are pleased with the outcomes. Research suggests that company executives need to know their own firm well, understand factors that determine the norms in different countries, know how the firm is seen by other partners in the venture, and learn to adapt while remaining consistent with their own company cultural values. Such a multifaceted and versatile approach has helped the GM and SAIC alliance to succeed.

Not all alliances are successful; in fact, many fail.[108] The primary reasons for failure include incompatible partners and conflict between the partners. International strategic alliances are especially difficult to manage. Several factors may cause a relationship to sour. Trust between the partners is critical and is affected by at least four fundamental issues: the initial condition of the relationship, the negotiation process to arrive at an agreement, partner interactions and external events.[109] Trust is also influenced by the country cultures involved in the alliance or joint venture.[110]

Research has shown that equity-based alliances, over which a firm has more control, tend to produce more positive returns.[111] (Strategic alliances are discussed in greater depth in Chapter 8) However, if trust is required to develop new capabilities in a research collaboration, equity can serve as a barrier to the necessary relationship building. If conflict in a strategic alliance or joint venture is not manageable, an acquisition may be a better option.[112] Alliances can also lead to an acquisition, which is discussed next.

## Acquisitions

As free trade has continued to expand in global markets, cross-border acquisitions have also been increasing significantly. In 2008, the number of cross-border acquisitions comprised about 40 per cent, down from 45 per cent of all acquisitions completed worldwide in previous years.[113] As explained in Chapter 8, acquisitions can provide quick access to a new market. In fact, acquisitions often provide the fastest and the largest initial international expansion of any of the alternatives.[114] Thus, entry is much quicker than by other modes. For example, Wal-Mart entered Germany and the UK by acquiring local firms, Asda in the latter case. Later, Wal-Mart withdrew from Germany.[115]

Although acquisitions have become a popular mode of entering international markets, they are not without costs. International acquisitions carry some of the disadvantages of domestic acquisitions (again see Chapter 8). In addition, they can be expensive and also often require debt financing, which carries an extra cost. International negotiations for acquisitions can be exceedingly complex and are generally more complicated than domestic acquisitions. For example, acquisitions are being used by emerging economy firms to enter developed economies. China has been buying firms in foreign countries that have assets in natural resources. For instance, China Minmetals, a state-owned mining firm, has tried to acquire Oz Minerals, the world's second largest zinc miner based in Australia. But this acquisition, like many others, has been opposed by the government because of the potential for a sovereign power to take control of important natural resources.[116]

Interestingly, acquirers make fewer acquisitions in countries with significant corruption, preferring to use international joint ventures instead. However, these ventures fail more often, although this is moderated by the acquiring firm's past experience with such deals. When acquisitions are made in such countries, acquirers commonly pay smaller premiums to buy the target firms.[117]

Problems frequently present themselves when dealing with the legal and regulatory requirements in the target firm's country and obtaining appropriate information to negotiate an agreement. Finally, the problems of merging the new firm into the acquiring firm are often more complex than in domestic acquisitions. The acquiring firm must deal not only with different corporate cultures, but also with potentially different social cultures and practices.[118] These differences make the integration of the two firms after the acquisition more challenging; it is difficult to capture the potential synergy when integration is slowed or stymied because of cultural differences.[119] Therefore, while international acquisitions have been popular because of the rapid access to new markets they provide, they also carry with them important costs and multiple risks.

SAIC acquired assets of the insolvent MG Rover Group, an historic UK automobile producer. This acquisition gave the Chinese firm an entry point into Europe and an opportunity to establish its own brand through the MG Rover label. SAIC had previously considered a joint venture but decided to make the acquisition bid, worth €81 million. However, SAIC experienced formidable government opposition in the UK and had to clear extra regulatory hurdles to receive approval. However, by 2008 it had not produced one of the intended MG roadsters because of apparent "quality issues".[120]

**Greenfield venture**

The establishment of a new wholly-owned subsidiary is referred to as a greenfield venture.

## New wholly-owned subsidiary

The establishment of a new wholly-owned subsidiary is referred to as a greenfield venture. The process of creating such ventures is often complex and potentially costly, but it affords maximum control to the firm and has the most potential to provide above-average returns. This potential is especially true of firms with strong intangible capabilities that might be leveraged through a greenfield venture.[121] A firm maintains full control of its operations with a greenfield venture. More control is especially advantageous if the firm has proprietary technology. Research also suggests that "wholly owned subsidiaries and expatriate staff are preferred" in service industries where "close contacts with end customers" and "high levels of professional skills, specialized know-how, and customization" are required.[122] Other research suggests that greenfield investments are more prominent where physical capital-intensive plants are planned and that acquisitions are more likely to be preferred when a firm is human capital intensive – that is, where a strong local degree of unionization and high cultural distance would cause difficulty in transferring knowledge to a host nation through a greenfield approach.[123]

The risks are also high, however, because of the costs of establishing a new business operation in a new country. The firm may have to acquire the knowledge and expertise of the existing market by hiring either host-country nationals, possibly from competitors, or consultants, which can be costly. However, the firm maintains control over the technology, marketing and distribution of its products. Furthermore, the company must build new manufacturing facilities, establish distribution networks, and learn and implement appropriate marketing strategies to compete in the new market.[124] Research also suggests that when the country risk is high, firms prefer to enter with joint ventures instead of greenfield investments in order to manage the risk. However, if they have previous experience in a country, they prefer to use a wholly-owned greenfield venture rather than a joint venture.[125]

The globalization of the air cargo industry has implications for companies such as UPS and FedEx. The impact of this globalization is especially pertinent to the China and the Asia Pacific region. China's air cargo market is expected to grow 11 per cent per year through 2023. Accordingly, in 2008, both UPS and FedEx opened new hub operations in Shanghai and Gangzhou, respectively; each firm has about 6000 employees in China. The hubs facilitated their distribution and logistics business during the Olympics in Beijing. These investments are wholly owned because the firms need to maintain the integrity of their IT and logistics systems in order to maximize efficiency. Greenfield ventures also help the firms to maintain the proprietary nature of their systems.[126]

## Dynamics of mode of entry

A firm's choice of mode of entry into international markets is affected by a number of factors.[127] Initially, market entry is often achieved through export, which requires no foreign manufacturing expertise and investment only in distribution. Licensing can facilitate the product improvements necessary to enter foreign markets, as in the Komatsu example. Strategic alliances have been popular because they allow a firm to connect with an experienced partner already in the targeted market. Strategic alliances also reduce risk through the sharing of costs. Therefore, all three modes – export, licensing, and strategic alliance – are good tactics for early market development. Also, the strategic alliance is often used in more uncertain situations, such as an emerging economy where there is significant risk, such as Venezuela and Columbia.[128] However, if intellectual property rights in the emerging economy are not well protected, the number of firms in the industry is growing fast, and the need for global integration is high, a joint venture or wholly owned subsidiary entry mode is preferred.[129]

To secure a stronger presence in international markets, acquisitions or greenfield ventures may be required. Large aerospace firms Airbus and Boeing have used joint ventures to facilitate entry, especially in large markets, while military equipment firms such as Thales SA have used acquisitions to build a global presence. Japanese automobile manufacturers, such as Toyota, have gained a presence in Europe through both greenfield ventures and joint ventures. Because of Toyota's highly efficient manufacturing process, despite recent problems with reliability, it wants to maintain control over its automobile manufacturing where possible. It has engaged in a joint venture in the US with General Motors,[130] but most of its manufacturing facilities are greenfield investments. It also has a joint venture with PSA Peugeot Citroën (called Toyota Peugeot Citroën Automobile Czech which is based in Kolín, in the Czech Republic) where it shares a plant producing the Peugeot 107s, Citroën C1s and Toyota Aygo.[131] Toyota opened a new plant in Canada in 2008 and plans to open a new plant in Mississippi in 2010, although this project may be delayed or postponed given the economic downturn[132] and recent recalls. Therefore, Toyota uses some form of foreign direct investment (e.g., greenfield ventures, joint ventures) rather than another mode of entry, although it may use exporting in new markets as it did in China. Both acquisitions and greenfield ventures are likely to come at later stages in the development of an international strategy.

Large diversified business groups, often found in emerging economies, not only gain resources through diversification but also have specialized abilities in managing differences in inward and outward flows of foreign direct investment.[133] For instance, in India such groups have facilitated the development of a thriving pharmaceutical industry.[134]

Therefore, to enter a global market, a firm selects the entry mode that is best suited to the situation at hand. In some instances, the various options will follow sequentially, beginning with exporting and ending with greenfield ventures. In other cases, the firm may use several, but not all, of the different entry modes, each in different markets. The decision regarding which entry mode to use is primarily a result of the industry's competitive conditions, the country's situation and government policies, and the firm's unique set of resources, capabilities and core competencies.

# Strategic competitive outcomes

After its international strategy and mode of entry have been selected, the firm turns its attention to implementation issues. Implementation is highly important, because international expansion is risky, making it difficult to achieve a competitive advantage (see Figure 9.1). The probability the firm will be successful with an international strategy increases when it is effectively implemented.

## International diversification and returns

**International diversification**

International diversification is a strategy through which a firm expands the sales of its goods or services across the borders of global regions and countries into different geographic locations or markets.

Firms have numerous reasons to diversify internationally.[135] International diversification is a strategy through which a firm expands the sales of its goods or services across the borders of global regions and countries into different geographic locations or markets. Because of its potential advantages, international diversification should be related positively to firms' returns. Research has shown that, as international diversification increases, firms' returns decrease initially but then increase quickly as they learn to manage international expansion.[136] In fact, the stock market is particularly sensitive to investments in international markets. Firms that are broadly diversified into multiple international markets usually achieve the most positive stock returns, especially when they diversify geographically into core business areas.[137] Many factors contribute to the positive effects of international diversification, such as private versus government ownership, potential economies of scale and experience, location advantages, increased market size and the opportunity to stabilize returns. The stabilization of returns helps reduce a firm's overall risk.[138] All of these outcomes can be achieved by smaller and newer ventures, as well as by larger and established firms.

Toyota has found that international diversification allows it to better exploit its core competencies, because sharing knowledge resources across subsidiaries can produce synergy. Also, a firm's returns may affect its decision to diversify internationally. For example, poor returns in a domestic market may encourage a firm to expand internationally in order to enhance its profit potential. In addition, internationally diversified firms may have access to more flexible labour markets, as the Japanese do in Europe, and may thereby benefit from scanning international markets for competition and market opportunities. Also, through global networks with assets in many countries, firms can develop more flexible structures to adjust to changes that might occur. "Offshore outsourcing" has created significant value-creation opportunities for firms engaged in it, especially as firms move into markets with more flexible labour markets. Furthermore, offshoring increases exports to firms that receive the offshoring contract.[139]

## International diversification and innovation

In Chapter 1, we indicated that the development of new technology is at the heart of strategic competitiveness. As noted in Porter's model (see Figure 9.2), a nation's competitiveness depends, in part, on the capacity of its industry to innovate. Eventually and inevitably, competitors outperform firms that fail to innovate and improve their operations and products. Therefore, the only way to sustain a competitive advantage is to upgrade it continually.[140]

International diversification provides the potential for firms to achieve greater returns on their innovations (through larger or more numerous markets) and reduces the often substantial risks of R&D investments. Therefore, international diversification provides incentives for firms to innovate. Additionally, the firm uses its primary resources and capabilities to diversify internationally and thus earn further returns on these capabilities (e.g., capability to innovate).[141]

In addition, international diversification may be necessary to generate the resources required to sustain a large-scale R&D operation. An environment of rapid technological obsolescence makes it difficult to invest in new technology and the capital-intensive operations necessary to compete in this environment. Firms operating solely in domestic markets may find such investments difficult because of the length of time required to recoup the original investment. If the time is extended, it may not be possible to recover the investment before the technology becomes obsolete. However, international diversification improves a firm's ability to appropriate additional returns from innovation before competitors can overcome the initial competitive advantage created by the innovation. In addition, firms moving into international markets are exposed to new products and processes. If they learn about those products and processes and integrate this knowledge into their operations, further innovation can be developed. To incorporate the learning into their own R&D processes, firms must manage those processes effectively in order to absorb and use the new knowledge to create further innovations[142] (see chapter 4).

The relationship among international diversification, innovation, and returns is complex. Some level of performance is necessary to provide the resources to generate international diversification, which in turn provides incentives and resources to invest in research and development. The latter, if done appropriately, should enhance the returns of the firm, which then provides more resources for continued international diversification and investment in R&D. Of course, these relationships have to be well managed by a firm's top level managers. Evidence suggests that more culturally diverse top management teams often have a greater knowledge of international markets and their idiosyncrasies, but their orientation to expand internationally can be affected by the nature of their compensation.[143] (Top management teams are discussed further in Chapter 11). Moreover, managing the diverse business units of a multinational firm requires skill, not only in managing a decentralized set of business but also coordinating diverse points of view derived from regionalized businesses without descending into chaos. Firms that are able to do this will challenge the best global industry incumbents.[144] This topic is addressed next.

## Complexity of managing multinational firms

Although firms can realize many benefits by implementing an international strategy, doing so is complex and can produce greater uncertainty.[145] For example, multiple risks are involved when a firm operates in several different countries. Firms can grow only so large and diverse before becoming unmanageable, or before the costs of managing them exceed their benefits. Managers are constrained by the complexity and sometimes by the culture and institutional systems within which they must operate.[146] The complexities involved in managing diverse international operations are shown in the problems experienced by even high-performing firms such as Toyota. Toyota became overly focused on sales in the North American market and began to experience quality problems (i.e., increased number of recalls) and reduced customer satisfaction. Toyota was also late in entering the Chinese market with manufacturing and as a result it was behind the market leaders, VW and GM. However, by 2008 it had recovered and actually was outselling Volkswagen and GM in China, but only in passenger cars.[147] Other complexities include the highly competitive nature of global markets, multiple cultural environments, potentially rapid shifts in the value of different currencies, and the instability of some national governments.

# Risks in an international environment

International diversification carries multiple risks. Because of these risks, international expansion is difficult to implement and manage. The chief risks are political and economic. Specific examples of political and economic risks are shown in Figure 9.4.

## Political risks

Political risks are risks related to instability in national governments and to war, both civil and international. Instability in a national government creates numerous problems, including economic risks and uncertainty created by government regulation; the existence of many, possibly conflicting, legal authorities or corruption; and the potential nationalization of private assets.[148] Foreign firms that invest in another country may have concerns about the stability of the national government and the effects of unrest and government instability on their investments or assets.[149]

Russia has experienced a relatively high level of institutional instability in the years following its revolutionary transition to a more democratic government. Decentralized political control and frequent changes in policies created chaos for

**FIGURE 9.4** Risk in the international environment

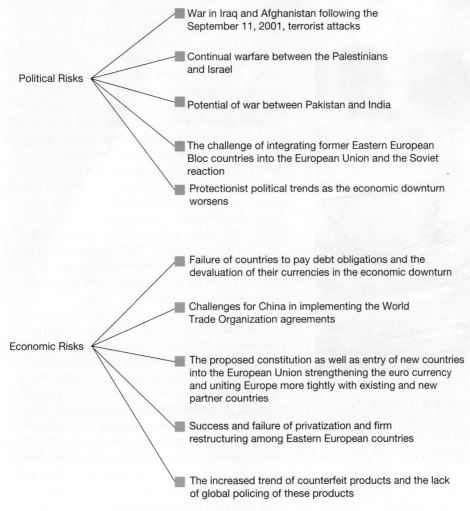

Sources: Sources 2009, Euro-Zone PPI posts biggest annual drop in 22 years, *Wall Street Journal*, www.online.wsj. com, May 5; 2009, The nuts and bolts come apart: As global demand contracts, trade is slumping and protectionism rising, *Economist*, www.economist.com, March 26; 2009, New fund, old fundamentals: Has the IMF changed or has the world? *Economist*, www.economist.com, April 30; 2009, Competitive devaluations, *Financial Times*, www.ft.com, March 14; D. Bilefsky, 2009, A crisis is separating Eastern Europe's strong from its weak, New York Times, www.ny-times.com, February 23; I. Dreyer, 2009, Mending EU-China trade ties, *Wall Street Journal*, www.online.wsj.com, May 6; J. Garten, 2009, The dangers of turning inward, *Wall Street Journal*, www.online.wsj.com, March 5; S. Levine, 2009, Emergency loans for European banks: Three international development banks pledged nearly $30 billion to shore up the troubled Eastern European banking system, *Businessweek*, www.businessweek.com, February 28; M. Singh, 2009, India launches a toy trade war with China, *Time*, www.time.com, February 6; 2008, The best way to do business with Russia, *Financial Times*, www.ft.com, August 21; 2008, Strong dollar, weak dollar, *Russia Today*, www.russiatoday. com, October 28; J. Barnham, 2008, China's pirates move up value chain, *Security Management*, June 44; L. Burkitt, 2008, Fighting fakes, *Forbes*, August 11, 44; B. Szlanko, 2008, Will the crisis spur Hungary to reform? *BusinessWeek*, www.businessweek.com, November, 13; B. Szlanko, Europe: Tougher than it looks on Russia, *BusinessWeek*, www. businessweek.com, September 4; C. C. Tschang, 2008, Currency stalemate at U.S.-China meeting, *BusinessWeek*, www.businessweek.com, December 5.

many, but especially for those in the business landscape. In an effort to regain more central control and reduce the chaos, Russian leaders took actions such as prosecuting powerful private firm executives, seeking to gain state control of firm assets, and not approving some foreign acquisitions of Russian businesses. The initial institutional instability, followed by the actions of the central government, caused some

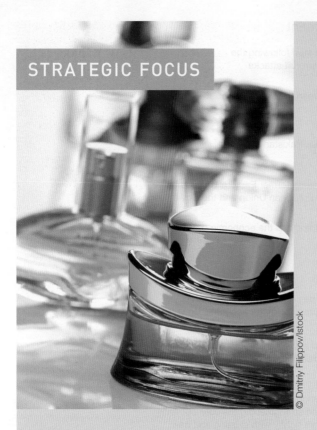

## STRATEGIC FOCUS

# The continuing threat for legitimate companies of counterfeit or fake products

The International Anti-Counterfeiting Coalition has estimated that counterfeit or fake products make up 7 per cent of the world's goods. This is an issue of growing importance (see chapter 5), especially for firms competing on a more global basis and for firms that have significant profit margins associated with intellectual property rights such as software makers, entertainment content businesses (i.e., music producers), and branded products. As businesses or governments implement solutions to overcome counterfeit products, the "pirates" often move up the value chain to copy more high-tech, high-margin products. China's rock bottom production costs have turned it into the "world's workshop and has empowered an economic boom;" however, China's environment, because of lax legal enforcement, creates an incentive for counterfeit product makers to create fake products and software and also to supply "nonstandard" electronic components which are less traceable.

For example, Philip Morris has filed a complaint with the International Trade Commission (ITC) to stop illegal imports of "grey market" cigarettes from China and other regions bearing Philip Morris's trademarks, including Marlboro. Charlie Whitaker, vice president, compliance and brand integrity, Philip Morris USA, suggests that "our brands are among our company's most valuable assets and we take many steps to protect them". The firm complains that Internet-based cigarette vendors are selling Philip Morris-labelled products in violation of intellectual property laws and the Lanham Act. Perhaps there is no worse victim of fake products than Burberry which *The Guardian* claims to be the "most copied designer label". Other statistics reveal the extremely high incidence of counterfeit manufacture but also worldwide distribution. For example, one study has estimated that one in every three designer watches purchased in the UK are counterfeit, with Cartier having the highest number of fake sales.

Many of the counterfeit products are sold on the Internet as the cigarette example indicates. French perfume producer, L'Oreal has mounted a legal challenge to eBay for sales of fake products using its brand. L'Oreal argues that by failing to police fake products, eBay is in fact acting in concert with the sellers of those goods. Of course, eBay denies the claim and says that it is simply providing a trading platform and that responsibility for looking after L'Oreal's trademarks should rest with L'Oreal. Interestingly, luxury goods manufacturers LVMH and Hermes have won rulings in French courts on similar issues against eBay, but eBay has triumphed in other cases such as one in a Belgium court.

Some counterfeit products are more than just a nuisance, they are dangerous. One firm identified bogus pesticides that have created problems when used in treating crops and could create both health risks and reduce farmer's livelihoods. Additionally, military forces are facing a growing threat of potentially fatal equipment failures and even foreign espionage through computer components that might be embedded in war planes, ships and communication networks. For instance, BEA Systems experienced field failures of some military equipment with bogus parts, and some defence contractors have traced fake microchips as well as tiny electronic circuits found in computer and other gears which have come through Chinese producers.

These and other problems illustrate the importance of protecting intellectual property and the risks associated with pursuing global trade and production. Firms might pursue legal challenges, but this is often difficult in emerging economies such as China and Russia, where there is weak legal protection. Some products such as fashion and clothing items can be protected with better labels that guard against counterfeiters. As firms pursue international strategies by using strategies based on intellectual property and which require significant R&D investments, the loss of such intellectual property to counterfeiting increases and proactive strategies must be taken to protect against significant losses.

**Sources:** Murphy, M. and Tait, N. (2009) "L'Oreal mounts legal challenges over eBay sales", *Financial Times*, March 10, 4; Barnham, J. (2008), "China's pirates move up value chain", *Security Management*, June, 44; Burkitt, L. (2008) "Fighting fakes", *Forbes*, August 11, 44; 2010 "Counterfeit fashion: the most copied designer labels", *The Guardian*, http://www.guardian.co.uk March 17; Fairley, M. (2008) "Brand protection: Label makers become vital security link in

anti-counterfeiting", *Converting Magazine*, August, 20; Grow, B., Tschang, C. C., Burnsed, B. and Epstein, K. (2008) "Dangerous fakes", *BusinessWeek*, October 13, 34–37; Slota, J. and Humphreys, M. (2008) "Connect the dots", *Pharmaceutical Executive*, July, 67–70; 2008 "Alarm at flood of bogus pesticides", *Financial Times*, May 20, 12.

## Questions

**1** Should counterfeiting be managed at the consumer level or at the points of manufacture and distribution?

**2** Within the global context, how can firms who are vulnerable to counterfeiting behaviour communicate the value of their premium consumer brands and distance themselves from counterfeit merchandise?

---

firms delay or negated significant foreign direct investment in Russia. Although leaders in Russia have tried to reassure potential investors about their property rights, prior actions, the fact that other laws (e.g., environmental and employee laws) are weak, and the fact that government corruption is common, makes firms wary of investing in Russia.[150]

## Economic risks

As illustrated in the example of Russian institutional instability and property rights, economic risks are interdependent with political risks. If firms cannot protect their intellectual property, they are highly unlikely to make foreign direct investments. Countries therefore need to create and sustain strong intellectual property rights and enforce them in order to attract desired foreign direct investment. As noted in the Strategic Focus on the continuing trend of counterfeit or fake products, this is a growing problem especially as the market for these products becomes globalized. Firms like eBay get caught when authentic producers desire to punish the counterfeit producers for selling these products on the Internet (see Strategic Focus).

Another economic threat is the perceived security risk of a foreign firm acquiring firms that have key natural resources or firms which may be considered strategic in regard to intellectual property. For instance, many Chinese firms have been buying natural resource firms in Australia and Latin America, as well as manufacturing assets in Europe and the US. This has made the governments of the key resource firms nervous about such strategic assets falling under the control of state-owned Chinese firms.[151] Terrorism has also been of concern. For example, concerns about terrorism have kept many firms from investing in Indonesia, compared to the faster growth of FDI in China and India, which have fewer perceived security risks.

As noted earlier, foremost among the economic risks of international diversification are the differences and fluctuations in the value of different currencies.[152] The value of the euro relative to other currencies determines the value of the international assets and earnings of European firms; for example, an increase in the value of the euro can reduce the value of European multinational firms' international assets and earnings in other countries. Furthermore, the value of different currencies can also, at times, dramatically affect a firm's competitiveness in global markets because of its effect on the prices of goods manufactured in

**KEY DEBATE**

# The limits to globalization

There is a compelling myth that successful firms must globalize. Since the late 1990s, the rush by firms to globalization has been incessant and we have witnessed foreign direct investment at record highs, cross-border alliances, partnerships and acquisitions growing, global sourcing of supply consistently increasing and new customers being sought in emerging markets as economies develop. Despite the recent economic downturn, the momentum behind globalization remains and the strategic development of many firms is toward greater internationalization leading to globalization.

There have been many critics of globalization and these range from some in the anti-globalization lobby who support national protectionism through to those that oppose neo-liberalism and all that comes with global integration activities. Fundamentally, firms that do not manage their globalization appropriately or do not anticipate the problems that can likely arise, perform poorly and there are many examples of this form of globalization fallout. To the same extent that firms with poorly planned diversification strategies became targets for hostile takeover bids in the past, nowadays firms with ill-conceived globalization strategies are likely to fall victim to break up or disinvestment.

For example, ABN Amro's failure of their globalization strategy was based on a flawed approach which was to seek a dominant market position in multiple regional bank retail markets. Many of these markets have since been crowded out by substantial competition and their rivals' consolidation attempts. Similarly, the integration mechanisms and economies of scope that ABN Amro anticipated did not materialize, which led ultimately to ABN Amro being broken up with divisions subsequently becoming parts of the Royal Bank of Scotland, Fortis and Banco Santander. ABN Amro is not alone in these global experiences. Kelda, which is a UK-based water utility firm, expanded into the US and subsequently sold the business six years after having purchased it on the basis that it struggled with pricing issues, environmental requirements and

water distribution became so challenging that the firm was unable to sustain its business. The Taiwanese consumer electronics firm BenQ acquired Siemens' mobile device division in 2005 in an ill-conceived international expansion move. Following problems with cultural integration, business processes and also troubled R&D integration, this business unit was declared bankrupt by BenQ in 2007.

Even though these accounts offer dramatic conclusions for these firms, expanding overseas can present challenges that are typically underestimated. For example, when Starbucks expanded rapidly throughout the world many of the margins that it had experienced in its home market could not be realized overseas. In fact, outside of the US, Starbucks has only been able to realize around half of its home margins.

Despite this, Rosabeth Moss Kanter (Harvard Business School) has suggested that many successful multinational firms are able to "shift organizational gears on a global basis and produce meaningful innovations quickly". In order to explore this hypothesis she and her research team studied dozens of multinational firms (such as IBM, Procter & Gamble, Omron, CEMEX, Cisco and Banco Real) across five continents which comprised 350 interviews. Kanter's conclusions are that these multinational firms are able to be as agile and responsive as smaller firms provided they are managed correctly.

**Sources:** Alexander, M. and Korine, H. (2008) "When you shouldn't go global", *Harvard Business Review*, 86(12): 70–77; Bhagat, R. S., McDevitt, A S. and McDevitt, I. (2010) "On improving the robustness of Asian management theories: Theoretical anchors in the era of globalization", *Asia Pacific Journal of Management*, 27(2): 179–192; Bellin, J. B. and Pham, C. T. (2007) "Global expansion: balancing a uniform performance culture with local conditions", *Strategy & Leadership*, 35(6): 44–50; Bouquet, C., Morrison, A. and Birkinshaw, J. (2009) "International attention and multinational enterprise performance", *Journal of International Business Studies*, 40(1): 108–132; Grant, R. M. and Venzin, M. (2010) "Strategic and organizational challenges of internationalization in financial services", *Long Range Planning*, 42 (5/6): 561–587; Kanter, R. M. (2008) "Transforming giants", *Harvard Business Review*, 86(1): 43–56.

## Questions

**1** Present a case outlining the potential dangers to firms of globalization.

**2** What recommendations would you make to a firm seeking to embark upon a globalization strategy for the first time?

different countries.[153] An increase in the value of the euro can harm European firms' exports to international markets because of the price differential of the products. Thus, government oversight and control of economic and financial capital in the country affect not only local economic activity, but also foreign investments in the country. Certainly, the political and policy changes in Eastern Europe have stimulated much more FDI due to the significant changes there since the early 1990s.[154]

Google is the market leader in the Internet search markets in Europe and the US. However, its expansion into Russia and Asian countries has experienced difficulties. As noted earlier, in the Strategic Focus (see page 325), it has dominant competitors in Russia (Yandex) and China (Baidu). It learned from its previous difficulties and is managing with a persistent strategy, but these competitors are dominating, especially given the additional help and support they receive from their local governments, formally and informally.

## Limits to international expansion: management problems

After learning how to operate effectively in international markets, firms tend to earn positive returns on international diversification. But, the returns often level off and become negative as the diversification increases past a certain point.[155] Several reasons explain the limits to the positive effects of international diversification. First, greater geographic dispersion across country borders increases the costs of co-ordination between units and the distribution of products. Second, trade barriers, logistical costs, cultural diversity and other differences by country (e.g., access to raw materials and different employee skill levels) greatly complicate the implementation of an international diversification strategy.

Institutional and cultural factors can present strong barriers to the transfer of a firm's competitive advantages from one country to another. Marketing programmes often have to be redesigned and new distribution networks established when firms expand into new countries. In addition, firms may encounter different labour costs and capital charges. In general, it is difficult to effectively implement, manage and control a firm's international operations.

The amount of international diversification that can be managed varies from firm to firm and according to the abilities of each firm's managers. The problems of central coordination and integration are mitigated if the firm diversifies into more friendly countries that are geographically close and have cultures similar to its own country's culture. In that case, the firm is likely to encounter fewer trade barriers, the laws and customs are better understood, and the product is easier to adapt to local markets.[156] For example, Western European firms may find it less difficult to expand their operations into the US and Canada than into Asian countries.

Management must also be concerned with the relationship between the host government and the multinational corporation.[157] Although government policy and regulations are often barriers, many firms, such as Toyota and GM, have turned to strategic alliances, as they did in China, to overcome those barriers. By forming interorganizational networks, such as strategic alliances (see Chapter 10), firms can share resources and risks but also build flexibility. However, large networks can be difficult to manage.[158]

**CLOSING CASE**

© B. O'Kane/Alamy

# Al Jazeera – successful transformation from a regional to global channel

"Be accurate, factual, be there first – that's not necessarily most important – and be with the human being all the time – you don't stay at the top getting the views of politicians and diplomats," says Ahmed al-Sheikh, editor-in-chief at Al Jazeera. This briefly describes the factors that made Al Jazeera successful. Founded in 1996 with its headquarters in Qatar, Al Jazeera television network nowadays is the most popular channel in the Arab world and its success, radical alternative journalism and enormous interest globally and politically has resulted in the creation of the term the "Al Jazeera Effect". Although there are numerous television channels in the Arab world, Al Jazeera is the only channel which has succeeded in becoming both a regional channel and one which has taken an important place in the global media world. This has not been achieved without a significant amount of controversy along the way.

In the Arab world, television channels are usually information channels of authoritarian regimes. The Arab world was dependent on national presses that were often monitored and controlled by regimes or Western media such as BBC and CNN. Despite the fact that Al Jazeera was founded by the Emir of Qatar, it was given freedom to carry out its journalism and allowed to act independently from governmental interference. Al Jazeera has been known to go one step further than its competitors and broadcast from geographical areas that no others had access to. Their close-up stories within these restricted areas has, in the past, gained the attention of political leaders who have criticized them for certain news items.

Al Jazeera was broadcast everywhere in the Arab world rather than staying in Qatar, a country of less than two million population. During the invasion of Afghanistan and Iraq by the US and allied forces, Al Jazeera succeeded in finding itself at the place of news and informing the Arab world instantly. What is more Al Jazeera opened offices in many countries such as Afghanistan, Palestinian Territory and Iraq in order to be the first in line with breaking news. By doing so, Al Jazeera was able to provide coverage of the US invasion of Afghanistan to the world. It also was able to provide graphical coverage of the Palestinian-Israeli conflict especially during the second Palestinian uprising. Due to its large network which covers larger parts of the Middle East and North Africa, Al Jazeera differentiated itself from other Arab channels.

Al Jazeera has been successful in altering the structure of the news industry and no longer is it dominated by Western countries. Its success was aided by advancements in technologies but is mostly attributable to being independent. This independence is credited to a range of factors. First, Al Jazeera maintains a high diversity of staff in order to achieve different voices. Second, and more importantly, Al Jazeera's independence comes from its programming which is not restricted to Arab and Muslim voices but also Israeli, American and European guests. The channel has broadcast many social, political and religious issues which never would have been allowed by Arab governments, such as secret relations between Arab and Israeli leaders and debates between secularists and fundamentalists on topics such as politics and polygamy. The result of such a programming style is that Al Jazeera has been praised for its free and open journalism but also accused of being the channel of fundamentalists and extremists of both Islamism and anti-Islamism. These accusations, however, do not stop Al Jazeera being diverse in terms of programming. By maintaining a varied portfolio schedule and voices, Al Jazeera covers many different opinions in the Arab world. As a consequence, people from different political, religious and cultural origins can find themselves on Al Jazeera.

Much of the ubiquitous media coverage in Tunisia and Egypt in early 2011, indicates that Al-Jazeera's coverage by the broadcaster of these anti-government riots and protests might have hastened the political outcomes. With both the Tunisian and Egyptian bureaus being closed during the protests, many commentators agree that Al Jazeera's style and approach to news gathering and reporting is creating new found popularity for the broadcaster.

In 2006 a revolutionary step was taken, the launch of an English language and international platform of Al Jazeera – "Al Jazeera English" which provided an audience with access to 24-hour news. It was the first global organization based in the Middle East to broadcasts news in English. In order to become a global station rather than remaining regional, Al Jazeera perceived this step as necessary. Additionally, in order to become a global player and compete with channels such as BBC and CNN, an English version was inevitable. The goal of Al Jazeera English is to reach global viewers rather than just the Arabic audience. Its positioning within the global media industry, of uniquely being based in the Middle East but broadcasting in English from around the globe, has helped achieve this goal. Shortly after launch, 40 million viewers were expected. At the end of 2007 the number of homes viewing Al Jazeera English reached 100 million and in 2008 they were awarded the "Best 24 Hour News Programme" from the Monte Carlo Television Festival. As well as the English television channel Al Jazeera also launched four other television channels, one broadcasting children's programmes, one for sports, one for broadcasting political conferences and one for broadcasting documentary programmes. By doing so, Al Jazeera provided the Arab world with a broad range of options.

Although there are many, the prominent opponent for Al Jazeera is the Al Arabiya television channel. Al Arabiya television tries to draw viewers from Al Jazeera by focusing more on business and financial news. "The subject all people care about in the Gulf now is the stock market, not Palestine, Iraq or terrorism", argues Abdelrahman al-Rashed, Al Arabiya's general manager. Although Al Arabiya gained market share from Al Jazeera it did not succeed in becoming the global television broadcaster that is now Al Jazeera with its broad portfolio of television channels.

Certain strategies have played a major role in Al Jazeera's success. These include being impartial in broadcasting news, being the first in reaching the place of news, going global by launching an international website and providing a wide range of options for viewers rather than broadcasting just news. This whole effort by Al Jazeera has led to positive responses. Besides having millions of viewers, changing the way in which information is provided to the Arab countries and in fact globally, Al Jazeera has been recorded, by Brand Channel, as the fifth most influential global brand following brands such as Apple and Google.

**Sources:** Al Jazeera English Website, Corporate Profile, 3 June 2009, http://www.english.aljazeera.net; Al Jazeera English Website: News Europe, Al Jazeera wins prestigious award, 14 June 2008, http://www.english.aljazeera.net; Anonymous (2005) Al Jazeera: A brand recognized the world over, Middle East, March; L. Barkho (date unknown), The Arabic Aljazeera vs Britain's BBC and America's CNN: who does journalism right?, *American Communication Journal*, 1–15, http://www.acjournal.org; Soliman, A. and Feuilherade, P. (2006) Al-Jazeera's Popularity and Impact, *BBC News*, 11 November, http://www.news.bbc.co.uk; O'Connor, C. (2008) "Al Jazeera moves from East to West", *PR week*, March 21; El-Nawawy, M. and Powers, S. (2008) "Mediating Conflict Al-Jazeera English and the Possibility of a Conciliatory Media", California: Figueroa Press, http://www.uscpublicdiplomacy.org; Esposito, J. L. (2003) "Al-Jazeera: How the Free Arab News Network Scooped the World and Changed the Middle East", *Political Science Quarterly*, Summer; Tischler, L. (2006) "Al Jazeera's (global) mission", *Fast Company*, April 2006; Rusch, R. D. (2004) Readers Choice Awards 2004, *Brand Channel*, http://www.brandchannel.com; Khalaf, R. (2005) "Stock market frenzy becomes the big news in Gulf region", *Financial Times*, December 3; Saghieh, H. (2004) "Al-Jazeera: the world through Arab eyes", *Open Democracy*, http://www.opendemocracy.net; Anon (2011) "Egypt Shuts Down Al Jazeera Bureau", Al Jazeera English, http://www.english.aljazeera.net, 30 January; Plunkett, J. and Halliday, J. (2011) "Al-Jazeera's Coverage of Egypt Protests May Hasten Revolution in World News", *The Guardian*, February 7, http://www/guardian.co.uk; Zayed, D. (2011) "Al Jazeera TV Makes Waves with Tunisia Coverage", MSN, 21 January, http://msnbc.msn.com.

## Questions

1 How do the target consumer markets for CNN differ to those of Al Jazeera English.

2 Why has Al Jazeera English been so successful in their internationalization strategy?

# SUMMARY

- The use of international strategies is increasing. Traditional motives include extending the product life cycle, securing key resources, and having access to low-cost labour. Emerging motives include the integration of the Internet and mobile telecommunications, which facilitates global transactions. Also, firms experience increased pressure for global integration as the demand for commodities becomes borderless, and yet they feel simultaneous pressure for local country responsiveness.

- An international strategy is commonly designed primarily to capitalize on four benefits: increased market size; earning a return on large investments; economies of scale and learning; and advantages of location.

- International business-level strategies are usually grounded in one or more home-country advantages, as Porter's model suggests. Porter's model emphasizes four determinants: factors of production; demand conditions; related and supporting industries; and patterns of firm strategy, structure and rivalry.

- There are three types of international corporate-level strategies. A multidomestic strategy focuses on competition within each country in which the firm competes. Firms using a multidomestic strategy decentralize strategic and operating decisions to the business units operating in each country, so that each unit can tailor its goods and services to the local market. A global strategy assumes more standardization of products across country boundaries; therefore, a competitive strategy is centralized and controlled by the home office. A transnational strategy seeks to integrate characteristics of both multidomestic and global strategies to emphasize both local responsiveness and global integration and coordination. This strategy is difficult to implement, requiring an integrated network and a culture of individual commitment.

- Although the transnational strategy's implementation is a challenge, environmental trends are causing many multinational firms to consider the need for both global efficiency and local responsiveness. Many large multinational firms, particularly those with many diverse products, use a multidomestic strategy with some product lines and a global strategy with others.

- The threat of wars and terrorist attacks increases the risks and costs of international strategies. Furthermore, research suggests that the liability of foreignness is more difficult to overcome than once thought.

- Some firms decide to compete only in certain regions of the world, as opposed to viewing all markets in the world as potential opportunities. Competing in regional markets allows firms and managers to focus their learning on specific markets, cultures, locations, resources and other factors.

- Firms may enter international markets in one of several ways, including exporting, licensing, forming strategic alliances, making acquisitions and establishing new wholly-owned subsidiaries, often referred to as greenfield ventures. Most firms begin with exporting or licensing, because of their lower costs and risks, but later they might use strategic alliances and acquisitions to expand internationally. The most expensive and risky means of entering a new international market is through the establishment of a new wholly-owned subsidiary. On the other hand, such subsidiaries provide the advantages of maximum control by the firm and, if it is successful, the greatest returns.

- International diversification facilitates innovation in a firm, because it provides a larger market to gain more and faster returns from investments in innovation. In addition, international diversification may generate the resources necessary to sustain a large-scale R&D programme.

- In general, international diversification is related to above average returns, but this assumes that the diversification is effectively implemented and that the firm's international operations are well managed. International diversification provides greater economies of scope and learning, which, along with greater innovation, help produce above-average returns.

- Several risks are involved with managing multinational operations. Among these are political risks (e.g., instability of national governments) and economic risks (e.g., fluctuations in the value of a country's currency).

- Some limits also constrain the ability to manage international expansion effectively. International diversification increases coordination and distribution costs, and management problems are exacerbated by, among other factors, trade barriers, logistical costs and cultural diversity.

## REVIEW QUESTIONS

1  What are the traditional and emerging motives that cause firms to expand internationally?

2  What are the four primary benefits of an international strategy?

3  What four factors provide a basis for international business-level strategies?

4  What are the three international corporate-level strategies? How do they differ from each other? What factors lead to their development?

5  What environmental trends are affecting international strategy?

6  What five modes of international expansion are available, and what is the normal sequence of their use?

7  What is the relationship between international diversification and innovation? How does international diversification affect innovation? What is the effect of international diversification on a firm's returns?

8  What are the risks of international diversification? What are the challenges of managing multinational firms?

## DISCUSSION QUESTIONS

1  Prepare a debate to speak on the motion that "Globalization benefits consumers, businesses, national economies and global society". Adopt the format of a speaker/team that proposes the motion and a speaker/team that opposes the motion. Take an audience vote of the class both before and after the debate to establish how many observers switched their initial support.

2  Develop a series of examples to illustrate each of the five modes of international market entry strategy; evaluate the success or failure of each.

3  Theodore Levitt, the legendary late Harvard Business School Professor, declared in 1983: "The world's needs and desires have been irrevocably homogenized. This makes the multinational corporation obsolete and the global corporation absolute."[159] Discuss to what extent this opinion is as applicable today.

4  Consider three liabilities of foreignness and illustrate how firms that are victim to these can overcome them by entering new international markets.

5  How can multinational corporations manage innovation strategies coherently?

## FURTHER READING

The rise of Brazilian, Chinese, Indian firms but also firms from Arabia, Israel, Mexico or Turkey is – similar to natural phenomena – fascinating to witness. From many previously less developed countries new firms have emerged and what markets and competition were yesterday seems to have completely changed. So much so that staying in control is challenging (e.g. A. P. Raman (2009) "The new frontiers", *Harvard Business Review*, 87(7/8): 130–137; S. Athreye and S. Kapur (2009) "Introduction: The internationalization of Chinese and Indian firms – trends, motivations and strategy", *Industrial and Corporate Change*, 18(2), Special Issue: 209–221; N. Kumar (2009) "How emerging giants are rewriting the rules of M&A", *Harvard Business Review*, 87(5): 115–121;

Y. Luo and R. L. Tung (2007) "International expansion of emerging market enterprises: A springboard perspective", *Journal of International Business Studies*, 38: 481–498; J. Li and D. R. Yue (2009) "Market size, legal institutions and international diversification strategies: Implications for the performance of multinational firms", *Management International Review*, 48(6): 667–688; K. Smith (2009) "Losing (ownership) control", *Harvard Business Review*, 87(6): 18–19). Especially the challenges of increasing internationalization, institutional change and institutional voids have been addressed by these leading scholars. Kurt Lewin's dictum "nothing is as practical as a good theory" again provides a way forward. The importance of institutional differences and the dynamic changes of rules and norms are being conceptualized in the current debate (e.g. P. Ghemawat (2007) *Redefining Global Strategy: Crossing Borders in a World Where Differences Still Matter*, Cambridge, MA: Harvard Business School Press; M. W. Peng and E. G. Pleggenkuhle-Miles (2009) "Current debates in global strategy",

*International Journal of Management Reviews*, 11(1): 51–68; G. Y. Gao, J. Y. Murray, M. Kotabe and J. Lu (2010) "A 'strategy tripod' perspective on export behaviours: Evidence from domestic and foreign firms based in an emerging economy", *Journal of International Business Studies*, 41(3): 377–396).

# EXPERIENTIAL EXERCISES

## Exercise 1: McDonald's: global, domestic or transnational strategy?

McDonald's is one of the world's best-known brands: The company has approximately 30000 restaurants located in more than 100 countries and serves 47 million customers *every day*. McDonald's opened its first international restaurant in Japan in 1971. Its Golden Arches are featured prominently in two former bastions of communism: Puskin Square in Moscow and Tiananmen Square in Beijing, China. What strategy has McDonald's used to achieve such visibility? For this exercise, each group will be asked to conduct some background research on the firm and then make a brief presentation to identify the international strategy (i.e., global, multidomestic, or transnational) McDonald's is implementing.

### Individual

Use the Internet to find examples of menu variations in different countries. How much do menu items differ for a McDonald's in Western Europe from other locations outside Western Europe?

### Groups

Review the characteristics of global, multidomestic, and transnational strategies. Conduct additional research to assess what strategy best describes the one McDonald's is using. Prepare a flip chart with a single page of bullet points to explain your reasoning.

### Whole class

Each group should have 5–7 minutes to explain its reasoning. Following Q&A for each group, ask class members to vote for the respective strategy choices.

## Exercise 2: Country analysis

Black Canyon Coffee is a Bangkok-based company that operates a chain of coffee shops. Black Canyon differentiates itself from other coffee chains (e.g., Starbucks, Caribou) by offering a broad menu of "fusion"

Asian foods as well as a range of coffee products. Although the company operates primarily in Thailand, it has retail shops in a number of neighbouring countries as well. For this exercise, assume that you have been hired by the Black Canyon management team as consultants. Your group has been retained by management to conduct a preliminary review of several countries. The purpose of this review is to help prioritize the areas that are the most promising targets for international expansion.

### Part One

Working in teams of 5–7 persons, select three countries from the following list:

Malaysia

Singapore

Cambodia

Japan

Indonesia

Australia

New Zealand

United Arab Emirates

Taiwan

Philippines

Conduct research on the selected countries for the following criteria:

Economic characteristics: Gross national product, wages, unemployment, inflation and so on. Trend analysis of this data (e.g., are wages rising or falling, rate of change in wages, etc.) is preferable to single point-in-time snapshots.

Social characteristics: Life expectancy, education norms, income distributions, literacy and so on.

Risk factors: Economic and political risk assessment.

The following Internet resources may be useful in your research:

- The Library of Congress has a collection of country studies.
- BBC News offers country profiles online.
- *The Economist* offers country profiles.
- Both the United Nations and International Monetary Fund provide statistics and research reports.
- The *CIA World Factbook* has profiles of different regions.
- The Global Entrepreneurship Monitor provides reports with detailed information about economic conditions and social aspects for a number of countries.
- Links can be found at http://www.countryrisk.com to a number of resources that assess both political and economic risk for individual countries.

### Part Two

Based on your research, prepare a memorandum (3–4 pages, single-spaced, maximum) that compares and contrasts the attractiveness of the three countries you selected. In your report, include a bullet-point list of other topics that Black Canyon management should consider when evaluating its international expansion opportunities.

## VIDEO CASE

**Understand the differences when doing business abroad**

**Andrew Sherman, co-founder, Grow Fast Grow Right**

http://www.cengage.com/management/webtutor/hittsm9e/video/ch08v.html

Andrew Sherman, co-founder of Grow Fast Grow Right, suggests that global business strategy is like the pizza business. There are four key elements: crust; cheese; sauce; and toppings.

Further, he argues that only one of these elements, the toppings, should vary by international location.

Before you watch the video consider the following concepts and questions and be prepared to discuss them in class:

**Concepts**

- International expansion
- Cultural differences
- Risks
- Organizational size
- Transnational strategy

## NOTES

1. E. Tse, 2010, "Is it too late to enter China?", *Harvard Business Review*, 88(4): 96–101.
2. W. He and M. A. Lyles, 2009, "China's outward foreign direct investment", *Business Horizons*, 51(6): 485–491.
3. B. C. Kho, R. M. Stulz and F. E. Warnock, 2009, "Financial globalisation, governance, and the evolution of the home bias", *Journal of Accounting Research*, 47(2): 597–635; S. Li, 2005, "Why a poor governance environment does not deter foreign direct investment: The case of China and its implications for investment protection", *Business Horizons*, 48(4): 297–302.
4. G. L. Ge, D. Z. Ding, 2009, "A strategic analysis of surging Chinese manufacturers: The case of Galanz", *Asia Pacific Journal of Management*, 25(4): 667–683; A. K. Gupta and H. Wang, 2007, "How to get China and India right: Western companies need to become smarter – and they need to do it quickly", *Wall Street Journal*, April 28, R4.
5. D. Kronborg and S. Thomsen, 2009, "Foreign ownership and long-term survival", *Strategic Management Journal*, 30(2): 207–220; H. J. Sapienza, E. Autio, G. George and S. A. Zahra, 2006, "A capabilities perspective on the effects of early internationalisation on firm survival and growth", *Academy of Management Review*, 31: 914–933; W. P. Wan, 2005, "Country resource environments, firm capabilities, and corporate diversification strategies", *Journal of Management Studies*, 42: 161–182.
6. P. Enderwick, 2009, "Large emerging markets (LEMs) and international strategy", *International Marketing Review*, 26(1): 7–16; F. T. Rothaermel, S. Kotha and H. K. Steensma, 2006, "International market entry by U.S. Internet firms: An empirical analysis of country risk, national culture and market size", *Journal of Management*, 32: 56–82; R. E. Hoskisson, H. Kim, R. E. White and L. Tihanyi, 2004, "A framework for understanding international diversification by business groups from emerging economies", in: M. A. Hitt and J. L. C. Cheng (eds.), *Theories of the Multinational Enterprise: Diversity, Complexity, and Relevance. Advances in International Management*, Oxford, UK: Elsevier/JAI Press, 137–163.
7. M. Javidan, R. Steers and M. A. Hitt (eds.), 2007, *The Global Mindset*, Oxford, UK: Elsevier Publishing; T. M. Begley and D. P. Boyd, 2003, "The need for a corporate global mind-set", *MIT Sloan Management Review*, 44(2):

25–32; H. W. Volberda, 2006, "Bridging IB theories, constructs, and methods across cultures and social sciences", *Journal of International Business Studies*, 37(2): 280–284.

8. M. W. Peng and E. G. Pleggenkuhle-Miles, 2009, "Current debates in global strategy", *International Journal of Management Reviews*, 11(1): 51–68; M. A. Hitt, L. Tihanyi, T. Miller and B. Connelly, 2006, "International diversification: Antecedents, outcomes and moderators", *Journal of Management*, 32: 831–867.

9. Y. Luo and R. L. Tung, 2007, "International expansion of emerging market enterprises: A springboard perspective", *Journal of International Business Studies* 38: 481–498; J. E. Ricart, M. J. Enright, P. Ghemawat, S. L. Hart and T. Khanna, 2004, "New frontiers in international strategy", *Journal of International Business Studies*, 35: 175–200; T. Hutzschenreuter, T. Pedersen and H. W. Volberda, 2007, "The role of path dependency and managerial intentionality: A perspective on international business research", *Journal of International Business Studies*, 38(7): 1055–1068.

10. R. Vernon, 1996, "International investment and international trade in the product cycle", *Quarterly Journal of Economics*, 80: 190–207.

11. W. He and M. A. Lyles, 2008, "China's outward foreign direct investment", *Business Horizons*, 51: 485–491; P. J. Buckley, L. J. Clegg, A. R. Cross, X. Liu, H. Voss and P. Zheng, 2006, "The determinants of Chinese outward foreign direct investment", *Journal of International Business Studies*, 38: 499–518.

12. L. Yu, 2003, "The global-brand advantage", *MIT Sloan Management Review*, 44(3): 13.

13. M. E. Lloyd, 2009, "Ikea sees opportunity during hard times – as expansion in U.S. continues, Swedish retailer expects its value furnishings to appeal to shoppers amid economic slump", *Wall Street Journal*, February 18, B5A.

14. X. Liu and H. Zou, 2008, "The impact of greenfield FDI and mergers and acquisitions on innovation in Chinese high-tech industries", *Journal of World Business*, 43(3): 352–364.

15. F. Fortanier and R. Van Tulder, 2009, "Internationalisation trajectories – a cross-country comparison: Are large Chinese and Indian companies different?", *Industrial and Corporate Change*, 18(2) Special Issue: 223–247.

16. K. Addae-Dapaah and W. T. Y. Hwee, 2009, "The unsung impact of currency risk on the performance of international real property investment", *Review of Financial Economics*, 18(1): 56–65; C. C. Y. Kwok and D. M. Reeb, 2000, "Internationalisation and firm risk: An upstream-downstream hypothesis", *Journal of International Business Studies*, 31: 611–629.

17. M. Wright, I. Filatotchev, R. E. Hoskisson and M. W. Peng, 2005, "Strategy research in emerging economies: Challenging the conventional wisdom", *Journal of Management Studies*, 42: 1–30; T. London and S. Hart, 2004, "Reinventing strategies for emerging markets: Beyond the transnational model", *Journal of International Business Studies*, 35: 350–370; R. E. Hoskisson, L. Eden, C. M. Lau and M. Wright, 2000, "Strategy in emerging economies", *Academy of Management Journal*, 43: 249–267.

18. P. Zheng, 2009, "A comparison of FDI determinants in China and India", *Thunderbird International Business Review*, 51(3): 263–279; H. Sender, 2005, "The economy"; "The outlook: India comes of age, as focus on returns lures foreign capital", *Wall Street Journal*, June 6, A2.

19. S. Athreye and S. Kapur, 2009, "Introduction: The internationalisation of Chinese and Indian firms – trends, motivations and strategy", *Industrial and Corporate Change*, 18(2) Special Issue: 209–221; M. A. Witt and A. Y. Lewin, 2007, "Outward foreign direct investment as escape to home country institutional constraints", *Journal of International Business Studies*, 38: 579–594; M. W. Peng, S. H. Lee and D. Y. L. Wang, 2005, "What determines the scope of the firm over time? A focus on institutional relatedness", *Academy of Management Review*, 30: 622–633.

20. J. W. Spencer, T. P. Murtha and S. A. Lenway, 2005, "How governments matter to new industry creation", *Academy of Management Review*, 30: 321–337; I. P. Mahmood and C. Rufin, 2005, "Government's dilemma: The role of government in imitation and innovation", *Academy of Management Review*, 30: 338–360.

21. B. Elango, 2009, "Minimizing effects of 'liability of foreignness': Response strategies of foreign firms in the United States", *Journal of World Business*, 44(1): 51–62; L. Eden and S. Miller, 2004, "Distance matters: Liability of foreignness, institutional distance and ownership strategy", in: M. A. Hitt and J. L. Cheng (eds.), *Advances in International Management*, Oxford, UK: Elsevier/JAI Press, 187–221.

22. S. Anand, 2008, "Japan M&A, prescription for growth", *BusinessWeek*, http://www.businessweek.com, November 17.

23. V. Bauerlein and G. Fairclough, 2009, "Beijing thwarts Coke's takeover bid", *Wall Street Journal*, http://www.wsj.com, March 19.

24. H. Barnard, 2008, "Uneven domestic knowledge bases and the success of foreign firms in the USA", *Research Policy*, 37(10): 1674–1683.

25. S. Shimizutani and Y. Todo, 2008, "What determines overseas R&D activities? The case of Japanese multinational firms", *Research Policy*, 37(3): 530–544; J. Cantwell, J. Dunning and O. Janne, 2004, "Towards a technology-seeking explanation of U.S. direct investment in the United Kingdom", *Journal of International Management*, 10: 5–20; W. Chung and J. Alcacer, 2002, "Knowledge seeking and location choice of foreign direct investment in the United States", *Management Science*, 48(12): 1534–1554.

26. F. Jiang, 2005, "Driving forces of international pharmaceutical firms' FDI into China", *Journal of Business Research*, 22(1): 21–39.

27. M. D. R. Chari, S. Devaraj and P. David, 2007, "International diversification and firm performance: Role of information technology investments", *Journal of World Business*, 42: 184–197; W. Chung, 2001, "Identifying technology transfer in foreign direct investment: Influence of industry conditions and investing firm motives", *Journal of International Business Studies*, 32: 211–229.

28. M. V. S. Kumar, 2009, "The relationship between product and international diversification: The effects of short-run constraints and endogeneity", *Strategic Management Journal*, 30(1): 99–116; K. J. Petersen, R. B. Handfield and G. L. Ragatz, 2005, "Supplier integration into new product development: Coordinating product process and supply chain design", *Journal of Operations Management*, 23: 371–388.

29. C. Rauwald, 2009, "Porsche chooses the China road; four-door Panamera's Shanghai debut signals focus on emerging markets", *Wall Street Journal*, April 20, B2; A. Webb, 2007, "China needs strong automakers – not more", *Automotive News*, http://www.autonews.com, July 20; "China's SAIC says first half sales up 23 percent 2007", *Reuters*, http://www.reuters.com, July 12; A. Taylor, 2004, "Shanghai Auto wants to be the world's next great car company", *Fortune*, October 4, 103–109.

30. K. D. Brouthers, L. E., Brouthers and S. Werner, 2008, "Resource-based advantages in an international context", *Journal of Management*, 34: 189–217; N. Karra, N. Phillips and P. Tracey, 2008, "Building the born global firm developing entrepreneurial capabilities for international new venture success", *Long Range Planning*, 41(4): 440–458; L. Zhou, W. P. Wu and X. Luo, 2007, "Internationalisation and the performance of born-global SMEs: The mediating role of social networks", *Journal of International Business Studies*, 38: 673–690; R. J. Meyer and H. W. Volberda, 1997, "Porter on Corporate Strategy", in: F. A. J. van den Bosch and A. P. de Man (eds.), *Perspectives on Strategy: Contributions of Michael E. Porter*, Boston: Kluwer Academic, 25–33.

31. H. Zou and P. N. Ghauri, 2009, "Learning through international acquisitions: The process of knowledge acquisition in China", *Management International Review*, 48(2): 207–226; H. Berry, 2006, "Leaders, laggards, and the pursuit of foreign knowledge", *Strategic Management Journal*, 27: 151–168.

32. J. Song and J. Shin, 2008, "The paradox of technological capabilities: A study of knowledge sourcing from host countries of overseas R&D operations", *Journal of International Business Studies*, 39: 291–303; J. Penner-Hahn and J. M. Shaver, 2005, "Does international research increase patent output? An analysis of Japanese pharmaceutical firms", *Strategic Management Journal*, 26: 121–140.

33. D. Strutton, 2009, "Horseshoes, global supply chains, and an emerging Chinese threat: Creating remedies one idea at a time", *Business Horizons*, 52(1): 31–43.

34. A. M. Rugman and A. Verbeke, 2009, "A new perspective on the regional and global strategies of multinational services firms", *Management International Review*, 48(4): 397–411; R. Tahir and J. Larimo, 2004, "Understanding the location strategies of the European firms in Asian countries", *Journal of American Academy of Business*, 5: 102–110.

35. R. Chakrabarti, S. Gupta-Mukherjee and N. Jayaraman, 2009, "Mars-Venus marriages: Culture and cross-border M&A", *Journal of International Business Studies*, 40(2): 216–236; D. Xu and O. Shenkar, 2004, "Institutional distance and the multinational enterprise", *Academy of Management Review*, 27: 608–618.

36. C. C. J. M. Millar and C. J. Choi, 2009, "Worker identity, the liability of foreignness, the exclusion of local managers and unionism: A conceptual analysis", *Journal of Organisational Change Management*, 21(4): 460–470; D. Xu, Y. Pan and P. W. Beamish, 2004, "The effect of regulative and normative distances on MNE ownership and expatriate strategies", *Management International Review*, 44(3): 285–307.

37. J. D. Stoll, 2009, "Corporate news: GM pushes the throttle in China – affiliate's plan to expand into cars is seen as a key to growth in Asia", *Wall Street Journal*, April 27, B3.

38. J. Li and D. R. Yue, 2009, "Market size, legal institutions, and international diversification strategies: Implications for the performance of multinational firms", *Management International Review*, 48(6): 667–688; D. A. Griffith and M. G. Harvey, 2001, "A resource perspective of global dynamic capabilities", *Journal of International Business Studies*, 32: 597–606; Y. Luo, 2000, "Dynamic capabilities in international expansion", *Journal of World Business*, 35(4): 355–378.

39. R. Morck, B. Yeung and M. Zhao, 2008, "Perspectives on China's outward foreign direct investment", *Journal of International Business Studies*, 39: 337–350; J. Gimeno, R. E. Hoskisson, B. D. Beal and W. P. Wan, 2005, "Explaining the clustering of international expansion moves: A critical test in the U.S. telecommunications industry", *Academy of Management Journal*, 48: 297–319.

40. A. Cuervo-Cazurra and M. Gene, 2008, "Transforming disadvantages into advantages: Developing-country MNEs in the least developed countries", *Journal of International Business Studies*, 39: 957–979; M. A. Hitt, L. Bierman, K. Uhlenbruck and K. Shimizu, 2006, "The importance of resources in the internationalisation of professional service firms: The good, the bad and the ugly", *Academy of Management Journal*, 49: 1137–1157.

41. P. Dastidar, 2009, "International corporate diversification and performance: Does firm self-selection matter?", *Journal of International Business Studies*, 40: 71–85; L. Nachum, 2001, "The impact of home countries on the competitiveness of advertising TNCs", *Management International Review*, 41(1): 77–98.

42. M. E. Porter, 1990, *The Competitive Advantage of Nations*, New York: The Free Press; A. P. De Man, F. A. J. van den Bosch and T. Elfring, 1997, "Porter on national and regional competitive advantage", in: F. A. J. van den Bosch and A. P. de Man (eds.), *Perspectives on Strategy: Contributions of Michael E. Porter*, Boston: Kluwer Academic, 25–33.

43. M. E. Porter, 1990, *The Competitive Advantage of Nations*, New York: The Free Press, 84.

44. C. Storz, 2008, "Dynamics in innovation systems: Evidence from Japan's game software industry", *Research Policy*, 37 (9): 1480–1491; Y. Aoyama and H. Izushi, 2003, "Hardware gimmick or cultural innovation? Technological, cultural, and social foundations of the Japanese video game industry", *Research Policy*, 32: 423–443; P. Reinmoeller, 1999, "Internationalization of Japanese Contents, The Age of Marketing Innovation: Product Development Innovation", in: M. Shimaguchi, H. Takeuchi, H. Katahira and J. Ishi (eds.), *The Age of Marketing Innovation: Product Development Innovation*, Tokyo: Yuhikaku, 388–414.

45. B. Powell, 2009, "China's new king of solar", *Fortune*, February 16, 94–97.

46. N. Karra, N. Phillips and P. Tracey, 2008, "Building the born global firm developing entrepreneurial capabilities for

international new venture success", *Long Range Planning*, 41(4): 440–458.

47. J. Ioffe, 2009, "Search wars; The Russians are coming", *Fortune*, February 16, 36–38.

48. A. Tempel and P. Walgenbach, 2007, "Global standardisation of organisational forms and management practices? What new institutionalism and business systems approach can learn from each other", *Journal of Management Studies*, 44: 1–24.

49. M. V. S. Kumar, 2009, "The relationship between product and international diversification: The effects of short-run constraints and endogeneity", *Strategic Management Journal*, 30(1): 99–116; W. P. Wan and R. E. Hoskisson, 2003, "Home country environments, corporate diversification strategies and firm performance", *Academy of Management Journal*, 46: 27–45; J. M. Geringer, S. Tallman and D. M. Olsen, 2000, "Product and international diversification among Japanese multinational firms", *Strategic Management Journal*, 21: 51–80.

50. M. V. S. Kumar, 2009, "The relationship between product and international diversification: The effects of short-run constraints and endogeneity", *Strategic Management Journal*, 30(1): 99–116; M. A. Hitt, R. E. Hoskisson and R. D. Ireland, 1994, "A mid-range theory of the interactive effects of international and product diversification on innovation and performance", *Journal of Management*, 20: 297–326.

51. D. A. Ralston, D. H. Holt, R. H. Terpstra and Y. Kai-Cheng, 2008, "The impact of national culture and economic ideology on managerial work values: A study of the United States, Russia, Japan, and China", *Journal of International Business Studies*, 39(1): 8–26; B. B. Alred and K. S. Swan, 2004, "Global versus multidomestic: Culture's consequences on innovation", *Management International Review*, 44: 81–105.

52. D. Grewal, G. R. Iyer, W. A. Kamakura, A. Mehrotra and A. Sharma, 2009, "Evaluation of subsidiary marketing performance: Combining process and outcome performance metrics", *Academy of Marketing Science Journal*, 37(2): 117–120; A. Ferner, P. Almond, I. Clark, T. Colling and T. Edwards, 2004, "The dynamics of central control and subsidiary anatomy in the management of human resources: Case study evidence from U.S. MNCs in the U.K.", *Organization Studies*, 25: 363–392.

53. B. Connelly, M. A. Hitt, A. S. DeNisi and R. D. Ireland, 2007, "Expatriates and corporate-level international strategy: Governing with the knowledge contract", *Management Decision*, 45: 564–581; L. Nachum, 2003, "Does nationality of ownership make any difference and if so, under what circumstances? Professional service MNEs in global competition", *Journal of International Management*, 9: 1–32.

54. M. W. Hansen, T. Pedersen and B. Petersen, 2009, "MNC strategies and linkage effects in developing countries", *Journal of World Business*, 44(2): 121–139; Y. Luo, 2001, "Determinants of local responsiveness: Perspectives from foreign subsidiaries in an emerging market", *Journal of Management*, 27: 451–477.

55. H. Kasper, M. Lehrer, J. Mühlbacher and B. Müller, 2009, "Integration-responsiveness and knowledge-management perspectives on the MNC: A typology and field study of cross-site knowledge-sharing practices", *Journal of Leadership and Organization Studies*, 15(3): 287–303.

56. J. Neff, 2008, "Unilever's CMO finally gets down to business", *Advertising Age*, July, 11; G. Jones, 2002, "Control, performance, and knowledge transfers in large multinationals: Unilever in the United States, 1945–1980", *Business History Review*, 76(3): 435–478.

57. P. J. Buckley, 2009, "The impact of the global factory on economic development", *Journal of World Business*, 44(2): 131–143; A. Tempel and P. Walgenbach, 2007, "Global standardisation of organisational forms and management practices? What new institutionalism and business systems approach can learn from each other", *Journal of Management Studies*, 44: 1–24; L. Li, 2005, "Is regional strategy more effective than global strategy in the U.S. service industries?" *Management International Review*, 45: 37–57.

58. H. C. Moon and M. Y. Kim, 2009, "A new framework for global expansion: A dynamic diversification-coordination (DDC) model", *Management Decision*, 46(1): 131–151.

59. B. Connelly, M. A. Hitt, A. S. DeNisi and R. D. Ireland, 2007, "Expatriates and corporate-level international strategy: Governing with the knowledge contract", *Management Decision*, 45: 564–581; J. F. L. Hong, M. Easterby-Smith and R. S. Snell, 2006, "Transferring organisational learning systems to Japanese subsidiaries in China", *Journal of Management Studies*, 43: 1027–1058.

60. B. C. Kho, R. M. Stulz and F. E. Warnock, 2009, "Financial globalisation, governance, and the evolution of the home bias", *Journal of Accounting Research*, 47(2): 597–635; R. G. Barker, 2003, "Trend: Global accounting is coming", *Harvard Business Review*, 81 (4): 24–25.

61. A. Yaprak, 2002, "Globalisation: Strategies to build a great global firm in the new economy", *Thunderbird International Business Review*, 44(2): 297–302; D. G. McKendrick, 2001, "Global strategy and population level learning: The case of hard disk drives", *Strategic Management Journal*, 22: 307–334.

62. P. Komiak, S. Y. X. Komiak and M. Imhof, 2008, "Conducting international business at eBay: The determinants of success of e-stores", *Electronic Markets*, 18(2): 187–204; V. Shannon, 2007, "eBay is preparing to re-enter the China auction business", *New York Times*, http://www.nytimes.com, June 22; B Einhorn, 2007, "A break in Yahoo's China clouds?", *BusinessWeek*, http://www.businessweek.com, June 20.

63. M. Demirbag and E. Tatoglu, 2009, "Competitive strategy choices of Turkish manufacturing firms in European Union", *The Journal of Management Development*, 27(7): 727–743; K. E. Meyer, 2006, "Globalfocusing: From domestic conglomerates to global specialists", *Journal of Management Studies*, 43: 1109–1144; A. Delios and P. W. Beamish, 2005, "Regional and global strategies of Japanese firms", *Management International Review*, 45: 19–36.

64. A. Delios, D. Xu and P. W. Beamish, 2008, "Within-country product diversification and foreign subsidiary performance", *Journal of International Business Studies*, 39(4): 706–724; S. Massini, A. Y. Lewin, T. Numagami and A. Pettigrew, 2002, "The evolution of organisational routines among large Western and Japanese firms", *Research Policy*, 31(8,9): 1333–1348.

65. J. Millman, 2008, "The fallen: Lorenzo Zambrano: Hard times for cement man", *Wall Street Journal*, December 11, A1; K. A. Garrett, 2005, "Cemex", *Business Mexico*, April 23.

66. B. Elango and C. Pattnaik, 2007, "Building capabilities for international operations through networks: A study of Indian firms", *Journal of International Business Studies*, 38: 541–555; T. B. Lawrence, E. A. Morse and S. W. Fowler, 2005, "Managing your portfolio of connections", *MIT Sloan Management Review*, 46(2): 59–65; C. A. Bartlett and S. Ghoshal, 1989, *Managing across Borders: The Transnational Solution*, Boston, MA: Harvard Business School Press.

67. A. M. Rugman and A. Verbeke, 2008, "A regional solution to the strategy and structure of multinationals", *European Management Journal*, 26(5): 305–313; A. Abbott and K. Banerji, 2003, "Strategic flexibility and firm performance: The case of U.S. based transnational corporations", *Global Journal of Flexible Systems Management*, 4(1/2): 1–7; J. Child and Y. Van, 2001, "National and transnational effects in international business: Indications from Sino-foreign joint ventures", *Management International Review*, 41(1): 53–75.

68. A. M. Rugman and A. Verbeke, 2008, "A regional solution to the strategy and structure of multinationals", *European Management Journal*, 26(5): 305–313.

69. A. M. Rugman and A. Verbeke, 2003, "Extending the theory of the multinational enterprise: Internalisation and strategic management perspectives", *Journal of International Business Studies*, 34: 125–137.

70. H. F. Cheng, M. Gutierrez, A. Mahajan, Y. Shachmurove and M. Shahrokhi, 2007, "A future global economy to be built by BRICs", *Global Finance Journal*, 18(2) 143–156; M. Wright, I. Filatotchev, R. E. Hoskisson and M. W. Peng, 2005, "Strategy research in emerging economies: Challenging the conventional wisdom", *Journal of Management Studies*, 42: 1–30.

71. B. Elango, 2009, "Minimizing effects of 'liability of foreignness': Response strategies of foreign firms in the United States", *Journal of World Business*, 44(1), 51–62.

72. N. Y. Brannen, 2004, "When Mickey loses face: Recontextualisation, semantic fit and semiotics of foreignness", *Academy of Management Review*, 29: 593–616.

73. A. M. Rugman and A. Verbeke, 2007, "Liabilities of foreignness and the use of firm-level versus country-level data: A response to Dunning et al.", (2007), *Journal of International Business Studies*, 38: 200–205; S. Zaheer and A. Zaheer, 2001, "Market microstructure in a global B2B network", *Strategic Management Journal*, 22: 859–873.

74. A. M. Rugman and A. Verbeke, 2004, "A new perspective on regional and global strategies of multinational enterprises", *Journal of International Business Studies*, 35: 3–18; S. R. Miller and L. Eden, 2006, "Local density and foreign subsidiary performance", *Academy of Management Journal*, 49: 341–355.

75. A. M. Rugman and A. Verbeke, 2004, "A new perspective on regional and global strategies of multinational enterprises", *Journal of International Business Studies*, 35: 3–18; C. H. Oh and A. M. Rugman, 2007, "Regional multinationals and the Korean cosmetics industry", *Asia Pacific Journal of Management*, 24: 27–42.

76. A. K. Bhattacharya and D. C. Michael, 2008, "How local companies keep multinationals at bay", *Harvard Business Review*, 86(3): 84–95; C. Pantzalis, 2001, "Does location matter? An empirical analysis of geographic scope and MNC market valuation", *Journal of International Business Studies*, 32: 133–155.

77. A. M. Rugman and S. Girod, 2003, "Retail multinationals and globalisation: The evidence is regional", *European Management Journal*, 21(1): 24–37.

78. D. E. Westney, 2006. "Review of the regional multinationals: MNEs and global strategic management" (book review), *Journal of International Business Studies*, 37: 445–449.

79. R. D. Ludema, 2002, "Increasing returns, multinationals and geography of preferential trade agreements", *Journal of International Economics*, 56: 329–358.

80. K. E. Meyer, 2006, "Globalfocusing: From domestic conglomerates to global specialists", *Journal of Management Studies*, 43: 1109–1144; A. Delios and P. W. Beamish, 2005, "Regional and global strategies of Japanese firms", *Management International Review*, 45: 19–36.

81. M. Aspinwall, 2009, "NAFTA-isation: Regionalisation and domestic political adjustment in the North American economic area", *Journal of Common Market Studies*, 47(1): 1–24.

82. T. L. Pett and J. A. Wolff, 2003, "Firm characteristic and managerial perceptions of NAFTA: An assessment of export implications for U.S. SMEs", *Journal of Small Business Management*, 41(2): 117–132.

83. R. Morck, B. Yeung and M. Zhao, 2008, "Perspectives on China's outward foreign direct investment", *Journal of International Business Studies*, 39: 337–350; W. Chung and J. Song, 2004, "Sequential investment, firm motives, and agglomeration of Japanese electronics firms in the United States", *Journal of Economics and Management Strategy*, 13: 539–560; D. Xu and O. Shenkar, 2002, "Institutional distance and the multinational enterprise", *Academy of Management Review*, 27(4): 608–618.

84. A. Ojala, 2008, "Entry in a psychically distant market: Finnish small and medium-sized software firms in Japan", *European Management Journal*, 26(2): 135–144.

85. K. D. Brouthers, L. E. Brouthers and S. Werner, 2008, "Real options, international entry mode choice and performance", *Journal of Management Studies*, 45(5): 936–960.

86. C. A. Cinquetti, 2009, "Multinationals and exports in a large and protected developing country", *Review of International Economics*, 16(5): 904–918.

87. Y. Luo, 2001, "Determinants of local responsiveness: Perspectives from foreign subsidiaries in an emerging market", *Journal of Management*, 27: 451–477.

88. S. Shankar, C. Ormiston, N. Bloch and R. Schaus, 2008, "How to win in emerging markets", *MIT Sloan Management Review*, 49(3): 19–23; M. A. Raymond, J. Kim and A. T. Shao, 2001, "Export strategy and performance: A comparison of exporters in a developed market and an emerging market", *Journal of Global Marketing*, 15(2): 5–29.

89. G. R. G. Clarke, 2008, "Has the internet increased exports for firms from low and middle-income countries?", *Information Economics and Policy*, 20(1): 16–37;

K. A. Houghton and H. Winklhofer, 2004, "The effect of website and e-commerce adoption on the relationship between SMEs and their export intermediaries", *International Small Business Journal*, 22: 369–385.

90. A. Haahti, V. Madupu, U. Yavas and E. Babakus, 2005, "Cooperative strategy, knowledge intensity and export performance of small and medium-sized enterprises", *Journal of World Business*, 40(2): 124–138.

91. S. Theil, 2010, "Why Europe will win", *Newsweek,* http://www.newsweek.com, April 10.

92. U. Lichtenthaler, 2008, "Externally commercializing technology assets: An examination of different process stages", *Journal of Business Venturing*, 23(4): 445–664; D. Kline, 2003, "Sharing the corporate crown jewels", *MIT Sloan Management Review*, 44(3): 83–88.

93. R. Bird and D. R. Cahoy, 2008, "The impact of compulsory licensing on foreign direct investment: A collective bargaining approach", *American Business Law Journal*, 45(2): 283–330; A. Arora and A. Fosfuri, 2000, "Wholly owned subsidiary versus technology licensing in the worldwide chemical industry", *Journal of International Business Studies*, 31: 555–572.

94. N. Byrnes and F. Balfour, 2009, "Philip Morris unbound", *BusinessWeek*, May 4, 38–42; N. Zamiska, J. Ye and V. O'Connell, 2008, "Chinese cigarettes to go global", *Wall Street Journal*, January 30, B4; N. Zamiska and V. O'Connell, 2005, "Philip Morris is in talks to make Marlboros in China", *Wall Street Journal*, April 21, B1, B2.

95. N. Zamiska, J. Ye and V. O'Connell, 2008, "Chinese cigarettes to go global", *Wall Street Journal*, January 30, B4.

96. S. Nagaoka, 2009, "Does strong patent protection facilitate international technology transfer? Some evidence from licensing contracts of Japanese firms", *Journal of Technology Transfer*, 34(2): 128–144.

97. M. Johnson, 2001, "Learning from toys: Lessons in managing supply chain risk from the toy industry", *California Management Review*, 43(3): 106–124.

98. U. Lichtenthaler and H. Ernst, 2007, "Business insight (a special report); Think strategically about technology licensing", *Wall Street Journal*, R4; D. Rigby and C. Zook, 2002, "Open-market innovation", *Harvard Business Review*, 80(10): 80–89.

99. C. A. Bartlett and S. Rangan, 1992, "Komatsu Limited", in: C. A. Bartlett and S. Ghoshal (eds.), *Transnational Management: Text, Cases and Readings in Cross-Border Management*, Homewood, IL: Irwin, 311–326.

100. T. Audi, 2008, "Last resort: Ailing Sheraton shoots for a room upgrade"; "Starwood to tackle biggest hotel brand"; "The 'ugly stepchild'", *Wall Street Journal*, March 25, A1.

101. T. W. Tong, J. J. Reuer and M. W. Peng, 2008, "International joint ventures and the value of growth options", *Academy of Management Journal*, 51: 1014–1029; A. A. Ziedonis, 2007, "Real options in technology licensing", *Management Science*, 53(10): 1618–1633.

102. H. K. Steensma, J. Q. Barden, C. Dhanaraj, M. Lyles and L. Tihanyi, 2008, "The evolution and internalisation of international joint ventures in a transitioning economy", *Journal of International Business Studies*, 39(3): 491–507; M. Nippa, S. Beechler and A. Klossek, 2007, "Success factors for managing international joint ventures: A review and an integrative framework", *Management and Organization Review*, 3: 277–310.

103. N. Rahman, 2008, "Resource and risk trade-offs in Guanxi-based IJVs in China", *Asia Pacific Business Review*, 14(2): 233–251; J. S. Harrison, M. A. Hitt, R. E. Hoskisson and R. D. Ireland, 2001, "Resource complementarity in business combinations: Extending the logic to organisation alliances", *Journal of Management*, 27: 679–690.

104. W. Zhan, R. Chen, M. K. Erramilli and D. T. Nguyen, 2009, "Acquisition of organisational capabilities and competitive advantage of IJVs in transition economies: The case of Vietnam", *Asia Pacific Journal of Management*, 26(2): 285–308; M. A. Hitt, D. Ahlstrom, M. T. Dacin, E. Levitas and L. Svobodina, 2004, "The institutional effects on strategic alliance partner selection in transition economies: China versus Russia", *Organization Science*, 15: 173–185.

105. E. Woyke, 2009, "ZTE's smart phone ambitions; The company is betting on advanced phones to crack the U.S. market", *Forbes*, http://www.forbes.com, March 16.

106. T. Chi and A. Seth, 2009, "A dynamic model of the choice of mode for exploiting complementary capabilities", *Journal of International Business Studies*, 40(3): 365–387; M. A. Lyles and J. E. Salk, 2007, "Knowledge acquisition from foreign parents in international joint ventures: An empirical examination in the Hungarian context", *Journal of International Business Studies*, 38: 3–18; E. W. K. Tsang, 2002, "Acquiring knowledge by foreign partners for international joint ventures in a transition economy: Learning-by-doing and learning myopia", *Strategic Management Journal*, 23(9): 835–854.

107. M. J. Robson, C. S. Katsikeas and D. C. Bello, 2008, "Drivers and performance outcomes of trust in international strategic alliances: The role of organisational complexity", *Organization Science*, 19(4): 647–668; S. Zaheer and A. Zaheer, 2007, "Trust across borders", *Journal of International Business Studies*, 38: 21–29; P. W. L. Vlaar, F. A. J. Van den Bosch and H. W. Volberda, 2007, "On the evolution of trust, distrust, and formal coordination and control in interorganizational relationships: Toward an integrative framework", *Group & Organization Management*, Special Issue Trust and Control Interrelations: New Perspectives on the Trust-Control Nexus, 32(4): 407–429; P. W. L. Vlaar, F. A. J. Van den Bosch and H. W. Volberda, 2007, "Towards a dialectic perspective on formalization in interorganizational relationships: How alliance managers capitalize on the duality inherent in contracts, rules, and procedures", *Organization Studies*, 28(4): 437–466; P. W. L. Vlaar, F. A. J. Van den Bosch and H. W. Volberda, 2006, "Coping with problems of understanding in interorganizational relationships: Using formalization as a means to make sense", *Organization Studies*, Special Issue on "Making Sense of Organizing: in Honor of Karl Weick", 27(11): 1617–1638.

108. M. H. Ogasavara and Y. Hoshino, 2009, "The effects of entry strategy and inter-firm trust on the survival of Japanese manufacturing subsidiaries in Brazil", *Asian Business & Management*, 7(3): 353–380; M. W. Peng and O. Shenkar, 2002, "Joint venture dissolution as corporate divorce", *Academy of Management Executive*, 16(2): 92–105.

109. Y. Luo, O. Shenkar and H. Gurnani, 2008, "Control-cooperation interfaces in global strategic alliances: A situational typology and strategic responses", *Journal of International Business Studies*, 9(3): 428–453; A. Madhok, 2006, "Revisiting multinational firms' tolerance for joint ventures: A trust-based approach", *Journal of International Business Studies*, 37: 30–43; J. Child and Y. Van, 2003, "Predicting the performance of international joint ventures: An investigation in China", *Journal of Management Studies*, 40(2): 283–320; J. P. Johnson, M. A. Korsgaard and H. J. Sapienza, 2002, "Perceived fairness, decision control, and commitment in international joint venture management teams", *Strategic Management Journal*, 23(12): 1141–1160.

110. X. Lin and C. L. Wang, 2008, "Enforcement and performance: The role of ownership, legalism and trust in international joint ventures", *Journal of World Business*, 43(3): 340–351; L. Huff and L. Kelley, 2003, "Levels of organisational trust in individualist versus collectivist societies: A seven-nation study", *Organization Science*, 14(1): 81–90.

111. D. Li, L. Eden, M. A. Hitt and R. D. Ireland, 2008, "Friends, acquaintances and strangers? Partner selection in R&D alliances", *Academy of Management Journal*, 51: 315–334; Y. Pan and D. K. Tse, 2000, "The hierarchical model of market entry modes", *Journal of International Business Studies*, 31: 535–554.

112. J. Wiklund and D. A. Shepherd, 2009, "The effectiveness of alliances and acquisitions: The role of resource combination activities", *Entrepreneurship Theory and Practice*, 33 (1): 193–212; P. Porrini, 2004, "Can a previous alliance between an acquirer and a target affect acquisition performance?", *Journal of Management*, 30: 545–562.

113. C. M. Sanchez and S. R. Goldberg, 2009, "Strategic M&As: Stronger in tough times", *Journal of Corporate Accounting & Finance*, 20(2): 3–7; K. Shimizu, M. A. Hitt, D. Vaidyanath and V. Pisano, 2004, "Theoretical foundations of cross-border mergers and acquisitions: A review of current research and recommendations for the future", *Journal of International Management*, 10: 307–353; M. A. Hitt, J. S. Harrison and R. D. Ireland, 2001, *Mergers and Acquisitions: A Guide to Creating Value for Stakeholders*, New York: Oxford University Press.

114. A. Boateng, W. Qian and Y. Tianle, 2008, "Cross-border M&As by Chinese firms: An analysis of strategic motives and performance", *Thunderbird International Business Review*, 50(4): 259–270; M. A. Hitt and V. Pisano, 2003, "The cross-border merger and acquisition strategy", *Management Research*, 1: 133–144.

115. International operational fact sheet, 2007, http://www.walmartfacts.com, July; J. Levine, 2004, "Europe: Gold mines and quicksand", *Forbes*, April 12, 76.

116. B. Powell, 2009, "Buying binge", *Time*, April 20, GB1.

117. P. X. Meschi, 2009, "Government corruption and foreign stakes in international joint ventures in emerging economies", *Asia Pacific Journal of Management*, 26(2): 241–261; U. Weitzel and S. Berns, 2006, "Cross-border takeovers, corruption, and related aspects of governance", *Journal of International Business Studies*, 37: 786–806.

118. R. Chakrabarti, S. Gupta-Mukherjee and N. Jayaraman, 2009, "Mars-Venus marriages: Culture and cross-border M&A", *Journal of International Business Studies*, 40(2): 216–236; A. H. L. Slangen, 2006, "National cultural distance and initial foreign acquisition performance: The moderating effect of integration", *Journal of World Business*, 41: 161–170.

119. S. F. S. Chen, 2008, "The motives for international acquisitions: capability procurements, strategic considerations, and the role of ownership structures", *Journal of International Business Studies*, 39(3): 454–471; I. Bjorkman, G. K. Stahl and E. Vaara, 2007, "Cultural differences and capability transfer in cross-border acquisitions: The mediating roles of capability complementarity, absorptive capacity, and social integration", *Journal of International Business Studies*, 38: 658–672; S. Spedale, F. A. J. Van den Bosch and H. W. Volberda, 2007, "Preservation and dissolution of the target firm's embedded ties in acquisitions", *Organization Studies*, 28(8): 1169–1196.

120. J. Reed, 2008, "SAIC plans U.K. comeback for MG TF roadster", *Financial Times*, April 21, 25; C. Buckley, 2005, "SAIC to fund MG Rover bid", *The Times of London*, http://www.timesonline.co.uk, July 18.

121. H. Raff, M. Ryan and F. Stähler, 2009, "The choice of market entry mode: Greenfield investment, M&A and joint venture", *International Review of Economics & Finance*, 18 (1): 3–10; A. W. Harzing, 2002, "Acquisitions versus greenfield investments: International strategy and management of entry modes", *Strategic Management Journal*, 23: 211–227.

122. C. Bouquet, L. Hebert and A. Delios, 2004, "Foreign expansion in service industries: Separability and human capital intensity", *Journal of Business Research*, 57: 35–46.

123. K. F. Meyer, S. Estrin, S. K. Bhaumik,and M. W. Peng, 2009, "Institutions, resources, and entry strategies in emerging economies", *Strategic Management Journal*, 30 (1): 61–80.

124. K. F. Meyer, M. Wright and S. Pruthi, 2009, "Managing knowledge in foreign entry strategies: a resource-based analysis", *Strategic Management Journal*, 30(5): 557–574.

125. Y. Park and B. Sternquist, 2008, "The global retailer's strategic proposition and choice of entry mode", *International Journal of Retail & Distribution Management*, 36(4): 281–299; S. Mani, K. D. Antia and A. Rindfleisch, 2007, "Entry mode and equity level: A multilevel examination of foreign direct investment ownership structure", *Strategic Management Journal*, 28: 857–866.

126. A. Roth, 2008, "Beijing Olympics 2008: UPS markets its delivery for China only"; "Company transports gear for the Games"; "Face-off with FedEx", *Wall Street Journal* (Europe), August 11, 29.

127. D. L. Paul and R. B. Wooster, 2008, "Strategic investments by U.S. firms in transition economies", *Journal of International Business Studies*, 39(2): 249–266; V. Gaba, Y. Pan and G. R. Ungson, 2002, "Timing of entry in international market: An empirical study of U.S. Fortune 500 firms in China", *Journal of International Business Studies*, 33(1): 39–55; S. J. Chang and P. Rosenzweig, 2001,

"The choice of entry mode in sequential foreign direct investment", *Strategic Management Journal*, 22: 747–776; T. Hutzschenreuter, T. Pedersen and H. W. Volberda, 2007, "The role of path dependency and managerial intentionality: A perspective on international business research", *Journal of International Business Studies*, 38(7): 1055–1068.

128. P. X. Meschi, 2009, "Government corruption and foreign stakes in international joint ventures in emerging economies", *Asia Pacific Journal of Management*, 26(2): 241–261; R. Farzad, 2007, "Extreme investing: Inside Colombia", *BusinessWeek*, May 28, 50–58; K. E. Myer, 2001, "Institutions, transaction costs, and entry mode choice in Eastern Europe", *Journal of International Business Studies*, 32: 357–367.

129. J. Che and G. Facchini, 2009, "Cultural differences, insecure property rights and the mode of entry decision", *Economic Theory*, 38(3): 465–484; S. Li, 2004, "Why are property rights protections lacking in China? An institutional explanation", *California Management Review*, 46(3): 100–115.

130. A. C. Inkpen, 2008, "Knowledge transfer and international joint ventures: the case of NUMMI and General Motors", *Strategic Management Journal*, 29(4): 447–453.

131. R. Lindsay, 2010, "Peugeot Citroën joins Toyota and Honda in recall", http://www.business.timesonline.co.uk, February 1.

132. D. Hannon, 2008, "Shorter is better for Toyota's supply chain", *Purchasing*, August, 46–47; M. Zimmerman, 2007, "Toyota ends GM's reign as car sales leader", *Los Angeles Times*, April 25, 2007, C1; L. J. Howell and J. C. Hsu, 2002, "Globalisation within the auto industry", *Research Technology Management*, 45(4): 43–49.

133. J. W. Lu and X. Ma, 2008, "The contingent value of local partners' business group affiliations", *Academy of Management Journal*, 51(2): 295–314; A. Chacar and B. Vissa, 2005, "Are emerging economies less efficient? Performance persistence and the impact of business group affiliation", *Strategic Management Journal*, 26: 933–946; R. E. Hoskisson, H, Kim, R. E. White and L. Tihanyi, 2004, "A framework for understanding international diversification by business groups from emerging economies", in: M. A. Hitt and J. L. C. Cheng (eds.), *Theories of the Multinational Enterprise: Diversity, Complexity, and Relevance. Advances in International Management*, Oxford, UK: Elsevier/JAI Press, 137–163.

134. R. Chittoor, M. B. Sarkar, S. Ray and P. S. Aulakh, 2009, "Third-world copycats to emerging multinationals: Institutional changes and organisational transformation in the Indian pharmaceutical industry", *Organization Science*, 20(1): 187–205.

135. M. F. Wiersma and H. P. Bowen, 2008, "Corporate international diversification: The impact of foreign competition, industry globalisation and product diversification", *Strategic Management Journal*, 29: 115–132.

136. P. Dastidar, 2009, "International corporate diversification and performance: Does firm self-selection matter? ", *Journal of International Business Studies*, 40: 71–85; L. Li, 2007, "Multinationality and performance: A synthetic review and research agenda", *International Journal of Management Reviews*, 9: 117–139; J. A. Doukas and O. B. Kan,

2006, "Does global diversification destroy firm value", *Journal of International Business Studies*, 37: 352–371; J. W. Lu and P. W. Beamish, 2004, "International diversification and firm performance: The S-curve hypothesis", *Academy of Management Journal*, 47: 598–609.

137. S. E. Christophe and H. Lee, 2005, "What matters about internationalisation: A market-based assessment", *Journal of Business Research*, 58: 536–643; J. A. Doukas and L. H. P. Lang, 2003, "Foreign direct investment, diversification and firm performance", *Journal of International Business Studies*, 34: 153–172.

138. H. Zou and M. B. Adams, 2009, "Corporate ownership, equity risk and returns in the People's Republic of China", *Journal of International Business Studies*, 39(7): 1149–1168; M. A. Hitt, L. Tihanyi, T. Miller and B. Connelly, 2006, "International diversification: Antecedents, outcomes and moderators", *Journal of Management*, 32: 831–867; C. C. Y. Kwok and D. M. Reeb, 2000, "Internationalisation and firm risk: An upstream-downstream hypothesis", *Journal of International Business Studies*, 31: 611–629.

139. A. Birnik and R. Moat, 2009, "Mapping multinational operations", *Business Strategy Review*, 20(1): 30–33; T. R. Holcomb and M. A. Hitt, 2007, "Toward a model of strategic outsourcing", *Journal of Operations Management*, 25: 464–481; J. P. Doh, 2005, "Offshore outsourcing: Implications for international business and strategic management theory and practice", *Journal of Management Studies*, 42: 695–704.

140. J. Song and J. Shin, 2008, "The paradox of technological capabilities: A study of knowledge sourcing from host countries of overseas R&D operations", *Journal of International Business Studies*, 39: 291–303; J. Penner-Hahn and J. M. Shaver, 2005, "Does international research and development increase patent output? An analysis of Japanese pharmaceutical firms", *Strategic Management Journal*, 26: 121–140.

141. S. Shimizutani and Y. Todo, 2008, "What determines overseas R&D activities? The case of Japanese multinational firms", *Research Policy*, 37(3): 530–544; M. A. Hitt, L. Bierman, K. Uhlenbruck and K. Shimizu, 2006, "The importance of resources in the internationalisation of professional service firms: The good, the bad and the ugly", *Academy of Management Journal*, 49: 1137–1157; L. Tihanyi, R. A. Johnson, R. E. Hoskisson and M. A. Hitt, 2003, "Institutional ownership differences and international diversification: The effects of board of directors and technological opportunity", *Academy of Management Journal*, 46: 195–211.

142. H. Zou and P. N. Ghauri, 2009, "Learning through international acquisitions: The process of knowledge acquisition in China", *Management International Review*, 48(2), 207–226; B. Ambos and B. B. Schlegelmilch, 2007, "Innovation and control in the multinational firm: A comparison of political and contingency approaches", *Strategic Management Journal*, 28: 473–486; K. Asakawa and M. Lehrer, "Managing local knowledge assets globally: The role of regional innovation relays", *Journal of World Business*, 38(1): 31–42.

143. E. Matta and P. W. Beamish, 2008, "The accentuated CEO career horizon problem: Evidence from international

acquisitions", *Strategic Management Journal*, 29(7): 683; D. S. Elenkov, W. Judge and P. Wright, 2005, "Strategic leadership and executive innovation influence: An international multi-cluster comparative study", *Strategic Management Journal*, 26: 665–682; P. Herrmann, 2002, "The influence of CEO characteristics on the international diversification of manufacturing firms: An empirical study in the United States", *International Journal of Management*, 19(2): 279–289.

144. H. L. Sirkin, J. W. Hemerling and A. K. Bhattacharya, 2009, "Globality: Challenger companies are radically redefining the competitive landscape", *Strategy & Leadership*, 36(6): 36–41; M. A. Hitt, R. E. Hoskisson and H. Kim, 1997, "International diversification: Effects on innovation and firm performance in product-diversified firms", *Academy of Management Journal*, 40: 767–798.

145. E. García-Canal and M. F. Guillén, 2009, "Risk and the strategy of foreign location choice in regulated industries", *Strategic Management Journal*, 29(10): 1097–1115; J. Child, L. Chung and H. Davies, 2003, "The performance of cross-border units in China: A test of natural selection, strategic choice and contingency theories", *Journal of International Business Studies*, 34: 242–254.

146. C. Crossland and D. C. Hambrick, 2007, "How national systems differ in their constraints on corporate executives: A study of CEO effects in three countries", *Strategic Management Journal*, 28: 767–789; M. Javidan, P. W. Dorfman, M. S. de Luque and R. J. House, 2006, "In the eye of the beholder: Cross-cultural lessons in leadership from Project GLOBE", *Academy of Management Perspectives*, 20(1): 67–90.

147. N. Shirouzu, 2008, "Corporate news: GM's car sales slide in China"; "Toyota, Honda zoom ahead as buyers concentrate on fuel economy, quality", *Wall Street Journal*, September 26, B1.

148. I. Alon and T. T. Herbert, 2009, "A stranger in a strange land: Micro political risk and the multinational firm", *Business Horizons*, 52(2): 127–137; P. Rodriguez. K. Uhlenbruck and L. Eden, 2005, "Government corruption and the entry strategies of multinationals", *Academy of Management Review*, 30: 383–396; J. H. Zhao, S. H. Kim and J. Du, 2003, "The impact of corruption and transparency on foreign direct investment: An empirical analysis", *Management International Review*, 43(1): 41–62.

149. F. Wu, 2009, "Singapore's sovereign wealth funds: The political risk of overseas investments", *World Economics*, 9(3): 97–122; P. S. Ring, G. A. Bigley, T. D'Aunno and T. Khanna, 2005, "Perspectives on how governments matter", *Academy of Management Review*, 30: 308–320; A. Delios and W. J. Henisz, 2003, "Policy uncertainty and the sequence of entry by Japanese firms, 1980–1998", *Journal of International Business Studies*, 34: 227–241.

150. A. Kouznetsov, 2009, "Entry modes employed by multinational manufacturing enterprises and review of factors that affect entry mode choices in Russia", *The Business Review*, Cambridge, 10(2): 316–323.

151. S. Globerman and D. Shapiro, 2009, "Economic and strategic considerations surrounding Chinese FDI in the United States", *Asia Pacific Journal of Management*, 26(1): 163–183.

152. I. G. Kawaller, 2009, "Hedging currency exposures by multinationals: Things to consider", *Journal of Applied Finance*, 18(1): 92–98; K. Addae-Dapaah and W. T. Y. Hwee, 2009, "The unsung impact of currency risk on the performance of international real property investment", *Review of Financial Economics*, 18(1): 56–65; T. Vestring, T. Rouse and U. Reinert, 2005, "Hedging your offshoring bets", *MIT Sloan Management Review*, 46(3): 26–29.

153. T. G. Andrews and N. Chompusri, 2005, "Temporal dynamics of crossvergence: Institutionalizing MNC integration strategies in post-crisis ASEAN", *Asia Pacific Journal of Management*, 22(1): 5–22; S. Mudd, R. Grosse and J. Mathis, 2002, "Dealing with financial crises in emerging markets", *Thunderbird International Business Review*, 44 (3): 399–430.

154. N. Bandelj, 2009, "The global economy as instituted process: The case of Central and Eastern Europe", *American Sociological Review*, 74(1): 128–149; L. Tihanyi and W. H. Hegarty, 2007, "Political interests and the emergence of commercial banking in transition economies", *Journal of Management Studies*, 44: 789–813.

155. J. W. Lu and P. W. Beamish, 2004, "International diversification and firm performance: The S-curve hypothesis", *Academy of Management Journal*, 47: 598–609; W. P. Wan and R. E. Hoskisson, 2003, "Home country environments, corporate diversification strategies and firm performance", *Academy of Management Journal*, 46: 27–45; M. A. Hitt, R. E. Hoskisson and H. Kim, 1997, "International diversification: Effects on innovation and firm performance in product-diversified firms", *Academy of Management Journal*, 40: 767–798.

156. A. Ojala, 2008, "Entry in a psychically distant market: Finnish small and medium-sized software firms in Japan", *European Management Journal*, 26(2): 135–144; D. W. Yiu, C. M. Lau and G. D. Bruton, 2007, "International venturing by emerging economy firms: The effects of firm capabilities, home country networks, and corporate entrepreneurship", *Journal of International Business Studies*, 38: 519–540; P. S. Barr and M. A. Glynn, 2004, "Cultural variations in strategic issue interpretation: Relating cultural uncertainty avoidance to controllability in discriminating threat and opportunity", *Strategic Management Journal*, 25: 59–67.

157. M. L. L. Lam, 2009, "Beyond credibility of doing business in China: Strategies for improving corporate citizenship of foreign multinational enterprises in China", *Journal of Business Ethics*: Supplement, 87: 137–146; W. P. J. Henisz and B. A. Zeiner, 2005, "Legitimacy, interest group pressures and change in emergent institutions, the case of foreign investors and host country governments", *Academy of Management Review*, 30: 361–382; T. P. Blumentritt and D. Nigh, 2002, "The integration of subsidiary political activities in multinational corporations", *Journal of International Business Studies*, 33: 57–77, 175.

158. D. Lavie and S. Miller, 2009, "Alliance portfolio internationalisation and firm performance", *Organization Science*, 19 (4): 623–646.

159. T. Levitt, 1983, "The globalisation of markets", *Harvard Business Review*, 61(3): 92–102.

# CHAPTER 10

# COOPERATIVE STRATEGY

## LEARNING OBJECTIVES

Studying this chapter should provide you with the strategic management knowledge needed to:

1   Define cooperative strategies and explain why firms use them.
2   Define and discuss three types of strategic alliances.
3   Name the business-level cooperative strategies and describe their use.
4   Discuss the use of corporate-level cooperative strategies in diversified firms.
5   Understand the importance of cross-border strategic alliances as an international cooperative strategy.
6   Explain cooperative strategies' risks.
7   Describe two approaches used to manage cooperative strategies.

© Jimmy Anderson/iStock

**OPENING CASE**

Image courtesy of IBM.

# Using cooperative strategies at IBM

A company widely known throughout the world, IBM has 350 000-plus employees who design, manufacture, sell and service advanced information technologies such as computer systems, storage systems, software and microelectronics. The firm's extensive line-up of products and services is grouped into three core business units – Systems and Financing, Software and Services.

As is true for all companies, IBM uses three means to grow – internal developments (primarily through innovation), mergers and acquisitions (such as the recent purchase of France-based ILOG, which produces software tools to automate and speed up a firm's decision-making process) and cooperative strategies. Interestingly, IBM had a ten year partnership with ILOG before making the acquisition. By cooperating with other companies, IBM is able to leverage its core competencies to grow and improve its performance.

Through cooperative strategies (e.g., strategic alliances and joint ventures, both of which are defined

and discussed in this chapter), IBM finds itself working with a variety of firms in order to deliver products and services. However, IBM has specific performance-related objectives it wants to accomplish as it engages in an array of cooperative arrangements. In regard to its systems business, IBM works to develop leading-edge chip technology. In order to do this it has formed five separate alliances to develop the most advanced semiconductor research and expand its facilities by purchasing the latest chip-making equipment. These allies provide brain power including more than 250 scientists and engineers that work alongside IBM's engineers and scientists to foster innovation. Some of these innovations come through new advances in materials and chemistry. For instance IBM signed an agreement with Japan's JSR, a Japanese firm engaged in materials science, to develop materials and processes for circuitry necessary to advance futuristic semi-conductors.

One of IBM's growing businesses even in the downturn is business analytics. The ILOG acquisition, noted previously, is an example of IBM's thrust into this area. IBM has created a new unit called IBM Business Analytics and Optimization Services. This business provides software solutions to help a firm better analyse data and make smarter decisions. It has four thousand consultants who examine IBM's research and software divisions for algorithms, applications and other innovations to help provide solutions to companies. This is just one aspect of the services business that IBM pursues with its consulting service operations. Of course it needs software to produce the solutions. Many of these solutions come through partnerships with small providers that IBM manages through cooperative agreements and often acquires, as it did ILOG.

However, other firms are entering into this space through their own acquisitions or alliances. For instance, Sun MicroSystems Inc. had an alliance with IBM to produce software in competition with Hewlett Packard. IBM bid for Sun in an acquisition attempt but was bested by Oracle that won with a €5.75 billion bid. Thus the competition for the solutions service and network business has heated up through acquisitions and especially through partnerships which IBM has used to facilitate its change from solely producing hardware to adding solution services and software. One study concluded that IBM was able to make this significant shift by managing its alliance of networks according to three principles. (1) Company alliance networks may be used not just for individual projects but to facilitate strategic change inside a company; (2) two principal mechanisms can bring about this change: (a) increasing speed of change through partners and (b) finding partners in areas outside existing competencies; (3) companies can shape their alliance networks by conscious actions. Other firms are observing IBM's actions and learning and seeking to catch up fast through their own partnerships as illustrated by a recent partnership between Cisco and the Japanese firm Fujitsu. These two firms are traditionally hardware firms building networks for phone companies, but are moving to increase their service options especially among mobile telephone providers.

As one might anticipate, a firm as large and diverse as IBM is involved with a number of cooperative relationships such as those already mentioned. Given the challenges associated with achieving and maintaining superior performance and in light of its general success with cooperative relationships, one might anticipate that IBM will continue to use cooperative strategies as a path toward growth and enhanced performance.

**Sources:** Agarwal, R. and Helfat, C. E. (2009) "Strategic renewal of organizations", *Organization Science*, 20(2): 281–293; Bulkeley, W. M. (2009) "Corporate News: IBM buoyed by its balance of business", *Wall Street Journal*, April 20, B3; Bulkeley, W. M. (2009) "IBM results are clouded by Oracle's deal for Sun", *Wall Street Journal*, April 21, B1; Hamm, S. (2009) "Big blue goes into analysis", *Business-Week*, April 27, 16; Menn, J. (2009) "IBM focuses on software and services to meet targets", *Financial Times*, April 21, 19; O'Brien, J. M. (2009) "IBM's grand plan to save the planet", *Fortune*, May 4, 84–91; SOA News Desk (2009) "IBM completes acquisition of ILOG", *2009 Journal OR-MS Today*, 36(1): 60; Bulkeley, W. M. (2008) "Business technology, A service rival looms for IBM"; "H-P deal for EDS to pose challenge for big blue unit", *Wall Street Journal*, May 20, B6; Dittrich, K., Duysters, D. and de Man, A. P. (2007) "Strategic repositioning by means of alliance networks: The case of IBM", *Research Policy*, 36: 1496–1511; Hamm, S. (2007) "Radical collaboration: Lessons from IBM's innovation factory", *BusinessWeek*, September 10, 16.

## Questions

**1** Describe the business analytics business for IBM.

**2** What future cooperative arrangements do you consider IBM might employ in the business analytics space?

As noted in the Opening Case, firms use three means to grow and improve their performance – internal development, mergers and acquisitions and cooperation. In each of these cases, the firm seeks to use its resources in ways that will create the greatest amount of value for stakeholders.[1]

Recognized as a viable engine of firm growth,[2] cooperative strategy is a strategy in which firms work together to achieve a shared objective.[3] Thus, cooperating with other firms is another strategy firms use to create value for a customer that exceeds the cost of providing that value and to establish a favourable position relative to competition.[4]

As explained in the Opening Case, IBM is involved with a number of cooperative arrangements. The intention of serving customers better than competitors and of gaining an advantageous position relative to competitors drives this firm's use of cooperative strategies. IBM's corporate level cooperative strategy in services and software is seeking to deliver server technologies in ways that maximize customer value while improving the firm's position relative to competitors. For example, Hewlett-Packard recently bought EDS to battle IBM for the leadership position in the global services market.[5] IBM has many business-level alliances with partner firms focusing on what they believe are better ways to improve services for customer firms such as the cooperative agreements that IBM has through its new division in business analytics.[6] The objectives IBM and its various partners seek by working together highlight the reality that in the twenty-first century landscape, firms must develop the skills required to successfully use cooperative strategies as a complement to their abilities to grow and improve performance through internal developments and mergers and acquisitions.[7]

**Cooperative strategy**

A cooperative strategy is a strategy in which firms work together to achieve a shared objective.

We examine several topics in this chapter. First, we define and offer examples of different strategic alliances as primary types of cooperative strategies. Next, we discuss the extensive use of cooperative strategies in the global economy and reasons for them. In succession, we then describe business-level (including collusive strategies), corporate-level, international and network cooperative strategies. The chapter closes with discussion of the risks of using cooperative strategies as well as how effective management of them can reduce those risks.

We focus on strategic alliances in this chapter because firms use them more frequently than other types of cooperative relationships. Although not often used, collusive strategies are another type of cooperative strategy discussed in this chapter. In a *collusive strategy*, two or more firms cooperate to increase prices above the fully competitive level.[8]

# Strategic alliances as a primary type of cooperative strategy

A strategic alliance is a cooperative strategy in which firms combine some of their resources and capabilities to create a competitive advantage.[9] Thus, strategic alliances involve firms with some degree of exchange and sharing of resources and capabilities to co-develop, sell and service goods or services.[10] Strategic alliances allow firms to leverage their existing resources and capabilities while working with partners to develop additional resources and capabilities as the foundation for new competitive advantages.[11] To be certain, the reality today is that "strategic alliances have become a cornerstone of many firms' competitive strategy".[12]

Consider the case for Kodak. CEO Antonio Perez stated, "Kodak today is involved with partnerships that would have been unthinkable a few short years ago."[13] His comment suggests the breadth and depth of cooperative relationships with which the firm is involved. Each of the cooperative relationships is intended to lead to a new competitive advantage as the source of growth and performance improvement. Kodak has changed from a firm rooted in film and imaging into a digital technology-oriented company.[14]

A competitive advantage developed through a cooperative strategy is often called a *collaborative* or *relational* advantage.[15] As previously discussed, particularly in Chapter 3, competitive advantages enhance the firm's marketplace success. Rapid technological changes and the global economy are examples of factors challenging firms to constantly upgrade current competitive advantages while they develop new ones to maintain strategic competitiveness.[16]

Many firms, especially large global competitors, establish multiple strategic alliances. Although we discussed only a few of them in the Opening Case, the reality is that IBM has formed hundreds of partnerships as it uses cooperative strategies. IBM is not alone in its decision to frequently use cooperative strategies as a means of competition. Focusing on developing advanced technologies, Lockheed Martin has formed more than 250 alliances with firms in more than 30 countries as it concentrates on its primary business of defence modernization and serving the needs of the air transportation industry. For instance, Lockheed Martin recently entered into an alliance with Northrop Grumman Corp. and Alliant Techsystems Inc. These three firms are contracted to develop multi-role missiles which have both air-to-air and air-to-ground capabilities. This missile would give aircraft much more flexibility in pursuing either air or ground targets and thus boost the target efficiency of each flight sortie.[17] For all cooperative arrangements, including those we are describing here, success is more likely when partners behave cooperatively. Actively solving

**Strategic alliance**

A strategic alliance is a cooperative strategy in which firms combine some of their resources and capabilities to create a competitive advantage.

problems, being trustworthy and consistently pursuing ways to combine partners' resources and capabilities to create value are examples of cooperative behaviour known to contribute to alliance success.[18]

## Three types of strategic alliances

The three major types of strategic alliances include joint venture, equity strategic alliance and nonequity strategic alliance. These alliance types are classified by their ownership arrangements; later, we classify alliances by strategic categorizations.

A joint venture is a strategic alliance in which two or more firms create a legally independent company to share some of their resources and capabilities to develop a competitive advantage. Joint ventures, which are often formed to improve firms' abilities to compete in uncertain competitive environments,[19] are effective in establishing long-term relationships and in transferring tacit knowledge. Because it cannot be codified, tacit knowledge is learned through experiences such as those taking place when people from partner firms work together in a joint venture.[20] As discussed in Chapter 3, tacit knowledge is an important source of competitive advantage for many firms.[21]

Typically, partners in a joint venture own equal percentages and contribute equally to the venture's operations. Germany's Siemens AG and Japan's Fujitsu Ltd equally own a joint venture named Fujitsu Siemens Computers. Although the joint venture has been losing money, Fujitsu has decided that it wants to increase its market share from 4 to 10 per cent. As such it is taking over the jointly owned venture between Fujitsu and Siemens. The new entity will be called Fujitsu Technology Solutions.[22] Overall, evidence suggests that a joint venture may be the optimal type of cooperative arrangement when firms need to combine their resources and capabilities to create a competitive advantage that is substantially different from any they possess individually and when the partners intend to enter highly uncertain markets.[23] These conditions influenced the two independent companies' decision to form the original venture, Fujitsu Siemens Computers.

An equity strategic alliance is an alliance in which two or more firms own different percentages of the company they have formed by combining some of their resources and capabilities to create a competitive advantage. Many foreign direct investments, such as those made by Japanese and European firms in China, are completed through equity strategic alliances.[24]

Interestingly, as many European banks have suffered poor results, foreign banks have been creating equity alliances to provide them with the necessary capital to survive and expand. For instance, in the US 21 per cent of Morgan Stanley's ownership was sold to Mitsubishi UFJ Financial Group in 2008. As a result Nobuyuki Hirano, a senior executive for Mitsubishi, took a seat on the board of directors of Morgan Stanley. This will enhance Mitsubishi's understanding of Morgan Stanley's US Strategy. The relationship may move towards combining Mitsubishi's and Morgan Stanley Japan's Securities Corporation into a single entity in Japan.[25]

A nonequity strategic alliance is an alliance in which two or more firms develop a contractual relationship to share some of their unique resources and capabilities to create a competitive advantage.[26] In this type of alliance, firms do not establish a separate independent company and therefore do not take equity positions. For this reason, nonequity strategic alliances are less formal and demand fewer partner commitments than do joint ventures and equity strategic alliances although the research evidence indicates that they create value for the firms involved.[27] The relative informality and lower commitment levels characterizing nonequity strategic alliances make them unsuitable for complex projects where success requires effective transfers of tacit knowledge between partners.[28]

---

*Handwritten margin note: tactic important for CA!*

**Joint venture**

A joint venture is a strategic alliance in which two or more firms create a legally independent company to share some of their resources and capabilities to develop a competitive advantage.

**Equity strategic alliance**

An equity strategic alliance is an alliance in which two or more firms own different percentages of the company they have formed by combining some of their resources and capabilities to create a competitive advantage.

**Nonequity strategic alliance**

A nonequity strategic alliance is an alliance in which two or more firms develop a contractual relationship to share some of their unique resources and capabilities to create a competitive advantage.

© Cubolmages srl/Alamy

## STRATEGIC FOCUS

# Pininfarina design and Ferrari – a nonequity design alliance

The alliance formed between Ferrari – the Italian luxury sports car manufacturing firm founded in Maranello in 1929, and Pininfarina – the Italian full service car company which started life under its original name "Carrozzeria" in Turin in 1930, is one which has now lasted nearly sixty years with no signs of ending soon. To date, Pininfarina has been involved in the design of approximately two hundred Ferrari models in the sixty years the two companies have worked alongside one another.

However, the coming together of Pininfarina and Ferrari was initially not expected to survive more than a few years by insiders in the motor industry in the 1950s, let alone as long as it has. Indeed, when the alliance was first formed some people said that it was akin to "putting two Prima Donnas in the same opera". This opinion appeared to be fairly accurate if the records made for the arrangement of the first meeting between Enzo Ferrari and Battista "Pinin" Farina, the founders of Ferrari and Pininfarina respectively, are to

be believed. For this meeting in 1951, each man was willing to invite the other to the headquarters of his company, yet was unwilling to travel to the other for the meeting. This appeared to be heading towards a result in which no meeting would be held and therefore no alliance formed. However, a compromise was reached, with the two company founders agreeing to meet at a neutral location approximately half-way between the two company locations at the time, a restaurant in Tortona.

This meeting, at least according to Farina, was one in which both sides immediately knew a mutually beneficial alliance could be formed: "At a certain point, it was clear that one of us was looking for a beautiful, famous woman to dress and the other a world-class couturier to deck her out". The alliance was confirmed in 1952.

Throughout the alliance to date, Pininfarina has provided Ferrari with both design and engineering services. Ferrari have their own design and engineering teams in place who have worked alongside the Pininfarina employees in creating many of the Ferrari models we have seen developed in the last sixty years, including the *Daytona* in 1968, the *F355* in 1994, the *550 Maranello* in 1996 and the *Enzo*, named after the founder of Ferrari, in 2002.

This is an example of a situation where two companies have managed to achieve a long and fruitful alliance in which both have significantly benefited from each other's resources and capabilities. Whereas Ferrari have been able to obtain high design and engineering skills by outsourcing some work on their models to Pininfarina, the design company has both been given the opportunity to demonstrate what it is able to achieve with significant financial support and budgets, and has benefited from association with one of the strongest and most reputable brands in the motor industry, helping it sell its services to other motor companies and companies in other industries such as mobile phones (they helped design the Motorola iDen i833 released in 2004) as a result.

We will never know whether either company would have been more or less successful if the alliance between them had not occurred, but we can safely say it has been one of the most successful alliances ever between a car manufacturer and a car design company with so many iconic models in its portfolio.

**Sources:** Pininfarina Online (2010) "Enzo Ferrari and 'Pinin' Farina: the birth of the myth", http://www.pininfarina.com, July 5; Pininfarina Online (2010) Pininfarina automotive

customer portfolio, http://www.pininfarina.com; July 5; Pininfarina Online (2010) Ferrari Cooperation timeline, http://www.
pininfarina.com, July 5; Chan R. (unknown year) "Alliance
Between Pininfarina and Aedas Architects", Entrepreneur
Online, http://www.entrepreneur.com/prnewswire/release/
232426.html, 14 January; Raja, S. (2004) "The Ferrari of Mobile Phones", http://www.mobileburn.com, 22 August.

### Questions

**1** Based on the Pininfarina Design and Ferrari alliance,
what does each partner offer the other?

**2** Does the length of this alliance reflect its success?
What factors sustain this alliance?

Forms of nonequity strategic alliances include licensing agreements, distribution agreements and supply contracts. Hewlett-Packard (HP), which actively "partners to create new markets . . . and new business models", licenses some of its intellectual property through strategic alliances.[29] Typically, outsourcing commitments are specified in the form of a nonequity strategic alliance. (Discussed in Chapter 3, *outsourcing* is the purchase of a value-creating primary or support activity from another firm.) Dell Inc. and most other computer firms outsource most or all of their production of laptop computers and often form nonequity strategic alliances to detail the nature of the relationship with firms to whom they outsource. Interestingly, many of these firms that outsource introduce modularity that prevents the contracting partner or outsourcee from gaining too much knowledge or from sharing certain aspects of the business the outsourcing firm does not want revealed.[30]

## Reasons firms develop strategic alliances

As our discussion to this point implies and the Pininfarina and Ferrari strategic focus exemplifies, cooperative strategies are an integral part of the competitive landscape and are important to many companies and even to educational institutions. In fact, many firms are cooperating with educational institutions to help commercialize ideas coming from basic research at universities.[31] In for-profit organizations, many executives believe that strategic alliances are central to their firm's success.[32] One executive's position that "you have to partner today or you will miss the next wave . . . and that . . . you cannot possibly acquire the technology fast enough, so partnering is essential"[33] highlights this belief.

Among other benefits, strategic alliances allow partners to create value that they couldn't develop by acting independently and to enter markets more quickly and with greater market penetration possibilities.[34] Moreover, most (if not all) firms lack the full set of resources and capabilities needed to reach their objectives, which indicates that partnering with others will increase the probability of reaching firm-specific performance objectives.[35] Dow Jones & Co., the publisher of *Wall Street Journal* and owned by News Corp., is forming a joint venture with SBI Holdings Inc. to create a Japanese edition of the *Wall Street Journal*'s website. It will primarily feature Japanese translations of news articles, videos, multi-media print and other features of online editions of the *Wall Street Journal*. In particular this venture will develop mobile products and services in conjunction with the website. This is the second news website launched by Dow Jones in Asia; the first was launched in 2002 in China.[36]

The effects of the greater use of cooperative strategies – particularly in the form of strategic alliances – are noticeable. In large firms, for example, alliances can account for 25 per cent or more of sales revenue. And many executives believe that alliances are a prime vehicle for firm growth.[37] In some industries, alliance versus alliance is becoming more prominent than firm versus firm as a point of competition.

In the global airline industry, for example, competition is increasingly between large alliances rather than between airlines.[38]

In summary, we can note that firms form strategic alliances to reduce competition, enhance their competitive capabilities, gain access to resources, take advantage of opportunities, build strategic flexibility and innovate. To achieve these objectives, they must select the right partners and develop trust.[39] Thus, firms attempt to develop a network portfolio of alliances in which they create social capital that affords them flexibility.[40] Because of the social capital, they can call on their partners for help when needed. Of course, social capital means reciprocity exists; partners can ask them for help as well (and they are expected to provide it).[41]

The individually unique competitive conditions of slow-cycle, fast-cycle and standard-cycle markets[42] find firms using cooperative strategies to achieve slightly different objectives (see Table 10.1). We discussed these three market types in Chapter 6 while examining competitive rivalry and competitive dynamics. *Slow-cycle markets* are markets where the firm's competitive advantages are shielded from imitation for relatively long periods of time and where imitation is costly. These markets are close to monopolistic conditions. Railways and, historically, telecommunications, utilities and financial services are examples of industries characterized as slow-cycle markets. In *fast-cycle markets,* the firm's competitive advantages are not shielded from imitation, preventing their long-term sustainability. Competitive advantages are moderately shielded from imitation in *standard-cycle markets,* typically allowing them to be sustained for a longer period of time than in fast-cycle market situations, but for a shorter period of time than in slow-cycle markets.

**Table 10.1** Reasons for strategic alliances by market type

| Market | Reason |
| --- | --- |
| Slow-Cycle | • Gain access to a restricted market |
| | • Establish a franchise in a new market |
| | • Maintain market stability (e.g., establishing standards) |
| Fast-Cycle | • Speed up development of new goods or services |
| | • Speed up new market entry |
| | • Maintain market leadership |
| | • From an industry technology standard |
| | • Share risky R&D expenses |
| | • Overcome uncertainty |
| Standard-Cycle | • Gain market power (reduce industry overcapacity) |
| | • Gain access to complementary resources |
| | • Establish better economies of scale |
| | • Overcome trade barriers |
| | • Meet competitive challenges from other competitors |
| | • Pool resources for very large capital projects |
| | • Learn new business techniques |

**Slow-cycle markets** Firms in slow-cycle markets often use strategic alliances to enter restricted markets or to establish franchises in new markets but the truth of the matter is that slow-cycle markets are becoming rare in the twenty-first century competitive landscape for several reasons. These include the privatization of industries and economies, the rapid expansion of the Internet's capabilities for the quick dissemination of information and the speed with which advancing technologies make quickly imitating even complex products possible.[43] Firms competing in slow-cycle markets, including steel manufacturers, should recognize the future likelihood that they will encounter situations in which their competitive advantages become partially sustainable (in the instance of a standard-cycle market) or unsustainable (in the case of a fast-cycle market). Cooperative strategies can be helpful to firms transitioning from relatively sheltered markets to more competitive ones.[44]

**Fast-cycle markets** Fast-cycle markets are unstable, unpredictable and complex; in a word, "hypercompetitive" (a concept that was discussed in Chapter 6).[45] Combined, these conditions virtually preclude establishing long-lasting competitive advantages, forcing firms to constantly seek sources of new competitive advantages while creating value by using current ones. Alliances between firms with current excess resources and capabilities and those with promising capabilities help firms compete in fast-cycle markets to effectively transition from the present to the future and to gain rapid entry into new markets. As such a "collaboration mindset" is paramount.[46]

The entertainment business is fast becoming a new digital market place as television content is now available on the Web. This has led the entertainment business into a fast-cycle market where collaboration is important not only to succeed but to survive. For example, during 2010 the BBC Trust approved the BBC-led TV Internet merger called Project Canvas which will be launched under the brand name: YouView. This is a merger between Independent Television (ITV), Channel 4 and BT plc and seeks to integrate online video and television – many analysts are predicting that this will be an important stage toward the convergence between the personal computer and television.[47]

Additionally, many of the firms that have digital video content have sought to make a profit also through digital music and have had difficulties in extracting profits from their earlier ventures. In 2007 GE's NBC Universal and News Corp.'s Fox formed a new website named Hulu.com. Walt Disney Corporation in 2009 became a third partner contributing content and capital in this joint venture along with an investment stake held by private equity firm Providence Equity Partners. Thus, this website will be co-owned by direct competitors. For instance ABC (owned by Disney) will shift much of its content to the Hulu site and viewers will be able stream ABC TV shows such as "*Lost*" and "*Grays Anatomy*". CBS will be the only major network not participating in the Hulu venture with NBC Universal, Fox and ABC. As digital video content moves on to the Web, it will be interesting to see how the competition and cooperation between all of these firms evolves.[48]

**Standard-cycle markets** In standard-cycle markets, alliances are more likely to be made by partners with complementary resources and capabilities. Even though airline alliances were originally set up to increase revenue,[49] airlines have realized that they can also be used to reduce costs. SkyTeam (chaired by AirFrance-KLM and Delta) developed an internal website to speed up joint purchasing and to swap tips on pricing. Managers at Oneworld (British Airways and American Airlines) say the alliance's members have already saved more than €157 million through joint purchasing and Star Alliance (Lufthansa and United Airlines) estimates that its member airlines save up to 25 per cent on joint orders.

Given the geographic areas where markets are growing, these global alliances are adding partners from Asia. China Southern Airlines joined the SkyTeam alliance, Air China and Shanghai Airlines were added to the Star Alliance and Dragonair joined as an affiliate of Oneworld. One of the competitive difficulties with the airline alliances is that often major partners switch between airlines. Recently for instance, Continental Airlines, which was part of SkyTeam, switched to the Star Alliance with United Airlines, Air Canada and Lufthansa. Although this move has been approved by the US Department of Transportation, it still lacks approval from the European Union regulators.[50] The fact that Oneworld, SkyTeam and Star Alliance account for more than 60 per cent of the world's airline capacity suggests that firms participating in these alliances have gained scale economies.

# Business-level cooperative strategy

A firm uses a business-level cooperative strategy to grow and improve its performance in individual product markets. As discussed in Chapter 5, business-level strategy details what the firm intends to do to gain a competitive advantage in specific product markets. Thus, the firm forms a business-level cooperative strategy when it believes that combining its resources and capabilities with those of one or more partners will create competitive advantages that it cannot create by itself and that will lead to success in a specific product market. The four business-level cooperative strategies are listed in Figure 10.1.

## Complementary strategic alliances

Complementary strategic alliances are business-level alliances in which firms share some of their resources and capabilities in complementary ways to develop competitive advantages.[51] The two types of complementary strategic alliances are vertical and horizontal (see Figure 10.1).

**Vertical complementary strategic alliance**   In a vertical complementary strategic alliance, firms share their resources and capabilities from different stages of the value chain to create a competitive advantage (see Figure 10.2).[52] Often, vertical complementary alliances are formed to adapt to environmental changes;[53] sometimes the changes represent an opportunity for partnering firms to innovate while adapting.[54]

An example of a vertical complementary alliance is Nintendo and its need for additional software and games for its Wii game console. To fulfil this need

> **Business-level cooperative strategy**
>
> A firm uses a business-level cooperative strategy to grow and improve its performance in individual product markets.

> **Complementary strategic alliances**
>
> Complementary strategic alliances are business-level alliances in which firms share some of their resources and capabilities in complementary ways to develop competitive advantages.

**FIGURE 10.1**  Business-level cooperative strategies

- Complementary strategic alliances
  - Vertical
  - Horizontal
- Competition response strategy
- Uncertainty-reducing strategy
- Competition-reducing strategy

**FIGURE 10.2** Vertical and horizontal complementary strategic alliances

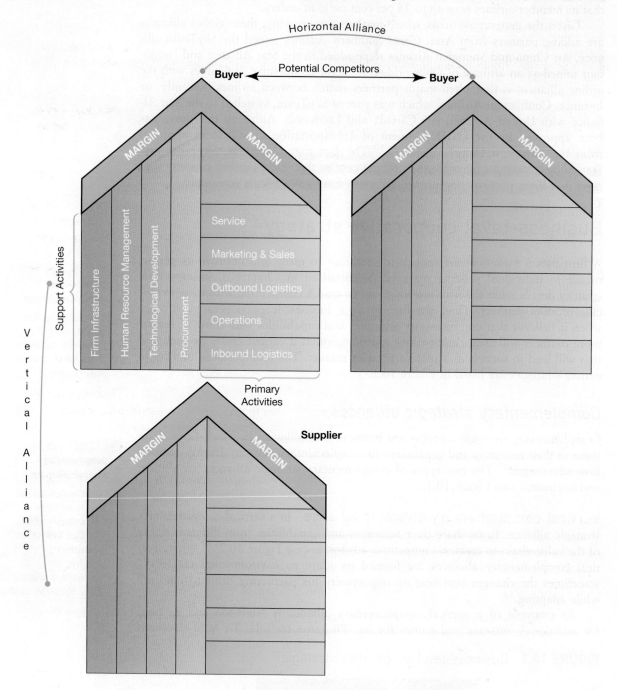

Nintendo has developed a partnership with Electronic Arts. Through this partnership it will lease two sports games before its brand new hardware accessory comes out; one game is Tiger Wood's PGA Tour 10 and the other is Grand Slam Tennis. Nintendo is allowing these games to be sold even before it releases more of its own games. Previously, Nintendo trailed other game platforms in its production of new releases because it stressed its own games over those of other game software

© David Coll Blanco/Alamy

**STRATEGIC FOCUS**

# Nissan and Renault – a horizontal complementary strategic alliance

In 2010, Nissan Motors was one of the three largest Japanese car manufacturers alongside Toyota and Honda, while Renault is the fourth largest automobile manufacturer in the world. For both of these companies their current position in the automotive market is owed significantly to a strategic alliance set up in 1999 to bring the two separate brands together.

The deal to set up the strategic alliance has allowed each separate company to retain its culture and brand identity over the last ten years, with the key link between the two sides being a cross-shareholding. Through this cross-shareholding Renault, the larger of the two companies prior to 1999, holds a 44 per cent stake in Nissan shares and Nissan a 15 per cent stake in Renault shares in 2010. This results in each company having a direct interest in the results of the other, leading to a freedom in communication and honesty between the two companies that might not be found in other strategic alliances in which the companies remain autonomous in financial performance, such as the failed deal between Chrysler and Daimler Benz.

Another key aspect that has been cited as a reason for the success of the Renault-Nissan alliance is the formation of Renault-Nissan b.v., a strategic management company set up to help create a common strategy and manage synergies between the two sides of the alliance. The company is jointly owned by Renault and Nissan and is therefore neutral in its decision making, keeping both sides satisfied that decisions are being made in the best interest of the alliance, not one side of it or the other. In addition, a number of committees made up of representatives from both Renault and Nissan exist which are coordinated by the Coordination Bureau. This includes a small dedicated team of six persons from Nissan and five from Renault, who apply their in-depth understanding of their own companies to help develop synergies at all levels of the alliance, pushing for greater standardization in the long term.

The alliance has set itself three key objectives:

- To be recognized by customers as being among the best three automotive groups in the quality and value of its products and services in each region and market segment.

- To be among the best three automotive groups in key technologies, each partner being a leader in specific domains of excellence.

- To consistently generate a total operating profit among the top three automobile groups in the world, by maintaining a high operating profit margin and pursuing growth.

As of 2008 the combined brands held under the alliance accounted for 9.4 per cent of global automobile sales, making the Renault-Nissan collaboration one of the world's top five car manufacturing companies in that year. This is slightly outside the key objectives outlined above, but is a clear step forward from what the two companies would be achieving if they had not been in collaboration over the last ten years.

**Sources:** Renault-Nissan Alliance: Structure, 2010, http://www.renault.com; July 5; Renault-Nissan Alliance: Corporate Information, 2010, http://www.nissan-global.com, July 5; Renault-Nissan Alliance: The Renault-Nissan Alliance, 2010, http://www.renault.com, July 5.

## Questions

1 Why is the Nissan and Renault case a good example of a horizontal complementary strategic alliance?

2 What are the main challenges confronting this alliance in the ever changing automobile sector?

producers and would not release its hardware details to them in advance. It has changed its policy to encourage more vertical relationships with game software producing firms such as Electronic Arts and Activision Blizzard, Inc.[55]

**Horizontal complementary strategic alliance** A horizontal complementary strategic alliance is an alliance in which firms share some of their resources and capabilities from the same stage (or stages) of the value chain to create a competitive advantage (see Figure 10.2). Commonly, firms use complementary strategic alliances to focus on joint long-term product development and distribution opportunities.[56] As previously noted in the example regarding Hulu.com, GE's Universal Pictures, Disney's ABC unit and News Corp's Fox Video Production have formed a joint website to distribute video content such as TV programmes. Recently, pharmaceutical companies have also been pursuing horizontal alliances. As the healthcare reform takes place, large pharmaceutical firms are seeking to have relationships with generic drug producers. For example, Pfizer has reached marketing agreements with two Indian generic-drug makers: Aurobindo Pharma Ltd and Claris Lifesciences Ltd. These two firms produce and sell 60 and 15 off-patent drugs and injectables, respectively. Similarly Novartis AG is acquiring Ebewe Pharma, an Austrian drug maker, which will partner with Novartis' generic drug subsidiary, Sandoz. These moves are targeted to tap into the growing generic drug market which was €2.75 billion in 2008 and is expected to be €7 billion by 2015.[57]

The automotive manufacturing industry is one in which many horizontal complementary strategic alliances are formed. In fact, virtually all global automobile manufacturers use cooperative strategies to form scores of cooperative relationships. The Renault-Nissan alliance, signed in March 1999, is a prominent example of a horizontal complementary strategic alliance. The challenge is to integrate the partners' operations to create value while maintaining their unique cultures.

## Competition response strategy

As discussed in Chapter 6, competitors initiate competitive actions to attack rivals and launch competitive responses to their competitors' actions. Strategic alliances can be used at the business level to respond to competitors' attacks. Because they can be difficult to reverse and expensive to operate, strategic alliances are primarily formed to take strategic rather than tactical actions and to respond to competitors' actions in a like manner.

Many complementary horizontal alliances are created in response to heavy competition. For instance, digital music producers have been trying to extract more value from their products beyond what they can collect through middlemen such as Apple's iTunes distribution outlet. Many music producers have sought to develop their own distribution outlets through joint partnership, in response to Apple's success, such as Blue Matter Press, Jimmy and Doug's Farm Club and eMusic, but most have failed. Now many of them are seeking online advertisements through websites that distribute music and video. For instance, Warner Music has invested in Lala Media and a start-up company called iMeem Inc. because MySpace Music, a joint venture between four major labels and News Corp., was not generating enough advertising revenue. In response to the focus on advertising, Universal Music, a division of Vivendi SA, through a joint venture with Google has created a new online site for music videos called Vevo. Most of these actions are attempts to bolster revenue because digital music downloads are increasing, but not quickly enough to offset the steep decline in CD sales.[58]

## Uncertainty-reducing strategy

Some firms use business-level strategic alliances to hedge against risk and uncertainty, especially in fast-cycle markets.[59] Also, they are used where uncertainty exists, such as in entering new product markets or emerging economies.

As large global automotive firms manufacture more hybrid vehicles there is insufficient capacity in the battery industry to meet future demand. Volkswagon AG is partnering with China's BYD Co. to produce hybrid and electric vehicles powered by lithium batteries. BYD is the one of the world's largest mobile phone battery producers and is also a fledgling auto producer as it moves to launch a plug-in car before more established rival firms. Volkswagon has also made agreements with Samuel Electric and Toshiba Corp. of Japan to reduce the uncertainty about the insufficient capacity for lithium-ion batteries used in hybrid vehicles.[60]

## Competition-reducing strategy

Used to reduce competition, collusive strategies differ from strategic alliances in that collusive strategies are often an illegal type of cooperative strategy. Two types of collusive strategies are explicit collusion and tacit collusion.

When two or more firms negotiate directly with the intention of jointly agreeing about the amount to produce and the price of the products that are produced, explicit collusion exists.[61] Explicit collusion strategies are illegal in Europe and most developed economies (except in regulated industries).

Firms that use explicit collusion strategies may find others challenging their competitive actions. In early 2009, for example, European officials joined forces with the US Department of Justice to investigate alleged "price coordination" between three air cargo carriers. Luxembourg's Cargolux, Japan's Nippon Cargo Airlines and Korea's Asiana Airlines pleaded guilty and paid criminal fines of €168 million for their role in a global conspiracy to fix prices on air freight. This investigation began in 2001 and the prosecution began in 2006. Throughout the history of the investigation more than 15 air cargo airlines have been prosecuted and fined over €1.26 billion. The investigation continues in the air freight industry and is one of the world's biggest cartel probes by competition officials around the world.[62] As this example suggests, any firm that may use explicit collusion as a strategy should recognize that competitors and regulatory bodies might challenge the acceptability of their competitive actions.

*Tacit collusion* exists when several firms in an industry indirectly coordinate their production and pricing decisions by observing each other's competitive actions and responses.[63] Tacit collusion results in production output that is below fully competitive levels and above fully competitive prices. Unlike explicit collusion, firms engaging in tacit collusion do not directly negotiate output and pricing decisions. However, research suggests that joint ventures or cooperation between two firms can lead to less competition in other markets in which both firms operate.[64]

Tacit collusion tends to be used as a business-level, competition-reducing strategy in highly concentrated industries, such as airline and breakfast cereals. Research in the airline industry suggests that tacit collusion reduces service quality and on-time performance.[65] Firms in these industries recognize that they are interdependent and that their competitive actions and responses significantly affect competitors' behaviour toward them. Understanding this interdependence and carefully observing competitors tends to lead to tacit collusion.

Four firms (Kellogg, General Mills, Post and Quaker) have accounted for as much as 80 per cent of sales volume in the ready-to-eat segment of the US cereal market.[66] Some believe that this high degree of concentration results in "prices for

*[handwritten margin note: Price or restrict demand]*

**Explicit collusion**

Explicit collusion is when two or more firms negotiate directly with the intention of jointly agreeing about the amount to produce and the price of the products that are produced.

**Tacit collusion**

Tacit collusion is when several firms in an industry indirectly coordinate their production and pricing decisions by observing each other's competitive actions and responses.

branded cereals that are well above [the] costs of production".[67] The *Wall Street Journal* reported in 2008 that prices were among the easiest to inflate for breakfast cereals when there are commodity shortages.[68] Prices above the competitive level in this industry suggest the possibility that the dominant firms use a tacit collusion cooperative strategy.

Discussed in Chapter 6, *mutual forbearance* is a form of tacit collusion in which firms do not take competitive actions against rivals they meet in multiple markets. Rivals learn a great deal about each other when engaging in multimarket competition, including how to deter the effects of their rival's competitive attacks and responses. Given what they know about each other as a competitor, firms choose not to engage in what could be destructive competitions in multiple product markets.[69]

In general, governments in free-market economies need to determine how rivals can collaborate to increase their competitiveness without violating established regulations.[70] However, this task is challenging when evaluating collusive strategies, particularly tacit ones. For example, regulation of pharmaceutical and biotech firms who collaborate to meet global competition might lead to too much price fixing and, therefore, regulation is required to make sure that the balance is right, although sometimes the regulation gets in the way of efficient markets.[71] Individual companies must analyse the effect of a competition-reducing strategy on their performance and competitiveness.

## Assessment of business-level cooperative strategies

Firms use business-level strategies to develop competitive advantages that can contribute to successful positions and performance in individual product markets. To develop a competitive advantage using an alliance, the resources and capabilities that are integrated through the alliance must be valuable, rare, imperfectly imitable and non-substitutable (see Chapter 3).

Evidence suggests that complementary business-level strategic alliances, especially vertical ones, have the greatest probability of creating a sustainable competitive advantage.[72] Horizontal complementary alliances are sometimes difficult to maintain because they are often between rival competitors. In this instance, firms may feel a "push" toward and a "pull" from alliances. Airline firms, for example, want to compete aggressively against others serving their markets and target customers. However, the need to develop scale economies and to share resources and capabilities (such as scheduling systems) dictates that alliances be formed so the firms can compete by using cooperative actions and responses while they simultaneously compete against one another through competitive actions and responses. This has lead to many changes in the large airline alliances, for instance with Continental recently aligning with United and Lufthansa rather than Delta and AirFrance-KLM.[73] The challenge in these instances is for each firm to find ways to create the greatest amount of value from both their competitive and cooperative actions. It seems that Nissan and Renault have learned how to achieve this balance.

Although strategic alliances designed to respond to competition and to reduce uncertainty can also create competitive advantages, these advantages often are more temporary than those developed through complementary (both vertical and horizontal) strategic alliances. The primary reason is that complementary alliances have a stronger focus on creating value than do competition-reducing and uncertainty-reducing alliances, which are formed to respond to competitors' actions or reduce uncertainty rather than to attack competitors.

Of the four business-level cooperative strategies, the competition-reducing strategy has the lowest probability of creating a sustainable competitive advantage. For example, research suggests that firms following a foreign direct investment strategy using alliances as a follow-the-leader imitation approach may not have strong strategic or learning goals. Thus, such investment could be attributable to tacit collusion among the participating firms rather than to forming a competitive advantage (which should be the core objective).

# Corporate-level cooperative strategy

*— M+A*

A firm uses a corporate-level cooperative strategy to help it diversify in terms of products offered or markets served, or both. Diversifying alliances, synergistic alliances and franchising are the most commonly used corporate-level cooperative strategies (see Figure 10.3).

Firms use diversifying alliances and synergistic alliances to grow and improve performance by diversifying their operations through a means other than a merger or an acquisition.[74] When a firm seeks to diversify into markets in which the host nation's government prevents mergers and acquisitions, alliances become an especially appropriate option. Corporate-level strategic alliances are also attractive compared with mergers and particularly acquisitions, because they require fewer resource commitments[75] and permit greater flexibility in terms of efforts to diversify partners' operations.[76] An alliance can be used as a way to determine whether the partners might benefit from a future merger or acquisition between them. This "testing" process often characterizes alliances formed to combine firms' unique technological resources and capabilities.[77]

## *Diversifying strategic alliance*

A diversifying strategic alliance is a corporate-level cooperative strategy in which firms share some of their resources and capabilities to diversify into new product or market areas. The spread of high-speed wireless networks and devices with global positioning chips and the popularity of website applications running on Apple's iPhone and Research in Motion's Blackberry (and other smart phones) shows that consumers are increasingly accessing mobile information. Equipped with this knowledge Alcatel Lucent is entering the market through mobile advertising which will allow a mobile phone carrier to alert customers about the location of a favourite store or the closest ATM. It is pursuing this diversification alliance with 1020 Placecast, a developer of mobile phone online advertisements associated with user locations. Hyatt, FedEx and Avis Rental Car Systems are especially interested in using the service. The advertisements will also include a link to coupons or other promotions. Other mobile phone producers have started to sell mobile phone display advertisements in other metropolitan areas through Nokia Phones. These networks are trying to gain a share of the profits that would normally be out of their reach through revenue-sharing models with companies that are advertising, as well as the advertisements-producing service companies.[78]

**Corporate-level cooperative strategy**

A firm uses a corporate-level cooperative strategy to help it diversify in terms of products offered or markets served, or both.

**Diversifying strategic alliance**

A diversifying strategic alliance is a corporate-level cooperative strategy in which firms share some of their resources and capabilities to diversify into new product or market areas.

**FIGURE 10.3** Corporate-level cooperative strategies

- Diversifying alliances
- Synergistic alliances
- Franchising

It should be noted that highly diverse networks of alliances can lead to poorer performance by partner firms.[79] However, cooperative ventures are also used to reduce diversification in firms that have overdiversified.[80] Japanese chipmakers Fujitsu, Mitsubishi Electric, Hitachi, NEC and Toshiba have been using joint ventures to consolidate and then spin off diversified businesses that were performing poorly. For example, Fujitsu, realising that memory chips were becoming a financial burden, dumped its flash memory business into a joint venture company controlled by Advanced Micro Devices. This alliance helped Fujitsu refocus on its core businesses.[81]

## Synergistic strategic alliance

A synergistic strategic alliance is a corporate-level cooperative strategy in which firms share some of their resources and capabilities to create economies of scope. Similar to the business-level horizontal complementary strategic alliance, synergistic strategic alliances create synergy across multiple functions or multiple businesses between partner firms. The most recent development for Disney's media segment is a partnership with Google's YouTube that will allow it to advertise its movies and products by showing short clips and selling advertisements.[82] This is an example of a synergistic diversification alliance.

In recent years, there has been much more competitive interaction between hardware and software firms. Cisco, traditionally a network telecommunications equipment manufacturer, is moving into computers – in particular, servers. After HP moved into selling network equipment, Cisco decided to move more fully into developing its server business. Although it is trying not to upset its former partners, HP and IBM, it needs to develop a service segment to drive its computer business. Both IBM and HP have large service businesses. As such, Cisco developed partnership agreements with Accenture Ltd and India-based Tata Consulting Services Ltd to help market Cisco's products to businesses around the world. These were synergistic alliances by Cisco to foster this diversification move.[83]

## Franchising

Franchising is a corporate-level cooperative strategy in which a firm (the franchisor) uses a franchise as a contractual relationship to describe and control the sharing of its resources and capabilities with partners (the franchisees).[84] A *franchise* is a "Contractual agreement between two legally independent companies whereby the franchisor grants the right to the franchisee to sell the franchisor's product or do business under its trademarks in a given location for a specified period of time."[85] Success is often determined in these strategic alliances by how well the franchisor can replicate its success across multiple partners in a cost-effective way.[86] Interestingly, research suggests that too much innovation results in difficulties for replicating this success.[87]

Franchising is a popular strategy. The European Franchise Federation report that there are 6500 distinct franchised brands which operate across 20 different European countries. Also, the International Franchise Association has observed that franchised brands accounted for 56.3 per cent of quick service restaurants, 18.2 per cent of lodging establishments, 14.2 per cent of retail food businesses and 13.1 per cent of table/full service restaurants. In sum, European franchises therefore employ nearly 10 million people with attributable revenue amounting to nearly €500 billion.[88] Franchising is a particularly attractive strategy to use in fragmented industries, such as retailing, hotels and motels, and commercial printing. In fragmented industries, a large number of small and medium-sized firms compete as rivals; however, no firm or small set of firms has a dominant share, making it possible for a company to gain

---

**Synergistic strategic alliance**

A synergistic strategic alliance is a corporate-level cooperative strategy in which firms share some of their resources and capabilities to create economies of scope.

**Franchising**

Franchising is a corporate-level cooperative strategy in which a firm (the franchisor) uses a franchise as a contractual relationship to describe and control the sharing of its resources and capabilities with partners (the franchisees).

a large market share by consolidating independent companies through contractual relationships.

In the most successful franchising strategy, the partners (the franchisor and the franchisees) work closely together.[89] A primary responsibility of the franchisor is to develop programmes to transfer to the franchisees the knowledge and skills that are needed to successfully compete at the local level.[90] In return, franchisees should provide feedback to the franchisor regarding how their units could become more effective and efficient.[91] Working cooperatively, the franchisor and its franchisees find ways to strengthen the core company's brand name, which is often the most important competitive advantage for franchisees operating in their local markets.[92]

## Assessment of corporate-level cooperative strategies

Costs are incurred with each type of cooperative strategy.[93] Compared with those at the business-level, corporate-level cooperative strategies commonly are broader in scope and more complex, making them relatively more costly. Those forming and using cooperative strategies, especially corporate-level ones, should be aware of alliance costs and carefully monitor them.

In spite of these costs, firms can create competitive advantages and value when they effectively form and use corporate-level cooperative strategies.[94] When successful alliance experiences are internalized it is more likely that the strategy will attain the desired advantages. In other words, those involved with forming and using corporate-level cooperative strategies can also use them to develop useful knowledge about how to succeed in the future. To gain maximum value from this knowledge, firms should organize it and verify that it is always properly distributed to those involved with forming and using alliances.[95]

We explained in Chapter 7 that firms answer two questions to form a corporate-level strategy: in which businesses will the diversified firm compete and how will those businesses be managed? These questions are also answered as firms form corporate-level cooperative strategies. Thus, firms able to develop corporate-level cooperative strategies and manage them in ways that are valuable, rare, imperfectly imitable and non-substitutable (see Chapter 3) develop a competitive advantage that is in addition to advantages gained through the activities of individual cooperative strategies. (Later in the chapter, we further describe alliance management as another potential competitive advantage.)

# International cooperative strategy

A cross-border strategic alliance is an international cooperative strategy in which firms with headquarters in different nations decide to combine some of their resources and capabilities to create a competitive advantage. Taking place in virtually all industries, the number of cross-border alliances continues to increase.[96] These alliances are sometimes formed instead of mergers and acquisitions (which can be riskier).[97] Even though cross-border alliances can themselves be complex and hard to manage,[98] they have the potential to help firms use their resources and capabilities to create value in locations outside their home market.

IMG Worldwide Inc. is one of the largest producers and distributors of sports entertainment in the world. It pursues its strategy through international joint ventures with other broadcasting firms. The events that it currently broadcasts for instance are the Wimbledon Tennis Tournament in the UK and the Australian Open Tennis Tournament. In an effort to expand into emerging economies, IMG recently

**Cross-border strategic alliance**

A cross-border strategic alliance is an international cooperative strategy in which firms with headquarters in different nations decide to combine some of their resources and capabilities to create a competitive advantage.

signed a twenty-year sporting event partnership with China Central Television, the main Chinese broadcasting organization. A national broadcast of this size could have an audience of 740 million viewers daily. The first two events this venture broadcast were the China Open Tennis Tournament in Beijing and the Chengdu Open Tennis Tournament in 2009. The Top 50 women players in the world were expected to play in the China Open tournament. Through this strategic alliance, IMG substantially broadened its international reach.[99]

Several reasons explain the increasing use of cross-border strategic alliances, including the fact that in general, multinational corporations outperform domestic-only firms.[100] What takes place with a cross-border alliance is that a firm leverages core competencies that are the foundation of its domestic success in international markets.[101] Nike provides an example as it leverages its core competence with celebrity marketing to expand globally with its diverse line of athletic goods and apparel. With a €1.57 billion celebrity endorsement budget, Nike has formed relationships with athletes who have global appeal. Tiger Woods and Michael Phelps are recent endorsers, while seven-time Tour de France winner Lance Armstrong, Michael Jordan and Magic Johnson are historic examples of these types of individuals. In addition, Nike has had endorsement relationships with star athletes and organizations outside the United States such as Brazilian soccer star Ronaldo Nazario and Manchester United, the world's most popular football team.[102] Coupling these alliances with Nike's powerful global brand name helps the firm apply its marketing competencies in markets worldwide. But the downturn in the economy is causing problems such that even these relationships are not protecting sales declines.[103]

Limited domestic growth opportunities and foreign government economic policies are additional reasons firms use cross-border alliances. As discussed in Chapter 7, local ownership is an important national policy objective in some nations. In India and China, for example, governmental policies reflect a strong preference to license local companies. Thus, in some countries, the full range of entry mode choices that we described in Chapter 9 may not be available to firms seeking to diversify internationally. Indeed, investment by foreign firms in these instances may be allowed only through a partnership with a local firm, such as in a cross-border alliance. Especially important, strategic alliances with local partners can help firms overcome certain liabilities of moving into a foreign country, such as lack of knowledge of the local culture or institutional norms.[104] A cross-border strategic alliance can also be helpful to foreign partners from an operational perspective, because the local partner has significantly more information about factors contributing to competitive success such as local markets, sources of capital, legal procedures and politics.[105] Interestingly, recent research suggests that firms with foreign operations have longer survival rates than domestic-only firms, although this is reduced if there are competition problems between foreign subsidiaries.[106]

In general, cross-border alliances are more complex and risky than domestic strategic alliances, especially in emerging economies.[107] However, the fact that firms competing internationally tend to outperform domestic-only competitors suggests the importance of learning how to diversify into international markets. Compared with mergers and acquisitions, cross-border alliances may be a better way to learn this process, especially in the early stages of the firms' geographic diversification efforts. Starbucks is a case in point.

When Starbucks sought overseas expansion, it wanted to do so quickly as a means of supporting its strong orientation to continuous growth. Thus, it agreed to a complex series of joint ventures in many countries in the interest of speed. While the company receives a percentage of the revenues and profits as well as licensing fees for supplying its coffee, controlling costs abroad is more difficult than in its home US market. Starbucks is learning from the results achieved from the collaborative relationships it initially established. In light of what it has learned, the firm continues to collaborate with others in different countries including China. At Starbuck's ten-year anniversary mark in China, one analyst noted that "China, conventionally a coffee exporter, may become a net importer in 2009 with demand outpacing supply, as Starbucks Coffee Co. and other coffee chains mushroom around the country."[108] Among other actions, Starbucks is seeking to take larger equity positions in some of the joint ventures with which it is now involved in different countries (such as China).

# Network cooperative strategy

In addition to forming their own alliances with individual companies, a growing number of firms are joining forces in multiple networks.[109] A network cooperative strategy is a cooperative strategy wherein several firms agree to form multiple partnerships to achieve shared objectives. As noted above Cisco has multiple cooperative arrangements with IBM and Hewlett Packard, but also with service providers, Accenture Ltd and Tata Consulting Services Ltd. Demonstrating the complexity of network cooperative strategies is the fact that Cisco has a set of unique collaborations with both IBM and Hewlett-Packard, but is also competing with them as they move into servers. The fact is that the number of network cooperative strategies being formed today continues to increase as firms seek to find the best ways to create value by offering multiple goods and services in multiple geographic (domestic and international) locations.

A network cooperative strategy is particularly effective when it is formed by geographically clustered firms,[110] as in California's Silicon Valley (where "the culture of Silicon Valley encourages collaborative webs"[111]) and Singapore's Biopolis (in the bio-medical sciences) and the now fusionopolist (collaborations in "physical sciences and engineering to tackle global science and technology challenges").[112] Effective social relationships and interactions among partners while sharing their resources and capabilities make it more likely that a network cooperative strategy will be successful,[113] as does having a productive *strategic centre firm* (we discuss strategic centre firms in detail in Chapter 13). Firms involved in networks gain information and knowledge from multiple sources. They can use these heterogeneous knowledge sets to produce more and better innovation. As a result, firms involved in networks of alliances tend to be more innovative.[114] However, there are disadvantages to participating in networks as a firm can be locked in to its partnerships, precluding the development of alliances with others. In certain types of networks, such as Japanese *keiretsus*, firms in the network are expected to help other firms in the network whenever they need aid. Such expectations can become a burden and reduce the focal firm's performance over time.[115]

## Alliance network types

An important advantage of a network cooperative strategy is that firms gain access to their partners' other partners. Having access to multiple collaborations increases the likelihood that additional competitive advantages will be formed as the set of shared resources and capabilities expands.[116] In turn, being able to develop new capabilities further stimulates product innovations that are critical to strategic competitiveness in the global economy.[117]

The set of strategic alliance partnerships resulting from the use of a network cooperative strategy is commonly called an *alliance network*. The alliance networks that companies develop vary by industry conditions. A stable alliance network is formed in mature industries where demand is relatively constant and predictable. Through a

**Network cooperative strategy**

A network cooperative strategy is a cooperative strategy wherein several firms agree to form multiple partnerships to achieve shared objectives.

*Good when formed by Geographics e.g Sillicon Valley*

**Stable alliance network**

A stable alliance network is formed in mature industries where demand is relatively constant and predictable.

stable alliance network, firms try to extend their competitive advantages to other settings while continuing to profit from operations in their core, relatively mature industry. Thus, stable networks are built primarily to exploit the economies (scale and/or scope) that exist between the partners such as in the airline industry.[118] **Dynamic alliance networks** Dynamic alliance networks are used in industries characterized by frequent product innovations and short product life cycles.[119] For instance, the pace of innovation in the information technology (IT) industry (as well as other industries that are characterized by fast-cycle markets) is too fast for any one company to be successful across time if it only competes independently. Another example is the movie industry which has a lot of collaborative ventures and networked firms to produce and distribute movies.[120] In dynamic alliance networks, partners typically explore new ideas and possibilities with the potential to lead to product innovations, entries to new markets and the development of new markets.[121] Often, large firms in such industries as software and pharmaceuticals create networks of relationships with smaller entrepreneurial start-up firms in their search for innovation-based outcomes.[122] An important outcome for small firms successfully partnering with larger firms in an alliance network is the credibility they build by being associated with their larger collaborators.[123]

> **Dynamic alliance networks**
>
> Dynamic alliance networks are used in industries characterized by frequent product innovations and short product life cycles.

## Competitive risks with cooperative strategies

Stated simply, many cooperative strategies fail. In fact, evidence shows that two-thirds of cooperative strategies have serious problems in their first two years and that as many as 50 per cent of them fail. This failure rate suggests that even when the partnership has potential complementarities and synergies, alliance success is elusive.[124] Although failure is undesirable, it can be a valuable learning experience, meaning that firms should carefully study a cooperative strategy's failure to gain insights with respect to how to form and manage future cooperative arrangements.[125] We show prominent cooperative strategy risks in Figure 10.4.

One cooperative strategy risk is that a partner may act opportunistically. Opportunistic behaviours surface either when formal contracts fail to prevent them or when an alliance is based on a false perception of partner trustworthiness. Not infrequently, the opportunistic firm wants to acquire as much of its partner's tacit knowledge as it can.[126] Full awareness of what a partner wants in a cooperative strategy reduces the likelihood that a firm will suffer from another's opportunistic actions.[127] The strategic focus on TNK-BP a 50/50 joint venture between three Russian oil tycoons and British Petroleum demonstrate potential opportunistic actions by parties involved and some of the potential risks of joint ventures, especially in an emerging economy like Russia.

*Opportunistic eg.*
*BP + TNK*

**FIGURE 10.4**  Managing competitive risks in cooperative strategies

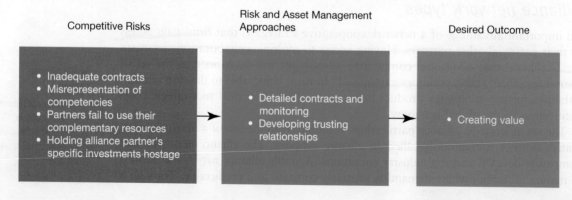

Competitive Risks
- Inadequate contracts
- Misrepresentation of competencies
- Partners fail to use their complementary resources
- Holding alliance partner's specific investments hostage

Risk and Asset Management Approaches
- Detailed contracts and monitoring
- Developing trusting relationships

Desired Outcome
- Creating value

Some cooperative strategies fail when it is discovered that a firm has misrepresented the competencies it can bring to the partnership. The risk of competence misrepresentation is more common when the partner's contribution is grounded in some of its intangible assets. Superior knowledge of local conditions is an example of an intangible asset that partners often fail to deliver. Asking the partner to provide evidence that it does possess the resources and capabilities (even when they are largely intangible) it aims to share in the cooperative strategy may be an effective way to deal with this risk.[128]

Another risk is a firm failing to make available to its partners the resources and capabilities (such as the most sophisticated technologies) that it committed to the cooperative strategy. For example, in the strategic focus, TNK-BP did not meet agreed-upon targets and this put them in a situation of weakness relative to both the powerful partners and the Russian government. This risk surfaces most commonly when firms form an international cooperative strategy, especially in emerging economies.[129] In these instances, different cultures and languages can cause misinterpretations of contractual terms or trust-based expectations.

A final risk is that one firm may make investments that are specific to the alliance while its partner does not. For example, the firm might commit resources and capabilities to develop manufacturing equipment that can be used only to produce items coming from the alliance. If the partner is not also making alliance-specific investments, the firm is at a relative disadvantage in terms of returns earned from the alliance, compared with investments made to earn the returns. This is certainly an issue in the TNK-BP alliance where BP is continuing to make investments, but losing power regarding the management of those investments.

## Managing cooperative strategies

Although cooperative strategies are an important means of firm growth and enhanced performance, managing these strategies is challenging. Learning how to effectively manage cooperative strategies is important however, in that being able to do so can be a source of competitive advantage.[130] Due to the fact that the ability to effectively manage cooperative strategies is unevenly distributed across organizations in general, assigning managerial responsibility for a firm's cooperative strategies to a high-level executive or to a team improves the likelihood that the strategies will be well managed.

Those responsible for managing the firm's set of cooperative strategies should take the actions necessary to coordinate activities, categorize knowledge learned from previous experiences and make certain that what the firm knows about how to effectively form and use cooperative strategies is in the hands of the right people at the right time. Also, firms must learn how to manage both the tangible assets and the intangible assets (such as knowledge) that are involved with a cooperative arrangement. Too often, partners concentrate on managing tangible assets at the expense of taking action to also manage a cooperative relationship's intangible assets.[131]

Two primary approaches are used to manage cooperative strategies – cost minimization and opportunity maximization[132] (see Figure 10.4). In the *cost minimization* management approach, the firm develops formal contracts with its partners. These contracts specify how the cooperative strategy is to be monitored and how partner behaviour is to be controlled. The TNK-BP joint venture discussed previously is managed through contractual agreements. The goal of the cost minimization approach is to minimize the cooperative strategy's cost and to prevent opportunistic behaviour by a partner. The focus of the second managerial approach – *opportunity maximization* – is on maximizing a partnership's value-creation opportunities. In this case, partners are prepared to take advantage of unexpected opportunities to learn from each other and

© Georgiy Shpade/iStock

# Troubles in the Russian oil joint venture, TNK-BP

The situation in 2009 with the joint venture that British Petroleum (BP) formed in 2003 with three Russian oil tycoons, Mikhail Fridman, Viktor Vekselberg and Leonard Blavatnik, seems to demonstrate opportunistic behaviour as well as political risks. These three oil oligarchs own 50 per cent of the venture labelled TNK-BP, and BP owns the remaining 50 per cent. The venture gave a Western company unprecedented access to vital Russian oil and gas resources. However, the Kremlin is becoming increasingly involved in the nation's energy production activities and it has claimed that TNK-BP failed to fulfil all terms of its licence regarding a particular oil field (the Kovykta field). This claim threatens the joint venture's viability. Part of the problem is that members of the Kremlin feel uncomfortable with the Russian tycoons having control of the state-owned assets and are even more uncomfortable with the fact that BP officials head the joint venture. It has been speculated that Gazprom, the state run gas giant, may join the venture as a partner to improve the production deficit in the main oil field. If Gazprom does indeed become part owner, it is questionable what it will compensate BP for its ownership position. Over the years, BP has tried to develop a good relationship with the Russian government and demonstrate its commitment by investing billions of dollars. BP has also invested in other ventures to drill in other oil fields such as with Rosneft as minority stakeholder.

This situation culminated with a battle over who would run TNK-BP, the third largest oil operation in Russia with 17 per cent of Russia's reserves. The Russian shareholders charged that BP was running TNK-BP as a BP subsidiary and thereby depressing its values. BP officials considered the conflict an attempt at "corporate raiding", accusing the rich Russian partners of hardball tactics. For example, Robert Dudley the nominated chief executive of TNK-BP was unable to get a visa and subsequently was banned by Russian courts from serving as CEO. BP officials suspected that this "paper-work problem" was orchestrated by Russian shareholders.

Mr. Fridman, one of the Russian owners, was appointed as the interim CEO, and all officials agreed to hire a new CEO who must be fluent in Russian and have business experience in Russia. New board members were appointed to help keep the peace on the board, including former German Chancellor Gerhard Schroder. Not only did Mr Dudley leave from the BP side, but the chief financial officer also felt pressure and resigned and left Russia. Thus, the bottom line appears to be that BP is conceding overall control to the Russians, but it is at least maintaining its 50 per cent ownership position. Although BP has realized a positive return on its investment, it faces continued risk because of the organization's power structure and it will probably be under the control of the Russian tycoons who are also subject to influence by government policy. As one can see from this example, firms that are pursuing international joint ventures need to be concerned about the opportunistic behaviour of their partners as well as the political risks involved. Interestingly, other firms have had less control than BP in Russian joint ventures and in fact have lost their ownership positions through pressure by the Russian partners. In this light BP has done better than others, but risks obviously remain. Coincidentally, on October 1, 2010, Robert Dudley became CEO of BP plc succeeding Tony Hayward in this role. The TNK-BP Executive Chairman is said to welcome Robert Dudley and has claimed that, "we fully support the nomination of Mr. Dudley".

**Sources:** Associated Press (2009) "TNK-BP names tycoon Mikhail Fridman interim CEO", *Forbes*, http://www.forbes.com, May 27; Belton, C. and Krooks, E. (2009)

"Schroder a vital link with Russian TNK-BP", *Financial Times*, January 16, 19; Gimbel, B. (2009) "Russia's king of crude", *Fortune*, February 2, 88; Gorst, I. (2009) "BP moves to settle TNK clash", *Financial Times*, May 26, 15; Herron, J. (2009) "Corporate news: Schroder to join TNK-BP board"; "Venture makes room for ex-German leader, two other independent directors", *Wall Street Journal*, January 16, B2; Reed, S. and Elder, M. (2008) "BP's dream deal hits a rough patch", *BusinessWeek*, August 11, 50; White, G. L. and Chazan, G. (2008) "International business: BP retains its stake in TNK-BP"; 2008 "BP pays price for staying in Russia: Company must take account of increased political risk", *Financial Times*, September 5, 8; 2010, "BP CEO Tony Hayward to step down and be succeeded by Robert Dudley" www.bp.com, 12 October; 2010, J. Gronholt-Pedersen, "Update: TNK-BP Shareholder Welcomes Dudley as Chief Despite Spat", *Wall Street Journal*, www.online.wsj.com, July 27.

### Questions

**1** Given the recent challenges that BP have faced in the Gulf of Mexico oil-spill, how might this affect future alliances for BP?

**2** Opportunistic behaviour is common to many alliances. How can it best be managed by all parties in the case of TNK-BP?

to explore additional marketplace possibilities. Less formal contracts, with fewer constraints on partners' behaviours, make it possible for partners to explore how their resources and capabilities can be shared in multiple value-creating ways.

Firms can successfully use both approaches to manage cooperative strategies. However, the costs to monitor the cooperative strategy are greater with cost minimization, in that writing detailed contracts and using extensive monitoring mechanisms is expensive, even though the approach is intended to reduce alliance costs. Although monitoring systems may prevent partners from acting in their own best interests, they also often preclude positive responses to new opportunities that surface to use the alliance's competitive advantages. Thus, formal contracts and extensive monitoring systems tend to stifle partners' efforts to gain maximum value from their participation in a cooperative strategy and require significant resources to put into place and use.[133]

The relative lack of detail and formality that is a part of the contract developed by firms using the second management approach of opportunity maximization means that firms need to trust each other to act in the partnership's best interests. A psychological state, trust in the context of cooperative arrangements is "the expectation held by one firm that another will not exploit its vulnerabilities when faced with the opportunity to do so".[134] When partners trust each other, there is less need to write detailed formal contracts to specify each firm's alliance behaviours,[135] and the cooperative relationship tends to be more stable. On the other hand, research shows that some level of formalization in terms formal documents and clear rules and procedures may also result in a virtuous cycle in which trust is further enhanced between partners over time.[136] On a relative basis, trust tends to be more difficult to establish in international cooperative strategies compared with domestic ones. Differences in trade policies, cultures, laws and politics that are part of cross-border alliances account for the increased difficulty. When trust exists, partners' monitoring costs are reduced and opportunities to create value are maximized. Essentially, in these cases, the firms have built social capital.[137] According to company officials, the alliance between Renault and Nissan is built on "mutual trust between the two partners ... together with operating and confidentiality rules".[138]

Research showing that trust between partners increases the likelihood of alliance success seems to highlight the benefits of the opportunity maximization approach to managing cooperative strategies. Trust may also be the most efficient way to influence and control alliance partners' behaviours. Research indicates that trust can be a capability that is valuable, rare, imperfectly imitable and often non-substitutable,[139] Thus, firms known to be trustworthy can have a competitive advantage in terms of how they develop and use cooperative strategies.[140] One reason is that it is impossible to specify all operational details of a cooperative strategy in a formal contract. Confidence that its partner can be trusted reduces the firm's concern about the inability to contractually control all alliance details.

**KEY DEBATE**

© sebastian-julian

# Using metrics to manage strategic alliances

Business managers and management consultants are all too familiar with the search for appropriate tools and techniques to employ in diagnosing strategic, operational and tactical realities in their firms. Strategic alliances have become a key focal area for such tools and techniques in recent years for a number of reasons, but the most important being the fact that only one in two alliances succeed. Considering the incidence of strategic alliances and the volume of business that goes through this organizational form annually, it is remarkable that managers still struggle to find suitable tools and techniques to assess, manage, diagnose and detect appropriate interventions for improving the chances of alliance success.

There are a number of reasons for the poor chances of success of strategic alliances but frequently many alliances perform poorly because of the way they are established and the manner in which they are assessed. All too often, strategic alliances are set up as a strategic initiative but managed as a set of operational problems. That is, there is a displacement of responsibility within the respective firms that compose the alliance and often mid-level managers manage the day-to-day activities of the alliance with little oversight at the strategic level. Invariably, alliance administration is drawn up with high level scrutiny and a strategic focus on key deliverables. In order to manage the alliance, the focus then tends to be on the specific service level agreements that determine the responsibilities of each alliance member so as to make transparent the key responsibilities that each partner needs to deliver to.

These service level agreements offer a snapshot at one point in time of what the alliance requires to deliver upon its objectives, but as the business environment changes so too strategic alliances evolve and their demands necessarily change. Without a focus on key metrics in specific areas of the alliance and strategic buy-in from senior management, the assessment of alliance performance is reduced to a small number of

key financial metrics. These financial metrics tend not to indicate the nature of dynamics within the alliance and the behaviours and relationship that affect performance. Usually, they are the outcomes of this process and are highly aggregated financial measures. All too often in working with companies, managers have told us that senior executives are only concerned with the summary financial metrics in gauging alliance success and this means that the strategic alliance is a "black box". That is, without a more complete appreciation of the inputs and dynamics, there is a disconnect with the anticipated outputs from the strategic alliance.

By focusing on the key financial measures, this not only deflects attention away from allowing the strategic alliance to flourish but it also leads to short term decision making which will cause the alliance to suffer prematurely. In extending the Balanced Scorecard, Kaplan, Norton and Rugelsjoen have adapted their framework to focus on managing strategic alliances. This is a framework that examines alliances from end-to-end: from employees and organization who execute business processes which deliver customer value that, in turn, drives stakeholder outcomes. By creating a causal map which can isolate key ingredients of the flows in which alliances develop, Kaplan, Norton and Rugelsjoen have been able to enable managers to appreciate the individual components and manage these areas so as to open up the "black box" of alliance success. In their 2010 *Harvard Business Review* article, they illustrate how Solvay Pharmaceuticals represent their alliance scorecard in executing their alliance strategy with their partners. Further, they explore how the alliance scorecard works with Quintiles, a biopharmaceutical services firm, which uses this technique to identify areas to maximize alliance value.

Developing a management diagnostic tool that enables improved insights into strategic alliance management is without doubt beneficial to managers, consultants and ultimately stakeholders. Nonetheless, alliance success will largely depend upon the fit between partners, the resource combinations that bring the alliance together and the value that each partner can demonstrate in providing complementarities to one another. Otherwise, diagnostic tools such as the alliance balance scorecard merely serve as a damage report when a firm has hit an iceberg rather than a tool that is used to manage a coherent alliance strategy in-life.

**Sources:** Kaplan, R. S., Norton, D. P. and Rugelsjoen, B. (2010) "Managing alliances with the balanced scorecard", *Harvard Business Review*, 88 (January): 114–120; Kaplan, R. S. and Norton, D. P. (2008) "Mastering the management system", *Harvard Business Review*, 86 (January): 62–77; Kaplan, R. S. and Norton, D. P. (2000) "Having trouble with your strategy? Then map it", *Harvard Business Review*, 78 (Sept–Oct): 167–176; Draulans J. A. J., De Man, A. P. and Volberda, H. W. 2003, "Building alliance capability: Management techniques for superior alliance performance", *Long Range Planning*, 36(2): 151–166.

## Questions

**1** Read further on the principles of the balance scorecard and to improve your understanding of how this technique can be applied in a strategic alliance context.

**2** If strategic alliances are so popular, why is it that so many of them are dissolved prematurely? Illustrate your response with examples.

© Kevin Foy/Alamy

# CLOSING CASE

# BT and HP – pursuing a successful strategic alliance

In order to successfully compete and grow in respect of market share and increased revenue and profitability, companies must have the ability to provide customers with products and/or services which will allow them to appear to offer better value than competitors in the eyes of their customers. In some markets and industries this may require adding extra aspects to the product or service being offered which competitors are not able to match easily, if at all.

In 2004 British Telecom plc (BT) and the Hewlett-Packard Company (HP) entered into a strategic alliance designed for just this purpose. Individually, these two firms work in separate but related markets. BT operates as a market leader in the UK telecommunications and network outsourcing industry, while HP provides outsourced information technology (IT) hardware and support services globally. The purpose of the alliance when it was formed in 2004 was to bring together the resources and capabilities of each company as a combined offering to customers in which BT's communications packages and HP's IT equipment and expertise could be integrated to offer a whole which would give more value than the two parts would when provided by the companies separately.

The alliance did not dictate that all BT customers must use the HP IT systems, or vice versa, but gave customers the opportunity to buy the offerings together as an integrated package; "Under a single service contract, our joint customers are able to benefit from an integrated approach that combines world-class IT and network capabilities from two market leaders. No one else offers this level of service integration." This is a quote given by Mark Hurd, the former CEO of HP, and one which demonstrates the unique competitive advantage both HP and BT have been able to generate in the market. Customers are now able to see the additional benefits of having a fully integrated communications network and IT package against buying from separate suppliers of each and trying to make these two systems work together when they were not originally designed to do so.

The alliance has proven very successful for both BT and HP, winning the 2007 Alliance Excellence Award from the Association of Strategic Alliance

Professionals. Following this award BT agreed to sell its UK datacentres to HP for approximately €1.65 billion in 2008, further strengthening the ties between the two companies.

This is an example of an alliance between two companies offering complementary products and who are not likely to ever directly compete. This has meant that decisions made for the alliance are all made in order to help the combined entity perform, as opposed to benefiting one of the involved parties or the other. In addition, the fact that BT and HP have both continued to operate autonomously in addition to working together has ensured that they are still able to operate as before for the most part in their activities, with their own best interests in mind. However, both companies have discovered increased opportunities through tapping into one another's resources and

capabilities, including innovations which allow them to develop unique selling points separately as well as a larger customer base than they had previously been able to access through cross selling.

**Sources:** Ashton, J. (2008) "BT in £1.5bn talks with Hewlett-Packard", *The Sunday Times*, May 11; Fay, J. (2008) "HP tipped to take over BT's datacentres in £1.5bn deal", *The Register*, http://www.theregister.co.uk, May 12; BT's Strategic Alliances: HP, 2010, http://www.btplc.com/thegroup/strategicpartnerships, July 5; The BT HP Alliance, 2010, http://www.btplc.com/thegroup/strategicpartnerships/HP, July 5.

*Questions*

**1** Why does this alliance work so well?

**2** To what extent is this alliance sustainable? What challenges might undermine this alliance?

## SUMMARY

- A cooperative strategy is one where firms work together to achieve a shared objective. Strategic alliances, where firms combine some of their resources and capabilities to create a competitive advantage, are the primary form of cooperative strategies. Joint ventures (where firms create and own equal shares of a new venture that is intended to develop competitive advantages), equity strategic alliances (where firms own different shares of a newly created venture) and nonequity strategic alliances (where firms cooperate through a contractual relationship) are the three basic types of strategic alliances. Outsourcing, discussed in Chapter 3, commonly occurs as firms form nonequity strategic alliances.

- Collusive strategies are the second type of cooperative strategies (strategic alliances being the other). In many economies, explicit collusive strategies are illegal unless sanctioned by government policies. Increasing globalization has led to fewer government-sanctioned situations of explicit collusion. Tacit collusion, also called mutual forbearance, is a cooperative strategy through which firms tacitly cooperate to reduce industry output below the potential competitive output level, thereby raising prices above the competitive level.

- The reasons firms use cooperative strategies vary by slow-cycle, fast-cycle and standard-cycle market conditions. To enter restricted markets (slow-cycle), to move quickly from one competitive advantage to another (fast-cycle) and to gain market power (standard-cycle) are among the reasons why firms choose to use cooperative strategies.

- Four business-level cooperative strategies are used to help the firm improve its performance in individual product markets. (1) Through vertical and horizontal complementary alliances, companies combine their resources and capabilities to create value in different parts (vertical) or the same parts (horizontal) of the value chain. (2) Competition-responding strategies are formed to respond to competitors' actions, especially strategic ones. (3) Competition-reducing strategies are used to avoid excessive competition while the firm marshals its resources and capabilities to improve its competitiveness. (4) Uncertainty-reducing strategies are used to hedge against the risks created by the conditions of uncertain competitive environments (such as new product markets). Complementary alliances have the highest probability of yielding a sustainable competitive advantage; competition-reducing alliances have the lowest probability.

- Firms use corporate-level cooperative strategies to engage in product and/or geographic diversification. Through diversifying strategic alliances, firms agree to share some of their resources and capabilities to enter new markets or produce new products. Synergistic alliances are ones where firms share resources and capabilities to develop economies of scope. This alliance is similar to the business-level horizontal complementary alliance where firms try to develop operational synergy, except that synergistic alliances are used to develop synergy at the corporate level. Franchising is a corporate-level cooperative strategy where the franchisor uses a franchise as a contractual relationship to specify how resources and capabilities will be shared with franchisees.

■ As an international cooperative strategy, a cross-border alliance is used for several reasons, including the performance superiority of firms competing in markets outside their domestic market and governmental restrictions on growth through mergers and acquisitions. Commonly, cross-border alliances are riskier than their domestic counterparts, particularly when partners aren't fully aware of each other's purpose for participating in the partnership.

■ In a network cooperative strategy, several firms agree to form multiple partnerships to achieve shared objectives. A primary benefit of a network cooperative strategy is the firm's opportunity to gain access to its partner's other partnerships. When this happens, the probability greatly increases that partners will find unique ways to share their resources and capabilities to form competitive advantages. Network cooperative strategies are used to form either a stable alliance network or a dynamic alliance network. Used in mature industries, partners use stable networks to extend competitive advantages into new areas. In rapidly changing environments where frequent product innovations occur, dynamic networks are primarily used as a tool of innovation.

■ Cooperative strategies are not risk free. If a contract is not developed appropriately, or if a partner misrepresents its competencies or fails to make them available, failure is likely. Furthermore, a firm may be held hostage through asset-specific investments made in conjunction with a partner, which may be exploited.

■ Trust is an increasingly important aspect of successful cooperative strategies. Firms recognize the value of partnering with companies known for their trustworthiness. When trust exists, a cooperative strategy is managed to maximize the pursuit of opportunities between partners. Without trust, formal contracts and extensive monitoring systems are used to manage cooperative strategies. In this case, the interest is to minimize costs rather than to maximize opportunities by participating in a cooperative strategy.

## REVIEW QUESTIONS

1 What is the definition of cooperative strategy and why is this strategy important to firms competing in the twenty-first century competitive landscape?

2 What is a strategic alliance? What are the three types of strategic alliances firms use to develop a competitive advantage?

3 What are the four business-level cooperative strategies and what are the differences between them?

4 What are the three corporate-level cooperative strategies? How do firms use each one to create a competitive advantage?

5 Why do firms use cross-border strategic alliances?

6 What risks are firms likely to experience as they use cooperative strategies?

7 What are the differences between the cost-minimization approach and the opportunity-maximization approach to managing cooperative strategies?

## DISCUSSION QUESTIONS

1 What are the key attributes that firms should seek in identifying an alliance partner?

2 When do firms potentially have more to lose than to gain from entering into a strategic alliance?

3 Although cooperative arrangements between firms vary in type, there is a commonly held management myth that successful cooperative strategies need to

sustain themselves over time. How would you argue against this notion?

4   Do you consider that vertical alliances are more successful than horizontal alliances? Justify your arguments.

5   Identify a case example of where multiple firms enter into a single alliance. How does this form of alliance management differ compared with a dyadic alliance amend?

## FURTHER READING

Smart companies know that besides acquisitions also alliances can be a good way to integrate resources but managing alliances requires skills and tools (e.g. R. S. Kaplan, D. P. Norton and B. Rugelsjoen (2010) "Managing alliances with the balanced scorecard", *Harvard Business Review*, 88(January): 114–120; H. Ness (2009) "Governance, negotiations and alliance dynamics: Explaining the evolution of relational practice", *Journal of Management Studies*, 46(3): 451–480; J. A. J. Draulans, A. P. De Man and H.W. Volberda (2003) "Building alliance capability: Management techniques for superior alliance performance",

*Long Range Planning*, 36(2): 151–166). Large firms with many alliances in different stages of the alliance life cycle need to develop capabilities to select the right partners, to map and manage the portfolio so to realize the promise of cooperative strategy (e.g. K. H. Heimeriks, E. Klijn and J. J. Reuer (2009) "Building capabilities for alliance portfolios", *Long Range Planning*, 42(1): 96–114; P.E. Bierly, III and S. Gallagher (2007) "Explaining alliance partner selection: Fit, trust and strategic expediency", *Long Range Planning*, 40: 134–153; D. Lavie (2009) "Capturing value from alliance portfolios" *Organizational Dynamics*, 38(1): 26–36).

## EXPERIENTIAL EXERCISES

### Exercise 1: What is it: TV, Internet, both?

Hulu (http://www.hulu.com) is a website and a cooperative alliance that offers commercial supported content of TV (video on demand) shows through the Internet. The name is derived from a Chinese word which translated means "holder of precious things". The alliance has many different partners related in interesting ways. The alliance additionally includes firms and partners from very different market types.

Working in groups, answer the following questions:

1   Describe the alliance partners. Characterize the market type for each (slow-cycle, fast-cycle, standard-cycle).

2   Characterize the type of strategic alliance Hulu has become.

3   In what type of market are they competing?

4   Why did this alliance form, list some competitive pressures that made this alliance a necessity for its partners?

5   What does the future hold for this alliance?

### Exercise 2: The Swatchmobile

Swatch is well-known for its line of stylish, affordable wristwatches. In the early 1990s, Swatch CEO Nicholas Hayek had a novel idea to diversify his company's product offerings: a stylish, affordable automobile. His vision was to create a two-seater car with minimal storage space. Fuel-efficient, he expected these cars would be highly attractive to younger European car buyers. Drawing on the company's watch designs, the Swatch car was intended to have removable body panels so that owners could change the car's look on a whim.

Swatch initially partnered with Volkswagen, but the alliance never reached production. In 1994, Swatch partnered with Mercedes-Benz. The vehicle was named SMART, which stood for "Swatch Mercedes Art."

Using Internet resources, answer the following questions:

1   What resources did each partner bring to the partnership?

2   How successful has the partnership been for each company?

3   Which company seems to be deriving the greatest benefit from the partnership and why?

## VIDEO CASE

### Cooperation vs competition

**Lynda Gratton, Professor of Management Practice, London Business School**

www.cengage.co.uk/volberda/students/video_cases

Lynda Gratton, Professor of Management Practice at the London Business School, talks about the role of co-operation coming from a profession that is really quite competitive. As you prepare for this video consider the concepts of cooperation and competition in dynamic environments. Are they complementary or contradictory?

Apply that logic to the following concepts and questions and be prepared to discuss them in class:

### Concepts

- Trust
- Networking
- Cooperation

### Questions

1 Cooperation vs competition. Which drives performance the most? Can we have one without the other?

2 Think about what you consider to be the firm of the future. What will it look like, how will employee roles shift?

3 Is cooperation necessary in today's environment or merely a nicety?

## NOTES

1. D. Lavie, 2009, "Capturing value from alliance portfolios", *Organizational Dynamics*, 38(1): 26–36; J. L. Morrow, Jr., D. G. Sirmon, M. A. Hitt and T. R. Holcomb, 2007, "Creating value in the face of declining performance: Firm strategies and organisational recovery", *Strategic Management Journal*, 28: 271–283.

2. T. W. Tong, J. J. Reuer and M. W. Peng, 2008, "International joint ventures and the value of growth options", *Academy of Management Journal*, 51: 1014–1029.

3. H. Ness, 2009, "Governance, negotiations and alliance dynamics: Explaining the evolution of relational practice", *Journal of Management Studies*, 46(3): 451–480; R. C. Fink, L. F. Edelman and K. J. Hatten, 2007, "Supplier performance improvements in relational exchanges", *Journal of Business & Industrial Marketing*, 22: 29–40.

4. M. J. Chen, 2008, "Reconceptualising the competition–cooperation relationship: A transparadox perspective", *Journal of Management Inquiry*, 17(4): 288–304; P. E. Bierly, III and S. Gallagher, 2007, "Explaining alliance partner selection: Fit, trust and strategic expediency", *Long Range Planning*, 40: 134–153; K. Singh and W. Mitchell, 2005, "Growth dynamics: The bidirectional relationship between interfirm collaboration and business sales in entrant and incumbent alliances", *Strategic Management Journal*, 26: 497–521.

5. W. M. Bulkeley, 2008, "Business technology, A service rival looms for IBM: H-P deal for EDS to pose challenges for big blue unit", *Wall Street Journal*, May 20, B6.

6. S. Hamm, 2009, "Big blue goes into analysis", *BusinessWeek*, April 27, 16.

7. R. Agarwal and C. E. Helfat, 2009, "Strategic renewal of organisations", *Organization Science*, 20(2): 281–293; P. M. Senge, B. B. Lichtenstein, K. Kaeufer, H. Bradbury and J. Carroll, 2007, "Collaborating for systemic change", *MIT Sloan Management Review*, 48(2): 44–53; R. Vassolo, J. Anand and T. B. Folta, 2004, "Non-additivity in portfolios of exploration activities: A real options-based analysis of equity alliances in biotechnology", *Strategic Management Journal*, 25: 1045–1061.

8. R. C. Marshall, L. M. Marx and M. E. Raiff, 2008, "Cartel price announcement: The vitamins industry", *International Journal of Industrial Organization*, 26(3): 762–802; T. L. Sorenson, 2007, "Credible collusion in multimarket oligopoly", *Managerial and Decision Economics*, 28: 115–128.

9. C. E. Ybarra and T. A. Turk, 2009, "The evolution of trust in information technology alliances", *Journal of High Technology Management Research*, 20(1): 62–74; R. D. Ireland, M. A. Hitt and D. Vaidyanath, 2002, "Alliance management as a source of competitive advantage", *Journal of Management*, 28: 413–446; J. G. Coombs and D. J. Ketchen, 1999, "Exploring interfirm cooperation and performance: Toward a reconciliation of predictions from the resource-based view and organisational economics", *Strategic Management Journal*, 20: 867–888.

10. M. A. Schilling, 2009, "Understanding the alliance data", *Strategic Management Journal*, 30(3): 233–260; J. J. Reuer and A. Arino, 2007, "Strategic alliance contracts: Dimensions and determinants of contractual complexity", *Strategic Management Journal*, 28: 313–330; M. R. Subramani and N. Venkatraman, 2003, "Safeguarding investments in asymmetric

interorganisational relationships: Theory and evidence", *Academy of Management Journal*, 46(1): 46–62.

11. S. Lahiri and B. L. Kedia, 2009, "The effects of internal resources and partnership quality on firm performance: An examination of Indian BPO providers", *Journal of International Management*, 15(2): 209–22; R. Krishnan, X. Martin and N. G. Noorderhaven, 2007, "When does trust matter to alliance performance?", *Academy of Management Journal*, 49: 894–917; P. Kale, J. H. Dyer and H. Singh, 2002, "Alliance capability, stock market response and long-term alliance success: The role of the alliance function", *Strategic Management Journal*, 23: 747–767.

12. K. H. Heimeriks and G. Duysters, 2007, "Alliance capability as a mediator between experience and alliance performance: An empirical investigation into the alliance capability development process", *Journal of Management Studies*, 44: 25–49; J. A. J. Draulans, A. P. De Man and H. W. Volberda, 2003, "Building alliance capability: Management techniques for superior alliance performance", *Long Range Planning*, 36(2): 151–166; J. J. Reuer, E. Klijn, F. A. J. Van den Bosch and H. W. Volberda, 2011, "Bringing corporate governance to international joint ventures", *Global Strategy Journal*, 1(1), Forthcoming.

13. R. E. Hoskisson, M. A. Hitt, R. D. Ireland and J. S. Harrison, 2008, *Competing for Advantage*, 2nd edn, Thomson/ Southwestern, 184.

14. B. S. Bulik, 2009, "Kodak develops as modern brand with digital shift", *Advertising Age*, April 27, 26.

15. R. Lunnan and S. A. Haugland, 2008, "Predicting and measuring alliance performance: A multi-dimensional analysis", *Strategic Management Journal*, 29(5): 545–556; R. Seppanen, K. Blomqvist and S. Sundqvist, 2007, "Measuring interorganisational trust – A critical review of the empirical research in 1990–2003", *Industrial Marketing Management*, 36: 249–265; T. K. Das and B. S. Teng, 2001, "A risk perception model of alliance structuring", *Journal of International Management*, 7: 1–29.

16. L. F. Mesquita, J. Anand and T. H. Brush, 2008, "Comparing the resource-based and relational views: Knowledge transfer and spillover in vertical alliances", *Strategic Management Journal*, 29: 913–941; F. F. Suarez and G. Lanzolla, 2007, "The role of environmental dynamics in building a first mover advantage theory", *Academy of Management Review*, 32: 377–392; M. A. Geletkanycz and S. S. Black, 2001, "Bound by the past? Experience-based effects on commitment to the strategic status quo", *Journal of Management*, 27: 3–21.

17. A. Pasztor and A. Cole, 2008, "New multirole missile is planned", *Wall Street Journal*, July 16, A13.

18. K. H. Heimeriks, E. Klijn and J. J. Reuer, 2009, "Building capabilities for alliance portfolios", *Long Range Planning*, 42 (1): 96–114; D. Gerwin, 2004, "Coordinating new product development in strategic alliances", *Academy of Management Review*, 29: 241–257; R. D. Ireland, M. A. Hitt and D. Vaidyanath, 2002, "Alliance management as a source of competitive advantage", *Journal of Management*,

28: 413–446; J. A. J. Draulans, A. P. De Man and H. W. Volberda, 2003, "Building alliance capability: Management techniques for superior alliance performance", *Long Range Planning*, 36 (2): 151–166.

19. X. Lin and C. L. Wang, 2008, "Enforcement and performance: The role of ownership, legalism and trust in international joint ventures", *Journal of World Business*, 43 (3): 340–351; Y. Luo, 2007, "Are joint venture partners more opportunistic in a more volatile environment?", *Strategic Management Journal*, 28: 39–60.

20. F. Evangelista and L. N. Hau, 2008, "Organisational context and knowledge acquisition in IJVs: An empirical study", *Journal of World Business*, 44(1): 63–73; S. L. Berman, J. Down and C. W. L. Hill, 2002, "Tacit knowledge as a source of competitive advantage in the National Basketball Association", *Academy of Management Journal*, 45: 13–31.

21. M. Becerra, R. Lunnan and L. Huemer, 2008, "Trustworthiness, risk and the transfer of tacit and explicit knowledge between alliance partners", *Journal of Management Studies*, 45(4): 691–713.

22. Y. Yamaguchi, 2009, "Leading the news: Fujitsu targets 10% share of markets for servers", *Asian Wall Street Journal*, March 31, 3.

23. A. Tiwana, 2008, "Do bridging ties complement strong ties? An empirical examination of alliance ambidexterity", *Strategic Management Journal*, 29(3): 251–272; R. E. Hoskisson and L. W. Busenitz, 2002, "Market uncertainty and learning distance in corporate entrepreneurship entry mode choice", in: M. A. Hitt, R. D. Ireland, S. M. Camp and D. L. Sexton (eds.), *Strategic Entrepreneurship: Creating a New Mindset*, Oxford, UK: Blackwell Publishers, 151–172.

24. J. Xia, J. Tan and D. Tan, 2008, "Mimetic entry and bandwagon affect: The rise and decline of international equity joint venture in China", *Strategic Management Journal*, 29(2): 195–217.

25. A. Tudor and A. Lucchetti, 2009, "MUFG's Hirano takes Morgan Stanley role", *Wall Street Journal*, March 12, C5.

26. Y. Wang and S. Nicholas, 2007, "The formation and evolution of nonequity strategic alliances in China", *Asia Pacific Journal of Management*, 24: 131–150.

27. N. Garcia-Casarejos, N. Alcalde-Fradejas and M. Espitia-Escuer, 2009, "Staying close to the core: Lessons of studying the cost of unrelated alliances in Spanish banking", *Long Range Planning*, 42(2): 194–215; S. C. Chang, S. S. Chen and J. H. Lai, 2008, "The wealth effect of Japanese-U.S. strategic alliances", *Financial Management*, 37(2): 271–301

28. C. Weigelt, 2009, "The impact of outsourcing new technologies on integrative capabilities and performance", *Strategic Management Journal*, 30(6): 595–616; S. Comino, P. Mariel and J. Sandonis, 2007, "Joint ventures versus contractual agreements: An empirical investigation", *Spanish Economic Journal*, 9: 159–175.

29. 2007, Intellectual property licensing, http://www.hp.com, August 30.

30. A. Tiwana, 2008, "Does interfirm modularity complement ignorance? A field study of software outsourcing alliances", *Strategic Management Journal*, 29(11): 1241–1252.

31. A.L. Sherwood and J. G. Covin, 2008, "Knowledge acquisition in university–industry alliances: An empirical investigation from a learning theory perspective", *Journal of Product Innovation Management*, 25: 162–179.

32. P. Beamish and N. Lupton, 2009, "Managing joint ventures", *Academy of Management Perspectives*, 23(2): 75–94.

33. A. C. Inkpen and J. Ross, 2001, "Why do some strategic alliances persist beyond their useful life?", *California Management Review*, 44(1): 132–148.

34. A. Al-Laham, T. L. Amburgey and K. Bates, 2008, "The dynamics of research alliances: Examining the effect of alliance experience and partner characteristics on the speed of alliance entry in the biotech industry", *British Journal of Management*, 19(4): 343–364; F. Rothaermel and D. L. Deeds, 2006, "Alliance type, alliance experience and alliance management capability in high-technology ventures", *Journal of Business Venturing*, 21: 429–460; L. Fuentelsaz, J. Gomez and Y. Polo, 2002, "Followers" entry timing: Evidence from the Spanish banking sector after deregulation", *Strategic Management Journal*, 23: 245–264; J. A. J. Draulans, A. P. De Man and H. W. Volberda, 2003, "Building alliance capability: Management techniques for superior alliance performance", *Long Range Planning*, 36 (2): 151–166.

35. L. F. Mesquita, J. Anand and T. H. Brush, 2008, "Comparing the resource-based and relational views: Knowledge transfer and spillover in vertical alliances", *Strategic Management Journal*, 29: 913–941; B. L. Bourdeau, J. J. Cronink, Jr and C. M. Voorhees, 2007, "Modeling service alliances: An exploratory investigation of spillover effects in service partnerships", *Strategic Management Journal*, 28: 609–622.

36. J. Murphy, 2009, "Dow Jones: Venture to launch site for newspaper in Japanese", *Wall Street Journal*, May 8, B3.

37. A. Arino, P. Olk and J. J. Reuer, 2008, *Entrepreneurial Strategic Alliances*, Upper Saddle River, New Jersey: Prentice Hall.

38. R. Fores-Fillol, 2009, "Allied alliances: Parallel or complementary?", *Applied Economic Letters*, 16(6): 585–590; S. G. Lazzarini, 2007, "The impact of membership in competing alliance constellations: Evidence on the operational performance of global airlines", *Strategic Management Journal*, 28: 345–367.

39. S. R. Holmberg and J. L. Cummings, 2009, "Building successful strategic alliance: Strategic process and analytical tools for selecting partner industries and firms", *Long Range Planning*, 42(2): 164–193; M. A. Hitt, D. Ahlstrom, M. T. Dacin, E. Levitas and L. Svobodina, 2004, "The institutional effects of strategic alliance partner selection in transition economies: China versus Russia", *Organization Science*, 15: 173–185; P. A. Saparito, C. C. Chen and H. J. Sapienza, 2004, "The role of relational trust in bank-small firm relationships", *Academy of Management Journal*, 47: 400–410; P. W. L. Vlaar, F. A. J. Van den

Bosch and H. W. Volberda, 2007, "On the evolution of trust, distrust, and formal coordination and control in interorganizational relationships: Toward an integrative framework", *Group & Organization Management*, Special Issue Trust and Control Interrelations: New Perspectives on the Trust-Control Nexus, 32(4): 407–429; P. W. L. Vlaar, F. A. J. Van den Bosch and H. W. Volberda, 2006, "Interorganizational governance trajectories: Towards a better understanding of the connections between partner selection, negotiation and contracting", Ch. 10 in: Africa Arino and Jeffrey J. Reuer (eds.), *Strategic Alliances: Governance and Contracts*, Houndmills: Palgrave, 98–110.

40. G. Padula, 2008, "Enhancing the innovation performance of firms by balancing cohesiveness and bridging ties", *Long Range Planning*, 41(4): 395–419; A. C. Inkpen and E. W. K. Tsang, 2005, "Social capital, networks and knowledge transfer", *Academy of Management Review*, 30: 146–165.

41. W. P. Wan, D. Yiu, R. E. Hoskisson and H. Kim, H. 2008, "The performance implications of relationship banking during macroeconomic expansion and contraction: A study of Japanese banks' social relationships and overseas expansion", *Journal of International Business Studies*, 39: 406–427; M. Hughes, R. D. Ireland and R. E. Morgan, 2007, "Stimulating dynamic value: Social capital and business incubation as a pathway to competitive success", *Long Range Planning*, 40(2): 154–177; T. G. Pollock, J. F. Porac and J. B. Wade, 2004, "Constructing deal networks: Brokers as network "architects" in the U.S. IPO market and other examples", *Academy of Management Review*, 29: 50–72.

42. J. R. Williams, 1998, *Renewable Advantage: Crafting Strategy Through Economic Time*, New York: The Free Press.

43. S. A. Zahra, R. D. Ireland, I. Gutierrez and M. A. Hitt, 2000, "Privatisation and entrepreneurial transformation: Emerging issues and a future research agenda", *Academy of Management Review*, 25: 509–524.

44. H. K. Steensma, J. Q. Barden, C. Dhanaraj, M. Lyles and L. Tihanyi, 2008, "The evolution and internalisation of international joint ventures in a transitioning economy", *Journal of International Business Studies*, 39(3): 491–507; I. Filatotchev, M. Wright, K. Uhlenbruck, L. Tihanyi and R. E. Hoskisson, 2003, "Governance, organisational capabilities and restructuring in transition economies", *Journal of World Business*, 38(4): 331–347.

45. H. L. Sirkin, 2008, "New world disorder", *Time*, October 27, GB1; J. Lash and F. Wellington, 2007, "Competitive advantage on a warming planet", *Harvard Business Review*, 85(3): 94–102; K. M. Eisenhardt, 2002, "Has strategy changed?", *MIT Sloan Management Review*, 43 (2): 88–91; H. W. Volberda, 1996, "Toward the flexible form: How to remain vital in hypercompetitive environments", *Organization Science*, 7(4): 359–387.

46. S. Lahiri, L. Perez-Nordtvedt and R. W. Renn, 2008, "Will the new competitive landscape cause your firm's decline? It depends on your mindset", *Business Horizons*, 51(4): 311–320.

47. B. Fenton, 2010, "BBC-led TV internet merger draws near", *Financial Times*, 26/27 June, 4.

48. S. Schechner and E. Holmes, 2009, "Disney teams up with other networks online, buying stake in Hulu site", *Wall Street Journal*, May 1, B1.

49. C. Czipura and D. R. Jolly, 2007, "Global airline alliances: Sparking profitability for a troubled industry", *Journal of Business Strategy*, 28(2): 57–64.

50. C. Conkey and P. Prada, 2009, "Corporate news: Continental wins nod to join Star Alliance", *Wall Street Journal*, April 8, B4.

51. S. G. Lazzarini, D. P. Claro and L. F. Mesquita, 2008, "Buyer-supplier and supplier-supplier alliances: Do they reinforce or undermine one another?", *Journal of Management Studies*, 45(3): 561–584; D. R. King, J. G. Covin and H. Hegarty, 2003, "Complementary resources and the exploitation of technological innovations", *Journal of Management*, 29: 589–606; J. S. Harrison, M. A. Hitt, R. E. Hoskisson and R. D. Ireland, 2001, "Resource complementarity in business combinations: Extending the logic to organisational alliances", *Journal of Management*, 27: 679–699.

52. T. E. Stuart, S. Z. Ozdemir and W. W. Ding, 2007, "Vertical alliance networks: The case of university-biotechnology-pharmaceutical alliance chains", *Research Policy*, 36(4): 477–498; F. T. Rothaermel, M. A. Hitt and L. A. Jobe, 2006, "Balancing vertical integration and strategic outsourcing: Effects on product portfolio, product success and firm performance", *Strategic Management Journal*, 27: 1033–1056.

53. Y. Yan, D. Ding and S. Mak, 2009, "The impact of business investment on capability exploitation and organisational control in international strategic alliances", *Journal of Change Management*, 9(1): 49–65; R. Gulati, P. R. Lawrence and P. Puranam, 2005, "Adaptation in vertical relationships beyond incentive conflict", *Strategic Management Journal*, 26: 415–440.

54. J. Wiklund and D. A. Shepherd, 2009, "The effectiveness of alliances and acquisitions: The role of resource combination activities", *Theory and Practice*, 31(1): 193–212; B. S. Teng, 2007, "Corporate entrepreneurship activities through strategic alliances: A resource-based approach toward competitive advantage", *Journal of Management Studies*, 44: 119–142; S. Spedale, F. A. J. Van den Bosch and H. W. Volberda, 2007, "Preservation and dissolution of the target firm's embedded ties in acquisitions", *Organization Studies*, 28(8): 1169–1196.

55. Y. I. Kane and D. Wakabayashi, 2009, "Nintendo looks outside the box", *Wall Street Journal*, May 27, B5.

56. F. A. Ghisi, J. A. G. da Silveira, T. Kristensen, M. Hingley and A. Lindgreen, 2008, "Horizontal alliances amongst small retailers in Brazil", *British Food Journal*, 110(4/5): 514–538; A. Tiwana, 2008, "Does technological modularity substitute for control? A study of alliance performance in software outsourcing", *Strategic Management Journal*, 29(7): 769–780; F. T. Rothaermel and M. Thursby, 2007, "The nanotech versus the biotech revolution: Sources of

productivity in incumbent firm research", *Research Policy*, 36: 832–849; T. H. Oum, J. H. Park, K. Kim and C. Yu, 2004, "The effect of horizontal alliances on firm productivity and profitability: Evidence from the global airline industry", *Journal of Business Research*, 57: 844–853.

57. A. Johnson and A. Greil, 2009, "Pfizer, Novartis disclose separate deals in generic drugs", *Wall Street Journal*, May 21, B3.

58. E. Smith, 2009, "Universal takes another stab online", *Wall Street Journal*, May 15, B8.

59. T. W. Tong, J. J. Reuer and M. W. Peng, 2008, "International joint ventures and the value of growth options", *Academy of Management Journal*, 51: 1014–1029; J. J. Reuer and T. W. Tong, 2005, "Real options in international joint ventures", *Journal of Management*, 31: 403–423; S. Chatterjee, R. M. Wiseman, A. Fiegenbaum and C. E. Devers, 2003, "Integrating behavioural and economic concepts of risk into strategic management: The twain shall meet", *Long Range Planning*, 36(1): 61–80; J. J. Reuer, E. Klijn, F. A. J. Van den Bosch and H. W. Volberda, 2011, "Bringing corporate governance to international joint ventures", *Global Strategy Journal*, 1(1), Forthcoming.

60. C. Rauwald and N. Shirouzu, 2009, "Volkswagon eyes China venture", *Wall Street Journal*, May 27, B4.

61. L. Tesfatsion, 2007, "Agents come to bits: Toward a constructive comprehensive taxonomy of economic entities", *Journal of Economic Behaviour & Organization*, 63: 333–346.

62. K. Done, 2009, "Cargo airlines fined $214m for price fixing", *Financial Times*, http://www.ft.com, April 12.

63. C. d'Aspremont, R. D. S. Ferreira and L. A. Gerard-Varet, 2007, "Competition for market share or for market size: Oligopolistic equilibria with varying competitive toughness", *International Economic Review*, 48: 761–784.

64. R. W. Cooper and T. W. Ross, 2009, "Sustaining cooperation with joint ventures", *Journal of Law Economics and Organisation*, 25(1): 31–54.

65. J. T. Prince and D. H. Simon, 2009, "Multi-market contact and service quality: Evidence from on-time performance in the U.S. airline industry", *Academy of Management Journal*, 52(2): 336–354.

66. G. K. Price and J. M. Connor, 2003, "Modeling coupon values for ready-to-eat breakfast cereals", *Agribusiness*, 19(2): 223–244.

67. G. K. Price, 2000, "Cereal sales soggy despite price cuts and reduced couponing", *Food Review*, 23(2): 21–28.

68. S. Kilman, 2008, "Food giants race to pass rising costs to shoppers", *Wall Street Journal*, August 8, A1.

69. S. Kilman, 2008, "Food giants race to pass rising costs to shoppers", *Wall Street Journal*, August 8, A1; J. Hagedoorn and G. Hesen, 2007, "Contract law and the governance of interfirm technology partnerships – An analysis of different modes of partnering and their contractual implications", *Journal of Management Studies*, 44: 342–366; B. R. Golden and H. Ma, 2003, "Mutual forbearance: The role of intrafirm integration and rewards", *Academy of Management Review*, 28: 479–493.

70. J. Apesteguia, M. Dufwenberg and R. Selton, 2007, "Blowing the whistle", *Economic Theory*, 31: 127–142.

71. J. D. Rockoff, 2009, "Drug CEOs switch tactics on reform; Pharmaceutical companies join health-care overhaul hoping to influence where costs are cut", *Wall Street Journal*, May 27, B1, B2; J. H. Johnson and G. K. Leonard, 2007, "Economics and the rigorous analysis of class certification in antitrust cases", *Journal of Competition Law and Economics*, http://jcle.oxfordjournals.org, June 26.

72. S. G. Lazzarini, D. P. Claro and L. F. Mesquita, 2008, "Buyer-supplier and supplier-supplier alliances: Do they reinforce or undermine one another?" *Journal of Management Studies*, 45(3): 561–584; P. Dussauge, B. Garrette and W. Mitchell, 2004, "Asymmetric performances: The market share impact of scale and link alliances in global auto industry", *Strategic Management Journal*, 25: 701–711.

73. C. Conkey and P. Prada, 2009, "Corporate news: Continental wins nod to join Star Alliance", *Wall Street Journal*, April 8, B4.

74. J. S. Harrison, M. A. Hitt, R. E. Hoskisson and R. D. Ireland, 2001, "Resource complementarity in business combinations: Extending the logic to organisational alliances", *Journal of Management*, 27: 679–699.

75. L. H. Lin, 2009, "Mergers and acquisitions, alliances and technology development: an empirical study of the global auto industry", *International Journal of Technology Management*, 48(3): 295–307; J. Wiklund and D. A. Shepherd, 2009, "The effectiveness of alliances and acquisitions: The role of resource combination activities", *Theory and Practice*, 31(1): 193–212; A. E. Bernardo and B. Chowdhry, 2002, "Resources, real options and corporate strategy", *Journal of Financial Economics*, 63: 211–234.

76. J. Li, C. Dhanaraj and R. L. Shockley, 2008, "Joint venture evolution: Extending the real options approach", *Managerial and Decision Economics*, 29(4): 317–336.

77. V. Moatti, 2009, "Learning to expand or expanding to learn? The role of imitation and experience in the choice among several expansion modes", *European Management Journal*, 27(1): 36–46; C. C. Pegels and Y. I. Song, 2007, "Market competition and cooperation: Identifying competitive/cooperative interaction groups", *International Journal of Services Technology and Management*, 2/3: 139–154.

78. S. Silver and E. Steel, 2009, "Alcatel gets into mobile ads; Service will target cell phone users based on location", *Wall Street Journal*, May 21, B9.

79. A. Goerzen and P. W. Beamish, 2005, "The effect of alliance network diversity on multinational enterprise performance", *Strategic Management Journal*, 333–354.

80. M. V. Shyam Kumar, 2005, "The value from acquiring and divesting a joint venture: A real options approach", *Strategic Management Journal*, 26: 321–331.

81. J. Yang, 2003, "One step forward for Japan's chipmakers", *BusinessWeek Online*, http://www.businessweek.com, July 7.

82. J. E. Vascellaro and E. Holmes, 2009, "YouTube seals deal on ABC, ESPN clips", *Wall Street Journal online*, http://www.wsj.com, March 31.

83. B. Worthen and J. Scheck, 2009, "As growth slows, ex-allies square off in a turf war", *Wall Street Journal*, March 16, A1.

84. A. M. Doherty, 2009, "Market and partner selection processes in international retail franchising", *Journal of Business Research*, 62(5): 528–534; M. Tuunanen and F. Hoy, 2007, "Franchising – multifaceted form of entrepreneurship", *International Journal of Entrepreneurship and Small Business*, 4: 52–67; J. G. Combs and D. J. Ketchen Jr, 2003, "Why do firms use franchising as an entrepreneurial strategy? A meta-analysis", *Journal of Management*, 29: 427–443.

85. F. Lafontaine, 1999, "Myths and strengths of franchising, 'Mastering Strategy'" (Part Nine), *Financial Times*, November 22, 8–10.

86. A. M. Hayashi, 2008, "How to replicate success", *MIT Sloan Management Review*, 49(3): 6–7.

87. G. Szulanski and R. J. Jensen, 2008, "Growing through copying: The negative consequences of innovation on franchise network growth", *Research Policy*, 37(10): 1732–1741; H. W. Volberda, E. Verwaal and N. P. Van der Weerdt, 2006, "Ownership structure, organizational flexibility and store performance in retail chains", *International Journal of Business Environment*, 1(3): 268–279.

88. European Franchising: Trends and Developments, 2010, http://www.franchiseeurope.com, July 5.

89. A. M. Doherty, 2009, "Market and partner selection processes in international retail franchising", *Journal of Business Research*, 62(5): 528–534; R. B. DiPietro, D. H. B. Welsh, P. V. Raven and D. Severt, 2007, "A message of hope in franchises systems: Assessing franchisees, top executives and franchisors", *Journal of Leadership & Organisational Studies*, 13(3): 59–66; S. C. Michael, 2002, "Can a franchise chain coordinate?", *Journal of Business Venturing*, 17: 325–342.

90. A. K. Paswan and C. M. Wittmann, 2009, "Knowledge management and franchise systems", *Industrial Marketing Management*, 38(2): 173–180.

91. J. Torikka, 2007, "Franchisees can be made: Empirical evidence from a follow-up study", *International Journal of Entrepreneurship and Small Business*, 4: 68–96; P. J. Kaufmann and S. Eroglu, 1999, "Standardisation and adaptation in business format franchising", *Journal of Business Venturing*, 14: 69–85.

92. B. Arruñada, L. Vázquez and G. Zanarone, 2009, "Institutional constraints on organisations: The case of Spanish car dealerships", *Managerial and Decision Economics*, 30(1): 15–26; J. Barthélemy, 2008, "Opportunism, knowledge and the performance of franchise chains", *Strategic Management Journal*, 29(13): 1451–1463.

93. A. Tiwana, 2008, "Does technological modularity substitute for control? A study of alliance performance in software outsourcing", *Strategic Management Journal*, 29(7): 769–780; M. Zollo, J. J. Reuer and H. Singh, 2002, "Interorganisational routines and performance in strategic alliances", *Organization Science*, 13: 701–714.

94. E. Levitas and M. A. McFadyen, 2009, "Managing liquidity in research-intensive firms: Signaling and cash flow effects of patents and alliance activities", *Strategic Management Journal*, 30(6): 659–678; R. D. Ireland, M. A. Hitt and D. Vaidyanath, 2002, "Alliance management as a source of competitive advantage", *Journal of Management*, 28: 413–446.

95. R. Durand, O. Bruyaka and V. Mangematin, 2008, "Do science and money go together? The case of the French biotech industry", *Strategic Management Journal*, 29(12): 1281–1299; A. V. Shipilov, 2007, "Network strategies and performance of Canadian investment banks", *Academy of Management Journal*, 49: 590–604; P. Almeida, G. Dokko and L. Rosenkopf, 2003, "Startup size and the mechanisms of external learning: Increasing opportunity and decreasing ability?", *Research Policy*, 32(2): 301–316.

96. H. Ren, B. Gray and K. Kim, 2009, "Performance of international joint ventures: What factors really make a difference and how?", *Journal of Management*, 35(3): 805–832; R. Narula and G. Duysters, 2004, "Globalisation and trends in international R&D alliances", *Journal of International Management*, 10: 199–218; M. A. Hitt, M. T. Dacin, E. Levitas, J. L. Arregle and A. Borza, 2000, "Partner selection in emerging and developed market contexts: Resource-based and organisational learning perspectives", *Academy of Management Journal*, 43: 449–467.

97. W. Zhan, R. Chen, M. K. Erramilli and D. T. Nguyen, 2009, "Acquisition of organisational capabilities and competitive advantage of IJVs in transition economies: The case of Vietnam", *Asia Pacific Journal of Management*, 26(2): 285–308; T. W. Tong, J. J. Reuer and M. W. Peng, 2008, "International joint ventures and the value of growth options", *Academy of Management Journal*, 51: 1014–1029; J. H. Dyer, P. Kale and H. Singh, 2004, "When to ally & when to acquire", *Harvard Business Review*, 81(7/8): 109–115.

98. Y. Yan, D. Ding and S. Mak, 2009, "The impact of business investment on capability exploitation and organisational control in international strategic alliances", *Journal of Change Management*, 9(1): 49–65; P. Ghemawat, 2007, "Managing differences: The central challenge of global strategy", *Harvard Business Review*, 85(3): 59–68.

99. L. Chao, 2009, "IMG China venture opens with tennis", *Wall Street Journal*, May 26, B10.

100. H. Ren, B. Gray and K. Kim, 2009, "Performance of international joint ventures: What factors really make a difference and how?", *Journal of Management*, 35(3): 805–832; L. Dong and K.W. Glaister, 2007, "National and corporate culture differences in international strategic alliances: Perceptions of Chinese partners", *Asia Pacific Journal of Management*, 24: 191–205; I. M. Manev, 2003, "The managerial network in a multinational enterprise and the resource profiles of subsidiaries", *Journal of International Management*, 9: 133–152.

101. P. H. Dickson, K. M. Weaver and F. Hoy, 2006, "Opportunism in the R&D alliances of SMEs: The roles of the institutional environment and SME size", *Journal of Business Venturing*, 21: 487–513; H. K. Steensma, L. Tihanyi, M. A. Lyles and C. Dhanaraj, 2005, "The evolving value of foreign partnerships in transitioning economies", *Academy of Management Journal*, 48: 213–235.

102. 2007, Branding and celebrity endorsements, *VentureRepublic*, http://venturerepublic.com, August 31.

103. 2009, "Nike winded", *Financial Times*, March 20, 14.

104. B. Elango, 2009, "Minimising effects of 'liability of foreignness': Response strategies of foreign firms in the United States", *Journal of World Business*, 44(1): 51–62; Y. Luo, O. Shenkar and M. K. Nyaw, 2002, "Mitigating the liabilities of foreignness: Defensive versus offensive approaches", *Journal of International Management*, 8: 283–300.

105. T. J. Wilkinson, A. R. Thomas and J. M. Hawes, 2009, "Managing relationships with Chinese joint venture partners", *Journal of Global Marketing*, 22(2): 109–210; S. R. Miller and A. Parkhe, 2002, "Is there a liability of foreignness in global banking? An empirical test of banks' x-efficiency", *Strategic Management Journal*, 23: 55–75; Y. Luo, 2001, "Determinants of local responsiveness: Perspectives from foreign subsidiaries in an emerging market", *Journal of Management*, 27: 451–477.

106. D. Kronborg and S. Thomsen, 2009, "Foreign ownership and long-term survival", *Strategic Management Journal*, 30(2): 207–220.

107. E. Rodríguez, 2008, "Cooperative ventures in emerging economies", *Journal of Business Research*, 61(6): 640–647; D. Li, L. E. Eden, M. A. Hitt and R. D. Ireland, 2008, "Friends, acquaintances or strangers? Partner selection in R&D alliances", *Academy of Management Journal*, 51: 315–334; J. E. Oxley and R. C. Sampson, 2004, "The scope and governance of international R&D alliances", *Strategic Management Journal*, 25: 723–749.

108. H. Sun, 2009, "China poised to be net importer of coffee", *Wall Street Journal*, January 20, C10; 2006, "Starbucks acquires control of China joint venture", *Apostille US*, http://apostille.us.com, October 25.

109. D. Lavie, 2009, "Capturing value from alliance portfolios", *Organisational Dynamics*, 38(1): 26–36; D. Lavie, C. Lechner and H. Singh, 2007, "The performance implications of timing of entry and involvement in multipartner alliances", *Academy of Management Journal*, 49: 569–604.

110. K. Atkins, J. Chen, V. S. A. Kumar, M. Macauley and A. Marathe, 2009, "Locational market power in network constrained markets", *Journal of Economic Behaviour & Organization*, 70(1/2): 416–430; A. Nosella and G. Petroni, 2007, "Multiple network leadership as a strategic asset: The Carlo Gavazzi space case", *Long Range Planning*, 40: 178–201.

111. K. Sawyer, 2007, "Strength in webs", *The Conference Board*, July/August, 9–11.

112. C. Yarbrough, 2008, "Singapore to open fusionopolis", *Research Technology Management*, 51(5): 4–5; A. H. Van de Ven, H. J. Sapienza and J. Villanueva, 2007, "Entrepreneurial pursuits of self- and collective interests", *Strategic Entrepreneurship Journal*, 1(3/4): 353–370.

113. D. Lavie, 2009, "Capturing value from alliance portfolios", *Organizational Dynamics*, 38(1): 26–36; D. Lavie, 2007, "Alliance portfolios and firm performance: A study of value creation and appropriation in the U.S. software industry", *Strategic Management Journal*, 28(12): 1187–1212; G. K. Lee, 2007, "The significance of network resources in the race to enter emerging product markets: The convergence of telephony communications and computer networking", 1989–2001, *Strategic Management Journal*, 28: 17–37.

114. R. Cowan and N. Jonard, 2009, "Knowledge portfolios and the organisation of innovation networks", *Academy of Management Review*, 34(2): 320–342; G. G. Bell, 2005, "Clusters, networks and firm innovativeness", *Strategic Management Journal*, 26: 287–295.

115. H. Kim, R. E. Hoskisson and W. P. Wan, 2004, "Power, dependence, diversification strategy and performance in keiretsu member firms", *Strategic Management Journal*, 25: 613–636.

116. A. V. Shipilov, 2009, "Firm scope experience, historic multimarket contact with partners, centrality and the relationship between structural holes and performance", *Organization Science*, 20(1): 85–106; M. Rudberg and J. Olhager, 2003, "Manufacturing networks and supply chains: An operations strategy perspective", *Omega*, 31(1): 29–39.

117. R. Cowan and N. Jonard, 2009, "Knowledge portfolios and the organisation of innovation networks", *Academy of Management Review*, 34(2): 320–342; E. J. Kleinschmidt, U. de Brentani and S. Salomo, 2007, "Programs: A resource-based view", *Journal of Product Innovation Management*, 24: 419–441; G. J. Young, M. P. Charns and S. M. Shortell, 2001, "Top manager and network effects on the adoption of innovative management practices: A study of TQM in a public hospital system", *Strategic Management Journal*, 22: 935–951.

118. J. T. Prince and D. H. Simon, 2009, "Multi-market contact and service quality: Evidence from on-time performance in the U.S. airline industry", *Academy of Management Journal*, 52(2): 336–354; E. Garcia-Canal, C. L. Duarte, J. R. Criado and A. V. Llaneza, 2002, "Accelerating international expansion through global alliances: A typology of cooperative strategies", *Journal of World Business*, 37(2): 91–107; F. T. Rothaermel, 2001, "Complementary assets, strategic alliances and the incumbent's advantage: An empirical study of industry and firm effects in the biopharmaceutical industry", *Research Policy*, 30: 1235–1251.

119. T. Kiessling and M. Harvey, 2008, "Globalisation of internal venture capital opportunities in developing small and medium enterprises' relationships", *International Journal of Entrepreneurship and Innovation Management*, 8(3): 233–253; V. Shankar and B. L. Bayus, 2003, "Network effects and competition: An empirical analysis of the home video game industry", *Strategic Management Journal*, 24: 375–384.

120. A. Schwab and A. S. Miner, 2008, "Learning in hybrid-project systems: The effects of project performance on repeated collaboration", *Academy of Management Journal*, 51(6): 1117–1149.

121. A. E. Leiponen, 2008, "Competing through cooperation: The organisation of standard setting in wireless telecommunications", *Management Science*, 54(11): 1904–1919; Z. Simsek, M. H. Lubatkin and D. Kandemir, 2003, "Inter-firm networks and entrepreneurial behaviour: A structural embeddedness perspective", *Journal of Management*, 29: 401–426.

122. H. W. Gottinger and C. L. Umali, 2008, "The evolution of the pharmaceutical-biotechnology industry", *Business History*, 50(5): 583–601; F. T. Rothaermel and W. Boeker, 2008, "Old technology meets new technology: Complementarities, similarities and alliance formation", *Strategic Management Journal*, 29(1): 47–77; P. Puranam and K. Srikanth, 2007, "What they know vs what they do: How acquirers leverage technology acquisitions", *Strategic Management Journal*, 28: 805–825; M. Moensted, 2007, "Strategic networking in small high-tech firms", *The International Entrepreneurship and Management Journal*, 3: 15–27; M. Hensmans, F. A. J. Van den Bosch and H. W. Volberda, 2001, "Clicks versus bricks in the emerging online financial services industry", *Long Range Planning* 34(2): 231–247.

123. P. Ozcan and K. M. Eisenhardt, 2009, "Origin of alliance portfolios: Entrepreneurs, network strategies and firm performance", *Academy of Management Journal*, 52(2): 246–279; C. T. Street and A. F. Cameron, 2007, "External relationships and the small business: A review of small business alliance and network research", *Journal of Small Business Management*, 45: 239–266.

124. M. Rod, 2009, "A model for the effective management of joint ventures: A case study approach", *International Journal of Management*, 26(1): 3–17; T. K. Das and R. Kumar, 2007, "Learning dynamics in the alliance development process", *Management Decision*, 45: 684–707.

125. A. Carmeli and Z. Sheaffer, 2008. "How learning leadership and organisational learning from failures enhance perceived organisational capacity to adapt to the task environment", *Journal of Applied Behavioural Science*, 44(4): 468–489; J. Y. Kim and A. S. Miner, 2007, "Vicarious learning from the failures and near-failures of others: Evidence from the U.S. commercial banking industry", *Academy of Management Journal*, 49: 687–714.

126. Y. Li, Y. Liu, M. Li and H. Wu, 2008, "Transformational offshore outsourcing: Empirical evidence from alliances in China", *Journal of Operations Management*, 26(2): 257–274; P. M. Norman, 2002, "Protecting knowledge in strategic alliances – Resource and relational characteristics", *Journal of High Technology Management Research*, 13(2): 177–202; P. M. Norman, 2001, "Are your secrets safe? Knowledge protection in strategic alliances", *Business Horizons*, November–December, 51–60.

127. K. H. Heimeriks, E. Klijn and J. J. Reuer, 2009, "Building capabilities for alliance portfolios", *Long Range Planning*, 42(1): 96–114; A. Al-Laham, T. L. Amburgey and K. Bates, 2008, "The dynamics of research alliances: Examining the

effect of alliance experience and partner characteristics on the speed of alliance entry in the biotech industry", *British Journal of Management*, 19(4): 343–364; J. Connell and R. Voola, 2007, "Strategic alliances and knowledge sharing: Synergies or silos?", *Journal of Knowledge Management*, 11: 52–66.

128. M. B. Sarkar, P. S. Aulakh and A. Madhok, 2009, "Process capabilities and value generation in alliance portfolios", *Organization Science*, 20(3): 583–600.

129. P. X. Meschi, 2009, "Government corruption and foreign stakes in international joint ventures in emerging economies", *Asia Pacific Journal of Management*, 26(2): 241–261.

130. M. H. Hansen, R. E. Hoskisson and J. B. Barney, 2008, "Competitive advantage in alliance governance: Resolving the opportunism minimisation-gain maximisation paradox", *Managerial and Decision Economics*, 29: 191–208; J. H. Dyer, P. Kale and H. Singh, 2001, "How to make strategic alliances work", *MIT Sloan Management Review*, 42(4): 37–43; J. J. Reuer, E. Klijn, F. A. J. Van den Bosch and H. W. Volberda, 2011, "Bringing corporate governance to international joint ventures", *Global Strategy Journal*, 1(1), Forthcoming.

131. J. Connell and R. Voola, 2007, "Strategic alliances and knowledge sharing: Synergies or silos?", *Journal of Knowledge Management*, 11: 52–66.

132. E. Levitas and M. A. McFadyen, 2009, "Managing liquidity in research-intensive firms: Signaling and cash flow effects of patents and alliance activities", *Strategic Management Journal*, 30(6): 659–678; M. H. Hansen, R. E. Hoskisson and J. B. Barney, 2008, "Competitive advantage in alliance governance: Resolving the opportunism minimisation-gain maximisation paradox", *Managerial and Decision Economics*, 29: 191–208; J. H. Dyer, 1997, "Effective interfirm collaboration: How firms minimise transaction costs and maximise transaction value", *Strategic Management Journal*, 18: 535–556.

133. L. Poppo, K. Z. Zhou and S. Ryu, 2008, "Alternative origins to interorganisational trust: An interdependence perspective on the shadow of the past and the shadow of the future", *Organization Science*, 19(1): 39–56; J. H. Dyer and C. Wujin, 2003, "The role of trustworthiness in reducing transaction costs and improving performance: Empirical evidence from the United States, Japan and Korea", *Organization Science*, 14: 57–69; P. W. L. Vlaar, F. A. J. Van den Bosch and H. W. Volberda, 2007, "Towards a dialectic perspective on formalization in interorganizational relationships: How alliance managers capitalize on the duality inherent in contracts, rules, and procedures", *Organization Studies*, 28(4): 437–466.

134. R. Krishnan, X. Martin and N. G. Noorderhaven, 2007, "When does trust matter to alliance performance?", *Academy of Management Journal*, 49: 894–917.

135. K. Langfield-Smith, 2008, "The relations between transactional characteristics, trust and risk in the start-up phase of a collaborative alliance", *Management Accounting Research*, 19(4): 344–364; M. Lundin, 2007, "Explaining cooperation: How resource interdependence, goal congruence and trust affect joint actions in policy implementation", *Journal of Public Administration Research and Theory*, 17(4): 651–672.

136. T. K. Das and R. Kumar, 2009, "Interpartner harmony in strategic alliances: Managing commitment and forbearance", *International Journal of Strategic Business Alliances*, 1(1): 24–52; V. Perrone, A. Zaheer and B. McEvily, 2003, "Free to be trusted? Boundary constraints on trust in boundary spanners", *Organization Science*, 14: 422–439; P. W. L. Vlaar, F. A. J. Van den Bosch and H. W. Volberda, 2006, "Coping with problems of understanding in interorganizational relationships: Using formalization as a means to make sense", *Organization Studies*, Special Issue on "Making Sense of Organizing: in Honor of Karl Weick", 27(11): 1617–1638; P. W. L. Vlaar, F. A. J. Van den Bosch and H. W. Volberda, 2007, "On the evolution of trust, distrust, and formal coordination and control in interorganizational relationships: Toward an integrative framework", *Group & Organization Management*, Special Issue Trust and Control Interrelations: New Perspectives on the Trust-Control Nexus, 32(4): 407–429.

137. J. W. Rottman, 2008, "Successful knowledge transfer within offshore supplier networks: A case study exploring social capital in strategic alliances", *Journal of Information Technology*: Special Issue: Global Sourcing, 23(1): 31–43; R. D. Ireland and J. W. Webb, 2007, "A multi-theoretic perspective on trust and power in strategic supply chains", *Journal of Operations Management*, 25: 482–497.

138. 2007, The principles of the alliance, http://www.renault. com, August 26.

139. C. E. Ybarra and T. A. Turk, 2009, "The evolution of trust in information technology alliances", *Journal of High Technology Management Research*, 20(1): 62–74; F. D. Schoorman, R. C. Mayer and J. H. Davis, 2007, "An integrative model of organisational trust: Past, present and future", *Academy of Management Review*, 344–354; J. H. Davis, F. D. Schoorman, R. C. Mayer and H. H. Tan, 2000, "The trusted general manager and business unit performance: Empirical evidence of a competitive advantage", *Strategic Management Journal*, 21: 563–576.

140. Y. Luo, 2008, "Procedural fairness and interfirm cooperation in strategic alliances", *Strategic Management Journal*, 29(1): 27–46; B. Hillebrand and W. G. Biemans, 2003, "The relationship between internal and external cooperation: Literature review and propositions", *Journal of Business Research*, 56: 735–744.

**PART III**

# IMPLEMENTATION OF STRATEGIC ACTIONS

**CHAPTER 11**

# STRATEGIC LEADERSHIP

## LEARNING OBJECTIVES

Studying this chapter should provide you with the strategic management knowledge needed to:

1   Define strategic leadership and describe top-level managers' importance.
2   Explain what top management teams are and how they affect firm performance.
3   Describe the managerial succession process using internal and external managerial labour markets.
4   Discuss the value of strategic leadership in determining the firm's strategic direction.
5   Describe the importance of strategic leaders in managing the firm's resources.
6   Define organizational culture and explain what must be done to sustain an effective culture.
7   Explain what strategic leaders can do to establish and emphasize ethical practices.
8   Discuss the importance and use of organizational controls.

We thank Ignacio Vaccaro for his contribution to this Chapter.

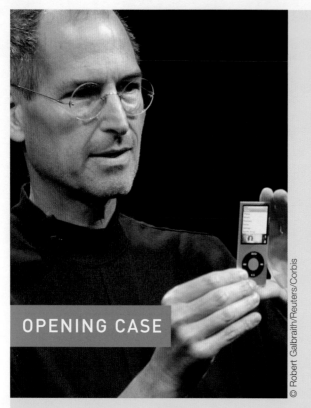

OPENING CASE

© Robert Galbraith/Reuters/Corbis

# Selecting a new CEO: the importance of strategic leaders

Evidence shows that the shelf life of a CEO is not long and it continues to get shorter. In the period 2000–2010 the global average tenure of CEOs decreased from 8.1 to 6.3 years.

The brevity of CEOs and top-level managers' tenure means that planning for and selecting new leaders should be continuous processes. Furthermore, the importance of strategic leaders to the firm's overall health and success makes selecting effective leaders a critical need. For example, in 2009, 357 CEOs of the global top 2500 public companies were replaced. Despite this high number of strategic leader departures, boards of directors are rarely effective in planning for and completing the succession. A survey of boards found that over 40 per cent of the firms had no succession plan. In another survey, directors rated their boards as ineffective in succession planning in more than 50 per cent of the firms. Often, changes in the CEO occur without warning. For example, the

CEOs at NXP, Toyota, SAP and Lenovo unexpectedly resigned or were replaced. In the cases of Toyota and Lenovo, the reasons for change related to the poor performance of the firm. Both suffered net losses in 2008 and Lenovo's market share declined from third to fourth place in the PC industry.

The importance of CEOs and planning for succession is clearly evident with Steve Jobs at Apple. Jobs took time off from the CEO role in 2009 due to illness. Analysts expressed major concerns about his ability to continue because of his importance to the success of the firm. He is believed to be especially important to Apple's innovation capability. While he does not design new products, he reviews each new project and serves as an internal champion for those he feels are worthy. For instance, Jobs supported the work on the iPod in its early stages despite the scepticism of several others in the company. Furthermore, Jobs will not accept compromises; he pushes project teams to do everything possible to make the "product right".

Jobs is a co-founder of Apple but left the company for 12 years. During that time, the company floundered. He returned in 1997 and Apple has had a number of market successes since that time. However, many fear the loss of Jobs and wonder if he can be replaced. One analyst referred to Apple without Jobs as similar to a John Wayne movie without John Wayne. Another stated that Apple without Jobs is Sony. While Jobs has trained and delegated authority to several others regarding innovation in Apple, few believe that he can be adequately replaced. Thus, the selection of a new CEO for Apple whenever Jobs leaves will be a critical one for the company.

Companies can develop effective succession plans. Usually such plans call for selecting one or more potential successors and helping them to build the capabilities necessary to perform the CEO job. For example, they may be given challenging assignments where they can build valuable knowledge of critical markets and/or establish relationships with important stakeholders. They can receive mentoring and 360 degree feedback to identify and work on positive and negative traits.

Identifying potential CEOs is a difficult assignment because of the many and varied capabilities needed for the job. Recent efforts to identify potential successors for CEOs focused on people who were innovative and championed innovation, who had vision and could gain others commitment to that vision, who nurtured important human capital and who built relationships with critical constituencies such as customers and suppliers.

**Sources:** Favaro, K., Karlsson, P. O. and Neilson, G. L. (2010) "CEO Succession 2000–2009: A decade of convergence and compression", *Strategy+business*, 59, May 25, 76-91, http://www.strategy-business.com; Tobak, S. (2009) "What happens when Steve Jobs leaves Apple?", BNET, http://www.blogs.bnet.com, May 26; Mikla, N. (2008) UPDATE 1-Chipmaker NXP unexpectedly replaces CEO, *Reuters*, http://www.reuters.com, December 31; Soble, J. (2009) "Toyota plans top-level overhaul", *Financial Times*, http://www.ft.com, May 14; Kjetland, R. (2010) "SAP CEO Apotheker unexpectedly leaves; CO-CEOs named", *Business Week*, http://www.businessweek.com, February 8; Boyle, M. (2009) "The art of succession", *Business Week*, May 11, 030-037; Boyle, M. (2009) "The art of CEO succession", *Business Week*, http://www.businessweek.com, April 30; Balfour, F. and Einhorn, B. (2009) "Lenovo CEO is out; Chinese execs return", *Business Week*, http://www.business week.com, February 5; Scheck, J. and Wingfield, N. (2008)

"How Apple could survive without Steve Jobs", *The Wall Street Journal*, http://www.wsj.com, December 19; Behan, B. (2008) "Shareholder proposals on CEO succession planning", *Business Week*, http://www.businessweek.com, January 24.

## Questions

**1** Why do you think succession plans are so important for companies?

**2** What does the case of Steve Jobs say about the relevance of leaders to both internal and external stakeholders?

**3** Do you think that analysts' focus on Steve Jobs' personal contribution to Apple is an asset or a liability for the company?

**4** What are, in your opinion, the key traits that would-be CEOs must possess?

As the Opening Case implies, strategic leaders' work is demanding, challenging and may last for a long period of time. Regardless of how long they remain in their positions, strategic leaders (and most prominently CEOs) can make a major difference to how a firm performs.[1] If a strategic leader can create a strategic vision for the firm using forward thinking, she/he may be able to energize the firm's human capital and achieve positive outcomes. However, the challenge of strategic leadership is significant. For example, replacing Steve Jobs at Apple will be difficult because of his special skills in identifying and nurturing creative new products that have significant market potential. Yet the transition at GlaxoSmithKline was smooth because a person was identified early and groomed to take over the CEO role when change was necessary (for more details see the Strategic Focus on page 411) .

A major message in this chapter is that effective strategic leadership is the foundation for successfully using the strategic management process. As is implied in Figure 1.1 (see page 7), strategic leaders guide the firm in ways that result in forming a vision and mission (see Chapter 1). Often, this guidance finds leaders thinking of ways to create goals that stretch everyone in the organization to improve performance.[2] Moreover, strategic leaders facilitate the development of appropriate strategic actions and determine how to implement them. As we show in Figure 11.1, these actions are the path to strategic competitiveness and above-average returns.[3]

We begin this chapter with a definition of strategic leadership; we then discuss its importance as a potential source of competitive advantage as well as effective strategic leadership styles. Next, we examine top management teams and their effects on innovation, strategic change and firm performance. Following this discussion, we analyse the internal and external managerial labour markets from which strategic leaders are selected. Closing the chapter are descriptions of the five key components of effective strategic leadership: determining a strategic direction; effectively managing the firm's resource portfolio (which includes exploiting and maintaining core competencies along with developing human capital and social capital); sustaining an effective organizational culture; emphasizing ethical practices; and establishing balanced organizational controls.

**FIGURE 11.1**  Strategic leadership and the strategic management process

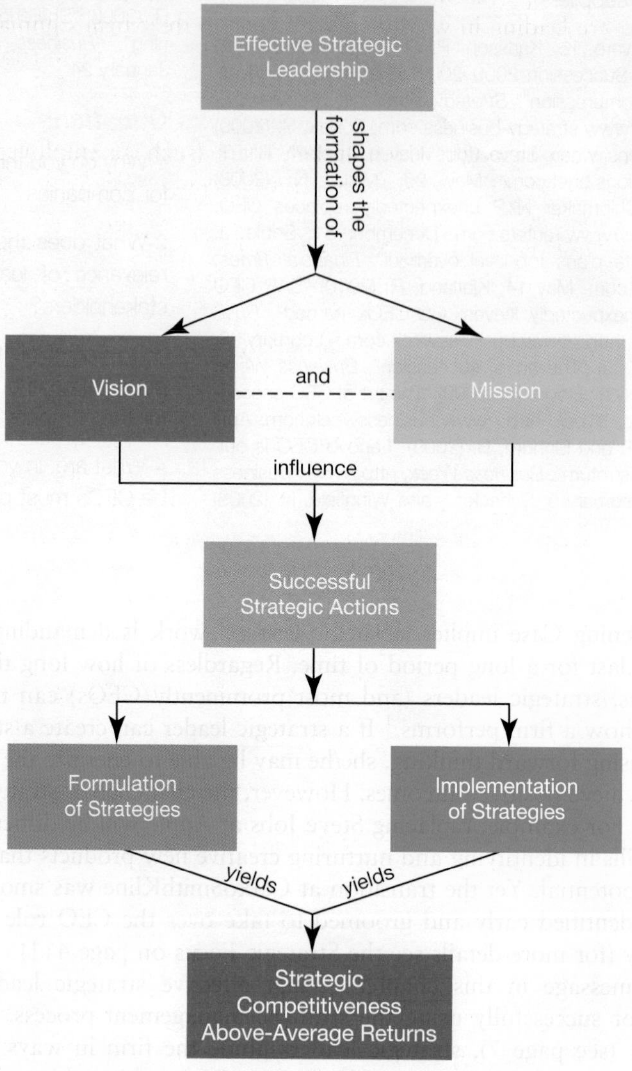

## Strategic leadership and style

**Strategic leadership**

Strategic leadership is the ability to anticipate, envision, maintain flexibility and empower others to create strategic change as necessary.

Strategic leadership is the ability to anticipate, envision, maintain flexibility and empower others to create strategic change as necessary. Multifunctional in nature, strategic leadership involves managing through others, managing an entire enterprise rather than a functional subunit, and coping with change that continues to increase in the global economy. Because of the global economy's complexity, strategic leaders must learn how to effectively influence human behaviour, often in uncertain environments. By word or by personal example, and through their ability to envision the future, effective strategic leaders meaningfully influence the behaviours, thoughts and feelings of those with whom they work.[4]

The ability to attract and then manage human capital may be the most critical of the strategic leader's skills,[5] especially because the lack of talented human capital constrains firm growth.[6] Increasingly, leaders throughout the global economy possess or are developing this skill. Some believe, for example, that leaders now surfacing in Chinese companies understand the rules of competition in market-based economies and are leading in ways that will develop their firm's human capital.[7]

In the twenty-first century, intellectual capital that the firm's human capital possesses, including the ability to manage knowledge and create and commercialize innovation, affects a strategic leader's success.[8] Effective strategic leaders also establish the context through which stakeholders (such as employees, customers and suppliers), can perform at peak efficiency.[9] Being able to demonstrate these skills is important, given that the crux of strategic leadership is the ability to manage the firm's operations effectively and sustain high performance over time.[10]

A firm's ability to achieve a competitive advantage and earn above-average returns is compromised when strategic leaders fail to respond appropriately and quickly to changes in the complex global competitive environment. The inability to respond or to identify the need for change in the competitive environment is one of the reasons some CEOs fail. Therefore, strategic leaders must learn how to deal with diverse and complex environmental situations. Individual judgement is an important part of learning about and analysing the firm's competitive environment.[11] In particular, effective strategic leaders build strong ties with external stakeholders to gain access to information and advice on the events in the external environment.[12]

The primary responsibility for effective strategic leadership rests at the top, in particular with the CEO. Other commonly recognized strategic leaders include members of the board of directors, the top management team, and divisional general managers. In truth, any individual with responsibility for the performance of human capital and/or a part of the firm (e.g., a production unit) is a strategic leader. Regardless of their title and organizational function, strategic leaders have substantial decision-making responsibilities that cannot be delegated.[13] Strategic leadership is a complex but critical form of leadership. Strategies cannot be formulated and implemented for the purpose of achieving above-average returns without effective strategic leaders.[14]

The styles used to provide leadership often affect the productivity of those being led. Researchers have studied top management leadership behaviour along a continuum of transactional and transformational leadership.[15] Transactional leadership entails engaging followers through an exchange between them and their leaders. This is typically done through the clarification and specification of what is expected of followers, as well as the leader's intervention to monitor and take action when expected standards are not met.[16] This leadership behaviour can lead to an increase in productivity and innovation as it promotes a sense of fairness and reward for clearly specified objectives.[17] Additionally, it can contribute to reinforce and refine learning within the organization.[18] Transformational leadership entails motivating followers to exceed the expectations others have of them, to continuously enrich their capabilities, and to place the interests of the organization above their own.[19] Transformational leaders develop and communicate a vision for the organization and formulate a strategy to achieve the vision. They make followers aware of the need to achieve valued organizational outcomes. And they encourage followers to continuously strive for higher levels of achievement. Additionally, transformational leaders have emotional intelligence. Emotionally intelligent leaders understand themselves well, have strong motivation, are empathetic with others, and have effective interpersonal skills.[20] As a result of these characteristics, transformational leaders are especially effective in promoting and nurturing innovation in firms.[21]

© MARKA/Alamy

## STRATEGIC FOCUS

## The man behind Diesel

Renzo Rosso is the president and innovator behind Diesel, the Italian-based international fashion brand with more than 10 000 points of sale and more than 200 privately owned stores in over 50 countries.

Rosso grew up in northeastern Italy on a farm near a village of 2000 people where there was only one car and one television. Rosso recalls, "I think this experience of growing up in a little town, of doing farm work, was important for me because I learned to respect the value of things. These sorts of experiences give you a real sense of the value of money, and over the years this has helped keep my feet on the floor."

When Rosso was 15 years old he decided to attend a newly-established Italian industrial textile manufacturing and fashion school where he thought graduation would be easier. There he discovered that he loved the fashion business and, after graduating in 1975, he started making clothes for himself and his friends. He dreamed of one day owning his own small business. In 1978 he joined forces with several other manufactures in his region to form the Genius

Group, which created many successful brands still widely known today, including Katherine Hamnett, Goldie, Martin Guy, Ten Big Boys and, of course, Diesel. In 1985 Rosso took complete control of Diesel by buying out the other partners and becoming the sole force behind the brand. Rosso was determined to make his company a leader, a company that took chances and carved out a niche for itself in its field. He surrounded himself with creative, talented and innovative people, people who looked like him. By 2003, Diesel had worldwide revenues in excess of $760 million. While the luxury brand's primary product is denim, particularly jeans, it designs, manufactures and markets trendy consumer products ranging from sunglasses to underwear.

Renzo is an idealistic, passionate man who has the motto: "Diesel is not my company, it's my life". Rosso describes himself as positive, simplistic and very demanding. Besides Diesel he enjoys yoga, soccer, jogging, snowboarding and wine-making. Colleagues note that Renzo Rosso never looked or acted like a chief executive. He attended corporate meetings and interviews in simple faded jeans and cowboy boots. Rosso never apologized for his attire nor his singular vision for Diesel, the company he founded and made into a multimillion-dollar fashion empire. His vision turned a small wholesale clothier into an international sensation.

**Sources:** Gail Amondson (2003) "Diesel is smokin", *BusinessWeek*, January 20; http://www.diesel.com; http://www.wikipedia.com; 2003 "The driving force behind Diesel", *BusinessWeek*, January 20; 2000 "Interview with Renzo Rosso", Designboom, November 22; 2003 *BusinessWeek*, February 10, 64; Colavita, C. (2003) "Diesel's engine; Renzo Rosso has a prescription for the fashion industry. Step one: Forget about the numbers", *Daily News Record*, September.

### Questions

1 How do you think Renzo Rosso's hiring and management of talent helped him realize his vision for Diesel?

2 What type of leadership behaviour is more prominent in Renzo Rosso: transactional or transformational leadership?

3 How does Rosso's leadership style affect the strategic leadership process?

# The role of top-level managers

Top-level managers play a critical role in that they are charged to make certain their firm is able to effectively formulate and implement strategies.[22] Top-level managers' strategic decisions influence how the firm is designed and how goals will be achieved. Thus, a critical element of organizational success is having a top management team with superior managerial skills.[23]

Managers often use their discretion (or latitude for action) when making strategic decisions, including those concerned with effectively implementing strategies.[24] Managerial discretion differs significantly across industries. The primary factors that determine the amount of decision-making discretion held by a manager (especially a top-level manager) are: (1) external environmental sources such as the industry structure, the rate of market growth in the firm's primary industry, and the degree to which products can be differentiated; (2) characteristics of the organization, including its size, age, resources and culture; and (3) characteristics of the manager, including commitment to the firm and its strategic outcomes, tolerance for ambiguity, skills in working with different people and aspiration levels (see Figure 11.2). Because strategic leaders' decisions are intended to help the firm gain a competitive advantage, how managers exercise discretion when determining appropriate strategic actions is critical to the firm's success.[25]

**FIGURE 11.2** Factors affecting managerial discretion

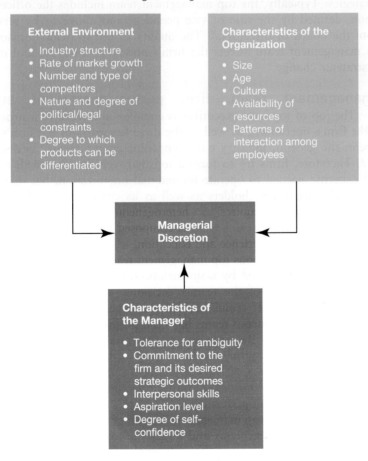

Source: Adapted from S. Finkelstein and D. C. Hambrick, 1996, *Strategic Leadership: Top Executives and Their Effects on Organizations,* St. Paul, MN: West Publishing Company.

In addition to determining new strategic initiatives, top-level managers develop a firm's organizational structure and reward systems. Top executives also have a major effect on a firm's culture. Evidence suggests that managers' values are critical in shaping a firm's cultural values.[26] Accordingly, top-level managers have an important effect on organizational activities and performance.[27] Because of the challenges top executives face, they often are more effective when they operate as top management teams.

## Top management teams

In most firms, the complexity of challenges and the need for substantial amounts of information and knowledge require strategic leadership by a team of executives. Using a team to make strategic decisions also helps to avoid another potential problem when these decisions are made by the CEO alone: managerial hubris. Research evidence shows that when CEOs begin to believe glowing press accounts and to feel that they are unlikely to make errors, they are more likely to make poor strategic decisions.[28] Top executives need to have self-confidence but must guard against allowing it to become arrogance and a false belief in their own invincibility.[29] To guard against CEO over-confidence and poor strategic decisions, firms often use the top management team to consider strategic opportunities and problems and to make strategic decisions. The top management team is composed of the key individuals who are responsible for selecting and implementing the firm's strategies. Typically, the top management team includes the officers of the corporation, defined by the title of vice president and above or by service as a member of the board of directors.[30] The quality of the strategic decisions made by a top management team affects the firm's ability to innovate and engage in effective strategic change.[31]

> **Top management team**
>
> The top management team is composed of the key individuals who are responsible for selecting and implementing the firm's strategies.

### Top management team, firm performance and strategic change
The job of top-level executives is complex and requires a broad knowledge of the firm's operations, as well as the three key parts of the firm's external environment: the general, industry and competitor environments, as discussed in Chapter 2. Therefore, firms try to form a top management team with the knowledge and expertise needed to operate the internal organization, but that also can deal with all the firm's stakeholders as well as its competitors.[32] To have these characteristics normally requires a heterogeneous top management team. A heterogeneous top management team is composed of individuals with different functional backgrounds, experience and education.

Members of a heterogeneous top management team benefit from discussing the different perspectives advanced by team members.[33] In many cases, these discussions increase the quality of the team's decisions, especially when a synthesis emerges within the team after evaluating the diverse perspectives.[34] The net benefit of such actions by heterogeneous teams has been positive in terms of market share and above-average returns. Research shows that more heterogeneity among top management team members promotes debate and facilitates the exchange of ideas regarding radical new products or new unchartered markets, which often leads to higher levels of innovation and better strategic decisions. In turn, better strategic decisions produce higher firm performance.[35]

> **Heterogeneous top management team**
>
> A heterogeneous top management team is composed of individuals with different functional backgrounds, experience and education.

It is also important for top management team members to function cohesively. In general, the more heterogeneous and larger the top management team is, the more difficult it is for the team to effectively implement strategies.[36] Comprehensive and long-term strategic plans can be inhibited by communication difficulties among top executives who have different backgrounds and different cognitive skills.[37] Alternatively, communication among diverse top management team members can be facilitated through electronic communications, sometimes reducing the barriers before face-to-face meetings.[38] However, a group of top executives with diverse backgrounds may inhibit the process of decision making if it is not effectively managed. In these cases, top management teams may fail to comprehensively examine threats and opportunities, leading to a suboptimal strategic decision. Thus, the CEO must attempt to achieve behavioural integration among the team members.[39]

Having members with substantive expertise in the firm's core functions and businesses is also important to a top management team's effectiveness.[40] In a high-technology industry, it may be critical for a firm's top management team members to have R&D expertise, particularly when growth strategies are being implemented. Yet their eventual effect on strategic decisions depends not only on their expertise and the way the team is managed but also on the context in which they make the decisions (the governance structure, incentive compensation, etc.).[41]

The characteristics of top management teams are related to innovation and strategic change.[42] For example, more heterogeneous top management teams are positively associated with innovation and strategic change. The heterogeneity may force the team or some of its members to "think outside of the box" and thus be more creative in making decisions.[43] Therefore, firms that need to change their strategies are more likely to do so if they have top management teams with diverse backgrounds and expertise. When a new CEO is hired from outside the industry, the probability of strategic change is greater than if the new CEO is from inside the firm or inside the industry.[44] Although hiring a new CEO from outside the industry adds diversity to the team, the top management team must be managed effectively to use the diversity in a positive way. Thus, to successfully create strategic change, the CEO should exercise transformational leadership.[45] A top management team with various areas of expertise is more likely to identify environmental changes (opportunities and threats) or changes within the firm, suggesting the need for a different strategic direction.

One knowledge stock important in the current competitive environment is understanding of international markets. However, recent research suggests that only about 15 per cent of the top executives in the *Fortune* 500 firms have global leadership expertise.[46] Executives generally gain this knowledge by working in one of the firm's international subsidiaries but can also gain some knowledge by working with international alliance partners.[47]

**The CEO and top management team power**  As will be discussed in Chapter 12, the board of directors is an important governance mechanism for monitoring a firm's strategic direction and for representing stakeholders' interests, especially those of shareholders.[48] In fact, higher performance normally is achieved when the board of directors is more directly involved in shaping a firm's strategic direction.[49]

Boards of directors, however, may find it difficult to direct the strategic actions of powerful CEOs and top management teams.[50] Often, a powerful CEO appoints a number of sympathetic outside members to the board or may have inside board members who are also on the top management team and report to her or him.[51] In either case, the CEO may significantly influence the board's actions. Thus, the amount of discretion a CEO has in making strategic decisions is related to the board of directors and how it chooses to oversee the actions of the CEO and the top management team.[52]

CEOs and top management team members can achieve power in other ways. A CEO who also holds the position of chairperson of the board usually has more power than the CEO who does not.[53] Some analysts and corporate "watchdogs" criticize the practice of CEO duality (when the CEO and the chairperson of the board are the same) because it can lead to poor performance and slow response to change.[54] Although it varies across industries, CEO duality occurs most commonly in larger firms. Increased shareholder activism, however, has brought CEO duality under scrutiny and attack in both US and European firms. In both the US and Europe more companies have split the function of the CEO and the chairman of the board. In 2000 almost half of the 2500 largest public companies had named its CEO chairman as well. Nowadays only 7.1 per cent of the European companies and only 16.5 per cent of the US companies applied a dual function for its CEO.[55] As will be discussed in Chapter 12, an independent board leadership structure in which the same person did not hold the positions of CEO and chair is commonly believed to enhance a board's ability to monitor top-level managers' decisions and actions, particularly with respect to financial performance.[56] On the other hand, if a CEO acts as a steward, holding the dual roles facilitates effective decisions and actions. In these instances, the increased effectiveness gained through CEO duality accrues from the individual who wants to perform effectively and desires to be the best possible steward of the firm's assets. Because of this person's positive orientation and actions, extra governance and the coordination costs resulting from an independent board leadership structure would be unnecessary.[57]

Top management team members and CEOs who have long tenure – on the team and in the organization – have a greater influence on board decisions. CEOs with greater influence may take actions in their own best interests, the outcomes of which increase their compensation from the company.[58] In Chapter 12, we will discuss that many people are angry about the excessive top executive compensation paid, especially during poor economic times when others are losing their jobs because of ineffective strategic decisions made by the same managers.

In general, long tenure is thought to constrain the breadth of an executive's knowledge base. Some evidence suggests that with the limited perspectives associated with a restricted knowledge base, long-tenured top executives typically develop fewer alternatives to evaluate in making strategic decisions.[59] However, long-tenured managers also may be able to exercise more effective strategic control, thereby obviating the need for board members' involvement because effective strategic control generally produces higher performance.[60] Intriguingly, recent findings suggest that "the liabilities of short tenure ... appear to exceed the advantages, while the advantages of long tenure – firm-specific human and social capital, knowledge, and power – seem to outweigh the disadvantages of rigidity and maintaining the status quo."[61] Overall then the relationship between CEO tenure and firm performance is complex, indicating that to strengthen the firm, boards of directors should develop an effective relationship with the top management team.

In summary, the relative degrees of power held by the board and top management team members should be examined in light of an individual firm's situation. For example, the abundance of resources in a firm's external environment and the volatility of that environment may affect the ideal balance of power between the board and the top management teams. Moreover, a volatile and uncertain environment may create a situation where a powerful CEO is needed to move quickly, but a diverse top management team may create less cohesion among team members and prevent or stall necessary strategic actions. With effective working relationships, boards, CEOs and other top management team members have the foundation required to select arrangements with the highest probability of best serving stakeholders' interests.[62]

# Managerial succession

The choice of top executives – especially CEOs – is a critical decision with important implications for the firm's performance.[63] Many companies use leadership screening systems to identify individuals with managerial and strategic leadership potential as well as to determine the criteria individuals should satisfy to be candidates for the CEO position.[64]

The most effective of these systems assess people within the firm and gain valuable information about the capabilities of other companies' managers, particularly their strategic leaders.[65] Titan cement is known for its elaborate leadership programmes. An important part of these programmes, next to the training of technological and leadership skills, is the development of behavioural skills as part of Titan Cement's strong value system.[66]

Organizations select managers and strategic leaders from two types of managerial labour markets – internal and external.[67] An internal managerial labour market consists of a firm's opportunities for managerial positions and the qualified employees within that firm. An external managerial labour market is the collection of managerial career opportunities and the qualified people who are external to the organization in which the opportunities exist.

Several benefits are thought to accrue to a firm when the internal labour market is used to select an insider as the new CEO. Because of their experience with the firm and the industry environment in which it competes, insiders are familiar with company products, markets, technologies and operating procedures. Internal hiring also produces lower turnover among existing personnel, many of whom possess valuable firm-specific knowledge. When the firm is performing well, internal succession is favoured to sustain high performance. It is assumed that hiring from inside keeps the important knowledge necessary to sustain performance.

The tendency of firms to select a CEO from insider candidates seems to be consistent for companies in Europe, Japan and the US. Over the last ten years, firms that appointed an insider to be the new CEO outperformed companies with outsider CEOs. Even though external candidates have broader perspective they can also create resistance to change within their new company. Consequently, it is more likely that external candidates may be forced out of the company in case of disappointing corporate performance. In general, CEO tenure increases by two years when insiders are selected for the executive job.[68]

Employees commonly prefer the internal managerial labour market when selecting top management team members and a new CEO. In the past, companies have also had a preference for insiders to fill top-level management positions because of a desire for continuity and a continuing commitment to the firm's current vision, mission and chosen strategies.[69] However, because of a changing competitive landscape and varying levels of performance, an increasing number of boards of directors are turning to outsiders to succeed CEOs. In rebuilding its management team, easyJet selected three outside candidates, CEO Carolyn McCall from Guardian Media Group, CFO Chris Kennedy from EMI and COO Dana Dunne from AOL in order to create a diversified perspective on how to lead the airline company.[70] Anders Moberg, the former CEO of IKEA, replaced Cees van der Hoeven as CEO of Ahold, a supermarket operator, after the company's accounting scandal in 2003. However, four years later the company announced that Moberg, who was hired as the person to give the company a positive turnaround, did not succeed and was subsequently let go.[71] A firm often has valid reasons to select an outsider as its new CEO. In some situations for example, long tenure with a firm may reduce strategic leaders' level of commitment to push

**Internal managerial labour market**

An internal managerial labour market consists of a firm's opportunities for managerial positions and the qualified employees within that firm.

**External managerial labour market**

An external managerial labour market is the collection of managerial career opportunities and the qualified people who are external to the organization in which the opportunities exist.

**FIGURE 11.3** Effects of CEO succession and top management team composition on strategy

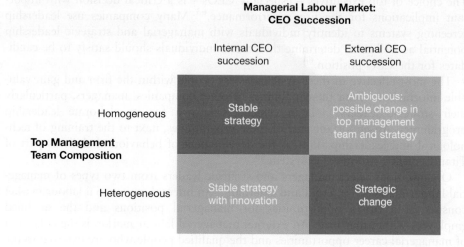

innovation throughout the firm. Given innovation's importance to firm success (see Chapter 14), this hesitation could be a liability for a strategic leader.

In Figure 11.3, we show how the composition of the top management team and the CEO succession (managerial labour market) interact to affect strategy. For example, when the top management team is homogeneous (its members have similar functional experiences and educational backgrounds) and a new CEO is selected from inside the firm, the firm's current strategy is unlikely to change. Alternatively, when a new CEO is selected from outside the firm and the top management team is heterogeneous, the probability is high that strategy will change. When the new CEO is from inside the firm and a heterogeneous top management team is in place, the strategy may not change, but innovation is likely to continue. An external CEO succession with a homogeneous team creates a more ambiguous situation. The selection of Sir Howard Stringer as CEO of Sony signalled major changes in that firm's future. He is not only an outsider but also a foreigner. He is making major changes in the hopes of turning around Sony's poor performance. His intent is to have Sony regain its traditional excellence in innovative products.[72]

Including talent from all parts of both the internal and external labour markets increases the likelihood that the firm will be able to form an effective top-management team. Evidence suggests that women are a qualified source of talent as strategic leaders that has been somewhat overlooked. In light of the success of a growing number of female executives, the foundation for change may be established. Trailblazers such as Catherine Elizabeth Hughes (the first African-American woman to head a firm that was publicly traded on a US stock exchange), Muriel Siebert (the first woman to purchase a seat on the New York Stock Exchange), and publisher Judith Regan made important contributions as strategic leaders. Recent years have produced several prominent female CEOs including Cynthia Carroll (Anglo American plc), Anne Lauvergeon (Areva), Nancy McKinstry (Wolters Kluwer), and Clara Furse (London Stock Exchange).

As noted earlier, managerial talent is critical to a firm's success and one area in which managerial talent is crucial is in the integration of an acquired firm into the acquiring business. In fact, the top management team of an acquired firm is integral to a successful integration process because they play a critical role in helping the

STRATEGIC FOCUS

gsk

GlaxoSmithKline

© imagebroker/Alamy

## GlaxoSmithKline's internal CEO succession model

GlaxoSmithKline, the world's second-largest pharmaceutical company, took a rigorous and controversial approach in selecting its new CEO. Three internal candidates, Chries Viehbacher, president of US pharmaceuticals, David Stout, president of global pharmaceutical operations and Andrew Witty, president of European pharmaceuticals competed publicly to become the new CEO. The "public horse race" organized by GSK implied the risk of fierce rivalry within the company, while Jean-Pierre Garnier, Glaxo's former CEO, argued that this process gave the company's board a full understanding of the candidates.

Dr Garnier supervised the year-long CEO-level projects, which were carried out by the candidates and the company's chairman, Sir Christopher Gent, who discussed the process with GSK's shareholders. Simultaneously, external consultants were hired to evaluate the candidates' leadership capabilities.

The candidates had to review the different functions of the company, including supply chain management, and marketing and sales, as a basis for competition. The company deducted 360-degree assessments although these were not found very helpful, as the basis

for comparison of the reviews was not clear. Additionally, a monitoring panel was installed consisting of 14 internal executives who had all worked directly with the candidates. Feedback from this panel was gathered by interviews called "450-degree analyses", which were consequently reported to Jean-Pierre Garner. The interviews had to conclude on the quality of decision making of the candidates, the suitability of their capabilities with the company's strategic needs, and their leadership qualities and characters. These interviews seemed an ideal method for data collection as they provided comparable information on the candidates.

The results complemented the findings from the year-long projects, enabling the company to select Andrew Witty as its top CEO candidate. Witty faces some tough challenges following his appointment. The company's shares have fallen as investors are not convinced that the company will grow its sales in the long term.

The selection process raised a lot of questions on the aftermath of the competition. How would the other two candidates react to Glaxo's final decision? How was Glaxo able to retain the "unsuccessful" candidates? Other companies such as Glaxo's main competitor Pfizer experienced similar difficulties when vice-chairman Karen Katen left the company after not getting the executive job. Although the two remaining contenders at Glaxo were offered a seat on the board and a substantial amount of shares in GSK, the two decided to leave the company.

**Sources:** Carey, D., Phelan, D. and Useem, M. (2009) "Picking the right insider for CEO succession", *Harvard Business Review*, 87(1), 24–26; Cave, A. (2010) "The man who keeps the GSK ball rolling", *The Daily Telegraph*, http://www.telegraph.co.uk, February 6; GlaxoSmithKline plc, (2007) "GlaxoSmithKline appoints Andrew Witty CEO designate", GlaxoSmithKline plc, http://www.gsk.com, October 8; Whalen, J. and Lublim, J. S. (2007) "An unusal race to become Glaxo's next CEO", *WallStreetJournal*, http://online.wsj.com, September 24; Hirschler, B. (2007) "New Glaxo CEO is in for the long haul", Reuters, http://www.reuters.com, October 8.

### Questions

**1** In looking for a new CEO, GlaxoSmithKline chose to focus on internal candidates. What were, at the outset, the potential benefits and detriments of this option?

**2** How do you think the "public horse race" aided the selection procedure for a new CEO?

**3** While the selection procedure yielded a new CEO, it also led to the departure of two top executives who didn't get the job. In hindsight, how does this reflect on GlaxoSmithKline's selection procedure?

change be implemented and accepted by the acquired firm's employees.[73] It is common for a major turnover among the top management team of acquired firms. Sometimes it occurs because the acquiring firm unwisely replaces them. In other cases, the managers depart voluntarily to seek other top management positions. Research shows that high turnover among the acquired firm's top managers often produces poor performance and perhaps even a failed acquisition.[74] Therefore, acquiring firms should work hard to avoid successions during the integration process and thereafter.

# Key strategic leadership actions

Certain actions characterize effective strategic leadership; we present the most important ones in Figure 11.4. Many of the actions interact with each other. For example, managing the firm's resources effectively includes developing human capital and contributes to establishing a strategic direction, fostering an effective culture, exploiting core competencies, using effective organizational control systems and establishing ethical practices. The most effective strategic leaders create viable options in making decisions regarding each of the key strategic leadership actions.[75]

## *Determining strategic direction*

**Determining the strategic direction**

Determining the strategic direction involves specifying the image and character the firm seeks to develop over time.

Determining the strategic direction involves specifying the image and character the firm seeks to develop over time.[76] The strategic direction is framed within the context of the conditions (i.e., opportunities and threats) strategic leaders expect their firm to face in roughly the next three to five years.

The ideal long-term strategic direction has two parts: a core ideology and an envisioned future. The core ideology motivates employees through the company's heritage, but the envisioned future encourages employees to stretch beyond their expectations of accomplishment and requires significant change and progress to be realized.[77] The envisioned future serves as a guide to many aspects of a firm's strategy implementation process, including motivation, leadership, employee empowerment and organizational design. The strategic direction could include such actions as entering new international markets and developing a set of new suppliers to add to the firm's value chain.[78]

**FIGURE 11.4** Exercise of effective strategic leadership

Most changes in strategic direction are difficult to design and implement; Olli-Pekka Kallasvuo faced a tough challenge as the successor of Jorma Ollila. At his appointment as Nokia's CEO, Kallasvuo was praised for his actions as COO of the company, although analysts questioned his strategic views. Ollila transformed Nokia from an average manufacturer of cables, tyres and rubber boots into a leading telecommunications company. Additionally, the competitive landscape has become more dynamic over the years putting pressure on Nokia's margins. Sustaining Nokia's dominant position was therefore an even more difficult task.[79]

A charismatic CEO may foster stakeholders' commitment to a new vision and strategic direction. Nonetheless, it is important not to lose sight of the organization's strengths when making changes required by a new strategic direction. Kallasvuo, for example, needed to use Nokia's strengths to ensure continued positive performance. In September 2010, he was replaced by the Canadian Stephen Elop. This first non-Finn to be named CEO of Nokia comes from Microsoft and has much experience in software which is of outmost importance for operating in the smart phone industry. The goal is to pursue the firm's short-term need to adjust to a new vision and strategic direction while maintaining its long-term survivability by effectively managing its portfolio of resources.

## Effectively managing the firm's resource portfolio

Effectively managing the firm's portfolio of resources may be the most important strategic leadership task. The firm's resources are categorized as financial capital, human capital, social capital and organizational capital (including organizational culture).[80]

Clearly, financial capital is critical to organizational success; strategic leaders understand this reality.[81] However, the most effective strategic leaders recognize the equivalent importance of managing each remaining type of resource as well as managing the integration of resources (e.g., using financial capital to provide training opportunities through which human capital is able to learn and maximize its performance). Most importantly, effective strategic leaders manage the firm's resource portfolio by organizing them into capabilities, structuring the firm to facilitate using those capabilities, and choosing strategies through which the capabilities are successfully leveraged to create value for customers.[82] Exploiting and maintaining core competencies and developing and retaining the firm's human and social capital are actions taken to reach these important objectives.

### Exploiting and maintaining core competencies
Examined in Chapters 1 and 3, core competencies are capabilities that serve as a source of competitive advantage for a firm over its rivals. Typically, core competencies relate to an organization's functional skills, such as manufacturing, finance, marketing, and research and development. Strategic leaders must verify that the firm's competencies are emphasized when implementing strategies. Intel, for example, has core competencies of competitive agility (an ability to act in a variety of competitively relevant ways) and competitive speed (an ability to act quickly when facing environmental and competitive pressures).[83] Capabilities are developed over time as firms learn from their actions and enhance their knowledge about specific actions needed. For example, through repeated interactions, some firms have formed a capability allowing them to fully understand customers' needs as they change.[84] Firms with capabilities in R&D that develop into core competencies are rewarded by the market because of the critical nature of innovation in many industries.[85]

In many large firms, and certainly in related diversified ones, core competencies are effectively exploited when they are developed and applied across different organizational units (see Chapter 7). For example, Richemont, the world's largest jewellery maker, purchased Net-A-Porter, an online fashion retailer. This step into e-commerce enabled Richemont to gain more insight into the online buying behaviour for luxury items. Richemont can use this competence to market the sales for its watches, jewellery and fashion. Additionally, Net-A-Porter's product offering can be enriched by Richemont's product portfolio.[86]

Firms must continuously develop and when appropriate, change their core competencies to outperform rivals. If they have a competence that provides an advantage but do not change it, competitors will eventually imitate that competence and reduce or eliminate the firm's competitive advantage. Additionally, firms must guard against the competence becoming a liability, thereby preventing change.

As we discuss next, human capital is critical to a firm's success. One reason it's so critical is that human capital is the resource through which core competencies are developed and used.

### Developing human capital and social capital
Human capital refers to the knowledge and skills of a firm's entire workforce. From the perspective of human capital, employees are viewed as a capital resource requiring continuous investment.[87]

Nestlé considers its people the most valuable asset of the company and at the centre of the company's success. The company uses different types of training programmes, development plans and international assignments as an investment in its human capital.[88]

Investments such as those being made at Nestlé are productive, in that much of the development of industry can be attributed to the effectiveness of its human capital. This fact suggests that "as the dynamics of competition accelerate, people are perhaps the only truly sustainable source of competitive advantage".[89] In all types of organizations – large and small, new and established – human capital's increasing importance suggests a significant role for the firm's human resource management activities.[90] As a support activity (see Chapter 3), human resource management practices facilitate people's efforts to successfully select and especially to use the firm's strategies.[91]

Effective training and development programmes increase the probability of individuals becoming successful strategic leaders.[92] These programmes are increasingly linked to firm success as knowledge becomes more integral to gaining and sustaining a competitive advantage.[93] Additionally, such programmes build knowledge and skills, inculcate a common set of core values and offer a systematic view of the organization, thus promoting the firm's vision and organizational cohesion. For example, Nestlé's development programme emphasizes its commitment to develop its employees' competencies through exposure to different countries and cultures, as well as different areas of its business.[94]

Effective training and development programmes also contribute positively to the firm's efforts to form core competencies.[95] Furthermore, they help strategic leaders improve skills that are critical to completing other tasks associated with effective strategic leadership, such as determining the firm's strategic direction, exploiting and maintaining the firm's core competencies and developing an organizational culture that supports ethical practices. Thus, building human capital is vital to the effective execution of strategic leadership. Indeed, some argue that the world's "best companies are realizing that no matter what business they're in, their real business is building leaders".[96]

Strategic leaders must acquire the skills necessary to help develop human capital in their areas of responsibility.[97] When human capital investments are successful, the result is a workforce capable of learning continuously. Continuous learning and leveraging the firm's expanding knowledge base are linked with strategic success.[98]

**Human capital**

Human capital refers to the knowledge and skills of a firm's entire workforce.

Learning also can preclude making errors. Strategic leaders tend to learn more from their failures than their successes because they sometimes make the wrong attributions for the successes.[99] For example, the effectiveness of certain approaches and knowledge can be context specific.[100] Thus, some "best practices' may not work well in all situations. We know that using teams to make decisions can be effective, but sometimes it is better for leaders to make decisions alone, especially when the decisions must be made and implemented quickly (e.g., in crisis situations).[101] Thus, effective strategic leaders recognize the importance of learning from success *and* from failure.

Learning and building knowledge are important for creating innovation in firms.[102] Innovation leads to competitive advantage. Overall, firms that create and maintain greater knowledge usually achieve and maintain competitive advantages. However, as noted with core competencies, strategic leaders must guard against allowing high levels of knowledge in one area to lead to myopia and overlooking knowledge development opportunities in other important areas of the business.[103]

When facing challenging conditions, firms sometimes decide to lay off some of their human capital. Strategic leaders must recognize that layoffs can result in a significant loss of the knowledge possessed by the firm's human capital. Research evidence shows that moderate-sized layoffs may improve firm performance, but large layoffs produce stronger performance downturns in firms because of the loss of human capital.[104] Although it is also not uncommon for restructuring firms to reduce their expenditures on or investments in training and development programmes, restructuring may actually be an important time to increase investments in these programmes. The reason for increased focus on training and development is that restructuring firms have less slack and cannot absorb as many errors; moreover, the employees who remain after layoffs may find themselves in positions without all the skills or knowledge they need to perform the required tasks effectively.

Viewing employees as a resource to be maximized rather than as a cost to be minimized facilitates successful implementation of a firm's strategies, as does the strategic leader's ability to approach layoffs in a manner that employees believe is fair and equitable.[105] A critical issue for employees is the fairness in the layoffs and in treatment in their jobs.[106]

Social capital involves relationships inside and outside the firm that help the firm accomplish tasks and create value for customers and shareholders.[107] Social capital is a critical asset for a firm. Inside the firm, employees and units must cooperate to get the work done. In multinational organizations, employees often must cooperate across country boundaries on activities such as R&D to achieve performance objectives (e.g., developing new products).[108]

External social capital is increasingly critical to firm success. The reason for this is that few if any companies have all of the resources they need to successfully compete against their rivals. Firms can use cooperative strategies such as strategic alliances (see Chapter 10) to develop social capital. Social capital can develop in strategic alliances as firms share complementary resources. However, resource sharing must be effectively managed to ensure that the partner trusts the firm and is willing to share the desired resources.[109]

Research evidence suggests that the success of many types of firms may partially depend on social capital. Large multinational firms often must establish alliances in order to enter new foreign markets. Likewise, entrepreneurial firms often must establish alliances to gain access to resources, venture capital, or other types of resources (e.g., special expertise that the entrepreneurial firm cannot afford to maintain in-house).[110] Retaining quality human capital and maintaining strong internal social capital can be strongly affected by the firm's culture.

**Social capital**

Social capital involves relationships inside and outside the firm that help the firm accomplish tasks and create value for customers and shareholders.

## Sustaining an effective organizational culture

In Chapter 1, we define organizational culture as a complex set of ideologies, symbols and core values that are shared throughout the firm and influence the way business is conducted. Evidence suggests that a firm can develop core competencies in terms of both the capabilities it possesses and the way the capabilities are leveraged when implementing strategies to produce desired outcomes. In other words, because the organizational culture influences how the firm conducts its business and helps regulate and control employees' behaviour, it can be a source of competitive advantage[111] and is a "critical factor in promoting innovation".[112] Given its importance, it may be that a vibrant organizational culture is the most valuable competitive differentiator for business organizations. Thus, shaping the context within which the firm formulates and implements its strategies – that is, shaping the organizational culture – is an essential strategic leadership action.[113]

**Entrepreneurial mindset** Especially in large organizations, an organizational culture often encourages (or discourages) strategic leaders from pursuing (or not pursuing) entrepreneurial opportunities.[114] This issue is important because entrepreneurial opportunities are a vital source of growth and innovation.[115] Therefore, a key role of strategic leaders is to encourage and promote innovation by pursuing entrepreneurial opportunities.[116]

One way to encourage innovation is to invest in opportunities as real options – that is, invest in an opportunity in order to provide the potential option of taking advantage of the opportunity at some point in the future.[117] For example, a firm might buy a piece of land to have the option to build on it at some time in the future should the company need more space and should that location increase in value to the company. Firms might enter strategic alliances for similar reasons. In this instance, a firm might form an alliance to have the option of acquiring the partner later or of building a stronger relationship with it (e.g., developing a joint new venture).[118]

In Chapter 14, we describe how large firms use strategic entrepreneurship to pursue entrepreneurial opportunities and to gain first-mover advantages. Small and medium-sized firms also rely on strategic entrepreneurship when trying to develop innovations as the foundation for profitable growth. In firms of all sizes, strategic entrepreneurship is more likely to be successful when employees have an entrepreneurial mindset.[119]

Five dimensions characterize a firm's entrepreneurial mindset: autonomy, innovativeness, risk taking, proactiveness and competitive aggressiveness.[120] In combination, these dimensions influence the actions a firm takes to be innovative and launch new ventures. In sum, strategic leaders with an entrepreneurial mindset are committed to pursuing profitable growth.[121]

*Autonomy*, the first of an entrepreneurial orientation's five dimensions, allows employees to take actions that are free of organizational constraints and permits individuals and groups to be self-directed. The second dimension, *innovativeness*, "reflects a firm's tendency to engage in and support new ideas, novelty, experimentation and creative processes that may result in new products, services, or technological processes'.[122] Cultures with a tendency toward innovativeness encourage employees to think beyond existing knowledge, technologies and parameters to find creative ways to add value. *Risk taking* reflects a willingness by employees and their firm to accept risks when pursuing entrepreneurial opportunities. Assuming significant levels of debt and allocating large amounts of other resources (e.g., people) to projects that may not be completed are examples of these risks. The fourth dimension of an entrepreneurial orientation, *proactiveness*, describes a

**STRATEGIC FOCUS**

© With kind permission from DSM

# Entrepreneurship at DSM helps deliver technological and management innovations

Dutch life science and material sciences company DSM exemplifies the entrepreneurial mindset needed to implement innovative changes. Faced with increasing competition – particularly from China – for its anti-infectives division, DSM undertook a series of changes spanning technology and management in order to retain its competitive edge. In the year 2000, it developed a radically new technique to produce the raw materials for antibiotics. This involved phasing out a resource-intensive chemical production process and implementing a much more efficient biotechnological process which required fewer resources and yielded lower volumes of waste and emissions. Having pioneered this key production process, in 2001 DSM organized its new anti-infectives plant in Delft to make the most of the possibilities afforded by the new technology. It was then that DSM began managing its Delft plant around self-managing teams, which had the autonomy and discretion to organize their work in the way they thought best. Members of these teams were forced to learn how to take charge of the different processes within the plant and to make important decisions based on their collective analysis of the situation. Gradually, process operators, technicians and maintenance operators began operating with a great degree of autonomy. The next step was to stimulate the exchange of knowledge and ideas for improvement of processes between the different constituencies. Besides technicians, both process and maintenance operators were explicitly invited to – and rewarded for – making suggestions for improvements. These could involve any aspect of the plant, be it a specific production process, or savings in other aspects such as energy consumption. In this way, operators proactively put forward propositions for improvements to the plant management, which implemented several of them.

Overall, the enhanced involvement of employees at DSM resulted in much more capable teams which, through their high involvement, contributed to a significant increase in productivity for the plant. To this day, DSM's anti-infectives plant in Delft is a very nimble organization, which actively seeks to harness its employees' intellect, and is ready to pursue innovative ideas in order to stay competitive in a very demanding environment. As a result, DSM's Dutch-based anti-infectives unit continues to be competitive and remains one of the very few producers of anti-infectives outside Asia.

**Sources:** DSM (2000) *DSM N.V. Annual Report 2000*; Gram, A., Treffenfeldt, W., Lange, U., McIntyre, T. and Wolf O. (eds.) (2001) *The Application of Biotechnology to Industrial Sustainability*, Paris: OECD; Manz, C. C. and Sims, H. P. (1987) "Leading workers to lead themselves: The external leadership of self-managing work teams", *Administrative Science Quarterly*, 32(1): 106–129; Vaccaro, I. G., Jansen, J. J. P., Van den Bosch, F. A. J. and Volberda, H. W. (2011) "Management innovation and leadership: The moderating role of organizational size", *Journal of Management Studies*, Forthcoming; Vacccaro, I. G. (2010) *Management Innovation*, Rotterdam: ERIM PhD Series in Research in Management.

## Questions

**1** How did DSM's use of its human capital affect its competitiveness?

**2** Besides a breakthrough technology, DSM introduced a new way of managing its plant. How did this affect its social capital?

**3** How, in your opinion, did the use of self-managed teams promote DSM's entrepreneurial mindset?

firm's ability to be a market leader rather than a follower. Proactive organizational cultures constantly use processes to anticipate future market needs and to satisfy them before competitors learn how to do so. Finally, *competitive aggressiveness* is a firm's propensity to take actions that allow it to consistently and substantially outperform its rivals.[123]

### Changing the organizational culture and restructuring

Changing a firm's organizational culture is more difficult than maintaining it; however, effective strategic leaders recognize when change is needed. Incremental changes to the firm's culture typically are used to implement strategies.[124] More significant and sometimes even radical changes to organizational culture support selecting strategies that differ from those the firm has implemented historically. Regardless of the reasons for change, shaping and reinforcing a new culture require effective communication and problem-solving, along with selecting the right people (those who have the values desired for the organization), engaging in effective performance appraisals (establishing goals and measuring individual performance toward goals that fit in with the new core values), and using appropriate reward systems (rewarding the desired behaviours that reflect the new core values).[125]

Evidence suggests that cultural changes succeed only when the firm's CEO, other key top management team members and middle-level managers actively support them.[126] To effect change, middle-level managers in particular need to be highly disciplined to energize the culture and foster alignment with the strategic vision.[127] In addition, managers must be sensitive to the effects of other major strategic changes on organizational culture. For example, major downsizings can have negative effects on an organization's culture, especially if it is not implemented in accordance with the dominant organizational values.[128]

## Emphasizing ethical practices

The effectiveness of processes used to implement the firm's strategies increases when they are based on ethical practices. Ethical companies encourage and enable people at all organizational levels to act ethically when doing what is necessary to implement strategies. In turn, ethical practices and the judgement on which they are based create "social capital" in the organization, increasing the "goodwill available to individuals and groups' in the organization.[129] Alternatively, when unethical practices evolve in an organization, they may become acceptable to many managers and employees.[130] One study found that in these circumstances, managers were particularly likely to engage in unethical practices to meet their goals when current efforts to meet them were insufficient.[131]

To properly influence employees' judgement and behaviour, ethical practices must shape the firm's decision-making process and must be an integral part of organizational culture. In fact, research evidence suggests that a value-based culture is the most effective means of ensuring that employees comply with the firm's ethical requirements.[132] As we will explain in Chapter 12, managers may act opportunistically, making decisions that are in their own best interests but not in the firm's best interests when facing lax expectations regarding ethical behaviour. In other words, managers acting opportunistically take advantage of their positions, making decisions that benefit themselves to the detriment of the firm's stakeholders.[133] But strategic leaders are most likely to integrate ethical values into their decisions when the company has explicit ethics codes, the code is integrated into the business through extensive ethics training and shareholders expect ethical behaviour.[134]

Firms should employ ethical strategic leaders – leaders who include ethical practices as part of their strategic direction for the firm, who desire to do the right thing, and for whom honesty, trust and integrity are important.[135] Strategic leaders who consistently display these qualities inspire employees as they work with others to develop and support an organizational culture in which ethical practices are the expected behavioural norms.[136] Strategic leaders can take several actions to develop an ethical organizational culture. Examples of these actions include (1) establishing and communicating specific goals to describe the firm's ethical standards (e.g., developing and disseminating a code of conduct); (2) continuously revising and updating the code of conduct, based on inputs from people throughout the firm and from other stakeholders (e.g., customers and suppliers); (3) disseminating the code of conduct to all stakeholders to inform them of the firm's ethical standards and practices; (4) developing and implementing methods and procedures to use in achieving the firm's ethical standards (e.g., using internal auditing practices that are consistent with the standards); (5) creating and using explicit reward systems that recognize acts of courage (e.g., rewarding those who use proper channels and procedures to report observed wrongdoings); and (6) creating a work environment in which all people are treated with dignity.[137] The effectiveness of these actions increases when they are taken simultaneously and thereby are mutually supportive. When strategic leaders and others throughout the firm fail to take actions such as these – perhaps because an ethical culture has not been created – problems are likely to occur. As we discuss next, formal organizational controls can help prevent further problems and reinforce better ethical practices.[138]

## Establishing balanced organizational controls

Organizational controls are basic to a capitalistic system and have long been viewed as an important part of strategy implementation processes.[139] Controls are necessary to help ensure that firms achieve their desired outcomes.[140] Defined as the "formal, information-based ... procedures used by managers to maintain or alter patterns in organizational activities", controls help strategic leaders build credibility, demonstrate the value of strategies to the firm's stakeholders, and promote and support strategic change.[141] Most critically, controls provide the parameters for implementing strategies as well as the corrective actions to be taken when implementation-related adjustments are required.

In this chapter, we focus on two organizational controls – strategic and financial – that will be discussed further in Chapter 13. Our discussion of organizational controls here emphasizes strategic and financial controls because strategic leaders, especially those at the top of the organization, are responsible for their development and effective use.

As we will explain in Chapter 13, financial control focuses on short-term financial outcomes. In contrast, strategic control focuses on the *content* of strategic actions rather than their *outcomes*. Some strategic actions can be correct but still result in poor financial outcomes because of external conditions such as a recession in the economy, unexpected domestic or foreign government actions, or natural disasters. Therefore, emphasizing financial controls often produces more short-term and risk-averse managerial decisions, because financial outcomes may be caused by events beyond managers' direct control. Alternatively, strategic control encourages lower-level managers to make decisions that incorporate moderate and acceptable levels of risk because outcomes are shared between the business-level executives making strategic proposals and the corporate-level executives evaluating them.

The challenge strategic leaders face is to verify that their firm is emphasizing financial and strategic controls so that firm performance improves. The balanced scorecard is a tool that helps strategic leaders assess the effectiveness of the controls.

**The balanced scorecard**  The balanced scorecard is a framework firms can use to verify that they have established both strategic and financial controls to assess their performance.[142] This technique is most appropriate for use when dealing with business-level strategies; however, it can also be used with the other strategies firms may choose to implement (e.g., corporate level, international and cooperative).

The underlying premise of the balanced scorecard is that firms jeopardize their future performance possibilities when financial controls are emphasized at the expense of strategic controls,[143] in that financial controls provide feedback about outcomes achieved from past actions, but do not communicate the drivers of future performance.[144] Thus, an overemphasis on financial controls has the potential to promote managerial behaviour that sacrifices the firm's long-term, value-creating potential for short-term performance gains.[145] An appropriate balance of strategic controls and financial controls, rather than an overemphasis on either, allows firms to effectively monitor their performance.

Four perspectives are integrated to form the balanced scorecard framework: *financial* (concerned with growth, profitability and risk from the shareholders' perspective), *customer* (concerned with the amount of value customers perceive as created by the firm's products), *internal business processes* (with a focus on the priorities for various business processes that create customer and shareholder satisfaction), and *learning and growth* (concerned with the firm's effort to create a climate that supports change, innovation and growth). Thus, using the balanced scorecard framework allows the firm to understand how it looks to shareholders (financial perspective), how customers view it (customer perspective), the processes it must emphasize to successfully use its competitive advantage (internal perspective), and what it can do to improve its performance in order to grow (learning and growth perspective).[146] Generally speaking, strategic controls tend to be emphasized when the firm assesses its performance relative to the learning and growth perspective, whereas financial controls are emphasized when assessing performance in terms of the financial perspective.

Firms use different criteria to measure their standing relative to the scorecard's four perspectives. We show sample criteria in Figure 11.5. The firm should select the number of criteria that will allow it to have both a strategic understanding and a financial understanding of its performance without becoming immersed in too many details.[147] For example, we know from research that a firm's innovation, quality of its goods and services, growth of its sales and its profitability are all interrelated.[148]

Strategic leaders play an important role in determining a proper balance between strategic controls and financial controls, whether they are in single-business firms or large diversified firms. A proper balance between controls is important, in that "wealth creation for organizations where strategic leadership is exercised is possible because these leaders make appropriate investments for future viability [through strategic control], while maintaining an appropriate level of financial stability in the present [through financial control]".[149] In fact, most corporate restructuring is designed to refocus the firm on its core businesses, thereby allowing top executives to re-establish strategic control of their separate business units.[150]

Successfully using strategic control is frequently integrated with appropriate autonomy for the various subunits so that they can gain a competitive advantage in their respective markets.[151] Strategic control can be used to promote the sharing of both tangible and intangible resources among interdependent businesses within a firm's portfolio. In addition, the autonomy provided allows the flexibility necessary

**FIGURE 11.5** Strategic controls and financial controls in a balanced scorecard framework

| Perspectives | Criteria |
|---|---|
| Financial | • Cash flow<br>• Return on equity<br>• Return on assets |
| Customer | • Assessment of ability to anticipate customers' needs<br>• Effectiveness of customer service practices<br>• Percentage of repeat business<br>• Quality of communications with customers |
| Internal Business Processes | • Asset utilization improvements<br>• Improvements in employee morale<br>• Changes in turnover rates |
| Learning and Growth | • Improvements in innovation ability<br>• Number of new products compared to competitors<br>• Increases in employees' skills |

to take advantage of specific marketplace opportunities. As a result, strategic leadership promotes simultaneous use of strategic control and autonomy.[152]

The balanced scorecard is being used by car manufacturer Porsche. After this manufacturer of sought-after sports cars regained its market-leader position, it implemented a balanced scorecard approach in an effort to maintain this position. In particular, Porsche used the balanced scorecard to promote learning and continuously improve the business. For example, knowledge was collected from all Porsche dealerships throughout the world. The instrument used to collect the information was referred to as "Porsche Key Performance Indicators'. The fact that Porsche is now the world's most profitable automaker suggests the value the firm gained and is gaining by using the balanced scorecard as a foundation for simultaneously emphasizing strategic and financial controls.[153]

As we have explained, strategic leaders are critical to a firm's ability to successfully use all parts of the strategic management process. The new CEO for Gucci Group, Robert Polet, has the strategic leadership skills to position him and his company for future success as described in the Closing Case. Certainly, the future for such strategic leaders as Polet is likely to be challenging. He transformed Gucci Group into a successful company that is increasing its market share and likely to grow in international markets where he now has significant experience and knowledge. Thus, with people like Robert Polet at the helm of companies, the work of strategic leaders will remain exciting and has a strong possibility of creating positive outcomes for all of a firm's stakeholders.

© sebastian-julian

## KEY DEBATE

# Leading for innovation

As companies seek to remain competitive in increasingly dynamic environments, innovation has remained on top of the corporate agenda. Scholars have long studied technological innovation as well as its relationship with leadership. However, an emergent dialogue in the management literature proposes that another type of hitherto under-researched innovation, may be essential in unlocking an organization's potential to achieve above-average returns.

Management innovation, that is the introduction of changes to an organization's practices, processes or structures, relates to the work of management and how it is performed, rather than the output of a production process. What's more, as opposed to technological innovation, management innovation typically emerges without a dedicated infrastructure (such as a research lab) and is relatively abstract and intangible. The implications for organizational performance, however, can be as powerful as any other type of innovation. Notable examples include Toyota's Lean Manufacturing and Procter & Gamble's introduction of Brand Management.

How, then, can organizations stimulate an entrepreneurial mindset that fosters experimentation and eventually changes in management practices, processes or structures? Many factors could arguably play a role: the type of industry, its competitive dynamics or the size of the organization. However, the specific actions of key individuals within the organization, such as the CEO, emerge as a key potential determinant in the pursuit of management innovation. Strategic leaders can engage in both transactional and transformational leadership behaviours to engage their followers. Transformational leadership behaviour fosters a sense of identification with the organization's goals and contributes to the development of a trusting relationship between leaders and followers in which

challenging the status quo is encouraged. Transactional leadership behaviour may aid the implementation of management innovation by clearly defining rules and rewarding behaviour associated with new practices, processes or structures. These seemingly opposing leadership behaviours may coexist within the organization's top management and be replicated throughout the organization.

**Sources:** Avolio, B. J., Bass, B. M. and Jung, D. I. (1999) "Re-examining the components of transformational and transactional leadership using the multifactor leadership questionnaire", *Journal of Occupational & Organizational Psychology*, 72(4): 441–462; Birkinshaw, J. (2010) *Reinventing Management: Smarter Choices for Getting Work Done*, Cornwall: John Wiley & Sons; Birkinshaw, J., Hamel, G. and Mol, M. J. (2008) "Management innovation", *Academy of Management Review*, 33(4): 825–845; Elenkov, D. S., Judge, W. and Wright, P. (2005) "Strategic leadership and executive innovation influence: An international multi-cluster comparative study", *Strategic Management Journal*, 26(7): 665–682; Hamel, G. (2006) "The why, what, and how of management innovation", *Harvard Business Review*, 84(2): 72–84; Mol, M. and Birkinshaw, J. (2008) *Giant Steps in Management: Innovations That Change the Way We Work*, Dorchester: FT/Prentice Hall; Mol, M. J. and Birkinshaw, J. (2006) "Against the flow: Reaping the rewards of management innovation", *European Business Forum* (27): 24–29; Vera, D. and Crossan, M. (2004) "Strategic leadership and organizational learning", *Academy of Management Review*, 29(2): 222–240; Vaccaro, I. G., Jansen, J. J. P., Van den Bosch, F. A. J. and Volberda, H. W. (2011) "Management innovation and leadership: The moderating role of organizational size", *Journal of Management Studies*, forthcoming.

## Questions

**1** What do you think is the role of strategic leaders in fostering management innovation within organizations?

**2** Do you think that promoting management innovation will be different to promoting technological innovation within an organization? How so?

**3** What sort of leadership behaviour do you think is more conducive to management innovation?

**4** Since management innovation is typically abstract and intangible, how would you go about measuring its impact on organizational performance?

© Picture Partners/Alamy

**CLOSING CASE**

# Robert Polet, the ice cream man who made Gucci hot again

July 2004: PPR's announcement gave the fashion industry another reason for scepticism. After acquiring Gucci Group earlier that year, spending €8bn, PPR, a luxury goods conglomerate owned by the French Pinault Family, did not renew the contracts of Gucci's star designer Tom Ford and the Italian CEO, Domenico De Sole, who had saved Gucci from bankruptcy. One month later the Pinaults introduced Robert Polet as Domenico De Sole's successor. PPR stock dropped. How could Polet, who used to be the head of the ice cream and frozen foods division at Unilever, be appointed as the new director of a fashion institute?

Robert Polet, who worked at Unilever for 26 years, was not the flamboyant type of CEO that Gucci had previously appointed, but he did know how to turn things around as president of his division, as he increased the unit's operation margin from only 3 per cent to 15 per cent. At Unilever, Polet was known as a pragmatic manager always encouraging people to advance. Unilever put him in charge of its Malaysian activities when Polet was only 35 years old. The difficult situation in which he started made him into the manager he was when a headhunter from Russell Reynolds approached him for the function at Gucci. When looking for a new CEO, PPR instructed the headhunter to look for someone with international experience and a strong track record of managing a multi-brand operation.

After his appointment, Robert Polet introduced some major changes at the company giving each brand serving under Gucci Group more autonomy. Gucci's eight brands, including jewellery brand Boucheron and haute couture brand Yves Saint Laurent, were losing money at the time Polet stepped into the company. All brand groups installed a creative and a financial director in order to make them more commercially viable and all support functions, such as IT and human resources were transferred to the head office in London. All employees were encouraged to break the status quo and think out of the box. For instance, in improving Boucheron's performance, Polet gave Jean-Christophe Bdos, the brand's executive, the assignment to "fix Boucheron" within three years. The brands were now fully responsible for their profits as well as their products.

Robert Polet's hands-off management style worked: in 2007 Gucci's sales increased by 30 per cent, all brands were profitable except for YSL, whose losses have been cut by more than 60 per cent, and Gucci was elected as the strongest fashion brand by Nielsen Company. *Fortune* even elected Robert Polet as Europe's Business Man of the Year in 2007. Although Gucci's corporate results increased and its operating income has doubled the company was not as profitable as its largest competitor, LVMH.

Two years later, Gucci was ready to face the global economic downturn as the company focused on its speed, flexibility and its innovative capacity, while constantly adapting to its customers' needs. According to Robert Polet it is essential for Gucci's management to show leadership, confidence and calmness in this economic climate. People will constantly look to the executive team for clues about the state of business. Furthermore, the economic crisis gives Gucci the opportunity to review its long-term goals and brand positioning while short-term adaptations are implemented to sustain its performance. The company's head office was moved from London to Cadempino, Switzerland. The main reason for this move was that the new Swiss location is closer to Gucci's key markets, France and Italy. Some supportive functions have been kept at the UK location. Each of the eight brands has set its own strategy varying from narrowing down the brands collection to the introduction of cheaper products.

The Internet presence of Gucci's brands has increased as a result of Polet imposing tough discipline on the brand's budgets. Additionally, Gucci has to improve its position in Asia. After the success of luxury brands in Japan, China seems to be the next big thing. In 2009 43.3 per cent Gucci's sales already came from the Asian continent. Sales in Asia, excluding Japan, increased from 17.7 per cent in 2001 to 27.8 per cent in 2009. Gucci's brands Boucheron and Yves Saint Laurent have a limited presence in China. Nevertheless, Gucci aims to spend 60 per cent of its investments on expanding in Asia in 2010. Mexico, Brazil and Chile, Latin America's emerging markets, are also being considered as targets for expansion. However, many challenges have to be faced as the company needs to adapt to new target markets in the coming period.

**Sources:** Gumbel. P. (2008) "Gucci Group: The ice cream man cometh", *Fortune*, http://money.cnn.com/fortune, January 9; Thomson Reuters (2008) "Polet, Gucci Group galvanizer, wins *Fortune* award", *Reuters*, http://www.reuters.com, January 9; Kouters, S. (2008) "Ik ben vrolijk geboren", *VKBanen*, http://www.vkbanen.nl, April 22; Mattack, C. (2009) "For the downturn Gucci downplays the logos", *BusinessWeek*, http://www.businessweek.com, October 15; Polet, R. (2009) "Making employee engagement fashionable", *BusinessWeek*, http://www.businessweek.com, April 24; Spanier, G. (2010) "Blow to London as Gucci bosses quit for Switzerland", *London Evening Standard,* http://www.thisislondon.co.uk, June 8; Daneshkhu, S. (2010) "Gucci eyes Asia as shoppers opt for discreet consumption", *Financial Times*, http://www.ft.com. March 6.

## Questions

**1** How can you explain the appointment of an outsider as the CEO of Gucci with no experience in the fashion industry?

**2** How do you think the appointment of Robert Polet affects the implementation of far-reaching changes to the company strategy and structure?

**3** How did Gucci's new CEO stimulate the company's entrepreneurial mindset?

**4** What attributes of transformational and transactional leadership did Robert Polet display at Gucci?

**5** How can Gucci sustain the organizational culture that has served it in achieving sustained growth during Robert Polet's tenure?

**6** In making a push into the Asian market, what sort of human and social capital will Gucci need to develop in order to be successful?

## SUMMARY

- Effective strategic leadership is a prerequisite to successfully using the strategic management process. Strategic leadership is the ability to anticipate events, envision possibilities, maintain flexibility and empower others to create strategic change.

- Top-level managers are an important resource for firms to develop and exploit competitive advantages. In addition, when they and their work are valuable, rare, imperfectly imitable, and non-substitutable, strategic leaders are also a source of competitive advantage.

- The top management team is composed of key managers who play a critical role in selecting and implementing the firm's strategies. Generally, they are officers of the corporation and/or members of the board of directors.

- The top management team's characteristics, a firm's strategies and its performance are all interrelated. For example, a top management team with significant marketing and R&D knowledge positively contributes to the firm's use of a growth strategy. Overall, having diverse skills increases most top management teams' effectiveness and innovation potential.

- Typically, performance improves when the board of directors is involved in shaping a firm's strategic direction. However, when the CEO has a great deal of power, the board may be less involved in decisions about strategy formulation and implementation. By appointing people to the board and simultaneously serving as CEO and chair of the board, CEOs increase their power.

- In managerial succession, strategic leaders are selected from either the internal or the external managerial labour market. Because of their effect on firm performance, selection of strategic leaders has implications for a firm's effectiveness. Companies use a variety of reasons for selecting the firm's strategic leaders either internally or externally. In most instances, the internal market is used to select the CEO; but the number of outsiders chosen is increasing. Outsiders are often selected to initiate major changes in strategy.

- Effective strategic leadership has five major components: determining the firm's strategic direction, effectively managing the firm's resource portfolio (including exploiting and maintaining core competencies and managing human capital and social capital), sustaining an effective organizational culture, emphasizing ethical practices and establishing balanced organizational controls.

- Strategic leaders must develop the firm's strategic direction. The strategic direction specifies the image and character the firm wants to develop over time. To form the strategic direction, strategic leaders evaluate the conditions (e.g., opportunities and threats in the external environment) they expect their firm to face over the next three to five years.

- Strategic leaders must ensure that their firm exploits its core competencies, which are used to produce and deliver products that create value for customers, when implementing its strategies. In related diversified and large firms in particular, core competencies are exploited by sharing them across units and products.

- The ability to manage the firm's resource portfolio and manage the processes used to effectively implement the firm's strategy are critical elements of strategic leadership. Managing the resource portfolio includes integrating resources to create capabilities and leveraging those capabilities through strategies to build competitive advantages. Human capital and social capital are perhaps the most important resources.

- As a part of managing the firm's resources, strategic leaders must develop a firm's human capital. Effective strategic leaders view human capital as a resource to be maximized – not as a cost to be minimized. Such leaders develop and use programmes designed to train current and future strategic leaders to build the skills needed to nurture the rest of the firm's human capital.

- Effective strategic leaders also build and maintain internal and external social capital. Internal social capital promotes cooperation and coordination within and across units in the firm. External social capital provides access to resources the firm needs to compete effectively.

- Shaping the firm's culture is a central task of effective strategic leadership. An appropriate organizational culture encourages the development of an entrepreneurial orientation among employees and an ability to change the culture as necessary.

- In ethical organizations, employees are encouraged to exercise ethical judgement and to act ethically at all times. Improved ethical practices foster social capital. Setting specific goals that reflect the firm's ethical standards, using a code of conduct, rewarding ethical behaviours and creating a work environment where all people are treated with dignity, facilitates and supports ethical behaviour.

- Developing and using balanced organizational controls is the final component of effective strategic leadership. The balanced scorecard is a tool that measures the effectiveness of the firm's strategic and financial controls. An effective balance between strategic and financial controls allows for flexible use of core competencies, but within the parameters of the firm's financial position.

## REVIEW QUESTIONS

1  What is strategic leadership? In what ways are top executives considered important resources for an organization?

2  What is a top management team, and how does it affect a firm's performance and its abilities to innovate and design and implement effective strategic changes? Why is its composition relevant?

3  How do the internal and external managerial labour markets affect the managerial succession process? What are the possible implications for organizational change and innovation of hiring a CEO from either labour market?

4  How can different leadership behaviours affect the firm's strategic actions?

5  How do strategic leaders effectively manage their firm's resource portfolio to exploit its core competencies and leverage the human capital and social capital to achieve a competitive advantage?

6  What is organizational culture? How can it be used to achieve above-average returns?

7  As a strategic leader, what actions could you take to establish and emphasize ethical practices in your firm?

8  What are organizational controls? Why are strategic controls and financial controls important aspects of the strategic management process?

## DISCUSSION QUESTIONS

1  Search for instances of CEOs as strategic leaders leading organizations through changes in, for instance, strategic focus, markets, structures, products, etc.

   a  How would you characterize their leadership behaviour?

   b  What was the role of the top management team in the implementation of such changes?

   c  What sort of human and social capital was required to implement these changes?

2  Companies routinely bring new top talent into their organizations to fill positions in senior management and occasionally the CEO position. Discuss examples of companies which have done so tapping into internal and external labour markets and consider:

   a  How successful were they?

   b  Were there differences in the level of entre-preneurship between organizations promoting their own employees to senior positions and those hiring from outside?

   c  Was the organizational culture affected? If so, how?

3  In this chapter we have said that, increasingly, human capital is a resource to maximize, rather than a cost to minimize. Seek examples of human capital development in company websites, business publications and media, and consider:

   a  What skills do companies develop in their employees? Are these skills the same across organizational levels?

   b  How do training and development programmes relate to the organization's core competencies?

   c  Having considered these examples, can you explain how human capital development relates to firm performance?

## FURTHER READING

The challenging work of leaders ultimately involves, to a large extent, tapping into its employees' abilities, talent and intellectual capital in order to meet demands and overcome challenges from competing firms. In *Reinventing Management* (Jossey-Bass/Wiley, 2010), Julian Birkinshaw explores the idea of *management models* as the choices made by leaders that define how work gets done within the firm. This involves not only new ways of making decisions, but also coordinating activities, defining objectives and motivating employees.

## EXPERIENTIAL EXERCISES

### Exercise 1: Executive succession

For this exercise, you will identify and analyse a case of CEO succession. Working in small groups, find a publicly-held firm that has changed CEOs. The turnover event must have happened at least twelve months ago, but no more than twenty-four months ago. Use a combination of company documents and news articles to answer the following questions:

1   Why did the CEO leave? Common reasons for CEO turnover include death or illness, retirement, accepting a new position, change in ownership or control, or termination. In cases of termination, there is often no official statement as to why the CEO departed. Consequently, you may have to rely on news articles that speculate why a CEO was fired, or forced to resign.

2   Did the replacement CEO come from inside the organization, or outside?

3   What are the similarities and differences between the new CEO and the CEO she or he replaced? Possible comparison items could include functional experience, industry experience, etc. If your library has a subscription to *Hoovers Online*, you can find information on top managers through this resource.

4   At the time of the succession event, how did the firm's financial performance compare to industry norms? Has the firm's standing relative to the industry changed since the new CEO took over?

5   Has the firm made major strategic changes since the succession event? For example, has the firm made major acquisitions or divestitures since the succession event? Launched or closed down product lines?

Create a PowerPoint presentation that presents answers to each of the above questions. Your presentation should be brief, consisting of no more than five to seven slides.

### Exercise 2: Strategic leadership is tough!!

Your textbook defines strategic leadership as "the ability to anticipate, envision, maintain flexibility and empower others ..." Accordingly, this exercise combines the practical elements of leadership in an experiential exercise. You are asked to replicate leaders and followers in the attainment of a defined goal.

The class is divided into teams of three to five individuals who are organized in teams throughout the classroom. Next each team chooses a leader and by that decision who will be the followers. It is important to choose wisely. The classroom instructor will then assign the task to be completed.

Students should be prepared to debrief the assignment when completed. Your instructor will guide this discussion.

## VIDEO CASE

### Leaders are made, not born
www.cengage.co.uk/volberda/students/video_cases
Sanjiv Ahuja, Chairman, Orange, UK

Sanjiv Ahuja, Chairman of Orange, UK, talks about leadership and in particular those who believe they have the desire and capability to be a leader and if this is a born trait or an acquired one. Much of what he talks about is having the right attitude.

Be prepared to discuss the following concepts and questions in class:

- Concepts
- Leadership traits
- Effectively managing your personal resource portfolio
- Entrepreneurial mindset

### Questions

1　Do you believe that one's propensity to become a leader is an acquired skill or that the ability to be a leader is something that individuals are born with?

2　How well do you know yourself? Think through a top five list of your personal strengths and weaknesses.

3　Once you have identified personal strengths and weaknesses, think through an action plan to either leverage your strengths or work on weaknesses.

## NOTES

1. A. Mackey, 2008, "The effect of CEOs on firm performance", *Strategic Management Journal*, 29: 1357–1367.
2. E. F. Goldman, 2007, "Strategic thinking at the top", *MIT Sloan Management Review*, 48(4): 75–81.
3. L. Bassi and D. McMurrer, 2007, "Maximizing your return on people", *Harvard Business Review*, 85(3): 115–123; R. D. Ireland and M. A. Hitt, 2005, "Achieving and maintaining strategic competitiveness in the 21st century: The role of strategic leadership", *Academy of Management Executive*, 19: 63–77.
4. J. P. Kotter, 2007, "Leading change: Why transformation efforts fail", *Harvard Business Review*, 85(1): 96–103.
5. M. A. Hitt, C. Miller and A. Collella, 2009, *Organizational Behaviour: A Strategic Approach*, 2nd edition, New York: John Wiley and Sons; M. A. Hitt and R. D. Ireland, 2002, "The essence of strategic leadership: Managing human and social capital", *Journal of Leadership and Organizational Studies*, 9: 3–14.
6. D. A. Ready and J. A. Conger, 2007, "Make your company a talent factory", *Harvard Business Review*, 85(6): 69–77.
7. D. Roberts and C. C. Tschang, 2007, "China's rising leaders", *BusinessWeek*, October 1, 33–35.
8. P. A. Gloor and S. M. Cooper, 2007, "The new principles of a swarm business", *MIT Sloan Management Review*, 48(3): 81–85; A. S. DeNisi, M. A. Hitt and S. E. Jackson, 2003, "The knowledge-based approach to sustainable competitive advantage", in: S. E. Jackson, M. A. Hitt and A. S. DeNisi (eds.), *Managing Knowledge for Sustained Competitive Advantage*, San Francisco: Jossey-Bass, 3–33.
9. L. Bossidy, 2007, "What your leader expects of you: And what you should expect in return", *Harvard Business Review*, 85(4): 58–65; J. E. Post, L. E. Preston and S. Sachs, 2002, "Managing the extended enterprise: The new stakeholder view", *California Management Review*, 45(1): 6–28.
10. A. McKee and D. Massimilian, 2007, "Resonant leadership: A new kind of leadership for the digital age", *Journal of Business Strategy*, 27(5): 45–49.
11. E. Baraldi, R. Brennan, D. Harrison, A. Tunisini and J. Zolkiewski, 2007, "Strategic thinking and the IMP approach: A comparative analysis", *Industrial Marketing Management*, 36: 879–894; C. L. Shook, R. L. Priem and J. E. McGee, 2003, "Venture creation and the enterprising individual: A review and synthesis", *Journal of Management*, 29: 379–399.
12. M. L. McDonald, P. Khanna and J. D. Westphal, 2008, "Getting them to think outside the circle: Corporate governance, CEOs' external advice networks and firm performance", *Academy of Management Journal*, 51: 453–475.
13. R. A. Burgleman and A. S. Grove, 2007, "Let chaos reign, then rein in chaos – repeatedly: Managing strategic dynamics for corporate longevity", *Strategic Management Journal*, 28: 965–979.
14. T. R. Holcomb, R. M. Holmes and B. L. Connelly, 2009, "Making the most of what you have: Managerial ability as a source of resource value creation", *Strategic Management Journal*, 30: 457–485.
15. B. M. Bass and R. E. Riggio, 2006, *Transformational Leadership*, Mahwah, NJ: Lawrence Earlbaum Associates.

16. B. M. Bass and B. J. Avolio, 1993, "Transformational leadership and organizational culture", *Public Administration Quarterly*, 17 (1): 112–121.

17. D. S. Elenkov, W. Judge and P. Wright, 2005, "Strategic leadership and executive innovation influence: An international multi-cluster comparative study", *Strategic Management Journal*, 26(7): 665–682; D. S. Elenkov and I. M. Manev, 2005, "Top management leadership and influence on innovation: The role of sociocultural context", *Journal of Management*, 31(3): 381–402; F. O. Walumbwa, C. Wu and B. Orwa, 2008, "Contingent reward transactional leadership, work attitudes, and organizational citizenship behaviour: The role of procedural justice climate perceptions and strength", *Leadership Quarterly*, 19(3): 251–265.

18. D. Vera and M. Crossan, 2004, "Strategic leadership and organizational learning", *Academy of Management Review*, 29(2): 222–240.

19. A. E. Colbert, A. L. Kristof-Brown, B. H. Bradley and M. R. Barrick, 2008, "CEO transformational leadership: The role of goal importance congruence in top management teams", *Academy of Management Journal*, 51: 81–96; S. Borener, S. A. Eisenbeliss and D. Griesser, 2007, "Follower behaviour and organizational performance: The impact of transformational leaders", *Journal of Leadership & Organizational Studies*, 13(3): 15–26.

20. D. Goleman, 2004, "What makes a leader?", *Harvard Business Review*, 82(1): 82–91.

21. Y. Ling, Z. Simsek, M. H. Lubatkin and J. F. Veiga, "Transformational leadership's role in promoting corporate entrepreneurship: Examining the CEO-TMT interface", *Academy of Management Journal*, 51: 557–576.

22. J. L. Morrow, Jr., D. G. Sirmon, M. A. Hitt and T. R. Holcomb, 2007, "Creating value in the face of declining performance: Firm strategies and organizational recovery", *Strategic Management Journal*, 28: 271–283; R. Castanias and C. Helfat, 2001, "The managerial rents model: Theory and empirical analysis", *Journal of Management*, 27: 661–678.

23. H. G. Barkema and O. Shvyrkov, 2007, "Does top management team diversity promote or hamper foreign expansion?", *Strategic Management Journal*, 28: 663–680; M. Beer and R. Eisenstat, 2000, "The silent killers of strategy implementation and learning", *Sloan Management Review*, 41(4): 29–40.

24. V. Santos and T. Garcia, 2007, "The complexity of the organizational renewal decision: The management role", *Leadership & Organization Development Journal*, 28: 336–355; M. Wright, R. E. Hoskisson, L. W. Busenitz and J. Dial, 2000, "Entrepreneurial growth through privatization: The upside of management buyouts", *Academy of Management Review*, 25: 591–601.

25. D. G. Sirmon, J. L. Arregle, M. A. Hitt and J. W. Webb, 2008, "The role of family influence in firms' strategic responses to threat of imitation", *Entrepreneurship Theory and Practice*, 32: 979–998; Y. L. Doz and M. Kosonen, 2007, "The new deal at the top", *Harvard Business Review*, 85(6): 98–104.

26. A. S. Tsui, Z. X. Zhang, H. Wang, K. R. Xin and J. B. Wu, 2006, "Unpacking the relationship between CEO leadership behaviour and organizational culture", *The Leadership Quarterly*, 17: 113–137; J. A. Petrick and J. F. Quinn, 2001, "The challenge of leadership accountability for integrity capacity as a strategic asset", *Journal of Business Ethics*, 34: 331–343.

27. D. G. Sirmon, S. Gove and M. A. Hitt, 2008, "Resource management in dyadic competitive rivalry: The effects of resource bundling and deployment", *Academy of Management Journal*, 51: 918–935; R. Martin, 2007, "How successful leaders think", *Harvard Business Review*, 85(6): 60–67.

28. M. L. A. Hayward, V. P. Rindova and T. G. Pollock, 2004, "Believing one's own press: The causes and consequences of CEO celebrity", *Strategic Management Journal*, 25: 637–653.

29. K. M. Hmieleski and R. A. Baron, 2008, "When does entrepreneurial self-efficacy enhance versus reduce firm performance?", *Strategic Entrepreneurship Journal*, 2: 57–72; N. J. Hiller and D. C. Hambrick, 2005, "Conceptualizing executive hubris: The role of (hyper-) core self-evaluations in strategic decision making", *Strategic Management Journal*, 26: 297–319.

30. A. M. L. Raes, U. Glunk, M. G. Heijltjes and R. A. Roe, 2007, "Top management team and middle managers", *Small Group Research*, 38: 360–386; I. Goll, R. Sambharya and L. Tucci, 2001, "Top management team composition, corporate ideology, and firm performance", *Management International Review*, 41(2): 109–129.

31. J. Bunderson, 2003, "Team member functional background and involvement in management teams: Direct effects and the moderating role of power and centralization", *Academy of Management Journal*, 46: 458–474; L. Markoczy, 2001, "Consensus formation during strategic change", *Strategic Management Journal*, 22: 1013–1031.

32. C. Pegels, Y. Song and B. Yang, 2000, "Management heterogeneity, competitive interaction groups, and firm performance", *Strategic Management Journal*, 21: 911–923.

33. R. Rico, E. Molleman, M. Sanchez-Manzanares and G. S. Van der Vegt, 2007, "The effects of diversity faultlines and team task autonomy on decision quality and social integration", *Journal of Management*, 33: 111–132.

34. A. Srivastava, K. M. Bartol and E. A. Locke, 2006, "Empowering leadership in management teams: Effects on knowledge sharing, efficacy, and performance", *Academy of Management Journal*, 49: 1239–1251; D. Knight, C. L. Pearce, K. G. Smith, J. D. Olian, H. P. Sims, K. A. Smith and P. Flood, 1999, "Top management team diversity, group process, and strategic consensus', *Strategic Management Journal*, 20: 446–465.

35. A. S. Alexiev, J. J. P. Jansen, F. A. J. Van den Bosch and H. W. Volberda, 2010, "Top management team advice

seeking and exploratory innovation: the moderating role of TMT heterogeneity", *Journal of Management Studies*, 47: 1343–1364; B. J. Olson, S. Parayitam and Y. Bao, 2007," Strategic decision making: The effects of cognitive diversity, conflict, and trust on decision outcomes", *Journal of Management*, 33: 196–222; T. Simons, L. H. Pelled and K. A. Smith, 1999, "Making use of difference, diversity, debate, and decision comprehensiveness in top management teams", *Academy of Management Journal*, 42: 662–673.

36. S. Finkelstein, D. C. Hambrick and A. A. Cannella, Jr, 2008, *Strategic Leadership: Top Executives and Their Effects on Organizations*, New York: Oxford University Press.

37. J. J. Marcel, 2009, "Why top management team characteristics matter when employing a chief operating officer: A strategic contingency perspective", *Strategic Management Journal*, 30: 647–658; S. Barsade, A. Ward, J. Turner and J. Sonnenfeld, 2000, "To your heart's content: A model of affective diversity in top management teams", *Administrative Science Quarterly*, 45: 802–836.

38. B. J. Avolio and S. S. Kahai, 2002, "Adding the 'e' to e-leadership: How it may impact your leadership", *Organizational Dynamics*, 31: 325–338.

39. Z. Simsek, J. F. Veiga, M. L. Lubatkin and R. H. Dino, 2005, "Modeling the multilevel determinants of top management team behavioural integration", *Academy of Management Journal*, 48: 69–84.

40. A. A. Cannella, J. H. Park and H. U. Lee, 2008, "Top management team functional background diversity and firm performance: Examining the roles of team member collocation and environmental uncertainty", *Academy of Management Journal*, 51: 768–784.

41. M. Jensen and E. J. Zajac, 2004, "Corporate elites and corporate strategy: How demographic preferences and structural position shape the scope of the firm", *Strategic Management Journal*, 25: 507–524.

42. R. Yokota and H. Mitsuhashi, "Attributive change in top management teams as a driver of strategic change", *Asia Pacific Journal of Management* , 25: 297–315; W. B. Werther, 2003, "Strategic change and leader-follower alignment", *Organizational Dynamics*, 32: 32–45.

43. H. Li and J. Li, 2009, "Top management team conflict and entrepreneurial strategy making in China", *Asia Pacific Journal of Management*, 26: 263–283; S. C. Parker, 2009, "Can cognitive biases explain venture team homophily?", *Strategic Entrepreneurship Journal*, 3: 67–83.

44. Y. Zhang and N. Rajagopalan, 2003, "Explaining the new CEO origin: Firm versus industry antecedents", *Academy of Management Journal*, 46: 327–338.

45. T. Dvir, D. Eden, B. J. Avolio and B. Shamir, 2002, "Impact of transformational leadership on follower development and performance: A field experiment", *Academy of Management Journal*, 45: 735–744.

46. J. P. Muczyk and D. T. Holt, 2008, "Toward a cultural contingency model of leadership", Journal of *Leadership and Organizational Studies*, 14: 277–286.

47. C. Bouquet, A. Morrison and J. Birkinshaw, 2009, "International attention and multinational enterprise performance", *Journal of International Business Studies*, 40: 108–131; H. U. Lee and J. H. Park, 2008, "The influence of top management team international exposure on international alliance formation", *Journal of Management Studies*, 45: 961–981.

48. C. Thomas, D. Kidd and C. Fernandez-Araoz, 2007, "Are you under-utilizing your board?", *MIT Sloan Management Review*, 48(2): 71–76.

49. F. Adjaoud, D. Zeghal and S. Andaleeb, 2007, "The effect of board's quality on performance: A study of Canadian firms", *Corporate Governance: An International Review*, 15: 623–635; L. Tihanyi, R. A. Johnson, R. E. Hoskisson and M. A. Hitt, 2003, "Institutional ownership and international diversification: The effects of boards of directors and technological opportunity", *Academy of Management Journal*, 46: 195–211.

50. B. R. Golden and E. J. Zajac, 2001, "When will boards influence strategy? Inclination times power equals strategic change", *Strategic Management Journal*, 22: 1087–1111.

51. M. Carpenter and J. Westphal, 2001, "Strategic context of external network ties: Examining the impact of director appointments on board involvement in strategic decision making", *Academy of Management Journal*, 44: 639–660.

52. M. A. Rutherford and A. K. Buchholtz, 2007, "Investigating the relationship between board characteristics and board information", *Corporate Governance: An International Review*, 15: 576–584.

53. X. Huafang and Y. Jianguo, 2007, "Ownership structure, board composition and corporate voluntary disclosure: Evidence from listed companies in China", *Managerial Auditing Journal*, 22: 604–619.

54. J. Coles, N. Sen and V. McWilliams, 2001, "An examination of the relationship of governance mechanisms to performance", *Journal of Management*, 27: 23–50; J. Coles and W. Hesterly, 2000, "Independence of the chairman and board composition: Firm choices and shareholder value", *Journal of Management*, 26: 195–214.

55. K. Favaro, P. O. Karlsson and G. L. Neilson, 2010, "CEO succession 2000–2009: A decade of convergence and compression", *Strategy+business*, 59, May 25, 76–91, http://www.strategy-business.com.

56. C. M. Daily and D. R. Dalton, 1995, "CEO and director turnover in failing firms: An illusion of change?", *Strategic Management Journal*, 16: 393–400.

57. D. Miller, I. LeBreton-Miller and B. Scholnick, 2008, "Stewardship vs stagnation: An empirical comparison of small family and non-family businesses", *Journal of Management Studies*, 51: 51–78; J. H. Davis, F. D. Schoorman and L. Donaldson, 1997, "Toward a stewardship theory of management", *Academy of Management Review*, 22: 20–47.

58. P. Kalyta, 2009, "Compensation transparency and managerial opportunism: A study of supplemental retirement plans", *Strategic Management Journal*, 30: 405–423; J. G. Combs and M. S. Skill, 2003,

"Managerialist and human capital explanations for key executive pay premiums: A contingency perspective", *Academy of Management Journal*, 46: 63–73.

59. E. Matta and P. W. Beamish, 2008, "The accentuated CEO career horizon problem: Evidence from international acquisitions", *Strategic Management Journal*, 29: 683–700; N. Rajagopalan and D. Datta, 1996, "CEO characteristics: Does industry matter?", *Academy of Management Journal*, 39: 197–215.

60. R. A. Johnson, R. E. Hoskisson and M. A. Hitt, 1993, "Board involvement in restructuring: The effect of board versus managerial controls and characteristics", *Strategic Management Journal*, 14 (Special Issue): 33–50.

61. Z. Simsek, 2007, "CEO tenure and organizational performance: An intervening model", *Strategic Management Journal*, 28: 653–662.

62. M. Schneider, 2002, "A stakeholder model of organizational leadership", *Organization Science*, 13: 209–220.

63. M. Sorcher and J. Brant, 2002, "Are you picking the right leaders?", *Harvard Business Review*, 80(2): 78–85; D. A. Waldman, G. G. Ramirez, R. J. House and P. Puranam, 2001, "Does leadership matter? CEO leadership attributes and profitability under conditions of perceived environmental uncertainty", *Academy of Management Journal*, 44: 134–143.

64. J. Werdigier, 2007, "UBS not willing to talk about departure of chief", *New York Times Online*, http://www.nytimes.com, July 7.

65. W. Shen and A. A. Cannella, 2002, "Revisiting the performance consequences of CEO succession: The impacts of successor type, postsuccession senior executive turnover, and departing CEO tenure", *Academy of Management Journal*, 45: 717–734.

66. B. Kowitt and K. Thai, 2009, "World's best companies for leaders, *Fortune*, 160(10), http://money.cnn.com, November 19."

67. G. A. Ballinger and F. D. Schoorman, 2007, "Individual reactions to leadership succession in workgroups", *Academy of Management Review*, 32: 116–136; R. E. Hoskisson, D. Yiu and H. Kim, 2000, "Capital and labor market congruence and corporate governance: Effects on corporate innovation and global competitiveness", in: S. S. Cohen and G. Boyd (eds.), *Corporate Governance and Globalization*, Northampton, MA: Edward Elgar, 129–154.

68. K. Favaro, P. O. Karlsson and G. L. Neilson, 2010, "CEO succession 2000–2009: A decade of convergence and compression", *Strategy+business*, 59, May 25, 76–91, http://www.strategy-business.com.

69. W. Shen and A. A. Cannella, 2003, "Will succession planning increase shareholder wealth? Evidence from investor reactions to relay CEO successions", *Strategic Management Journal*, 24: 191–198.

70. P. Sandle and G. Prodhan, 2010. "EasyJet picks Carolyn McCall as new CEO", *Reuters*, http://www.reuters.com, March 24.

71. I. Bickerton, 2007, "Moberg to step down as Ahold chief, *Financial Times*, http://www.ft.com, April 27.

72. Y. Tanokura, 2009, "Special interview: Sony chairman, CEO Howard Stringer", *Nikkei Electronics Asia*, http://www.techon.nikkeibp.co.jp, May 26.

73. T. Kiessling, M. Harvey and J. T. Heames, 2008, "Operational changes to the acquired firm's top management team and subsequent organizational performance", *Journal of Leadership and Organizational Studies*, 14: 287–302.

74. J. A. Krug and W. Shill, 2008, "The big exit: Executive churn in the wake of M&As", *Journal of Business Strategy*, 29(4): 15–21.

75. J. O"Toole and E. E. Lawler, Jr, 2006, "The choices managers make – or don"t make", *The Conference Board*, September/October, 24–29.

76. S. Nadkarni and P. S. Barr, 2008, "Environmental context, managerial cognition, and strategic action: An integrated view", *Strategic Management Journal*, 29: 1395–1427; M. A. Hitt, B. W. Keats and E. Yucel, 2003, "Strategic leadership in global business organizations", in: W. H. Mobley and P. W. Dorfman (eds.), *Advances in Global Leadership*, Oxford, UK: Elsevier Science, Ltd., 9–35.

77. I. M. Levin, 2000, "Vision revisited", *Journal of Applied Behavioural Science*, 36: 91–107.

78. E. Verwaal, H. Commandeur and W. Verbeke, 2009, "Value creation and value claiming in strategic outsourcing decisions: A resource contingency perspective", *Journal of Management*, 35: 420–444; S. R. Miller, D. E. Thomas, L. Eden and M. Hitt, 2008, "Knee deep in the big muddy: The survival of emerging market firms in developed markets", *Management International Review*, 48: 645–666.

79. Reinhardt, A., 2005. "Can Nokia read the signals?", *BusinessWeek*, http://www.businessweek.com, August 2.

80. J. Barney and A. M. Arikan, 2001, "The resource-based view: Origins and implications", in: M. A. Hitt, R. E. Freeman and J. S. Harrison (eds.), *Handbook of Strategic Management*, Oxford, UK: Blackwell Publishers, 124–188.

81. E. T. Prince, 2005, "The fiscal behaviour of CEOs", *Managerial Economics*, 46(3): 23–26.

82. T. R. Holcomb, R. M. Holmes and B. L. Connelly, 2009, "Making the most of what you have" *Strategic Management Journal*, 30: 457–485; D. G. Sirmon, S. Gove and M. A. Hitt, 2008, "Resource management in dyadic competitive rivalry", *Academy of Management Review*, 51:919–935.

83. R. A. Burgelman, 2001, *Strategy Is Destiny: How Strategy-Making Shapes a Company's Future*, New York: The Free Press.

84. D. J. Ketchen, Jr., G. T. M. Hult and S. F. Slater, 2007, "Toward greater understanding of market orientation and the resource-based view", *Strategic Management Journal*, 28: 961–964; S. K. Ethiraj, P. Kale, M. S. Krishnan and J. V. Singh, 2005, "Where do capabilities come from and how do they matter? A study in the software services industry", *Strategic Management Journal*, 26: 25–45.

85. S. K. Ethiraj, 2007, "Allocation of inventive effort in complex product systems", *Strategic Management Journal*, 28: 563–584; S. Dutta, O. Narasimhan and S. Rajiv, 2005, "Conceptualizing and measuring capabilities: Methodology and empirical application", *Strategic Management Journal*, 26: 277–285.

86. T. Mulier and A. Roberts, 2010, "Richemont buys Net-a-Porter, online fashion retailer (update4)", *BusinessWeek*, http://www.businessweek.com, April 1.

87. M. Larson and F. Luthans, 2006, "Potential added value of psychological capital in predicting work attitudes", *Journal of Leadership & Organizational Studies*, 13: 45–62; N. W. Hatch and J. H. Dyer, 2004, "Human capital and learning as a source of sustainable competitive advantage", *Strategic Management Journal*, 25: 1155–1178.

88. Nestlé SA, 2010, Nestlé careers – welcome, http://careers.nestle.com/, June.

89. M. A. Hitt, L. Bierman, K. Uhlenbruck and K. Shimizu, 2006, "The importance of resources in the internationalization of professional service firms: The good, the bad and the ugly", *Academy of Management Journal*, 49: 1137–1157; M. A. Hitt, L. Bierman, K. Shimizu and R. Kochhar, 2001, "Direct and moderating effects of human capital on strategy and performance in professional service firms: A resource-based perspective", *Academy of Management Journal*, 44: 13–28.

90. S. E. Jackson, M. A. Hitt and A. S. DeNisi (eds.), 2003, *Managing Knowledge for Sustained Competitive Advantage: Designing Strategies for Effective Human Resource Management*, Oxford, UK: Elsevier Science Ltd.

91. B. E. Becker and M. A. Huselid, 2007, "Strategic human resources management: Where do we go from here?", *Journal of Management*, 32: 898–925.

92. R. E. Ployhart, 2007, "Staffing in the 21st century: New challenges and strategic opportunities", *Journal of Management*, 32: 868–897.

93. R. A. Noe, J. A. Colquitt, M. J. Simmering and S. A. Alvarez, 2003, "Knowledge management: Developing intellectual and social capital", in: S. E. Jackson, M. A. Hitt and A. S. DeNisi (eds.), 2003, *Managing Knowledge for Sustained Competitive Advantage: Designing Strategies for Effective Human Resource Management*, Oxford, UK: Elsevier Science Ltd, 209–242.

94. Nestle Careers – Career development, http://www.careers.nestle.com/Career+Development.htm

95. G. P. Hollenbeck and M. W. McCall Jr. 2003, "Competence, not competencies: Making a global executive development work", in: W. H. Mobley and P. W. Dorfman (eds.), *Advances in Global Leadership*, Oxford, UK: Elsevier Science, Ltd, 101–119; J. Sandberg, 2000, "Understanding human competence at work: An interpretative approach", *Academy of Management Journal*, 43: 9–25.

96. G. Colvin, 2007, "Leader machines", *Fortune*, October 1, 100–106.

97. Y. Liu, J. G. Combs, D. A. Ketchen, Jr and R. D. Ireland, 2007, "The value of human resource management for organizational performance", *Business Horizons*, 50, 503–511.

98. T. R. Holcomb, R. D. Ireland, R. M. Holmes and M. A. Hitt, 2009, "Architecture of entrepreneurial learning: Exploring the link among heuristics, knowledge and action", *Entrepreneurship, Theory & Practice*, 33: 173–198; J. S. Bunderson and K. M. Sutcliffe, 2003, "Management team learning orientation and business unit performance", *Journal of Applied Psychology*, 88: 552–560.

99. R. J. Thomas, 2009, "The leadership lessons of crucible experiences", *Journal of Business Strategy*, 30(1): 21–26; J. D. Bragger, D. A. Hantula, D. Bragger, J. Kirnan and E. Kutcher, 2003, "When success breeds failure: History, hysteresis, and delayed exit decisions", *Journal of Applied Psychology*, 88: 6–14.

100. M. R. Haas and M. T. Hansen, 2005, "When using knowledge can hurt performance: The value of organizational capabilities in a management consulting company", *Strategic Management Journal*, 26: 1–24; G. Ahuja and R. Katila, 2004, "Where do resources come from? The role of idiosyncratic situations", *Strategic Management Journal*, 25: 887–907.

101. M. A. Hitt, C. C. Miller and A. Colella, 2005, *Organizational Behaviour*, New York: Wiley.

102. A. Carmeli and B. Azeroual, 2009, "How relational capital and knowledge combination capability enhance the performance of work units in a high technology industry", *Strategic Entrepreneurship Journal*, 3: 85–103; J. W. Spencer, 2003, "Firms' knowledge-sharing strategies in the global innovation system: Empirical evidence from the flat-panel display industry", *Strategic Management Journal*, 24: 217–233.

103. K. D. Miller, 2002, "Knowledge inventories and managerial myopia", *Strategic Management Journal*, 23: 689–706.

104. R. D. Nixon, M. A. Hitt, H. Lee and E. Jeong, 2004, "Market reactions to corporate announcements of downsizing actions and implementation strategies", *Strategic Management Journal*, 25: 1121–1129.

105. R. D. Nixon, M. A. Hitt, H. U. Lee and E. Jeong, (2004) "Market reactions to corporate announcements of down-sizing actions", *Strategic Management Journal*, 25: 1121–1129.

106. T. Simons and Q. Roberson, 2003, "Why managers should care about fairness: The effects of aggregate justice perceptions on organizational outcomes", *Journal of Applied Psychology*, 88: 432–443; M. L. Ambrose and R. Cropanzano, 2003, "A longitudinal analysis of organizational fairness: An examination of reactions to tenure and promotion decisions", *Journal of Applied Psychology*, 88: 266–275.

107. C. L. Luk, O. H. M. Yau, L. Y. M. Sin, A. C. B. Tse, R. P. M. Chow and J. S. Y. Lee, 2008, "The effects of social capital and organizational innovativeness in different institutional contexts", *Journal of International Business Studies*, 39: 589–612; P. S. Adler and S. W. Kwon, 2002, "Social

capital: Prospects for a new concept", *Academy of Management Review*, 27: 17–40.

108. J. J. Li, L. Poppo and K. Z. Zhou, 2008, "Do managerial ties in China always produce value? Competition, uncertainty, and domestic vs foreign firms", *Strategic Management Journal*, 29: 383–400; S. Gao, K. Xu and J. Yang, 2008, "Managerial ties, Absorptive capacity and innovation", *Asia Pacific Journal of Management*, 25: 395–412.

109. P. Ozcan and K. M. Eisenhardt, 2009, "Origin of alliance portfolios: Entrepreneurs, network strategies, and firm performance", *Academy of Management Journal*, 52: 246–279; W. H. Hoffmann, 2007, "Strategies for managing a portfolio of alliances", *Strategic Management Journal*, 28: 827–856.

110. H. E. Aldrich and P. H. Kim 2007, "Small worlds, infinite possibilities? How social networks affect entrepreneurial team formation and search", *Strategic Entrepreneurship Journal*, 1: 147–165; P. Davidsson and B. Honig, 2003, "The role of social and human capital among nascent entrepreneurs", *Journal of Business Venturing*, 18: 301–331.

111. C. M. Fiol, 1991, "Managing culture as a competitive resource: An identity-based view of sustainable competitive advantage", *Journal of Management*, 17: 191–211; J. B. Barney, 1986, "Organizational culture: Can it be a source of sustained competitive advantage?", *Academy of Management Review*, 11: 656–665.

112. 2006, "Connecting the dots between innovation and leadership", *Knowledge@Wharton*, http://www.knowledge.wharton.upenn.edu, October 4.

113. V. Govindarajan and A. K. Gupta, 2001, "Building an effective global business team", *Sloan Management Review*, 42(4): 63–71; S. Ghoshal and C. A. Bartlett, 1994, "Linking organizational context and managerial action: The dimensions of quality of management", *Strategic Management Journal*, 15: 91–112.

114. R. D. Ireland, J. G. Covin and D. F. Kuratko, 2008, "Conceptualizing corporate entrepreneurship strategy", *Entrepreneurship Theory and Practice*, 33: 19–46; D. F. Kuratko, R. D. Ireland and J. S. Hornsby, 2001, "Improving firm performance through entrepreneurial actions: Acordia's corporate entrepreneurship strategy", *Academy of Management Executive*, 15(4): 60–71.

115. J. H. Dyer, H. B. Gregersen and C. Christensen, 2008, "Entrepreneur behaviours, opportunity recognition and the origins of innovative ventures", *Strategic Entrepreneurship Journal*, 2: 317–338; R. D. Ireland and J. W. Webb, 2007, "Strategic entrepreneurship: Creating competitive advantage through streams of innovation", *Business Horizons*, 50: 49–59.

116. S. A. Alvarez and J. B. Barney, 2008, "Opportunities, organizations and entrepreneurship", *Strategic Entrepreneurship Journal*, 2: 171–174; D. S. Elenkov, W. Judge and P. Wright, 2005, "Strategic leadership and executive innovation influence: An international multi-cluster comparative study", *Strategic Management Journal*, 26: 665–682.

117. R. E. Hoskisson, M. A. Hitt, R. D. Ireland and J. S. Harrison, 2008, *Competing for Advantage* (2nd edition), Mason, OH: Thomson Publishing; R. G. McGrath, W. J. Ferrier and A. L. Mendelow, 2004, "Real options as engines of choice and heterogeneity", *Academy of Management Review*, 29: 86–101.

118. Y. Luo, 2008, "Structuring interorganizational cooperation: The role of economic integration in strategic alliances", *Strategic Management Journal*, 29: 617–637; R. S. Vassolo, J. Anand and T. B. Folta, 2004, "Non-additivity in portfolios of exploration activities: A real options analysis of equity alliances in biotechnology", *Strategic Management Journal*, 25: 1045–1061.

119. P. G. Kein, 2008, "Opportunity discovery, entrepreneurial action and economic organization", *Strategic Entrepreneurship Journal*, 2: 175–190; R. D. Ireland, M. A. Hitt and D. Sirmon, 2003, "A model of strategic entrepreneurship: The construct and its dimensions", *Journal of Management*, 29: 963–989.

120. G. T. Lumpkin and G. G. Dess, 1996, "Clarifying the entrepreneurial orientation construct and linking it to performance", *Academy of Management Review*, 21: 135–172; R. G. McGrath and I. MacMillan, 2000, *The Entrepreneurial Mindset*, Boston, MA: Harvard Business School Press.

121. C. Heath and D. Heath, 2007, "Leadership is a muscle", *Fast Company*, July/August, 62–63.

122. G. T. Lumpkin and G. G. Dess, 1996, "Clarifying the entrepreneurial orientation construct and linking it to performance", *Academy of Management Review*, 21: 142.

123. G. T. Lumpkin and G. G. Dess, 1996, "Clarifying the entrepreneurial orientation construct and linking it to performance", *Academy of Management Review*, 21: 137.

124. D. D. Bergh, R. A. Johnson and R. Dewitt, 2008, "Restructuring through spinoff or sell-off: Transforming information asymmetries into financial gain", *Strategic Management Journal*, 29: 133–148; P. Pyoria, 2007, "Informal organizational culture: The foundation of knowledge workers' performance", *Journal of Knowledge Management*, 11(3): 16–30.

125. M. Kuenzi and M. Schminke, 2009, "Assembling fragments into a lens: A review, critique, and proposed research agenda for the organizational work climate literature", *Journal of Management*, 35: 634–717; C. M. Christensen and S. D. Anthony, 2007, "Put investors in their place", *BusinessWeek*, May 28, 10.

126. D. D. Bergh and E. N. K. Lim, 2008, "Learning how to restructure: Absorptive capacity and improvisational views of restructuring actions and performance", *Strategic Management Journal*, 29: 593–616; J. S. Hornsby, D. F. Kuratko and S. A. Zahra, 2002, "Middle managers' perception of the internal environment for corporate entrepreneurship: Assessing a measurement scale", *Journal of Business Venturing*, 17: 253–273.

127. D. F Kuratko, R. D. Ireland, J. G. Covin and J. S. Hornsby, 2005, "A model of middle-level managers' entrepreneurial behaviour", *Entrepreneurship Theory and Practice*, 29: 699–716.

128. E. G. Love and M. Kraatz, 2009, "Character, conformity, or the bottom line? How and why downsizing affected corporate reputation", *Academy of Management Journal*, 52: 314–335; H. W. Volberda, 1998, *Building the flexible firm: How to remain competitive*, Oxford: Oxford University Press.

129. P. S. Adler and S. W. Kwon, 2002, "Social Capital: Prospects for a New Concept", *Academy of Management Review*, 27: 17–40.

130. J. Pinto, C. R. Leana and F. K. Pil, 2008, "Corrupt organizations or organizations of corrupt individuals? Two types of organization-level corruption", *Academy of Management Review*, 33: 685–709.

131. M. E. Scheitzer, L. Ordonez and M. Hoegl, 2004, "Goal setting as a motivator of unethical behaviour", *Academy of Management Journal*, 47: 422–432.

132. D. C. Kayes, D. Stirling and T. M. Nielsen, 2007, "Building organizational integrity", *Business Horizons*, 50: 61–70; L. K. Trevino, G. R. Weaver, D. G. Toffler and B. Ley, 1999, "Managing ethics and legal compliance: What works and what hurts", *California Management Review*, 41(2): 131–151.

133. X. Zhang, K. M. Bartol, K. G. Smith, M. D. Pfaffer and D. M. Khanin, 2008, "CEOs on the edge: Earnings manipulation and stock-based incentive misalignment", *Academy of Management Journal*, 51: 241–258; M. A. Hitt and J. D. Collins, 2007, "Business ethics, strategic decision making, and firm performance", *Business Horizons*, 50: 353–357.

134. J. M. Stevens, H. K. Steensma, D. A. Harrison and P. L. Cochran, 2005, "Symbolic or substantive document? Influence of ethics codes on financial executives' decisions", *Strategic Management Journal*, 26: 181–195.

135. Y. Zhang and M. F. Wiersema, 2009, "Stock market reaction to CEO certification: The signaling role of CEO background", *Strategic Management Journal*, 30: 693–710; C. Driscoll and M. McKee, 2007, "Restorying a culture of ethical and spiritual values: A role for leader storytelling", *Journal of Business Ethics*, 73: 205–217.

136. C. Caldwell and L. A. Hayes, 2007, "Leadership, trustworthiness, and the mediating lens", *Journal of Management Development*, 26: 261–281.

137. B. E. Ashforth, D. A. Gioia, S. L. Robinson and L. K. Trevino, 2008, "Re-viewing organizational corruption", *Academy of Management Review*, 33: 670–684; M. Schminke, A. Arnaud and M. Kuenzi, 2007, "The power of ethical work climates", *Organizational Dynamics*, 36: 171–186; L. B. Ncube and M. H. Wasburn, 2006, "Strategic collaboration for ethical leadership: A mentoring framework for business and organizational decision making", *Journal of Leadership & Organizational Studies*, 13: 77–92.

138. J. Welch and S. Welch, 2007, "Flying solo: A reality check", *BusinessWeek*, June 4, 116.

139. A. Weibel, 2007, "Formal control and trustworthiness", *Group & Organization Management*, 32: 500–517; G. Redding, 2002, "The capitalistic business system of China and its rationale", *Asia Pacific Journal of Management*, 19: 221–249.

140. B. D. Rostker, R. S. Leonard, O. Younassi, M. V. Arena and J. Riposo, 2009, "Cost controls: How the government can get more bag for its buck", *Rand Review*, http://www.rand.org/publications/randreview/issues/spring2009; A. C. Costa, 2007, "Trust and control interrelations", *Group & Organization Management*, 32: 392–406.

141. M. D. Shields, F. J. Deng and Y. Kato, 2000, "The design and effects of control systems: Tests of direct- and indirect-effects models", *Accounting, Organizations and Society*, 25: 185–202.

142. R. S. Kaplan and D. P. Norton, 2009, "The balanced scorecard: Measures that drive performance" (HBR OnPoint Enhanced Edition), *Harvard Business Review*, March; R. S. Kaplan and D. P. Norton, 2001, "The strategy-focused organization", *Strategy and Leadership*, 29(3): 41–42; R. S. Kaplan and D. P. Norton, 2000, *The Strategy-Focused Organization: How Balanced Scorecard Companies Thrive in the New Business Environment*, Boston, MA: Harvard Business School Press.

143. B. E. Becker, M. A. Huselid and D. Ulrich, 2001, *The HR Scorecard: Linking People, Strategy, and Performance*, Boston: Harvard Business School Press, 21.

144. R. S. Kaplan and D. P. Norton, 2001, "The strategy-focused organization", *Strategy and Leadership*, 29(3): 41–42.

145. R. S. Kaplan and D. P. Norton, 2001, "Transforming the balanced scorecard from performance measurement to strategic management: Part I", *Accounting Horizons*, 15(1): 87–104.

146. R. S. Kaplan and D. P. Norton, 1992," The balanced scorecard – measures that drive performance", *Harvard Business Review*, 70(1): 71–79.

147. M. A. Mische, 2001, *Strategic Renewal: Becoming a High-Performance Organization*, Upper Saddle River, NJ: Prentice Hall, 181.

148. H. J. Cho and V. Pucik, 2005, "Relationship between innovativeness, quality, growth, profitability and market value", *Strategic Management Journal*, 26: 555–575.

149. G. Rowe, 2001, "Creating wealth in organizations: The role of strategic leadership", *Academy of Management Executive*, 15(1): 81–94.

150. R. E. Hoskisson, R. A. Johnson, D. Yiu and W. P. Wan, 2001, "Restructuring strategies of diversified business groups: Differences associated with country institutional environments", in: M. A. Hitt, R. E. Freeman and J. S. Harrison (eds.), *Handbook of Strategic Management*, Oxford, UK: Blackwell Publishers, 433–463.

151. J. Birkinshaw and N. Hood, 2001, "Unleash innovation in foreign subsidiaries", *Harvard Business Review*, 79(3): 131–137.

152. R. D. Ireland and M. A. Hitt, 2005, "Achieving and maintaining strategic competitiveness in the 21st century: The role of strategic leadership", *Academy of Management Executive*, 19: 63–77.

153. G. Edmondson, 2007, "Pedal to the metal at Porsche", *BusinessWeek*, September 3, 68; J. D. Gunkel and G. Probst, 2003, "Implementation of the balanced scorecard as a means of corporate learning: The Porsche case", European Case Clearing House, Cranfield, UK.

# CHAPTER 12

# CORPORATE GOVERNANCE

## LEARNING OBJECTIVES

Studying this chapter should provide you with the strategic management knowledge needed to:

1. Define corporate governance and explain why it is used to monitor and control managers' strategic decisions.
2. Explain why ownership has been largely separated from managerial control in the corporation.
3. Define an agency relationship and managerial opportunism and describe their strategic implications.
4. Explain how three internal governance mechanisms – ownership concentration, the board of directors and executive compensation – are used to monitor and control managerial decisions.
5. Discuss the types of compensation executives receive and their effects on strategic decisions.
6. Describe how the external corporate governance mechanism – the market for corporate control – acts as a restraint on top level managers' strategic decisions.
7. Discuss the use of corporate governance in international settings, especially in Germany, Japan and China.
8. Describe how corporate governance fosters ethical strategic decisions and the importance of such behaviours on the part of top-level managers.

We thank Pieter-Jan Bezemer for his contribution to this Chapter
© Dan Moore/iStock

# CHAPTER

# CORPORATE GOVERNANCE

## LEARNING OBJECTIVES

OPENING CASE

© imagebroker/Alamy

## Siemens: Bribery

"Siemens is closing a painful chapter in its history", Gerhard Cromme, the Siemens chairman, said in announcing the agreements with US authorities at a news conference. More than three years after Siemens, Europe's largest engineering firm, was rocked to the core by the largest bribery scandal in Germany, the conglomerate can see calmer waters ahead. Prosecutors found €1.3bn of suspected payments by hundreds of managers to officials around the world designed to win contracts. Although bribery is not a unique phenomenon in the business world, in Siemens' case bribery is notable for its worldwide breadth, the sums of money involved, and the organizational intensity with which the company deployed bribes to secure contracts.

Bribery practices at Siemens are not a phenomenon of this decade. After World War II Siemens turned to markets in less developed countries to compete, and bribery became a useful technique. In order to win contracts Siemens paid huge amounts of money to government officials. Each year units at Siemens set aside millions of dollars for the payments of bribes.

Siemens particularly used these budgets to secure government contracts. The telecommunications unit, for example, paid €309 million in bribes to the son of the prime minister at the time and other senior officials, to secure a mobile phone contract in Bangladesh. In Argentina, a Siemens subsidiary paid at least €31.5 million in bribes to win a €0.8 billion contract to produce national identity cards. In Israel it was €15.7 million to senior government officials for building power plants. In Venezuela, the company provided €12.6 million for urban rail lines. In China it was €11 million for medical equipment.

Bribing as a company was not too difficult. The most common method of bribery involved hiring an outside consultant to help "win" a contract. This was a local resident with ties to ruling leaders. Siemens paid a fee to the consultant, who in turn delivered the cash to the ultimate recipient. Before 1999, bribes were deductible as business expenses under the German tax code, and paying off a foreign official was not a criminal offence. However, in 1999, when Germany joined the international convention banning foreign bribery, a pact signed by most of the world's industrial nations, Siemens had to change the way of doing its "business". According to US Justice Department and the Securities and Exchange Commission Siemens used several methods to conceal bribes, including sham consulting contracts. The Justice Department also claims that Siemens used "removable Post-It notes" with affixed signatures to obscure audit trails and "cash desks" where employees could fill "empty suitcases" with as much as €1 million ($1.3 million) to pay bribes. Money was transferred through offshore firms, which were controlled by executives of Siemens. Instead of German bank accounts, Siemens usually used bank accounts from Liechtenstein and Switzerland as secrecy laws in these countries provided greater cover and anonymity.

This "business model" of Siemens began to collapse as various countries like Liechtenstein traced suspicious transactions. Prosecutors in Italy, Liechtenstein and Switzerland sent requests for help to counterparts in Germany. Accordingly, German authorities decided to raid several offices of Siemens in November 2006. As Siemens is listed on the New York Stock Exchange, US authorities also became involved in the case and started an investigation. Investigations were initiated in Germany and in the US whereby Siemens was alleged to have made bribery payments between 1999 and 2007 in order to secure contracts worldwide. In the meantime, Siemens hired an American law firm, Debevoise & Plimpton, to conduct an internal investigation and to work with federal investigators. Siemens officials "made it crystal clear that they wanted us to get to the bottom of this and follow it wherever the evidence led", said Bruce E. Yannett, a Debevoise partner. The Securities and Exchange Commission claims Siemens made at least 4283 bribe payments totalling €1.1 billion between March 2001 and September 2007. Both investigations resulted in huge fines: €600 million to US authorities and €596 million to German authorities. Various managers were arrested and the investigation is still ongoing.

This downturn has posed a challenge to Peter Löscher, who is the first outsider to head the company. Mr. Löscher vowed to transform Siemens through "state of the art" anticorruption measures. The new chief executive brought in radical measures to make Siemens both an ethical and profitable company. "Operational excellence and ethical behaviour are not a contradiction of terms," the company said in a statement. "We must get the best business – and the clean business." Siemens has said that the internal inquiry and related restructurings have cost it more than €0.8 billion. Many measures have been taken such as banning the use of external advisors, replacing 100 top managers, introducing a new compliance system, linking compliance issues to bonuses and revamping the group's structure, focusing it on energy, healthcare and industry segments and selling non-core subsidiaries.

**Sources:** 2008 "The Siemens scandal: Bavarian baksheesh", *The Economist*, http://www.economist.com, December 17; Schäfer, D. (2008) "Siemens fines set group on a path to normality", http://www.ft.com, December 15; Schäfer, D. (2008) "Siemens to pay €1bn fines to close bribery scandal", http://www.ft.com, 15 December; Schubert, S. and Miller, C. (2008) "At Siemens, bribery was just a line item", *New York Times*, http://www.nytimes.com, December 20; Milne, R. (2009) "Siemens issues a ban on external advisers", *Financial Times*, http://www.ft.com, February 11; Crawford, D. and Esterl, M. (2007) "Inside bribery probe of Siemens: Liechtenstein Bank triggered an international hunt", *Wall Street Journal*, http://online.wsj.com, December 28; Crawford, D. and Esterl, M. (2008) "Siemens to pay huge fine in bribery inquiry", *Wall Street Journal*, http://online.wsj.com, December 15.

## Questions

**1** What are the ethical responsibilities of firms doing business in contexts with different societal values and norms? Should they give preference to their home or host values and norms?

**2** Do you think that Siemens responded to the bribery scandals in an appropriate fashion?

As the Opening Case illustrates, designing governance mechanisms to ensure effective leadership of firms to develop and implement strategies that create value for stakeholders is challenging. However, corporate governance is critical to firms' success and thus has become an increasingly important part of the strategic management process.[1] If the board makes the wrong decisions in selecting, governing and compensating the firm's strategic leader (e.g., CEO), the shareholders and the firm suffer. When CEOs are motivated to act in the best interests of the firm – in particular, the shareholders – the firm's value should increase.

National differences may complicate the board's ability to do so.[2] As suggested in the Opening Case, bribery may be a common strategy to attract business in certain areas of the globe, it is highly contested in others. Similar tensions are apparent in the way in which nation states and corporations deal with issues such as executive compensation, environmental pollution, employee representation and regulatory compliance. In particular, the globalization and liberalization of financial markets seem to have added an extra layer of complexity, as multinationals are increasingly exposed to varied national regulatory initiatives and diverse governance demands of large international stakeholders.[3]

Corporate governance is the set of mechanisms used to manage the relationship between stakeholders and to determine and control the strategic direction and performance of organizations.[4] At its core, corporate governance is concerned with identifying ways to ensure that strategic decisions are made effectively.[5] Governance can also be thought of as a means to establish harmony between parties (the firm's

**Corporate governance**

Corporate governance is the set of mechanisms used to manage the relationship among stakeholders and to determine and control the strategic direction and performance of organizations.

owners and its top level managers) whose interests may conflict. In modern corporations – especially those in the United States and the United Kingdom – a primary objective of corporate governance is to ensure that the interests of top level managers are aligned with the interests of the shareholders. Corporate governance involves oversight in areas where owners, managers and members of boards of directors may have conflicts of interest. These areas include the election of directors, the general supervision of CEO pay and more focused supervision of the corporation's overall structure and strategic direction.[6]

Recent emphasis on corporate governance stems mainly from the failure of corporate governance mechanisms to adequately monitor and control top level managers' decisions. This situation results in changes in governance mechanisms in corporations throughout the world, especially with respect to efforts intended to improve the performance of boards of directors. A second and more positive reason for this interest is based on evidence that a well-functioning corporate governance and control system can create a competitive advantage for an individual firm.[7] Thus, in this chapter, we describe actions designed to implement strategies that focus on monitoring and controlling mechanisms designed to ensure that top level managerial actions contribute to the firm's strategic competitiveness and its ability to earn above-average returns.

Effective corporate governance is also of interest to nations.[8] Although corporate governance reflects company standards, it also collectively reflects country societal standards.[9] As with these firms and their boards, nations that effectively govern their corporations may gain a competitive advantage over rival countries. In a range of countries, but especially in the United States and the United Kingdom, the fundamental goal of business organizations is to maximize shareholder value.[10] Traditionally, shareholders are treated as the firm's key stakeholders, because they are the company's legal owners. The firm's owners expect top level managers and others influencing the corporation's actions (e.g., the board of directors) to make decisions that will maximize the company's value and, hence, the owners' wealth.[11] However not all countries maintain this Anglo-Saxon model. In many European and Asian countries, business organizations attempt to maintain a stakeholder approach rather than a shareholder approach. By maintaining a pluralistic approach, business organizations try to pursue the interests of all involved stakeholders rather than those of shareholders only.[12] Research shows that these varying national models of corporate governance influence firms' decision to invest and operate in different countries.[13]

In the first section of this chapter, we describe the relationship that is the foundation on which the modern corporation is built: the relationship between owners and managers. The majority of this chapter is used to explain various mechanisms owners use to govern managers and to ensure that they comply with the responsibility to pursue shareholders' interests. Three internal governance mechanisms and a single external one are used in the modern corporation. The three internal governance mechanisms we describe are (1) ownership concentration, represented by types of shareholders and their different incentives to monitor managers; (2) the board of directors; and (3) executive compensation. We then consider the market for corporate control, an external corporate governance mechanism. Essentially, this market is a set of potential owners seeking to acquire undervalued firms and earn above-average returns on their investments by replacing ineffective top level management teams.[14]

The chapter's focus then shifts to the issue of international corporate governance. We briefly describe governance approaches used in German, Japanese and Chinese firms whose traditional governance structures are being affected by the realities of global competition. In part, this discussion suggests that the structures used to govern global companies in many different countries, including Germany, Japan, the United Kingdom and the United States, as well as emerging economies such as China and India, are converging. Closing our analysis of corporate governance is a consideration of the need for these control mechanisms to encourage and support ethical behaviour in organizations.

Importantly, the mechanisms discussed can positively influence the governance of the modern corporation, which has placed significant responsibility and authority in the hands of top level managers. With multiple governance mechanisms operating simultaneously, however, it is also possible for some of the governance mechanisms to be in conflict.[15] Later, we review how these conflicts can occur.

# Separation of ownership and managerial control

Historically, firms were managed by the founder-owners and their descendants. In these cases, corporate ownership and control resided in the same persons. As firms grew larger, "The managerial revolution led to a separation of ownership and control in most large corporations, where control of the firm shifted from entrepreneurs to professional managers while ownership became dispersed among thousands of unorganized stockholders who were removed from the day-to-day management of the firm."[16] These changes created the modern public corporation, which is based on the efficient separation of ownership and managerial control. Supporting the separation is a basic legal premise suggesting that the primary objective of a firm's activities is to increase the corporation's profit and, thereby, the financial gains of the owners.[17]

The separation of ownership and managerial control allows shareholders to purchase stock, which entitles them to income (residual returns) from the firm's operations after paying expenses. This right, however, requires that they also take a risk that the firm's expenses may exceed its revenues. To manage this investment risk, shareholders maintain a diversified portfolio by investing in several companies to reduce their overall risk.[18] The poor performance or failure of any one firm in which they invest has less overall effect on the value of their portfolio of investments. Thus, shareholders specialize in managing their investment risk.

In small firms, managers are often high percentage owners, which means less separation between ownership and managerial control. In fact, in a large number of family-owned firms, ownership and managerial control are not separated. And family-owned firms perform better when a member of the family is the CEO than when the CEO is an outsider.[19] In the United States at least one-third of the S&P 500 firms have substantial family ownership stakes, in many countries outside the United States, family-owned firms represent the dominant form.[20] For example, in Europe and Asia around 40 per cent of the listed companies used to be family owned.[21] The primary purpose of most of these firms is to increase the family's wealth, which explains why a family CEO often is more common and better than an outside CEO.

Family-controlled firms face at least two critical issues. First, as they grow, they may not have access to all of the skills needed to effectively manage the firm and maximize its returns for the family. Thus, they may need outsiders. Second, as they grow, they may need to seek outside capital and thus give up some of the ownership. In these cases, protection of the minority owners' rights becomes important.[22] To avoid these potential problems, when these firms grow and become more complex, their owner-managers may contract with managerial specialists. These managers make major decisions in the owners' firm and are compensated on the basis of their decision-making skills. As such, recent research suggests that firms in which families own enough equity to have influence without major control tend to make the best strategic decisions.[23]

Without owner (shareholder) specialization in risk bearing and management specialization in decision making, a firm may be limited by the abilities of its owners to manage and make effective strategic decisions. Thus, the separation and specialization of ownership (risk bearing) and managerial control (decision making) should produce the highest returns for the firm's owners.

## Agency relationships

The separation between owners and managers creates an agency relationship. An agency relationship exists when one or more persons (the principal or principals) hire another person or persons (the agent or agents) as decision-making specialists to perform a service.[24] Thus, an agency relationship exists when one party delegates decision-making responsibility to a second party for compensation (see Figure 12.1).[25] In addition to shareholders and top level managers, other examples of agency relationships are consultants and clients and insured and insurer. Moreover, within organizations, an agency relationship exists between managers and their employees, as well as between top level managers and the firm's owners.[26] However, in this chapter we focus on the agency relationship between the firm's owners (the principals) and top level managers (the principals' agents), because these managers formulate and implement the firm's strategies that in turn have major effects on firm performance.[27]

The separation between ownership and managerial control can be problematic. Research evidence documents a variety of agency problems in the modern corporation.[28] Problems can surface because the principal and the agent have different interests and goals, or because shareholders lack direct control of large publicly traded corporations. Problems also arise when an agent makes decisions that result

> **Agency relationship**
>
> An agency relationship exists when one or more persons (the principal or principals) hire another person or persons (the agent or agents) as decision-making specialists to perform a service.

**FIGURE 12.1** An agency relationship

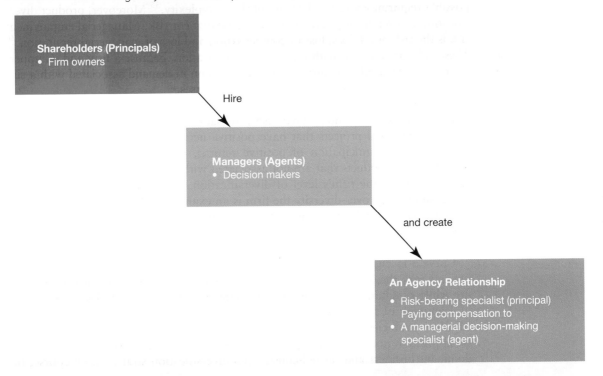

in the pursuit of goals that conflict with those of the principals. Thus, the separation of ownership and control potentially allows divergent interests (between principals and agents) to surface, which can lead to managerial opportunism.

Managerial opportunism is the seeking of self-interest with guile (i.e., cunning or deceit).[29] Opportunism is both an attitude (e.g., an inclination) and a set of behaviours (i.e., specific acts of self-interest).[30] It is not possible for principals to know beforehand which agents will or will not act opportunistically. The reputations of top level managers are an imperfect predictor, and opportunistic behaviour cannot be observed until it has occurred. Thus, principals establish governance and control mechanisms to prevent agents from acting opportunistically, even though only a few are likely to do so. Interestingly, research suggests that when CEOs feel constrained by governance mechanisms, they are more likely to seek external advice that in turn helps them to make better strategic decisions.[31] Any time that principals delegate decision-making responsibilities to agents, the opportunity for conflicts of interest exists. Top level managers, for example, may make strategic decisions that maximize their personal welfare and minimize their personal risk.[32] Decisions such as these prevent the maximization of shareholder wealth. Decisions regarding product diversification demonstrate this alternative.

## Product diversification as an example of an agency problem

As explained in Chapter 7, a corporate-level strategy to diversify the firm's product lines can enhance a firm's strategic competitiveness and increase its returns, both of which serve the interests of shareholders and the top level managers. However, product diversification can result in benefits to managers that shareholders do not enjoy, so top level managers may prefer product diversification more than shareholders do.[33] Increased product diversification provides an opportunity for top level managers to increase their compensation,[34] as diversification usually increases the size of a firm, and size is positively related to executive compensation. Also, diversification increases the complexity of managing a firm and its network of businesses, possibly requiring more pay because of this complexity.[35] Moreover, product diversification can reduce top level managers' employment risk. Managerial employment risk is the risk of job loss, loss of compensation and loss of managerial reputation.[36] These risks are reduced with increased diversification, because a firm and its upper-level managers are less vulnerable to the reduction in demand associated with a single or limited number of product lines or businesses.

A related potential agency problem is a firm's free cash flows over which top level managers have control. Free cash flows are resources remaining after the firm has invested in all projects that have positive net present value within its current businesses.[37] In anticipation of positive returns, managers may decide to invest these funds in products that are not associated with the firm's current lines of business to increase the firm's level of diversification. The managerial decision to use free cash flows to over-diversify the firm is an example of self-serving and opportunistic managerial behaviour. In contrast to managers, shareholders may prefer that free cash flows be distributed to them as dividends, so they can control how the cash is invested.[38]

Curve S in Figure 12.2 depicts the shareholders' optimal level of diversification. Owners seek the level of diversification that reduces the risk of the firm's total failure while simultaneously increasing the company's value through the development of economies of scale and scope (see Chapter 7). Of the four corporate-level diversification strategies shown in Figure 12.2, shareholders are likely to prefer the diversified position noted by point A on curve S – a position that is located between the dominant business and related-constrained diversification strategies. Of course, the

**FIGURE 12.2** Manager and shareholder risk and diversification

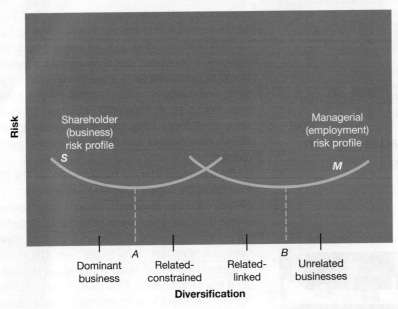

optimum level of diversification owners seek varies from firm to firm.[39] Factors that affect shareholders' preferences include the firm's primary industry, the intensity of rivalry among competitors in that industry, and the top management team's experience with implementing diversification strategies and its effects on other firm strategies such as its entry into international markets (see Chapter 9).[40]

Top level managers – as agents – also seek an optimal level of diversification. Declining performance resulting from too much product diversification increases the probability that corporate control of the firm will be acquired in the market. After a firm is acquired, the employment risk for the firm's top level managers increases substantially. Furthermore, a manager's employment opportunities in the external managerial labour market (discussed in Chapter 11) are affected negatively by a firm's poor performance. Therefore, top level managers prefer diversification, but not to a point that it increases their employment risk and reduces their employment opportunities.[41] Curve M in Figure 12.2 shows that top level managers prefer higher levels of product diversification than do shareholders. Top level managers might prefer the level of diversification shown by point B on curve M.

As illustrated in the Strategic Focus, the varying preferences of shareholders and managers might result in conflict and actions by owners to regain control of a firm's strategy. In general, shareholders prefer riskier strategies and more focused diversification. They reduce their risk through holding a diversified portfolio of equity investments. Alternatively, managers cannot balance their employment risk by working for a diverse portfolio of firms, and therefore may prefer a level of diversification that maximizes firm size and their compensation while also reducing their employment risk. Product diversification, therefore, is a potential agency problem that could result in principals incurring costs to control their agents' behaviours.

## Agency costs and governance mechanisms

The potential conflict illustrated by Figure 12.2, coupled with the fact that principals cannot easily predict which managers might act opportunistically, demonstrates

# STRATEGIC FOCUS

## STORK®

**Algemene Vergadering van Aandeelhouders**

© AFP/Getty Images

# The influence of hedge funds on Stork's strategy

In September 2006, Centaurus Capital and Paulson & Co, two hedge funds and large shareholders of Stork, demanded the break-up of the Dutch industrial conglomerate. They perceived that the value of the sum of Stork's diversified business units exceeded the value of the company as a whole. Stork's management, however, rejected the proposal to sell off all its technical services and food processing divisions and to continue as an aerospace company, as it stated that the funds' proposition was not credible and unrealistic.

While Stork faced litigation by continuously refusing the offer, it organized an extraordinary shareholders' meeting enabling other shareholders to vote on the motion by Centaurus and Paulson. The two shareholders, who jointly have a 31.5 per cent stake in Stork, consequently tried to mobilize more investors to vote for their proposal by launching an advertising campaign in the Dutch media. As a countermove Stork requested a court to investigate whether the two funds breached stock market disclosure regulations. It suspected that the investors acted in concert before formally declaring that they had signed a

protocol to jointly exercise voting rights. On October 12 the motion, which was not binding, was accepted by Stork's shareholders, but still rejected by its management. It concluded that breaking up the company would be irresponsible as it led to "significant uncertainty and execution risks". At this point it became even more likely that the affair could end up in court since it was not likely that a settlement between Stork's management and the two investors could be reached.

Several weeks later the battle heated up. The Stork foundation, the company's preventive measure for hostile take-over bids, exercised its option to buy preference shares in the same amount as other outstanding shares minus one. This measure diminished the joint stake of Centaurus and Paulson to 15 per cent. The investors considered this move as an act of war and sought a court injunction to prevent the foundation from using its voting rights linked to its preference shares. In advance of the court case the funds requested a shareholder meeting to formally put the management team to a confidence vote as they stated that Stork's supervisory board failed in managing the issue. The court outlawed the use of Stork's defence by the foundation related to the Dutch company. Nevertheless, it also barred the confidence vote that had been set up for the dismissal of the company's supervisory board. Eventually the Dutch court appointed three renowned non-executive directors in the Netherlands, Wim Kok, the former Dutch prime minister who serves as a non-executive board member of ING and Royal Dutch Shell, Dudley Eustace, former finance director at Philips and food retailer Ahold, and Kees van Lede, the chairman of Heineken, to resolve the lengthy conflict.

Several months later the issue finally came to its end. Marel, a competitor of Stork from Iceland, expanded its share in the company to 43 per cent in order to combine forces with Centaurus and Paulson. Having a joint stake of almost 75 per cent the break-up of Stork became more likely, allowing Marel to acquire Stork's food processing division. A British private equity fund, Candover, later announced that it intended to purchase the remainder of the company for €1.5 billion. In the first two months of 2008 the deals were settled, Storks public listing was terminated and Candover became Stork's new owner.

**Sources:** Bickerton, I. (2006) "Activists demand break-up of Stork", *Financial Times*, http://www.ft.com. September 8; Bickerton, I. (2006) "Stork may face legal challenge", *Financial Times*, http://www.ft.com. September 15; 2006 "Stork resists disposal calls", *Financial Times*, http://www.ft.com. September 19; Bickerton, I. (2006) "Stork investors step up campaign", *Financial Times*, http://www.ft.com. October 2; Bickerton, I. (2006) "Stork asks court to look into investors' conduct.", *Financial Times*, http://www.ft.com. October 5; Bickerton, I. (2006) "Stork facing battle over break-up plan", *Financial Times*, http://www.ft.com. October 12; Bickerton, I. (2006) "Compromise at Stork 'being hatched'", *Financial Times*, http://www.ft.com October 16; Bickerton, I. (2006) "Stork set for showdown with investors", *Financial Times*, http://www.ft.com. November 15; Spikes, S. (2006) "Funds' battle with Stork heat up", *Financial Times*, http://www.ft.com. November 24; Bickerton, I. (2006) "Stork in appeal to activist investors", *Financial Times*, http://www.ft.com. December 15; Bickerton, I. (2006) "Outrage over triggering of Stork poison pill", *Financial Times*, http://www.ft.com. December 21; Bickerton, I. (2007) "Hedge fund try to block Stork foundation's vote", *Financial Times*, http://www.ft.com. January 6; Bickerton, I. (2007) "Court to hear injunction on Stork", *Financial Times*, http://www.ft.com. January 10; Bickerton, I. (2007) "Stork in court clash with investors", *Financial Times*, http://www.ft.com. January 13; Bickerton, I. (2007) "Court upholds calls for probe into Stork", *Financial Times*, http://www.ft.com. January 18; Bickerton, I. (2007') Trio get job of resolving Stork conflict', *Financial Times*, http://www.ft.com. January 27; Daling, T. and Gossink, W. (2008) "Medezeggenschapraad Stork 'Gecharmeerd' van private-equity maatschappij Candover", *Het Financieele Dagblad*, http://www.fd.nl. July 8; 2007 "Candover convinces opponents to deliver Stork", *New York Times,* http://www.nytimes.com. November 30; 2008 "Settlement of offer for Stork completed", Stork BV, http://www.stork.com. January 22; 2008 "99.5 per cent of outstanding shares Stork committed to London Acquisition", Stork BV, http://www.stork.com. February 4.

## Questions

**1** How much influence should (minority) shareholders and top level managers respectively have when it comes to determining a firm's scope and strategy?

**2** Do you think that Stork's top level managers and board have chosen the "right" strategy to manage and cope with the activist moves made by Centaurus Capital and Paulson & Co?

why they establish governance mechanisms. However, the firm incurs costs when it uses one or more governance mechanisms. Agency costs are the sum of incentive costs, monitoring costs, enforcement costs and individual financial losses incurred by principals because governance mechanisms cannot guarantee total compliance by the agent. If a firm is diversified, agency costs increase because it is more difficult to monitor what is going on inside the firm.[42]

In general, managerial interests may prevail when governance mechanisms are weak; this is exemplified in situations where managers have a significant amount of autonomy to make strategic decisions. If, however, the board of directors controls managerial autonomy, or if other strong governance mechanisms are used, the firm's strategies should better reflect the interests of the shareholders. More recently, governance observers have been concerned about more egregious behaviour beyond inefficient corporate strategy.

Due to fraudulent behaviour such as that found at Enron, WorldCom, Parmalat and Ahold, concerns regarding corporate governance continue to grow. As a result, numerous regulatory initiatives have been introduced throughout the world.[43] For example, the US Congress enacted the Sarbanes-Oxley (SOX) Act in 2002, which increased the intensity of corporate governance mechanisms.[44] While the implementation has been controversial to some, most believe that the results of it have been generally positive. Section 404 of SOX, which prescribes significant transparency improvement on internal controls associated with accounting and auditing, has arguably improved the internal auditing scrutiny and thereby trust in such financial reporting. Furthermore, the OECD and European Union refined their principles and directives multiple times to restore the general public's trust and ensure that appropriate checks and balances were put in place in the regulatory systems of nations.[45]

Whereas the focus in the United States has been on "hard law" (i.e., binding laws that are legally enforceable), Europe favoured "soft law", (i.e., commitments made by negotiating parties that are not legally binding). Over the last decade,

**Agency costs**

Agency costs are the sum of incentive costs, monitoring costs, enforcement costs and individual financial losses incurred by principals because governance mechanisms cannot guarantee total compliance by the agent.

most European countries have introduced corporate governance codes based on self-regulation to cope with the lack of trust in financial markets after the wave of corporate governance scandals.[46] Well-known examples include among others the Combined Code (United Kingdom), Cromme Code (Germany) and Vienot Reports (France). In the wake of the financial crisis, most of these initiatives have been significantly revised recently.

The more intensive application of governance mechanisms may produce significant changes in strategies. For example, because of more intense governance, firms may take on fewer risky projects and thus decrease potential shareholder wealth. Next, we explain the effects of different governance mechanisms on the decisions managers make about the choice and the use of the firm's strategies.

## Ownership concentration

Both the number of large-block shareholders and the total percentage of shares they own define ownership concentration. Large-block shareholders typically own at least 5 per cent of a corporation's issued shares. Ownership concentration as a governance mechanism has received considerable interest because large-block shareholders are increasingly active in their demands that corporations adopt effective governance mechanisms to control managerial decisions.[47]

In general, diffuse ownership (a large number of shareholders with small holdings and few, if any, large-block shareholders) produces weak monitoring of managers' decisions. For example, diffuse ownership makes it difficult for owners to effectively coordinate their actions. Diversification of the firm's product lines beyond the shareholders' optimum level can result from ineffective monitoring of managers' decisions. Higher levels of monitoring could encourage managers to avoid strategic decisions that harm shareholder value. In fact, research evidence shows that ownership concentration is associated with lower levels of firm product diversification.[48] Thus, with high degrees of ownership concentration, the probability is greater that managers' strategic decisions will be designed to maximize shareholder value.[49]

As noted, such concentration of ownership has an influence on strategies and firm value, mostly positive but perhaps not in all cases. For example, when large shareholders have a high degree of wealth, they have power relative to minority shareholders in extracting wealth from the firm, especially when they are in managerial positions. The importance of boards of directors in mitigating expropriation of minority shareholder value has been found in firms with strong family ownership wherein family members have incentive to appropriate shareholder wealth, especially in the second generation after the founder has departed.[50] Such expropriation is often found in countries such as Korea where minority shareholder rights are not as protected as they are in the United States.[51]

### The growing influence of institutional owners

A classic work published in the 1930s argued that the "modern" corporation was characterized by a separation of ownership and control.[52] The change occurred primarily because growth prevented founders-owners from maintaining dual positions in their increasingly complex companies. More recently, another shift has occurred: Ownership of many modern corporations is now concentrated in the hands of institutional investors rather than individual shareholders.[53]

---

**Ownership concentration**

Both the number of large-block shareholders and the total percentage of shares they own define ownership concentration.

---

**Large-block shareholders**

Large-block shareholders typically own at least 5 per cent of a corporation's issued shares.

Institutional owners are financial institutions such as stock mutual funds and pension funds that control large-block shareholder positions. Because of their prominent ownership positions, institutional owners, as large-block shareholders, are a powerful governance mechanism. Institutions of these types now own more than 60 per cent of the stock in large US corporations. Pension funds alone control at least one-half of corporate equity.[54] Although firms in Europe are most commonly family-controlled, institutional investors such as banks and pension funds also have significant ownership stakes.[55]

These ownership percentages suggest that as investors, institutional owners have both the size and the incentive to discipline ineffective top level managers and can significantly influence a firm's choice of strategies and overall strategic decisions.[56] Research evidence indicates that institutional and other large-block shareholders are becoming more active in their efforts to influence a corporation's strategic decisions, unless they have a business relationship with the firm. Initially, these shareholder activists and institutional investors concentrated on the performance and accountability of CEOs and contributed to the dismissal of a number of them. As illustrated in the Stork Strategic Focus, these investors often target the actions of boards more directly via proxy vote proposals that are intended to give shareholders more decision rights because they believe board processes have been ineffective.[57]

To date, research suggests that institutional activism may not have a strong effect on a firm's financial performance, but that its influence may be indirect through its effects on important strategic decisions, such as those concerned with international diversification and innovation.[58] With the increased intensity of governance associated with regulation and the latest economic crisis largely created by poor strategic decisions in the financial services industry, institutional investors and other groups have been emboldened in their activism.

## Board of directors

Shareholders typically monitor the managerial decisions and actions of a firm through the board of directors. Shareholders elect members to their firm's board. Those who are elected are expected to oversee managers and to ensure that the corporation is run in the best interests of all involved stakeholders. Even with large institutional investors having major equity ownership, diffuse ownership continues to exist in many firms, which means that in large corporations, monitoring and control of managers by individual shareholders is limited. These conditions highlight the importance of the board of directors for corporate governance.

Unfortunately, over time, boards of directors have not been highly effective in monitoring and controlling top management's actions.[59] Given the recent problems with top level managers making less than ethical decisions, boards are experiencing increasing pressure from shareholders, lawmakers, and regulators to become more forceful in their oversight role and thereby forestall inappropriate actions by top level managers. Furthermore, boards not only serve a monitoring role, they also provide resources to firms. These resources include their personal knowledge and expertise as well as their access to resources of other firms through their external contacts and relationships.[60]

The board of directors is a group of elected individuals whose primary responsibility is to act in the owners' best interests by formally monitoring and controlling the corporation's top level managers.[61] Boards have the power to direct the affairs of the organization, punish and reward managers, and protect shareholders' rights and interests. Thus, an appropriately structured and effective board of directors

**Institutional owners**

Institutional owners are financial institutions such as stock mutual funds and pension funds that control large-block shareholder positions.

**Board of directors**

The board of directors is a group of elected individuals whose primary responsibility is to act in the owners' interests by formally monitoring and controlling the corporation's top-level managers.

protects owners from managerial opportunism such as that found at Ahold, Parmalat and Vivendi Universal and at financial services firms including the Royal Bank of Scotland, Fortis and others, where shareholders and employees encountered significant losses. Board members are seen as stewards of their company's resources, and the way they carry out these responsibilities affects the society in which their firm operates. For instance, research suggests that better governance produces more effective strategic decisions leading to higher firm performance.[62]

Generally, board members (often called directors) are classified into one of three groups (see Table 12.1). *Insiders* are active top level managers in the corporation who are elected to the board because they are a source of information about the firm's day-today operations.[63] *Related outsiders* have some relationship with the firm, contractual or otherwise, that may create questions about their independence, but these individuals are not involved with the corporation's day-to-day activities. *Outsiders* provide independent counsel to the firm and may hold top level managerial positions in other companies or may have been elected to the board prior to the beginning of the current CEO's tenure.[64]

Historically, boards of directors are organized differently around the globe. Most investors are familiar with the one-tier board model in which a combination of insiders, related outsiders and outsiders are jointly responsible for ensuring that top level managers act in the interests of shareholders. In contrast, the two-tier board model provides for a formal separation of insiders and outsiders who operate in separate boards with their own specific roles. Insiders are responsible for the day-to-day operations of the firm and (related) outsiders are responsible for the supervision of top level managers and for providing advice and counselling to insiders.[65]

A widely accepted view is that a board with a significant percentage of its membership from the firm's top level managers provides relatively weak monitoring and control of managerial decisions.[66] Thus, corporate governance is becoming more intense especially with the oversight of the board of directors. Critics advocate reforms to ensure that independent outside directors represent a significant majority of the total membership of a board, which research suggests has been accomplished.[67] On the other hand, others argue that having outside directors is not enough to resolve the problems; it depends on the power of the CEO. One proposal to reduce the power of the CEO is to separate the chairperson's role and the CEO's role on the board so that the same person does not hold both positions.[68] However, having a board that actively monitors top executive decisions and actions does not ensure high performance. The value that the directors bring to the company also influences the outcomes. For example, boards with members having significant

**Table 12.1** Classifications of board of director members

| Insiders |
| --- |
| ● The firm's CEO and other top-level managers |

| Related outsiders |
| --- |
| ● Individuals not involved with the firm's day-to-day operations, but who have a relationship with the company |

| Outsiders |
| --- |
| ● Individuals who are independent of the firm in terms of day-to-day operations and other relationships |

relevant experience and knowledge are the most likely to help the firm formulate effective strategies and to implement them successfully.[69]

Alternatively, having a large number of outside board members can also create some problems. Outsiders do not have contact with the firm's day-to-day operations and typically do not have easy access to the level of information about managers and their skills that is required to effectively evaluate managerial decisions and initiatives.[70] Outsiders can, however, obtain valuable information through frequent interactions with inside board members, during board meetings and otherwise. Insiders possess such information by virtue of their organizational positions. Thus, boards with a critical mass of insiders typically are better informed about intended strategic initiatives, the reasons for the initiatives, and the outcomes expected from them.[71] Without this type of information, outsider-dominated boards may emphasize the use of financial, as opposed to strategic, controls to gather performance information to evaluate managers' and business units' performances. A virtually exclusive reliance on financial evaluations shifts risk to top level managers, who, in turn, may make decisions to maximize their interests and reduce their employment risk. Reductions in R&D investments, additional diversification of the firm, and the pursuit of greater levels of compensation are some of the results of managers' actions to achieve financial goals set by outsider-dominated boards.[72] Additionally, boards can make mistakes in CEO succession decisions because of the lack of important information about candidates as well as specific needs of the firm. So knowledgeable and balanced boards are likely to be the most effective over time.[73]

## Enhancing the effectiveness of the board of directors

Because of the importance of boards of directors in corporate governance and as a result of increased scrutiny from shareholders – in particular, large institutional investors – the performances of individual board members and of entire boards are being evaluated more formally and with greater intensity as explained in the Strategic Focus below.[74] Given the demand for greater accountability and improved performance, many boards have initiated voluntary changes (e.g., those described at Candover, PME and EasyJet). Among these changes are (1) the strengthening of internal management and accounting control systems, and (2) the establishment and consistent use of formal processes to evaluate the board's performance.[75] Additional changes include (3) the creation of a "lead director" role that has strong powers with regard to the board agenda and oversight of non-management board member activities, and (4) modification of the compensation of directors, especially reducing or eliminating stock options as a part of the package.

Boards are increasingly involved in the strategic decision-making process, so they must work collaboratively. Some argue that improving the processes used by boards to make decisions and monitor managers and firm outcomes is important for board effectiveness.[76] Moreover, because of the increased pressure from owners and the potential conflict among board members, procedures are necessary to help boards function effectively in facilitating the strategic decision-making process.

Increasingly, outside directors are being required to own significant equity stakes as a prerequisite to holding a board seat. In fact, some research suggests that firms perform better if outside directors have such a stake; the trend is toward higher pay for directors with more stock ownership, but with fewer stock options.[77] However, other research suggests that too much ownership can lead to lower independence for board members.[78] Additionally, other research suggests that diverse boards help firms make more effective strategic decisions and perform better over time.[79] Although questions remain about whether more independent and diverse boards

**STRATEGIC FOCUS**

# Where have all of the good directors gone?

The global economic crisis, largely the result of extremely poor strategic decisions made by top level managers in the financial services industry, laid bare the holes in the global corporate governance system. In particular, the outcomes showed that many boards of directors were very weak. Boards of directors had suffered significant criticism for the failures in monitoring executive actions in companies including Enron, Ahold, Parmalat and others in the early 2000s. With more recent failures, boards are now experiencing substantial amounts of public animosity. Many people do not understand how top level managers were allowed to take the extreme risks that have melted away corporate value when the debt became too heavy for most of the firms. Moreover, the reckless behaviour of executives triggered the debate on the (excessive) compensation of executive board members. The weakness of corporate boards is exemplified by the "nationalization" of banks such as the Royal Bank of Scotland and Fortis in 2008.

As a result of the economic meltdown, the obviously poor strategic decisions leading to it and the

inability of previous boards to prevent the problems, many boards are now changing. Old board members are resigning or being replaced and many new members are joining boards. For example, in 2008, Fred Goodwin resigned as chief executive of the Royal Bank of Scotland Group. Goodwin was held accountable for the RBS's loss of £28.8bn, the biggest loss in British corporate history. Public outrage resulted from his pension plan worth €835,000 a year. Furthermore, the Dutch pension fund PME changed its board structure as a direct result of the financial crisis. The Dutch National Bank insisted on downsizing the fund's board from fourteen to six executives as the national bank claimed that the executive board was incompetent.

Boardroom shakeups are also occurring outside the financial services industry. For example, EasyJet announced that it had appointed a new chairman of its board to replace the current chairman, Colin Chandler. The new chairman, Michael Rake, formerly headed the BT Group.

Interestingly, research suggests that smaller boards are more effective in governing companies than are larger boards. For instance, Candover, a British private equity firm, resized its board as part of its restructuring after being hit hard by the financial crisis. Changes are being made in the processes used by many boards in order to improve their monitoring function. These changes extend to the balance of independent and inside members, renewed emphasis on audit and compensation committees and ensuring that outside board members spend an adequate amount of time on board business so that they can make informed decisions. Furthermore there are other moves afoot to change the governance practices in firms. These include new rules and a renewed scrutiny by financial regulatory authorities and other governmental agencies. For instance, the Financial Reporting Council in the UK introduced a completely revised version of the Combined Code, a template of corporate governance used by investors and listed companies. In fact, the code is commonly used by institutional investors to evaluate the boards of companies. The Institute of Company Secretaries announced plans to strengthen the norms for corporate governance practices in India. Furthermore, in the US a financial reform bill, which will be implemented as the Wall Street Reform and Consumer Protection Act, has been submitted as a proposal for the regulation of financial firms and financial markets, the protection of consumers and investors and as a tool kit for crisis management.

The financial crisis of 2007–2010 also triggered the debate on executive compensation. The general observation was that there was no clear connection between corporate performance and executive pay and that the risk-taking activities of CEOs were only rewarded by high salaries. The first measure against the "reckless behaviour" of managers was to regulate the (excessive) bonus system in the financial industry. The public debate resulted in a global effort to regulate bankers' bonuses. Future restrictions on bonuses imply bonuses can only be paid for 30 per cent in cash and that at least fifty per cent of the bonus will have to be deferred for a minimum of three years.

**Sources:** Kellogg School of Management Faculty Members (2010) "Executive compensation and public outrage", *BusinessWeek*, http://www.businessweek.com. February 26; Treanor, J. (2009) "RBS record losses raise prospect of 95% state ownership", *The Guardian*, http://www.guardian.co.uk. February 26; Preesman, L. (2010) "Hard-hit PME changes board structure", *Investment & Pensions Europe*, http://www.ipe.com. January 29; Espinoza, J. (2009) "EasyJet shakes up boardroom", *Forbes*, http://www.forbes.com. April 6; 2009 "ICSI plans governance norms", *Business Standard*, http://www.business-standard.com. April 5; Serchuk, D.

(2009) "Where are Wall Street's directors?", *Forbes*, http://www.forbes.com. March 31; Costello, M. (2009) "New boardroom code to 'draw on lessons' from bank crisis", *The Times*, http://www.business.timesonline.co.uk. March 18; 2009 "Directors under fire", *Stuff*, http://www.stuff.co.nz. March 10; Groom, B. (2010) "Executive pay rises out of line with results", *Financial Times*, http://www.ft.com. July 5; Morris, N. and Savage, M. (2009) "Excessive bonuses to be banned in war on greed", *The Independent*, http://www.independent.co.uk. September 28; Aldrick, P. (2010) "Brussels backs down on bonus caps for bankers", *The Daily Telegraph*, http://www.telegraph.com. July 1; Bollen, J. (2010) "Candover reduces board size", *Financial News*, http://www.efinancialnews.com. March 1; Byrd, R. (2010) "Financial regulation: Not all on the same page", *The Economist*. http://www.economist.com. July 1.

### Questions

**1** Do you think that the role and structure of boards of directors of companies has to be redefined in order to improve the monitoring of top level managers?

**2** How can companies create a reward system that controls the risk-taking behaviour of top level managers?

enhance board effectiveness, the trends for greater independence and increasing diversity among board members are likely to continue. Clearly, the corporate failures in the first decade of the twenty-first century suggest the need for more effective boards.

## Executive compensation

As the Strategic Focus above highlights, the compensation of top level managers, and especially of CEOs, generates a great deal of interest and strongly-held opinions. One reason for this widespread interest can be traced to a natural curiosity about extremes and excesses. Another stems from a more substantive view that CEO pay is tied in an indirect but tangible way to the fundamental governance processes in large corporations. Some believe that while highly paid, CEOs are not overpaid.[80] Others argue that not only are they highly paid, they are overpaid. These critics are especially concerned that compensation is not as strongly related to performance as some believe.[81]

Executive compensation is a governance mechanism that seeks to align the interests of managers and owners through salaries, bonuses and long-term incentive compensation, such as stock awards and options.[82] Long-term incentive plans have become a critical part of compensation packages in US and European firms. The use of longer-term pay theoretically helps firms cope with or avoid potential agency problems by linking managerial wealth to the wealth of common shareholders.[83]

Sometimes the use of a long-term incentive plan prevents major stockholders (e.g., institutional investors) from pressing for changes in the composition of the board of directors, because they assume the long-term incentives will ensure that

**Executive compensation**

Executive compensation is a governance mechanism that seeks to align the interests of managers and owners through salaries, bonuses and long-term incentive compensation, such as stock awards and options.

top executives will act in shareholders' best interests. Alternatively, stockholders largely assume that top-executive pay and the performance of a firm are more closely aligned when firms have boards that are dominated by outside members. However, research shows that fraudulent behaviour can be associated with stock option incentives, such as earnings manipulation.[84]

Effectively using executive compensation as a governance mechanism is particularly challenging to firms implementing international strategies. For example, the interests of owners of multinational corporations may be best served by less uniformity among the firm's foreign subsidiaries' compensation plans.[85] Developing an array of unique compensation plans requires additional monitoring and increases the firm's potential agency costs. Importantly, levels of pay vary by regions of the world. For example, managerial pay is highest in the United States and much lower in Asia. Compensation is lower in India partly because many of the largest firms have strong family ownership and control.[86] As corporations acquire firms in other countries, the managerial compensation puzzle for boards becomes more complex and may cause additional governance problems.[87]

## The effectiveness of executive compensation

Executive compensation – especially long-term incentive compensation – is complicated for several reasons. First, the strategic decisions made by top level managers are typically complex and nonroutine, so direct supervision of executives is inappropriate for judging the quality of their decisions. The result is a tendency to link the compensation of top level managers to measurable outcomes, such as the firm's financial performance. Second, an executive's decision often affects a firm's financial outcomes over an extended period, making it difficult to assess the effect of current decisions on the corporation's performance. In fact, strategic decisions are more likely to have long-term, rather than short-term, effects on a company's strategic outcomes. Third, a number of other factors affect a firm's performance besides top level managerial decisions and behaviour. Unpredictable economic, social or legal changes (see Chapter 2) make it difficult to identify the effects of strategic decisions. Thus, although performance-based compensation may provide incentives to top management teams to make decisions that best serve shareholders' interests; such compensation plans alone cannot fully control managers. Incentive compensation represents a significant portion of many executives' total pay.

Although incentive compensation plans may increase the value of a firm in line with shareholder expectations, such plans are subject to managerial manipulation.[88] Additionally, annual bonuses may provide incentives to pursue short-run objectives at the expense of the firm's long-term interests. Although long-term, performance-based incentives may reduce the temptation to under-invest in the short run, they increase executive exposure to risks associated with uncontrollable events, such as market fluctuations and industry decline. The longer-term the focus of incentive compensation, the greater are the long-term risks borne by top level managers. Also, because long-term incentives tie a manager's overall wealth to the firm in a way that is inflexible, such incentives and ownership may not be valued as highly by a manager as by outside investors who have the opportunity to diversify their wealth in a number of other financial investments.[89] Thus, firms may have to over-compensate for managers using long-term incentives.

Even though some stock option-based compensation plans are well designed with option strike prices substantially higher than current stock prices, some have been designed with the primary purpose of giving executives more compensation. Research of stock option repricing where the strike price value of the option has been lowered from its original position suggests that action is taken more frequently in high-risk situations.[90] However, repricing also happens when firm performance is poor, to restore the incentive effect for the option. Evidence also suggests that politics are often involved, which has resulted in "option backdating".[91] While this evidence shows that no internal governance mechanism is perfect, some compensation plans accomplish their purpose. For example, recent research suggests that long-term pay designed to encourage managers to be environmentally friendly has been linked to higher success in preventing pollution.[92]

Stock options became highly popular as a means of compensating top executives and linking pay with performance, but they also have become controversial of late. Because all internal governance mechanisms are imperfect, external mechanisms are also needed. One such governance device is the market for corporate control.

# Market for corporate control

The market for corporate control is an external governance mechanism that becomes active when a firm's internal controls fail.[93] The market for corporate control is composed of individuals and firms that buy ownership positions in or take over potentially under-valued corporations so they can form new divisions in established diversified companies or merge two previously separate firms. Because the undervalued firm's top level managers are assumed to be responsible for formulating and implementing the strategy that led to poor performance, they are usually replaced. Thus, when the market for corporate control operates effectively, it ensures that managers who are ineffective or act opportunistically are disciplined.[94]

The takeover market as a source of external discipline is used only when internal governance mechanisms are relatively weak and have proven to be ineffective. Alternatively, other research suggests that the rationale for takeovers as a corporate governance strategy is not as strong as the rationale for takeovers as an ownership investment in target candidates where the firm is performing well and does not need discipline.[95] A study of active corporate raiders in the 1980s showed that takeover attempts often were focused on above-average performance firms in an industry.[96] Taken together, this research suggests that takeover targets are not always low performers with weak governance. As such, the market for corporate control may not be as efficient as a governance device as theory suggests.[97] At the very least, internal governance controls are much more precise relative to this external control mechanism.

Hedge funds have become a source of activist investors as noted in Chapter 8. An enormous amount of money has been invested in hedge funds, and because it is significantly more difficult to gain high returns in the market, hedge funds turned to activism. Likewise in a competitive environment characterized by a greater willingness on the part of investors to hold under-performing managers accountable, hedge funds have been given licence for increased activity.[98] Traditionally, hedge funds are a portfolio of stocks or bonds, or both, managed by an individual or a team on behalf of a large number of investors. Activism allows them to influence the market by taking a large position in seeking to drive the stock price up in a short period of time and then sell.

Although the market for corporate control may be a blunt instrument for corporate governance, the takeover market continues to be active even in the economic crisis. In fact, the more intense governance environment has fostered an increasingly active takeover market. At the same time, managers who have ownership positions or stock options are likely to gain in making a transaction with an acquiring firm. Even more evidence indicates that this type of gain may be the case, given the

**Market for corporate control**

The market for corporate control is an external governance mechanism that becomes active when a firm's internal controls fail.

increasing number of firms that have golden parachutes that allow up to three years of additional compensation plus other incentives if a firm is taken over. These compensation contracts reduce the risk for managers if a firm is taken over. Private equity firms often seek to obtain a lower price in the market through initiating friendly takeover deals. The target firm's top level managers may be amenable to such "friendly" deals because not only do they get the payout through a golden parachute, but at their next firm they may get a "golden hello" as a signing bonus to work for the new firm.[99] Golden parachutes help them leave, but "golden hellos are increasingly needed to get them in the door" of the next firm.[100] Although the 1980s had more defences put up against hostile takeovers, the more recent environment has been much friendlier. However, the recent economic crisis has led to significant criticism of defence mechanisms and their abolishment throughout Europe.

The market for corporate control governance mechanisms should be triggered by a firm's poor performance relative to industry competitors. A firm's poor performance, often demonstrated by the firm's below-average returns, is an indicator that internal governance mechanisms have failed; that is, their use did not result in managerial decisions that maximized shareholder value. However, even though these acquisitions often involve highly underperforming firms and the changes needed may appear obvious, there are no guarantees of success. The acquired firm's assets still must be integrated effectively into the acquiring firm's operation to earn positive returns from the takeover. And, integration is an exceedingly complex challenge.[101] Even active acquirers often fail to earn positive returns from some of their acquisitions. Yet, some acquirers are successful and earn significant returns from the assets they acquire.[102] Target firm managers and members of the boards of directors are commonly sensitive about hostile takeover bids (see the Stork Strategic Focus). It frequently means that they have not done an effective job in managing the company. If they accept the offer, they are likely to lose their jobs; the acquiring firm will insert its own management. If they reject the offer and fend off the takeover attempt, they must improve the performance of the firm or risk losing their jobs as well.[103]

## Managerial defence tactics

Hostile takeovers are the major activity in the market for corporate control governance mechanism. Not all hostile takeovers are prompted by poorly performing targets, and firms targeted for hostile takeovers may use multiple defence tactics to fend off the takeover attempt. Historically, the increased use of the market for corporate control has enhanced the sophistication and variety of managerial defence tactics that are used in takeovers. The market for corporate control tends to increase risk for managers. As a result, managerial pay is often augmented indirectly through golden parachutes (wherein a CEO can receive up to three years' salary if his or her firm is taken over). Golden parachutes, similar to most other defence tactics, are controversial.

Among other outcomes, takeover defences increase the costs of mounting a takeover, causing the incumbent management to become entrenched, while reducing the chances of introducing a new management team.[104] One takeover defence is traditionally known as a "poison pill". This defence mechanism usually allows shareholders (other than the acquirer) to convert "shareholders' rights" into a large number of common shares if anyone acquires more than a set amount of the target's stock (typically 10–20 per cent). This move dilutes the percentage of shares that the acquiring firm must purchase at a premium and in effect raises the cost of the deal for the acquiring firm.

Table 12.2 lists a number of additional takeover defence strategies. Some defence tactics necessitate only changes in the financial structure of the firm, such as

## Table 12.2 Hostile takeover defence strategies

| Defence strategy | Category | Popularity among firms | Effective-ness as a defence | Stockholder wealth effects |
|---|---|---|---|---|
| **Poison pill** Preferred stock in the merged firm offered to shareholders at a highly attractive rate of exchange. | Preventive | High | High | Positive |
| **Corporate charter amendment** An amendment to stagger the elections of members to the board of directors of the attacked firm so that all are not elected during the same year, which prevents a bidder from installing a completely new board in the same year. | Preventive | Medium | Very low | Negative |
| **Golden parachute** Lump-sum payments of cash that are distributed to a select group of senior executives when the firm is acquired in a takeover bid. | Preventive | Medium | Low | Negligible |
| **Litigation** Lawsuits that help a target company stall hostile attacks; areas may include antitrust, fraud, inadequate disclosure. | Reactive | Medium | Low | Positive |
| **Greenmail** The repurchase of shares of stock that have been acquired by the aggressor at a premium in exchange for an agreement that the aggressor will no longer target the company for takeover. | Reactive | Very low | Medium | Negative |
| **Standstill agreement** Contract between the parties in which the pursuer agrees not to acquire any more stock of the target firm for a specified period of time in exchange for the firm paying the pursuer a fee. | Reactive | Low | Low | Negative |
| **Capital structure change** Dilution of stock, making it more costly for a bidder to acquire; may include employee stock option plans (ESOPs), recapitalization, new debt, stock selling, share buybacks. | Reactive | Medium | Medium | Inconclusive |

Source: J. A. Pearce II & R. B. Robinson, Jr., 2004, Hostile takeover defenses that maximize shareholder wealth, *Business Horizons,* 47(5): 15–24.

repurchasing shares of the firm's outstanding stock.[105] Some tactics require shareholder approval, but the greenmail tactic, wherein money is used to repurchase stock from a corporate raider to avoid the takeover of the firm, does not. Some firms use rotating board member elections as a defence tactic where only one-third of members are up for re-election each year. Research shows that this results in managerial entrenchment and reduced vulnerability to hostile takeovers.[106]

Many institutional investors also oppose severance packages (golden parachutes).[107] But, as previously noted, an advantage to severance packages is that they may encourage top level managers to accept takeover bids that are attractive to shareholders.[108] Alternatively, recent research has shown that the use of takeover defences reduces pressure experienced by managers for short-term performance gains. As such, managers engage in longer-term strategies and pay more attention to the firm's stakeholders. In turn, when they do this, the firm's market value increases, which rewards the shareholders.[109]

A potential problem with the market for corporate control is that it may not be totally efficient. A study of several of the most active corporate raiders in the 1980s showed that approximately 50 per cent of their takeover attempts targeted firms with above-average performance in their industry – corporations that were neither undervalued nor poorly managed.[110] The targeting of high-performance businesses may lead to acquisitions at premium prices and to decisions by managers of the targeted firm to establish what may prove to be costly takeover defence tactics to protect their corporate positions.[111]

Although the market for corporate control lacks the precision of internal governance mechanisms, the fear of acquisition and influence by corporate raiders is an effective constraint on the managerial growth motive. The market for corporate control has been responsible for significant changes in many firms' strategies and, when used appropriately, has served shareholders' interests. But this market and other means of corporate governance vary by region of the world and by country. Accordingly, we next address the topic of international corporate governance.

# International corporate governance

Understanding the corporate governance structure of the United Kingdom and the United States is inadequate for a multinational firm in the current global economy.[112] The stability associated with German and Japanese governance structures has historically been viewed as an asset, but the governance systems in these countries are changing, similar to other parts of the world. And, the importance of these changes has been heightened by the global economic crisis.[113] These changes are partly the result of multinational firms operating in many different countries and attempting to develop a more global governance system.[114] Although the similarity among national governance systems is increasing, significant differences remain evident, and firms employing an international strategy must understand these differences in order to operate effectively in different international markets.[115]

## Corporate governance in Germany and Japan

In many private German firms, the owner and manager are still the same individual. In these instances, agency problems are not present.[116] Even in publicly-traded German corporations, a single shareholder is often dominant. Thus, the concentration of ownership is an important means of corporate governance in Germany, as it is in the United States.[117]

Historically, banks occupied the centre of the German corporate governance structure, as is also the case in many other European countries, such as Italy and France. As lenders, banks become major shareholders when companies they financed earlier seek funding on the stock market or default on loans. Although the stakes are usually less than 10 per cent, banks can hold a single ownership position that can be up to, but not exceed, 15 per cent of the bank's capital. Although shareholders can tell the banks how to vote their ownership position, they generally do not do so. The banks monitor and control managers, both as lenders and as shareholders, by electing representatives to supervisory boards.

German firms with more than 2000 employees are required to have a two-tiered board structure that places the responsibility for monitoring and controlling managerial (or supervisory) decisions and actions in the hands of a separate group.[118] All the functions of strategy and management are the responsibility of the management board (the *Vorstand*), but appointment to the *Vorstand* is the responsibility of the supervisory tier (the *Aufsichtsrat*). Employees, union members and shareholders appoint members to the *Aufsichtsrat*. Proponents of the German structure suggest that it helps prevent corporate wrongdoing and rash decisions by "dictatorial CEOs". However, critics maintain that it slows decision making and often ties a CEO's hands. The corporate governance framework in Germany has made it difficult to restructure companies as quickly as can be done in the United States when performance suffers. Because of the role of local government (through the board structure) and the power of banks in Germany's corporate governance structure, private shareholders rarely have major ownership positions in German firms. Large institutional investors, such as pension funds and insurance companies, are also relatively insignificant owners of corporate stock. Thus, at least historically, German executives generally have not been dedicated to the maximization of shareholder value that occurs in many countries.[119]

However, corporate governance in Germany is changing, at least partially, because of the increasing globalization of business. Many German firms are beginning to gravitate toward the US system. Recent research suggests that the traditional system produced some agency costs because of a lack of external ownership power. Interestingly, German firms with listings on the US stock exchange have increasingly adopted executive stock option compensation as a long-term incentive pay policy.[120] Attitudes toward corporate governance in Japan are affected by the concepts of obligation, family and consensus.[121] In Japan, an obligation "May be to return a service for one rendered or it may derive from a more general relationship, for example, to one's family or old alumni, or one's company (or Ministry), or the country. This sense of particular obligation is common elsewhere but it feels stronger in Japan."[122] As part of a company family, individuals are members of a unit that envelops their lives; families command the attention and allegiance of parties throughout corporations. Moreover, a *keiretsu* (a group of firms tied together by cross-shareholdings) is more than an economic concept; it, too, is a family. Consensus, an important influence in Japanese corporate governance, calls for the expenditure of significant amounts of energy to win the hearts and minds of people whenever possible, as opposed to top executives issuing edicts.[123] Consensus is highly valued, even when it results in a slow and cumbersome decision-making process.

As in Germany, banks in Japan play an important role in financing and monitoring large public firms.[124] The bank owning the largest share of stocks and the largest amount of debt – the main bank – has the closest relationship with the company's top executives. The main bank provides financial advice to the firm and also closely monitors managers. Thus, Japan has a bank-based financial and corporate governance structure, whereas the United States has a market-based financial and governance structure.[125]

Aside from lending money, a Japanese bank can hold up to 5 per cent of a firm's total stock; a group of related financial institutions can hold up to 40 per cent. In many cases, main-bank relationships are part of a horizontal *keiretsu*. A *keiretsu* firm usually owns less than 2 per cent of any other member firm; however, each company typically has a stake of that size in every firm in the *keiretsu*. As a result, somewhere between 30 and 90 per cent of a firm is owned by other members of the *keiretsu*. Thus, a *keiretsu* is a system of relationship investments.

As is the case in Germany, Japan's structure of corporate governance is changing. For example, because of Japanese banks' continuing development as economic organizations, their role in the monitoring and control of managerial behaviour and firm outcomes is less significant than in the past.[126] Also, deregulation in the financial sector reduced the cost of mounting hostile takeovers.[127] As such, deregulation facilitated more activity in Japan's market for corporate control, which was nonexistent in past years.[128] Interestingly, however, recent research shows that CEOs of both public and private companies in Japan receive similar levels of compensation and their compensation is tied closely to observable performance goals.[129]

## Corporate governance in China

Corporate governance in China has changed dramatically in the first decade of 2000, along with the privatization of business and the development of the equity market. The stock markets in China are young. In their early years, these markets were weak, having significant insider trading. But, research has shown that they have improved with stronger governance in recent years.[130] The Chinese institutional environment is unique. While there has been a gradual decline in the equity held in state-owned enterprises and the number and percentage of private firms have grown, the state still dominates the strategies employed by most firms through direct or indirect controls.

Recent research shows that firms with higher state ownership tend to have lower market value and more volatility in those values over time. This is because of agency conflicts in the firms and because the executives do not seek to maximize shareholder returns. They also have social goals they must meet placed on them by the government.[131] This suggests a potential conflict between the principals, particularly the state owner and the private equity owners of the state-owned enterprise.[132]

The Chinese governance system has been moving toward the Western model in recent years. For example, China YCT International recently announced that it was strengthening its corporate governance with the establishment of an audit committee within its board of directors and appointed three new independent directors.[133] Additionally, recent research shows that the compensation of top executives of Chinese companies is closely related to prior and current financial performance of the firm.[134] And, while state ownership and indirect controls complicate governance in Chinese companies, research in other countries suggests that some state ownership in recently privatized firms provides some benefits. It signals support and seems to help stock prices. However, continued state ownership and involvement over time tend to have negative effects on the stock price.[135] Thus, the corporate governance system in China and the heavy oversight of the Chinese government will need to be observed over time to determine the long-term effects.

# Global corporate governance and ethical behaviour

As noted in the Strategic Focus on the Indian IT company Satyam, corporate governance is becoming an increasingly important issue in economies around the world, even in emerging economies. The problems evidenced with Satyam in India and Siemens in Asia (see Opening Case) could be repeated in other parts of the world if diligence in governance is not exercised. And this concern is stronger because of the globalization in trade, investments and equity markets. Countries and major companies based in them want to attract foreign investment. To do so, the foreign investors must be confident of adequate corporate governance. Truthfully, effective corporate governance is also required to attract domestic investors. Although many

**STRATEGIC FOCUS**

© Alex Segre/Alamy

# The Satyam truth: CEO fraud and corporate governance failure

In 2008, Satyam was India's fourth largest IT company, well-known and respected. It had clients across the world. The firm provided IT services to more than one-third of the *Fortune* 500 companies. The Founder and CEO, Ramalinga Raju, was highly respected. On September 2008, he was named the Ernst & Young Entrepreneur of the Year. On December 16, 2008, he was given the Golden Peacock Award for Corporate Governance and Compliance. But his term as CEO started to unravel.

On December 17, 2008, Raju announced plans to acquire two companies, Maytas Infra and Maytas Properties, both owned by members of his family. The rationale was to diversify Satyam's business portfolio to avoid being so tied to the IT services market. However, the stockholders enacted major protests over these acquisitions. They believed that only Raju and his family would benefit from the acquisition but Satyam would not.

On December 23, 2008, the World Bank announced that Satyam was barred from doing business with the bank because of alleged malpractices in securing previous contracts (e.g., paying bribes). In turn, Satyam requested

an apology from the World Bank. Shortly thereafter, the price of Satyam's stock declined to a four-year low. On December 26 three major outside directors resigned from Satyam's board of directors.

Worst of all on January 7, 2009, Raju sent a letter to the Satyam Board of directors and the India's Securities and Exchange Commission. In this letter, he admitted his involvement in overstating the amount of cash held by Satyam on its balance sheet. The overstatement was by approximately €0.8 billion. Furthermore, Satyam had a liability for €199 million arranged for his personal use and he overstated Satyam's September 2008 quarterly revenues by 76 per cent and the quarterly profits by 97 per cent. This announcement sent shockwaves through corporate India and through India's stock market. Not only did Satyam's stock price suffer greatly (78 per cent decline) but the overall market decreased by 7.3 per cent on the day of the announcement.

Sadly, Satyam means "truth" in Sanskrit. While the CEO was arrested and charged, others worked hard to save the company. And, it appears that Satyam will be saved. Tech Malindra outbid two other firms to acquire an eventual 51 per cent of Satyam and thus will have controlling interest in the company. The sale was due partly to swift government intervention to arrange a sale and save the company. But even though Satyam has been saved, corporate governance in India has taken a big hit. Its reputation for good governance has been tarnished.

**Sources:** Thakurta, P. G. (2009) "Satyam scam questions corporate governance", IPS Inter Press Service, http://www.ipsnews.net. April 21; Anand, G. (2009) "How Satyam was saved", *Wall Street Journal*, http://www.wsj.com. April 14; 2009 "Satyam-chronology", Trading Markets, http://www.tradingmarkets.com. April 7; Timmons, H. and Wassener, B. (2009) "Satyam chief admits huge fraud", *New York Times*, http://nytimes.com. January 8; Arakali, H. (2009) "Satyam chairman resigns after falsifying accounts", Bloomberg, http://bloomberg.com. January 7; Kripalani, M. (2009) "India's Madoff? Satyam scandal rocks outsourcing industry", *BusinessWeek*, http://www.businessweek.com. January 7; Riberiro, J. (2008) "Satyam demands apology from World Bank", Network World, http://www.networkworld.com. December 26.

## Questions

1 Which factors might explain why the Satyam scandal could unfold in spite of the sound corporate governance framework and strong legislation in India?

2 Do you think that the various corporate governance mechanisms discussed in this chapter could have prevented the Satyam scandal?

# KEY DEBATE

## Shareholder value or stakeholder value?

The purpose of the public corporation is a topic for debate among scholars and practitioners around the world. Coordinated market economies (e.g., Germany and Japan) used to conceptualize firms as communities of interests whose stakeholders should be served. In contrast, liberal market economies (e.g., the United States) used to view firms as instruments to create value for its shareholders. There is, however, growing evidence that both economic systems are converging and that top level managers in contexts with an emphasis on stakeholder value, ranging from France and Japan to Denmark and Sweden, are struggling with pressures for shareholder value.

As illustrated in Figure 12.3, many firms throughout Europe have started to refer to shareholder value as an important financial objective during the last two decades. Some scholars have suggested that the importance of this development must not be overstated, because firms might only be paying lip-service to shareholder value. The growing popularity of the use of stock option plans, share buyback programmes and techniques for creating economic value (EVA), however, suggests that the European economies are changing substantially. However, the rationale for the spread of

the Anglo-American shareholder value model is subject to inquiry. Scholars have suggested that the rise of shareholder value is driven by global capital- and product-market pressures. Others have pointed at sociopolitical processes, such as the role of preferences of major owners and (international) business ties.

An important question is what effect this will have on the competitiveness of European firms. Mintzberg (2000: 38) already commented that "if others are stupid enough to do it [adopting the shareholder value model], that will only help North American businesses". While the global financial crisis has highlighted the inherent dangers of short-term oriented capitalism and research has found some support for a negative relationship of the shareholder model and financial performance in Europe, other scholars have pointed at the possibilities of attaining the best of both worlds by tailoring new corporate governance practices to the old institutional context.

In fact, this discussion suggests that the structures used to govern global companies in many different countries, including Germany, Japan, the United Kingdom and the United States, as well as emerging economies such as China and India, are becoming more similar. Yet, important national differences remain as a result of path dependencies, economic nationalism and varying cultural norms and values. Only time will tell whether we will observe more convergence in corporate governance practices.

**Sources:** Bezemer, P. (2010) "Diffusion of corporate governance beliefs: Board independence and the emergence of a shareholder value orientation in the Netherlands", Rotterdam: ERIM doctoral thesis; Fiss, P. C. and Zajac, E. J. (2004) "The diffusion of ideas over contested terrain: The (non-)adoption

**FIGURE 12.3** The adoption of a shareholder value orientation in Germany and the Netherlands

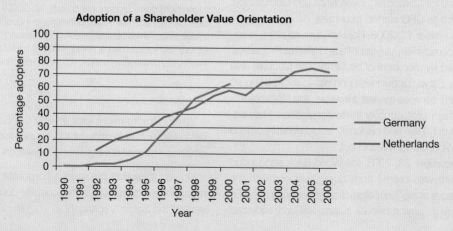

Bezemer, P., Van den Bosch, F.A.J and Volberda, H.W., 2010, *INSCOPE: Research for Innovation.*

of a shareholder value orientation among German firms", *Administrative Science Quarterly*, 49: 501–534; Fiss, P. C. and Zajac, E. J. (2006) "The symbolic management of strategic change: Sensegiving via framing and decoupling", *Academy of Management Journal*, 49: 1173–93; Freeman, R. E., Wicks, A. C. and Parmar, B. (2004) "Stakeholder theory and 'the corporate objective revisited'", *Organization Science*, 15: 364–369; Kwee, Z., Van Den Bosch, F. A. J. and Volberda, H. W. (forthcoming) "The influence of top management team's corporate governance orientation on strategic renewal trajectories: A longitudinal analysis of Royal Dutch Shell plc, 1907–2004", *Journal of Management Studies*; Lazonick, W. and O'Sullivan, M. (2000) "Maximizing shareholder value: A new ideology for corporate governance", *Economy & Society*, 29: 13–35; Mintzberg, H. (2000) "View from the top: Henry Mintzberg on strategy and management", *Academy of Management Executive*, 14: 31–39; Sanders, W. G. and Tuschke, A. C. (2007) "The adoption of the institutionally contested organizational practices: The emergence of stock option pay in Germany", *Academy of Management Journal*, 57: 33–56; Sundaram, A. K. and Inkpen, A. C. (2004) "The corporate objective revisited", *Organization Science*, 15: 350–363; Yoshikawa, T. and Rasheed, A. A. (2009) "Convergence of corporate governance: Critical review and future directions", *Corporate Governance: An International Review*, 17: 388–404.

## Questions

**1** In the light of the global financial crisis, do you think that the tide is now turning against shareholder value or that this trend will persist over the coming years?

**2** What is your position in the debate on the convergence/divergence of global corporate governance structures and practices? What are the long-term strategic consequences of this development?

times domestic shareholders will vote with management, as activist foreign investors enter a country it gives domestic institutional investors courage to become more active in shareholder proposals, which will increase shareholder welfare.

The governance mechanisms described in this chapter are designed to ensure that the agents of the firm's owners – the corporation's top level managers – make strategic decisions that best serve the interests of the entire group of stakeholders, as described in Chapter 1. The importance of various stakeholders varies around the globe (see the Key Debate). In the United States, shareholders are recognized as a company's most significant stakeholder. Thus, governance mechanisms focus on the control of managerial decisions to ensure that shareholders' interests will be served, but product market stakeholders (e.g., customers, suppliers and host communities) and organizational stakeholders (e.g., managerial and non-managerial employees) are important as well.[136] Therefore, at least the minimal interests or needs of all stakeholders must be satisfied through the firm's actions. Otherwise, dissatisfied stakeholders will withdraw their support from one firm and provide it to another (e.g., customers will purchase products from a supplier offering an acceptable substitute).

The firm's strategic competitiveness is enhanced when its governance mechanisms take into consideration the interests of all stakeholders. Although the idea is subject to debate, some believe that ethically responsible companies design and use governance mechanisms that serve all stakeholders' interests. The more critical relationship, however, is found between ethical behaviour and corporate governance mechanisms. The Enron disaster, Siemens scandal (described in the Opening Case) and the sad affair at Satyam (described in the Strategic Focus, see page 459) illustrate the devastating effect of poor ethical behaviour not only on a firm's stakeholders, but also on other firms. This issue is being taken seriously in other countries. The trend toward increased governance scrutiny continues to spread around the world.[137]

The mentioned examples show that all corporate owners are vulnerable to unethical behaviours and very poor judgements exercised by their employees, including top level managers – the agents who have been hired to make decisions that are in a firm's best interests. The decisions and actions of a corporation's board of directors can be an effective deterrent to these behaviours. In fact, some believe that the most effective boards participate actively to set boundaries for their firms' business ethics and values.[138] Once formulated, the board's expectations related to ethical decisions and actions of all of the firm's stakeholders must be clearly communicated to its top level managers. Moreover, as shareholders' agents, these managers must understand that the board will hold them fully accountable for the development and support of an organizational culture that allows unethical decisions and behaviours. As was explained in Chapter 11, CEOs can be positive role models for improved ethical behaviour.

Only when the proper corporate governance is exercised can strategies be formulated and implemented that will help the firm achieve strategic competitiveness and earn above-average returns. As the discussion in this chapter suggests, corporate governance mechanisms are a vital, yet imperfect, part of firms' efforts to select and successfully use strategies.

© Richard Levine/Alamy

## CLOSING CASE

## Europe's Enron – Parmalat

At the end of 2003, the Italian food-giant Parmalat ran into financial problems. While the producer of dairy products and beverages ought to have more than 4 billion euros in liquidity, it appeared that the company could not repay a 150 million euros bond in time. This only turned out to be the tip of the iceberg: during the weeks that followed the black hole in the company accounts increased to over 14 billion, resulting in one of Europe's largest bankruptcies.

Parmalat was founded in 1961 when Calisto Tanzi, a 22-year-old university dropout, took over a small, regional family firm after his father's death. In the following years the company expanded rapidly and employed 36 000 staff in 30 countries at the time that the scandal went public. From being one of Italy's corporate success stories, Parmalat's accounting fraud ruined the savings of more than 100 000 private investors, resulted in serious reputation damage for the Bank of America, Citicorp, Grant Thornton, and Deloitte and Touche, and caused financial problems for dairy farmers across the globe. Interestingly, and in line with other scandals such as Enron and Ahold, only a few analysts had foreseen the problems at the dairy manufacturer and publicly voiced their concerns.

As the scandal unfolded, more and more problems were exposed. First, while the books displayed a Parmalat account of 4 billion euros at a subsidiary of the Bank of America in the Cayman Islands, this money appeared not to exist. Second, Calisto Tanzi admitted that he had funnelled about 500 million euros away into other (family) companies and falsified the company accounts. In a response he stated: "I apologize to all who have suffered so much damage as a result of my schemes to make my dream of an industrial project come true." Third, the board of directors turned out to be not fully independent (e.g., one of the non-executive directors used to work for Parmalat) and Calisto Tanzi combined the position of CEO and chairman of the board of directors.

Given the huge failure of the corporate governance system as a whole, Italian prosecutors ordered trials for more than 20 people, ranging from the former CEO and CFO to several bank officials and accountants. In 2005, the first 11 officials submitted a plea to prevent jail sentences. In 2008 former CEO Tanzi was sentenced to

10 years in prison. According to his attorney "his client is 'a broken man' who knew nothing about finance and simply wanted to provide for himself and the community". The judge did not convict officials from any of the involved banks and accountancy firms, as it could not be proven that they knew or could have known the deplorable financial state of the Parmalat books.

In the meantime, the bankrupt group of Parmalat firms has been restructured. The Italian Prime Minister, Silvio Berlusconi, appointed Enrico Bondi to manage the firm's rescue. In October 2005, the new Parmalat Group was established and on 6 October the new corporation was listed on the Milan Stock Exchange.

**Sources:** Solomon, J. (2007) *Corporate Governance and Accountability*, Chichester: John Wiley & Sons; Hooper, J. (2003) "Parmalat 'is Europe's Enron'", *The Guardian*, 20 December; Willan, P. and Wachman, R. (2003) "Parmalat goes bankrupt as new scandal emerges", *The Observer*, 28 December; Hooper, J. (2003) "Tanzi 'has admitted diverting €500m'", *The Guardian*, 30 December; Arie, S. (2004) "Parmalat admits real debt is 14bn Euros", *The Guardian*, 27 January; Tran, M. and Jay, A. (2004) "Parmalat: All you need to know about the collapse of the Italian dairy giant", *Guardian Unlimited*, 6 October; BBC News, 2005, "Parmalat founder offers apology", http://www.news.bbc.co.uk, 16 January; Hooper, J. (2005) "Parmalat fraudsters to avoid prison", *The Guardian*, 29 June; Hooper, J. (2008) "Parmalat founder gets 10 years' prison for market rigging", *The Guardian*, 19 December.

## Questions

**1** The court ruled that officials of the involved banks and accounting firms were not to blame for the financial scandal at Parmalat. In your view, what is the extent to which the responsibilities of both groups of actors should range (i.e., did they get off the hook too easily or not)?

**2** One could argue that the presence of corporate governance scandals such as Parmalat and Ahold are simply the excesses of market capitalism. To what extent do you think that we should reconsider our economic models to prevent such crises?

**3** Compare and contrast this case with the others provided in the Opening Case and the Strategic Focus of this chapter. What are the communalities? And how do they inform us about the effectiveness of the various discussed external and internal corporate governance mechanisms in this chapter?

**4** Search for background information about the Italian corporate governance context. To which extent do you think that the institutional context and national culture have facilitated this crisis?

## SUMMARY

- Corporate governance is a relationship among stakeholders that is used to determine a firm's direction and control its performance. How firms monitor and control top level managers' decisions and actions affects the implementation of strategies. Effective governance that aligns managers' decisions with shareholders' interests can help produce a competitive advantage.

- Three internal governance mechanisms in the modern corporation include (1) ownership concentration, (2) the board of directors, and (3) executive compensation. The market for corporate control is the single external governance mechanism influencing managers' decisions and the outcomes resulting from them.

- Ownership is separated from control in the modern corporation. Owners (principals) hire managers (agents) to make decisions that maximize the firm's value. As risk-bearing specialists, owners diversify their risk by investing in multiple corporations with different risk profiles. As decision-making specialists, owners expect their agents (the firm's top level managers) to make decisions that will help to maximize the value of their firm. Thus, modern corporations are characterized by an agency relationship that is created when one party (the firm's owners) hires and pays another party (top level managers) to use its decision-making skills.

- Separation of ownership and control creates an agency problem when an agent pursues goals that conflict with principals' goals. Principals establish and use governance mechanisms to control this problem.

- Ownership concentration is based on the number of large-block shareholders and the percentage of shares they own. With significant ownership percentages, such as those held by large mutual funds and pension funds, institutional investors often are able to influence top level managers' strategic decisions and actions. Thus, unlike diffuse ownership, which tends to result in relatively weak monitoring and control of managerial decisions, concentrated ownership produces more active and effective monitoring. Institutional investors are becoming a powerful force across the globe and actively use their positions of concentrated ownership to force managers and boards of directors to make decisions that maximize a firm's value.

- A firm's board of directors, composed of insiders, related outsiders and outsiders, is a governance mechanism expected to represent the interests of all stakeholders affected by the firm, most notably the owners (shareholders). The percentage of outside directors on many boards now exceeds the percentage of inside directors. Through several regulatory initiatives, outsiders are expected to be more independent of a firm's top level managers compared with directors selected from inside the firm.

- Executive compensation is a highly visible and often criticized governance mechanism. Salary, bonuses and long-term incentives are used to strengthen the alignment between managers' and shareholders' interests. A firm's board of directors is responsible for determining the effectiveness of the firm's executive compensation system. An effective system elicits managerial decisions that are in the shareholders' best interests.

- In general, evidence suggests that shareholders and boards of directors have become more vigilant in their control of managerial decisions. Nonetheless, these mechanisms are insufficient to govern managerial behaviour in many large companies as shown in the latest economic crisis brought on by poor strategic decisions made by top level managers in financial services firms. Therefore, the market for corporate control is an important governance mechanism. Although it, too, is imperfect, the market for corporate control has been effective in causing corporations to combat inefficient diversification and to implement more effective strategic decisions.

- Corporate governance structures used in Germany, Japan and China differ from each other and from the structure used in the United States. Historically, the US governance structure focused on maximizing shareholder value. In Germany, employees, as a stakeholder group, take a more prominent role in governance. By contrast, until recently, Japanese shareholders played virtually no role in the monitoring and control of top level managers. However, now Japanese firms are being challenged by "activist" shareholders. China's governance system is the youngest and has a number of characteristics that mirror those in the US. However, the central government still plays a major role in governance in China as well. Internationally, all these systems are becoming increasingly similar, as are many governance systems both in developed countries, such as France and Spain, and in transitional economies, such as Russia and India.

- Effective governance mechanisms ensure that the interests of all stakeholders are served. Thus, long-term strategic success results when firms are governed in ways that permit at least minimal satisfaction of capital market stakeholders (e.g., shareholders), product market stakeholders (e.g., customers and suppliers), and organizational stakeholders (managerial and non-managerial employees; see Chapter 2). Moreover, effective governance produces ethical behaviour in the formulation and implementation of strategies.

## REVIEW QUESTIONS

1 What is corporate governance? What factors account for the considerable amount of attention corporate governance receives from several parties, including shareholder activists, business press writers and academic scholars? Why is governance necessary to control managers' decisions?

2 What is meant by the statement that "ownership is separated from managerial control in the corporation"? Why does this separation exist?

3 What is an agency relationship? What is managerial opportunism? What assumptions

do owners of corporations make about managers as agents?

4 How is each of the three internal governance mechanisms – ownership concentration, boards of directors and executive compensation – used to align the interests of managerial agents with those of the firm's owners?

5 What trends exist regarding executive compensation? What is the effect of the increased use of long-term incentives on executives' strategic decisions?

6 What is the market for corporate control? What conditions generally cause this external governance mechanism to become active? How does the mechanism constrain top level managers' decisions and actions?

7 What is the nature of corporate governance in Germany, Japan and China?

8 How can corporate governance foster ethical strategic decisions and behaviours on the part of managers as agents?

## DISCUSSION QUESTIONS

1 As discussed in this chapter, corporate governance regulation, such as the Sarbanes-Oxley Act and various corporate governance codes, are becoming more important in today's economy.

  a What purpose does corporate governance regulation serve? And what kind of problems might regulation create?

  b Different types of regulation exist across the globe, varying from self-regulation (soft law) to explicit government regulation (hard law). Which factors should be taken into account while choosing the appropriate type of regulation?

2 Search for a corporate governance scandal in the newspapers. Examples include, among others, accounting fraud, insider trading, excessive remuneration or empire building by CEOs.

  a Which internal and external corporate governance mechanisms failed in this case?

  b What is the significance of your case and how have financial markets responded?

  c How does your scandal relate to the national culture of the home country of the company?

3 In this chapter we have said that companies vary in the extent to which they try to maximize either shareholder value or stakeholder value. Seek examples of both approaches in the annual reports of companies and consider:

  a What are key differences in the business approach between organizations promoting shareholder value and those emphasizing stakeholder value?

  b Having considered these examples, do you think that this strategic decision relates to firm performance in the long run?

## FURTHER READING

In this chapter, it has been highlighted that the effectiveness of the three discussed corporate governance mechanisms widely varies across national boundaries. Monks and Minow's *Corporate Governance* (Blackwell Business, 2004), Tricker's *Corporate Governance: Principles, Policies, and Practices* (Oxford University Press, 2009) and Solomon's *Corporate Governance and Accountability* (John Wiley & Sons, 2007) provide excellent further introductions to this theme. Furthermore, Huse's *Boards, Governance and Value Creation* (Cambridge University Press, 2007) provides a thorough description of the functioning of boards of directors and offers an analytic framework to analyze them.

Finally, as worldwide changes in corporate governance are progressively taking place over the last years, scholars and practitioners are increasingly confronted with new and complex corporate governance challenges. Two papers, authored by Hambrick, Von Werder and Zajac (*Organization Science*, 2008) and Filatotchev and Boyd (*Corporate Governance* 2009), provide thought-provoking reflections on the current stance of scholarly research and highlight new avenues for future studies.

# EXPERIENTIAL EXERCISES

## Exercise 1: International governance codes

As described in this chapter, numerous regulatory initiatives aimed at improving corporate governance have been undertaken since the nineties. These initiatives varied from hard law (SOX) to soft law (self-regulatory corporate governance codes) and established (mandatory) "best practices" for both board composition and processes. The first code was developed by the Cadbury Committee for the London Stock Exchange in 1992. The Australian Stock Exchange developed its guidelines in the Hilmer Report, released in 1993. The Toronto Stock Exchange developed its guidelines the following year in the Dey Report. Today, most major stock exchanges have governance codes.

Working in small groups, find the governance codes of two stock exchanges. Prepare a short (2–3 pages, single-spaced) bullet point comparison of the similarities and differences between the two codes. Be sure to include the following topics in your analysis:

- How are the guidelines structured? Are they rules (i.e., required) or recommendations (i.e., suggestions)? What mechanism is included to monitor or enforce the guidelines?

- What board roles are addressed in the guidelines? For example, some codes may place most or all of their emphasis on functions derived from the importance of the agency relationship illustrated in Figure 12.1 on p.441, such as monitoring, oversight and reporting. Codes might also mention the board's role in supporting strategy, or their contribution to firm performance and shareholder wealth.

- What aspects of board composition and structure are covered in the guidelines? For instance, items included in different codes include the balance of insiders and outsiders, committees, whether the CEO also serves as board chair, director education and/or evaluation, compensation of officers and directors, and ownership by board members.

## Exercise 2: Governance and personal investments

Governance mechanisms are considered to be effective if they meet the needs of all stakeholders, including shareholders. As an investor, how much weight, if any, do you place on a firm's corporate governance? If you currently own any stocks, select a firm that you have invested in. If you do not own any stocks, select a publicly traded company that you consider an attractive potential investment. Working individually, complete the following research on your target firm:

- Find a copy of the company's most recent proxy statement. Proxy statements are mailed to shareholders prior to each year's annual meeting and contain detailed information about the company's governance and present issues on which a shareholder vote might be held. Proxy statements are typically available from a firm's website (look for an "Investors" sub-menu).

- Conduct a search for news articles that address the governance of your target company. Using different keywords (e.g., "governance", "directors", or "board of directors") in combination with the company name may be helpful.

Some of the topics that you should examine include:

- Compensation plans (for both the CEO and board members)
- Board composition (e.g., board size, insiders and outsiders)
- Committees
- Stock ownership by officers and directors
- Whether the CEO holds both CEO and board chairperson positions
- Is there a lead director who is not an officer of the company?
- Board seats held by blockholders or institutional investors
- Activities by activist shareholders regarding corporate governance issues of concern

Prepare a one-page single-spaced memo that summarizes the results of your findings. Your memo should include the following topics:

- Summarize what you consider to be the key aspects of the firm's governance mechanisms.
- Based on your review of the firm's governance, did you change your opinion of the firm's desirability as an investment? Why or why not?

## VIDEO CASE

### A panel discussion chaired by Jim Quigley, global CEO of Deloitte

www.cengage.co.uk/volberda/students/video_cases

Before you watch the video, consider the following concepts:

- Stakeholder value
- Shareholder value
- Financial crisis
- Ethical values

During the Davos Annual Meeting 2010, an international panel chaired by Jim Quigley (Deloitte) discussed whether and how contemporary values have contributed to the worldwide economic crisis. Watch the video and answer the questions below.

1 Do you agree with the result of the web-based survey of the Forum that the current financial crisis is foremost a crisis of values? Why (not)?

2 Identify the different views the various panellist put forward to prevent the recurrence of the financial crisis. Which one is most compelling to you?

3 To what extent should the various internal and external corporate governance mechanisms mentioned in this chapter be revisited in the post-crisis world?

4 Reflect on the desirability of a set of globally accepted (economic) values. In your view, what values should be included in such set?

## NOTES

1. B. W. Heineman, Jr, 2009, "Redefining the CEO role", *BusinessWeek*, http://www.businessweek.com, April 16; C. Thomas, D. Kidd and C. Fernández-Aráoz, 2007, "Are you underutilizing your board?", *MIT Sloan Management Review*, 48(2): 71–76; D. C. Carey and M. Patsalos-Fox, 2006, "Shaping strategy from the boardroom", *McKinsey Quarterly*, (3): 90–94.

2. R. Aguilera and G. Jackson, 2003, "The cross-national diversity of corporate governance: Dimensions and determinants", *Academy of Management Review*, 28: 447–465; R. Aguilera, I. Filatotchev, H. Gospel and G. Jackson, 2008, "An organizational approach to comparative corporate governance: Costs, contingencies, and complementarities", *Organization Science*, 19: 475–492; I. Filatotchev and B. K. Boyd, 2009, "Taking stock of corporate governance research while looking to the future", *Corporate Governance: An International Review*, 17: 257–265; M. A. Witt and G. Redding, 2009, "Culture, meaning, and institutions: Executive rationale in Germany and Japan", *Journal of International Business Studies*, 40: 859–885.

3. R. Aguilera, I. Filatotchev, H. Gospel and G. Jackson, 2008, "An organizational approach to comparative corporate governance: Costs, contingencies, and complementarities", *Organization Science*, 19: 475–492; D. C. Hambrick, A. Von Werder and E. J. Zajac, 2008, "New directions in corporate governance research", *Organization Science*, 19: 381–385; A. Pugliese, P. Bezemer, A. Zattoni, M. Huse, F. A. J. Van Den Bosch and H. W. Volberda, 2009, "Boards of directors' contribution to strategy: A literature review and research agenda", *Corporate Governance: An International Review*, 17: 292–306.

4. C. Crossland and D. C. Hambrick, 2007, "How national systems differ in their constraints on corporate executives: A study of CEO effects in three countries", *Strategic Management Journal*, 28: 767–789; M. D. Lynall, B. R. Golden and A. J. Hillman, 2003, "Board composition from adolescence to maturity: A multitheoretic view", *Academy of Management Review*, 28: 416–431.

5. M. A. Rutherford, A. K. Buchholtz and J. A. Brown, 2007, "Examining the relationships between monitoring and incentives in corporate governance", *Journal of Management Studies* 44: 414–430; C. M. Daily, D. R. Dalton and A. A. Cannella, 2003, "Corporate governance: Decades of dialogue and data", *Academy of Management Review*, 28: 371–382; P. Stiles, 2001, "The impact of the board on strategy: An empirical examination", *Journal of Management Studies*, 38: 627–650.

6. D. R. Dalton, M. A. Hitt, S. T. Certo and C. M. Dalton, 2008, "The fundamental agency problem and its mitigation: Independence, equity and the market for corporate control", in: J. P. Walsh and A. P. Brief (eds.), *The Academy of Management Annals*, New York: Lawrence Erlbaum Associates, 1: 1–64; E. F. Fama and M. C. Jensen, 1983, "Separation of ownership and control", *Journal of Law and Economics*, 26: 301–325.

7. I. Le Breton-Miller and D. Miller, 2006, "Why do some family businesses out-compete? Governance, long-term orientations, and sustainable capability", *Entrepreneurship Theory and Practice*, 30: 731–746; M. Carney, 2005,

"Corporate governance and competitive advantage in family-controlled firms", *Entrepreneurship Theory and Practice*, 29: 249–265; R. Charan, 1998, *How Corporate Boards Create Competitive Advantage*, San Francisco: Jossey-Bass; I. Filatotchev and S. Toms, 2003, "Corporate governance, strategy and survival in a declining industry: A study of UK cotton textile companies", *Journal of Management Studies*, 40: 895–920.

8. X. Wu, 2005, "Corporate governance and corruption: A cross-country analysis", *Governance*, 18(2): 151–170; J. McGuire and S. Dow, 2002, "The Japanese keiretsu system: An empirical analysis", *Journal of Business Research*, 55: 33–40.

9. R. E. Hoskisson, D. Yiu and H. Kim, 2004, "Corporate governance systems: Effects of capital and labor market congruency on corporate innovation and global competitiveness", *Journal of High Technology Management*, 15: 293–315.

10. C. Crossland and D. C. Hambrick, 2007, "How national systems differ in their constraints on corporate executives", *Strategic Management Journal*, 28: 767–789; R. Aguilera and G. Jackson, 2003, "The cross-national diversity of corporate governance: Dimensions and determinants", *Academy of Management Review*, 28: 447–465; W. Lazonick and M. O'Sullivan, 2000, "Maximizing shareholder value: A new ideology for corporate governance", *Economy & Society*, 29: 13–35.

11. R. P. Wright, 2004, "Top managers' strategic cognitions of the strategy making process: Differences between high and low performing firms", *Journal of General Management*, 30(1): 61–78.

12. R. E. Freeman, A. C. Wicks and B. Parmar, 2004, "Stakeholder theory and 'the corporate objective revisited'", *Organization Science*, 15: 364–369; B. De Wit and R. Meyer, 2004, *Strategy: Process, content, context*, London: ITP Press.

13. X. Luo, C. N. Chung and M. Sobczak, 2009, "How do corporate governance model differences affect foreign direct investment in emerging economies?", *Journal of International Business Studies*, 40: 444–467; A. Bris and C. Cabous, 2006, "In a merger, two companies come together and integrate their distribution lines, brands, work forces, management teams, strategies and cultures", *Financial Times*, October 6, 1.

14. S. Sudarsanam and A. A. Mahate, 2006, "Are friendly acquisitions too bad for shareholders and managers? Long-term value creation and top management turnover in hostile and friendly acquirers", *British Journal of Management: Supplement*, 17(1): S7–S30; T. Moeller, 2005, "Let's make a deal! How shareholder control impacts merger payoffs", *Journal of Financial Economics*, 76(1): 167–190; M. A. Hitt, R. E. Hoskisson, R. A. Johnson and D. D. Moesel, 1996, "The market for corporate control and firm innovation", *Academy of Management Journal*, 39: 1084–1119.

15. R. E. Hoskisson, M. A. Hitt, R. A. Johnson and W. Grossman, 2002, "Conflicting voices: The effects of ownership heterogeneity and internal governance on corporate strategy", *Academy of Management Journal*, 45: 697–716.

16. G. E. Davis and T. A. Thompson, 1994, "A social movement perspective on corporate control", *Administrative Science Quarterly*, 39: 141–173.

17. R. Bricker and N. Chandar, 2000, "Where Berle and Means went wrong: A reassessment of capital market agency and financial reporting", *Accounting, Organizations, and Society*, 25: 529–554; M. A. Eisenberg, 1989, "The structure of corporation law", *Columbia Law Review*, 89(7): 1461, as cited in R. A. G. Monks and N. Minow, 1995, *Corporate Governance*, Cambridge, MA: Blackwell Business, 7.

18. R. M. Wiseman and L. R. Gomez-Mejia, 1999, "A behavioural agency model of managerial risk taking", *Academy of Management Review*, 23: 133–153.

19. T. Zellweger, 2007, "Time horizon, costs of equity capital, and generic investment strategies of firms", *Family Business Review*, 20(1): 1–15; R. C. Anderson and D. M. Reeb, 2004, "Board composition: Balancing family influence in S&P 500 firms", *Administrative Science Quarterly*, 49: 209–237.

20. M. Carney, 2005, "Corporate governance and competitive advantage in family-controlled firms", *Entrepreneurship Theory and Practice*, 29: 249–265; N. Anthanassiou, W. F. Crittenden, L. M. Kelly and P. Marquez, 2002, "Founder centrality effects on the Mexican family firm's top management group: Firm culture, strategic vision and goals and firm performance", *Journal of World Business*, 37: 139–150.

21. M. Faccio, L. H. P. Lang and L. Young, 2001, "Dividends and expropriation", *American Economic Review*, 91: 54–78; M. Faccio and L. H. P. Lang, 2002, "The ultimate ownership of Western European corporations", *Journal of Financial Economics*, 65: 365–395.

22. M. Santiago-Castro and C. J. Brown, 2007, "Ownership structure and minority rights: A Latin American view", *Journal of Economics and Business*, 59: 430–442; M. Carney and E. Gedajlovic, 2003, "Strategic innovation and the administrative heritage of East Asian family business groups", *Asia Pacific Journal of Management*, 20: 5–26; D. Miller and I. Le Breton-Miller, 2003, "Challenge versus advantage in family business", *Strategic Organization*, 1: 127–134.

23. D. G. Sirmon, J. L. Arregle, M. A. Hitt and J. Webb, 2008, "Strategic responses to the threat of imitation", *Entrepreneurship Theory and Practice*, 32: 979–998.

24. M. A. Rutherford, A. K. Buchholtz and J. A. Brown, 2007, "Examining the relationships between monitoring and incentives in corporate governance", *Journal of Management Studies*, 44: 414–430; D. Dalton, C. Daily, T. Certo and R. Roengpitya, 2003, "Meta-analyses of financial performance and equity: Fusion or confusion?", *Academy of Management Journal*, 46: 13–26; M. Jensen

and W. Meckling, 1976, "Theory of the firm: Managerial behaviour, agency costs, and ownership structure", *Journal of Financial Economics*, 11: 305–360.

25. G. C. Rodríguez, C. A. D. Espejo and R. Valle Cabrera, 2007, "Incentives management during privatization: An agency perspective", *Journal of Management Studies*, 44: 536–560; D. C. Hambrick, S. Finkelstein and A. C. Mooney, 2005, "Executive job demands: New insights for explaining strategic decisions and leader behaviours", *Academy of Management Review*, 30: 472–491.

26. T. G. Habbershon, 2006, "Commentary: A framework for managing the familiness and agency advantages in family firms", *Entrepreneurship Theory and Practice*, 30: 879–886; M. G. Jacobides and D. C. Croson, 2001, "Information policy: Shaping the value of agency relationships", *Academy of Management Review*, 26: 202–223.

27. A. Mackey, 2008, "The effects of CEOs on firm performance", *Strategic Management Journal*, 29: 1357–1367; Y. Y. Kor, 2006, "Direct and interaction effects of top management team and board compositions on R&D investment strategy", *Strategic Management Journal*, 27: 1081–1099.

28. D. R. Dalton, M. A. Hitt, S. T. Certo and C. M. Dalton, 2008, "The fundamental agency problem and its mitigation: Independence, equity and the market for corporate control", in: J. P. Walsh and A. P. Brief (eds.), *The Academy of Management Annals*, 1: 1–64; A. Ghosh, D. Moon and K. Tandon, 2007, "CEO ownership and discretionary investments", *Journal of Business Finance & Accounting*, 34: 819–839.

29. S. Ghoshal and P. Moran, 1996, "Bad for practice: A critique of the transaction cost theory", *Academy of Management Review*, 21: 13–47; O. E. Williamson, 1996, *The Mechanisms of Governance*, New York: Oxford University Press, 6.

30. B. E. Ashforth, D. A. Gioia, S. L. Robinson and L. K. Trevino, 2008, "Re-viewing organizational corruption", *Academy of Management Review*, 33: 670–684; E. Kang, 2006, "Investors' perceptions of managerial opportunism in corporate acquisitions: The moderating role of environmental condition", *Corporate Governance*, 14: 377–387; R. W. Coff and P. M. Lee, 2003, "Insider trading as a vehicle to appropriate rent from R&D", *Strategic Management Journal*, 24: 183–190.

31. M. L. McDonald, P. Khanna and J. D. Westphal, 2008, "Getting them to think outside the circle: Corporate governance, CEOs' external advice networks, and firm performance", *Academy of Management Journal*, 51: 453–475.

32. E. F. Fama, "Agency problems and the theory of the firm", *Journal of Political Economy*, 88: 288–307.

33. P. Jiraporn, Y. Sang Kim, W. N. Davidson and M. Singh, 2006, "Corporate governance, shareholder rights and firm diversification: An empirical analysis", *Journal of Banking &*

*Finance*, 30: 947–963; R. C. Anderson, T. W. Bates, J. M. Bizjak and M. L. Lemmon, 2000, "Corporate governance and firm diversification", *Financial Management*, 29(1): 5–22; R. E. Hoskisson and T. A. Turk, 1990, "Corporate restructuring: Governance and control limits of the internal market", *Academy of Management Review*, 15: 459–477.

34. S. W. Geiger and L. H. Cashen, 2007, "Organizational size and CEO compensation: The moderating effect of diversification in downscoping organizations", *Journal of Managerial Issues*, 9(2): 233–252; Y. Grinstein and P. Hribar, 2004, "CEO compensation and incentives: Evidence from M&A bonuses", *Journal of Financial Economics*, 73: 119–143.

35. G. P. Baker and B. J. Hall, 2004, "CEO incentives and firm size", *Journal of Labor Economics*, 22: 767–798; R. Bushman, Q. Chen, E. Engel and A. Smith, 2004, "Financial accounting information, organizational complexity and corporate governance systems", *Journal of Accounting & Economics*, 7: 167–201; M. A. Geletkanycz, B. K. Boyd and S. Finkelstein, 2001, "The strategic value of CEO external directorate networks: Implications for CEO compensation", *Strategic Management Journal*, 9: 889–898.

36. S. Rajgopal, T. Shevlin and V. Zamora, 2006, "CEOs' outside employment opportunities and the lack of relative performance evaluation in compensation contracts", *Journal of Finance*, 61: 1813–1844; L. R. Gomez-Mejia, M. Nunez-Nickel and I. Gutierrez, 2001, "The role of family ties in agency contracts", *Academy of Management Journal*, 44: 81–95.

37. M. S. Jensen, 1986, "Agency costs of free cash flow, corporate finance, and takeovers", *American Economic Review*, 76: 323–329.

38. A. V. Douglas, 2007, "Managerial opportunism and proportional corporate payout policies", *Managerial Finance*, 33(1): 26–42; M. Jensen and E. Zajac, 2004, "Corporate elites and corporate strategy: How demographic preferences and structural position shape the scope of the firm", *Strategic Management Journal*, 25: 507–524; T. H. Brush, P. Bromiley and M. Hendrickx, 2000, "The free cash flow hypothesis for sales growth and firm performance", *Strategic Management Journal*, 21: 455–472.

39. J. Lunsford and B. Steinberg, 2006, "Conglomerates' conundrum", *Wall Street Journal*, September 14, B1, B7; K. Ramaswamy, M. Li and B. S. P. Petitt, 2004, "Who drives unrelated diversification? A study of Indian manufacturing firms", *Asia Pacific Journal of Management*, 21: 403–423; K. Ramaswamy, M. Li and R. Veliyath, 2002, "Variations in ownership behavior and propensity to diversify", *Strategic Management Journal*, 23: 345–358.

40. M. V. S. Kumar, 2009, "The relationship between product and international diversification: The effects of short-run constraints and endogeneity", *Strategic Management Journal*, 30: 99–116; M. F. Wiersema and H. P. Bowen, 2008, "Corporate diversification: The impact of foreign

competition, industry globalization and product diversification", *Strategic Management Journal*, 29: 115–132.

41. D. D. Bergh, R. A. Johnson and R. L Dewitt, 2008, "Restructuring through spin-off or sell-off: Transforming information asymmetries into financial gain", *Strategic Management Journal*, 29: 133–148; K. B. Lee, M. W. Peng and K. Lee, 2008, "From diversification premium to diversification discount during institutional transitions", *Journal of World Business*, 43: 47–65.

42. T. K. Berry, J. M. Bizjak, M. L. Lemmon and L. Naveen, 2006, "Organizational complexity and CEO labor markets: Evidence from diversified firms", *Journal of Corporate Finance*, 12: 797–817; R. Rajan, H. Servaes and L. Zingales, 2001, "The cost of diversity: The diversification discount and inefficient investment", *Journal of Finance*, 55: 35–79; A. Sharma, 1997, "Professional as agent: Knowledge asymmetry in agency exchange", *Academy of Management Review*, 22: 758–798.

43. R. Aguilera and A. Cuervo-Cazurra, 2004, "Codes of good governance worldwide: What is the trigger?", *Organization Studies*, 25: 415–443; P. Bezemer, G. F. Maassen, F. A. J. Van Den Bosch and H. W. Volberda, 2007, "Investigating the development of the internal and external service tasks of non-executive directors: The case of the Netherlands (1997–2005)", *Corporate Governance: An International Review*, 15: 1119–1129; C. M. Daily, D. R. Dalton and A. A. Cannella, 2003, "Corporate governance: Decades of dialogue and data", *Academy of Management Review*, 28: 371–382; A. Enrione, C. Mazza and F. Zerboni, 2006, "Institutionalizing codes of governance", *American Behavioural Scientist*, 49: 961–973.

44. V. Chhaochharia and Y. Grinstein, 2007, "Corporate governance and firm value: The impact of the 2002 governance rules", *Journal of Finance*, 62: 1789–1825; A. Borrus, L. Lavelle, D. Brady, M. Arndt and J. Weber, 2005, "Death, taxes and Sarbanes-Oxley? Executives may be frustrated with the law's burdens, but corporate performance is here to stay", *BusinessWeek*, January 17, 28–31.

45. C. M. Daily, D. R. Dalton and A. A. Cannella, 2003, "Corporate governance: Decades of dialogue and data", *Academy of Management Review*, 28: 371–382.

46. R. Aguilera and A. Cuervo-Cazurra, 2004, "Codes of good governance worldwide: What is the trigger?", *Organization Studies*, 25: 415–443; A. De Jong, V. Douglas, G. Mertens and C. E. Wasley, 2005, "The role of self-regulation in corporate governance: Evidence and implications from the Netherlands", *Journal of Corporate Finance*, 11: 473–503; A. Zattoni and F. Cuomo, 2008, "Why adopt codes of good governance? A comparison of institutional and efficiency perspectives", *Corporate Governance: An International Review*, 16: 1–15.

47. F. Navissi and V. Naiker, 2006, "Institutional ownership and corporate value", *Managerial Finance*, 32: 247–256; A. de Miguel, J. Pindado and C. de la Torre, 2004, "Ownership structure and firm value: New evidence from Spain",

*Strategic Management Journal*, 25: 1199–1207; J. Coles, N. Sen and V. McWilliams, 2001, "An examination of the relationship of governance mechanisms to performance", *Journal of Management*, 27: 23–50.

48. P. Jiraporn, Y. S. Kim, W. N. Davidson and M. Singh, 2006, "Corporate governance, shareholder rights and firm diversification", *Journal of Banking and Finance*, 30: 947–963; M. Singh, I. Mathur and K. C. Gleason, 2004, "Governance and performance implications of diversification strategies: Evidence from large US firms", *Financial Review*, 39: 489–526; R. E. Hoskisson, R. A. Johnson and D. D. Moesel, 1994, "Corporate divestiture intensity in restructuring firms: Effects of governance, strategy, and performance", *Academy of Management Journal*, 37: 1207–1251.

49. G. Iannotta, G. Nocera and A. Sironi, 2007, "Ownership structure, risk and performance in the European banking industry", *Journal of Banking & Finance*, 31: 2127–2149.

50. B. Villalonga and R. Amit, 2006, "How do family ownership, control and management affect firm value?", *Journal of Financial Economics*, 80: 385–417; R. C. Anderson and D. M. Reeb, 2004, "Board composition: Balancing family influence in S&P 500 firms", *Administrative Science Quarterly*, 49: 209–237.

51. M. Fackler, 2008, "South Korea faces question of corporate control", *New York Times*, http://www.nytimes.com, April 24; S. J. Chang, 2003, "Ownership structure, expropriation and performance of group-affiliated companies in Korea", *Academy of Management Journal*, 46: 238–253.

52. A. Berle and G. Means, 1932, *The Modern Corporation and Private Property*, New York: Macmillan.

53. M. Gietzmann, 2006, "Disclosure of timely and forward-looking statements and strategic management of major institutional ownership", *Long Range Planning*, 39(4): 409–427; B. Ajinkya, S. Bhojraj and P. Sengupta, 2005, "The association between outside directors, institutional investors and the properties of management earnings forecasts", *Journal of Accounting Research*, 43: 343–376.

54. K. Schnatterly, K. W. Shaw and W. W. Jennings, 2008, "Information advantages of large institutional owners", *Strategic Management Journal*, 29: 219–227; R. E. Hoskisson, M. A. Hitt, R. A. Johnson and W. Grossman, 2002, "Conflicting voices: The effects of ownership heterogeneity and internal governance on corporate strategy", *Academy of Management Journal*, 45: 697–716; A. Brav, W. Jiang, F. Partnoy and R. Thomas, 2008, "Hedge fund activism, corporate governance, and firm performance", *Journal of Finance*, 63: 1729–1775.

55. M. Faccio, L. H. P. Lang and L. Young, 2001, "Dividends and expropriation", *American Economic Review*, 91:54–78; M. Faccio and L. H. P. Lang, 2002, "The ultimate ownership of Western European corporations", *Journal of Financial Economics*, 65: 365–395; S. Thomsen and T. Pedersen, 2000, "Ownership structure and economic

performance in the largest European companies", *Strategic Management Journal*, 21: 689–706.

56. S. D. Chowdhury and E. Z. Wang, 2009, "Institutional activism types and CEO compensation: A time-series analysis of large Canadian corporations", *Journal of Management*, 35: 5–36; M. Musteen, D. K. Datta and P. Herrmann, 2009, "Ownership structure and CEO compensation: Implications for the choice of foreign market entry modes", *Journal of International Business Studies*, 40: 321–338; R. Dharwadkar, M. Goranova, P. Brandes and R. Khan, 2008, "Institutional ownership and monitoring effectiveness: It's not just how much but what else you own", *Organization Science*, 19: 419–440.

57. T. W. Briggs, 2007, "Corporate governance and the new hedge fund activism: An empirical analysis", *Journal of Corporation Law*, 32(4): 682-737; K. Rebeiz, 2001, "Corporate governance effectiveness in American corporations: A survey", *International Management Journal*, 18(1): 74–80; C. P. Clifford, 2008, "Value creation or destruction? Hedge funds as shareholder activists", *Journal of Corporate Finance*, 14: 323–336.

58. S. Thurm, "When investor activism doesn't pay", *Wall Street Journal*, September 12, A2; S. M. Jacoby, 2007, "Principles and agents: CalPERS and corporate governance in Japan", *Corporate Governance*, 15(1): 5–15; L. Tihanyi, R. A. Johnson, R. E. Hoskisson and M. A. Hitt, 2003, "Institutional ownership differences and international diversification: The effects of boards of directors and technological opportunity", *Academy of Management Journal*, 46: 195–211; R. E. Hoskisson, M. A. Hitt, R. A. Johnson and W. Grossman, 2002, "Conflicting voices: The effects of ownership heterogeneity and internal governance on corporate strategy", *Academy of Management Journal*, 45: 697–716; P. David, M. A. Hitt and J. Gimeno, 2001, "The role of institutional investors in influencing R&D," *Academy of Management Journal*, 44: 144–157.

59. D. R. Dalton, M. A. Hitt, S. T. Certo and C. M. Dalton, 2008, "The fundamental agency problem and its mitigation: Independence, equity and the market for corporate control", in: J. P. Walsh and A. P. Brief (eds.), *The Academy of Management Annals*, 1: 1–64; C. M. Dalton and D. R. Dalton, 2006, "Corporate governance best practices: The proof is in the process", *Journal of Business Strategy*, 27(4): 5–7; R. V. Aguilera, 2005, "Corporate governance and director accountability: An institutional comparative perspective", *British Journal of Management*, 16(S1), S39–S53.

60. R. H. Lester, A. Hillman, A. Zardkoohi and A. A. Cannella, 2008, "Former government officials as outside directors: The role of human and social capital", *Academy of Management Journal*, 51: 999–1013; M. L. McDonald, J. D. Westphal and M. E. Graebner, 2008, "What do they know? The effects of outside director acquisition experience on firm acquisition performance", *Strategic Management Journal*, 29: 1155–1177; A. J. Hillman and T. Dalziel, 2003, "Boards of directors and firm performance", *Academy of Management Review*, 28: 383–396;

A. Pugliese, P. Bezemer, A. Zattoni, M. Huse, F. A. J. Van Den Bosch and H. W. Volberda, 2009, "Boards of directors' contribution to strategy: A literature review and research agenda", *Corporate Governance: An International Review*, 17: 292–306; W. Ruigrok, S. Peck and H. Keller, 2006, "Board characteristics and involvement in strategic decision making: Evidence from Swiss companies", *Journal of Management Studies*, 43: 1201–1226.

61. L. Bonazzi and S. M. N. Islam, 2007, "Agency theory and corporate governance: A study of the effectiveness of board in their monitoring of the CEO", *Journal of Modeling in Management*, 2(1): 7–23; K. Rebeiz, 2001, "Corporate governance effectiveness in American corporations: A survey", *International Management Journal*, 18: 74–80.

62. E. Kang, 2008, "Director interlocks and spillover effects of reputational penalties from financial reporting fraud", *Academy of Management Journal*, 51: 537–555; N. Chipalkatti, Q. V. Le and M. Rishi, 2007, "Portfolio flows to emerging capital markets: Do corporate transparency and public governance matter?", *Business and Society Review*, 112(2): 227–249.

63. V. Krivogorsky, 2006, "Ownership, board structure, and performance in continental Europe", *International Journal of Accounting*, 41: 176–197; R. E. Hoskisson, M. A. Hitt, R. A. Johnson and W. Grossman, 2002, "Conflicting voices: The effects of ownership heterogeneity and internal governance on corporate strategy", *Academy of Management Journal*, 45: 697–716; B. D. Baysinger and R. E. Hoskisson, 1990, "The composition of boards of directors and strategic control: Effects on corporate strategy", *Academy of Management Review*, 15: 72–87.

64. Y. Y. Kor and V. F. Misangyi, 2008, "Outside directors' industry-specific experience and firms' liability of newness", *Strategic Management Journal*, 29: 1345–1355; E. E. Lawler III and D. Finegold, 2006, "Who's in the boardroom and does it matter: The impact of having non-director executives attend board meetings", *Organizational Dynamics*, 35(1): 106–115.

65. R. Hooghiemstra and J. Van Manen, J, 2004, "The independence paradox: (Im)possibilities facing non-executive directors in the Netherlands", *Corporate Governance: An International Review*, 12: 314–324; G. F. Maassen, 1999, *An International Comparison of Corporate Governance Models*, Amsterdam: Spencer Stuart Amsterdam; T. McNulty and A. M. Pettigrew, 1999, "Strategists on the board", *Organization Studies*, 20: 47–74.

66. E. M. Fich and A. Shivdasani, 2006, "Are busy boards effective monitors?", *Journal of Finance*, 61: 689–724; J. Westphal and L. Milton, 2000, "How experience and network ties affect the influence of demographic minorities on corporate boards", *Administrative Science Quarterly*, 45 (2): 366–398.

67. S. K. Lee and L. R. Carlson, 2007, "The changing board of directors: Board independence in S&P 500 firm", *Journal of Organizational Culture, Communication and Conflict*, 11(1): 31–41.

68. R. C. Pozen, 2006, "Before you split that CEO/Chair", *Harvard Business Review*, 84(4): 26–28; J. W. Lorsch and A. Zelleke, 2005, "Should the CEO be the chairman", *MIT Sloan Management Review*, 46(2): 71–74.

69. M. Kroll, B. A. Walters and P. Wright, 2008, "Board vigilance, director experience and corporate outcomes", *Strategic Management Journal*, 29: 363–382.

70. E. M. Fich and A. Shivdasani, 2006, "Are busy boards effective monitors?", *Journal of Finance*, 61: 689–724; J. Roberts, T. McNulty and, P. Stiles, 2005, "Beyond agency conceptions of the work of the non-executive director: Creating accountability in the boardroom", *British Journal of Management*, 16(S1): S5–S26.

71. E. M. Fich and A. Shivdasani, 2006, "Are busy boards effective monitors? ", *Journal of Finance*, 61: 689–724; S. Zahra, 1996, "Governance, ownership and corporate entrepreneurship among the *Fortune* 500: The moderating impact of industry technological opportunity", *Academy of Management Journal*, 39: 1713–1735.

72. B. D. Baysinger and R. E. Hoskisson, 1990, "The composition of boards of directors and strategic control: Effects on corporate strategy", *Academy of Management Review*, 15: 72–87; G. F. Maassen, 1999, *An International Comparison Of Corporate Governance Models*. Amsterdam: Spencer Stuart Amsterdam.

73. Y. Zhang, 2008, "Information asymmetry and the dismissal of newly appointed CEOs: An empirical investigation", *Strategic Management Journal*, 29: 859–872.

74. E. E. Lawler III and D. Finegold, 2006, "Who's in the boardroom and does it matter: The impact of having non-director executives attend board meetings", *Organizational Dynamics*, 35: 106–115; E. E. Lawler III and D. L. Finegold, 2005, "The changing face of corporate boards", *MIT Sloan Management Review*, 46(2): 67–70; A. Conger, E. E. Lawler and D. L. Finegold, 2001, *Corporate Boards: New Strategies for Adding Value at the Top*, San Francisco: Jossey-Bass; J. A. Conger, D. Finegold and E. E. Lawler III, 1998, "Appraising boardroom performance", *Harvard Business Review*, 76(1): 136–148.

75. A. L. Boone, L. C. Field, J. M. Karpoff and C. G. Raheja, 2007, "The determinants of corporate board size and composition: An empirical analysis", *Journal of Financial Economics*, 85(1): 66–101; J. Marshall, 2001, "As boards shrink, responsibilities grow", *Financial Executive*, 17(4): 36–39; M. Huse, 2007, *Boards, Governance and Value Creation*, Cambridge: Cambridge University Press.

76. T. Long, 2007, "The evolution of FTSE 250 boards of directors: Key factors influencing board performance and effectiveness", *Journal of General Management*, 32(3): 45–60; S. Finkelstein and A. C. Mooney, 2003, "Not the usual suspects: How to use board process to make boards better", *Academy of Management Executive*, 17: 101–113.

77. J. L. Koors, 2006, "Director pay: A work in progress", *The Corporate Governance Advisor*, 14(5): 25–31; W. Shen, 2005, "Improve board effectiveness: The need for incentives", *British Journal of Management*, 16(S1): S81–S89; M. Gerety, C. Hoi and A. Robin, 2001, "Do shareholders benefit from the adoption of incentive pay for directors?", *Financial Management*, 30: 45–61; D. C. Hambrick and E. M. Jackson, 2000, "Outside directors with a stake: The linchpin in improving governance", *California Management Review*, 42(4): 108–127.

78. Y. Deutsch, T. Keil and T. Laamanen, 2007, "Decision making in acquisitions: the effect of outside directors' compensation on acquisition patterns", *Journal of Management*, 33(1): 30–56.

79. A. J. Hillman, C. Shropshire and A. A. Cannella, Jr. 2007, "Organizational predictors of women on corporate boards", *Academy of Management Journal*, 50: 941–952; I. Filatotchev and S. Toms, 2003, "Corporate governance, strategy and survival in a declining industry: A study of UK cotton textile companies", *Journal of Management Studies*, 40: 895–920.

80. S. N. Kaplan, 2008, "Are US CEOs overpaid?", *Academy of Management Perspectives*, 22 (2): 5–20.

81. J. P. Walsh, 2009, "Are US CEOs overpaid? A partial response to Kaplan", *Academy of Management Perspectives*, 23(1): 73–75; J. P. Walsh, 2008, "CEO compensation and the responsibilities of the business scholar to society", *Academy of Management Perspectives*, 22 (3): 26–33.

82. K. Rehbein, 2007, "Explaining CEO compensation: How do talent, governance, and markets fit in?", *Academy of Management Perspectives*, 21(1): 75–77; J. S. Miller, R. M. Wiseman and L. R. Gomez-Mejia, 2002, "The fit between CEO compensation design and firm risk", *Academy of Management Journal*, 45: 745–756.

83. M. Larraza-Kintana, R. M. Wiseman, L. R. Gomez-Mejia and T. M. Welbourne, 2007, "Disentangling compensation and employment risks using the behavioural agency model", *Strategic Management Journal*, 28: 1001–1019; J. McGuire and E. Matta, 2003, "CEO stock options: The silent dimension of ownership", *Academy of Management Journal*, 46: 255–265.

84. X. Zhang, K. M. Bartol, K. G. Smith, M. D. Pfarrer and D. M. Khanin, 2008, "CEOs on the edge: Earnings manipulations and stock-based incentive misalignment", *Academy of Management Journal*, 51: 241–258; J. P. O'Connor, R. L. Priem, J. E. Coombs and K. M. Gilley, 2006, "Do CEO stock options prevent or promote fraudulent financial reporting?", *Academy of Management Journal*, 49: 483–500.

85. S. O'Donnell, 2000, "Managing foreign subsidiaries: Agents of headquarters, or an interdependent network?", *Strategic Management Journal*, 21: 521–548; K. Roth and S. O'Donnell, 1996, "Foreign subsidiary compensation: An agency theory perspective", *Academy of Management Journal*, 39: 678–703.

86. A. Ghosh, 2006, "Determination of executive compensation in an emerging economy: Evidence from India", *Emerging Markets, Finance and Trade*, 42(3): 66–90; K. Ramaswamy, R. Veliyath and L. Gomes, 2000, "A study of the determinants of CEO compensation in India", *Management International Review*, 40(2): 167–191.

87. C. L. Staples, 2007, "Board globalization in the world's largest TNCs 1993–2005", *Corporate Governance*, 15(2): 311–32.

88. P. Kalyta, 2009, "Compensation transparency and managerial opportunism: A study of supplemental retirement plans", *Strategic Management Journal*, 30: 405–423.

89. L. K. Meulbroek, 2001, "The efficiency of equity-linked compensation: Understanding the full cost of awarding executive stock options", *Financial Management*, 30(2): 5–44.

90. C. E. Devers, R. M. Wiseman and R. M. Holmes Jr, 2007, "The effects of endowment and loss aversion in managerial stock option valuation", *Academy of Management Journal*, 50: 191–208; J. C. Bettis, J. M. Biziak and M. L. Lemmon, 2005, "Exercise behaviour, valuation and the incentive effects of employee stock options", *Journal of Financial Economics*, 76: 445–470.

91. M. Klausner, 2007, "Reducing directors' legal risk", *Harvard Business Review*, 85(4), 28; T. G. Pollock, H. M. Fischer and J. B. Wade, 2002, "The role of politics in repricing executive options", *Academy of Management Journal*, 45: 1172–1182; M. E. Carter and L. J. Lynch, 2001, "An examination of executive stock option repricing", *Journal of Financial Economics*, 59: 207–225; D. Chance, R. Kumar and R. Todd, 2001, "The 'repricing' of executive stock options", *Journal of Financial Economics*, 59: 129–154.

92. P. Berrone and L. R. Gomez-Mejia, 2009, "Environmental performance and executive compensation: An integrated agency-institutional perspective", *Academy of Management Journal*, 52: 103–126.

93. R. Sinha, 2006, "Regulation: The market for corporate control and corporate governance", *Global Finance Journal*, 16(3): 264–282; R. Coff, 2002, "Bidding wars over R&D intensive firms: Knowledge, opportunism and the market for corporate control", *Academy of Management Journal*, 46: 74–85; M. A. Hitt, R. E. Hoskisson, R. A. Johnson and D. D. Moesel, 1996, "The market for corporate control and firm innovation", *Academy of Management Journal*, 39: 1084–1119.

94. D. N. Iyer and K. D. Miller, 2008, "Performance feedback, slack, and the timing of acquisitions", *Academy of Management Journal*, 51: 808–822; R. W. Masulis, C. Wang and F. Xie, 2007, "Corporate governance and acquirer returns", *Journal of Finance*, 62(4), 1851–1889; R. Sinha, 2004, "The role of hostile takeovers in corporate governance", *Applied Financial Economics*, 14: 1291–1305.

95. K. Ruckman, 2009, "Technology sourcing acquisitions: What they mean for innovation potential", *Journal of Strategy and Management*, 2: 56–75; R. W. Masulis, C. Wang and F. Xie, 2007, "Corporate governance and acquirer returns", *Journal of Finance*, 62, 1851–1889.

96. J. P. Walsh and R. Kosnik, 1993, "Corporate raiders and their disciplinary role in the market for corporate control", *Academy of Management Journal*, 36: 671–700.

97. J. Haleblian, C. E. Devers, G. McNamara, M. A. Carpenter and R. B. Davison, 2009, "Taking stock of what we know about mergers and acquisitions: A review and research agenda", *Journal of Management*, 35: 469–502; B. Kalpic, 2008, "Why bigger is not always better: The strategic logic of value creation through M&As" *Journal of Business Strategy*, 29 (6): 4–13.

98. T. W. Briggs, 2007, "Corporate governance and a new hedge fund activism", *Empirical Analysis*, 32(4): 681–723.

99. N. Goodway, 2009, "Credit Suisse pays 25 million pounds golden hellos", *Evening Standard*, http//:www.standard.co.uk, March 24; R. B. Adams and D. Ferreira, 2007, "A theory of friendly boards", *Journal of Finance*, 62: 217–250.

100. J Cresswell, 2006, "Gilded paychecks: Pay packages allow executives to jump ship with less risk", *New York Times*, http://www.nyt.com, December 29.

101. H. G. Barkema and M. Schijven, 2008, "Toward unlocking the full potential of acquisition: The role of organizational restructuring", *Academy of Management Journal*, 51: 696–722; M. Cording, P. Chritmann and D. R. King, 2008, "Reducing causal ambiguity in acquisition integration: Intermediate goals as mediators of integration decisions and acquisition performance", *Academy of Management Journal*, 51: 744–767.

102. T. Laamanen and T. Keil, 2008, "Performance of serial acquirers: Toward an acquisition program perspective", *Strategic Management Journal*, 29: 663–672; G. M. McNamara, J. Haleblian and B. J. Dykes, 2008, "The performance implications of participating in an acquisition wave: Early mover advantages, bandwagon effects, and the moderating influence of industry characteristics and acquirer tactics", *Academy of Management Journal*, 51: 113–130.

103. J. A. Krug and W. Shill, 2008, "The big exit: Executive churn in the wake of M&As", *Journal of Business Strategy*, 29(4): 15–21; J. Harford, 2003, "Takeover bids and target directors' incentives: The impact of a bid on directors' wealth and board seats", *Journal of Financial Economics*, 69: 51–83; S. Chatterjee, J. S. Harrison and D. D. Bergh, 2003, "Failed takeover attempts, corporate governance, and refocusing", *Strategic Management Journal*, 24: 87–96.

104. E. Webb, 2006, "Relationships between board structure and takeover defenses", *Corporate Governance*, 6(3): 268–280; C. Sundaramurthy, J. M. Mahoney and J. T. Mahoney, 1997, "Board structure, antitakeover provisions, and stockholder wealth", *Strategic Management Journal*, 18: 231–246.

105. W. G. Sanders and M. A. Carpenter, 2003, "Strategic satisficing? A behavioural-agency theory perspective on stock repurchase program announcements", *Academy of Management Journal*, 46: 160–178; J. Westphal and E. Zajac, 2001, "Decoupling policy from practice: The case of stock repurchase programs", *Administrative Science Quarterly*, 46: 202–228.

106. O. Faleye, 2007, "Classified boards, firm value, and managerial entrenchment", *Journal of Financial Economics*, 83: 501–529.

107. 2007, Leaders: Pay slips; management in Europe, *Economist*, June 23, 14: A. Cala, 2005, "Carrying golden parachutes; France joins EU trend to reign in executive severance deals", *Wall Street Journal*, June 8, A13.

108. J. A. Pearce II and R. B. Robinson Jr., 2004, "Hostile takeover defenses that maximize shareholder wealth", *Business Horizons*, 47(5): 15–24.

109. A. Kacperzyk, 2009, "With greater power comes greater responsibility? Takeover protection and corporate attention to stakeholders", *Strategic Management Journal*, 30: 261–285.

110. J. P. Walsh and R. Kosnik, 1993, "Corporate raiders and their disciplinary role in the market for corporate control", *Academy of Management Journal*, 36: 671–700.

111. A. Chakraborty and R. Arnott, 2001, "Takeover defenses and dilution: A welfare analysis", *Journal of Financial and Quantitative Analysis*, 36: 311–334.

112. M. Wolf, 2007, "The new capitalism: How unfettered finance is fast reshaping the global economy", *Financial Times*, June 19, 13: C. Millar, T. I. Eldomiaty, C. J. Choi and B. Hilton, 2005, "Corporate governance and institutional transparency in emerging markets", *Journal of Business Ethics*, 59: 163–174; D. Norburn, B. K. Boyd, M. Fox and M. Muth, 2000, "International corporate governance reform", *European Business Journal*, 12(3): 116–133.

113. 2009, "China YCT International strengthens corporate governance with establishment of audit committee and appointments of three new independent directors", *Quamnet.com Stock News*, http//:www.quamnet.com, April 13; P. Aldrick, 2009, "RBS investors threaten to vote down pay report", *Daily Telegraph*, http//:www.telegraph.co.uk, March 24.

114. P. Witt, 2004, "The competition of international corporate governance systems—A German perspective", *Management International Review*, 44: 309–333; L. Nachum, 2003, "Does nationality of ownership make any difference and if so, under what circumstances? Professional service MNEs in global competition", *Journal of International Management*, 9: 1–32.

115. C. Crossland and D. C. Hambrick, 2007, "How national systems differ in their constraints on corporate executives", *Strategic Management Journal*, 28: 767–789; R. Aguilera and G. Jackson, 2003, "The cross-national diversity of corporate governance: Dimensions and determinants", *Academy of Management Review*, 28: 447–465; M. A. Witt and G. Redding, 2009, "Culture, meaning, and institutions: Executive rationale in Germany and Japan", *Journal of International Business Studies*, 40: 859–885; K. Van Veen and J. Elbertsen, 2008, "Governance regimes and nationality diversity in corporate boards: A comparative study of Germany, the Netherlands and the United Kingdom", *Corporate Governance: An International Review*, 16: 386–399.

116. Carney, "Corporate governance and competitive advantage in family-controlled firms"; S. Klein, 2000, "Family businesses in Germany: Significance and structure", *Family Business Review*, 13: 157–181.

117. A. Tuschke and W. G. Sanders, 2003, "Antecedents and consequences of corporate governance reform: The case of Germany", *Strategic Management Journal*, 24: 631–649; J. Edwards and M. Nibler, 2000, "Corporate governance in Germany: The role of banks and ownership concentration", *Economic Policy*, 31: 237–268; E. R. Gedajlovic and D. M. Shapiro, 1998, "Management and ownership effects: Evidence from five countries", *Strategic Management Journal*, 19: 533–553.

118. P. C. Fiss, 2006, "Social influence effects and managerial compensation evidence from Germany", *Strategic Management Journal*, 27: 1013–1031; S. Douma, 1997, "The two-tier system of corporate governance", *Long Range Planning*, 30(4): 612–615.

119. P. C. Fiss and E. J. Zajac, 2004, "The diffusion of ideas over contested terrain: The (non)adoption of a shareholder value orientation among German firms", *Administrative Science Quarterly*, 49: 501–534; S. M. Ansari, P.C. Fiss and E. J. Zajac, "Made to fit: how practices vary as they diffuse", *Academy of Management Review*, 35(1): 67–92.

120. W. G. Sanders and A. C. Tuschke, 2007, "The adoption of the institutionally contested organizational practices: The emergence of stock option pay in Germany", *Academy of Management Journal*, 57: 33–56.

121. T. Hoshi, A. K. Kashyap and S. Fischer, 2001, *Corporate Financing and Governance in Japan*, Boston, MA: MIT Press.

122. J. P. Charkham, 1994. *Keeping Good Companies: A Study of Corporate Governance in Five Countries*, New York: Oxford University Press, 70.

123. M. A. Hitt, H. Lee and E. Yucel, 2002, "The importance of social capital to the management of multinational enterprises: Relational networks among Asian and Western firms", *Asia Pacific Journal of Management*, 19: 353–372.

124. W. P. Wan, D. W. Yiu, R. E. Hoskisson and H. Kim, 2008, "The performance implications of relationship banking during macroeconomic expansion and contraction: A study of Japanese banks' social relationships and overseas expansion", *Journal of International Business Studies*, 39: 406–427.

125. S. M. Jacoby, 2005, *The embedded corporation: Corporate governance and employment relations in Japan and the United States*, Princeton, NJ: Princeton University; P. M. Lee and H. M. O'Neill, 2003, "Ownership structures and R&D investments of US and Japanese firms: Agency and stewardship perspectives", *Academy of Management Journal*, 46: 212–225.

126. I. S. Dinc, 2006, "Monitoring the monitors: The corporate governance in Japanese banks and their real estate lending in the 1980s", *Journal of Business*, 79(6): 3057–3081; A. Kawaura, 2004, "Deregulation and governance: Plight of Japanese banks in the 1990s", *Applied Economics*, 36: 479–484; B. Bremner, 2001, "Cleaning up the banks—finally", *BusinessWeek*, December 17, 86; 2000,

"Business: Japan's corporate-governance U-turn", *The Economist*, November 18, 73.

127. N. Isagawa, 2007, "A theory of unwinding of cross-shareholding under managerial entrenchment", *Journal of Financial Research*, 30: 163–179.

128. C. L. Ahmadjian and G. E. Robbins, 2005, "A clash of capitalisms: Foreign shareholders and corporate restructuring in 1990s Japan", *American Sociological Review*, 70: 451–471; T. Yoshikawa, L. S. Tsui-Auch and J. McGuire, 2007, "Corporate governance reform as institutional innovation: The case of Japan", *Organization Science*, 18: 973–988.

129. J. M. Ramseyer, M. Nakazato and E. B. Rasmussen, 2009, "Public and private firm compensation: Evidence from Japanese tax returns", Harvard Law and Economics Discussion Paper, February 1.

130. S. R. Miller, D. Li, L. Eden and M. A. Hitt, 2008, "Insider trading and the valuation of international strategic alliances in emerging stock markets", *Journal of International Business Studies*, 39: 102–117.

131. H. Zou and M. B. Adams, 2008, "Corporate ownership, equity risk and returns in the People's Republic of China", *Journal of International Business Studies*, 39: 1149–1168.

132. Y. Su, D. Xu and P. H. Phan, 2008, "Principal-principal conflict in the governance of the Chinese public corporation", *Management and Organization Review*, 4: 17–38.

133. China YCT International strengthens corporate governance with establishment of audit committee and appointments of three new independent directors, 2009, *Quamnet.com Stock News*, http//:www.quamnet.com, April 13.

134. China YCT International strengthens corporate governance with establishment of audit committee and appointments of three new independent directors, 2009, *Quamnet.com Stock News*, http//:www.quamnet.com, April 13.

135. P. M. Vaaler and B. N. Schrage, 2009, "Residual state ownership, policy stability and financial performance following strategic decisions by privatizing telecoms", *Journal of International Business Studies*, 40: 621–641.

136. C. Shropshire and A. J. Hillman, 2007, "A longitudinal study of significant change in stakeholder management", *Business and Society*, 46(1): 63–87; S. Sharma and I. Henriques, 2005, "Stakeholder influences on sustainability practices in the Canadian Forest products industry", *Strategic Management Journal*, 26: 159–180; A. J. Hillman, G. D. Keim and R. A. Luce, 2001, "Board composition and stakeholder performance: Do stakeholder directors make a difference?", *Business and Society*, 40: 295–314.

137. D. L. Gold and J. W. Dienhart, 2007, "Business ethics in the corporate governance era: Domestic and international trends in transparency, regulation, and corporate governance", *Business and Society Review*, 112(2): 163–170; N. Demise, 2005, "Business ethics and corporate governance in Japan", *Business and Society*, 44: 211–217.

138. R. V. Aguilera, D. E. Rupp, C. A. Williams and J. Ganapathi, 2007, "Putting the S back in corporate social responsibility: A multilevel theory of social change in organizations", *Academy of Management Review*, 32(3): 836–863; C. Caldwell and R. Karri, 2005, "Organizational governance and ethical systems: A covenantal approach to building trust", *Journal of Business Ethics*, 58: 249–259; A. Felo, 2001, "Ethics programs, board involvement, and potential conflicts of interest in corporate governance", *Journal of Business Ethics*, 32: 205–218.

# CHAPTER 13

# ORGANIZATIONAL STRUCTURE AND CONTROLS

### LEARNING OBJECTIVES

Studying this chapter should provide you with the strategic management knowledge needed to:

1 Define organizational structure and controls and discuss the difference between strategic and financial controls.
2 Describe the relationship between strategy and structure.
3 Discuss the functional structures used to implement business-level strategies.
4 Explain the use of three versions of the multidivisional (M-form) structure to implement different diversification strategies.
5 Discuss how organizational structure transforms when four main international strategies are implemented.
6 Define strategic networks and discuss how strategic centre firms implement such networks at the business, corporate and international levels.

We thank Ernst Verwaal for his contribution to this Chapter

## OPENING CASE

© Joe Biafore/iStock

## Restructuring Nestlé

Nestlé, the world's largest food nutrition, health and wellness company from Switzerland, is often considered as a "true" multinational company as 98 per cent of its revenue comes from sales outside of Switzerland. Employing 278 000 people in 449 factories in almost every country in the world, the company has to find a balance between decentralization, local adaptation, strategic direction and financial control.

As the company argues that homogenous customer preferences do not exist, its organizational structure has been decentralized in order to accommodate local demand. However the existence of overall company culture and principles is also considered highly important.

Nestlé's major challenge is to reduce bureaucracy, as one of the company's biggest handicaps is its size. The magnitude of the firm has led to slow decision making; the company organized responsibility by country for many of its functions. Additionally, the firm's complicated portfolio, its many brands with many product variations, required the company to take a good look at its structure.

Peter Brabeck, the company's chairman and former CEO, continued the work of his predecessor, Helmut Maucher, by consolidating the business. Brabeck and Maucher identified two unique features of Nestlé that shouldn't change: decentralization and the relatively low importance of IT in its daily operations.

As the company does not believe in homogeneous customer preferences it does not believe in a "global consumer", particularly when it comes to food and beverages, since taste is based on local culture and traditions. For example, Nestea, Nestlé's iced tea brand, has many variations: In the Philippines one can buy calamansi-flavoured iced tea whereas in Ukraine one can buy watermelon-flavoured iced tea. In order to cater to these local demands the company believes that decisions need to be made at a local level. On the other hand, a high degree of decentralization can lead to a complex situation as production, logistics and supply chain management need to be centralized in order to be efficient.

Brabeck sees Nestlé's people, products and brands as more important to its strategy than technology as he argues that the company is not a systems company. Technology is considered more as a supportive tool than a strategic target.

The transformation process implied a change from a geographic and functionally focused organization to an organization that is also product-oriented. Brabeck wanted to transform Nestlé from a task-orientated hierarchical organization to a result-orientated network. The main objectives of this transformation were to increase the organization's overall efficiency and to increase its margins.

Today, the company is organized into three geographic zones (Europe, Americas and Asia/Oceania/Africa) for most of its food business. Nestlé Waters, Nestlé Nutrition, Nespresso, Nestlé's pharmaceutical products and its joint ventures are managed on a global scale. Furthermore, the company has twelve SBUs (Strategic Business Units). These SBUs, for instance the Ice Cream SBU, develop strategies for selected market clusters and develop strategic brands. Before the restructuring of the company, Nestlé was structured by zones. In the 1990s SBUs complementary to the geographic zones were introduced to increase business focus, and in 2004 a structure was proposed where some activities were managed globally and some zones were divided into regional businesses. Subsidiaries operate interdependently in order to leverage knowledge and activities between divisions.

Nestlé reduced its number of factories from over 500 to 449, as the management of these factories was integrated. Several programmes were launched to increase the organization's global efficiency: Shared Service Centres have been established in order to centralize back-office functions for each geographic region; GLOBE was introduced as the company's ERP system as a mean to standardize the company's information systems infrastructure and FitNes was an initiative to improve "white-collar" productivity in order to lower its selling, general and administrative expenses.

Nestlé's transformation had the desired effect on the firm's performance. The company's earnings before interest and taxes (EBIT) margin increased from 10.3 per cent to 14.6 per cent from 1997 to 2009, although sales in 2009 were affected by the global financial crisis. In 2008 Paul Bulcke was appointed as Nestlé's new CEO. As Brabeck's successor he did not plan to make major changes to the company. He argued that a revolutionary change might do more bad than good for Nestlé. However, his main challenge is to improve Nestlé's profitability compared to its competitors. Initiatives such as Globe will support Bulcke in reaching his targets as second and improved generations of the information system will be implemented in 2010.

**Sources:** Nestlé SA (2010) *Introduction*. Nestlé SA. http://www.nestle.com/, July, 12; Nestlé SA (2010) *Annual Report 2009*. Nestlé SA. http://www.nestle.com, March 26; Nestlé SA (2009) *The Nestlé Management and Leadership Principles*. Nestlé SA. http://www.nestle.com, July; Maucher, H. (1989) "Global Strategies of Nestlé", *European Management Journal*, 7(1): 92–96; Wetlaufer, S. (2001) "The Business Case Against Revolution: An Interview with Nestle's Peter Brabeck", *Harvard Business Review*, 79(2): 112–121; Nestlé SA (2010) *Organisational Chart*. Nestlé SA. http://www.nestle.com, January; Gelnar, M. and Berton, E. (2007) "Nestlé's New Boss Has a Long To-Do List", *Barron's*, 87(39). M9; Reichenberger, W. (2002) "Delivering Growth", *Nestlé Investor Seminar*. http://www.nestle.com, October 8; Brabeck, P. (2004) "Business focus and the organization", *Nestlé Investor Seminar*. http://www.nestle.com, June 16; Sibun, J. (2010) "Nestlé chief executive Paul Bulcke is not one for a break, but he loves his Kit Kat", *The Daily Telegraph*. http://www.telegraph.co.uk. February 21.

## Questions

**1** Describe Nestlé's initial structure. How did this structure change?

**2** What has changed in the way Nestlé manages its foreign subsidiaries?

**3** How can a possible diversification into new markets (e.g. pharmaceuticals or cosmetics) be governed in Nestlé's organizational structure?

**4** Can you provide an update on Nestlé's international organizational structure?

As we explain in Chapter 5, all firms use one or more business-level strategies. In Chapters 7–10, we discuss other strategies firms may choose to use (corporate-level, international, and cooperative). Once selected, strategies are not implemented in a vacuum. Organizational structure and controls, this chapter's topic, provide the framework within which strategies are used in both for-profit organizations and not-for-profit agencies.[1] However, as we explain, separate structures and controls are required to successfully implement different strategies. In all organizations, top-level managers have the final responsibility for ensuring that the firm has matched each of its strategies with the appropriate organizational structure and that changes to both occur when necessary. Thus, Peter Bulcke, the CEO of Nestlé, is responsible for changing Nestlé's organizational structure if the firm decides to use a different business or corporate-level strategy. The match or degree of fit between strategy and structure influences the firm's attempts to earn above-average returns.[2] Thus, the ability to select an appropriate strategy and match it with the appropriate structure is an important characteristic of effective strategic leadership.[3]

This chapter opens with an introduction to organizational structure and controls. We then provide more details about the need for the firm's strategy and structure to be properly matched. Affecting firms' efforts to match strategy and structure is their influence on each other.[4] As we discuss, strategy has a more important influence on structure, although once in place, structure influences strategy.[5] Next, we describe the relationship between growth and structural change that successful firms experience. We then discuss the different organizational structures firms use to implement the separate business-level, corporate-level, international and cooperative strategies. A series of figures highlights the different structures firms match with strategies. Across time and based on their experiences, organizations, especially large and complex ones, customize these general structures to meet their unique needs.[6] Typically, the firm tries to form a structure that is complex enough to facilitate use of its strategies but simple enough for all parties to understand and implement.[7] When, for instance, a company has to combine its local awareness with global efficiency as with Nestlé in the Opening Case, a firm must adjust its structure to deal with the increased complexity.

# Organizational structure and controls

Research shows that organizational structure and the controls that are a part of the structure affect firm performance.[8] In particular, evidence suggests that performance declines when the firm's strategy is not matched with the most appropriate structure and controls.[9] Even though mismatches between strategy and structure do occur, research indicates that managers try to act rationally when forming or changing their firm's structure.[10] Jan Hommen, chief executive of ING, focused on maintaining the fit between strategy and structure by splitting the company's banking and insurance activities as a direct result of the economic downturn.[11]

## *Organizational structure*

Organizational structure specifies the firm's formal reporting relationships, procedures, controls, and authority and decision-making processes.[12] Developing an organizational structure that effectively supports the firm's strategy is difficult, especially because of the uncertainty (or unpredictable variation[13]) about cause-effect relationships in the global economy's rapidly changing and dynamic competitive environments.[14] When a structure's elements (e.g., reporting relationships, procedures, etc.) are properly aligned with one another, the structure facilitates effective use of the firm's strategies.[15] Thus, organizational structure is a critical component of effective strategy implementation processes.[16]

A firm's structure specifies the work to be done and how to do it, given the firm's strategy or strategies.[17] Thus, organizational structure influences how managers work and the decisions resulting from that work.[18] Supporting the implementation of strategies, structure is concerned with processes used to complete organizational tasks.[19] Having the right structure and process is important. For example, many product-oriented firms have been moving to develop service businesses associated with their produced goods. Siemens, Europe's largest engineering company, offers a broad range of services related to its products. However, research suggests that developing a separate division for such services in product-oriented companies, rather than managing the service business within the product divisions, leads to additional growth and profitability in the service business.[20]

Effective structures provide the stability a firm needs to successfully implement its strategies and maintain its current competitive advantages while simultaneously providing the flexibility to develop advantages it will need in the future.[21] *Structural stability* provides the capacity the firm requires to consistently and predictably manage its daily work routines[22] while *structural flexibility* provides the opportunity to explore competitive possibilities and then allocate resources to activities that will shape the competitive advantages the firm will need to be successful in

**Organizational structure**

Organizational structure specifies the firm's formal reporting relationships, procedures, controls, and authority and decision-making processes.

the future.[23] An effectively flexible organizational structure allows the firm to *exploit* current competitive advantages while *developing* new ones that can potentially be used in the future.[24] For example, H&M's use of its network of suppliers and manufacturers allows the company to be more efficient and flexible than its competitors.[25]

Modifications to the firm's current strategy or selection of a new strategy call for changes to its organizational structure. However, research shows that once in place, organizational inertia often inhibits efforts to change structure, even when the firm's performance suggests that it is time to do so.[26] In his pioneering work, Alfred Chandler found that organizations change their structures when inefficiencies force them to do so.[27] Firms seem to prefer the structural status quo and its familiar working relationships until the firm's performance declines to the point where change is absolutely necessary.[28] For instance, the financial crisis's impact on ING's results forced the company to restructure.[29]

In addition to the issues we already mentioned, it is important to note that top-level managers hesitate to conclude that the firm's structure (or its strategy, for that matter) are the problem, in that doing so suggests that their previous choices were not the best ones. Because of these inertial tendencies, structural change is often induced instead by actions from stakeholders (e.g., those from the capital market and customers – see Chapter 2) who are no longer willing to tolerate the firm's performance. Evidence shows that appropriate timing of structural change happens when top-level managers recognize that a current organizational structure no longer provides the coordination and direction needed for the firm to successfully implement its strategies.[30] Interestingly, many organization changes are taking place in the current economic downturn, apparently because low performance reveals organization weaknesses.

Chandler's contributions to our understanding of organizational structure and its relationship to strategies and performance are quite significant. Indeed, some believe that Chandler's emphasis on "organizational structure" so transformed the field of business history that some call the period before Dr Chandler's publications "BC", meaning "before Chandler".[31] As we discuss next, effective organizational controls help managers recognize when it is time to adjust the firm's structure.

## Organizational controls

**Organizational controls**

Organizational controls guide the use of strategy, indicate how to compare actual results with expected results, and suggest corrective actions to take when the difference is unacceptable.

Organizational controls are an important aspect of structure.[32] Organizational controls guide the use of strategy, indicate how to compare actual results with expected results, and suggest corrective actions to take when the difference is unacceptable. When fewer differences separate actual from expected outcomes, the organization's controls are more effective.[33] It is difficult for the company to successfully exploit its competitive advantages without effective organizational controls.[34] Properly designed organizational controls provide clear insights regarding behaviours that enhance firm performance.[35] Firms use both strategic controls and financial controls to support using their strategies.

**Strategic controls**

Strategic controls are largely subjective criteria intended to verify that the firm is using appropriate strategies for the conditions in the external environment and the company's competitive advantages.

Strategic controls are largely subjective criteria intended to verify that the firm is using appropriate strategies for the conditions in the external environment and the company's competitive advantages. Thus, strategic controls are concerned with examining the fit between what the firm *might do* (as suggested by opportunities in its external environment) and what it *can do* (as indicated by its competitive advantages). Effective strategic controls help the firm understand what it takes to be successful.[36] Strategic controls demand rich communications between managers responsible for using them to judge the firm's performance and those with primary responsibility for implementing the firm's strategies (such as middle and first-level managers). These frequent exchanges are both formal and informal in nature.[37]

Strategic controls are also used to evaluate the degree to which the firm focuses on the requirements to implement its strategies. For a business-level strategy, for example, the strategic controls are used to study primary and support activities (see Tables 3.6 and 3.7, on page 113) to verify that the critical activities are being emphasized and properly executed.[38] With related corporate-level strategies, strategic controls are used to verify the sharing of appropriate strategic factors such as knowledge, markets and technologies across businesses. To effectively use strategic controls when evaluating related diversification strategies, executives must have a deep understanding of each unit's business-level strategy.[39]

As we described in the Opening Case, Nestlé's SBUs are mainly concerned with issues related to strategic control. These SBUs are on the interface of Nestlé's external interface and its businesses. They assist Nestlé's divisions in achieving their business and brand objectives by developing strategies for market clusters, promoting innovation and renovation and by brand equity management. The market clusters are grouped by similarities such as consumer preferences or market developments.[40]

Financial controls are largely objective criteria used to measure the firm's performance against previously established quantitative standards. Accounting-based measures such as return on investment (ROI) and return on assets (ROA) as well as market-based measures such as economic value added are examples of financial controls. Partly because strategic controls are difficult to use with extensive diversification,[41] financial controls are emphasized to evaluate the performance of the firm using the unrelated diversification strategy. The unrelated diversification strategy's focus on financial outcomes (see Chapter 7) requires using standardized financial controls to compare performances between units and managers.[42]

> **Financial controls**
>
> Financial controls are largely objective criteria used to measure the firm's performance against previously established quantitative standards.

When using financial controls, firms evaluate their current performance against previous outcomes as well as against competitors' performance and industry averages. In the global economy, technological advances are being used to develop highly sophisticated financial controls, making it possible for firms to more thoroughly analyse their performance results and to assure compliance with regulations. Companies such as Oracle and SAP sell software tools that automate processes firms can use to meet the financial reporting requirements specified by the Sarbanes-Oxley Act. (As noted in Chapter 12, this act requires a firm's principal executive and financial officers to certify corporate financial and related information in quarterly and annual reports submitted to the Securities and Exchange Commission.)

Both strategic and financial controls are important aspects of each organizational structure, and as we noted previously, any structure's effectiveness is determined by using a combination of strategic and financial controls. However, the relative use of controls varies by type of strategy. For example, companies and business units of large diversified firms using the cost leadership strategy emphasize financial controls (such as quantitative cost goals), while companies and business units using the differentiation strategy emphasize strategic controls (such as subjective measures of the effectiveness of product development teams).[43] As previously explained, a corporate-wide emphasis on sharing among business units (as called for by related diversification strategies) results in an emphasis on strategic controls, while financial controls are emphasized for strategies in which activities or capabilities are not shared (e.g., in an unrelated diversification strategy).

As firms consider controls, the important point is to properly balance the use of strategic and financial controls. Indeed, overemphasizing one at the expense of the other can lead to performance declines. According to Peter Brabeck, Nestlé has never focused solely on short-term results, even though financial analysts and managers put pressure on the company to maximize shareholder value. The company believes that long-term optimization of shareholder value only results from its corporate strategy, not from an over-emphasis on financial targets.[44]

# Strategy and structure

Strategy and structure have a reciprocal relationship.[45] This relationship highlights the interconnectedness between strategy formulation (Chapters 5–10) and strategy implementation (Chapters 11–15). In general, this reciprocal relationship finds structure flowing from or following selection of the firm's strategy. Once in place though, structure can influence current strategic actions as well as choices about future strategies. Consider, for example, the possible influences of Nestlé's structure and control system in influencing its strategy as illustrated in the Opening Case.

The general nature of the strategy/structure relationship means that changes to the firm's strategy create the need to change how the organization completes its work. In the "structure influences strategy" direction, firms must be vigilant in their efforts to verify that how their structure calls for work to be completed, remains consistent with the implementation requirements of chosen strategies. Research shows, however, that "strategy has a much more important influence on structure than the reverse".[46]

Regardless of the strength of the reciprocal relationships between strategy and structure, those choosing the firm's strategy and structure should be committed to matching each strategy with a structure that provides the stability needed to use current competitive advantages as well as the flexibility required to develop future advantages. Therefore, when changing strategies, the firm should simultaneously consider the structure that will be needed to support use of the new strategy; properly matching strategy and structure can create a competitive advantage.[47]

# Evolutionary patterns of strategy and organizational structure

Research suggests that most firms experience a certain pattern of relationships between strategy and structure. Chandler[48] found that firms tend to grow in somewhat predictable patterns: "first by volume, then by geography, then integration (vertical, horizontal), and finally through product/business diversification"[49] (see Figure 13.1). Chandler interpreted his findings as an indication that firms' growth patterns determine their structural form.

As shown in Figure 13.1, sales growth creates coordination and control problems that the existing organizational structure cannot efficiently handle. Organizational growth creates the opportunity for the firm to change its strategy to try to become even more successful. However, the existing structure's formal reporting relationships, procedures, controls, and authority and decision-making processes lack the sophistication required to support using the new strategy.[50] A new structure is needed to help decision makers gain access to the knowledge and understanding required to effectively integrate and coordinate actions to implement the new strategy.[51]

Firms choose from among three major types of organizational structures – simple, functional and multidivisional – to implement strategies. Across time, successful firms move from the simple to the functional to the multidivisional structure to support changes in their growth strategies.[52]

## Simple structure

The simple structure is a structure in which the owner-manager makes all major decisions and monitors all activities while the staff serve as an extension of the manager's supervisory authority.[53] Typically, the owner-manager actively works in the business on a daily basis. Informal relationships, few rules, limited task specialization,

**Simple structure**

The simple structure is a structure in which the owner-manager makes all major decisions and monitors all activities while the staff serve as an extension of the manager's supervisory authority.

STRATEGIC FOCUS

© Caro/Alamy

# Towards one Philips: simplifying the organizational structure

The foundations of Philips were laid in 1891 when Anton and Gerard Philips established Philips & Co. in Eindhoven, the Netherlands. Currently Philips is one of the biggest electronic firms in the world. In 2008 Philips employed 121 000 people and had sales of €24.4 million. Since the beginning, Philips has placed R&D and innovation at the core of its activities, generating many breakthrough inventions, such as the Compact Cassette and the CD. But innovative products need great brand strategies and until the mid-1990s Philips lacked representation as a global company. Advertising and marketing campaigns were carried out at product level on a local market basis. People weren't getting the message that Philips was the key behind all those technological products. With the huge range of products and services offered by rivals such as General Electric and Siemens, Philips was losing ground to the giants.

When Gerard Kleisterlee took control at Royal Philips Electronics in 2001, he introduced his new branding strategy, "Sense and Simplicity", to make a link between technology and business success. The idea was to create a "health care, lifestyle and technology"

company, whose products promised innovation but were easy to use and designed around consumers. Kleisterlee hired a new marketing executive, Andrea Ragnetti, and quickly moved to ensure the company's strategy was executed properly. Those changes in branding strategy have been remarkably successful: In the 2006 annual *BusinessWeek*/Interbrand global brand study, Philips was one of the top gainers, registering a 14 per cent increase in the value of its brand, up to €5.3 billion, and jumping five places in the rankings to place 48.

As part of the "Vision 2010" strategy, Kleisterlee made big changes in the structure of Philips. He introduced "Towards One Philips" to simplify business structure. He streamlined 14 product divisions down to four product divisions, which included the sales of Philips' semiconductors division. Today, all businesses are even organized under three sectors; Healthcare, Lighting and Consumer Lifestyle, internalizing the brand positioning "Sense and Simplicity" launched in 2004. The Vision 2010-strategy was introduced in 2007 which included the main goals for Philips to annually increase its revenue by 6%, to increase its EBITA from 7.8% of sales in 2007, to 10–11% of sales in 2010, and to double its EBITA per share by 2010. The aforementioned restructuring of the company into three divisions was one of the direct actions set by Vision 2010. One year later, in 2008, these targets were adjusted as Gerard Kleisterlee stated that the original targets were set for a company operating in a "normal" economic climate, not a financial crisis. The adjustment of targets, which basically was the adjustment of the time frame for its targets, was announced after Philips was hit by the global economic crisis. However, due to some serious cost cutting in 2009, the outlook for Philip's results was positive again. Where the company's EBITA in 2009 was only 4.5% of sales, the EBITA for 2010 was estimated at 10% of sales, which coincided with the targets of the Vision 2010 strategy.

At the time Kleisterlee became CEO, the medical division was the laggard, accounting for 8 per cent of Philips' revenue and less than 4 per cent of its operating income. Kleisterlee spent billions on acquisitions, adding medical companies such as Witt Biomedical and Stentor. In 2006, medical systems accounted for 21 per cent of Philips' revenue and 38 per cent of operating income. Furthermore by the end of 2006, Philips sold its semiconductor division, Europe's third-largest chipmaker. Kleisterlee has outsourced operations, including Philips' entire components division, lowering the overall headcount by 60 000 workers. Even as he unloaded units whose future he didn't feel was promising, Kleisterlee has continued to shut factories and move manufacturing in profitable divisions like lighting to lower-cost locales such as Poland, Mexico and China. A decade ago Philips had 110 factories for bulbs and other lighting products; in 2007 it had fewer than 70, and 60 per cent of its 50 000 employees are in low-wage countries.

Kleisterlee has been making acquisitions both in Europe and the US to kick-start the change. In 2006–2007 Philips had spent more than €1.2 billion buying smaller lighting-technology firms, such as Lumileds, a Silicon Valley company that makes specialty diodes that go into cars and computers and high-end stores. On the health front Philips has spent nearly €1.6 billion acquiring US-based companies like Intermagnetics, a maker of components for MRI machines.

In 2011 Kleisterlee's term as CEO will end. The company has already announced that Frans van Houten, the former CEO of NXP, Philips' semiconductor spin-off, will be Kleisterlee's successor. The targets as described in the Vision 2010 strategy were not fully reached, mainly because of the financial crisis. Philips has to create a new strategic plan, Vision 2015, as Vision 2010 will come to an end in 2010. N.V., 2010.

*Q3-2010 Quarterly Report.* N.V. http://www.philips.com, October 18.

**Sources:** 2006 "The world's best brands", *BusinessWeek.* http://www.businessweek.com, August 7; Arndt, M. (2005) "The new face of Philips", *BusinessWeek.* http://www.businessweek.com, December 1; Ang, J. (2008) TAXI: The Brand Central Station – Philips: Sense and Simplicity. *TAXI Design Network.* http://www.taxidesign.com. June 30; http://www.philips.com; Schwartz, N. D. (2007) "Lighting up Philips" (cont.). *Fortune,* January 12; Elfrink, R. (2010) "Nieuw strategisch plan bij concern – Mouwen bij Philips weer opgestroopt", *Eindhovens Dagblad.* http://www.ed.nl. March 26; Bökkerink, I. (2010) 'Philips komt na de zomer met nieuwe CEO en "Vision 2015", *Het Financieele Dagblad.* http://www.fd.nl. March 26; Royal Philips N.V. (2010) *Annual Report 2009,* Royal Philips N.V. http://www.philips.com. March 1; Royal Philips N.V. (2010) *Q3-2010 Quarterly Report,* Royal Philips N.V. http://www.philips.com, October 18.

## Questions

1 Describe Philips' original organizational structure.

2 How did the new organizational structure of Philips facilitate the new "Sense and Simplicity" branding strategy?

3 Can you provide an update on Philips' strategy and structure?

and unsophisticated information systems characterize this structure. Frequent and informal communications between the owner-manager and employees make coordinating the work to be done relatively easy. The simple structure is matched with focus strategies and business-level strategies, as firms implementing these strategies commonly compete by offering a single product line in a single geographic market. Local restaurants, repair businesses and other specialized enterprises are examples of firms using the simple structure.

As the small firm grows larger and becomes more complex, managerial and structural challenges emerge. For example, the amount of competitively relevant information requiring analysis substantially increases, placing significant pressure on the owner-manager. Additional growth and success may cause the firm to change its strategy. Even if the strategy remains the same, the firm's larger size dictates the need for more sophisticated work-flows and integrating mechanisms. At this evolutionary point, firms tend to move from the simple structure to a functional organizational structure.[54]

## Functional structure

**Functional structure**

The functional structure consists of a chief executive officer and a limited corporate staff, with functional line managers in dominant organizational areas such as production, accounting, marketing, R&D, engineering and human resources.

The functional structure consists of a chief executive officer and a limited corporate staff, with functional line managers in dominant organizational areas such as production, accounting, marketing, R&D, engineering and human resources.[55] This structure allows for functional specialization,[56] thereby facilitating active sharing of knowledge within each functional area. Knowledge sharing facilitates career

**FIGURE 13.1** Strategy and structure growth pattern

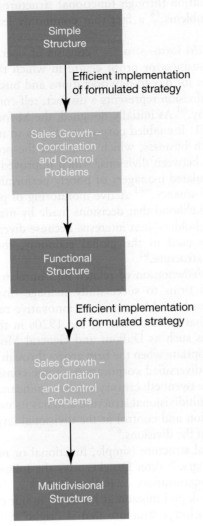

paths as well as professional development of functional specialists. However, a functional orientation can negatively affect communication and coordination among those representing different organizational functions. For this reason, the CEO must work hard to verify that the decisions and actions of individual business functions promote the entire firm rather than a single function. The functional structure supports implementing business-level strategies and some corporate-level strategies (e.g., single or dominant business) with low levels of diversification. When changing from a simple to a functional structure, firms want to avoid introducing value-destroying bureaucratic procedures such as failing to promote innovation and creativity.[57]

## Multidivisional structure

With continuing growth and success, firms often consider greater levels of diversification. Successfully using a diversification strategy requires analysing substantially greater amounts of data and information when the firm offers the same products in different markets (market or geographic diversification) or offers different products in several markets (product diversification). In addition, trying to manage high levels of diversification through functional structures creates serious coordination and control problems,[58] a fact that commonly leads to a new structural form.[59]

The multidivisional (M-form) structure consists of operating divisions, each representing a separate business or profit centre in which the top corporate officer delegates responsibilities for day-to-day operations and business unit strategy to division managers. Each division represents a distinct, self-contained business with its own functional hierarchy.[60] As initially designed, the M-form was thought to have three major benefits: "(1) It enabled corporate officers to more accurately monitor the performance of each business, which simplified the problem of control; (2) it facilitated comparisons between divisions, which improved the resource allocation process; and (3) it stimulated managers of poorly performing divisions to look for ways of improving performance."[61] Active monitoring of performance through the M-form increases the likelihood that decisions made by managers heading individual units will be in stakeholders' best interests. Because diversification is a dominant corporate-level strategy used in the global economy, the M-form is a widely adopted organizational structure.[62]

Used to support implementation of related and unrelated diversification strategies, the M-form helps firms to successfully manage diversification's many demands.[63] Chandler viewed the M-form as an innovative response to coordination and control problems that surfaced during the 1920s in the functional structures then used by large firms such as DuPont and General Motors.[64] Research shows that the M-form is appropriate when the firm grows through diversification.[65] Partly because of its value to diversified corporations, some consider the multidivisional structure to be one of the twentieth century's most significant organizational innovations.[66] However, the multidivisional structure also has its weaknesses. For example, the improved coordination and control at the divisional level may come at the expense of synergy between the divisions.[67]

No one organizational structure (simple, functional or multidivisional) is inherently superior to the others.[68] Peter Drucker says the following about this matter: "There is no one right organization. ... Rather the task ... is to select the organization for the particular task and mission at hand."[69] In our context, Drucker is saying that the firm must select a structure that is "right" for successfully using the chosen strategy. Because no single structure is optimal in all instances, managers concentrate on developing proper matches between strategies and organizational structures rather than searching for an "optimal" structure. This matching of structure and strategy is taking place at Nestlé. As noted in the opening case, Peter Bulcke and Peter Brabeck aimed to increase the company's efficiency and as such they have adjusted its structure to match the company's ability to adapt to local preferences and to be globally efficient.

Next we describe the strategy/structure matches that evidence shows positively contribute to firm performance.

## Matches between business-level strategies and the functional structure

Firms use different forms of the functional organizational structure to support implementing the cost leadership, differentiation and integrated cost leadership/ differentiation strategies. The differences in these forms are accounted for primarily by different uses of three important structural characteristics: *specialization* (concerned with the type and number of jobs required to complete work[70]), *central-*

---

**Multidivisional (M-form) structure**

The multidivisional (M-form) structure consists of operating divisions, each representing a separate business or profit centre in which the top corporate officer delegates responsibilities for day-to-day operations and business unit strategy to division managers.

*ization* (the degree to which decision-making authority is retained at higher managerial levels[71]), and *formalization* (the degree to which formal rules and procedures govern work).

## Using the functional structure to implement the cost leadership strategy

Firms using the cost leadership strategy sell large quantities of standardized products to an industry's typical customer. Simple reporting relationships, few layers in the decision-making and authority structure, a centralized corporate staff, and a strong focus on process improvements through the manufacturing function rather than the development of new products by emphasizing product R&D, characterize the cost leadership form of the functional structure[72] (see Figure 13.2). This structure contributes to the emergence of a low-cost culture – a culture in which employees constantly try to find ways to reduce the costs incurred to complete their work.[73]

In terms of centralization, decision-making authority is centralized in a staff function to maintain a cost-reducing emphasis within each organizational function (engineering, marketing, etc.). While encouraging continuous cost reductions, the centralized staff also verifies that further cuts in costs in one function won't adversely affect the productivity levels in other functions.[74]

Jobs are highly specialized in the cost leadership functional structure; work is divided into homogeneous subgroups. Organizational functions are the most common subgroup, although work is sometimes batched on the basis of products produced or clients served. Specializing in their work allows employees to increase their efficiency, reducing costs as a result. Guiding individuals' work in this

**FIGURE 13.2** Functional structure for implementing a cost leadership strategy

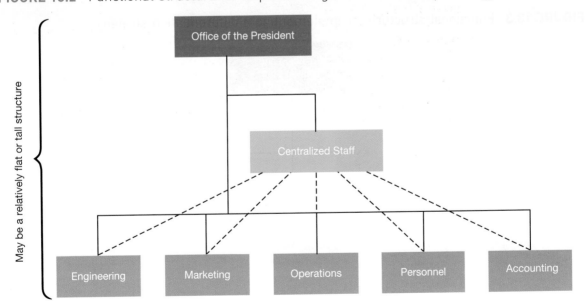

Notes:

- Operations is the main function
- Process engineering is emphasized rather than new product R&D
- Relatively large centralized staff coordinates functions
- Formalized procedures allow for emergence of a low-cost culture
- Overall structure is mechanistic; job roles are highly structured

structure are highly formalized rules and procedures, which often emanate from the centralized staff.

Ryanair, the Irish low cost carrier, uses the functional structure to implement a cost leadership strategy. The responsibility and authority of functional roles are clearly defined. The company's organization is centralized and has seven divisions: Legal & Regulatory Affairs; Flight Operations and Ground Operations; Customer Service; Engineering; Pilots; Personnel and In-Flight.[75]

## Using the functional structure to implement the differentiation strategy
Firms using the differentiation strategy produce products customers perceive as being different in ways that create value for them. With this strategy, the firm wants to sell non-standardized products to customers with unique needs. Relatively complex and flexible reporting relationships, frequent use of cross-functional product development teams, and a strong focus on marketing and product R&D rather than manufacturing and process R&D (as with the cost leadership form of the functional structure) characterize the differentiation form of the functional structure (see Figure 13.3). From this structure emerges a development-oriented culture in which employees try to find ways to further differentiate current products and to develop new, highly differentiated products.[76]

Continuous product innovation demands that people throughout the firm interpret and take action based on information that is often ambiguous, incomplete and uncertain. Following a strong focus on the external environment to identify new opportunities, employees often gather this information from people outside the firm (e.g., customers and suppliers). Commonly, rapid responses to the possibilities indicated by the collected information are necessary, suggesting the need for decentralized decision-making responsibility and authority. To support creativity and the

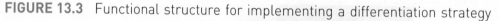

**FIGURE 13.3**  Functional structure for implementing a differentiation strategy

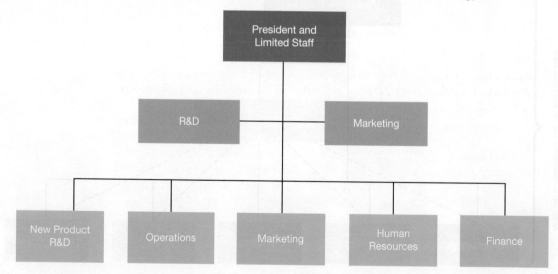

Notes:

- Marketing is the main function for keeping track of new product ideas
- New product R&D is emphasized
- Most functions are decentralized, but R&D and marketing may have centralized staffs that work closely with each other
- Formalization is limited so that new product ideas can emerge easily and change is more readily accomplished
- Overall structure is organic; job roles are less structured

continuous pursuit of new sources of differentiation and new products, jobs in this structure are not highly specialized. This lack of specialization means that workers have a relatively large number of tasks in their job descriptions. Few formal rules and procedures also characterize this structure. Low formalization, decentralization of decision-making authority and responsibility, and low specialization of work tasks combine to create a structure in which people interact frequently to exchange ideas about how to further differentiate current products while developing ideas for new products that can be crisply differentiated.

**Using the functional structure to implement the integrated cost leadership/differentiation strategy** Firms using the integrated cost leadership/differentiation strategy sell products that create value because of their relatively low cost and reasonable sources of differentiation. The cost of these products is low "relative" to the cost leader's prices while their differentiation is "reasonable" when compared with the clearly unique features of the differentiator's products.

Although challenging to implement, the integrated cost leadership/differentiation strategy is used frequently in the global economy. The challenge of using this structure is due largely to the fact that different primary and support activities (see Chapter 3) are emphasized when using the cost leadership and differentiation strategies. To achieve the cost leadership position, production and process engineering are emphasized, with infrequent product changes. To achieve a differentiated position, marketing and new product R&D are emphasized while production and process engineering are not. Thus, effective use of the integrated strategy depends on the firm's successful combination of activities intended to reduce costs with activities intended to create additional differentiation features. As a result, the integrated form of the functional structure must have decision-making patterns that are partially centralized and partially decentralized. Additionally, jobs are semi-specialized, and rules and procedures call for some formal and some informal job behaviour.

## Matches between corporate-level strategies and the multidivisional structure

As explained earlier, Chandler's research shows that the firm's continuing success leads to product or market diversification or both.[77] The firm's level of diversification is a function of decisions about the number and type of businesses in which it will compete, as well as how it will manage the businesses (see Chapter 7). Geared to managing individual organizational functions, increasing diversification eventually creates information processing, coordination, and control problems that the functional structure cannot handle. Thus, using a diversification strategy requires the firm to change from the functional structure to the multidivisional structure to develop an appropriate strategy/structure match.

As defined in Figure 7.1 (see page 243), corporate-level strategies have different degrees of product and market diversification. The demands created by different levels of diversification highlight the need for a unique organizational structure to effectively implement each strategy (see Figure 13.4).

**Using the cooperative form of the multidivisional structure to implement the related constrained strategy** The cooperative form is a structure in which horizontal integration is used to bring about interdivisional cooperation. Divisions in a firm using the related constrained diversification strategy commonly are formed around products, markets, or both. In Figure 13.5, we use

**Cooperative form**

The cooperative form is a structure in which horizontal integration is used to bring about interdivisional cooperation.

**FIGURE 13.4** Three variations of the multidivisional structure

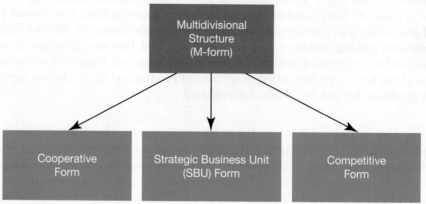

product divisions as part of the representation of the cooperative form of the multi-divisional structure, although market divisions could be used instead of or in addition to product divisions to develop the figure.

ASML, a Dutch manufacturer of lithography systems, applies such a multidivisional structure to implement the related constrained strategy. The company's operational functions, such as R&D, and support functions (e.g. marketing) are being shared across its business segments.[78] Sharing divisional competencies facilitates the corporation's efforts to develop economies of scope. As explained in Chapter 7, economies of scope (cost savings resulting from the sharing of competencies developed in one division with another division) are linked with successful use of the related constrained strategy. Interdivisional sharing of competencies depends on cooperation, suggesting the use of the cooperative form of the multidivisional structure.[79] Increasingly, it is important that the links resulting from effectively using integrating mechanisms support the cooperative sharing of both intangible resources (such as knowledge) and intangible resources (such as facilities and equipment).

The cooperative structure uses different characteristics of structure (centralization, standardization and formalization) as integrating mechanisms to facilitate interdivisional cooperation. Frequent, direct contact between division managers, another integrating mechanism, encourages and supports cooperation and the sharing of competencies or resources that could be used to create new advantages. Sometimes, liaison roles are established in each division to reduce the time division managers spend integrating and coordinating their unit's work with the work occurring in other divisions. Temporary teams or task forces may be formed around projects whose success depends on sharing competencies that are embedded within several divisions. Nestlé has used these devices to develop new cooperative strategies as illustrated in the Opening Case. Formal integration departments might be established in firms frequently using temporary teams or task forces.

Ultimately, a matrix organization may evolve in firms implementing the related constrained strategy. A *matrix organization* is an organizational structure in which there is a dual structure combining both functional specialization and business product or project specialization.[80] Although complicated, an effective matrix structure can lead to improved coordination among a firm's divisions.[81] From the 1960s up to the 1990s Royal Dutch Shell used a three-dimensional matrix structure for its service companies, the organizations that provided counsel and services to Shell's operating companies. The matrix consisted of a functional dimension, a regional dimension and a sector dimension. The main flaw however was that it lacked proper coordination of Shell's operating companies.[82]

**FIGURE 13.5** Cooperative form of the multidivisional structure for implementing a related constrained strategy

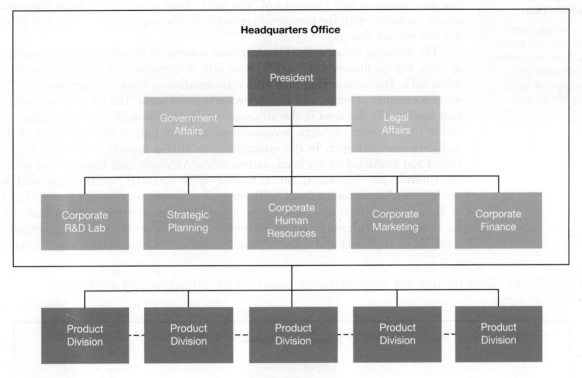

Notes:

- Structural integration devices create tight links among all divisions
- Corporate office emphasizes centralized strategic planning, human resources, and marketing to foster cooperation between divisions
- R&D is likely to be centralized
- Rewards are subjective and tend to emphasize overall corporate performance in addition to divisional performance
- Culture emphasizes cooperative sharing

The success of the cooperative multidivisional structure is significantly affected by how well divisions process information. However, because cooperation among divisions implies a loss of managerial autonomy, division managers may not readily commit themselves to the type of integrative information-processing activities that this structure demands. Moreover, coordination among divisions sometimes results in an unequal flow of positive outcomes to divisional managers. In other words, when managerial rewards are based at least in part on the performance of individual divisions, the manager of the division that is able to benefit the most by the sharing of corporate competencies might be viewed as receiving relative gains at others' expense. Strategic controls are important in these instances, as divisional managers' performance can be evaluated at least partly on the basis of how well they have facilitated interdivisional cooperative efforts. In addition, using reward systems that emphasize overall company performance, besides outcomes achieved by individual divisions, helps overcome problems associated with the cooperative form.

## Using the strategic business unit form of the multidivisional structure to implement the related linked strategy

Firms with fewer links or less constrained links among their divisions use the related linked diversification strategy. The strategic business unit form of the multidivisional structure supports implementation of this strategy. The strategic business unit (SBU) form consists of three levels: corporate headquarters, strategic business units (SBUs), and SBU divisions (see Figure 13.6). The SBU structure is used by large firms and can be complex, with the complexity reflected by the organization's size and product and market diversity.

The divisions within each SBU are related in terms of shared products or markets or both, but the divisions of one SBU have little in common with the divisions of the other SBUs. Divisions within each SBU share product or market competencies to develop economies of scope and possibly economies of scale. The integrating mechanisms used by the divisions in this structure can be equally well used by the divisions within the individual strategic business units that are part of the SBU form of the multidivisional structure. In this structure, each SBU is a profit centre that is controlled and evaluated by the headquarters office. Although both financial and strategic controls are important, on a relative basis financial controls are vital to headquarters' evaluation of each SBU; strategic controls are critical when the heads of SBUs evaluate their divisions' performances. Strategic controls are also critical to the headquarters' efforts to determine whether the company has formed an effective portfolio of businesses and whether those businesses are being successfully managed.

**FIGURE 13.6**  SBU form of the multidivisional structure for implementing a related linked strategy

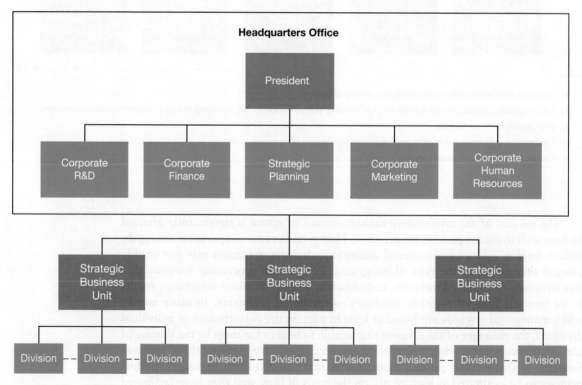

Notes:

- Structural integration among divisions within SBUs, but independence across SBUs
- Strategic planning may be the most prominent function in headquarters for managing the strategic planning approval process of SBUs for the president
- Each SBU may have its own budget for staff to foster integration
- Corporate headquarters staff members serve as consultants to SBUs and divisions, rather than having direct input to product strategy, as in the cooperative form

Philips' restructuring in 2006 resulted in a company that consisted of only three SBUs; Healthcare, Lighting and Consumer Lifestyle.[83] This allowed for related businesses to work together to focus on their distinct customer sets, but also provided for better control for headquarters in order to evaluate performance of each strategic business unit and division within the SBU. As can be read in the Strategic Focus, LVMH implemented the SBU form of the multidivisional structure to manage the great diversity of its brands.

Sharing competencies among units within an SBU is an important characteristic of the SBU form of the multidivisional structure (see the notes to Figure 13.6). A drawback to the SBU structure is that multifaceted businesses often have difficulties in communicating this complex business model to stockholders.[84] Furthermore, if coordination between SBUs is needed, problems can arise because the SBU structure, similar to the competitive form discussed next, does not readily foster cooperation across SBUs.

### Using the competitive form of the multidivisional structure to implement the unrelated diversification strategy

Firms using the unrelated diversification strategy want to create value through efficient internal capital allocations or by restructuring, buying, and selling businesses.[85] The competitive form of the multidivisional structure supports implementation of this strategy.

The competitive form is a structure characterized by complete independence among the firm's divisions (see Figure 13.7). Unlike the divisions included in the

> **Competitive form**
>
> The competitive form is a structure characterized by complete independence among the firm's divisions.

**FIGURE 13.7** Competitive form of the multidivisional structure for implementing an unrelated strategy

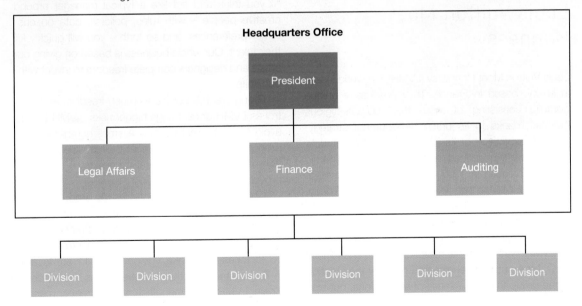

Notes:

- Corporate headquarters has a small staff
- Finance and auditing are the most prominent functions in the headquarters office to manage cash flow and assure the accuracy of performance data coming from divisions
- The legal affairs function becomes important when the firm acquires or divests assets
- Divisions are independent and separate for financial evaluation purposes
- Divisions retain strategic control, but cash is managed by the corporate office
- Divisions compete for corporate resources

STRATEGIC FOCUS

© Caro/Alamy

# Louis Vuitton Moët Hennessy

Louis Vuitton Moët Hennessy (LVMH) is a world leader in luxury, based in France. They possess a unique portfolio consisting of more than 60 prestigious brands. Thanks to its brand development strategy, and the expansion of its international retail network, LVMH has experienced a strong growth dynamic since its creation in 1987 as the result of a merger between Moët Hennessy and Louis Vuitton. Today, they possess more than 2400 stores worldwide and employ more than 77 000 employees, 74 per cent of whom are based outside France.

LVMH was largely a reflection of its charismatic CEO, Mr Arnault. He engineered not only the creation of the group through a series of acquisitions, but also defined the fundamental strategic direction that the company would take in its evolution to become a global player. He became CEO in 1990 and in less than a decade had transformed the company through a spree of acquisitions and opportunistic expansion into overseas markets. By early 2001, the company had been reorganized around five divisions, covering several famous brands, wines and spirits (Dom Pérignon,

Moët & Chandon, Veuve Clicquot and Hennessy), perfumes (Christian Dior, Guerlain and Givenchy), cosmetics (Bliss, Fresh and BeneFit), fashion and leather goods (Christian Lacroix, Donna Karan, Givenchy, Kenzo and Louis Vuitton), watches and jewellery (TAG Heuer, Ebel, Chaumet and Fred). Diversification has been emphasized by LVMH's organization structure in order to manage the great diversity of brands. Each division functions as a strategic business unit with its own general manager and top management team. These divisions also manage overseas sales of their respective lines.

This decentralized structure is chosen to keep the creativity in the company. Creativity and innovation are synonymous with success in the fashion business. As two analysts recently observed, "Luxury brands must foster an appreciation for creativity that is unconstrained by commercial or production constraints." In almost all of its acquisitions, LVMH had maintained the creative talent as an independent pool without attempting to generate synergies across product lines or brands. To maintain the creativity in the company, LVMH has a decentralized structure and a very small cadre of managers. Mr Arnault, CEO of LVMH stated: "If you think and act like a typical manager around creative people – with rules, policies, data on customer preferences, and so forth – you will quickly kill their talent. Our whole business is based on giving our artists and designers complete freedom to invent without limits."

Giving creative people as much freedom and control as LVMH does, brings bigger risks. LVMH tries to avoid those by making only a small number of new products. Only 15 per cent of their business comes from new products, the rest comes from traditional, proven products, the classics.

Contrary to innovation activities the production process hasn't a decentralized structure at all. The manufacturing mostly takes place in France, one of the world's most expensive labour markets. Of the 13 factories that make Vuitton bags, 11 are located in France and the other two are across the border in Spain. LVMH is not manufacturing in cheaper markets because they feel more confident of quality control in France.

But despite this control over the production, LVMH faced control challenges in pricing. For example, its Louis Vuitton handbags are 40 per cent more expensive in Japan than they are in France. This imperfection had encouraged an arbitrage business in handbags run by groups from Japan who flew into France with the sole purpose of buying Louis Vuitton handbags for resale through parallel channels in Japan. Counterfeit handbags and accessories were another big problem that had persisted for a very long time. In fashion centres such as Milan, Venice and Florence, it was not uncommon to see hawkers peddling fake goods in the very same exclusive market zones where the designers had their boutiques. As counterfeiting affects LVMH's brands, taking protective measures against imitation goods is one of LVMH's priorities. For instance, the company attempted to control the grey market of counterfeit goods by maintaining a database, identifying customers through their passport numbers, and thus making it difficult for the arbitrageurs. Anti-counterfeiting measures have been organized for each brand. However, the actions against imitation products are being managed centrally, since the company employs a special unit which works full time on anti-counterfeiting. These efforts have appeared to be helpful: fake products have been seized; factories and stores selling counterfeit items have been shut down and law suits have been filed, not only against producers and sellers but also against online wholesalers. In February 2010, eBay was sentenced to pay LVMH €200 000 million in damages as the court found that eBay harmed the image of Louis Vuitton as counterfeits were sold on the online auction.

Sales have gone up over the recent years to €17 053 million in 2009. However, the financial crisis of 2007–2010 has put a lot of pressure on its profit margins. In time of recession people are becoming more price conscious and consequently delay their expensive purchases. Simultaneously, LVMH faces the challenge of focusing on developing markets, such as Asia, and increasing its leading position in the luxury goods industry. LVMH expanded to China and South Korea in 1990 and it entered India in 2000. LVMH acknowledges that it has to adapt to its new customer base in order to maintain its growth.

**Sources:** Reena Jana (2007) "Louis Vuitton's Life of Luxury", *BusinessWeek*. http://www.businessweek.com. August 6; Moffet, M. H. and Ramaswamy, K. (2003) "Fashion faux pas: Gucci and LVMH", *Thunderbird International Business Review*, 45(2), 225–239; Wetlaufer, S. (2001) "The perfect paradox of star brands: an interview with Bernard Arnault of LVMH", *Harvard Business Review*, 79(9): 116–123; LVMH S.A. (2010) *Annual Report 2009*, LVMH S.A. http://www.lvmh.com. February 26; LVMH S.A. (2008) *Brand Protection*, LVMH S.A. http://www.lvmh.com; Colchester, M. (2010) "eBay to pay damages to unit of LVMH", *Wall Street Journal*, http://www.wsj.com, February 12; 2009 "The substance of style: LVMH in the recession", *The Economist*, 293(8469): 79.

## Questions

**1** Concerning the history of LVMH, how did the company evolve into its current structure?

**2** What effect does the combination of centralization and decentralization in LVMH's structure have on LVMH's brand values?

**3** How can LVMH structure its organization to respond to its focus on new markets?

**4** How can LVMH effectively implement its anti-counterfeiting activities into the organization?

cooperative structure, divisions that are part of the competitive structure do not share common corporate strengths. Because strengths are not shared, integrating devices are not developed for use by the divisions included in the competitive structure.

The efficient internal capital market that is the foundation for using the unrelated diversification strategy requires organizational arrangements emphasizing divisional competition rather than cooperation.[86] Three benefits are expected from the internal competition. First, internal competition creates flexibility (e.g., corporate headquarters can have divisions working on different technologies and projects to identify those with the greatest potential). Resources can then be allocated to the division appearing to have the most potential to fuel the entire firm's success. Second, internal competition challenges the status quo and inertia, because division heads know that future resource allocations are a product of excellent current performance as well as superior positioning in terms of future performance. Finally, internal competition motivates effort in that the challenge of competing against internal peers can be as great as the challenge of competing against external rivals.[87] In this structure, organizational controls (primarily financial controls) are used to emphasize and support internal competition among separate divisions and as the basis for allocating corporate capital based on divisions' performances.

Tata Group, the large Indian conglomerate, operates in seven different industries: engineering, communications and IT, materials, services, energy, consumer products and chemicals. Every business related to an industry functions independently within Tata Group as they each have an executive board and shareholders as they are all publicly listed. Tata Sons, an additional independent subsidiary, acts as the main shareholder of the seven businesses. The company created "business review committees" and a "group executive office" as an instrument for control and portfolio management.

To emphasize competitiveness among divisions, the headquarters office maintains an arm's-length relationship with them, intervening in divisional affairs only to audit operations and discipline managers whose divisions perform poorly. In emphasizing competition between divisions, the headquarters office relies on strategic controls to set rate-of-return targets and financial controls to monitor divisional performance relative to those targets. The headquarters office then allocates cash flow on a competitive basis, rather than automatically returning cash to the division that produced it. Thus, the focus of the headquarters' work is on performance appraisal, resource allocation, and long-range planning to verify that the firm's portfolio of businesses will lead to financial success.[88]

The three major forms of the multidivisional structure should each be paired with a particular corporate-level strategy. Table 13.1 shows these structures' characteristics. Differences exist in the degree of centralization, the focus of the performance appraisal, the horizontal structures (integrating mechanisms), and the incentive compensation schemes. The most centralized and most costly structural form is the cooperative structure. The least centralized, with the lowest bureaucratic costs, is the competitive structure. The SBU structure requires partial centralization and involves some of the mechanisms necessary to implement the relatedness between divisions. Also, the divisional incentive compensation awards are allocated according to both SBUs and corporate performance.

**Table 13.1** Characteristics of the structures necessary to implement the related constrained, related linked, and unrelated diversification strategies

| Structural Characteristics | Overall Structural Form | | |
|---|---|---|---|
| | Cooperative M-Form (Related Constrained Strategy)[a] | SBU M-Form (Related Linked Strategy)[a] | Competitive M-Form (Unrelated Diversification Strategy)[a] |
| **Centralization of operations** | Centralized at corporate office | Partially centralized (in SBUs) | Decentralized to divisions |
| **Use of integration mechanisms** | Extensive | Moderate | Nonexistent |
| **Divisional performance appraisals** | Emphasize subjective (strategic) criteria | Use a mixture of subjective (strategic) and objective (financial) criteria | Emphasize objective (financial) criteria |
| **Divisional incentive compensation** | Linked to overall corporate performance | Mixed linkage to corporate, SBU, and divisional performance | Linked to divisional performance |

[a] Strategy implemented with structural form.

## Matches between international strategies and worldwide structure

As explained in Chapter 9, international strategies are becoming increasingly important for long-term competitive success[89] in what continues to become an increasingly borderless global economy.[90] Among other benefits, international strategies allow the firm to search for new markets, resources, core competencies and technologies as part of its efforts to outperform competitors.[91] The success of pursuing an international strategy is exemplified by Nestlé, as this company's domestic market only counts for two per cent of its revenue base. We will now describe the organizational structures needed to execute these international strategies.

The combination of a company's business-level international strategy and its corporate-level international strategy is based on the need for global integration and the need for local responsiveness.[92] As mentioned earlier, strategic leadership results from a proper fit between a firm's strategy and structure. Thus, similar to business-level and corporate-level strategies, unique organizational structures are necessary to successfully implement the different international strategies.[93] Forming proper matches between international strategies and organizational structures facilitates the firm's efforts to effectively coordinate and control its global operations. More importantly, research findings confirm the validity of the international strategy/structure matches we discuss here.[94] As an example, the Strategic Focus on IKEA points out how this Swedish home products company struggled with adjusting its organizational structure to its international strategy.

When a firm aims to expand its activities internationally its (domestic) structure needs to be adapted in order to govern the international strategy. Chandler highlighted the need for the organization structure to adapt as a company extends its domestic focus to an international focus through the geographical dispersion of the company. He stressed the fact that a central division is needed to manage local business units. Figure 13.8 shows that the company's structure evolves together with the international strategy a company pursues and that a mismatch between strategy and structure (no change in structure after the newly implemented strategy) eventually leads to coordination and control problems.

When choosing an international corporate-level strategy a company can follow a multidomestic strategy, which fits a diversification business-level strategy or a global strategy, which fits a cost-leadership business-level strategy. Preliminary to this step, firms usually start their international activities by pursuing an international growth strategy to complement their domestic business. However, such an ad-hoc international corporate strategy is likely to forgo the specific needs of local markets.

The multidomestic strategy focuses on high local adaptation in its international operations. Firms using this strategy try to isolate themselves from global competitive forces by establishing protected market positions or by competing in industry segments that are most affected by differences among local countries. The multidomestic strategy fits best with a worldwide geographic area structure, however a key disadvantage of the multidomestic strategy/worldwide geographic area structure match is that this setting disables the company's ability to create strong global efficiency.

A global strategy focuses on efficiency by global integration. For instance, economies of scale and scope can be reached by standardizing products and processes. However this strategy is based on the notion of homogenized global demand. The worldwide product divisional structure supports use of the global strategy. The disadvantages of the global strategy/worldwide structure combination are the difficulty involved with coordinating decisions and actions across country borders and the inability to quickly respond to local needs and preferences.

**FIGURE 13.8** International strategy and structure growth pattern

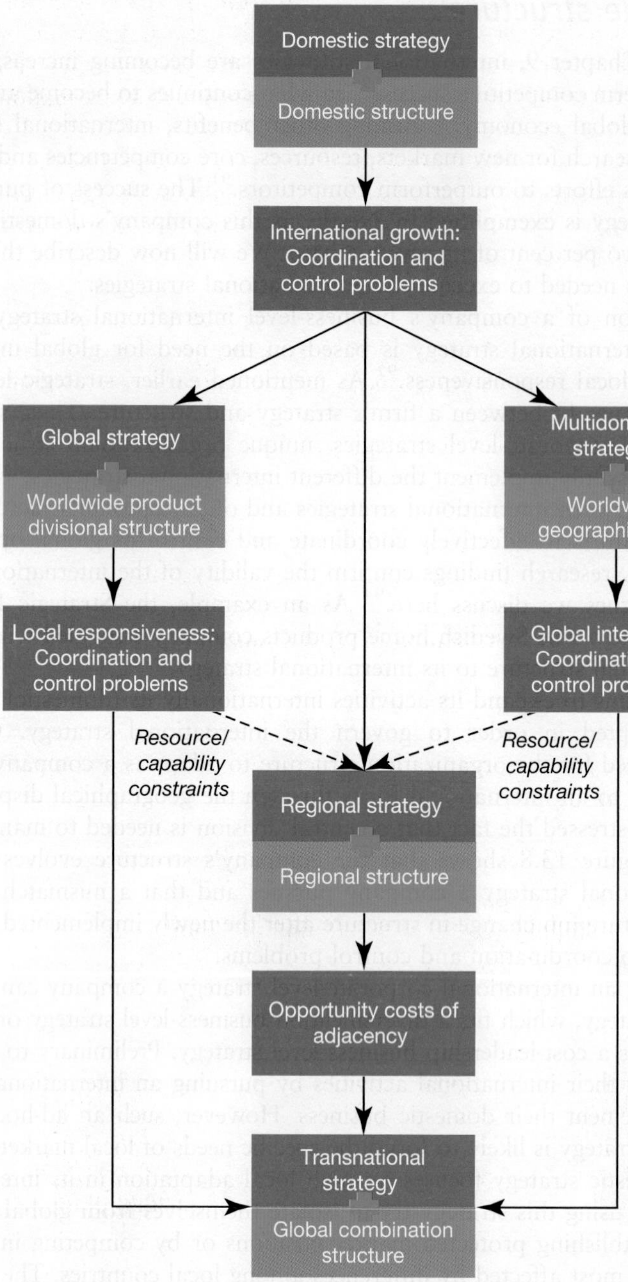

Domestic strategy

Domestic structure

International growth:
Coordination and
control problems

Global strategy

Worldwide product
divisional structure

Multidomestic
strategy

Worldwide
geographic area

Local responsiveness:
Coordination and
control problems

Global integration:
Coordination and
control problems

*Resource/
capability
constraints*

*Resource/
capability
constraints*

Regional strategy

Regional structure

Opportunity costs of
adjacency

Transnational
strategy

Global combination
structure

The intensified competitive landscape of the foreign location may pressure the company to follow a combined strategy where local adaptation and differentiation are combined with global integration and cost leadership. However, a lack of resources and capabilities to enter global markets or a low transferability of these resources and capabilities to the new location may cause the company to focus on a particular region.[95] The company may not understand the market it competes in or may be incapable of creating economies in a wide variety of global locations.[96] It is important to make a distinction between resources and capabilities when considering a mismatch between strategy and structure. For instance, competitors' efforts to duplicate the success of Wal-Mart's cost leadership strategies have generally failed, partly because of their lack of capabilities in matching the strategy and structure in each of the firm's segments effectively. Rugman highlighted the importance of a regional strategy to a firm's international success as opposed to a transnational strategy.[97] The successful execution of a transnational strategy on the other hand does combine global integration with local responsiveness in many global markets and creates more potential for profit generation due to its extended scale. One of the major drawbacks of pursuing a regional strategy is therefore the opportunity costs of not using the potential of the global market.[98]

**Using the worldwide geographic area structure to implement the multidomestic strategy** The multidomestic strategy decentralizes the firm's strategic and operating decisions to business units in each country so that product characteristics can be tailored to local preferences. The worldwide geographic area structure is used to implement this strategy. The worldwide geographic area structure emphasizes national interests and facilitates the firm's efforts to satisfy local differences (see Figure 13.9).

The multidomestic strategy/worldwide geographic area structure match evolved as a natural outgrowth of the multicultural European marketplace. Friends and family members of the main business who were sent as expatriates into foreign countries to develop the independent country subsidiary often used this structure

> **Worldwide geographic area structure**
>
> The worldwide geographic area structure emphasizes national interests and facilitates the firm's efforts to satisfy local differences.

**FIGURE 13.9** Worldwide geographic area structure for implementing a multidomestic strategy

Notes:

- The perimeter circles indicate decentralization of operations
- Emphasis is on differentiation by local demand to fit an area or country culture
- Corporate headquarters coordinates financial resources among independent subsidiaries
- The organization is like a decentralized federation

for the main business. The relationship to corporate headquarters by divisions took place through informal communication among "family members".[99]

Using the multidomestic strategy requires little coordination between different country markets, meaning that integrating mechanisms among divisions in the worldwide geographic area structure are not needed. Hence, formalization is low, and coordination among units in a firm's worldwide geographic area structure is often informal, limiting the firm in creating a global efficient innovation.

A typical example that illustrates this disadvantage is the case of Ahold, a Dutch retailing concern. In the 1970s the company expanded to the US as it acquired a local supermarket chain. In the succeeding thirty years Ahold grew internationally by acquiring companies in the US, Latin America, Central Europe, Southern Europe, Scandinavia and Asia.[100] This acquisition strategy resulted in a decentralized organization which was locally adaptive but poorly coordinated. In 2003 it became clear that one of Ahold's US subsidiaries, US Foodservice, had underperformed over the years. More importantly, it was announced that Ahold's financial statements had to be reviewed as fraud was suspected.[101] Several months later another bookkeeping scandal was found at a different subsidiary, Tops Market.[102] These accounting scandals hit Ahold so hard that the company eventually withdrew its activities in Latin America and Asia, and the majority of its activities in the US.

**Using the worldwide product divisional structure to implement the global strategy** With the corporation's home office dictating competitive strategy, the global strategy is one through which the firm offers standardized products across country markets. The firm's success depends on its ability to develop

**FIGURE 13.10** Worldwide product divisional structure for implementing a global strategy

Notes:

■ The headquarters' circle indicates centralization to coordinate information flow among worldwide products

■ Corporate headquarters uses many intercoordination devices to facilitate global economies of scale and scope

■ Corporate headquarters also allocates financial resources in a cooperative way

■ The organization is like a centralized federation

economies of scope and economies of scale on a global level. Decisions to outsource or maintain integrated subsidiaries may in part depend on the country risk and institutional environment into which the firm is entering.[103]

The worldwide product divisional structure is the structural match for the global strategy. In the worldwide product divisional structure, decision-making authority is centralized in the worldwide division headquarters to coordinate and integrate decisions and actions among divisional business units (see Figure 13.10). This structure is often used in rapidly growing firms seeking to manage their diversified product lines effectively.

Integrating mechanisms are important in the effective use of the worldwide product divisional structure. Direct contact between managers, liaison roles between departments, and temporary task forces as well as permanent teams, are examples of these mechanisms. One researcher describes their use in the worldwide structure: "There is extensive and formal use of task forces and operating committees to supplement communication and coordination of worldwide operations."[104] As a result of the misconception that homogeneous products and services can be developed for the world market, the firm that pursues a global strategy will be unable to be properly adapt to local standards. Local competition has an advantage over the corporation as they have this specified knowledge. ABN AMRO's stagnating profit margins in the period 2000–2005 were influenced by its choice of a global strategy. This is illustrated by its former global product division that designed services for its subsidiary in Brazil, Banco Real.[105] Products for the Brazilian market were designed in Amsterdam. The failing performance of this subsidiary and ABN AMRO as a whole eventually contributed to the split-up of the bank, as activist shareholders initiated the takeover process.[106]

## Using the regional structure to implement the regional strategy

The competitive environment of the company may require a firm to be both locally adaptive and efficient in its operations. However, a combination of the multidomestic strategy's local responsiveness with the global strategy's efficiency may not work if the company pursues this combination at a global level, i.e. the transnational strategy.

A lot of companies do not have the capability or resources to compete in a wide variety of international locations. In fact, most of the corporate activities in America, Western Europe and Japan are local or regional.[107] Instead of applying a global scope firms need to be responsive to local customers. These customers are usually located in regions adjacent to the domestic market of the company or in the triad of Western Europe, the US and Japan. Rugman and Collison defined a global company as a company that derives at least 20 per cent per cent of its sales in each of the three regions of the triad of the US, the EU and Japan. The main part of Fiat Group's sales, for instance, 60.7 per cent, comes from inter-regional activities.[108]

As companies follow a regional strategy, the benefits of applying a "real" global scope are implicitly being acknowledged. The need for a combination of global integration and local responsiveness is recognized, and the benefits of pursuing such a strategy acknowledged. The capabilities and specific advantages developed by first acting regionally can later be applied in different regions.[109] The structure that is needed to successfully implement a regional strategy is similar to the combination structure discussed in the next section. The only differentiating factor is the company's regional or global scope.

## Using the combination structure to implement the transnational strategy

The transnational strategy calls for the firm to combine the multidomestic strategy's local responsiveness with the global strategy's efficiency. Firms

**Worldwide product divisional structure**

In the worldwide product divisional structure, decision-making authority is centralized in the worldwide division headquarters to coordinate and integrate decisions and actions among divisional business units.

## STRATEGIC FOCUS

© Ken Welsh/Alamy

# IKEA expands all over the world

The Swedish home products company IKEA is one of the largest in their industry with revenues in 2009 of €22.7bn and 301 stores worldwide. IKEA was one of the first in their industry who moved to globalization.

The furniture industry is an example of a business that did not lend itself to globalization before the 1960s. The fact that the furniture industry was not internationalized can be explained by several reasons. Furniture relatively takes up a lot of space compared to its value and can be damaged easily. Those two factors led to high transportation costs. Furthermore, government trade barriers were also unfavourable.

IKEA's furniture was not assembled and therefore could be shipped more economically. IKEA also lowered costs by involving the customer in the value chain; the customer carried the furniture home and assembled it himself. IKEA successfully expanded in Europe by moving to Norway in 1963 and to Switzerland in 1973. Since customers in different countries were willing to purchase similar designs, IKEA expanded to other European countries, and Australia and Canada followed. IKEA applied the same formula

to its international expansion, but after successfully expanding to several countries, ran into difficulties in the US market because of differences in taste and culture. IKEA moved to the US in 1985 and over the following six years, six more stores were opened. Many of the products sold in these stores were manufactured in Sweden and shipped to the US. Some of these products did not match the local preferences in the US. IKEA had learned from the move to the US that consumption patterns and the way of life regarding household equipment, furniture and related items remain significantly different, according to the consumers' cultural backgrounds. Routines were adapted as IKEA started to make use of local suppliers. The aforementioned can be witnessed by comparing IKEA customers in Germany with their counterparts in Singapore and Malaysia, where customers perceive IKEA as a prestigious European brand and prefer not to assemble the furniture themselves as wished for by IKEA. On the contrary, IKEA acknowledges its perception as a European status brand, and offers all electric goods with European sockets in order to enhance its up-market image by appearing distinctly European (although these electric goods are manufactured outside Europe). In the 1990s IKEA expanded into economies that were now open due to the fall of the Berlin Wall (e.g. Hungary and Poland). These markets were rapidly growing as well as customer spending.[111] This expansion created another big challenge for IKEA. Difficulties in the US were mainly due to product characteristics that did not fit local preferences, However, these new markets required more adaptation.

In 2009, IKEA faced problems with extending globally. IKEA already sources textiles from India for its global stores. However, for almost two years they failed to persuade the Indian government to raise its foreign ownership limit on single-brand retail businesses to 100 per cent, up from the current 51 per cent. In June 2009 IKEA abandoned their plans to enter the Indian retail market because of those stringent foreign direct investment norms. However, the company said it would continue sourcing supplies from the country for its international operations. "We would have liked the government to allow 100 per cent FDI in retail. As it is not forthcoming, we have stopped all plans for our retail business in India," an IKEA official said. "Our sourcing business has no links with our retail plans in India. The sourcing of goods and raw materials will continue from India," the official added. The company has been active in India for two years and is sourcing business that is worth around Rs 1800 core (€ 295 billion). He said the company has a policy of not operating retail chains through joint ventures or other routes. Under the existing rules, foreign investment of up to 51 per cent is allowed in single-brand retail, while for wholesale cash-and-carry business, 100 per cent FDI is allowed. No FDI is currently allowed in multibrand retail business.

This illustrates the problems a globalization strategy brings, based on the rather different customer needs and local governments. In conclusion, IKEA succeeds globally by relying on the match between their strategy and structure as the key driver of profitable growth.

**Sources:** Flynn, J. and Bongiornom, L. (1997) "IKEA's new game plan", *BusinessWeek*. http://www.businessweek.com. October 6; Inter IKEA Systems B.V. (2006) *Grundsteinlegung für neues IKEA Einrichtungshaus in Spreite*, Inter IKEA Systems B.V. http://www.ikea.com. March 10; 1994 "Management brief: Furnishing the world", *The Economist*, 333 (7890): 79–80; Lloyd, M. E. (2009) "IKEA sees opportunity in slump", *Wall Street Journal Online*, http://online.wsj.com, February 17; Baraldi, E. (2008) "Strategy in industrial networks: Experiences from IKEA", *California Management Review*, 50(4): 99–126; Kazmin, A. (2009) "Ikea abandons efforts to invest in India" *Financial Times* http://www.ft.com. June 11; Inter IKEA Systems B.V. (2010) *Facts & Figures*. Inter IKEA Systems B.V. http://www.franchisor.ikea.com. July 13.

### Questions

1 How did IKEA evolve in its international expansion?

2 Identify the main problems IKEA faced in its international strategy and describe how these problems relate to IKEA's organizational structure.

3 Can you provide an update on IKEA's international organizational structure?

using this strategy are trying to gain the advantages of both local responsiveness and global efficiency. The combination structure is used to implement the transnational strategy. The combination structure is a structure drawing characteristics and mechanisms from both the worldwide geographic area structure and the worldwide product divisional structure. The transnational strategy is often implemented through two possible combination structures: a global matrix structure and a hybrid global design.[111]

The global matrix design brings together both local market and product expertise into teams that develop and respond to the global marketplace. The global matrix design (the basic matrix structure was defined earlier) promotes flexibility in designing products and responding to customer needs. However, it has severe limitations in that it places employees in a position of being accountable to more than one manager. At any given time, an employee may be a member of several functional or product group teams. Relationships that evolve from multiple memberships can make it difficult for employees to be simultaneously loyal to all of them. Although the matrix places authority in the hands of managers who are most able to use it, it creates problems in regard to corporate reporting relationships that are so complex and vague that it is difficult and time-consuming to receive approval for major decisions.

We illustrate the hybrid structure in Figure 13.11. In this design, some divisions are oriented toward products while others are oriented toward market areas. Thus, in some cases when the geographic area is more important, the division managers are area-oriented. In other divisions where worldwide product coordination and efficiencies are more important, the division manager is more product-oriented.

The fits between the multidomestic strategy and the worldwide geographic area structure and between the global strategy and the worldwide product divisional structure are apparent. However, when a firm wants to implement the multidomestic and the global strategies simultaneously through a combination structure, the appropriate integrating mechanisms are less obvious. The structure used to implement the transnational strategy must be simultaneously centralized and decentralized; integrated and nonintegrated; formalized and nonformalized. IKEA has faced difficulties balancing these organization aspects in implementing the transnational

**Combination structure**

The combination structure is a structure drawing characteristics and mechanisms from both the worldwide geographic area structure and the worldwide product divisional structure.

**FIGURE 13.11** Hybrid form of the combination structure for implementing a transnational strategy

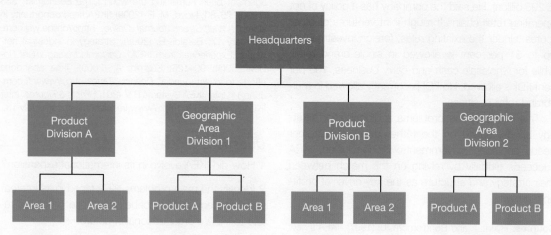

strategy.[112] IKEA focuses on lowering its costs and also understanding its customers" needs. It has been aiming to manage these seemingly opposite characteristics through is structure and management process. Over the years the company encouraged its employees to understand the effects of cultural and geographic diversity on firm's operations. IKEA's system also has internal network attributes which will be discussed next in regard to external inter-organizational networks.

## Matches between cooperative strategies and network structures

As discussed in Chapter 10, a network strategy exists when partners form several alliances in order to improve the performance of the alliance network itself through cooperative endeavours.[113] The greater levels of environmental complexity and uncertainty facing companies in today's competitive environment are causing more firms to use cooperative strategies such as strategic alliances and joint ventures.[114]

The breadth and scope of firms' operations in the global economy create many opportunities for firms to cooperate.[115] In fact, a firm can develop cooperative relationships with many of its stakeholders, including customers, suppliers and competitors. When a firm becomes involved with combinations of cooperative relationships, it is part of a strategic network, or what others call an alliance constellation or portfolio.[116]

A strategic network is a group of firms that has been formed to create value by participating in multiple cooperative arrangements. An effective strategic network facilitates discovering opportunities beyond those identified by individual network participants.[117]

A strategic network can be a source of competitive advantage for its members when its operations create value that is difficult for competitors to duplicate and that network members can't create by themselves.[118] Strategic networks are used to implement business-level, corporate-level and international cooperative strategies.

Commonly, a strategic network is a loose federation of partners participating in the network's operations on a flexible basis. At the core or centre of the strategic network, the strategic centre firm is the one around which the network's cooperative relationships revolve (see Figure 13.12).

**FIGURE 13.12** A strategic network

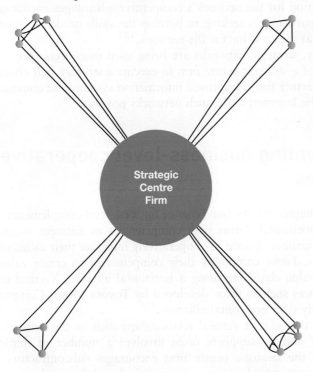

Because of its central position, the strategic centre firm is the foundation for the strategic network's structure. Concerned with various aspects of organizational structure, such as formal reporting relationships and procedures, the strategic centre firm manages what are often complex, cooperative interactions between network partners. To perform the tasks discussed next, the strategic centre firm must make sure that incentives for participating in the network are aligned so that network firms continue to have a reason to remain connected.[119] The strategic centre firm is engaged in four primary tasks as it manages the strategic network and controls its operations:[120]

*Strategic outsourcing* The strategic centre firm outsources and partners with more firms than do other network members. At the same time, the strategic centre firm requires network partners to be more than contractors. Members are expected to find opportunities for the network to create value through its cooperative work.

*Competencies* To increase network effectiveness, the strategic centre firm seeks ways to support each member's efforts to develop core competencies with the potential of benefiting the network and secures adequate alignment of the transaction attributes with the strategic outsourcing relationships.[121]

*Technology* The strategic centre firm is responsible for managing the development and sharing of technology-based ideas among network members. The structural requirement that members submit formal reports detailing the technology-oriented outcomes of their efforts to the strategic centre firm facilitates this activity.[122]

*Race to learn.* The strategic centre firm emphasizes that the principal dimensions of competition are between value chains and between networks of value chains. Because of this interconnection, the strategic network is only as strong as its weakest value-chain link. With its centralized decision-making authority and responsibility, the strategic centre firm guides participants in efforts to form network-specific competitive advantages. The need for each participant to have capabilities that can be the foundation for the network's competitive advantages encourages friendly rivalry among participants seeking to develop the skills needed to quickly form new capabilities that create value for the network.[123]

Interestingly, strategic networks are being used more frequently, partly because of the ability of a strategic centre firm to execute a strategy that effectively and efficiently links partner firms. Improved information systems and communication capabilities (e.g., the Internet) make such networks possible.[124]

# Implementing business-level cooperative strategies

As noted in Chapter 10, the two types of business-level complementary alliances are vertical and horizontal. Firms with competencies in different stages of the value chain form a vertical alliance to cooperatively integrate their different, but complementary, skills. Firms combining their competencies to create value in the same stage of the value chain are using a horizontal alliance. Vertical complementary strategic alliances such as those developed by Toyota Motor Company are formed more frequently than horizontal alliances.[125]

A strategic network of vertical relationships such as the network in Japan between Toyota and its suppliers often involves a number of implementation issues.[126] First, the strategic centre firm encourages subcontractors to modernize their facilities and provides them with technical and financial assistance to do so, if necessary. Second, the strategic centre firm reduces its transaction costs by promoting longer-term contracts with subcontractors, so that supplier-partners increase their long-term productivity. This approach is diametrically opposed to that of continually negotiating short-term contracts based on unit pricing. Third, the strategic centre firm enables engineers in upstream companies (suppliers) to have better communication with those companies with whom it has contracts for services. As a result, suppliers and the strategic centre firm become more interdependent and less independent.[127]

The lean production system (a vertical complementary strategic alliance) pioneered by Toyota and others has been diffused throughout the global auto industry.[128] However, no auto company has learned how to duplicate the manufacturing effectiveness and efficiency Toyota derives from the cooperative arrangements in its strategic network.[129]

A key factor accounting for Toyota's manufacturing-based competitive advantage is the cost other firms would incur to imitate the structural form used to support Toyota's application. In part, then, the structure of Toyota's strategic network that it created as the strategic centre firm, facilitates cooperative actions among network participants that competitors can't fully understand or duplicate.

In vertical complementary strategic alliances, such as the one between Toyota and its suppliers, the strategic centre firm is obvious, as is the structure that firm establishes. However, the same is not always true with horizontal complementary strategic alliances where firms try to create value in the same part of the value chain, as with airline alliances that are commonly formed to create value in the marketing and sales primary activity segment of the value chain (see Table 3.6). Because air carriers commonly participate in multiple horizontal complementary alliances such as the Star Alliance between Lufthansa, United, Continental, US Airways, Thai, Air Canada, SAS and others, it is difficult to determine the strategic centre firm. Moreover, participating in several alliances can

© sebastian-julian

# KEY DEBATE

## Structure follows strategy or strategy follows structure?

As discussed in this chapter, a proper match between strategy and organizational structure can lead to competitive advantage, particularly in dynamic environments. However, what needs to be adjusted first to regain fit is a classic debate in the strategic management literature, and relevant to managerial practice. Ideally, a strategy is first formulated and subsequently an appropriate organizational structure is designed in order to successfully implement the corporate strategy. For example, Royal Friesland Campina first formulated an international strategy and then redesigned its cooperative organizational structure to remove organizational barriers for its international strategy. Royal Friesland Campina is today a very successful international cooperative organization and realized many of the opportunities in emerging markets, whereas most other competing cooperatives missed these opportunities and are still nationally oriented.

On the other hand organizations are more than only structures. For example, the organizational culture or capabilities may not support the structural change of the organization. Under such circumstances it may be wise to reformulate the strategy in the light of the limitations of organizational reality. Successful strategic management is not only about identifying entrepreneurial opportunities but also takes into account the limitations of the organizational reality, such as cognitive limitations and conflict of interests between organizational stakeholders, that hinder

strategy implementation with calculated or opportunistic behaviour. Ultimately, successful strategic management is a permanent process of rebalancing between the search and development of new opportunities and organizational limitations such as organizational structure, bounded rationality and conflict of interests.

**Sources:** Chandler, A. (1962) *Strategy and Structure*, Cambridge, MA: MIT Press; Crozier, M. (1964) *The Bureaucratic Phenomenon*. Chicago: University of Chicago Press; Jarzabkowski, P. (2008) "Shaping strategy as a structuration process", *Academy of Management Journal*, 51(4): 621–650; Levinthal, D. (2004) "Bounded rationality and the search for organizational architecture: An evolutionary perspective on the design of organizations and their evolvability", *Administrative Science Quarterly*, 49: 404–437; Rivkin. J. and Siggelkow, N. (2003) "Balancing search and stability: Interdependencies among elements of organizational design", *Management Science*, 49: 290–321; Verwaal, E., Commandeur, H. R. and Verbeke, W. J. M. I. (2009) "Value creation and value claiming in strategic outsourcing decisions: A resource-contingency perspective", *Journal of Management*, 35(2): 420–444; Volberda, H. W. (1998) *Building the Flexible Firm: How to Remain Competitive*. Oxford: Oxford University Press.

### Questions

1 International strategies need to be adjusted to the conditions in the external environment and the company's competitive advantages. Similarly, a company's organization structure needs to be adjusted to its international strategy. Seek examples of at least two companies in the same industry that operate internationally.

2 Describe the firm's international strategy and relate it to its organization structure. What are the advantages/disadvantages of the pursued international strategy and does it match with the organization's structure?

3 Relate the changes strategy/structure from the viewpoint of different stakeholders of the organization. How did these changes influence the position of the different stakeholders?

cause firms to question partners' true loyalties and intentions. Also, if rivals band together in too many collaborative activities, one or more governments may suspect the possibility of illegal collusive activities. For these reasons, horizontal complementary alliances are used less often and successfully than their vertical counterpart, although there are examples of success, for instance, among auto and aircraft manufacturers.[130]

# Implementing corporate-level cooperative strategies

Corporate-level cooperative strategies, such as franchising, are used to facilitate product and market diversification. As a cooperative strategy, franchising allows the firm to use its competencies to extend or diversify its product or market reach, but without completing a merger or an acquisition.[131] Research suggests that knowledge embedded in corporate-level cooperative strategies facilitates synergy.[132] For example, Accor Hospitality, the hotels division of the French Accor Group, pursues a franchising strategy for a considerable part of its 4100 hotels in 90 countries. The franchised hotels are operated by the franchisee. The hotels make use of Accor's booking and distribution system and carry Accor's brands in exchange for a fee. Accor's franchising system is a strategic network, which keeps the company more flexible than its previous structure where its hotels were owned by the group or operated under fixed-rent leases. Accor's headquarters office serves as the strategic centre firm for the network's franchisees, helping them to increase revenue, optimize their cost-structure and also providing assistance with employee training.[133]

# Implementing international cooperative strategies

Strategic networks formed to implement international cooperative strategies result in firms competing in several countries.[134] Differences among countries' regulatory environments increase the challenge of managing international networks

**FIGURE 13.13** A distributed strategic network

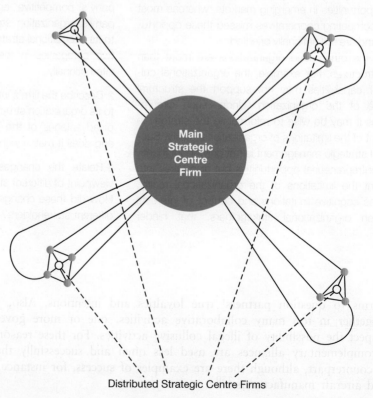

Distributed Strategic Centre Firms

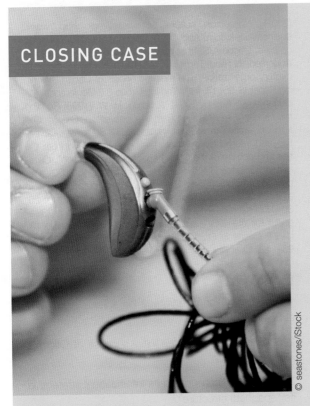

© seastones/iStock

# Oticon's "Spaghetti Organization"

In 1904 Hans Demant started his hearing devices importing business in Denmark. The Second World War prevented the company from importing the Acousticon devices from General Acoustic Co., so it decided to manufacture a copy of the original device for the Danish market. Six years later, William Demant, Hans' son who took over the company, entered into a partnership with an American hearing-aid manufacturer and the Oticon Corporation was established. Almost twenty years later, the Danish hearing-aid manufacturer made its first international move into the US, which was followed by global expansion into Europe, Japan, New Zealand and China. Nowadays, the company is known for its unique organizational structure, the "spaghetti organization", an extreme form of the matrix organization.

By the 1980s Oticon had become a traditional hierarchical organization. However, although it was the leading hearing-aid supplier the company faced some financial and organizational issues. At his appointment in 1988 Lars Kolind, Oticon's CEO, imposed a strict cost control system at Oticon. In 1989 this policy

seemed to have worked as Oticon performed better, but, Kolind realized that the benefits of cost cutting were limited. His challenge became to transform Oticon into an organization that fosters innovation and is responsive to customer demands while at the same time increasing the firm's productivity.

In 1991 Lars Kolind and Niels Jacobsen (who became CEO in 1998), led the transformation process into the firm's new structure. This new project-based structure was similar to the "original" matrix structure; however its uniqueness was defined by how projects were managed in the company. All departments at the company's headquarters were merged into one department in order to eliminate intra-departmental competition. Tasks were organized into projects. Employees managed the selection and execution themselves instead of Oticon's management: projects were managed bottom-up as opposed to top-down project management. This structure had no hierarchical reporting relationships, but project managers were appointed by Oticon's top management. Employees could freely choose which team they would join and what projects they wanted to carry out, so project managers had to market their projects in order to form a team. The system of voluntary subscription was implemented as Kolind believed that people are more motivated if they choose their tasks themselves. Consequently, the company could save on monitoring and coordination. The company did not make use of formal functions and even prohibited employees from focusing on one job. This measure was taken in order to promote diversity into projects. The company's physical layout was designed as open-plan so that innovation could prosper. Oticon's headquarters were moved to a new location where nobody had a permanent office; furniture could be freely moved around so that project teams could sit together; meeting rooms were not furnished. Kolind named his newly-implemented structure a spaghetti structure as it resembled chaos which was somehow connected. Information technology played an important role in Oticon's new structure since the company became "paperless". Employees were equipped with computers at home to speed up the staff members' familiarity with computers. All documents were stored on to the company's server and could be accessed from the employees' workstations.

The transformation process was promoted by an internal campaign using slogans including "think the unthinkable" and visual symbols, such as a large transparent chute in the middle of the building.

In the years following the reorganization very few employees resigned and the company grew and went public. The firm's profit margin increased from 1.8 per cent in 1991 to 17.9 per cent in 1999 and more innovations were introduced as product development time was reduced by 50 per cent. Nonetheless, in 1996, the company shaped its structure into a more traditional form. The head office was divided into three groups and a competence centre which was responsible for project management and the company's supportive functions. The company's radical approach was considered a key driver behind the company's success. After co-managing the company with Lars Kolind, Niels Jacobsen succeeded him as CEO in 1998. Eventually Oticon's project management structure professionalized as becoming a project leader became an official function, requiring an employee to advance in her/his career and follow training in project management. Employees were no longer entirely free to work on the projects of their choice and instead reported to a superior. The company created a human resources department led by a HR director and expertise in functional areas was grouped in more traditional business units. The head office, however, still doesn't have cubicles or proper meeting rooms.

**Sources:** Mol, M. J. and Birkinshaw, J. (2008) *Giant Steps in Management: Innovations That Change the Way We Work.* Harlow, UK: Pearson Education. 100, 183–184; Jack Ewing

(2007) "No-cubicle culture", *BusinessWeek.* http://www.businessweek.com. August 20; Oticon A/S (2010) *Founded on care.* Oticon A/S. http://www.oticon.com. July 13; Bjørn-Andersen, N. and Turner, J. A. (1994) "Creating the 21st century organization: The metamorphosis of Oticon", Working Paper IS-95–13, IFIP Working Group 8.2 Conference, Michigan, USA August 1994; Volberda, H. W. (1998) *Building the Flexible Firm: How to Remain Competitive.* Oxford: Oxford University Press; Foss, N. J. (2003) "Selective intervention and internal hybrids: Interpreting and learning from the rise and decline of the Oticon spaghetti organization", *Organization Science,* 14(3): 331–349; Larsen, H. H. (2002) "Oticon: Unorthodox project-based management and careers in a 'spaghetti organization'", *Human Resource Planning,* 25: 30–37; Eskerod, P. and Darmer, P. (1994) "Oticon – Spaghetti for the ears", in: Adam-Smith, D. and Peacock, A. (1994) *Cases in Organisational Behaviour,* London: Pitman 98–102.

## Questions

**1** How can Oticon's strategy be linked to its new structure?

**2** What contributed to the initial success of Oticon's reorganization?

**3** How can Oticon govern its international strategy in its "spaghetti structure"?

**4** How can Oticon's eventual transformation to a more traditional matrix organization be explained?

and verifying that at a minimum, the network's operations comply with all legal requirements.[135]

Distributed strategic networks are the organizational structure used to manage international cooperative strategies. As shown in Figure 13.13, several regional strategic centre firms are included in the distributed network to manage partner firms' multiple cooperative arrangements.[136]

Hewlett Packard acquired EDS, a large information technology consulting firm. One of EDS' assets is the EDS Agility Alliance, which is an example of a distributed strategic network. "The Agility Alliance is EDS" premiere partner program bringing together industry-leading technology providers to build and deliver end-to-end IT solutions."[137] EDS is the main strategic centre firm in this alliance and has two dedicated centres that are the hubs for jointly developing initiatives with its partners. Cisco, SAP, Sun, Xerox, Oracle, EMC and Microsoft are members of this distributed strategic network. Symantec, an Internet anti-virus and security firm, was recently added as a partner to respond to clients, needs "for more innovative security products and solutions that help them better secure their mission-critical business data and address specific enterprise security issues".[138] EDS's partners each work with their own networks to complete projects that are a part of the Agility Alliance. As this example demonstrates, the structure used to implement the international cooperative strategy is complex and demands careful attention to be used successfully.

## SUMMARY

- Organizational structure specifies the firm's formal reporting relationships, procedures, controls, and authority and decision-making processes. Essentially, organizational structure details the work to be done in a firm and how that work is to be accomplished. Organizational controls guide the use of strategy, indicate how to compare actual and expected results, and suggest actions to take to improve performance when it falls below expectations. A proper match between strategy and structure can lead to a competitive advantage.

- Strategic controls (largely subjective criteria) and financial controls (largely objective criteria) are the two types of organizational controls used to implement a strategy. Both controls are critical, although their degree of emphasis varies based on individual matches between strategy and structure.

- Strategy and structure influence each other although, overall, strategy has a stronger influence on structure. Research indicates that firms tend to change structure when declining performance forces them to do so. Effective strategic managers anticipate the need for structural change and quickly modify structure to better accommodate the firm's strategy when evidence calls for that action.

- The functional structure is used to implement business-level strategies. The cost leadership strategy requires a centralized functional structure – one in which manufacturing efficiency and process engineering are emphasized. The differentiation strategy's functional structure decentralizes implementation-related decisions, especially those concerned with marketing, to those involved with individual organizational functions. Focus strategies, often used in small firms, require a simple structure until such time that the firm diversifies in terms of products and/or markets.

- Unique combinations of different forms of the multidivisional structure are matched with different corporate-level diversification strategies to properly implement these strategies. The cooperative M-form, used to implement the related constrained corporate-level strategy, has a centralized corporate office and extensive integrating mechanisms. Divisional incentives are linked to overall corporate performance. The related linked SBU M-form structure establishes separate profit centres within the diversified firm. Each profit centre may have divisions offering similar products, but the centres are unrelated to each other. The competitive M-form structure, used to implement the unrelated diversification strategy, is highly decentralized, lacks integrating mechanisms, and utilizes objective financial criteria to evaluate each unit's performance.

- The multidomestic strategy, implemented through the worldwide geographic area structure, emphasizes decentralization and locates all functional activities in the host country or geographic area. The worldwide product divisional structure is used to implement the global strategy. This structure is centralized in order to coordinate and integrate different functions' activities so as to gain global economies of scope and economies of scale. Decision-making authority is centralized in the firm's worldwide division headquarters.

- The transnational strategy – a strategy through which the firm seeks the local responsiveness of the multidomestic strategy and the global efficiency of the global strategy – is implemented through the combination structure. Because it must be simultaneously centralized and decentralized, integrated and nonintegrated, and formalized and nonformalized, the combination structure is difficult to organize and successfully manage. However, two structural designs are suggested: the matrix and the hybrid structure with both geographic and product-oriented divisions.

- Increasingly important to competitive success, cooperative strategies are implemented through organizational structures framed around strategic networks. Strategic centre firms play a critical role in managing strategic networks. Business level strategies are often employed in vertical and horizontal alliance networks. Corporate level cooperative strategies are used to pursue product and market diversification. Franchising is one type of corporate strategy that uses a strategic network to implement this strategy. This is also true for international cooperative strategies where distributed networks are often used.

## REVIEW QUESTIONS

1    What is organizational structure and what are organizational controls? What are the differences between strategic controls and financial controls? What is the importance of these differences?

2    What does it mean to say that strategy and structure have a reciprocal relationship?

3    What are the characteristics of the functional structures used to implement the cost leadership, differentiation, integrated cost leadership/differentiation and focused business-level strategies?

4    What are the differences among the three versions of the multidivisional (M-form) organizational structures that are used to implement the related constrained, the related linked, and the unrelated corporate-level diversification strategies?

5    What organizational structures are used to implement the multidomestic, global and transnational international strategies?

6    What is a strategic network? What is a strategic centre firm? How is a strategic centre used in business-level, corporate-level and international cooperative strategies?

## DISCUSSION QUESTIONS

1    Search for instances of public companies that have recently changed their corporate strategies.

    a    Specify what financial and strategic controls these firms use in order to successfully execute their strategies.

    b    Describe how the firm's organization structure relates to its intended strategy.

    c    Is there a fit between the firm's structure and strategy? How would you restructure the company to achieve a fit between strategy and structure?

2    In this chapter the evolutionary pattern of an organization's structure has been described. Find examples of companies that have gone through similar paths and describe:

    a    How the organization structure is currently governed and how it relates to its corporate strategy.

    b    How did the organization evolve in its current form (e.g. by volume, by geography, through product/business diversification)?

    c    Describe the critical points in the firm's evolutionary path? What (mis)fit of the organization's structure and strategy can be observed?

3    The functional structure can be used to implement various strategies.

    a    Explain how the functional structure can implement a cost leadership strategy, a differentiation strategy, and an integrated cost leadership/differentiation strategy.

    b    What are the differences among the three versions of the multidivisional form (M-form) and explain how they can influence the position of different stakeholders of the organization.

4    In this chapter we discussed the strategy and structure growth pattern in internationalization.

    a    Explain how international growth can lead to a worldwide product divisional structure.

    b    Explain how international growth can lead to a worldwide geographic structure.

    c    Explain what may bring a global firm to restructure a worldwide structure into a regional structure.

## FURTHER READING

Alfred P. Sloan presents a fascinating insider's perspective on how he as CEO managed General Motors's transition to a multidivisional structure in response to the changing demands of the car market. This managerial innovation was decisive in GM's strategy to become the world's largest car maker (A. P. Sloan Jr (1964) *My Years with General Motors*, New York: Doubleday).

A historic analysis of this transition can be found in the classic study of Chandler's Strategy and Structure (A. D. Chandler (1962) *Strategy and Structure*, Cambridge, MA: MIT Press). When you are interested in how firms deal with the paradoxes of stability and renewal in increasingly changing environments, an insightful and extensive study on this dilemma can be found in Henk Volberda's *Building the Flexible Firm* (H. W. Volberda (1998) *Building the Flexible Firm: How to Remain Competitive*, Oxford: Oxford University Press).

Bartlett and Ghoshal propose – based on an elaborate case analysis of leading multinational firms – a new organizational model on how to deal with the conflicting demands of the international business environment (C. Bartlett and S. Ghoshal (2007) *Transnational Management: Text, Cases, and Readings in Cross-Border Management*, New York: McGraw-Hill Companies). In recent years, global competition is however shifting from the firm level to the level of the global supply chain.

You can find an insightful perspective on how to manage and design organizational structures that can successfully compete in international supply networks in V. K. Fung, W. F. Fung and Y. J. Wind (2007) *Competing in a Flat World: Building Enterprises for a Borderless World*, Upper Saddle River, New Jersey: Wharton School Publishing.

## EXPERIENTIAL EXERCISES

### Exercise 1: Organizational structure and business level strategy

The purpose of this exercise is to apply the concepts introduced in this chapter to live examples of business level strategies and how various firms actually structure their organizations to compete. In teams, you will be assigned by the instructor a business level strategy such as differentiation or cost leader. Once you have your category assigned you are to identify a firm that exemplifies this strategy and pictorially draw out its corporate structure. You will need to present the results of your investigation by comparing your firm's organizational chart with that in your text identified for your particular business level strategy. (See text for figures labelled "Functional Structure for Implementing a Differentiation (or Cost Leadership) Strategy"). Be prepared to address the following issues:

1   Describe your firm's business level strategy. Why do you consider it to be a cost leader or a differentiator?

2   What is the mission statement and/or vision statement of this firm? Are there specific goals this firm is targeting that you can identify?

3   Using the text examples for a functional structure, how does your firm differ, if it does?

4   Summarize your conclusions. Does your team believe that this firm is structured appropriately considering its goals for the future?

### Exercise 2: Burger Buddy and Ma Maison

Assume that it is a few months before your college graduation. You and some classmates have decided to become entrepreneurs. The group has agreed on the restaurant industry, but your discussions thus far have gone back and forth between two different dining concepts: Burger Buddy and Ma Maison. Details about these two concepts follow.

Burger Buddy would operate near campus in order to serve the student market. Burger Buddy will be a 1950s-themed hamburger outlet, emphasizing large portions and affordable prices.

Ma Maison is the alternate concept. One of your partners has attended cooking school and has proposed the idea of a small, upscale French restaurant. The menu would have no set items, but would vary on a daily basis instead. Ma Maison would position itself as a boutique restaurant providing superb customer service and unique offerings.

Working in small groups, answer the following questions:

1   What is the underlying strategy for each restaurant concept?

2   How would the organizational structure of the two restaurant concepts differ?

3   How would the nature of work vary between the two restaurants?

4   If the business concept is successful, how might you expect the organizational structure and nature of work at each restaurant to change in the next five to seven years?

# VIDEO CASE

## Organizational Structure and Accountability

### Roger Parry, former chairman and CEO, Clear Channel International

www.cengage.co.uk/volberda/students/video_cases

Roger Parry, former chairman and CEO of Clear Channel International, describes the topic of structure and control inside an organization. Before you view the video think through your concept of an organizational chart and its role in the modern corporation.

Be prepared to discuss the following concepts and questions in class:

### Concepts

- Organizational structure
- Organizational control

- Strategy and structure
- Performance alignment

### Questions

1  Do you think it is important for an organization to have an organizational chart?

2  How can organizations use structure to allow business units to meet business unit goals as well as corporate goals?

3  How important is it for everyone in the organization to know precisely their responsibility and that proper control is in place to ensure that responsibility is being met?

# NOTES

1.  P. Jarzabkowski, 2008, "Shaping strategy as a structuration process", *Academy of Management Journal*, 51(4): 621–650; B. Ambos and B. B. Schlegelmilch, 2007, "Innovation and control in the multinational firm: A comparison of political and contingency approaches", *Strategic Management Journal*, 28: 473–486; S. Kumar, S. Kant and T. L. Amburgey, 2007, "Public agencies and collaborative management approaches", *Administration & Society*, 39: 569–610.

2.  R. Gulati and P. Puranam, 2009, "Renewal through reorganization: The value of inconsistencies between formal and informal organization", *Organization Science*, 20 (2): 422–440; R. E. Miles and C. C. Snow, 1978, *Organizational Strategy, Structure and Process*, New York: McGraw-Hill.

3.  S. T. Hannah and P. B. Lester, 2009, "A multilevel approach to building and leading learning organizations", *Leadership Quarterly*, 20(1): 34–48; E. M. Olson, S. F. Slater and G. T. M. Hult, 2007, "The importance of structure and process to strategy implementation", *Business Horizons*, 48(1): 47–54; D. N. Sull and C. Spinosa, 2007, "Promise-based management", *Harvard Business Review*, 85(4): 79–86.

4.  R. Ireland, J. Covin and D. Kuratko, 2009, "Conceptualizing corporate entrepreneurship strategy", *Entrepreneurship Theory and Practice*, 33(1): 19–46; T. Amburgey and T. Dacin, 1994, "As the left foot follows the right? The dynamics of strategic and structural change", *Academy of Management Journal*, 37: 1427–1452.

5.  L. F. Monteiro, N. Arvidsson and J. Birkinshaw, 2008, "Knowledge flows within multinational corporations: Explaining subsidiary isolation and its performance implications", *Organization Science*, 19(1): 90–107;

P. Ghemawat, 2007, "Managing differences: The central challenge of global strategy", *Harvard Business Review*, 85 (3): 59–68; B. Keats and H. O'Neill, 2001, "Organizational structure: Looking through a strategy lens", in: M. A. Hitt, R. E. Freeman and J. S. Harrison (eds.), *Handbook of Strategic Management*, Oxford, UK: Blackwell Publishers, 520–542.

6.  R. E. Hoskisson, C. W. L. Hill and H. Kim, 1993, "The multidivisional structure: Organizational fossil or source of value?", *Journal of Management*, 19: 269–298.

7.  P. Jarzabkowski, 2008, "Shaping strategy as a structuration process", *Academy of Management Journal*, 51(4): 621–650; E. M. Olson, S. F. Slater, G. Tomas and G. T. M. Hult, 2005, "The performance implications of fit among business strategy, marketing organization structure, and strategic behavior", *Journal of Marketing*, 69(3): 49–65.

8.  T. Burns and G. M. Stalker, 1961, *The Management of Innovation*, London: Tavistock; P. R. Lawrence and J. W. Lorsch, 1967, *Organization and Environment*, Homewood, IL: Richard D. Irwin; J. Woodward, 1965, *Industrial Organization: Theory and Practice*, London: Oxford University Press.

9.  A. M. Rugman and A. Verbeke, 2008, "A regional solution to the strategy and structure of multinationals", *European Management Journal*, 26(5): 305–313; H. Kim, R. E. Hoskisson, L. Tihanyi and J. Hong, 2004, "Evolution and restructuring of diversified business groups in emerging markets: The lessons from chaebols in Korea", *Asia Pacific Journal of Management*, 21: 25–48.

10. R. Kathuria, M. P. Joshi and S. J. Porth, 2007, "Organizational alignment and performance: Past, present and future", *Management Decision*, 45: 503–517.

11. NRC Handelsblad – International, 2009, "ING to split banking and insurance operations", *NRC Handelsblad— International*, October 26.

12. A. Tempel and P. Walgenbach, 2007, "Global standardization of organizational forms and management practices: What new institutionalism and the business-systems approach can learn from each other", *Journal of Management Studies*, 44: 1–24; B. Keats and H. O'Neill, 2006, "Organizational structure: Looking through a strategy lens", in: M. A. Hitt, R. E. Freeman and J. S. Harrison (eds.), *Handbook of Strategic Management*, Oxford, UK.

13. Tieying Yu, M. S. Insead and R. H. Lester, 2008, "Misery loves company: The spread of negative impacts resulting from an organizational crisis", *Academy of Management Review*, 33(2): 452–472; R. L. Priem, L. G. Love and M. A. Shaffer, 2002, "Executives" perceptions of uncertainty sources: A numerical taxonomy and underlying dimensions', *Journal of Management*, 28: 725–746; H.W. Volberda, 1998, *Building the flexible firm: How to remain competitive*, Oxford: Oxford University Press.

14. A. N. Shub and P. W. Stonebraker, 2009, "The human impact on supply chains: Evaluating the importance of "soft" areas on integration and performance", *Supply Chain Management*, 14(1): 31–40; S. K. Ethiraj and D. Levinthal, 2004, "Bounded rationality and the search for organizational architecture: An evolutionary perspective on the design of organizations and their evolvability", *Administrative Science Quarterly*, 49: 404–437.

15. R. Khadem, 2008, "Alignment and follow-up: steps to strategy execution", *Journal of Business Strategy*, 29(6): 29–35; J. G. Covin, D. P. Slevin and M. B. Heeley, 2001, "Strategic decision making in an intuitive versus technocratic mode: Structural and environmental consideration", *Journal of Business Research*, 52: 51–67.

16. J. R. Maxwell, 2008, "Work system design to improve the economic performance of the firm", *Business Process Management Journal*, 14(3): 432–446; E. M. Olson, S. F. Slater and G. T. M. Hult, 2005, "The importance of structure and process to strategy implementation", *Business Horizons*, 48(1): 47–54.

17. L. Donaldson, 2001, *The Contingency Theory of Organizations*, Thousand Oaks, CA: Sage; P. Jenster and D. Hussey, 2001, *Company Analysis: Determining Strategic Capability*, Chichester: John Wiley and Sons, 135–171.

18. M. A. Schilling and H. K. Steensma, 2001, "The use of modular organizational forms: An industry-level analysis", *Academy of Management Journal*, 44: 1149–1168.

19. P. Legerer, T. Pfeiffer, G. Schneider and J. Wagner, 2009, "Organizational structure and managerial decisions", *International Journal of the Economics of Business*, 16(2): 147–159; C. B. Dobni and G. Luffman, 2003, "Determining the scope and impact of market orientation profiles on strategy implementation and performance", *Strategic Management Journal*, 24: 577–585.

20. H. Gebauer and F. Putz, 2009, "Organizational structures for the service business in product-oriented companies", *International Journal of Services Technology and Management*, 11(1): 64–81; M. Hammer, 2007, "The process audit", *Harvard Business Review*, 85(4): 111–123.

21. H. W. Volberda, 1998. *Building the Flexible Firm: How to Remain Competitive*. Oxford: Oxford University Press; T. J. Andersen, 2004, "Integrating decentralized strategy making and strategic planning processes in dynamic environments", *Journal of Management Studies*, 41: 1271–1299.

22. J. Rivkin and N. Siggelkow, 2003, "Balancing search and stability: Interdependencies among elements of organizational design", *Management Science*, 49: 290–321; G. A. Bigley and K. H. Roberts, 2001, "The incident command system: High-reliability organizing for complex and volatile task environments", *Academy of Management Journal*, 44: 1281–1299; H. W. Volberda, 1997, "Building flexible organizations for fast-moving markets", *Long Range Planning*, 30: 169–183.

23. L. F. Monteiro, N. Arvidsson, J. Birkinshaw, 2008, "Knowledge flows within multinational corporations: Explaining subsidiary isolation and its performance implications", *Organization Science*, 19(1): 90–107. S. Nadkarni and V. K. Narayanan, 2007, "Strategic schemas, strategic flexibility, and firm performance: The moderating role of industry clockspeed", *Strategic Management Journal*, 28: 243–270; K. D. Miller and A. T. Arikan, 2004, "Technology search investments: Evolutionary, option reasoning, and option pricing approaches", *Strategic Management Journal*, 25: 473–485; H. W. Volberda, 1996, "Toward the flexible firm: How to remain vital in hypercompetitive environments", *Organization Science* 7(4): 359–387.

24. S. Raisch and J. Birkinshaw, 2008, "Organizational ambidexterity: Antecedents, outcomes, and moderators", *Journal of Management* 34: 375–409; C. Zook, 2007, "Finding your next core business", *Harvard Business Review*, 85(4): 66–75; J. J. P. Jansen, M. P. Tempelaar, F. A. J. Van den Bosch and H. W. Volberda, 2009, "Structural differentiation and ambidexterity: The mediating role of integration mechanisms", *Organization Science*, 20: 798–811; J. J. P. Jansen, F. A. J. Van den Bosch and H. W. Volberda, 2006, "Exploratory innovation, exploitative innovation, and performance: Effects of organizational antecedents and environmental moderators", *Management Science*, 52: 1661–1674. P. Reinmoeller (2011), The Ambidextrous Organization, Routledge (forthcoming).

25. Capell, K, 2008. "H&M defies retail gloom", *BusinessWeek*, http://www.businessweek.com, September 3.

26. S. K. Maheshwari and D. Ahlstrom, 2004, "Turning around a state owned enterprise: The case of Scooters India Limited", *Asia Pacific Journal of Management*, 21(1–2): 75–101; B. W. Keats and M. A. Hitt, 1988, "A causal model of linkages among environmental dimensions, macro-organizational characteristics, and performance", *Academy of Management Journal*, 31: 570–598.

27. A. Chandler, 1962, *Strategy and Structure*, Cambridge, MA: MIT Press.

28. R. E. Hoskisson, R. A. Johnson, L. Tihanyi and R. E. White, 2005, "Diversified business groups and corporate refocusing in emerging economies", *Journal of Management*, 31: 941–965; J. D. Day, E. Lawson and

K. Leslie, 2003, "When reorganization works", *The McKinsey Quarterly,* (2), 20–29.

29. The Daily Telegraph, 2009, "ING to split, launch €7.5bn rights issue, and repay state aid", *The Daily Telegraph,* http://www.telegraph.co.uk, October 26.

30. S. K. Ethiraj, 2007, "Allocation of inventive effort in complex product systems", *Strategic Management Journal,* 28: 563–584.

31. D. Martin, 2007, "Alfred D. Chandler, Jr., a business historian, dies at 88", *New York Times Online,* http://www.nytimes.com, May 12.

32. A. M. Kleinbaum and M. L. Tushman, 2008, "Managing corporate social networks", *Harvard Business Review,* 86 (7): 26–27; A. Weibel, 2007, "Formal control and trustworthiness", *Group & Organization Management,* 32: 500–517; P. K. Mills and G. R. Ungson, 2003, "Reassessing the limits of structural empowerment: Organizational constitution and trust as controls", *Academy of Management Review,* 28: 143–153.

33. C. Rowe, J. G. Birnberg and M. D. Shields, 2008, "Effects of organizational process change on responsibility accounting and managers" revelations of private knowledge', *Accounting, Organizations and Society,* 33(2/3): 164–198; M. Santala and P. Parvinen, 2007, "From strategic fit to customer fit", *Management Decision,* 45: 582–601; R. Reed, W. J. Donoher and S. F. Barnes, 2004, "Predicting misleading disclosures: The effects of control, pressure, and compensation", *Journal of Managerial Issues,* 16: 322–336.

34. P. Greve, S. Nielsen and W. Ruigrok, 2009, "Transcending borders with international top management teams: A study of European financial multinational corporations", *European Management Journal,* 27(3): 213–224; T. Galpin, R. Hilpirt and B. Evans, 2007, "The connected enterprise: Beyond division of labor", *Journal of Business Strategy,* 28(2): 38–47; C. Sundaramurthy and M. Lewis, 2003, "Control and collaboration: Paradoxes of governance", *Academy of Management Review,* 28: 397–415.

35. M. A. Desai, 2008, "The finance function in a global corporation", *Harvard Business Review,* 86(7): 108–112; Y. Li, L. Li, Y. Liu and L. Wang, 2005, "Linking management control system with product development and process decisions to cope with environment complexity", *International Journal of Production Research,* 43: 2577–2591.

36. I. Filatotchev, J. Stephan and B. Jindra, 2008**, "**Ownership structure, strategic controls and export intensity of foreign-invested firms in transition economies", *Journal of International Business Studies,* 39(7): 1133–1148; G. J. M. Braam and E. J. Nijssen, 2004, "Performance effects of using the balanced scorecard: A note on the Dutch experience", *Long Range Planning,* 37: 335–349; S. D. Julian and E. Scifres, 2002, "An interpretive perspective on the role of strategic control in triggering strategic change", *Journal of Business Strategies,* 19: 141–159.

37. J. H. Burgers, J. J. P. Jansen, F. A. J. Van den Bosch and H. W. Volberda, 2009, "Structural differentiation and corporate venturing: The moderating role of formal and informal integration mechanisms", *Journal of Business Venturing,* 24: 206–220; J. Kratzer, H. G. Gemünden and C. Lettl, 2008, "Balancing creativity and time efficiency in multi-team R&D projects: the alignment of formal and informal networks", *R & D Management,* 38(5): 538–549; D. F. Kuratko, R. D. Ireland and J. S. Hornsby, 2004, "Corporate entrepreneurship behavior among managers: A review of theory, research, and practice", in: J. A. Katz and D. A. Shepherd (eds.), *Advances in Entrepreneurship: Firm Emergence and Growth: Corporate Entrepreneurship,* Oxford, UK: Elsevier Publishing, 7–45.

38. Y. Doz and M. Kosonen, 2008, "The dynamics of strategic agility: Nokia's rollercoaster experience", *California Management Review,* 50(3): 95–118.

39. Y. Liu and T. Ravichandran, 2008, "A comprehensive investigation on the relationship between information technology investments and firm diversification", *Information Technology and Management,* 9(3): 169–180; K. L. Turner and M. V. Makhija, 2006, "The role of organizational controls in managing knowledge", *Academy of Management Review,* 31: 197–217; M. A. Hitt, R. E. Hoskisson, R. A. Johnson and D. D. Moesel, 1996, "The market for corporate control and firm innovation", *Academy of Management Journal,* 39: 1084–1119.

40. P. Brabeck, 2004, "Business focus and the organization", *Nestlé Investor Seminar.* http://www.nestle.com, June 16;

41. M. A. Desai, 2008, "The Finance Function in a Global Corporation", *Harvard Business Review,* 86(7/8): 108–112; M. A. Hitt, L. Tihanyi, T. Miller and B. Connelly, 2006, "International diversification: Antecedents, outcomes, and moderators", *Journal of Management,* 32: 831–867; R. E. Hoskisson and M. A. Hitt, 1988, "Strategic control and relative R&D investment in multiproduct firms", *Strategic Management Journal,* 9: 605–621.

42. S. Lee, K. Park and H-H. Shin, 2009, "Disappearing internal capital markets: Evidence from diversified business groups in Korea", *Journal of Banking & Finance,* 33(2): 326–334; D. Collis, D. Young and M. Goold, 2007, "The size, structure, and performance of corporate headquarters", *Strategic Management Journal,* 28: 383–405.

43. X. S. Y. Spencer, T. A. Joiner and S. Salmon, 2009, "Differentiation strategy, performance measurement systems and organizational performance: Evidence from Australia", *International Journal of Business,* 14(1): 83–103; K. Chaharbaghi, 2007, "The problematic of strategy: A way of seeing is also a way of not seeing", *Management Decision,* 45: 327–339; J. B. Barney, 2002, *Gaining and Sustaining Competitive Advantage,* 2nd edition, Upper Saddle River, NJ: Prentice Hall.

44. S. Wetlaufer, 2001, "The business case against revolution: An interview with Nestle's Peter Brabeck", *Harvard Business Review,* 79(2): 112–121.

45. H. Gebauder and F. Putz, 2009, "Organizational structures for the service business in product-oriented companies", *International Journal of Services Technology and Management,* 11(1): 64–81; X. Yin and E. J. Zajac, 2004, "The strategy/governance structure fit relationship: Theory and evidence in franchising arrangements", *Strategic Management Journal,* 25: 365–383.

46. B. Keats and H. O'Neill, 2006, "Organizational structure: Looking through a strategy lens", in: M. A. Hitt, R. E. Freeman and J. S. Harrison (eds.), *Handbook of Strategic Management*, Oxford, UK.

47. H. W. Volberda and T. Elfring, 2001, *Rethinking Strategy*, London: Sage; K. Wakabayashi, 2008, "Relationship between business definition and corporate growth: The effect of functional alignment", *Pacific Economic Review*, 13(5): 663–679; K. M. Green, J. G. Covin and D. P. Slevin, 2008, "Exploring the relationship between strategic reactiveness and entrepreneurial orientation: The role of structure-style fit", *Journal of Business Venturing*, 23(3): 356–383; E. M. Olson, S. F. Slater and G. T. M. Hult, 2005, "The importance of structure and process to strategy implementation", *Business Horizons*, 1: 47–54; D. Miller and J. O. Whitney, 1999, "Beyond strategy: Configuration as a pillar of competitive advantage", *Business Horizons*, 42(3): 5–17.

48. A. D. Chandler, 1962, *Strategy and Structure*, Cambridge, MA: MIT Press.

49. B. Keats and H. O'Neill, 2006, "Organizational structure: Looking through a strategy lens", in: M. A. Hitt, R. E. Freeman and J. S. Harrison (eds.), *Handbook of Strategic Management*, Oxford, UK: Blackwell.

50. E. Rawley, 2010, "Diversification, coordination costs and organizational rigidity: Evidence from microdata", *Strategic Management Journal*, 31(8): 873–891; M. E. Sosa, S. D. Eppinger and C. M. Rowles, 2004, "The misalignment of product architecture and organizational structure in complex product development", *Management Science*, 50: 1674–1689.

51. J. W. Yoo, R. Reed, S. J. Shin and D. J. Lemak, 2009, "Strategic choice and performance in late movers: Influence of the top management team's external ties", *Journal of Management Studies*, 46(2): 308–335; S. Karim and W. Mitchell, 2004, "Innovating through acquisition and internal development: A quarter-century of boundary evolution at Johnson & Johnson", *Long Range Planning*, 37: 525–547.

52. H. W. Volberda, 1998, *Building the Flexible Firm: How to Remain Competitive*, Oxford: Oxford University Press; I. Daizadeh, 2006, "Using intellectual property to map the organizational evolution of firms: Tracing a biotechnology company from startup to bureaucracy to a multidivisional firm", *Journal of Commercial Biotechnology*, 13: 28–36.

53. C. Levicki, 1999, *The Interactive Strategy Workout*, 2nd edition, London: Prentice Hall.

54. E. E. Entin, F. J. Diedrich and B. Rubineau, 2003, "Adaptive communication patterns in different organizational structures", *Human Factors and Ergonomics Society Annual Meeting Proceedings*, 405–409; H. M. O'Neill, R. W. Pouder and A. K. Buchholtz, 1998, "Patterns in the diffusion of strategies across organizations: Insights from the innovation diffusion literature", *Academy of Management Review*, 23: 98–114.

55. X. S. Y. Spencer, T. A. Joiner, S. Salmon, 2009, "Differentiation strategy, performance measurement systems and organizational performance", *International Journal of Business*, 14(4): 83–104; 2007, "Organizational structure", *Wikipedia*, http://en.wikipedia.org; J. R. Galbraith, 1995, *Designing Organizations: An executive guide to strategy, structure, and process*, San Francisco: Jossey-Bass, 25.

56. B. Keats and H. O'Neill, 2006, "Organizational structure: Looking through a strategy lens", in: M. A. Hitt, R. E. Freeman and J. S., Harrison (eds.), *Handbook of Strategic Management*, Oxford, UK: Blackwell.

57. C. M. Christensen, S. P. Kaufman and W. C. Shih, 2008, "Innovation killers", *Harvard Business Review*: Special HBS Centennial Issue, 86(1): 98–105; J. Welch and S. Welch, 2006, "Growing up but staying young", *BusinessWeek*, December 11, 112.

58. O. E. Williamson, 1975, *Markets and Hierarchies: Analysis and Anti-Trust Implications*, New York: The Free Press.

59. S. H. Mialon, 2008, "Efficient horizontal mergers: The effects of internal capital reallocation and organizational form", *International Journal of Industrial Organization*, 26(4): 861–877; A. D. Chandler, 1962, *Strategy and Structure*, Cambridge, MA: MIT Press.

60. R. Inderst, H. M. Muller and K. Warneryd, 2007, "Distributional conflict in organizations", *European Economic Review*, 51: 385–402; J. Greco, 1999, "Alfred P. Sloan Jr. (1875–1966): The original organizational man", *Journal of Business Strategy*, 20(5): 30–31.

61. R. Hoskisson, C. Hill and H. Kim, 1993, "The multidivisional structure: Organizational fossil or source of value?", *Journal of Management*, 19(2), 269–298.

62. S. H. Mialon, 2008, "Efficient horizontal mergers: The effects of internal capital reallocation and organizational form", *International Journal of Industrial Organization*, 26(4): 861–877; H. Zhou, 2005, "Market structure and organizational form", *Southern Economic Journal*, 71: 705–719; W. G. Rowe and P. M. Wright, 1997, "Related and unrelated diversification and their effect on human resource management controls", *Strategic Management Journal*, 18: 329–338.

63. C. E. Helfat and K. M. Eisenhardt, 2004, "Inter-temporal economies of scope, organizational modularity, and the dynamics of diversification", *Strategic Management Journal*, 25: 1217–1232; A. D. Chandler, 1994, "The functions of the HQ unit in the multibusiness firm", in: R. P. Rumelt, D. E. Schendel and D. J. Teece (eds.), *Fundamental Issues in Strategy*, Cambridge, MA: Harvard Business School Press, 327.

64. O. E. Williamson, 1994, "Strategizing, economizing, and economic organization", in: R. P. Rumelt, D. E. Schendel and D. J. Teece (eds.), *Fundamental Issues in Strategy*, Cambridge, MA: Harvard Business School Press, 361–401.

65. R. Hoskisson, C. Hill and H. Kim, 1993, "The multidivisional structure: Organizational fossil or source of value?", *Journal of Management*, 19(2), 269–298; R. M. Burton and B. Obel, 1980, "A computer simulation test of the M-form hypothesis", *Administrative Science Quarterly*, 25: 457–476.

66. O. E. Williamson, 1985, *The Economic Institutions of Capitalism: Firms, Markets, and Relational Contracting*, New York: Macmillan.

67. S. Ansari, M. Schouten and E. Verwaal, 2006, "Unlocking synergies between business units: internal value

creation at Royal Vopak", *Strategic Change,* 15(7/8): 353–360.

68. H. W. Volberda and A. Y. Lewin, 2003, "Co-evolutionary dynamics within and between firms: From evolution to co-evolution", *Journal of Management Studies*, 40: 2111–2136; A. Y. Lewin and H. W. Volberda, 1999, "Prolegomena on coevolution: A framework for research on strategy and new organizational forms", *Organization Science*, 10: 519–534; H. W. Volberda, 1998, *Building the Flexible Firm: How to Remain Competitive*, Chapter 6, Oxford: Oxford University Press; B. Keats and H. O'Neill, 2006, "Organizational structure: Looking through a strategy lens", in: M. A. Hitt, R. E. Freeman and J. S. Harrison (eds.), *Handbook of Strategic Management,* Oxford, UK: Blackwell.

69. M. F. Wolff, 1999, "In the organization of the future, competitive advantage will be inspired", *Research Technology Management,* 42(4): 2–4.

70. R. H. Hall, 1996, *Organizations: Structures, Processes, and Outcomes,* 6th edition, Englewood Cliffs, NJ: Prentice Hall, 13; S. Baiman, D. F. Larcker and M. V. Rajan, 1995, "Organizational design for business units", *Journal of Accounting Research,* 33: 205–229.

71. L. G. Love, R. L. Priem and G. T. Lumpkin, 2002, "Explicitly articulated strategy and firm performance under alternative levels of centralization", *Journal of Management,* 28: 611–627.

72. J. B. Barney, 2006, *Gaining and Sustaining Competitive Advantage*, Upper Saddle River, NJ: Prentice Hall, 257.

73. H. Karandikar and S. Nidamarthi, 2007, "Implementing a platform strategy for a systems business via standardization", *Journal of Manufacturing Technology Management,* 18: 267–280.

74. E. M. Olson, S. F. Slater, G. T. M. Hult, 2005, "The importance of structure and process to strategy implementation", *Business Horizons*, 1: 47–54.

75. 2010, "Ryanair Holdings business profile", *The Financial Times*, http://markets.ft.com, July 12; Ryanair Holdings, 2009, "Annual Report 2009", *Ryanair Holdings plc*, July 29.

76. E. M. Olson, S. F. Slater, G. T. M. Hult, 2005, "The importance of structure and process to strategy implementation", *Business Horizons*, 1: 47–54.

77. A. D. Chandler, 1962, *Strategy and Structure*, Cambridge, MA: MIT Press.

78. ASML N.V., 2010, *ASML Organization*, ASML N.V. http://www.asml.com. July 12.

79. C. C. Markides and P. J. Williamson, 1996, "Corporate diversification and organizational structure: A resource-based view", *Academy of Management Journal,* 39: 340–367; C. W. L. Hill, M. A. Hitt and R. E. Hoskisson, 1992, "Cooperative versus competitive structures in related and unrelated diversified firms", *Organization Science,* 3: 501–521. J. Robins and M.E. Wiersema, 1995, "A resource-based approach to the multibusiness firm: Empirical analysis of portfolio interrelationships and corporate financial performance", *Strategic Management Journal*, 16: 277–299.

80. S. H. Appelbaum, D. Nadeau and M. Cyr, 2008, "Performance evaluation in a matrix organization: A case study (part two)", *Industrial and Commercial Training*, 40(6): 295–299; J. Robins and M. E. Wiersema, 1995, "A resource-based approach to the multibusiness firm: Empirical analysis of portfolio interrelationships and corporate financial performance", *Strategic Management Journal*, 16: 277–299.

81. S. H. Appelbaum, D. Nadeau and M. Cyr, 2009, "Performance evaluation in a matrix organization: A case study (part three)", *Industrial and Commercial Training*, 41(1): 9–14; M. Goold and A. Campbell, 2003, "Structured networks: Towards the well designed matrix", *Long Range Planning,* 36(5): 427–439.

82. R. M. Grant, 2008, *Contemporary Strategy Analysis*, 6th edition, Malden: Blackwell Publishing, 121–145.

83. Royal Philips Electronics N.V., 2007, "Philips communicates "Vision 2010" strategic plan and raises profitability target", *Royal Philips Electronics N.V.*, http://www.philips.com, September 10.

84. N. M. Schmid and I. Walter, 2009, "Do financial conglomerates create or destroy economic value?", *Journal of Financial Intermediation*, 18(2): 193–216; P. A. Argenti, R. A. Howell and K. A. Beck, 2005, "The strategic communication imperative", *MIT Sloan Management Review,* 46(3): 84–89.

85. M. F. Wiersema and H. P. Bowen, 2008, "Corporate diversification: The impact of foreign competition, industry globalization, and product diversification", *Strategic Management Journal*, 29: 115–132; R. E. Hoskisson and M. A. Hitt, 1990, "Antecedents and performance outcomes of diversification: A review and critique of theoretical perspectives", *Journal of Management,* 16: 461–509.

86. C. W. L. Hill, M. A. Hitt, R. E. Hoskisson, 1992, "Cooperative versus competitive structures in related and unrelated diversified firms", *Organization Science*, 3(4): 501–521.

87. S. Lee, K. Park and H. Shin, 2009, "Disappearing internal capital markets: Evidence from diversified business groups in Korea", *Journal of Banking & Finance*, 33(2) 326–334; J. Birkinshaw, 2001, "Strategies for managing internal competition", *California Management Review*, 44(1): 21–38.

88. M. Maremont, 2004, "Leadership; more can be more: Is the conglomerate a dinosaur from a bygone era? The answer is no – with a caveat", *Wall Street Journal,* October 24, R4; T. R. Eisenmann and J. L. Bower, 2000, "The entrepreneurial M-form: Strategic integration in global media firms", *Organization Science,* 11: 348–355.

89. T. Yu and A. A. Cannella, Jr, 2007, "Rivalry between multinational enterprises: An event history approach", *Academy of Management Journal*, 50: 665–686; S. E. Christophe and H. Lee, 2005, "What matters about internationalization: A market-based assessment", *Journal of Business Research*, 58: 636–643; Y. Luo, 2002, "Product diversification in international joint ventures: Performance implications in an emerging market", *Strategic Management Journal*, 23: 1–20.

90. M. Mandel, 2007, "Globalization versus immigration reform", *BusinessWeek*, June 4, 40.

91. T. M. Begley and D. P. Boyd, 2003, "The need for a corporate global mind-set", *MIT Sloan Management Review*, 44(2): 25–32; S. Tallman, 2006, "Global Strategic Management", in: M. A. Hitt, R .E. Freeman and

J. S. Harrison (eds.), *Handbook of Strategic Management,* Oxford, UK: Blackwell, 467; T. Hutzschenreuter, T. Pedersen and H. W. Volberda, 2007, "The role of path dependency and managerial intentionality: a perspective on international business research", *Journal of International Business Studies,* 38: 1055–1068.

92. C. A. Bartlett and S. Ghoshal, 1989, *Managing Across Borders: The Transnational Solution,* Boston: Harvard Business School Press; T. Hutzschenreuter, T. Pedersen and H. W. Volberda, 2007, "The role of path dependency and managerial intentionality: A perspective on international business research", *Journal of International Business Studies,* 38: 1055–1068.

93. T. Kostova and K. Roth, 2003, "Social capital in multinational corporations and a micro-macro model of its formation", *Academy of Management Review,* 28: 297–317.

94. J. Jermias and L. Gani, 2005, "Ownership structure, contingent-fit, and business-unit performance: A research model and evidence", *The International Journal of Accounting,* 40: 65–85; J. Wolf and W. G. Egelhoff, 2002, "A reexamination and extension of international strategy-structure theory", *Strategic Management Journal,* 23: 181–189.

95. A. Verbeke, 2009, *International Business Strategy,* Cambridge: Cambridge University Press.

96. A. Rugman and S. Girod, 2003, "Retail multinationals and globalization: The evidence is regional", *European Management Journal,* 21(1): 24–37.

97. A. Rugman and S. Collinson, 2006, *International Business,* 4th edition, Harlow: Pearson Education Limited.

98. B. Kogut, 1985, "Designing global strategies: Comparative and competitive value-added chains", *MIT Sloan Management Review,* 26(4): 15–28.

99. C. A. Bartlett and S. Ghoshal, 1989, *Managing Across Borders: The Transnational Solution,* Boston: Harvard Business School Press.

100. Royal Ahold N.V., 2010, *History,* Royal Ahold N.V. http://www.ahold.com, July 13.

101. 2007, *Chronologie fraude Ahold,* Nederlandse Omroep Stichting. http://www.nos.nl. October, 5.

102. D. M. Katz, 2003, "Another Hole at Royal Ahold", *CFO.* http://www.cfo.com. May, 29.

103. S. Feinberg and A. Gupta, 2009, "MNC subsidiaries and country risk: Internalization as a safeguard against weak external institutions", *Academy of Management Journal* 52 (2): 381–399; S. T. Cavusgil, S. Yeniyurt and J. D. Townsend, 2004, "The framework of a global company: A conceptualization and preliminary validation", *Industrial Marketing Management,* 33: 711–716.

104. T. W. Malnight, 2001, "Emerging structural patterns within Multinational Corporations: Towards process-based structures", *Academy of Management Journal,* 44: 1187–1210.

105. J. Smit, 2008, *De Prooi,* Amsterdam: Prometheus.

106. K. Worthington, 2007, "Does Barclays, the Consortium, Bank of America or ABN shareholders win in this deal?", *GLG News,* Gerson Lehrman Group, http://www.glgroup.com, April, 25.

107. A. Rugman and R. Hodgetts, 2001, "The end of global strategy", *European Management Journal,* 19(4): 333–343.

108. Fiat S.p.A., 2010, *Annual Report 2009,* Fiat S.p.A, http://www.fiatgroup.com. March 15.

109. A. Verbeke, 2009, *International Business Strategy.* Cambridge: Cambridge University Press.

110. R. Jungbluth, 2006, *Die 11 Geheimnisse des IKEA-Erfolgs,* Frankfurt: Campus.

111. B. Connelly, M. A. Hitt, A. DeNisi and R. D. Ireland, 2007, "Expatriates and corporate-level international strategy: Governing with the knowledge contract", *Management Decision,* 45: 564–581.

112. M. E. Lloyd, 2009, "IKEA sees opportunity in slump", *Wall Street Journal Online,* http://online.wsj.com, February 17; E. Baraldi, 2008, "Strategy in industrial networks: Experiences from IKEA, *California Management Review,* 50(4): 99–126.

113. D. Lavie, 2009, "Capturing value from alliance portfolios", *Organizational Dynamics,* 38(1): 26–36; S. G. Lazzarini, 2007, "The impact of membership in competing alliance constellations: Evidence on the operational performance of global airlines", *Strategic Management Journal,* 28: 345–367; Y. L. Doz and G. Hamel, 1998, *Alliance Advantage: The Art of Creating Value through Partnering,* Boston: Harvard Business School Press, 222.

114. J. Li, C. Zhou and E. J. Zajac, 2009, "Control, collaboration, and productivity in international joint ventures: Theory and evidence", *Strategic Management Journal,* 30: 865–884; Y. Luo, 2007, "Are joint venture partners more opportunistic in a more volatile environment?", *Strategic Management Journal,* 28: 39–60; K. Moller, A. Rajala and S. Svahn, 2005, "Strategic business nets – their type and management", *Journal of Business Research,* 58: 1274–1284.

115. D. Li, L. E. Eden, M. A. Hitt and R. D. Ireland, 2008, "Friends, acquaintances, or strangers? Partner selection in R&D alliances", *Academy of Management Journal,* 51(2): 315–334.

116. D. Lavie, 2009, "Capturing Value from Alliance Portfolios", *Organizational Dynamics,* 38(1): 26–36; B. Comes-Casseres, 2003, "Competitive advantage in alliance constellations", *Strategic Organization,* 1: 327–335; T. K. Das and B. S. Teng, 2002, "Alliance constellations: A social exchange perspective", *Academy of Management Review,* 27: 445–456.

117. T. Vapola, P. Tossavainen and M. Gabrielsson, 2008, "The battleship strategy: The complementing role of born globals in MNC's new opportunity creation", *Journal of International Entrepreneurship:* 6(1): 1–21; S. Tallman, M. Jenkins, N. Henry and S. Pinch, 2004, "Knowledge, clusters, and competitive advantage," *Academy of Management Review,* 29: 258–271.

118. V. Moatti, 2009, "Learning to expand or expanding to learn? The role of imitation and experience in the choice among several expansion modes", *European Management Journal,* 27(1): 36–46; A. Capaldo, 2007, "Network structure and innovation: The leveraging of a dual network as a distinctive relational capability", *Strategic Management Journal,* 28: 585–608; A. Zaheer and G. G. Bell, 2005, "Benefiting from network position: Firm capabilities, structural holes, and performance", *Strategic Management Journal,* 26: 809–825.

119. J. Wiklund and D. A. Shepherd, 2009, "The effectiveness of alliances and acquisitions: The role of resource

combination activities", *Theory and Practice*, 31(1): 193–212; R. D. Ireland and J. W. Webb, 2007, "A multi-theoretic perspective on trust and power in strategic supply chains", *Journal of Operations Management,* 25: 482–497; V. G. Narayanan and A. Raman, 2004, "Aligning incentives in supply chains", *Harvard Business Review,* 82(11): 94–102.

120. S. Harrison, 1998, *Japanese Technology and Innovation Management,* Northampton, MA: Edward Elgar.

121. E. Verwaal, H. R. Commandeur and W. J. M. I. Verbeke, 2009, "Value creation and value claiming in strategic outsourcing decisions: A resource-contingency perspective", *Journal of Management,* 35(2), 420–444.

122. M. H. Hansen, R. E. Hoskisson and J. B. Barney, 2008, "Competitive advantage in alliance governance: Resolving the opportunism minimization-gain maximization paradox", *Managerial and Decision Economics*, 29: 191–208; T. Keil, 2004, "Building external corporate venturing capability", *Journal of Management Studies,* 41: 799–825.

123. T. J. Vapola, P. Tossavainen and M. Gabrielsson, 2008, "The battleship strategy: The complementing role of born globals in MNC's new opportunity creation", *Journal of International Entrepreneurship*, 6: 1–21; P. Dussauge, B. Garrette and W. Mitchell, 2004, "Learning from competing partners: Outcomes and duration of scale and link alliances in Europe, North America and Asia", *Strategic Management Journal,* 21: 99–126; G. Lorenzoni and C. Baden-Fuller, 1995, "Creating a strategic center to manage a web of partners", *California Management Review,* 37(3): 146–163.

124. S. R. Holmberg and J. L. Cummings, 2009, "Building successful strategic alliances: Strategic process and analytical tools for selecting partner industries and firms", *Long Range Planning,* 42(2): 164–193; B. J. Bergiel, E. B. Bergiel and P. W. Balsmeier, 2008, "Nature of virtual teams: A summary of their advantages and disadvantages", *Management Research News*, 31(2): 99–110.

125. A. C. Inkpen, 2008, "Knowledge transfer and international joint ventures: The case of NUMMI and General Motors", *Strategic Management Journal*, 29(4): 447–453; T. A. Stewart and A. P. Raman, 2007, "Lessons from Toyota's long drive", *Harvard Business Review*, 85(7/8): 74–83; J. H. Dyer and K. Nobeoka, 2000, "Creating and managing a high-performance knowledge-sharing network: The Toyota case", *Strategic Management Journal,* 21: 345–367.

126. L. F. Mesquita, J. Anand and J. H. Brush, 2008, "Comparing the resource-based and relational views: Knowledge transfer and spillover in vertical alliances", *Strategic Management Journal*, 29: 913–941; M. Kotabe, X. Martin and H. Domoto, 2003, "Gaining from vertical partnerships: Knowledge transfer, relationship duration and supplier performance improvement in the US and Japanese automotive industries", *Strategic Management Journal,* 24: 293–316.

127. T. Nishiguchi, 1994, *Strategic Industrial Sourcing: The Japanese Advantage,* New York: Oxford University Press.

128. S. G. Lazzarini, D. P. Claro and L. F. Mesquita, 2008, "Buyer-supplier and supplier-supplier alliances: Do they reinforce or undermine one another?", *Journal of Management Studies*, 45(3): 561–584; P. Dussauge, B. Garrette and W. Mitchell, 2004, "Asymmetric performance: The market share impact of scale and link alliances in the global auto industry", *Strategic Management Journal,* 25: 701–711.

129. J. Shook, 2009, "Toyota's secret: The A3 report", *MIT Sloan Management Review*, 50(4): 30–33; C. Dawson and K. N. Anhalt, 2005, "A 'China price' for Toyota", *BusinessWeek,* February 21, 50–51; W. M. Fruin, 1992, *The Japanese Enterprise System,* New York: Oxford University Press. E. Ohsono, H. Takeuchi, N. Shimizu, 2008, *Extreme Toyota: Radical Contradictions That Drive Success at the World's Best Manufacturer*, John Wiley & Sons.

130. B. Garrette, X. Castañer and P. Dussauge, 2009, "Horizontal alliances as an alternative to autonomous production: Product expansion mode choice in the worldwide aircraft industry 1945–2000", *Strategic Management Journal*, 30(8): 885–894.

131. A. M. Hayashi, 2008, "How to replicate success", *MIT Sloan Management Review*, 49(3): 6–7; M. Tuunanen and F. Hoy, 2007, "Franchising: Multifaceted form of entrepreneurship", *International Journal of Entrepreneurship and Small Business,* 4: 52–67.

132. J. Li, C. Dhanaraj and R. L. Shockley, 2008, "Joint venture evolution: Extending the real options approach", *Managerial and Decision Economics*, 29(4): 317–336; B. B. Nielsen, 2005, "The role of knowledge embeddedness in the creation of synergies in strategic alliances", *Journal of Business Research,* 58: 1194–1204.

133. Accor Group S.A., 2010, *Annual Report 2009*, Accor Group S.A. http://www.accor.com. May 21.

134. T. W. Tong, J. J. Reuer and M. W. Peng, 2008, "International joint ventures and the value of growth options", *Academy of Management Journal*, 51: 1014–1029; P. H. Andersen and P. R. Christensen, 2005, "Bridges over troubled water: Suppliers as connective nodes in global supply networks", *Journal of Business Research,* 58: 1261–1273; C. Jones, W. S. Hesterly and S. P. Borgatti, 1997, "A general theory of network governance: Exchange conditions and social mechanisms", *Academy of Management Review*, 22: 911–945.

135. M. W. Hansen, T. Pedersen and B. Petersen, 2009, "MNC strategies and linkage effects in developing countries", *Journal of World Business*, 44(2): 121–139; A. Goerzen, 2005, "Managing alliance networks: Emerging practices of multinational corporations", *Academy of Management Executive,* 19(2): 94–107.

136. L. H. Lin, 2009, "Mergers and acquisitions, alliances and technology development: An empirical study of the global auto industry", *International Journal of Technology Management*, 48(3): 295–307; R. E. Miles, C. C. Snow, J. A. Mathews, G. Miles and J. J. Coleman Jr, 1997, "Organizing in the knowledge age: Anticipating the cellular form", *Academy of Management Executive,* 11(4): 7–20.

137. 2009, EDS Agility Alliance: Collaboration for better business outcomes, http://www.eds.com, July 16.

138. 2009, EDS Agility Alliance reaches milestone, *Wireless News,* June 3.

# CHAPTER 14

# STRATEGIC ENTREPRENEURSHIP

## LEARNING OBJECTIVES

Studying this chapter should provide you with the strategic management knowledge needed to:

1 Define strategic entrepreneurship and corporate entrepreneurship.
2 Define entrepreneurial opportunities and explain their importance.
3 Define potential hurdles for established firms to pursue entrepreneurship.
4 Define invention, innovation and imitation, and describe the relationship among them.
5 Explain the difference between autonomous and induced strategic behaviour.
6 Describe how firms internally develop innovations.
7 Describe start-up entrepreneurship and venture capital.
8 Explain how strategic entrepreneurship helps firms create value.

We thank Sebastiaan van Doorn for his contribution to this Chapter

© fotoVoyager/iStock

© Alex Segre/Alamy

# The continuing innovation revolution at Nokia: the case of car navigation

Nokia has consistently shown its potential in terms of devising entrepreneurial solutions in response to environmental requirements. Originally founded as a processing plant for woodpulp, then venturing in the rubber industry and finally becoming a leading player in the industry of telecommunication, Nokia has shown incredible stamina in its quest for entrepreneurship. The latest addition to their successful line of mobile phones is the ability to use mobile phones as navigation devices, hence circumventing the need to buy a separate device such as traditional navigation devices by TOMTOM or Garmin. This is a classic example of strategic entrepreneurship, venturing into a market previously outside the scope of current activities, but offering a premium to customers by integrating functions into one simple solution.

The first attempts made by Nokia were rather unsatisfactory, with considerably lower quality than its competitors, but with the use of suboptimal solutions for attaching the device in the car in such a way that similar functions could be obtained as with the Garmin and TOMTOM device. However, after acquiring NAVTEQ in 2007, a specialist firm in the development of digital maps, as well as the addition of new design features, quality is now up to industry standards.

Its newest features enable users to follow the latest news, receive up-to-date traffic information, watch movies, call through Skype and many more. In this way the newest generation of Nokia smartphones ticks many boxes previously divided over several distinct products. However the market of navigation is constantly developing and competition has been active in realizing joint ventures, e.g. TOMTOM and Renault have far-reaching agreements about offering TOMTOM navigation as a standard option in each new Renault, which could undermine the current position of Nokia. Continuous scanning of market opportunities therefore remains a vital part of strategic entrepreneurship, as competitive advantages are usually shortlived in the current dynamic business environment.

**Sources:** http://www.nokia.com; annual report Nokia 2009, Annual report Nokia 2008, Annual reports TOMTOM, Renault 2009.

## Questions

**1** With the Nokia case in mind, why is it important to be proactive in a dynamic industry?

**2** How was Nokia able to enter the market of navigation devices? What was their competitive edge?

**3** Think of future developments in the market, how will Nokia be able to sustain their competitive advantage?

This Chapter's Opening Case explains that Nokia's entrepreneurial orientation encourages and supports continuous product innovation. Increasingly, a firm's ability to engage in innovation makes the difference in gaining and maintaining a competitive advantage and achieving performance targets. Nokia is clearly an entrepreneurial and innovative company and has radically transformed itself over time. From reading this chapter, you will understand that Nokia's ability to innovate shows that it successfully practices Strategic Entrepreneurship.

Strategic entrepreneurship is the process of taking entrepreneurial actions using a strategic management perspective. In this effort, organizational actors attempt to identify opportunities in the external environment that can be readily exploited through internal adaptation and innovation. The search dimension, characterized by intensified scanning activities constitutes the *entrepreneurship* dimension of strategic entrepreneurship. The *strategy* dimension involves internal selection that determines the best way to manage the firm's adaptation and innovation process in the light of emerging entrepreneurial opportunities. Thus, firms engaging in strategic entrepreneurship integrate their actions to find opportunities, anticipate their future value and implement timely internal adaptation in order to reap future benefits.[1] In the twenty-first century competitive landscape, firm survival and success depend heavily on a firm's ability to continuously find new opportunities and quickly produce innovations to pursue them.[2]

To examine strategic entrepreneurship, we consider several topics in this chapter. First, we examine the scanning behaviour of organizational actors: How do entrepreneurial opportunities first get recognized and how do they become part of corporate reality? Second, we assess how firms react to selected opportunities: How are emerging opportunities utilized to keep the firm fit for the future and what is the relation with existing activities? Third, we investigate start-up entrepreneurship and the function of venture capital.

A major portion of the material in this chapter is on innovation and entrepreneurship within established organizations. This phenomenon is called corporate entrepreneurship, which is "the process by which organizational actors within an established company conceive, foster, launch and manage a new business that is distinct from the parent company".[3] Corporate entrepreneurship has become critical to survival and success of established organizations.[4] Indeed, established firms use entrepreneurship to strengthen their performance and to enhance growth opportunities.[5] Of course, opportunity recognition, valuation and strategic management also play a critical role in the degree of success achieved by start-up ventures and venture capital investments.[6] Start-up ventures are new ventures that emerge without the consolidated support of a parent firm. These types of ventures often draw heavily on the entrepreneurial character of the original initiator as they are especially risky and gaining support from external sources such as banks and/or venture capitalists is rather difficult. Venture capital investments are financial investments in external companies, venture capital firms are at the forefront of the entrepreneurship dimension of strategic entrepreneurship, continuously scanning the environment for investment opportunities. The strategy dimension, however, is limited to their financial risk assesments regarding future benefits and subsequent financial support. Venture capital has become a rather common practice in highly volatile markets and industries, such as biotechnology and pharma. In the past two decades we have witnessed a remarkable rise in venture capital investments; hence these developments call for further attention in this chapter.

In this chapter we emphasize that innovation and entrepreneurship are vital for young and old as well as large and small firms; similarly it is deemed to be important for service companies, manufacturing firms and high-technology ventures.[7] In the global competitive landscape, the long-term success of new ventures and established firms is a function of the ability to meld entrepreneurship with strategic management.[8]

# Entrepreneurship and entrepreneurial opportunities

Entrepreneurship is the process by which individuals, teams or organizations identify and pursue entrepreneurial opportunities, without immediately being constrained by the resources they currently control.[9] This last notion is very important as incumbent firms are always bound by existing activities and vested interests,

**Strategic entrepreneurship**

Strategic entrepreneurship is taking entrepreneurial actions using a strategic perspective.

**Corporate entrepreneurship**

Corporate entrepreneurship is the use or application of entrepreneurship within an established firm.

**Entrepreneurship**

Entrepreneurship is the process by which individuals, teams or organizations identify and pursue entrepreneurial opportunities without being immediately constrained by the resources they currently control.

hence truly entrepreneurial behavior is difficult to initiate. Not only ambiguity and uncertain pay-offs need to be overcome, internal resistance to change may in fact prove to be one of the major forces hampering corporate entrepreneurship.

Entrepreneurial opportunities are conditions in which new goods or services can satisfy a need in the market. These opportunities exist because of competitive imperfections in markets and some firms are better at recognizing potential value in emerging opportunities, will be more proactive in selecting them and appropriating perceived value.[10] Entrepreneurial opportunities come in many forms such as the chance to develop and sell a new product, or the chance to sell an existing product in a new market.[11] Firms should be receptive to the pursuit of entrepreneurial opportunities whenever and wherever they may surface.[12] Timing is an essential aspect of entrepreneurship as it ensures that firms secure first mover advantage on market opportunities.

As the definition suggests, the essence of entrepreneurship is to identify and exploit entrepreneurial opportunities – that is, opportunities others do not see, or for which they do not recognize the commercial potential.[13] The Virgin Group Ltd as discussed in the Strategic Focus, is a nice example of a truly entrepreneurial company that is highly successful in exploring entrepreneurial opportunities. As a process, entrepreneurship results in the "creative destruction" of existing products (goods or services) or methods of producing them and replaces them with new products and production methods.[14] Thus, firms engaging in entrepreneurship place high value on individual innovations as well as the ability to continuously innovate across time.[15] The difficulty with continuous innovation within established firms is threefold. First, organizational actors are focused on existing activities and often refrain from entrepreneurial efforts because of their uncertain nature and potential penalties in case of failure. Second, if organizational actors do decide to develop an outward-looking notion, they are heavily constrained by vested interests and the current portfolio of activities, hence most of the time they are responsive only to entrepreneurial opportunities that are in line with current activities limiting the scope of their search effort. Third, once the decision is made to act upon selected opportunities, only a reported 5–10 per cent of efforts pursued turn out successful in the end.[16] This rate may seem low but research has also suggested that failed ventures often translate into new entrepreneurial efforts over time; learning from failure is a widespread phenomenon in unsuccessful ventures.

Firms therefore have to actively manage the process of entrepreneurship. For example they should instill an internal climate conducive to entrepreneurial behaviour. This means that organizational actors should be enabled to spend a certain percentage of their time on scanning and evaluation of entrepreneurial opportunities. Moreover, organizational actors should feel confident to pursue emerging opportunities without experiencing major drawbacks in terms of penalties for failed efforts. In addition, support and trust of management is vital for firms that aim to be entrepreneurial. It is only when organizational actors perceive sufficient support and trust, e.g. in the allocation of resources or legitimacy to dedicated projects that they act upon opportunities.

Although a focused portfolio is always to be preferred over a heavily scattered chain of activities, too narrow a focus will hamper the entrepreneurial activities of the firm. As the spectrum of the scanning and search process becomes too narrow, the level of newness of entrepreneurial efforts is reduced. Firms always need to balance the level of newness in relation to existing activities with the risk profile related to selected opportunities. More novel pathways will typically be characterized by higher risks as firm expertise in the specific area of interest has not yet been well developed. Conversely, more incremental entrepreneurial efforts will have lower risks but also lower expected returns in the long term.

Finally, firms should embrace entrepreneurial potential within the environment. Although failure rates are high, evidence suggests that firms focusing on the pursuit of entrepreneurial opportunities have up to 15 per cent higher performance levels than firms that largely refrain from entrepreneurial efforts.[17] Dedicated management

**Entrepreneurial opportunities**

Entrepreneurial opportunities are conditions in which new goods or services can satisfy a need in the market.

© Trinity Mirror/Mirrorpix/Alamy

**STRATEGIC FOCUS**

## How Virgin Group Ltd mastered the process of scanning and search

A striking example of a company that seems to experience few problems with continuously reinventing itself and venturing into unknown territory is Virgin Group Ltd. Virgin reframed the air travel business by turning flying into a lifestyle commodity. Moreover, they were able to transcend traditional industry boundaries by opening retail stores and providing mobile phone services. Virgin can truly be considered an entrepreneurial company as it continuously renews, takes risks and

attacks weak spots of traditional service providers. Established in 1968 as a trading company, the Virgin conglomerate now consists of over 200 distinct companies with 35 000 employees. The latest and most remarkable addition to the Virgin group is offering flights in outer space. How did Virgin become this successful, and more importantly, what was the driving force behind their successful diversification policy?

Chairman of the Virgin Group, billionaire Richard Branson, is one of the most successful entrepreneurs of our times. However, he could not have been this successful without the creation of a specific business philosophy that drives all Virgin Group businesses. Managers within Virgin Group companies use the concept of innovation to inspire employees to be creative as well as competitive in all respects. They are required to add to the cutting edge of all products that the company creates and aim for an increase in overall efficiency by scoping the environment for new business opportunities. Moreover, employees of Virgin Group are led through transformational leadership which grants them a great deal of independence, autonomy and room to manoeuvre in pursuit of entrepreneurial opportunities. For more information on transformational leadership refer to Chapter 11.

**Sources:** Grant R. M. (2004) Richard Branson and the Virgin Group of Companies; Annual Report Virgin Group 2008, 2009, http://www.blackwellpublishing.com/grant/docs/15Virgin.pdf.

### Questions

**1** What do you think are the origins of the diversification strategy at Virgin Group?

**2** How would transformational leadership help in realizing internal innovations?

**3** Think of another company with an innovation philosophy and trace how they first implemented it.

of entrepreneurial efforts, including the spin down of failed efforts and categorizing of acquired information may help in future search and internal innovation activities.

## Innovation

Peter Drucker has argued that "innovation is the specific function of entrepreneurship, whether in an existing business, a public service institution, or a new venture started by a lone individual".[18] Moreover, Drucker suggested that innovation is "the means by which the entrepreneur either creates new wealth-producing resources or endows existing resources with enhanced potential for creating wealth".[19]

Thus, entrepreneurship and the innovation resulting from it are critically important for all firms. The realities of competition in the competitive landscape of the twenty-first century suggest that to be market leaders, companies must regularly develop innovative products desired by customers. This means that innovation should be an intrinsic part of virtually all of a firm's activities.[20]

Innovation is a key outcome firms seek through entrepreneurship and is often the source of competitive success, especially in turbulent, highly competitive environments.[21] For example, research results show that firms competing in global industries that invest more in innovation also achieve the highest returns.[22] In fact, investors often react positively to the introduction of a new product, thereby increasing the price of a firm's stock. Furthermore, "innovation may be required to maintain or achieve competitive parity, much less a competitive advantage in many global markets".[23] Investing in the development of new technologies can increase the performance of firms that operate in different but related product markets (see discussion of related diversification in Chapter 7); moreover, it increases capacity for action should entrepreneurial opportunities arise. In this way, the ability to innovate internally is a necessary condition for reaping the benefits of external market opportunities.

In his classic work, Schumpeter argued that firms engage in three types of innovative activity.[24] Invention is the act of creating or developing a new product or process. Innovation is the process of creating a commercial product from an invention. Innovation begins after an invention is chosen for development.[25] Thus, an invention brings something new into being, while an innovation brings something new into use. Accordingly, technical criteria are used to determine the success of an invention, whereas commercial criteria are used to determine the success of an innovation.[26] Finally, imitation is the adoption of a similar innovation by different firms. Imitation usually leads to product or process standardization, and products based on imitation often are offered at lower prices, but without as many features. Entrepreneurship is critical to innovative activity in that it acts as the linchpin between invention and innovation.[27]

Innovation is the most critical of the three types of innovative activity. Many companies are able to create ideas that lead to inventions, but commercializing those inventions has, at times, proved difficult.[28] This difficulty is suggested by the fact that approximately 80 per cent of R&D occurs in large firms, but these same firms produce fewer than 50 per cent of the patents.[29] Patents are a strategic asset and the ability to regularly produce them can be an important source of competitive advantage, especially for firms competing in knowledge-intensive industries.[30] It seems that in the twenty-first century competitive landscape, R&D may be the most critical factor in gaining and sustaining a competitive advantage in some industries (e.g., pharmaceuticals). Larger, established firms, certainly those competing globally, often try to use their R&D labs to create competence-destroying new technologies and products. Being able to innovate in this manner can create a competitive advantage for a firm in many industries.[31] Although critical to long-term corporate success, the outcomes of R&D investments are uncertain and often not achieved in the short term, meaning that patience is required as firms evaluate the outcomes of their R&D efforts.[32]

## Incremental and radical innovation

Firms produce two types of internal innovations – incremental and radical innovations – when using their R&D activities. Most innovations are incremental – that is, they build on existing knowledge bases and provide small improvements in the current product lines. Incremental innovations are evolutionary and linear in nature.[33] "The markets for incremental innovations are well-defined, product characteristics are well understood, profit margins tend to be lower, production

**Invention**

Invention is the act of creating or developing a new product or process.

**Innovation**

Innovation is the process of creating a commercial product from an invention.

**Imitation**

Imitation is the adoption of a similar innovation by different firms.

technologies are efficient, and competition is primarily on the basis of price."[34] Adding a different kind of whitening agent to a soap detergent is an example of an incremental innovation, as are improvements in televisions over the last few decades. Companies launch far more incremental innovations than radical innovations because they are cheaper, easier and faster to produce and they involve less risk.[35]

In contrast to incremental innovations, radical innovations usually provide significant technological breakthroughs and create new knowledge.[36] Radical innovations, which are revolutionary and nonlinear in nature, typically use new technologies to serve newly created markets. The development of the original personal computer (PC) was a radical innovation at the time. Reinventing the computer by developing a "radically new computer-brain chip" (e.g., with the capability to process a trillion calculations per second) is an example of a radical innovation. Obviously, such a radical innovation would seem to have the capacity to revolutionize the tasks computers could perform.

Because they establish new functionalities for users, radical innovations have strong potential to lead to significant growth in revenue and profits. Developing new processes is a critical part of producing radical innovations. Both types of innovation can create value, meaning that firms should determine when it is appropriate to emphasize either incremental or radical innovation. However, radical innovations have the potential to contribute more significantly to a firm's efforts to earn above-average returns.[37]

Radical innovations are rare because of the difficulty and risk involved in developing them. The value of the technology and the market opportunities are highly uncertain.[38] Because radical innovation creates new knowledge and uses only some or little of a firm's current product or technological knowledge, creativity is required. However, creativity does not produce something from nothing. Rather, creativity discovers, combines, or synthesizes current knowledge, often from diverse areas.[39] This knowledge is then used to develop new products that can be used in an entrepreneurial manner to move into new markets, capture new customers, and gain access to new resources.[40] Such innovations are often developed in separate business units that start internal ventures.[41]

Internally developed incremental and radical innovations result from deliberate efforts. These deliberate efforts are called internal corporate venturing, which is the set of activities firms use to develop internal inventions and especially innovations.[42] As shown in Figure 14.1, autonomous and induced strategic behaviours are the two types of internal corporate venturing. Each venturing type facilitates incremental and radical innovations. However, a larger number of radical innovations spring from autonomous strategic behaviour while the greatest percentage of incremental innovations come from induced strategic behaviour.

## Autonomous strategic behaviour

Autonomous strategic behaviour is a bottom-up process in which product champions pursue new ideas, often through a political process, by means of which they develop and coordinate the commercialization of a new good or service until it achieves success in the marketplace. A product champion is an organizational member with an entrepreneurial vision of a new good or service who seeks to create support for its commercialization. Product champions play critical roles in moving innovations forward. Indeed, in many corporations, "Champions are widely acknowledged as pivotal to innovation speed and success."[43] Champions are vital to sell the ideas to others in the organization so that the innovations will be commercialized. Commonly, product champions use their social capital to develop informal networks within the firm. As progress is made, these networks become more formal

FIGURE 14.1   Model of internal corporate venturing

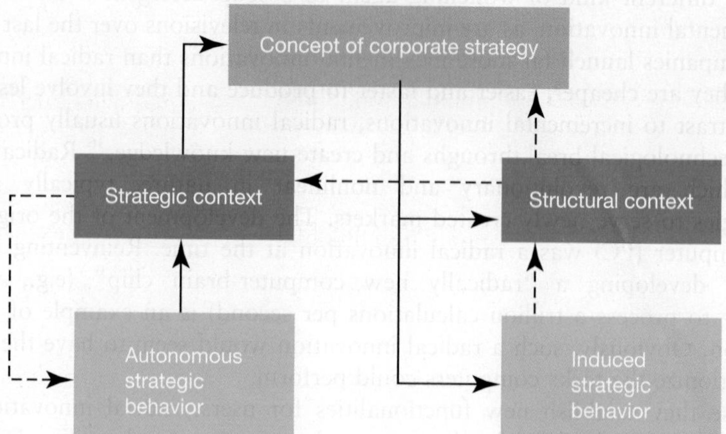

Source: Adapted from R. A. Burgelman, 1983, "A model of the interactions of strategic behavior, corporate context, and the concept of strategy", *Academy of Management Review*, 8: 65.

as a means of pushing an innovation to the point of successful commercialization.[44] Internal innovations springing from autonomous strategic behaviour frequently differ from the firm's current strategy, taking it into new markets and perhaps new ways of creating value for customers and other stakeholders. Autonomous strategic behaviour is based on a firm's wellspring of knowledge and resources that are the sources of the firm's innovation (See Strategic Focus on Henkel's autonomous innovation teams). Thus, a firm's technological capabilities and competencies are the basis for new products and processes.[45]

Changing the concept of corporate-level strategy through autonomous strategic behaviour results when a product is championed within strategic and structural contexts (see Figure 14.1). Such a transformation occurred with the development of new ways to utilize organic waste for the production of biofuel at DSM (global life sciences and materials sciences company based in the Netherlands). The strategic context is the process used to arrive at strategic decisions (often requiring political processes to gain acceptance). The best firms keep changing their strategic context and strategies because of the continuous changes in the current competitive landscape. Thus, some believe that the most competitively successful firms reinvent their industry or develop a completely new one across time as they compete with current and future rivals.[46]

To be effective, an autonomous process for developing new products requires that new knowledge be continuously diffused throughout the firm. In particular, the diffusion of tacit knowledge is vital for development of more effective new products.[47] Interestingly, some of the processes important for the promotion of autonomous new product development behaviour vary by the environment in which a firm operates. Although dynamic markets warrant strong focus on autonomous strategic behaviour, they are also characterized by high levels of uncertainty. Hence, it depends on the industry whether firms will indeed focus on autonomous behaviour versus more induced ways of pursuing entrepreneurship. Next to delegation of responsibilities to lower levels of the firm, setting the stage for autonomous behaviour requires conscientious support strategies from higher management. As discussed earlier, the allocation of resources and trust and legitimacy play an important role in the success of corporate ventures. Without dedicated support from higher level management, organizational actors will refrain from entrepreneurial behaviour due to fear of failure, rejection or other types of penalties.

## STRATEGIC FOCUS

© Philipp Hympendahl/Alamy

## Autonomous innovation teams at Henkel

At Henkel, a German-based company, some of its brightest employees are placed in dedicated innovation units that enjoy high levels of autonomy and are placed relatively outside company boundaries to ensure restrictions to entrepreneurial efforts are low. In this way entrepreneurial and existing activities are structurally separated and do not harm each other as much as when they would be more tightly knit together.

This recently resulted in the development of new ways to utilize enzymes in washing detergents. Scientists of Henkel were literally sent on a quest to locate enzymes that would allow low washing temparatures without the loss of cleaning power. They collected soil samples from cool habitats, crawled into bat caves and visited penguins in the zoo to isolate bacteria which naturally produce enzymes that are active at room temperature. The Henkel researchers investigated over 10 000 bacteria and subsequently took the most active ones to their laboratories for further investigation. After extensive washing tests they replaced the conventional "high temperature active" enzyme mix in Persil with the new enzyme mix and the results were satisfactory. The open approach towards innovation and the autonomous nature of the research project enabled the researchers to reinvent the product development process and come up with new innovative products. The result is apparent, the new product is more environmentally friendly and reduces the cost for customers as it is no longer necessary to wash with hot water.

**Sources:** Annual report Henkel 2009; http://www.henkel.com; http://www.henkel.com/innovation/cool-laundry.

### Questions

1 How does employee autonomy help in developing new business solutions?

2 Do you think employee autonomy is always good? What type of informal control mechanisms may be utilized to steer autonomous behaviour?

3 Think of another company with high levels of employee autonomy, trace the development process of a recent innovation and explain how autonomy influenced its effectiveness.

## Induced strategic behaviour

The second of the two forms of internal corporate venturing, induced strategic behaviour, is a top-down process whereby the firm's current strategy and structure foster innovations that are closely associated with that strategy and structure.[48] In this form of venturing, the strategy in place is filtered through a matching structural hierarchy. In essence, induced strategic behaviour results in internal innovations that are highly consistent with the firm's current strategy. Thus, the top management team play a key role in induced strategic behaviour, suggesting that the composition and the effectiveness of the team is important.[49] Such induced behaviour is especially common within industries that draw heavily on the status quo where firms have high vested interests that have to be protected in the face of new developments.

For example, the major oil companies, such as Exxon Mobil, Shell and BP have huge oil supplies all over the world and their value has to be protected from more novel solutions to energy supply. Therefore they have been behaving quite hesitantly in their investments towards new energy solutions. Only a reported 5 per cent of current profits of the major oil companies are invested in renewable energy solutions, which makes sense given the internal rationale of these firms. The non-destructive character of induced strategic behaviour together with the incremental nature of its innovations makes it ideal for companies protecting vested interests. Although the pursuit of incremental innovations remains vital to stay competitive with rivals, the overall idea is to retain the status quo. In the oil industry we have witnessed increases primarily in efficiency, small changes to fuel composition, such as Shell "fuel save" and BP "ultimate", and increasing interest for carbon dioxide storage. Major innovations, however, remain few in numbers which is also partly due to the embeddedness of the industry in everyday life.

In the end, we all drive cars that use petrol or diesel, many homes in Europe, Africa and the Middle East still have individual oil tanks for daily energy consumption and most commercial products are made partly or wholly of plastic composites. The way strategic entrepreneurship in the oil industry is organized is therefore mainly focused on exploitation of current competencies and less on the pursuit of radical innovations. Industries that pursue strategic entrepreneurship through induced strategic behaviour will only change when breakthrough innovations are created by start-up and smaller companies within the same industry. These companies are less restricted by their vested interests and therefore represent the drivers of innovation within these industries. We will discuss the importance of start-up companies for established industries at the end of this chapter.

## Implementing internal innovations

**Entrepreneurial mindset**

The person with an entrepreneurial mindset values uncertainty in the marketplace and seeks to continuously identify opportunities with the potential to lead to important innovations.

An entrepreneurial mindset is required to be innovative and to develop successful internal corporate ventures. The person with an entrepreneurial mindset values uncertainty in the marketplace and seeks to continuously identify opportunities with the potential to lead to important innovations. Because of environmental and market uncertainty, individuals and firms must be willing to take risks to commercialize innovations. Although they must continuously attempt to identify opportunities, they must also select and pursue the best opportunities and do so with discipline. Employing an entrepreneurial mindset entails not only developing new products and markets but also execution in order to do these things effectively. Often, firms provide incentives to managers to be entrepreneurial and to commercialize innovations.[50]

Having processes and structures in place through which a firm can successfully implement the outcomes of internal corporate ventures and commercialize the innovations is critical. Indeed, the successful introduction of innovations into the marketplace reflects implementation effectiveness.[51] In the context of internal corporate ventures, managers must allocate resources, coordinate activities, communicate with many different parties in the organization, and make a series of decisions to convert the innovations resulting from either autonomous or induced strategic behaviours into successful market entries.[52] As we described in Chapter 13, organizational structures are the sets of formal relationships that support processes managers use to commercialize innovations.

Effective integration of the various functions involved in innovation processes – from engineering to manufacturing and, ultimately, market distribution – is required to implement the incremental and radical innovations resulting from internal corporate ventures.[53] Increasingly, product development teams are being used to integrate the activities associated with different organizational functions. Such integration involves coordinating and applying the knowledge and skills of different functional areas in order to maximize innovation.[54] Teams must help to make decisions as to which projects should be commercialized and which ones should end. Although ending a project is difficult because of emotional commitments to innovation-based projects, effective teams should recognize when conditions change such that the innovation cannot create value as originally anticipated.

## Cross-functional product development teams

Cross-functional teams facilitate efforts to integrate activities associated with different organizational functions, such as design, manufacturing and marketing. These teams may also include representatives from major suppliers and/or customers because they can help in making the firm's innovation processes more effective.[55] In addition, new product development processes can be completed more quickly and the products more easily commercialized when cross-functional teams work effectively.[56] Using cross-functional teams, product development stages are grouped into parallel or overlapping processes to allow the firm to tailor its product development efforts to its unique core competencies and to the needs of the market.

Horizontal organizational structures support the use of cross-functional teams in their efforts to integrate innovation-based activities across organizational functions.[57] Therefore, instead of being designed around vertical hierarchical functions or departments, the organization is built around core horizontal processes that are used to produce and manage innovations. Some of the core horizontal processes that are critical to innovation efforts are formal; they may be defined and documented as procedures and practices. More commonly, however, these processes are informal: "They are routines or ways of working that evolve over time."[58] Often invisible, informal processes are critical to successful innovations and are supported properly through horizontal organizational structures more so than through vertical organizational structures.[59]

Two primary barriers that may prevent the successful use of cross-functional teams as a means of integrating organizational functions are independent frames of reference of team members and organizational politics.[60] Team members working within a distinct specialization (e.g., a particular organizational function) may have an independent frame of reference typically based on common backgrounds and experiences. They are likely to use the same decision criteria to evaluate issues such as product development efforts as they do within their functional units. Research suggests that functional departments vary along four dimensions: time orientation, interpersonal orientation, goal orientation and formality of structure.[61] Thus, individuals from different functional departments having different orientations on these dimensions can be expected to perceive product development activities in different ways. For example, a design engineer may consider the characteristics that make a product functional and workable to be the most important for product development. Alternatively, a person from the marketing function may be primarily interested in characteristics that satisfy customer needs. These different orientations, although not always mutually exclusive, can create barriers to effective communication across functions and even produce conflict in the team at times.[62]

Organizational politics is the second potential barrier to effective integration in cross-functional teams. In some organizations, considerable political activity may centre on allocating resources to different functions. Inter-unit conflict may result from aggressive competition for resources among those representing different organizational functions. This dysfunctional conflict between functions creates a barrier to their integration.[63] Methods must be found to achieve cross-functional integration without excessive political conflict and without changing the basic structural characteristics necessary for task specialization and efficiency.

Shared values and effective leadership are also imperative for achieving cross-functional integration and implementing innovation.[64] Highly effective shared values are framed around the firm's vision and mission, and become the glue that promotes integration between functional units. Thus, the firm's culture promotes unity and internal innovation.[65] This type of strategic leadership is highly important for achieving cross-functional integration and promoting innovation. Leaders set the goals and allocate resources. The goals include integrated development and commercialization of new goods and services. Effective strategic leaders also ensure a high-quality communication system to facilitate cross-functional integration. A critical benefit of effective communication is the sharing of knowledge among team members. Effective communication thus helps create synergy and gains team members' commitment to an innovation throughout the organization. Shared values and leadership practices shape the communication systems that are formed to support the development and commercialization of new products.[66]

## Creating value from internal innovation

The model in Figure 14.2 shows how firms can create value from the internal corporate venturing processes they use to develop and commercialize new goods and services. An entrepreneurial mindset is necessary so that managers and employees will consistently try to identify entrepreneurial opportunities the firm can pursue by developing new goods and services and new markets. Cross-functional teams are important for promoting integrated new product design ideas and commitment to their subsequent implementation. Effective leadership and shared values promote integration and vision for innovation and commitment. The end result for the firm is the creation of value for the customers and shareholders by developing and commercializing new products.[67] We should acknowledge that not all entrepreneurial efforts succeed, even with effective management. Sometimes managers must decide to exit the market to avoid value decline.[68]

Newer entrepreneurial firms often are more effective than larger established firms in the identification of entrepreneurial opportunities.[69] As a consequence, entrepreneurial ventures often produce more radical innovations than do their larger, more established counterparts. Entrepreneurial ventures' strategic flexibility and

**FIGURE 14.2** Creating value through internal innovation processes

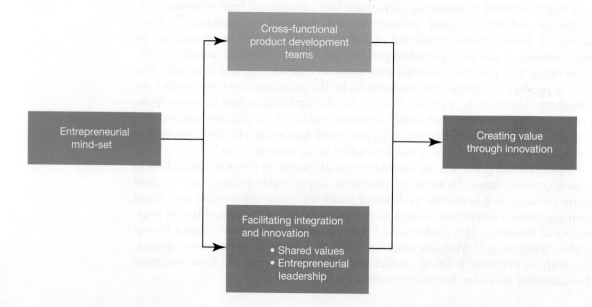

willingness to take risks at least partially account for their ability to identify opportunities and then develop radical innovations to exploit them.

Alternatively, larger and well established firms often have more resources and capabilities to exploit identified opportunities.[70] Younger, entrepreneurial firms generally excel in the opportunity-seeking dimension of strategic entrepreneurship while more established firms generally excel in the advantage-seeking dimension. However, to compete effectively in the twenty-first century competitive landscape, firms must not only identify and exploit opportunities but do so while achieving and sustaining a competitive advantage.[71] Thus, on a relative basis, newer entrepreneurial firms must learn how to gain a competitive advantage (advantage-seeking behaviours), and older, more established firms must relearn how to identify entrepreneurial opportunities (opportunity-seeking skills).

To be entrepreneurial, firms must develop an entrepreneurial mindset among their managers and employees. Managers must emphasize the management of their resources, particularly human capital and social capital.[72] The importance of knowledge to identify and exploit opportunities, as well as to gain and sustain a competitive advantage, suggests that firms must have strong human capital.[73] Social capital is critical for access to complementary resources from partners in order to compete effectively in domestic and international markets.[74]

Many entrepreneurial opportunities continue to surface, a reality that is contributing to firms' willingness to engage in entrepreneurship. By entering new markets, firms can learn new technologies and management practices and diffuse this knowledge throughout the entire enterprise. Furthermore, the knowledge firms gain can contribute to their innovations. Research has shown that firms operating in different markets tend to be more innovative.[75] Entrepreneurial ventures and large firms now regularly enter new markets. Both types of firms must also be innovative to compete effectively. Thus, by developing resources (human and social capital), taking advantage of opportunities in existing and new markets, and using the resources and knowledge gained in these markets to be innovative, firms achieve competitive advantages.[76] In so doing, they create value for their customers and shareholders.

After identifying opportunities, entrepreneurs must develop capabilities that will become the basis of their firm's core competencies and competitive advantages. In this connection, entrepreneurs are individuals, acting independently or as part of an organization, who perceive an entrepreneurial opportunity and then take risks to develop an innovation to exploit it. The process of identifying opportunities is entrepreneurial, but this activity alone is not sufficient to create maximum wealth or even to survive over time.[77] As we learned in Chapter 3, to successfully exploit opportunities, a firm must develop capabilities that are valuable, rare, difficult to imitate and non-substitutable. When capabilities satisfy these four criteria, the firm has one or more competitive advantages to exploit the identified opportunities (as described in Chapter 3). Without a competitive advantage, the firm's success will be only temporary (as explained in Chapter 1). An innovation may be valuable and rare early in its life, if a market perspective is used in its development. However, competitive actions must be taken to introduce the new product to the market and protect its position against competitors to gain a competitive advantage.[78] These actions combined represent strategic entrepreneurship of incumbent firms.

Strategic entrepreneurship helps established firms to renew their product and service base and venture into markets previously unexplored. However, there are major hurdles incumbent firms need to overcome to establish strategic entrepreneurship within firm boundaries. Internal retention pressures as well as path dependent portfolios of activities do not help in the exploration process of new entrepreneurial opportunities, and often reduce the level of newness of selected entrepreneurial pathways.

**Entrepreneurs**

Entrepreneurs are individuals, acting independently or as part of an organization, who perceive an entrepreneurial opportunity and then take risks to develop an innovation to exploit it.

## KEY DEBATE

# Researching strategic entrepreneurship

Researchers on the topic of strategic entre- preneurship are increasingly interested in the appropriate mix for incumbent firms of internal devel- opment versus the acquisition of start-up ventures and venture capital strategies. Most researchers agree that acquisition of start-ups and venture capital is mostly useful in highly dynamic markets. However, in- ternal development and awareness of environmental changes remain imperative in tracing and selecting interesting candidate firms for acquisition, and to allocate venture capital to viable innovation efforts. Re- alizing an appropriate mix is often regarded as an ad- hoc process that is heavily dependent on market de- velopments and emerging innovation within any given industry. Continuous scanning and acting when the time is right are vital for success of either of the ap- proaches to strategic entrepreneurship.

## Questions

**1** Consider two companies, a large incumbent operat- ing in a relatively stable environment and a medium sized company operating in a dynamic environment. Discuss in class the most appropriate mix in pursuing corporate entrepreneurship.

**2** Discuss in class on which managerial level deci- sions on the appropriate mix should be taken. Is this mainly a topic for top management, or should middle and line managers be involved as well, and why?

As well as internal corporate venturing there are also two important types of stra- tegic entrepreneurship: start-up entrepreneurship and venture capital. Whereas they are primarily concerned with their individual success, they also play an important role at industry level due to their unrestricted pursuit of new business solutions. Start-up entrepreneurship is seen as one of the most important drivers of economic growth and constitutes the start of an entirely new firm, without the support of a parent firm. Research has shown start-up entrepreneurship to add significantly to the level of competitiveness and innovativeness of countries.[79] Venture capital also plays an important role as it ensures ample support for early stage entrepreneurial endeavours within start-up companies as well as established firms. Whereas estab- lished firms often have sufficient funds to support their own entrepreneurial efforts, they still like to share risks in the early stages of development. For start-up compa- nies, venture capital is one of the few ways to attract sufficient funds to get started. Lacking support of a parent firm, start-up ventures often experience difficulty attract- ing funds, especially in the current business environment following the credit crunch.

# The functions of start-up entrepreneurship and venture capital

## Start-up entrepreneurship

Next to the corporate activities previously discussed, entrepreneurship can also emerge as a stand alone activity by a founding entity. In this case it arises without the support of a parent company and usually the founding entity is found to take on considerable risk as start-ups are typically surrounded by even more uncertainty than corporate venturing activities. The reason for heightened uncertainty lies in the absence of prior knowledge, prior experience and a steady cash flow to support

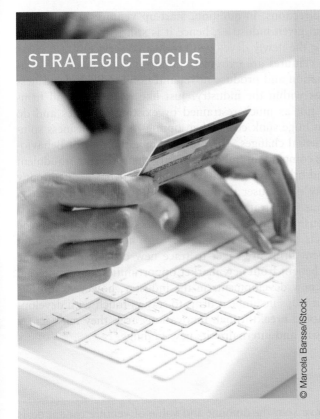

## STRATEGIC FOCUS

© Marcela Barsse/iStock

# The case of BehavioSec: new solutions to Internet security

Since BehavioSec was founded its mission has been to transform the world of Internet security through the use of biological and behavioural parametrics. Incumbent firms active on the Internet all use passwords, pincodes, automated codes and codes generated by mobile phones to enhance the security of the Internet environment for their customers. Although it has been successful for many years, we have witnessed a rise in fraudulent transactions as codes are prone to hacking activities. BehavioSec has developed a programme that investigates behavioural patterns in computer use; more specifically they trace key flight, key press and key sequence as well as mouse acceleration, mouse click and mouse speed. By doing so they are able to establish beyond doubt whether the individual

on the Internet is indeed who he or she claims to be. Given the great rise in Internet sales and transactions in the past two decades it is imperative that firms offer customers a safe environment on the Internet.

It is with great interest that the activities of BehavioSec are monitored by large firms active on the Internet. Most specifically banks are among the major players that are willing to invest in the future safety of their business. Banks have become more and more Internet-based and are experiencing both the benefits and drawbacks of this increased digitalization of the banking business. However, they are embedded in fixed security structures that command code-based security. They also lack the specific skills and expertise to develop novel solutions such as security systems based on behavioural patterns. A start-up company such as BehavioSec plays an important role in renewing the realm of Internet security and offers incumbent firms a chance to increase their Internet security.

In future, cyber crime will become more widespread and today its total impact is already estimated at a stunning one trillion euro a year. And the extent of security breaches is also growing, stretching from transaction fraud to intellectual property theft. It is therefore expected that high technology firms will gain interest in the usage of behaviometric security for their R&D and related departments.

**Sources:** http://www.behaviosec.com; Baker, C. Richard (1999) "An analysis of fraud on the Internet", *Internet Research*, 9(5): 348–360; Grazioli, S. and Jarvenpaa, S. (2002) "Perils of Internet fraud: An empirical investigation of deception and trust with experienced Internet consumers", *IEEE Transactions on Systems, Man, and Cybernetics – Part A: Systems and Humans*, 30(4): 395–410.

## Questions

1 Why are start-up companies important for established industries?

2 Explain how the absence of restrictions enabled BehavioSec to develop novel ways of Internet security.

3 Think of another industry where start-up firms may revolutionize the industry standard and explain why the incumbent firms do not develop it themselves.

emerging efforts. The founding entity is required to quickly grasp different types of knowledge that it was previously unfamiliar with, moreover the mere set-up of a stand-alone business requires all kinds of organizational know-how, such as the hiring of employees, the marketing of the developed product or service and setting the strategy for future business directions. In addition, start-up ventures are typically exploring new territory within given industries, hence it is still to be seen whether there are indeed customers for the newly developed product or service.[80]

At the same time start-up ventures are extremely important at industry level as they create the necessary variation and produce novel and non-established business solutions to existing problems within the industry. Just like relatively small firms within an industry, they are not as much restrained by existing activities and do not have to take into account huge sunk costs when opting for new business solutions in the light of environmental changes. Take for example the case of Behaviosec, a young but fast growing company in Internet security that prevents fraudulent transactions, identity theft and other malign behaviour online. It has created many applications that trace identity of the user through their use of the computer, e.g. keyboard and mouse behaviour (see Strategic Focus).

Such new approaches to business not only offer customers an alternative to the status quo in terms of products on the market, but they also act as a guiding light for incumbent firms. Incumbent firms are eager to trace new developments in the field, but are often unable to benefit from new market opportunities due to internal constraints. Making sense of new developments in the industry, however, still has an important function. First, it helps incumbent firms to stay in touch with developments in the field, second, should breakthrough innovations arise they may act by acquiring the small start-up firm and internalize its new findings.[81]

## Venture capital

In the past two decades we have seen the amount and value of venture capital deals steadily rising and it has become an essential element in the pursuit of entrepreneurship. Venture capitalists invest in companies and projects they believe will bring substantial profit. In this way, similar to start-up ventures, they are not bound by existing activities and/or sunks costs. Although they tend to invest in specific areas in which they build up expertise and experience, they are more free than incumbent firms who are bound by major vested interests and internal retention politics with regard to activities already in place. Venture capitalists have a significant role for established firms and start-up companies. They have experienced risk evaluation officers with broad industry experience who will test viability of entrepreneurial opportunities and subsequently offer financial support to those opportunities with highest risk return ratios. In addition most venture capital firms nowadays also provide skilled management for selected ventures, but mostly when it concerns start-up ventures.[82]

Venture capital can be allocated to early stages in entrepreneurial efforts, which ensures that more entrepreneurial efforts are pursued than without the existence of venture capital. This is especially true for high-technology industries with relatively costly innovation processes, such as biotechnology and pharma. Failure rates are high, investment decisions often ambiguous and potential returns difficult to predict. In these types of industry many projects would not come into existence without the support of venture capital.[83]

Venture capital investments also significantly reduce time-to-market of newly developed products by speeding up the development cycle. Most venture capital is allocated to the so-called expansion phase of new ventures. This means that although the venture firm was probably already involved in the early stage with minor investment, after discovery and more certain future benefits they invest heavily in the quick production, marketing and distribution of the newly invented product. This in turn enables first mover advantage, allowing the firm to gain significant market share and demand a premium for its products.[84]

In recent times we have also witnessed incumbents taking the role of venture capitalists and opting for a real option approach to innovation. They take stakes in small innovative firms, allowing them to stay informed with regard to new developments in the field. Should the small firm realize a breakthrough innovation that fits well with activities in place at the incumbent firm, they may also acquire the small firm as a whole and internalize the externally developed innovation.

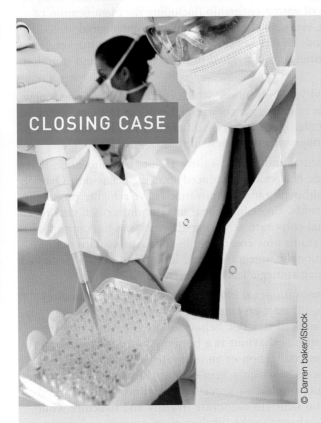

## CLOSING CASE

© Darren baker/iStock

## The case of the Dutch life sciences sector

Venture capital has had a profound impact on the development of the life sciences sector in the Netherlands. Life sciences encompass the industries of pharma and biotechnology and are considered a highly dynamic sector. Over the past decade we have seen a major rise in the amount and value of venture capital investments in the life sciences industry. The upward trend has been consistent and shows venture capital investments growing from 20 million euro in 2000 to 120 million euro in 2007. In 2007 11 per cent of total investments in R&D in the sector were funded by venture capital. Of these investments 30 per cent was allocated to start-up and early stage projects, delineating the importance of venture capital to boost experimentation and discovery. Another 20 per cent was allocated to buy-outs and 50 per cent to projects in the expansion phase. The latter phase consists of projects that have already proven their worth and consist of setting up production facilities and exploitation of new findings. A good example of a firm that has been relying on venture capital is Octoplus, a pharmaceutical company specializing in the development of drugs that enable a more fluent distribution of medicines through the human body. Before establishing their IPO (initial public offering), they were jointly owned by a consortium of internationally diverse venture capital firms that together enabled the research activities of the firm. After years of uncertain results, they now have several drugs approved by the European and American food and drug administration, and produced their first profits in 2009. The use of venture capital has not only helped the initial research efforts of Octoplus, later stages of development and expansion phases have also received ample support from venture capital firms. Although first discovery is sufficient in most industries, the pharmaceutical industry is characterized by slow and tedious approval schemes that require much patience and sufficient financial backing.

**Sources:** Jansen, J. J. P., Van de Vrande, V. and Volberda, H.W. (2008) "More return on R&D: Life Sciences and Medical Technology in The Netherlands", Rotterdam School of Management, Erasmus University; Thomson One Banker, Annual report Octoplus 2009.

### Questions

1 What are the uses of venture capital? Which ones hold for Octoplus especially?

2 Which phase in innovation development do you think is best suited to attracting venture capital?

3 Do you think venture capital is useful in all industries? Compare static and dynamic industry environments.

4 If you were to start a company would you consider venture capital as a potential business partner?

## SUMMARY

- Strategic entrepreneurship is taking entrepreneurial actions using a strategic perspective. Firms engaging in strategic entrepreneurship simultaneously engage in opportunity-seeking and advantage-seeking behaviours. The purpose is to continuously find new opportunities and quickly develop innovations to exploit them.

- Entrepreneurship is a process used by individuals, teams and organizations to identify entrepreneurial opportunities without being immediately constrained by the resources they control. Corporate entrepreneurship is the application of entrepreneurship (including the identification of entrepreneurial opportunities) within ongoing, established organizations. Entrepreneurial opportunities are conditions in which new goods or services can satisfy a need in the market. Increasingly, entrepreneurship positively contributes to individual firms' performance and stimulates growth in countries' economies.

- Firms engage in three types of innovative activity: (1) invention, which is the act of creating a new good or process; (2) innovation, or the process of creating a commercial product from an invention; and (3) imitation, which is the adoption of similar innovations by different firms. Invention brings something new into being while innovation brings something new into use.

- Firms create two types of innovation – incremental and radical – through internal innovation that takes place in the form of autonomous strategic behaviour or induced strategic behaviour. Overall, firms produce more incremental innovations although radical innovations have a higher probability of significantly increasing sales revenue and profits. Cross-functional integration is often vital to a firm's efforts to develop and implement internal corporate venturing activities and to commercialize the resulting innovation. The cross-functional teams now commonly include representatives from external organizations such as suppliers. Additionally, integration and innovation can be facilitated by developing shared values and effectively using strategic leadership.

- Three basic approaches are used to produce innovation: (1) internal innovation, which involves R&D and forming internal corporate ventures; (2) start-up entrepreneurship; and (3) venture capital. Autonomous strategic behaviour and induced strategic behaviour are the two forms of internal corporate venturing. Autonomous strategic behaviour is a bottom-up process through which a product champion facilitates the commercialization of an innovative good or service. Induced strategic behaviour is a top-down process in which a firm's current strategy and structure facilitate the development and implementation of product or process innovations. Thus, induced strategic behaviour is driven by the organization's current corporate strategy and structure while autonomous strategic behaviour can result in a change to the firm's current strategy and structure arrangements.

- Entrepreneurs see or envision entrepreneurial opportunities and then take actions to develop innovations and exploit them. The most successful entrepreneurs (whether they are establishing their own venture or are working in an ongoing organization) have an entrepreneurial mindset, which is an orientation that values the potential opportunities available because of market uncertainties.

- Start-up entrepreneurship refers to new start-ups without the support of the parent firm. Because it is not related to existing firms they are not as much restricted to industry standards and activities as incumbents. As such they play an important role in development of novel business solutions to existing problems.

- Venture capital refers to external funding for entrepreneurial efforts of existing firms or start-up ventures. We have witnessed a significant rise in venture capital investments over the past two decades and it has helped innovation efforts, especially in highly dynamic and capital intensive industries.

## REVIEW QUESTIONS

1   What is strategic entrepreneurship? What is corporate entrepreneurship?

2   What is entrepreneurship, and what are entrepreneurial opportunities? Why are they important for firms competing in the twenty-first century competitive landscape?

3   What are potential hurdles for firms aiming to pursue entrepreneurial opportunities?

4   What are invention, innovation and imitation? How are these concepts interrelated?

5   How do firms develop innovations internally?

6   What is autonomous/induced strategic behaviour?

7   How do firms realize integration between entrepreneurial efforts and existing activities?

8   What is start-up entrepreneurship and how may entrepreneurship help at industry level?

9   What is venture capital, what are its functions?

10  How does strategic entrepreneurship help firms to create value?

## DISCUSSION QUESTIONS

1   To be entrepreneurial, firms must develop an entrepreneurial mindset among their managers and employees.

   a   Discuss in class if and how an entrepreneurial mindset can be developed
   b   Discuss in class why new small firms are more effective than large established firms in the identification of entrepreneurial opportunities

2   Discuss in class the benefits of autonomous versus induced strategic behaviour and its association with newness of entrepreneurial efforts, and try to come up with an industry to fit both entrepreneurial pathways.

3   Discuss in class the benefits for established industries of a large contingent of start-up companies within the same industry. Discuss implications for development of new technologies and/or new new product and service development.

4   Consider the Closing Case on the Dutch life sciences sector; discuss why venture capital was most useful in this particular industry and prepare an example of a recent case where venture capital was key in business development.

5   Consider the different types of entrepreneurship, i.e. corporate, start-up and venture capital and provide a well developed argument which type you would choose in your future career.

## FURTHER READING

Dynamic capabilities allow firms to quickly change activities when commanded by the environment. For example, the ability to recognize and assess arising opportunities will enable firms to become more proactive in their pursuit of entrepreneurial pathways. For further reading on dynamic capabilities and entrepreneurship we advise you to read the following articles: S. A. Zahra, H. J. Sapienza and P. Davidsson (2006) "Entrepreneurship and dynamic capabilities: A review, model and research agenda", *Journal of Management Studies*, 43: 917–955; Ch. Baden-Fuller and H. W. Volberda (1996) "Strategic renewal in large complex organisations: A competence based view", in: R. Sanchez, A. Heene and H. Thomas (eds.), *Dynamics of Competence-Based Competition: Theory and Practice in the New Strategic Management*, Oxford, UK: Pergamon; J. H. Burgers, F. A. J. Van den Bosch and H. W. Volberda (2008) "Why new business development projects fail:

Coping with the differences of technological versus market knowledge", *Long Range Planning*, 41(1): 55–73.

At the same time firms need to develop a dedicated innovation function within the firm that allows quick and successful development of new products and services. Simultaneous pursuit of exploratory and exploitative innovations has proven a major challenge for most companies. The following articles provide some clues regarding how to overcome potential pitfalls: J. J. P. Jansen, F. A. J. Van den Bosch and H. W. Volberda (2006) "Exploratory innovation, exploitative innovation, and performance effects of organizational antecedents and environmental moderators", *Management Science*, 52: 1661–1674; J. S. Sidhu, H. R. Commandeur and H. W. Volberda (2007) "The multifaceted nature of exploration and exploitation: Value of supply, demand and spatial search for innovation", *Organization Science*, 18(1): 20–38.

# EXPERIENTIAL EXERCISES

## Exercise 1: What would be a viable entrepreneurial avenue for company X?

Imagine Company X, a large multinational company in the car manufacturing industry. Company X has just finalized a three-year project which has resulted in a whole line of new fuel-based, but relatively efficient engines. The project has cost over €300 million and it is time to start mass-production of the new generation of cars. At the same time, all major competitors have started investing heavily in hybrid cars, combining the benefits of fuel-based and electric engines. Others have made their engines fit for bio-fuel consumption, or have started experimenting with hydrogen-based engines but results have been inconsistent. It seems that while the use of hybrid technology and biofuel adaptations is a viable opportunity in the short term, hydrogen solutions seem interesting in the long run. Assess the options for Company X. What would be a good entrepreneurial strategy?

## Exercise 2: Do firms walk the walk when it comes to strategic entrepreneurship?

In teams pick a company that is well represented on the Internet and trace their statements on strategic entrepreneurship in their annual reports of the last three years.

1　Provide an overview of their announced activities.

2　What is unique about their activities when compared to industry standards?

3　Use additional information, newspaper articles, company magazines, folders etc., to trace whether they have indeed succeeded in what was announced.

4　If successful, try to map how the road to success was paved, if not provide an overview of the hurdles that prevented the firm from reaching its intended target.

5　Discuss in class the different findings and try to establish why some companies are better in realizing corporate entrepreneurship than others.

# VIDEO CASES

## Inspiring entrepreneurs in Africa
www.cengage.co.uk/volberda/students/video_cases
Consider the following video which taps into opportunities and hurdles for entrepreneurship in Africa. Tabeisa, a not-for-profit organization, offers expert advice and training through its Enterprise Centres and supports local entrepreneurs and business initiatives to help sustain disadvantaged communities throughout Africa. Although depicted from the perspective of a non-for-profit organization, the video offers some interesting insights into the world of entrepreneurship in Africa. As can also be inferred from the results of Tabeisa, there might be an interesting role for venture capitalists in Africa. After watching the video please consider the following questions and prepare them for discussion in class.

1　What are the major hurdles and/or opportunities for entrepreneurship in Africa?

2　What are the major drivers of entrepreneurship in Africa?

3　What are the benefits and risks for Africa if the role of an organization such as Tabeisa was taken over by professional capitalist firms?

4　List the main differences for African entrepreneurs versus European entrepreneurs in setting up a new business.

5　Would you like to become involved in entrepreneurship in Africa? What role would interest you?

# NOTES

1.　R. D. Ireland and J. W. Webb, 2007, "Strategic entrepreneurship: Creating competitive advantage through streams of innovation", *Business Horizons*, 50(4): 49–59; M. A. Hitt, R. D. Ireland, S. M. Camp and D. L. Sexton, 2002, "Strategic entrepreneurship: Integrating entrepreneurial and strategic management perspectives", in: M. A. Hitt, R. D. Ireland, S. M. Camp and D. L. Sexton (eds.), *Strategic Entrepreneurship: Creating a New Mindset*, Oxford, UK: Blackwell Publishers, 1–16; M. A. Hitt, R. D. Ireland,

S. M. Camp and D. L. Sexton, 2001, "Strategic entrepreneurship: Entrepreneurial strategies for wealth creation", *Strategic Management Journal*, 22(Special Issue): 479–491.

2.　R. Durand, O. Bruyaka and V. Mangematin, 2008, "Do science and money go together? The case of the French biotech industry", *Strategic Management Journal*, 29: 1281–1299; R. K. Sinha and C. H. Noble, 2008, "The adoption of radical manufacturing technologies and firm survival", *Strategic Management Journal*, 29: 943–962.

3.  R. C. Walcott and M. J. Lippitz, 2007, "The four models of corporate entrepreneurship", *Sloan Management Review,* 49(1): 75–82.

4.  M. H. Morris, S. Coombes and M. Schindehutte, 2007, "Antecedents and outcomes of entrepreneurial and market orientations in a non-profit context: Theoretical and empirical insights", *Journal of Leadership and Organizational Studies*, 13(4): 12–39; H. A. Schildt, M. V. J. Maula and T. Keil, 2005, "Explorative and exploitative learning from external corporate ventures", *Entrepreneurship Theory and Practice*, 29: 493–515.

5.  J. Uotila, M. Maula, T. Keil and S. A. Zahra, 2009, "Exploration, exploitation and financial performance: Analysis of S&P 500 corporations", *Strategic Management Journal*, 30: 221–231; G. T. Lumpkin and B. B. Lichtenstein, 2005, "The role of organizational learning in the opportunity-recognition process", *Entrepreneurship Theory and Practice*, 29: 451–472; J. S. Sidhu, H. W. Volberda and H. Commandeur, 2004, "Exploring exploration orientation and its determinats: Some empirical evidence", *Journal of Management Studies*, 41: 913–932.

6.  B. A. Gilbert, P. P. McDougall and D. B. Audretsch, 2006, "New venture growth: A review and extension", *Journal of Management*, 32: 926–950.

7.  J. L. Morrow, D. G. Sirmon, M. A. Hitt and T. R. Holcomb, 2007, "Creating value in the face of declining performance: Firm strategies and organizational recovery", *Strategic Management Journal*, 28: 271–283; K. G. Smith, C. J. Collins and K. D. Clark, 2005, "Existing knowledge, knowledge creation capability, and the rate of new product introduction in high-technology firms", *Academy of Management Journal*, 48: 346–357.

8.  D. F. Kuratko, 2007, "Entrepreneurial leadership in the 21st century", *Journal of Leadership and Organizational Studies*, 13(4): 1–11; R. D. Ireland, M. A. Hitt and D. G. Sirmon, 2003, "A model of strategic entrepreneurship: The construct and its dimensions", *Journal of Management*, 29: 963–989.

9.  B. R. Barringer and R. D. Ireland, 2006, *Entrepreneurship: Successfully Launching New Ventures*, Upper Saddle River, NJ: Pearson/Prentice Hall; S. A. Zahra, H. J. Sapienza and P. Davidsson, 2006, "Entrepreneurship and dynamic capabilities: A review, model and research agenda", *Journal of Management Studies*, 43: 917–955.

10.  S. A. Alvarez and J. B. Barney, 2008, "Opportunities, organizations and entrepreneurship", *Strategic Entrepreneurship Journal*, 2: 265–267; S. A. Alvarez and J. B. Barney, 2005, "Organizing rent generation and appropriation: Toward a theory of the entrepreneurial firm", *Journal of Business Venturing*, 19: 621–635.

11.  P.G. Klein, 2008, "Opportunity discovery, entrepreneurial action and economic organization", *Strategic Entrepreneurship Journal*, 2: 175–190; W. Kuemmerle, 2005, "The entrepreneur's path to global expansion", *MIT Sloan Management Review*, 46(2): 42–49.

12.  R. K. Mitchell, J. R. Mitchell and J. B. Smith, 2008, "Inside opportunity formation: Enterprise failure, cognition and the creation of opportunities", *Strategic Entrepreneurship Journal*, 2: 225–242; C. Marquis and M. Lounsbury, 2007, "Vive la resistance: Competing logics and the consolidation of US community banking", *Academy of Management Journal*, 50: 799–820.

13.  S. A. Zahra, 2008, "The virtuous cycle of discovery and creation of entrepreneurial opportunities", *Strategic Entrepreneurship Journal*, 2: 243–257; N. Wasserman, 2006, "Stewards, agents, and the founder discount: Executive compensation in new ventures", *Academy of Management Journal*, 49: 960–976.

14.  J. Schumpeter, 1934, *The Theory of Economic Development*, Cambridge, MA: Harvard University Press.

15.  J. H. Dyer, H. B. Gregersen and C. Christensen, 2008, "Entrepreneur behaviors and the origins of innovative ventures", *Strategic Entrepreneurship Journal*, 2: 317–338; R. Greenwood and R. Suddaby, 2006, "Institutional entrepreneurship in mature fields: The big five accounting firms", *Academy of Management Journal*, 49: 27–48.

16.  OECD Data entrepreneurship indicators program.

17.  Erasmus competition and innovation monitor 2005–2010.

18.  P. F. Drucker, 1998, "The discipline of innovation", *Harvard Business Review*, 76(6): 149–157.

19.  M. Hitt, R. Nixon, R. Hoskisson and R. Kochhar, 1999, Corporate entrepreneurship and cross-functional fertilization: activation, process and disintegration of a new product design team', *Entrepreneurship Theory and Practice,* 23(3): 145–167.

20.  A. Leiponen, 2008, "Control of intellectual assets in client relationships: Implications for innovation", *Strategic Management Journal*, 29: 1371–1394; M. Subramaniam and M. A. Youndt, 2005, "The influence of intellectual capital on the types of innovative capabilities", *Academy of Management Journal*, 48: 450–463.

21.  F. F. Suarez and G. Lanzolla, 2007, "The role of environmental dynamics in building a first mover advantage theory", *Academy of Management Review*, 32: 377–392.

22.  M. J. Leiblein and T. L. Madsen, 2009, "Unbundling competitive heterogeneity: Incentive structures and capability influences on technological innovation", *Strategic Management Journal*, 30: 711–735; R. Price, 1996, "Technology and strategic advantage", *California Management Review*, 38(3): 38–56.

23.  M. A. Hitt, R. D. Nixon, R. E. Hoskisson and R. Kochhar, 1999, "Corporate entrepreneurship and cross-functional fertilization: Activation, process and disintegration of a new product design team", *Entrepreneurship: Theory and Practice*, 23(3): 145–167.

24.  J. A. Schumpeter, 1912, *The Theory of Economic Development*, Leipzig: Duncker and Humblot.

25.  R. Katila and S. Shane, 2005, "When does lack of resources make new firms innovative?", *Academy of Management Journal*, 48: 814–829.

26.  P. Sharma and J. L. Chrisman, 1999, "Toward a reconciliation of the definitional issues in the field of corporate entrepreneurship", *Entrepreneurship: Theory and Practice*, 23(3): 11–27; R. A. Burgelman and L. R. Sayles, 1986, *Inside Corporate Innovation: Strategy, Structure, and Managerial Skills*, New York: Free Press; J. H. Burgers, F. A. J. Van den Bosch and H. W. Volberda, 2009, "Why new business development projects fail: Coping with the differences of technological versus market knowledge", *Long Range Planning*, 41: 55–73.

27.  D. G. Sirmon, J. L. Arregle, M. A. Hitt and J. W. Webb, 2008, "The role of family influence in firms' strategic responses to the threat of imitation", *Entrepreneurship Theory and Practice*, 32: 979–998; D. K. Dutta and M. M. Crossan, 2005, "The nature of entrepreneurial opportunities: Understanding the process using the 4I organizational learning framework", *Entrepreneurship Theory and Practice*, 29: 425–449.

28.  S. F. Latham and M. Braun, 2009,' Managerial risk, innovation and organizational decline", *Journal of Management*, 35: 258–281; J. H. Burgers, F. A. J. Van den Bosch and H. W. Volberda, 2008, "Why New Business Development Projects Fail: Coping with the Differences of Technological versus Market Knowledge", *Long Range Planning*, 41: 55–73.

29.  R. E. Hoskisson and L. W. Busenitz, 2002, "Market uncertainty and learning distance in corporate entrepreneurship entry mode choice", in: M. A. Hitt, R. D. Ireland, S. M. Camp and D. L. Sexton (eds.), *Strategic Entrepreneurship: Creating a New Mindset*, Oxford, UK: Blackwell Publishers, 151–172.

30.  S. Thornhill, 2006, "Knowledge, innovation, and firm performance in high- and low-technology regimes", *Journal of Business Venturing*, 21: 687–703; D. Somaya, 2003, "Strategic determinants of decisions not to settle patent litigation", *Strategic Management Journal*, 24: 17–38.

31.  W. Chung and S. Yeaple, 2008, "International knowledge sourcing: Evidence from US firms expanding abroad", *Strategic Management Journal*, 29: 1207–1224; J. Santos, Y. Doz and P. Williamson, 2004, "Is your innovation process global?", *MIT Sloan Management Review*, 45(4): 31–37.

32.  Y. S. Su, E. W. K. Tsang and M. W. Peng, 2009, "How do internal capabilities and external partnerships affect innovativeness?", *Asia Pacific Journal of Management*, 26: 309–331; J. A. Fraser, 2004, "A return to basics at Kellogg", *MIT Sloan Management Review*, 45(4): 27–30.

33.  P. A. M. Vermeulen, F. A. J. Van den Bosch and H. W. Volberda, 2007, "Complex incremental product innovation in established service firms: A micro institutional perspective, *Organization Studies*, 28: 1523–1546; H. W. Volberda and C. Baden-Fuller, 2003, "Strategic renewal processes in multi-unit firms: Generic journeys of change" in: B. Chakravarthy, G. Mueller-Stewens, P. Lorange and C. Lechner (eds.), *Strategy Process: Shaping the Contours of the Field*, Oxford, UK: Blackwell: 208–232; F. K. Pil and S. K. Cohen, 2006, "Modularity: Implications for imitation, innovation, and sustained advantage", *Academy of Management Review*, 31: 995–1011; S. Kola-Nystrom, 2003, "Theory of conceptualizing the challenge of corporate renewal", Lappeenranta University of Technology, working paper.

34.  J. J. P. Jansen, F. A. J. van den Bosch and H. W. Volberda, 2006, "Exploratory innovation, exploitative innovation, and performance effects of organizational antecedents and environmental moderators", *Management Science*, 52: 1661–1674.

35.  E. Xu and H. Zhang, 2008, "The impact of state shares on corporate innovation strategy and performance in China", *Asia Pacific Journal of Management*, 25: 473–487; W. C. Kim and R. Mauborgne, 2005, "Navigating toward blue oceans", *Optimize*, February, 44–52.

36.  A. Phene and P. Almieda, 2008, "Innovation in multinational subsidiaries: The role of knowledge assimilation and subsidiary capabilities", *Journal of International Business Studies*, 39: 901–919; G. Ahuja and M. Lampert, 2001, "Entrepreneurship in the large corporation: A longitudinal study of how established firms create breakthrough inventions", *Strategic Management Journal*, 22 (Special Issue): 521–543; H. W. Volberda, N. J. Foss and M. A. Lyles, 2010, "Absorbing the concept of absorptive capacity: How to realize its potential in the organization field", *Organization Science*, 21: 931–951.

37.  J. J. P. Jansen, F. A. J. van den Bosch and H. W. Volberda, 2006, "Exploratory innovation, exploitative innovation, and performance effects of organizational antecedents and environmental moderators", *Management Science*, 52, 1661–1674.

38.  A. J. Chatterji, 2009, "Spawned with a silver spoon? Entrepreneurial performance and innovation in the medical device industry", *Strategic Management Journal*, 30: 185–206; J. Goldenberg, R. Horowitz, A. Levav and D. Mazursky, 2003, "Finding your innovation sweet spot", *Harvard Business Review*, 81(3): 120–129.

39.  C. E. Shalley and J. E. Perry-Smith, 2008, "The emergence of team creative cognition: The role of diverse outside ties, socio-cognitive network centrality, and team evolution", *Strategic Entrepreneurship Journal*, 2(1): 23–41; R. I. Sutton, 2002, "Weird ideas that spark innovation", *MIT Sloan Management Review*, 43(2): 83–87.

40.  K. G. Smith and D. Di Gregorio, 2002, "Bisociation, discovery, and the role of entrepreneurial action", in: M. A. Hitt, R. D. Ireland, S. M. Camp and D. L. Sexton (eds.), *Strategic Entrepreneurship: Creating a New Mindset*, Oxford, UK: Blackwell Publishers, 129–150; J. S. Sidhu, H. R. Commandeur and H. W. Volberda, 2007, "The multifaceted nature of exploration and exploitation: Value of supply, demand and spatial search for innovation", *Organization Science*, 18(1): 20–38.

41.  S. A. Hill, M. V. J. Maula, J. M. Birkinshaw and G. C. Murray, 2009, "Transferability of the venture capital model to the corporate context: Implications for the performance of corporate venture units", *Strategic Entrepreneurship Journal*, 3: 3–27; R. E. Hoskisson and L. W. Busenitz, 2002, Market uncertainty and learning distance in corporate entrepreneurship entry mode choice, in: M. A. Hitt, R. D. Ireland, S. M. Camp and D. L. Sexton (eds.), *Strategic Entrepreneurship: Creating a New Mindset* (Strategic Management Society), Oxford, UK: Blackwell Publishing, 151–172.

42.  S. Hill, M. Maula, J. Birkinshaw and G. Murray, 2009, "Transferability of the venture capital model to the corporate context: Implications for the performance of corporate venture units", *Strategic Entrepreneurship Journal*, 3(1): 3–27; R. A. Burgelman, 1995, *Strategic Management of Technology and Innovation*, Boston: Irwin; R. E. Hoskisson and L. W. Busenitz, 2002, "Market uncertainty and learning distance in corporate entrepreneurship entry mode choice", in: M. A. Hitt et al. (eds.), *Strategic Entrepreneurship: Creating a New Mindset*, Oxford, UK: Blackwell, 151–172.

43.  M. W. Wielemaker, T. Elfring and H. W. Volberda, 2001, "How well-established firms prepare for the new economy:

An empirical study on the development of new economy initiatives", *International Studies of Management & Organization*, 31: 7–29; J. M. Howell, 2005, "The right stuff: Identifying and developing effective champions of innovation", *Academy of Management Executive*, 19(2): 108–119.

44. M. D. Hutt and T. W. Seph, 2009, *Business Marketing Management: B@B*, 10th edition, Mason, OH: Cengage South-Western.

45. S. K. Ethiraj, 2007, "Allocation of inventive effort in complex product systems", *Strategic Management Journal*, 28: 563–584; M. A. Hitt, R. D. Ireland and H. Lee, 2000, "Technological learning, knowledge management, firm growth and performance", *Journal of Engineering and Technology Management*, 17: 231–246.

46. V. Gaba and A. D. Meyer, 2008, "Crossing the organizational species barrier: How venture capital practices infiltrated the information technology sector", *Academy of Management Journal*, 51: 976–998; H. W. Chesbrough, 2002, "Making sense of corporate venture capital", *Harvard Business Review*, 80(3): 90–99.

47. M. Subramaniam and N. Venkatraman, 2001, "Determinants of transnational new product development capability: Testing the influence of transferring and deploying tacit overseas knowledge", *Strategic Management Journal*, 22: 359–378.

48. B. Ambos and B. B. Schegelmilch, 2007, "Innovation and control in the multinational firm: A comparison of political and contingency approaches", *Strategic Management Journal*, 28: 473–486; T. Hutzschenreuter, T. Pedersen and H. W. Volberda, 2007, "The role of path dependency and managerial intentionality: A perspective on international business research", *Journal of International Business Studies*, 38: 1055–1068.

49. H. Li and J. Li, 2009, "Top management team conflict and entrepreneurial strategy in China", *Asia Pacific Journal of Management*, 26: 263–283; S. C. Parker, 2009, "Can cognitive biases explain venture team homophily", *Strategic Entrepreneurship Journal*, 3: 67–83.

50. M. Makri, P. J. Lane and L. R. Gomez-Mejia, 2006, "CEO incentives, innovation and performance in technology-intensive firms: A reconciliation of outcome and behavior-based incentive schemes", *Strategic Management Journal*, 27: 1057–1080.

51. A. Tiwana, 2008, "Does technological modularity substitute for control? A study of alliance performance in software outsourcing", *Strategic Management Journal*, 29: 769–780.

52. C. Zhou and J. Li, 2008, "Product innovation in emerging market-based international joint ventures: An organizational ecology perspective", *Journal of International Business Studies*, 39: 1114–1132; E. Danneels, 2007, "The process of technological competence leveraging", *Strategic Management Journal*, 28: 511–533.

53. F. T Rothaermel and W Boeker, 2008, "Old technology meets new technology: Complementarities, similarities and alliance formation", *Strategic Management Journal*, 29: 47–77; L. Yu, 2002, "Marketers and engineers: Why can't we just get along?", *MIT Sloan Management Review*, 43(1): 13; S. Spedale, F. A. J. Van den Bosch and H. W. Volberda, 2007, "Preservation and dissolution of the target's firm embedded ties in acquisitions", *Organization Studies*, 28: 1169–1196.

54. T. Mom, F. A. J. Van den Bosh and H. W. Volberda, 2007, "Investigating managers' exploration and exploitation activities: The influence of top-down, bottom-up, and horizontal knowledge inflows", *Journal of Management Studies*, 44: 910–931; R. Cowan and N. Jonard, 2009, "Knowledge portfolios and the organization of innovation networks", *Academy of Management Review*, 34: 320–342; A. Somech, 2006, "The effects of leadership style and team process on performance and innovation in functionally hetergeneous teams", *Journal of Management*, 32: 132–157.

55. A. Azadegan, K. J. Dooley, P. L. Carter and J. R. Carter, 2008, "Supplier innovativeness and the role of interorganizational learning in enhancing manufacturer capabilities", *Journal of Supply Chain Management*, 44(4): 14–34; P. Evans and B. Wolf, 2005, "Collaboration rules", *Harvard Business Review*, 83(7): 96–104.

56. B. Fischer and A. Boynton, 2005, "Virtuoso teams", *Harvard Business Review*, 83(7): 116–123.

57. M. Hitt, R. Nixon, R. Hoskisson and R. Kochhar, 1999, "Corporate entrepreneurship and cross-functional fertilization: activation, process and disintegration of a new product design team", *Entrepreneurship Theory and Practice,* 23(3): 145–167.

58. C. M. Christensen and M. Overdorf, 2000, "Meeting the Challenge of Disruptive Change", *Harvard Business Review*, 78: 67–76.

59. J. H. Burgers, J. J. P. Jansen, F. A. J. Van den Bosch and H. W. Volberda, 2009, "Structural differentiation and corporate venturing: The moderating role of formal and informal integration mechanisms", *Journal of Business Venturing*, 24: 206–220.

60. M. Hitt, R. Nixon, R. Hoskisson and R. Kochhar, 1999, "Corporate entrepreneurship and cross-functional fertilization: activation, process and disintegration of a new product design team", *Entrepreneurship Theory and Practice,* 23(3): 145–167.

61. A. C. Amason, 1996, "Distinguishing the effects of functional and dysfunctional conflict on strategic decision making: Resolving a paradox for top management teams", *Academy of Management Journal*, 39: 123–148; P. R. Lawrence and J. W. Lorsch, 1969, *Organization and Environment*, Homewood, IL: Richard D. Irwin.

62. M. A. Cronin and L. R. Weingart, 2007, "Representational gaps, information processing, and conflict in functionally heterogeneous teams", *Academy of Management Review*, 32: 761–773; D. Dougherty, L. Borrelli, K. Muncir and A. O'sullivan, 2000, "Systems of organizational sensemaking for sustained product innovation", *Journal of Engineering and Technology Management*, 17: 321–355.

63. M. Hitt, R. Nixon, R. Hoskisson and R. Kochhar, 1999, "Corporate entrepreneurship and cross-functional fertilization: activation, process and disintegration of a new product design team", *Entrepreneurship Theory and Practice,* 23(3): 145–167.

64. J. J. P. Jansen, G. George, F. A. J. Van den Bosch and H. W. Volberda, 2008. "Senior team attributes and organizational ambidexterity: The moderating role of transformational leadership", *Journal of Management Studies*, 45: 982–1007; J. J. P. Jansen, M. P. Tempelaar, F. A. J. Van den

Bosch and H. W. Volberda, 2009, "Structural differentiation and ambidexterity: The mediating role of integration mechanisms", *Organization Science*, 20(4): 798–811.

65. Gary Hamel, 2000, *Leading the Revolution*, Boston: Harvard Business School Press.

66. P. H. Kim, K. T. Dirks and C. D. Cooper, 2009, "The repair of trust: A dynamic bilateral perspective and multilevel conceptualization", *Academy of Management Review*, 34: 401–422; Q. M. Roberson and J. A. Colquitt, 2005, "Shared and configural justice: A social network model of justice in teams", *Academy of Management Review*, 30: 595–607.

67. H. W. Volberda, 2003, Strategic flexibility: "Creating dynamic competitive advantages", Ch. 32 in: D. Faulkner and A. Campbell (eds.), *The Oxford Handbook of Strategy*, volume 2, *Corporate Strategy*, Oxford: Oxford University Press: 447–506; N. Stieglitz and L. Heine, 2007, "Innovations and the role of complementarities in a strategic theory of the firm", *Strategic Management Journal*, 28: 1–15; S. W. Fowler, A. W. King, S. J. Marsh and B. Victor, 2000, "Beyond products: New strategic imperatives for developing competencies in dynamic environments", *Journal of Engineering and Technology Management*, 17: 357–377.

68. J. C. Short, A. McKelvie, D. J. Ketchen and G. N. Chandler, 2009, "Firm and industry effects on firm performance: A generalization and extension for new ventures", *Strategic Entrepreneurship Journal*, 3: 47–65; M. B. Sarkar, R. Echamabadi, R. Agarwal and B. Sen, 2006, "The effect of the innovative environment on exit of entrepreneurial firms", *Strategic Management Journal*, 27: 519–539.

69. R. D. Ireland, M. A. Hitt and D. G. Sirmon, 2003, "A model of strategic entrepreneurship: The construct and its dimensions", *Journal of Management*, 29: 963–989.

70. A. Afuah, 2009, *Strategic Innovation: New game strategies for Competitive Advantage*, New York: Routledge.

71. M. A. Hitt, R. D. Ireland, S. M. Camp and D. L. Sexton, 2001, "Strategic entrepreneurship: Entrepreneurial strategies for wealth creation", *Strategic Management Journal*, Special Issue, 22, 479–491; J. H. Burgers, F. A. J. Van den Bosch and H. W. Volberda, 2008, "Why new business development projects fail: Coping with the differences of technological versus market knowledge", *Long Range Planning*, 41(1): 55–73; H. W. Volberda, 1998, *Building The Flexible Firm: How to Remain Competitive*, Oxford: Oxford University Press.

72. D. G. Sirmon, M. A. Hitt and R. D. Ireland, 2007, "Managing firm resources in dynamic environment to create value: Looking inside the black box", *Academy of Management Review*, 32: 273–292.

73. D. G. Sirmon, S. Gove and M. A. Hitt, 2008, "Resource management in dyadic competitive rivalry: The effects of resource bundling and deployment", *Academy of Management Journal*, 51: 918–935; M. A. Hitt, L. Bierman, K. Shimizu and R. Kochhar, 2001, "Direct and moderating effects of human capital on strategy and performance in professional service firms: a resource-based perspective", *Academy of Management Journal*, 44(1): 13–28.

74. A. Tiwana, 2008, "Do bridging ties complement strong ties? An empirical examination of alliance ambidexterity", *Strategic Management Journal*, 29(3): 251–272; M. A. Hitt, L. Bierman, K. Uhlenbrock and K. Shimizu, 2006, "The importance of resources for the internationalization of professional service firms: The good, the bad, and the ugly," *Academy of Management Journal*, 49: 1137–1157.

75. K. Asakawa and A. Som, 2008, "Internationalization of R&D in China and India: Conventional wisdom versus reality", *Asia Pacific Journal of Management*, 25: 375–394; M. A. Hitt, R. E. Hoskisson and H. Kim, 1997, "International diversification: Effects on innovation and firm performance in product diversified firms", *Academy of Management Journal*, 40: 767–798.

76. M. A. Hitt and R. D. Ireland, 2002, "The essence of strategic leadership: Managing human and social capital", *Journal of Leadership and Organization Studies*, 9(1): 3–14.

77. P. A. M. Vermeulen, F. A. J. Van den Bosch and H. W. Volberda, 2007, "Complex incremental product innovation in established service firms: A micro institutional perspective", *Organization Studies*, 28: 1523–1546; C. W. L. Hill and F. T. Rothaermel, 2003, "The performance of incumbent firms in the face of radical technological innovation", *Academy of Management Review*, 28: 257–274.

78. D. G. Sirmon and M. A. Hitt, 2009, "Contingencies within dynamic managerial capabilities: Interdependent effects of resource investment and deployment on firm performance", *Strategic Management Journal*, 30(13): 1375–1394.

79. K. Schwab, 2010, *The Global Competitiveness Report* 2010–2011, Geneva: World Economic Forum.

80. G. C. Reid and J. A. Smith, 2000. "What makes a new business start-up successful?", *Small Business Economics*, 14(3): 165–182.

81. Terpstra, D. E. and P. D. Olsen, 1993, "Entrepreneurial start-up and growth: A classification of problems", *Entrepreneurial Theory and Practice*, 17(3): 5–20.

82. G. N. Gregoriou, M. Kooli and R. Kräussl, *Venture capital in Europe*, Boston, MA: Butterworth-Heinemann; T. Hellman and Manju Puri, 2002, "Venture capital and the professionalization of start-up firms: Empirical evidence", *Journal of Finance* 57(1): 169–197.

83. Engel, D. and M. Keilbach, 2007, "Firm-level implications of early stage venture capital investment: An empirical investigation", *Journal of Empirical Finance*, 14: 150–167.

84. H. W. Volberda, 2005, "Rethinking the strategy process: A co-evolutionary approach", in: S. W. Floyd, J. Roos, C. D. Jacobs and F. W. Kellermans (eds.), *Innovating Strategy Process*, Oxford, UK: Blackwell, 81–87; H. W. Volberda, Ch. Baden-Fuller and F. A. J. Van den Bosch, 2001, "Mastering strategic renewal: Mobilizing renewal journeys in multi-unit firms", *Long Range Planning*, 34: 159–178; Ch. Baden-Fuller and H. W. Volberda, 2003, "Dormant capabilities, complex organizations, and renewal", in: R. Sanchez (ed.), *Knowledge Management and Organizational Competence*, Oxford, UK: Oxford University Press, 114–136; Ch. Baden-Fuller and H. W. Volberda, 1996, "Strategic renewal in large complex organizations: A competence-based view", in: R. Sanchez, A. Heene and H. Thomas (eds.), *Dynamics of Competence-Based Competition: Theory and Practice in the New Strategic Management*, Oxford, UK: Pergamon.

# CHAPTER 15

# STRATEGIC RENEWAL

## LEARNING OBJECTIVES

Studying this chapter should provide you with the strategic management knowledge needed to:

1. Understand path dependence, inertia and why firms find it difficult to adapt.
2. Define strategic renewal and explain why it is important for organizational survival.
3. Understand the managerial intentionality and environmental selection perspectives on strategic renewal and explain the debate between both perspectives.
4. Describe the flexibility paradox and discuss the tensions between exploration and exploitation.
5. Describe four ideal types of organizational forms for dealing with hypercompetition.
6. Describe strategic renewal trajectories of routinization and revitalization.
7. Understand the concept of ambidexterity and describe different ways of balancing exploration and exploitation.
8. Describe different strategic renewal journeys and explain the roles of top, middle and front-line management.
9. Explain the key principles of sustained strategic renewal.

We thank Shiko M. Ben-Menahem and Mariano Heyden for their contributions in creating this new Chapter

© Julian Brooks/Alamy

OPENING CASE

## Sustained strategic renewal at Royal Dutch Shell plc 1907–2009

Royal Dutch originates from the former Dutch concessions in their colonies in the Far East, while Shell gloried as a private trading and transport company named after the famous yellow pecten (seashell). At the beginning of the twentieth century, Shell had lost much of its initial competitive advantages in transportation and trade. The European alliance between Royal Dutch and Shell was formed in 1907 to join forces to compete against the powerful Standard Oil Company. Henri Deterding, president of Royal Dutch, and Walter Samuel, founder of Shell Transport and Trading, agreed on an historic alliance with a 60:40 division of interest between Royal Dutch and Shell. Royal Dutch and Shell entered their first alliance in the Asian Petroleum Company in 1906. While Sir Henri Deterding was the uncontested leader of the company, Shell outwardly remained a British company. The Group adopted the Shell brand name and the yellow pecten logo for Group-wide products and operations. Shell Transport and Trade retained Marcus Samuel as figurehead and CEO from 1907 until 1921 when he was succeeded by his son Walter.

In the early years, Shell showed resilience during the price war with Standard in 1910–11, and especially during the First World War. In the 1920s, Shell became the undisputed leader of the international oil industry which eventually led to the famous cartel agreement of Achnacarry. During these years, Shell emphasized rationing of oil supplies and stabilizing of prices and market shares. The US and Venezuela were Shell's most important sources of crude oil supply between the world wars.

Shell's initial key success factors were the booming and undeveloped nature of the oil industry, and its integrated value chain, geographical spread, attention to human resources and best practice technology. Due to technological innovations in production (e.g. rotary drilling), process (e.g. cracking, petrochemicals) and exploration (e.g. geophysics, seismic surveying), the Group gradually emerged as market leader.

The Second World War was a major environmental disturbance for Shell. The company suffered from large tanker losses and loss of production output and processing capacity. Royal Dutch moved its headquarters to Willemstad, Curaçao. After the war, several major changes took place in Shell's organization. The management structure of the parent companies was aligned and the general attitude towards staff management changed to more inhouse selection and training. Furthermore, under the presidency of Loudon in the 1950s, Shell established a listing on the New York Stock Exchange and approached an external consultant to review its management structure. A review by McKinsey led to remodelling of the organization; decentralized operating companies were established and responsibilities and authorities were delegated. A matrix-organization structure was implemented and a formal Committee of Managing Directors (CMD) was established to reach consensus and coordination in the TMT (Top Management Team).

After the Second World War, the large oil companies created market stability through strategic partnering and interlocked directorships. An account of Shell's history notes that "it was a resilient coalition because the parties to it were each other's economic hostage".[1] The industry's centre of gravity became the eastern hemisphere. In particular in the Middle East the companies divided concessions and joined forces in the process of negotiations of long-term supply contracts with oil-producing governments. New firms entered the industry, supply usually exceeded demand, and prices remained constant in the 1950s and the 1960s. Shell, however, remained a crude-short business in the 1950s and the 1960s as it did not gain a major foothold in the Middle East concessions. With regard to Shell's performance, the sharp decline in return on assets after 1955 showed the Group was struggling with rising competition. One could argue that Shell missed an opportunity to establish itself in the vast Middle East crude oil resources, but the company responded with a dual strategy, economies of scale combined with product differentiation. Shell always retained an open attitude towards the OPEC after its formation in 1960. The company could do so as it relied less on Middle East oil than its competitors.

Next to geographical dispersion of its oil supplies upstream, Shell radically diversified its product portfolio in the post-war period. In line with the business philosophy of that time, Shell explored new business sectors to generate growth, amid concerns about the longevity of the oil industry. After the 1973 oil shock, the company diversified into alternative energy sources (e.g. nuclear energy and coal), metals and even forestry. Shell's interest in new technology initially created competitive advantages through a diversified product portfolio. Unfortunately, different businesses required different business approaches and unrealistic expectations about their profitability caused many of these diversifications to fail. No business could match the performance of oil.

When competition intensified and the economic environment changed in the 1980s and 1990s, Shell stepped back from its diversified and decentralized strategy and gradually focused on base chemicals only. Emphasis was shifted towards profitability, increasing return on capital and delivering shareholder value. Projects with high profit potential were allowed to go ahead while underperforming non-core activities such as forestry and mining were gradually disposed of in the 1990s. Currently, Shell is primarily involved in two businesses: energy (mainly oil and gas products) and petrochemicals.

Several environmental shocks at the end of the twentieth century influenced the behaviour and performance of organizations in the oil and gas industry. For instance, the 1997 financial crisis in Asia and the decline of the Russian ruble in 1998 strongly affected global stock markets. The technology bubble, apparent accounting scandals and the 9/11 terrorist attack in New York further inhibited economic growth and changed the way organizations would do business in the twenty-first century. Moreover, oil industry consolidation impacted the current outlook for global energy companies. Illustrative of how Shell handled industry consolidation were the acquisitions of Fletcher in Australia, Pennzoil Quaker in the US and DEA in Germany. Shell considered participating in a large takeover, but ultimately decided to seek growth organically and through relatively small – compared to the Exxon-Mobile, BP-Amoco and Chevron-Texaco deals – acquisitions of local companies.

In 2004, Shell's reputation suffered from an overestimation of oil reserves. Ultimately, this event and the long-lasting internal disturbances led to the unification of the parent companies Royal Dutch and Shell Transport in 2005. Incorporated in England and Wales, and headquartered and resident in the Netherlands, Royal Dutch Shell plc was born and Jeroen van der Veer was appointed the Company's first CEO.

In response to the latest global recession, a reorganization was initiated in 2009 under the leadership of a new CEO, Peter Voser (the same year it was ranked first in *Fortune*'s annual ranking of the world's leargest corporations, with revenues exceeding €360 bn.). "Transition 2009", as the reorganization programme was called, was aimed at enhancing accountability for operating performance and technology development within Shell's organization, thereby improving decision making and execution speed and reducing costs. The firm's five businesses – Exploration & Production, Gas & Power, Oil Products, Chemicals and Renewables – were restructured into four businesses: Upstream International, Upstream Americas, Downstream and Projects & Technology, which are now operating in more than 90 countries with 101 000 employees.

By exploiting its existing skills and exploring other innovative opportunities, Shell is trying to keep its favourable competitive position against competitors such as Exxon Mobile, BP, ChevronTexaco, and Total. As Shell is now experiencing a challenging period in exploring new growth opportunities and sustaining its competitive advantage under changing economic, regulatory and political conditions, the question that remains is whether Shell still possesses the capabilities to renew itself in the future.

**Sources**: Royal Dutch Shell plc http://www.shell.com; Grant, R. M. (2003) "Strategic planning in a turbulent environment: Evidence from the oil majors", *Strategic Management* 24(6): 491–517; Van Zanden, J. L., Howarth, S., Jonker, J. and Sluijterman, K. (2007) *A History of Royal Dutch Shell. From Challenger to Joint Industry Leader, 1890–1939, 1939–1973, 1973–2007*, 3 volumes and appendices. New York: Oxford University Press; Kwee, Z., Van den Bosch, F. A. J. and Volberda, H. W. (2011) "The influence of top management team's corporate governance orientation on strategic renewal trajectories: A longitudinal analysis of Royal Dutch Shell plc, 1907–2004", *Journal of Management Studies* (forthcoming).

*Questions*

1 Identify the main changes in Shell's environment. How did the company react?

2 Compare Shell's current operations with activities it undertook in the past. What are the (dis)advantages of its contemporary range of businesses? Consider how this may change in the future.

3 Considering Shell's history, which elements do you deem to be most important for organizational longevity?

Modern-day organizations operate in extremely challenging environments. In many industries, competition is increasingly characterized by temporary advantages punctuated by frequent disruptions rather than long, stable periods in which firms can achieve sustainable competitive advantages. As the Shell Case illustrates, many situations firms face now involve strategic surprises that do not give sufficient warning to permit deliberate formulation and execution of strategy. Constant change has become the norm modern managers must cope with. Surviving under these conditions requires firms to continuously renew by revitalizing and transforming their core activities, and seeking new avenues for growth.

As will become clear from this chapter, renewing incumbent firms is far from straightforward. As organizations grow older, larger and more complex, structures, systems and routines slowly become rooted in the organization.[2] This is due to the firm's effort to best leverage its existing knowledge and competencies and deliver customer value with maximum efficiency.[3] Simultaneously, future organizational developments become highly dependent on past decisions related to resource allocation and relations with stakeholders. Particular courses of action, once introduced, can be virtually impossible to reverse. This property is known as path dependence and can be defined as the causal relevance of preceding stages in a temporal sequence.[4] Path dependence is problematic as environments change, and can hinder firms in maintaining a fit with their environment, or worse, threaten firm survival.[5]

Two conflicting forces become apparent here. On the one hand, there is a need for an efficient, stable structure enabling optimal exploitation of available knowledge and competencies to deal with short term competitive forces (i.e. stability). In this connection, exploitation refers to refinement, choice, production, efficiency, selection, implementation and execution using existing knowledge. On the other hand, environmental change forces established firms to be flexible, transform stagnant businesses and explore new sources of wealth through new resource combinations[6] (i.e. change). Exploration here implies search, variation, risk-taking, experimentation, play, flexibility, discovery and innovation using new learning. This tension between stability and change and its underlying forces of exploitation and exploration is fundamental to understanding organizational survival and strategic renewal.[7] Accordingly, the present chapter focuses on how firms can resolve the tension between stability and change as environments change.

In the first section of this chapter the concept of strategic renewal is introduced. We discuss its importance for firm survival, taking into account different theoretical perspectives that form the core of the academic debate between managerial intentionality versus environmental selection. We then proceed to explain the distinction between the three dimensions constituting the concept of strategic renewal, and describe the flexibility paradox and generic ways in which the underlying tensions of exploration versus exploitation can be balanced for long-term survival.

**Path dependence**

Path dependence is the (constraining) influence of past stages in organizational development on future decisions and actions.

**Exploitation**

Exploitation refers to refinement, choice, production, efficiency, selection, implementation and execution using existing knowledge.

**Exploration**

Exploration refers to search, variation, risk-taking, experimentation, play, flexibility, discovery and innovation using new learning.

In the second section we proceed to discuss ways of developing strategic flexibility by considering the managerial design task and organizational design tasks. We subsequently analyse different organizational forms that enable firms to cope with different levels of competition, and how the strategic renewal trajectories relate to these different forms. Next, we discuss how multi-unit firms can balance exploration and exploitation using various forms of ambidexterity as more permanent solutions for strategic renewal. The roles of managers at different levels are brought to light, and the way they interact in relation to the environment will be linked to several journeys of renewal within multi-unit firms. We finalize the chapter by reverting back to the Key Debate within on what matters most for strategic renewal: managerial intentionality or environmental pressures?

## Strategic renewal: definition, theoretical perspectives and dimensions

**Strategic renewal**

Strategic renewal refers to the adaptive choices and actions a firm undertakes to alter its path dependence and maintain a dynamic strategic fit with changing environments over time.

At the core of strategic thinking rests the premise that a fit should exist between organizational structure, processes, competencies and resources on the one hand, and opportunities and threats arising in the organization's external environment on the other (see also Chapters 1–3).[8] As environments change over time – because of ever-increasing rates of technological developments, globalization, government interventions, tightening resource constraints, changing customer preferences, new entrants and shorter product life cycles – organizations need to adapt to change. In other words, the fit between a firm and its environment should be dynamic and firms have to continuously renew their strategies to maintain fit. Strategic renewal can be understood as the adaptive choices and actions a firm undertakes to alter its path dependence and maintain a dynamic strategic fit with changing environments over time. This involves the changing, replacing, or refreshing of one or more core organizational attributes which have the potential to affect the firm's long-term performance, and ultimately, survival.[9]

### Selection and adaptation perspectives on strategic renewal

**Dynamic strategic fit**

Dynamic strategic fit refers to firm-specific fit over time between environmental factors and organizational contingencies.

How do firms renew themselves over time? Why do some firms survive for centuries while others cease to exist? Theories explaining organizational renewal and survival abound and still form a core debate in the field of strategy. However, two main theoretical perspectives can be distinguished in the body of literature: selection and adaptation perspectives. The key difference between selection and adaptation perspectives relates to the extent to which organizations are believed to be able to renew in the face of environmental change. We describe the selection and adaptation perspectives and eight associated theories according to their view on renewal and survival.[10]

**Selection**    The selection perspective has a deterministic approach to viewing the interaction between firms and their environment. From a selection perspective, firms are assumed to be limited in their ability and agility for adaptation. Strategic renewal can be achieved, yet only in relatively familiar ways. The more prominent theories associated with this perspective are population ecology theory, evolutionary theory, the resource-based view and institutional theory.

*Population ecology theory* views renewal at the level of populations of firms. At this level, environmental factors favour or "select" organizations that are reliable and specialized. Such firms exhibit unique forms, resources, competencies and routines that match the environmental niche they occupy, and thereby account for competitive advantages.[11] Organizations which survive the selection process gradually build up structural inertia. Structural inertia is generated by structures and procedures that organizations accumulate over time and constrain adaptability to environmental change.[12] Inertia is the opposite of fitness, which refers to the capacity to learn and change behavioural characteristics or capabilities to fit to new circumstances in organizational environments.[13] Sources of inertia can stem both from within and outside the firm (see Table 15.1).

According to some population ecologists, attempts to adapt the organization are futile and can even decrease survival chances.[14] In a simple (stable, uncompetitive) environment, inertia may enable a more effective and economical use of managerial skills and resources and allow managers to focus on the most important decisions.[15] However, when the environment changes, inertia will be difficult to overcome and can result in deteriorating performance, and eventually in "selecting out" of firms whose competencies have become outdated. These firms will subsequently be replaced by new entrants exhibiting new organizational forms that better match the new environmental conditions, thereby engendering renewal at the population level.

Less radical representations of population ecology recognize that variations and change can occur,[16] yet contend that long-term survival is only feasible when the speed of the organization's response is commensurate with temporal patterns of change of the environment. However, despite the potential to adapt, organizations often respond too slowly to threats and opportunities in their environments. This

**Inertia**

Inertia is a persistent resistance to changing organizational features.

**Fitness**

Fitness is the organizational capacity to learn and change behavioural characteristics or capabilities to fit to new circumstances in organizational environments.

**Table 15.1** Internal and external sources of organisational inertia

| | Type of constraint | Locus of constraint | Examples |
|---|---|---|---|
| INTERNAL | **Prior investments** | Intra-firm | Sunk costs; investments in property, plant, specialized equipment and personnel; long-term investments; formalized structures and policies |
| | **Behavioural predispositions** | Individual and teams | Commitment to status quo; risk averseness; intolerance for ambiguity; bounded rationality; satisficing behaviour |
| | **Established social structures** | Relation between individuals | Shared identity; organizational culture; strong social ties; organizational politics; shared norms and values; normative contracts; established expectations about roles |
| EXTERNAL | **Resource dependencies** | Relation between firms and providers of key resources | Long-term contracts with customers and suppliers; interlocking directorates; established customer base; long-term debts/obligations |
| | **Normative expectations** | Firm at interface with society/stakeholders | Collective rationality; industry recipes; cognitive inertia; normative metrics of reliability; societal expectations; legitimacy-seeking; accreditations and certifications |
| | **Legal and fiscal barriers** | Firm at interface with regulatory agencies | Anti-trust regulations; protectionist policies; barriers to entry and exit |

phenomenon is known as relative inertia,[17] referring to the comparison between the organization's internal rate of change and the rate of change in the environment.[18]

The notion of relative inertia implies that a firm's efforts to adapt to the changing environment are negated by higher levels of environmental change, competition and selection. Competitive advantages are continuously eroded by actions of other players which lead again to higher levels of competition and the need to react faster (see also the discussion on fast-cycle markets, temporary advantages and the Opening Case in Chapter 6). In other words, companies adapt faster and faster, but as a consequence of the resulting increase in competition they do not make any progress. In the end, these dynamic interactions between firm adaptation on the one hand and higher levels of competition and selection on the other, cancel each other out. This condition is known in management theory as hypercompetition, or "the Red Queen effect"[19], after a passage from Lewis Carroll's *Through the Looking Glass* (see Figure 15.1).

*Evolutionary theory* shares a number of elements with population ecology: (1) a limited role for organizational adaptability, (2) a population level of analysis, and (3) the importance of environmental selection. However, whereas organizational form is the main focus point of population ecology, routines take centre stage in evolutionary theory. Routines are the regular and predictable behaviour patterns of firms with which day-to-day operations get done. They develop over time as organizations accumulate know-how. In the course of their existence, organizations become repositories of skills that are unique and often difficult to transfer. Routines may therefore create opportunities for producing distinctive competitive advantages and further improving organizational know-how. The potential benefits include greater reliability in delivering a sound and comprehensible product and economies of efficiency.[20]

The same routines suppress attention span and the capacity to absorb new information by spelling out behaviour that permits search only for new ideas that are consistent with prior ones. This results from entrenched social structures, and organization members becoming attached to cognitive styles, behavioural dispositions and decision heuristics. As organizations age, radical change therefore becomes increasingly difficult. Adaptation occurs either when routines which are not used for some time disappear, or through evolutionary modification.

In a similar way, the *resource-based theory* views the firm as a bundle of tangible and intangible resources and tacit know-how that must be identified, selected, developed and deployed to generate superior performance (see Chapter 3 for a

**Relative inertia**

Relative inertia is the notion that organizations' internal rate of change is too slow to respond to the rate of change in the external environment (e.g. threats and opportunities).

**Hypercompetition**

Hypercompetition is an environmental condition characterized by rapidly escalating competition, high uncertainty, heterogeneity of players, and constant disequilibrium and change.

**Routines**

Routines are the regular and predictable behaviour patterns of firms with which day-to-day operations get done.

## FIGURE 15.1  The Red Queen effect

"Now! Now!" cried the Queen. "Faster! Faster!" And they went so fast that at last they seemed to skim through the air, hardly touching the ground with their feet till, suddenly, just as Alice was getting quite exhausted, they stopped, and she found herself sitting on the ground, breathless and giddy.

The Queen propped her up against a tree, and said kindly, "You may rest a little now." Alice looked round her in great surprise. "Why, I do believe we've been under this tree the whole time! Everything's just as it was!"

"Of course it is," said the Queen. "What would you have it?"

"Well, in *our* country," said Alice, still panting a little, "you'd generally get to somewhere else – if you ran very fast for a long time, as we've been doing."

"A slow sort of country!" said the Queen. "Now, *here*, you see, it takes all the running *you* can do to keep in the same place. If you want to get somewhere else, you must run at least twice as fast as that!"

(Lewis Carroll, *Through the Looking Glass*, 1946: 178–179)

detailed discussion of resources, competencies and capabilities).[21] Competitive advantage originates from heterogeneity in the distribution of resources across firms.[22] At the firm level, firms should therefore seek out resources that are valuable, rare, inimitable and non-substitutable (i.e. so-called VRIN attributes as discussed in Chapter 3, 108).[23] These resources, and the unique way they are used – competencies – take time to develop and are complexly intertwined within the organization.[24] In other words, a firm's resource endowments are "sticky" and difficult to change. When firms lack the capacity to develop new resources and competencies quickly altogether, core competencies can turn into "core rigidities" or "competence traps".[25] Thus, as we saw in population ecology and evolutionary theory, the resource-based theory assumes that, at least for the short term, firms are "stuck with what they have and have to live with what they lack".[26] For this reason, the theory has been criticized for being of limited value in explaining how and why certain firms adapt in pursuit of competitive advantage.

Finally, *institutional theory* focuses on why organizations within a population exhibit isomorphism, or similar strategies and characteristics. A core argument is that the embeddedness of organizations in their institutional context informs the direction of firm adaptation. The core proposition is that firms are inclined or forced to resemble other firms in a population due to three types of isomorphism:[27]

> **Isomorphism**
>
> Isomorphism is similarity in strategy and behavioural characteristics between firms.

- *Coercive* isomorphism stems from political influence and legitimacy constrains that firms, or individuals within firms, face. For instance, hospitals and educational institutions may conform their strategies to the role they are expected to fulfil by their stakeholders. These roles may for instance be governed by (in)formal rules (e.g. regulations or agreements) or social convention. Regulatory policy can directly shape, structure, and constrain the conduct and strategic decision-making of organizations. A notable example is the stronger regulations imposed on the European and American financial sector throughout followed by the recent financial crisis.[28]

- *Normative* isomorphism relates to professionalization and conforming to dominant industry values and norms. Whereas coercive forces mainly concern written rules, normative forces are associated with unwritten ones. This may apply to individuals within organizations, where social obligations for instance influence how people perform and interact. At the firm level, normative forces are visible in the filtering of personnel. Many organizational fields hire individuals with a narrow range of training and professional experience. Such practices may make managers view the world around them in a highly similar way.

- *Mimetic* isomorphism results from standard responses to uncertainty. Firms may for instance mimic the strategic behaviour of competitors that are perceived to be successful or legitimate. Mimetic isomorphism is reflected in the *bandwagon phenomenon*,[29] which is the tendency of firms to follow the behaviour and beliefs of others. Mimicry can for instance be noticed in price wars between supermarkets in e.g. the Netherlands, France and the UK, and the internationalization of professional service firms.

Combined, these isomorphic forces may cause firms to homogenize their strategic choices by conforming to industry rules, norms and shared logics.

**Adaptation**   While many companies drift from industry leadership to obscurity, this path is not followed by all companies. Royal Dutch Shell (see the Opening Case to this chapter) is an example of a company that has ranked among the world's top ten industrial companies for almost a century. Such long-lived complex organizations form a major challenge to the pessimistic connotation surrounding the concept of inertia.[30]

Compared to the selection perspective, the adaptation perspective has a more voluntaristic approach to strategic renewal. The intentional actions organizations undertake to adapt to changing environmental conditions take centre stage.[31] Moreover, organizations are considered to be able to change in unfamiliar ways rather than only in familiar ways. Theories associated with this perspective are strategic choice theory, dynamic capabilities theory, organizational learning theory and behavioural theory.

As opposed to most selection theories, *strategic choice theory* argues that organizations are not always passive recipients of environmental influence, but have the power and opportunity to drive strategic renewal and reshape their environment.[32] Strategic renewal is viewed as a dynamic interaction between managerial action and environmental forces.[33] Decision makers play an intermediary role between the firm and its environment and have leeway in the choice of strategic renewal actions.

*Dynamic capabilities theory* is an extension of the resource-based theory of the firm. It focuses on the dynamics of resource deployments within firms over time.[34] As we saw earlier in this chapter, a limited repertoire of available routines severely limits the range of strategic choices when environmental conditions change. Highly specialized resources and core competencies enhance profits, but simultaneously have the risk of becoming sources of rigidities and inflexibility.[35] Consequently, to remain viable in changing environments organizations have to repeatedly seek out possibilities to develop and dissipate new skills and capabilities. Organizations should remain in a so-called *dynamic capability-building mode* and continuously renew themselves by exploring opportunities arising in their environment.[36] Accordingly, we define dynamic capabilities as "the firm's processes that use resources – specifically the processes to integrate, reconfigure, gain and release resources – to match and even create market change. Dynamic capabilities thus are the organizational and strategic routines by which firms achieve new resource configurations as markets emerge, collide, split, evolve, and die."[37] Organizational learning plays an important role in the development of dynamic capabilities.

*Organizational learning theory* focuses on how organizational members notice, interpret and use information and knowledge to reconsider the fit of firms within their environment. Organizational learning and the firm's absorptive capacity for new external knowledge are considered principal drivers of strategic renewal in strategy research. As discussed in Chapter 4, absorptive capacity is a firm's ability to value, assimilate and utilize new external knowledge.[38] The balance between the extent to which organizations explore new knowledge domains and their exploitation of existing knowledge domains is of crucial importance to effective learning and organizational survival.[39] "Where exploration is rooted in variance-increasing activities, learning by doing, and trial and error, exploitation is rooted in variance-decreasing activities and disciplined problem solving. Where exploitation builds on an organization's past, exploration creates futures that may be quite different from the organization's past."[40] Organizational learning will play a key role in further treatments of renewal in this chapter.

*Behavioural theory* views organizations as coalitions of individuals with their own objectives that need to be satisfied by balancing resource allocation processes. The theoretical building blocks developed in Cyert and March's *A Behavioural Theory of the Firm*[41] became the foundations for current research in organizational learning theory and evolutionary theory. For example, the theory's explanation of operating procedures had a strong impact on the development of the theory of routines central to evolutionary theory.[42] Other important notions of the theory are that decision makers are boundedly rational and seek to avoid uncertainty by

**Dynamic capabilities**

Dynamic capabilities are the firm's processes to integrate, reconfigure, gain and release resources to match and even create market change.

**Absorptive capacity**

Absorptive capacity is a firm's ability to value, assimilate and utilize new external knowledge.

STRATEGIC FOCUS

© Chris Cooper-Smith/Alamy

# Blocking the bust: Blockbuster's struggle for survival in the film rental industry

As consumer demand in home entertainment has radically changed over the past decade, Blockbuster, once a thriving global provider of in-home retail and rental film and game entertainment, has fallen on hard times.

Founded in 1985 and headquartered in Dallas, Texas, Blockbuster expanded rapidly during the 1990s through the opening of new video stores and a series of takeovers of film rental chains across the Americas, Europe, Australia and Asia. Soon, it became one of the most recognized entertainment brands in the world, and a primary outlet for the major Hollywood studios. In 2009, the company operated over 7400 video and game stores in the US and 20 other countries under the Blockbuster brand and other brand names including Xtra-Vision (in the Republic of Ireland and Northern Ireland) and Game Rush (Canada, Italy, Mexico and Denmark).

While Blockbuster continues to be a leader in the US DVD and video rental market, its struggle to adapt to changing consumer needs and fight off competitors resembles a horror scenario. Caused by continual falls in the price of DVDs, consumers progressively prefer to buy rather than rent movies, squeezing the company's profit margins. In addition, competition faced by new entrants offering more flexible and cheaper forms of distribution is rapidly increasing.

One of these competitors is Netflix Inc., a company which started life as a provider of film rental subscription services delivering DVDs directly to its member's address by mail with a postage-paid return envelope. Two years after its incorporation in 1997, Netflix had 100 000 subscribers. Just 10 years later, the company boasts over 12 million subscribers to which it now offers a variety of services including instant online access to films, and a market capitalization of €3 billion compared to Blockbuster's €49 million. Estimates are that since 2007, Blockbuster has lost over €0.8 billion in revenues to Netflix and comparable online competitors. Yet another example is the Redbox division of competitor Coinstar Inc. Redbox offers DVDs at a "$1-a-day" rental price through its vast network of 20 000 vending machines at locations including Wal-Mart, the largest US retailer by sales, and leading drug stores.

In 2004, the company's majority shareholder, Viacom, sold the company. In an effort to restore profitability, Blockbuster initiated a plan involving a move out of peripheral markets. This included a retreat from the UK – its largest market outside the US – and Spain. However, despite its efforts to focus on its core market and adapt to the new retailing landscape at home, Blockbuster's efforts to renew its business and re-win its customers have proven of little help to date. While it too has started offering Internet-based subscription services – though arguably not in time – the lingering threat of a bankruptcy continues to rise. The remaining question is whether the radical turn-around operation planned for 2010–2012, consisting of the closure of another 1500 stores in the US and the slashing of advertising budgets, will produce a Hollywood ending.

**Sources**: Grover, R. (2010) "The last picture at Blockbuster?", *BusinessWeek*, http://www.businessweek.com, March 26; Birchall, J. (2009) "DVD business shift hits Blockbuster", *Financial Times*, http://www.ft.com, September 17; Steverman, B. (2007) "Netflix battle with Blockbuster gets ugly", *BusinessWeek*, http://www.businessweek.com, July 24; Verdict Research (2006) "Blockbuster: DVD giant beats predictable retreat from Europe", *Marketline*, http://www. marketlineinfo.com, June 26.

*Questions*

**1** How has path dependence affected the ability of Blockbuster to adapt to increasing competition?

**2** Which adaptation or selection theories are most suitable for describing the challenges Blockbuster faces?

**3** Do you think the current efforts of Blockbuster to turnaround the company will be successful? Justify your position.

satisficing decision making, maintaining firm performance within industry average, and seeking stability. Furthermore, change is considered to be the result of unsatisfactory firm performance in relation to aspiration levels leading to a search for adaptive solutions or "*problemistic search*". Because of inherent short-sightedness, this search often leads to exploitative rather than explorative adaptive solutions. Finally, the strategic allocation of organizational slack (i.e. excess capacity maintained by an organization) is considered a key aspect of innovativeness.

## Dimensions of strategic renewal

Strategic renewal can be considered as a multidimensional construct. In order to renew, choices have to be made with regard to what needs to be changed to alter path dependencies, where to seek the necessary knowledge, and how to manage the interactions and knowledge flows necessary in the process. Accordingly, three dimensions can be distinguished: the content, context and process of strategic renewal.[43]

The *content* dimension of strategic renewal relates to the question which core attributes of the current strategy need to be changed, replaced or refreshed.[44] It pertains to whether renewal actions can be thought of as doing more of what is already being done by the organization (exploitation) or doing new things (exploration). Examples include the organization's product market scope, technologies to be applied, organizational design and administrative systems, geographic markets to be considered, and services to be provided. In the case of Shell, the diversification into alternative energy sources and forestry can be considered as a decision relating to the content dimension of strategic renewal.

The *context* dimension in turn relates to the "where" question, and reflects whether the learning underlying strategic renewal actions is internally developed through experimental learning or externally acquired through acquisitive learning.[45] *Internal strategic renewal* takes place within the boundaries of the firm and is driven by experience and experimentation with internal resources, (re)combinations of these, and internal development of capabilities. Examples are corporate entrepreneurship initiatives, investments in research and development (R&D), and employee training. *External strategic renewal* involves using external resources and acquiring or cooperating with outside parties. These include mergers, acquisitions, joint ventures, and other forms of cooperative agreements.[46] In the case of Shell, the strategy to seek organic growth rather than engaging in large takeovers (as done by its main competitors) is an example of a decision related to the context dimension of strategic renewal.

Finally, the *process* dimension relates to the question how and when effective strategies are shaped, validated and implemented efficiently within the firm.[47] This dimension incorporates the temporal sequence of events that unfold as organizational change occurs and is fundamentally concerned with the timing, frequency, interaction and volatility of strategic renewal actions and actors during a particular time period.[48] As was evident from the Opening Case, the number of strategic renewal actions introduced at Shell differs between periods. An example is the reorganization in reaction to the most recent economic downturn. Such increased internal variety in strategic renewal actions exemplifies a development related to the process dimension of strategic renewal.

## Incremental and discontinuous strategic renewal

Discussions of strategic renewal have further distinguished between *incremental* and *discontinuous* transformations of core attributes.[49] Incremental perspectives assume that adaptation is the outcome of relatively small iterative interactions between path dependent choices and environmental feedback over time.[50] Discontinuous perspectives see renewal as revitalizing the company's operations by drastically redefining the scope of its business, its competitive approach, or both.[51]

At times, the distinction between incremental and discontinuous is clear-cut, for instance with strategic reorientation and turnaround initiatives. IBM's transformation from a computer processor and hardware company, to a professional service organization, is a clear example of discontinuous renewal. However, most of the time the distinction between whether path altering decisions are incremental or discontinuous can only be understood by taking a longitudinal perspective towards a firm's strategic renewal path. "A series of small incremental changes can accumulate into a much larger change when viewed over a longer time span. Thus, not only discontinuous transformations but also continuous incremental strategic renewal efforts hold the potential for major strategic change."[52] A key aspect of the distinction is based on the *renewal pattern* that emerges over a long period of time resulting from strategic renewal actions that a firm undertakes towards incremental path dependence or discontinuous path creation.[53] Thus, to differentiate between the two types of renewal one must consider the magnitude of deviation from a specific reference point, within a specified window of observation.

## Organizational learning in strategic renewal

For the organization to renew successfully and ensure its long-term survival, it must manage its learning trajectories.[54] Learning takes place when an entity, through its processing of information, experiences change in the range of its potential behaviours.[55] Two generic types of learning orientations can be defined: exploratory and exploitative learning.[56]

Exploratory learning ("exploration") has a bearing on the long-term renewal of the organization and adds new attributes to the organization's current portfolio of activities and competencies. Outcomes include launching new products and services, starting up new businesses, and entering new markets or new geographic regions. Exploratory learning is the process underlying discontinuous path creations and inevitably entails unlearning of much of what the firm has done before as it replaces previous competencies. Exploitative learning ("exploitation") denotes a shorter-term orientation and encompasses those actions that lie in line with the organization's current activities and competencies in existing domains. Exploitative learning is the process underlying more incremental paths of renewal and builds on the cumulative knowledge and capabilities of the firm.

Figure 15.2 gives a representation of the ratio between Shell's exploratory and exploitative strategic renewal actions over a large part of its history (the gap between 1938 and 1945 is a consequence of missing data due to the Second World War). As becomes evident from this chart, the company oscillated between periods dominated by exploration and periods dominated by exploitation. During the post-war period (1950s through to the 1970s), Shell's diversification strategy is reflected

**Exploratory learning**

Exploratory learning adds new attributes to the organization's current portfolio of activities and competencies.

**Exploitative learning**

Exploitative learning encompasses those actions that lie in line with the organization's current activities and competencies in existing domains.

**FIGURE 15.2**  Royal Dutch Shell's exploratory and exploitative strategic renewal trajectories

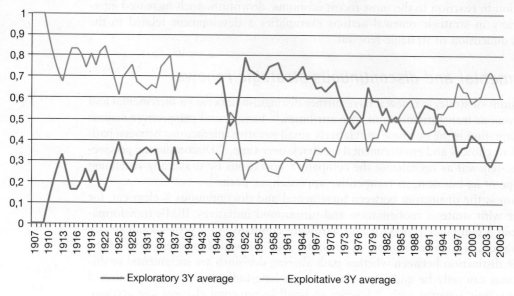

— Exploratory 3Y average       — Exploitative 3Y average

Source: Adapted with the permission of Kwee, Z. (2009), "Investigating three key principles of sustained strategic renewal: A longitudinal study of long-lived firms", *ERIM PhD series in Management*, Rotterdam School of Management.

in the increased attention towards exploration over exploitation. Interestingly, in recent periods – characterized by increased demand and tight supply of oil – the company gradually overemphasizes exploitation in its strong focus on oil, gas and petrochemicals. This raises the question whether Shell will still be able to renew in the future, or is slowly on its way to developing detrimental core rigidities threatening its market leadership and survival.

In sum, to remain successful, firms must constantly renew themselves by breaking out of path dependencies and adapting to their environment.[57] To achieve this, they must not only learn new knowledge, but also be able to unlearn redundant or dysfunctional capabilities, relearn, and combine old and partially useful skill sets into novel combinations. This renewed knowledge should then serve to replenish traditional and obsolete systems with life and vigour through new sets of skills and competencies.[58] The challenge confronting the strategist becomes one of a balancing act.

# The flexibility paradox: tensions between exploration and exploitation

The distinction between selection and adaptation highlights the tension between environmental and path-dependence forces that drive organizations towards inertia, and the adaptive choices decision makers can enact. It highlights a tension between stability versus change. Accordingly, the basic problem confronting an organization becomes to engage in sufficient exploitation to ensure its current viability and, at the same time, to devote enough energy to exploration to ensure its future viability.[59] However, exploring and exploiting are associated with different and inconsistent organizational architectures and processes. Moreover, the returns associated with exploration are distant in time and highly variable, while the returns associated with exploitation are proximate in time and more certain.[60] These inconsistencies

and their associated contradictory logics create fundamental organizational challenges and tensions as both exploration and exploitation compete for scarce organizational resources and managerial attention – a flexibility paradox.

Firms that neither explore nor exploit are surely to fade away quickly. However,
a skewed tendency to overexplore or overexploit also has its perils. "Systems that
engage in exploitation to the exclusion of exploration are likely to find themselves
trapped in suboptimal stable equilibria while adaptive systems that engage in exploration to the exclusion of exploitation are likely to find that they suffer the costs of
experimentation without gaining many of its benefits."[61] Too much exploitation
drives inertia and dynamic conservatism; exploitation crowds out exploration.[62]
Similarly, too much exploration drives out efficiencies and prevents gaining economies of scale or learning by doing.[63] Firms that engage in either too much exploration (i.e. overexploration) or exploitation (i.e. overexploitation) at the expense of
the other can fall victim to several "traps".

*Overexploitation.* When firms in dynamic environments overexploit competencies and highly specialized resources without focusing sufficiently on exploration,
core competencies can become core rigidities and cause a competence trap.[64] The
strong focus on exploitation of existing opportunities leads to the proliferation of
routines that become institutionalized in planning and control systems and shared
norms and values. Adaptive solutions, driven by learning and search processes,
only take place within narrow norms and values and result in small, incremental
changes. This eliminates variety in strategic options: the organization is doing
what it had been doing more efficiently, but is unable to question the appropriate-
ness of its actions. Consequently, planning strategies are reinforced and errors in
beliefs and norms remain. The organization is dominated by a tendency towards
conservatism, delay in decision-making and ossification. The accumulated inertia
may well be so significant that it threatens the firm's survival when environments
change irreversibly.

General Motors' core competence throughout the 1980s and early 1990s is illustrative. Following the first oil shocks in the 1970s and the entrance of Japanese imports of smaller cars, it reinforced the mistaken belief that cars are status symbols
and that styling and volume is more important than quality. Consequently, the
company remained focused on the production of large, fuel-inefficient vehicles. Further, finance exerted a tremendous dominance over the entire organization. Money
became a substitute for innovation, past success turned into dogma and maintenance of the status quo became the measure of success. General Motors' narrow
frame of learning during the past 30 years hampered search and filtered away significant amounts of relevant uncertainty, diversity and change signals. Consequently, the organization was motivated to transform ill-defined problems into a
form that could be handled with existing routines. The inability of the organization
to solve new, significantly different problems derived from this retardation of organizational learning. Mistaken perceptions of the customer and the tight financial instruments led to complacency, myopia, and, ultimately, the long-expected
bankruptcy of the world's largest carmaker in 2009.[65]

*Overexploration.* High levels of exploration combined with insufficient exploitation creates instability as a consequence of overreactions and excessive information
searches. The organization exaggerates the importance of local errors and becomes
overresponsive to fads and fashions. It creates a vicious circle that results in a
renewal trap characterized by potentially serious problems with conflict of authority, unclear responsibilities, inadequate controls, lack of direction, identity and
shared ideology, and a greater scope for chaos and inefficiency.[66] The continuous
adjustments may waste resources on "noise" in environmental signals. Consequently,
value of existing approaches is continuously destroyed rather than exploited.

**Competence trap**

An overexploitation of
existing competencies
and specialized resources
that is threatening firm's
survival when
environments change

**Renewal trap**

Overexploration of
resources by overreaction
and excessive search
resulting in destroyed
value.

An example of overexploration is evident in the early days of Apple Computer Inc. Apple created the legend of two kids (Steve Wozniak and Steve Jobs) in a garage inventing a computer and then building a company where the old corporate rules were scrapped: no dress or hair codes, no formal meetings. This anarchic culture facilitated renewal, but also fostered chaos and conflict. It led to many clashes between the creators, or the "technical wizards", and the experienced managers hired to run marketing and finance. Year after year, key decisions such as licensing the Mac operating system were postponed, reversed, or avoided completely as various executives and factions tried to push their own agendas.[67]

## A strategic framework of flexibility

Competitive changes force firms to move more quickly and boldly and to experiment in ways that do not conform to traditional administrative theory. In order not to be competed away by the Red Queen effect, firms have to continuously develop and adapt new sources of advantage, and thus become the fastest runner in the Red Queen race. This dynamic process requires new modes of managing and organizing to enable firms to explore new opportunities effectively as well as exploit those opportunities efficiently, to change their strategic focus easily as well as develop some strategic direction, and to change their dominating norms and values as well as correct deviations from essential norms and values. How can firms reconcile these conflicting forces?

The framework proposed here (see Figure 15.3) suggests two important tasks required to resolve the paradox of flexibility.[68] First, it is argued that flexibility is a *managerial task*. Can managers respond at the right time in the right way? In this connection, the concern is with the variety and speed of managerial capabilities that endow the firm with flexibility; for example, manufacturing flexibility to expand the number of products the firm can profitably offer in *task*. Can the organization react at the right time in the directed way? The concern here is with the controllability or changeability of the organization, which depends on the creation of the right conditions to foster flexibility. For instance, manufacturing flexibility requires a technology with multipurpose machinery, universal equipment and an extensive operational production repertoire.[69] Similarly, innovation flexibility requires a structure of multifunctional teams, few hierarchical levels and few process regulations.[70]

Combining the managerial and organization design tasks involves a process of matching and resolving paradoxes. Management must develop dynamic capabilities that enhance flexibility, and the firm must have an adequate organizational design to utilize those capabilities. Consequently, management must cope with a constructive tension between developing capabilities and preserving organizational conditions, which can be considered the building blocks of flexibility. Different companies put these building blocks together in very different ways. From this framework we can therefore obtain several alternative flexible forms, each of which reflects a particular way of coping with the paradox of change and preservation. First, we elaborate on the management and organization design task of flexibility and subsequently we will distinguish various flexible forms.

**The managerial task: developing dynamic capabilities** As a managerial task, flexibility involves the creation or promotion of capabilities for situations that generate unexpected disturbance. The managerial task consists of two core components, variety and speed.

*Variety of managerial capabilities.* The possible emergence of opportunities or threats requires managers to have some potential capabilities as insurance against

## FIGURE 15.3 A strategic framework of flexibility

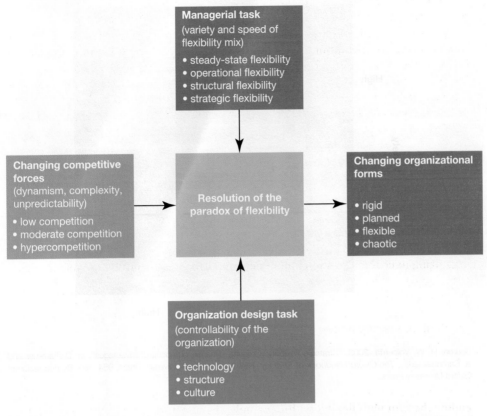

Source: H. W. Volberda, 2003, "Strategic flexibility: Creating dynamic competitive advantages", in: D. Faulkner and A. Campbell (eds.), *The Oxford Handbook of Strategy*, New York: Oxford University Press, 954–955. By permission of Oxford University Press.

risk. To be able to respond to all circumstances, a firm must have a variety of capabilities at least as great as the variety of disturbances in the environment. In a turbulent environment, managers will need an extensive, multidimensional collection of capabilities. Variety can be in terms of either the quantity (the number) of capabilities or the quality of capabilities (e.g. temporary versus durable flexibility-increasing capabilities). For instance, the training of multi-skilled personnel results in a durable improvement in flexibility, whereas the contracting out of certain peripheral activities or "hire-and-fire" employment practices results in a temporary improvement in flexibility. Temporary flexibility-increasing capabilities lead to a reduction of the potential for use once allocated, but durable flexible capabilities are not restricted in use.

*Speed.* Management may have the necessary capabilities, but may not be able to activate them in a timely fashion. Flexibility is not a static condition, but a dynamic process. Speed is therefore an essential factor of organizational flexibility.

The dynamic capabilities that endow the firm with flexibility are manifested in the flexibility mix. Combining different levels of variety and speed of dynamic capabilities, four types of flexibility can be distinguished: steady-state, operational, structural and strategic (see Figure 15.4). Each type represents a simple combination of more/less variety of capabilities and fast/slow response.

Steady-state flexibility (low variety, low speed) consists of static procedures to optimize the firm's performance when the levels of throughput and the nature of

**Steady-state flexibility**

Steady-state flexibility consists of static procedures to optimize the firm's performance when the level of throughput and the nature of throughput remain relatively stable over time.

**FIGURE 15.4** Types of flexibility

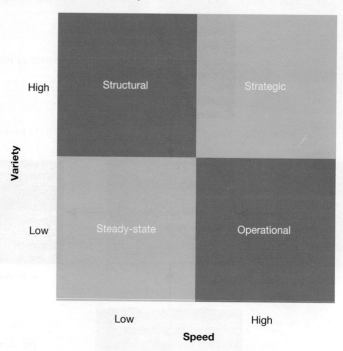

Source: H. W. Volberda, 2003, "Strategic flexibility: Creating dynamic competitive advantages", in: D. Faulkner and A. Campbell (eds.), *The Oxford Handbook of Strategy*, New York: Oxford University Press, 954–955. By permission of Oxford University Press.

throughput remain relatively stable over time. It hardly seems to be a real type of flexibility because under steady-state conditions there is only minor change and a relatively low premium on speed of response to external conditions.

For the other three types of flexibility, a distinction can be made between internal and external flexibility.[71] Internal flexibility is defined as management's capability to adapt to the demands of the environment. External flexibility is defined as management's capability to influence the environment so that the firm becomes less vulnerable to environmental changes. Examples of these types of flexibility are provided in Table 15.2. The table shows that the variety and speed of managerial capabilities may result in various levels of managerial manoeuvring capacity, which can be both internal and external.

Operational flexibility (low variety, high speed) consists of routine capabilities that are based on present structures or goals of the organization. It is the most common type of flexibility and relates to the volume and mix of activities rather than the kinds of activities undertaken within the firm. The routines used are directed primarily at the operational activities and are reactive. Operational flexibility provides rapid response to changes that are familiar. Such changes typically lead to temporary, short-term fluctuations in the firm's level of activity. Although the variety in the environment may be high, the combinations of conditions are sufficiently predictable for management to develop routine capabilities to reduce uncertainty.

Operational flexibility can be internal or external. Examples of internal operational flexibility are the variation of production volume, the building up of inventories and the maintenance of excess capacity. For instance, vertically integrated fashion apparel firms like Benetton have developed "quick-response" capabilities aimed at shortening the manufacturing cycle, reducing inventory levels and enabling

**Operational flexibility**

Operational flexibility consists of routine capabilities based on present structures and goals of the organization, providing the firm with a capacity to respond to dynamic changes in the environment.

**Table 15.2** Examples of internal and external types of flexibility

| | Internal | External |
|---|---|---|
| **Routine manoeuvring capacity** | Internal operational flexibility<br>• variation of production volume<br>• building up of inventories<br>• use of crash teams | External operational flexibility<br>• use of temporary labour<br>• multi-sourcing<br>• reserving of capacity with suppliers |
| **Adaptive manoeuvring capacity** | Internal structural flexibility<br>• creating multifunctional teams<br>• changing managerial roles<br>• alternations in control systems | External structural flexibility<br>• purchasing of components from suppliers with a short delivery time (JIT)<br>• purchasing of subassemblies from suppliers (co-makership)<br>• developing of subcomponents together with suppliers (co-design) |
| **Strategic manoeuvring capacity** | Internal strategic flexibility<br>• dismantling of current strategy<br>• applying new technologies<br>• fundamentally renewing products | External strategic flexibility<br>• creating new product-market combinations<br>• using market power to deter entry and control competitors<br>• engaging in political activities to counteract trade regulations |

Source: H. W. Volberda, 2003, "Strategic flexibility: Creating dynamic competitive advantages", in: D. Faulkner and A. Campbell (eds.), *The Oxford Handbook of Strategy*, New York: Oxford University Press, 954–955. By permission of Oxford University Press.

manufacture in response to sales during the season.[72] These routine capabilities in rapid learning, communication and coordination supplant traditional core competencies in design and fashion sense. Rather than bet on a few designs from the most savvy designers, these firms try out many designs, quickly imitate others and continue to produce what sells. Though product innovations and demand changes are rapid and somewhat unpredictable, introducing new products and responding to changing demands are routine manoeuvring in fashion apparel. New styles and designs do not usually require new types of inputs or process technologies. The object of this kind of internal operational flexibility is a more efficient, less risky operation in a volatile end market. In addition to these internal types, external operational flexibility can be achieved by contracting out certain peripheral activities, using temporary labour to adjust the size of the workforce to shifts in product demand, or obtaining resources from more than one supplier.

Structural flexibility (high variety, low speed) consists of managerial capabilities for adapting the organization structure, and its decision and communication processes, to suit changing conditions in an evolutionary way. When faced with revolutionary changes, management needs great internal structural flexibility or intraorganizational leeway to facilitate the renewal or transformation of current structures and processes. Examples of internal structural flexibility are horizontal or vertical job enlargement; the creation of small production units or work cells within a production line; changes in organizational responsibilities; alterations in

**Structural flexibility**

Structural flexibility consists of managerial capabilities for adapting the organization structure and its decision and communication processes, providing the firm with a capacity to respond to complex changes in the environment.

control systems; the use of project teams; and the transformation from a functional grouping to a market-oriented grouping with interchangeable personnel and equipment.

Structural flexibility can also be external in terms of interorganizational leeway in supporting and sheltering new technologies or developing new products or markets. Examples include various forms of JIT purchasing, co-makership, co-design, or even joint ventures and other co-alignments. By increasing structural relations with outsiders, the organization can engage more easily in new developments. Examples of superior external structural flexibility include large dominating firms or strategic centres such as Nike, Nintendo, Sun Microsystems, and Toyota. These firms responded to increasing competition by forming tight network organizations in which they perform only a few unique functions along the value chain and outsource the remaining functions to specialist partners. Such relationships can be temporary, as in the case of a past alliance between IBM, Intel and Microsoft in the computer industry, or it can endure, as in the long-standing relationships between Nike and its production partners in the athletic footwear and apparel industry. From the focal firm's standpoint, external structural flexibility raises interesting questions about the relative efficacy of internal versus external avenues toward new products, technologies and knowledge. When management retains the opportunity to modify the structural relationship and leave a relationship that no longer meets its needs (external structural flexibility), external avenues can be very attractive. If not, internal avenues by means of internal structural flexibility are more appropriate.

Strategic flexibility (high variety, high speed) consists of managerial capabilities related to the goals of the organization or the environment.[73] This most radical type of flexibility involves changes in the nature of organizational activities. It is necessary when the organization faces unfamiliar changes that have far-reaching consequences and needs to respond quickly. The issues and difficulties relating to strategic flexibility are by definition unstructured and nonroutine. The signals and feedback received from the environment tend to be indirect and open to multiple interpretations, "soft" and "fuzzy". Because the organization usually has no specific experience and no routine answer for coping with the changes, management may have to change its game plans, dismantle its current strategies,[74] apply new technologies, or fundamentally renew its products. Its response may also be external, for example influencing consumers through advertising and promotions, creating new product market combinations, using market power to deter entry and control competitors, or engaging in political activities to counteract trade regulations. New values and norms are necessary and past experience may not provide any advantage. The creation of new activities in new situations may be very important. For instance, regional Bell operating companies that were spun off from AT&T[75] developed strategic flexibility from international expansion activities because the international managers in the unregulated side of the business questioned past practices, raised new assumptions about the organization and promoted significant changes in strategy. The transfer of strategic capabilities from international operations to domestic network operations was helpful in awakening wireline operations to the realities of future competition and the need for employees to be flexible, strategic thinkers.

**Strategic flexibility**

Strategic flexibility consists of dynamic capabilities for adapting the goals of the organization, providing the firm with a capacity to respond to unpredictable changes in the environment.

## The organization design task: creating adequate organizational conditions
The ability to initiate the repertoire of managerial capabilities depends on the design adequacy of organizational conditions, such as the organization's technology, structure and culture. These conditions determine the

organization's controllability or responsiveness. If management tries to increase the flexibility repertoire beyond the limits of organizational conditions, the controllability of the organization will diminish.

Designing the appropriate organizational conditions requires identifying the type of technological, structural or cultural changes necessary to ensure effective utilization of managerial capabilities. For many service and manufacturing organizations, recent developments in organizational technology have created a range of programmable automation systems and general information systems that seem to afford much greater flexibility potential.[76] In this connection, "technology" refers to the hardware (such as machinery and equipment) and the software (knowledge) used in the transformation of inputs into outputs, as well as the configuration of the hardware and software. The design of technology can range from routine to non-routine, corresponding to the opportunities for routine capabilities. In the fashion apparel industry, for instance, those firms that redesigned their technology by implementing new information technologies such as CAD/CAM equipment and EDI developed a much greater potential for operational flexibility.

Increases in controllability might also involve changes in organizational structure (see Chapter 13). Organizational structure comprises not only the actual distribution of responsibilities and authority among the organization's personnel (basic form), but also the planning and control systems and the process regulations of decision-making, coordination, and execution. The structural design of the organization can range from mechanistic to organic,[77] corresponding to the opportunities for adaptive capabilities. Many large corporations such as Shell and Unilever are undertaking organizational restructuring to increase their responsiveness. For instance, Unilever is able to better exploit its superior innovation and market capabilities after fundamentally changing its organizational architecture by creating business divisions with self-organizing teams and developing new reward and recognition systems.

Not only structural changes, but also changes in organizational culture may be necessary to increase the controllability of the firm. Organizational culture can be defined as the set of beliefs and assumptions held relatively commonly throughout the organization and taken for granted by its members. Essential features of such beliefs are that they are implicit in the minds of organization members and to some extent shared. These beliefs may constrain managerial capabilities by specifying broad, tacitly understood rules for appropriate action in unspecified contingencies.[78] The organizational culture can range from conservative to innovative, depending on the slack within the current norms and value systems for strategic capabilities.

The beliefs and assumptions of the organizational culture also play a central role in the interpretation of environmental stimuli and the configuration of organizationally relevant strategic responses.[79] Does the organization see new strategic options? Can it deviate from present patterns? The more innovative the culture, the greater the leeway for strategic flexibility within the organization. Hence, many large Western corporations such as GE, Philips, ABB and Unilever have not only restructured themselves, but also tried to change their corporate cultures. After downsizing and delayering, GE started its famous workout programme, best-practice sessions and change acceleration programme. In the same way, Philips' Centurion programme started with an efficiency drive but was followed by a cultural revitalizing module initiated by the concern committee, Values and Behaviour (the Philips Way). An even more radical cultural change was attempted by ABB, which developed a 21-page "Mission, Values, and Policy" booklet referred to inside the company as the policy bible when it formed its global matrix structure. Also, Unilver's new CEO Paul Polman argued that Unilever's renewal will fail if they only change the structure but try to run the company the way they used to do.

**Organizational technology**

Organizational technology refers to the hardware and the software used in the transformation of inputs into outputs, as well as the configuration of the hardware and software.

**Organizational structure**

Organizational structure comprises the actual distribution of responsibilities and authority among the organization's personnel (basic organizational form), the planning and control systems as well as the process regulations of decision-making, coordination, and execution.

**Organizational culture**

Organizational culture refers to the set of beliefs and assumptions held relatively commonly throughout the organization and taken for granted by its members.

Unilever's new architecture is thus based on changes in the hardware of the company (structure and reward systems) along with changes in the software in the company (leadership, workpractices and values).

# A typology of organizational forms for coping with competitive environments

The strategic framework of flexibility[80] (see Figure 15.3) shows that the managerial task and the organization design task have to be matched with various levels of competition to achieve effective flexibility. Building on this framework four ideal types can be distinguished: the *rigid*, *planned*, *flexible*, and the *chaotic* form. Each type represents a particular way of structurally addressing the flexibility paradox of exploration versus exploitation, and some are more effective than others.

## The rigid form: strategic programming

In a rigid organization management has a very restricted flexibility mix dominated by simple procedures (steady-state flexibility). Its choice and variation possibilities are limited; improvisation is all but forbidden in the organization. Organizational design is characterized by a mature, routine technology and a mechanistic (i.e. centralized and hierarchical) structure. The monotonous and narrow-minded culture (conservative) does not allow potential for flexibility and results in a fragile and vulnerable organization.

The rigid form is often found in static, simple and predictable (i.e. noncompetitive) environments where firms have established positions that enable them to develop absolute sustainable competitive advantages and generate excessive profit potential. In such environments, there is little need for managers to expend effort on a flexibility mix or for the organizational conditions to generate potential for flexibility. Too much flexibility is a nuisance. Strategy is in the rigid form limited to the development of strategic programmes, which are mainly based on extrapolation of existing trends.

## The planned form: strategic planning

The planned form is adequate for firms coping with moderate competition. For survival in such dynamic and complex but largely predictable environments, managers must activate many sophisticated routines. This requires an extensive information-processing capacity and a potential for operational flexibility originating from non-routine technology. The flexibility mix in the planned form therefore consists mainly of specific rules and detailed procedures. Strategic management in the planned firm involves scanning the environment, reducing rivalry and systematically developing strategic plans.

As long as the organization encounters no unexpected changes, its controllability is high. However, if changes occur that are not anticipated in the planning repertoire and are threatening to the idea system shared by its members, the result is a situation known as strategic drift in which consciously managed incremental changes do not necessarily keep pace with environmental changes.[81] The incremental changes result in further attempts by the firm to perfect its process regulations and basic beliefs and assumptions. These attempts increase organizational inertia, and rigidity sets in. The rigidity of this organizational form is not a result of the technology or the basic organizational structure, but of strong process regulations

**Strategic drift**

A process towards rigidity due to the fact that consciously managed incremental changes in the organization do not keep pace with more radical environmental changes.

such as standardization, formalization and specialization, and very detailed planning and control systems. Also, the shared cultural beliefs and assumptions of its members give very little leeway for deviant interpretations of the environment, and dissonance is potentially threatening to the organization's integrity.

## The flexible form: adaptive strategies

In contrast to the planned form, the *flexible form* has an extensive flexibility mix dominated by strategic and structural flexibility. In addition, its ability to change its organizational conditions is reasonably high. It effectively adapts to disturbances without the organization losing its distinctiveness. The innovative culture helps the firm to constructively incorporate new perspectives. They can be implemented easily through adaptations within the current (nonroutine) technology and (organic) structure. At the same time, it develops some dominance over its environment to preserve its identity, and effects a balance between exploration and exploitation.

Flexible forms are effective in fundamentally unpredictable environments, which may also be dynamic and complex. In such hypercompetitive environments, management must activate both strategic flexibility and structural flexibility, which originate from innovative culture and organic structure. The escalating degree of competition results in short periods of advantage punctuated by frequent disruptions, which are associated with departures from current approaches that reduce the value of established commitments and competence and require fundamentally new capabilities. Hypercompetition is facilitated by the disequilibrium-creating activities of firms that are capable of breaking new ground, pioneering new fields, promoting radical innovation, and partially or completely transforming the organization in the process. Instead of building on current routines as a part their operational flexibility, such firms develop high levels of structural and strategic flexibility.

Strategic management in flexible firms therefore requires intelligence-gathering and information-processing directed towards enhancing the receptiveness to new environments and increasing the learning capacity of management. The signals and feedback received in such unpredictable environments are very indirect and open to multiple interpretations. The problems are by definition unstructured and nonroutine and the scarce information is very soft and fuzzy. Extrapolation or other conventional management tools are not useful in this context. New values and norms are necessary and past experience may not provide any advantage. It involves a change in the criteria of evaluation; past practices need to be questioned, new assumptions about the organization have to be raised, and significant changes in strategy have to be considered.

## The chaotic form: spontaneous strategies

Finally, the *chaotic form* has a very extensive flexibility mix dominated by strategic flexibility, but is totally uncontrollable. In organizations with this form, the possibilities for variation are unlimited because there is no anchorage within a set of basic organizational conditions. The innumerable initiatives for change are impossible to implement. Chaotic organizations have no distinct technology, stable administrative structure, or basic shared values stemming from their organizational culture. Consequently, the environment can push a chaotic organization in any direction. A chaotic organization's lack of administrative stability is caused by strategic neglect, which denotes the deliberate tendency of managers not to pay attention to the administrative structure of the organization.[82] As a consequence of the lack of strong strategic orientation and a stable structure, managers' decision-making capacity is greatly reduced. Decisions are delayed although the situation requires an immediate decision.

**Strategic neglect**

A process towards chaos and reduction of decision-making capacity due to the deliberate tendency of management not to pay attention to a shared strategic orientation or a stable structure.

On the basis of our framework we can argue that flexible modes are most likely to prosper in dynamic rugged landscapes with many peaks, planned modes in sloping hilly landscapes with moderate competition, while rigid modes seem only to survive in quiet valleys with stable competition. The chaotic mode seems to be locked in a Red Queen race, without being able to sustain competitive advantages. The chaotic mode tries to move faster than the company can actually achieve. Management overreacts to competitive change and the organization is unable to respond. Although the chaotic form has a negative connotation, this mode can however be helpful for regulated firms that are confronted with increasing competition. To unlearn old routines and existing monopolistic mindsets, the chaotic mode can be an effective temporary alternative. In particular, resource-rich firms can use chaotic forms to quickly develop new capabilities in their unregulated business.

## Single and dual trajectories of renewal

Each of the four discussed organizational forms enable firms to initiate or respond successfully to different levels of competition. None of these forms however create a permanent solution. Shift may occur in the level of competition, and the organization has to prevent itself from overshooting and becoming extremely rigid or chaotic. On the basis of the extensiveness of the flexibility mix (simple routines versus dynamic capabilities) and the controllability or responsiveness of the organization (low versus highly controllable), we distinguish various renewal trajectories for coping with changing levels of competition: the natural trajectory of routinization, and the reverse trajectory of revitalization (see Figure 15.5).

**FIGURE 15.5**  A typology of organizational forms for coping with hypercompetition

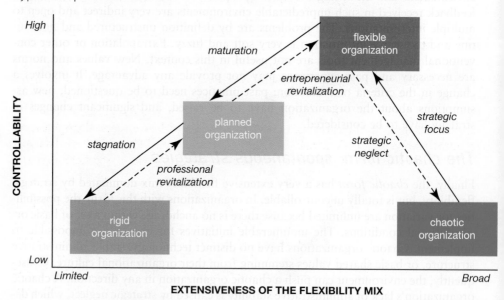

Source: H. W. Volberda, 1998, *Building the flexible firm: How to remain competitive*, Oxford: Oxford University Press. By permission of Oxford University Press.

## The natural trajectory of routinization: decreasing levels of competition

The most likely trajectory firms go through is a transition from a chaotic state to flexible, planned and rigid forms. During this process of decreasing levels of competition, management's increased capacity to process information facilitates the rapid increase of routines, thus creating natural trajectories of evolution towards static fit.[83] These trajectories correspond with those in evolutionary theory,[84] which holds that radical change becomes less possible as the organization ages.

The natural trajectory of routinization suggests that starting entrepreneurial firms and new ventures operate chaotically in order to develop new capabilities. This state of loose and unsettled relationships is organic and responds easily to environmental change, but necessarily has slack and is inefficient.[85] To "get off the ground", this form must be sufficiently well organized to change from a chaotic state of random, disconnected and uncoordinated impulses. This transition requires a capacity for achieving some degree of *strategic focus*.

As the level of competition decreases, the flexible organization faces a crisis. It must become more efficient in its operations to extract greater benefit from the changes that it introduced previously, and to exploit its existing knowledge and opportunities. These change efforts are particularly important if the organization is to stay ahead of its imitators and other competitors, which are busy enhancing their competencies. The transition from a flexible form toward a planned form can be portrayed as a process of *maturation*.[86] Maturation requires a greater need for the firm to professionalize and institutionalize its intelligence-gathering and information-processing functions, and to integrate efforts of its decision makers by formal means (process regulations). Whereas managers in the flexible form may have gathered information quite informally on their own, the firm must now set up systems and departments to gather certain types of information routinely and to disseminate this information to appropriate decision makers.

However, in the process of adapting and refining the organizational conditions to efficiently exploit time and response opportunities, the planned organization runs the risk of losing its strategic and structural flexibility as it concentrates increasingly on accumulating and optimizing a large number of operational procedures and routines (operational flexibility). In such circumstances, it may become progressively more rigid. In this progression toward *stagnation*,[87] the routinization and systematization of organizational conditions bring bureaucratic momentum, traditions, and resistance to change. These all play an important role in boosting conservatism. As a result, the rigid form is characterized by a reduced emphasis on product-market innovation, risk-taking and proactiveness. The rigid form has pursued the development of specialized routines at the cost of decreased flexibility and innovative capacity.

Many large corporate giants such as GE, IBM and Philips realized years ago that they went too far with this process of routinization and created extremely rigid organizations. They want to be revitalized in more flexible or even chaotic forms. As discussed previously, many theorists doubt, however, that large, established firms can self-consciously change themselves very much or very often, or that conscious initiatives by management are likely to succeed (see the prior discussion on selection theories). They argue that older, larger corporations must die-off, like dinosaurs, to be succeeded by a new breed better adapted to its environment. Others[88] have demonstrated that mature firms can become flexible enough to balance corporate discipline with entrepreneurial creativity (see the prior discussion of adaptation theories). In fact, there are many routes mature corporations might take to effect

**Natural trajectory of routinization**

A process of accumulation of specialized routines and fine-tuning of organizational conditions when firms age and competition decreases.

this goal. On the basis of our typology, we will provide a more systematic analysis of alternative renewal trajectories directed towards "revitalization" of mature or declining organizations. Such trajectories are most likely to be effective in extremely competitive environments.

## The reversed trajectory of revitalization: escalating levels of competition

For many organizations, the transition from a chaotic state toward a rigid organization can be regarded as a natural trajectory. A transition in the reverse direction can also be perceived as a trajectory, though it may not be as easy to achieve or seem as "natural" as the former process. Such trajectories of revitalization, initiated for creating temporary disequilibria, are most likely to be effective under situations of hypercompetition.

The dangers for rigid organizations in non-competitive environments stem from their increasing vulnerability to the occurrence of major change in their environments, and from the exhaustion of profitable opportunities obtainable in these niches. As organizations are confronted by low and diminishing returns from established product lines and rapidly escalating competition from numerous rivals in the same field, they must seek to exploit opportunities flowing from more unstable environments, or attempt to generate major innovations. Confronted with escalating levels of competition, they face the task of shifting back toward the flexibility mix and the organizational conditions of the planned organization. This transition, or *professional revitalization*, involves the comprehensive and often dramatic movement away from traditions, conservatism and rigidity, and toward adaptiveness, vigilance and diversification.[89] Such a trajectory was evident within ING's former Postbank division. In the past, its main line of business had been retail banking because of restrictions imposed by the Dutch government. It provided mostly standardized services to more than six million account holders. After its acquisition by ING, it intended to provide more customized services as a part of corporate banking. It was confronted, however, with increasing national and international competition, new information technologies in banking, increased pressure on interest margins, and the introduction of new banking-related services. The Postbank division, which was bureaucratically organized for a non-competitive environment, had to adopt a more comprehensive flexibility mix dominated by operational flexibility, which in turn originated from a more adaptive technology (broadly applicable information systems) and a larger operational skill repertoire by employees.

When professional revitalization proves inadequate, the planned organization must transform itself further into a more flexible form. Although planned forms have developed a great number of complex routine capabilities, they are seriously handicapped when confronted with hypercompetition. This change in the composition of the flexibility mix can be realized only if the organization moves toward even more flexible or multipurpose technologies, develops a more organic structure, and adopts a more heterogeneous, open and externally oriented culture. Such efforts help to promote asymmetry within the previous organizational form while propelling the organization toward the creation of new temporary advantages better suited to hypercompetitive environments. This process of *entrepreneurial revitalization* is promoted by such changes as new leadership composed of visionary entrepreneurs, reduction of process regulations (specialization, formalization), loose organizational forms (grouping by target market, flat structure and broad management tasks), a more open external orientation and a high tolerance for ambiguity.

**Trajectories of revitalization**

A process of developing dynamic capabilities and transforming organizational conditions to cope with increasing levels of competition.

A transition of entrepreneurial revitalization occurred within Philips Semiconductors. The rapidly escalating competition in cost and quality (price erosion and unforeseen volume developments) and in timing and know-how (introduction of plastic diodes, release of higher voltages version, new crystal types and the advance of integrated circuits in the application markets), forced the firm to increase its structural and strategic flexibility to more easily exploit unknown opportunities in those hypercompetitive areas. It effected this entrepreneurial revitalization by radically transforming itself from a bureaucratic, conservative company into an innovative and responsive one. Managers initiated autonomous task groups, created interdisciplinary marketing-production-development teams, used less formal planning and control systems, developed a unique logo for the plant, and organized social events, special training and a news bulletin for employees. The combination of these efforts made the transformation possible.

If the organization successfully transforms itself, it faces the opposite danger of overshooting its target and becoming chaotic. For example, the R&D department of the Dutch National Gas Corporation had unlimited potential for flexibility, but managers could not capitalize on it. In other words, the department was too flexible. The department had many initiatives for new research, but it could not implement them because it had no clear administrative structures or shared values stemming from its culture. Nor did it have adequate information about man-hours, costs, or technical progress per project. The schizophrenia of the department resulted in distorted information that managers could not use to make appropriate decisions. Consequently, various environmental forces (board, internal clients) could force the department in any direction. This *strategic neglect* resulted in a lack of decisiveness about research priorities, a fragmented structure and a loose constellation of subcultures. Creating change requires some stability. Organizational structures and cultures must allow continuity and preserve the organization in the midst of change. In particular, strong social ties and strong beliefs in fundamental values create stability for the organization. If successful revitalization is not anchored in stability, it runs the danger of provoking chaos.[90]

## Dual renewal trajectories in multi-unit organizations

So far, the typology of various flexible forms has been applied to a division or business unit with only one line of business. However, evidence of corporate transformations in regulated companies suggests that if multiple levels or multiple parts are considered, dual renewal trajectories for coping with hypercompetition can be found in a single company. We will consider these dual renewal trajectories because they illustrate how large established firms can create flexibility to successfully cope with increasing competition. Such a dual-trajectory model of organizational transformation may be of value to regulated companies, such as electric utilities, railway and post companies that must address dramatically changing competitive forces. In increasingly competitive environments (e.g. the introduction of competition in a nearly monopolistic industry), areas of chaos should perhaps be created or tolerated by top management, while core activities should move along a revitalization path.

**Dual migration paths** Such dual migration paths were found in TNT. TNT Post was made up of several business units (letters, parcel service, mediaservice, international, EMS, logistics, philately) and joint ventures (Post Offices, GD Express Worldwide, Interpost Group of Companies). It was preparing itself for the transition from a highly regulated environment to a more competitive one. To revitalize

**STRATEGIC FOCUS**

© Steven May/Alamy

# Radical transformation of KLM Cargo

KLM Cargo, a division of Air France KLM, is one of the world's leading air cargo carriers. It intends to rank among the top three customer-driven suppliers of high-quality transport, distribution and information services worldwide. It has embarked on a radical change programme, turning itself inside out in the process, to fulfil this mission.

A major step in this endeavour occurred in 1989 with the development of the KLM corporate programme vision '93, which led to the reconfirmation of the airline's core activities and the creation of two divisions: passenger and cargo. In 1994, KLM Cargo launched the "division in transition" programme, which incorporated not only issues of strategy and structure but the determination to effect behavioural change throughout the organization. Until then, KLM's main cargo activities were made up of predominantly generic transport services, which are packaged and supplied to the end-user. The margin on these generic services has been slowly eroded: carriers can provide

these services only if the highest priority is given to efficiency. Moreover, KLM Cargo did not know who its clients were, and their customers – the freight forwarding agents – frequently turned out to be their competitors. KLM Cargo's new strategy was therefore based on end-customers that are prepared to pay extra for value-added products, the exact nature of which differs from client to client. This move towards an organization that will be able to offer yet more added value to clients required a shift from air network, which offers a distributed network with a central hub, to air logistics or even full logistics. Essentially, all providers of base commodities (airlines, truckers, shipping lines) find that the further they move downstream towards the customer, the more their perspectives need to shift from mono-modal to multi-modal, and from basic transportation services to more complete logistics service options.

In realizing this fundamental change, the creation of an entirely different mindset was most important. It now had to perceive itself as provider of integrated logistics instead of an airline operator with only transport and distribution services. This unlearning of its old strategic schema and relearning of a new one required it to invest heavily in flexible capabilities to provide a variety of customized added-value services. Furthermore, it decided to fundamentally redesign the organization. Thus, it flattened the organization and arranged its functions into three disciplines (operations, sales and customer service), five business units (cargo service centres, which perform handling activities; mail; IT; logistics; and a special cargo unit, which is responsible for such cargoes as perishables, valuables and live animals); and seven staff departments. The obvious reason for this structural change was to get closer to customers, cutting down the bureaucracy, and empowering people to act innovatively and swiftly.

In less than a year, it had managed to change its geographic hierarchical structure into a flat dual structure with central functional departments and autonomous business units. Everybody had to reapply for new management positions and managers often had to move from one continent to another. Furthermore, it created self-organizing teams in the factory. In order to facilitate these fundamental changes, management organized awareness courses, training seminars and interactive workshops.

Although this radical change from a rigid towards a chaotic state created momentum for change, it also

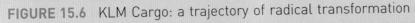

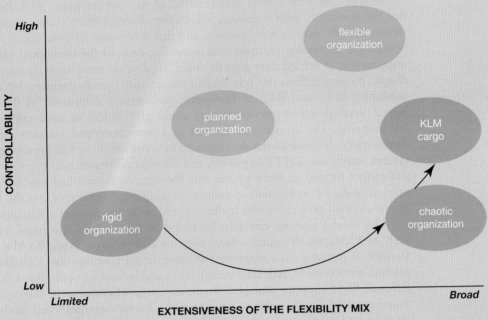

**FIGURE 15.6** KLM Cargo: a trajectory of radical transformation

caused some major problems. First, the applicability of both information systems and the skill repertoire of employees (rigidity of technology) to new services was very limited. Moreover, the splitting of the division into functional departments (sales, operations and customer service) and five business units (cargo service centre, mail, IT, logistics, and special cargo) resulted in large sequential interdependencies and fights about who owns the customer. Furthermore, there was much resistance from lower-level managers who were not involved in the change process (cultural values). In order to exploit its newly developed capabilities, management standardized the service portfolio (commodities, specialties and customized) and developed a more transparent structure in which a new department business system was responsible for more efficient coordination. In addition, management tightened its strategic vision and developed a code of conduct for communicating the common cultural values in KLM Cargo. After the transformation, KLM Cargo

could be positioned somewhere between the flexible and the chaotic mode (see figure 15.6).

**Sources**: Volberda, H. W. (1998) *Building the Flexible Firm: How to Remain Competitive*, Oxford; Oxford University Press; Volberda, H. W. (2003) "Strategic flexibility: Creating dynamic competitive advantages" in: Faulkner, D. O. and Campbell, A. (eds.), *The Oxford Handbook of Strategy*, Oxford: Oxford University Press, 939–998.

## Questions

1 Why did KLM Cargo not follow a less risky trajectory of sequential revitalization from a rigid to a planned to a flexible mode?

2 What were the problems the management of KLM Cargo faced when they chose to radically transform the division from a rigid to a chaotic state?

3 Analyse the required roles of management for these dual trajectories to succeed.

its core activities and exploit new growth opportunities, it initiated several change projects such as Mail 2000, Tele-present, and New Formulas for the Post Office network. In the Mail 2000 project it worked together with A.T. Kearny on improving its competencies in physical transport and distribution of mail, still its core business. By automating the sorting process and reducing the number of sorting hubs, it increased the steady-state and operational flexibility of its primary process. In the Post Office project, it adopted a McDonald's formula to focus on the client.

Despite this professional revitalization of its core activities, TNT Post realized that the amount of mail it delivers will further decrease due to other communication means, that its margins will diminish, and that wages and inflation increase. To compensate for decreasing revenues and increasing costs of the traditional planned post organization, it needed new growth areas. To develop these areas, it started various chaotic projects such as the Tele-Present project with outside partners, VNU (a Dutch publishing firm) and RTL (a European mediaservice company). In this project it helped develop a new service: clients could give orders to send gifts, a kind of tele-shopping. The service was located in a new developed business unit, namely mediaservice. It required the development of a call centre, a tele-present information system, warehousing (PTT Logistics), and distribution (Parcel Service). For TNT Post, this project formed an entry avenue into the electronic super-highway and the development of data distribution capabilities. In addition, this venture was the forerunner of a multi-mall project, in which clients could order products in a virtual store.

This dual trajectory can also be found in firms facing less-regulated markets such as KLM, which actually faces extreme competition. While KLM's Passenger Division is working on a trajectory of professional revitalization (continuously improving service levels, reducing overall costs and increasing operational flexibility in terms of flight capacity and personnel), its Cargo Division went through a radical transformation from a rigid to an extremely chaotic organizational mode (offering an increased number of value-added services to customers, attracting new customers, and providing non-transport related logistic services) and is now slowly shifting towards a more flexible mode (categorizing the service portfolio, a more transparent structure, tightening the strategic vision, and developing Cargo values and a code of conduct).

For these dual trajectories to succeed, top managers must be able to tolerate the presence of initially chaotic modes so that learning takes place. On the other hand, they should have some business intuition of when to intervene, focus on certain activities, give additional resources, or terminate activities. Moreover, one may ask when it is appropriate for management to choose a sequential revitalization from a rigid to a planned to a flexible mode, and when it should choose to radically transform the organization from a rigid to a chaotic to a flexible mode. A radical transformation is less time-consuming, but more risky because the scope of change is large and the content of change is most difficult. It requires the organization to transform quickly and in a holistic manner, which carries severe dangers. There is a risk that the organization will disintegrate into chaos. Sequential revitalization will therefore be most effective when the firm is not concerned with speedy reaction. By contrast, radical transformation will be more effective when there is a pressing need for the organization to respond collectively.

## Towards sustained strategic renewal: permanent solutions for the multi-unit firm

From our typology, trajectories of organizational "success and failure" in meeting various levels of competition were obtained. In the old mode of competition in which firms' attention is directed toward reducing the level of competition, a natural trajectory of routinization is most likely. In the new mode of rapid, escalating hypercompetition, a trajectory of revitalization is more likely to be successful.

To be front runner in hypercompetitive environments of the Red Queen, firms must continuously increase the variety and speed of their flexible capabilities as well as their organizational responsiveness. Of course, we have to realize that both trajectories have their pitfalls.

The risk of a trajectory of routinization is that it will transform the firm into a rigid form as a result of strategic drift. The surplus of operational flexibility, consisting of sophisticated routines, creates inertia in the form of a very mechanistic structure and a very narrowly focused culture. Growing resistance in an organization to "deviant" interpretations of the environment reflects a tendency toward "overbalance" of the rigid form. On the other hand, a trajectory of revitalization risks turning a firm into a "chaotic form" as a result of "strategic neglect". The surplus of structural and strategic flexibility in this situation can lead to unfocused actions with dysfunctional results. The chaotic form's lack of administrative structures, sense of direction, shared beliefs and institutional leadership is characteristic of a tendency towards "underbalance" of the chaotic form.

Thus, in the long run, neither of these trajectories seems to provide permanent solutions for competing in hypercompetitive environments. Firms have to cope with different levels of competition at the same time and need efficient exploitation as well as superior exploration. In terms of our typology, these organizations need properties of the flexible, planned, or even chaotic forms at the same time or in different portions of the corporation. Is there a more permanent solution? What can firms do to reconcile, or at least relax, the seemingly irreconcilable tensions between exploration and exploitation in the long run?

Recent studies have identified various organizational forms in which firms can successfully balance sufficient levels of both exploration and exploitation without having to undergo continuous structural change. This term has been coined ambidexterity, as an analogy with reference to the ability (of a person) to use both hands with equal dexterity. Figure 15.7 provides a framework for understanding different modes of balancing exploration and exploitation by juxtaposing the underlying temporal and structural dimensions.[91]

## Organizational ambidexterity: generic modes of balancing exploration and exploitation

Contextual ambidexterity entails managing the tensions of exploration and exploitation concurrently within organizational units. The link between exploration and exploitation is also assumed to be orthogonal, that is, high levels of both types of activities can be achieved simultaneously. To achieve this balancing mode involves "building a set of processes or systems that enable and encourage individuals to make their own judgments about how to divide their time between conflicting demands [for exploration and exploitation]".[92] Large corporations such as 3M and HP have developed structures and cultures to achieve this balancing act. Against their minimal structures, they developed a strong culture dominated by corporate values like trust, respect for individuals, uncompromising integrity and teamwork.

3M, for example, continually reassesses the barriers to flexibility that tend to develop over time. In order to overcome core rigidities, 3M has a formal goal of having 30 per cent of its sales derived from products that are new or have been substantially modified in the past four years. HP is also pursuing structures and cultures that are more focused on building new competencies. Like 3M, HP decentralized decision making at the team and divisional level, and encouraged spin-off projects. In addition, the company constantly seeks ways of making its current technology obsolete in order to push the innovation envelope of its assets. For example,

**Ambidexterity**

Ambidexterity is the ability to achieve high levels of exploration and exploitation.

**Contextual ambidexterity**

Simultaneous pursuit of exploitation and exploration within an organizational unit by creating an organizational context that stimulates individuals to do both.

**FIGURE 15.7**  Generic modes of balancing exploration and exploitation

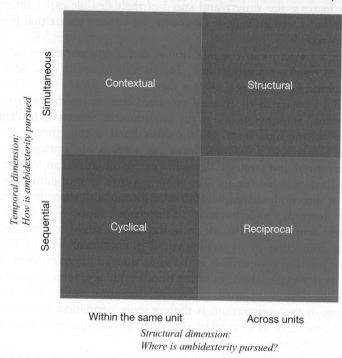

Source: Adapted from Z. Simsek, C. Heavy, J. F. Veiga and D. Souder, 2009, "A typology for aligning organizational ambidexterity's conceptualizations, antecedents, and outcomes", *Journal of Management Studies*, 46: 864–894. Reproduced by permission of John Wiley & Sons.

70 per cent of HP's sales are represented by products introduced or substantially modified in the past two years.[93]

Structural ambidexterity entails designing the organization in such a form that it consist of highly differentiated units with targeted structural integration. It is considered as an interdependent, simultaneous phenomenon, involving the compartmentalizing and synchronizing of exploitation and exploration within different structural units or divisions of an organization. Thus high levels of both exploration and exploitation are possible and each unit exhibits internal consistency in tasks, culture and organizational arrangements, but across units there is inconsistency in the activities being pursued. The main managerial challenge is to coordinate the integration of the various inputs and outputs between units that, by design, will have the inclination to become disconnected silos. Mechanisms for integration include cross-functional interfaces, informal connectedness between members of different units, job rotation, social integration at senior team level and periodic reorganizations.[94]

In almost every diversified firm, one sees asymmetry between high-growth businesses and older, mature operations. That is, mature divisions confronted with moderate competition operate in a planned mode, whereas some new divisions developed to create or counter hypercompetitive disruption may operate in a flexible or even chaotic mode.[95] We can distinguish separation by location in different degrees, varying from the creation of skunk works,[96] corporate ventures,[97] to even completely new venture departments. At the simplest level, we can think of isolating a flexible unit from a rigid operating core. This principle was applied at IBM when the IBM PC was developed, as the mainframe logic was strongly preserved in IBM's culture and prevented entry into the new PC market. While at first IBM was very successful with this isolation strategy, it found that transferring these new capabilities from the flexible mode to the rigid operating core was very difficult. IBM could not exploit these capabilities in its operating core because it lacked communication channels and common mental frames. Similarly, Eastman Kodak, Philips and Xerox have had only modest success from their internal venturing and new business development programmes.

A more complicated form of separation involves the continuous splitting off of groups into separate organizations. Hewlett Packard, Johnson & Johnson and Origin are examples of corporations that have developed a system of small, semi-autonomous units, and encourage entrepreneurs to pursue their ideas in new separate divisions, while the older, more established divisions provide continuity and stability.[98] Overall, the organization appears to be in a perpetual stage of adaptation, never really rigid or planned as long as new units are being regularly spun off from the older ones. This process is best described as a regular cell fission, characterized by ongoing entrepreneurial revitalization. However, the downside to this cell structure is that such corporations may become overly divisionalized, and have problems with exploiting synergies across certain businesses. Because of continuous fission, these organizations risk losing their identity and becoming uncontrollable.

Cyclical ambidexterity finds the firm focusing the allocation of resources and attention to exploration and exploitation in oscillating fashion. This mode of balancing assumes exploration and exploitation as polar opposites and involves a system of temporal cycling in which organizations alternate between long periods of exploitation and short potent bursts of exploration. It enables organizations to balance exploration and exploitation by shifting from one activity to the other over time. A key challenge in this form is managing of the transition between the various states, as the organization is most vulnerable during the transitional phase.

For small entrepreneurial firms, this dynamic alternation between flexible and planned organizational modes (for respectively exploration and exploitation) is part of their existence and competitive advantage. Their lack of tight commitments and relatively low sunk costs enable them to easily undertake radical change. For large corporations, complete transformations are much more complicated and nearly impossible. However, Microsoft provides an illustration that large organizations can also change. The company initiates a corporate redesign every eight months in order to remain competitive because in the software industry the fully flexible company of today will be the rigid organization of tomorrow. Case histories of large capital-intensive corporations such as DSM Chemicals, Shell and Unilever that operate in cyclical industries also give us examples of firms that have been successful in managing alternate cycles of convergence and divergence. In the process of frequent change, however, oscillating corporations have to prevent themselves from "overshooting" and becoming extremely rigid or chaotic.

Reciprocal ambidexterity requires that organizations strive towards balance across domains of activity. In this mode they do not need to reconcile exploration and exploitation within each domain, as long as an overall balance is maintained across domains. This implies that for instance, a firm may explore upstream and exploit downstream, or vice versa.[99] This mode is characterized by relationships that embody ongoing information exchange, collaborative problem solving, joint decision making, and resource flows between the managers in charge of the different domains responsible for exploitation and exploration. An emerging view of this mode is balancing activities by hierarchical separation of explorative and exploitative conditions. Responsibility for exploration can, for instance, increase and decrease with organizational rank.[100]

**Cyclical ambidexterity**

Sequential pursuit of exploitation and exploration within an organizational unit over time.

**Reciprocal ambidexterity**

Sequential pursuit of exploitation and exploration across domains, functions and hierarchical levels.

An example of a *hierarchical distinction* can be found in the traditional multi-unit (M-) form, in which top management operates in a flexible mode and has a high absorptive capacity for exploring new business opportunities (see also Chapter 13). In this setting, the divisions operate best in the planned mode for maximally exploiting these business opportunities; they change only as a result of the strategic intent of top management. The new corporate form of GE emerging from Jack Welch's redesign efforts is a more sophisticated version of such a hierarchically divisionalized structure.[101] Yet, we can also think of corporations in which the strategic exploration of new opportunities takes place at the lowest level; interactions with the market and demanding clients cause front-line managers to call into question their norms, objectives and basic policies. Corporate management operates in the planned mode, which permits it to persist in its set policies and achieve formulated objectives, which change as a result of autonomous behaviour of front-line managers. This reversed hierarchy can be found in 3M.

Another form of separation, namely by *function*, can be found in nearly all corporations. Usually, production departments operate in a rigid or planned mode for reasons of efficiency and scale, marketing departments operate in a more flexible mode since they are exposed to various customer demands, while R&D departments that are engaged in highly unpredictable research projects operate in a chaotic mode. More extreme examples of functional separation for solving the flexibility paradox can be found in Honda and KLM Cargo. In order to make functional tensions visible, Honda broke itself apart in a far more radical fashion than had ever occurred in its industry.[102] R&D and Engineering were split into two separate companies. While Honda Motor Company (with sales and manufacturing) is the parent and primary customer, each of the three companies now has its own distinct identity and specific organizational mode. The tensions between these companies, each highly independent, yet interdependent, are not suppressed, but serve as the engine of change and renewal.

Similarly, KLM Cargo decided to split its Cargo Factory (handling, warehouse management and flight network control), in which volume and efficiency are most important, from the business units, in which service, market penetration and the development of new logistic services dominate. The functional separation allows each business unit to respond to various well-defined markets, but still share in processes and technologies. Yet, dividing a corporation into its functional parts can result in dysfunctional tensions and a fragmented organization that has lost its synergies. In Honda, the shared culture is strong enough to handle stress without tearing. In KLM Cargo, the lack of this increased the need for setting rules and guidelines on how to use shared assets. Management thus decided to create a new unit, Cargo Business Systems, which is responsible for coordination, systemization and organization of the core processes.

Finally, in the context of alliances, firms can differentially explore or exploit within and across three domains namely: value chain function (upstream versus downstream alliances), network structure (existing versus new partners), and partner attributes (similar versus dissimilar to prior partners).[103] When organizations engage in recurrent R&D alliances with their existing partners, exploration in the function domain is traded off with exploitation in the structure domain.

In sum, extremity in either exploration or exploitation may create dysfunctions in the form of rigidity or chaos. Only flexible firms that somehow solve the seemingly paradoxical combination of exploration and exploitation may win the Red Queen race of dynamic competition. Table 15.3 summarizes the core elements of the different balancing modes.

Table 15.3 Overview of balancing modes

| Balancing mode | Contextual | Structural | Cyclical | Reciprocal |
|---|---|---|---|---|
| **Locus of balance** | Individual and group levels | Organizational level | Organizational level | Aggregate across domains |
| **Mechanisms** | Mutual adjustment and employee empowerment; No buffers between concurrent exploration and exploitation | Separate units dedicated/division of labour and structure dedicated to either exploration or exploitation, simultaneously coordinated at the corporate level | Sequential shifts over time from exploration to exploitation and vice versa | Exploring in one domain while simultaneously exploiting in another |
| **Main challenges** | Managing contradictions within organizational units; Managing conflict; Measuring individual performance/ contribution; Staffing qualified individuals with high tolerance for ambiguity | Coordinating across units and managing contradictions at the senior team level; Determining levels of differentiation and integration necessary between units; Comparability of performance indicators across different units | Managing transitions between exploration and exploitation; Dislodging from inertial pressures | Identifying applicable domains; Deciding whether to explore or exploit in any given domain |
| **Tension between exploration/ exploitation assumed** | Orthogonal | Orthogonal | Continuum | Continuum (within domain); orthogonal between |

Source: Adapted from D. Lavie, U. Stettner and M. L. Tushman, 2010, "Exploration and exploitation within and across organizations", *The Academy of Management Annals*, 4: 109–155. Used by kind permission of the Academy of Management.

# Mastering strategic renewal journeys within multi-unit firms: exploring the different roles of managers

In previous sections, strategic renewal has been conceptualized as a firm's strategic development path of explorative and exploitative strategic renewal actions to align the company to the changing environment. We have considered various renewal trajectories and discussed various multi-unit forms to deal with the tensions between exploitation and exploration. However, we have not explicitly detailed the various roles of management in these renewal processes. Scholars[104] have argued that these strategic renewal trajectories are conjointly driven by two forces: (1) external selection forces

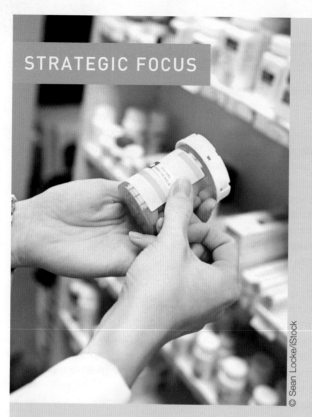

## STRATEGIC FOCUS

© Sean Locke/iStock

# Balancing on the edge of the patent cliff

The global pharmaceutical industry is one of the most profitable sectors in the world. The large knowledge-intensive incumbents are built around a model of drug discovery, development and commercialization. These so-called "Big Pharma" companies – multibillion pharmaceutical corporations like Pfizer, Merck, Eli Lilly and GlaxoSmithKline (GSK) – rely on "blockbuster" drugs that generate billions of euros in annual sales. On average, it takes about €500 million to develop a drug. This amount covers everything from early pre-clinical trials, the three phases of the Food and Drug Administration (FDA) approvals and marketing costs. Only one in 10 early-stage drugs eventually make it to the market, with the odds rising to 20 per cent at Phase II and 50 per cent at Phase III.

Alhough Big Pharma companies spend a third of their R&D budget on early-stage drug development, the established industry model has become one where their core competencies have shifted away from new drug discovery. Nowadays, they acquire knowledge from outside parties, integrating them into therapeutic packages or drugs, fund the clinical trials,

manage regulators and commercialize the drugs. These partners are often smaller, flexible, biotech firms, universities and other research institutions which specialize in exploring new avenues and discovering the breakthrough molecular and genetic components for potentially new blockbuster drugs, which Big Pharma can subsequently exploit under patent exclusivity.

Patent exclusivity is essential within the pharmaceutical industry, where the market exclusivity enables companies to enjoy a period of high profitability necessary to justify the high costs of development for a novel therapeutic. New drugs are patented for 20 years from initial patent filing. However, since it takes about a decade to get a drug on the market, firms effectively have about 7–10 years to recoup their investment. Generic drug makers wait for the patents to expire, take the formula that costs hundreds of billions of dollars to develop, and reproduce. Since they have none of the up-front invested research costs to recover, they can easily undercut the prices of the original developer of the drug. Consequently, generics can cost as much as 90 per cent less than brand name drugs. According to EvaluatePharma, a London-based consulting firm, blockbuster drugs, generating over a €100 billion in annual sales, are threatened by generics between 2011 and 2014 as patents expire,. According to IMH Health, more than €40 billion worth of drugs are going "off patent" by 2011. Key expiries within the pharmaceutical sector will intensify from 2011 onwards, affecting some of the biggest brands in the industry, such as Pfizer's Lipitor, and almost three-quarters of Eli Lilly's patents within the next seven years. As Big Pharma approaches this "patent cliff", desperate incumbents run to the market to acquire specialized biotech firms with novel breakthroughs, inflating the price of novel therapy acquisitions due to competitive bidding. "We have the challenge of replenishing our product portfolio from our pipeline," said John Lechleiter, CEO of Eli Lilly in an interview in 2010.

Take the British drugmaker GSK for instance. Ten of its medicines have accounted for 65 per cent of revenues in 2008. When one of these drugs – Avandia, a diabetes treatment – was linked with an increased risk of heart attack, GSK lost over €10 billion from its market value. Next to that, GSK lost patent exclusivity to several blockbuster drugs from 2006 to 2008, including Wellbutrin XL, Lemactil, Zofran, Valtrex and Coreg. By the second quarter of 2008, sales of Coreg, a heart medication, fell 97 per cent after the introduction of generic competition in September 2007. GSK's Advair came off patent in February, 2008. Advair accounted for 15 per cent of annual sales for GSK in the previous years. Their major genital herpes therapy Valtrex, which brought in €1.2 billion in 2008, lost patent exclusivity at the end of 2009, and their blockbuster asthma therapy, Advair, which earned over €4.1 in 2008, is set to lose exclusivity in 2010 and the diabetes drug Avandia expires in 2012. By 2011, 43 per cent of GSK's 2008 revenue will be represented by drugs that will face generic competition, given its current portfolio. Though GSK has been trying to be active on the market for acquisitions in an effort to replace revenue that will be lost to generic competition, prices have been driven up by competitors, making the premiums too high, said Moncef Slaoui, head of R&D in an interview in 2009.

To cope with the challenges facing the industry in general, but GSK in particular, they have started pursuing several avenues to renew their strategy. Among the important changes, GSK is shifting the focus from reliance on a few blockbuster drugs, in favour of more targeted drugs that earn modest incomes. "The pharmaceutical industry needs to look at lots of ways of doing business in the future," said Nick Cammack, head of development in GSK's Spanish facilities, in a *Wall Street Journal* article in 2010. CEO Andrew Witty is pushing the company to pursue drugs that it wouldn't have in the past. Mr Slaoui noted that GSK would be entering into orphan or even super-orphan medicines – treatments aimed at rare diseases such as swine flu and malaria – which give the medicines a speedier review and up to seven years of market exclusivity in the US. One such initiative the company launched in May 2010 is based on open-source principles which would involve a patent pool and more transparent collaborations on an online platform, where volunteer researchers can interact, free of charge, to try to discover new ways of treating malaria. However, GSK has yet to fully address the intellectual property implications if a breakthrough were to be achieved.

Another development is GSK's shift to a biotech-like approach, creating small outfits of up to 80 scientists to pursue development programmes. To stimulate innovation and emulate the competitive pressures from the environment, GSK developed a system in which outfits have a three-year window to come up with breakthroughs and apply for continued funding through a competitive internal venture fund, or face being shut down. However, some industry leaders, such as Sanofi-Aventis CEO Chris Viehbacher, have cautioned against this approach. They argue

that biotechs have entirely different cultures and working environments. Viehbacher notes: "Just because you have the same size as a team, that's the same size of a biotech, doesn't mean you within pharma are like a biotech."

GSK is also considering new domains. The company will make its first move into the branded generics market through an alliance with Aspen Pharmacare Holdings, a South African group, in a sign that it is trying to target emerging markets as the West becomes more challenging. To cater to these markets, GSK also will cap the prices of patented medicines it sells in the poorest countries to no more than 25 per cent of the cost in wealthy nations. The measures are targeted at 50 nations considered the world's least developed, many of them in Africa, a relatively unattractive market given the high margins on branded drugs in the current business model of Big Pharma.

**Sources:** Kelley, T. (2009) "Glaxo search for acquisitions hampered by 'desperate' rivals'", *Bloomberg*. http://www.bloomberg.com. September 24; Chu, K. (2010) "A conversation with John Lechleiter: Lilly CEO sizes up challenges, lessons Learned", *Usa Today*, http://www.indystar.com. July 21; Whalen, J. (2010) "Glaxo tries biotech model to spur drug innovations", *Wall Street Journal*. http://www.wsj.com. July 1; Boyle, C. (2008) "Glaxosmithkline to break up research and development operations", *The Times*. http://business.timesonline.co.uk. July 24; Guth, R. (2010) "Glaxo tries a Linux approach: Drug maker shares its research data online in test of open-source principles", *Wall Street Journal*. http://www.wsj.com. May 26; Kelly, T. (2010) "Glaxo profit beats estimates as savings plan expanded", *Bloomberg*. http://www.bloomberg.com. February 4; *Gsk Annual Report*, http://www.gsk.com/investors/annual-reports.htm; Pal, S. (2007) "Trends in FDA approval of generic drugs", *Us Pharmacist* http://www.uspharmacist.com; Jack, A. (2008) "GSK to shake-up research strategies", *Financial Times*. http://www.ft.com. June 9.

## Questions

1 Identify the most important components of the content and context of GSK's renewal. Which forms of learning do you recognize in GSK's old strategy and which ones in their renewed one?

2 Would you classify GSK's renewal as incremental or discontinuous? Why?

3 Which modes of balancing exploration and exploitation do you recognize in GSK's renewed strategy, compared to the old one?

4 What are the main managerial challenges you can foresee in GSK's new way of balancing exploration and exploitation?

at the industry level, and (2) internal forces influenced by managers. To better understand this issue, we first discuss managerial roles in strategic renewal at three different levels, i.e. top-, middle- and front-line management. Subsequently, we explore how these managerial levels interact between each other and the environment, reflecting the tension between forces of environmental selection and intentional adaptation.

## Managerial roles of top-, middle- and front-line management

Actors at different levels in the renewing organization have different roles that are manifested in different behaviours. Managers face different, and oftentimes inconsistent, behavioural expectations (roles) based on the need to efficiently deploy existing competencies and the need to experiment with new ones. Though any actor is likely to enact several roles at any given point in the renewal process, a distinction can be made between passive or active roles of managers with regard to whether their behaviours are geared towards driving and initiating change in light of changing environments or implementing change directives. Though the roles and behaviours of top managers have by far received the most academic attention, the roles of middle and lower-level managers has been shown to be of crucial importance as well.[105]

**Top management**   Within their overarching strategic decision-making role, the more passive roles of top managers in driving renewal include orchestrating,[106] retroactive legitimizing,[107] and judging or arbiting.[108] As *orchestrators*, top managers influence initiatives for renewal only indirectly, creating the right structures and climate for general innovation and change. As *retroactive legitimizers*, top managers endorse only those courses of action that are proven successes, and then only after they have established themselves as such (see quote from former CEO of Shell). Next to this, they can also act as *judges or arbiters* between those who champion initiatives for change and those who criticize it.[109]

In a more active role top managers are entrusted to search, direct and endorse. Top management actively scan the internal and external environment in their *searching* role in an attempt to identify and define what is needed to ensure alignment between the competencies and the environment, for instance, whether exploitative choices are necessary or more diverging explorative ones. In their *directing* roles, top management outline courses of action, command those involved, and allocate resources accordingly. As *endorsers* they openly advocate change as they provide support, legitimacy and mentor managers lower down in the hierarchy.

**Middle management**   The term *middle management* refers to managers located below top managers and above supervisors in the hierarchy.[110] The overarching role of middle management is to function as a critical "vertical link" within the hierarchy of an organization but also an important "horizontal connector" for disseminating knowledge-based resources throughout the organization.[111] As a nexus for information flows, the distinction between active and passive is more complex for middle managers. Clearly, they play an active role in *championing* initiatives for change as they devote their reputation and skills towards selling issues to top management and navigating initiatives for change through the social, cognitive and political barriers of the organization (see also Chapter 14 on autonomous and induced initiatives). A more passive role finds the middle manager as an *implementor* enacting mandates for change received from their superiors. However, some of their roles are also contingent on the phase of change. In their *facilitating* roles middle managers encourage discourse, new perspectives and divergence in interpretations of managers across hierarchical levels during early stages of the interpretation process.

As *synthesizers*, they guide sensemaking, blend and articulate the divergent interpretations of managers during later stages.[112]

**Front-line management**   Those who come from the lower levels of the organization are likely both to be closer to the technological and market interfaces and to have the most current specialized knowledge and expertise.[113] They act as reactors to, and extractors of, information from both environments *and* higher level managers. Because of this they are expected to play an active role in *experimenting* with new technologies, improve current approaches, propose new initiatives and identify radically new avenues for change. They also have to *observe* trends, threats and opportunities for growth or change that might otherwise go unnoticed by top and middle managers and ensure these get the attention of managers higher up. More passive roles include *conforming* to prescribed policies and acting in accordance with preset rules and also *adjustment* of their behaviours and those of their subordinates to the new requirements of the change.

## Idealized strategic renewal journeys: interactions between levels of analysis

By combining the passive and active attitudes of top-, middle- and front-line managers to change in relation to the environment, four idealized strategic renewal journeys (i.e. patterns of strategic renewal) can be distinguished: emergent, directed, facilitated and transformational journeys (see Figure 15.8). Each of these journeys is relevant to the multi-unit firms, but offers different approaches to managing the interactions between the front-line/middle and top management, and between the overall firm and the environment.

**The emergent renewal journey: follow the market**   In the emergent renewal journey, management is essentially passive regarding the environment. Top managers believe that their role is to amplify market forces and market signals for the benefit of middle and unit management. They often take a trader's attitude, engaging in acquisition and sales of businesses in the firm's portfolio in reaction or anticipation of market trends. At the unit level, meeting profit targets is emphasized and rewarded, while internal processes such as speed, product development, or extensive search for new ideas and business models are discouraged. Existing

**FIGURE 15.8**   Idealized renewal journeys of multi-unit firms

| | Top management is PASSIVE with respect to environment | Top management is ACTIVE with respect to environment |
|---|---|---|
| **Frontline and middle management are PASSIVE (stable competition)** | **Emergent renewal** <br><br> *'Follow the market'* | **Directed renewal** <br><br> *'Top management should be in control'* |
| **Frontline and middle management are ACTIVE (hypercompetition)** | **Facilitated renewal** <br><br> *'Increase variety of renewal initiatives'* | **Transformational renewal** <br><br> *'Mobilize company-wide renewal process'* |

Source: Based on H. W. Volberda, Ch. Baden-Fuller and F. A. J. Van den Bosch, 2001, "Mastering strategic renewal: mobilizing renewal journeys in multi-unit firms", *Long Range Planning*, 34: 159–178.

businesses are evaluated based on a profit-driven, market-orientated approach: those that cannot meet benchmark targets are sold or closed.

The emergent journey is commonly seen in many high-performing conglomerates operating in stable, mature environments. These companies select units based on their ability to achieve synergies and yield high returns in the short run. More often than not, such synergies hardly materialize due to a lack of effective coordination across functional and organizational boundaries requiring active management (see also Chapter 7 on corporate level strategy).[114] The British Barclays Bank's behaviour during the 1990s is an example of an emergent renewal journey. During this period, it cut thousands of jobs, scaled down its investment banking activities and avoided splurging on risks.[115]

### The directed renewal journey: top management should be in control

The ideal directed journey of renewal assumes that top managers believe they have some form of power over their environment, and that the multi-unit firm is purposeful and adaptive to changes in the competitive environment. Strategy making is therefore regarded as a rational and intentional process in which management performs extensive analyses before it respectively formulates and implements strategy by issuing directives top-down. Top managers explicitly manage the balance of exploration and exploitation by introducing new competencies to some units while utilizing well-developed competencies in others. To this end, top managers should hold a considerable amount of power on the unit level and have access to complete information.

The directed renewal journey is particularly appropriate in firms experiencing steady growth or decline. In these situations the benefits of formal planning and control can be fully realized. The typical tight control and hierarchical style makes this journey less suited for firms in highly turbulent environments. The emergent and directed renewal journeys represent ideal types that are in line with traditional approaches to management thinking in mature environments. Front-line and middle managers are expected to take on a passive, following role in such environments. In more hypercompetitive landscapes, front-line and middle management are required to takes a more active stand, creating a more complex and subtle approach to management.

### The facilitated renewal journey: increase variety of renewal initiatives

In the facilitated renewal journey lower levels of management play an active role in enabling renewal. This approach recognizes these levels of management have the most current knowledge and expertise as they are closer to the routines and sources of information critical to innovative outcomes. Top management's role is to facilitate front-line and middle management entrepreneurship by creating a strategic context for nurturing and selecting promising renewal initiatives. Top managers should therefore be seen as retrospective legitimizers or judges of renewal actions.

Compared to the emergent renewal journey, the facilitated journey business portfolio exhibits a better balance between exploration and exploitation. Attention is more directed towards frequency of new product and service introductions, rather than pure profit maximization. To this end, top management can intervene in guiding the structure of units, suggesting or directing forms of organizing. This involves splitting innovative units from more rigid parts of the organization, in order to facilitate entrepreneurs to pursue their ideas in separate divisions away from forces of inertia (i.e. structural ambidexterity, see section on generic balancing modes).

The continuous creation of new units from within the firm (i.e. internal selection process) enables a perpetual stage of adaptation making facilitated renewal journeys particularly appropriate in highly complex and dynamic markets. However, top management's lack of control over the organization may hamper the multi-unit firm to engage in large-scale developments that require some form of central coordination or synergy across units.

### The transformational renewal journey: mobilize a company-wide renewal process
The transformational renewal journey can be described as a holistic process in which top management believes it can influence the environment, and lower level managers are closely involved. Renewal is driven by collective sense-making and the development of shared strategic schemas across organizational levels.[116] Through social interaction, organizational participants socially construct their reality and actively form or enact their environment, which in turn affects future enactments.

This process is best illustrated when applied to a small setting, e.g. a start-up firm. Here, a single entrepreneur drives the innovation process by inspiring and motivating the entire enterprise. The lack of tight commitments and relatively low sunk costs enable these units to undertake radical change easily. Similar processes can be seen in larger organizations such as Novotel, one of the largest hotel chains in the world. Novotel's renewal processes were led from the top, but involved close involvement from all organizational levels in the change process itself as well as in shaping the direction of the process. Following this transformational path improved the quality of the result and increased the speed of the process (see the Closing Case on "Novotel's transformational renewal journey").[117]

Transformational renewal journeys involve the whole multi-unit firm and require systematic rather than piecemeal changes. Consequently, organizations can move in renewal cycles between exploration and exploitation. This journey may therefore prove particularly suitable in evolutionary moving environments punctuated by occasional radical shifts.

## Renewal journeys of the future

We have posed four basic journeys of renewal: market selection pressures propelling emergent renewal journeys; top management intentions pushing directed renewal journeys; deliberate variety generation and internal selection driving facilitated renewal journeys; and collective sense-making allowing transformational renewal journeys. These journeys of renewal differ fundamentally, each implying a different solution to the tensions between top, middle and front line management. Although these are ideal, understanding their implications and appreciating the differences between them can be a potent source of understanding for managers of firms in the real world, whose journey of renewal may by hybrid forms of two or more of the ideals. Another reason why firms may be hard to categorize is that they may move through different periods, each characterized by a different renewal journey. Such meta or development journeys of renewal form part of the portfolio of strategic choice.

Consider Shell's corporate revitalization guided by Peter Voser, Unilever's corporate change initiated by Paul Polman, or Novotel's renewal led by Gérard Pélisson (see the Strategic Focus on Novotel, 588). The starting point of these companies seemed to be a period of stasis where both top and front line managers had been passive and where the financial community was threatening to impose market selection. New CEOs arrived and pushed directed renewal. Typically they began with a process of competence development led by the CEO, which introduced new concepts, communicated them in an understandable manner through the use of metaphors and analogies, and reiterated them repeatedly. Consequently, new capabilities such as speed, simplicity and market responsiveness were passed down the organization almost as an order or instruction to be followed. Following these periods of top-down directed renewal, the organizations have moved on to another period, where top management shows more transformational leadership and other management levels are involved in order to create system-wide change (transformational renewal). Finally, top management becomes more of an orchestrator, facilitating decentralized entrepreneurship, and the journey is more like that of facilitated renewal.

© sebastian-julian

## KEY DEBATE

# What matters most? Managerial intentionality versus environmental selection

Throughout this chapter, we have treated strategic renewal as being driven by either environmental selection or reactive adaptive choices. However, the emerging view of co-evolution considers strategic renewal to be jointly influenced by environmental selection forces and managerial intentionality.[118] This perspective acknowledges that environments are not exogenously defined, but must be malleable – at least to some extent – by individual firms. In a population of learning, connected and mutually influencing

interactions between firms,[119] *path creating* actions of individual firms ahead in the Red Queen race come to influence the environment.

Combining the previously discussed theoretical perspectives of environmental selection and managerially driven adaptation, from a co-evolution perspective, sustained strategic renewal can be considered to rest on three key principles:[120]

1 Self-renewing organizations manage requisite variety by regulating internal rates of change to equal or exceed relevant external rates change (e.g. competitors, technology, customers, etc.).

2 Self-renewing organizations optimize self-organization by delegating decision making to the lowest possible level to maximize search depth and scope throughout the organization.

3 Self-renewing organizations synchronize concurrent exploitation and exploration (i.e. ambidexterity).

Figure 15.9 shows these three principles in a three-dimensional space. The red cloud represents firms in the "denial range". These are rigid organizations suffering from retarded internal rates of change, overexploitation

**FIGURE 15.9** Three principles of sustained strategic renewal

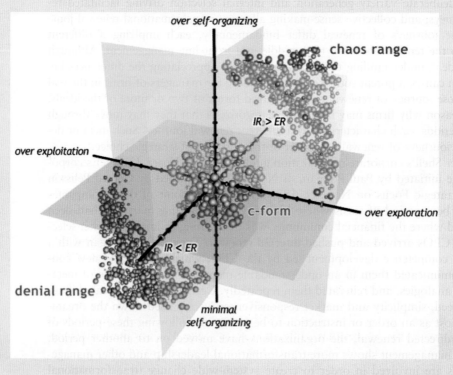

and an insufficient ability to self-organize. In contrast, the blue cloud represents firms in the "chaotic range", which are characterized by internal rates of change that outstrip external rates of change at an unfavourable pace, over-explore (wasting valuable resources), and are self-organized to an uncontrollable extent. Finally, the green spot represents organizations with a co-evolutionary (i.e. C-) form. These organizations succeed in the challenge of matching internal rates of change to external rates of change, balancing exploration and exploitation, and achieving a suitable level of self-organization.

## Questions

1 If you had to pick one side of the selection versus adaptation debate, which side would you choose, and why?

2 What do you think are the strengths and weaknesses of a co-evolutionary view of strategic renewal?

3 What challenges can you foresee in attempting to integrate the three principles of sustained renewal into everyday organizational life?

4 To what extent do you personally believe survival to be a matter of chance or "luck"? If so, how can firms increase their "luck"?

5 Think of an ongoing real-life example in which, in your view, instead of reacting adaptively to changing environments, a firm is proactively shaping it. Describe the adaptation and selection elements in this case.

Should any of these idealized journeys be preferred over the other? Of course, the *emergent renewal* journey represents an extreme, where top management amplifies market pressures, often enforcing more rigorous standards than would otherwise be imposed. There is no doubt, however, that for substantial periods of time, firms may benefit by adopting such emergent journeys.

In contrast, in *transformational renewal* where the cooperation between front-line managers and top managers is the strongest, learning is intense and diversity among levels and groups leads to learning, exploration and rejuvenation. Here, top management sees its role as overcoming market forces of selection, forcing fast-track adaptive and learning behaviour. While it sounds ideal as a development model, the resulting path appears to have drawbacks. For instance, it is poor at dealing with technological discontinuities, and the journey may not sustain over time because of the effort required of all the parties involved. The firm lurches from states of high exploration to high exploitation, placing severe demands on managerial capacity.[121]

The *facilitated renewal* may be very effective in the future business landscape. Scholars have argued that renewal proceeds most rapidly when top management cause small probes in a characteristic rhythm, recombining the portfolio of units, so that renewal is generated without destroying the best elements of past experience (see the earlier discussion on incremental renewal). Top management operates on unit managers indirectly, taking advantage of the tendency for myriad local interactions to self-organize into a coherent pattern. Rather than shaping the pattern that constitutes strategic renewal (*directed renewal*), managers shape the context within which it emerges, speeding up adaptive processes.

Finally, these renewal journeys point to important lessons for practicing strategists. By setting up the benchmark of "selection" where managers are seen as passive actors driven by path dependency in a biological game, these journeys point out that there are real choices that strategists can be make. Each of these is distinctive from the other having different competitive advantages and costs. Each may respond differently to different environmental stimuli. Each implies differences in roles of top, middle-line and front-line management.

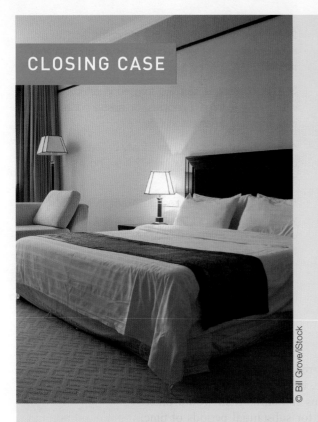

## CLOSING CASE

© Bill Grove/iStock

# Novotel's transformational renewal journey

Novotel was founded in 1967 by two entrepreneurs, Paul Dubrule and Gérard Pélisson, as the first division of the Accor group, nowadays one of the world's largest hotel managers and market leader in the European hotel industry. Since its incorporation, Accor has been rapidly expanding by starting up and acquiring other hotel and restaurant chains. Today, the Group's hotel division operates in 90 countries with 145 000 employees, and offers a total of 500 000 rooms in 4100 hotels (of which 2300 are in Europe). Its extensive offering consists of 15 complementary brands – from luxury to economy – including Ibis (a two-star hotel chain), Mercure (a three-star hotel chain), Sofitel (a luxury hotel chain), and Formule 1 (a one-star budget hotel).

During the 1970s and 1980s, Novotel based its growth – adding one hotel per month on average – on a unique market positioning formula offering four-star service at a three-star rate. This was achieved by applying standardization and siting hotels on inexpensive land outside city centres, near motorways and airports.

By the early 1990s Novotel had become market leader in Europe with 191 hotels in 18 European countries (1991) and 50 more hotels outside Europe. However, the company's outlook seemed unfavourable. With the effects of an economic recession becoming visible, companies' travel budgets were cut and fewer business trips were permitted. Moreover, with the Iraqi occupation of Kuwait in late 1990 and the Gulf war in early 1991, the threat of terrorist activity in European cities further diminished international travel. Consequently, competition among hotels increased and room rates were slashed.

During large-scale "open-space" meetings in 1992, hotel managers aired their concerns that things were going wrong and requested more autonomy. Influenced by the recent success of Accor's new concept, the Formule 1 budget hotel, the Group's top management recognized that the Novotel proposition was losing its edge and should be revitalized to better fit the transformed business environment. As a result of the company's growth and bureaucratization in the 1980s, the business had become too inward looking, and lacked adequate marketing knowledge as well as operational and strategic flexibility. Moreover, the company faced managerial rigidities reflected by its highly hierarchical structure. Dubrule and Pélisson took action and appointed Gilles Pélisson (Gérard's nephew) and Philippe Brizon as new co-presidents of Novotel to lead a renewal project. Each of the new co-presidents brought different and complementary skills and management styles to the table, and together they quickly assembled their core management team consisting of innovation minded individuals they could trust.

The project had a dual objective of cost reduction and improved flexibility to increase differentiation. However, Novotel's top management intended to preserve the best from the organization's past to build a platform for the future. Accordingly, the project was named "Back to the Future", referring to the entrepreneurial innovative epoch of the company's co-founders 25 years ago. In December 1992 the two co-presidents outlined their draft strategy to "Re-Novotelize Novotel", using a simple framework covering concepts with respect to "clients, administration (costs) and people".

To further enable the change project, Novotel designed its communication so as to ensure a balance between top-down and bottom-up flows of knowledge. To guide the formulation of strategies from the corporate level to the level of each hotel (top-down), 12 three-day meetings were organized in spring 1993. These meetings were organized by each director of operations and his or her 25 hotel general managers and were attended by the co-presidents. The project plan was described in a few pages that outlined the new identity of the company in terms of competitive advantage, key resources, organizational formula and norms of behaviour. Additionally, "progress groups" were set up across geographical areas and functions to improve service, reduce costs and improve management. Bottom-up "reflective clubs" were organized within and across hotels by hotel managers who shared problems and could share solutions. Meetings at the regional level and so-called "open space" meetings between hotel managers and top management continued to ensure experimentation, variation and information sharing across levels.

Another important aspect of Novotel's renewal journey involved the development of new competencies and capabilities. This encompassed a personal development trajectory for the 280 hotel general managers, who played a critical role in the hotel's rejuvenation. By delegating more responsibilities to the hotel level, hotel managers and the rest of the front line staff was empowered to take leadership of their unit. Consequently, the units were enabled to tailor their responses to fit the reservoirs of unique skills and local environment, thereby greatly increasing the flexibility of the organization as a whole and better enabling it to survive environmental shifts in the future.

**Sources:** Accor SA corporate website http://www.accor.com; Baden-Fuller, Ch. and Volberda, H. W. (2001) "Dormant capabilities, complex organizations, and renewal", in: R. Sanchez (ed.), *Knowledge Management and Organizational Competence*, Oxford, UK: Oxford University Press, 114–136; Calori, R., Baden-Fuller, Ch. and Hunt, B. (2000) "Managing change at Novotel: Back to the future", *Long Range Planning* 33, 779–804; Volberda, H. W., Baden-Fuller, Ch. and Van den Bosch, F. A. J. (2001) "Mastering strategic renewal, mobilising renewal journeys in multi-unit firms", *Long Range Planning* 34, 159–178.

## Questions

**1** What was the main reason for renewal at Novotel?

**2** Describe the predominant mix of roles of top-, middle-, and front-line management in Novotel's renewal journey. Classify them as passive or active and explain your choice.

**3** Reflect on the renewal approach by Novotel's top management and identify the elements of a transformational renewal journey. Was this journey suitable in your opinion?

## SUMMARY

- Organizations face conflicting forces of stability and change. On the one hand, there is a need for an efficient, stable structure enabling optimal exploitation of available knowledge and competencies to deal with short term competitive forces. On the other hand, environmental change forces established firms to be flexible, transform stagnant businesses and explore new sources of wealth through new resource combinations.

- Strategic renewal refers to the adaptive choices and actions a firm undertakes to overcome path dependence – the firm's attachment to past decisions and actions – and maintain a dynamic strategic fit with changing environments over time. It encompasses the changing, replacing, or refreshing of one or more core organizational attributes which have the potential to affect the firm's long-term performance, and ultimately, survival.

- Theoretical perspectives differ with regard to the extent to which firms are believed to self-renew. The selection perspective on strategic renewal is deterministic and assumes that firms are limited in their ability to adapt to changing environmental conditions. By contrast, the adaptation perspective is more voluntaristic and assumes that strategic choice and managerial intentionality enable organizational adaptation to changing environments.

■ Strategic renewal can be conceived as a three-dimensional construct consisting of a content, context and process dimension. The content dimension pertains to which core attributes of the current strategy need to be changed, replaced or refreshed. The context dimension reflects whether the learning underlying strategic renewal actions are internally developed through experimental learning or externally acquired through acquisitive learning. Finally, the process dimension relates to the question how and when effective strategies are shaped, validated and implemented within the firm.

■ The dimensions of strategic renewal interact and result in two types of renewal – incremental and discontinuous. Incremental perspectives on strategic renewal assume that adaptation is the outcome of relatively small iterative interactions between path dependent choices and environmental feedback over time. Discontinuous perspectives see renewal as revitalizing the company by drastically redefining the scope of its business, its competitive approach, or both.

■ For the organization to renew successfully and ensure its long-term survival, it must manage its learning trajectories. Two generic types of learning orientations can be defined: exploratory and exploitative learning. Exploratory learning has a bearing on the long-term renewal of the organization and adds new attributes to the organization's current portfolio of activities and competencies. Exploitative learning denotes a shorter-term orientation and encompasses those actions that lie in line with the organization's current activities and competencies in existing domains. Firms should seek to balance exploration and exploitation. A skewed tendency to overexplore or overexploit can have negative consequences. Too much exploitation drives inertia and dynamic conservatism; exploitation crowds out exploration. Similarly, too much exploration drives out efficiencies and prevents gaining economies of scale or learning by doing.

■ To facilitate strategic renewal, organizations need to have certain levels of flexibility consistent with the competitive forces in the environment. Four different types of flexibility can be distinguished, namely steady-state, operational, structural, and strategic flexibility. Strategic flexibility is the highest level and refers to a mix of dynamic capabilities providing the firm with a capacity to respond to unpredictable changes in the environment. By combing the managerial task (i.e. managing the variety of capabilities and their speed of response) and the organization design task (i.e. redesigning technology, organizational structure and organizational culture), various organizational forms with different levels of flexibility can be developed.

■ Multi-unit firms can introduce various generic modes or organizational forms to balance sufficient levels of both exploration and exploitation – i.e. ambidexterity – without having to undergo continuous structural change. These modes thus provide more permanent solutions for mastering strategic renewal. Four forms of ambidexterity are distinguished: contextual, structural, cyclical and reciprocal.

■ Strategic renewal actions are conjointly driven by two forces: (1) external selection forces at the industry level, and (2) internal forces influenced by managers (i.e. co-evolution). To understand a firm's strategic renewal path these adaptation and selection forces should be combined. Accordingly, a conceptual distinction can be made between an active and a passive role of top-, middle- and front-line managers to change, yielding four idealized strategic renewal journeys, i.e. patterns of strategic renewal: emergent, directed, facilitated and transformational.

## REVIEW QUESTIONS

1   Describe the relationship between path dependence and inertia and why they can be problematic over time.

2   Explain how the "Red Queen" metaphor applies to the tension between strategic renewal and survival.

3   What is the flexibility paradox? Elaborate on its causes and consequences.

4   What is strategic renewal and how does it relate to organizational learning?

5 What is the difference between incremental and discontinuous renewal?

6 What is ambidexterity and what is its role in strategic renewal?

7 Explain the role of strategic flexibility in the journeys of renewal.

8 Considering the repertoire of passive and active managerial roles, which specific mix of roles is most suitable for each journey of renewal? Justify your choice.

9 Juxtapose the key debate between selection and adaptation and state the strengths, weaknesses, similarities, and differences of both schools of thought.

10 How do the three principles of sustained renewal relate to strategic flexibility?

11 How does self-organizing affect the managerial roles described previously?

12 Examining Figure 15.2, what do you consider to be future challenges for Shell?

# DISCUSSION QUESTIONS

Find the *Global Fortune 500* ranking list (or another similar one) for the year 1990. From this list, select two comparable companies from the *same* primary industry based on at least *two* attributes (e.g. age, size, rank, revenues, profits, market capitalization). Now look for the same two companies in the last available listing and answer the relevant questions pertaining to the scenario that best describes the companies you chose.

1 Both companies are on the latest list:

a Graph their relative ranking and other key financial metrics annually for the period of observation. How did their rank change on the list over this time period? Explain any notable changes in ranking.

b What was the rate of industry growth (or decline) during this period and how is this related to the annual rankings? Include this rate in your graph.

c Look for at least three other firms in your selected industry listed on the latest list that were also on the list in 1990. Add these to your graph, as you did for the two previous companies, and identify periods of stability versus periods of change. Consult news archives, annual reports and other sources to identify how these companies balanced exploration and exploitation during these periods. What are the similarities and differences between their approaches?

d Would you attribute survival, as per the list, *primarily* to clever managerial choices or to favourable industry conditions? Explain why in terms of adaptation or selection theories.

2 *Only one* company is on the latest list:

a Graph their relative ranking and other key financial metrics annually for the period of observation. When did one of the companies drop from the list and why?

b What was the rate of industry growth (or decline) during this period and how was this related to their annual ranking? Include this rate in your graph.

c Consult news archives, annual reports and other sources to identify the managerial choices that contributed to the success of the active firm and the demise of the other, as per the list. To what extent did these choices foster, or hamper, strategic flexibility for both firms?

d Explain why these comparable firms reacted differently to the same environmental pressures in their industry invoking theories of adaptation.

3 *Neither* company is on the latest list:

a Graph their relative ranking and other key financial metrics annually for their active duration on the list. Did both disappear about the same time or did one significantly outlive the other? Why?

b What was the rate of industry growth (or decline) during this period and how was this related to their disappearance from the list? Include this rate in your graph. Elaborate on whether their demise can be attributed to industry level selection forces or poor managerial choices.

c    Identify the main internal and external constraints these firms were confronted with. How
would you have relieved the company from
these constraints? How did these companies
balance exploration and exploitation?

d    Are there new entrants in the industry which
replaced these firms on the list? If so, describe
their organizational forms and how the content
of their strategies differs from the original two
firms you selected. If not, explain why invoking
theories of selection.

# FURTHER READING

For an exposition on the characteristics of strategic renewal and its impact on firms, industries and economies
we refer readers to R. Argawal and C. Helfat (2009) "Strategic renewal of organizations", *Organization Science,* 20:
281–293.

A comprehensive explanation of strategic renewal journeys can be found in H. W. Volberda, Ch. Baden-Fuller
and F. A. J. Van den Bosch (2001) "Mastering strategic

renewal: Mobilizing renewal journeys in multi-unit firms",
*Long Range Planning,* 34: 159–178.

For a synthesis of strategic and organizational flexibility,
and more information on what types of flexibility are effective under different organizational conditions and environmental characteristics, we refer to H. W. Volberda (1998)
*Building the Flexible Firm: How to Remain Competitive,*
Oxford, UK: Oxford University Press.

# EXPERIENTIAL EXERCISES

## Exercise 1: Reviving the dead

In practice, firms that fail typically go bankrupt. However,
in some countries, such as the US, these firms can
sometimes get a second chance. As liquidation would
destroy all the residual value of a firm for its stakeholders
and could have negative macro-economical consequences (e.g. unemployment), regulators protect them
for a short period from creditors to give managers a
chance to resurrect the company.[122]

Assume this is the case for this exercise, and identify a
bankruptcy filing of a large firm within the last five years.
The firm is to be granted protection from creditors for one
year provided it can devise a sound strategy to revive the
company. Your team has been nominated as the new top
management team and the board of directors has put
you in charge of this task.

### Assignment

1    Form teams of 3–5 students.

2    Devise a plan with a concrete timeline and key performance indicators in which you outline and specify
the elements of a discontinuous renewal strategy
that can save the firm. Your plan should cover at the
very least:

a    Sources of problem and how to avoid these in
the future

b    Renewed mission and vision

c    Three dimensions of renewal

d    How you intend to allocate resources to
exploration and exploitation

e    Environmental contingencies that need to be
taken into account

f    How you intend to build-in strategic flexibility

g    Roles key actors throughout the firm will have to
play

h    Renewed organizational form

i    Main managerial challenges, risks and trade-offs
inherent in your strategy

j    Expected outcomes and sustainability of your
strategy

k    How you intend to raise capital to fund the
changes (bonus)

3    Present the proposal to the group as if it were a
general assembly of shareholders. The audience
should scrutinize the proposal on its *suitability* and
*feasibility* and decide if you can keep your job.

## Exercise 2: Small- and medium-sized firms: a view from within

Like much of this chapter, the previous exercise has dealt
with large incumbent firms. However, the challenges
identified throughout are not endemic to these types

of firms. For this exercise, select one of two options below and answer the questions pertaining to your choice.

1 Identify a *small- or medium-sized* company in your community (according to your local Chamber of Commerce classification) and interview one or more of its executives. The company must have existed for at least 10 years.

2 Identify an *entrepreneurial start-up* in your community and interview its founder(s). The company must not employ more than 25 full-time equivalents and must have been founded within the last five years.

### Assignment

a Profile the industry-level environmental forces by considering at the very least: technological changes and paradigm shifts, changes in customer preferences and intensity of competitive activities (e.g. entries, exits, [de]escalation).

b Provide an overview of the company's mission, vision, strategy and structure. How have these changed over the last few years?

c Describe how the company balances exploration and exploitation.

d Which elements of strategic and operational flexibility are evident?

e Has the company undergone any transformation of its core atributes? If so, which ones, and how did they do this?

f How would you describe their organizational form and what are its strengths and weaknesses compared to the form of large(r) incumbents in their industry?

g Which roles do different managers play, and how do these relate to the roles described previously in the chapter?

h What advice would you give to this firm to increase its likelihood of survival?

## VIDEO CASE

### A conversation with A. G. Lafley, Chairman and CEO, Procter & Gamble plc

www.cengage.co.uk/volberda/students/video_cases
Before you watch the video consider the following concepts:

- Strategic flexibility
- Explorative innovation
- Exploitative innovation
- Ambidexterity

Alan Lafley, Chairman and CEO of Procter & Gamble (P&G), discusses how his company addresses the challenge of continuous innovation in a rapidly changing environment. Watch the video and answer the questions below.

1 Would you typify P&G's approach to strategic renewal as incremental or more discontinuous?

2 Identify how P&G puts elements of the managerial task and the organizational design task in action in order to become flexible.

3 Identify key environmental changes in P&G's environment and discuss how the company responded to these changes.

4 Reflect on Lafley's role as CEO and his attitude towards this role. What elements of the four strategic renewal trajectories do you recognize at P&G?

## NOTES

1. J. L. Van Zanden, S. Howarth, J. Jonker and K. Sluijterman, 2007, *A History of Royal Dutch Shell. From Challenger to Joint Industry Leader, 1890–1939, 1939–1973, 1973–2007*, 3 volumes and Appendices, New York: Oxford University Press.

2. M. S. Feldman and J. G. March, 1981, "Information in organizations as signal and symbol", *Administrative Science Quarterly*, 26: 171–186; R. Nelson and S. Winter, 1982, *An Evolutionary Theory of Economic Change*, Cambridge MA: The Belknap Press of Harvard University;

P. C. Nystrom and W. H. Starbuck, 1984, "To avoid organizational crises, unlearn", *Organizational Dynamics*, 12(4): 53–65.

3.  S. W. Floyd and P. J. Lane, 2000, "Strategizing throughout the organization: Managing role conflict in strategic renewal", *The Academy of Management Review*, 25(1), 154–177.

4.  A. Y. Lewin, C. P. Long and T. N. Carroll, 1999, "The coevolution of new organizational forms", *Organization Science,* 10: 535–50; W. H. Sewell, 1996, "Three temporalities: Toward an eventful sociology", in: J. T. Macdonald (ed.), *The Historic Turn in the Human Sciences*, Ann Arbor: University of Michigan Press, 245–280; A. Y. Lewin and H. W. Volberda, 1999, "Prolegomena on Coevolution: A Framework for Research on Strategy and New Organizational Forms". *Organization Science*, 10: 519–534.

5.  B. Levitt and J. G. March, 1988, "Organizational learning", in: W. R. Scott, *Annual Review of Sociology,* 14: 319–340; S. J. Liebowitz and S. E. Margolis, 1995, "Path dependence, lock-in, and history", *Journal of Law Economics and Organization*, 11(1): 205–226.

6.  W. D. Guth and A. Ginsburg, 1990, "Corporate entrepreneurship", *Strategic Management Journal*, 11: 5–15.

7.  J. O. Huff, A. S. Huff and H. Thomas, 1992, "Strategic renewal and the interaction of cumulative stress and inertia", *Strategic Management Journal*, 13(Special Issue: Strategy Process: Managing Corporate Self-Renewal): 55–75.

8.  R. E. Miles and C. C. Snow, 1978, *Organizational Strategy, Structure, and Process*, New York: McGraw-Hill; N. Venkatraman and J. C. Camillus, 1984, "Exploring the concept of 'fit' in strategic management", *Academy of Management Review,* 9(3): 513–525.

9.  R. Agarwal and C. E. Helfat, 2009, "Strategic renewal of organizations", *Organization Science*, 20: 281–293; H. W. Volberda, Ch. Baden-Fuller and F. A. J. Van den Bosch, 2001, "Mastering strategic renewal: mobilizing renewal journeys in multi-unit firms", *Long Range Planning*, 34: 160; J. Lamberg, H. Tikkanen, T. Nokelainen and H. Suur-Inkeroinen, 2008, "Competitive dynamics, strategic consistency, and organizational survival", *Strategic Management Journal*, 30: 45–60; D. Miller, 1992, "Environmental fit versus internal fit", *Organization Science*, 3: 159–78; E. J. Zajac, M. S. Kraatz and R. K. F. Bresser, 2000, "Modeling the dynamics of strategic fit: A normative approach to strategic change", *Strategic Management Journal,* 21(4): 429–453.

10. This discussion is based on A. Y. Lewin and H. W. Volberda, 1999, "Prolegomena on coevolution: A framework for research on strategy and new organizational forms", *Organization Science* 10(5): 519–534; H. W. Volberda and A. Y. Lewin, 2003, "Co-evolutionary dynamics within and between firms: From evolution to co-evolution", *Journal of Management Studies*, 40(8): 2111–2136; A. Y. Lewin and H. W. Volberda, 2003, "Beyond adaptation vs. selection research: Organizing self-renewal in co-evolving environments", *Journal of Management Studies*, 40 (8): 2109–2110; H. W. Volberda and Ch. Baden-Fuller, 1999, "Strategic Renewal and

Competence Building: Four Dynamic Mechanisms", in: G. Hamel, C. K. Prahalad, H. Thomas and D. O'Neal (eds.), *Strategic Flexibility: Managing in a Turbulent Economy*, Chichester: Wiley, 371–389; H. W. Volberda, 2005, "Rethinking the Strategy Process: A Co-evolutionary Approach", in: S. W. Floyd, J. Roos, C. D. Jacobs and F. W. Kellermans (eds.), *Innovating Strategy Process*, Oxford: Blackwell, 81–87.

11. H. E. Aldrich and J. Pfeffer, 1976, "Environments of organizations", *Annual Review of Sociology*, 2: 79–105.

12. J. Freeman, G. R. Carroll and M. T. Hannan, 1983, "The liability of newness: Age dependence in organizational death rates", *American Sociological Review*, 48(5): 692–710; M. T. Hannan and J. Freeman, 1977, "The population ecology of organizations", *American Journal of Sociology,* 82: 929–964.

13. M. Beer, S. C. Voelpel, M. Leibold and E. D. Tekie, 2005, "Strategic management as organizational learning: Developing fit and alignment through a disciplined process", *Long Range Planning*, 38: 445–465; M. T. Hannan and J. Freeman, 1984, "Structural inertia and organizational change", *American Sociological Review*, 49 (2): 152.

14. M. T. Hannan and J. Freeman, 1984, "Structural inertia and organizational change", *American Sociological Review*, 49(2): 152.

15. D. Miller and P. H. Friesen, 1984, "A longitudinal study of the corporate life cycle", *Management Science*, 30(10): 1161–1183.

16. H. E. Aldrich and J. Pfeffer, 1976, "Environments of organizations", *Annual Review of Sociology*, 2: 79–105.

17. M. T. Hannan and J. Freeman, 1989, *Organizational Ecology*, Cambridge, MA: Harvard University Press.

18. S. M. Ben-Menahem, F. A. J. Van den Bosch, H. W. Volberda and Z. Kwee, 2010, "Investigating the temporal dimension of strategic renewal: Managing absorptive capacity for aligning internal and external rates of change", Research Paper presented at the European Academy of Management annual meeting in Rome, Italy.

19. L. Van Valen, 1973, "A new evolutionary law", *Evolutionary Theory*, 1: 1–30; L. Carroll, 1946, *Through the Looking Glass and What Alice Found There*, New York: Grosset & Dunlap, 178–179.

20. R. Nelson and S. Winter, 1982, *An Evolutionary Theory of Economic Change*, Cambridge MA: The Belknap Press of Harvard University; D. Miller and M. Chen, 1994, "Sources and consequences of competitive inertia: A study of the US airline industry", *Administrative Science Quarterly*, 39: 1–23.

21. E. T. Penrose, 1959, *The Theory of Growth of the Firm*, New York: Wiley; E. P. Learned, C. R. Christensen, K. R. Andrews and W. Guth, 1969, *Business Policy: Text and Cases*, Homewood, IL: R. Irwin; B. Wernerfelt, 1984, "A resource-based view of the firm", *Strategic Management Journal*, 5: 171–180.

22. S. A. Lippman and R. P. Rumelt, 1982, "Uncertain imitability: An analysis of interfirm differences in efficiency under competition", *The Bell Journal of Economics,* 13: 418–438; M. A. Peteraf, 1993, "The cornerstones of

competitive advantage: A resource-based view", *Strategic Management Journal*, 14(3): 179–191.

23. J. B. Barney, 1991, "Firm resources and sustained competitive advantage", *Journal of Management,* 17: 99–120.

24. For an exposition on this subject refer to a discussion on time compression diseconomies, asset mass efficiencies, asset stock interconnectedness, and causal ambiguity in: I. Dierckx and K. Cool, 1989, "Asset stock accumulation and sustainability of competitive advantage", *Management Science*, 35(12): 1504–1511.

25. D. Leonard-Barton, 1992, "Core capabilities and core rigidities: A paradox in managing new product development", *Strategic Management Journal*, 13(Special Issue): 111–125; D. A. Levinthal and J. G. March, 1993, "The myopia of learning", *Strategic Management Journal*, 14(Special Issue): 95–112.

26. D. J. Teece, G. Pisano and A. Shuen, 1997, "Dynamic capabilities and strategic management", *Strategic Management Journal*, 18(7): 514.

27. P. J. DiMaggio and W. W. Powell, 1991, "The iron cage revisited: Institutional isomorphism, and collective rationality in organizational fields", in: W. W. Powell and P. J. DiMaggio (eds.) *The New Institutionalism in Organisational Analysis,* University of Chicago Press: Chicago.

28. *The Economist*, "A decent start", 1 July 2010, http://www.economist.com; *The Economist*, "Not all on the same page", 1 July 2010; http://www.economist.com.

29. E. Abrahamson and L. Rosenkopf, 1993, "Institutional and competitive bandwagons: Using a mathematical modelling as a tool to explore innovation diffusion", *Academy of Management Review*, 18(3): 487–517.

30. Ch. Baden-Fuller and H. W. Volberda, 2003, "Dormant capabilities, complex organizations, and renewal", in: R. Sanchez (ed.), *Knowledge Management and Organizational Competence*, Oxford University Press, 114–136; M. W. Wielemaker, T. Elfring, T. and H. W. Volberda, 2000, Strategic renewal in large European firms: Investigating viable trajectories of change, *Organization Development Journal*, 18(4): 49–68.

31. A. Y. Lewin and H. W. Volberda, 1999, "Prolegomena on coevolution: A framework for research on strategy and new organizational forms", *Organization Science*, 10(5): 519–534; Ch. Baden-Fuller and H. W. Volberda, 1997, "Strategic renewal: How large complex organizatons prepare for the future", *ISMO, International Studies of Management & Organization*, 27 (2): 95–120.

32. Ch. Baden-Fuller and J. Stopford, 1994, *Rejuvenating the Mature Business*, Harvard Business School Press: Boston; M. Stienstra, M. G. Baaij, F. A. J. Van den Bosch and H. W. Volberda, 2004, "Strategic renewal of Europe's largest telecom operators (1999–2001): From herd behaviour towards strategic choice?", *European Management Journal*, 22 (3): 273–280.

33. J. Child, 1972, "Organization structure, environment and performance: The role of strategic choice", *Sociology*, 1–22; J. Child, 1997, "Strategic choice in the analysis of action structure, organizations and environment:

Retrospect and prospect", *Organization Studies*, 18(1): 43–76; L. G. Hrebiniak and W. F. Joyce, 1985, "Organizational adaptation: Strategic choice and environmental determinism", *Administrative Science Quarterly*, 30(3): 336–349.

34. R. Sanchez, 2001, "Building blocks for strategy theory: Resources, dynamic capabilities and competences", in: H. W. Volberda and T. Elfring (eds.) *Rethinking Strategy,* Sage Publications: London, 143–157.

35. H. W. Volberda, 1996, "Toward the flexible form: How to remain vital in hypercompetitive environments", *Organization Science*, 7(4): 359–374; H. W. Volberda, 1998, *Building the Flexible Firm: How to Remain Competitive*, Oxford: Oxford University Press.

36. D. J. Teece, G. Pisano and A. Shuen, 1997, "Dynamic capabilities and strategic management", *Strategic Management Journal*, 18: 509–533.

37. K. M. Eisenhardt and J. A. Martin, 2000, "Dynamic capabilities, what are they?", *Strategic Management Journal*, 21(Special Issue): 1105–1121.

38. W. M. Cohen and D. A. Levinthal, 1990, "Absorptive capacity: A new perspective on learning and innovation", *Administrative Science Quarterly*, 35(1): 128–152; M. M. Crossan, H. W. Lane and R. E. White, 1999, "An organizational learning framework: From intuition to institution", *Academy of Management Review*, 24(3): 522–537; P. J. Lane, B. R. Koka and S. Pathak, 2006, "The reification of absorptive capacity: A critical review and rejuvenation of the construct", *The Academy of Management Review*, 31(4): 833–863; J. J. J. Jansen, F. A. J. Van den Bosch and H. W. Volberda, 2005, "Managing potential and realized absorptive capacity: How do organizational antecedents matter?", *Academy of Management Journal*, 48(6): 999–1015; H. W. Volberda, N. J. Foss and M. A. Lyles, 2010, "Absorbing the concept of absorptive capacity: How to realize its potential in the organization field", *Organization Science*, 21: 931–951.

39. J. G. March, 1991, "Exploration and exploitation in organizational learning", *Organization Science*, 2(1): 71–87. Other important literatures make a comparable distinction between single-loop and double-loop learning (see C. Argyris and D. A. Schön, 1978, *Organizational Learning: A Theory of Action Perspective*, Addison-Wesley: Reading), and incremental and step-function learning (see C. E. Helfat and R. S. Raubitschek, 2000, "Product sequencing: Co-evolution of knowledge, capabilities and products", *Strategic Management Journal*, 21(Special Issue): 961–979.

40. W. K. Smith and M. L. Tushman, 2005, "Managing strategic contradictions: A top management team model for managing innovation streams", *Organization Science,* 16: 522–536.

41. R. M. Cyert and J. G. March, 1963, *A Behavioural Theory of the Firm*, Englewood Cliffs, NJ: Prentice-Hall.

42. L. Argote and H. R. Greve, 2007, "A behavioural theory of the firm – 40 years and counting: Introduction and impact", *Organization Science*, 18(3): 337–349.

43. A. Pettigrew, 1988, *The Management of Strategic Change*, Oxford: Blackwell; H. Mintzberg, 1990, "Strategy

formation: Schools of thought", in: J. Frederickson (ed.), *Perspectives on Strategic Management*, New York: Harper & Row, 105–235; H. W. Volberda, F. A. J. Van den Bosch, B. Flier and E. R. Gedajlovic, 2001, "Following the herd or not?: Patterns of renewal in the Netherlands and the UK", *Long Range Planning*, 34: 209–229.

44. R. Agarwal and C. E. Helfat, 2009, "Strategic renewal of organizations", *Organization Science*, 20: 281–293.

45. G. G. Dess, R. D. Ireland, S. A. Zahra, S. W. Floyd, J. J. Janney and P. J. Lane, 2003, "Emerging issues in corporate entrepreneurship", *Journal of Management*, 29(3): 356; M. L. M. Heyden, J. S. Sidhu, F. A. J. Van den Bosch and H. W. Volberda, "Top management team attributes and strategic renewal: How managerial attention to local and non-local search drives adaptive change", Research Paper presented at the Strategic Management Society (SMS) Conference in Rome (September, Italy 2010).

46. L. Capron and W. Mitchell, 2009, "Selection capability: How capability gaps and internal social frictions affect internal and external strategic renewal", *Organization Science*, 20(2): 294–312.

47. B. S. Chakravarthy and Y. Doz, 1992, "Strategy process research: Focusing on corporate self-renewal", *Strategic Management Journal*, 13(1, Special Issue): 5–14.

48. B. Flier, F. A. J. Van den Bosch and H. W. Volberda, 2003, "Co-evolution in strategic renewal behaviour of British, Dutch and French financial incumbents: Interaction of environmental selection, institutional effects and managerial intentionality", *Journal of Management Studies*, 40: 2163–2187.

49. R. Agarwal and C. E. Helfat, 2009, "Strategic renewal of organizations", *Organization Science*, 20: 281–293.

50. S. W. Floyd and P. J. Lane, 2000, "Strategizing throughout the organization: Managing role conflict in strategic renewal", *The Academy of Management Review*, 25(1), 154–177.

51. T. K. Lant and S. J. Mezias, 1990, "Managing discontinuous change: A simulation study of organizational learning and entrepreneurship", *Strategic Management Journal*, 11: 147–179; E. Romanelli and M. L. Tushman, 1994, "Organizational transformation as punctuated equilibrium: An empirical test", *The Academy of Management Journal*, 37(5): 1141–1166; J. Markard and B. Truffer, 2006, "Innovation processes in large technical systems: Market liberalization as a driver for radical change?", *Research Policy*, 35(5): 609–625; S. A. Zahra, 1996, "Governance, ownership, and corporate entrepreneurship: The moderating impact of industry technological opportunities", *Academy of Management Journal*, 39: 1713–1735.

52. R. Agarwal and C. E. Helfat, 2009, "Strategic renewal of organizations", *Organization Science*, 20: 281–293.

53. Z. Kwee, F. A. J. Van den Bosch and H. W. Volberda, 2011, "The influence of top management team's corporate governance orientation on strategic renewal trajectories, A longitudinal analysis of Royal Dutch Shell plc, 1907–2004", *Journal of Management Studies*, (Special Issue), forthcoming.

54. G. G. Dess, R. D. Ireland, S. A. Zahra, S. W. Floyd, J. J. Janney and P. J. Lane, 2003, "Emerging issues in

corporate entrepreneurship", *Journal of Management*, 29(3): 356.

55. G. P. Huber, 1991, "Organizational learning: The contributing processes and the literature", *Organization Science*, 2: 88–115.

56. J. G. March, 1991, "Exploration and exploitation in organizational learning", *Organization Science*, 2(1): 71–87.

57. H. W. Volberda, C. Baden-Fuller and F. A. J. Van den Bosch, 2001, "Mastering strategic renewal: mobilizing renewal journeys in multi-unit firms", *Long Range Planning*, 34: 160.

58. F. T. Azmi, 2008, "Mapping the learn-unlearn-relearn model: Imperatives for strategic management", *European Business Review*, 20(3): 240–259; C. M. Fiol and M. A. Lyles, 1985, "Organization learning", *Academy of Management Review*, 10(4): 803–813; P. C. Nystrom and W. H. Starbuck, 1984, "To avoid organizational crises, unlearn", *Organizational Dynamics*, 12(4) 53–65.

59. D. A. Levinthal and J. G. March, 1993, "The myopia of learning", *Strategic Management Journal*, 14(Special Issue): 95–112.

60. W. K. Smith and M. L. Tushman, 2005, "Managing strategic contradictions: A top management team model for managing innovation streams", *Organization Science*, 16: 522–536.

61. J. G. March, 1991, "Exploration and exploitation in organizational learning", *Organization Science*, 2(1): 71.

62. D. N. Sull, 1999, "Why good companies go bad", *Harvard Business Review*, 77: 42–51; M. J. Benner and M. L. Tushman, 2002, "Process management and technological innovation: a longitudinal study of the photography and paint industries", *Administrative Science Quarterly*, 47: 676–706.

63. Z. He and P-K. Wong, 2004, "Exploration and exploitation: An empirical test of the ambidextrous hypothesis", *Organization Science*, 15: 481–96; W. K. Smith and M. L. Tushman, 2005, "Managing strategic contradictions: A top management team model for managing innovation streams", *Organization Science*, 16: 522–536.

64. D. Leonard-Barton, 1992, "Core capabilities and core rigidities: A paradox in managing new product development", *Strategic Management Journal*, 13(Special Issue): 111–125; R. A. Burgelman, 1994, "Fading memories: A process theory of strategic business exit in dynamic environments", *Administrative Science Quarterly*, 39(1): 24–56; B. Levitt and J. G. March, 1988, "Organizational learning", in: W. R. Scott, *Annual Review of Sociology*, 14: 319–340; D. A. Levinthal and J. G. March, 1993, "The myopia of learning", *Strategic Management Journal*, 14(Special Issue): 95–112.

65. *The Economist*, "A giant falls; The bankruptcy of General Motors", 6 June 2009, http://www.economist.com; *The Economist*, "Leaders: Detroitosaurus wrecks; The decline and fall of General Motors", 6 June 2009, http://www.economist.com; H. W. Volberda, 2003, "Strategic flexibility: Creating dynamic competitive advantages", in: D. Faulkner and A. Campbell (eds.), *The Oxford Handbook of Strategy*, New York: Oxford University Press, 954–955.

66. H. W. Volberda, 1996, "Toward the flexible form: How to remain vital in hypercompetitive environments", *Organization Science*, 7(4): 359–374; H. W. Volberda, 1998, *Building the Flexible Firm: How to Remain Competitive*, Oxford: Oxford University Press.

67. *BusinessWeek*, "The fall of an American icon", 5 February 1996, http://www.businessweek.com.

68. H. W. Volberda, 1996, "Toward the flexible form: How to remain vital in hypercompetitive environments", *Organization Science*, 7(4): 359–374; H. W. Volberda, 1998, *Building the Flexible Firm: How to Remain Competitive*, Oxford: Oxford University Press.

69. P. S. Adler, 1988, "Managing Flexible Automation", *California Management Review*, Spring: 34–56.

70. J. B. Quinn, 1985, "Managing Innovation: Controlled Chaos", *Harvard Business Review*, 63: 73–84.

71. H. I. Ansoff, 1965, *Corporate Strategy*, New York: McGraw Hill.

72. J. Richardson, 1996, "Vertical integration and rapid response in fashion apparel", *Organization Science*, 7: 400–412.

73. D. A. Aaker and B. Mascarenhas, 1984, "The need for strategic flexibility", *The Journal of Business Strategy*, 5(2): 74–82.

74. K. R. Harrigan, 1985, *Strategic Flexibility*, Massachusetts/Toronto: Lexington Books.

75. A. D. Smith and C. Zeithaml, 1996, "Garbage cans and advancing hypercompetition: the creation and exploitation of new capabilities and strategic flexibility in two regional bell operating companies", *Organization Science*, 4: 388–399.

76. P. S. Adler, 1988, "Managing flexible automation", *California Management Review*, 34–56; C. D. Ittner and B. Kogut, 1995, "How control systems can support organizational flexibility", in: E. Bowman and B. Kogut (eds.), *Redesigning the Firm*, New York: Oxford University Press, 155–180.

77. T. Burns and G. M. Stalker (1961), *The Management of Innovation*, London: Tavistock.

78. C. Camerer and A. Vepsalainen, 1988, "The economic efficiency of corporate culture", *Strategic Management Journal*, 9: 115–126.

79. G. Johnson, 1987, *Strategic Change and the Management Process*, Oxford: Basil Blackwell.

80. H. W. Volberda, 1996, "Toward the flexible form: How to remain vital in hypercompetitive environments", *Organization Science*, 7(4): 359–374; H. W. Volberda, 1998, *Building the Flexible Firm: How to Remain Competitive*, Oxford: Oxford University Press.

81. G. Johnson, 1988, "Rethinking incrementalism", *Strategic Management Journal*, 9: 75–91.

82. R. A. Burgelman, 1983, "A process model of internal corporate venturing in the diversified major firm", *Administrative Science Quarterly*, 28: 223–244.

83. N. Siggelkow, 2002, "Evolution toward fit", *Administrative Science Quarterly*, 47: 125–159.

84. R. Nelson and S. Winter, 1982, *An Evolutionary Theory of Economic Change*, Cambridge MA: The Belknap Press of Harvard University.

85. J. M. Utterback and W. J. Abernathy, 1975, "A dynamic model of process and product innovation", *Omega*, 3(6): 639–656.

86. D. Miller and P. Friesen, 1980, "Archetypes of organizational transition", *Administrative Science Quarterly*, 25(2): 268–300.

87. D. Miller and P. Friesen, 1980, "Archetypes of organizational transition", *Administrative Science Quarterly*, 25(2): 283–284.

88. See for example, R. M. Kanter, 1994, *When Giants Learn to Dance: Mastering the Challenge of Strategy, Management and Careers in the 1990s*, London: Routledge (Reprint); Ch. Baden-Fuller and J. Stopford, 1994, *Rejuvenating the Mature Business*, Boston: Harvard Business School Press.

89. D. Miller and P. Friesen, 1980, "Archetypes of organizational transition", *Administrative Science Quarterly*, 25(2): 281.

90. R. M. Kanter, 1988, "When a thousand flowers bloom: Structural, collective, and social conditions for innovation in organization", in: B. M. Staw and L. L. Cummings (eds.), *Research in Organizational Behaviour*, 10, Greenwich, Connecticut: JAI Press, 169–211.

91. This framework and discussion on modes of balancing exploration and exploitation is based on Z. Simsek, 2009, "Organizational ambidexterity: Towards a multilevel understanding", *Journal of Management Studies*, 46(4): 597–624; Z. Simsek, C. Heavey, J. F. Veiga and D. Souder, 2009, "A typology for aligning organizational ambidexterity's conceptualizations, antecedents, and outcomes", *Journal of Management Studies*, 46(5): 864–894; D. Lavie, U. Stettner and M. I. Tushman, 2010, "Exploration and exploitation within and across organizations", *Academy of Management Annals*, 4(1): 109–155; S. Raisch, J. Birkinshaw, G. Probst and M. L. Tushman, 2009, "Organizational ambidexterity: Balancing exploitation and exploration for sustained performance", *Organization Science*, 20(4): 685–695; H. W. Volberda, 2003, "Strategic flexibility: Creating dynamic competitive advantages", in: D. Faulkner and A. Campbell (eds.), *The Oxford Handbook of Strategy*, New York: Oxford University Press, 954–955.

92. C. B. Gibson and J. Birkinshaw, 2004, "The antecedents, consequences, and mediating role of organizational ambidexterity", *Academy of Management Journal*, 47(2): 209–226.

93. H. W. Volberda, 2003, "Strategic flexibility: Creating dynamic competitive advantages", in: D. Faulkner and A. Campbell (eds.), *The Oxford Handbook of Strategy*, New York: Oxford University Press, 954–955.

94. J. J. P. Jansen, M. P. Tempelaar, F. A. J. Van den Bosch and H. W. Volberda, 2009, "Structural differentiation and ambidexterity: The mediating role of integration mechanisms", *Organization Science*, 20(4): 797–811.

95. D. C. Galunic and K. M. Eisenhardt, 1996, "The evolution of intracorporate domains: Divisional charter losses in high-technology, multidivisional corporations", *Organization Science*, 7(3): 255–282.

96. T. J. Peters and R. H. Waterman Jr, 1982, *In Search of Excellence*, New York: Warner Books.

97. N. D. Fast, 1979, "The future of industrial new venture departments", *Industrial Marketing Management*, 8: 264–273; R. A. Burgelman, 1983, "A process model of internal

corporate venturing in the diversified major firm", *Administrative Science Quarterly*, 28: 223–244.

98. H. Mintzberg and F. Westley, 1992, "Cycles of organizational change", *Strategic Management Journal*, 13: 39–59.

99. J. S. Sidhu, H. R. Commandeur and H. W. Volberda, 2007, "The multifaceted nature of exploration and exploitation: Value of supply, demand and spatial search for innovation", *Organization Science*, 18(1): 20–38.

100. T. J. M. Mom, F. A. J. Van Den Bosch and H. W. Volberda, 2009, "Understanding variation in managers' ambidexterity: Investigating direct and interaction effects of formal structural and personal coordination mechanisms", *Organization Science*, 20(4): 812–828; T. J. M. Mom, F. A. J. Van Den Bosch and H. W. Volberda, 2007, "Investigating managers' exploration and exploitation activities: The influence of top-down, bottom-up and horizontal knowledge inflows", *Journal of Management Studies*, 44(6): 910–931.

101. R. E. Miles, H. J. Coleman, Jr and W. E. D. Creed, 1995, "Keys to success in corporate redesign", *California Management Review*, 37(3): 128–145.

102. R. T. Pascale, 1984, "Perspectives on strategy: The real story behind Honda's success", *California Management Review*, 26(3): 47–86.

103. D. Lavie and L. Rosenkopf, 2006, "Balancing exploration and exploitation in alliance formation", *Academy of Management Journal*, 49(4): 797–818.

104. H. W. Volberda, Ch. Baden-Fuller and F. A. J. Van den Bosch, 2001, "Mastering strategic renewal: Mobilizing renewal journeys in multi-unit firms", *Long Range Planning*, 34: 160; H. W. Volberda, 2004, "Mastering strategic renewal", in: S. Chowdhury (ed.), *Next Generation Business Handbook: New Strategies from Tomorrow's Thought Leaders*, Ch. 19, Hoboken, New Jersey: Wiley, 333–357; H. W. Volberda and Ch. Baden-Fuller, 2003, Strategic renewal processes in multi-unit firms: Generic journeys of change, Ch. 10 in: B. Chakravarthy, G. Mueller-Stewens, P. Lorange and C. Lechner (eds.), *Strategy Process: Shaping the Contours of the Field*, Oxford: Blackwell, 208–232.

105. This section builds on S. W. Floyd and P. J. Lane, 2000, "Strategizing throughout the organization: Managing role conflict in strategic renewal", *The Academy of Management Review*, 25(1), 154–177.

106. J. R. Galbraith, 1982, "Designing the innovating organization", *Organizational Dynamics*, 10: 5–25.

107. R. A. Burgelman, 1983, "A process model of internal corporate venturing in the diversified major firm", *Administrative Science Quarterly*, 28: 223–244.

108. H. L. Angle and A. H. Van de Ven, 1989, "Suggestions for managing the innovation journey", in: A. H. Van de Ven, H. L. Angle and M. S. Poole (eds.), *Research on the Management of Innovation*, New York: Harper & Row, 663–97.

109. For a similar treatment of these roles see also D. L. Day, 1994, "Raising radicals: Different processes for championing innovative corporate ventures", *Organization Science*, 5(2): 148–172.

110. J. E. Dutton and S. J. Ashford, 1993, "Selling issues to top management", *Academy of Management Review*, 18(3): 397–428.

111. C. A. Barlett and S. Goshal, 1993, "Toward a managerial theory of the firm", *Strategic Management Journal*, 14 (Special Issue: Organizations, Decision Making and Strategy): 23–46; Q. N. Huy, 2002, "Emotional balancing of organizational continuity and radical change: The contribution of middle managers", *Administrative Science Quarterly*, 47(1): 31–69.

112. T. E. Beck and D. A. Plowman, 2009, "Experiencing rare and unusual events richly: The role of middle managers in animating and guiding organizational interpretation", *Organization Science*, 20(5): 909–924.

113. M. A. Maidique, 1980, "Entrepreneurs, champions and technological innovation", *Sloan Management Review*, 21(2): 59–76; D. L. Day, 1994, "Raising radicals: Different processes for championing innovative corporate ventures", *Organization Science*, 5(2): 148–172.

114. For a more extensive discussion see also A. Andrews and M. Goold, 1998, *Synergy: Why Links Between Business Units Often Fail and How To Make Them Work*, Oxford: Capstone.

115. Lex Column, 1996, "Pick of Lex: A selection of comments from this week's FT", *Financial Times*, 10 August.

116. K. E. Weick (1979) describes this sense making as *enactment* in *The Social Psychology of Organizing*, Reading, MA: Addison-Wesley; P. S. Barr, J. L. Stimpert and A. S. Huff, 1992, "Cognitive change, strategic action, and organizational renewal", *Strategic Management Journal*, 13(6): 15–36. For a further discussion of top management cognition and renewal see: J. P. Eggers and S. Kaplan, 2009, "Cognition and renewal: comparing CEO and organizational effects on incumbent adaptation to technical change", *Organization Science*, 20(2): 461–477.

117. See R. Calori, Ch. Baden-Fuller and B. Hunt, 2000, "Managing change at Novotel: Back to the future", *Long Range Planning*, 33: 779–804.

118. A. Y. Lewin and H. W. Volberda, 1999, "Prolegomena on coevolution: A framework for research on strategy and new organizational forms", *Organization Science*, 10(5): 523.

119. B. McKelvey, 2002, "Managing coevolutionary dynamics", Paper presented at the 18th Egos Colloquium, Subtheme 11: Adaptation, Selection and Long Lived Organizations, 4–6 July, Barcelona, Spain.

120. H. W. Volberda and A. Y. Lewin, 2003, "Co-evolutionary dynamics within and between firms: From evolution to coevolution", *Journal of Management Studies*, 40(8).

121. T. J. M. Mom, F. A. J. Van Den Bosch and H. W. Volberda, 2009, "Understanding variation in managers' ambidexterity: Investigating direct and interaction effects of formal structural and personal coordination mechanisms", *Organization Science*, 20(4): 812–828; T. J. M. Mom, F. A. J. Van Den Bosch and H. W. Volberda, 2007, "Investigating managers' exploration and exploitation activities: The influence of top-down, bottom-up and horizontal knowledge inflows", *Journal of Management Studies*, 44(6): 910–931.

122. See the US Security Exchange Commission (http://www.sec.gov) on "Chapter 11 Filings".

© BIM/iStock

# INTEGRATIVE CASES

| Case List | 1. Strategic management and strategic competitiveness | 2. The external environment: opportunities, threats, industry competition and competitor analysis | 3. The internal organization: resources, capabilities, core competencies and competitive advantages | 4. Integrating internal and external resources: open innovation, absorptive capacity and integration approaches | 5. Business-level strategy | 6. Competitive rivalry and competitive dynamics | 7. Corporate-level strategy | 8. Strategic acquisition and restructuring | 9. International strategy | 10. Cooperative strategy | 11. Strategic leadership | 12. Corporate governance | 13. Organizational structure and contols | 14. Strategic entrepreneurship | 15. Strategic renewal |
|---|---|---|---|---|---|---|---|---|---|---|---|---|---|---|---|
| 1. ABN AMRO in the Volvo Ocean Race: A Bank Learning to Sail as One Team | X | | | X | | | X | | | | | | | X | X |
| 2. A Perfect Marriage for all the Right Reasons: P&G and Gillette | | X | | X | | | | X | X | | | | X | | |
| 3. Carrefour in Asia | | X | | | | | | | X | | | | | | |
| 4. China's Home Improvement Market: Should Home Depot Enter or Will it Have a Late-Mover (dis)advantage? | X | | | | X | | | | X | | | | | | |
| 5. Corporate Environmental Responsibility: Microsoft's Partnership Programs | | | X | X | | | | | X | | X | | | | X |
| 6. eBay Inc.: Bidding for the Future | X | | | X | | X | X | | | X | | | | | |
| 7. Huawei: Cicso's Chinese Challenger | | | | X | | | | | X | | X | | | X | |
| 8. ING Direct: Rebel in the Banking Industry | | | | X | | X | | | | | X | | | X | X |
| 9. Lufthansa: Going Global, but How to Manage Complexity? | | | | X | | | | X | X | | | | X | | X |
| 10. Nestlé: Divesting Perrier? | | | X | | | X | | X | X | | | X | | | |
| 11. Nintendo's Distributive Strategy: Implications for the Video Game Industry | | X | X | | | | | | | | X | X | X | | |
| 12. PSA Peugeot Citroën: Strategic Alliances for Competitive Advantage? | | X | X | | | | | | | X | | X | X | X | |
| 13. Tesco versus Sainsbury's: Growth Strategies and Corporate Competitiveness | X | X | X | | | | X | | X | | | | X | | |
| 14. Toyota: The Once-in-a-Century Challenge | | X | X | | | | | | X | | | X | X | | X |
| 15. Vodafone: Out of Many, One | X | X | X | | | | | | X | | | X | X | | |

# INTEGRATIVE CASE 1

# 1

# ABN AMRO IN THE VOLVO OCEAN RACE: A BANK LEARNING TO SAIL AS ONE TEAM

Henk W. Volberda

*Rotterdam School of Management, Erasmus University Rotterdam*

## Introduction

On November 12th, 2005, two state-of-the-art sailing boats called ABN AMRO ONE and ABN AMRO TWO headed off from Vigo, Spain to Cape Town, in one of the most prestigious sailing races in the world. The Volvo Ocean Race (VOR) finished 216 days and 31,250 nautical miles later in Gothenburg, Sweden.

Although ABN AMRO had been active in sports sponsoring and local sailing events (such as the North Sea Regatta) for some time, the magnitude of the VOR was unprecedented. This was the first time the bank had participated in a global sporting event, let alone one with a world-wide client hospitality programme, including a huge travelling pavilion that attracted over a million spectators in nine countries.

Furthermore, the bank took the decision not just to sponsor an existing sailing team, but to actively participate in the race. Through an embedded organisation called ABN AMRO Brand & Sail Company, the bank organised two new sailing teams in-house; designed and built its own boats; and developed an extensive branding and marketing campaign. Considering the size of the ABN AMRO logos on the sails, the sides of the boats, and the impressive amount of media attention the race generated worldwide, one would expect that the bank was pretty sure they would not mess this up. But what were the reasons behind the bank's participation in the sailing race in the first place?

## The one bank strategy of ABN AMRO N.V.

ABN AMRO (AA) is a leading international bank whose Dutch origins date back to 1824. Based on total assets, amounting to EUR 999 billion,[1] AA ranks 8th in Europe and 13th in the world and employs staff of over 110,000 full-time equivalents. With the appointment of Rijkman Groenink as CEO in 2000, AA's new focus was to be on the upper-segment with a key role for BU Wholesale Clients. However, fierce competition from large players in the whole-sale segment, such as Goldman Sachs and Morgan Stanley, led AA to reverse this decision in 2001 and redirect its focus to pension-funding and asset-gathering in the private market and to medium-size enterprises as its business clients.

Within this segment, AA believes it distinguishes itself most from its competitors[2] (see Exhibit 1a). The new strategic focus on the mid-market segment was accompanied by a strong need to reduce costs. Together, these factors laid the basis for what would become a continuing process of organisational restructuring, which in itself has received quite a bit of critique from business analysts.[3]

This business case for educative purposes was prepared by Henk W. Volberda, professor of Strategic Management and Business Policy, together with research-assistants Martin Dongelmans, Michiel de Man and Thiemen P. Vermeulen at Rotterdam School of Management, Erasmus University. We would like to thank ABN AMRO for its generous support and in particular Sandor Brouwer and Jan Berent Heukensfeldt Jansen for their helpful suggestions.

**EXHIBIT 1a**  ABN AMRO's client focus

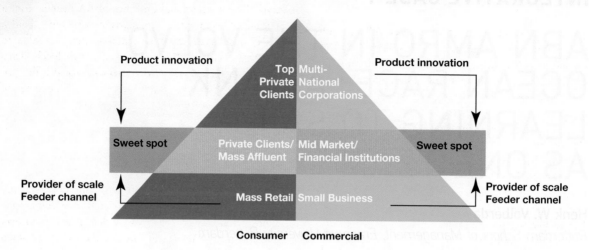

**Source:** ABN AMRO N.V., 2005.

**EXHIBIT 1b**  ABN AMRO's BU-structure

| Netherlands | Europe | North America | Latin America | Asia | Private Clients | Global Clients |
|---|---|---|---|---|---|---|
| Consumer Client Segment | | | | | | |
| Commercial Client Segment | | | | | | |
| Local Products | Local Products | Local Products | Local Products | Local Products | Local Products | M&A ECM |
| Global Markets | | | | | | |
| Transaction Banking | | | | | | |
| Asset Management | | | | | | |
| Services | | | | | | |
| Group Functions | | | | | | |

**Source:** ABN AMRO N.V., 2005.

Another often heard complaint is that the reduction of wholesale activities – which are generally viewed as depressing AA's overall performance – is not going fast enough.[4] Since the 1st of January 2006, AA has consisted of a number of Business Units (BUs). These units are responsible for managing a distinct region, client segment or product segment (see Exhibit 1b for an organisational overview). Five regional Client BUs, namely the Netherlands, Europe, North America, Latin America and Asia, serve about 20 million consumer clients and small to larger businesses worldwide. Two BUs serve clients with global needs: the BU Private Clients provides private banking services to individuals, while the BU Global Clients serves multinational corporations.

Additionally, three BUs serve the product segments Global Markets, Transaction Banking and Asset Man-agement. Global Markets develops products for commercial clients across the globe, Transaction Banking covers payments and trade in the bank for retail, private client, and commercial markets, while Asset Management focuses on the management of assets for private investors and institutional clients. A separate Service organisation was established as a vital infrastructure to the BUs and the duties of the BU Wholesale Clients were partially placed under the responsibility of the separate regional Client BUs. By means of this structure, AA is able to create value through a wide range of banking services for a comprehensive spectrum of clients. To date, the bank's main focus remains on mid-market clients, both at the private and the commercial markets: the 'sweet spot' for the bank.

# Internationalization

Starting as a small Dutch trading society, AA has evolved into a global financial player, with more than 4500 branches in 60 countries. AA's internationalisation strategy is based on setting up its own international branches worldwide, as well as on acquisitions of a number of retail banks.

The most notable acquisitions include LaSalle Bank in Chicago in 1979; Brazilian Banco Real in 1998; and recently the much-discussed takeover of Italian Antonveneta in 2005. These acquisitions represent AA's most important international markets: the Midwest of the US; Brazil and Northeastern Italy, served by respectively BU North America, BU Latin America and BU Europe.

BU North America (BU NA) is the 13th largest bank in the US with assets exceeding US$ 110 billion, and is the 20th largest in terms of deposits. The core of BU NA is LaSalle Bank, serving approximately 3.5 million consumer and commercial clients. BU NA's mission is to be the premier relationship-driven bank based in the US Midwest. To achieve this objective, BU NA maintains a varied portfolio of businesses designed to meet the sophisticated and changing needs of consumer and commercial clients.

AA has been present in Brazil since 1917. With the acquisition of retail banks Banco Real, Bandepe and Paraiban in 1998 and Banco Sudameris in 2003, it strongly increased its stake in the Brazilian retail and commercial banking industry, serving around 10 million clients. AA aims to be one of the most efficient and valued banks in the Brazilian market. It seeks to grow its business by optimising its segmented approach to the mid-market consumer and commercial clients.

The acquisition of Banca Antonveneta is envisaged as offering AA a strong presence in Italy's wealthy north-eastern region and to serve as an ideal platform to expand its presence in the mid-market segment. Currently, AA is transforming Antonveneta's organisational structure to a matrix organisation, enhancing its ties with the Group function while maintaining client-focus. Investor relations officer Alexander Mollerus says: "The international branches of AA benefit from a unique selling point. In comparison with other banks, AA's subsidiaries stand out in that they are able to link their long-standing relationships with local clients to a powerful global network, which provides the private and commercial clients access to a unique set of products and service."

# One bank

Although ABN AMRO also grew organically, its acquisition strategy was the major driver to it becoming the major global player it is today, with subsidiaries in over 60 countries. AA had, in most countries, opted for a 'laissez-faire' approach with regard to most of the activities of the acquired subsidiaries and this approach appeared to work well. However, around the year 2000, negative coverage increased as a consequence of disappointing growth of earnings per share. Investment analysts argued that even though the internal organisational structure of AA and its international subsidiaries had been quite homogeneous over time, AA failed to invest in a cohesive global entity and was not reaping the benefits of corresponding synergy-advantages. Alexander Mollerus explains: "One of the main reasons for the disappointing financial results was the lack of synergy within the AA group. Although some collaboration existed, it was organised ad hoc and limited in scope."

The lack of synergy resulted in suboptimal value creation and a lower valuation per share. In 2001, this so-called 'conglomerate discount' was estimated to account for 10 to 15% of the total value of the company. Between 2000 and 2002, AA held extensive discussions about how to improve internal alignment of activities as well as transparency to external stakeholders. Reorganisation processes were initiated that focused on improving internal communication, alignment and cooperation between business units worldwide. Aligning the organisation's structure, management, training and human resources, as

---

*Box 1: Horizon*

"An interesting program promoting the 'one bank strategy' is the Horizon project, which is still running today. Horizon is a collective name for a broad range of knowledge sharing initiatives across ABN AMRO. The premise is that recognizing and developing new collaboration opportunities within and between businesses which, for example, stimulate productivity and improve the time a product or service takes to come to market, will improve efficiency and serve customers better."

## EXHIBIT 2  The renewal journey of ABN AMRO

### A strategic reflection

In 2001, AA changed its strategic focus from wholesale to the mid-market segment in both the private and business market. This decision was taken at the corporate level. However, even though it was recognised by the board that AA would not be able to compete in the wholesale segment, the bank only gradually reduced its investments in this division which, according to analysts, has depressed the performance of the bank.

To date, large scale operations in the wholesale segment continue, despite the strategic intent disseminated by the bank to focus on the 'sweet spot'. This has led to fierce criticism from investors and analysts, arguing the bank leaves (too) much strategic decision authority to the separate BUs. AA had also opted for a 'laissez-faire strategy' towards the acquired international BUs. This loose governance structure enabled the BUs to be highly responsive to their own markets. Market-driven changes were made on an ad hoc and emergent basis without either top management or frontline managers actively and fundamentally altering the organisation's processes. Even though the international BUs were performing well, shareholders demanded synergies resulting from 'parenting advantages'.[1]

Strategic renewal actions aimed at improving communication and cooperation between BUs and achieving learning effects and economies of scale, without compromising the local responsiveness of the BUs were needed. However, these proved not easy to achieve, and especially in the short run. For example, as a result of institutional, cultural, demographic and legal factors, the demand for financial products is very country-specific, especially in the retail market. As a result, scale advantages at the product portfolio are difficult to achieve. Branding and cultural alignment were identified as areas where synergies could potentially create value and projects in these areas were initialised.

Large-scale organisational restructuring to improve efficiency constituted the bulk of the work, however. An important element was the implementation of a large offshoring programme in India, consolidating the supporting units of the bank and cutting service costs. Yet most of these reorganisations, like other large investments such as the takeover of Antonveneta, impose high initial costs and take time to release value. As a result of these and other factors, AA's performance has been lagging behind the industry average, and year after year the bank failed to reach its goal to be among the top five of a group of 20 selected competitors. In February 2007, shareholder pressure mounted with a direct letter from hedge fund TCI to AA's board, urging the company to split up: a unique event in financial business history. The fact that value creation is expected from splitting up (in other words: the sum of parts is expected to be worth more than the whole) can be seen as a worrisome indication of conglomerate discount continuing up to today.

### Idealized Renewal Journeys of Multi-Unit Firms[2]

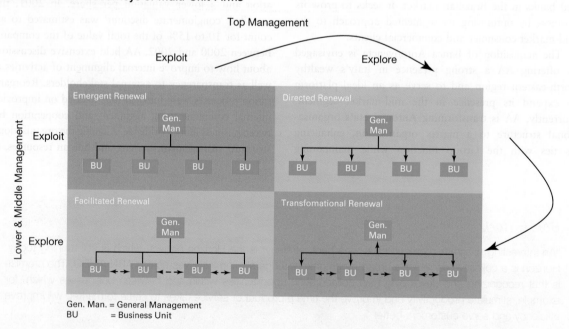

Gen. Man. = General Management
BU         = Business Unit

|  | Top management is *passive* with respect to environment | Top management is *active* with respect to environment |
| --- | --- | --- |
| **Frontline and Middle Management are** *Passive* **(stable competition)** | **Emergent Renewal**<br>1) Market<br>2) External selection environment<br>3) Unbalanced: Strong bias towards exploitation<br>4) Market knows best: No organisational knowledge integration (less connected units)<br>5) Following Industry rules | **Directed Renewal**<br>1) Hierarchy<br>2) Top Management<br>3) Balanced: Matching exploitative and explorative units<br>4) Top Management knows best and orchestrates organisational knowledge integration (reasonably coupled units)<br>5) Adapting to industry rules |
| **Frontline and Middle Management are** *Active* **(hypercompetition)** | **Facilitated Renewal**<br>1) Co-evolution<br>2) Internal selection environment<br>3) Balanced: exploitative and explorative units<br>4) Front and middle management challenge 'market knows best' and orchestrate organisational knowledge integration (loosely connected units)<br>5) Influencing industry rules | **Transformational Renewal**<br>1) Shared sense-making<br>2) Top-, middle- and frontline management<br>3) Unbalanced: from strong exploitation towards strong exploration and vice versa<br>4) Organisation knows best: High organisational knowledge integration (tightly coupled units)<br>5) Changing industry rules |

Theoretical differences regarding (1) source of variation; (2) locus of unit selection; (3) exploitation/exploration balance; (4) knowledge design; (5) competitive positioning.

### Notes

1. See Goold *et al.* 1994.

2. Adapted from Volberda *et al.*, 2001: 164.

well as consolidating the supportive units should all contribute to more synergy advantages and eventually a reduction of conglomerate discount.[5]

The structural reorganisation accompanying this one bank strategy was directed top-down to the BUs globally (see Exhibit 2). International integration also aimed to align the business culture among employees of the bank globally, which was expected to enhance employee performance and commitment to the bank's overall objectives. Being able to cooperate as one team at the group level constitutes the basic idea behind this so-called 'One Bank philosophy', which has become one of the core elements of AA's business culture.[6]

# Endorsement campaign: one brand

In line with the one bank strategy, AA's managing board decided that the bank should reconsider its global brand positioning. In the financial services sector, the importance and value of a strong company brand has steadily increased in recent decades. In 2005, the brand ABN AMRO was estimated to account for 18.9 % of the total market capitalisation of AA, which means its brand value is more than US$ 9 billion, underscoring the importance of professional brand management (see Exhibits 3 and 4).

**EXHIBIT 3**  Brand architecture

| | Monolithic | Endorsed | Pluralistic |
|---|---|---|---|
| **Definition** | One name and visual identity | Different brands are endorsed with a group name and visual identity | Different brands live side by side, unrelated to either each other or the group name and visual identity |
| **Example** | HSBC | ABN·AMRO<br>BANCO REAL (ABN AMRO)<br>LaSalle Bank (ABN AMRO)<br>Antonveneta (ABN AMRO) | HBOS plc<br>BANK OF SCOTLAND<br>HALIFAX |
| **Advantages** | Clear and consistent<br>Strong and memorable<br>Equity transfer<br>Economies of scale | Cohesive<br>Mutually supportive<br>Flexibility<br>Best of both worlds | Simple consumer proposition<br>Clear individual identity<br>Defined areas of competence<br>Creative flexibility |
| **Disadvantages** | Repetitive<br>Unsubtle<br>Inflexible<br>Hard to segment | Potential confusion<br>Requires strong parent equity<br>Possible 'guilt by association'<br>Duplicated cost | Vulnerable to me-too's<br>Lacks 'family' security<br>Limits brand extension<br>Fragmented cost |

Brand Architecture is the hierarchy within which corporate and sub-brand in a company's portfolio are related to each other, differentiated from each other and supported by each other. The characteristics shared by strong brands today are as follows:

| | |
|---|---|
| **Clarity** | The brand is a single entity with a common vision, mission and set of values, which are distinctive and relevant, and which are recognised and understood by staff, the trade, the financial community, the media and the customers. |
| **Consistency** | The brand adopts, embeds and manifests its values wherever it appears and in whatever form (from the visual identity and advertising to the way the phone is answered). |
| **Leadership** | To achieve a truly global leadership status, the brand must lead and exceed expectations and take people into new territories and new areas of product and service. |

**Source:** Adapted from Brand-Finance, 2006: 12–13.

**EXHIBIT 4** The global banking brand index (1–30)

| Rank | Companies | Country | Brand value[1] | Market Cap[2] | Brand Value/ Market Cap | Brand Rating[3] |
|---|---|---|---|---|---|---|
| 1 | Citi | US | 35,148 | 245,512 | 14,3% | AAA– |
| 2 | HSBC | GB | 33,495 | 181,703 | 18,4% | AAA |
| 3 | Bank of America | US | 31,426 | 185,342 | 17,0% | AAA– |
| 4 | American Express | US | 18,109 | 63,897 | 28,3% | AAA– |
| 5 | Santander Central Hispano | ES | 17,063 | N.A. | N.A. | AA– |
| 6 | UBS | SW | 15,137 | 103,522 | 14,6% | AA– |
| 7 | Wells Fargo & CO | US | 14,277 | 105,067 | 13,6% | AA |
| 8 | BNP Paribas | FR | 12,278 | 67,796 | 18,1% | A |
| 9 | Barclays | GB | 12,182 | 67,955 | 17,9% | A |
| 10 | Chase | US | 12,083 | N.A. | N.A. | AA– |
| 11 | Credit Suisse | US | 11,519 | 61,851 | 18,6% | A– |
| 12 | ABN AMRO | NL | 9,434 | 49,919 | 18,9% | AA– |
| 13 | Wachovia Corp | US | 9,430 | 82,116 | 11,5% | AA– |
| 14 | Merrill Lynch | US | 8,835 | 62,116 | 14,2% | A+ |
| 15 | Morgan Stanley | US | 8,732 | 60,012 | 14,6% | A |
| 16 | Goldman Sachs | US | 8,712 | 59,263 | 14,7% | A+ |
| 17 | Deutsche Bank | DE | 8,240 | 53,605 | 15,4% | A– |
| 18 | Societe Generale | FR | 7,856 | 53,300 | 14,7% | A– |
| 19 | BBVA | ES | 7,553 | 60,507 | 12,5% | A+ |
| 20 | JP Morgan | US | 6,383 | N.A. | N.A. | A |
| 21 | Lloyds TSB | GB | 6,169 | N.A. | N.A. | A+ |
| 22 | Mizuho Financial | JP | 6,090 | 95,242 | 6,4% | AA |
| 23 | Credit Agricole | FR | 5,820 | 47,147 | 12,3% | A– |
| 24 | Natwest | GB | 5,705 | N.A. | N.A. | A |
| 25 | Capital One | US | 5,701 | 25,877 | 22,0% | AA+ |
| 26 | ING | NL | 5,354 | N.A. | N.A. | A+ |
| 27 | National Australia Bank | AU | 5,274 | 37,959 | 13,9% | BBB |
| 28 | Royal Bank of Scotland | GB | 4,997 | N.A. | N.A. | A |
| 29 | Halifax | GB | 4,918 | N.A. | N.A. | A+ |
| 30 | Lehman Bros | US | 4,424 | 34,785 | 12,7% | A+ |

**Source:** Adapted from Brand-Finance, 2006: 7.

**Notes**

1. In million US Dollars, in 2005.

2. In Million US Dollars as at 31/12/05.

3. Based on BrandBeta analysis; AAA = Extremely Strong; AA; Very Strong; A = Strong; BBB Average.

At AA, the '*laissez-faire* strategy' had also been applied to the branding: after the acquisitions, the bank's international branches kept their original names (LaSalle, Banco Real, etc.) and overall customer interface. "Our practice in most markets where we acquired local banks was to keep them unchanged. The logos represented traditions and positive reputations, based on a strong history in their markets. Such brands are valuable assets", global brand director Bob Van Gessel explains.

The destruction of brand capital is a major concern for international organisations that consider rebranding of their subsidiaries. In general, the main risks of re-branding include a waste of the subsidiaries' brand value; negative effects on customer loyalty and employee commitment; and uncertainty about whether the expected surplus value to result from re-branding will actually be attained.[7] At the same time, communicating uniformity to all customer segments, shareholders, and employees was considered very important: "AA needed to be seen as an entity rather than some sort of broad investment fund and the lack of visible unity was seen as an important obstacle to the external communication of the 'one bank' image", Bob explains. Also, separate brand identities limited the potential for cooperation and realizing cost synergies between different parts of the group, due to the interconnectedness between brand connotation and organisation culture. One global positioning strategy could facilitate communication towards customers and shareholders, as well as align the complete company with the central strategy.[8] Worldwide uniformity in brand name, visual identity and customer interface were expected to appeal to international clients, both private and commercial. Also, one brand would facilitate economies of scale in branding costs, such as advertising.[9]

In line with these pros and cons, divergent views existed at AA's branding department about what branding strategy to follow. Some managers envisaged a full monolithic re-branding strategy including the renaming of all worldwide subsidiaries to AA and a shared visual identity to be the best solution. Others pointed at the risk that a sudden shift would alienate the customers from their local branches and lead to a run out of customers.

Early in 2003, AA decided to opt for 'the best of both worlds' by means of an 'endorsement campaign' to re-brand the relationship banking businesses. While retaining the brand name, subsidiaries' logos were changed to the AA shield, followed by the original name and the AA endorsement (see Figure 1). LaSalle Bank and Standard Federal Bank of the US, Alfred Berg of Sweden, Hoare Govett of the United Kingdom, and Dellbrück & Co of Germany participated in the programme. Banque

**FIGURE 1**   Endorsed branding

NSMD and Banque OBC, both France, followed in early 2004. Late 2006 AA announced the rebranding of its Italian subsidiary Antonveneta.

As a result of the consolidation trend in the financial services industry, many banks are now dealing with their (global) branding strategy. AA's endorsement campaign, often termed 'glocal positioning' is but one path towards global brand management. For example, Fortis Bank has recently fully re-branded several of its subsidiaries and HSBC completely centralised its brand positioning by opting for a uniform global brand. This is often a preferred strategy if global markets are perceived homogeneous. ING, another leading European bank, is currently examining the possibilities of re-branding its daughter Postbank. Interestingly, Postbank's brand value is even higher than its mother's. Contrary, Royal Bank of Scotland and its affiliates treat its global markets as a portfolio of national opportunities, like AA did before.[10] As Exhibits 3 and 4 demonstrate, the balance between global integration and national responsiveness could prove to be contingently successful for different companies.

## "Making more possible" through one global tagline

Another important element of the re-branding strategy followed in February 2005 with the introduction of a global tagline. Taglines, the memorable phrases summing up the tone and premise of a brand, have become widespread in the financial sector. Global players, such as UBS, USBC, Citibank, Deutsche Bank and Bank of America have all adopted this marketing trend.

As a core element in the global branding strategy, it was important to find a tagline that would fit all of AA's markets. After rigorous marketing research in all of AA's markets, 'Making more possible' was put forward as AA's worldwide motto and promoted intensively through television advertisements: "This tagline encapsulates the way we work in close partnership with our customers to tackle challenges and achieve goals together. It also emphasises that we are one group with the same business methodology and the same high quality of service all over the world, while – internally – it unites our staff and helps us to focus on our common vision. 'Making more possible' will appear in English, Dutch, French, German and Portuguese."[11]

## Internalising the one bank philosophy

Internally, the re-branding campaign had the objective of aligning the different cultures among the bank's employees. According to AA, "employees are critical to knowledge sharing and achieving synergy. In order to achieve this, employees need to be stimulated by creating a culture in which sharing knowledge is stimulated and rewarded."[12] Shared social knowledge, trust and identification with the mother company have been identified as important factors contributing to the adoption of desired organisational practices by the subsidiary.[13] To promote the one bank philosophy on AA's shop floor, management training, presentations and several programmes within the bank were organised (see Box 1 for an example). However, acquiring cultural changes is widely known to be a complex and slow process while progress is difficult to measure. Given the fact that even within one organisation this may be very difficult as departments are generally reluctant to change their attitudes and routines, it is evident that aligning the business cultures of its international subsidiaries poses a major challenge to AA until today. As Bob puts it, "It's difficult to ensure the one bank philosophy is actually internalised at the foreign branches. PowerPoint presentations and workshops only get you so far. To succeed, you need to appeal to the emotions of the employees."

## The VOR as a marketing platform

Marketing experts concluded that an active sponsorship could "appeal to people's emotions, as it transcends cultural and geographical borders and creates brand experience with impact",[14] especially when it involves leisure and sports activities. Obviously, brand exposure to the outside world was another important reason to opt for a sponsorship.

Together with IMG – a media company specialised in sports and entertainment – the corporate sponsoring department analysed several sponsorship opportunities. Global sporting events were identified as "potentially powerful means to communicate the new brand identity both externally and internally; to build bridges between business units (BUs); and to demonstrate the board's commitment to the global brand and to being a major international banking force."[15]

Research shows that image transfer is stimulated when the sponsored event matches the company's image or when the event matches the company's functionality.[16] In this line of thought, several events within football, sailing, golf, Formula One and tennis, as well as stand-alone events such as the Olympics were evaluated. Finally, the VOR was identified as a strong marketing platform offering the most opportunities (see Box 2 for the history of the VOR). "The story of sailing is comparable to daily life at work: you are challenged and performance is influenced by your strategy, tactics and commitment; communicating is essential to be successful. The VOR fits perfectly with our brand values of integrity, professionalism, teamwork and respect, as well as fitting our (top-) clients profile."[17]

Comparison with other potential sponsorship events also topped the VOR: "It is one of the few team sports with a global appeal (besides Formula One and football). Furthermore, it has a unique brand positioning compared to the Olympic Games, Football World Cup and a F1 team, where there is presence of other brands; here you have your own boat(s), an exposure period of the race of 9 months and full commercial control. On top of that, with stopovers planned in Rio de Janeiro, New York, Baltimore and Rotterdam, the VOR offers a perfect opportunity to engage local BUs, employees and customers in AA's three most important markets."[18]

## Calculated risk or risky business?

Even though the VOR was expected to provide an effective platform for the bank, the risks were not to be overlooked. First, the media success of the campaign would strongly depend on the performance of the team: losing the VOR was obviously not what AA intended to become known for. Furthermore, even though AA had a long experience with sports sponsorships (e.g. being head sponsor of football club Ajax and the AA Tennis Tournament), participation in the VOR would be nothing like AA had done before and only two years earlier,

## Box 2: History of the Volvo Ocean Race

Colonel Bill Whitbread, of the Whitbread Brewing family and Admiral Otto Steiner, of the Royal Naval Sailing Association, founded the race in 1973. The Whitbread around the World race, since 1998 known as the Volvo Ocean Race, was the world's first round the world yacht race and attracted seventeen boats. During the first race, there was a mix of amateur and professional sailors, many different types of yachts, and a sense of pioneering adventure. Nowadays, the traditional yachts have developed into dedicated high tech racing machines crewed by multi-national teams bristling with Olympic medal winners and America's Cup campaigners. The VOR 2005/6 consisted of nine legs, starting in Vigo, Spain and ultimately finishing in Goteborg, Sweden. This edition introduced a new scoring system; teams can score points via mid-leg scoring gates, leg finishes and in-port races, which in sum counts for the overall result. Seven points are being awarded to the winner of each leg, and half the points are rewarded to the winner of the scoring gates as well as for the in port races (see Exhibit 5 for an overview).

**EXHIBIT 5**   Race overview

| VENUE | LEG | DATE | DISTANCE |
|---|---|---|---|
| | In-port race | 05-Nov-05 | |
| VIGO | Leg 1 START | 12-Nov-05 | Distance 6,400 nm |
| CAPE TOWN | Leg 1 FINISH | 04-Dec-05 | |
| | In-port race | 26-Dec-05 | |
| | Leg 2 START | 02-Jan-06 | Distance 6,100 nm |
| MELBOURNE | Leg 2 FINISH | 19-Jan-06 | |
| | In-port race | 04-Feb-06 | |
| | Leg 3 START | 12-Feb-06 | Distance 1,450 nm |
| WELLINGTON (Pitstop) | Leg 3 FINISH | 17-Feb-06 | |
| | Leg 4 START | 19-Feb-06 | Distance 6,700 nm |
| RIO DE JANEIRO | Leg 4 FINISH | 13-Mar-06 | |
| | In-port race | 25-Mar-06 | |
| | Leg 5 START | 02-Apr-06 | Distance 5,000 nm |
| BALTIMORE/ANNAPOLIS | Leg 5 FINISH | 20-Apr-06 | |
| | In-port race | 29-Apr-06 | |
| | Leg 6 START | 07-May-06 | Distance 400 nm |
| NEW YORK (Pitstop) | Leg 6 FINISH | 09-May-06 | |
| | Leg 7 START | 11-May-06 | Distance 3,200 nm |
| PORTSMOUTH | Leg 7 FINISH | 23-May-06 | |
| | In-port race | 29-May-06 | |
| | Leg 8 START | 03-Jun-06 | Distance 1,500 nm |

| VENUE | LEG | DATE | DISTANCE |
|---|---|---|---|
| **ROTTERDAM** | Leg 8 FINISH | 09-Jun-06 | |
| | In-port race | 11-Jun-06 | |
| | Leg 9 START | 15-Jun-06 | Distance 500 nm |
| **GOTHENBURG** | Leg 9 FINISH | 17-Jun-06 | |

| IN PORT RACES | DATE |
|---|---|
| SANXENXO (GALICIA) | 5-Nov-05 |
| CAPE TOWN (SOUTH AFRICA) | 26-Dec-05 |
| MELBOURNE (AUSTRALIA) | 4-Feb-06 |
| RIO DE JANEIRO (BRAZIL) | 25-Mar-06 |
| BALITMORE/ANNAPOLIS (USA) | 29-Apr-06 |
| PORTSMOUTH (UK) | 29-May-06 |
| ROTTERDAM (NED) | 11-Jun-06 |

| SCORING GATES | |
|---|---|
| Archipelago of Fernando de Noronha | LEG 1 |
| Kerguelen and Eclipse Islands | LEG 2 |
| Cape Horn | LEG 4 |
| Archipelago of Fernando de Noronha | LEG 5 |
| Lizard Point | LEG 7 |

**Source:** Internal documentation.

Rijkman Groenink had rejected an earlier proposal to participate in the VOR 2001/2.[19]

It was decided that to achieve the ambitious goals of the campaign, including worldwide brand exposure – promoting employee's commitment; business unit involvement; and customer satisfaction[20] (see Figure 2)[21] – the bank would have to become 'owner' of the team, rather than just a sponsor. Given the total lack of experience in organising global events, let alone competing in a nine-month sailing race and fully organising a bulky

'marketing circus', the VOR would definitely stretch the bank's competences.

Nonetheless, on the 11th of March 2004, AA publicly announced its participation in the around the world sailing race. Member of the managing board Tom de Swaan stated: "We are an international bank with subsidiaries located in all continents the VOR calls at. This is one of the reasons we enter this race. We are convinced that the worldwide publicity will make this investment worth every penny. Banking is about taking

FIGURE 2   AA's objectives to participate in the VOR

| | | |
|---|---|---|
| 1. | Brand exposure: | remove conglomerate discount and convey one bank philosophy |
| 2. | Employee perception: | increase employee cohesion, motivation and involvement |
| 3. | Business unit involvement: | develop synergies |
| 4. | Customer satisfaction: | increase client recognition and enforce AA community |
| 5. | Business tracking: | new business generation and wallet enlargement |

calculated risks. This is also counts for a sailing race around the world."[22]

## Organising the business of sailing

A former member of the board of directors of the Dutch insurance company RVS, Jan Berent Heukensfeldt Jansen joined AA as a director of Insurances in December 1998. In 2002 he successfully led AA Insurances into a joint venture with Delta Lloyd, to achieve volume growth for AA's insurance activities. In 2003 corporate Executive Vice President (EVP) and sailing aficionado Jan Berent was approached to lead a very different, but not less challenging project: directing AA's participation in the VOR.

At that time, even at AA's managing board the scope of the sponsorship could not be fully foreseen. It was member of the managing board Dolf Collee who realised the importance of not underestimating the impact and the potential break-down risk of the event and persisted in attracting the executive vice president Jan Berent as a 'heavyweight' manager.

By then the budget for the VOR had been approved by members of the managing board under the condition that the participation would serve a strong business purpose. Together with Sandor Brouwer, who as a planning and operations manager was responsible for the budgeting of the project, Jan Berent engaged in establishing the organisation for the participation in the VOR, developing a business plan and planning the budget allocations.

The business plan outlined the objectives of the campaign as well as the structure and governance of the organisation. Furthermore, dependency of nautical and marketing activities were clarified and prioritised and

risks were identified to be mitigated. The budget was planned for a three-year period and was also broken down to departments. This also included a scheme for cost allocations across BU's within ABN AMRO based on assumed activation per BU and region. Together the business plan and budget formed the fundamentals for further preparations and organisation of the business of sailing.

## Organisational structure[23]

A separate administrative construction was created to organise the race: ABN AMRO Brand and Sail Company (AABS) would operate as a fully-owned subsidiary of AA, with the freedom of an autonomous company. Control over the management team and AABS, and the ultimate responsibility for the performance of AABS were with the supervisory board, consisting of three members of the managing board and two other executive vice presidents of AA.

CFO[24] of AA Tom de Swaan was assigned as chairman to clinically monitor AABS' performance. The fact that three members of the AA's managing board were assigned to the board of AABS helped to communicate throughout the bank that AA was taking its participation in the VOR seriously and was determined to make the race a success, also as a business enterprise.

It is useful to look at AABS as consisting of three major parts: a nautical side, a marketing side and a support side (see Exhibit 6 for organisational chart AABS). Team Heiner (TH), named after Roy Heiner – the world famous ocean race sailor who set up his own company in 1996 – is a firm specialised in organising professional sailing races. TH was already well known to the members of AA's board, since AA had co-sponsored Heiner's Brunel Sunergy team in the Whitbread Round the World Race 1997–1998. TH would be largely responsible for

**EXHIBIT 6** Organisational chart of AABS

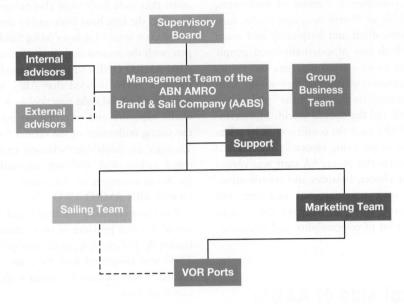

**Source:** Internal documentation.

the nautical part of AA's participation in the VOR and was integrated into AABS.

The 'marketing side' consisted of AA employees from different departments as well as a much larger number of externally hired professionals for the various activities. The general organisation of the marketing side was with the BUs as a middle-layer, serving as a platform to activate the marketing activities for the VOR on a local scale. The business-oriented support side was concerned with planning and control, reporting, business cases, partner selection etc.

Taking care of these apparently natural tasks was indispensable and the support side consisted mainly of people from within AA's Finance, Tax, Audit, Insurance, ICT, HR and Legal departments. The information system of AA appeared not to match the AABS requirements for global accessibility – also at remote places – and bandwidth to send large chunks of (video and audio) data. Therefore, AABS also developed its own 24/7 accessible information system that was needed to administrate and support the worldwide activities of the VOR, including the media campaign, financial management, and logistics.

## Staffing AABS

Jan Berent: "To organise an organisation within an organisation, stimulate support and convey a brand, you need well-defined objectives, a powerful organisational

and management structure, a strong management process and people with accountability." Between the start of preparations and the finish of the race, AABS on average consisted of around 110 employees, of which only 10 members came from within the bank. As a financial institution AA clearly lacked the know-how of ocean racing, so the large share of externally-hired people within the nautical side of AABS is hardly surprising.

The marketing programme, including the organisation and execution of the port events; the media activities; an internal branding campaign, etc., also proved to be beyond the bank's existing capabilities and expert consultants were attracted. It was also easier to hire professionals from outside AA for contractual reasons: "One of the goals was to outsource to the max for AABS, because we didn't want to carry the responsibility to find 100 people new jobs within AA once the project was finished. Also, since most employees had no clear view of what they could expect from the VOR or simply were not interested in participating in a two-year project, there was a reluctance to join the team. So in May 2004 we started to look for skilled and experienced people from outside AA," Jan Berent explains.

Among the companies that were attracted to join Team AA were IMG; ATP, an agency specialised in business travels and events, was responsible for overall hospitality management at the stopover locations; Pitch PR, consisting of an enthusiastic team of young sports-PR professionals; several logistic service providers; as well as a considerable number of freelancers, with expertise in fields as diverse as sports media, hospitality and communication; and hospitality and event management. The high rate of externally-hired people that were unfamiliar to the overall practices and values of AA, raised the question of whether they would actually be able to communicate the 'one bank' philosophy throughout the bank and the outside world. More critically, how would AABS meet the conditions to be taken seriously by the rest of the bank, especially the international BUs? To address this point, AA staff was placed in key positions for checks, balances and coordination. "We created a strong organisational structure and stayed in tight control. Doing so we were able to give all team members a lot of responsibility and freedom," Jan Berent adds.

## The nautical side of AABS: off the beaten track

As soon as the decision to participate in the VOR was taken, AABS' nautical side jump-started preparations, starting from scratch. The goal was attractively simple: winning the race. Nonetheless, the content of AABS' strategy *how* to win the race was not so self-evident.

For the 2005–2006 edition of the VOR the 'Volvo 70'-concept, with the so-called canting keel, was introduced. The concept specifies the maximum dimensions of the boat, and leaves the individual teams free to come up with their own design within a predetermined set of rules. AABS decided to hire the young and relatively unknown Argentinean boat designer Juan Kouyoumdjian to design a wholly new type of boat, an innovative design that redefined the technical state-of-the-art in sailing. The choice of skipper was Mike Sanderson, also a highly talented yet young and little-known professional, and the implicit choice not to opt for a world famous skipper with the best track record, exemplifies AA's off-the-beaten-track strategy.

In the process of building the boat, the idea arose to build a second boat that, after rigorous testing of the first design, was expected to offer important improvements in terms of speed, durability etc. Roy Heiner judged that this would substantially increase the chance to win the race. Building a second boat would cost significantly less than the first one since economies of scale could be achieved. In addition, the lessons learned from building the first boat could be implemented for the next boat resulting in lower labour and material costs and so AA got in the unique position to build a second boat.

However, since Volvo's regulations determined that all boats that were built were also obliged to participate in the race, the first boat built had to compete as well. The world class team of skipper Mike Sanderson would compete with the second built boat that was now called the ABN AMRO ONE and was presumed to be the faster of the two. AABS decided that ABN AMRO TWO (the boat first built) should function as a vehicle for getting media exposure and receiving sympathy through being the young underdogs of the race: a 'likeability strategy'. Through an 'Idols'-like selection campaign young talented sailors with different nationalities, representing the home countries of AA, were selected to form the crew of ABN AMRO TWO. This would keep the media within these countries interested and strengthen the image of AA as a provider of opportunities for young professionals. For example, in the Netherlands ABN AMRO TWO was associated with the career opportunities and tailored products that AA offers with its Young Professional package.

## The marketing side of AABS

AABS' main goal was to use the VOR as a platform to promote the 'One Bank' philosophy both to AA employees and the general public in the main markets of AA. The internal and external branding campaigns were built on three main pillars: 'PR and communications', 'branding and merchandising' and 'events and hospitality' (see Exhibit 7: Organisational Chart Marketing Team). Subsidiaries, especially in Brazil and the USA, that had recently been 're-branded' as part of the endorsement campaign still had to get used to visibly carrying the name and being part of the AA family.

One of the main goals of participation in the VOR was to involve, inspire and commit the employees, and subsequently influence their behaviour in line with the bank's values (the one bank philosophy). An employee who is committed to the organisation tends to be loyal and will work harder to accomplish his objectives,[25] while involvement generally generates positive attitudes towards work.[26] This also holds for employees who care about and believe in their company's *brand*, while linking internal and external marketing by sending out the same message is regarded to be important to improve employees' brand understanding.[27]

The VOR appeared to be an effective platform to promote this employee commitment: the idea of being part of a winning team is appealing and creates team spirit. Participation in the VOR would hopefully stimulate this (winning) team-feeling among bank employees and was envisaged to boost 'company pride'.

**EXHIBIT 7**  Organisational chart marketing team

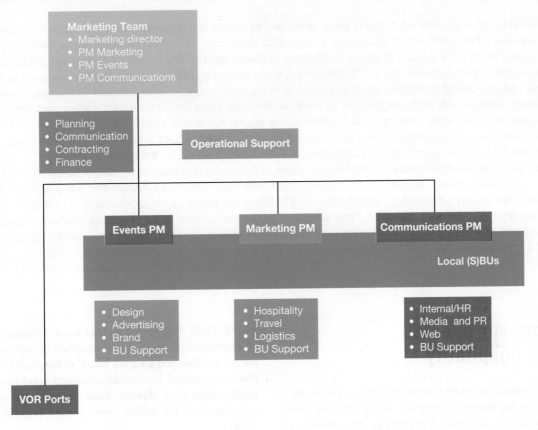

**Source:** Internal documentation.

In turn, bank-wide employee engagement to the VOR was also crucial to communicate the one bank philosophy to the customers: "you can't afford a client of the bank inquiring about the latest leg in the VOR, while the desk clerk uninterestedly shrugs his shoulders", Jan Berent exemplifies. Getting the employees involved in the VOR was therefore strongly promoted through the elaborate internal branding and media campaign before and during the race. Jan Berent comments: "Given the business purpose of the race and the intrinsic uncertainties of sailing, you can't let the success of the internal marketing campaign depend on the success of the race. Quite practically, AABS had invested € 4 million in merchandise. This had to be sold within the bank, regardless of the outcome of the race to stay out of trouble! Thus, the marketing race had to be successful before the sailing race had even started."

To promote *and preserve* enthusiasm for the nine-month VOR among its worldwide employees, AABS organised various activities, utilising all available communication systems. For example, the crew selection and the christening of ABN AMRO ONE on the 17th of January 2005 (ten months before the start) were broadcasted on the intranet. The intranet was also used to provide employees with more information about the race commentary of the legs, news of upcoming events, specials about the crew, and more insight in the stopovers. Furthermore, a monthly internal magazine 'Forty knots', was especially set up to cover all aspects of the race. The company website contained a web shop selling merchandise ranging from bags and branded sports clothing to watches and scale models of the boats. The merchandise was popular among AA's personnel. Also, an interactive sailing game was developed that could be accessed by all employees via the intranet (see Box 3).

To inform and gain full attention from all employees, the Team ABN AMRO day was held on 4th November 2005, the day before the start of the race. The highlight of this day was the introduction of the two AA teams. Nearly all of AA's approximately 110,000 employees around the world were wearing a VOR T-shirt and connected through live satellite, showing images of colleagues from all over the world, which generated a very energetic atmosphere and a feeling of unity bank-wide.

### Box 3: Sail2Win

Sail2win is an interactive virtual sailing game developed to involve and engage employees, and to teach them more about the organisation stimulated by a competitive aspect. To win the virtual race, nautical miles have to be collected by solving sailing dilemmas comparable to issues faced in daily banking activities, and gather facts about their parent company and own business unit. Every sailing leg deals with a different theme related to the corporate values of teamwork, professionalism, integrity and respect. Cross-business unit relations were strengthened through team assignments, as more nautical miles could be obtained by forming a team with colleagues working in other business units. Furthermore, everyone was able to identify participating fellow-workers. This stimulated engagement, as it is much more fun beating a familiar colleague from your own department. To further encourage engagement and participation, rewards were given out by the board of directors to the winner as well as the most creative or best team solution or best team approach, consisting of tickets to the next port stop and a meet and greet with the crew. Project coordinator with Team AA, Chantal van Sparrentak explains the ambition of Sail2Win: "Our ambition was to make 50 percent of the approximately 110,000 employees participate. We sent out questionnaires to participants and received a lot of positive feedback." Sandor Brouwer: "the initial goal of 50,000 participating employees proved overambitious. In total, around 20 percent of the worldwide employees participated."

## Stopover events and hospitality

Client entertainment and hospitality activities were organised at the stopover locations, where the race boats finished a leg and started a new leg. At a number of stop-over locations, including the ports of the AA's main markets Rio, Rotterdam, and Baltimore, in-port races were organised that were followed by large numbers of spectators on the dockside. The AA pavilion – a large branded tent – was always prominently present and a lot of effort was put into promoting the visibility of the bank.

In some places, such as in Rio, AA merchandise and advertisements, including full scale posters of the ABN

AMRO ONE were spread all over town. Different types of entertainment events were organised in and around the AA pavilion and a varied 'menu' of hospitality events that were tailored for specific customers segments – including boat trips, dinners, hotel accommodation and meetings with the sailing crew – were organised by AABS.

## Media campaign

As outlined in the business plan, media exposure and internal and external communication of the bank's values were the main objectives of AA's participation in the VOR. Again, this was especially important in Brazil and the US, where the BUs were recently re-branded as

### Box 4: Protecting the brand

The development of the VOR brand manual provides an interesting example of how AABS balanced between control and delegation. The local BUs were responsible for their own marketing and branding activities supporting the VOR. However, when BU Brazil enthusiastically started designing very exotic posters, merchandise, mugs, etc., AABS feared that a proliferation of branding styles and marketing products would put at risk the 'one brand' image of AA. It was concluded that it was necessary to secure the uniformity in the marketing efforts. For this purpose, a brand manual was formulated in cooperation with professional marketing agencies, in which extensive guidelines and examples of possible marketing and advertisement expressions were provided. By fixing standards and strictly scrutinizing all new marketing initiatives and branding designs centrally, the brand image would not become diluted.

part of the endorsement campaign and – as a result – brand awareness of AA still had to be further promoted among the general public. Although sailing is recently getting more popular as a spectator sport, the amount of media attention it receives is still low. At the same time, "if you are broadcasted on television as a participant in the VOR, it is very important to get a positive story. For these reasons you want to have full control over the media", Jan Berent explains.

Being able to control the content of the media coverage about ABN AMRO ONE and TWO to a large extent was important to be able to accentuate the 'one team' philosophy and the values of the bank. Although achieving full control would be very difficult, the bank decided to organise a professional media team in-house that would create footage of the teams of ABN AMRO ONE and TWO. Since the media only paid limited attention to the VOR and high costs were involved with producing quality material, AABS managed to acquire an oligopoly position in terms of providing footage about

the VOR. Getting the footage broadcasted was probably the main challenge for the media team and therefore AABS invested a lot of efforts in carefully managing its relationships with the local media agencies in the different home markets. "The media could have possibly turned us down, but they didn't because we had such good contact with them and we've always been straightforward and transparent," says Jan Berent.

For example, journalists from newspapers and TV stations were invited at the stop-over locations to interview the sailors or shoot an item for a sports programme. "By providing access to the state-of-the-art production and editing equipment and offering the service of AABS' cameraman, it became a lot more attractive for media people to come over. Furthermore, our highly advanced mobile production centre – which was especially developed for the VOR and enabled broadcasting of the material on the same day – discomfited several giant television stations," production manager Yvo Janssen adds.

---

### Box 5: Hans Horrevoets (April 26, 1974 – May 18, 2006)

Only 22 years old, Hans Horrevoets was the youngest sailor on the Whitbread round the world race 1997/1998 – the predecessor of the VOR – on the Dutch Brunel Synergy boat. Nine years later he would be the eldest and most experienced sailor amongst the young crew of the ABN AMRO TWO as a helmsman/trimmer.

In the seventh leg of the VOR between New York and Portsmouth, a wave washed back down the deck and when the water cleared Hans was no longer on deck. The other nine members of ABN AMRO TWO turned the boat around, took the sails down and mounted a search and rescue effort. After around 40 minutes Hans was found but despite getting him back on board, they could not save him. Horrevoets was married and father of an infant daughter.

The accident would soon become part of the public opinion and front-page coverage in several Dutch media, followed by cover-stories worldwide. Utmost integrity and flawless communication with the media were thus essential to handling the delicate situation.

At AABS an elaborate contingency plan was in place to manage emergency situations and risky events in general. It was decided that the best way to inform the media about the tragedy would be to let the crew of ABN AMRO TWO explain what had happened. In a press conference skipper Sebastien Josse said: "We are all devastated by the events that took place this morning and all our thoughts are with Hans' family. I would like to stress that throughout the whole man overboard procedure, the crew handled themselves calmly, professionally and with the utmost maturity. It is with deep regret that we were unable to resuscitate Hans."

Also, AA's top-management was directly involved to present AA's first official response. CEO Rijkman Groenink stated: "We are all devastated by this terrible accident. Over the past year and a half, from preparation to where we are now, the crew members of TEAM ABN AMRO have become an integral part of the ABN AMRO family. We shared in the excitement leading up to the race and celebrated our achievements since the race began. Now, in this tragic moment, our thoughts are with Hans' family, and also with his fellow crew members."

The accident will remain a black day in the memories of all the people involved. Even at AA's head office in Amsterdam a depressed atmosphere could be felt amongst all employees for a week. Fortunately, the professionalism and integrity with which AA handled the situation was lauded by the people involved.

By actively stimulating the local media to pay attention to the race, often through providing them with high quality material, AABS managed to get the positive media exposure it hoped for. Producing its own footage offered more interesting opportunities: the media team would not only supply footage to local and international media agencies and television stations, but it would provide material to be used within the bank, including for the company website, intranet, material for management training, etc. Says Yvo: "The media team used footage to strengthen internal communication, motivate and mobilise employees and promote company pride."

AA's website provided a lot of information and news about the race, the boat, the crew and AA's role. The intention was to have the best-informed website, aiming to provide news faster and better than the main website hosted by Volvo. It was even possible to follow the race in real-time through a 'virtual spectator' application. To obtain the attention from all potential clients and employees, it was vital to gain interest beyond the sailing fraternity and sport-minded people. "Therefore, we also focused on the personal stories of the sailors, their families, their daily emotions and touching moments," Yvo explains.

# All hands on deck: Team ABN AMRO at the operational level

## The start

The decision to participate in the VOR was taken in November 2003, two years before the start of the race. Within one year from the public announcement in the beginning of 2004, AABS was raised; the business case was formulated; and around a hundred dedicated professionals joined AABS.

As mentioned before, the nautical part of AABS was able to start preparations as early as 2003. Even though the challenge to win the race would remain huge until the final sailing leg and demanded full devotion from the team, it was clear that the nautical side was able to build on many years of professional experience in the full organisation – and winning – of world class sailing races. The fact that the bank offered sufficient financial support also helped AABS' nautical operations run quite smoothly. As a result, the sailing team enjoyed an absolute advantage in terms of preparation time and financial resources as compared to their opponent sailing teams in the race.

At the marketing side of AABS, the starting phase was characterised by a lot of creative 'intrapreneurial' activity. Countless ideas were generated, projects formulated and the Team AA members developed several products for the internal and external branding campaigns and operational plans. However, this creative surge came at a cost. At times the organisation could best be described as chaotic and key elements of the campaign were lagging behind schedule. For example, two 'travelling' pavilions were needed to be set up at the different stopover locations of the race for the hospitality events and the crew. With little more than half a year until the start of the race, the design for the two large AA-tents remained unfinished, while the planning for the complex logistical operations was largely nonexistent.

Communication was hardly organised: every day managers from different business units from Brazil to Cape Town were calling the AABS head office, with questions ranging from what the VOR was actually about and how big it would be, to what menu would be included in the hospitality package the local branches could offer to their invited customers. Thousands of emails piled up. Many questions often could not be answered since AABS' employees had lost oversight of what was happening within the organisation.

During the pre-race period it had also become clear that different types of skills were needed at different stages of the organisation lifecycle of AABS. For example, inventive people with bright ideas about how to design the branding campaign – although strongly needed in the first phases of the campaign – were not by default the best people to bring these plans to practice. This posed another challenge to the management, since having the right people in the wrong places and vice versa made it even more difficult to control the processes and outcomes of the team. Together this resulted in ideas being revised over and over again, but often not actually scheduled and implemented. The fact that the marketing side was lagging behind schedule also caused coordination problems with the nautical side of AABS.

## Getting organised

At the beginning of 2005, it had become clear to the management of AABS that a number of main targets of the marketing campaign were at risk and urgent action was needed. AA ran the risk that it would win the nautical battle, while losing the marketing war.

In February, the consulting programme director was replaced by Pauline van Esterik. Her strong reputation as a skilled project manager from within the bank and as a person who loves to create order out of chaos seemed to provide a perfect fit with the situation. As Jan Berent puts it, "Pauline's job was to win the marketing race.

Her knowledge about the bank, as well as her network and reputation were very important to get things done."

However, taking over the lead of the marketing campaign at this late stage was not easy. "It was a chaos of well-meaning people," Pauline says. "Even though most employees were very skilled at their job and many valuable ideas had been generated, due to the lack of focus and coordination their functioning as 'One Team' with 'one goal' was not efficient."

A major weakness Pauline encountered when she joined Team AA was that "it was unclear to the employees at the marketing side of AABS when the race could be called a success." As opposed to the nautical part of AABS, where winning the race was the clear goal and the operational agenda was pretty much 'set' from the start, the marketing team lacked both strategic focus and – largely as a result – clarity about which activities should be organised to make the media campaign, the brand management projects, and the employee and hospitality programmes a success.

"The first thing I did was read the business plan and I took out all the numbers," Pauline recalls. The business plan of May 2004 included clear financial targets for all elements of the race, but only limited operational guidance, especially for the marketing campaign. For example, the plan stated that 'media value' – probably *the* critical element of the marketing campaign – should at least account to € 60.6 million at the end of the race, but it provided little clue as to how to achieve this value.

Translating the generic quantitative goals into an operational activity agenda was therefore the second important step Pauline undertook. Together with Graham Fleet, managing director of IMG, she went through all the existing ideas that were generated over the last year and made quick decisions about which ideas would be carried out – often after some adaptations – and those that would not. This resulted in a structurally-layered agenda in which the activities for the different disciplines (hospitality, internal engagement, media, branding) during the different phases of the race were outlined in detail from March 2005 (8 months before the start of the race) to October 2006 (well after the final leg).

Uncertainties about responsibilities among employees were also discussed and eliminated, so everybody had a shared goal of where to go and a clear agenda of what to do. Importantly, Key Performance Indicators (KPIs) for every three months were attached to the different activities within the different disciplines. The KPIs also specified the expected value creation of the activities. This allowed the managers as well as all team members to keep track of the performance of the campaign and

make timely adjustments (See Exhibit 8 for the project plans top sheet).

Another important step was to organise professional training sessions to make AABS' employees aware of how their own cultural backgrounds differed from those of AAs employees in the international BUs. These sessions were necessary, since prejudices and communication problems of the team at times impeded constructive and effective cooperation. For example, "to get things done in Brazil, an informal and enthusiastic approach was likely to work, while a more hierarchical delegation of tasks was more suitable for the US," says Sandor. Also, solutions were sought for the employees who were not doing what they liked or were underperforming. Initially, Jan Berent aimed to carry out the whole project with the same group of people. As the time pressure rose, however, a culture of 'hiring and firing' became more dominant and even at key positions managers were replaced, often at the most pressing moments. Given the high pressure, high performance environment, this was considered a necessity.

## During the race: day-to-day management

At the start of the first leg in Vigo on November 12th 2005, Team AA had already been on location for about a month. Even though on paper a clear trajectory had been made explicit, the daily operations were quite messy. The main reasons were that hardly anyone had prior knowledge about how to organise such an event in a foreign country and the fact that the exact responsibilities of the employees within the different disciplines still had to be settled.

Sandor Brouwer adds that "there were simply too many people to do the job", which further reduced controllability, since as a result people started to interfere with all sorts of ongoing activities they had not been hired for. An internal evaluation showed that the different disciplines were not communicating – let alone cooperating – effectively. Therefore, learning by doing, a radically different approach was developed for the stopover events to come.

The new operational strategy closely resembled a military approach. Pauline introduced daily morning meetings, to be punctually attended by all managers of the different disciplines. A daily agenda, often containing a long list of topics, was discussed and – in deliberation – tasks were delegated to the various disciplines. Apart from the activities that had to be carried out that day or that week, the morning sessions were utilised to prepare the stopover of the next destination.

**EXHIBIT 8**   Project plans top sheet

| Objectives | A. Win the race | B. Build equity of the ABN AMRO brand internationally in association with the corporate centre | C. Create effective marketing platforms to enable BUs to hit business and brand targets | D. Involve, inspire and influence the behaviour of employees | E. Create a cohesive marketing team – focused and efficient delivering results on budget and on time |
|---|---|---|---|---|---|
| **Core Projects** | **A1. Sailing preparation** <br> Maintain momentum, focus and progress of sail team | **B1. Develop corporate brand personality** <br> – brand theme <br> – brand characteristics <br> – tone-of-voice <br><br> Develop corporate brand campaign to unify the bank behind one shield <br><br> – corporate branding initiatives (guidelines, merchandise, signage) <br><br> – corporate above-the-line campaign <br><br> Ongoing communications/servicing of corporate centre | **C1. Secure total BU involvement and activation** <br> Internal marketing plan <br><br> Develop campaign planner tool-kit built on base campaign and 8 campaign modules (below-the-line campaigns and product development) <br><br> Develop BU activation plans/management of campaign modules <br><br> Ongoing communications/servicing of BUs | **D1. Employee communications** <br> Mapping network and channels <br><br> Develop corporate initiative <br><br> Producing and selling in BU initiatives as part of toolkit <br><br> Servicing content needs, push and pull | **E1. Personal/team development** <br> Setting goals <br><br> Creating environment <br><br> Develop office signing toolkit <br><br> Building the team spirit |
| | **A2. Adding value to the sailing team** <br> Create a high performance environment; train the team to new levels; teach new skills <br><br> Create a team-ship philosophy and rules | **B2. Centralised media plan** <br> Create efficient content team and distribution network <br><br> Create and execute corporate PR plan <br><br> Develop AABS web-site as an instrument of information and distribution to several levels (Greater public, Employees and Press) | **C2. Local market media plan** <br> Integration of central and local teams, closely co-operating, facilitating, directing the local teams in concordance with the central goals <br><br> Identifying and establishing key partners/developing a BU media plan for inclusion within campaign planner tool-kit | **D2. Corporate Lessons** <br> Identifying AABS legacy and briefing team <br><br> Producing specific content | **E2. Operational management** <br> Management, communication logistics across all internal and external specialist groups and partners i.e. tax, legal. |

Cooperate closely with Volvo media service (TV, radio, web, print) as a source and as supplier

Developing and delivering content, in white label and in specialised form

**A3. Partner programmes**
Build strong working relationships with all key internal and external partners

**B3. Corporate events plan**
Develop VVIP events calendar for key stakeholders pre, during and post race

**C3. Port activation**
Hospitality: creation and delivery of gold, silver and bronze packages for inclusion within campaign planner tool-kit

AA branding and presence marketing

**E3. Budget**
Budget management, process and control

**A4. Secure co-sponsorship**
Delivery of value and building relationships with partners/sponsors

**C4. Lead generation**
Identifying sales targets from within sailing community

**E4. Measurement and evaluation**
Develop research plan and implement

Assist BUs in development of their own research needs

**E5. Project planning and process**
Planning & traffic

Activities alignment with wet/dry/shore/marketing

Central receiving/filing point for all documentation

Manager team space

**EXHIBIT 8**  *continued*

| Objectives | A. Win the race | B. Build equity of the ABN AMRO brand internationally in association with the corporate centre | C. Create effective marketing platforms to enable BUs to hit business and brand targets | D. Involve, inspire and influence the behaviour of employees | E. Create a cohesive marketing team – focused and efficient delivering results on budget and on time | | |
|---|---|---|---|---|---|---|---|
| | Jan Berent Heukensfeldt Jansen | Pauline van Esterik (Base campaign 4) | Philippe (Base campaign 2) | Chantal van Sparrentak (Overall campaign) | Frank During (Base campaign 3) | Sijmen de Hoogh (Base campaign 1) | Sandor Brouwer |
| | A1. Sailing preparation<br>A2. Adding value to the sailing team<br>A3. Partner programmes<br>C4. Lead Generation | C1. Secure total BU Involvement and Activation<br>D1. Employee Communications<br>D2. Corporate lessons<br>E1. Personal/Team Development<br>E4. Measurement and evaluation | B2. Centralised media Plan<br>C2. Local market media<br>D2. (part) Servicing content needs<br>D2. (part) Producing specific content for corporate lessons | E5. Project planning and process e.g. Project office | B1. Create a brand campaign<br>C1. (part) Produce campaign planner Tool-kit; Ongoing communications/Servicing;<br>C3. (part) AA branding and presence marketing<br>D1. (part) Producing and selling in BU initiatives as part of tool-kit | B1. Create a brand campaign<br>C1. (part) Produce campaign planner Toolkit; Ongoing communications/Servicing;<br>C3. (part) AA branding and presence marketing<br>D1. (part) Producing and selling in BU initiatives as part of tool-kit | A4. Secure co-sponsorship<br>E2. Operations<br>E3. Budget |

**Source:** Internal documentation.

This approach proved highly effective in terms of improving coordination and quickly became popular with the team. Still, the organisation and coordination of the stopover events, including the arrangement of hotels and boat trips, the organisation of the pavilion, the branding activities, the in-port races, the media activities, etc. was a daunting task. Says hospitality manager Majella Blok: "The scheduling of activities was almost always last-minute. For example, even though the local BUs were responsible to pass on their final reservations for their clients' hotel bookings one month ahead, in practice we often were calling all day to make sure the rooms would be filled up to a few days before the race would arrive. At times we had the feeling that someone was juggling eggs and we were there to catch the ones that were falling."

Time pressure was also a costly issue. As head of Financial Services, Pieter van den Broek indicates that often there was not enough time to find the best deals or to bargain with suppliers. Many purchase decisions had to be taken ad hoc, sidestepping the regular procurement procedures of the bank. According to Sandor, "this resulted in hundreds of thousands of Euros of unnecessary costs."

Also, "many of the consultants – in the heat of their own tasks – did not take into account the bank's office procedures which had enormous administrative consequences," Pieter adds. Stef van 't Zand, AABS' events and hospitality manager and responsible for the logistics and content of the hospitality programme, also believes efficiency could have been a lot higher: "The basis for this project is damn good planning. If specialised knowledge would have been attracted from the start, this would have saved a lot of money." While Sandor states that "we could have achieved 95% of the results with two-thirds of the number of employees."

This said, the achievements of Team AA should not be played down. To organise successful stopovers at all ports, including top-class hospitality and visitor events for thousands of people; maximising exposure through intensive management of media, branding and merchandise; handling the logistical and technical affairs; as well as developing the impressive portfolio of employee engagement activities, all within two years, can be seen as an impressive example of project management.

This especially holds taking into account the fact that many of AABS' members were away from home for nine months, having to adapt to new local cultures and customs over and over again and work under continuous pressure. A big advantage was AABS' good relationship with the sailors. Close cooperation between sailing teams and their sponsors – albeit desirable – is often difficult to achieve for a sponsor, but at Team AA taking photos, having interviews and chatting with customers all came

very easily. "The sailors were sitting in the pavilion, eating and drinking with their wives and children and chatting with our invited clients. That was fun and effective of course," Pauline says. Shore director Tom Touber: "As consultants, we got a lot of freedom to organise and execute the nautical aspects, but all major decisions were taken in close collaboration with AABS staff. They've continuously expressed criticism and asked the difficult questions, but that is only a good thing. On the other hand, even though we were not directly in charge of the marketing aspect, we did well at promoting the AA brand name and values during the race. This came quite naturally." Stef van 't Zand: "The clients loved the activities. Getting the opportunity to personally experience the race, attend the in-port race and see the boats, or even meet the crew of one of the teams offered a fantastic experience to many people."

Of the major markets of AA, the stopover in Rio de Janeiro stood out as the most festive event. The fact that the ABN AMRO ONE won the in-port race added to the success and enthusiasm and tens of thousands of people visited the AA pavilion. At AA LaSalle in the US, the overall popularity of the VOR was limited. The fact that LaSalle operated in the mid west, while the stopover port was located in New York made it difficult for customers to go and see the race. According to marketing director of AA North America Mark Nystuen "the VOR has been quite successful and was promoted and managed professionally by AABS." Nonetheless, "the event did not provide an opportunity to get thousands of clients."

## Managing the project-based organisation

In retrospect, it is possible to distinguish an organisational life cycle with at least four different stages in the race, each with very different management challenges and characteristics (see Figure 3).

When Pauline joined AABS in February 2005, the operations at the team could be described as chaotic: the lack of a clear structure, the absence of formal rules, and low regulation of goals and priorities caused low controllability. The transition from such a preparatory phase towards a more structured organisation allowing for practical planning and execution is part of the typical life-cycle of most project based organisations.[28] Some employees argue that the marketing side of AABS got stuck in the preparatory process – causing loss of precious time – and that the management of AABS should have taken a more prominent role in directing the embedded company through the different phases. Given the short managerial lines in the flat organisational structure of AABS, the transition from one phase to the other

**FIGURE 3** AABS' life-cycle

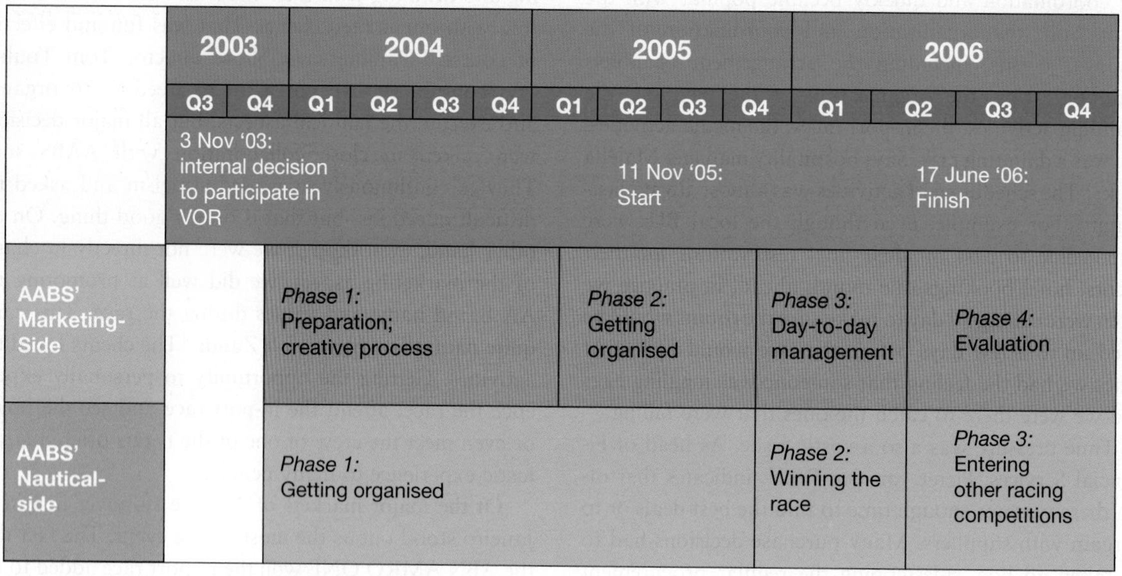

| | 2003 | | 2004 | | | | 2005 | | | | 2006 | | | |
|---|---|---|---|---|---|---|---|---|---|---|---|---|---|---|
| | Q3 | Q4 | Q1 | Q2 | Q3 | Q4 | Q1 | Q2 | Q3 | Q4 | Q1 | Q2 | Q3 | Q4 |
| | 3 Nov '03:<br>internal decision<br>to participate in<br>VOR | | | | | | 11 Nov '05:<br>Start | | | | 17 June '06:<br>Finish | | | |
| AABS'<br>Marketing-<br>Side | | | Phase 1:<br>Preparation;<br>creative process | | | | Phase 2:<br>Getting<br>organised | | | | Phase 3:<br>Day-to-day<br>management | Phase 4:<br>Evaluation | | |
| AABS'<br>Nautical-<br>side | | | Phase 1:<br>Getting organised | | | | | | | | Phase 2:<br>Winning the<br>race | Phase 3:<br>Entering<br>other racing<br>competitions | | |

## Box 6: Business unit involvement: the hospitality challenge

An interesting example of a 'product' of AABS causing quite some management trouble was the development of hospitality packages by AABS to be sold to the different BUs, who in turn would offer these packages to their clients. Initially, AABS' managers attempted to co-develop different types of tailor-made packages in close cooperation with the event managers of the different BUs. This proved to be a nerve-wrecking job, since each BU had its own specific and diverging wishes about the type of hospitality programme to offer to its clients. Another factor was the 'not invented here' problem. Little uniformity could be reached, impeding scale advantages in planning and designing of products. With time running out, it was decided that co-development was too difficult and AABS would design a line of packages for the different BUs. However, many BUs were reluctant to allocate their marketing budgets to purchasing the packages and inviting their valuable customers to this unknown event. Reasons included the perception that AABS did not offer a 'clear product' and could not provide any guarantee that the race would become a success. Also, the initial consultation rounds by AABS' managers to promote the VOR among the event managers of the different BUs was done by hired people who were foreign to the bank, which caused the level of trust between the BUs and AABS to be less than optimal. Also, some managers of AABS experienced that the event managers felt being 'passed' in the sense that they were not in control of the development and planning process.

On behalf of the Managing Board, Sandor and Jan Berent had specified in detail for each BU how much budget had to be allocated per stopover, per event and even per type of package. However, the worldwide BUs proved to have a high level of decisive power, in the sense that they would often simply not purchase the required amount of packages. Oftentimes, AABS had to persuade the local BUs as late as a week before the stopover to finalise their bookings (of hotel rooms, boats, dinners etc.). Since the logistic operations demanded up-front planning and speed, this time-consuming last-minute management was unpractical and costly. As hospitality manager Majella Blok points out, the first step to a solution lay in more effective communication: once the BUs got a clearer picture of what to expect they would become more enthusiastic. This is why, during the race, the decision was taken for AABS' marketing managers to travel all over the world to prepare the stopover activities in all countries and demonstrate what the race was about and point out the success in other locations. Together with the fact that AABS was performing well in the race, this helped most BUs to overcome their initial scepticism. "By telling the people at the local BUs what to do, you adversely motivate them to do it. So, we tried our best to make them really enthusiastic, show them the critical 'elements' and let them dive into it in order to make the project a success," Jan Berent says of the method to involve all BUs.

The appointment of a new programme director who knew the bank and was well-known within the bank proved to be important in increasing trust among the BUs. Combined, these measures proved largely successful. Nonetheless, to the frustration of AABS' hospitality managers, a number of BUs did not follow the order of the Managing Board and got away with it at that point in time. The financial aspects of this problem – including a budget deficit at AABS – were settled after the race.

could *in principle* be made quite fast. Indeed, the strategic turnaround directed by Pauline could be implemented within just weeks.[29]

## The final leg

ABN AMRO ONE achieved overall race victory when it arrived in Gothenburg on 17th June 2006 with six offshore leg wins out of nine, and five out of seven in-port race victories. It was one of the most outstanding performances in the history of the Volvo Ocean Race. ABN AMRO TWO finished in fourth place overall, and broke the world 24 hour speed record during the event. A delighted skipper Mike Sanderson commented: "I am very happy to be here, to finally be able to lift this trophy is a fantastic moment. We have won the Volvo Ocean Race – this is a dream come true. What an amazing opportunity we have had and that was what has made this team unique. Today belonged to everyone: what happens on the water is a small part of the overall result and every person in every part of this campaign has been important."[30]

After the big party it was time to clean up. Within a few weeks after the finish the team shrunk from a medium-size enterprise to a sleeping organisation with only 10% of its original number of employees. An important remaining task for the leaving consulting members was to settle their bills with the AABS's financial department. Altogether, this proved to be a huge task, which took months to finalise. For the media team there was still a lot of work to do in terms of providing material for internal use, such as presentations, management training etc. Apart from this, the choice to keep a small number of key AABS members actively engaged resulted from the fact that there was a real possibility that AA would also participate in the next VOR of 2008. An internal evaluation was being prepared to back up this decision. Exhibit 9 contains a section of AA's evaluation of the VOR.

On October 18th 2006, AA announced it would not participate in the next VOR of 2008; a decision taken by the managing board. AA's press report stated: "This was ABN AMRO's first global sponsorship project aimed at uniting the worldwide territories of the bank, raising global awareness of the brand and introducing the global tagline 'Making more possible'. The campaign's primary objectives were to involve employees from all key territories around the world, achieve worldwide brand exposure, create a platform for client hospitality, communicate the core values of the bank to a global audience, and win the race."

## FIGURE 4   Final results

| Position | Team | Total points |
|---|---|---|
| 1. | ABN AMRO ONE | 96.0 |
| 2. | Pirates of the Caribbean | 73.0 |
| 3. | Brazil 1 | 67.0 |
| 4. | ABN AMRO TWO | 58.5 |
| 5. | Ericsson Racing Team | 55.0 |
| 6. | Movistar | 48.0 |
| 7. | Brunel | 27.0 |

## EXHIBIT 9.1  Media exposure

Before the start of the 2005/2006 Volvo Ocean Race a target of €60.6 million of media exposure was set for TEAM ABN AMRO's participation. This target was based upon the media returns generated by the winning boat from the last race, Illbruck, and to reflect the fact that ABN AMRO had entered two boats.

| Exposure | | Value | |
|---|---|---|---|
| **Television** | Pre-race | € 31,172 | € 37,355,660 |
| | During-race | € 37,324,488 | |
| **Press** | Pre-race | € 643,222 | € 12,242,771 |
| | During-race | € 11,599,549 | |
| **Web** | US Web value | € 9,425,050 | € 10,963,586 |
| | Volvooceanrace.com | € 1,339,391 | |
| | Teamabnamro.com | € 199,145 | |
| **Various** | Database value | € 16,802 | € 1,420,874 |
| | Ambient value | € 82,254 | |
| | Mobile | € 143,656 | |
| | Radio | € 1,178,162 | |
| **Total TEAM ABN AMRO Media Value** | | **€ 61,982,891** | |

**Source:** Internal documentation.

## EXHIBIT 9.2  Brand equity analysis

Brand research was conducted in two waves in two markets – Brazil and Chicago – and in four waves in the Netherlands. The first wave in each market was conducted prior to each stopover and sets a benchmark. The full effect of the impact on the brand was determined when the boats had visited the markets.

### Sample

#### Netherlands:
Fieldwork: continuously week 1 – week 52, Online from capi@home panel TNS Nipo.
The analysis in Holland is taking place over four waves on a quarterly basis.
Three waves are complete. Results are compared with Q1, 2006. Significant changes are mentioned.
n=1,187, representative of Dutch population.

Among these:
n=344 customers

n=207 primary customers (those who consider ABN AMRO their most important bank)

n=313 primary target group (20–49 years, social class A/B1)

*Brazil:*

1600 CATI interviews (telephone) targeting banking customers, of which 20% are Banco Real clients belonging to classes AB, from between ages 18 and 70 years old; Male and Female; Class: A1, A2, B1 and B2 with (individual) income higher than R$2.500,00.

The study was divided in two waves as follows:

1st wave sample = 800 (December 2005)

2nd wave sample = 800 (March 2006)

*Chicago:*

Online interviews were conducted in two waves among consumers in the Chicago metropolitan area:

| | |
|---|---|
| Wave One: | Between 15 December—22 December 2005 (post- 1st Leg) |
| | A total of 507 interviews were completed |
| | 113 respondents reported LaSalle is their primary bank |
| Wave Two: | Between 27 May—12 June 2006 (post- 6th Leg to US) |
| | A total of 501 interviews were completed |
| | 113 respondents reported LaSalle is their primary bank |
| Consumers selected: | Adults; P18+; Household income $50,000+ |

## Results Netherlands and Brazil

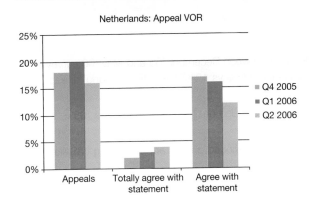

Netherlands: Appeal VOR

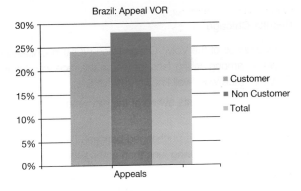

Brazil: Appeal VOR

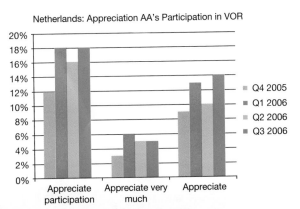

Netherlands: Appreciation AA's Participation in VOR

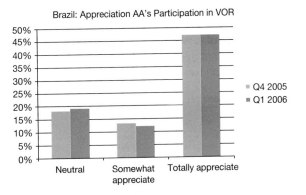

Brazil: Appreciation AA's Participation in VOR

## EXHIBIT 9.2 *continued*

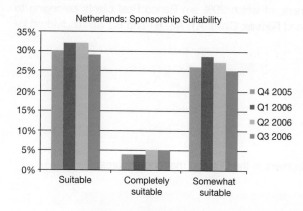

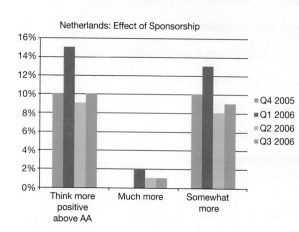

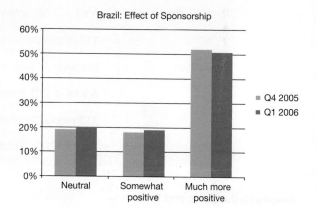

## Results Chicago

– Awareness of the Volvo Ocean Race (VOR) in Chicago declined between December '05 and May '06 survey waves among sailing fans for whom the race was 'vaguely known' (25% vs 12%) rather than among fans for whom race was 'well known' (9% vs 6%).

– Among respondents aware of the race, the percent following it 'often' also declined from December '05 to May '06 (9% vs 1%).

– The VOR appeal is unchanged between December and May, with continued greater appeal among LaSalle customers and sailing fans than among the total sample.

– While aided awareness of ABN AMRO's participation in the VOR remained relatively low in Chicago (3%), LaSalle customers and sailing fans continued to have a positive view toward ABN AMRO's involvement in the VOR.

– In Chicago, awareness of LaSalle sponsorships continues to be much higher than awareness of ABN AMRO sponsorships.

– Awareness of ABN AMRO's participation in the Volvo Ocean Race in the Chicago area was comparatively low due to the fact that the route took the race mainly outside the US and when in the US, it was along the East Coast— Baltimore and New York, which are outside the LaSalle Bank customer base.

**Source:** Internal documentation.

## EXHIBIT 9.3 Employees' perception

An online questionnaire was sent in 7 waves to a selection (1/7 per unit) of email addresses of employees of the ABN AMRO Group, where in each employee participated only once.

| Wave 1 | July 2004 |
|--------|-----------|
| Wave 2 | October 2004 |
| Wave 3 | February 2005 |
| Wave 4 | July 2005 |
| Wave 5 | December 2005 |
| Wave 6 | April 2005 |
| Wave 7 | July 2005 |

### Interest

- 74% (up slightly from 72% in wave 6) wishes to be informed about future developments regarding the participation in the Volvo Ocean Race which is still much more than previous wave results of around 55% of all employees, and 43% of employees (up from 37% last wave) actively follow news on the race.

- Since the Volvo Ocean Race started, more employees have followed the news: in wave 6 37% of the employees followed somewhat too intensively the news about the Volvo Ocean Race since being aware of ABN AMRO's participation, now this is 43% (only 33% in wave 5 and 18% in wave 4).

- BU Latin America (58%) and BU Global Clients (44%) want to be informed more than other units. In the previous wave BU Asia had a high percentage that wanted to be informed about the race. However, this has decreased dramatically to 37%, the second lowest percentage recorded.

- As in all other waves, Intranet (rather than the website) is the most important source of information about ABN AMRO's participation in the Volvo Ocean Race (78%), followed by the internal magazine (58%). However, as in wave 6, an exception must be made for BU Netherlands, whose main source of information is television (79%), with Intranet mentioned 2nd most important (75%).

- The number of employees that have been approached or have been asked questions by people outside the bank regarding ABN AMRO's participation in the Volvo Ocean Race is still increasing. In July 2005 (before the race started) 12% of employees were approached by people outside the bank, in December 2005 (after the race had started) this was 32% and in wave 6 this had increased to 40%. Now this has increased to 46%, an excellent result versus last July.

### Employees' involvement

- 52% of all employees (who are aware of the Volvo Ocean Race) are aware of events or activities related to the Volvo Ocean Race (compared to 43% in April), whilst only 46% of them have actually participated in these events or activities. This is a bit less than in wave 6, in which 52% actually participated in events or activities.

- Compared to other BUs, awareness of activities is rather low in BU North America (38%) and BU Latin America (40%). In BU Netherlands, participation in events or activities is lower than in other BUs, with only 29% of those aware of activities admitting they have participated in any events or activities.

- One of the activities ABN AMRO organised was Sail2Win, a game launched in November 2005 which could be played throughout the Volvo Ocean Race. 30% of all employees who are aware of the race said they had never heard of this game before and only 5% played the game in every leg. 51% of all employees that played the game rated it good/very good, whilst 15% rated it bad/very bad.

**EXHIBIT 9.3** *continued*

– Most employees are very proud of working for ABN AMRO. Employees of BU Latin America are by far the proudest (93%), as in wave 6. As in April, the majority of BU Latin America thinks that ABN AMRO is a united group (59%), although this is less than in wave 6. BU Asia is also rather positive (58%).

– Since the Volvo Ocean Race started, more and more employees have become interested in participating (again) in activities related to the race. However, compared to wave 6, less are now interested in participating (again) and the figure has decreased significantly to 30%, compared to 45% in wave 6 and 32% in wave 5.

– Employees in BU Latin America are more positive about participating in events or activities than employees in other BUs (44% indicate they want to participate), however, they are far less positive than they were in April of this year (when this was 70%).

– 11% of all employees is involved in a project related to the Volvo Ocean Race as part of a day job (this is about the same as in the previous waves, rising by 2% since wave 6).

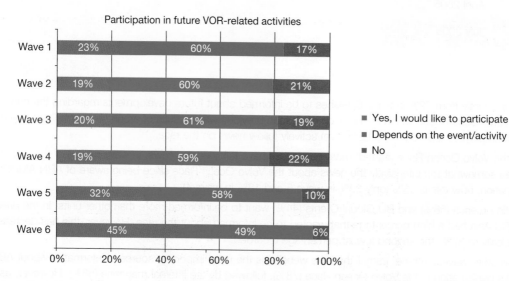

**Impact on the brand**

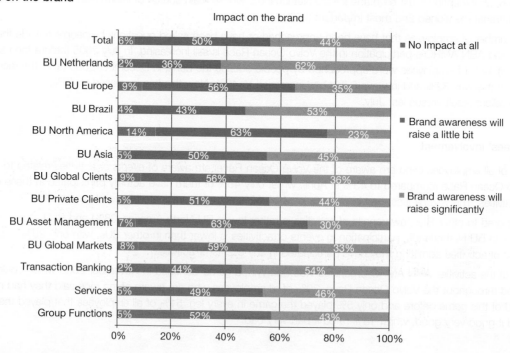

46% of employees believe the race will significantly raise brand awareness. This has increased from 43% in April, 35% in December 2005 and 20% in July 2005 before the race started. BU Netherlands are most confident that the race will significantly raise brand awareness (62%). As in wave 6, 63% (up from 55% in wave 5) believe the race accurately reflects 'teamwork' and 49% (up from 46%) professionalism.

Targets were set at 90% and these will not be reached but there has been a continual positive trend throughout the race.

Source: Internal documentation; research conducted by Motivaction, an company specialized in research and strategy.

## EXHIBIT 9.4   Hospitality evaluation

Research was undertaken among the customers attending the hospitality events held in Vigo (wholesale customers) and Rotterdam (private customers).

**Results**

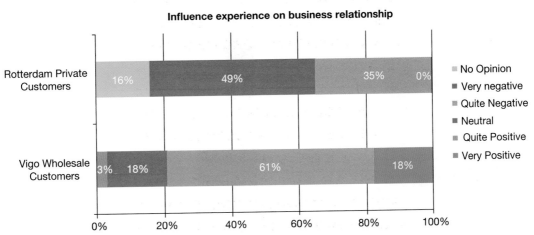

**EXHIBIT 9.4** *continued*

### Reflection teamwork in VOR participation

'From what you have experienced, to what extent do you believe that ABN AMRO's participation in the Volvo Ocean Race reflects teamwork?'

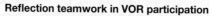

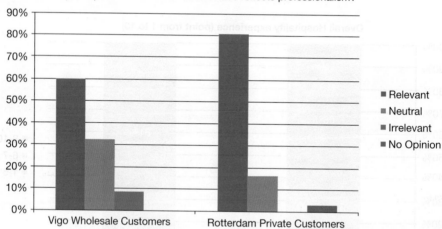

### Reflection Professionalism in VOR participation

'From what you have experienced, to what extent do you believe that ABN AMRO's participation in the Volvo Ocean Race reflects professionalism?'

### Reflection 'Making More Possible' in VOR participation

'From what you have experienced, to what extent do you believe that ABN AMRO's participation in the Volvo Ocean Race reflects "Making More Possible"?'

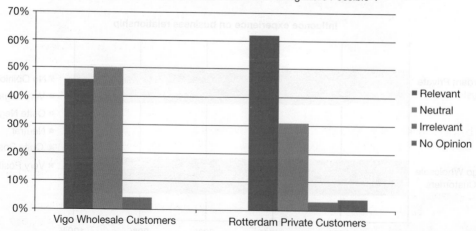

**Source:** Internal documentation.

Jan Berent commented: "The Volvo Ocean Race has been a great marketing platform for us and its impact will continue long into the future. We entered the Volvo Ocean Race as a three year, one-off campaign to meet specific objectives, promoting the unity and strength of the AA brand to a global audience. We did everything we could to win the race, and with a combination of teamwork and professionalism TEAM AA travelled the world reflecting all that the bank stands for. The results of the campaign confirm that all our objectives have been met, which is largely thanks to the outstanding effort made by the large number of people involved."[31]

Apart from communicating that the main objectives had been met, the bank provided little details about the reasons not to race the VOR 2008. A Dutch newspaper[32] speculated that the departure of managing board member Dolf Collee – one of the driving forces behind the event – , the tragic accident of Hans Horrevoets, as well as resistance among international subsidiaries could be behind the decision. Whatever the reasons, as illustrated by shore director Tom Touber, lack of enthusiasm by the sailing team was clearly not a factor: "we're obviously very disappointed. We had the best boat and a strong lead to the rest."[33]

## REFERENCES

ABN AMRO Holding N.V., 2005. *Annual Report 2005.* Amsterdam: ABN AMRO Holding N.V.

ABN AMRO Press Relations, 2006. *ABN AMRO announces it will not enter the next Volvo Ocean Race.* Amsterdam. Available from: http://www.abnamro.com/pressroom/releases/2006/2006-10-18-en.jsp.

Aaker, D.A. and Joachimsthaler, E., 1999. The Lure of Global Branding. *Harvard Business Review*, 77(6): 137–144.

Bartlett, C.A. and Ghoshal, S., 1989. *Managing Across Borders: The Transnational Solution.* Boston: Harvard Business School Publishing.

Bartlett, C.A. and Ghoshal, S., 1992. What is a Global Manager? *Harvard Business Review*, 70(5): 124–132.

Bartlett, C.A., Ghoshal, S. and Birkinshaw, J., 2004. *Transnational Management.* New York: McGraw-Hill.

Brand-Finance, 2006. *Global 100 Brands Valuable Banking Brands – 2006.* Available from: http://www.brandfinance.com/Uploads/pdfs/Global%20100%20Banking%20Brands%202006.pdf

Clark, K.B. and Wheelwright, S.C., 1992. Organizing and Leading 'Heavyweight' Development Teams. *California Management Review*, 34(3): 9–28. In Clark, K.B. and Wheelwright, S.C., 1992. *Revolutionizing Product Development: Quantum leaps in Speed, Efficiency, and Quality.* New York: Free Press.

Financieel Dagblad, 2005. Zwakke plek. *Financieel Dagblad*, 2nd August.

Financieel Dagblad, 2006a. AA werkt aan efficiency; Nieuwe business unit 'Europa' moet anders gaan functioneren. *Financieel Dagblad*, 1st August.

Financieel Dagblad, 2006b. ABN's Vruchteloze Snijden. *Financieel Dagblad*, 20th October.

Financieel Dagblad, 2007. ABN Amro lijkt weer op bank van Jan Kalff, *Financieel Dagblad*, 9th February.

Fem Business, 2006. Venture Capital: Wat ziet de Bank in Pieper? *Fem Business*, 41: 18–20.

Grant, R.M., 1996. Towards a Knowledge-Based Theory of the Firm. *Strategic Management Journal*, 17(1): 109–122.

Goold, M., Campbell, A. and Alexander, M., 1994. *Corporate Level Strategy: Creating Value in the Multibusiness Company.* New York: John Wiley.

Greiner, L., 1972. Evolution and Revolution as Organizations Grow. *Harvard Business Review*, 50(4): 37–46.

Gwinner, K.P. and Eaton, J., 1999. Building Brand Image through Event Sponsorship: The Role of Image Transfer. *Journal of Advertising*, 28(4): 47–57.

Holan, P.M. de, Phillips, N. and Lawrence, T.B., 2004. Managing Organizational Forgetting. *Sloan Management Review*, 45(2), 45–51.

Kostova, T. and Kendall, R., 2002. Adoption of an Organizational Practice by Subsidiaries of Multinational Corporations: Institutional and Relational Effects. *Academy of Management Journal*, 45(1): 215–233.

Kotler, P. 2003. *Marketing Management.* Upper Saddle River: Pearson Educational.

Kumar, N., 2003. Kill a Brand, Keep a Customer. *Harvard Business Review*, 8(12): 86–95.

Leana, C.R., Ahlbrandt, R.S. and Murrell, A.J., 1992. The Effects of Employee Involvement Programs on Unionized Workers' Attitudes, Perceptions, and Preferences in Decision Making. *The Academy of Management Journal*, 35(4): 861–873.

Mitchel, C., 2002. Selling the Brand Inside. *Harvard Business Review*, 80(1): 99–105.

NRC, 2006. ABN Amro zet punt achter Ocean Race; Teleurstelling bij zeilteam Roy Heiner. *NRC*, 19th October.

Pinto, J.K. and Prescott, J.E., 1988. Variations in Critical Success Factors Over the Stages in the Project Life Cycle. *Journal of Management*, 14(1), 5–18.

Porter, L.W., Steers, R.M., Mowday, R.T. and Boulian, P.V., 1974. Organizational Commitment, Job Satisfaction, and Turnover among Psychiatric Technicians. *Journal of Applied Psychology*, 59(5): 603–609.

Sanderson, M., 2006. *ABN AMRO wins the Volvo Ocean Race 2005–2006.* Available from: http://www.mike-sanderson.com/default.asp?m=da&id=37283.

Sydow, J., Lindkvist, L. and DeFillippi, R., 2004. Project-Based Organizations, Embeddedness and Repositories of Knowledge: Editorial. *Organization Studies*, 25 (9): 1475–1489.

Telegraaf, 2005. Groei ABN Amro moet nu uit Midden-segment komen. *Telegraaf*, February 8th.

Telegraaf, 2007. Miljonair zoekt sponsors. *Telegraaf*, January 16th.

Venkatesan, R., 1992. Strategic Sourcing: to Make or Not to Make. *Harvard Business Review*, 70 (6): 98–107.

Volberda, H.W., 1996. Towards The Flexible Form: How To Remain Vital in Hypercompetitive Environments, *Organization Science*, 7 (4): 359–387.

Volberda, H.W., 1999. *Building the Flexible Firm: How to Remain Competitive*. Oxford: Oxford University Press.

Volberda, H.W., Baden-Fuller, C. and Van den Bosch, F.A.J., 2001. Mastering Strategic Renewal: Mobilising Renewal Journeys in Multi-unit Firms. *Long Range Planning*, 34(2): 159–178.

## INTERVIEWS

| Name | Function | Date interview |
| --- | --- | --- |
| Majella Blok | Hospitality manager | February 19 2007 |
| Robin Boon | Head of Corporate Communications | November 9 2006 |
| Pieter S. van den Broek | Head of Financial Services | July 27 2006 |
| Sandor Brouwer | Planning & Operations Manager | June 30 2006 (and more) |
| Pauline van Esterik | Marketing Director | November 1 2006 |
| Bob van Gessel | Global Brand Manager | July 26 2006 |
| Jan Berent Heukensfeldt Jansen | CEO | July 25 2006 (and more) |
| Yvo Janssen | PR & Communications Manager | July 26 2006 |
| Alexander Mollerus | Investor Relations Officer | November 1 2006 |
| Mark Nystuen | Head of Marketing LaSalle | February 21 2007 |
| Tom Touber | Shore Director | July 26 2006 |
| Simon Schoon | Internal Auditing | July 27 2006 |
| Sander Schuurman | Marketing Manager | July 26 2006 |
| Chantal van Sparrentak | Project Coordinator Partners & Sail2Win | July 27 2006 |
| Stef van 't Zand | Events & Hospitality Manager | July 25 2006 |

## NOTES

1. As of September 2006.
2. Financieel Dagblad, 2006.
3. Financieel Dagblad, 2003; Financieel Dagblad, 2007.
4. e.g. Financieel Dagblad, 2005; Telegraaf, 2005.
5. Goold *et al.* (1994) mention four types of 'parental' value creation: 1) Stand alone influence: Each subsidiary is viewed as a separate profit center, controlled and monitored using basic performance targets. Value creation based on making strategic decisions such as the appointment of managers and approving capital expenditures. 2) Linkage influence: improved cooperation and synergy benefits. 3) Central functions and services: the provision of managerial or administrative services to the businesses. 4) Corporate development: value creation through portfolio management.
6. ABN AMRO Holding N.V., 2005.
7. Kumar, 2003.
8. See also Kotler, 2003.
9. Aaker and Joachimsthaler, 1999.
10. For discussion on global positioning strategies see Bartlett and Ghoshal, 1989.
11. ABN AMRO Holding N.V., 2005.
12. ABN AMRO Holding N.V., 2005.
13. Kostova *et al.*, 2002.
14. Internal documentation of AA.
15. Internal documentation of AA.
16. Gwinner and Eaton, 1999.
17. Internal documentation of AA.
18. Internal documentation of AA.
19. Fem Business, 2006.
20. Internal documentation of AA.
21. Internal documentation of AA.
22. Telegraaf, 2004.
23. See also Clark and Wheelwright (1992) for a discussion on different organizational structures, and specifically their discussion of 'heavyweight' development teams for effective product and process development.
24. Chief Financial Officer.
25. Porter *et al.*, 1974.
26. Leana *et al.*, 1992.
27. Mitchel, 2002.
28. For example, Greiner's (1972) growth phases model describes 5 phases of organizational development. Even though AABS did not operate in a typical business environment, the phases are similar. Pinto *et al.* (1988) specifically focus on a managing a project life cycle.
29. Volberda (1999) discusses how different organizational forms, with varying levels of structural, strategic and operational flexibility are optimal within different business contexts.
30. http://www.mike-sanderson.com.
31. http://www.abnamro.com.
32. De Telegraaf, January 16 2007.
33. NRC, October 19 2006.

# INTEGRATIVE CASE 2

**2**

# P&G GILLETTE WELCOME TO THE BEST CONSUMER PRODUCTS COMPANY IN THE WORLD

## Ali Tayfun Erguven, Nikolai Khlystov, Natalie Noetzli, Professor Gilbert Probst

*HEC – University of Geneva*

## A perfect marriage for all the right reasons: P&G and Gillette

*"This combination of two best-in-class consumer products companies, at a time when they are both operating from a position of strength, is a unique opportunity"*

A.G. Lafley, Chairman and CEO, P&G in the *New York Times*, 29th of January 2005

*"... I have a simple formula. Strength plus strength equals success"*

James M. Kilts, Chairman and CEO, Gillette in *BusinessWeek* in 2005

## Introduction

It was a sunny, spring day in May. The CEO and Chairman of Procter & Gamble (P&G) A.G. Lafley (see Exhibit 1) had just finished reading a very interesting article in the *Financial Times* about Microsoft's second bid to acquire Yahoo. Standing at the window of his office, he could not help but feel a great sense of accomplishment with the $57 billion acquisition of the Gillette Company (Gillette). He, together with his friend and former president of Gillette, J. Kilts (see Exhibit 1), had orchestrated this acquisition, which many considered one of the most successful of its size.

The CEOs knew each other well as both served on the board of the Grocery Manufacturers of America (GMA). Nevertheless, everything had really begun in November 2004 with a telephone call from Kilts to Lafley. During this call, the idea of a *"merger"* had been broached. From the beginning, the negotiations were therefore very friendly. No lawyers or bankers were brought in during the first discussions, as Lafley was intent on making the deal as easy and collaborative as possible. The next step (November 17), brought the two companies' senior management together with representatives from Merrill Lynch, UBS, and Goldman Sachs to discuss the possible deal in more detail (Merrill Lynch represented P&G, while UBS and Goldman Sachs represented Gillette). Lafley had also met with his close friend Rajat Gupta and other consultants from McKinsey & Company for their assessment of a combined firm.

When all the involved parties gave the go ahead, the two companies appeared close to completing the

# EXHIBIT 1 P&G's and Gillette's CEOs

## Alan G. Lafley

### Vital statistics

- Born on June 13, 1947, in Keene, New Hampshire

### Education

- Graduated in 1969 with BA in history from Hamilton College
- Graduated in 1977 with MBA from Harvard Business School

### Career highlights

- P&G (1977–Present)

  - Chairman of the board, president and chief executive (2002–present)
  - President and chief executive (2000–02)
  - President, global beauty care and North American Market Development (1999–2000)
  - Executive vice president, P&G; president, P&G North America (1998–99)
  - Executive vice president, P&G; president, P&G Asia (1995–98)
  - Group vice president, P&G; president, P&G Far East (1994–95)
  - Group vice president, P&G; president, laundry and cleaning products, P&G USE (1992–94)

### Fast facts

- Served in the US Navy (1970–75)
- Serves on board of directors of numerous institutions and companies including GE, United Nations College Fund, Hamilton College, Business Council, Business Roundtable
- Served on board of directors of GM
- Member of Harvard Club of Cincinnati

## James M. Kilts

### Vital statistics

- Born on February 10, 1948, in Chicago, Illinois

### Education

- Graduated in 1970 with BA in history from Knox College
- Graduated in 1974 with MBA from University of Chicago

### Career highlights

- Gillette (2001–05) – Chief executive (2001–05) – President and chief executive (2003–05)
- Nabisco (1998–99) – President and chief executive
- Philip Morris (1994–97) – Executive vice president worldwide food (1994–97)
- Kraft Foods (1970–94) – President of Kraft USA (1989–94)

transaction. However, just when the Christmas holidays were around the corner, the deal fell through due to valuation differences – the Gillette leadership wanted a better price for its shares. It was not the end though and a couple of days after New Year, Hank Paulson (at the time board chairman and CEO of Goldman Sachs) reminded Lafley of the long-term strategic value of the merger. Furthermore, each of the three banks assisting in the transaction would receive a $30 million acquisition completion fee for their advisory services. One week later, Lafley's board authorized him to resume discussions with Gillette. Rajat Gupta (the former managing director of McKinsey & Company) was asked to call Kilts on behalf of Lafley and explore the possibility of reaching an agreement.

Paulson and Gupta were therefore instrumental in bridging the gap between the two companies. The public announcement of the acquisition came on January 28, 2005. With the exception of a few people at the very top, almost all of the two companies' employees heard the news through the press (see Exhibit 4).

## Strategic considerations

Kilts had just spent four years restructuring the company. Gillette was now generating $2 billion in cash per year, five times more than before Kilts's arrival. It was estimated that he had created $20 billion in shareholder value. Nevertheless, he realized that Gillette lacked scale. It was, for example, only present in China's four largest cities; by the 1990's, P&G, which had entered China in 1988, had a presence in the country's 500 largest cities through a sub-distributor network. Kilts realized that his company would experience similar difficulties in other high-growth emerging markets, such as India, though it did have certain market expertise there. Lafley, whose company was missing specific capabilities in Brazil and India, offered Gillette a possibility to increase market complementarities.

In addition, Kilts considered his company's options regarding getting into skin care although it lacked the technological expertise as well as the capital to invest in a viable R&D program. P&G, on the other hand, was very interested in the product complementarities that Gillette would bring to the table. Its success in male personal care (hair and skin) would open up vast opportunities for P&G. Lafley summarized the idea, *"They have the brand. We have the technology … We're using the Gillette acquisition to move into male personal care."* Gillette's very strong marketing capabilities in the male market segment were mainly due to its male razors, while P&G was particularly skilled in marketing various product categories

to women, which also included the razor market segment. There were also high expectations regarding another pair of products that the deal would combine: the world's No. 1 toothbrush and the world's No. 2 toothpaste. In addition, P&G did not mind entering a completely new market: through Gillette's Duracell brand, a merger would instantaneously make P&G a major player in the batteries market (see Exhibits 2 & 3).

Most consumer product and retail experts regarded the move as more beneficial for P&G. During the previous decade and a half, the giant retailer chains had increasingly dominated their relationships with product suppliers such as P&G, Unilever or Nestlé. The manufacturers had valid reasons for regarding the huge merger with concern as the retail giants regularly demanded that their suppliers provide products at decreased prices, introduced private-label products that cut into the margins of national brands, and even required special pallet arrangements. P&G, for example, generated 17% of its annual sales through Wal-Mart and Gillette a quarter. Combined, these sales still represented less than 10% of the discounter's total sales. According to Lafley, however, the *retailers' shoppers* were the real target of the deal, which would provide them with more products and innovation. Increasing the two companies' combined relationship with the shopper was the important objective, not gaining power with respect to the retailers.

Initially, many of the two companies' managers, especially those of Gillette, were concerned and anxious. It was also clear that there would be cuts. A Latin America manager commented, *"There is going to be blood on the walls."* To the surprise of many though, the company announced that it would be cutting a mere 4% of the combined workforce. Although P&G wanted to retain as many of the two companies' employees as possible, some did have to leave after the deal had been completed.

From the financial markets perspective, many shareholders were worried that the two companies' stock prices would fall. From the Gillette side, shareholders were worried that they will not get a fair price for their shares and that their votes would be diluted after the deal. From the P&G side, there was concern that its stock price will fall if the deal was considered too risky. Warren Buffet, Gillette's largest shareholder, who had saved the company from several takeover attempts during the 1980's, was very optimistic about the acquisition. Calling it a *'dream deal,'* he calmed the concerns of the investors from both sides, thus helping to finalize the deal. Although concluded at the end of January 2005, the deal was only officially completed on October 1 of that year. This delay was due to a series of regulatory issues primarily focused on antitrust laws, which were

**EXHIBIT 2**  P&G's product categories and main products in 2005

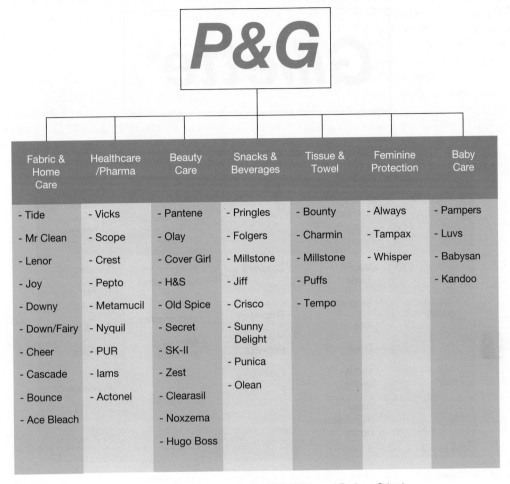

| Fabric & Home Care | Healthcare /Pharma | Beauty Care | Snacks & Beverages | Tissue & Towel | Feminine Protection | Baby Care |
|---|---|---|---|---|---|---|
| - Tide | - Vicks | - Pantene | - Pringles | - Bounty | - Always | - Pampers |
| - Mr Clean | - Scope | - Olay | - Folgers | - Charmin | - Tampax | - Luvs |
| - Lenor | - Crest | - Cover Girl | - Millstone | - Millstone | - Whisper | - Babysan |
| - Joy | - Pepto | - H&S | - Jiff | - Puffs | | - Kandoo |
| - Downy | - Metamucil | - Old Spice | - Crisco | - Tempo | | |
| - Down/Fairy | - Nyquil | - Secret | - Sunny Delight | | | |
| - Cheer | - PUR | - SK-II | - Punica | | | |
| - Cascade | - Iams | - Zest | - Olean | | | |
| - Bounce | - Actonel | - Clearasil | | | | |
| - Ace Bleach | | - Noxzema | | | | |
| | | - Hugo Boss | | | | |

**Source:** Piskorski M.J., Spadini A.L., 2007. "Procter & Gamble: Organization 2005 (A)" Harvard Business School.

resolved by both P&G and Gillette divesting from certain market segments around the world.

The acquisition did not overly excite the local Boston press and politicians, where Gillette was situated. A possible investigation into the merger even threatened the deal. Attitudes changed, however, when Lafley visited Boston and showed his commitment to the city by speaking with the community leaders. He announced that the company would grant scholarships, make donations to hospitals, sign research agreements with local tech firms, and would make a large investment in the South Boston facility to which all the Gillette employees would eventually be relocated.

The Massachusetts government was a greater obstacle: the State Secretary tried to subpoena Gillette regarding its acquisition by P&G as the state harbored real economic and social concerns regarding its well being.

But the arguments that Kilts raised to defend the acquisition were sufficient. The state court ruled in favor of the acquisition. Kilts did not, however, get off scot-free; he was subjected to a great deal of criticism regarding his compensation for the successful completion of the deal.

Kilts' total compensation was hard to decipher, as it included stock options and rights, a large 'change-of-control' payment, as well as stock options from P&G, but it was estimated to be a total of $153–185 million. The compensation was highly contested and often regarded as inappropriate.[1] However, to some business leaders this did not seem so unreasonable since this amount represented only about 1% of the total value that he had created as the CEO of Gillette.

Standing at the window and gazing out, Lafley remembered that at the time, the reasons for the acquisition of

**EXHIBIT 3**  Gillette's product categories and main products in 2005

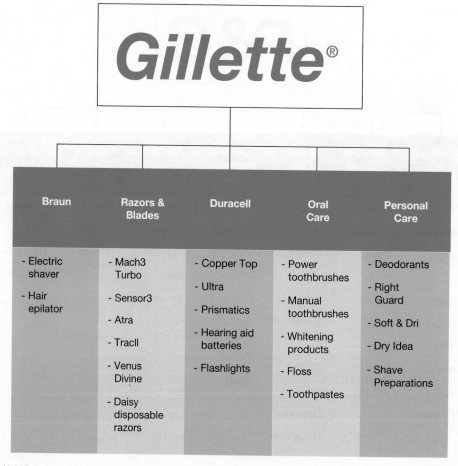

**Source:** Lorsch J.W., Robertson A.C., 2005. "The P&G Acquisition of Gillette", Harvard Business School.

Gillette seemed obvious. Deciding to "*merge*" the two companies was therefore also the easy part. Figuring out how to integrate the two structures successfully and do it in a way that would build on the two distinct cultures – so compatible and yet so different – was the more challenging part. The hard work was only about to begin …

# The two organizational designs

## P&G's structure before the acquisition (see Exhibit 5)

Lafley was proud of P&G for being relatively open even though it was a global giant in the consumer products market. When he took over the company – the very day Durk Jager suddenly resigned in June 2000 – an aggressive restructuring program, called Organization 2005, was in full swing. The new design comprised three interdependent organizations – one organized by product category, one by geography, and one by business process – linked together by a matrix-type structure. The main idea of this new organizational design was not only to improve the speed with which P&G innovated and brought these innovations to market globally, but also to increase its numerous functions' economies of scale.

**Global Business Units (GBUs)**  There were seven Global Business Units, each focusing on a different product category, such as Beauty Care or Baby Care. Each

## EXHIBIT 4   Timeline of the acquisition

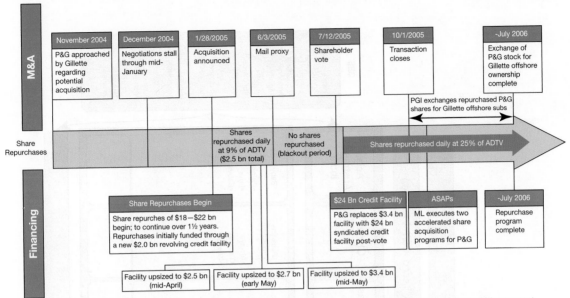

Source: Stowell D.P., 2007. "The Best Deal Gillette could get?: Procter & Gamble's Acquisition of Gillette". Kellogg School of Management.

GBU was responsible for everything that had to do with product development, its brand design, business strategy, and any new business development. Each of them had complete profit responsibility. Their presidents, reporting directly to the CEO, were also members of the global leadership council (which determined the overall company strategy). Since this structure meant that the GBUs no longer required the regional managers' approval, the global rollouts of innovations and new brands would be faster.

### Market Development Organizations (MDOs)

Conversely, in the Market Development Organizations, compensation was based on sales growth. The MDOs were responsible for local market adaptations of the company's global programs by using their knowledge of local consumers and retailers. Customer Business Development functions were consolidated regionally and reflected the line functions in each MDO. The seven MDOs were each led by a president, who reported directly to the CEO. The MDO presidents, like the GBU presidents, were members of the global leadership council.

### Global Business Services (GBS)

Representing the third leg of the new structure, the Global Business Services unit was given the task of standardizing and consolidating the various business processes and platforms across the company. Before the GBS units were established, many services and IT systems across the globe had been duplicated and had functioned differently. Centralizing these processes would achieve economies of scale (by 2008, cost savings of $600 million had been realized through the consolidation of all back-office functions and outsourcing of many non-strategic activities). Compensation was based on cost savings with the head of GBS reporting directly to the CEO.

Consensus on decisions was key in the P&G organization, which led to a relatively stiff system. Every decision took a great deal of time: everything was done in teams. Therefore everyone's opinion and consent were required to move on to the next stage in the process. Consequently, meetings were an extremely important aspect of the decision-making process. Some employees even joked that at P&G people would have pre-meetings about meetings. Team members would work together with members from other teams to consult them or simply obtain their opinions. Having a network was therefore a crucial component of the structure. Furthermore, the directors still had to approve all the decisions.

Partly because he wanted to counter the slow decision-making process within the structure, Lafley wanted his managers to take on the responsibility of making tough strategic choices. That not only shortened the

**EXHIBIT 5**  P&G's structure before the integration (2005)

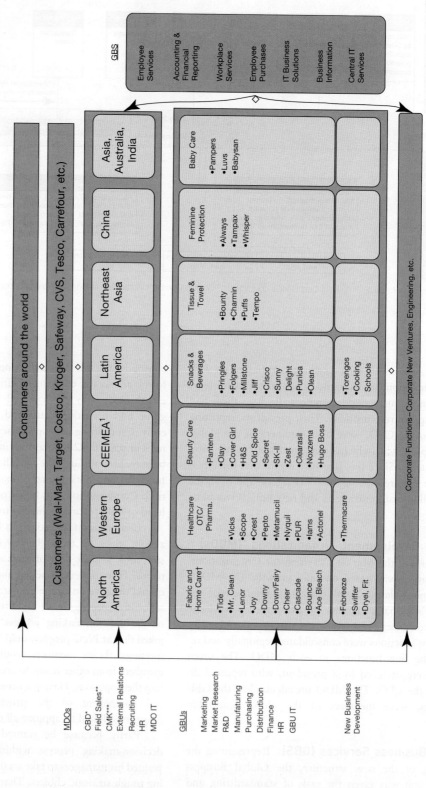

| | | | | | | |
|---|---|---|---|---|---|---|
| **GBS** | | | | | | |

Employee Services
Accounting & Financial Reporting
Workplace Services
Employee Purchases
IT Business Solutions
Business Information
Central IT Services

Consumers around the world

Customers (Wal-Mart, Target, Costco, Kroger, Safeway, CVS, Tesco, Carrefour, etc.)

| North America | Western Europe | CEEMEA[1] | Latin America | Northeast Asia | China | Asia, Australia, India |
|---|---|---|---|---|---|---|

**Fabric and Home Care†**
•Tide
•Mr. Clean
•Lenor
•Joy
•Downy
•Down/Fairy
•Cheer
•Cascade
•Bounce
•Ace Bleach

**Healthcare OTC/ Pharma.**
•Vicks
•Scope
•Crest
•Pepto
•Metamucil
•Nyquil
•PUR
•Iams
•Actonel

**Beauty Care**
•Pantene
•Olay
•Cover Girl
•H&S
•Old Spice
•Secret
•SK-II
•Zest
•Clearasil
•Noxzema
•Hugo Boss

**Snacks & Beverages**
•Pringles
•Folgers
•Millstone
•Jiff
•Crisco
•Sunny Delight
•Punica
•Olean

**Tissue & Towel**
•Bounty
•Charmin
•Puffs
•Tempo

**Feminine Protection**
•Always
•Tampax
•Whisper

**Baby Care**
•Pampers
•Luvs
•Babysan

•Thermacare

•Torengos
•Cooking Schools

•Febreeze
•Swiffer
•Dryel, Fit

Corporate Functions–Corporate New Ventures, Engineering, etc.

**MDOs**
CBD*
Field Sales**
CMK***
External Relations
Recruiting
HR
MDO IT

**GBUs**
Marketing
Market Research
R&D
Manufaturing
Purchasing
Distributiuon
Finance
HR
GBU IT

New Business Development

**Source:** Piskorski M.J., Spadini A.L., 2007. "Procter & Gamble: Organization 2005 (A)". Harvard Business School.

whole process's timeframe, but also greatly increased accountability in the organization. Consequently, managers sometimes found themselves responsible for making decisions that they were not necessarily comfortable making; however, it also forced them to think and come up with creative ideas by exercising their entrepreneurial spirit.

## Gillette's structure before the acquisition (see Exhibit 6)

Under Jim Kilts's leadership, Gillette underwent a very drastic makeover between 2001 and 2005. This change was far more severe than the Organization 2005, which took place at P&G during almost the same period. Gillette, however, needed that kind of transformation far more at the time. The matrix structure chosen for Gillette consisted of four legs.

### Global Business Units (GBUs)

With the exception of Duracell and Braun (which respectively would keep their headquarters in Connecticut and Germany after the acquisition), Gillette's five GBUs operated out of Boston. The GBUs' focus was on the consumer; they handled strategic marketing and product development. When Kilts had moved manufacturing out of the GBUs and into a separate unit, some managers ended up losing a certain amount of power and influence. As the Grooming GBU president, Peter Hoffman, for example, had gone from having 8,000 people in his organization to fewer than one hundred.

### Commercial Operations

These organizations were responsible for sales and services to Gillette's customers across all of the product areas. Like the GBUs, there were five Commercial Operations, comprising the five commercial operations regions. Each region had a president to whom the marketing, sales, HR, and finance directors reported. Each region was further sub-divided into smaller geographic areas.

### Manufacturing and Technology

The other two organizations comprised the Manufacturing and Technology Operation (MTO) and the corporate staff functions.

Kilts liked seeing his company functioning first hand and having conversation with the employees. He regularly left Boston to visit the field offices; however, there were simply too many facilities to visit every single one. Nevertheless, managers often saw him during their visits to Boston. All decisions in the company were validated by the GBU heads, and later reviewed by Kilts himself. Global coordination was also typical of Gillette.

Kilts, along with his operating committee, demanded weekly business overviews from all the functional groups and business units. This resulted in managers sometimes failing to respond to corporate requests or providing only partial information. In contrast to the previous reporting structure in which the GBUs and commercial operations groups reported to the COO, they now reported directly to Kilts. This change was applied during Kilts's first month on the job.

Kilts was instrumental in turning the company around. He did this not only through obvious ways, such as reducing costs and finding less expensive vendors, but also by reducing the number of SKUs and eliminating trade loading. Although Kilts wanted to know everything that was going on in the company, and would make all the final important decisions, he wanted the managers to work through the different issues themselves. "... *when you come to see me at a quarterly budget presentation, I expect you to have a common recommendation on what the numbers should be,*" said Hoffman, the grooming GBU president, mimicking Kilts talking to the executives.

Kilts started creating a performance culture shortly after his arrival. He was a strong advocate of job descriptions, through which he wanted to bring commitment and accountability back into the organization. On his arrival in the organization, he found that many people had no idea what their specific job entailed other than just showing up and doing something, "*I expect outstanding performance, that we achieve our projected figures and that we do what we say we are going to do.*" Consequently, he wanted to change the evaluation system by disposing of the old system that simply rewarded people for their effort. Effort was not enough for him; people had to perform, had to achieve the goals set out for them. Some employees feared his performance culture. An employee who did not know him well commented: "*Part of the stress in the organization is due to the idea passed down to us that Jim Kilts is very unforgiving. You have to deliver the numbers, and if you don't, you are dead meat.*" This performance culture did, however, create an organization that was flexible, agile, and responsive.

## The structural integration

When the official control of the Gillette Company was passed to P&G on October 1, 2005, Lafley knew that it would take roughly three years to complete the integration. At the beginning of the process, senior leaders traveled extensively. "*Get in as many talks as possible, talk about what P&G's like, talk about our purpose and our principles, allow people to put a face to the company,*" said Bob McDonald, the future COO. Roisin Donnelly, the UK's chief marketing officer and a member of the country integration team, concurred. He felt that

**EXHIBIT 6**  Gillette's structure before the integration (2005)

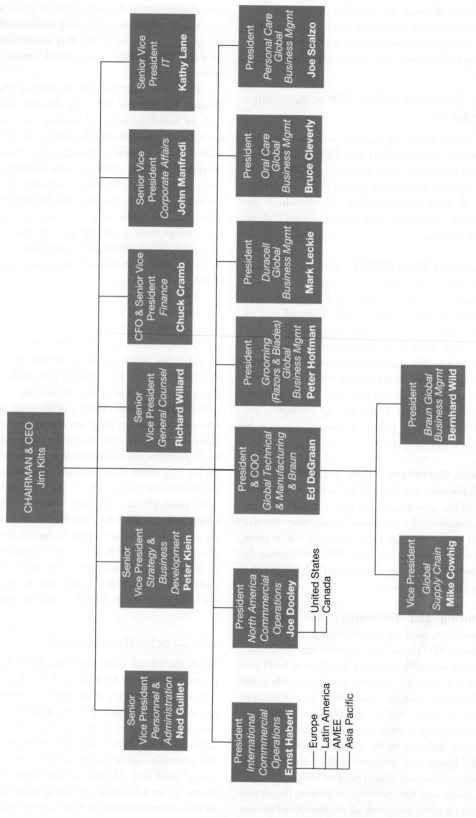

**Source:** Kanter R.M., Weber J., 2005. "Gillette Company (B): Leadership for Change". Harvard Business School.

Lafley's presentation helped win over the doubters: *"He talked about himself as a person and his values before mentioning the P&G values. The Gillette people said that this was a huge ah-ha moment, that we were a human, caring company."* He added: *"I have had several people say that the moment they decided that P&G was the right place for them was after his first town hall meeting."*

**GBU integration**  The key decision taken right away was to maintain the Gillette categories in their global business unit, as that would help preserve the strong business momentum. The only exceptions were with regard to oral care and personal beauty care. For the duration of the integration, the Gillette GBU would be based in Boston, while Duracell would remain in Connecticut, and Braun in Germany. Although the integration team leaders did not want to disrupt the Gillette model, they had no choice but to integrate the reporting systems. No cross-fertilization (placing Gillette people in P&G business units and vice versa) was initiated. With the benefit of hindsight, certain Gillette GBU team leaders observed that teams should have been cross-fertilized as this would have provided additional support and helped educate Gillette leaders on the new processes. Bringing in key Gillette people and giving them important jobs from the start was vital to accessing Gillette's knowledge. Having direct access to the top management talent was one of the reasons that had attracted P&G to Gillette in the first place. Consequently, Bruce Cleverly of Gillette headed the business merger between the two oral care divisions. Lafley likewise appointed Ed Shirley of Gillette as the new Group President of North America. The idea was to upgrade P&G's talent by replacing low performing employees with top performers from Gillette, while remaining fair to those who were displaced.

By July 2007 – one year ahead of schedule – the Gillette GBUs were fully integrated into the other GBUs at P&G.

**MDO-GBS integration**  The MDO-GBS integration included two main components – systems and people – and accounted for 70% of the total merger efforts. The leaders of the integration process staggered the mergers, as there weren't sufficient resources for a simultaneous integration (84 subsidiaries in seven regions). This process also allowed for learning during each of the steps and for leveraging the lessons learned by carrying out subsequent steps more efficiently. The integration started in the Latin American countries. The second wave included much of Asia, followed by North America and a few European countries. Finally, the rest of Europe was

merged. Each of the steps had its specific difficulties and unexpected obstacles. Despite these, all countries underwent the same integration phases.

Regional and country integration teams were formed early in the process – within two months of the merger announcement. The 84 subsidiary teams reported to the seven regional teams, who in turn partnered the integration lead team in Cincinnati. The GBS unit retained three regional teams with service centers in Costa Rica, the UK, and the Philippines. Consequently, support was available 24 hours per day. Moheet Nagrath, the MDO integration leader (and future global HR officer), set up bi-weekly global conference calls to provide regional leaders with a forum for addressing issues and sharing insights. In turn, the regional leaders hosted their own regular conference calls with the country leaders. Furthermore, the regional leaders often had to mediate between country and corporate demands. Sub-integration teams created ad hoc project groups as the need arose along the way.

## Picking the best flowers

*"The brilliance in how A.G. had led the integration with Gillette is he's used Gillette as a catalyst for change. It was such a pinnacle point."*[2]

Ed Shirley Group President, P&G North America

The idea of creating the best team from the combined organizations meant the creation of a stronger, more capable company. It promised to rejuvenate the P&G organization with new talent, skills, and knowledge. Right after the acquisition announcement, the human resources department was told to identify top talent in Gillette. As soon as the official control of Gillette had passed into the hands of P&G in October 2005, Gillette employees began receiving transitional and permanent job offers. HR started at the top, and moved down the organizational levels. All the employees had been contacted by March 2006. The *"field the best team"* (see Exhibit 7) principle clearly had its drawbacks. *"Obviously, some people in our company were not promoted or even had to go, as some of the Gillette leaders were given their positions. There is just a limited number of positions available as you move up the [corporate] ladder,"* stated Carolina Klüft, a P&G brand manager. Another manager responded by citing the value of trust: *"... we trust that the talent in this organization that we're bringing in is exceptional. It is a much tougher thing to have to sell. ... How do you look P&G people in the eyes and tell them that, as a result of the acquisition, they need to go?"*

At the beginning, the challenge was to convince the Gillette organization's managers not to 'jump ship' before P&G had worked its way down through the Gillette

**EXHIBIT 7** "Fielding the best team communication"

## FIELDING THE BEST TEAM, DICK ANTOINE, GLOBAL HUMAN RESOURCES OFFICER 18 MAY 2005

A few weeks ago, a P&G/Gillette Transition Team update outlined the guiding principles for the integration process. One key principle is fielding the best team. Completing this work will be a critical factor in the ultimate success of our future Company.

So what does *"fielding the best team"* mean?

It means we will create a stronger, more capable organization from the combined talents of P&G and Gillette. Importantly, we will do this while still building our current business. We'll do this work in a way that allows us to:

- Maintain continuity of talent in both organizations, at and after the date of the merger
- Minimize the loss of talent in any part of P&G or Gillette and where possible, increase the diversity of company talent going forward
- Look for opportunities to integrate Gillette talent within P&G
- Identify and retain employees needed during the transition process

As we move forward with the merger, we will bring *"fielding the best team"* to life. Senior leaders from P&G and Gillette are already meeting in *"top-to-top"* discussions to focus on the following elements:

### 1. TRANSFER KEY GILLETTE TALENT INTO P&G'S ORGANIZATION. This will:

- Retain continuity of key leadership and resources to support the ongoing business
- Provide positions, as appropriate and available, for high performers, technical masters and institutional knowledge-holders
- Incorporate the best of Gillette, including its unique business knowledge, technical mastery and culture, into the ongoing operations of P&G
- Provide Gillette employees and leaders opportunities to learn the P&G business

### 2. PLACE A SMALL NUMBER OF P&G EMPLOYEES INTO THE GILLETTE ORGANIZATION. These people will:

- Learn the Gillette business from Gillette managers
- Foster the transfer of P&G learning and perspectives to Gillette
- Supplement Gillette talent in leadership roles

### 3. CREATE CAPACITY WITHIN P&G TO ABSORB GILLETTE PEOPLE. To accomplish this, we will:

- Identify current and anticipated vacancies within P&G, looking first to fill these positions with Gillette or other P&G employees before hiring externally
- Identify opportunities for filling gaps in P&G's *"bench strength"* by adding Gillette employees and leaders
- Identify positions for which Gillette employees have stronger qualifications than incumbents

When we announced the proposed merger in January, we estimated there would be reductions of approximately 6,000 employees, or 4% of the combined workforce of 140,000. These reductions could occur anywhere in the P&G or Gillette organizations, not just in areas of overlap.

All employees affected by the workforce reduction will be notified as soon as possible, although much of this work cannot progress until the merger closes. Also, the staffing work is likely to move forward on different timings based on organization, function and geography. To the extent possible, employees will be given another employment option to pursue. Those who will not have positions within the company will be provided appropriate notice and severance. There will be no employee-initiated separation program.

Within the next month, we expect to announce those senior Gillette managers who have accepted roles in the post-merger P&G organization. These managers will, in turn, work with their P&G colleagues to identify further opportunities to *"field the best team."* In addition, our goal is to notify all employees of their employment status within six months of the closing. This work excludes P&G and Gillette manufacturing operations. They will continue to follow their normal staffing processes.

We will work as quickly as possible to minimize the disruptions to employees, their families and the business. We'll conduct this process in the fairest and most respectful way possible, and in compliance with all relevant employment laws, regulations and legal obligations to works councils. People will always be our most important asset. That's why our staffing plans are among the highest-priority integration work. We are committed to finding and keeping the best talent in every function, operation and geography. By fielding the best possible team, we will be able to recognize our shared vision of being the best consumer products company in the world.

**Source:** SEC 425 Filing, Business Combination-Transaction Communication, see http://www.secinfo.com/d2eH7.z1g.htm. Consulted on 25/04/09.

ranks and had a chance to make an offer. Although the hot labor markets made persuading these managers more difficult, they simultaneously made it easier for P&G to float employees to other firms. *"While most jobs would go to P&G-ers, we were going to make sure that there was enough room in the P&G system to allow Gillette folks to come in and create an environment in which they could be successful,"* commented Ed Shirley, the future Group President of North America.

# Culture

*"Gillette and P&G have similar cultures and complementary core strengths in branding, innovation, scale and go-to-market capabilities, making it a terrific fit"*

A.G. Lafley, Chairman and CEO, P&G in the *New York Times*, 29th of January 2005

## P&G's culture

With approximately 110,000 employees across the world, P&G was an extremely large company. When Lafley arrived in 2000, he tuned up the company in terms of strategy and put it back on the growth track, achieving attractive financial performance figures. On the whole, very few companies equaled P&G's success. The company subsequently adjusted its organizational culture. Though Lafley did want to improve P&G's notorious bureaucracy, he did not want to change the values. He therefore emphasized the company's purpose, its value system, and the six guiding principles from the beginning. The purpose, values, and principles (PVP) were a key concept within the P&G organization (see Exhibit 8). All decisions were made with these in mind.

Even though P&G was a very large company, it was not run as a top-down organization. Team collaboration was rewarded and obtaining consensus on any decision was very important. Lafley insisted that the businesses define their own future, while he acted more as a coach.

Although P&G was considered a well structured organization, it had numerous fragmented processes with multiple owners. Consequently, obtaining consensus required multiple people's consent, which made social networking extremely important. It mattered who you knew, how you knew them, and the type of relationship you had with them. This clearly created trust over time and potentially better decisions; however, it came at the cost of slower decision making and reduced response times due to a certain level of rigidity. Furthermore, outsiders found it difficult to follow the company meetings, as P&G employees were known for using many acronyms in their communication. One outside board member even maintained that she needed a glossary to follow meetings.

The company was also famous for its promote-from-within policy, which defined the organizational culture for many years. Even though 40% of its employees had entered through recent acquisitions, the top 200 executives did not reflect the same proportion of new employees. Employees usually took a bit of time getting used to the company culture, while one needed to spend some time on the inside before being promoted to a managerial position, even if one had achieved an outstanding performance somewhere else. A P&G spokeswoman declared that the only time somebody is hired at the brand-manager level is during acquisitions. Owing to the size of its workforce and the scope of operations, the company had no problem finding people from within for future manager and executive positions.

## Gillette's culture

Within a few hours of his arrival at Gillette on February 12, 2001, Jim Kilts had his first operating committee staff meeting, while all the company employees received his first communication. From the outset, he made it clear that while everyone would be evaluated, people would not be eliminated unless they did not perform. At the first meeting, he described the detailed process for setting yearly and quarterly objectives; weekly meetings and company off-sites were also announced.

## EXHIBIT 8   Comparison of P&G and Gillette values

**P&G Values**

Consumers

Integrity
Leadership
Ownership
Passion for Winning
Trust

P&G Brands          P&G People

P&G Brands and P&G People are the
foundation of P&G's success.
P&G People bring the values to life
as we focus on improving
the lives of the world's consumers.

**Gillette Values**

**ACHIEVEMENT**
We are dedicated to the highest standards
of achievement in all areas of our business.
We strive to consistently exceed the
expectations of both external and internal
Customers.

**INTEGRITY**
Mutual respect and ethical behavior are the
Basis for our relationship with colleagues,
Customers and the community. Fair practice
is the hallmark of the company.

**COLLABORATION**
We work closely together as one global
team to improve the way we do business
everyday. We communicate openly and
establish clear accountability for making
Decisions, identifying issues and solutions,
and maximizing business opportunities.

**Source:** Kanter R.M., Bird M., 2008. "Procter & Gamble in the 21st Century (B): Welcoming Gillette (Abridged)". Harvard Business School.

He even mentioned the behavior he expected from every-body during meetings (punctuality, full attention, and jokes allowed). Kilts described himself as an open, straightforward, what-you-see-is what-you-get kind of guy. His managers' first impression of him was of a forthright person, an excellent communicator, somebody who knew where he wanted to be and how to get there.

Kilts expected his employees to perform (see Exhibit 8). In the fall of 2001, a new performance-based apprai-sal system was introduced that would reward perfor-mance and not effort, as had been the case previously. Many employees – including senior executives – who had been rated *"highly effective"* before, were merely rated as 'effective' when they received their next bonus. Mike Cowhig, a senior VP of supply chain and business development, observed: *"Jim began ... to measure to make sure you were on track towards your commit-ments. ... The performance culture was clear. If you de-livered, then he was happy, and if you didn't, he wasn't."*

During the years of Kilts's reign, the company became a highly responsive and performing unit. Employees knew exactly what they had to do; they knew what suc-cess or failure entailed. Decisions were taken relatively quickly, which was also one of the reasons why Gillette could roll out its new products within a few weeks. Em-ployees felt strongly about their culture, as they had spent several years working very hard to try and meet

all the goals and objectives of the CEO; they felt com-fortable with it.

## Cultural integration

Both companies were American business icons. Never-theless, there were notable differences between the two. During its previous acquisitions, like that of Wella in 2003, P&G would usually wipe the company's identity slate clean, making it part of its own culture. Gillette's acquisition was, however, different.

When the CEO of Gillette, Jim Kilts, called the CEO of P&G, Alan Lafley, to offer his company for sale, the two leaders had a friendly conversation. After first dis-cussing the price and Kilts's commitment to leadership, Lafley raised the question of culture. Both men agreed that the two organizations would make a great fit. This was a major issue, however, clearly a major issue that had to be considered carefully, as both companies were over a century old. The whole process of negotiations was one of collaboration. Important signs of trust were exchanged between the two men, like having no lawyers or bankers present at their first meetings!

Though there were many similarities between the two old American companies, there were also subtle, but impor-tant, differences. Kilts summarized these as: *"P&G was like a family and Gillette was like a team."* With clear decision

**EXHIBIT 9**   Gillette's presentation to its employees

# Gillette – Procter & Gamble

P&G wants to field the *best possible* team ... with members from BOTH companies

- There will be job losses

- Losses are estimated at approximately 4% of the combined company's work force of 140,000

- Many will occur at the corporate office ... but NO decisions have been made

- We've implemented special severance protection

  ☐ Change of control measures

  ☐ Fully vested stock option plan

**Source:** Stowell, D.P., 2007. "The Best Deal Gillette Could Get". Kellogg School of Management.

rights and responsibilities due to its newly instilled performance and commitment culture, Gillette set clear goals and accomplished them. This gave the organization agility. Following their principle of consensus, P&G-ers lacked decision-making speed. "*Have pre-meetings about meetings*" was a common observation among Gillette employees when getting a taste of the new environment. Michelle Stacey, who headed Gillette's sales to dental professionals and kept her job in the merged operation, observed that at P&G, people tended to put everything on paper, while they would have meetings at Gillette. She was accustomed to giving PowerPoint presentations and "*... had not written a memo in 10 to 15 years.*"

Bringing the two companies together on the cultural level was the most complicated task of all. According to Carolina Klüft, a brand manager at P&G, "*... everything else is relatively easy, but if you cannot integrate the employees on the cultural level, the whole operation will be a failure.*" The integration leaders used several mechanisms to integrate Gillette employees into P&G. Selected employees had already been brought in during the first week of October in order to reinforce the commitment signals; they would also facilitate other Gillette employees' future integration. During site merging, for example, Gillette employees were assigned peer buddies and mentors, thus giving them a go-to-person on horizontal and vertical levels. Early cross-fertilization between the two organizations also helped share the culture, while simultaneously fostering the transfer of

knowledge. Klüft adds that cultural session meetings (see Exhibit 9) were very useful to acclimatize newcomers to the P&G culture. HR organized these meetings, which would last several hours and during which initial learnings from cultural clashes were studied: the goal was to stimulate conversation.

The various instruments were all very helpful, because the Gillette people had at first felt at a disadvantage during the discussions. P&G employees would always reference the company's Purpose, Values, and Principles (PVP) statement during meetings, in documents and when taking decisions. "*Some got it pretty quickly. They saw that it was actually to their advantage to do this,*" Madalyn Brooks, a member of the Western Europe regional integration team, remembers. "*The quicker they got on to the PVP, the quicker they would be integrated into the company.*"

Among other organizational cultural differences, there were divergences in marketing philosophies. P&G has long made segmentation a science, with the consumer being referred to as '*she*' across the whole company (the primary consumers were female). Conversely, one of the key Gillette executives reportedly said that the company has no segments, and that they are for all men.

After the announcement of the deal, communication played a major role in calming the fears and anxieties of the Gillette employees. By showing that full collaboration was the only way to go, the P&G leaders were able to win over most of the Gillette people. Although this was the biggest acquisition in P&G's history, both sides framed the deal as a '*merger.*' And this was not all talk. P&G did not only place Gillette managers in key positions, but the company was also interested in learning from the highly effective Gillette culture. Lafley declared from the start that P&G would adopt some of Gillette's business strategies. Ultimately, this was not only helpful for the Gillette employees coming in, but on the P&G side, it was easier to justify letting some people go if the deal was called a merger.

The biggest difficulty arose when the businesses had to be physically integrated to truly leverage the various synergies. Many Boston employees were reluctant to move to Cincinnati. Consequently, P&G organized a weekend event in Cincinnati to promote the city to Gillette employees. Nonetheless, retention issues did come up. Although 95% of Gillette employees agreed to join the new company, the percentage was smaller with regard to the top management. Of Gillette's top executives, only two remained after completion of the deal. Overall, 60% of top managers had decided to stay by December 2005. Most of those who left, had received substantial compensation; others had personal reasons (age, not wanting to move, difficulty in adjusting to the new culture) for going.

Although the Gillette employees' decision to stay on after the deal was important to P&G, their full integration into the company was equally important. If they were ultimately unable to integrate into the P&G culture, the knowledge that they held would not be fully transferred. Carolina Klüft confirmed that some had not been able to fully integrate, and thus had to leave. These managers had often occupied more senior positions at

Gillette but had to assume lower ones when they went to P&G; not everyone could manage that.

Some Gillette managers were given plum jobs at P&G, which shocked P&G employees, as they were replacing colleagues who had to leave. Some of these P&G employees were not impressed with their new Gillette bosses. Several mentioned the PVP: "*How can you choose this person over me? You've known me for 20 years!*" P&G, which had once been a promote-from-within company, had to wake up to a few hard facts. After the Gillette deal (and the earlier purchases of Clairol and Wella), 40% of P&G employees were "outsiders". The Gillette leaders were also paid a lot more than their P&G counterparts for running a much smaller business. Kilts's compensation also appeared to be an issue during the initial negotiations. Furthermore, it was unclear what the salaries of the Gillette managers coming into P&G would be.

## Conclusion

Almost four years had passed since he listened to Jim Kilts's message. Lafley still could not fully believe that the integration process was over – the ceremony had been held, the honeymoon was over, and real family life was in full swing. He felt like making a call to his old friend Kilts to discuss Microsoft's bid for Yahoo and reminisce about their undertaking. The ringing of the phone brought the CEO of Procter & Gamble back to the reality of a working day. He had to get back to running the best consumer products company in the world.

## REFERENCES

### Interviews

Klüft C., Brand Manager at P&G. Interview conducted on March 19, 2009. P&G headquarters, Geneva. Second interview conducted by phone on April 6, 2009.

### Articles & Books

Aiken C., Keller S., 2009. "The irrational side of change management". *The McKinsey Quarterly*, Vol. 2, pp. 101–105.

Balogun J., Hailey V.H., Johnson G., Scholes K., 2003. "*Exploring Strategic Change*". Financial Times / Prentice Hall, 2nd edition, 280 pages.

Burns T., Stalker G.M., 1966. "*The Management of Innovation*". Oxford University Press, USA, Revised edition, 312 pages.

Byrnes N., Berner R., Zellner W., Symonds W.C., 2005. "Branding: Five New Lessons". *BusinessWeek*, Issue 3920, February, p. 26.

Byron E., 2007. "Paired Up: Merger Challenge: Unite Toothbrush, Toothpaste – P&G and Gillette find creating synergy can be harder than it looks". *The Wall Street Journal*, 24 April 2007.

Ghosn C., 2007. "Will she, won't she?" *Economist*, Vol. 384, Issue 8541, pp. 61–66

Gupta R., Wendler J., 2005. "Leading change: An interview with the CEO of P&G". *The McKinsey Quarterly,* July 2005, pp. 1–6.

Hays C.L., Dash E., 2005. "A household giant: in the store; What's behind the Procter Deal? Wal-Mart". *The New York Times*, 29 January 2005 issue.

Kotter J.P., 1996. *"Leading Change"*. Harvard Business School Press, 1st edition, 187 pages.

Lafley A.G., Sellers P., 2005. "It was a no-brainer". *Fortune*, Vol. 151, Issue 4, pp. 60–64.

Lewin, K., 1951. *"Field theory in social science; selected theoretical papers"*. D. Cartwright (ed.). New York: Harper & Row.

Metais E., Meschi, P.X., 2008. "The failure of Merger & Acquisitions: Myth or Reality?" *EDHEC Business School*.

Miles S.A., Watkins M.D., 2007. "The Leadership Team: Complementary Strengths or Conflicting Agendas?" *Harvard Business Review*, Vol. 85, No. 4, pp. 90–98.

Nahavandi A., Malekzadeh A.R., 1988. "Acculturation in Mergers and Acquisitions." *Academy of Management Review*, Vol. 13, No. 1, pp. 79–90.

Neff J., Johnson, B., 2005. "P&G bids for domination". *Advertising Age*, Vol. 76, Issue 5, pp. 1–37.

Neff J., 2005. "Cash clash could prove a P&G, Gillette obstacle". *Advertising Age*, Vol. 76, Issue 39, p. 8.

Neff, J., 2006. "Ogling talent beyond its ranks? Surely not P&G". *Advertising Age,* Vol. 77, Issue 30, p. 8.

Neff, J., 2007. "P&G struggles to hang on to top Gillette talent". *Advertising Age*, Vol. 78, Issue 22, pp. 4–28.

Pomeroy A., 2005. "A Fitting Role". *HR Magazine*, June 2005 issue, pp. 54–60.

Strebel P., 1994. "Choosing the Right Change Path". *California Management Review*, Vol. 36, Issue 2, pp. 29–51.

Thornton, E., Symonds, W., Barrett, A., Foust, D., and Grow, B., 2005. "Fat Merger Payouts For CEOs". *BusinessWeek*, 12.12.2005.

## Study Cases

Kanter R.M., Weber J., 2005. "Gillette Company (A): Pressure for Change". *Harvard Business School Case*.

Kanter R.M., Weber J., 2005. "Gillette Company (B): Leadership for Change". *Harvard Business School Case*.

Kanter R.M., Weber J., 2005. "Gillette Company (C): Strategies for Change". *Harvard Business School Case*.

Kanter R.M., 2005. "Gillette Company (D): Implementing Change". *Harvard Business School Case*.

Kanter R.M., Bird M., 2005. "Gillette Company (E): Procter & Gamble". *Harvard Business School Case*.

Kanter R.M., Bird M., 2008. "Procter & Gamble in the 21st Century (B): Welcoming Gillette (Abridged)". *Harvard Business School Case*.

Kanter R.M., Bird M., 2008. "Procter & Gamble in the 21st Century (C): Integrating Gillette". *Harvard Business School Case*.

Lorsch J.W., Robertson A.C., 2005. "The P&G Acquisition of Gillette". *Harvard Business School Case*.

Piskorski M.J., Spadini A.L., 2007. "Procter & Gamble: Organizing 2005 (A)". *Harvard Business School Case*.

Stowell D.P., 2007. "The Best Deal Gillette Could Get? Procter & Gamble's Acquisition of Gillette". *Kellogg School of Management Case*.

## NOTES

1. Thornton et al. (2005).
2. Kanter R.M., Bird M., 2008. "Procter & Gamble in the 21st Century (C): Integrating Gillette". *Harvard Business School Case*, p.12.

# INTEGRATIVE CASE 3

# CARREFOUR IN ASIA

**Neil Jones, and Philippe Lasserre**
*INSEAD*

*"China represents a huge market and now it has acquired its WTO membership. But there is no easy way to stand out a winner here. China is nearly as big as Europe and all areas differ from each other,"* declared Jean-Luc Chereau, president of Carrefour China, at the opening of the first Carrefour store in Urumqi, Xinjiang province. The Urumqi hypermarket was the forty-second to be opened by the company in China where Carrefour was the leading mass retailer, despite mounting competition.

## History

In 2003 Carrefour was the second-largest mass retailer in the world with net sales totaling €70.5 billion (US$84 billion) and net profits of €1.6 billion. It operated 10,378 stores in 29 countries and employed more than 410,000 people.

Although primarily known as a hypermarket pioneer, Carrefour also operated supermarkets, hard discounts and other formats, such as convenience stores (see Exhibits 1 and 2).

**EXHIBIT 1** Carrefour's key figures

| Year | Revenue (in million euros) | Net Income (in million euros) | Net Profit Margin (%) | Employees | Sales Area (m²) | Annual Sales/ m² in Euros |
|------|------|------|------|------|------|------|
| 2003 | 70,486 | 1,629 | 2.3% | 410,000 | 13,207 | 5,337 |
| 2002 | 68,728 | 1,347 | 2.0 | 396,662 | 9,767 | 7,037 |
| 2001 | 69,486 | 1,265 | 1.8 | 382,821 | 9,151 | 7,593 |
| 2000 | 64,802 | 1,065 | 1.6 | 330,247 | 8,130 | 7,971 |
| 1999 | 51,948 | 898 | 1.7 | 297,290 | 6,569 | 7,908 |
| 1998 | 27,408 | 647 | 2.4 | 132,875 | 3,721 | 7,366 |
| 1997 | 25,804 | 546 | 2.1 | 113,289 | 3,075 | 8,392 |
| 1996 | 23,615 | 476 | 2.0 | 103,600 | 2,727 | 8,660 |
| 1995 | 22,046 | 539 | 2.4 | 102,900 | 2,378 | 9,271 |
| 1994 | 20,778 | 324 | 1.6 | 95,900 | 2,129 | 9,760 |
| 1993 | 18,708 | 448 | 2.4 | 81,500 | 1,920 | 9,744 |

This case was written by Claudia Gehlen, Research Associate, under the supervision of Neil Jones and Philippe Lasserre, both professors at INSEAD. It is intended to be used as a basis for class discussion rather than to illustrate either effective or ineffective handling of an administrative situation.

**EXHIBIT 2** Carrefour formats worldwide

| Format | Number of Stores | Sales (incl. taxes in million euros) | Sales % of Total | Sales Area (1000 m²) | Sales Incl. Taxes/m² in Euros |
|---|---|---|---|---|---|
| Hypermarkets | 823 | 51,060 | 57.60% | 6,985 | 7,310 |
| Supermarkets | 2,380 | 22,592 | 25.50 | 3,394 | 6,656 |
| Hard discounts | 4,456 | 6,692 | 7.60 | 1,459 | 4,586 |
| Other stores | 2,718 | 8,229 | 9.30 | 1,369 | 6,010 |
| Total | 10,378 | 88,572 | 100.00 | 13,207 | |

Note: Those figures relate to all stores operated under Carrefour's banner, including the franchises.
**Source:** Carrefour Annual Report, 2003.© Don Hammond/Design Pics/Corbis

It has always been significantly more international than most of its competitors (see Exhibit 3). Carrefour's international operations are located in three major geographical zones: Europe and the Middle East, Latin America, and Asia. In 2003, 49 percent of its hypermarket revenues were derived from markets outside France (see Exhibit 4). In Europe and China, Carrefour is the number one retailer in terms of size.

Carrefour developed the hypermarket concept of bringing nearly all types of consumer goods under one roof in 1959, when the Defforey and Fournier families created their first hypermarket in the suburbs of Paris. It built a reputation as the retailer that offered the most variety and freshness at low prices. For years its claim to fame was to offer a massive array of quality goods in one place, at reasonable prices rather than bargain-basement value.

The retailer operated exclusively in France until the late 1960s before expanding into Spain, where under the name of Pryca, it became the country's second-largest retailer. It then successfully entered Portugal, Argentina, and Brazil. However, in more mature markets its results were not so conclusive and it had to pull out of the United Kingdom, Switzerland, the United States, and Belgium (although it was later to reenter Switzerland and Belgium).

As in France during the 1960s, Carrefour was generally successful when it entered new markets that had seen dramatic changes in consumer buying habits, coupled with high growth in *per capita* GNP, suburbanization, greater participation of women in the labor force, and a large increase in the ownership of cars and refrigerators.

During the 1980s and 1990s, Carrefour continued its international expansion through a combination of organic growth and acquisitions, extending its reach into Latin America. The 1990s were characterized by a

move into Asia, starting with Taiwan in 1989 and a few years later expanding to Malaysia, China, South Korea, Thailand, Singapore, Indonesia, and Japan. In all the Asian markets, hypermarkets emerged as the winning format (see Exhibit 5).

In France, due to regulatory constraints, Carrefour merged in 1999 with rival Promodès, the number two in the French market. The merger may also have been motivated by Wal-Mart's acquisition of Asda in the United Kingdom that same year. From 2000 to 2003 Carrefour wrestled with integrating Promodès'

**EXHIBIT 3** Level of internationalization of global retailers in 2003

| Retailer | Number of Countries | Net Sales (in million US$) | Foreign Sales % |
|---|---|---|---|
| Carrefour | 29 | 84,000 | 50 |
| Metro | 22 | 46,900 | 45 |
| Ito-Yokado | 12 | 27,238 | 41 |
| Tesco | 11 | 39,521 | 18 |
| Aeon | 10 | 24,677 | 17 |
| Costco | 7 | 37,993 | 16 |
| Wal-Mart | 11 | 205,500 | 16 |
| Daiei | 3 | 17,717 | 1 |

**Source:** http://www.siamfuture.com; companies reports.

**EXHIBIT 4** Carrefour worldwide operations

| Region | Number of Stores | Net Sales (in million euros) | Sales (% of total) | Investments million € | % Sales | Operating Million € | Margin % |
|---|---|---|---|---|---|---|---|
| France | 1,448 | 35,704 | 50.65% | 818 | 2.3% | 2144 | 6.0% |
| Europe | 3,606 | 25,526 | 36.21 | 1169 | 4.6 | 952 | 3.7 |
| Latin America | 814 | 4,619 | 6.55 | 295 | 6.4 | 13 | 0.3 |
| Asia | 199 | 4,637 | 6.58 | 436 | 9.4 | 143 | 3.1 |
| Total | 6,067 | 70,486 | 100.00 | 2717 | 3.9 | 3251 | 4.6 |

**Source:** Carrefour Annual Report, 2003.

businesses into its existing operations. As a result, its performance and organic growth rate slipped during this period. Carrefour focused intensely on integration and repairing weak domestic sales and by the end of the year it had successfully repositioned itself to continue its international expansion at its historically fast pace.

Carrefour also has a foothold in the Middle East. In the United Arab Emirates (UAE), the joint venture company between Majid al Futtaim and Carrefour was the most dynamic and fast-moving hypermarket chain, with a total of eight stores in 2004. Thanks to its massive buying power, Carrefour could guarantee low prices while permanently offering about 50,000 items in stock.

In February 2004 shares in Carrefour SA jumped in value, renewing market speculation that its larger rival, Wal-Mart, was planning a bid. Wal-Mart had coveted the French market for years but its attempts to buy a French subsidiary had been stymied since its abortive courtship of the Auchan and Carrefour chains in 1999.

Adding to the speculation over Carrefour's future was the death in a plane crash in December 2003 of a member of the Halley family group, Carrefour's largest shareholder with an approximate 11.5 percent stake. Such speculation highlighted that Carrefour was vulnerable to a takeover, or at least to increased competition from international competitors like Wal-Mart and Tesco that were posting stronger domestic growth. In 2003 Carrefour's hypermarkets had a 13.9 percent share of the "fast-moving consumer goods" category in its French home market (which included food as well as household goods and health and beauty products), down from 14.4 percent in 2002. The company might have considered a defensive merger with another European retailer had Wal-Mart set its sights on Carrefour, although any

merger or takeover might well run into culture clashes, integration headaches, and antitrust concerns. As CEO Daniel Bernard put it, "Hostile bids in a 'people' sector simply don't work."

Another threat came from the growth of hard-discounters like Aldi from Germany that sold goods at rock-bottom prices. In order to fight back against the hard-discounters, Carrefour expanded its own hard discount chain, ED.

# Carrefour's approach

The basics of Carrefour's concept are (1) one-stop shopping, (2) low prices, (3) self-service, (4) quality products, (5) freshness, and (6) free parking.

Before entering a new international market, local conditions are analyzed against a set of socio-economic criteria. The size and maturity of the market, the legal framework and the openness to foreign investors are major aspects. For instance, Carrefour postponed its entry into India due to a lack of clarity on direct foreign investment. Basic figures regarding population, per capita GDP, transport networks, the level of motorization, urbanization, real estate prices, and so forth are also taken into account. However, Carrefour does not believe only in extensive market research, as Jean-Michel Arlaud, head of its Romanian operations, put it in an interview:

> When we decided to set up stores in Romania, it was more an instinctive feeling than the results of a market study. If we had based our decisions on studies, we would never have come.

Once the feasibility study is conclusive, Carrefour focuses on selecting the format best suited to the particular

**EXHIBIT 5** Carrefour formats by region

| Sales Incl. Taxes in 2003 (in million euros) | | | | |
| --- | --- | --- | --- | --- |
| | Hypermarkets | Supermarkets | Hard Discounts | Others | Total |
| France | 23,948 | 13,151 | 2,037 | 5,576 | 44,912 |
| Europe | 17,900 | 8,302 | 4,405 | 2,453 | 33,060 |
| Latin America | 4,059 | 1,139 | 245 | – | 5,444 |
| Asia | 5,152 | – | 4 | – | 5,157 |
| | 51,060 | | | | – |
| Total | 50,509 | 22,592 | 6,692 | 2,719 | 88,572 |

| Number of Stores in 2003 | | | | |
| --- | --- | --- | --- | --- |
| | Hypermarkets | Supermarkets | Hard Discounts | Others | Total |
| France | 216 | 1,005 | 588 | 1,766 | 3,575 |
| Europe | 315 | 1,121 | 3,381 | 953 | 5,770 |
| Latin America | 147 | 254 | 432 | – | 833 |
| Asia | 145 | – | 55 | – | 200 |
| Total | 823 | 2,380 | 4,456 | 2,719 | 10,378 |

| Sales Area in 2002 (thousand m²) | | | | |
| --- | --- | --- | --- | --- |
| | Hypermarkets | Supermarkets | Hard Discounts | Others | Total |
| France | 1,864 | 1,577 | 343 | 945 | 4,729 |
| Europe | 2,584 | 1,367 | 959 | 425 | 5,335 |
| Latin America | 1,316 | 449 | 141 | – | 1,907 |
| Asia | 1,220 | – | 16 | – | 1,236 |
| Total | 6,985 | 3,393 | 1,459 | 1,370 | 13,207 |

**Source:** Carrefour Annual Report, 2003.

market and adapting that format to local needs. Unprecedented in its history, Carrefour has opted in many Asian countries for an urban location for its stores due to the population density, and has positioned its hypermarkets as proximity stores rather than suburban stores, offering a limited product range but producing greater volume.

Carrefour tries to establish as many stores as possible in major urban areas in order to achieve economies of scale. Its challenge in each new market is to recreate the virtuous circle of "freshness + variety + low prices → high volume → high bargaining power → low costs → low prices" (see Exhibit 6).

For Carrefour, price is not simply a competitive advantage but an essential means of survival. In order to drive down prices in response to competition while maintaining high-quality brands, Carrefour advertises new

## EXHIBIT 6  Carrefour's virtuous circle

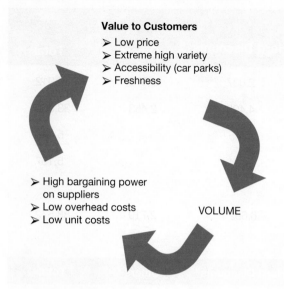

**Value to Customers**
➢ Low price
➢ Extreme high variety
➢ Accessibility (car parks)
➢ Freshness

➢ High bargaining power
  on suppliers
➢ Low overhead costs
➢ Low unit costs

VOLUME

**Source:** Carrefour Annual Report, 2003; EIU Data Services.

promotions and discounts every day, reminding customers that they will be refunded if they find the same product cheaper elsewhere.

Taking local constraints into account, Carrefour has added new services in developing markets, such as free shuttle services for customers and play areas for children, as well as home delivery. In some markets, such as China, Carrefour has launched its own product line in home appliances and spices.

Because Carrefour operates on tiny margins (6.9 percent gross margin and 2.5 percent net margin), the slightest improvement in these translates into significant growth for the bottom line.

One important factor in cost management is its sourcing strategy. In China, for instance, more than 95 percent of its merchandise is locally sourced and the remainder is sourced through local importers or the trading office in Hong Kong. Carrefour has built big global procurement centers coordinated through Shanghai and Hong Kong.

The centralization of its IT systems and administrative procedures achieves further savings. Shared processes and systems increase operational efficiency and the introduction of international product ranges complements its locally sensitive strategy. In order to increase its profitability, in 2000 Carrefour created the GNX online supply platform with Oracle and Sears, whereby suppliers and retailers can exchange information via the Internet and optimize the flow of merchandise, thus reducing their administrative costs. Other retailers have since joined GNX including Metro (Germany), Sainsbury's (U.K.), Kroger (U.S.) and Coles Myer (Australia).

Carrefour also works actively with local governments and nonprofit organizations to protect the environment. In 2002 Carrefour and the Chinese Packaging Corporation initiated actions to globally reduce pollution from packaging. Worldwide, Carrefour requested that its stores make less use of plastic in packaging, thereby gaining a reputation as a model in the retailing industry.

While venturing into new markets, Carrefour's human resource policy has relied on a small number of expatriates. In 2002 Carrefour employed about 200 expatriate executives with solid experience of adapting Carrefour's retailing concept to local contexts. They were mainly recruited in France but also in countries that were considered Carrefour strongholds, such as Taiwan.

When opening a new market, Carrefour operates a dual system for employing expatriates and local executives. Initially, store and department heads are experienced expatriates. Local managers receive six months' training in a country of the region where Carrefour is already successfully operating. Thereafter they work hand-in-hand: the expatriates contributing their expertise and experience and the local executives sharing their know-how of the local business environment. Carrefour's aim is to eventually promote local talent to top management.

As early as 1969 Carrefour was the first mass retailer to measure performance on the return on invested capital instead of the classic concept of gross profit margin used in traditional trade. In terms of remuneration it has a reputation for paying employees well: Department heads earn 20 percent more than they would with other supermarkets, and can earn a bonus linked to the results of the department. The pressure for sales and profit is put on department heads, as each store is a profit center. In Asia, department heads are much more autonomous than in France and are also in charge of recruiting employees and negotiating salaries.

In China, Carrefour employs 95 percent of local Chinese managers and invests heavily in their training. In 2002 Carrefour employed a total of 18,000 local employees, and 1,000 Chinese department heads were trained in retail techniques and business management.

## Carrefour in Asia

In 2003 Carrefour was present in eight Asian markets, operating 144 hypermarkets and 55 hard discount stores (see Exhibits 7 and 8). The Asian zone represented 13 percent of the group's hypermarket sales and 6.7 percent of the total. Net sales revenues totaled €4,637 million and profits €143 million (4.7 percent of the total).

**EXHIBIT 7** Carrefour's Asian presence

| | Year of Entry | Sales in 2002 (in million euro) | Sales growth (%) | GDP Growth in 2002 (%) | Population (millions) in 2002 | Urban population (%) |
|---|---|---|---|---|---|---|
| Taiwan | 1989 | 1,381.00 | 1.6 | 3.0 | 22.50 | N.A. |
| Malaysia | 1994 | 225.90 | −1.7 | 3.5 | 24.00 | 58.7 |
| China | 1995 | 1,369.50 | 6.1 | 7.5 | 1,282.10 | 33.1 |
| South Korea | 1996 | 1,242.90 | 1.7 | 6.3 | 48.10 | 83.0 |
| Thailand | 1996 | 416.40 | 21.0 | 4.5 | 63.40 | 22.4 |
| Singapore | 1997 | 86.00 | 6.0 | 2.2 | 3.60 | 100.0 |
| Indonesia | 1998 | 313.20 | 48.6 | 3.5 | 217.10 | 42.9 |
| Japan | 2000 | 156.90 | 6.1 | 0.9 | 127.20 | 79.1 |
| **Total** | | **5,191.80** | | | | |

When first moving into Asia, Carrefour opted for joint ventures and partnerships to make up for its lack of knowledge of the Asian market. Later on it worked with financial or industrial partners only when national regulations made it necessary, as in China, Thailand, Malaysia, and Indonesia.

With the exception of Japan, Carrefour chose those countries that, despite their low GDP, had reached a sufficient level of maturity to make the transition to mass consumption. Timing was crucial to Carrefour's success because it entered these markets earlier than its competitors, who had delayed entry due to the Asian crisis. Local competition was also slow to react to this new phenomenon and was often thwarted by the onset of the Asian crisis, especially in Korea, Thailand, and Indonesia.

According to Gérard Clerc, the vice president who led Carrefour's Asian expansion, the Asian crisis did not affect the company; on the contrary, Carrefour benefited, thanks to its low price policy and emerged even stronger from the crisis with a higher market share than expected. Until the year 2000 international competition had been rather timid but was now progressing fast. International players such as Makro, Metro, Tesco, and Wal-Mart had shown a big appetite for the region.

Even though Asian customers still tended to shop daily at wet markets or "mom & pop" stores, buying patterns were slowly changing and a certain degree of Westernization of local tastes was apparent in most countries. Moreover, impulse buying was on the rise and replacing necessity purchasing. Shopping as a form of leisure was an increasing phenomenon: a visit to the French hypermarket had turned into a Sunday outing.

## Carrefour in Taiwan

"It was as if the Huns had arrived in Taiwan," Gérard Clerc said of the reaction of local retailers in Taiwan to Carrefour's arrival.

In 1987 Carrefour selected Taiwan as the entry point into the vast, mainly untapped market space for hypermarkets. As René Brillet, director of the Asia region, put it: "This explains why we have roots on this continent, offering us the potential for tremendous growth, because of its size, its cultural diversity and its enormous population." Another advantage of the Taiwanese experience was that it served as a human resource hub for other Asian markets, especially China.

However, Carrefour did not have an easy start in Taiwan and it was almost two years before it finally set up a hypermarket in 1989. Carrefour, with Makro, was the first foreign retailer to establish the hypermarket concept in Taiwan. The retailer entered a partnership with a local food and retailing conglomerate, the President Group, which held 40 percent of the shares. The President Group is a dominant figure on the Taiwanese business landscape, ranking number two in size. Right from the start it accepted the role of a dormant partner but played a big role in introducing Carrefour to the political and economic establishment.

**EXHIBIT 8** Carrefour in Asia

Expansion of Stores and Surface

| | 1993 | 1994 | 1995 | 1996 | 1997 | 1998 | 1999 | 2000 | 2001 | 2002 | 2003 | Surface (1000 m²) | Tesco 2002 | Macro 2002 | Wal-Mart 2002 |
|---|---|---|---|---|---|---|---|---|---|---|---|---|---|---|---|
| **China** | | | 2 | 3 | 7 | 14 | 20 | 24 | 24 | 36 | **95** | **337** | 12 | 5 | 25 |
| Hypermarkets | | | | | | | | | | | 40 | 321 | | | |
| Hard Discounts | | | | | | | | | | | 55 | 15 | | | |
| **South Korea** | | | | 3 | 5 | 6 | 12 | 20 | 22 | 25 | 27 | **253** | 20 | | 9 |
| **Hong Kong** | | | | 1 | | 4 | 4 | | | | | | | | |
| **Indonesia** | | | | | | 1 | 5 | 7 | 8 | 10 | **11** | **73** | | 12 | |
| **Japan** | | | | | | | | 1 | 3 | 4 | **7** | **65** | | | |
| **Malaysia** | | 1 | 1 | 2 | 3 | 5 | 6 | 6 | 6 | 6 | **7** | **69** | 1 | 8 | |
| **Singapore** | | | | | 1 | 1 | 1 | 1 | 1 | 1 | **2** | **15** | | | |
| **Taiwan** | 7 | 8 | 10 | 13 | 17 | 21 | 23 | 24 | 26 | 28 | **31** | **243** | 3 | 8 | |
| **Thailand** | | | | 2 | 6 | 7 | 9 | 11 | 15 | 17 | **19** | **172** | 41 | 21 | |
| **Total** | 7 | 9 | 13 | 24 | 39 | 59 | 80 | 94 | 105 | 126 | **199** | **1228** | **77** | **54** | **34** |
| Hypermarkets | | | | | | | | | | | 144 | 1212 | | | |
| Hard Discounts | | | | | | | | | | | 55 | 15 | | | |

During this period real estate prices skyrocketed, making some adaptation of Carrefour's policy necessary. Traditionally, Carrefour had set up much bigger stores in suburban areas. Instead of buying the sites, Carrefour rented space to operate hypermarkets in Kaohsiung and Taipei on a much smaller scale (3,500 m$^2$) in urban centers on two stories instead of the classic one-floor layout. In addition, in urban areas some kind of "protection" from the local secret societies had to be negotiated.

All stores consistently had pilot departments to introduce new product ranges. Study conclusions were then introduced on a national scale across all Carrefour stores in Taiwan. This cross-learning was vitally important as it spread the know-how within the company. Subsequently, Carrefour increased the size of its new stores.

In certain cases Carrefour chose industrial and commercial parks to develop the hypermarkets. Wholesale stores or "green stores" were built in industrial areas, and general retailing or "blue stores" in residential areas. By adopting this strategy Carrefour could capture both big and small accounts and grow much faster than its rival Makro.

Carrefour is pronounced Jia Le Fu in Chinese, which means "luck and happiness for the whole family." This fortunate phonetic translation unexpectedly contributed to Carrefour's success in Taiwan and later in China, where foreign names often remain unpronounceable.

However, Carrefour still had to tackle different business approaches, especially to negotiation. "For Europeans, Chinese are known to be difficult negotiators. They consider the negotiation process as a refined art which they master with intelligence and patience," Gerard Clerc explained. Managing the supply chain was another major challenge. Taiwanese suppliers lacked rigor, organization, equipment, and aggressiveness, but they were much more flexible than their Western counterparts. They sold products, not services, and often lacked information regarding basic data on their sales, inventory level, and even internal accounting.

Communication was another challenge. In Taiwan, all documents were written in Chinese while Carrefour's documentation was in English. Corporate culture, training, and company goals, among other factors, were difficult to communicate to all staff members, and promotions were only possible for English-speaking staff.

The cultural gap was also a source of misunderstanding amongst management. Rather than sharing their knowledge with their staff, local managers had the tendency to withhold information. According to one French local store manager, Philippe Ravelli, the French and the Chinese cultures do not give the same priority to the three basic elements in daily life. For the Chinese, emotion (quing) comes first, followed by reason (li), and law (fa). For the French, law comes first (the company policy), reason second, emotion last. Despite such differences, thanks to its adaptive capabilities Carrefour became the largest mass retailer on the island.

Fortunately, Taiwan was relatively spared by the Asian crisis and consumption levels continued to increase. Carrefour continued to reinforce its lead over Makro, sometimes opening new stores near existing Makro stores. By 2003 Carrefour was operating 31 stores in Taiwan, which continued to be its most important Asian market with net sales of €1,322 million.

# Carrefour in South Korea

Since the liberalization of the Korean retail market in 1996, local and foreign retailers, such as Carrefour, Makro, Costco, Wal-Mart, and Metro, had struggled to stake out their territory. Local conglomerates raised the stakes and invested massively to protect the local industry. But the Asian crisis forced these local retailers to freeze their expansion plans, and some even had to file for bankruptcy. As a consequence, Carrefour further reinforced its position and recorded its first profit in 1997. Restructuring and modernization of existing stores started in 2001. Carrefour introduced a new feature with the creation of cultural centers in two stores in partnership with Korea's leading newspaper. These offered women and children weekly courses in English, dance, cooking, drawing, and other subjects. In 2003 Carrefour, now the number four food retailer, operated 27 stores, posting net sales of €1,149 million.

# Carrefour in Thailand

As with Korea, Thailand seemed to present all the conditions for Carrefour to succeed and the crisis offered an opportunity to expand while costs were lower and the competition reduced. Carrefour opened two stores there in 1996. However, unlike Korea, the chain operated with two local partners and this postponed their expansion plans for a year and reduced the number of stores to be opened from five to two in 1999.

Foreign ownership laws in Thailand allowed foreign companies – except American companies – to hold no more than 49 percent of the shares. Carrefour argued that this law would favor its rival, Wal-Mart. When the Central Retail Corp. sold its 40 percent shareholding in 1998, this law made it impossible for Carrefour to purchase the shares.

In 2002 Carrefour introduced a number of sales innovations that proved successful. The fresh product concept was redesigned in order to reproduce the atmosphere and merchandising style found in street markets, while emphasizing hygienic conditions. As an example, the "pork quality line" covered the entire cycle from breeding selection and reproduction to stocking the shelves. In 2003 Carrefour Thailand counted 19 stores with net sales of €392 million.

# Carrefour in Indonesia

With a population of 202 million, Indonesia was an attractive market for retailers, which Carrefour entered in 1998 at the peak of the Asian crisis. Just before the merger with Carrefour, Promodès had opened two stores in the country in 1998 and 1999, and these were subsequently integrated.

Indonesia's recovery from the Asian crisis had not been swift, unlike Korea and Thailand. The country was still facing major problems of financial sector fragility and private sector debt. Carrefour took advantage of the Indonesian crisis with its low prices. In order to offer a larger section of the population its first opportunity to purchase durable household goods, Carrefour organized two "free credit" campaigns in 2002, which were a resounding success, given that the household appliance segment represented 21 percent of total sales revenues.

In 2003 Carrefour was Indonesia's leading foreign hypermarket with 11 stores and net sales of €286 million. In addition to consolidating its position in Jakarta, Carrefour also planned to enter other provinces in 2003.

# Carrefour in Malaysia

When Carrefour entered the Malaysian market in 1994 it met with little competition. Before the Asia crisis Malaysia had experienced one of the strongest growth rates of all the Asian nations. The strong contraction of the economy after 1998 did not jeopardize Carrefour's expansion. In 1999 it opened its sixth store, and in 2003 its seventh. In 2004 it planned to open a hypermarket in Kepong, Kuala Lumpur, on three stories with 46,450m$^2$ of floorspace.

Illustrating the local adjustments necessary for this market, all products within its stores were "halal" in compliance with prevailing food requirements. Nevertheless, in order to cater to the large ethnic Chinese community it also operated a separate "non-halal" store outside its catchment zone. Alcoholic beverages received a distinct label clearly indicating the alcohol content.

In 2003 Carrefour was the number three food retailer in Malaysia but was facing increasing competition from strong local and foreign retailers, such as Tesco. Carrefour's net sales represented €226 million in 2003.

# Carrefour in Singapore

Since entering this mature and sophisticated market in 1997, Carrefour succeeded in modifying both shopping habits and price expectations among the small population of 4 million Singaporeans. However, local competition remained strong and professional (NTUC) and local suppliers resisted Carrefour's methods. Singapore was not overly affected by the Asian crisis, posting a rise of more than 2 percent in GDP in 1999.

Backed by a dynamic commercial strategy with frequent and original promotional campaigns, Carrefour, No. 5 in food retail, adapted well to the local economic environment. Monthly theme promotions were introduced (French Week, Wine Fair, Japanese Week, Bicycle Week, etc). In particular, products imported from France, both fine foods and fresh produce, recorded continuing success. Its hypermarket in Suntec City registered significant sales growth, and a second store was opened in Plaza Singapura in December 2003. Net sales in 2003 amounted to €83 million (see Exhibit 9).

# Carrefour in Hong Kong

Initially, Carrefour thought Hong Kong would help it penetrate the Chinese market. In contrast to Taiwan, Hong Kong's retail industry was hard hit by the Asian crisis and had yet to return to strong growth. The price slump and suppliers' concerns over retailers' insolvency worked in Carrefour's favor and the company opened four stores by 1998. But in 1999 it experienced fierce competition and had to modify its activity. Despite its efforts, Carrefour failed to find large sites suitable for developing its hyper-market concept and to acquire a significant market share. It disposed of its four stores in 2000.

# Carrefour in China

Based on the lessons learned in Taiwan, Carrefour moved into China in 1995 with its first store opening in Shanghai. In 2003 it was ranked the top foreign retailer with net sales of €1,031 million, operating 40 hypermarkets and 55 hard discount stores in all major cities. The continental Chinese market is quite different from those of Taiwan and Hong Kong because urbanization, consumption and purchasing power are steadily increasing (see Exhibit 10).

As in Taiwan, Carrefour had to deal with a different negotiation culture and at first used Taiwanese negotia-

**EXHIBIT 9** Carrefour advertisement in Singapore

tors for its suppliers in China. Since 1992, foreign participation in retailing had been permitted through joint ventures with Chinese companies. At first, Carrefour's strategy was to look for a strong local partner who could help it overcome the hurdles while keeping the majority stake and assigning a non-operational role to the partner. Its relationship with Lianhua, one of the two major local retailers, helped Carrefour to establish its leadership in China. In different provinces it used different partners.

In 1999 China's central government ruled that foreign companies could not own more than 65 percent of any retailing enterprise in China. Carrefour, which wholly owned many of its stores, was subsequently ordered to sell its excess shares (above the regulatory 65 percent limit) and in 2002 signed a deal to sell stakes to local partners.

China's retail scene differs substantially from one store type to another as well as geographically. Convenience stores and supermarkets are dominated by domestic chains such as Lianhua, whereas hypermarkets are in the firm hands of big international players. In the Shanghai region, foreign retailers such as Carrefour, Makro, Wal-Mart, and Metro generate about a third of total supermarket sales. Because most retailers concentrate their efforts in this part of China, competition is steadily increasing. As a result, Royal Ahold, which operated 46 stores until 2002, withdrew from China and eventually divested all its activities in the Asian region.

In 2000 Carrefour experienced legal tribulations due to the intricate network of central, provincial, and local authorities that resulted in lengthy negotiation procedures at many different levels. "Sometimes, we may have problems in understanding Chinese laws and regulations, but we always respond positively to the government's requirements when problems arise, by rectifying our operations to make sure that the law is fully observed," commented Jean-Luc Chereau. Even though China is officially a centralized country, local authorities seek to enforce their own sphere of influence. In its rush to achieve economies of scale, Carrefour set up hypermarkets and operated stores based on licenses obtained from local authorities, which were not approved by the central authorities. Subsequently, the SETC (State

**EXHIBIT 10** Per capita annual disposable income of China's 10 richest cities, 2002–2003

| | Income (in US$) | Population (in million) |
|---|---|---|
| **Shenzhen** | 2,887 | 1.3 |
| **Guangzhou** | 1,812 | 7.1 |
| **Shanghai** | 1,796 | 13.3 |
| **Ningbo** | 1,724 | 5.4 |
| **Beijing** | 1,677 | 11.3 |
| **Xiamen** | 1,560 | 1.3 |
| **Hangzhou** | 1,557 | 6.3 |
| **Jinan** | 1,330 | 5.7 |
| **Tianjin** | 1,246 | 9.2 |
| **Nanjing** | 1,231 | 5.5 |

**Sources:** National Statistics Bureau; Ministry of Public Security.

Economic and Trade Commission) threatened to shut down all the stores if Carrefour did not comply with central government regulations. As a result Carrefour had to re-apply to obtain proper licenses from the central regulator, a delay that enabled its closest foreign competitor, Wal-Mart, to make inroads into the market.

Thus from 2000 to 2002 Carrefour was not allowed to open any new stores until it had first restructured its existing outlets. "Through two-and-a-half years of effort, we have completed our revamp in China, and now we are heading into a fast growth period in the country," said Chereau. Legal restructuring was performed in collaboration with the Chinese authorities and allowed expansion to resume. In this respect, the Chinese authorities were pragmatic with regard to legislation, having first evaluated the benefits an industrial player could bring to the country.

In 2002 and 2003 Carrefour stepped up its expansion in a bid to move faster than its competitors. It opened more hypermarkets in existing and new cities as well as 55 new Dia discount stores.

In 2004 Carrefour opened its forty-second hypermarket in one of the most remote regions in China. The new Urumqi store in Xinjiang province in the northwestern part of the country shared a 6,500 m$^2$ shopping center with five other stores. For religious reasons it could not sell fresh pork, but focused on beef and lamb. This shopping center was the first to be built by a retail chain in a province earmarked by the authorities as a development priority. The store was served by 17 different bus lines. Carrefour's aim had always been to pioneer urban centers that had been ignored by competitors, as with Wuhan and Shenyang, where it opened hypermarkets in 1999 despite a 30 percent rate of unemployment.

Carrefour opened its first Champion store in Zhongguancun Beijing. This was its fifth store in Beijing, and regarded as Carrefour's flagship store in Asia after three years of dormancy in the capital. Located in an area dubbed Beijing's Silicon Valley, the outlet has floorspace of 11,600 m$^2$, much bigger than any other Carrefour store in the country. As an area lacking big shopping centers and supermarkets, Zhongguancun is attracting foreign retailers such as PriceSmart, one of Carrefour's major rivals. In the wake of the Zhongguancun store opening, Carrefour planned to open one or two more stores in Beijing in 2004 as well as a store in Jinan, the capital of east China's Shandong Province.

Carrefour is one of the world's major exporters of Chinese products. It purchased US$1.6 billion worth of goods in China in 2002 and US$2.15 billion in 2003. Since 2002 a new organization within the group has aimed to expand market outlets for its suppliers and enhance its product offering in its European stores. An "export service" was established in Shanghai, and 10 liaison offices were set up with the objective of doubling export volumes by 2005.

Carrefour also sought to participate in public welfare projects and to contribute to local communities, while cooperating closely with local authorities. Among other things, the company set up Hope primary schools, donated to disaster-hit areas, and contributed face masks during the SARS outbreak.

In 2004 China announced that it would honor its pledges to open the booming retail sector to foreign players such as Wal-Mart and Carrefour, abolishing joint-venture requirements before the end of the year. Beijing also promised to end restrictions on the location and number of foreign-owned chain stores.

With China's entry into the WTO, its main trade barriers such as import taxes had to be abolished, but non-tariff trade barriers might still be put in place. Although officially welcomed, the press often blames foreign retail operations for destroying jobs and killing the local retail industry. In recent years Shanghai-based major retailers have started to defy foreign competition. In 2004 the Bailian Group, which controlled Lianhua Supermarket Holdings, announced plans to merge with Hualian into China's largest retailer, the Brilliance Group, with the aim of creating a local giant with assets of US$721.4 million.

Carrefour has only just started making profits in all its stores, while Wal-Mart is still witnessing losses in some outlets. The company's aim is to operate 70 hypermarkets in a few years' time, but political risk remains high in China.

# Carrefour in Japan

Being a different market in cultural and economic terms, Carrefour postponed entering Japan until 2000. By then, compared to the 1990s, real estate prices had become more affordable, loans more attractive, and the traditional clout of wholesalers was slowly being reduced to a more logistic function.

Compared to other Asian markets many differences still remain. Although Japan's GDP and purchasing power are much higher, refrigerators and storage space in Japanese homes are limited, so housewives tend to go shopping more often. They make it their daily routine to visit a nearby supermarket where other friends congregate, rather than to drive to a hypermarket to stock up on groceries for a week.

In addition, the Japanese have a sound marketing culture and are perfectionists. Japan is a much more advanced market with established consumer trends, local brands, and supplier networks. Consumers are sophisticated and look for quality and service.

Despite the spectacular bankruptcies of local players such as Mycal in 2002, Japan's retail sector has remained overcrowded and competition quite fierce. Japan was left with five major general merchandise store chains, namely Ito-Yokado, Aeon (parent company of Jusco), Daiei, Uny, and Seiyu, of which Wal-Mart was the largest shareholder in 2002 (see Exhibit 11).

Ito-Yokado, Japan's largest supermarket chain, had no plans to copy Carrefour or to open hypermarkets because land costs remained too high. Ito-Yokado did not reduce prices but instead emphasized higher quality.

Aeon, the parent company of Jusco, was Japan's second-largest supermarket chain and took a more aggressive and innovative approach. It operated 368 stores in 2002. Daiei, for years Japan's largest retailer, had been on the edge of bankruptcy for some time. Uny, the smallest of the four, had not been able to keep up with the rapid expansion pace of Jusco and Ito-Yokado.

One concrete barrier to entry into the Japanese market was the close network of multiple layers of intermediaries. Carrefour fell short of its original plan to persuade all of its Japanese suppliers to adopt the Carrefour direct-purchasing system, which was revolutionary by Japanese standards. Instead, local distributors launched lawsuits against Carrefour as the company opted to purchase directly rather than conform to the long-established distribution channels. After the Japanese distributors lost their case, Carrefour resumed its expansion.

When Carrefour opened its first megastore in a Tokyo suburb in December 2000, so many shoppers poured into the store that managers had to restrict entry. Two other stores, set up in Tokyo and Osaka, were similarly clogged. Junichi Kanamori, a retail analyst at Société Générale Securities Ltd. in Tokyo, explained that Carrefour's arrival was portrayed as "a foreign attack on the Japanese retail market. That made people think something French was going to arrive. Then they discovered it wasn't different from other supermarkets." It was not surprising, therefore, that after a month customers evaporated because shoppers had initially shown up purely out of curiosity.

Like other Western megastores, Carrefour had apparently swept into the Japanese market with much fanfare and little sensitivity to Japan's retail culture. The company did not adequately adjust its business to the purchasing patterns of Japanese consumers, nor did it capitalize on the curiosity of local consumers regarding products hailing from France.

**EXHIBIT 11**  Main Japanese retailers, February 2003

|  | Revenue (in million US$) | Net income (in million US$) | Net Profit Margin % | Employees |
|---|---|---|---|---|
| **Ito-Yokado** | 28,435.50 | 178.80 | 0.6 | 125,400 |
| **Aeon** | 24,274.40 | 436.00 | 1.8 | 42,376 |
| **Daiei** | 18,692.20 | 1,151.60 | 6.2 | 26,589 |
| **Uny** | 8,736.90 | 106.70 | 1.2 | 25,095 |

**Source:** Hoover's Online.

There was some misconception that Carrefour was a general merchandise store that competed on price alone. Japanese supermarkets chains began slashing prices in anticipation of the "foreign threat." Thus its three stores were showing major losses and Carrefour had to review its ambitious plans to expand to 13 stores by 2003.

In 2003 Carrefour continued its adaptation to the specific requirements of the local market. Along with demonstrating its professionalism in fresh produce, the company established its first sales space specializing in French household goods at its fully renovated store in Chiba Prefecture. Named "La Maison," the 110m² store-within-a-store offered 1,000 items ranging from fragrant soaps to trendy tableware and other sundry goods, all made in France. The French-themed corner came into being after a pilot sales space in Carrefour's

fourth hypermarket store at Saitama Prefecture was well received by housewives. The corner was established to grow consumer interest in certain categories of French products that were not available in Japanese supermarkets, and bring the "French touch" loved by the Japanese.

This approach was a clear departure from Carrefour Japan's existing policy of localizing its merchandise and the highly successful store would serve as a benchmark for future store openings. In 2003 Carrefour's stores recorded net sales of €225 million. However, rumors circulated in October 2004 in the *Asian Wall Street Journal* that, according to a consultant, Carrefour was planning to sell its eight stores in Japan due to "difficulties in acquiring real estate for new stores and the lack of touch with Japanese consumers' tastes."

## NOTES

1. *EuroMonitor.*
2. *Asian Wall Street Journal*, March 2004.
3. CSFB report, October 10, 2003.
4. INSEAD case Carrefour's Entry into Asia (A1), (A2), 10 years later.
5. Interview Gérard Clerc, *Reflets ESSEC* magazine.
6. Carrefour Worldwide.
7. *China Business Weekly*, March 2004.
8. Comparative Study of Asia Strategy: Wal-Mart versus Carrefour.
9. *Forbes*, March 2004.
10. *China Online*, March 2004.
11. *International Herald Tribune*, 2001.
12. *Retail Asia Online*, March 2000.

# INTEGRATIVE CASE 4

# CHINA'S HOME IMPROVEMENT MARKET: SHOULD HOME DEPOT ENTER OR WILL IT HAVE A LATE-MOVER (DIS)ADVANTAGE?

R. Muthu Kumar, Nagendra Chowdary

*ICFAI University*

China, the fastest-growing economy in the world, is witnessing rapid growth in the private housing market after its introduction of housing reforms in 1998. As the Chinese people's income and purchasing power increases, their property investment is also on the rise. In 2005, real estate investment accounted for 8.65 percent of China's GDP and it is expected to rise to 9.3 percent in 2006.[1] As a result, the total value of property under construction in 2005 was RMB 5.1 trillion ($637.42 billion), contributing to 28 percent of China's GDP.[2] Consequently, China's home improvement market also projected great potential for growth. Many foreign home improvement retailers such as B&Q and IKEA have established their strong presence along with the domestic home improvement players.

"The home improvement market on the mainland is the most promising in the world: $50 billion in sales in 2005 and growing at 12% a year. Homeownership has skyrocketed, from near zero two decades ago, when there was virtually no private property, to 70% of all housing today," *BusinessWeek* reported.[3] However, China's home improvement market is not that easy to navigate although the potential is highly tempting.

U.S.-based Home Depot has not yet started its operations in China and its "China Strategy" is in progress. Some think it missed the bus by not being an early entrant and therefore will suffer from late mover disadvantage. Others think the delay will help shorten its learning curve and it will rise rapidly.

## China's economy and real estate

China is the second-largest economy in the world (see Exhibit 1) when measured by Purchasing Power Parity, with a GDP (PPP) of $9.412 trillion in 2005. When measured in USD-exchange rate terms, it is the fourth largest in 2005 (Exhibit 1) with $2.25 trillion. It is the world's fastest-growing major economy with a population of 1.3 billion (see Exhibit 2). Its per capita GDP was $1,703 in

**EXHIBIT 1** World economies GDP rankings

| | List of Countries by GDP (PPP) | | | List of Countries by GDP (Nominal) | | Economy of China: 2005 Statistics | |
|---|---|---|---|---|---|---|---|
| Rank | Country | GDP (in $ billion) | Rank | Country | GDP (in $ billion) | | |
| 1 | United States | 12277.583 | 1 | United States | 12485.725 | GDP (Nominal) Ranking | 4 |
| **2** | **China** | **9412.361** | 2 | Japan | 4571.314 | GDP (PPP) Ranking | 2 |
| 3 | Japan | 3910.728 | 3 | Germany | 2797.343 | GDP (Nominal) | $2.22 trillion |
| 4 | India | 3633.441 | **4** | **China** | **2224.811** | GDP (PPP) | $9.412 trillion |
| 5 | Germany | 2521.699 | 5 | United Kingdom | 2201.473 | GDP per capita | $1,703 |
| 6 | United Kingdom | 1832.792 | 6 | France | 2105.864 | GDP per capita (PPP) | $6,200 |
| 7 | France | 1830.11 | 7 | Italy | 1766.16 | GDP growth rate | 9.90% |
| 8 | Italy | 1668.151 | 8 | Canada | 1130.208 | | |
| 9 | Brazil | 1576.728 | 9 | Spain | 1126.565 | | |
| 10 | Russia | 1575.561 | 10 | Korea | 793.07 | | |

**Source:** Compiled from "International Monetary Fund, World Economic Outlook Database," http://www.imf.org/external/pubs/ft/weo/2006/01/data/dbcoutm.cfm? April 2006.

**EXHIBIT 2** Population of China (2000–2004)

| | 2000 | 2001 | 2002 | 2003 | 2004 |
|---|---|---|---|---|---|
| Male | 654.4 | 656.7 | 661.1 | 665.6 | 669.8 |
| Female | 613.1 | 619.6 | 623.4 | 626.7 | 630.1 |
| **Total (million)** | **1,267.4** | **1,276.3** | **1,284.5** | **1,292.3** | **1,299.9** |
| % change, year on year | 0.8 | 0.7 | 0.6 | 0.6 | 0.6 |
| Urban (million) | 459.1 | 480.6 | 502.1 | 532.8 | 542.8 |
| % of total | 36.2 | 37.7 | 39.1 | 40.5 | 41.7 |
| Rural (million) | 808.4 | 795.6 | 782.4 | 768.5 | 757.1 |
| % of total | 63.8 | 62.3 | 60.9 | 59.5 | 58.2 |

**Source:** "Country Profile 2006," http://www.eiu.com.

**EXHIBIT 3**   China GDP per person by province, 2005

**Source:** "Coming out," http://www.economist.com/surveys/displaystory.cfm?story_id=5623226, March 23, 2006.

2005 and varied for each region in China (see Exhibit 3, above).

# Economic growth

China's economic evolution happened over a period of four generations (see Exhibit 4, on page 70). To speed up the industrialization process, the central government invested heavily in the 1960s and 1970s. A large share of the country's economic output was controlled by the government, which set production goals, controlled prices, and allocated resources. As a result, by 1978 nearly three-fourths of industrial production was manufactured by state-owned enterprises based on centrally planned output targets. The central government's major goal was to make China's economy self-sufficient. Foreign trade was restricted to obtain only those goods that could not be manufactured in China. Only countries that maintained diplomatic relations with China could participate in foreign trade. Though China's real GDP grew at an average annual rate of 5.3 percent from 1960 to 1978, the economy was almost inactive due to the huge population base and lack of competition. In addition, the economy was inefficient because of the few

profit incentives for enterprises and workers. Price and production controls also caused widespread distortions in China's economy.[4]

Since 1978, the government had been devising strategies to shift from a centrally planned economy to a more market-oriented economy. China's economic development had occurred in two phases. The first phase began in 1979, when the then Chairman Deng Xiaoping launched a series of reforms, including decollectivization of agriculture and a return to household farming.

In the 1980s, China tried to combine central planning with market-oriented reforms to increase productivity, living standards, and technological quality without exacerbating inflation, unemployment, and budget deficits. The country pursued agricultural reforms, dismantling the commune system and introducing household farming that authorized peasants with greater decision-making powers in agricultural activities. The government also encouraged non-agricultural activities, such as setting up of village enterprises in rural areas, promoting more self-management of state-owned enterprises, and increasing competition in the marketplace.

These reforms led to average annual rates of growth of 10 percent in agricultural and industrial output. Rural per capita real income doubled. Industry posted major

## EXHIBIT 4 Four generations of China's economic growth

### Mao Era, 1949–1976

After the Communist victory in 1949, China had a strong central government for the first time since the fall of the Qing dynasty in 1911. But a succession of political campaigns, including the Great Leap Forward and the Cultural Revolution, brought famine and upheaval. Agriculture was collectivized and industry nationalized. Economic growth suffered. China largely cut itself off from the world, and relations with the United States were hostile until President Richard Nixon's 1972 visit.

### Deng Era, 1978–1990s

Deng Xiaoping launched his famous economic reforms in 1978, which led to the flourishing of private enterprise in the 1980s. U.S.-China ties blossomed following the normalization of relations in 1979 and amid mutual distrust of the Soviet Union. Killings of pro-democracy Tiananmen protesters in 1989 tarnished Deng's legacy, bruised ties with the United States, and slowed reform. But Deng's 1992 call for faster reforms reignited economic growth.

### Jiang Era, 1990s–2002

Catapulted from relative obscurity, Jiang consolidated his power as Deng's influence waned in the years before his death in 1997. Jiang jettisoned Marxist ideology and fostered the shift to a market-oriented economy. He expanded social freedoms for the urban elite and curbed military clout. His attempts to make the state sector more competitive and clean up the financial sector were less successful. In 2002, he oversaw China's entry into the World Trade Organization.

### Fourth Generation, 2003–

Lacking revolutionary experience, this generation is the best-educated to date. Hu Jintao may be president, but no one leader will dominate, and consensus will be the rule. On the economic front, the leadership will likely focus on reforming agriculture, state-owned enterprises, and the financial sector. There is disagreement between those who favor maintaining an authoritarian approach and those who insist economic reform must be accompanied by limited democracy.

**Source:** Roberts Dexter and Clifford Mark L., "China's Power Shift," http://www.businessweek.com/magazine/content/02_08/b3771018.htm, February 25, 2002.

gains especially in coastal areas, where foreign investment helped drive output of both domestic and export goods. However, beginning in 1985, agricultural output witnessed a steady decline due to subsidy cuts and rising costs of inputs.

From the 1990s, during the second phase of China's growth, as the country further opened up, many foreign companies began entering China. China's economy boomed in the early 1990s. During 1993, output and prices were accelerating, and economic expansion was fueled by the introduction of more than 2,000 special economic zones (SEZs) and the influx of foreign capital that the SEZs facilitated. But the economy slowed down in the late 1990s, influenced in part by the Asian Financial Crisis of 1998–1999. Economic growth fell from 13.6 percent in 1992 to 7.1 percent in 1999 (see Exhibit 5, on page 71). From 1995 to 1999 inflation dropped sharply, reflecting the tighter monetary policy of central banks and stronger measures to control food prices.

However, the average annual growth rate of China's GDP through 2001 had been 8.9 percent since its

economic reforms. The pace of GDP growth in different regions was uneven due to variation in their incomes. Based on geographical location and government regulations, China can be divided into three areas – eastern coastal, central and western. The average growth rate of GDP in these areas during 1978–2001 were 10.2 percent, 9.08 percent, and 8.19 percent, respectively. The GDP share of eastern area in the total national GDP increased from 52 percent to 60 percent, while the other two areas' share decreased (see Exhibit 6).

Between 1978 and 2001, the ratio of GDP per capita in the eastern area to the average GDP per capita nationwide increased from 1.28 to 1.42, while for the other areas it decreased (see Exhibit 7).

In addition, economic inequalities between rural and urban regions were high in China. From 1994, a steep rise in unemployment had turned many rural farmers into absolute economic losers. Meanwhile, the inflow of foreign direct investment and the rise of industrial joint ventures had increased the urban-rural disparity. China's levels of inequality surpassed that of Eastern European

**EXHIBIT 5** China's GDP percentage

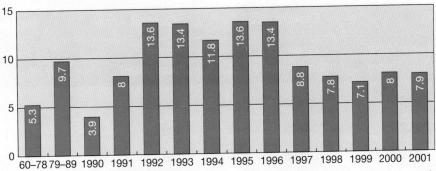

**Source:** Ye Xiannian, "China Real Estate Market – Economic Development," http://www.china-window.com/china_market/china_real_estate/china-real-estatemarket-2.shtml, August 20, 2004.

transition economies, Western European industrialized nations, and other Asian developing nations such as India, Pakistan, and Indonesia. Since the inception of reforms in 1978, the disparities had witnessed a cyclical pattern (Appendixes I(a) and I(b)) that was attributed to urban-biased industrial development strategy over agricultural development. Since the reforms, the politically powerful urban population had pressured the government for fast income growth. As a result, the government followed an urban bias in order to preserve regime stability and political legitimacy.

The people's response to such urban-based policies has been rural social unrest and mass migration to cities in search of jobs. Many other countries including the United States had faced similar dilemmas of human displacement in the course of their development. The significant urban-rural income disparity led to massive rural-to-urban migration. Numbers of migrants peaked during the planting and harvesting seasons, desperate for jobs.

As China joined the WTO in 2001, the import quotas, subsidies, and tariffs that had traditionally protected Chinese agriculture disappeared. Some experts commented that entry into the WTO would further exacerbate the issues of unemployment and inequality. But the Chinese government hoped that the WTO membership would induce more foreign investment and much-needed technology that would sustain long-term growth and would reduce the income disparity and unemployment rates. GDP growth accelerated again in early 2000s, reaching 9.3 percent in 2003, 9.4 percent in 2004, and 9.8 percent in 2005 (see Exhibits 8(a) and 8(b)).

In 2005, China's GDP grew by 9.8 percent. China's economy is expected to grow further with an increase in trade and the expected huge investment for the 2008 Olympics. Industry observers said that high GDP growth is coming at the expense of a gaping chasm between the rich and the poor.[5] Joe O'Mara, partner-in-charge of KPMG's

North America's China practice said, "It's one of the fastest-growing economies with 1.3 billion people. There is a growing middle class – over the last 20 years, per capita income has ballooned more than 700 percent."[6]

# Real estate

After the founding of the People's Republic of China in 1949, the first Chairman Mao Zedong (Mao) seized land from private landowners (killing thousands of them in the process) and redistributed it to peasants.[7] To facilitate the mobilization of agricultural resources, improve the efficiency of farming, and increase government access to agricultural products in the 1950s, private land ownership was eliminated. Mao took the land away from them and put it under the "collective" ownership of communes. Peasants had become property-less members of "People's Communes."[8] Private ownership of housing in the urban areas was nearly extinguished.

The communes were dismantled in the early 1980s, a few years after Mao's death. Peasants were allocated land for farming, but ownership remained collective. Under Deng Xiaoping, agricultural production soared for the first time as peasants were allocated (but not given full ownership of) plots of land to farm independently, and marked the start of the economic transformation in the rural areas.

Since the 1990s, leases of 30 years have been granted for these tiny plots, but the peasants were not allowed to use the land as collateral for loans or to sell it. They could rent it out, but this arrangement often involved paying a fee to the village administration.

So whereas trade in land and property had become an important engine of growth in urban China (where residential leases run for 70 years and others for 40 or 50), farmers had been far removed from the effects of this

**EXHIBIT 6** China's GDP and the percentage share of GDP in total GDP for the three areas (1978-2001)

| | National GDP (million yuan) | Eastern Area | | Central Area | | Western Area | |
|---|---|---|---|---|---|---|---|
| | | GDP (million yuan) | % | GDP (million yuan) | % | GDP (million yuan) | % |
| 1978 | 346,354 | 181,832 | 52.5 | 106,466 | 30.7 | 58,056 | 16.8 |
| 1979 | 394,275 | 203,873 | 51.7 | 123,687 | 31.4 | 66,715 | 16.9 |
| 1980 | 439,596 | 229,585 | 52.2 | 136,908 | 31.1 | 73,103 | 16.6 |
| 1981 | 479,347 | 250,961 | 52.4 | 151,041 | 31.5 | 77,345 | 16.1 |
| 1982 | 533,108 | 279,868 | 52.5 | 166,131 | 31.2 | 87,109 | 16.3 |
| 1983 | 595,085 | 311,019 | 52.0 | 189,495 | 31.7 | 97,571 | 16.3 |
| 1984 | 712,537 | 373,412 | 52.4 | 223,875 | 31.4 | 115,250 | 16.2 |
| 1985 | 862,066 | 455,246 | 52.8 | 267,538 | 31.0 | 139,282 | 16.2 |
| 1986 | 965,648 | 511,314 | 53.0 | 300,087 | 31.1 | 154,247 | 16.0 |
| 1987 | 1,144,177 | 612,845 | 53.6 | 352,365 | 30.8 | 178,967 | 15.6 |
| 1988 | 1,445,266 | 786,501 | 54.4 | 434,060 | 30.0 | 224,705 | 15.5 |
| 1989 | 1,635,691 | 895,790 | 54.8 | 489,251 | 29.9 | 250,650 | 15.3 |
| 1990 | 1,833,023 | 989,966 | 54.0 | 547,920 | 29.9 | 295,137 | 16.1 |
| 1991 | 2,110,312 | 1,164,293 | 55.2 | 605,130 | 28.7 | 340,889 | 16.2 |
| 1992 | 2,584,738 | 1,459,328 | 56.5 | 725,345 | 28.1 | 400,065 | 15.5 |
| 1993 | 3,422,001 | 1,981,049 | 57.9 | 931,780 | 27.2 | 509,172 | 14.9 |
| 1994 | 4,521,683 | 2,652,547 | 58.7 | 1,212,823 | 26.8 | 656,313 | 14.5 |
| 1995 | 5,763,278 | 3,361,540 | 58.3 | 1,586,764 | 27.5 | 814,974 | 14.1 |
| 1996 | 6,730,552 | 3,970,377 | 59.0 | 1,916,757 | 28.5 | 843,418 | 12.5 |
| 1997 | 7,547,520 | 4,445,350 | 58.9 | 2,164,300 | 28.7 | 937,870 | 12.4 |
| 1998 | 8,106,540 | 4,807,090 | 59.3 | 2,287,150 | 28.2 | 1,012,300 | 12.5 |
| 1999 | 8,619,170 | 5,156,430 | 59.8 | 2,397,450 | 27.8 | 1,065,290 | 12.4 |
| 2000 | 9,527,990 | 5,752,720 | 60.4 | 2,625,020 | 27.6 | 1,150,250 | 12.1 |
| 2001 | 10,501,650 | 6,362,436 | 60.6 | 2,867,045 | 27.3 | 1,272,169 | 12.1 |

**Source:** Zhang Wei, "Can the Strategy of Western Development Narrow Down China's Regional Disparity", *Asia Economic Paper*, 2005, 3.

**EXHIBIT 7** China's GDP per capita and the ratio of GDP per capita to national GDP per capita for the three areas, 1978–2001

| | National GDP per Capita (yuan) | Eastern Area | | Central Area | | Western Area | |
|---|---|---|---|---|---|---|---|
| | | GDP per Capita (yuan) | R* | GDP per Capita (yuan) | R* | GDP per Capita (yuan) | R* |
| 1978 | 361.4 | 462.2 | 1.28 | 311.0 | 0.86 | 260.7 | 0.72 |
| 1979 | 406.0 | 511.3 | 1.26 | 356.1 | 0.88 | 296.3 | 0.73 |
| 1980 | 447.4 | 569.0 | 1.27 | 389.2 | 0.87 | 321.5 | 0.72 |
| 1981 | 481.1 | 612.6 | 1.27 | 423.8 | 0.88 | 335.8 | 0.70 |
| 1982 | 527.1 | 672.4 | 1.28 | 459.3 | 0.87 | 373.1 | 0.71 |
| 1983 | 585.0 | 739.0 | 1.26 | 517.9 | 0.89 | 414.1 | 0.71 |
| 1984 | 689.6 | 877.4 | 1.27 | 604.8 | 0.88 | 485.1 | 0.70 |
| 1985 | 824.9 | 1,058.0 | 1.28 | 714.2 | 0.87 | 580.1 | 0.70 |
| 1986 | 911.3 | 1,172.0 | 1.29 | 790.2 | 0.87 | 633.1 | 0.69 |
| 1987 | 1,063.5 | 1,383.3 | 1.30 | 913.9 | 0.86 | 723.8 | 0.68 |
| 1988 | 1,322.7 | 1,750.1 | 1.32 | 1,107.2 | 0.84 | 894.4 | 0.68 |
| 1989 | 1,474.8 | 1,965.8 | 1.33 | 1,227.4 | 0.83 | 983.8 | 0.67 |
| 1990 | 1,611.0 | 2,104.0 | 1.31 | 1,345.7 | 0.84 | 1,134.6 | 0.70 |
| 1991 | 1,835.2 | 2,451.8 | 1.34 | 1,468.4 | 0.80 | 1,296.5 | 0.71 |
| 1992 | 2,225.2 | 3,042.4 | 1.37 | 1,741.7 | 0.78 | 1,507.3 | 0.68 |
| 1993 | 2,918.3 | 4,093.2 | 1.40 | 2,215.2 | 0.76 | 1,899.9 | 0.65 |
| 1994 | 3,819.3 | 5,436.9 | 1.42 | 2,854.0 | 0.75 | 2,421.3 | 0.63 |
| 1995 | 4,816.3 | 6,812.0 | 1.41 | 3,698.7 | 0.77 | 2,972.9 | 0.62 |
| 1996 | 5,548.9 | 7,946.8 | 1.43 | 4,421.2 | 0.80 | 3,014.5 | 0.54 |
| 1997 | 6,327.6 | 8,821.9 | 1.39 | 4,952.2 | 0.78 | 3,723.8 | 0.59 |
| 1998 | 6,743.0 | 9,474.2 | 1.41 | 5,194.2 | 0.77 | 3,977.6 | 0.59 |
| 1999 | 7,114.8 | 10,089.5 | 1.42 | 5,406.8 | 0.76 | 4,145.7 | 0.58 |
| 2000 | 7,737.7 | 10,728.3 | 1.39 | 5,974.1 | 0.77 | 4,497.4 | 0.58 |
| 2001 | 8,490.6 | 12,070.6 | 1.42 | 6,400.9 | 0.75 | 4,858.4 | 0.57 |

*R is the ratio of the GDP per capita for a given area to the national GDP per capita.

**Source:** Zhang Wei, "Can the Strategy of Western Development Narrow Down China's Regional Disparity", *Asia Economic Paper*, 2005, 4.

**EXHIBIT 8(a)** China's gross domestic product (at market prices), 2000–2004

|  | 2000 | 2001 | 2002 | 2003 | 2004 |
|---|---|---|---|---|---|
| **Total (US$ bn)** | | | | | |
| At current prices | 1,080 | 1,159 | 1,304 | 1,471 | 1,720 |
| **Total (Rmb bn)** | | | | | |
| At current prices | 8,940 | 9,593 | 10,790 | 12,173 | 14,239 |
| At constant (1990) prices | 4,857 | 5,221 | 5,639 | 6,164 | 6,744 |
| % change, year on year | 8.0 | 7.5 | 8.0 | 9.3 | 9.4 |
| **Per Head (Rmb)** | | | | | |
| At current prices | 7,054 | 7,517 | 8,400 | 9,420 | 10,954 |
| At constant (1990) prices | 3,832 | 4,091 | 4,390 | 4,770 | 5,188 |
| % change, year on year | 7.2 | 6.8 | 7.3 | 8.7 | 8.8 |

**Source:** "Country Profile 2006," http://www.eiu.com.

**EXHIBIT 8(b)** China's GDP (% increase on a year earlier), 1990–2005

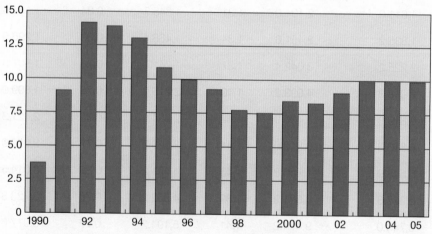

**Source:** "Coming out," http://www.economist.com/surveys/displaystory.cfm?story_id=5623226, March 23, 2006.

boom. When land was seized, peasants were compensated for its agricultural value, which averaged about one-tenth of its market value. Out of that village administration took a cut, and so the amount received by the peasants was far less. However, in the cities, the privatization of housing since the late 1990s had created a middle class that was utilizing its property as collateral to borrow. Trading in property had become a huge source of urban wealth.

The government was alarmed that creating a free market in rural land would prompt peasants to sell their holdings to pay their debts. As a result a flood of landless farmers fled to cities that had no social security infrastructure to deal with the influx. In order for rural land reform to work, fiscal transfers from the center to the provinces required fairer reforms. This required considerable political will because richer provinces would be reluctant to lose their privileges. However, in 1998, the government ordered written land-use contracts to be issued to peasants. A law introduced in 2003 restricted the right of collectives to reassign land within villages and provided a legal basis for transfer of land between peasants for farming.[9]

The leasing of land to households in the early 1980s began as an initiative that gradually gained official support. Under the 1982 Constitution, urban land in China is owned by the state and the collectives own the rural land. Since the local and central governments administer the rural collectives, it can be construed that all land ownership is under the control of the state. However, the Constitution's Amendment Act of 1988 to Article 10 adopted on April 12, 1988, states that a land use right may be transferred in accordance to law. Accordingly, a land use right was accorded with a sort of land ownership, thus making land use right likely to be privatized. Individuals, including foreigners, were allowed to hold long-term leases for land use. They were eligible to own buildings, apartments, and other structures on land, as well as own personal property.[10]

In the 1980s, almost all urban housing was owned by the state. Most of the people in China's urban centers had patronized the welfare housing system in which the government provided nearly free housing to urban residents. All employees from government agencies, academic and public institutions, and state-owned companies, received housing facilities from the government or their work units. In March 1998, Chinese Premier Zhu Rongji introduced a package of reforms that included a series of housing reforms intended to stimulate the domestic economy. He declared that subsidized housing traditionally available to Chinese workers would be phased out and that workers would be encouraged to buy their own homes or pay rent closer to real market prices. The reforms intended for workers to utilize their savings, along with the one-time housing subsidies they received, to purchase their own houses. *The Economist* observed, "In one of the most dramatically successful economic reforms of the past quarter century in China, most housing is now privately owned. This has fostered the growth of a middle class that wants guarantees that its new assets are safe from the party's whims. Property owners are electing their own landlord committees – independent of the party – to protect their rights. A new breed of lawyers, not party stooges as most once were, is emerging to defend those whose properties are threatened by the state. Property

owners want a clean environment around their homes. Green activism, which hardly existed in China a decade ago, is spurring the development of a civil society."[11]

In the 1990s, with the emergence of better public housing, improved incomes, and raised expectations of the community at large, the housing market had grown beyond the provision of shelter to the quest to provide pleasant homes tailored to the community needs.

The Chinese government began to divest state housing and create a class of homeowners, primarily in the larger cities but gradually across the country. With the proposed development of a secondary housing market in the future, eventually it is envisaged that the Chinese housing market will come to resemble that of mature private property markets.

In August 1999, the government announced that all vacant residential housing units built after January 1, 1999, were to be sold, not allocated. Since then, the private housing market has seen tremendous growth. The Chinese people, faced with a local stock market offering low returns and high-risk and looking for other ways to invest their money, poured their money into property.

The investment in China's real estate development in 1999 was RMB 401 billion ($48.43 billion), up 10 percent from 1998. From January to November of 2000, the total investment in the real estate sector reached RMB 374.4 billion ($45 billion). In 2000, commercial housing construction had increased by 17.9 percent, finished construction area increased by 22.3 percent, sales volume increased by 38.8 percent, and housing purchase increased by 44.5 percent over the same period in 1999.[12]

A study by the *Sinomonitor* and the British Market Research Bureau indicated that from 1999 to 2000 the percentage of homeowners in China's urban areas rose by nearly 10 percent, from 49.9 percent to 59 percent. The study also commented that the housing reform had boosted home purchase and construction in China.[13]

China's state banks also started lending to home buyers. From 1998 to 2003, mortgage and consumer credit liabilities rose from virtually zero to 11.6 percent of GDP.

As many middle-class families started investing in property, the real estate prices started increasing. Some believed that in some cities it was rising too fast. The government announced that it would reduce the prices in favor of construction of more affordable housing for relatively low-income earners. The government had ordered in 2005 its city leaders to contain the rising housing prices. The main target of this order was Shanghai, which had the largest and most expensive housing market in China. This order resulted in the price reduction in the range of 15 to 20 percent on average.

Consequently, the local Shanghai property speculators started moving to other cities such as Beijing and

**EXHIBIT 9**  China property price increase by city, first quarter 2006 (% change over 2005)

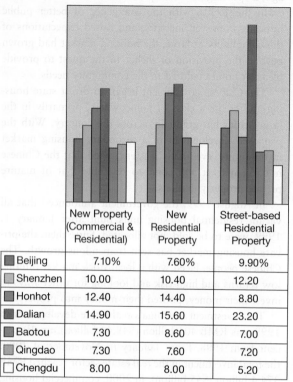

| | New Property (Commercial & Residential) | New Residential Property | Street-based Residential Property |
|---|---|---|---|
| Beijing | 7.10% | 7.60% | 9.90% |
| Shenzhen | 10.00 | 10.40 | 12.20 |
| Honhot | 12.40 | 14.40 | 8.80 |
| Dalian | 14.90 | 15.60 | 23.20 |
| Baotou | 7.30 | 8.60 | 7.00 |
| Qingdao | 7.30 | 7.60 | 7.20 |
| Chengdu | 8.00 | 8.00 | 5.20 |

**Source:** Compiled from Browne Andrew, "China reins in real-estate sector," *Wall Street Journal*, May 19–21, 2006, 3.

Chongqing in the west. "The problem is that China has built up this huge pile of wealth and there is nowhere else for it to go, other than into property," said Sam Crispin, a Shanghai-based property consultant.[14]

The National Bureau of Statistics says that new house prices in Beijing have gone up by 7.6 percent in the first quarter of 2006 (see Exhibit 9). Some economists argue that China faces a risky property bubble. While urban property prices are rising fast, so are incomes, and hence property is generally affordable.

# China's home improvement market

Since the mid-1990s, the home improvement market had grown rapidly, as housing reform encouraged home ownership in China. In 1998, the Chinese government made changes in its home ownership policy by getting state companies out of the business of providing housing facilities to their workers. Instead, these companies had to extend financial assistance to the employees for housing purposes, which for many raised their incomes by

half. The employee could buy the work-unit flat he was already living in at a heavy discount.[15] It encouraged people to buy homes, offering low-cost mortgages or bargain prices on older apartments. Coupled with rising urban incomes, the private housing market boom in the late 1990s in Beijing, Shanghai, and other cities ushered in a new revolution in the Chinese housing sector.

New apartments were built, largely for private buyers. Private buyers bought 88 percent of the homes, compared with about 50 percent before 1995. In Shanghai, China's most sophisticated city, 10 percent of households owned their own homes in 1997, while the figure was about 25 percent in 2000.[16] However, the Chinese construction industry operates quite differently.

Newly constructed homes in China do not have bathrooms, kitchens, and even interior walls. These features do not come with the new house. The Chinese contractors do not do any finishing work; they just hand over concrete shells. Chinese homeowners have to fix up these shells themselves. They have to install everything with the help of locally hired workers. The home improvement stores operating in China undertake to provide the necessary workforce. As a result, home purchases generated significant sales of appliances and other home improvement items. Many foreign retailers such as IKEA (1998) and B&Q[17] (1999) entered China.

China has proven to be a huge market for foreign home improvement players for more than one reason. In China, retailing is overspecialized; one store sells door handles, another paint, and yet another paintbrushes. Decorating takes loads of energy, requiring the homeowners to make trips to scores of stores, and hunt for a reliable contractor. Foreign stores profit from this activity, providing end-to-end "home solutions" under one roof with a do-it-yourself (DIY) model. B&Q can fit out an entire house, including furniture, and guarantee all the work. Another key advantage that foreign chains have is trust reposed in them by the Chinese consumers. "Chinese shoppers are used to being sold shoddy goods backed by dodgy guarantees," observed *The Economist*.[18] Chinese homeowners trust international retailers when they promise "no fakes" and money-back guarantees. B&Q even takes Chinese customers to workshops to reassure them about quality.

As a result, the homeowners began focusing on decorating and even handling home-decoration projects themselves. The sales of DIY products were on the rise compared to other home improvement products (Exhibits 10(a) and 10(b)). The DIY sector has become the major area of growth in the market, due to increasing demand for basic tools for household repair and decorating, as well as decorative products, such as paint, wallpaper, and tiles.

**EXHIBIT 10(a)** China's home improvement market: percentage breakdown by sector, 1996–2000

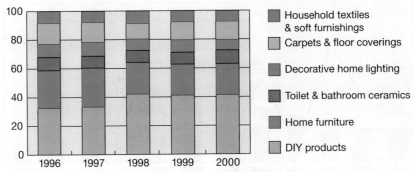

**Source:** "Doing it for themselves," *The Economist Intelligence Unit (Business China)*, 27(21), September 24, 2001, 9.

**EXHIBIT 10(b)** China's home improvement market: growth of DIY products, 1994–2000

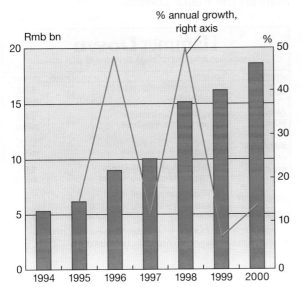

**Source:** "Doing it for themselves," *The Economist Intelligence Unit (Business China)*, 27(21), September 24, 2001, 9.

Statistics from the Ministry of Construction indicated that the business volume of interior renovation and decoration registered a 50 percent year-on-year rise in 1998 to more than RMB 75 billion. More than 60 percent of urban households had spruced up their houses, with the average cost reaching RMB 20,000 per household. In 1998, Beijing residents spent more than RMB 2 billion on housing improvements.[19] It was reported that only 70 percent of the market demand was supplied in 1999.[20]

Based on a national development plan on housing construction, China will build at least 200 million square meters of residential housing annually by 2010. The plan is aimed to help 4.5 million residents to have spacious living space.[21]

In a survey, *McKinsey* found that nearly three-quarters of the respondents upgraded their furniture and home appliances when they moved into a new apartment.[22] New homeowners dug into their savings to add flooring, plumbing, and furniture to the unfinished units they had purchased. In 2000, total market value of the home-improvement market was RMB 43 billion ($5.2 billion) (see Exhibit 11).[23]

In 2004, *China Construction magazine* reported that about 59 percent of the urban residents in China owned their own homes. It was also reported that 21.9 percent of the residents would like to purchase new houses within five years. Family savings were the main source of financing, which was at RMB 6700 billion ($1 trillion).[24] China is expected to build 70 million houses in the coming 10 years.[25]

Home ownership has been the catalyst behind the home improvements market and has encouraged consumers to engage in home improvement/decorating activities. Industry analysts said, "As living standards improve in China and the government opens up the property market, interior decoration, design, and DIY are becoming popular pastimes in certain key markets. In line with the interest in home decoration and improvement has come a desire for better quality materials."[26] Additionally, this growth in private housing has resulted in fierce competition among domestic and foreign retailers.

Sweden-based IKEA, which opened its first store in Shanghai in 1998, opened outlets in Beijing and in the southern city of Guangzhou a year later. IKEA also plans to open a total of 10 stores within 2010, including expansion to the country's west with an outlet being built in the city of Chengdu.[27]

B&Q, which opened a store in Shanghai in 1999, later expanded to Beijing and increased its stores to 14.

**EXHIBIT 11** Growth of total home improvement market of China, 1994–2005

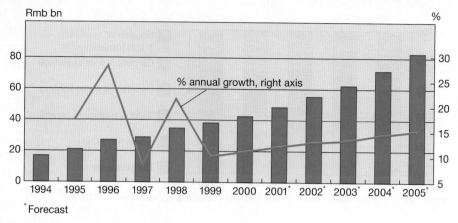

*Forecast

**Source:** "Doing it for themselves," *The Economist Intelligence Unit (Business China)*, 27(21), September 24, 2001, 9.

Its sales have doubled each year since it opened its first store in China. B&Q estimates that one-tenth of China's 400 million households have disposable income of $1,000 or more a year to spend on home improvements and it is increasing rapidly. Government deregulation is boosting home ownership by 30 percent a year. Increased home ownership coupled with "western" levels of disposable income and lifestyles have ushered in a demand for decor. "Chinese people have the money, intention and desire to improve their homes," said David Wei, head of B&Q China.[28]

B&Q bought five outlets from PriceSmart China in November 2004 and took over the mainland operations of rival, German-based OBI, which had 13 stores in April 2005. B&Q became the biggest decorative building materials retailer in China in April 2005 (see Exhibit 12). It dominates China's home improvement market. B&Q's sales rose by nearly 48 percent to 313 million pounds ($547 million) in 2005.[29] As of early 2006, the company had 49 stores in eight Chinese cities, including Shenzhen. B&Q plans to have 75 stores in 30 Chinese cities by the end of 2008.[30] Wei said, "In the past five years, we have enjoyed average double-digit like-for-like growth and we continue to see double-digit as a trend and our forecast for our next five years. The company's market share has risen sharply, from 0.8 percent at the beginning of 2005, as B&Q has opened new stores and sales have increased at existing ones. Getting statistics in China is really difficult, but whatever figures you quote as the national market, we will probably be at 2 to 3 percent."[31] He wants to double B&Q's store count in China by 2010.

Local competitors include Home Mart, controlled by retail conglomerate Friendship Co., with about 20 outlets, and Orient Home, a part of Orient Group Inc. Foreign competition is also heating up. France's Leroy Merlin

**EXHIBIT 12** China home improvement market: the major players

## Hammer Down
Competition is building in China's do-it-yourself retail market

| COMPANY | DESCRIPTION | NO. OF STORES | 2005 SALES |
|---|---|---|---|
| B&Q | British-owned retailer dominates the big coastal cities | 49 | $542 million |
| ORIENT HOME | Beijing-based chain is possible takeover target for Home Depot | 30 | $350 million* |
| HOMEMART | State-owned Shanghai chain has good locations but indifferent service | 27 | $300 million* |
| HOMEWAY | Tianjin-based retailer benefited from training cooperation with Home Depot | 11 | $215 million |
| HOME DEPOT | Has two global sourcing centers in China but no stores—yet | 0 | 0 |

*Estimate Data: Business Week, companies

**Source:** Frederik Balfour and Brain Grow, "One Foot In China," http://www.businessweek.com/magazine/content/06_18/b3982068.htm, May 1, 2006.

opened its first China store in Beijing in 2004 and said that it would have 20 outlets across the country by 2010. German franchiser OBI (owned by Tengelmann Warenhandelsgesellschaft) also operates four stores in China.

"The growth has been very strong between IKEA, B&Q, even local brands like Orient Home. It's very competitive. Over 100 cities in China have more than 1 million people. If even a small percentage of these people are able to purchase home furnishings, it would be really promising," said Anna Kalifa, head of research in Beijing for consulting firm Jones Lang LaSalle.[32]

In China, housing construction is growing by 33 percent a year. In 2006, Chinese banks relaxed controls on loans to purchase houses. This would result in the growth of the home improvement market estimated at

$50 billion annually.[33] It is projected that the China's home improvement market will have growth rate of 10 to 20 percent a year.[34] Wei said that it is a highly fragmented industry dotted with mom-and-pop outfits, niche stores that stock one product type, and a few budding domestic one-stop shops.

After witnessing the growth of the home improvement market in China and B&Q's success, Atlanta-based Home Depot, the world's biggest DIY group, also planned to set up shops in China.[35] In June 2005, *Reuters* announced that Home Depot was seeking to buy a stake in Chinese peer Orient Group Inc. for up to $500 million to win a foothold in the country's fast-growing home improvement market. An agreement would mark the U.S. group's entry into the Chinese home improvement market. However, it already has an indirect interest in China through its links with the Homeway chain. In 2004, Home Depot opened a business-development office in China and named Bill E. Patterson for the newly created position of president, The Home Depot Asia. Home Depot runs two procurement centers in China. Home Depot announced plans in mid-2004 to start opening retail stores in China, but has yet to set up shop.

## Should Home Depot enter or will it have a late-mover (dis)advantage?

Amid many speculations about the Home Depot's foray into China, the company remained tight-lipped. Home Depot's China head said, "China is an incredibly exciting opportunity. We're going to make the prudent decision. We're going to make sure we have the right business model."[36] For Home Depot's CEO Robert Nardelli, China is a top priority and he said, "A successful strategy there would offset the challenge of sustaining strong sales growth back home and could even boost the stock."[37] He added, "China's economy is over $1 trillion. It has GDP growth of 7% to 8%. No one has dominance there. It's a unique opportunity to get a footprint, to really be part of the expansiveness and the growth. Sixty percent of the world concrete is being consumed in China today. Surveys say that Chinese consumers are looking for Westernized products and brands."[38]

However, there are many challenges in China's home improvement market. Some of them concern Chinese consumer behavior while others have more to do with the market (competition) dynamics. Unless addressed with a clear strategic intent (as opposed to short-term), the potential virtue can become mere wishful thinking, not converting into a reality.

The big challenge facing Home Depot and its rivals in China is that most customers are not doing home improvement themselves. "Chinese DIY is still really BIY – buy it yourself,"[39] admits Wei. He added, "You need time for DIY. There aren't many public holidays or paid leave. And you need the incentive to do it. Labor is so cheap in China there's no incentive to save money by doing your own work."[40] Since the government policy is to build homes that are more finished, the foreign players have to convert DIY into more of a hobby and the Chinese into a nation of home improvers, like the Americans and British. Yet, for many middle-class Chinese, it is not befitting to build a cabinet or fit a shelf by themselves. Thanks to abundant cheap labor, they've never had to do it themselves, nor do they have the skills. "Many Chinese don't know how to wire a plug or rise to the challenge of scumble painting,"[41] observed *The Economist*. B&Q, for instance, conducts training sessions for customers, showing them how to use a drill and even teaching children the mysteries and the fun of DIY. However, to utilize the potential, B&Q has initiated CIY (create-it-yourself) that helps customers to be involved in the process of creation. B&Q staffers help customers design a floor plan and choose materials and then perform all the installation work. In Beijing and Shanghai, B&Q started to build a DIY culture starting with a DIY kids club, where at the weekends people who do not have DIY skills could come and learn some basic skills. It is provided free of cost to attract kids and parents to the stores. Also, Chinese shoppers like to handle the merchandise before buying. However, products were stacked high on shelves. They still believe that foreign retailers display the most expensive products. They are intimidated by the exorbitant rates.

Another challenge for foreign home improvement players in China is managing their supply chain. Efficient suppliers are the key to success in a low-margin industry like retailing. Getting goods into stores in China is costly and expensive. B&Q's gross margins in China are half of those of its international division. *The Economist* observed, "China's huge size and enormous regional variations mean retailers struggle to establish a national infrastructure, let alone a national brand."[42] It is almost like operations in different countries. In humid summers, laminated wood cannot survive in Shenzhen. During a winter in Beijing, aquariums freeze. (Chinese believe fish bring good luck.) The biggest retailers, therefore, "remain in thrall to regional manufacturers – and their middlemen – which raises costs."[43] For 15 of B&Q's China stores, it has 1,800 vendors, while its 350 British stores have only 600 vendors. Moreover, these middlemen enter into deals clandestinely. Even on the shop floor, vendor representatives regularly offer customers "special" prices. "This is a state-controlled economy. Price fixing is endemic. Retailers are at the bottom of the food chain in China. They have far less power than manufacturers. It is the opposite of the rest of the world,"[44] said Steve Gilman, head of B&Q International.

Another concern for foreign home improvement retailers is regarding the treatment meted out to them in China in sales tax imposition and allocation of land. Foreign retailers face discrimination. Foreign home improvement retailers are forced to pay much more sales tax than the domestic counterparts. Using *Guanxi* (connections), the tiny stores avoid paying sales tax. They are often offered the poorest sites to carry out their business operations. For instance, B&Q had to build its new Shenzhen store under a residential tower block. Low-cost labor does not translate into quality labor either, forcing the foreign home improvement retailers to employ more workers to meet the greater service levels expected and continue to win the customers' trust.

Home Depot is studying the industry environment, competitors, and searching for suitable locations. According to the company, China has few large-format home improvement stores, and the country is largely served by small outdoor markets and shopping malls. Patterson said, "About 70 percent of home improvement spending in China is for completion of interior space in new homes. We see that as a solid growth opportunity given The Home Depot's strength in merchandise and services geared to finishing out a home."[45] However, experts say that due to the urban-rural divide and income disparity, requirements for houses are quite different due to different regions and culture. Housing consumption witnesses strong regional and multilevel characteristics.[46]

Home Depot's major rivals such as B&Q and IKEA were early entrants to the Chinese home improvement market. It has helped them gain better traction in many areas, such as government connections for getting approvals for zoning and licensing. Wei said, "Also, we have had the opportunity to recruit the best people and train them. New entrants may nick a few people, but it won't damage our management team and forces. And we understand product mix. Building relationships with suppliers and getting the pricing and supply chain right take time."[47]

In the United States, Home Depot has benefited from high labor prices for skilled labor, which encourages Americans to improve their own homes. But in China labor is low-cost and plentiful, and is often the single cost-effective element in home improvement. For this reason, some analysts say Home Depot's largest customers might not be homeowners, but interior designers and construction contractors.[48] If Home Depot decides to enter China, it has to train its employees to do installations also.

Home Depot faces stiff competition from foreign players such as B&Q and IKEA and domestic players

including Homemart, Homeway, and Orient Home. Homeway, which had a brief alliance with Home Depot in the mid-1990s, adopted much of the Home Depot model, including the orange work aprons. These retail chains spent many years cultivating relationship with local suppliers and are already located in prime retail locations in the big cities. B&Q has already learned many lessons about operating in China. B&Q attracts consumers with stylish brands and more fashionable products, with an improved decorative-lighting section. Homeowners in China started switching from small local retailers to B&Q and other warehouse chains to buy flooring, cabinets, and curtain rods.

In China, due to increasing urbanization, most customers of home improvement chains are urban residents and the stores had to be located in urban centers. Locating in urban centers will require new strategies for its stores (in the United States, its stores are mostly in the suburbs). Home Depot needs to meet the unique demands of these urban customers and a multitude of challenges related to dealing with large urban markets. Analysts say, "It will be good if companies such as Home Depot learn from their experiences in China's urban markets. In Connecticut, as well as in many other parts of the United States, large retailers tend to overlook or avoid the large urban market due to what they perceive as potential problems. Perhaps companies that have learned strategies in China will be able to bring back some of the lessons and be more willing to invest in the potentially lucrative inner city markets."[49]

About the foray of Home Depot into China, *BusinessWeek* says, "Is Home Depot blowing it? Or is it biding its time for the right reasons? The China home improvement market is a lot trickier to navigate than those hot growth numbers would indicate. For starters, it barely resembles the do-it-yourself market back in America, where Home Depot workers dispense advice, then send customers back home to lay their own tiles and install some track lighting."[50]

As Home Depot executives try to gauge the risks and rewards in China, they do not want to get off on the wrong foot either. Home Depot's foreign forays have yielded mixed results. Although it was successful in Canada and Mexico, it had to close its stores in Chile and Argentina in 2001.

Goldman Sachs analyst Matthew Fassler said that Home Depot's reported interest in the Chinese home improvement market was "consistent" with Home Depot's goals and Wall Street expectations. He added, "We believe that an alliance … or minority investment with option for increased ownership would enable Home Depot to participate in China's economic development without the difficulties associated with navigating its political and cultural challenges alone."[51] Keith Davis, analyst at investment managers Farr Miller Washington, said, "It's going to take a long time to see any effects to the bottom line from an expansion into China, but in the more near term it will hopefully alleviate some concerns about opportunities for growth going forward."[52] Tian Guanyong, CEO of CGen Media,[53] said, "Home Depot had better make up its mind about China before it's too late."[54]

However, some analysts are skeptical whether Home Depot will suffer from any late-mover disad-

vantage and whether the early movers will enable Home Depot to compete more effectively and efficiently against them. *BusinessWeek* says, "It's likely that Home Depot will try some mix of building its own stores and buying share in China through an acquisition. Yet the longer it waits, the tougher it will be to break in. Securing the best locations requires good government connections. Getting to know the market and forging relationships with local suppliers can take years."[55]

**APPENDIX 1(a)** Per capita consumption of rural and urban residents of China, 1952–1997 (units: nominal yuan per year; ratio: rural = 1)

| Year | National Average | Rural Residents | Urban Residents | Ratio (Nominal) | Ratio (Real) |
|------|-----------------|-----------------|-----------------|-----------------|--------------|
| 1952 | 76 | 62 | 149 | 2.4 | |
| 1953 | 87 | 69 | 181 | 2.6 | |
| 1954 | 89 | 70 | 183 | 2.6 | |
| 1955 | 94 | 76 | 188 | 2.5 | |
| 1956 | 99 | 78 | 197 | 2.5 | |
| 1957 | 102 | 79 | 205 | 2.6 | |
| 1958 | 105 | 83 | 195 | 2.4 | |
| 1959 | 96 | 65 | 206 | 3.2 | |
| 1960 | 102 | 68 | 214 | 3.2 | |
| 1961 | 114 | 82 | 225 | 2.8 | |
| 1962 | 117 | 88 | 226 | 2.6 | |
| 1963 | 116 | 89 | 222 | 2.5 | |
| 1964 | 120 | 95 | 234 | 2.5 | |
| 1965 | 125 | 100 | 237 | 2.4 | |
| 1966 | 132 | 106 | 244 | 2.3 | |
| 1967 | 136 | 110 | 251 | 2.3 | |
| 1968 | 132 | 106 | 250 | 2.4 | |
| 1969 | 134 | 108 | 255 | 2.4 | |
| 1970 | 140 | 114 | 260 | 2.3 | |
| 1971 | 142 | 116 | 267 | 2.3 | |
| 1972 | 147 | 116 | 295 | 2.6 | |
| 1973 | 155 | 123 | 306 | 2.5 | |

## APPENDIX 1(a)  Continued

| Year | National Average | Rural Residents | Urban Residents | Ratio (Nominal) | Ratio (Real) |
|------|------------------|-----------------|-----------------|-----------------|--------------|
| 1974 | 155 | 123 | 313 | 2.6 | |
| 1975 | 158 | 124 | 324 | 2.6 | |
| 1976 | 161 | 125 | 340 | 2.7 | |
| 1977 | 165 | 124 | 360 | 2.9 | |
| 1978 | 175 | 132 | 383 | 2.9 | 2.9 |
| 1979 | 197 | 152 | 406 | 2.7 | 2.6 |
| 1980 | 227 | 173 | 468 | 2.7 | 2.5 |
| 1981 | 249 | 194 | 487 | 2.5 | 2.3 |
| 1982 | 267 | 212 | 500 | 2.4 | 2.1 |
| 1983 | 289 | 234 | 531 | 2.3 | 2.0 |
| 1984 | 329 | 266 | 599 | 2.3 | 2.0 |
| 1985 | 406 | 324 | 747 | 2.3 | 1.9 |
| 1986 | 451 | 353 | 850 | 2.4 | 2.0 |
| 1987 | 513 | 393 | 997 | 2.5 | 2.0 |
| 1988 | 643 | 480 | 1288 | 2.7 | 2.1 |
| 1989 | 700 | 518 | 1404 | 2.7 | 2.2 |
| 1990 | 803 | 571 | 1686 | 3.0 | 2.4 |
| 1991 | 896 | 621 | 1925 | 3.1 | 2.5 |
| 1992 | 1070 | 718 | 2356 | 3.3 | 2.5 |
| 1993 | 1331 | 855 | 3027 | 3.5 | 2.7 |
| 1994 | 1781 | 1138 | 3979 | 3.5 | 2.6 |
| 1995 | 2311 | 1479 | 5044 | 3.4 | 2.6 |
| 1996 | 2677 | 1756 | 5620 | 3.2 | 2.4 |
| 1997 | 2936 | 1930 | 6048 | 3.1 | 2.3 |

**Source:** Yang Dennis Tao and Fang Cai, "The Political Economy of China's Rural-Urban Divide," http://scid.stanford.edu/pdf/credpr62.pdf, August 2000.

## APPENDIX 1(b) Real per capita total income for rural and urban residents of China, 1978–1997 (units: nominal yuan per year; ratio: rural = 1)

| Year | Urban per Capita Income | Rural per Capita Income | Ratio of Urban to Rural Income |
|------|------|------|------|
| 1978 | 454 | 134 | 3.4 |
| 1979 | 523 | 160 | 3.3 |
| 1980 | 560 | 190 | 3.0 |
| 1981 | 567 | 219 | 2.6 |
| 1982 | 597 | 261 | 2.3 |
| 1983 | 620 | 296 | 2.1 |
| 1984 | 690 | 330 | 2.1 |
| 1985 | 692 | 358 | 1.9 |
| 1986 | 784 | 360 | 2.2 |
| 1987 | 801 | 369 | 2.2 |
| 1988 | 783 | 370 | 2.1 |
| 1989 | 778 | 343 | 2.3 |
| 1990 | 855 | 374 | 2.3 |
| 1991 | 916 | 378 | 2.4 |
| 1992 | 989 | 399 | 2.5 |
| 1993 | 1073 | 413 | 2.6 |
| 1994 | 1133 | 443 | 2.6 |
| 1995 | 1179 | 487 | 2.4 |
| 1996 | 1217 | 551 | 2.2 |
| 1997 | 1252 | 584 | 2.1 |

**Source:** Yang Dennis Tao and Fang Cai, "The Political Economy of China's Rural-Urban Divide," http://scid.stanford.edu/pdf/credpr62.pdf, August 2000.

## NOTES

1.  A. Browne, 2006, China reins in real-estate sector, *Wall Street Journal*, May 19–21, 3.
2.  Ibid.
3.  F. Balfour & B. Grow, 2006, One foot in China, http://www.businessweek.com/magazine/content/06_18/b3982068.htm, May 1.
4.  Ye Xiannian, 2004, China real estate market – Economic development, http://www.china-window.com/china_market/china_real_estate/china-real-estate-market-2.shtml, August 20.
5.  2004, Market for luxury brands booms in Shanghai, http://www.chinadaily.com.cn/english/doc/2004-03/13/content_314462.htm, March 13.

6.  2004, Chinese consumer markets: Exploding demand, worries, http://www.kpmginsiders.com/display_analysis. asp?cs_id=107803, July 2.

7.  A peasant is a farm worker who does not own the land he farms, but pays part of the crops he grows to the owner of the land as rent. Peasants cannot ever prosper, because, if they work hard and grow a surplus, the landowner will inevitably raise the amount of the crop to be paid in "rent."

8.  People's communes, in the People's Republic of China, were formerly the highest of three administrative levels in rural areas in the period from 1958 to 1982–85, when they were replaced by townships. Communes, the largest collective units, were divided in turn into production brigades and production teams. The communes had governmental, political, and economic functions.

9.  2006, Fat of the land, http://www.economist.com/surveys/displaystory.cfm?story_id=5623357, March 23.

10. China real estate market – Economic development, op. cit.

11. 2006, How to make China even richer, http://www.economist.com/opinion/displaystory.cfm?story_id=5660833, March 23.

12. Ye Xiannian, 2004, China real estate market – Housing reforms, http://www.china-window.com/china_market/china_real_estate/china-real-estate-market-4.shtml, August 12.

13. China real estate market – Housing reforms, op. cit.

14. R. McGregor, 2006, Beijing confronts calls for ceiling on spiralling property prices, http://www.ft.com, May 19.

15. 2000, Housing's great leap forward, http://www.economist.com, September 28.

16. Ibid.

17. It is a subsidiary of Europe-based Kingfisher plc, the largest home improvement retailer in Britain. It is the world's third-largest home improvement chain, with more than 650 stores in 10 countries in Europe and Asia.

18. 2003, Doing up the Middle Kingdom, http://www.economist.com, October 9.

19. 1999, Home improvement boom in China, http://www.hartford-hwp.com/archives/55/279.html, June 11.

20. Ibid.

21. Ibid.

22. K. P. Lane & I. St-Maurice, 2006, The Chinese consumer: To spend or to save? The McKinsey Quarterly, 1, 1, 6–8.

23. 2001, Doing it for themselves, The Economist Intelligence Unit (Business China), 27(21), September 24, 9.

24. China real estate market – Economic development, op.cit.

25. 2004, China's real estate industry in a boom, http://www.china-window.com/china_market/china_real_estate/chinas-real-estate-indust.shtml, March 24.

26. 2001, Home improvement in China: A market analysis, http://www.the-infoshop.com/study/ae8399_home_china.html, August.

27. J. McDonald, 2006, IKEA happily feeds China's hungry home-improvement market, http://the.honoluluadvertiser.com/article/2006/Apr/11/bz/FP604110318.html, April 11.

28. Doing up the Middle Kingdom, op. cit.

29. 2006, B&Q expects more double-digit growth, http://en.ce.cn/Business/Enterprise/200603/21/t20060321_6435244.shtml, March 21.

30. Doing up the Middle Kingdom, op. cit.

31. B&Q expects more double-digit growth, op. cit.

32. IKEA happily feeds China's hungry home-improvement market, op. cit.

33. J. Beystehner, 2005, Asia's ideas market, http://www.pressroom.ups.com/execforum/op-eds/op-ed/0,1399,52,00.html, June 1.

34. IKEA happily feeds China's hungry home-improvement market, op. cit.

35. Home Depot, which was started in the late 1970s, has grown from a single-store operation in Atlanta to a network that now boasts more than 1,700 stores with a revenue of $60 billion in 2004.

36. One foot in China, op. cit.

37. Ibid.

38. M. A. Schwarz, 2004, Fixer-uppers spruce up profit at Home Depot, http://www.usatoday.com/money/companies/management/2004-07-05-insana-nardelli_x.htm, July 7.

39. Doing up the Middle Kingdom, op. cit.

40. F. Balfour, 2006, B&Q Stores: Renovating China's attitudes, http://www.businessweek.com/globalbiz/content/apr2006/gb20060425_120572.htm?campaign_id=search, April 25.

41. Doing up the Middle Kingdom, op. cit.

42. Ibid.

43. Ibid.

44. Ibid.

45. Home Depot to establish China business operation, http://www.buildingonline.com/news/viewnews.pl?id=320306/10/2004.

46. China's real estate industry in a boom, op. cit.

47. 2006, B&Q stores: Renovating China's attitudes, http://www.businessweek.com/globalbiz/content/apr2006/gb20060425_120572.htm?campaign_id=search, April 25.

48. P. Denlinger, 2004, Home depot plans China strategy, http://www.china-ready.com/news/June2004/HomeDepotPlansChinaStrategy060804.htm, June 8.

49. Y. Zhang, 2003, Learning to pay more attention to urban consumers: What home improvement companies could learn in China, www.cerc.com/pdfs/home_improve.pdf.

50. One foot in China, op. cit.

51. 2006, Home Depot mum on China chain, http://www.foxnews.com/story/0,2933,184699,00.html, February 13.

52. 2004, U.S. DIY store in China expansion, http://news.bbc.co.uk/2/hi/business/3785871.stm, June 8.

53. A company that installs flat-panel screens that play ads in retail outlets.

54. One foot in China, op. cit.

55. Ibid.

# CORPORATE ENVIRONMENTAL RESPONSIBILITY

## MICROSOFT'S PARTNERSHIP PROGRAMS

**Sushree Das**
*Amity Research Center*

**Abstract:** Corporate environmental responsibility is a part of corporate governance and more specifically it is a part of corporate social responsibility. An organisation that has the ability to implement an effective environmental management system will be able to reduce environmental waste and natural resource use, while at the same time improve the economic bottom line. Adoption of appropriate environmental practices and technologies can help a business in gaining a competitive advantage over its immediate competitors. Once this is understood, companies can find the most effective approach to assess a business bottom line by implementing a strategic environmental management system coupled with an environmental auditing and reporting process. Microsoft, one of the leading software services and solutions companies, is committed to being a responsible environmental leader and has implemented a number of programs to reduce its environmental footprint. This case focuses on the initiatives taken up by Microsoft in collaboration with other global organisations to uphold environmental sustainability. It also tries to concentrate on the benefits derived from these initiatives and assess whether Microsoft would continue to shoulder its responsibility for the benefit of the environment as a whole or only to retain its image as a responsible organisation.

## Pedagogical objectives

- To understand the importance of Corporate Environmental Responsibility (CER) and the tools for practicing CER.
- To understand the vehicles and barriers in implementing CER initiatives.
- To focus on the initiatives taken by Microsoft towards environmental sustainability.
- To assess the benefits emanating from these initiatives.

## Case study

*"At Microsoft, success comes from our passion for creating value – value for customers, shareholders, and partners; value for our employees and the communities around the world where we do business. Underlying our success is an approach to corporate governance that extends beyond simple compliance with legal requirements. I believe that corporate governance must provide a framework for establishing a culture of business integrity, accountability, and responsible business practices."*

Bill Gates, Chairman, Microsoft Corporation

This case was written by Sushree Das, Amity Research Center. It is intended to be used as the basis for class discussion rather than to illustrate either effective or ineffective handling of a management situation. The case was compiled from published sources.

© 2009, Amity Research Centers HQ, Bangalore.

Contributing to partnerships for development is an integral part of corporate citizenship and an essential part of conducting responsible business. The Corporate Environmental Responsibility (CER) program of an organization reflects its social conscience and commitments to the community and society at large. Today, Corporate Environmental Responsibility has become a universal concept, wherein organizations consider the interests of society by taking responsibility for the impact of their activities on customers, employees, shareholders, communities and the environment in all aspects of their operations. Today's complex environmental challenges such as climate change and pollution, increasingly require a comprehensive global response from both the public and private sectors, because of which, CER has become one of the most important global issues with serious challenges and implications. Corporate Environmental Responsibility has been adopted by many companies globally, as a strategic move to address the challenges of climate and environmental sustainability. Microsoft, one of the leading software services and solutions companies, was committed to being a responsible environmental leader and has implemented a number of programs to reduce its carbon footprint.[1] It sought to leverage information and communication technology to help address climate change and other complex global environmental challenges. As part of broader efforts to build global partnerships for development, Microsoft joined hands with various organizations. Its main areas of co-operation included: providing access to research and scientific information on the environment; building integrated knowledge platforms to enable better cooperation between environmental scientists, policymakers, NGOs, and other stakeholders; and supporting the development of applications for environmental sustainability management. However, the various environmental efforts adopted by Microsoft raised the question whether it would sustain the initiatives for the benefit of the society or would it remain only a strategy to maintain its image as a world leader.

# CER: significance, drivers and barriers

While CER continued to evolve in many countries, some businesses started to view it as a tool to enhance their competitiveness and increase their exports to markets with strong environmental regulations and environmentally conscious consumers. Corporate environmental responsibility added value to the bottom line of a business by integrating its environmental programs into the mainstream operations to provide sustainability.

It differed from company to company and from sector to sector. While manufacturing based businesses dealt with a wide range of environmental challenges, small or service-sector businesses usually came across a narrow range. Businesses of all sizes and sectors improved environmental performance and realised a wide range of benefits. Whether it was an automotive industry, manufacturing industry, retail or a service industry, managing issues such as waste minimisation, water quality and conservation, energy efficiency, air quality, pollution prevention, spill management and regulatory compliance helped to tackle the environmental challenges faced by them. Good environmental practices of leading companies led others to emulate such practices in their own premises. Many businesses in emerging markets were involved in areas such as social development or environmental improvements, and achieved cost savings, revenue growth and other business benefits. In terms of the nature of assurance, most companies followed the same steps for addressing the environmental issues, such as corporate environmental policy, environmental audit,[2] employee involvement, green procurement,[3] green products,[4] ecolabeling[5] and environmental management system[6] standards. Corporate environmental responsibility being an important aspect of corporate social responsibility (CSR) played a vital role among Indian corporate houses. India had been one of the world's richest traditions of CSR, even before the MNCs established base here. Being a fast growing economy, India was booming with national and multinational firms opening up new opportunities. At the same time, India also faced a number of social and environmental challenges. Therefore, in order to create an environment of equitable partnership between civil society and business, it became important to view CER in the right perspective. Some of the leading Indian companies like Tata Group,[7] Aditya Birla Group,[8] Jindal Steel,[9] Hindustan Lever Ltd.,[10] ITC,[11] Maruti Udyog,[12] Bharat Heavy Electricals Ltd.,[13] National Thermal Power Corporation,[14] Oil and Natural Gas Corporation[15] and Sony Corporation[16] included social and environmental obligations as an integral part of their business despite privatisation.[17]

The major factors that motivated companies to become aware of their environmental responsibilities and develop policies accordingly included – the business/environment context; global trade; requirements through the supply chain to Small and Medium Enterprises (SME), and the informal sector; pressure and support stemming from government actions such as regulations and financial incentives; and demand from civil society.[18] The general business conditions or factors such as reputation, risk, relationship with stakeholders, customers and suppliers, and market opportunities were often seen as drivers behind CER implementation, because companies carried out such activities to improve their future outlook by proactively addressing issues such as environmental damages, regulatory costs, accountability and transparency. Implementing CER could make a difference in an increasingly competitive global market by helping the companies to gain faster and easier access to export markets. At times, large companies were found to work with their suppliers in implementing CER practices. Government actions, laws and regulations as well as incentives were also identified as drivers for CER. Governments made it mandatory for companies to disclose their environmental information to the public so that their feedback could help the company to improve its performance. Civil society actions in the form of campaigns, public disclosure programs and CER indexes helped in raising awareness and activism among citizens and communities about a company's environmental performance. NGOs and industrial associations played an important role in developing various CER related standards.

Despite the various initiatives to promote CER, barriers still existed, which included – lack of demand and poor awareness about CER; limitations of CER tools such as environmental reporting and ISO standards; and financial and technical constraints to implement CER.[19] Citizens might not be aware of the company's performance which depends on the availability of sufficient technical or financial incentives and infrastructure to carry out such activities. The presence of a large number of SMEs and companies in the informal sector failed to put an impact on the media as well as its stakeholders, thereby posing a challenge for its growth. Some voluntary initiatives such as environmental reporting do not ensure that the company will have good environmental records. Companies in developing countries, particularly SMEs, might experience financial and technical difficulties in implementing CER. The entire process in obtaining ISO certification that involved a substantial amount of time and cost went through various stages like performance measurement and evaluation, documentation, training of staff, development of process controls, followed by an external audit. Financial and technical constraints could be eased if governments provide financial assistance and support to companies that adopt cleaner production systems.

# CER: evolution and initiatives at Microsoft

Microsoft Corporation was founded in 1975 by Bill Gates and Paul Allen.[20] Since its inception, Microsoft Corporation strengthened its position as a worldwide

leader in providing software services and solutions to help people realise their full potential. Its business model, which included more than 600,000[21] partners worldwide, and its commitment to invest in Research & Development (more than \$9 billion in 2009)[22] generated millions of jobs and helped make the IT industry one of the most vibrant sectors of the global economy. Microsoft's core mission was to popularise computing by making IT affordable and accessible, so that there would be a PC on every desk. While focusing on the future generation of computing, Microsoft was committed to foster innovation and advance global prosperity through technology solutions, implement responsible leadership practices, and create partnerships that enhanced economic and social opportunities for everyone. Microsoft followed a global culture of accountability through its core values and codes of conduct. It conducted its business through its three core divisions such as Platform Products and Services Division, Business Division and Entertainment and Devices Division. Its operation centers were spread throughout the world. Of all its business segments, Microsoft earned its revenue primarily from its Online Services Division. Revenue was generated from online advertising which included web search, displays, email and messaging services. From the very beginning, the fundamental component of Microsoft's business success was its strong corporate governance. It provided support to communities in three ways: technology skills training, strengthening non-governmental organizations through technology, and engaging its employees in their communities.

Microsoft worked in collaboration with its stakeholders, governments and leading environmental organisations to apply the power of software and information technology with the objective of supporting environmental sustainability. Key areas where it partnered to promote positive environmental outcomes included: applying information technology to maximise energy efficiency; focusing on research and scientific breakthroughs to solve vital issues concerning society such as energy, climate, and environment; and practicing responsible environmental leadership and citizenship in its own premises, operations, and supply chain.[23]

Microsoft worked with various leading non-governmental organisations, academic researchers and public institutions to improve the use of energy in its own facilities as well as across the economy. (Annexure I)

Microsoft also focused on research and scientific breakthroughs to solve vital issues concerning society such as energy, climate, and environment. It had a growing portfolio of collaborations with governments and

## ANNEXURE I  Microsoft's initiatives to maximize energy efficiency

| Year/Name of the Initiative | Partnership/ Collaboration with | Objectives |
| --- | --- | --- |
| Since 2007. Climate Savers Computing Initiative[24] | IT companies like Google, Dell, Lenovo, HP, Intel, World Wild Life Fund | 1. To promote development deployment and adoption of smart technologies which can not only improve the efficiency of a computer's power delivery but also reduce the energy consumed when the computer is in an inactive state.<br>2. To reduce the global carbon emissions by over 50 million tones per year, by 2010 |
| The Green Grid[25] | Consortium of major IT companies and professionals | 1. To develop standard metrics and best practices to measure and improve energy efficiency in data centers. |
| ENERGY STAR program[26] | Joint initiative of U.S. Environmental Protection Agency (EPA) and U.S. Department of Energy | 1. To develop specific operational requirements for data centers, personal computers and servers.<br>2. To create a special System Center configuration pack that allowed organizations to easily configure their IT systems in accordance with the guidelines laid down by ENERGY STAR.<br>3. To help IT professionals manage the physical and virtual environments across data centers, desktops and other devices from one central location. |
| EU Code of Conduct for Data Centers[27] | | 1. To spread awareness among data center operators and owners to use energy in a cost effective manner without disturbing the critical functions of data centers.<br>2. To maximize the energy efficiency of data centers so that the carbon emissions and other environmental, economic and energy supply security impacts such as strain on infrastructure caused as a result of rising energy consumption are prevented. |
| Project 2°[28] | Clinton Climate Initiative[29] | 1. To enable cities to accurately monitor, compare and reduce their greenhouse gas emissions through the development of a free web-based application thereby making it the first global, multilingual emissions measurement toolset available 24 hours a day, seven days a week via the Web. |
| Web-based carbon scenario planning tool[30] | World Wildlife Fund[31] | 1. To frame policies promoting telework/virtual meeting solutions in U.S., Europe, India, China, and Japan.<br>2. To encourage green technology and support computer monitoring of a forest reserve in Italy. |

| Year/Name of the Initiative | Partnership/ Collaboration with | Objectives |
|---|---|---|
| Digital Energy Solutions Campaign (DESC)[32] | Reputed ICT companies and environmental NGOs | 1. To spread awareness among the policymakers about the role of ICT in improving the energy efficiency of the global economy. 2. To framing public policies that promote the use of ICT solutions as a means for dealing with the energy challenge, fostering innovation, and advocating practical strategies for mitigating climate change. |
| Global e-Sustainability Initiative (GeSI)[33] and the Smart 2020 report[34] | Leading IT companies and the United Nations Environment Programme (UNEP) and International Telecommunication Union (ITU) | 1. To prepare report on ways IT can address climate change. |
| Pecan Street project | Public-private partnership with Austin Energy and the City of Austin and Environmental Defense Fund[35] | 1. To develop a cutting-edge clean energy distribution system. 2. Help cities map out the creation of the infrastructure it will take to power their economies and preserve the environment. |
| | Green IT Alliance (GITA)[36] | 1. To provide software worth $250,000 to help GITA promote its work to facilitate energy efficient data center design and other green IT solutions. |

Source: Compiled by the author from various sources.

individuals to help society make use of environmental information. (Annexure II)

Apart from practicing environmental leadership at a global level, Microsoft demonstrated environmental leadership and citizenship in its own premises, operations, and supply chain. The organisation worked to measure, report, and reduce its environmental impacts across all its operations. The main area where it focused was to reduce its carbon emissions per unit of revenue by at least 30 percent compared with 2007 levels by 2012.[37] To achieve this, Microsoft collaborated with external groups. (Annexure III)

Apart from the above initiatives, since 1983, Microsoft and its employees provided over $3.4 billion[38] in cash, services and software to non-profit organisations including numerous environmental groups around the world through localised company-sponsored volunteer campaigns. Reports also showed that Microsoft provided strategic software grants worth $200,000 to the Green IT Alliance, $700,000 to the Kenya-based

Greenbelt Movement[39] and $2.5 million to The Nature Conservancy.[40,41] As a partner with the Net Hope coalition,[42] Microsoft provided IT capacity building to a coalition of leading global humanitarian and environmental groups, including The Nature Conservancy, Water Aid,[43] and Wildlife Conservation Society.[44] Microsoft also served on the steering committee of Freedom to Roam, a coalition of corporations, governments, and non-governmental organizations that work to find solutions to the threats to wildlife arising out of global warming.[45]

# Assessment of success and failures

Microsoft's Global Foundation Services' team implemented a number of best practices and policy guidelines to run its construction and facility operations around the

**ANNEXURE II** Microsoft's initiatives on environmental sustainability

| Year/Name of the Initiative | Partnership/ Collaboration with | Objectives |
|---|---|---|
| Digital Watershed[46] | Hydrology scientists at the University of California, Berkeley Water Center and the Lawrence Berkeley National Laboratory | 1. To help researchers create models and forecasts that can be used by a wide range of water interests by efficiently using and visualizing existing disparate data sets.<br>2. To acquire and curate existing hydrologic data to understand historic conditions on key watersheds in California. |
| Project Trident[47] | University of Washington and the Monterey Bay Aquarium Research Institute | 1. To enable scientists to explore and visualize instant oceanographic data captured from sensors and computer simulations and then compose, visualize and interpret data for important experiments and data analysis. |
| 2009 | Signed an MoU with United Nations Environment Programme (UNEP)[48] | 1. To apply ICT for dealing with problems arising from climate change and other global environmental challenges.<br>2. To provide access to research and scientific information on the environment; to build integrated knowledge platforms to link environmental scientists, policymakers, NGOs. and other stakeholders.<br>3. To support the development of applications for environmental sustainability management. |
| 2009 | Microsoft Research's Computational Science Laboratory in Cambridge, UK, tied up with UNEP's World Conservation Monitoring Centre | 1. To conduct advanced studies on new computational modeling for biodiversity and conservation, and more priority on climate change, biodiversity, human activity and sustainability. |
| 2009 | UN's Climate Neutral Network | 1. To share best practices about reducing their carbon footprint. |
| For five years, Eye on Earth online environmental observatory | European Environment Agency (EEA)[49] | 1. To merge critical information such as European soil, air and ozone indicators, into one online location.<br>2. To deliver environmental information to more than 500 million citizens across Europe. |

| Year/Name of the Initiative | Partnership/ Collaboration with | Objectives |
|---|---|---|
| | | 3. To help the community and member countries make informed decisions about improving the environment, integrate environmental considerations into economic policies and move towards sustainability, and to coordinate the European environment information and observation network. |

**Source:** Compiled by the author from various sources.

world. It included benchmarks for the design, construction, and operation of high performance green buildings, high efficiency electric motors for pumps and fans, electronic variable speed drives, electronic ballasts for fluorescent lamps, and occupancy dimmers. At the Microsoft campus in Hyderabad, India, double-glazed windows and sunshades helped in reducing reliance on air conditioning, automatic switches were installed to turn off lights if offices were unoccupied for more than 10 minutes, and a reservoir recycled 36,000 cubic meters of rainwater to irrigate the 48-acre campus and to run energy-efficient, water-cooled AC units.[50] The Microsoft data center in San Antonio, Texas, used approximately eight million gallons[51] of recycled water a month from the city's waste water system during peak cooling months. The Microsoft data center in Quincy, Washington, derived 10 percent of its peak capacity by using 100 percent[52] renewable hydropower from the Columbia Basin River. The Dublin, Ireland data center utilised outside air for cooling, while reducing the need for energy-intensive coolers. An example of Microsoft's focus on reducing waste was the company's transition to use standard shipping containers to accommodate thousands of servers. This eliminated the need for large amounts of packaging and other materials required earlier when servers were delivered separately or in batches.[53]

According to a climate report by the World Wildlife Fund, the IT industry had the maximum potential to reduce its carbon footprint.[54] Microsoft's own use of its unified communications virtual meeting and telework software already reduced its employee travel by approximately 1 million air miles a year, and the carbon footprint by 17,000 metric tons annually.[55] It sponsored its own free commute service called the Microsoft Connector for employees in its corporate headquarters at Redmond, Washington. This service helped in reducing

traffic in the greater Seattle area by over ten million car miles each year.[56] It was extended to an R&D center in Vancouver, B.C. and they were also exploring options to extend it to other locations globally. Their intra-campus shuttle service used around 60 hybrid vehicles.[57] Microsoft also offered free public transportation passes to its employees and vendors, provided a subsidised vanpool and carpool system, and encouraged bike/walk commuting. Microsoft worked with its business customers and platform partners on creative consumer solutions.

Its EcoDrive[58] collaboration with Fiat used an in-car USB[59] stick tool that analysed the users' driving style and provided recommendations on more energy efficient driving.[60]

Climate Savers Computing Initiative[61] began in the spirit of World Wildlife Fund (WWF). Climate Savers program had pooled together over a dozen companies[62] since 1999 with a mission to cut carbon dioxide emissions. As per the CSCI's specifications, a number of reputed companies and organisations joined the Initiative, and thousands of individuals pledged their support. By joining the Initiative, individuals and businesses became a part of a powerful group, which demanded high volumes of energy-efficient computers, thereby lowering the cost penalty associated with it. CSCI started functioning in India with initial local partners such as TERI,[63] CII-ITC Centre of Excellence for Sustainable Development,[64] Manufacturers Association of Information Technology (MAIT)[65] and National Association of Software and Services Companies (NASSCOM).[66] According to Interactive Data Corporation's (IDC)[67] Worldwide Quarterly PC Tracker for 4Q08, "there were 4.1 million more desktop PCs and 2.4 million more notebook PCs in use in India in 2009 than in the previous year. It also predicted that by 2010, India will have 47 million installed PCs making it a priority to educate its

## ANNEXURE III  Microsoft demonstrating responsible environmental leadership

| Year/Name of the Initiative | Partnership/ Collaboration with | Objectives |
|---|---|---|
| | U.S. EPA Low Carbon IT Campaign[68] | 1. It is committed to use energy-saving power management features on monitors and computers in its premises.<br>2. To save energy for reducing air pollution associated with the burning of fossil fuels, and ultimately lower the risk of global warming. |
| Since 2004. Carbon Disclosure Project[69] | Microsoft is a voluntary participant of the annual Carbon Disclosure Project (CDP) | 1. To necessitate companies to disclose their strategies to measure, manage, and reduce emissions and respond to climate change. |
| Global Reporting Initiative[70] | Microsoft is an official Organizational Stakeholder of this global network | 1. To provide guidance on corporate reporting on environment and other CSR issues. |
| Sustainable Packaging Coalition[71] | Microsoft is also an Executive Committee Member. | 1. To provide education, resources, and tools to promote more environmentally sustainable packaging design, use, and recycling. 2. To promote reuse and end-of-life recycling of its hardware products like Xbox and computers produced by its partners. |
| Solving the E-waste Problem (STEP)[72] | United Nations Initiative | 1. To optimize the life cycle of electric and electronic equipment and utilize these resources for other purposes. |
| 2006 | UN Industrial Development Organization (UNIDO)[73] | 1. To refurbish used computers for discount sale to the local market to promote sustainable development in developing countries.<br>2. To promote the development and growth of SMEs through the application of ICTs, support the e-business and e-government initiatives and assist governments in developing national ICT strategies. |
| 2008, Digital Green | | 1. To educate farmers in India on how to use azolla – an aquatic fern fed to cows, yielding increased milk production.[74] |

**Source**: Compiled by the author from various sources.

growing population about energy-efficient computing that can save money, energy and in turn, the planet".[75]

By adhering to the guidelines of the Clinton Climate Initiative,[76] the Project 2° Emissions Tracker[77] software made it possible for many cities to set up a baseline of their greenhouse gas emissions, create action plans; track the effectiveness of their emissions reduction programs, and share experiences with each other. According to a recent study by Gartner,[78] the Information and Communication Technology sector accounted for 2% of global greenhouse gas emissions.[79] Windows Vista was their most energy efficient operating system which had been possible, through significant enhancements to power management infrastructure, functionality, and default settings. Windows Vista added new power management features according to the Natural Resources Defense Council.[80] According to a senior scientist in the United States, those features helped eliminate 3 million tons[81] of carbon emissions annually in the U.S. alone. Windows Server 2008 offered virtualisation and power management settings that optimised energy efficiency. As per the Windows Server 2008 Power Savings document, Windows Server 2008 achieved power savings of up to 10 percent over Windows Server 2003 at comparable levels throughout.[82]

Microsoft also considered its contribution to e-waste in a significant way. It helped in refurbishing discarded functional computers and provided affordable solutions to millions of people. Microsoft Authorised Refurbisher Program (MAR) with the help of TechTurn, a computer overhauling company in Texas, helped revamp old computers and made it ready for the user. Through the MAR programs and by supporting other programs such as Digital Pipeline (DP), Microsoft helped extend the life of older computers by providing low-cost licenses for Microsoft software.[83] Those computers were then bought by low income families, non profit organisations and charitable organisations, thereby extending the life of computers. This prevented the environment from getting polluted even more by stopping every part of the computer to be disposed in a landfill. Microsoft also sponsored free computer recycling events in collaboration with other software giants such as Dell[84] and Intechra.[85]

Though Microsoft was successful in implementing a number of projects effectively, there were certain areas where its performance was not satisfactory (Exhibit I). As per the report published by Greenpeace International,[86] Microsoft remained in 15th position but with an increased score of 2.7 points, up from 2.5 points, as it was then engaged in a coalition with the European

## EXHIBIT 1   Microsoft overall score

| | | | | |
|---|---|---|---|---|
| Precautionary Principle | | | | |
| Chemicals Management | | | | |
| Timeline for PVC & BFR phaseout | | | | |
| Timeline for additional substances phaseout | | | | |
| PVC-free and/or BFR-free models (companies score double on this criterion) | | | | |
| Individual producer responsibility | | | | |
| Voluntary take-back | | | | |
| Information to individual customers | | | | |
| Amounts recycled | | | | |
| Use of recycled plastic content | | | | |
| Global GHG emissions reduction support | | | | |
| Carbon Footprint disclosure | | | | |
| Own GHG emissions reduction commitment | | | | |
| Amounts of renewable energy used | | | | |
| Energy efficiency of new models (companies score double on this criterion) | | | | |

**Source:** "GUIDE TO GREENER ELECTRONICS", www.greenpeace.org/greenerelectronics, September 2009.

## ANNEXURE IV  Microsoft's detailed scoring on chemicals

| Precautionary Principle | Chemicals Management | Timeline for PVC- and BFR phaseout | Timeline for additional substances phaseout | PVC free and/or BFR-free models (double points) |
|---|---|---|---|---|
| **GOOD (3+)** | **GOOD (3+)** | **GOOD (3+)** | **PARTIALLY BAD (1+)** | **BAD (0)** |
| Microsoft has a definition of the Precautionary Principle, as defined in the UN Rio declaration. | Microsoft lists its Chemical specifications and a procedure for identifying future substances for elimination. | Microsoft is committed to eliminating PVC and brominated flame retardants from all of its hardware products by or before 2010. | Microsoft provides a timeline till the end of 2010 for removing phthalates. It currently restricts certain phthalates and antimony in line with the EU Toys Directive, for use in selected products such as game controllers, etc. | Microsoft offers phthalate and/or BFR free electronic products with the exception of the printed circuit board, and gives an example of the Xbox 360 Wireless Microphone product. |

**Source:** Compiled by the author from: "GUIDE TO GREENER ELECTRONICS", www.greenpeace.org/greenerelectronics, September 2009.

## ANNEXURE V  Microsoft's detailed scoring on e-waste

| Support for Individual Producer Responsibility | Provides voluntary take-back where no EPR laws exist | Provides info for individual customers on take-back in all countries where products are sold | Reports on amount of e-waste collected and recycled | Use of recycled plastic content in products – and timelines for increasing content |
|---|---|---|---|---|
| **BAD (0)** | **BAD (0)** | **BAD(O)** | **BAD (0)** | **BAD(O)** |
| Although Microsoft now states that it "supports the mandatory collection and recycling of consumer electronics funded by individual producers...", for any marks, it needs to support the principle of Individual Producer Responsibility more explicitly. | Microsoft refurbishes computers and other devices to keep them in use and out of the waste stream as long as possible – so that they can be recycled properly at the end of life, however it provides no voluntary take-back and recycling services for products that reach the end of their life. | Microsoft provides links to various recycling initiatives by Microsoft (MAR, Digital Pipeline), other organizations (eg. CEA's my Green Electronics) and other electronic manufacturers but it still does not provide free take-back for its own products. | In 2008, Microsoft funded the collection and recycling of more than 5.82 million kgs of e-waste, representing some 15% of the world wide sales volume.[87] However, it is unclear if the 15% is calculated on current or past sales and whether weight contracted – is the weight of products actually recycled or just the weight that potentially could be recycled in those installations? | Microsoft is using recycled plastics in product packaging films but no details are given about its use in hardware products. |

**Source:** Compiled by the author from: "GUIDE TO GREENER ELECTRONICS", www.greenpeace.org/greenerelectronics, September 2009.

Union supporting Individual Producer Responsibility. Most of Microsoft's points were earned on the toxic chemicals criteria. (Annexure IV) The company was committed to removing Polyvinyl Chloride (PVC)[88] and brominated flame retardants (BFRs)[89] from its hardware products by or before 2010 and phthalates by the end of 2010. However, analysts felt that it might need to put products on the market that are free from BFRs in printed circuit boards before it can score points for this criterion. On other e-waste criteria, Microsoft failed to score any points (Annexure V). On energy, the company got points for reporting its total carbon dioxide equivalent emissions from its own operations, and for sourcing 24.4% of all the electricity used in 2007 from renewable sources (Annexure VI). Further, it was also required to provide more information on the Renewable Energy Certificates (RECs) that it was buying and commit to increase its use of renewable energy with a timeline.[90]

# Microsoft's CER practices: is it only an eye wash?

Microsoft made significant progress in key areas of product development and technology innovation. It also took initiatives in controlling e-wastes which were highly toxic and harmful for health and environment. However, some analysts felt that, for long term survival, a corporate leader like Microsoft would need to be very careful in the case of waste minimisation, otherwise, all its environmental sustainability programs would be considered an eye wash. They also felt that Microsoft should fully commit towards sustainable development of the company as well as society in order to prevent the negative effects on the company's bottom line. Some industry observers pointed out that the rapid growth of Microsoft Corporation spawned continuous product creation and their

## ANNEXURE VI  Microsoft's detailed scoring on energy

| Support for global mandatory reduction of GHG emissions | Company carbon footprint disclosure | Commitment to reduce own direct GHG emissions | Amount of renewable energy used | Energy efficiency of New Models (double points) |
|---|---|---|---|---|
| BAD (0) | PARTIALLY BAD (1+) | BAD (0) | PARTIALLY GOOD (2+) | BAD (0) |
| Microsoft now has a Climate Change Policy Statement which supports government actions to transition to a low- carbon economy. However, the need for mandatory reduction of GHG emission is not mentioned. | Microsoft reports its total CO2 equivalent emissions in 2007 at 15100 metric tonnes (scope 1), 152480 metric tonnes (scope 2) and 255370 metric tonnes from employee business travel (scopes),but these are not third party verified. | Microsoft has set a goal to reduce its carbon emissions per unit of revenue at least 30% below 2008 levels by 2012. However, there is no commitment for absolute cuts of GHG emissions. | Microsoft reports that in 2007, renewable energy supplied 24.4% of its total electricity load associated with its facilities and data centres; it is currently trying to boost this percentage. But, it is unclear if there is additionally in its purchasing of renewable and which sources of renewable energy it considers renewable. To keep these points. Microsoft needs to address these concerns and commit to increase its use of renewable energy with a timeline. | Microsoft does not report on Energy Star compliance but states that it is collaborating with the Natural Resources Defense Council to help make the Xbox 360 more energy-efficient.[91] It has committed to reduce energy consumption of the Xbox 360 by an additional 10% by 2010. |

**Source:** Compiled by the author from: "GUIDE TO GREENER ELECTRONICS", www.greenpeace.org/greenerelectronics, September 2009.

subsequent obsolescence. While Microsoft funded the collection and recycling of e-waste that represented 15%[92] of worldwide sales volume, experts raised doubts on the method as well as the parameters used for its calculation. There were also uncertainties regarding Microsoft's existing e-waste management system as to whether it was sufficient enough to purify the huge amount of waste that was getting dumped on a regular basis. Though it provided links to various recycling initiatives of consumer electronics funded by other producers, it did not provide any voluntary take back measures for its own products. Critics analysed that Microsoft needed to support the principle of Individual Producer Responsibility more explicitly, which meant that it had to support individualised financing for the end-of-life costs of its own brand.

On the energy issue, Microsoft used the electricity in its data centers by generating renewable sources of energy. However, analysts were skeptical about the company's categorisation of renewable sources of energy. They were of the opinion that Microsoft should clarify these concerns and also increase its use of renewable energy within a fixed timeline. Though Microsoft had a Climate Change Policy statement to show its support to the government in its transition to a low-carbon economy, it did not make any commitment for mandatory reduction of GHG emissions. Microsoft committed to make its products more energy efficient, but did not report on the Energy Star compliance, which gave sufficient scope for analysts to criticise such initiative.

Microsoft gained points mostly on the chemicals criteria, with exception on using certain reportable substances.[93] However, it remained to be seen as to whether Microsoft would continue these initiatives for the benefit of society or as a step to retain its image as a world leader. There is a common belief that out of the very few companies who contribute to the overall development, the main purpose is not to ensure the good of the nation, but rather a business strategy to evade the tax net. In fact, the credibility of companies is determined to a great extent by their consciousness of social responsibility. Therefore, the question that arises is whether CSR has become a business strategy to help establish the credibility of the company or is it a responsibility undertaken genuinely?

## REFERENCES

1. A carbon footprint is the total set of greenhouse gas (GHG) emissions caused by an organization, event or product.
2. Environmental auditing is a systematic, documented, periodic and objective process in assessing an organization's activities and services in relation to the environment.
3. Green procurement is the selection of products and services that minimise environmental impacts.
4. Green products are made from organic, recycled, or bio-based (biodegradable) materials that lessen our impact on the environment.
5. Eco-labeling is a voluntary method of environmental performance certification and labelling that is practiced around the world.
6. Environmental management system (EMS) refers to the management of an organisation's environmental programs in a comprehensive, systematic, planned and documented manner. It includes the organisational structure, planning and resources for developing, implementing and maintaining policy for environmental protection.
7. The Tata Group of Companies is one of the premier business conglomerates of India and was founded by Jamsetji Tata in the second half of the 19th century.
8. The Aditya Birla Group is a multinational conglomerate based in Mumbai, India with operations in 25 countries.
9. Jindal Steel and Power Limited is the most valuable private steel producer in India, also involved in manufactures and sells sponge iron, mild steel slabs, ferro chrome, iron ore, mild steel, structural, hot rolled plates & coils, coal based sponge iron plant and power production.
10. Hindustan Unilever Limited (HUL) is India's largest Fast Moving Consumer Goods Company, touching the lives of two out of three Indians with over 20 distinct categories in Home & Personal Care Products and Foods & Beverages.
11. ITC is one of India's foremost private sector companies having a diversified presence in Cigarettes, Hotels, Paperboards & Specialty Papers, Packaging, Agri-Business, Packaged Foods & Confectionery, Information Technology, Branded Apparel, Personal Care, Stationery, Safety Matches and other FMCG products.
12. Maruti Udyog Ltd is India's largest automobile company in collaboration with Suzuki of Japan.
13. Bharat Heavy Electricals Limited (BHEL) is the largest engineering and manufacturing enterprise in India in the energy-related and infrastructure sector which includes Power, Railways, Telecom, Transmission and Distribution, Oil and Gas sectors and many more.
14. NTPC Limited, a premier Public Sector Enterprise of Navratna status, established in 1975 is the largest power utility of India.
15. ONGC is one of Asia's largest and most active public sector petroleum companies involved in exploration and production of oil.
16. Sony Corporation is one of the world's largest multinational conglomerate corporations engaged in business through

its five operating segments – electronics, games, entertainment (motion pictures and music), financial services and other.

17. "Corporate Social Responsibility", http://www.eleaarningbuzz.com/knowledge-management/corporate-socialresponsibility, September 2009.

18. Corporate Environmental and Social Responsibility in the East Asia and Pacific Region, Review of Emerging Practice, www.worldbank.org/eapenvironment, May 2006.

19. Corporate Environmental and Social Responsibility in the East Asia and Pacific Region, Review of Emerging Practice, www.worldbank.org/eapenvironment, May 2006.

20. Alfred Randy, "Bill Gates, Paul Allen Form a Little Partnership", http://www.wired.com/science/discoveries/news/2008/04/dayintech_0404.

21. "Partnering to Strengthen Economies, Address Societal Challenges and Promote a Healthy Online Ecosystem", www.microsoft.com/publicpolicy, June 2009.

22. "Microsoft Corporation – Annual Report 2009", www.microsoft.com/Public_Policy_Agenda.pdf, 2009.

23. "Microsoft Corporate Environmental Partnerships Overview", www.microsoft.com/environment.

24. The Climate Savers Computing Initiative is a nonprofit group of eco-conscious consumers, businesses and conservation organizations dedicated to improving the power efficiency and reducing the energy consumption of computers.

25. The Green Grid is a global consortium of IT companies and professionals seeking to improve energy efficiency in data centers and business computing ecosystems around the globe.

26. ENERGY STAR is a government-backed program helping businesses and individuals protect the environment through superior energy efficiency.

27. EU Code of Conduct for Data Centers provides guidelines, recommendations and examples of best practice which could lead to a reduction in energy consumption by data centres in Europe of up to 20%, http://re.jrc.ec.europa.eu/energyefficiency/html/standby_initiative_data%20centers.htm.

28. According to the United Nations, "2° Celsius is the maximum allowable change in global temperatures without catastrophic consequences".

29. The William J. Clinton Foundation launched the Clinton Climate Initiative (CCI) to create and advance solutions to the core issues driving climate change and focuses on three strategic program areas: increasing energy efficiency in cities, catalyzing the large-scale supply of clean energy, and working to stop deforestation.

30. "Microsoft Corporate Environmental Partnership overview" Op. cit.

31. World Wildlife Fund is the leading organization in wildlife conservation and endangered species.

32. DESC is a consortium of IT & telecom companies, trade associations and environmental NGOs that promote ICT as part of the solution to our energy and climate challenges.

33. The Global eSustainability Initiative (GeSI) – an initiative of Information and Communications Technology (ICT) companies aimed at improving the sustainability impact of the ICT industry.

34. According to the findings of the Smart 2020 Report, "Emissions from the ICT sector will represent an estimated 2.8% of total global emissions by 2020. But ICT will enable others to achieve significant emissions reductions, helping other industries and consumers avoid an estimated 7.8 gigatonnes of $CO_2$ emissions by 2020, http://www.gesi.org/Initiatives/ClimateChange/tabid/71.Default.aspx.

35. Environmental Defense Fund is a US-based nonprofit environmental advocacy group. The group is known for its work on issues including global warming, ecosystem restoration, oceans, and human health.

36. GITA is a non-profit Clean Technology Center of Excellence in U.S which focuses on public-private interdisciplinary research on green IT issues, and aims for the integration of technologies through real-world pilot projects and laboratory testing.

37. "According to the findings of the Smart 2020 Report, "Emissions from the ICT sector will represent an estimated 2.8% of total global emissions by 2020. But ICT will enable others to achieve significant emissions reductions, helping other industries and consumers avoid an estimated 7.8 gigatonnes of $CO_2$ emissions by 2020", op. cit.

38. "Microsoft Environmental Partnerships Overview", download.microsoft.com/.../Microsoft_Corporate_Environmental_Partnerships_Overview.doc.

39. The Green Belt Movement is an indigineous grassroots non-governmental organization based in Nairobi, Kenya that takes an holistic approach to development by focusing on environmental conservation, community development and capacity building.

40. The Nature Conservancy of Canada (NCC) is a leading national land conservation organization that partners with corporate and individual landowners to achieve the direct protection of its most important natural treasures through property securement and long-term stewardship of its portfolio of properties.

41. "Microsoft Environmental Partnerships Overview", op. cit.

42. NetHope is an interagency collaboration of IT executives and managers from 25 of the world's largest international NGOs.

43. WaterAid is an international NGO dedicated exclusively to the provision of safe domestic water, sanitation and hygiene education to the world's poorest.

44. The Wildlife Conservation Society (WCS) saves wildlife and wild places worldwide. They do so through science, global conservation, education and the management of the world's largest system of urban wildlife parks, led by the flagship Bronx Zoo.

45. "Microsoft Environmental Partnerships Overview", op. cit.

46. A digital watershed is that area of land, a bounded hydrologic system, within which all living things are inextricably linked by their common water course and where, as humans settled, simple logic demanded that they become part of a community. http://www.microsoft.com/environment/our_commitment/articles/digital_watershed.aspx.

47. Project Trident is a scientific workflow workbench for oceanography. www.microsoft.com/mscorp/tc/trident.mspx.

48. UNEP's mission is to provide leadership and encourage partnership in caring for the environment by inspiring, informing, and enabling nations and peoples to improve their quality of life without compromising that of future generations.

49. The aim of the EEA is to ensure that decision-makers and the general public are kept informed about the state and outlook of the environment.

50. "Microsoft Commitment to Environmental Sustainability – Fact Sheet", http://download.microsoft.com/download/7/1/b/71b42457-99b2-4c3a-ad85-00fc7e86c5a2/Sustainability_Fact_Sheet_updatedOct08.docx, Oct 2009.

51. Arne, Josefsberg, et al., "Microsoft's Top 10 Business Practices for Environmentally Sustainable Data Centers" www.microsoft.com/environment/our.../datacenter_bp.aspx, accessed on 23rd Oct, 2009.

52. Ibid.

53. Ibid.

54. "Applying the Potential of Software to Address Climate Change", UNEP Climate Neutral Network, http://www.unep.org/climateneutral/Participants/Companies/Microsoft/tabid/566/Default.aspx.

55. "Why Earth Day Matters to Microsoft – Microsoft On The Issues". microsoftontheissues.com/.../why-earth-day-mattersto-microsoft.aspx.

56. 'Microsoft on the Topic: Climate Change', www.microsoft.com/about/corporatecitizenship/citizenship/businesspractices/environmentalimpact.mspx.

57. Ibid.

58. EcoDrive is the very latest in digital integrated technology. It is an easy-to-use computer application that connects your car to your PC.

59. Launched by Fiat at the 2008 Paris Motor Show, eco:Drive is a free-of-charge tool that helps drivers understand the impact of their driving style on fuel consumption and CO2 emissions.

60. "Microsoft Corporate Citizenship" www.microsoft.com/about/corporatecitizenship/citizenship/businesspractices/environmentalimpact.mspx.

61. The Climate Savers Computing Initiative is a nonprofit group of eco-conscious consumers, businesses and conservation organizations dedicated to improving the power efficiency and reducing the energy consumption of computers.

62. "Green IT: Taking the First Step" An address by Dr. Dileep Bhandarkar, Distinguished Engineer, Microsoft, at the 2008 CeBIT Conference.

63. TERI – The Energy and Resources Institute. Formally established in 1974, its mission is to work towards global sustainable development, creating innovative solutions for a better tomorrow. Website can be accessed from www.teriin.org.

64. The CII – ITC Centre of Excellence for Sustainable Development is an institution that creates a conducive, enabling climate for Indian businesses to pursue sustainability goals. It creates awareness, promotes through leadership and builds capacity to achieve sustainability across a broad spectrum of issues.

65. MAIT was set up in 1992 for purposes of scientific, educational and IT industry promotion. Its charter is to develop a globally competitive Indian IT Industry, promote the usage of IT in India. Website can be accessed from www.mait.com.

66. The National Association of Software and Services Companies (NASSCOM), the Indian chamber of commerce is a consortium that serves as an interface to the Indian software industry and Indian BPO industry.

67. IDC is the premier global provider of market intelligence, advisory services, and events for the Information technology, telecommunications, and consumer technology markets.

68. The ENERGY STAR Low Carbon IT Campaign is a nationwide effort to assist and recognize organizations for reducing the energy consumed by their computers and monitors.

69. Microsoft was categorically included in CDP's 2007 Climate Disclosure Leadership Index. www.cdproject.net/online_response.asp?cid=1152&year=2.

70. Sustainability reports based on the GRI framework are used to benchmark organizational performance with respect to laws, norms, codes, performance standards and voluntary initiatives; demonstrate organizational commitment to sustainable development; and compare organizational performance over time. http://www.globalreporting.org/AboutGRI/WhatIsGRI/.

71. The Sustainable Packaging Coalition is an industry working group inspired by cradle to cradle principles and dedicated to transforming packaging into a system that encourages economic prosperity and a sustainable flow of materials. www.sustainablepackaging.org.

72. StEP is an initiative of various UN organizations with the overall aim to solve the e-waste problem. www.step-initiative.org.

73. UNIDO is the specialized agency of the United Nations that promotes industrial development for poverty reduction, inclusive globalization and environmental sustainability.

74. Ashlee, Vance, "Microsoft Goes Far Afield to Study Emerging Markets", The New York Times, Oct. 27, 2008.

75. "Global IT Majors Band Together; Launch Energy Saving Initiative", http://www.climatesaverscomputing.org/news/press-releases, June 2009.

76. The William J. Clinton Foundation launched the Clinton Climate Initiative (CCI) to create and advance solutions to the core issues driving climate change and focuses on three strategic program areas: increasing energy efficiency in cities, catalyzing the large-scale supply of clean energy, and working to stop deforestation.

77. According to the United Nations, "2° Celsius is the maximum allowable change in global temperatures without catastrophic consequences.

78. Gartner, Inc. is the world's leading information technology research and advisory company. They deliver the technology-related insights necessary for their clients to make the right decisions, every day.

79. "Future emissions reductions in the ICT Sector", Responding to Climate Change 2009, http://www.rtcc.org/2009/html/help-consumers-8.html, 2009.

80. The Natural Resources Defense Council works to protect wildlife and wild places and to ensure a healthy environment for all life on earth.

81. Ibid.

82. "Windows Server 2008 Power Savings", download.microsoft.com/.../Windows_Server_2008_Power_Savings.docx, June 2008.

83. "Microsoft Commitment to Environmental Sustainability", Fact Sheet, download.microsoft.com/download/.../Sustainability_-Fact_Sheet_updatedOct08.docx, October 2008.

84. Dell Inc. is a multinational technology corporation that develops, manufactures, sells, and supports personal computers and other computer-related products.

85. Intechra is a Microsoft Authorised Refurbisher. It refurbishes and recycles computers and hardware for businesses and government agencies, ensuring maximum value recovery while eliminating the risks surrounding data security, compliance, and environmental impact.

86. Greenpeace International is a non-profit organization with involvement in issues spanning forty countries worldwide.

87. It is calculated by dividing the weight of worldwide hardware products for which recycling is contracted by Microsoft by the weight of worldwide hardware product sales.

88. PVC (polyvinyl chloride) plastic, commonly referred to as vinyl, is one of the most hazardous consumer products ever created.

89. Brominated flame retardants (BFRs) are a group of flame retardants that consist of organic compounds containing bromine.

90. "Guide to Greener Electronics – Microsoft", www.greenpeace.org/greenerelectronics, September 2009, accessed on 22nd October 2009.

91. Energy use has been lowered by 34% from product launch in 2005 through 2008.

92. "GUIDE TO GREENER ELECTRONICS", www.greenpeace.org/greenerelectronics, September 2009.

93. Ibid.

# INTEGRATIVE CASE 6

# EBAY INC: BIDDING FOR THE FUTURE

**Kazi Ahmed, Phillip Feller, Tara Ferrin, Jeffrey Fletcher, Fidel Rodriguez, Juliet Taylor, Robin Chapman**
*Arizona State University*

*"Our purpose is to pioneer new communities around the world built on commerce, sustained by trust and inspired by opportunity."*[1]

## Introduction

John Donahoe took over as president and CEO of eBay in March, 2008, during an unfavorable time for the company.[2] Since its inception in 1995, eBay has experienced revenue and earnings growth year after year, but the growth rate has slowed since 2006. For the first time, eBay's revenues fell from the previous year, 7 percent in fourth quarter 2008.[3] Although eBay is still the industry leader for online retailing with 17 percent market share, it has lost market share to innovative key competitors such as Amazon, Yahoo!, and Google. The expensive acquisition of Skype (a communications software company), did not have the outcome former CEO, Meg Whitman, expected. The company's venture into China failed, and changes in seller fees have not provided the results that eBay executives had anticipated. Additionally, there have been lawsuits related to counterfeit products. In March 2008, Meg Whitman stepped down as CEO and was succeeded by John Donahoe who has to confront the current situation. In a fast-cycle market such as online retailing, how can Donahoe discover new competitive advantages and regain its market share and growth rate, while confronting a more complex international and legal environment? In particular, Donahoe now faces a global economic downturn, a struggling ecommerce industry, and company shares trading between $10 and $11 below their prior year price of $40.

## Company leaders and overview

Shortly after conducting a successful online auction for a broken laser pointer for $14.83 in 1995, Pierre Omidyar realized that the Internet enabled market efficiency by allowing millions of buyers and sellers to view products and conduct transactions and he launched Auctionweb, an online marketplace for buyers and sellers.[4] Auctionweb officially became eBay in 1997 and hosted more auctions per month in that year than it did in all of 1996. Within four years and with the help of Meg Whitman, eBay grew from a programmer's experiment into a major publicly-traded company, trading on NASDAQ with the symbol EBAY[5] (see Exhibit 1 for more details on eBay's history).

Meg Whitman was recruited as eBay's second president and CEO in 1998 and helped bring eBay public in September of that year. At the time eBay's registered users had grown six-fold, to over 2 million, from the prior year. Under Whitman's leadership the company grew to over two hundred million users globally and over $7 billion in revenues. During her tenure, Whitman helped eBay enter China, integrated globally recognized brands like PayPal and Skype into the eBay portfolio, and most notably, successfully steered the company through the dot-com bust by staying focused on its core users and core competency – online auctions. She continues to serve on eBay's board of directors.

After a 20 year career at Bain & Company, Donahoe joined eBay in February 2005 as president of eBay marketplaces, where he served for three years. Donahoe's prior executive experience made him an ideal candidate

The authors would like to thank Professor Robert E. Hoskisson for his support under and whose direction the case was developed. This case is not intended to illustrate either effective or ineffective handling of managerial situations. The case is solely intended for class discussion.

to help expand marketplaces, eBay's core business. Under his leadership eBay acquired Shopping.com, StubHub, Gumtree, and LoQUo, giving it a strategic presence in the growing online comparison shopping industry, ticket sales, and classifieds. At the time of this transition to CEO eBay market share was declining and it had failed to gain in its number of unique visitors. In an attempt to reinvigorate growth, Donahoe helped by shifting eBay's emphasis closer to other competitors from auctions to fixed price listing, which has been the profit engine for Wal-Mart.com, Amazon.com, and Yahoo!.com. He also streamlined the organization with a 10 percent workforce reduction and the acquisition of Bill Me Later, a transaction-based credit business with a

## EXHIBIT 1   eBay history

| 1995: | Pierre Omidyar successfully conducted an online auction for a broken laser pointer which cost $14.83. Omidyar realized the Internet enabled market efficiency by allowing millions of buyers and sellers to view products and interact. It was this experiment that led Omidyar to found AuctionWeb, an online marketplace for buyers and sellers. |
|---|---|
| 1996: | AuctionWeb expanded greatly, with revenue topping which cost $10,000. In June Omidyar hired Jeff Skoll as president. |
| 1997: | AuctionWeb officially became eBay and hosted more auctions per month than it did in all of 1996. |
| 1998: | Meg Whitman joined as president and CEO and in September; eBay went public listing on NASDAQ under the symbol EBAY. |
| 1999: | eBay started its international expansion with marketplaces in the United Kingdom, Germany, and Australia. |
| 2000: | eBay became the number one e-commerce Web site, acquired Half.com to enter into the fixed price market, and continued international expansion with marketplaces in Austria, Canada, France, and Taiwan. |
| 2001: | eBay dramatically accelerated its international expansion through marketplaces in Ireland, Italy, Korea, New Zealand, Singapore, and Switzerland. |
| 2002: | eBay boosted revenues by acquiring Paypal.com, the primary payment method used on eBay. |
| 2003: | eBay expanded into Hong Kong; integrated PayPal Buyer Protection Services, protecting buyers and sellers in the eBay marketplace. |
| 2004: | eBay expanded into Malaysia and the Philippines, started strategic alliance in China, and acquired Rent.com. eBay purchased 28 percent ownership in online marketplace rival Craigslist.com for a reported $15 million. |
| 2005: | eBay diversified by acquiring Shopping.com, Skype, and foreign classified Web sites LoQUo and Gumtree while launching U.S. classified Web site Kijiji.com. |
| 2006: | Launched eBay express adding brand new fixed-price items to its marketplace, thereby further enhancing eBay as a primary shopping location. |
| 2007: | eBay acquired online ticket Web site Stubhub.com and Stumbleupon.com, which enhanced its Web presence while strategically partnering to enter India. eBay also partnered with Wal-Mart and Myspace.com to market Skype, and Northwest and Southwest Airlines to make PayPal a payment option. Major League Baseball named StubHub as its official provider of secondary tickets. In June, eBay cancelled its advertising on Google as a result of Google's push for Google Checkout as an eBay payment option. |

## EXHIBIT 1 Continued

2008: eBay announced that large-volume sellers with the highest feedback ratings will have preferential search locations and lower fees. eBay removed the option for buyers to receive negative feedback. On March 31, Meg Whitman stepped down as CEO and John Donahoe took over as president and CEO. On October 6, eBay announced a massive streamlining process which entailed laying off 10 percent of its workforce and restructuring charges of $70 to 80 million. It acquired Bill Me Later and two Danish classified ad Web sites. In mid-2008 eBay signed a deal with Buy.com allowing some sellers to directly negotiate their seller fees, dramatically increasing its items listed, but angering many of its smaller "powersellers." On July 15, a U.S. District Court judge ruled that eBay did not bear legal responsibility for sales of counterfeit goods in its marketplace. On September 16, eBay lowered fees on fixed-cost auctions by more than 70 percent in an effort to better compete with Amazon.com while also eliminating the use of checks and money orders as payments, and shifted to PayPal as the sole payment option for most auctions.

**Sources:** 2008, eBay history, http://www.ebay.com, November 3; J. Swartz, 2008, eBay to lay off 1,600 employees, cites economy, *USA Today*, October 7, 2B; 2008, eBay 2007 Form 10-K, http://www.ebay.com, November 25, 51; 2008, eBay major direct shareholders, http://finance.yahoo.com, November 26; B. Stone, 2008, Buy.com deal with eBay angers sellers, *New York Times*, July 14, 1; C. Wolf, 2008, eBay cuts fixed-price sales fees by 70%, *Washington Post*, August 21, D03; J. Schofield, 2008, Technology, *The Guardian*, February 21, 3; J. Swartz, 2008, Listings down 13% in boycott of eBay, *USA Today*, February 28, 3B; D. Rushe, 2008, Silicon Valley culture clash as eBay sues Craigslist, *The Times (London)*, April 27, B9; 2008, Judge rules for eBay over fake Tiffany jewelry sales, *International Herald Tribune*, July 15, F12; 2008, Google cancels 'Freedom' party to appease eBay, http://www.techweb.com, June 14; 2008, eBay Fact Sheet, http://www.ebay.com, November 28; 2008, eCommerce marketsize and trends, www.goecart.com/ecommerce_solutions_facts.asp, November 30; 2008, World's most valuable general retailers, http://galenet.galegroup.com. November 30.

total payment volume of over $1 billion, as a complementary payment method to PayPal.

Consisting of over 88 million active users in thirty-nine global markets (see Exhibit 2 for eBay marketplace locations), eBay offers anyone the opportunity to be an entrepreneur.[6] The company's marketplace segment operates online auctions, classified ad sites, and other sites where people can conduct commercial transactions. Unlike other ecommerce companies, eBay does not operate the online equivalent of a store; it is more like an online mall or flea market. Its payment segment provides ways for individuals to transfer money, particularly, although note solely, in order to complete an ecommerce transaction. Its third segment communications offer technology that enables voice and video communications between computers, and from a computer to an ordinary telephone.[7]

The ecommerce industry is attractive because it is relatively simple to enter. Most of the major players in the industry, including Yahoo!, Google and eBay, began as small entrepreneurial ventures with little more than an Internet connection and lines of code. Despite relatively low entry barriers, growth is difficult due to strong industry rivalry.

## Competitors

### Amazon.com Inc.

Amazon.com Inc. (Amazon) was founded in 1994 as an online bookstore. Over the years it expanded to include items ranging from books and CDs to clothing and electronics. This expansion occurred through partnerships with companies including Toys "R" Us, AOL and Hoovers.[8] Amazon sells other companies' products on its Website and uses its distribution network to ensure prompt and accurate delivery. After a relatively unsuccessful attempt to add an auction component, Amazon created the Amazon marketplace, which allows sellers to place used items on the site, featuring them alongside identical new items sold by Amazon.[9]

Amazon aims to be the low-cost leader in the ecommerce industry. In order to continue attracting new customers, Amazon continues to add innovative value-added services such as "frustration-free packaging" – which eliminates difficult-to-open product containers – and the ability for customers to pay with installment payment plans.[10] Amazon is also attempting to vertically integrate as a supplier of kitchenware through its new division, Pinzon.

In 2008, even though third quarter profit was up 48 percent, Amazon reduced fourth quarter projections, citing expectations, along with the rest of the retail sector, for a bleak holiday season.[11]

### Yahoo! Inc.

Originally known primarily as a search engine, Yahoo! Inc. ventured into the ecommerce industry in 1998 with the purchase of Viaweb. In addition to ecommerce services, Yahoo! products include advertising, email, news and information, photo sharing, and Internet browser

## EXHIBIT 2  Locations of eBay marketplaces

| | |
|---|---|
| Argentina | Malaysia |
| Australia | Mexico |
| Austria | Netherlands |
| Belgium | New Zealand |
| Brazil | Panama |
| Canada | Peru |
| Chile | Philippines |
| China | Poland |
| Colombia | Switzerland |
| Costa Rica | Singapore |
| Dominican Republic | Sweden |
| Ecuador | Taiwan |
| France | Thailand |
| Germany | Turkey |
| Hong Kong | United Kingdom |
| India | United States |
| Ireland | Uruguay |
| Italy | Venezuela |
| Korea | Vietnam |

**Source:** 2008, eBay Web site, http://www.ebay.com.

toolbars and add-ins.[12] It is present in over 20 countries. It appeals to advertisers by creating a Website that users go to for all of their needs, thereby creating the most exposure for its ads.[13]

While the company currently operates a Yahoo! Shopping site, it discontinued its auction site in the United States and Canada in June 2007. However Yahoo! still runs auction Websites in Hong Kong, Singapore, and Taiwan.[14]

In recent years, Yahoo! was involved in a takeover bid by Microsoft. The software giant saw Yahoo! as a way to compete with Google for advertising dollars. After a friendly acquisition was rejected, Microsoft attempted and failed at an unsolicited takeover. Investors have criticized Yahoo!'s board for not dealing more

effectively with Microsoft and for not acting in their interest.[15] Although Microsoft is reportedly no longer interested in a full takeover, analysts speculate that it may still pursue the purchase of Yahoo!'s search engine segment.[16]

### Google, Inc.

Google Inc. (Google) is a search engine site that was founded in 1998. It uses proprietary software to "understand exactly what you mean and give back exactly what you want" when searching on the Internet.[17] While Google continually adds applications, such as email and file sharing, 70 percent of its resources are directed toward improving search engine capabilities. Google's strength in this industry comes from its popularity as a search engine. Google also has a strong international presence, with its site available in 116 languages.[18]

From an ecommerce perspective, Google Product Search is an application that will search for items available for purchase on the Internet and display a side-by-side comparison. Google does not have an auction site available, although sellers do have the option of setting a negotiable price for their products. In order to compete with eBay's financial service segment, PayPal, Google launched Google Checkout in 2006 and began charging for its use in February of 2008.[19]

### Craigslist

A successful new entrant in the ecommerce industry is Craigslist. A private company, Craigslist began in San Francisco as a way for local residents to list events and classified ads. Craigslist differentiates itself by not charging to list or sell products on its Website. All revenue comes from fees for job postings and brokered apartment listings in selected cities such as New York. Craigslist keeps its overheads low in many ways, such as by continuing to operate out of a house instead of an office building and by having a staff of only twenty-five employees.[20] While confirmed financials are not available, some experts estimate the value of Craigslist to be near $5 billion.[21] As part of eBay's growth and acquisition strategy it has *acquired* a portion, roughly 28 percent, of Craigslist. (See Exhibit 3 and Exhibit 4 for competitor's financial data.)

## Acquisitions

eBay's revenue growth has come largely through acquisitions. The acquisitions have also allowed it to increase its geographic reach, move into related businesses such as on-line payments, and obtain technology that will

## EXHIBIT 3  Key competitor financials

| | eBay | Google | Amazon | Yahoo! | Overstock | Craigslist |
|---|---|---|---|---|---|---|
| Annual Sales (in Billions) | 8.69 | 20.92 | 18.14 | 7.32 | 0.873 | N/A |
| Employees | 15,500 | 16,805 | 17,000 | 14,300 | 844 | 25 |
| Market Value (in Billions) | 6.57 | 86.99 | 17.84 | 13.87 | 0.166 | N/A |
| Total Cash (in Billions) | 3.64 | 14.41 | 2.32 | 3.21 | 0.07 | N/A |
| Beta | 1.54 | 1.57 | 1.84 | 1.2 | 2.54 | N/A |
| Gross Profit Margin (in Billions) | 5.91 | 9.94 | 3.35 | 4.13 | 0.124 | N/A |
| EBITDA (in Billions) | 2.93 | 7.62 | 1.06 | 1.29 | 0.001 | N/A |
| Net Income (in Billions) | 1.94 | 5.05 | 0.627 | 0.933 | −0.02 | N/A |
| Return on Equity | 18.0% | 20.8% | 38.1% | 8.94% | −148% | N/A |
| Return on Assets | 9.7% | 14.4% | 8.8% | 2.51% | −9.03% | N/A |
| Total Debt/Equity | N/A | N/A | 0.172 | 0.005 | N/A | N/A |
| Market Capitalization (in Billions) | 16.34 | 80.99 | 18.23 | 14.16 | 0.16 | N/A |

**Sources:** 2008, Yahoo! Finance, http://finance.yahoo.com, November 24; 2008, Craigslist Fact Sheet, http://www.craigslist.org/about/factsheet, November 24

strengthen its product differentiation.[22] eBay has completed many acquisitions, but some of the more noteworthy ones are discussed below.

Half.com was one of eBay's first acquisitions and allowed eBay to enter the fixed price marketplace. It was acquired in 2000 for $312.8 million. Half.com allows eBay users to sell used books, games, CDs and DVDs at fixed prices. Sellers are paid directly by Half.com and eBay operates the Half.com Website separate from eBay.com, but allows eBay.com user profiles to be shared between the Websites.

In 2002 eBay purchased PayPal for $1.5 billion enabling sellers of any size to receive online payments from a buyer's credit card or checking account. This greatly reduced the payment and shipment time-frames and provided another source of revenue for eBay. PayPal's transaction fee for transactions of less than $3,000 is 2.9 percent of the amount transferred.[23] Revenues for PayPal in 2008 were $2.4 billion, making up 28 percent of eBay's total revenue.[24] In September 2008, eBay announced that PayPal was the sole payment option for a majority of its marketplace listings.[25]

In 2004 eBay acquired Shopping.com, Rent.com, and 28 percent ownership of Craigslist. It purchased

Shopping.com for $620 million. Shopping.com allows people to search for products and compare prices (similar to Google's product search formerly known as Froogle). This acquisition gave eBay a new channel for buyers and sellers to interact and a new medium for ad revenue.[26]

eBay acquired Rent.com for $415 million. Rent.com joins landlords with tenants online, charging property owners for each lease produced.[27] The acquisition of Rent.com gave eBay entry into the online classifieds market, while increasing revenue streams and online exposure.

eBay acquired its partial ownership of Craigslist for an undisclosed amount. eBay's relationship with Craigslist has always been somewhat 'icy'. eBay purchased its shares from an owner that went against the other stock holders' wishes to not sell to a public company. Craigslist alleges that eBay placed a variety of excessive demands on it, such as giving eBay 'blocking rights on all forms of corporate transactions.' In 2008 eBay accused Craigslist of diluting eBay's ownership interest by more than 10 percent; Craigslist countersued a month later accusing eBay of unlawful competition and copyright infringement because it launched the international

**EXHIBIT 4** Historical financial overview of eBay and its competitors

| eBay.com | 2003 | 2004 | 2005 | 2006 | 2007 | 2008 Q1 | 2008 Q2 | 2008 Q3 |
|---|---|---|---|---|---|---|---|---|
| Net Revenues | $2,165,096 | $3,271,309 | $4,552,401 | $5,969,741 | $7,672,329 | $2,192,223 | $2,195,661 | $2,117,531 |
| Cost of Net Revenues | 416,058 | 614,415 | 818,104 | 1,256,792 | 1,762,972 | 525,412 | 562,103 | 560,963 |
| Net Income (Loss) | 441,771 | 778,223 | 1,082,043 | 1,125,639 | 348,251 | 459,718 | 460,345 | 492,219 |
| **Google.com** | **2003** | **2004** | **2005** | **2006** | **2007** | **2008 Q1** | **2008 Q2** | **2008 Q3** |
| Net Revenues | $1,465,934 | $3,189,223 | $6,138,560 | $10,604,917 | $16,593,986 | $5,186,043 | $5,367,212 | $5,541,391 |
| Cost of Net Revenues | 1,123,470 | 2,549,031 | 4,121,282 | 7,054,921 | 11,509,586 | 3,639,808 | 3,789,247 | 2,173,390 |
| Net Income (Loss) | 105,648 | 399,119 | 1,465,397 | 3,077,446 | 4,203,720 | 1,307,086 | 1,247,391 | 1,289,939 |
| **Amazon.com** | **2003** | **2004** | **2005** | **2006** | **2007** | **2008 Q1** | **2008 Q2** | **2008 Q3** |
| Net Revenues | $5,264,000 | $6,921,000 | $8,490,000 | $10,711,000 | $14,835,000 | $4,135,000 | $4,063,000 | $4,265,000 |
| Cost of Net Revenues | 4,007,000 | 5,319,000 | 6,451,000 | 8,255,000 | 11,482,000 | 3,179,000 | 3,096,000 | 3,266,000 |
| Net Income (Loss) | 35,000 | 588,000 | 359,000 | 190,000 | 476,000 | 143,000 | 158,000 | 119,000 |
| **Yahoo.com** | **2003** | **2004** | **2005** | **2006** | **2007** | **2008 Q1** | **2008 Q2** | **2008 Q3** |
| Net Revenues | $1,625,097 | $5,257,668 | $6,425,679 | $6,969,274 | $6,969,274 | $1,817,602 | $1,798,085 | $1,786,426 |
| Cost of Net Revenues | 358,103 | 2,096,201 | 2,675,723 | 2,675,723 | 2,838,758 | 755,083 | 765,911 | 772,227 |
| Net Income (Loss) | 237,879 | 1,896,230 | 751,391 | 660,000 | 660,000 | 542,163 | 131,215 | 54,348 |
| **Overstock.com** | **2003** | **2004** | **2005** | **2006** | **2007** | **2008 Q1** | **2008 Q2** | **2008 Q3** |
| Net Revenues | $234,603 | $490,621 | $794,975 | $780,137 | $765,902 | $202,814 | $188,836 | $186,855 |
| Cost of Net Revenues | 209,320 | 424,183 | 678,502 | 690,333 | 641,352 | 168,843 | 155,627 | 154,736 |
| Net Income (Loss) | (11,981) | (4,414) | (25,212) | (106,762) | (48,036) | (4,724) | (7,359) | (1,589) |

**Sources:** 2008, http://www.ebay.com; http://www.google.com; http://www.yahoo.com; http://www.overstock.com; http://finance.yahoo.com; http://www.amazon.com

classified-ad site Kijiji.[28] The outcome of these lawsuits is still anticipated by the public.

eBay acquired Skype in 2005 for $2.6 billion. Skype is an Internet phone provider, allowing users to make calls to almost every country with their computers using Voice Over Internet Protocol (VOIP).[29] eBay's plan for Skype was to integrate it to allow buyers and sellers to communicate prior to transactions.[30] Skype is a free service if both parties are using Skype, but it charges non-Skype users for in-and-out calls.[31] The number of Skype users has increased from 57 million in 2005 to 400 million in 2008.[32] In 2007, eBay declared a $1.4 billion asset impairment for Skype, meaning that either eBay overpaid for Skype or that the strategic integration of Skype is not going as planned. Thus, to maximize Skype's potential, eBay has announced that it plans to make Skype a stand alone business and will conduct an initial public offering in the first half of 2010.[33]

eBay acquired Stubhub.com in 2007 for $310 million. Stubhub.com is a secondary ticket marketplace that integrates guaranteed fulfillment and shipment using FedEx.[34] Stubhub partners with American Express for concert tickets and over sixty teams for sporting events.[35] In 2007 Stubhub was named the official secondary market for tickets by Major League Baseball.[36] Stubhub features a season-ticketholder option, encouraging customer loyalty, and an easy method for season ticket holders to re-sell tickets.[37] eBay operates Stubhub.com independently from eBay.com.

eBay's purchase of Fraud Sciences Ltd. for $169 million in 2008 adds to its technology portfolio. eBay has long operated on the notion that trust is the key to its success, and it has announced plans to improve the level of trust that it provides. Fraud Sciences has developed ways to detect fraudulent purchases and provides eBay with the technology that it needs but lacks the capability to develop.

Also, eBay has expanded into Europe and Asia through acquisitions. It increased its auction reach with Alando in Germany, iBazar in France, Tradera in Sweden, Internet Auction in South Korea, and Baazee in India. eBay incorporated international classified ad Websites into its portfolio with purchases of Loquo in Spain, Gumtree in the United Kingdom, Marktplaats in the Netherlands, and Den Bla Avis in Denmark. Each international acquisition allows eBay to expand and diversify its revenue base by purchasing established Websites that the local culture understands.[38] This is an extremely important element when developing any sort of presence in a foreign country as eBay learned through its experience in China (discussed in the Customer demographics and international experience subsection below).

# Alliances

In addition to acquisitions, eBay uses alliances with small entrepreneurs and large companies to increase revenues and enhance the number of items available in the marketplace.

In 2004, eBay established a certified provider program consisting of exams, references, and an annual fee.[39] Partners provide services and products that sellers might need and eBay itself does not wish to offer, such as inventory management software, outbound logistics, or a full consignment business.[40] This helps eBay to attract sellers that might not otherwise use its services, or who wish to conduct a high number of transactions but lack expertise in certain areas. Having these services and products available helps sellers move more product than they would otherwise.[41] Activia is one of the best-known certified companies, providing marketplace listing tools to sellers of multiple items.[42] This alliance allows entrepreneurs to use the eBay name to grow their business while providing eBay fee revenue.

In 2006, eBay aligned with Yahoo! in a marketing alliance to promote revenue growth for both companies. Under the alliance Yahoo! became the exclusive advertising provider on eBay, the companies have a co-branded toolbar, and PayPal became Yahoo!'s preferred payment provider.[43] eBay also aligned with Google in 2006, making Google the primary advertiser on eBay's Websites outside of the United States.[44] Google has sought to integrate Skype into the alliance as a method to further sales from Web advertising, but details are not yet available.

In 2007, eBay aligned with Northwest and Southwest Airlines enabling PayPal as a payment option, and Wal-Mart and Myspace.com to promote the growth of Skype.[45] The alliance with Wal-Mart will allow eBay to sell Skype phone equipment in 1,800 retail locations.[46] These alliances help expand the brand name of both PayPal and Skype while also increasing revenue for eBay.

Although initially many smaller sellers were angered by eBay's alliance with Buy.com in 2008 because Buy.com does not pay listing fees and its volume, free shipping, and ability to take returns hurts smaller sellers, this alliance is one of the largest potential revenue generators for eBay. Buy.com is a middle-of-the-market tool that links retailers with buyers, and it immediately added five million fixed-price listings to the eBay marketplace.[47] eBay executives have responded to the objections about its alliance with Buy.com by stating, "eBay is aggressively using price as a lever to improve the value and selection on eBay.com. Consistent with our goals, we have entered into a partnership with Buy.com to bring their new-in-season merchandise onto eBay.com. We expect to learn a great deal from this partnership and we will build upon the results."[48]

It appears that eBay will continue to use partnerships as a large part of its growth strategy. Alliances with online competitors such as Yahoo! have allowed online exposure growth, and certified provider programs have given eBay the opportunity to fill the gaps that they are unable or unwilling to fill.

eBay also seeks growth through internal innovation. Product development accounts for almost 18 percent of the company's operating expenses.

## Internal innovation

eBay's early innovations include My eBay,[49] the feedback forum,[50] and final value fees.[51, 52] In 2005, eBay unveiled Kijiji.com, an online classified Website resembling Craigslist. By 2008, Kijiji attracted five million unique monthly visitors and was available in over 1,000 cities across the globe.[53] In 2006, eBay launched eBay Express in the United States, the United Kingdom, and Germany, providing buyers with the ability to buy multiple items, much like Amazon.com. However, due to feedback from both buyers and sellers, eBay closed eBay Express in all three markets in 2008 to focus more on its main eBay site.[54] David Hsu, a management professor at Wharton describes eBay's internal innovation as, "a poor job of identifying synergistic opportunities ... eBay's research group has not been able to drive much growth by internal innovation." eBay, "has to get that spark the company had in the early days."[55]

## Economic downturn

When it makes its acquisition, alliance, and innovation decisions, eBay first considers the environmental factors that may influence its success. The current unemployment rate (6.5 percent) and the mortgage crisis have also contributed to a decline in disposable income. This may increase the number of sellers on eBay as those who are unemployed seek ways to earn money, but fewer people are buying, and those who are demand low prices.[56] Thus, in September 2008 eBay lowered fees on fixed-cost sales by more than 70 percent in an effort to better compete with Amazon.com;[57] and starting in June 2009 infrequent sellers will be able to offer up to five items every 30 days without paying a listing fee.[58]

## Customer demographics and international experience

An aging population poses potential challenges. Currently, 50 percent of eBay buyers are over the age of forty-five, 53 percent are male, and 72 percent earn more than $50,000 per year; but as baby boomers age, the number of consumers in this age group will decline.[59]

Additionally, significant shifts in ethnic composition are occurring in the United States. For example, the Hispanic population is growing and is expected to triple over the next forty years. This will likely alter the type of products desired for purchase on eBay.[60] Furthermore, as eBay continues to pursue international expansion the products in demand will change and it will need to broaden its understanding of business practices and levels of service that are required to attract consumers in specific countries.

eBay did not succeed in its first attempt to establish a presence in China most likely because it lacked insight into the Chinese culture. eBay entered China in 2002 by purchasing a third of China's principal online auction site, Eachnet.com. In 2003 eBay purchased and became the sole owner of Eachnet.com, but by 2005 it had lost significant market share to Taobao, the consumer auction segment of China's largest ecommerce company.[61] eBay failed to understand that its popularity in the United States would not automatically make it successful in China. Some of the complaints were that eBay did not provide phone service or allow bartering, and it did not react quickly enough when Taobao entered the market without charging user fees.[62] Despite its failure with Eachnet.com, eBay is in China for the long haul, as Whitman said, "market leadership in China will be a defining characteristic of leadership globally," and failure to establish itself there would be an "astronomical" setback for the company as a whole.[63] Therefore in 2007 it established a partnership with a Beijing based Internet company, Tom Online Inc., taking a 49 percent stake in the company and possessing administration rights. This allows eBay to have strong local management that understands the culture and consumer desires. Tom eBay has done much to win the trust of Chinese consumers such as using an escrow service to hold payments until the buyer confirms satisfaction with the product. Whitman stated, "Whatever we do elsewhere to assure trust and safety, in China we have to do more."[64] eBay has had some success in China with Skype; Skype has grown faster in China than anywhere else.[65]

# Technology and competitive challenges

Various technological trends may pose challenges for eBay. Staying aware of the trends and if not being the leader in introducing new technology then responding quickly is essential as eBay learned from its misfortune in Japan. eBay lost significant market share to Yahoo! and pulled out of Japan in 2002 mostly due to failing to be up-to-date with the technology that Japanese users expected to be available on an auction site.[66]

Skype's technology may threaten eBay's profitability by giving buyers and sellers an opportunity to conduct the transaction without using eBay and therefore circumventing eBay's fees.

Another aspect related to technology that poses a challenge is that retailers have put great effort into improving their Websites to make online shopping easier for consumers. Stores such as Best Buy, Nordstrom, Target, and Wal-Mart carry items in four out of five of eBay's top volume categories (electronics, computers, clothing/accessories, and home/garden). Consumers may prefer retailers over eBay because they have greater confidence in their ability to return items and to have some sort of recourse if a purchased item is never received or is broken upon receipt.

However, eBay was founded on its judicious use of technology and it has recently developed some technology to help it limit the number of legal proceedings related to counterfeit products.

# Legal issues

Fashion fakes constitute a $600 billion industry worldwide[67] and despite eBay's efforts to crack down on counterfeit merchandise, some eBay users continue to sell it. This has led to law suits against eBay from companies such as Rolex, Tiffany & Co., Hermes, Louis Vuitton, and L'Oreal. Lawsuit results have been mixed. Rolex first instigated a trial against eBay in 2001. The original ruling was overturned by a German court in 2007 because the judge believed that eBay could not be held liable for damages, but it should monitor its site to prevent fakes from being sold. Again in early 2009 Rolex brought a case against eBay, but the judge ruled in favor of eBay.[68] In the case against Tiffany & Co. in July 2008, a U.S. District Court judge ruled that eBay did not bear legal responsibility for sales of counterfeit goods in its marketplace and that "it is the trademark owner's burden to police its mark."[69] However eBay was not as fortunate in the French courts in the cases against

Hermes and Louis Vuitton. It was ordered to pay Hermes $30,000 in damages on the account that "by failing to act within [its] powers to prevent reprehensible use of the site, both the seller and eBay committed acts of counterfeiting;"[70] eBay was also instructed to compensate Lois Vuitton $63 million for "culpable negligence," and an additional $20 million in damages for unauthorized sales of its perfume.[71] Most recently though, the Paris courts have ruled in favor of eBay in a case against L'Oreal, stating that "preventing the sale of counterfeit goods on the eBay platform encounters major difficulties when it comes to perfumes and cosmetics."[72]

eBay is dedicated to thwarting the sale of counterfeit products on its site. It has developed a filter program that detects offerings that blatantly violate trademark rights, established a team that works closely with law enforcement agencies, and even launched an anti-counterfeit campaign that aimed to educate buyers on how to avoid counterfeit products.

Tax law also may present challenges for eBay. Currently, if a consumer orders merchandise from a company that does not operate in his or her state of residence, no sales tax is paid on the item.[73] However, there is a possibility that legislation will pass requiring Internet purchases to be taxed. The IRS has also proposed that certain types of Internet companies, including eBay, should be required to collect and report individuals' earnings, allowing the IRS to ensure income taxes are being paid.[74] If this legislation passes, eBay users may move their business to sites that are not required to adhere to this policy.

To this point, eBay has been able to successfully navigate the company through environmental obstacles; hopefully it will continue to do so in order to remain profitable.

# Financial results

eBay derives most of its income from transaction costs associated with online sales. The product category that brings in the most revenue for eBay is vehicles (Exhibit 5). Revenues from its businesses outside of marketplaces have grown to 44 percent of total revenue. Of its $8.5 billion in 2008 total net revenues, PayPal made up $2.3 billion (27 percent), Skype made up $551 million (6 percent), and marketplace transactions made up $5.6 billion (66 percent); 46 percent came from the United States and 54 percent came from international sources.[75] Year over year, more of eBay's revenue is generated from international operations (Exhibit 6).

In 2008 eBay was ranked second among the world's most valuable retail Websites, trailing Amazon according to unique visitors and year-over-year growth.[76] In

**EXHIBIT 5** eBay categories and trends

| | $1 billion categories trend data (in millions) | | | | | | | | | |
|---|---|---|---|---|---|---|---|---|---|---|
| | 30-Sep-06 | 31-Dec-06 | 31-Mar-07 | 30-Jun-07 | 30-Sep-07 | 31-Dec-07 | 31-Mar-08 | 30-Jun-08 | 30-Sep-08 |
| Vehicles | 12,376 | 11,552 | 11,832 | 13,536 | 13,328 | 12,424 | 12,672 | 13,532 | 11,688 |
| Parts and Accessories | 3,764 | 4,172 | 4,680 | 5,016 | 4,596 | 4,768 | 5,348 | 5,392 | 4,620 |
| Consumer Electronics | 3,876 | 5,872 | 4,880 | 4,608 | 4,620 | 6,788 | 5,796 | 5,200 | 4,992 |
| Computers | 3,600 | 3,996 | 4,052 | 3,688 | 3,688 | 4,132 | 4,248 | 3,656 | 3,500 |
| Clothing and Accessories | 3,704 | 4,744 | 4,540 | 4,496 | 4,340 | 5,564 | 5,348 | 5,288 | 4,652 |
| Home and Garden | 3,036 | 3,496 | 3,584 | 3,640 | 3,700 | 4,120 | 4,244 | 4,184 | 3,840 |
| Collectibles | 2,208 | 2,804 | 2,684 | 2,388 | 2,380 | 2,948 | 2,772 | 2,468 | 2,232 |
| Books/Movies/Music | 2,780 | 3,032 | 3,124 | 2,720 | 3,000 | 3,288 | 3,456 | 2,952 | 2,864 |
| Sports | 2,496 | 2,668 | 2,584 | 2,892 | 2,836 | 2,884 | 2,940 | 3,232 | 2,992 |
| Business & Industrial | 1,752 | 2,012 | 2,232 | 2,220 | 2,140 | 2,300 | 2,584 | 2,452 | 2,212 |
| Toys | 1,700 | 2,564 | 2,136 | 1,940 | 1,940 | 2,748 | 2,396 | 2,144 | 1,952 |
| Jewelry & Watches | 1,644 | 2,184 | 1,972 | 1,960 | 1,924 | 2,508 | 2,332 | 2,216 | 1,988 |
| Cameras & Photo | 1,404 | 1,636 | 1,524 | 1,548 | 1,504 | 1,752 | 1,672 | 1,672 | 1,508 |
| Antiques & Art | 1,012 | 1,304 | 1,352 | 1,248 | 1,164 | 1,484 | 1,508 | 1,364 | 1,096 |
| Coins & Stamps | 900 | 1,044 | 1,320 | 1,068 | 1,028 | 1,192 | 1,428 | 1,188 | 1,032 |
| Tickets & Travel | 972 | 916 | 1,088 | 1,336 | 1,772 | 1,980 | 1,496 | 2,012 | 2,260 |
| Total | 47,224 | 53,996 | 53,584 | 54,304 | 53,960 | 60,880 | 60,240 | 58,952 | 53,428 |
| Percentage Growth | | 14% | −1% | 1% | −1% | 13% | −1% | −2% | −9% |

**Source:** 2008, eBay Annual Report, http://www.ebay.com

## EXHIBIT 6   eBay growth: US. vs. international

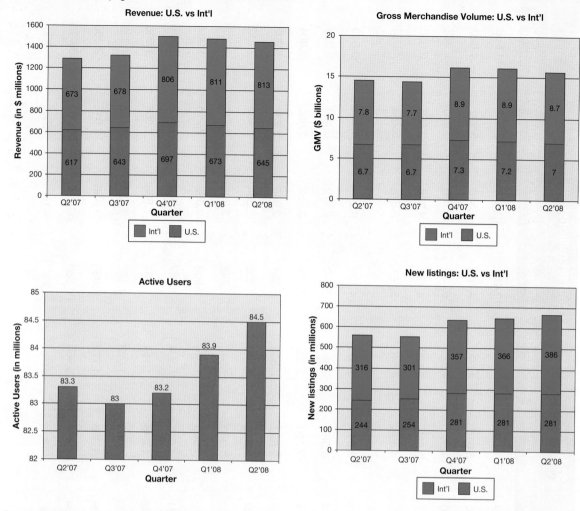

**Source:** 2008, Investor Relations, eBay company website, http://www.ebay.com.

annual sales, eBay trails Google ($20.92 billion) and Amazon ($18.14 billion), beating Yahoo! ($7.32 billion) and Overstock ($.873 billion) (see Exhibit 3 and 4). Craigslist is not a public company and thus its sales data is not public information.

Marketplace revenue depends on gross merchandise volume (GMV). eBay decomposes GMV into the number of listings multiplied by the conversion rate (the percentage of items that sold) multiplied by the average sale price.[77] New-listing and GMV growth in 2008 came primarily from the international marketplace (Exhibit 6). In 2008 eBay marketplaces had 86.3 million active users and 140 million listings at any given time.[78] Vehicles, parts, and accessories made up 31.5 percent of the top sixteen GMV categories for the years 2006–2008, while consumer electronics and computers composed 16.4 percent, clothing and accessories was 8.5 percent and home and garden was 6.8 percent (Exhibit 5). eBay's expansion into

fixed-price sales is positive, as this area increased to 45 percent of total GMV in 2008.[79] Regardless of the positive financial results that eBay posted in 2008, there are some significant challenges for which the new CEO and other leaders must determine solutions.

## Overview of challenges

eBay is currently in a fast-cycle market, causing it to experience extreme external competitive pressure. This competitive pressure is from both dominant Internet companies such as Amazon, Yahoo!, and Google was well as small private companies such as Craigslist. eBay faces the challenge of differentiating itself from these competitors, while at the same time striving to attract buyers, and increase revenues on each transaction. In an effort to attract more listings and higher revenues, eBay's alliance with

Buy.com has sparked boycotts and a loss of some its core customers. eBay needs to find a balance between satisfying buyers and creating economically beneficial cost structures for large strategic alliance partners.

Given the current budget deficits of many states, they may push to overturn the 1992 Supreme Court ruling that liberated mail-order merchants from having to collect sales tax from a consumer in a state in which they do not have a physical presence. This would result in eBay having to ensure that sales tax is collected on each transaction – leading to increased costs and more bookkeeping for eBay.[80]

Counterfeit merchandise affects eBay's image as a trustworthy auction site and poses the threat of more time and money spent in lawsuits. Current competition is fierce in the fast-cycle VOIP marketplace and potential government regulations of the VOIP industry could further affect the Skype brand. Additionally, Skype's technology is licensed from third parties and although there are contracts in place, future license renewals could increase costs or make it illogical for eBay to use this third party software.[81]

eBay is currently at a unique period in company growth as its acquisition strategy has created a large conglomerate of companies which intertwine within the online marketplace arena, while looking for new avenues to gain market share and revenue. The ecommerce industry as a whole is in a growth-stage and competitors are gaining market share as they innovate at a faster pace than eBay. With Meg Whitman's retirement, and the company's recent shift towards focusing on the fixed price marketplace, eBay has entered a defining phase of its business.

## NOTES

1. 2008, eBay: The world's online marketplace, http://pages.ebay.com/aboutebay/thecompany/companyoverview.html, December 4.
2. A. Schmidt, 2008, eBay CEO Meg Whitman to retire, MSNBC, www.msnbc.com, January 23.
3. R. Waters, 2008, eBay revenue to decline for first time, *Financial Times*, October 16; F. Ross, 2009, eBay's 4th quarter earnings – The recession? *All Business*, www.all-business.com, February 14.
4. 2008, eBay History, www.ebay.com, November 3.
5. Ibid.
6. 2008, eBay Form 10-K, www.ebay.com.
7. 2008, eBay Form 10-K, www.ebay.com.
8. 2008, Hoovers Company Records: Amazon.com Inc., November 1.
9. T. Wolverton, 2000, Amazon, Sotheby's closing jointly operated auction site, *Cnet News*, http://news.cnet.com/, October 10.
10. 2008, Amazon announces beginning of multi-year frustration-free packaging initiative, *Forbes*, www.forbes.com, November 3.
11. B. Stone, 2008, Profit is up at Amazon, but outlook is reduced, *The New York Times*, October 23, B3.
12. 2008, Hoovers Company Records: Yahoo! Inc., November 25.
13. 2008, 2007 Yahoo! Inc. Form 10K, www.yahoo.com, February 27.
14. 2007, Yahoo! to close North American auction site, *MSNBC*, www.msnbc.msn.com, May 9.
15. A. Sorkin & S. Lohr, 2008, Pursuing Yahoo! again, Microsoft shows need for a Web franchise, *The New York Times*, May 19, A1.
16. B. Stone, 2008, Now comes the hard part as Yahoo! wrestles with a question of direction, *The New York Times*, November 18, B1.
17. 2008, Corporate Information: Our Philosophy, http://www.google.com, November 28.
18. Ibid.
19. 2007, Google Inc., Form 10K, www.google.com.
20. 2008, craigslist fact sheet, www.craigslist.org, November 16.
21. J. Fine, 2008, Can Craigslist stay oddball? *Business Week*, May 19, 75.
22. 2008, The Portfolio Story, http://ebayinkblo6g.com/wp-content/uploads/ThePortfolioStory_24Oct08.pdf, October.
23. 2008, Transaction fees domestic transactions, PayPal company Website, www.paypal.com, December 3.
24. 2008, eBay 2007 Form 10-K, 51.
25. C. Wolf, 2008, eBay cuts fixed-price sales fees by 70%.
26. 2008, eBay to buy Shopping.com for $620 million, http://news.cnet.com, December 3.
27. 2008, eBay to buy Rent.com for $415 million, http://news.cnet.com, December 3.
28. 2008, eBay files corporate governance suit to protect its investment in Craigslist, *eBay News*, www.news.ebay.com, April 22; 2008, Craigslist-eBay suit details icy relationship, *PC Magazine*, www.pcmag.com, May 13; 2008, eBay goes public with Craigslist complaint, USA Today, www.usatoday, May 1.
29. 2008, About Skype, Skype company Website, www.skype.com, December 3.
30. 2008, eBay to buy Skype in $2.6bn deal, http://news.bbc.co.uk, December 3.
31. 2008, About Skype.
32. 2009, Skype available on Apple App store, *About Skype*, www.skype.com, March 31; 2008, What to do with Skype, http://news.cnet.com, December 3.
33. 2009, eBay Inc. announces plan for 2010 initial offering of Skype, *About Skype*, http://www.skype.com/, April 14.
34. 2008, Is Stubhub the ticket for eBay, *BusinessWeek*, www.businessweek.com, December 3.

35. 2008, About Stubhub, Stubhub company Website, www. stubhub.com/, December 3.

36. 2008, eBay 2007 Form 10-K.

37. 2008, About Stubhub.

38. 2008, The Portfolio Story.

39. Ibid.

40. 2008, eBay certified provider program, www.ebay.com, November 16.

41. 2008, Inside eBay's Innovation Machine – Case Studies, *CIO Insight*, www.cioinsight.com, November 16.

42. 2008, Certified providers program.

43. 2008, Yahoo!, eBay in Web advertising pact, *MSNBC*, www.msnbc.msn.com, December 3.

44. 2008, Google and eBay form an alliance to tailor adds to every customer, www.guardian.co.uk, December 3.

45. 2008, eBay 2007 Form 10-K, www.ebay.com, November 25, 51.

46. 2008, Wal-Mart to sell Skype phone gear, *MSNBC*, www. msnbc.msn.com, December 3.

47. B. Stone, 2008, Buy.com deal with eBay angers sellers, *The New York Times*, July 14, 1.

48. R. Smythe, 2008, eBay partners with Buy.com, www. ebayinkblog.com, May 3.

49. My eBay is a personal account on eBay that allows users to track their buying and selling activity, send and receive emails, update personal information, and view feedback reports.

50. The feedback forum is intended to form trust between buyers and sellers. Each eBay member has a feedback profile that consists of three main elements, 1. The feedback score, 2. The feedback percentage, 3. The feedback reports. The feedback score is the number of good reports about a member minus the number of bad reports in regard to their trade history. The feedback percentage is the percent of users that have reported a positive feedback experience with a seller in a given year. The feedback report displays both positive and negative reports from buyers and sellers who have traded with a member and includes information about each transaction.

51. The final value fees are the portion that eBay takes when an item sales or ends with a winning bid. For items less than $25, the Final Value Fee is 8.75 percent; items between $25 and $1000, the Final Value Fee is 8.75 percent of the initial $25 plus 3.5 percent of the remaining value; items over $1000, the Final Value Fee is 8.75 percent of the initial $25 plus 3.5 percent of the initial $25 to $1000 plus 1.5 percent of the remaining value.

52. A. Hsiao, 2009, Understanding the eBay feedback system, *About.com*, www.ebay.about.com, May 20; 2009, Final Value Fees, www.ebay.com, May 20; 2009, Using My eBay, www.ebay.com, May 20.

53. 2008, About Kijiji, http://bayarea.kijiji.com, December 3.

54. 2008, About eBay express, www.ebay.com, December 3.

55. 2008, eBay, After Meg, *Forbes*, www.forbes.com, December 3.

56. R. Waters, 2008, Add eBay to the cart, *Financial Times*, www.ft.com, October.

57. C. Wolf, 2008, eBay cuts fixed-price sales fees by 70%, *The Washington Post*, August 21, D03.

58. R. Metz, 2009, eBay cuts auction listing fees for casual sellers, *The Boston Globe*, www.boston.com, May 12.

59. 2008, eBay Seller Central, ebay.com, November; 2008, The changing nature of retail: Planting the seeds for sustainable growth, *Deloitte Consulting*, www.deloitte.com, November 18.

60. 2005, Changing demographics result in shifting consumer habits, www.retailforward.com, November 4.

61. K. Hafner & B. Stone, 2006, eBay is expected to close its auction site in China, *The New York Times*, www.nytimes.com, December 19.

62. Ibid; R. Hof, 2006, eBay's China challenge, *BusinessWeek*, www.businessweek.com, December 19.

63. K. Hafner & B. Stone, eBay is expected to close its auction site in China; B. Powell & J. Ressner, 2005, Why eBay must win in China, *Time*, www.time.com, August 22.

64. V. Shannon, 2007, eBay is planning to re-enter the China auction business, *The New York Times*, www.nytimes.com, June 22.

65. Ibid.

66. B. Powell & J. Ressner, Why eBay must win in China; 2001, How Yahoo! Japan beat eBay at its own game, *BusinessWeek*, www.businessweek.com, June 4.

67. A. Szustek, 2009, eBay victorious over Rolex in latest counterfeiting lawsuit, *Finding Dulcinea*, www.finding dulcinea.com, February 27.

68. D. Woollard, 2009, Rolex loses eBay lawsuit, www.luxist.com, February 26.

69. 2008, Judge rules for eBay over fake Tiffany jewelry sales, *The International Herald Tribune*, July 15, F12.

70. C. Matlack, 2008, Hermes beats eBay in counterfeit case, *BusinessWeek*, www.businessweek.com, June 6.

71. R. Waters, 2008, eBay wins court battle with Tiffany, *Financial Times*, www.ft.com, July 14; R.Waters, 2008, Moment of truth for eBay on luxury goods, *Financial Times*, www.ft.com, June 30.

72. I. Steiner, 2009, eBay fends off L'Oreal's counterfeiting lawsuit, *Auction Bytes*, www.auctionbytes.com, May 13.

73. A. Broache, 2008, Tax-free Internet shopping days could be numbered, *CNET News*, www.cnetnews.com, April 15.

74. 2008, Internet broker tax reporting, eBay Government Relations, www.ebay.com, November, 20.

75. 2008, eBay 2007 Form 10-K, http://investor.ebay.com/ annuals.cfm, page 51, November 25.

76. 2009, eBay narrows the gap, but Amazon tops in traffic again, Nielsen says, *Internet Retailer*, www.internetretailer.com, February 27.

77. 2008, Q3 20008 Earnings Slides, eBay company Website, www.ebay.com, November 16.

78. 2008, eBay 2007 Form 10-K, www.ebay.com, 51.

79. 2008, eBay Fact Sheet, www.ebay.com, November 28.

80. 2008, Sales tax on the Internet, http://www.nolo.com, December 4.

81. 2008, eBay 2007 Form 10-K, 29.

# INTEGRATIVE CASE 7

# HUAWEI: CISCO'S CHINESE CHALLENGER

Phoebe Ho, Ali F. Farhoomand

*The University of Hong Kong*

*Users are looking for a challenger [to Cisco] and value for money. Huawei has got the channel strategy and the pricing is right.*[1]

Immaculately trimmed green lawns, basketball courts, swimming pools, ergonomically designed office spaces set in a casual yet high-tech atmosphere – images frequently associated with technology parks in Silicon Valley – were found on the outskirts of Shenzhen, China, where Huawei Technologies housed its corporate headquarters. The 1.8-square-kilometer property signified the state of exponential growth the company had gone through since its inauguration in 1988.

Huawei (pronounced Hua-way) was incorporated in 1988 as a private enterprise manufacturing telecommunications equipment for local Chinese companies at a fraction of the price of its international rivals. By 2002, the company overtook Shanghai Bell, an Alcatel joint venture, to become the dominant supplier of digital switches and routers in China. It then entered the low-end international markets, supplying routers that were 40 percent cheaper than its competitors. The company had developed a full product portfolio consisting of wireless and fixed-line networking equipment, handsets, optical communications platforms, data networking, products for virtual private networks (VPNs), and Internet protocol (IP) telephony. It boasted an annual revenue of US$6.7 billion in 2005, of which 60 percent came from international sales.[2] With 55 branch offices worldwide, eight regional headquarters, world-scale research institutes in strategic locations, and a host of customer support and training centers, the company came to be known as the Cisco of China.

In early 2006, Huawei Technologies was among the ranks of China's "National Champions," along with Haier, Lenovo TCL, and the Wanxiang Group, poised to compete with global leaders in the international marketplace.[3] As concluded by an industry analyst, Huawei's threat came not from low-cost manufacturing, but from low-cost engineering.[4] With an inexpensive and highly qualified research and development (R&D) workforce, the company was able to deliver customized, innovative solutions to global enterprises looking to reduce their capital expenditures. Could Huawei climb up the technology value chain, replicating its success in low-end telecom networking in high-technology products and services? Could it build a global brand? If so, how profound was this threat to established global leaders in the telecom equipment sector? Were there any lessons for other Chinese companies in their respective paths to globalization?

## The global telecom equipment industry

The global telecom equipment industry had gone through a series of changes within the past few decades. In the 1960s and 1970s, network equipment suppliers were few and were categorized by the types of products they specialized in, primarily through in-house development.

Manufacturing was largely decentralized as suppliers operated independent subsidiaries to serve different countries and regional markets around the world. With the introduction of digital technology in the 1980s, product lines proliferated and country-specific operations were integrated into single, global organizations. Manufacturing tended to become more centralized to increase production volumes and decrease unit costs. By the 1990s, the pace of technological advances, commercialization of the Internet, and privatization of telecom service providers worldwide had created an unprecedented level of competition in the industry. Telecom equipment suppliers took on the role of broad-based system integrators, building extensive product lines through third-party contracts, original equipment manufacturers (OEMs) and other partnership arrangements.[5] Service providers used acquisition-based strategies to keep pace with consumer demand and drove the market for global networking products to US$50 billion by the end of 2000, up from US$15 billion in 1995.[6]

The dotcom bubble burst in 2001 and devastated the overheated telecom industry on a global scale. Service providers had difficulty accessing capital and the industry as a whole suffered from overcapacity. Global networking suppliers had to scale back and reposition themselves in light of the market slowdown. However, technological advances in the Internet boom had persisted up to 2006, and the technology choices and service requirements of service providers such as AT&T, AOL, and PCCW were more diverse than ever (see Exhibit 1 for the worldwide equipment capital expenditures by segment). Telecom equipment suppliers could be broadly divided into five subsectors and global players tended to align themselves with two or more of these subsectors: optical transmission systems, switch systems, access systems, data communications, and mobile communications (see Table 1.).

# China's telecom equipment industry

In the 1980s, China's telecom industry achieved substantial double-digit growth, and by the end of 2002, China surpassed the United States to become the largest telecom market in the world. Overall, China's telecom industry recorded US$112 billion in business transactions in 2004, with an annual growth rate of 34.9 percent, 3.7 times China's GDP growth rate of 9.5 percent.[8] Phone subscriptions had increased to 390 million mobile phone users and 348 million fixed-line users by October 2005.[9] Telecom service providers were shifting their focus from

**EXHIBIT 1**  Worldwide equipment CAPEX spending by segment, 2004

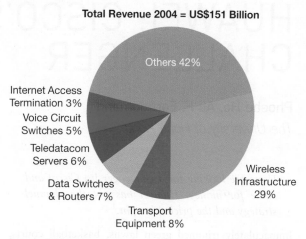

**Total Revenue 2004 = US$151 Billion**

- Others 42%
- Internet Access Termination 3%
- Voice Circuit Switches 5%
- Teledatacom Servers 6%
- Data Switches & Routers 7%
- Transport Equipment 8%
- Wireless Infrastructure 29%

**Source:** 2005, In-Stat, June.

**TABLE 1**  Leading firms in the global telecom equipment industry, 2001[07]

| Subsectors | Leading Firms |
|---|---|
| Optical Transmission Systems | Alcatel, Lucent, Nortel |
| Switch Systems | 3Com, Cisco |
| Access Systems | DSL: Alcatel, Siemens, Lucent Cable Modem: Motorola, Toshiba, Ambit |
| Data Communications | Routers: Cisco, Juniper Networks Ethernet Switches: Cisco, Nortel, Enterasys |
| Mobile Communications | Ericsson, Motorola, Nokia, Lucent |

infrastructure development to network improvement and value-added service offerings. According to the Gartner research group, China's telecom equipment market would continue to grow at a compound annual rate of 10.9 percent between 2004 and 2008, from US$30 billion to US$45 billion.[10]

As the market grew, most of the leading global telecom equipment firms started operations in China in the 1980s and 1990s. Due to ownership restrictions, most foreign firms entered the market by setting up joint ventures with local Chinese companies, usually involving equity investments. They leveraged their Chinese partners' local market knowledge and distribution networks in order to reduce investment risk.[11] Among the leading multinationals in China (Motorola, Siemens, Nokia, Alcatel, Lucent Technologies, and Ericsson), Cisco was a latecomer. Cisco first entered the Chinese market in 1994, but it was not until 1998 that the company intensely focused its attention on China[12] (see Cisco's story in the next section). High-end networking products were the traditional strongholds of foreign players, with the market divided between North American, European, and Japanese vendors. American companies accounted for 75 percent of the telecom equipment market in China in 2001, within which Cisco accounted for 62 percent and 26 percent of the routers and switching markets respectively.[13]

Even though the entry of these multinational telecom enterprises had facilitated the building of China's telecom infrastructure, they had also contributed to the growth of domestic manufacturers in China. Domestic firms had progressed from being far behind foreign companies in every subsector of the industry in the 1980s, to catching up in the switch market in the middle 1990s, to capturing the access market in the late 1990s, and finally to becoming competitive in the optical transmission, data communications, and mobile technology in the new millennium. Domestic Chinese vendors started to emerge, most notably the four companies, Huawei, ZTE, DTT, and GDT, collectively known as "Great China."[14] According to the CRC-Pinnacle market research firm, domestic Chinese equipment manufacturers occupied a combined 32 percent of the Chinese market by 2005, of which Huawei Technologies became the market leader with 13.5 percent market share (see Table 2).

# The Cisco story[15]

Cisco started as a one-product company in 1984 when two Stanford computer scientists, Len Bosack and Sandy Lerner, a married couple, built a multi-protocol router for networking between different types of computers. The couple ran the business out of their living room and sold to networking-intensive customers such as Hewlett-Packard, the U.S. Defense Department, and American universities. By 1987, the company had outgrown its capacity and, after a period of legal battles with Stanford University, managed to secure a sizable venture capital from Silicon Valley for its large-scale expansion.

**TABLE 2** Telecom equipment market share by leading vendors in China, 2005[16]

| Company Name | Market Share (%) |
| --- | --- |
| Huawei* | 13.5 |
| ZTE* | 12 |
| Ericsson | 12 |
| Alcatel Shanghai Bell | 7 |
| Motorola | 6.9 |
| Nokia | 6.2 |
| UTStarcom* | 6.1 |
| Siemens | 5.3 |
| Lucent | 4.7 |
| Nortel | 4 |
| Cisco | 4 |
| Others | 18.3 |
| Total | 100% |

* Denotes domestic Chinese companies.

The phenomenal growth of the Internet in the 1990s precipitated the building of the Cisco empire. As communication networks grew in complexity and size, Cisco expanded from a one-product router company into a comprehensive, service-based leader in the networking business. John Chambers, Cisco's president and CEO since 1995, recognized that the company could not rely on its own R&D departments to prevail as a leader in multiple product categories. He began to take on a series of acquisitions to broaden the company's service and product portfolios. The acquisitions consisted primarily of small companies developing leading technologies in different areas within the networking industry. To move into new market segments, Cisco formed extensive strategic alliances, frequently with equity investments, with companies in the networking value chain. Chambers used these acquisitions and strategic alliances as a way to accommodate the rapid market shifts in the exploding IT sector. By the end of the 1990s, Cisco had become a virtual manufacturer of networking products, running a network of outsourced operations.

As the Internet expanded its footprint across the globe, Cisco also began to develop its global presence. Cisco opened its first offices outside of the United States in 1991, in Britain and France initially, then Canada, Japan, Belgium, Mexico, and Hong Kong. Cisco entered these markets as foreign governments invested in their public Internet infrastructures, domestic telecom markets were liberalized, and commercial investments in the sector increased. To meet global demand for its products, Cisco made alliances with local original equipment manufacturers (OEMs) and distributors, but maintained a centralized management structure by region. The Netherlands, for example, was chosen as Cisco's regional headquarters to manage its European, African, and Middle Eastern markets.

Cisco entered China in 1994 with the opening of its first office in Beijing. Its original intention was simply to establish a presence and sell its equipment in China. In 1998, the company began to intensely focus its attention on China and announced a capital expenditure of $100 million over two years to expand its business in China. Cisco's strategy in China was to focus on recruiting and training employees to service the high-end markets of telecom service providers and enterprise markets. Instead of forming joint ventures with local partners (like most of its international competitors did in China), Cisco opened its own subsidiary in China, Cisco Networking Technology Co. Ltd, to promote education, demonstration, and development of network technology. It provided its market-leading switches and routers to all the major telecom service providers in China, including China Telecom, China Unicom, and China Mobile. Cisco also embarked on a number of education initiatives to develop favorable relations with Chinese authorities and to cultivate new areas of business within China. The Cisco Network Academy was one such initiative where 157 university-based, technical schools offered free network technology education to more than 7,000 students. On the business solution side, Cisco established its Internet Business Solutions Group to help top business leaders transform their own businesses into e-businesses, enhancing their business operations using supply chain management, customer care, or workforce optimization. Recognizing the large, low-cost, and skilled labor force in China, Cisco made further commitments to invest in a new R&D center in Shanghai. The facility would employ more than 100 people after its launch in 2005. Chambers's plans for the research facility were to allow Cisco access to technology and local talent so as to buy into the local Chinese market.

In all these endeavors, Cisco insisted on maintaining its leadership position in cutting-edge technology and single-system images (SSI) throughout the world. Most of its applications, and its Web site, were hosted in the United States. The company's entire data center was constantly replicated between San Jose, California and Raleigh, North Carolina. Global standards and consistencies were maintained such that applications were designed from a structural point of view and local content was dumped into a standardized functional design.

Cisco was by far the largest telecom networking company in the world, with 35,000 employees and an annual revenue of US$22 billion in 2003–2004. Its broadened service and product portfolio meant that it was not competing head-on with Huawei; rather they were competing in the data communications subsector. Cisco's leadership position in the telecommunications equipment sector was, however, not entirely insurmountable. Chinese competitors were using their aggressive pricing strategies to expand into the international markets, and were rapidly using their low-cost advantage to move up the value chain. Both Huawei and ZTE were expected to make further inroads into international markets in the next few years, competing head-to-head with the established Western players for the same global accounts. In Chambers's own words, "China will provide even stiffer competition over the next decade. ... Half of our top 12 competitors will be Chinese vendors."[17]

# Huawei: the home-grown Chinese multinational

Huawei, meaning "China achievement," was considered the model home-grown multinational company in China. Founded in 1988, Huawei Technologies was almost single-handedly created by Ren Zhengfei, a former People's Liberation Army officer and telecom engineer. Since the outset, Zhengfei's vision was to build innovation capability into the company. Contrary to the country's policy of "exchanging market for technology,[18] Zhengfei believed that joint venturing with foreign companies would not enable the Chinese to obtain foreign technologies, and they might end up losing the domestic market to foreign players. He stated his goals as:

> ... to develop the national industry, not to set up joint ventures with foreign companies, to closely follow global cutting-edge technology, and to insist on self-development, to gain domestic market share, and to explore the international market and compete against international rivals.[19]

# R&D powerhouse

In accordance with these goals, Huawei focused its resources on building itself into an R&D powerhouse. In the early years, the company started with 500 R&D staff and only 200 production staff. By the end of 2005, of its 24,000 employees, 48 percent were engaged in R&D. Huawei had a policy of investing no less than 10 percent of its total annual revenue in R&D (compared to 15 percent in leading foreign technology companies). Yet it was still able to establish the early winning formula for the company as its development leapfrogged into the Global Systems for Mobile Communications (GSM), obtaining almost 90 percent of the Chinese domestic market in mobile network equipment by 2002. Because of the low labor cost in China, Huawei's focused R&D strategy became a significant competitive advantage over its international competitors.

Another major foresight was its early and heavy investment in the third-generation (3G) mobile communications technology. Huawei started its own R&D in Code-Division Multiple Access (CDMA) in 1995. In the next few years, it invested more than US$370 million[20] in wide-band CDMA (WCDMA) technologies with a dedicated R&D staff of 3,500 scattered through its research centers in China and overseas. In 2006, Huawei had a 21-story research center at its corporate headquarters in Shenzhen; six other research laboratories in Beijing, Shanghai, Nanjing, Huangzhou, Xi'an, and Chengdu; a software development center in Bangalore (India) with 1,500 engineers working on-site; and research facilities in Moscow (Russia), Stockholm (Sweden), and the Silicon Valley in California (see Exhibit 2 for Huawei's R&D Institutes).

Also noteworthy was the education level of the company's employees. Huawei frequently boasted about having the most educated workforce in all of mainland China. Among its 24,000 employees, more than 85 percent had a bachelors or higher degree, and about 60 percent had a master's or PhD. As a result of its generous R&D spending and high-caliber labor pool, Huawei held an impressive record of patent ownership. By the end of 2004, its patent applications had totaled more than 8,000, of which 800 were applied for in more than 20 countries and territories, including the United States and Europe. In 2004 alone, its patent applications reached 2,000, on par with its international rivals in the telecom equipment sector.

In addition to internal development, Huawei had actively undertaken joint R&D laboratories with foreign companies, including Texas Instruments, Motorola, IBM, Intel, Sun Microsystems, and Microsoft, focusing on various telecom technologies. To Huawei, these joint development efforts were used as a complementary approach to enhancing its innovation capabilities. As one of Huawei's senior R&D officers pointed out:

> Huawei does not view R&D cooperation with foreign companies as an effective mechanism to gain technological competitiveness. There is no reason for foreign firms to transfer their most advanced core technologies to a Chinese partner over whom they do not have management control.[21]

# The military-styled wolf-pack enterprise

Ren Zhengfei's history with the Chinese military was a topic of much interest (and concern) in the Western world. Zhengfei's connection to the army had

**EXHIBIT 2** Huawei's R&D institutes

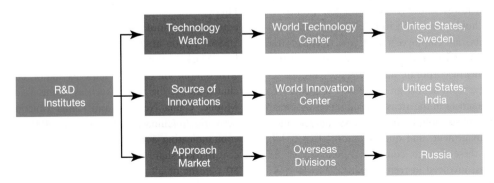

**Source:** J. Chen, 2005, Towards Indigenous Innovation: Pathways for Chinese Firms, Workshop of Technology Innovation and Economic Development, Zhejiang University, China, May 25–27.

undoubtedly created a guanxi (relationship) network few other competitors could match. In fact, in its early years the company had relied on big contract orders from the military to secure a foothold in the telecom network market. The company visitors' book contained such influential names as Jiang Zemin, Zhu Rongji, Li Peng, Hu Jintao, Wen Jiabao, and other central military dignitaries. The company received financial support from the state-owned Chinese Development Bank in the form of a US$10 billion facility for Huawei's international expansions over five years, and an additional US$600 million from the official Export-Import Bank of China. Zhengfei was reluctant to speak of his relationship with Beijing, but did give credit to the favorable industry policies his company benefited from:

> Huawei was somewhat naïve to choose telecom-equipment as its business domain in the beginning. Huawei was not prepared for such intensified competition when the company was just established. The rivals were internationally renowned companies with assets valued at tens of billions of dollars. If there had been no government policy to protect [nationally owned companies], Huawei would no longer exist.[22]

Ren Zhengfei's military background had also instilled a unique corporate culture within Huawei. He was known to frequently extol patriotism and cite Mao Zedong's thoughts in speeches and internal publications. All new employees were put through intensive military-style training for a few months. Zhengfei urged his employees to learn from the behavior of wolves, who had a keen sense of smell, were aggressive, and, most importantly, hunted in packs. In Zhengfei's own words, "An enterprise needs to develop a pack of wolves. Huawei's marketing arm has to focus on organizational aggressiveness."[23]

Over time, the company developed a national recruitment system with exceptionally high pay by Chinese standards (see Exhibit 3). According to a Huawei ex-employee, the lowest monthly salary in 2000 for a bachelors degree holder was US$500.[24] With housing and other benefits, an employee's first-year compensation could total as much as US$12,500.[25] To replicate a Western model of corporate management, the company had engaged a team of foreign experts to adopt international best practices in the areas of product development, supply chain integration, human resources management, financial management, and quality control (see Exhibit 4). Among these foreign consulting firms, IBM had been the most involved in reengineering Huawei's business processes and supply chains. For a while, 70 IBM

**EXHIBIT 3**  2004 average annual wage of staff and workers by sector and region, 2004

| Region | IT and Computer Service and Software Sector |
|---|---|
| Beijing | 57,412 RMB |
| Tianjin | 38,257 |
| Liaoning | 36,976 |
| Heilongjiang | 28,554 |
| Shanghai | 58,874 |
| Jiangsu | 36,754 |
| Zhejiang | 47,690 |
| Hubei | 19,451 |
| Guangdong | 45,624 |
| Chongqing | 30,607 |
| Yunnan | 21,855 |
| Shaanxi | 30,085 |
| Xinjiang | 24,032 |

**Source:** 2005, *Chinese Statistics Year Book.*

consultants were working at the Huawei headquarters alongside Huawei employees and manufacturing facilities worldwide.

# A strong and integrated Chinese network

Huawei was undisputedly the largest Chinese telecom equipment manufacturer, with an annual revenue of US$6.7 billion in 2005, and a net profit of US$470 million. Market capitalization was estimated to be up to US$10 billion. In China, Huawei's major customers included all the big names such as China Telecom, China Mobile, China Netcom, and China Unicom. Huawei's networks in China served more than 400 million people communicating across the country,[26] occupied 25 percent market share in the mobile networks, and supplied 80 percent of all short messaging services from China Mobile.[27] The company had been selected as one of the

**EXHIBIT 4**  Huawei's corporate management systems

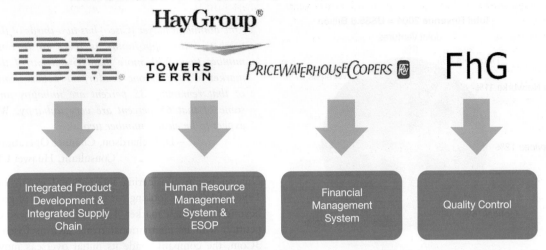

**Source:** J. Chen, 2005, Towards Indigenous Innovation: Pathways for Chinese Firms, Workshop of Technology Innovation and Economic Development, Zhejiang University, China, May 25–27.

**EXHIBIT 5**  Huawei's products lines

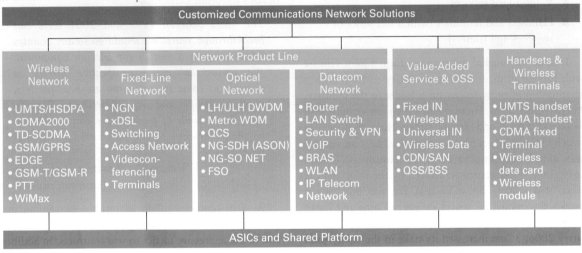

**Source:** J. Chen, 2005, Towards Indigenous Innovation: Pathways for Chinese Firms, Workshop of Technology Innovation and Economic Development, Zhejiang University, China, May 25–27.

major equipment suppliers for China Telecom's China-Net Next Carrying Network, or CN2, the core network for the country's next-generation business and consumer services, paving the way for China Telecom's entry into the 3G mobile market. In addition to the inexpensive R&D labor pool in China, the company had the advantage of integrating its marketing people into its core R&D team. The needs of service providers and telephone companies could thus be communicated through the marketers to the R&D headquarters in a timely and responsive manner.

Huawei's products could be divided into the following categories (see Exhibit 5 and Exhibit 6):

■ Wireless network

■ Fixed-line network

## EXHIBIT 6   Huawei's sales by technology

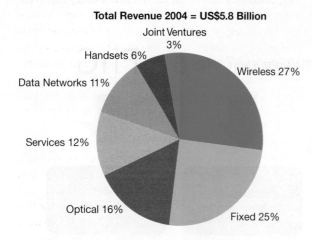

**Total Revenue 2004 = US$5.8 Billion**

Joint Ventures 3%

Handsets 6%

Data Networks 11%

Wireless 27%

Services 12%

Optical 16%

Fixed 25%

**Source:** EuroLAN.

- Optical network
- Data communications network
- Value-added services
- Handsets and terminals (with a full series of switches and routers)

Despite the original desire to not form a joint venture with foreign firms, it became necessary to form such a relationship in order to remain a leader in the industry. In November 2003, Huawei entered a joint venture with 3Com in China and Japan, called Huawei-3Com, in which Huawei held a 51 percent stake. The joint venture was aimed at selling to corporate customers, Cisco's stronghold. Products manufactured by the joint venture were sold under the individual Huawei and 3Com brands throughout the world, except in China and Japan where the joint Huawei-3Com brand was used. In February 2006, 3Com increased its stake in the equity joint venture to 51 percent. The joint venture had captured about 35 percent of the Chinese corporate market and was expected to overtake Cisco to be the largest network equipment provider in China.

As part of the joint venture arrangement, 3Com contributed US$160 million in cash, assets related to its operations in China and Japan, and licences to certain intellectual property. Moreover, the main reason Huawei entered into the joint venture with 3Com was that it wanted to leverage the latter's strong brand to increase profitability. Already a strong OEM with efficient production facilities, good R&D capabilities, and an extensive worldwide distribution network, what Huawei needed was a global name, because building a brand like 3Com's would be expensive and take a long time.

## Path to globalization

*One dominant player [Cisco] has two-thirds of the market – the opportunity is there to become number two. With more than 65 percent of the market looking at one vendor, we believe some of that remaining 35 percent are unhappy and some of that 65 percent are very unhappy. We expect to be clearly number two.*

– D. Richardson, Channel Operations Consultant, Huawei UK

Huawei began considering international expansion in 1996 when it was looking for diverse sources of growth beyond the Chinese market. To avoid head-to-head competition with its international rivals such as Cisco and 3Com, the company made its initial overseas move in the markets of developing countries. Huawei made its first significant international sale to a Russian telecom service provider in 2000, which was quickly followed by Advanced Info Service, Thailand's largest mobile service provider, and Tele Norte Leste Participacoes, Brazil's fixed-line carrier.

*The years between 1999 and 2001 were our breakthrough years. We would go to any country where we saw a market for telecom equipment. We invited as many prospective buyers as possible to come to our corporate headquarters, meet our people and see our products. We also went to all kinds of trade shows and exhibitions to show ourselves to the international customer base.*

– William Xu, President of Huawei's European region[28]

As a newcomer battling against the perception that Chinese products were cheap and unreliable, Huawei had to use aggressive tactics to win contracts. In addition to unbeatable pricing (typically 30 percent lower than those of established suppliers), Huawei went out of its way to offer powerful incentives. To win the Neuf Telecom contract in France in 2001, Huawei offered to build part of the customer's network free of charge and to run it for three months such that Neuf's engineers could test it before committing to buy it. Hiring local personnel was also part of Huawei's strategy to tailor technologies and services to customer's specific needs.

Major contracts won in recent years included the network upgrade contract with Etissalat, the telecommunications carrier of the United Arab Emirates, making UAE the first Arab country with 3G wireless communications. In 2004, Huawei became one of the first global communications suppliers to set up a CDMA network in Europe when it completed the construction of a project in Portugal for Denmark-based Radiometer A/S. In December that year, Huawei was selected by Telfort, the Dutch mobile operator, to build its 3G mobile phone network, signifying the company's first win in Europe's intensely competitive 3G market, and its arrival in the big league of telecom equipment suppliers. In late 2005, Huawei was selected as one of the four preferred suppliers to British Telecom's US\$19 billion, five-year-long 21st Century Network upgrade project, along with the U.S.-based Ciena Corporations and Lucent Technologies, and Germany's Siemens AG. It had also signed a global framework agreement with the Vodafone Group to supply mobile phone networks to any Vodafone company worldwide. In all these countries, Huawei had taken business from global giants in the rank of Siemens and Alcatel. In 2004, of the 19 licences awarded around the world for 3G wireless networks, Huawei was involved in building 14 of them.

# Struggles in the United States

Compared to Huawei's footprint in the European and other overseas markets, Huawei's presence in the United States was more limited. When it opened its first office in 2001 in Plano, Texas, the company made every effort to blend into the local culture. It shared the building with law offices, realtors, and the regional office of the lingerie company Victoria's Secret. A Texas state flag and an American receptionist welcomed visitors on the ground-floor lobby. Shortly after the U.S. launch, Huawei executives realized that Americans had difficulty pronouncing the company's name and came up with a working name, Futurewei. The new name, however, was never consistently adopted or promoted effectively. Magazines would still advertise Huawei, while trade shows, brochures, and other materials would feature Futurewei. Even though Americans had an easier time pronouncing the new name, they were confused by two different names belonging to the same company. In addition, the Chinese employees had a difficult time adapting to the Texas accent and other aspects of the local culture. The company sought to make its public face as American as possible, and hired local telecom talent in the area to that effect, but the relationship between its U.S. employees and Huawei executives was sometimes strained.

Contrary to its success in winning deals in developing countries, Huawei had run into snags in making deals in the United States. In a mature market where phone companies and their equipment suppliers had long-term ties, customers looked for exceptional leading-edge technology and a compelling reason to switch. One telecom service provider suggested that they would consider Huawei only after putting it through exhaustive trials, a common procedure for sourcing from an unknown company. Huawei management admitted that it was not prepared for the time and effort needed to break into the U.S. market, where lower prices were often not enough to land a deal.

Six months after setting up its subsidiary in the United States, Huawei was sued by Cisco for having allegedly infringed a number of Cisco's patents and copyrights by copying Cisco's user interface, user manuals, and source code for running its low-end routers. According to Cisco, the copying was so "lavish" that Huawei's router software contained the same bugs as Cisco's.[29] Cisco was seeking stiff penalties in the lawsuit, including the discontinuation of the production of Huawei's Quidway routers, as well as impoundment and destruction of all Huawei routers and manuals in the United States. At the same time, Cisco launched a "cease and desist" order against Huawei's UK distributor, Spot Distribution. Analysts observed that Huawei's steep discounting of Cisco products in its home turf, the U.S. market, had prompted the lawsuit, which was Cisco's first intellectual property lawsuit despite its huge intellectual portfolio.

Huawei initially denied the allegations, asserting its respect of intellectual property rights and its own focus on original R&D. The company then acknowledged that it had inadvertently obtained a small amount of Cisco's source code and used it in its own products. After Huawei agreed to withdraw its Quidway routers and other related products from sale in the United States, Cisco finally dropped the lawsuit in July 2004. In the midst of the legal proceedings, numerous sales contracts that Huawei was trying to close were killed. When the allegations were finally cleared, the company stumbled again. In June 2004, a Huawei employee was caught taking pictures of the insides of some high-tech equipment from Fujitsu in a Chicago trade show. Huawei later explained that it never used those photos and that it was the employee's first time in the United States.

After these blunders, Huawei landed the first contract with a U.S. wireless carrier in February 2004. It subsequently secured several other contracts with small wireless carriers in the United States. Huawei had serious intensions for the U.S. market, but results were yet to be seen. As Albert Lin, Huawei's head of R&D for North America, explained, "We need to present ourselves better. We also have to make it clear that we are not just testing the waters in the United States."[30]

# 3G and Huawei's future

The industry was of the opinion that Huawei's success as a global company eventually hinged on its performance at home.[31] China, with its huge and rapidly growing telecom market, would be the ultimate battleground for the world's telecom infrastructure suppliers. Core to the battle was the much-anticipated launch of 3G mobile phone services in early 2006. According to an estimate by China's Institute of Telecommunications Science and Technology, China's 3G users would reach 200 million by 2010, with associated revenue in the range of US$124 billion.[32] Confirmation of the 3G technology standards and the issue of licences were the two imminent issues for all players in China's much-coveted telecom market.

China was conducting standardized on-site testing on all three internationally recognized 3G technologies: the Chinese home-grown TD-SCDMA standard, the European-origined WCDMA standard, and the American CDMA2000 standard. Huawei had made heavy investments in WCDMA since 1995, formed a 3G research joint venture with Japan's NEC and Matsushita in 2003, and had deliberately entered the mobile handset market in early 2004 to prepare itself for the 3G market down the road. Concurrently, Huawei had formed a joint venture with Siemens, called TD-Tech, to test TD-SCDMA handsets and network gears. Huawei had been investing one-third of its R&D spending in 3G technologies for the past two years. To Huawei and other telecom players in China, the stakes were enormous as the launch of 3G services was expected to push the company onward to its next wave of growth and expansion.

# Conclusion

*It's like the global automotive industry in the 1970s and 1980s when the Japanese started to penetrate Europe and the United States with lower-cost products and then started to work their way up.*

— K. Deutsch, Vice President, A. T. Kearney[33]

*Incumbent Western firms should be very scared of Huawei. Its reputation as a low-cost vendor is only the visible part of the iceberg.*

— J. Doineau, Ovum IT Consultants[34]

*The low price is not the only reason that our customers choose us. Equipment reliability, service quality, and the company's association*

*with long-term development are elements of its success.*

— Johnson Hu, Vice President, Corporate Branding and Communications, Huawei Technologies[35]

To distance itself from its low-cost image, Huawei launched its first global image-building campaign in mid-2004. To emphasise the reliability of its telecommunication networks, one print media boasted that Huawei's networks were able to withstand Siberian winters and Saharan summers.[36] In early 2005, a survey report of 100 telecom operators worldwide ranked Huawei eighth among wireline-equipment suppliers, up from eighteenth the previous year. In addition, Huawei ranked fourth in service and support. The report called Huawei's ascendancy "astounding" as it surpassed several incumbent vendors in perceived market leadership.[37] Huawei's threat to the international telecom equipment suppliers was not to be overlooked (see Exhibit 7 for select financial performance of Huawei and its global competitors).

However, the battle could only become more intense. Huawei's track record was disappointing in the United States, just short of solid distribution networks to break into the lucrative enterprise markets; the network of choice in the developed countries was still Cisco. Huawei and other Chinese peers would have a difficult time matching the brand recognition and level of service provided by Cisco and other U.S. counterparts. Network security was another major concern expressed by service providers and enterprise customers. As stated by Cisco's CEO John Chambers, "Networks would have to be capable of responding to intrusions and viruses before human operators become aware of them. And security will be the most effective and efficient if a common strategy extends through all of a corporation's wired and mobile networks." During a two year period, Cisco acquired over 14 companies involved in network security and aspired to be "not just a vendor, but a trusted business advisor."[38]

In Asia, according to research firm IDC, Cisco's share of the Asian market (excluding Japan) in routers and LAN switches was still going strong at 62 percent versus Huawei's 6.2 percent.[39] In mobile handsets, Chinese suppliers were losing ground to their foreign counterparts; market shares of the Chinese companies of the local market fell from 50 percent in 2004 to 38 percent in the first six months of 2005. Foreign suppliers were also dominating the mobile switching infrastructure market.

Huawei was a privately owned global company. The industry speculated that the company could raise up to

**EXHIBIT 7** Select performance of Huawei and its global competitors

### Huawei

| Calendar year | 2004 | 2003 | 2002 |
|---|---|---|---|
| Net sales (billions of $) | 5.6 | 3.8 | 2.7 |
| Net profit (billions of $) | 0.47 | 0.38 | 0.11 |
| Number of employees | 22 000 | | |

### Cisco Systems

| Fiscal year through | July 2004 | July 2003 | July 2002 |
|---|---|---|---|
| Net sales (billions of $) | 22.0 | 18.9 | 18.9 |
| Net income (billions of $) | 4.4 | 3.6 | 1.9 |
| Number of employees | 35 000 | | |

### 3Com

| Fiscal year through | May 2004 | May 2003 | May 2002 |
|---|---|---|---|
| Net sales (billions of $) | 0.699 | 0.933 | 1.259 |
| Net income (loss) (billions of $) | (0.349) | (0.284) | (0.596) |

### Alcatel

| Calendar year | 2003 | 2002 | 2001 |
|---|---|---|---|
| Net sales (billions of $) | 9.4 | 12.4 | 19.1 |
| Net income (loss) (billions of $) | (1.5) | (3.6) | (3.7) |

### Juniper Networks

| Calendar year | 2003 | 2002 | 2001 |
|---|---|---|---|
| Total sales (billions of $) | 0.701 | 0.547 | 0.887 |
| Net income (loss) (billions of $) | 0.039 | (0.120) | (0.013) |

### Motorola

| Calendar year | 2003 | 2002 | 2001 |
|---|---|---|---|
| Net sales (billions of $) | 27.1 | 27.3 | 30.0 |
| Net profit (loss) (billions of $) | 0.9 | (2.5) | (3.9) |

### Nokia

| Calendar year | 2003 | 2002 | 2001 |
|---|---|---|---|
| Net sales (billions of $) | 22.1 | 22.6 | 23.5 |
| Net profit (billions of $) | 2.7 | 2.5 | 1.7 |

Note: For Nokia and Alcatel, Euros were converted into U.S. dollars at the rate of €1.33 = US$1, as per the U.S. Federal Reserve Bank exchange rate on December 21, 2004.

**Source:** D. Normile, 2005, Chinese Telecom Companies Come Calling, *Electronic Business,* 31(2): 38–43.

US$1.5 billion in an initial public offering on the back of its strong growth and high penetration in international telecommunications markets. Huawei stated that it had no intention to go public before 2008 because it had no urgent need for funds. The vice president of Huawei, however, expressed that the company was preparing to save more capital to look for good opportunities for overseas mergers and acquisitions in order to enhance its technical strength. The company's position was that it would seek acquisitions overseas to compete with its international rivals such as Nokia, Motorola, Alcatel, and NEC. Buying 3Com was always a possibility as the U.S. company continued to stumble in its global sales.

The general feeling was that Chinese vendors were mostly using Western engineering and not inventing much of their own. As with earlier technology migration from the United States to the Far East in the consumer electronics and personal computer businesses, Asian manufacturers were turning complex and high-profit products into standard commodities. Some had observed that Huawei's products appeared to be derived from those of other companies, either through patent-mining or reverse engineering. To become a serious global contender, Huawei would have to move beyond low-cost versions of Western gear. Its low-cost strategy seemed increasingly untenable because its reliance on local service partners in foreign markets would ultimately raise its cost of running the business. At the same time, foreign companies were increasing their manufacturing base and R&D facilities in China and would soon become equally competitive in terms of pricing.

Last but not least, Huawei's connection to the Chinese army continued to cast a shadow around Huawei's image for some overseas customers. A number of U.S. distributors remained skeptical about the potential military influence the company was subject to and were wary of any implication to international business relationships. Zhengfei's military background and the company's recent sales to Iraq had created suspicion in the eyes of the Western world. In 2005, Huawei lost its bid to acquire British telecom equipment provider Marconi to the world giant Ericsson largely because of Huawei's baffling connection with the Chinese military. Although the company was trying to improve its corporate image and increase transparency, questions of trust and reputation could undermine its efforts to win contracts with governments and international enterprises in the long run. Facing so many thorny challenges, Huawei's management had to draft a sustainable global strategy.

## NOTES

1. C. Walton, 2005, Huawei moves in on Cisco, MicroScope, September 5.
2. R. McGregor, 2005, Huawei reaches foreign sales milestone, Financial Times, London, November 30.
3. M. Zeng & P. Williamson, 2003, The hidden dragons, Harvard Business Review, October.
4. D. Normille, 2005, Chinese telecom companies come calling, Electronic Business, 31(2): 38–42.
5. K. Nissen, 2005, New world telecom: A survival guide for global equipment suppliers, Business Communications Review, September.
6. F.W. McFarlan, G. Chen, & D. Kiron, 2001, Cisco China, Harvard Business School Case, Harvard Business School.
7. P. Fan, 2004, Catching up through developing innovation capability: Evidence from China's telecom-equipment industry, Department of Urban Studies and Planning, MIT, November 11.
8. Annual Report, China's post and telecommunications industry 2005, Ministry of Information Industry, China.
9. 2005, China to have over 440 Million mobile phone users by end of next year, http://www.today.com.
10. A. Harney, 2005, The challenger from China: Why Huawei is making the telecoms world take notice, Financial Times, London, January 11.
11. A. Farhoomand, Z. Tao, Y. Jiang, & T. X. Liu, 2005, China's telecommunications industry in 2004, Asia case research center case, University of Hong Kong.
12. F. W, McFarlan, G. Chen, & D. Kiron, 2001, op. cit.
13. Ibid.
14. When the first characters of the four companies were arranged in reverse order (Ju-Great Dragon, Da-DTT, Zhong-ZTT, Hua-Huawei), the phrase "Great China" was created.
15. Information in this section was extracted from the following Harvard Business School cases: F. W., McFarlan, G. Chen, & D. Kiron, 2001, Cisco China, Harvard Business School Case; and G. Jones, & D. Kiron, 2005, Cisco goes to China: Routing an emerging economy, Harvard Business School Case.
16. 2006, China's telecommunications market 2005, CRC-Pinnacle Consulting Co. Ltd., http://www.buyusainfo.net/docs/x_8130085.pdf November 13.
17. G. Long, 2005, Power Shift, Telecom Asia, March.
18. China's "exchanging market for technology" policy encouraged foreign companies with the desired technological expertise to develop business in China, on the condition that they would share certain technical knowledge with their Chinese counterparts.
19. P. Fan, 2004, Catching up through developing innovation capability: Evidence from China's telecom-equipment in-

dustry, Department of Urban Studies and Planning, MIT, November 11.

20. US$1 = RMB 8.07 on December 29, 2005.

21. A. Smith-Gillespie, 2001, Building China's high-tech telecom equipment industry: A study of strategies in technology acquisition for competitive advantage, Masters Thesis, MIT.

22. P. Fan, 2004, Catching up through developing innovation capability: Evidence from China's telecom-equipment industry, Department of Urban Studies and Planning, MIT, November 11.

23. R. Tang, 2004, Hungry like a wolf, *The Standard*, September 24.

24. US$1 = RMB 8.07 on December 29, 2005.

25. R. Tang, Hungry like a wolf.

26. Refers to networks built with Huawei equipment in China, as noted by J. Hu, the company's vice president, corporate branding and communications.

27. J. Chen, 2005, Giant rises in the east, *National Post*, June 10.

28. C. Wu, 2004, Huawei reveals its difficult journey to globalization, http://tech.sina.com.cn/it/t/2004-08-06/0751399261/shtml.

29. 2003, A New Global technology player, *Exchange*, March 14.

30. C. Rhoads & R. Buckman, 2005, Trial and error: A Chinese telecom powerhouse stumbles on road to the U.S., *Wall Street Journal*, July 28.

31. A. Harney, 2005, The challenger from China: Why Huawei is making the telecoms world take notice, *Financial Times*, London, January 11.

32. A. Farhoomand, Z. Tao, Y. Jiang, & T. X. Liu, 2005, China's telecommunications industry in 2004, Asia case research centre case, University of Hong Kong.

33. 2003, A new global technology player, *Exchange*, March 14.

34. 2005, Business: See Huawei run, *The Economist*, March 5.

35. J. Chen, 2005, Giant rises in the east, *National Post*, June 10.

36. R. Flannery, 2004, An air of mystery, *Forbes* Online, http://www.forbes.com/business/global/2004/1129/030.html.

37. 2005, Business: See Huawei run, *The Economist*, March 5.

38. D. Normile, 2005, Chinese telecom companies come calling, *Electronic Business*, 31(2): 38–43.

39. 2005, Business: See Huawei run, *The Economist*, March 5.

# INTEGRATIVE CASE 8

# ING DIRECT: REBEL IN THE BANKING INDUSTRY

## Dr. Kurt Verweire, Dr. Lutgart A. A. Van den Berghe

*Vlerick Leuven Gent Management School*

*ING DIRECT USA is built on the foundation of being unconventional. We aren't like other banks. We've not only developed a unique business model, but the way we look at the business is different than how our competitors look at it. Our purpose is to be a servant of the average person. Rather than getting people to spend more – which is what most banks do – our approach is to get Americans to save more – to return to the values of thrift, self-reliance, and building a nest egg.*

*ING DIRECT was born in an age of broken promises. The last thing America needed was another bank, but that didn't mean America didn't need us. ING DIRECT's mission is to make it easy to save by offering the same great values to all Americans.*

> – Arkadi Kuhlmann, President and CEO, ING
> DIRECT (United States and Canada)

Many organizations have tried to enter the banking industry with innovative business models. But incumbents have always been able to defend their markets successfully. Today, ING DIRECT is changing the odds. Arkadi Kuhlmann, founder of ING DIRECT, is clear about his goals: "There's no such thing as an industry that can't be reenergized!"

Customers welcomed the company with open arms. In just five years, ING DIRECT has become the largest Internet-based bank – passing E*TRADE Bank – in the United States, and one of the 30 largest banks of any sort in the country. The company adds an astonishing 100,000 customers and $1 billion in deposits every month, and in 2005 (its fifth year of operations)

generated a profit of $360 million. And above all, 90 percent of the ING DIRECT customers believe it provides a much better service than the competitors.

## Profile of the ING group

ING DIRECT is one of the six business lines of ING Group, a major international financial services group. ING Group is active in more than 50 countries and is often cited as the example of an integrated financial services provider, offering a wide array of insurance, banking, and asset management services to a broad customer base: individuals, families, small businesses, large corporations, and institutions and governments.

ING Group is a financial conglomerate founded in 1991 by the merger between Nationale-Nederlanden, the Netherlands' largest insurance company, and NMB Postbank Group, one of the largest banking groups in the Netherlands. NMB Postbank Group itself was the result of a merger between the very entrepreneurial NMB Banking Group and the Postbank. Postbank had been split off from the Dutch Post Office and was privatized. Many people within ING believe that Postbank has been the true inspiration for ING DIRECT.

The merger between Nationale-Nederlanden and NMB Postbank Group created the first bancassurer in the Netherlands. Since 1991, ING has developed from a Dutch financial institution with some international businesses to a multinational with Dutch roots. It acquired banks and insurance companies in the United Kingdom (Barings Bank, 1995), Belgium (Bank Brussels

---

Lambert, 1998), Germany (BHF-Bank, 1999), United States (Equitable of Iowa, 1997; ReliaStar, 2000; Aetna Financial Services, 2000), Canada (Wellington, 1995; Canadian Group Underwriters, 1998; Allianz of Canada, 2004), and other countries. Some of these financial institutions were sold later, such as parts of Barings and BHF-Bank. As such, ING Group has become one of the 15 largest financial institutions worldwide and top-10 in Europe (in market capitalization). Exhibit 1 provides an overview of the 20 largest financial institutions, measured by market capitalization.

ING also used greenfields to grow the business. Greenfields were set up in the emerging markets, where ING leveraged the bancassurance concept it continued to refine in its home markets. ING Group also set up other initiatives to fuel the group's revenue and profit growth. It created a new international retail/direct banking division, which was composed of a team of Postbank's best marketing and IT people. Hans Verkoren, CEO of Postbank, became the head of this new division. This new venture was to explore to what extent Postbank's strategy could be expanded outside its Dutch home market. Postbank operated in a "branchless" manner for many years, offering simple checking accounts, savings, mortgages, consumer loans, and investment products.

This new division operated autonomously from the rest of the company. The parent company gave the new organization the necessary freedom to experiment. After detailed marketing research, the team introduced to

Canada ING's first foreign direct banking experiment in 1996.

ING chose Canada because it had no presence there, and the market was dominated by a small number of players. ING agreed it was important for this new experiment to survive or fail on its own. It created optimal conditions for success by providing it with adequate financial means and a brand new management team, lead by Arkadi Kuhlmann.

# A growing success story in the banking industry

Arkadi Kuhlmann, a Harley-riding painter and poet, was a professor of International Finance and Investment Banking at the American Graduate School of International Management (Thunderbird) in Phoenix, Arizona. He also served as president of North American Trust, CEO of Deak International Incorporated, and held various executive positions at the Royal Bank of Canada. When Hans Verkoren asked him in 1996 whether he was interested to start up a new foreign bank in Canada, he accepted the challenge.

Arkadi had noticed that few foreign banks had successfully entered the North American banking industry and had built a sustainable competitive position in that market. But he realized that those incumbents were not invincible.

**EXHIBIT 1**   20 Largest financial institutions worldwide

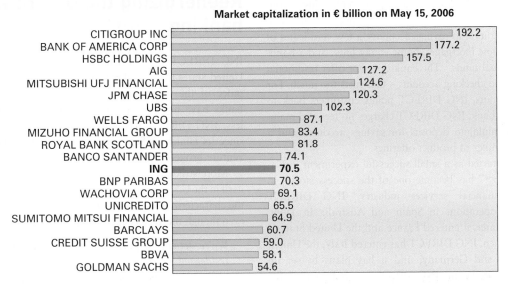

Market capitalization in € billion on May 15, 2006

|  |  |
| --- | --- |
| CITIGROUP INC | 192.2 |
| BANK OF AMERICA CORP | 177.2 |
| HSBC HOLDINGS | 157.5 |
| AIG | 127.2 |
| MITSUBISHI UFJ FINANCIAL | 124.6 |
| JPM CHASE | 120.3 |
| UBS | 102.3 |
| WELLS FARGO | 87.1 |
| MIZUHO FINANCIAL GROUP | 83.4 |
| ROYAL BANK SCOTLAND | 81.8 |
| BANCO SANTANDER | 74.1 |
| **ING** | **70.5** |
| BNP PARIBAS | 70.3 |
| WACHOVIA CORP | 69.1 |
| UNICREDITO | 65.5 |
| SUMITOMO MITSUI FINANCIAL | 64.9 |
| BARCLAYS | 60.7 |
| CREDIT SUISSE GROUP | 59.0 |
| BBVA | 58.1 |
| GOLDMAN SACHS | 54.6 |

**Source:** http://www.bloomberg.com

*Traditional banks are stuck. They have high fixed costs and use technology in an inefficient way. They have rigid distribution systems. And they charge too high prices. The customer always loses. When we came in, we said: "How can we do something different?" We looked at other industries and copied some ideas from successful players in the retail and airline industry. It is true that we actually haven't defined something new. In the context of Southwest Airlines or Wal-Mart, there are similarities. For decades, Southwest Airlines has defied the industry's standard approaches to economics and customer service, and has achieved good results. And we are on our way to do the same in the banking industry. Most companies, especially in our industry, are truly boring. If you do things the way everybody else does, why do you think you're going to be any better?*

ING DIRECT differentiates itself from traditional banks in many ways. But in essence, its differentiation lies in being direct.

*Our biggest advantage in standing out in the financial service market from all other players is that we are direct. Anyway we can emphasize that we are direct, thereby cutting out the middleman, is a way of saving money. So being a retail business, being simple, focused and direct adds up to good value. This is a retail trend that consumers know and one we should emphasize in everything we do.*

ING DIRECT is a direct-to-the-customer operation, an Internet-based savings bank, although customers can also bank by mail or telephone.

The bank operates no branches, no ATMs, just a couple of cafés in big cities where it sells coffee and mountain bikes in addition to savings accounts, a few certificates of deposit, home mortgages, home equity lines, and a handful of mutual funds.[1] The bank does not offer traditional paper-based checking accounts – that costs too much. For these accounts, ING DIRECT points customers back to their local bank. ING DIRECT charges no fees and maintains no minimum deposits for savings accounts and a limited number of product offerings.

What started as a small successful experiment in Canada in 1997 has become one of the success stories in today's financial services industry. ING DIRECT launched operations in Spain and Australia in 1999. One year later, it entered France and the United States.

Since then, ING DIRECT has entered Italy, the United Kingdom, and Germany, and it has plans to set up operations in Japan. ING DIRECT globally ended the

**EXHIBIT 2** ING DIRECT's clients and funds base

| | 2005 Profit (in € millions) | Deposits (in € millions) | Customers |
|---|---|---|---|
| Canada | 69.4 | 12,579 | 1,360,588 |
| Spain | 51.0 | 13,726 | 1,341,759 |
| Australia | 73.8 | 10,757 | 1,282,459 |
| France | 23.9 | 11,389 | 555,922 |
| USA | 162.9 | 39,031 | 3,785,927 |
| Italy | 29.0 | 13,426 | 699,603 |
| Germany | 242.1 | 57,654 | 5,488,865 |
| UK | (27.7) | 33,704 | 1,038,650 |
| Austria | (15.6) | 2,475 | 210,808 |
| Total ING DIRECT | 612.3 | 194,741 | 15,764,581 |

**Source:** ING DIRECT, http://www.ingdirect.com

first quarter of 2006 with €194 billion in deposits and 15,7 million customers (see Exhibit 2). In 2005, ING DIRECT's profits constituted 7 percent of ING's total profits. Exhibit 3 shows ING DIRECT's global profit progression from its creation to 2005.

# Reenergizing the U.S. retail banking industry

ING DIRECT has attracted a lot of attention in the United States for several reasons. Despite the wide acceptance of the Internet in American households, online banks have not been particularly successful. Nevertheless, ING DIRECT has experienced a meteoric growth since its launch in September 2000. What is more, the venture broke-even after only two years.

More striking is the way that ING DIRECT positions itself in the U.S. banking industry. Arkadi Kuhlmann rejects the characterization of ING DIRECT as an Internet bank, even though the Web is its primary customer channel.

*We're actually a pure savings bank, focusing on residential mortgages and savings accounts. You can't get any more old-fashioned than that.*

**EXHIBIT 3** ING DIRECT's global profit progression (in € millions)

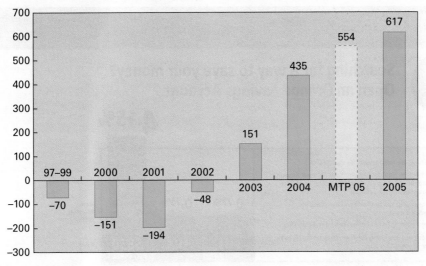

**Source:** ING DIRECT, http://www.ingdirect.com.

In all of its communication, ING DIRECT points out that it is a federally chartered bank and that its savings are FDIC insured in order to guarantee credibility with its customers.[2] But that is where the comparison with typical retail banks stops. In fact, there is nothing typical about ING DIRECT.

## ING DIRECT's product offering and value proposition

In a typical bank, first and foremost, the focus is on payments services. Once you get the payment services – such as checking, face-to-face teller services, and ATMs (automatic teller machines) – you're "owned" by the bank. But Arkadi Kuhlmann's strategy is different. The last thing he wants is to hold the traditional demand deposit accounts (i.e., checking account). These accounts typically have a large number of transactions per month and require a physical branch and a great deal of internal labor to process them. All this activity is too costly. Rather ING DIRECT wants to be "your other bank," offering a simple, high-return savings account, called the Orange Savings Account – ING's theme colour is orange. Customers are encouraged to shift money back and forth between their ING DIRECT savings account and their checking accounts with their existing bank. The account generates one of the highest rates in the market; sometimes the rate is four times higher than the industry average (see Exhibit 4). ING DIRECT sells its products

with the simple slogan: "Great rates, no fees, no minimums."

ING DIRECT also offers a limited number of mutual funds. And the bulk of the assets of the bank consists of simple residential mortgages and a small percentage of home equity lines of credit and customer loans. Nearly 90 percent of the loan portfolio consists of mortgages. All products have low fees and few requirements.

But what's so unique about high rates? Arkadi Kuhlmann comments:

*Nothing. ... What is unique is that we offer consistently great rates and at the same time a high quality service. The key to deliver high quality service is simplicity: no tricks, no catches. Customers must immediately understand ING DIRECT products. Educating people about financial products is very expensive.*

Although some banking professionals consider mortgages a difficult product to standardize and to sell via the Internet, Arkadi Kuhlmann disagrees:

*You can turn mortgages into simple products too. But it requires that you reengineer the product and the processes behind it. And to some extent, you need to reengineer the customer as well.*

And that strategy did not only attract many new customers, but also allowed the company to retain most of them.

Savings accounts can be set up in five minutes online. Mortgages take seven minutes to close (with all customer documentation available), as is demonstrated in

**EXHIBIT 4** "Great rates, no fees, no minimums"

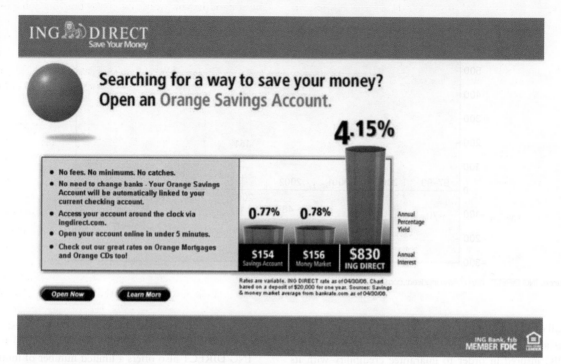

**Source:** ING DIRECT Web site, May 2006, http://www.ingdirect.com.

**EXHIBIT 5** Online banking: it's as easy as …

**Source:** Picture taken at ING DIRECT Café (New York), May 2006.

Exhibit 5. The company tries to avoid customer contact over the phone. The Web site plays a crucial role in informing customers how to deal with the bank. ING DIRECT makes opening a savings account and transferring money extremely simple and straightforward. On the Web site, it posts: "It's that simple to earn more!" For the people who prefer human contact, ING DIRECT's U.S. operations have more than 500 call center associates in three call centers. Those associates are trained to provide fast response and prompt service to the customers. The company strives to get 80 percent of the calls answered in 20 seconds. As a matter of fact, employees have their bonuses tied to achieving this goal. In order to reach that goal, employees receive extensive training – about 20 days for five products (which is a lot compared to traditional banks). Overall, the brand strategy of ING DIRECT is best described by the acronym GRASP, "Great deals, Responsive, Accessible, Simple and easy, and Passionate."

## The target customers

The first order of business for ING DIRECT is to introduce products that make it easy and financially rewarding for customers to save more. But part of the strategy is choosing the products it won't offer and the customers it won't serve. Unlike its traditional competitors, the company is not interested in rich Americans (unless they do what it wants them to do). "We want to *serve* the average American" as long as he/she behaves in the way ING DIRECT wants. In 2004, the company "fired" more than 3,500 customers who didn't play by the bank rules. Those customers relied too much on the call centers, or asked for too many exceptions from the standard operating procedures.

*People should not come and explain their financial problems. We sell products and commodities, not solutions.*

# Communicating the message

So far ING DIRECT USA has managed to communicate well the message about its rules and target customers. In five years, the bank has attracted more than 3.5 million customers. This growth can partially be explained by the huge efforts the company undertook to build the ING DIRECT brand: One third of its budget is allocated to marketing programs. Many customers are attracted by the combination of rates and a hip brand. ING DIRECT's marketing campaigns project a differentiated brand and "unbankness." They have a simple, clear message, and feature the bright colour orange, capturing

customers' attention by communicating in a humorous, "anti-establishment" tone. Exhibit 6 presents some outdoor advertising ING DIRECT used in 2006. Some of those campaigns were locally adapted to the target markets (see Exhibit 7). (Exhibit 8 presents some marketing campaigns of ING DIRECT in other countries.) The purpose of the guerrilla marketing tactics is clear, according to Arkadi Kuhlmann:

*People are sleeping. You have to shock people a little bit to get them to think differently about how they manage their money. So we wake them up with one of our marketing campaigns. They switch their money and go back to sleep.*

ING DIRECT does not restrict itself to the more traditional marketing campaigns. The bank continuously organizes innovative promotion campaigns to attract new customers. The company's "Save your money at the movies" campaign attracted many spectators and publicity in the press. In Baltimore and Washington, D.C., ING DIRECT surprised more than 8,000 people with a free movie at two participating Regal Cinemas. In a similar way, it offered free gas in Baltimore to 1,000 drivers at three

**EXHIBIT 6**   Outdoor advertising from ING DIRECT USA

**Source:** ING DIRECT, http://www.ing.com.

**EXHIBIT 7** Local marketing campaigns, ING DIRECT USA

### Washington D.C.

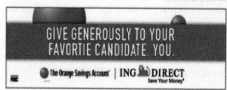

### New York

### Phoenix & Philadelphia

**Source:** ING DIRECT, http://www.ing.com.

selected Shell stations, and asked them to put that money into an Orange Savings Account. By the end of the three-hour promotion campaign cars lined up for more than three kilometres. ING Direct also let commuters ride the Boston "T" lines for free one morning, while ING representatives danced around in orange Paul Revere costumes. Those kinds of events certainly do wake people up.

Another uncommon feature of the marketing strategy is ING DIRECT's cafés. The cafés, each located in a big city of the targeted countries – such as New York, Washington, Philadelphia, Los Angeles – are not substitutes for branches. Rather they introduce the customers to the ING DIRECT brand. When ING DIRECT started its marketing and operations in Canada, early prospects were somewhat suspicious about the new brand. So they began visiting the company's call center in Toronto to check out the new bank to verify its physical existence. The employees from ING DIRECT Canada offered those prospectors a cup of coffee in the coffee corner of the call center. That is how the idea emerged. It took Arkadi Kuhlmann some time to convince the managers at ING in Amsterdam to set up "coffee shops,"[3] but now the cafés are a typical element of ING DIRECT's marketing strategy. Pictures of the ING DIRECT cafés are shown in Exhibit 9.

The cafés sustain ING DIRECT's atypical bank image, and they offer the customers a place to go to speak with an ING DIRECT café member, each a trained banker, and experience the simplicity the brand denotes. While serving coffee, the café staff members – called sales associates – can discuss financial products or help check information on one of the online terminals located on the premises. Consistent with the brand, the coffee is much less expensive than similar coffee at Starbucks, and Internet usage at the cafés is free.

*We believe saving money should be as simple as getting a cup of coffee. So we invite you to come in and experience just how refreshing it is to sip a latte, surf the Internet for free, and talk to us about how we can help Save Your Money.*

## Managing a rebellious organization

Obviously, the cafés have helped to build the brand. But it requires more than a handful of cafés to achieve the revenue and profit figures ING DIRECT has achieved

**EXHIBIT 8** Marketing campaigns, ING DIRECT in countries outside of the United States

**Source:** ING DIRECT, http://www.ing.com.

so far. Behind that rebellious image is a well-oiled machine, designed to deal with high-volume, low-margin commodity products. Exhibit 10 shows the key components of the company's strategy execution. Although significant attention is paid to understand demand and increase revenues, the execution challenge also involves cost control and efficiency improvement. Even though most retail banks in the United States operate at a margin spread of 250 basis points (2.50 percentage points), ING DIRECT operates on a spread of 175 basis points. ING DIRECT is able to operate at lower costs by managing both the "front and back" offices.

# Managing the front and back office

A big part of its lower cost structure stems from the things that it doesn't offer, and where it doesn't have to invest. The company does not invest in an ATM network or in traditional branches. It encourages customers to open accounts online or by using an interactive voice response (IVR) system. Online servicing of accounts and mortgage applications cuts down on costs. The company's acquisition costs are estimated to be lower than

**EXHIBIT 9**   Pictures of ING DIRECT Cafés in New York, Los Angeles, Philadelphia, and Wilmington

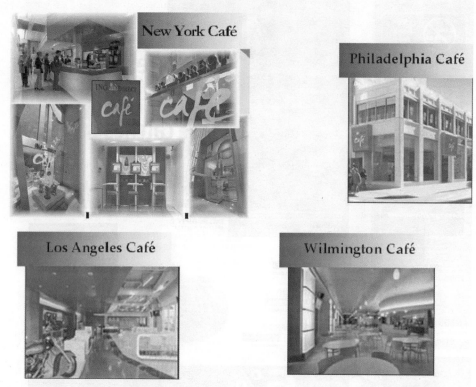

**Source:** ING DIRECT, http://www.ing.com.

**EXHIBIT 10**   Strategy execution at ING DIRECT

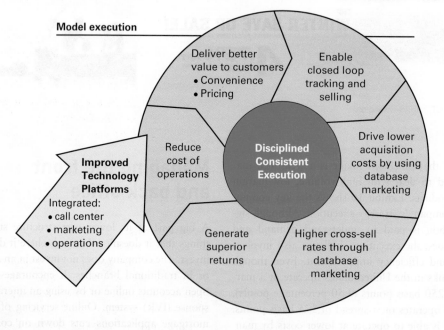

**Source:** ING Group, http://www.ing.com.

$100. According to Jim Kelly, chief marketing officer for ING DIRECT: "It is not unusual for a bank to have customer acquisition costs of about $300–400."[4] Similarly, maintenance costs are kept low as well. Says Arkadi Kuhlmann:

> If you don't have any activity in a month, we're not sending you a statement. Savings account customers who insist on a paper statement should go back to Chase.

The company also communicates to its customers that a high number of calls to the call center will lead to higher fees or lower interest rates. So customers should understand why ING DIRECT discourages telephone calls to (expensive) operators at the call center. To further discourage the use of these operators, customers who call frequently are put at the end of the operator's queue.

All of these aspects require that ING DIRECT manages its processes in a rigorous way. Processes are documented, and a large number of guidelines and procedures exist for the core processes within the organization. The company is constantly looking to simplify financial products and financial transactions, and uses tools such as Lean Six Sigma to achieve the efficiency of the manufacturing industry. In 2004, ING DIRECT Canada won a Canadian Information Productivity Award of Excellence for its Mortgage Application Processing Solution (MAPS). This solution enabled ING DIRECT to simplify the process of obtaining a mortgage dramatically. And this new solution is also leveraged in the other ING DIRECT entities.

The sharing of best practices and materials is common within the ING DIRECT business units. For example, ING DIRECT shares marketing campaigns across all of the countries in which it has operations and reuses marketing concepts and graphic designs.

## Information technology

ING DIRECT benefited from the absence of "legacy" information technology systems. ING DIRECT started from scratch, which helped the company significantly to operate with a higher performing IT architecture at a lower cost. The challenge was to develop a flexible IT architecture providing brand uniformity across borders, but allowing for adaptation to local banking regulations.

ING DIRECT buys the IT hardware centrally, exploiting its buying power, and then makes it available to the various country organizations. For software, the company's strategy is to "re-use (from sister companies) before buy, and buy before build." This approach saves

an enormous amount of money, and at the same time helps to insure a high level of service and ease in accommodating growing numbers of accounts. A central IT Group develops and maintains the IT policies and standards across the company, and works with the various countries to update and improve the systems.

ING DIRECT also strives to have its different departments in close contact with each other. The process flow is specified for the whole organization and takes into account all processes from the various departments simultaneously. Streamlining processes is a key element in ING DIRECT's business architecture, and business process orientation is a necessary element, says Arkadi Kuhlmann.

> We put our marketing and IT departments in one area. If your core competencies are marketing and IT, you really have to do both of them together.

## Product development

Product development is also done in close coordination with marketing and IT. To develop and introduce a new product, a country unit would first develop a business plan that includes forecasts of demand and marketing expenditures. The plan also evaluates the operational, financial, and legal risks associated with the launch of the product. And it specifies clearly what IT and operational requirements are necessary to support the product. The hurdles for a new product are high. Brunon Bartkiewicz (former manager at ING DIRECT, now heading ING's banking operations in Poland) explains:[5]

> Every new product reduces our simplicity, increases our risk and defocuses our people. A person who is working on marketing seven products cannot know all the details, all the figures, all the logic that a person focused on one product does. In the end, the whole game is efficiency: efficiency in marketing, in operations, and in systems.

## Performance measurement

Another important element of ING DIRECT's business model is the obsession for measuring how customers react to marketing campaigns and online advertising. But ING DIRECT's performance measurement doesn't stop at the marketing department. The company's operations centers compete against each other for recognition and monthly bonuses based on their ability to meet sales and service goals. Everybody in ING DIRECT measures and is measured. Some performance measures are posted daily on an intranet site, accessible to everyone within the company. The performance measures are continuously analyzed and are the input for action plans, allowing new product and process initiatives.

All operational performance measures have a direct impact on the company's five high-level targets. These targets are: (1) total profit, (2) nonmarketing expenses/ending assets, (3) net-retail funds entrusted (on balance sheet) growth, (4) net mortgage growth, and (5) call-center service level. Efficiency and cost effectiveness are monitored carefully. Exhibit 11 presents the evolution of the operational costs of ING DIRECT (all countries) from 1999 to March 2006. There we can see that the expense-to-assets ratio (excluding marketing expenses) for ING DIRECT (all countries) decreased from 96 basis points in 2001 to 40 basis points in 2006. An average branch bank has an expense-to-asset ratio of about 250 basis points. In a similar way, total assets per employee for ING DIRECT are $48 million, whereas traditional branch-based banks have an average of $5–$6 million per employee.

Those figures are impressive. But equally impressive is how ING DIRECT has "structured" its measurement processes. ING DIRECT used Microsoft Excel spreadsheets to create annual reports summarizing the company's performance until the company's fast growth necessitated a more structured approach toward measuring company performance. In 2004, the company hired a consultant who helped it set up a performance measurement system, generating enterprise-wide, relevant management information that steers the company's future growth. The powerful reporting and analysis tools help identify further cost-saving opportunities and gain in-depth visibility into the key performance metrics. In addition, the performance measurement system allows ING DIRECT to measure the effectiveness of marketing campaigns, to track market and risk exposure, and to gain a better understanding of its new and existing customer base. Arkadi Kuhlmann agrees that ING DIRECT has been getting more efficient with customer acquisition and with lowering customer acquisition costs due to the introduction of the new performance measurement system.

## Leadership, people, and culture

What really sets ING DIRECT apart from its competitors is its people. You can't be a rebel if you have all traditional bankers in your organization. That is why ING DIRECT tries to hire people who do not come from the big banks. Only for functions such as risk management, treasury, or asset-liability management does the bank hire employees with a banking background. Of course, ING DIRECT can benefit from ING's expertise in these technical matters. CEO Arkadi Kuhlmann himself is an experienced banker with a deep knowledge of all core functions within the bank. But he profiles himself as the outsider – even the bad guy – of the industry: "When the rest of the banking industry decides to zig, I zag," he says. And he ensures that the entire organization zags with him.

Arkadi Kuhlmann truly is a visionary and inspiring leader. You won't hear Arkadi talk a lot about financial metrics. Arkadi Kuhlmann is out for a more inspiring mission and vision.

*We are leading the Americans back to saving. One way or another, most financial companies are telling you to spend more. That's not what we want.*

**EXHIBIT 11** Evolution of ING DIRECT's operational cost base to assets (excluding marketing)

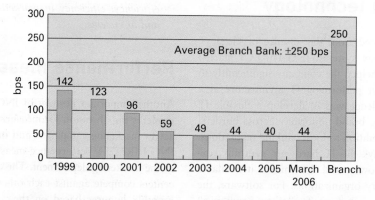

**Source:** ING Group, http://www.ing.com.

In all communication, the focus is on saving. And that's why credit cards and traditional checking accounts don't fit in the product portfolio.

Above all, it is the way that Arkadi conveys the message that makes him an inspiring leader: "You can't do meaningful things without passion and a powerful idea about what you're trying to do," he argues. In the United States, he has about 1,300 people who help him on his crusade. What is striking is that the employees of ING DIRECT are as determined as the CEO himself.

But then ING DIRECT spends a lot of time and effort to ensure that it hires people willing to do things differently from the industry, and inspires them with the same set of values that it uses to connect with its customers. The company hires people with the right attitude, who can easily be trained and introduced to a competitive selling culture. But above all, people are selected based on whether their personal values fit with the values of ING DIRECT. Rick Perles, head of human resources at ING DIRECT, comments:

> Everyone, no matter what level, starts in the new hire program. The new hire program used to be three days but we have expanded it to five, which is a big investment in our people and not something most companies do. All new hires take customer calls. During those first days, they'll hear a lot about culture and what ING stands for. Some people don't subscribe to it, but they realize it even before the five days are up.
>
> The Maiden Voyage refers to the next 90 days, where we spend another week or two facilitating technical training with our sales associates. During those first 90 days, there are things the new hire has to do before coming back for the second part of new hire training. These activities include volunteering in the community, working in one of our Cafés, and reading The Alchemist by Paulo Coelho.[6]

Values and culture are not idle concepts within ING DIRECT. Arkadi Kuhlmann is aware that the most differentiating aspect of the whole company is situated in what is called the "Orange Code." The Orange Code specifies in 13 statements what ING DIRECT is all about and what it stands for. The Orange Code brings the vision to life and provides employees with common goals. For example, one of those statements is "We will be for everyone." In the company, this vision is made concrete by removing all titles and offices. Everybody is in the bonus program, and the metrics are the same for everybody.

The reward strategy is also particular. Employees can earn substantial bonuses, based on how they perform relative to some well-specified financial, customer, and operational targets. Bonuses can be up to half of the fixed salary. Interestingly enough, the employees' fixed salary is also higher than the industry average. Although a cost leader, the company prides itself on paying at the 75th percentile or higher. Maybe that's why in a recent employee survey, 99 percent of the employees were proud to say that they are part of ING DIRECT. The survey indicated however that the employees' positive attitude is based on other facets than the reward policy. In particular, the employees consider ING DIRECT an attractive employer for the strength of its business model, and its "nonbanking" culture. ING DIRECT is a flat organization with few management layers. And employees can provide input in the many action plans that the organization sets up. Arkadi Kuhlmann describes it as follows: "I make sure that managers tell the employees what to do, but not how to do things. This is the starting point for real empowerment."

The growth of the company and the support of the ING Group is another driving force for the employees to help fulfill ING DIRECT's ambitious goals.

The Orange Code also ensures that the employees don't become too complacent. One of the statements reads as follows: "We aren't conquerors. We are pioneers. We are not here to destroy. We are here to create!"

## Challenges

The market has been created and ING DIRECT has developed an attractive position within that market. But the easy success of the online savings bank has attracted other newcomers. MetLife launched an Internet bank in late 2002 and has been heavily promoting high interest rates. And in 2006, HSBC's Internet Bank stepped in with higher rates than those of ING DIRECT. Other banks are soon to follow.

Arkadi Kuhlmann acknowledges that he will have to cope with more challenging competitors in the future. At the same time, the success of ING DIRECT has also created even higher expectations on the financial potential of its business model. A key question for the management team will be how the company can sustain its growth. What products should the company introduce? And which markets should it enter?

The company carefully analyzes what other ING DIRECT products customers will desire. In line with the general philosophy of the company, such an offer will only be made with the customers' consent. But only a small number of customers have opted into the permission marketing program. Should the company more aggressively try to cross-sell?

ING DIRECT also has to manage internal challenges. One of these challenges is how to cope with the growth the company has experienced. More customers mean increased pressure on the systems and processes. In the banking industry, size quite often implies *dis*economies of scale. Furthermore, will the company find employees who embrace its unique culture? Managing a unique culture is easier if the company is small. But it gets more challenging as the company grows.

One of the internal challenges also relates to the relationship that ING DIRECT has with its parent organization, ING Group. ING Group, known as the integrated financial services group, actively stimulates synergies between its banking, insurance, and investment entities across different countries. But Arkadi Kuhlmann has

always been able to limit ING DIRECT's participation in the Mandated Synergies program to what he calls the "low hanging fruit." ING DIRECT will help to exploit the benefits of cooperation with sister companies, but not at all costs. How long will ING DIRECT's management benefit from that exceptional status? And what will be the implications if ING DIRECT becomes more integrated and incorporated within the traditional ING businesses.

One of those synergies is to integrate brand development. ING DIRECT positions itself as the rebel in the banking industry, but at the same time it wears the brand of one of the most respected, traditional financial institutions, ING. The more that ING DIRECT contributes to ING's profit increases, the greater the dilemma.

## NOTES

1. ING DIRECT has opened cafés in Toronto, Vancouver, Sydney, Barcelona, Madrid, New York, Philadelphia, Los Angeles, Wilmington, and a couple of other cities.
2. The Federal Deposit Insurance Corporation (FDIC) is a governance institution that insures deposits in thrift institutions and commercial banks.
3. Coffee shops have a different connotation in the Netherlands than in the United States.

4. Would you like a mortgage with your mocha? *Fast Company*, March, 68, 110.
5. ING DIRECT: Your other bank, IMD Case, IMD-3-1343, 7.
6. 2005, Interview with Rick Perles by Irene Monley, *Delaware Society for Human Resource Management*, October, 2(4).

# INTEGRATIVE CASE 9

# LUFTHANSA: GOING GLOBAL, BUT HOW TO MANAGE COMPLEXITY?

Simon Tywuschik, Ulrich Steger

*International Institute for Management Development*

In the glamorous, but financially not so glorious, airline industry, Lufthansa is one of the three companies world-wide whose debt is rated as investment-grade. For most of the other companies, if they are not already in bank-ruptcy procedures or being bailed out by the govern-ment, the financial situation is simply a nightmare. Since World War II the industry has never earned its cost of capital over the business cycle. Especially after the deregulation (beginning in 1978 in the United States), which increasingly replaced the government-organized IATA cartel,[1] the situation got worse. By 2005, the cu-mulative losses of airlines since 2001 amounted to about

US$40.7 billion.[2] As mergers are still legally prevented across many country borders, the airlines' response to globalization was to form alliances (refer to Exhibit 1 for an overview).

Lufthansa is the leading, probably pivotal, member of the largest alliance, the Star Alliance. If globalization means increasing complexity (refer to Exhibits 2 and 3 for the characteristics of globalization and how it relates to complexity), alliances are even more complex to man-age than individual companies because they lack the hi-erarchical conflict resolution mechanisms that individual companies can employ.

**EXHIBIT 1** Key facts for the main airline alliances

| Key Features | Star Alliance | One World | Sky Team |
|---|---|---|---|
| Year of formation | 1997 | 1999 | 2000 |
| Members | 18 | 8 | 10 |
| Passengers (in millions) | 425 | 258 | 373 |
| Destinations | 842 | 605 | 728 |
| Fleet Size | 2800 | 2161 | 2151 |
| Market Share (Rev.) | 28.4% | 15.8% | 23.9% |
| Headquarters | Frankfurt (Ger) | Vancouver (Can) | None |
| Organization type | Formalized organization | Governing Board | Committee |

**Sources:** Web sites of the alliances, 2006; PATA, 2006. www.staralliance.com; www.oneworld.com; www.skyteam.com.

But despite their pride in mastering the turmoil of the past, some nagging questions remain for Lufthansa's management as the globalization of the airline industry moves full speed ahead.

- Is the current strategy sufficient to maintain Lufthansa's position as one of the few profitable airline companies, given the uncertainties and dynamics in the highly competitive but cyclical market?

- Has Lufthansa done enough to reduce complexity in the right places and to survive the competition, especially against the background of customer satisfaction and high value added?

- Are all employees in the corporation embraced culturally?

- Is Lufthansa prepared for the sustainability challenges – in particular global warming – which create new uncertainties?

# Surviving the changes in the airline industry

In 1992 Lufthansa – similar to other airlines – was close to bankruptcy, as the first Iraq war reduced international air traffic. It became obvious that the massive European and global expansion strategy that Lufthansa had been pursuing since the early 1980s was not economically viable (refer to Exhibits 4 and 5 for an overview of passenger sales and growth rate).

The fixed costs were too high for a cyclical business. On the other hand, strong reasons supported the belief that the "network effect" and economies of scale were leading to a global airline industry, dominated by a handful of key players (similar to the car industry).

However, the deregulation process had not gone far enough to allow for major mergers (in the United States, foreigners can own only 25 percent of an airline; in the EU non-European ownership is limited to 49 percent; in

**EXHIBIT 2** The six features of globalization

| Feature | Explanation |
|---|---|
| **(1) Eroding Borders** | Never before in history have so many boundaries in the social, political, and economic realm been weakened or abolished. However, boundaries fulfill two core functions: First, they contain effects (inside a certain entity); and second, they define the difference between "us" and others (identify creation). As a consequence of the erosion of boundaries, complexity increases (see also Exhibit 3). |
| **(2) Mobility** | The erosion of boundaries facilitates greater mobility of goods, capital, knowledge/ technology, and people. |
| **(3) Heterarchy** | Organizations across all industries are not structured hierarchically (top down), but rather heterarchically (i.e., changing dependencies and interdependent influencing channels are common). Due to the interdependency between different organizational layers, the process of power exertion has become more costly. |
| **(4) Erosion of Legitimacy** | Because it is almost impossible to clearly identify one-way cause-and-effect relationships within complex systems, responsibilities (institutional as well as personal) are difficult to establish. This process leads to the erosion of legitimacy within many organizations, in particular of democratically elected governments. Although they can no longer provide for the welfare of nation states, they remain the only addressee of the voter, which therefore leads to disenchantment with politics. |
| **(5) Variety of Options** | In complex systems no foreseeable and stable structures are evident (from a person's choice of profession to a global player's determination of corporate strategy), but the number of options can (on a personal and institutional level) also lead to information overload and failure (anxiety). |
| **(6) Asymmetry between Past and Future** | Asymmetry between past and future: The future is not a smooth continuation of the past; rather abrupt breaks are characteristic of development of the economic, social, and political spheres. |

**EXHIBIT 3** Complexity and consequences for corporations

| | Situation | Challenge | Approach |
|---|---|---|---|
| **Definition and Key Concepts** | In systems theory, complexity is defined by the number of different potential states of a system that depend on certain complexity drivers (see below for drivers). | Ashby's Law of Variety suggests that organizations can handle high external complexity only by a similar internal complexity. The internal implementation of such complexity would create problems particularly for multi-business line corporations. Hence, these corporations look for drivers that *decrease* complexity (see below). | The more open and globally spread out a system is, the greater the velocity of change. The main challenge of corporations is to manage complexity. A global company must be characterized by certain features in order to manage complexity and survive competition (see below). |
| **Key Drivers and Features** | ■ Difference and diversity of values, aims, interests, cultures, and types of behaviors.<br>■ Interdependence that provides for greater interaction.<br>■ Ambiguity of situations and of information in its meaning.<br>■ Fast flux: Through eroding borders, the number of actors and interdependencies increases. The different interests and information uncertainty increase the number and intensity of actions that influence a system. It means that adjustment processes occur continuously, which again cause interventions. | ■ A common business culture and values and one clearly formulated and focused business strategy should help to establish one clear direction.<br>■ Standardized processes decrease variations (and hence complexity) in the course of business and create more transparency.<br>■ Focus on certain activities (such as "core" competencies).<br>■ Decentralization of decision power reduces the need for coordination (and hence of interaction) and early warning systems allow for more time to adjust. | ■ Activities in several world regions provide for a certain homogeneity of demand on the one hand and advantages for corporations on the other hand, among others economies of scale.<br>■ One global strategy for the fulfillment of common aims.<br>■ Employees of different ethical and professional backgrounds.<br>■ Standardized norms and processes. |

most of Asia any acquisition of a major airline might not be illegal, but it is practically impossible). But deregulation and the erosion of the IATA cartel went far enough to allow for scores of new competitors. No-frills low-cost airlines spread from the United States to Europe and then Asia, nurtured by the abundance of used aircraft and leasing opportunities (e.g., easyJet was started with less than £5 million). Unlike the "flag carriers," with their hubs, they offered point-to-point connections on high traffic density routes. Also business class passengers were targeted with new offerings (such as Virgin

Airlines). Overcapacity and persisting government subsidies (especially in southern Europe, Asia, and Latin America) combined to create permanent price pressure: From the early 1990s, a minimum of 3 percent reduction in costs was needed every year, which was likely to continue.

Economic and political developments did not have a positive effect on the airline industry either. After recovering from the effects of the first Iraq war, air traffic was once again slowed down by the Asian financial crisis – starting in 1997 – followed by similar events in Russia

**EXHIBIT 4**  Lufthansa's passenger transportation turnover by region, 1980, 1990, and 2000

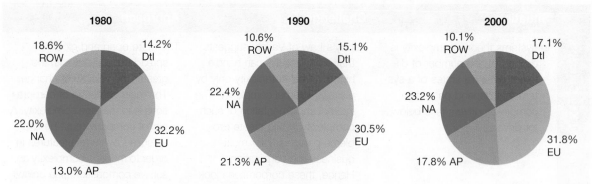

Note: Data for 1980 and 1990 also include cargo and mail services. Data for 2000 excludes CityLine.

Abbreviations: NA = North America; AP = Asia Pacific; ROW = Rest of the World; EU = Europe; Dtl = Germany

**Sources:** Lufthansa's annual reports; author's calculations.

**EXHIBIT 5**  Lufthansa's annual turnover growth rate in passenger transportation, 1981–2005

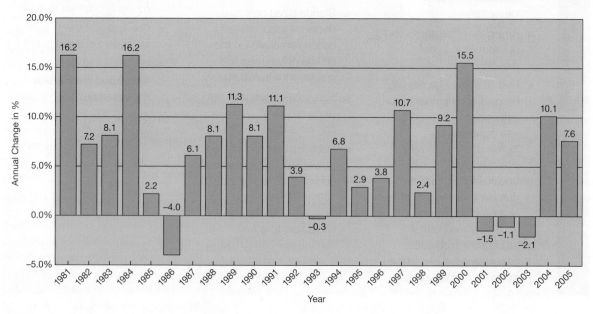

Note: From 1995, only passenger revenue is considered (excludes mail and cargo). Figures represent net sales.

**Sources:** Lufthansa's annual reports from 1981 to 2005; author's calculations.

and Latin America. However, everything the airline industry had experienced so far was dwarfed when terrorists used airplanes as flying bombs on September 11, 2001.

The succeeding "War on Terror" – especially the second Iraq war – along with spreading tensions through the Middle East and the SARS scare delivered a three-year nightmare for the industry, which was in a cyclical business downturn anyway: Worldwide air passenger volumes fell by 3.3 percent and 2.4 percent in 2001

and 2003, respectively, and remained flat in 2002.[3] Lufthansa's traffic turnover even decreased between 2001 and 2003 by 4.6 percent.[4]

Then, once passenger demand began to recover, oil prices escalated dramatically in 2005–2006. Currently, fuel costs are the second-highest cost category per seat kilometer, accounting for 26 percent of operating costs in Europe airlines (labor costs account for approximately 30 percent).[5]

Add in the issue above and the traffic jams and queues at major airports – which makes high-speed trains a more attractive alternative for journeys up to 500 kilometers – and a picture emerges. As such, the airline industry appears as a "high-growth–low-profit" industry. Everybody expects air traffic to grow – despite a highly volatile environment – but nobody expects a similar surge in profits. Because airline companies are now mostly privatized (Lufthansa since 1996, with about 40 percent held by diverse foreign owners), they have to fight for survival on their own. The bankruptcies of Swissair and Varig, for example, and the financial difficulties of Japan Airlines (JAL) indicate that the former flag carriers cannot bank on governments coming to their rescue. The fate of Pan Am – once the dominant international carrier and now defunct – is a sobering lesson for everyone.

# Lufthansa: continued challenges

Since Lufthansa's turnaround in 1992–1993, in only one year have no new cost-cutting initiatives been launched, implemented, or (after 2001) even accelerated. In fact, a certain management routine on how to implement and control such cost-cutting initiatives has even been established. Compared to 1992, the cost base has been reduced by approximately 40 percent, despite rising wages, security and airport fees and the roller coaster of fuel prices.

Lufthansa needed to ensure cash flow (especially after 2001), and it needed to reduce costs (e.g., by hiring foreign crew members). Lufthansa transformed fixed costs into variable costs (by outsourcing), and rationalized every step in the value chain, especially via electronic processes which is very tricky when it comes to interfacing with the customer.

The "art" of the endeavor was to push the cost-cutting through, without losing consensus with the employees – who, like everywhere in the industry, are highly unionized[6] – and the strong work-councils, who had several levers to derail the whole process or at least slow it down considerably. With one exception of the strike in early summer 2001 by the pilots who have a separate union and felt "disrespected," the magic worked. But employers always face the risk of a "burn out" syndrome, when everybody asks: Will this ever stop?

However, sometimes Lufthansa executives think that cost-cutting is easier, relatively speaking, than managing the Star Alliance (refer to Exhibit 6 for an overview of its

18 members), now the biggest of the global airline alliances, with 28.4 percent market share and 842 destinations in 152 countries.[7] Many think of Lufthansa as the leader and integrator, because the biggest member, United Airlines, was preoccupied for more than three years with emerging from Chapter 11 bankruptcy procedures in the United States.[8] From the beginning, Lufthansa's strategy was to drive the Star Alliance from the revenue side by keeping more passengers in the network. This idea of "seamless" travel is implemented through "code-sharing," coordinated flight schedules, common lounges, baggage handling, and so forth, leading to a higher utilization of planes and infrastructure (lower cost per unit), and sometimes also to economies of scale in purchasing and sales.

A constant balancing act is necessary between the alliance members' independence (including the right to leave) and the need for common processes, especially in IT, and quality insurance. Another constant point of debate centers on the needs and expectations of global customers. Are they the same or do they differ by culture (e.g., in terms of greeting during the boarding process)? A crisis of individual members (especially Varig and United) could endanger the whole alliance, and Lufthansa was pushed to save Air Canada from bankruptcy in 1999, but could not prevent the Australian partner Anselt from going out of service (Varig and United still flew during the bankruptcy process and received only technical aid from Lufthansa). In any case, Lufthansa management tries to avoid too much involvement in the affairs (and risks) of the other airline members and creates the perception that Lufthansa is seeking a role as a dominant force (e.g., looking for shareholdings in other airlines), a factor that contributed considerably to the downfall of SWISSair in 2001. However, when its new incarnation, SWISS, was "up for grabs" in 2005, Lufthansa violated this principle and acquired the airline to prevent it falling into the hands of arch rival British Airways and the OneWorld Alliance. And more acquisitions may be in the cards: Lufthansa maintains 10 percent of its own shares (the legal maximum) for the purpose of a "reserve."

For Lufthansa – trained in the art of consensus more than others – it seems to be easier to accept only an 80 percent workable solution, if everybody is behind it and has bought into the compromise. Nevertheless, it was a learning process over several years; many compromises ran counter to a Lufthansa culture that takes pride in engineering excellence and maintaining standards, not only in back-office processes like IT, but also with customer interfaces (e.g., Lufthansa thought that the electronic check-in should be completed in half the time than the other alliance members found acceptable for

## EXHIBIT 6  Global airline alliances and their members

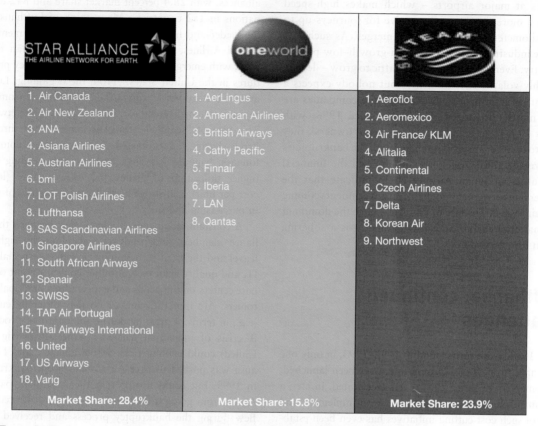

| STAR ALLIANCE THE AIRLINE NETWORK FOR EARTH. | oneworld | SKYTEAM |
| --- | --- | --- |
| 1. Air Canada | 1. AerLingus | 1. Aeroflot |
| 2. Air New Zealand | 2. American Airlines | 2. Aeromexico |
| 3. ANA | 3. British Airways | 3. Air France/ KLM |
| 4. Asiana Airlines | 4. Cathy Pacific | 4. Alitalia |
| 5. Austrian Airlines | 5. Finnair | 5. Continental |
| 6. bmi | 6. Iberia | 6. Czech Airlines |
| 7. LOT Polish Airlines | 7. LAN | 7. Delta |
| 8. Lufthansa | 8. Qantas | 8. Korean Air |
| 9. SAS Scandinavian Airlines | | 9. Northwest |
| 10. Singapore Airlines | | |
| 11. South African Airways | | |
| 12. Spanair | | |
| 13. SWISS | | |
| 14. TAP Air Portugal | | |
| 15. Thai Airways International | | |
| 16. United | | |
| 17. US Airways | | |
| 18. Varig | | |
| **Market Share: 28.4%** | **Market Share: 15.8%** | **Market Share: 23.9%** |

Note: The membership structure of the alliances and market share undergo continuous changes.

**Sources:** Web sites of alliances, 2006; PATA, 2006. www.stralliance.com; www.oneworld.com; www.skyteam.com.

their customers). Sometimes alliance initiatives run counter to the interests of Lufthansa divisions: The idea of creating a common Star Alliance IT infrastructure would rob the IT systems' divisions of most of their customers.

Despite the time-consuming negotiation and consensus-building processes in the Star Alliance management superstructure (refer to Exhibit 7) and despite the higher transaction costs, Lufthansa executives remained strong supporters of the alliance. The reason is quite simple: Because no alternatives (mostly M&As) are (legally) available, alliances are the only way to operate in a global network without increasing one's own investments in an economically unsustainable way (a lesson learned the hard way). It is estimated that for Lufthansa the net operating profit increase through the Star Alliance is about €500 million per year, which roughly corresponds to the profits for 2005. Hence, in the overall profitability equation for flag carriers, the regional business seems to fulfill a marketing activity for international routes rather than being a profit source of its own.

Although the Star Alliance is great for intercontinental and business travel, it does not provide an answer to the onslaught of the low-cost carriers. Alongside some second-tier partnerships outside the Star Alliance, Lufthansa created "Lufthansa Regional" (refer to Exhibit 8 for the organizational structure), which carries out approximately 50 percent of the company's German and European flights. Within Lufthansa Regional, Eurowings and CityLine (partially) belong to the Lufthansa Group.[9] However, the planes from the other partners are operated via "wetleasing," whereby Lufthansa leases the aircraft complete with crew and maintenance contracts. In this case the planes are integrated into Lufthansa's scheduling and the company carries the risk of the revenue side only.

Operating in a high-price competitive market, Lufthansa Regional needs a lower-cost structure than Lufthansa's core fleet. The cost savings at Lufthansa Regional come partly from the slightly lower wages, the smaller planes adjusted to the traffic density, a reduced service level, an operating base in second-tier airports, and point-to-point-service so that the time

INTEGRATIVE CASE 9: LUFTHANSA: GOING GLOBAL, BUT HOW TO MANAGE COMPLEXITY?

743

**EXHIBIT 7** Organizational structure of Star Alliance

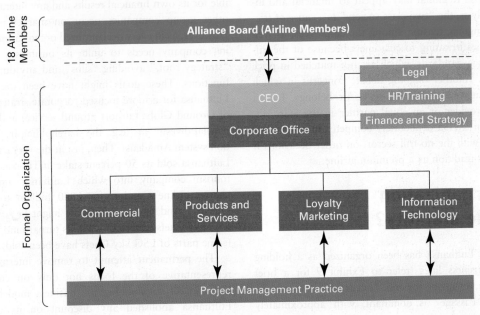

**Source:** Star Alliance, 2005. http://www.staralliance.com.

**EXHIBIT 8** Structure of Lufthansa holding and Lufthansa regional

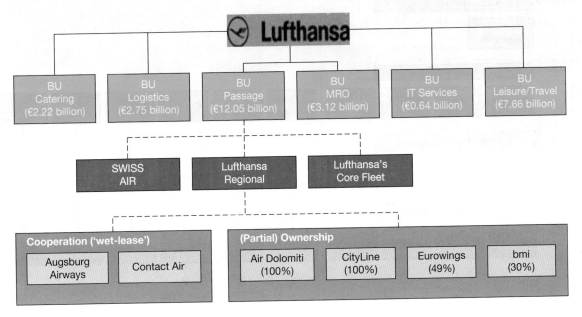

Note: Revenue figures refer to 2005.

**Source:** Company information, 2006. http://www.lufthansa.com.

in the air is greater than for "network" airplanes. On the revenue side, Lufthansa gains through the "feeder function" to intercontinental flights (otherwise passengers might go via other big hubs) and the density of the connections: Only a few attractive routes can be developed by low-cost carriers without facing competition from the outset directly with Lufthansa (and its ability to cut prices when needed, a source of continuous controversy with the antitrust authorities).

However, as compelling as the business logic for Lufthansa Regional may appear to financial and industry analysts, the "two-class society" is a cause of friction and ongoing tension among the employees, as well as sometimes irritating to customers because of the different service standards, which are not matched in price differences. Another ongoing debate concerns in which category the newly acquired SwissAir belongs. Is it a low-cost provider or an equal partner in the Star Alliance? Often SWISS deliberately competes in its marketing efforts with the no-frill sector; on other occasions it refers to its tradition as a premium airline.

## Can organization provide stability?

Since 1996 Lufthansa has been organized as a holding with six business lines (refer to Exhibit 9 for a brief description), dissolving the once "integrated" corporation. Although "Passage" is dominant, with approximately

two-thirds of the turnover, each division is fully responsible for its own financial results and any interactions with other group companies occur on market price terms. However, as in every decentralized organization, the holding company needs to unite its businesses under one "strategy roof," avoiding "silos" and any duplication of functions. These goals might have been the drivers at Lufthansa for a more focused corporate strategy, the sale of Ground Globe (airport ground service) and several financial divestments (e.g., the shareholding in the reservation system Amadeus). Then, just at the very end of 2006, Lufthansa sold its 50 percent stake in Thomas Cook, the tourism company into which Lufthansa integrated its charter airline Condor, for €800 million to Karstadt-Quelle.[10] And finally, even more might be for sale with LSG Sky Chefs (catering) when its turnaround is finalized (some parts of LSG Sky Chefs have been sold).

The permanent attempt to remove intermediaries is representative of the focus not only on cost cutting but also on streamlining the business model. In 2005 Lufthansa abolished any discount on its tickets for

**EXHIBIT 9**  Evolution of the organizational structure of Lufthansa

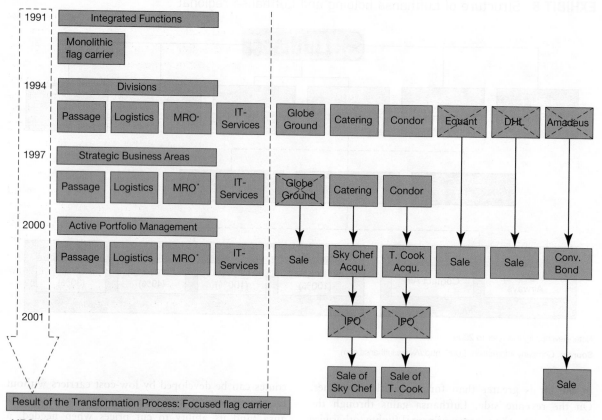

* MRO: Maintenance, repair, and overhaul

**Sources:** Company information; author's illustration, 2006.

independent travel agencies (they now have to charge their customers for issuing tickets) and promotes direct booking via the Web or call centers or controlled distribution channels (e.g., LH City Centers, a franchise travel agency chain with 540 offices in 49 countries as of 2006).

# Above all: maintaining financial discipline

Every business cycle challenges the precious investment-grade rating that Lufthansa enjoys. In the crisis from 2001 to 2004, the gearing increased from 36 percent in 2000 to 85.4 percent in 2005, despite an increase in shareholder capital.[11] As a result, financial operating goals are dominant and Lufthansa has learned to focus its cost cutting on the cash flow impact. Depreciation of airplanes is higher than British Airways for example (12 vs. 20 years) to ensure a rapid capital recovery and reduce debt service as quickly as possible. Leasing part of the fleet allows for quicker adjustment of capacity (after 2001 approximately 20 percent of plane capacity was taken out of operation; now it is building up again).

# Corporate culture in transition

Lufthansa was once known for its strong culture, based on pride in being a "Lufthanseat," the positive image of the company in Germany and its reputation for engineering excellence, underpinned by ongoing training and educational activities. Now approximately one-third of the workforce is non-German, and it has become more fragmented in its interests, perceptions, communication channels, and expectations. The pilots' strike in 2001, which put the pilots in confrontation with the ground personnel (who suffered the brunt of passenger anger), was not only about money. It was also about the pilots' feeling that they were no longer sufficiently appreciated, a lack of integration into the "normal" flow of communication and consensus building.

Management has tried to improve the situation; ongoing "town hall" meetings with members of the management board and the CEO are held, as well as an extensive written communication flow about the development of the company. Such initiatives are state-of-the-art in the industry today and Lufthansa has included them in the "leadership values" for its employees. As a result, every employee has individual targets and managers of all levels are evaluated on an annual basis (in a dialogue with his/her boss).

Continuous education and training is also high on the agenda, not only for employees but also for management. Among German-based companies, Lufthansa pioneered a "corporate university" in 1998. The "Lufthansa School of Business" is recognized worldwide as one of the best in the industry.

To increase employees' identification with the company and to help passengers "feel valued" (despite the high fuel consumption), Lufthansa is embarking on a wide range of social and environmental activities – from supporting children in need (via the "Help Alliance") to protecting endangered animals and recycling or introducing fuel efficiency initiatives (see http://konzern.lufthansa.com/en/html/ueber_uns/balance/index.html).

But Lufthansa management knows that past efforts are now being challenged by an issue of a completely new dimension – global warming. Although the airline industry claims that only 3 percent of global $CO_2$ emissions come from air traffic, the whole impact on global warming is approximately twice that factor (e.g., through $NO_x$ emissions at high altitude) and rapidly growing. Given current growth rates, the share of $CO_2$ emissions from air traffic might increase to approximately 20 percent by 2020.

Unlike many other energy sources in developed countries, fuel for airlines is not taxed – a point constantly raised in public criticism. So far the industry has avoided taxation because it would require some sort of international agreement, but the pressure is rapidly growing to price the "externalities" of air transport into travel costs. The industry is considering a kind of emission trading to avoid taxation, but even this approach would increase fuel prices considerably and may end the era of "cheap flights."

## NOTES

1.   As of 2006, IATA (International Air Transport Association) represents 261 airlines comprising 94 percent of international scheduled air traffic.

2.   IATA, 2006. The figure represents the sum of the net profits between 2001 and 2005 for all IATA member companies. These are (in US$ billion): −13.0 (2001), −11.3 (2002), −7.6 (2003), −5.6 (2004), −3.2 (2005). The estimated value for 2006 is US$ −1.7 billion.

3.   Datamonitor, Airline Report, 2005; IATA Air Transport Statistics, 2001, 2002, and 2003.

4.   Lufthansa's annual reports between 2000 and 2003. These figures represent the total passage revenue (including cargo and mail), which dropped from €12.55 billion for the year 2000 to €11.66 billion for the year 2003.

5.   IATA, 2005, 2006. In the United States and Asia, the share of labor costs in operating costs is 38 percent and 20 percent, respectively.

6.   Furthermore, in Lufthansa's case the chairman of the (Civil) Service and Transportation Union is the deputy chairman of the supervisory board due to the co-determination law.

7.   Star Alliance; PATA, November 2006. PATA data are calculated on the basis of IACO data.

8.   The formal bankruptcy procedure began on December 9, 2002, and closed on February 1, 2006.

9.   The low-cost airline Germanwings is a 100% subsidiary of Eurowings.

10.  Before this deal, KarstadtQuelle held the other 50% of Thomas Cook. Further, the deal that was announced in December 2006 makes Lufthansa a minority stakeholder in Condor.

11.  Gearing is calculated as the ratio of a company's long-term funds with fixed interest to its total capital. A high gearing is generally considered speculative.

# INTEGRATIVE CASE 10

# NESTLÉ: DIVESTING PERRIER?

Olivier Furrer, Rimy Koostra, Tom Meijer

*Radboud Universiteit Nijmegen*

*Perrier accounts for less than 5% of Nestlé Waters' sales, and less than 1% of total Nestlé food sales, so the effect on our business would be nil if we sold it. Perrier has always been loss producing – it has never contributed anything to profits as part of the Nestlé Group. So we would in fact be better off if we sold it.*

*– François-Xavier Perroud, Nestlé spokesman, October 21, 2004[1]*

In February 2006, Peter Brabeck, CEO and Chairman of Nestlé S.A., met with Carlo Donati, the new Chairman and CEO of the Nestlé Waters division. Before releasing Nestlé Waters' annual sales report for 2005, the two men wanted to discuss the long term future of the Perrier brand within the division's 75 bottled water brand portfolio (see Exhibit 8: Nestlé Waters' Brand Structure). Even if the long-standing dispute at the Perrier plant was effectively resolved in May 2005 through an agreement with the unions, the performance of the brand was still worrisome for Nestlé. The year 2005 had been marked by strong growth for Nestlé Waters.[2]

Overall sales increased by 9.3%, reaching CHF 8.8 billion (approximately € 5.7 billion). In addition, Nestlé Waters consolidated its position as the leading player in the worldwide bottled water market, gaining a market share of 18% in terms of value and recovering a leadership position from Danone in volume. With regard to its operating margin, Nestlé Waters' EBITA (Earnings Before Interest, Taxes, and Amortization of goodwill) for 2005 rose to CHF 709 million (€ 459 million), representing 8.1% of sales. Even more impressively, this performance came about in a difficult context marked by a steep rise in the price of PET (PolyEthylene Teraphthalate) resin, secondary packaging, and energy, as well as intense pressure on prices due to fierce competition in North America. Despite this unfavourable context, Nestlé Waters successfully increased its margin by 6.1% compared with 2004 – mostly by improving its operational efficiency.

**EXHIBIT 8** Nestlé waters' brand structure

| Sales | 2002 | 2003 | 2004 | 2005 | 2006[*] |
|---|---|---|---|---|---|
| **Local Brands** | 75.7% | 72.1% | 68.5% | 65.0% | 63.1% |
| **International Brands** (*Acquo Panna, San Pellegrino, Perrier, Vittei, Contrex*) | 21.8% | 25.0% | 23.6% | 23.0% | 22.4% |
| **Nestlé Brands** (*Nestlé Pure Life, Nestlé Aquarel, Vera*) | 2.5% | 2.9% | 7.9% | 12.0% | 14.5% |
| **Total Number of Brands** | 77 | 77 | 77 | 75 | 72 |

[*] Forecasts.

This case was written by Associate Professor Olivier Furrer, with the help of Rimy Koostra and Tom Meijer, Radboud Universiteit Nijmegen. It is intended to be used as the basis for class discussion rather than to illustrate either effective or ineffective handling of a management situation. The case was made possible by the co-operation of Nestlé and Nestlé Waters and from published sources.

The Nestlé brand, which is used in 35 countries worldwide and enjoys sales of more than CHF 1 billion (€ 648 million), accounts for 12% of Nestlé Waters' sales. Nestlé Pure Life and Nestlé Aquarel posted strong organic growth in 2005, confirming the Nestlé brand's ambition to become the leading worldwide bottled water brand. Nestlé Pure Life, already Nestlé Waters' leading brand in volume, entered three new markets that year: Indonesia, Nigeria, and Qatar. The brand held a solid position as number one in Pakistan, Lebanon, Canada, and Uzbekistan, as well as in the Home and Office Delivery (HOD) segment[3] in Russia. For its part, Nestlé Aquarel competed in 14 countries and posted organic growth of better than 50%. This performance confirmed the success of the price repositioning strategy implemented in Europe at the beginning of 2005.

On the international brands front, Vittel modernized its style by adopting both a new visual identity and a new design for its packaging. The new design, pretested in the French and German markets, received a unanimous welcome. Furthermore, Contrex introduced two innovative dessert varieties to its flavored water range: Lemon Meringue and Strawberry Melba. In the area of industrial developments, the two-year modernization program targeting Contrex and Vittel sites in France was continuing, with the aim of improving productivity by merging the plants to form a single production site that would make it the largest bottling site in the world. The plants could produce the two brands of natural mineral water according to format (i.e., bottle size), no longer just according to brand.

However, the performance of Perrier, one of Nestlé Waters' strongest international brands, appeared less positive – if not a value destroyer. In 2005, Perrier sales grew at less than the overall growth rate for Nestlé Waters. Its positions in the U.S. and European markets, the largest bottled water markets, continued to be strong, but its productivity remained low, it was barely making any profit, and the problematic restructuring of the Perrier production unit continued to move slower than expected.

# Nestlé S.A.

Nestlé S.A., headquartered in Vevey (Switzerland), is the biggest food and beverage company in the world. At the end of 2005, its sales of CHF 91 billion (€58.3 billion) created a net profit of CHF 8 billion (€5.13 billion).[4] Nestlé employs approximately 250,000 people worldwide and maintains factories or operations in almost every country in the world. Most Nestlé brands maintain top ranks in every segment and market in

which they operate. As a truly global firm, Nestlé's sales spread almost evenly around the globe (30.3% in Europe, 33.8% in the Americas, 17.2% Africa, Asia, and Oceania, less than 2% in Switzerland). Nestlé also is a publicly owned company with about 250,000 registered shareholders, none of whom own more than 3%. The main large shareholders are Swiss investors (36%) and U.S. investors (33%); remaining shares are divided among British (6%), German (5%), and French (3%) shareholders.

## Nestlé's history[5]

Nestlé was established in 1867 by Henri Nestlé, who developed a wheat-based formula product for the infants of mothers unable to breastfeed, *Farine Lactée Henri Nestlé*. After the stunning success of this innovative product, Nestlé sold his products in several European countries. In 1905, Nestlé merged with its largest competitor, the Anglo-Swiss Condensed Milk Company, which was active in both Europe and the United States. By adding more food activities, Nestlé grew throughout the century into Switzerland's largest company, building largely on internal growth and a steady stream of acquisitions. For example, in 1929, Nestlé bought Cailler-Peter-Kohler, the first firm to produce milk chocolate. Following a request from Brazilian coffee growers to develop a water-soluble coffee, Nescafé was launched in 1938. After World War II, Nestlé merged with Alimentana S.A., the manufacturer of Maggi, seasonings, and soups.

In 1968, Pierre Liotard-Vogt became Nestlé's CEO, marking the beginning of the most dynamic phase in Nestlé's history. The period was characterized by a strategy based on diversification in food and other sectors in the United States. Many new products were developed within the company and through national and foreign acquisitions. In 1969, Nestlé bought a 30% share in Société Générale des Eaux Minérales de Vittel, which laid the foundation for Nestlé Waters SA. A year later, it strengthened its position in the water sector by buying several German springs through acquiring Blaue Quellen A.G. and Rietenauer.

In 1981,[6] Helmut Maucher became Nestlé's new CEO and immediately started to undertake a radical change program to slash inefficiencies, revive cash flows, reorganize top management, reinvigorate Nestlé's culture of quality, emphasize the value of the Nestlé corporate brand, and refocus the firm's energies on remaining the world's leading branded food company. Maucher also divested a number of non-strategic or unprofitable businesses. During his tenure, the financial situation of Nestlé improved, and new strategic acquisitions were made.

Maucher led Nestlé on a campaign of impressive and occasionally hostile acquisitions, beginning with

Carnation in 1985 and followed by Buitoni, Rowntree, Perrier, and Alpo, among others. In pursuit of growth opportunities, Maucher extended the reach of the company beyond its core business of milk products, coffee and other soluble beverages, culinary products and confectionery to new corners of the globe and new product categories (e.g., ice cream, mineral water, pet foods). Furthermore, Maucher initiated major joint ventures with powerful partners such as Coca-Cola, General Mills, and Baxter Health. This phase of expansion also featured a more strategic use of Nestlé's corporate brand name and image. On a more selective basis, it began using the Nestlé brand name as an umbrella.

In 1997, Maucher retired as CEO and was replaced by Peter Brabeck. Brabeck focused first on improving performance and fostering internal growth. He believed that businesses could improve their positions and reduce costs by increasing the efficiency of manufacturing operations. Brabeck began his effort to improve efficiency by consolidating management and engaging in vigorous cost cutting. For example, he consolidated the management of Nestlé's factories in individual countries into regions and combined the operations of similar products into *Strategic Business Units* (SBU). He also expanded regional production to cut shipping costs. Between 1999 and 2001, he closed or sold 150 underperforming factories, for a saving of CHF 4 billion (€ 2.6 million). Subsequently, he launched three consecutive programs aimed to achieve cost savings of approximately CHF 6 billion (€ 3.6 million) by 2006: *Target 2004+* was designed to lower manufacturing costs; *FitNes* aimed to cut administrative costs to the tune of CHF 1 billion (€ 600 000) by 2006. Most ambitious of all, the *Global Business Excellence* (GLOBE) focused on boosting efficiency by introducing best practices across all countries and businesses by unifying and updating all data and introducing a common IT infrastructure.

## Nestlé's organizational structure and brand portfolio

Exhibit 1. depicts Nestlé's organizational structure and executive board. Using a matrix structure, businesses are organized by both product groups and geographic areas (see Exhibit 2.: Nestlé 2005 Sales). The six product groups are (1) beverages; (2) milk products, nutrition, and ice cream; (3) prepared dishes and cooking aids; (4) chocolate, confectionery, and biscuits; (5) pet care; and (6) pharmaceutical products, whereas the geographic zones refer to (1) Europe; (2) the Americas; and (3) Asia, Oceania, and Africa.[7] Nestlé Waters and Nestlé Nutrition are managed as separate SBUs. Exhibit 3

presents Nestlé's main brands; the five-year financial figures for the company appear in Exhibit 4.

# Nestlé 2005 sales by business segment and geographic region

## Nestlé Waters

Nestlé entered the bottled water business in 1969 with a 30% stake in the French *Société Générale des Eaux Minérales de Vittel*.[8] To develop this business, Nestlé acquired the German *Blaue Quellen* group in 1974 and then a controlling interest in Vittel in 1987. In May 1992, Nestlé also acquired the *Source Perrier S.A.* group and become the leading player on the world bottled water market, under the name Nestlé Sources International (NSI). In 1996, NSI changed its name to accelerate its international development and became *Perrier Vittel S.A.* Very quickly, Nestlé internationalized its bottled water business unit. By the end of 1997, the Perrier-Vittel Group competed on every continent, and the purchase of San Pellegrino in 1998 gave it a leadership position in the Italian market. The same year, it launched Nestlé Pure Life, the first multisite bottled water under the Nestlé brand. Two years later, Perrier-Vittel simultaneously launched Nestlé Aquarel, a pan-European, multisite spring water, into six markets. Then in April 2002, Nestlé changed the name Perrier-Vittel to Nestlé Waters to benefit from the Nestlé brand name. The newly named division pursued expansion into the HOD market by acquiring Europe's leading HOD company, the *Powwow Group* in 2003, and expanded its international activities in Asia and Africa.

By 2005,[9] Nestlé Waters accounted for 9.6% of the Nestlé Group's consolidated sales, managed a portfolio of 75 brands (63.1% local, 22.4% international, and 14.5% Nestlé brands in terms of sales) marketed in 130 countries and bottled at 103 production sites, and employed a workforce of 30,000 people. Nestlé Waters also had become the number one bottled water company worldwide. By geographical zone, Nestlé Waters sales covered North America (50%), Europe (42.7%), Africa and the Middle East (3.0%), Asia (2.1%), and Latin America (2.2%).

The fierce competition in the global bottled water market became especially difficult in the United States after Coca-Cola and PepsiCo moved aggressively into the market, slashing prices to gain market share. However, in most regions, Nestlé Waters still possesses the first or second market position in value compared with its main rivals Danone, Coca-Cola, and PepsiCo (see

**EXHIBIT 1**   Nestlé organizational structures in January 2006

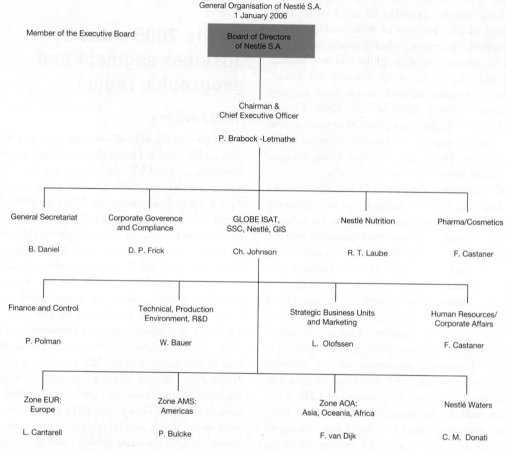

General Organisation of Nestlé S.A.
1 January 2006

**Source:** www.nestlé.com.

Exhibit 5: Nestlé Waters' Relative Market Share in the Worldwide Bottled Water Market). The world's top four bottled water companies (Danone, Nestlé, Coca-Cola, and PepsiCo) held a combined 32% share of total volume in 2005. Danone owns four of the top 10 brands by volume, including the number one Aqua from Indonesia. Nestlé and PepsiCo each keep two brands in the top 10, and Coca-Cola has one.

In terms of brand value, Nestlé Waters possesses 6 of the 10 most valuable mineral water global brands, according to the 2005 *BrandZ* ranking.[10] Perrier ranked third, after Danone's Evian and Pepsico's Aquafina, with an estimated brand value of $ 516 million; Poland Spring ranked sixth with a brand value of $ 331 million, followed, in positions 7–10, by Nestlé Pure Life ($324 million), Vittel ($ 298 million), and Contrex and Levissina ($ 212 million each) (see Exhibit 6).

The global bottled water market advanced by 8.3% in 2005, and bottled water volumes reached 173 billion liters that year. With an 8.8% compound annual growth

rate in the years 2000 to 2005, bottled water clearly remains a drink force to be reckoned with. Sustained growth patterns forecast a doubling of the bottled water market by 2012. In growth terms, Asia and North America have taken a sizable lead. In the United States, volumes continue to be boosted by sustained price competition. Meanwhile, emerging Asian economies have increased their worldwide consumption; though per capita bottled water consumption remains low, it is growing rapidly among a substantial population base. In China and India, for example, 2005 registered double-digit growth rates. As the rise of bottled water consumption illustrates, health appears to have become an increasingly influential factor in consumers' choice of drink.

# Perrier

Compared with Contrex, Vittel, San Pellegrino, and Acqua Panna, Perrier is the most valuable of Nestlé Waters'

**EXHIBIT 2**  Nestlé 2005 sales by business segment and geographic region

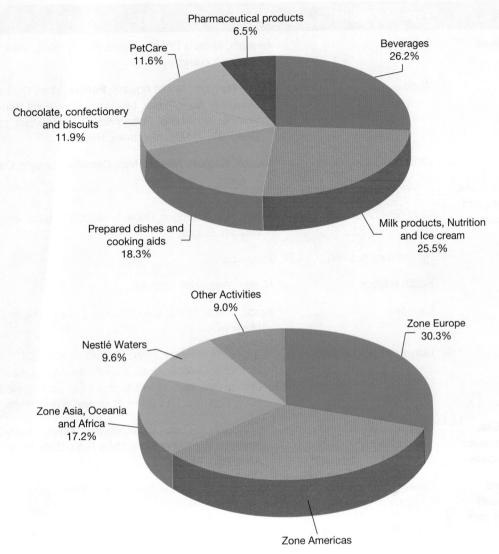

**Source:** Nestlé Quick Facts, 2006.

International Brands and a clear contributor to the division's number one position. However, Perrier constitutes only a small part of Nestlé Waters' brand portfolio – less than 5% in 2005.

## Perrier's history[11]

In 1769, the Granier family purchased the Bouillens estate. Alphonse Granier was the first to take an interest in the spring in 1841, but commercial operation only really started in 1863, when Napoleon III signed a decree acknowledging that the spring produced natural mineral water. After a bankruptcy, Louis Rouvière, a Vergèze landowner and businessman, purchased the spring in

1888. By 1894, he had leased the spring, with an option to purchase, to a doctor from Nîmes: Louis Perrier. In 1898, Dr. Perrier took over ownership of the Bouillens estate, and the same year, the *Établissement Thermal de Vergèze* became the *Société des Eaux Minérales, Boissons et Produits Hygiéniques de Vergèze*. Suffering financial difficulties, Dr. Perrier leased the property to Sir John Harmsworth in 1903 and later sold it to him. Sir John immediately renamed the spring Perrier after its former owner. His intention was to serve the entire British Empire with the water from this spring by connecting his plant to the local railway station. Harmsworth could ship 5 million bottles annually, and by 1933, production had increased to 19 million bottles, 10 million of which

## EXHIBIT 3 Nestlé's main brands

| | Type of Product | Brands |
|---|---|---|
| **Beverages** | Coffee | Nescafé, Taster's Choice, Ricoré, Ricoffy, Nespresso, Bonka, Zoégas, Loumidis |
| | Water | Nestlé Pure Life, Nestlé Aquarel, **Perrier**, Vittel, Contrex, San Pellegrino, Aqua Panna, Levissima, Vera, Fürst Bismarck, Viladrau, Arrowhead, Poland Spring, Santa Maria, La Vie, Deer Park, Al Manhal, Ozarka, Hépar |
| | Other drinks/beverages | Nestea, Nesquik, Nescau, Milo, Carnation, Libby's, Caro |
| **Milk products, nutrition, and ice cream** | Cereal (breakfast products) | Nestlé |
| | Child nutrition or baby food | Nestlé, Nan, Lactogen, Beba, Nestogen, Cérélac, Neslac, Nestum, Guigoz |
| | Performance nutrition | Power Bar |
| | Health nutrition | Nutren, Peptamen, Modulen |
| | Ice cream | Nestlé, Frisco, Motta, Camy, Savory, Peters, Haägen Dasz, Mövenpick |
| | Dairy (milk) products | Nestlé, Nido, Nespray, Ninho, Carnation, Milkmaid, La Lechera, Moça, Klim, Gloria, Svelty, Molico, Nestlé Omega Plus, Bear Brand, Coffee-mate (chilled): Nestlé, LC 1, Chamyto, La Laitière, Sveltesse, Yoco, Svelty, Molico |
| **Chocolate, confectionery, and biscuits** | Chocolate, confectionery, and biscuits | Nestlé, Crunch, Cailler, Galak/Milkybar, KitKat, Quality Street, Smarties, Baci, After Eight, Baby Ruth, Butterfinger, Lion, Aero, Polo, Frutips |
| **Prepared dishes and cooking aids** | Cooking products (bouillon, soup, pâté, sauce) | Maggi, Buitoni, Crosse&Blackwell, Thorny, Winiary |
| | Frozen products | Nestlé, Buitoni, Herta, Toll House |
| | Prepared dishes and cooking aids | Maggi, Buitoni, Stouffler's, Hot Pockets |
| | Restauration and professional products | Chef, Davigel, Minor's, Santa Rica |
| **Pet care** | Animal food/pet care | Friskies, Fancy Feast, Alpo, Mighty Dog, Gourmet, Mon Petit, Felix, Purina Dog Chow, Pro Plan, ONE, Beneful, Tidy Cats |
| **Pharmaceutical products** | Pharmaceuticals | Alcon, Galderma |
| | Cosmetics | L'Oreal, Laboratoires Innéov |

\* Forecasts

**Source:** www.nestlé.com

## EXHIBIT 4 Nestlé group's five-year figures

| In millions of CHP | 2006[*] | 2005 | 2004 | 2003 | 2002 |
|---|---|---|---|---|---|
| CHF per 1 Euro | 1.57 | 1.55 | 1.54 | 1.52 | 1.47 |
| **Results** | | | | | |
| Sales | 98,458 | 91,115 | 84,690 | 87,979 | 89,160 |
| EBIT (Earnings Before Interest, Taxes, restructuring and impairments) | 13,302 | 11,876 | 10,760 | 11,006 | 10,940 |
| as % of sales | 13.5% | 13.0% | 12.7% | 12.5% | 12.3% |
| Taxes | 3,293 | 2,647 | 2,404 | 2,307 | 2,295 |
| Net profit (Profit for the period attributable to shareholders of the parent) | 9,197 | 8,081 | 6,621 | 6,213 | 7,564 |
| as % of sales | 9.3% | 8.9% | 7.8% | 7.1% | 8.5% |
| as % of average equity | 18.7% | 18.6% | 17.4% | 17.3% | 22.1% |
| Total amount of dividend | 4,044 | 3,471 | 3,114 | 2,800 | 2,705 |
| Depreciation of property, plant and equipment | 2,581 | 2,382 | 2,454 | 2,408 | 2,542 |
| as % of sales | 2.6% | 2.6% | 2.9% | 2.7% | 2.9% |
| Amortization of goodwill | - | - | 1,583 | 1,571 | 1,438 |
| **Balance sheet and Cash flow statement** | | | | | |
| Current assets | 35,305 | 41,765 | 35,285 | 36,233 | 35,342 |
| of which liquid assets | 11,475 | 17,393 | 15,282 | 15,128 | 14,291 |
| Non-current assets | 66,500 | 60,953 | 51,832 | 53,328 | 52,010 |
| Total assets | 101,805 | 102,718 | 87,117 | 89,561 | 87,352 |
| Current liabilities | 32,479 | 35,854 | 29,075 | 30,365 | 33,737 |
| Non-current liabilities | 16,478 | 17,796 | 17,743 | 21,373 | 17,983 |
| Equity attributable to shareholders of the parent | 50,991 | 47,498 | 39,236 | 36,880 | 34,819 |
| Minority interests | 1,857 | 1,570 | 1,063 | 943 | 813 |
| Operating cash flow | 11,676 | 10,205 | 10,412 | 10,125 | 10,248 |
| Free cash flow | 7,018 | 6,557 | 6,640 | 6,361 | 6,278 |

**EXHIBIT 4** Continued

| In millions of CHP | 2006* | 2005 | 2004 | 2003 | 2002 |
|---|---|---|---|---|---|
| Capital expenditure | 4,200 | 3,375 | 3,260 | 3,337 | 3,577 |
| as % of sales | 4.3% | 3.7% | 3.8% | 3.8% | 4.0% |
| **Data per share (in CHF)** | | | | | |
| Weighted average number of shares outstanding (in millions) | 384.80 | 388.81 | 388.45 | 387.02 | 387.64 |
| Basic earnings per share from continuing operations | 23.71 | 20.82 | 16.97 | 16.05 | 19.51 |
| Basic earnings per share from discontinued operations | 0.19 | (0.04) | 0.07 | – | – |
| Equity attributable to shareholders of the parent | 132.51 | 122.16 | 101.01 | 95.29 | 89.82 |
| Dividend | 10.40(f) | 9.00 | 8.00 | 7.20 | 7.00 |
| Pay-out ratio (based on Total basic earnings per share) | 43.5% | 43.3% | 46.9% | 44.8% | 35.9% |
| Stock exchange prices (high/low) | 448.3/355.0 | 404.3/298.3 | 346.0/276.0 | 314.5/233.3 | 397.0/271.0 |
| Yield | 2.3/2.9% | 2.2/3.0% | 2.3/2.9% | 2.3/3.1% | 1.8/2.6% |
| **Market capitalization** | 166 | 152 | 115 | 119 | 113 |
| | 152 | 576 | 237 | 876 | 368 |
| **Number of personnel** (in thousands) | 265 | 250 | 244 | 253 | 254 |

* Forecasts

**Source:** Nestlé.

were exported. After his death in 1933, Harmsworth left the company with a strong image and identity.

In 1947, Gustave Leven, a young Parisian stockbroker, acquired the spring and decided to modernize the entire organization, including the production process, and therefore developed a new strategy based on manufacturing all the bottle components. To increase plant productivity, Leven imported high-quality machines from the United States and, between 1948 and 1952, massively expanded the factory area and completely modernized the plant. Perrier kept growing. Beginning in 1954, Perrier S.A. acquired other mineral water springs, such as Contrexéville, and launched an

extensive diversification program to secure the company's lead in the bottled water market. It launched the Pschitt brand and obtained the Pepsi-Cola license for France. Perrier also acquired various regional springs before starting its internationalization. In 25 years, Perrier became market leader in France and other European markets, and by early 1976, it was headed across the Atlantic to conquer North America, beginning with its office in New York. Quickly, Perrier captured 85% of the U.S. imported mineral water market, 55% of the French market, and 40% of the U.K. market. Perrier's stable position and good name enabled it to sell 300 million bottles in the United States in 1988. By 1990, Perrier

**EXHIBIT 5**  Nestlé Waters' relative market share in the worldwide bottled water market

| | Bottled Water Global Players % Value | | | | |
|---|---|---|---|---|---|
| **VALUE** | **2001** | **2002** | **2003** | **2004** | **2005** |
| **Nestlé** | 17.8 | 19.4 | 19.4 | 19.4 | 19.8 |
| **Danone** | 13.3 | 11.1 | 10.8 | 10.5 | 8.9 |
| **Coca-Cola** | 5.2 | 7.5 | 8.4 | 8.8 | 9.4 |
| *– own brands* | *3.9* | *6.2* | *7.1* | *7.4* | *7.9* |
| *– bottler brands* | *1.3* | *1.3* | *1.3* | *1.4* | *1.5* |
| **PepsiCo** | 3.8 | 4.5 | 4.5 | 4.7 | 4.8 |
| *– own brands* | *2.5* | *3.3* | *3.4* | *3.6* | *3.8* |
| *– bottler brands* | *1.3* | *1.2* | *1.1* | *1.1* | *1.0* |
| **Others** | 59.9 | 57.5 | 56.9 | 56.6 | 57.1 |
| **TOTAL** | 100.0 | 100.0 | 100.0 | 100.0 | 100.0 |
| | % volume | | | | |
| **VOLUME** | **2001** | **2002** | **2003** | **2004** | **2005** |
| **Nestlé** | 13.9 | 14.3 | 14.3 | 14.5 | 14.6 |
| **Danone** | 11.4 | 10.8 | 10.7 | 10.6 | 9.0 |
| **Coca-Cola** | 3.8 | 5.4 | 6.4 | 6.9 | 7.2 |
| *– own brands* | *2.6* | *4.0* | *5.0* | *5.4* | *5.7* |
| *– bottler brands* | *1.2* | *1.4* | *1.4* | *1.5* | *1.5* |
| **PepsiCo** | 2.6 | 3.1 | 3.2 | 3.5 | 3.6 |
| *– own brands* | *1.6* | *2.1* | *2.3* | *2.6* | *2.7* |
| *– bottler brands* | *1.0* | *1.0* | *0.9* | *0.9* | *0.9* |
| **Others** | 68.3 | 66.4 | 65.4 | 64.5 | 65.6 |
| **TOTAL** | 100.0 | 100.0 | 100.0 | 100.0 | 100.0 |

\* Market excludes HOD (10.1 liters plus) but includes jug (3-10 liters). Still and sparkling.

**Source:** Zenith International. Ltd., 2006.

had become the world leader in the mineral water market.

## The benzene incident

On February 11, 1990, *The New York Times* reported that Perrier had halted its production worldwide.[12] A laboratory in North Carolina had discovered traces of benzene (an industrial solvent and carcinogen) in 12 bottles of Perrier mineral water. Perrier initially claimed the contamination was an isolated incident and recalled 72 million Perrier bottles from North America. Later, when traces of benzene appeared in Perrier bottled water in Europe, Perrier announced a worldwide recall of Perrier

**EXHIBIT 6** Global Top 10 most valuable mineral water brands in 2005

| # | Brand | Parent | Value in £m |
|---|---|---|---|
| 1 | Evian | Danone | 651 |
| 2 | Aquafina | PepsiCo | 618 |
| 3 | Perrier | Nestlé | 516 |
| 4 | Dasani | Coca Cola | 451 |
| 5 | Volvic | Danone | 409 |
| 6 | Poland Spring | Nestlé | 331 |
| 7 | Nestlé Pure Life | Nestlé | 324 |
| 8 | Vittel | Nestlé | 298 |
| 9 | Contrex | Nestlé | 212 |
| 10 | Levissima | Nestlé | 212 |

**Source:** MillwardBrown Optimor' BrandZ 2005.

and withdrew 280 million bottles from the market. The problem was caused by a carbon filter system at the bottling plant, and on March 7, 1990, Perrier placed a full-page advertisement in several newspapers explaining that all the problems had been fixed. The ad asserted the contamination was never a health or safety concern and that the spring itself never was the problem – it was still as pure as it had been 1000 years ago. Yet the incident cost Perrier a total of $ 262.9 million.

Relaunched in April 1990, Perrier was required to drop the words "naturally sparkling" from its packaging, and the image and sales of Perrier dropped dramatically. Perrier's stock price initially fell by 15% and then by 37% within six months. In June 1990, Gustave Leven resigned from his position as president of the group, and by the end of 1990, Evian by BSN (which changed its name to Danone in 1994) replaced Perrier as the top brand in the United States.

# Nestlé's acquisition of Perrier

Two years after the benzene incident, Nestlé achieved its goal of buying Perrier. In 1992, the drive to acquire Perrier became a struggle among Nestlé, its competitor BSN, and the Italian Agnelli family. Nestlé and BSN joined forces to defeat their rival Agnelli and divided the Perrier brands into two companies: Volvic (second-largest brand of the Perrier group) became a part of BSN (for 20% of the price Nestlé paid for Perrier), whereas Nestlé would keep the other brands, which it most desired, including Perrier, Vittel, and Contrex.[13]

However, the European Commission (EC) challenged the agreement on the grounds that it would give Nestlé and BSN a duopoly position on the French bottled water market; both companies together would gain an extremely dominant 68% of the French bottled water market. However, according to the EC on March 26, 1992, "We're dealing with something that comes from springs in the ground, so it is a product with finite resources." The water market demands big brands and heavy resources to promote those brands, as Perrier had done. But as a result, the EC noted, entrance barriers to new competitors are extremely high, and the import-penetration rate in France is very low. These facets make the case rather complex.

To determine if the acquisition would create an overly dominant position for Nestlé, the EC examined multiple factors. First, it looked at the degree of supply concentration, because if Nestlé acquired Perrier, there would only remain two major suppliers with massive market share in France. Second, the EC addressed transparency and prices in the market. The commission believed that transparency would lessen if only two companies remained. Before the acquisition, three companies monitored one another in terms of their prices and volumes sold. If only two large companies with a market share of 68% remained, they could easily increase prices without fear of offsetting volume losses. Third, the EC noted that consumers buy and drink mineral water on a daily basis and do not have access to perfect substitutes. Therefore, an increase of prices would have a relatively small impact on quantities demanded, which would lead to increases of total revenues and profits. The commission believed that this development would reinforce the likelihood of such a strategy, as well as encourage tacit collusion.

However, because the EC could not prove that Nestlé would use Perrier for tacit collusion or a disputable strategy, it approved the acquisition with one important condition: Nestlé had to restructure its bid with the provision that it would sell Volvic, one of the top brands in the Perrier portfolio, to BSN so that Nestlé and BSN would have an equal market share in France. As a result of this deal, Nestlé would own 36.8% of the French market and BSN 30.9%. The EC agreed, based on the agreement that Nestlé would control 20% of France's mineral water capacity by selling eight smaller springs, including Vichy, Thonon, Pierval, and Saint-Yorre to a single buyer and must agree not to buy back the brands for

10 years and delaying the sale of Perrier's Volvic unit to BSN until the commission had approved the sale of the springs.[14] The springs to be sold accounted for approximately 7% of Perrier's turnover, excluding Volvic's revenues. When the dust settled, Nestlé had won control over Perrier; BSN (owner of Evian Mineral Waters) had received the Volvic brand; and the Agnellis settled for cash profit on their stock, plus the Châteaux Margaux vineyards in Bordeaux, the Caves de Roquefort cheese company, and some valuable Paris real estate. Nestlé's CEO Maucher asserted that with this acquisition, global market leadership was at stake: "It was simply a question of who won them. It was a too valuable an asset for Nestlé to let it slip away."

## Restructuring Perrier

With the acquisition of Perrier, Nestlé became the market leader in not only France but worldwide. To stay in that position, Nestlé had to deal with the consequences of the benzene incident. After a decade of excellent results and a big U.S. breakthrough, Perrier's financial position actually began to falter just after the acquisition. Nestlé had paid more than € 2 billion for Perrier, a price that seemed relatively high. Competitors were already trying to capture market share in important markets. In response, Nestlé had to restructure Perrier and reduce production costs. Exhibit 7 depicts the evolution of the relationship between Nestlé and Perrier.

Since the sale of Perrier to Gustave Leven in 1947, it had been managed in collaboration with the labor unions. In order to be able to respond to the sales' explosion and to avoid any trouble at the Perrier plant, Leven accepted pay rises, social benefits, and extra holiday demanded by the labor unions, financing the cost from Perrier's profits. The workers even won the right to be described as "co-manager" of the plant. Leven even established low-price stores for his employees and managed to produce Perrier's green glass bottles near the water source, which created more jobs in the region. Leven was immensely popular among workers; even employees who did not know him personally or did not work under his management seemed well disposed toward him. But with the arrival of Nestlé, employees grew afraid that their own corporate values would be exchanged for foreign multinational ones. The collaborative management structure might disappear, leaving them to be treated like just numbers. From this moment, labor unions started to play an important role in representing the workers and defending their rights.

Three months after the acquisition, Nestlé implemented its first redundancy plan, offering early retirements and voluntary departures for 428 workers, about 13% of Perrier's entire workforce. After this successful implementation, Nestlé announced a second redundancy plan in 1995 to eliminate 275 (10%) jobs in Perrier. In October 1998, after a year of conflicts between Nestlé's management and the trade unions, a third redundancy plan was developed to stop significant losses. Both parties accepted a redundancy plan that affected 349 (14%) full-time positions at the Perrier plant, and Nestlé committed to internally filling all vacant positions, giving priority to those who had lost their jobs. Nestlé also set up training programs for those employees who needed them. Within 10 years, Nestlé had reduced the workforce of Perrier by one-third in its efforts to create a profitable organization.

## Nestlé Waters' new strategy

As a result of the acquisition of Perrier in 1992, Nestlé became the world market leader in bottled waters. Its presence concentrated in the United States and Europe, where it was second behind Danone, because of brands such as Perrier, Vittel, Valvert, Contrex, and Fürst Bismarck.

Spring water brands had long been associated with specific springs, but by the late 1990s, the actual source of bottled water had become more and more irrelevant.[15] In France, Nestlé Waters faced new competition from a fast-growing new private brand, Cristalline, which was based on a new multisite concept that applied the same brand to water bottled at several different sites around France. With this concept, Cristalline had slashed its logistics costs and could sell its water at a price far lower than that of the premium brands represented by Nestlé and Danone. Other competitors emerged during the same period, and the large-scale retail distributors began to roll out their own private-label bottled waters.

Nestlé Waters responded in 1998 by launching its own multisite brand, Nestlé Pure Life, targeted at nascent markets in developing countries such as Pakistan, which became the first to test the Nestlé Pure Life brand.[16] Other markets followed quickly, including China, Thailand, and the Philippines. The Nestlé Pure Life rollout continued into South America, including Argentina and Mexico in 2000, then the Middle East, including Lebanon and Jordan in 2001 and Egypt, Uzbekistan, and Turkey in 2002, among others. By 2005, Nestlé Pure Life had reached South Africa, Russia, Canada, the United States, Qatar, United Arab Emirate, Bahrain, and Indonesia. Nestlé expected the brand to become the first truly global bottled water brand and initiated plans to develop it into the world leader by 2010.[17] The success of Nestlé Pure Life encouraged the company

## EXHIBIT 7  Chronology of Perrier and Nestlé

| | |
|---|---|
| 1984 | Perrier becomes number 1 mineral water company in the world with presence in Canada, the Gulf countries. South Africa, Australia, Japan, the U.S., and the U.K. |
| 1988–1990 | Perrier captures 85% of the U.S. imported mineral water market, 55% of the French market, and 40% of the U.K. market. By 1990, Perrier becomes the world leader in the mineral water market. |
| 1990 | The benzene incident. In February 1990, traces of benzene appear in bottles of Perrier, well above the maximum permitted quantity. Apparently, the problem was contained in the filter system used at the bottling plant to filter the water and add the "bubbles" artificially. It became a worldwide problem, and Nestlé was forced to recall and destroy all the contaminated bottles and hold sales for about 10 weeks.<br>April: The relaunched Perrier removed the words "naturally sparkling" and suffered significant drops in its image, sales, and stock prices.<br>June: Gustave Leven resigned as the president of the group.<br>End of the year: Evian replaced Perrier as the number one bottled water brand in the U.S. |
| 1992 | Nestlé took over Perrier with a hostile $2.7 billion bid and invested massively to bring the company back to profitability, emphasizing increasing productivity through redundancy plans. The first plan led to the early retirement of 428 workers out of 2,400 total. |
| 1995 | Sales had not been recuperated but fell to one-half the 1989 figure. Nestlé planned the second round of early retirements for 275 employees. |
| 1998 | The third round of early retirements, for 334 jobs. |
| 2002 | By gradual cuts since 1992. the number of employees at the Vergeze plant was reduced by one-third. |
| 2003 | Nestlé management and its shareholders are not satisfied with Perrier's productivity and present the fourth early retirement program for 356 employees to retire early.<br>The plan was accepted by two French unions, the CFE-CGC (Confédération Française de l'Encadrement-Confédération Générate des Cadres) and the CFDT (Confédération Française Democratique du Travail), but lacked the support of the CGT, supported by 93% of Perrier's workers. |
| 2004 | Continued conflict between the CGT and Nestlé–Perrier. |
| 2005 | Nestlé started restructuring Perrier's plant. |

to roll out another multisite brand specific to the European market. For the first time in its history, Nestlé associated its name with bottled water, then did so again with Nestlé Aquarel in 2000. From seven production sites around Europe, Nestlé Aquarel quickly reached Belgium, France, Germany, Hungary, Luxembourg, Poland, Portugal, and Spain, with plans to expand the brand to the entire European market in the second half of the decade. By the beginning of 2005, Nestlé Waters achieved a global market share of 18%, and the division had grown to become one of parent company Nestlé's most important business units, accounting for about 10% of its total sales.

Following this trend towards more economic multisite brands, Nestlé Waters invested more in Nestlé brands than in its other brands and started to divest itself of some local brands. Within the Nestlé Waters brand portfolio in 2005, local brands took up the major portion with a 65% share (down from 75.7% in 2002), and the share of the international brands has been relatively stable at 23%. But with its new branding strategy, the Nestlé brand (Nestlé Aquarel and Nestlé Pure Life) earned sales of more than 1 billion Swiss francs (approximately € 680 million) in 35 countries and accounted for 12% of Nestlé Waters' sales (up from 2.5% in 2002, see Exhibit 8) page 149, making it the primary growth driver. Nestlé Pure Life and Nestlé Aquarel posted strong organic growth in 2005, confirming the brand's ambition to become the leading worldwide bottled water brand within a few years. Remarkably, Nestlé Aquarel, in 14 countries, posted organic growth of greater than 50% in 2005.

Since September 8, 2004, its different water brands have shared a research and development (water) centre, in which Nestlé Waters experiments with new industrial processes to improve plant performances, shares water-related information, and quickly develops new products and packaging.[18] To further its organization and streamline costs, Nestlé Waters was also thinking about selling the Perrier division or grouping the Vittel and Contrex organizations into a single structure.

## Perrier's performance

Despite its profitable year in 2000, Nestlé remained unsatisfied with Perrier's results. An average Perrier worker produces 600,000 bottles a year in France, but an Italian worker for San Pellegrino produces 1.8 million bottles per year. As another example of Perrier's low productivity, the production of one bottle of Perrier, from the beginning to end, passes through 22 workers' hands; at the San Pellegrino plant in Italy, the production of one bottle takes only 12 workers.[19] Low productivity in France represented a significant concern because of the 35-hour workweek (see Exhibit 9), high social charges, and income tax. Absenteeism also was notably very high. Overall, the Perrier plants produced one-third as much as San Pellegrino's. Although mineral water was a booming market, Nestlé was suffering from the rigidity of French laws that made the plant less productive.

Then on February 6, 2003, 61-year-old Alain Dorfner, the CEO of Nestlé Waters France, announced that he would leave the company in a few months to retire. An engineer graduate from the *École Centrale* in Paris, Dorfner had joined the Nestlé Group over 32 years before and spent 17 years within the bottled water division. At his retirement, Richard Girardot took charge of the strategic development of the international brands (Perrier, Vittel, Contrex), as well as the industrial sites of all brands produced in France. On the same basis, he took responsibility for the Belgian brand Valvert and soon had been appointed CEO of Nestlé Waters France. At 47 years of age, married and the father of two children, and a law graduate from the University of Paris, Girardot has much experience in the bottled water sector, starting with the Source Perrier Group in 1987. After holding different marketing and sales positions, this brand management expert became Senior Vice-President

of the Perrier Business Unit for two years, during which time he obtained excellent results.

By 2003, Perrier's workforce had been cut by one-third since 1992. Yet on June 30, 2004, Perrier announced, after nine months of negotiation with trade unions, a fourth round of redundancies. Faced with a difficult competitive environment, the French subsidiary's inferior industrial performance compared with competitors, and access to the group's other production sites, Nestlé Waters France announced it would embark on an industrial reorganization of the French sites.

One-quarter of employees would be eligible for early retirement during the next five years, so Nestlé Waters France, after dialogue with its labor partners, chose a reorganization plan that did not resort to layoffs but used instead a GPEC/CATS program (Management Planning of Jobs & Skills and Early Departures). The program would improve organizational efficiency without requiring sudden layoffs or resorting to a redundancy plan. The proposed agreement provided for (1) voluntary early retirement for employees aged 55 years old and over (nearly 360 employees at the Vergèze plant by 2007, though the plant would hire about 120 new employees to replace them); (2) a gradual refocus on production operations by subcontracting peripheral services (e.g. security, cleaning services); (3) productivity gains by revising standards, production line start-up times, and so forth; and (4) personnel training and support in conjunction with long-term skills planning. The main goal of this version was to increase annual production by 600,000 bottles per employee.

On July 23, 2004, a central works council (*comité central d'entreprise*) was held to gather the opinion of the council members about the proposed agreements and have them signed by the labor unions. The agreement was signed by the *Confédération Française de l'Encadrement-Confédération Générale des Cadres* (CFE-CGC) and *Confederation Française Démocratique du Travail* (CFDT). But unlike its response to previous redundancy plans, the *Confédération Générale du Travail* (CGT) (related to the French Communist Party), which represents 83% of Perrier's workers, expressed an unfavorable opinion and refused to sign. Labor regulations require an eight-day waiting period before agreements may take effect, to allow the majority labor unions to exercise their right to object. Beyond this period, if the right to object is not exercised, the agreement is considered accepted by all of the labor unions.

On July 29, the CGT announced it would use its rights to challenge the redundancy plan, based on a law that barely passed the French Parliament in April 2004. The "Fillon" law (see Exhibit 9) states that collective agreements must have the support of a majority of the

# EXHIBIT 9   Employment laws in France

Provisions of French and European Union law govern virtually every aspect of the employer/employee relationship in France. It is not possible to operate a business in France or to buy or sell a business activity in France without effective labor and employment law representation. The legal relationship between employer and employee in France is very formal and highly regulated, and the majority of direct and indirect legislation leans in favor of the absolute protection of the interests of employee rather than employer. All workers in France are protected by the social and work legislation. Employment Law provisions are laid down by codified statute (*Code du Travail*).

The standard French working week is 35 hours, reduced from 39 hours. The 35-hour week came into effect on January 1, 2000, for businesses with more than 20 employees and on January 1, 2002, for businesses with 20 employees or fewer. This legislation was "watered down" in 2003; it is now possible for companies to insist employees work up to 39 hours (or more) per week for a negotiable extra cost. Employees may not waive their rights under the statutory provisions by contract. However, very senior management executives within a company may be exempted from all restrictions on working time.

Employment in France is not "at will" and thus dismissals may only come about on demonstrably and limited objective grounds, which must be brought to the attention of the employee in writing. Dismissals are subject to stringent, and often bureaucratic, procedural statutory constraints. Redundancies or layoffs on economic grounds are subject to separate and complex procedural and substantive constraints, particularly in the case of multiple dismissals. Legislative changes in 2002 have moved French Law toward a situation in which in essence the French entity (as opposed to the group to which it may belong) must be in a sufficiently severe economic situation to justify laying off staff or making them redundant. Various French states agencies have the statutory right to be advised of, and in some cases authorize, proposed dismissals by private sector employers. It is extremely easy and virtually costless for an employee to start litigation against an (ex-)employer in separate Labor Courts.

Furthermore, the lack of "at will" statutes means a hired employee may be dismissed only for a specific reason that has been recognized by French statute (i.e., *Code du Travail*) or French case law. The dismissal procedure on disciplinary grounds is very formalized, and failure to follow the procedural steps, even when the dismissal is justified on the merits, may result in the courts overturning the dismissal and ordering the reinstatement of the employee.

Restructuring refers to change in an enterprise's structure. It may be legal in nature and result, for example, in a merger or transfer of business as a going concern. The principle whereby contracts of employment are transferred to the new employer is applicable in such cases. Alternatively, restructuring may be purely technical, economic, or administrative. In these circumstances, the works council must, by law, be informed and consulted regarding the proposed restructuring.

Collective bargaining may apply nationally or only at a very localized level. In April 2004, the French Parliament passed the Fillon Law to reform collective bargaining by introducing a major innovation: Collective agreements must have the support of (or not be opposed by) a majority of representative trade unions or of unions representing a majority of employees to be valid. The legislation has introduced a "majority principle" before collective agreements may be regarded as valid. Previously, it was sufficient for an agreement to have been signed by at least one trade union with representative status. At the national level, a government decree dating from 1966 granted an irrefutable assumption of representativeness to five union confederations: the French Democratic Confederation of Labor (*Confédération française démocratique du travail*, CFDT), the French Christian Workers' Confederation (*Confédération française des travailleurs chrétiens*, CFTC), the French Confederation of Professional and Managerial Staff-General Confederation of Professional and Managerial Staff (*Confédération française de l'encadrement-Confédération générale des cadres*, CFE-CGC), the General Confederation of Labor (*Confédération générale du travail*, CGT), and the General Confederation of Labor-Force Ouvrière (*Confédération générale du travail-Force Ouvrière*, CGT-FO).

trade unions or unions that represent the majority of the employees, whereas previously, it had been adequate for an agreement to have been signed by at least one union with representative status. Nestlé Waters quickly announced that the CGT's decision demonstrated its opposition to a negotiated organizational restructuring and a performance improvement process that would be socially acceptable to all Nestlé Waters France employees. The CGT responded that it did not want to use its right but that the agreement forced it to do so. If the purpose of the agreement was changed from forced redundancy to voluntary redundancy for those over the age of 55, the CGT would sign the agreement. Furthermore, the group deemed the 1:3 replacement ratio, negotiated over several months, unsatisfactory, even though it had been 1:6 in the beginning.

Following the CGT's decision to challenge the agreement, Nestlé Waters France announced that after nine months of negotiations, it deeply regretted that it would have to definitively terminate the proposed plan, which would have allowed the company to continue to develop and contend with its increasing competition. It also announced that it would be forced to consider other approaches for the future of the company, the brands, and the sites, which it would announce in September 2004.

On September 15, Nestlé Waters issued its announcement:[20] It would turn the various industrial facilities and headquarters into subsidiaries. This reorganization would allow them to become more autonomous and thus develop specific organizational and productivity programs. The brand also informed the central works council that it was considering selling the Perrier division or grouping the Vittel and Contrex organizations into a single structure.

# The social conflict

From this moment, a power struggle began between an "old school" labor union and a global multinational. It seemed that the CGT was trying to keep things as they were after World War II and that Nestlé was a brutal and soulless, global megacorporation. In June 2004, Perrier's management put bottles of Badoit Rouge in the factory cafeteria, effectively declaring "war," because Badoit Rouge had just been launched by Nestlé Waters main competitor's Danone to compete with Perrier's new brand, *Eau de Perrier*.[21] Perrier employees found it a massive insult and a punch below the belt. The atmosphere became electric. As one Perrier truck driver reported, "It was a provocation. We took the bottles and dumped them in front of the factory director's door, so he could not get into his office." Perrier's head of human resources, André Sembelie, countered that it had not been a provocation: "It was to make the trade unions realize that there was a competitor under our nose." Perrier needed to change its structure to improve its productivity. Yet after several meetings, none of the parties wanted to compromise on the issue, so Nestlé threatened to move production to another country, claiming the restrictive labor laws in France and the hostile trade unions made it too complicated for Perrier to bring jobs in line with financial growth. As a response, the CGT searched for a patent believed to have been filed in the early 1990s, giving the right to use the Perrier brand only to mineral water from the source in Vergèze.

Moving the production of the "champagne of table water" to another country would mean that France would lose an important icon, and Nestlé Waters claimed it would rather divest itself of Perrier if the negotiations collapsed. Nestlé Waters easily could imagine living without Perrier if productivity were not to improve. Brabeck even said that selling Nestlé would be a strategic option. Richard Girardot, the CEO of Nestlé Waters France, also mentioned that Nestlé Waters had a global market share of 17%. Losing Perrier would definitely mean a loss of market share, but the company would still have market share it could use to compete with other global suppliers. Selling Perrier appeared to be the division's real option, even though doing so would reverse Nestlé Waters strategy of extending its business area.

In an attempt to put the company's early retirement plan back on the table, Richard Girardot told the *Agence France Presse* on the September 15, 2004: "We refuse to return to the negotiating table. The CGT must indicate that it 'rejects its right of refusal,' approve the original project, and create no obstacles to its application." In response, CGT delegate Jean-Paul Franc, the head of the CGT at the Perrier plant, called the position "blackmail," adding: "We remain at their disposal for negotiations aimed at reaching an acceptable agreement."

To avoid a catastrophic result, the French government decided to intervene in an attempt to bring both parties back to the table and end the conflict. It was Nicolas Sarkozy, then French Minister of State for Economy, Finance and Industry, who called both sides in for negotiations.[22] There were several reasons for Sarkozy to get involved. The first reason involved unemployment rates in Vergèze and its surroundings, sitting at 13.8% versus 9.7% nationally in 2003. The departure of Nestlé from the town would have significant consequences for the inhabitants, leaving the people of Vergèze terrified about brinkmanship between Nestlé and the CGT. René Balana, the mayor of Vergèze, told the *Financial Times* on September 18[23] that at least two-thirds of Vergèze's income derived from taxes levied on Perrier's plants. The second reason to intervene was the reputation of a world-renowned brand that functioned as a source of national pride. Sarkozy thought it important for France to maintain such an iconic brand. "In the Nestlé affair, the bitter-enders at a certain union are doing great damage to the image international investors have of France," Sarkozy told a French radio station.[24] The third and most important reason related to fear about French businesses fleeing the country, a problem that had become a significant trend. The "all or nothing" resistance of the CGT also communicated an image of France that discouraged international investors. If France wanted to compete with other countries, it had to keep multinationals satisfied. This incident was not the first time French workers had to deal with global corporations; for example, Bosch,[25] the German producer of car parts, forced its French employees to work longer for less money and fewer benefits after threatening to close its plant in Lyon. Although Bosch's situation provides a good example of a struggle between a multinational and its employees, it cannot cover the full scope of the Nestlé/Perrier issue. This battle raged on a different scale, involving the world's largest food company and the world's most famous mineral water. Those monitoring the situation included not just Nestlé's competitors but the entire world.

At the request of the Minister of State, representatives of Nestlé Waters France, led by CEO Richard Girardot, met on September 21 with Nicolas Sarkozy and key members of his staff. During the meeting, Girardot recalled the circumstances that had led to the negotiation of an early retirement plan, intended to sustainably improve Nestlé Waters' industrial efficiency in France, and presented the new strategy, under which it would transform the different industrial sites into subsidiaries to provide each with the autonomy and flexibility it needed to deal with its specific conditions. Nestlé Waters also stated it had favored the possible divestment of the Perrier component. The Minister of State then issued a press release, which reminded the management of Nestlé Waters France that the government wished to see Nestlé Waters maintain and further develop its sites in France, particularly in the Gard region. Nestlé Waters France noted that it was ready to resume discussions about maintaining Perrier activities – on the condition that the majority union's right to oppose the agreement, signed at the end of July, be immediately revoked. Under no circumstances would it renegotiate the content of the agreement already signed by two unions.

However, Nestlé's management also warned that under no circumstances could the early agreement be renegotiated. As a response, CGT official Jean-Paul Franc recognized that negotiations were necessary to get out of this impasse. The French government was willing to finance a small part of the early agreement, largely in an attempt to persuade the CGT to drop its opposition plan. In addition, Nestlé Waters France's management promised it would invest massively in the Perrier plant, on the condition that the profitability improves.

On September 27, the CGT agreed to lift its right to oppose the agreements, while also reaffirming its rejection of the project and refusal to back its implementation. Nestlé Waters France responded that under these conditions, it had no guarantee of the effective implementation of the agreements and could not anticipate investments to ensure the productivity levels needed to guarantee the company's durable, long-term future. The next day, Nestlé Waters France announced that it would go ahead and implement its restructuring, productivity improvement, early retirement, and hire plans, as outlined in the agreements. However, improving performance was a prerequisite of investing in any of the sites, Vergèze in particular. Under the restructuring deal,[26] 356 of the 1,650 staff at the Vergèze factory will leave on early-retirement packages, giving them 80% of their final net salaries, over the next two years. The French government has agreed to finance part of the early retirement program, while Nestlé has promised to continue recruiting seasonal workers, to maintain existing pay levels, and to "invest massively" in the site.

Nestlé started its early retirement program, narrowing overcapacity and loss of EBITA. But two months later, on November 29, 2004, Peter Brabeck said to CNN: "We have come to the point where the development of the Perrier brand is endangered by stubbornness of the CGT."[27] For his part, Jean-Paul Franc, the CGT official, replied, "Nestlé can not do whatever it likes. There are men and women who work here." Richard Girardot still believes that the CGT is likely to block any restructuring measure. As Perrier's co-general manager in charge of production, he thinks Nestlé already invested enough in the company, including, since 2000, more than $250 million to launch new products and developing new techniques: "From a technical point of view, we are in a good position."

## Divesting Perrier?

Although Perrier is a clear contributor to Nestlé Waters' impressive market position, the company derives 95% of its mineral water revenues from the combined sales of its other brands. The part Perrier contributes to Nestlé Waters' brand portfolio is rather small, but its position in the U.S. and European markets remains strong. Next to the local brands, Perrier is the market leader in the sparkling bottled water segment in the United States (13.6% market share in 2005). Still, its low productivity levels and minimal profits pushed Perrier sales below the overall growth level of Nestlé Water sales in 2005. Nestlé Waters is not prepared to maintain the status quo for much longer and has once again threatened to sell the business. But would anyone be interested in buying such a "hot potato," in such dire need of restructuring but with a workforce adamant that no changes are necessary? Yes, according to François-Xavier Perroud,[28] Nestlé's spokesperson, though a buyer from the bottled water industry is looking increasingly unlikely. "Perrier, with all its problems, might not be of interest to another drinks group," he acknowledges, "but what about a financial investor? If Peter Brabeck decides to put the company up for sale, then it will be because he believes that there is sufficient interest from financial bidders."

Nestlé also mentioned that producing Perrier elsewhere was theoretically possible, throwing specialists in France into a tizzy.[29] "It would be like making Bordeaux in Czechoslovakia!" complains Georges Lepré, a former sommelier at the Ritz Hotel in Paris. "It's unthinkable!" Some market analysts also agree; "Taking it outside of France is a big risk," says Stephen Williamson, research manager at Euromonitor International, a London-based market research firm. "Finding out it is produced in the Czech Republic [rumors have circulated that Nestlé would like to produce Perrier in Eastern Europe or Asia] would be a huge problem for Perrier's French market," he continued. "The only way they could overcome that one would be by putting a lot of money into it." Benoit Moreau, a bottled water specialist and editor-in-chief of the French drink trade monthly, *Rayon Boissons* (*Drink Aisle*), agrees that moving production outside of France will not work, because it would "kill the brand. You kill Perrier in France." Thus, he claims, "It's a big bluff." With 55% of Perrier's consumers in its homeland and its biggest markets among an older, more origin-conscious clientele, the idea of moving the production outside of the country is nothing to snicker at. Moreau also takes into account Perrier's French consumers. Outside of the country, Perrier is a symbol of luxury; within France, it is a mixed bag. Although it has lost some of its cachet in France, becoming more of mass-market drink than one consumed by society's elite, its biggest markets remain in the north and west of the country, where relatively older drinkers continue to be conscious of its origin.

"It would definitely have an impact on the French market if they made it elsewhere," asserted Gary Hemphill, senior vice president at Beverage Marketing Corporation, a New York research and consulting firm. Yet despite Perrier's "transporting imagery," he is not convinced that either the struggle between the two sides or where the water is bottled will make much difference on the world market. He noted, "Some people who buy Perrier might imagine themselves sitting in a café on the Champs Elysées, but [Nestlé] can probably work around that, but if people like a product, does the union and the [parent] company not getting along make much difference?"

Hubert Genieys, external communications director for Nestlé Waters, confidently asserts, "There is no negative effect on the sales. I think that each consumer reading [daily stories about the CGT/Perrier struggle] is really able to differentiate the messages and to consider that there is absolutely no link in this issue with the quality image of the product." As for a happy ending to the CGT/Perrier rift, Genieys takes a Swiss-style, numbers-first approach: "We don't want to be happy, we just want to be ready to react efficiently to a very stringent competitive environment." Though Genieys clearly states that Nestlé's goal for Perrier "is not to produce it elsewhere," he places productivity and efficiency over everything. Therefore, "If we don't succeed, we will need to think of other hypotheses. Anything is possible."

On this day in February 2006, Nestlé and Nestlé Waters face several difficult questions about the future of Perrier. Does Perrier fit within Nestlé Waters' portfolio? Does Perrier contribute to Nestlé Waters' portfolio? Should Nestlé divest or relocalize Perrier? Would this divestment or relocalization affect Nestlé's image and reputation? In France? Globally? If Nestlé Waters decides to sell Perrier, to which company should it offer it? Danone, Coca-Cola, PepsiCo, a private financial group? What would be the risks of each choice?

## NOTES

1. Bevaragedaily.com, October 21, 2004 (http://beveragedaily.com/news.asp?id=55582).
2. Nestlé Waters Press Release, March 7, 2006 (http://www.press.nestle-waters.com/en).
3. The HOD market segment consists of larger bottles and containers (10 liters and more), delivered to offices, shopping centers, institutions, department stores, and homes.
4. Nestlé at a Glance (http://www.nestle.com/AllAbout/AtGlance/Introduction/Introduction.htm).
5. Nestlé's History (http://www.nestle.com/AllAbout/History/HistoryList.htm).
6. The Economist (2004), "Daring, Defying, to Grow: Nestlé," *The Economist* (U.S. Edition), August 7, 2004 (http://www.economist.com).
7. Nestlé Group 2006: Company Profile (http://www.nestle.com).
8. Nestlé Waters History (http://www.nestle-waters.com/en/Menu/MeetUs/OurHistory/).
9. Nestlé Waters Key Data (http://press.nestle-waters.com/en/Menu/KeyData/).
10. *BrandZ* Top Brand Ranking: Water (http://www.millwardbrown.com).

11. The Perrier Story (http://www.perrier.com/EN/entrezbulle/rubrique10.asp).

12. James, George (1990), "Perrier Recalls Its Water in U.S. After Benzene Is Found in Bottles," *The New York Times*, February 10, 1990 (http://www.nytimes.com).

13. *The New York Times*, January 21, 1992 (http://www.nytimes.com).

14. *The New York Times*, "European Commission Puts Conditions on Perrier Deal," July 23, 1992 (http://www.nytimes.com).

15. Cohen M. L. (2005), "Nestlé Waters," *Answers.com* (http://www.answers.com/topic/nestl-waters).

16. Nestlé Pure Life press kit (http://www.nestle-purelife.com/press_room.htm).

17. Nestlé Waters Press Release, March 7, 2006 (http://www.press.nestle-waters.com/en).

18. Nestlé Waters Press Release, September 8, 2004, "Nestlé Waters Inaugurates Its Product Technology Centre, Water–Nestlé's First Research and Development Centre Entirely Devoted to Water (http://www.press.nestle-waters.com/en).

19. Tomlinson, Richard (2004), "Troubled Waters at Perrier," *Fortune*, November 29, 2004, p. 173.

20. Nestlé Waters Press Release, September 15, 2004 "Nestlé Waters in France: New Directions" (http://www.press.nestle-waters.com/en).

21. Tomlinson, Richard (2004), "Troubled Waters at Perrier."

22. Johnson, Jo (2004a), "Paris Steps in over Perrier Dispute," *Financial Times*, September 17, 2004, p. 29; Groom, Brian (2004), "Nestlé Strangled by Paris's Red Tap," *Financial Times*, September 17, 2004, p.17; LExpansion.com, "Sarkozy arrache un sursis pour Perrier," September 21, 2004 (http://www.lexpansion.com/Pages.asp?ArticleId=78375).

23. Johnson, Jo (2004b), "Threatened Move Worries Town Dependent on Perrier Plants: Mineral Water from the Famous Source Could Be Dropped for Supplies from a Lower-Cost Country," *Financial Times*, September 18, 2004, p. 6.

24. Johnson, Jo (2004a), "Paris Steps in over Perrier Dispute."

25. Johnson, Jo (2004b), "Threatened Move Worries Town Dependent on Perrier Plants: Mineral Water from the Famous Source Could Be Dropped for Supplies from a Lower-Cost Country."

26. Arnold, Martin (2005), "Closure Threat Ends Nestlé Waters Impasse," *Financial Times*, May 4, 2005, p. 27.

27. Tomlinson, Richard (2004), "Troubled Waters at Perrier."

28. FoodNavigator.com (2004), "Nestlé still threatening Perrier Sale," October 21, 2004 (http://foodnavigator.com/news.asp?id=55582).

29. Ray, Joy (2004), "Perrier: Nestled in Controversy?" *brandchannel.com*, Interbrand, November 8, 2004 (http://www.brandchannel.com/features_effect.asp?pf_id=237).

# INTEGRATIVE CASE 11

# NINTENDO'S DISRUPTIVE STRATEGY: IMPLICATIONS FOR THE VIDEO GAME INDUSTRY

## Ali Farhoomand

*ACRC, The University of Hong Kong*

*For some time we have believed the game industry is ready for disruption. Not just from Nintendo, but from all game developers. It is what we all need to expand our audience. It is what we all need to expand our imaginations.*

*– Satoru Iwata, president of Nintendo Co. Ltd*[1]

In the 2008 BusinessWeek–Boston Consulting Group ranking of the world's most innovative companies, Nintendo Co. Ltd ("Nintendo") was ranked seventh, up from 39th the previous year.[2] This recognised Nintendo's significant transformation into an innovative design powerhouse that had challenged the prevailing business model of the video game industry.

In 2000, when Sony, Microsoft and Nintendo (the "big three" of the video game console manufacturers) released their latest products, Sony's PlayStation 2 ("PS2") emerged as the clear winner, outselling Microsoft's Xbox and Nintendo's GameCube. In 2006, a new generation of video game consoles was introduced by these players, precipitating a new competitive battle in the industry. Microsoft and Sony continued with their previous strategies of increasing the computing power of their newest products and adding more impressive graphical interfaces. However, Satoru Iwata, president of Nintendo, believed that the video game industry had been focusing far too much on existing gamers and completely neglecting non-gamers. Armed with this insight, the company repositioned itself by developing a radically different console, the Wii (pro-

nounced "we"). The Wii was a nifty machine that used a wand-like remote controller to detect players' hand movements, allowing them to emulate the real-life gameplay of such games as tennis, bowling and boxing.

The new console proved to be a runaway success. By September 2007, Nintendo had become Japan's most valuable listed company after Toyota, and its market value had tripled since the launch of the Wii. In spite of this initial success, however, it was not clear whether Nintendo had really disrupted the industry and changed the name of the game.

## History of Nintendo – 1889 to 2002

Nintendo's roots[3] could be traced all the way back to 1889 in Kyoto, Japan, when Yamauchi, the founder of the company, started manufacturing playing cards. In 1907, the company began producing Western playing cards, and by 1951, it had become the Nintendo Playing Card Company. In 1959, it began making theme cards under a licensing agreement with Disney, and by 1963, the company had gone public and taken its current name.

During the period 1970 to 1985, Nintendo began focusing on the manufacture of electronic toys and entered the budding field of video games [see Exhibit 1].

Havovi Joshi and Samuel Tsang prepared this case under the supervision of Prof. Ali Farhoomand for class discussion. This case is not intended to show effective or ineffective handling of decision or business processes.

Interestingly, 1991, the year when Nintendo launched the highly popular Super NES in the US, was also the year that saw Nintendo's vision become Sony's opportunity – and the creation of what could be described as Nintendo's "greatest challenge" for over a decade – the Sony PlayStation ("PS"). Nintendo had wanted to incorporate CD-ROM into their Super NES, and Sony had agreed to create the PS for this purpose. However, over the next two years, conflicts of vision between Nintendo and Sony continued, and the two

## EXHIBIT 1  The history of Nintendo – 1889 to 2002

| | |
|---|---|
| 1889 | Fuerjiro Yamauchi, the founder of the company, began manufacturing and selling Japanese playing cards. |
| 1902 | The company began producing Western playing cards. |
| 1951 | It was named the Nintendo Playing Card Company Ltd. |
| 1959 | Nintendo began making theme cards under a licensing agreement with Disney. |
| 1962–63 | The company went public and took its current name. |
| 1970 | Nintendo began focusing on the manufacture of electronic toys and entered the budding field of video games by licensing Magnavox's Pong technology. |
| 1977 | Nintendo developed its first home video game machine, TV Game 15 and TV Game G. |
| 1980 | Nintendo established its US subsidiary, Nintendo of America. Developed and started selling the first portable LCD video games with microprocessor. |
| 1981 | One of Nintendo's most famous coin-operated games, Donkey Kong, appeared and was an instant hit in both the US and Japan. |
| 1983 | Nintendo decided to expand its product range from games and arcade machines to home consoles, and the company released Famicom, a technologically advanced home video game system in Japan. With its high-quality sound and graphics. Famicom was a huge hit, dominating the Japanese market. |
| 1985 | Nintendo successfully launched Famicom in the US as the Nintendo Entertainment System ("NES") The company then marketed a follow-up version of Super Mario Bros for the NES, and this classic game helped the NES become a resounding success. |
| 1989 | Nintendo released a new console: the Game Boy. The Game Boy was the first major product in the handheld game console industry and became immensely popular on account of its portability and accessibility. |
| 1990–92 | In 1990, Nintendo launched the Super Family Computer game system in Japan which also did very well. A year later, the same product was launched as the Super NES in the US. In 1992, Super NES was released in Europe. |
| 1994 | Nintendo formed design alliances with companies such as Silicon Graphics. Released the Super Game Boy, a peripheral for the Super NES, which enabled Game Boy software to be played on the TV screen. |
| 1995 | Introduced a 32bit Virtual Immersion System. Know as the "Virtual Boy". |
| 1996 | Nintendo launched its 64-bit N64 game system. It launched Pokemon on the Game Boy: the game involved trading and training virtual monsters and was the first in a hugely popular video-game series. The company also released another blockbuster video game, The Legend of Zeldor: Ocarina of Time. In Just six weeks, 2.5 million units of the game were sold. |

| 1997 | It introduces the innovative "Rumble Pak" attachment for the N64 controller, which enabled the gameplayers to feel vibrations while playing the game. |
|------|---|
| 1998 | Release of Game Boy Colour. Pokemon is introduced overseas and becomes a smash hit. |
| 2000 | Nintendo acquired a 3% stake of convenience store operator Lawson in order to leverage Lawson's online operations and network to sell video games. |
| 2001 | Launched the new version of the Game Boy, with a 32 bit CPU. Nintendo GameCube is launched in Japan and the US. |
| 2002 | GameCube is launched in the European and Australian markets. |

**Source:** Nintendo Co. Ltd (2008) "Annual Report", http://www.nintendo.co.jp/ir/pdf/2008/annual0803e.pdf (accessed 3 October 2008).

finally parted ways. Nintendo went ahead with Philips technology,[4] and Sony was left with the PS, which the company decided to continue developing. Given Sony's clout and resources, when the PS and its wide range of games were finally released in Japan in 1994, the console was an instant resounding success. In 1995, Sony released the PS in the US, totally uprooting Nintendo's established name in the industry.

For many years, Nintendo had been a dominant player in the video game industry. It had sold more than two billion games since 1985. Its top-selling series included non-violent and easy-to-play games such as Super Mario Bros and The Legend of Zelda. The huge success of its games portfolio could be attributed to its appeal to all age groups across different cultures. The title of a book published in 1993 summed up Nintendo's supremacy: "Game Over: How Nintendo Zapped an American Industry, Captured Your Dollars, and Enslaved Your Children". Now it was no longer the leader of the video game industry.

Nintendo tried various strategies to counter Sony. However, competition continued to intensify, and the PS2 quickly captured a significant portion of the video game market, taking over the dominant position in the industry. In May 2001, Microsoft too entered the video game market by introducing the Xbox console, leaving Nintendo with an even smaller piece of the pie.

In 2002 Nintendo appointed Iwata[5] as president of the company to bring a change in the company's senior leadership. It was hoped that, with his experience and deep insights into how the market evolved, Iwata would help the company develop a brand-new vision and approach.[6]

# The video game industry

## History

The video game industry was born in the 1970s. In the early days, notable players such as Atari from the US and Namco from Japan brought video games to teenagers in the form of arcade games found in malls and video game arcades. With the introduction of home consoles, video games began to make their way into households around the globe.

In the 1980s and early 1990s, many new players came to the market. With the increasing popularity of personal computers ("PCs"), gamers were no longer limited to playing their favourite video game titles on proprietary consoles. Although the market was impacted by the introduction of PCs, video game makers achieved steady growth.

Nevertheless, the target customer group of video game consoles was narrowly confined to teenagers. Armed with insightful targeting and positioning, image-conscious branding, and superb graphics technologies, Sony introduced the PS in the mid-1990s. The Japanese electronics giant revolutionised the perception of video game consoles and successfully captured new players, thereby helping the industry grow substantially. Video gaming suddenly became the new hype entertainment. It was especially well received by young adults, who were mostly male and in their late 20s or early 30s and had substantial disposable incomes. By the time Sony launched the PS2 in 2000, technology giant Microsoft realised that it could no longer ignore the runaway success of this product or the impact that the booming video game market may have on its traditional PC and software domains. Thus Microsoft's video game console, the Xbox, was launched in 2001.

Since the early 2000s, the convergence of information technology, telecommunications, media and entertainment had brought about dramatic social and technological changes. With the new socio-technological movement and a wider audience base, the big video game console makers such as Sony and Microsoft began to realise that there were new opportunities for their video gaming and console product offerings, which would play a far greater role in people's lives than mere entertainment.

## Trends in the industry

With the broad availability of broadband internet, increasing sophistication of high-definition ("HD") video technologies and decreasing cost of hard-drive storage, video game console manufacturers saw that their products should no longer be for gaming only. In fact, many players such as Sony and Microsoft had envisioned their game consoles as becoming all-encompassing home entertainment centres. Further, given the increasing speed achieved by broadband connections, internet users were increasingly able to access large quantities of data files, especially those containing HD audio and video. Consequently, these console producers developed and offered online libraries as a new service enabling users to download and stream a variety of movies, music and television shows through their consoles.

As top-quality video materials became more easily available through HD broadcasting and internet downloads, a new recording medium with increased storage capacity was required. Two formats, the Blu-ray format[7] developed by a consortium led by Sony, and the HD-DVD format developed by a consortium led by Toshiba, were engaged in fierce competition in order to become the de facto standard in this area.

By offering online games based on new and existing titles, console makers could provide similar social-networking or virtual-world services to get online gamers to play, connect and form loyal communities. Such communities were expected to help create a perpetual demand for services and products created by the video game makers and their alliance partners. In fact, in-game advertising had already started and offered a new revenue stream to video game developers.

## Nintendo – innovation and the launch of the Wii

Traditionally, Sony, Microsoft and Nintendo would go into a new cycle or a new battle every five to six years, and in 2000, Sony's PS2 had emerged as the clear winner.[8] Since then, the focus of the industry had turned even more to the technological advancement of the console hardware, particularly in terms of faster processing speed, higher definition of video quality and increasing complexity of the games. The relentless pursuit of superior technologies became the convention that drove the industry's dynamics.

However, the former leader in the video game industry, Nintendo, adopted a vastly different viewpoint about the future development of the industry. Some years before the battle that began in 2006, Iwata saw the potential threats facing the industry. He observed that the video game market in Japan was shrinking. Based on various market trends and data, the key cause for this reduction appeared to be the increasing complexity of video games, which required players to invest a significant amount of their time to learn and play these games using increasingly complicated controllers with combinations of buttons and joysticks. Consequently, occasional gamers with busy lives had stopped playing. Further, for novices and non-gamers, the time required to learn and play these games was a big deterrent for potential newcomers to join the camp. Iwata also saw that the video game industry had largely ignored non-gamers and was focused on the existing ones. Armed with these insights, Iwata decided to lead Nintendo down an unorthodox path by devising a radically new strategy.

The objective of this strategy was quite simply to reach out to non-gamers in order to create a bigger market. Iwata's mandate was for simpler games to be developed, targeting all customers, irrespective of age, gender or gaming experience. These new games were to take no more than a few minutes to set up and play. In addition, they would require an easy-to-use controller. He also wanted the game scenarios to be largely based on real-life situations rather than fantasies.

In order to pilot Iwata's idea, Nintendo first developed a new handheld gaming device called the DS, which stood for "double screen" and was launched in 2004. The DS was positioned as "the machine that enriches the owner's daily life".[9] One of the key features of this device was a touch-screen that gamers could tap or write on with a stylus. This innovative design enabled gamers to play without using complicated sets of buttons or a mini-joystick. The company then launched the Nintendo Wi-Fi Connection, an innovative service that allowed DS system players to play with other users through a wireless network. Ever since its rollout, the DS had been a huge success and by April 2008, Nintendo had sold more than 70 million units worldwide.[10]

Among the many DS game titles, the most popular was Nintendogs, particularly among female gamers.

Players of Nintendogs could interact with their virtual pets through the DS's built-in microphone and "touch" them via the touch-screen. They could take these dogs for walks, teach them tricks and enter them into competitions. Another popular game was Brainage, which featured brain-training games that were basically puzzles.

Following the success of the DS, Nintendo rolled out the DS Lite in 2006. With its mature Game Boy and innovative DS systems, Nintendo remained the leader in the handheld console segment and continued to retain well over 90% of the handheld device market that it had captured since 1989.

However, the deciding factor for Nintendo's success was the video game console segment. Since 2000, Nintendo had lost control of the fixed console market to Sony's PS. With its new strategy to capture non-gamers and expand the market, coupled with the lessons learnt from the DS handheld device, Nintendo developed its new console, the Wii, which arrived about the same time as the rollout of Microsoft's Xbox 360 and Sony's PS3, and just in time for the 2006 holiday shopping season [see Exhibit 2 for a timeline of the video game console industry].

*Our goal was to come up with a machine that moms would want – easy to use, quick to start up, not a huge energy drain, and quiet while it was running. Rather than just picking new technology, we thought seriously about what a game console should be. Iwata wanted a console that would play every Nintendo game ever made.*

– Shigeru Miyamoto, member of the
Wii development team[11]

The Wii was an impressive, well-designed and tiny machine controlled with a wand-like controller that resembled a TV remote control. Without an elaborate joypad and wire, gamers could navigate the system simply by moving the controller. Motion detectors would then translate the movement of the wand into on-screen action, enabling simulation of real-life games such as tennis, bowling and even boxing. The games were sold on optical discs similar to DVDs. The Wii could also be connected to the internet for online news and weather updates and to access Nintendo's classic game catalogue (eg, the Super Mario series), which could be downloaded from the web. To do this, players could access the Virtual Console service, whereby games originally released

## EXHIBIT 2  Significant milestones in the video game console industry

| | |
|---|---|
| 1967 | German engineer Baer and co-workers designed the first video game console and developed the first set of games, the Brown Box. |
| 1972 | Magnavox approved of the above 'Brown Box', and developed Magnavox Odyssey, the first commercial video game console. |
| 1975 | Atari, a company founded by Bushnell in 1972, had its first major hit with the arcade game Pong. Pong introduced at-home video games to the masses and Atari became hugely popular. |
| 1977 | With Warner Bros having bought Atari in 1976, the Atari VCS, a cartridge-based system that played multiple games, was developed and released, and became a resounding success. |
| 1980 | Mattel entered the market and released Intellivision, a console featuring synthesised voices. |
| 1983–84 | Unlicensed games flooded the market and, with many new home systems such as the Atari 5200, the video game industry crashed. Nintendo launched Famicom in Japan. |
| 1985 | Nintendo released the NES in the US. |
| 1989 | Nintendo released its second smash hit, the Game Boy. |
| 1991 | Nintendo released the Super NES in the US, a year after its launch in Japan. |
| 1995 | Sony launched the PS. |
| 1996 | The N64, the last mass-market system to use cartridges, was released by Nintendo. |
| 2000 | Sony released the PS2. |

**EXHIBIT 2**  Continued

| 2001 | Microsoft released the Xbox. |
|---|---|
| 2002 | Nintendo released the Game Boy Advance. |
| 2004 | Nintendo launched the DS. |
| 2005 | In early 2005, Sony released the PSP. |
| November 2005 | Microsoft released the Xbox 360. |
| November 2006 | Nintendo launched the Wii.<br>Sony launched the PS3. |

**Source:** Time (2005) "Video Game Console Timeline – Video Game History – Xbox 360", www.time.com/covers/1101050523/console_timeline/ (accessed 13 August 2008).

for the SNES and N64 could be downloaded from the Wii Shop Channel and accessed from the Wii. Nintendo positioned the Wii as "a machine that puts smiles on surrounding people's faces", encouraging communication among family members as each of them found something personally relevant and were motivated to turn on the console every day in order to enjoy "the new life with Wii".[12] To promote the Wii, Nintendo adopted the same word-of-mouth strategy that had proved successful in promoting the DS. The company "recruited a handful of carefully chosen suburban housewives to spread the word among their friends that the Wii was a gaming console the whole family could enjoy together".[13] The Wii was also featured in the gamers' self made video, which was then shared through YouTube and social networking sites. This once experimental approach had proven to be more effective than the traditional advertising or mass-media campaigns used by Sony and Microsoft.

In addition to becoming the home gaming system for the family, Wii also helped expand "exergaming", which was the combination of on-screen action with physical exercise. The origins of exergaming could be traced back to 1989, when Nintendo released the Power Pad and Power Glove, two accessories for its gaming console. The Power Pad was a "large plastic platform that plugged into the console and contained pressure sensors on which gamers could step or jump to play sports games".[14] The Power Glove was a "glove-like controller that translated various gestures into on-screen movements".[15] However, these two accessories had not sold well. Now, with the introduction of the Wii into millions of households, boxing, tennis, bowling, golf and baseball games would require players to act out the physical movements involved in these sports. Consequently, it was predicted that the Wii would spawn a whole new generation of exergaming that would go far beyond the existing games that used dance mats or video cameras to

detect players' actions, as the Wii's controller could detect more subtle movements and could be used to record and analyse these movements through intelligent software to determine the players' physical fitness levels.[16]

The Wii proved to be a runaway success and, by September 2007, Nintendo became Japan's most valuable listed company after Toyota, having zipped past US$72 billion in market value and almost tripling in value since the launch of the Wii the previous year [see Exhibit 3 and Exhibit 4].[17]

# Key players in the video game industry

## Video game hardware

Other than Nintendo, the video game hardware industry (essentially comprising the manufacture of consoles and devices) was dominated by Sony with its PS family and Microsoft with the Xbox 360.

**Sony**[18]  For decades, Sony had defined the leading edge in gadgetry, producing transistor radios in the 1950s, Trinitron TVs in the 1960s and the revolutionary Walkman in the 1970s.[19]

Similarly, when the company introduced the PS in Japan in March 1994 and in the US in 1995, it brought the technology of video gaming to a whole new level [see Exhibit 5]. With Sony's strategy of attracting late teens and young adults (who had significantly more disposable income) by offering more sophisticated and often more violent games, the PS dominated the market.

In 2000, the PS2 was released and completely won over the video game market. The PS2 was not only backward-compatible with the PS, but could also be used to play CDs and DVDs. For most people who

**EXHIBIT 3**  Nintendo's income statement from 2006 to 2008 (US$ millions)

| | 31 March 2006 Restated | 31 March 2007 Restated | 31 March 2008 |
|---|---|---|---|
| Revenues | 4,736.0 | 8,988.8 | 15,553.5 |
| Cost of Goods Sold | 2,735.4 | 5,289.1 | 9,043.0 |
| Gross Profit | 2,000.6 | 3,699.7 | 6,510.6 |
| Selling, General and Administrative Expenses | 850.4 | 1,219.0 | 1,602.0 |
| R&D Expenses | 284.5 | 350.7 | 344.1 |
| Depreciation | 16.4 | 24.8 | 31.7 |
| Other Operating Expenses | 1,151.3 | 1,594.4 | 1,977.8 |
| OPERATING INCOME | 849.3 | 2,105.2 | 4,532.8 |
| Interest Expense | 0.0 | – | – |
| Interest and Investment Income | 209.2 | 316.1 | 410.7 |
| Currency Exchange Gains | 423.3 | 269.4 | −858.8 |
| Other Non-Operating Income | 22.3 | 28.7 | 16.5 |
| Earnings Before Tax (excluding unusual items) | 1,504.1 | 2,689.3 | 4,101.1 |
| Gain on Sale of Investments | 32.8 | 5.2 | −101.2 |
| Gain on Sale of Assets | −0.2 | −1.2 | 34.1 |
| Other Unusual Items, Total | 11.5 | – | – |
| Earning Before Tax (including unusual items) | 1,548.2 | 2,693.3 | 4,034.1 |
| Income Tax Expense | 633.7 | 1,072.7 | 1,641.7 |
| Earnings from Continuing Operations | 914.9 | 1,620.9 | 2,393.3 |
| NET INCOME | 914.9 | 1,620.9 | 2,393.3 |

**Source:** Adapted from *BusinessWeek* (4 August 2008) "Financial Results for Nintendo Co. Ltd", investing.businessweek.com/research/stocks/ financials (accessed 4 August 2008).

bought the PS2, it was their first DVD player. By July 2008, Sony had announced that worldwide PS2 console sales had exceeded 140 million.[20] This would make the PS2 the best-selling console in history.

In order to compete against Nintendo, the ruler of the handheld video game market, Sony introduced the PlayStation Portable ("PSP") in 2004.

In the meantime, Sony continued to release other electronics: such as Sony Connect, an online music ser-

vice, Vaio Pocket, a portable music player designed to compete with Apple's iPod, and Network Walkman, which was its first Walkman with a hard drive.

Although the PS product line dominated the market, the sales of Sony's other electronics (eg, DVD recorders, TVs and computers) and music products dropped significantly. The consumer demand remained weak, there was a battle over prices, Apple's iPod undermined the sales of Sony's CD- and MiniDisc Walkmans, as well as their TV

**EXHIBIT 4** Nintendo's consolidated sales information for the six months ending 30 September 2007 (US$ millions)

| | | Year ending 31 March 2007 | Six months ending 30 September 2006 | Six months ending 30 September 2007 |
|---|---|---|---|---|
| Hardware | Handheld | 3,241 | 1,349 | 1,827 |
| | Console | 1,356 | 33 | 1,741 |
| | Others | 470 | 79 | 355 |
| | Total | 5,068 | 1,461 | 3,923 |
| Software | Handheld | 2,530 | 1,019 | 1,322 |
| | Console | 714 | 93 | 719 |
| | Others | 46 | 10 | 44 |
| | Total | 3,289 | 1,121 | 2,085 |
| Total Electronic Entertainment Products Division | | 8,357 | 2,582 | 6,008 |
| Others (playing cards, etc) | | 19 | 7 | 13 |
| **TOTAL** | | 8,376 | 2,589 | 6,021 |

(US$1–¥115.4 on 31 March 2008)

**Source:** Nintendo Co. Ltd (25 October 2007) "Consolidated Financial Statements For The Six Months Ending 30 September 2007", http://www.nintendo.com/corp/report/FY07FinancialResults.pdf (accessed 1 August 2008).

products. These challenges, in addition to the costs incurred in streamlining operations, had significantly decreased Sony's market value and, in 2004, the company reported a loss. Sony, once acknowledged globally for its cutting-edge technological innovations, was coming to be perceived as a bureaucratic conglomerate.

In order to rectify the situation, in 2005, Sony brought in Sir Howard Stringer to replace Nobuyuki Idei as chairman and chief executive. Stringer was the first non-Japanese chief of the company and, prior to this post, had been the head of the company's US and electronics divisions. After taking over, Stringer announced Project Nippon, a corporate restructuring plan designed to revamp Sony's electronics business and foster better collaboration between the company's divisions. His plan called for eliminating 10,000 jobs (the company had 150,000 employees) and closing 11 of Sony's 65 factories. Stringer also revealed plans for a concrete research-and-development ("R&D") scheme with a focus on consumer demand, aiming to re-establish Sony's leading presence in Japan. Sony's

emphasis became HD products for consumers and broadcasters and semiconductors that aimed to improve performance in the company's products. As one of the major weapons in Sir Stringer's grand plan, Sony planned to introduce and leverage the PS3 to regain its position in the electronics industry. The PS3 was designed to be a multimedia entertainment hub. Thus, people would buy the PS3 to watch movies in addition to playing games. Its computing power would also allow users to chat online, listen to music and view high-quality animations. The machine would also be backward-compatible with games designed for previous PSs. Sony hoped that it would be able to utilize the Cell computer chip, jointly developed with IBM and Toshiba, in other products too, such as selling home servers broadband and high-definition television ("HDTV") systems. This powerful chip would power the new PS3, whose games would also be the first mass utilisation of the Blu-ray format.[21]

In November 2006, after several delays, Sony's PS3 was released nearly a year after Microsoft's Xbox 360

**EXHIBIT 5** Evolution of technology in the video game console industry's war for supremacy

| | |
|---|---|
| First Generation 1972–1977 | Simple gameplay and basic visuals, such as Atari's Pong. |
| Second Generation 1977–1984 | Consoles such as the Atari 2600 were launched. The 8-bit cartridge appeared. This era ended with the video game market crashing. |
| Third Generation 1983–1987 | The 8-bit cartridge continued. The first console war took place between Nintendo's NES and Sega's Sega Master System, with Nintendo emerging as the leader. Games such as Super Mario Bros and Metal Gear were launched and became huge successes. The handheld market, allowing mobility while playing games, was introduced with Nintendo's Game Boy and Sega's Game Gear. |
| Fourth Generation 1987–1996 | The 16-bit cartridge arrived. Graphics became increasingly well-defined. Nintendo again won the war against Sega, with its SNES sales exceeding those of the Sega Mega Drive. |
| Fifth Generation 1995–2002 | 32-bit, 64-bit and 3D graphics were introduced. In this era, Sony launched the PS and the CD format arrived – two events that completely revolutionised the industry. In the format war of CD versus cartridge, the cartridge just did not have the capacity of the CD to store games, which were increasingly complex and featured high-quality graphics. Further, while there was a threat that the CD could easily be pirated, it had the advantage of being cheaper than the cartridge. Nintendo's N64 was the last cartridge-based console to be produced. |
| Sixth Generation 1998–2004 | The 128-bit era began. Sony launched the PS2, which used the DVD format and got exclusive licences for games such as GTA and Metal Gear Solid 2, making it the winner of this round of competition. Microsoft launched the Xbox and took second place. Nintendo's Game Cube trailed in third. Sega's Dreamcast lagged at fourth place. |
| Seventh Generation 2004–2008 | The Xbox 360 and the PS3 introduced HD gaming and graphics. The PS3 had now moved ahead from the DVD to the Blu-ray format, and this combination of HD and Blu-Ray implied far superior storage capacity and graphics. Nintendo's Wii had motion sensors. |

**Source:** Adapted from Lero, D. (14 November 2007) "A History of Gaming" www.gamespot.com/pages/unions/home.php?union_id-Contributions (accessed 13 August 2008).

and within a week of the debut of Nintendo's Wii. However, the results were largely disappointing. Supply problems and the high price tag of the PS3 resulted in Sony losing its dominant position in the console market to Nintendo. To boost sales, the company slashed the price of the PS3 in mid-2007. Around the same time, due to continuous setbacks in terms of delays and inability to ramp up production, Sony fired the chief architect of the PS product line, Ken Kutaragi.

In July 2008, 20 months after the release of the PS3, the console had barely achieved 10% of its target. Sales by the end of Sony's fiscal year in March 2008 were 12.85 million, and the company expected to sell just about 10 million in the fiscal year ending March 2009.[22] Sony's more pressing need was to steer the PS3 to profitability, which was only estimated to happen by 2009 [see Exhibit 6 and Exhibit 7]. Given the shaky situation, Sony had no plans to cease development of games for the older PS2 system and planned to continue rolling out titles specifically for it.[23]

**Microsoft** Entering the video game business in 2001 was one of Microsoft's diversification moves when the company recognised the remarkable success of Sony's PS2 and the potential threat the video game market was posing to its stronghold in the PC market.

**EXHIBIT 6** Sony's income statement from 2006 to 2008 (US$ millions)

|  | 31 March 2006 | 31 March 2007 | 31 March 2008 |
|---|---|---|---|
| Revenue | 63,541.2 | 70,513.4 | 89,601.3 |
| Cost of Goods Sold | 43,786.9 | 54,652.4 | 68,885.3 |
| Gross Profit | 19,754.3 | 15,861.0 | 20,716.0 |
| Gross Profit Margin | 31.1% | 22.5% | 23.1% |
| Selling, General and Administrative Expenses | 12,446.4 | 8,719.8 | 9,525.6 |
| Depreciation | 5,682.2 | 6,531.3 | 7,408.1 |
| Operating Income | 1,625.7 | 609.9 | 3,782.3 |
| Operating Margin | 2.6% | 0.9% | 4.2% |
| Non-Operating Income | 1,054.6 | 489.3 | 1,159.1 |
| Non-Operating Expenses | 246.5 | 231.9 | 231.6 |
| Income Before Taxes | 2,433.8 | 867.3 | 4,709.8 |
| Income Taxes | 1,500.4 | 458.0 | 2,055.1 |
| Net Income After Taxes | 933.4 | 409.3 | 2,654.7 |
| Continuing Operations | 1,050.7 | 1,073.8 | 3,731.3 |
| Total Net Income | 1,050.7 | 1,073.8 | 3,731.3 |
| Net Profit Margin | 1.7% | 1.5% | 4.2% |

**Source:** Adapted from Colbert, C. (2008) "Sony Corporation", Hoover's Company Information.

The Xbox was the company's first foray into the industry and was launched to compete directly with Sony's PS2 and Nintendo's GameCube. In November 2002, the company launched Xbox Live, allowing subscribers to play online Xbox games with other subscribers around the world. By mid-2005, the service had attracted about two million subscribers worldwide.

However, by May 2005, the software giant had sold only 21.3 million Xbox units, which put the company in a distant second place behind Sony's PS2 (which had sold 83.5 million units) and slightly ahead of Nintendo's GameCube (with sales of 18.3 million units).[24] By August 2005, Microsoft's Xbox division had cost the company US$4 billion.[25] Soon after, production of the Xbox ceased in favour of the Xbox 360.

Microsoft was determined to capture the top spot in the market with the launch of the Xbox 360 in November 2005, several months ahead of its rivals (Sony's PS3

appeared in the market in late 2006, about a week after Nintendo's Wii). Some believed that the previous success of Sony's PS2 was partly due to its advantage in reaching the market earlier than its rivals; thus, Microsoft had copied this marketing strategy by becoming the first game console in the new business cycle. Further, having learnt a hard lesson from the flop of the original Xbox in Japan, Microsoft had worked closely with the producers of Japanese games, hoping to neutralise the traditional advantages of its two main rivals. The company had also abandoned its previous approach of using off-the-shelf parts provided by Intel and Nvidia to build its consoles because, while such an approach was efficient, it lacked the flexibility that Microsoft's rivals had enjoyed in reducing costs and increasing profit margins during a console's lifetime.[26] (For instance, Sony had gradually reduced the number of chips required by its PS2 without sacrificing its performance in its lifetime.) Subsequently, Microsoft adopted a new design for its

**EXHIBIT 7** Analysis of Sony's income statement for the year ending 31 March 2008

Sony's increase in revenues was largely due to the group's electronics segment, comprising televisions and digital cameras, among which there was an 8.9% increase in sales. The video game segment increased sales by 26.3% to US$12.2 billion, largely due to an increase in sales of the PS3. In all, 9.24 million PS3 units were sold in the year, an increase of 5.63 million units over the previous year. With Sony increasing software sales to 57.9 million units (from 44.6 million) and reducing hardware costs, the losses in the PS3 segment declined to US$1.18 billion from US$2.21 billion in the previous year.

PSP sales increased by 4.36 million units to 13.89 million, and PSP software sales rose by 0.8 million to 55.5 million units. PS2 sales declined by 0.98 million units to 13.73 million, with PSP software sales decreasing by 39.5 million units to 154 million.

For the year ending 31 March 2009, Sony expected game segment sales to decline and the PS2 business to shrink. However, the company was optimistic that profitability would increase with more titles available for the PS3 and reductions in hardware costs. There would be an estimated 22% reduction in profits, taking into account the one-off increase in March 2008's financials due to property sales and the floating of the group's financial services segment.

**Source:** Adapted from Jenkins, D. (14 May 2008) "Sony's Game Division See 26% Sales Jump", http://www.gamasutra.com/php-bin/news-index.php?story=18638 (accessed 11 August 2008).

Xbox 360, in the hope that this would achieve a new degree of manufacturing flexibility that could help integrate various components and increase profitability in the future [see Exhibit 8].[27]

### Video game software

The computer game industry, one of the biggest money-spinners in the global entertainment industry, routinely spent amounts ranging from US$12 million to US$20 millions in developing each game. As the consoles became more expensive, the cost of developing games for them also increased. However, Nintendo turned its lower-cost hardware into another competitive advantage. By focusing on characters rather than special effects, developing Wii games cost the company about half what its competition was expending on Xbox and PS games, and thus the expense could be recouped at much lower volumes of sales. Nintendo had also thrown in five simple but highly addictive games, Wii Sports, with each console so that the buyer was getting a 'complete' product at a great price. Sony and Microsoft, on the other hand, incurred losses on the consoles they sold, despite their high price tags. To compensate for these losses, they sold their games with high licensing royalties. As of July 2008, six of the 10 most popular games worldwide were for Nintendo consoles [see Exhibit 9].

Nintendo also focused on developing first-party titles. Nintendo had placed its top software designers at the helm of hardware design. Thus, while Sony and Microsoft relied heavily on third parties to develop titles, Nintendo's consoles were designed to suit the concepts of the games that would run on them, allowing the creation of early first-party titles that really showcased the hardware, including low-profit and offbeat games like Brainage. Such games would have been impossible on another company's hardware.[28]

The sales of hardware consoles, such as Wii, Xbox and PS, were seen to be highly correlated to the launch and sale of the video games that could be played on them. For instance, in March 2008, Nintendo launched its exclusive hit game Super Smash Bros Brawl for the Wii and, in that month, along with selling 2.7 million copies of the game, the company sold more video game consoles in the US than Sony and Microsoft combined.[29]

## The battle had begun

Until the launch of the Wii at the end of 2006, competition in the video game market had been straightforward. The leader was the company that introduced a wider array of games with high-quality graphics and increasingly complex gameplay. Then Microsoft introduced the Xbox 360 in November 2005, and Nintendo and Sony followed about a year later with the Wii and PS3. It was apparent that the rules of the game had changed.

Sony continued to claim success in selling the ageing PS2 console. Given its long history in the market, the PS2 had outsold both the Xbox 360 and the Wii. Microsoft too remained confident about its Xbox 360. As of May 2008, Microsoft announced its Xbox 360 game machine had beaten the Wii and PS3 to reach 10 million units in US sales.[30] The head start of several months in selling the Xbox 360 had given Microsoft an edge over Sony's PS3 and Nintendo's Wii. The lead time had also helped

**EXHIBIT 8** Microsoft's income statement from 2005 to 2007 (US$ millions)

| | 30 June 2005 | 30 June 2006 | 30 June 2007 |
|---|---|---|---|
| Revenue | 39,788 | 44,282 | 51,122 |
| Cost of Goods Sold | 6,200 | 7,650 | 10,693 |
| Gross Profit | 33,588 | 36,632 | 40,429 |
| Gross Profit Margin | 84.4% | 82.7% | 79.1% |
| Selling, General and Administrative Expenses | 18,172 | 19,257 | 20,465 |
| Depreciation | 855 | 903 | 1,440 |
| Operating Income | 14,561 | 16,472 | 18,524 |
| Operating Margin | 36.6% | 37.2% | 36.2% |
| Non-Operating Income | 2,067 | 1,572 | 1,577 |
| Income Before Taxes | 16,628 | 18,262 | 20,101 |
| Income Taxes | 4,374 | 5,663 | 6,036 |
| Net Income After Taxes | 12,254 | 12,599 | 14,065 |
| Net Profit Margin | 30.8% | 28.5% | 27.5% |

**Source:** Adapted from Schafer, S. (2008) "Microsoft Corporation", Hoover's Company Information.

Microsoft and its partners build a vast library of games, which was a major factor for consideration when gamers chose a particular console.

However, within a month of Microsoft's announcement of being the leader in the US console war, the June 2008 figures were released and it was evident that the Wii had usurped the Xbox 360 as the leader. A total of 10.9 million Wiis had sold in the US since its launch in November 2006, whereas a total of 10.4 million Xbox 360s had sold since its launch an entire year earlier.[31] The PS3 came in a distant third with 4.8 million units sold. In the US, which was Nintendo's largest market,[32] the Wii had taken off the fastest by selling 600,000 units in the first eight days, generating US$190 million in sales.[33] In fact, because of its high demand and market buzz, many consumers found it difficult to get their hands on the machine even months after the launch [see Exhibit 10]. The same story was being repeated in different parts of the world where the Wii had been launched, and it was Nintendo, the erstwhile third-ranker in the gaming industry, which had emerged as the clear month-on-month leader with the outstanding success of its new console [see Exhibit 11].

In terms of profitability, Nintendo was in an enviable position of making a profit on each Wii console sold from the first day [see Exhibit 12]. Sony, on the other hand, had already slashed the price of the PS3 by US $100 to US$499 to help boost sales of the console. This was still US$20 more than Microsoft's most expensive version of the Xbox 360 and about twice the price of Nintendo's Wii.[34]

It was becoming clear that, in this latest battle between the Xbox 360, PS3 and Wii, the Wii was the clear winner of the game.

# Nintendo's disruptive strategy

It was not just the video game industry that had felt the impact of the innovative Wii. With the December 2007 release of Wii Fit (an extension of the Wii for exercise activities utilising the Wii Balance Board peripheral), the potential for capturing yet another class of non-gamers was significantly increased. Wii Fit aimed to

**EXHIBIT 9** Top 10 games worldwide, July 2008 (approximate number of units in thousands)

| Rank | Console | Game | Publisher | Number of weeks since launch | Sales for the week ending 25 July 2008 | Sales since launch by 25 July 2008 |
|------|---------|------|-----------|------|------|------|
| 1 | Wii | Wii Sports | Nintendo | 88 | 333 | 26,826 |
| 2 | Wii | Wii Fit | Nintendo | 35 | 206 | 6,010 |
| 3 | DS | Dragon Quest V | Square Enix | 2 | 181 | 861 |
| 4 | Wii | Mario Kart Wii | Nintendo | 16 | 167 | 6,604 |
| 5 | Wii | Wii Play | Nintendo | 87 | 144 | 13,840 |
| 6 | DS | Pokemon Mysterious Dungeon 2 | Nintendo | 46 | 117 | 2,919 |
| 7 | DS | Guitar Hero: On Tour | Activision | 3 | 116 | 740 |
| 8 | Wii | Super Smash Bros Brawl | Nintendo | 26 | 95 | 6,430 |
| 9 | PS2 | Powerful Pro Baseball 15 | Konami | 1 | 88 | 88 |
| 10 | Xbox 360 | NCCA Football 09 | Electronic Arts | 2 | 84 | 374 |

**Source:** Adapted from VGChartz (25 Jully 2008) "Worldwide Chart for Week Ending July 25, 2008", http://www.vgchartz.com (accessed 4 August 2008).

integrate health and entertainment and featured approximately 40 different activities, including yoga, push-ups and other exercises. It was described as a way to help get families to exercise together. Within six months of being released, the product had sold two million copies in Japan and had long queues waiting for its delivery in many parts of the world. Its impact on the health industry was already evident in these few months, with doctors and therapists recommending it for various purposes, such as body balance, strength training, keeping patients interested in performing repetitive and tedious exercises, and for the elderly to enjoy expanding their range of motion.

Nintendo's business model was also exciting for small, independent software producers. In a strategic move in May 2008, Nintendo loosened its traditional tight control over content and WiiWare, an online channel for distributing downloadable games, was launched in the US and Europe. With WiiWare, users could download new games by independent developers.

*Independent developers armed with small budgets and big ideas will be able to get their original games into the marketplace to see if we can find the next smash hit. WiiWare brings new levels of creativity and value to the ever-growing population of Wii owners.*

– Reggis Fils-Aime, president of Nintendo of America.[35]

While it was still too early to predict which way the competitors were headed, it seemed that Nintendo's Wii had revolutionised and changed the name of the game, and interestingly, not just in the video-game industry alone. Would this disruptive transformation of the video game industry leave the competitors in the cold? What course of action was available to them?

# Appendix

## Disruptive technology

The term "disruptive technology" was coined by Clayton M. Christensen, a professor at the Harvard Business School. Christensen believed that leading companies, despite having followed all the right practices (ie, keeping a

**EXHIBIT 10**  Sales figures of Wii, PS3 and Xbox 360 units in the US (approximate number of units in thousands)

| | Xbox 360 | Nintendo Wii | Sony PS2 | Sony PS3 |
|---|---|---|---|---|
| September 2006 | 259 | 0 | 300 | 0 |
| October 2006 | 217 | 0 | 235 | 0 |
| November 2006 | 511 | 476 | 664 | 197 |
| December 2006 | 1,132 | 604 | 1,400 | 491 |
| January 2007 | 294 | 436 | 299 | 244 |
| February 2007 | 228 | 335 | 295 | 127 |
| March 2007 | 199 | 259 | 280 | 130 |
| April 2007 | 174 | 360 | 194 | 82 |
| May 2007 | 155 | 338 | 188 | 82 |
| June 2007 | 198 | 382 | 270 | 95 |
| July 2007 | 170 | 425 | 222 | 159 |
| August 2007 | 277 | 404 | 202 | 131 |
| September 2007 | 528 | 501 | 215 | 119 |
| October 2007 | 366 | 519 | 184 | 121 |
| November 2007 | 770 | 981 | 496 | 466 |
| December 2007 | 1,260 | 1,350 | 1,100 | 798 |
| January 2008 | 230 | 274 | 264 | 269 |
| February 2008 | 254 | 432 | 352 | 281 |
| March 2008 | 262 | 721 | 216 | 257 |
| April 2008 | 188 | 714 | 124 | 187 |
| May 2008 | 187 | 675 | 133 | 209 |
| June 2008 | 220 | 667 | 189 | 406 |
| TOTAL | 8,079 | 10,853 | 7,822 | 4,851 |

*Cumulative sales of the Xbox 360 from the launch date in November 2005 to September 2006 equalled 2,414 units, bringing the total from launch to June 2008 to 10.5 million units.

**Source:** Adapted from PVC Forum (17 July 2008) "Games Sales Chart – Monthly Console Hardware Sales in America", forum.pcvsconsole.com (accessed 11 August 2008).

close watch on competition, listening to their customers and investing aggressively in new technologies), still lost their top positions when confronted with disruptive changes in technology and market structure. He suggested that, while keeping close to customers was critical for current success, it was paradoxically also the cause for companies' failure to meet the technological demands of customers in the future. *To remain at the top of their*

**EXHIBIT 11**  Worldwide sales figures of Wii, PS3 and Xbox 360 units (approximate number of units in thousands)

| | Xbox 360 | Nintendo Wii | Sony PS2 | Sony PS3 |
|---|---|---|---|---|
| September 2006 | 446 | 0 | 859 | 0 |
| October 2006 | 431 | 0 | 793 | 0 |
| November 2006 | 1,263 | 1,068 | 2,016 | 516 |
| December 2006 | 2,028 | 2,418 | 3,282 | 843 |
| January 2007 | 692 | 1,308 | 981 | 546 |
| February 2007 | 648 | 1,315 | 954 | 389 |
| March 2007 | 438 | 900 | 708 | 954 |
| April 2007 | 395 | 1,060 | 648 | 530 |
| May 2007 | 482 | 1,522 | 746 | 418 |
| June 2007 | 392 | 1,245 | 647 | 298 |
| July 2007 | 350 | 1,371 | 735 | 419 |
| August 2007 | 636 | 1,612 | 882 | 609 |
| September 2007 | 837 | 1,149 | 754 | 428 |
| October 2007 | 1,007 | 1,234 | 699 | 632 |
| November 2007 | 1,516 | 2,698 | 1,334 | 1,525 |
| December 2007 | 2,215 | 4,267 | 2,456 | 2,389 |
| January 2008 | 1,064 | 2,296 | 1,271 | 1,480 |
| February 2008 | 648 | 1,606 | 830 | 948 |
| March 2008 | 710 | 1,730 | 765 | 929 |
| April 2008 | 886 | 2,545 | 668 | 1,189 |
| May 2008 | 796 | 2,331 | 488 | 939 |
| June 2008 | 618 | 1,921 | 499 | 995 |
| TOTAL | 18,498 | 35,596 | 23,015 | 15,981 |

**Source:** Estimated data adapted from VGChartz (July 2008) "World Hardware Sales – Weekly Comparison", www.vgchartz.com/aweekly.php (accessed 16 August 2008).

industries, managers must first be able to spot disruptive technologies. To pursue these technologies, managers must protect them from the processes and incentives that are geared to serving mainstream customers. And the only way to do that is to create organizations that are completely independent of the mainstream business.[36] Disruptive technology was described as an innovation that used a 'disruptive strategy' rather than a 'sustaining' strategy (one which improved the performance of an established product) or a 'revolutionary' strategy (one which introduced products with dramatically improved features). Christensen argued that

## EXHIBIT 12   The economics of the game – Wii, PS3 and the Xbox 360

Microsoft and Sony had been prepared for initial losses in producing their Xbox 360 and PS3 in the hope that there would be a long-term profit from software sales. However, by integrating hardware and software development, Nintendo made profits on both from the very start. In the US and Europe, where the Wii's retail price was higher than Japan and it came bundled with Wii Sports, it was estimated that it made a healthy gross profit margin per console of US$49 in the US and US$74 in Europe, factoring in currency conversions.[37]

Nintendo also outsourced nearly all production of the Wii and the DS. Its strategy of having more than one supplier for the same part meant that it got the parts cheaper and increasing production was not difficult. Sony, on the other hand, was estimated to produce nearly 40% of its components in-house.[38] The massive costs of investing in the game console, which was equipped with a Blu-ray player and the powerful Cell chip, meant that Sony continued to incur a loss on each PS3 sold.[39] Electronics supply chain researcher iSuppli's analysis in November 2006 showed that Sony's selling price of US$499 per 20GB PS3 resulted in a unit loss of about US$306.85, not including packaging, controller and cables.[40]

As for Microsoft, at launch the Xbox 360 was estimated to have made a loss of about US$125 per console.[41] By November 2006, the company streamlined processes and reduced manufacturing costs by almost 40%, thereby making an estimated profit of US$75.70 on the retail price of US$399.[42] However, the year ending 2007 remained difficult for the company's Xbox 360 division, which managed both hardware and software sales. The division posted a net loss of US$2 billion. This was primarily due to Microsoft incurring costs exceeding US$1.1 billion by extending the warranty on the product from one year to three years, mainly due to "red ring o' death" issues (a problem that arose due to a defective graphic chip which caused the console to die while in use). It was only for the year ending 30 June 2008 that a yearly operating profit – amounting to US$426 million – was reported.

Finally, unlike Sony's and Microsoft's reliance on third-party development of games, Nintendo's focus on in-house titles had a pronounced impact on revenues. These were far more profitable than third-party titles, for which the console manufacturer might get only 10–15% of the price of the game.[43]

following good business practices could ultimately weaken a great company; it had been observed that truly important and breakthrough technologies had been invariably rejected by mainstream customers because they could not immediately use them. Companies with a strong customer focus would thus reject those strategically important innovations. As a result, it was left to the more nimble, entrepreneurial companies to pursue those disruptive opportunities, which might result in worse product performance in the short term, but in the long run were of strategic importance in creating new markets and finding new customers for future products.

## NOTES

1.  Iwata, S. (23 March 2006) "GDC Keynote Address", *Nintendo World Report*, http://www.nintendoworldreport.com/newsArt.cfm (accessed 31 July 2008).

2.  McGregor, J. (17 April 2008) "The World's Most Innovative Companies", *Business Week*, http://www.businessweek.com/magazine/content/08 (accessed 10 July 2008).

3.  "Nintendo", loosely translated from Japanese, means "leave luck to heaven".

4.  Under this deal, Philips, one of Sony's principal rivals, would produce an add-on device for Nintendo game players allowing them to use optical compact discs with greater storage capacities than game cartridges.

5.  Iwata joined HAL Laboratories in 1982 and shortly after became the company's co-ordinator for software production, where he helped create video games such as Kirby. In 1993, he became president of HAL, a post he

held until 2000, when he joined Nintendo as head of the corporate planning division. When Yamauchi retired in 2002, Iwata became president of Nintendo.

6.  Colbert, C. (2007) "Nintendo Co. Ltd", Hoover's Company Information; Sanchanta, M. (26 September 2007) "Nintendo Market Cap Rockets", *Financial Times*; The Economist (26 October 2006) "Playing a Different Game".

7.  Blu-ray was a new DVD format derived from the blue laser, which had a short wavelength of 405nm. Blu-ray Discs could store substantially more data than the DVD format, which was derived from red-laser (650 nm) technology.

8.  The PS2 had been updated since introduction and was available in a much smaller format than the original.

9.  Nintendo (25 October 2007) "Consolidated Financial Statements for the six months ending 30 September

2007", http://www.nintendo.com/corp/report/FY07Finan-cialResults.pdf (accessed 1 August 2008).

10. Data sourced from VGChartz.com (week ending 5 April 2008) "Hardware Table", www.vgchartz.com (accessed 1 August 2008).

11. Hall, K. (16 November 2006) "The Big Ideas behind Nintendo's Wii", *Business Week*, http://www.businessweek.com/technolgy/content/nov2006 (accessed 25 June 2008).

12. Nintendo (25 October 2007) "Consolidated Financial Statements for the six months ending 30 September 2007", http://www.nintendo.com/corp/report/FY07Finan-cialResults.pdf (accessed 1 August 2008).

13. The Economist (7 April 2007) "Building Buzz: Marketing" 383(8525), pp. 64.

14. http://www.wordspy.com/words/exergaming.asp?r=16.9423217396108&svr=9&lang=en_us& (accessed 1 August 2008).

15. Ibid.

16. Colbert. C. (2007) "Nintendo Co. Ltd", Hoover's Company Information; The Economist (8 March 2007) "Let's Get Physical".

17. Takenaka, K. (25 September 2007) "Nintendo Becomes Japan's Second Most Valuable Company", *Reuters*, www.reuters.com/article/technology-media-telco (accessed 1 August 2008).

18. This chapter contains excerpts from: Farhoomand, A. and Tsang, S. (2006) "Microsoft's Diversification Strategy", Asia Case Research Centre, The University of Hong Kong.

19. Stahl, L. (8 January 2006) "Sir Howard Stringer: Sony's Savior", *CBS News 60 Minutes*, http://www.cbsnews.com/stories/2006/01/06/60minutes/main1183023_page3.shtml (accessed 25 June 2008).

20. Nutall, C. (20 July 2008) "Sony Sets 150m Sales Target for PS3", *Financial Times*, http://www.ft.com/cms/s/0/1c46ad2e-5678 (accessed 14 August 2008).

21. Sony had joined Matsushita and Samsung, plus a few other companies, to jointly develop the Blu-ray Disc. The alliance formed in 2004 aimed to establish the new DVD format for optical storage media. In late 2004, Disney agreed to use the Blu-ray format.

22. Nutall, C. (20 July 2008) "Sony Sets 150m Sales Target for PS3", *Financial Times*, http://www.ft.com/cms/s/0/1c46ad2e-5678 (accessed 14 August 2008).

23. Colbert, C. (2007) "Nintendo Co. Ltd", Hoover's Company Information.

24. Data sourced from VGChartz.com (28 May 2005) "Hardware Table", www.vgchartz.com (accessed 30 July 2008).

25. Murphy, V. (13 September 2005) "Microsoft's Midlife Crisis", *Forbes*, www.forbes.com/2005/09/12 (accessed 1 August 2008).

26. Lifetime refers to the complete stages of the product's life cycle: from conception, through design and production, to its service and finally disposal.

27. This paragraph has been taken from: Farhoomand, A. and Tsang S. (2006) "Microsoft's Diversification Strategy", Asia Case Research Centre, The University of Hong Kong.

28. Ehrenberg, R. (3 May 2007) "Game Console Wars II: Nintendo Shaves Off Profits, Leaving Competition Scruffy", *Seeking Alpha*, http://seekingalpha.com/article/34357-game-console-wars-ii-nintendo-shaves-off-profits-leaving-competition-scruffy (accessed 14 August 2008).

29. McDougall, P. (18 April 2008) "Nintendo Wii Sales Trounce Xbox 360, Playstation 3", *Information Week*, www.informationweek.com/news/hardware/ (accessed 15 July 2008).

30. Wakabayashi, D. (15 May 2008) "Xbox 360 Sales Surpass Wii, PS3", *Reuters*, http://www.reuters.com/article/technologyNews (accessed 25 June 2008).

31. Ricker, T. (18 July 2008) "NPD: Wii Usurps Xbox as Best Selling US Game Console, Pulling Away", *Engadget*, www.engadget.com/2008/07/18/npd-wii-usurps-xbox-360-as-best-selling-us-game-console (accessed 11 August 2008).

32. The US comprised 36% of Nintendo's total sales for the year ending March 2007, followed by Japan with 34%.

33. Colbert. C. (2007) "Nintendo Co. Ltd", Hoover's Company Information.

34. CNN (9 July 2007) "Sony Slashes PS3 Price Tag by About $100", www.cnn.com/2007/TECH/fun.games/07/09/sony.prie.reut/index (accessed 11 August 2008).

35. Mokey, N. (27 June 2007) "Nintendo Launches WiiWare Channel", *Digital Trends*, http://news.digitaltrends.com/news-article/13401/nintendo-launches-wiiware-channel (accessed 4 August 2008).

36. Bower, J.L. and Christensen, C. (1 January 1995) "Disruptive Technologies: Catching the Wave", *Harvard Business Review*, www.hbsp.harvard.edu/b01/en/common/item_detail.jhtml (accessed 11 August 2008).

37. Sanchanta, M. (16 September 2007) "Nintendo Wii Success Helps Component Makers Score", *Financial Times*, http://ft.com/cms/s/0/4f9a9108-6467-11dc-90ea-00009fd2ac.html (accessed 14 August 2008).

38. Ibid.

39. Nutall, C. (20 July 2008) "Sony Sets 150m Sales Target for PS3", *Financial Times*, http://www.ft.com/cms/s/0/1c46ad2e-5678 (accessed 14 August 2008).

40. Edge Online (16 November 2006) "iSuppli: 60GB PS3 Costs US$840 to Produce", http://www.edge-online.com/news/isuppli-60gb-ps3-costs-840-produce (accessed 14 August 2008).

41. Ibid.

42. Mann, J. (20 November 2006) "Microsoft Makes Tiny Profit on Xbox 360 Hardware", TechSpot News, http://www.techspot.com/news/23612-microsoft-makes-a-tiny-profit-on-xbox-360-hardware.html (accessed 14 August 2008).

43. Ehrenberg, R. (3 May 2007) "Game Console Wars II: Nintendo Shaves Off Profits, Leaving Competition Scruffy", Seeking Alpha, http://seekingalpha.com/article/34357-game-console-wars-ii-nintendo-shaves-off-profits-leaving-competition-scruffy (accessed 14 August 2008).

**INTEGRATIVE CASE 12**

12

# PSA PEUGEOT CITROËN: STRATEGIC ALLIANCES FOR COMPETITIVE ADVANTAGE?

Sachin Govind, S. Sam George

*ICFAI Center for Management Research*

*I don't want to boast, but I can say that we are probably the champions in the sphere of the joint projects.*[1]

– Jean-Martin Folz,
President, Board of Directors,
PSA Peugeot Citroën, in 2003

## Introduction

In February 2005, PSA Peugeot Citroën (PSA) entered into an agreement with Mitsubishi Motor Corp.,[2] the ailing Japanese car maker. According to the terms of the deal, Mitsubishi agreed to supply 30,000 units of a new sports utility vehicle (SUV) every year to PSA, which would then be sold under the Peugeot and Citroën marques. The deal enabled Mitsubishi to utilize its idle production capacity, and PSA to fill a major gap in its product range.

The deal with Mitsubishi was typical of PSA's strategy of entering into alliances with other major automobile makers. Over the years, PSA has entered into long-term relationships with Renault S.A,[3] Fiat Auto SpA,[4] Ford Motor Co.,[5] Toyota Motor Corp.,[6] and BMW AG.[7] Such alliances have helped PSA share costs, risks, and investment. At the same time, PSA was also pursuing R&D independently to sharpen its competitive edge.

In January 2006, PSA announced that its profits for the year 2005 would be less than previously estimated. This profit warning – the second in three months –

reflected the poor sales performance of the company's cars in Europe. The competition in the automobile market in Europe remained intense, which contributed to lower margins. PSA launched several new models in 2005. Even so, worldwide sales of Peugeot branded cars in 2005 fell by 1.5 percent. However, Citroën car sales were 3.5 percent higher in the same period.

The Peugeot arm of PSA expected to sell 2 million cars in 2006. The company hoped to sell, by the end of 2007, half a million units of its new model, the 207, a compact car launched in January 2006.

## Background note

### About Peugeot

The history of PSA dates back to the nineteenth century. In 1810, Jean-Frederic Peugeot, together with his brother Jean-Pierre Peugeot, transformed their textile mill in Alsace, France, into a foundry. The brothers invented a new process of making sprung steel. Using this new technology, they started making saws, watch springs, and other products. In 1858, Peugeot adopted the now familiar lion logo as its symbol (refer to Exhibit 1 A for the logo). In the 1880s, Peugeot was managed by Armand Peugeot, Jean-Pierre's grandson. In 1885, Peugeot started producing bicycles. In 1889, Peugeot unveiled its first automobile – a steam-powered three-wheeler. However, almost immediately, the steam engine was dropped in favor of the petrol engine patented by

**EXHIBIT 1**   Company logos

**A. Peugeot Logo**

**B. Citroën Logo**

Source: http://www.psa-peugeot-citroen.com.

Gottlieb Daimler. The first "customer" car was delivered in 1891. In 1892, Peugeot made 29 cars and by 1899, production had increased to 300 cars a year.

Peugeot established a presence in several rallies and competitions in the 1890s. The first appearance of a Peugeot in a race was in the 1894 Paris–Rouen Trial (which is widely considered the world's first motor race). Peugeot tasted its first success in the 1895 Paris-Bordeaux-Paris race.

In 1896, Peugeot started making its own engines. The same year, Societe Anonyme des Automobiles Peugeot, a separate automobile company, was set up by Peugeot. In 1900, the company's first small car christened Bebe was launched. In 1902, the company opened a new factory in Lille. Soon, the factory started making motorbikes as well. With the success of its products, yet another factory was opened in 1910 in Sochaux. All this time, the company's cars continued to do well at motor races.

After World War I, the company began to concentrate on making diesel-powered cars. In 1922, Peugeot Quadrilette, a diesel car, replaced the Bebe. The Quadrilette was a huge success. In subsequent years, Peugeot acquired several companies including the Bellanger Car Company in Neuilly, and De Dion Bouton factory in Puteaux. In 1929, Peugeot launched the 201 model. The 1930s saw the launch of the 202 and 402 models, which went on to become bestsellers.

No new model launches occurred during World War II. In 1947, the 203 model was launched. During this period new acquisitions were made such as Chenard-Walcker and Hotchkiss. In 1955, the company launched the 403, which sold 1.2 million units in a decade.

## About Citroën

In 1912, André Citroën paid a visit to Ford's plant in the United States and learned the operational details of mass producing cars. In 1913, André established the Société des Engrenages Citroën headquartered at Quai de Grenelle in Paris. Soon he made preparations to transform an armaments plant into an automobile factory. In 1919, the company launched its first car, the Type A, the first mass-produced model in Europe. Around this time, the chevron[8] shape of its gear teeth was adopted as the company logo (refer to Exhibit 1 B for the logo). In 1921, a second model – the B2 – was launched, replacing the Type A. In 1922, a Citroën achieved the unique distinction of being the first car to cross the Sahara desert.

In 1924, a new company, Société Anonyme André Citroën, was created. The same year, sales subsidiaries were opened at Brussels, Cologne, Milan, Amsterdam, and other important cities in Europe. In 1924–1925, Citroën became popular for a motor expedition referred to as the black cruise.[9] In 1927, the C4 was launched. In 1931–1932, Citroën organized yet another motor expedition called the yellow cruise.[10] In 1934, the company launched the 7A, which incorporated several innovative features including front wheel drive, torsion bar suspension, aerodynamic body, hydraulic brakes, and so on. However, during this period the company faced financial problems. In 1934–1935, Michelin, the French tire maker, acquired a major stake in Citroën and started a restructuring exercise that included layoffs. Michelin was able to wipe off Citroën's debts and improve its efficiency. In 1935, André passed away.

During World War II, the Citroën factory was bombed, which led to a drastic fall in production. However, the company soon rebuilt the plant. In 1948, the 2CV van was launched. In 1953, the company entered into an agreement with Panhard, an armored vehicle maker, to partially merge the two companies' sales networks. In 1958, the company set up a new plant at Vigo, Spain, to manufacture its 2CV vans. In 1965, Citroën acquired Panhard. In 1967, the company acquired a majority stake in Berliet, another automobile company. In 1968, a parent company – Citroën SA, which owned Citroën, Panhard, and Berliet – was formed. In 1974, Peugeot acquired a 38.2 percent stake in Citroën SA.

## PSA Peugeot Citroën

In May 1976, Peugeot took complete control of Citroën SA, and PSA Peugeot Citroën was formed. PSA, the holding company, was the full owner of both the companies (Automobiles Peugeot S.A and Automobiles Citroën S.A). In the same year, the 10 millionth Peugeot car rolled out of the factory premises (refer to Exhibit 2 for new model launches during 1977–2005). In 1977, Société Mécanique Automobile de l'Est (SMAE) was established to manufacture gear boxes and engines. In the same year, SAMM, an aeronautics component manufacturer, was also acquired by the group. In 1978, the European arm of Chrysler[11] (Chrysler France, Chrysler UK, and Chrysler Spain) was acquired by PSA. PSA sold the models of the former Chrysler's European subsidiaries, including Simca[12] and Sunbeam[13] under the Talbot marque. In 1980, Peugeot and Talbot merged and a single dealership for both marques was established. The marketing for both product ranges was handled by Peugeot.

In 1982, Citroën shifted its headquarters to Neuilly, France. In the same year, a new plant to manufacture gear boxes was inaugurated at Valenciennes. In 1986, the Talbot models were discontinued. In 1990, Peugeot

celebrated its 100th year as an automaker. In 1991, Peugeot established its subsidiary, Peugeot do Brasil. In 1992, the group entered China and Egypt through partnership agreements.

In 1994, Citroën celebrated its 75th anniversary. In 1998, the group unveiled its new high-pressure direct injection (HDi) engine, which was incorporated in all its models. In 2001, the group received ISO 14001 certification for several of its facilities. In the same year, the group entered into an agreement with two French technology research institutions – Scientific Research Center (CNRS) and Atomic Energy Commission (CEA) – for joint research on fuel cells. In 2005, the group sold Panhard.

In 2005, PSA worldwide sales reached 3,389,900 units, with sales of the Peugeot marque totaling 1,995,450 units and the Citroën marque another 1,394,450 (refer to Exhibit 3 for region-wide sales of

## EXHIBIT 2  New model launches, 1977–2005

| Year | Models | Year | Models | Year | Models |
|------|--------|------|--------|------|--------|
| 1977 | Peugeot 305 | 1986 | 205 convertible, 309 GTI, Citroën AX | 1998 | 206, Partner Electric, Xsara Coupe, Xsara Estate, Berlingo Electric |
| 1978 | Citroën Visa, Simca Horizon | 1987 | 405 | 1999 | 206 S16 |
| 1979 | 505, 604 turbo diesel | 1989 | 605, Citroën XM | 2000 | Xsara Picasso, 607, 206 CC |
| 1980 | 305 Station Wagon, 505 turbo, Talbot Solara | 1991 | 106, Citroën ZX | 2001 | 307, C5 |
| 1981 | Peugeot J5, Samba, Tagora, Visa II, C25 | 1993 | 306, Citroën Xantia | 2002 | 206 SW, 307 SW, 307 Estate, 807, C3, C8 |
| 1982 | Citroën BX, 505 | 1994 | 806, 306 Convertible, Citroën Synergie, Relay | 2003 | 307 CC, Citroën C2, C3 Pluriel |
| 1983 | 205 | 1995 | 406, 106 electric, Peugeot Expert, Citroën Xantia Activa, AX Electric, Jumpy | 2004 | 407 |
| 1984 | 205 GTI | 1996 | Citron Saxo, Berlingo, Saxo Electric, Peugeot Partner, 406 Estate | 2005 | 107, C1, 1007, 407 Coupe |
| 1985 | 309, BX Estate | 1997 | 306 Estate, 406 Coupe, Xantia LPG, Berlingo Multispace, Xsara | | |

**Source:** http://www.psa-peugeot-citroen.com.

## EXHIBIT 3  Regional sales* for PSA, 2005

| Region | Sales (in units) |
|---|---|
| France | 777,000 |
| Other Western European countries | 1,583,400 |
| Central Europe and Turkey | 209,700 |
| Africa | 83,600 |
| The Americas | 194,500 |
| Asia-Pacific | 511,900 |
| Other | 29,800 |
| **TOTAL** | **3,389,900** |

\* Sales include passenger cars and light commercial vehicles.
**Source:** http://www.psa-peugeot-citroen.com.

## EXHIBIT 4  List of models, February 2006

| Peugeot | 107, 206, 206cc, 207, 307, 307cc, 407, 607, 807, 1007, Partner Combi |
|---|---|
| Citroën | C1, C2, C3, C3 Pluriel, C4, C5, C6, C8, Berlingo, Xsara Picasso |

**Source:** http://www.peugeot.com and www.citroen.com.

PSA). As of 2006, the group was selling more than 22 models (refer to Exhibit 4 for a list of models of Peugeot and Citroën as of 2006).

# Forging alliances

PSA could be considered the pioneer of strategic alliances in the automobile industry. Its first alliance with Renault started in 1966. Over the years, the company benefited considerably from its strategic alliances with several automobile and auto component companies. Subsequently, other automobile companies took the cue from PSA and entered into alliances and partnerships with their competitors (refer to Exhibit 5 for alliances in the auto industry).

## PSA and Renault S.A.

PSA and Renault had a series of agreements that involved several joint industrial and technological projects. As noted above, Peugeot and Renault first collaborated in 1966 when the two companies entered into a cooperation agreement for the joint production of mechanical subassemblies. In 1969, the two companies further strengthened their partnership by establishing a joint venture – La Française de Mécanique (LFM) – to produce long-series components and engines that were to be used in Peugeot and Renault cars. The 50:50 joint venture was located in Douvrin, in northern France. In the same year a limited company called Société de Transmissions Automatiques (STA), owned 80 percent by Renault and 20 percent by Peugeot, was founded. STA was established primarily to produce automatic transmissions for Renault and rear-axle assemblies for Peugeot. The STA plant was located in Ruitz in northern France.

In 1971, Peugeot, Renault, and Volvo[14] came together to design a V6 engine.[15] The three automobile makers formed an equally owned company called Peugeot Renault Volvo (PRV). The engines were manufactured by LFM and by 1974, they were being used in the Peugeot 504 and 604, and the Renault 30. However, in 1989, Volvo pulled out from PRV. As a result, Peugeot and Renault became 50 percent partners in the company.

In 1992, PSA entered into a fresh technological and industrial agreement with Renault to develop a new series of automatic transmissions. Meanwhile, LFM continued to develop improved versions of the V6 engines. In 1996, LFM introduced the new V6 ES 9 engine for mid-range and high-end Renault cars, the Peugeot 406, and the Citroën Xantia and XM models. Again in 1997, the self-acting automatic transmission – BVA – was jointly developed by PSA and Renault, with each company bearing FRF 2.8 billion as development costs. The transmission was manufactured at the STA plant in Ruitz and Peugeot's plant in Valenciennes.

In 2000, PSA and Renault launched an improved three-liter version of the V6 ES 9 engine. The new engine was installed in mid-range and high-end Renault, Peugeot, and Citroën cars and multipurpose vehicles. The LFM plant manufactured about 27,000 V6 ES 9 engines in 2000.

## Fiat Auto SpA

PSA's strategic relationship with Fiat started in 1978 when the two companies signed their first cooperation agreement to design and manufacture a light commercial vehicle. A joint venture, Société Européenne de Véhicules Légers (Sevel SpA), owned 50 percent by Fiat, 25 percent by Automobiles Peugeot, and 25 percent by Automobiles Citroën, was established for this purpose. The production of the vehicles (Fiat Ducato, Peugeot J5, and Citroën C25) began at Val di Sangro facility, near Pescara, Italy, in 1981. In 1988, the scope of the joint venture with Fiat was expanded to include the design and production of multipurpose vehicles (MPVs).

**EXHIBIT 5**  Some strategic alliances in the automobile industry

| No | Companies | Year | Remarks |
|----|-----------|------|---------|
| 1 | Fiat Auto and Tata Motors | 2006 | Tata Motors was to manage distribution and after-sales service for Fiat in India. Fiat, in turn, would provide access for Tata Motors to world markets. |
| 2 | Fiat Auto and Suzuki | 2005 | Fiat Motors and Suzuki co-developed an SUV. Suzuki was to use Fiat's 1.9 l diesel engines for its version of the SUV. |
| 3 | Nissan and Mitsubishi Motors | 2000 | Integration of forklift business of both companies – from product development to marketing. |
| 4 | Fiat Auto and General Motors | 2000 | Share engines as well as platforms and pool purchase and finance operations in Europe and Latin America. |
| 5 | Toyota and General Motors | 1999 | Joint research on fuel cell technology, joint operation of auto manufacturing plant in California. |
| 6 | Suzuki and General Motors | 1987 | Joint establishment and management of a company in Ingersoll, Canada. The objective of the alliance for Suzuki was to gain entry into the North American market, while GM attempted to gain insights into Japanese manufacturing methods and management. |

**Source:** Compiled from various sources.

In 1993, the Val di Sangro plant started the production of the Peugeot Boxer, and the Citroën Dispatch, both light commercial vehicles. The plant continued to manufacture Fiat Ducatos as well. In 1994, a new plant at Sevelnord, Valenciennes, France, began operations for the production of the Peugeot 806, the Citroën Synergie, and the Fiat Ulysses and Lancia Z (Zeta). The agreement between PSA and Fiat required the partners to manage the plants located in their country of origin (i.e., the Val di Sangro plant was managed by Fiat and the Sevelnord plant was managed by PSA). PSA and Fiat owned 50 percent in each plant and shared the production capacity equally. In 1995, the Sevelnord plant started production of the Peugeot Expert, the Citroën Relay, and the Fiat Scudo light commercial vehicles.

In 2002, PSA declared that its collaboration with Fiat in the development of light commercial vehicles would be extended through 2017 making it one of the most enduring alliances in the automobile industry. PSA and Fiat signed a major framework agreement that outlined various aspects of the collaboration. PSA and Fiat were to invest around €1.7 billion to manufacture two lines of light commercial vehicles.

In 2005, Tofas, a Turkey-based automobile manufacturer, entered into an agreement with PSA and Fiat, making it a three-way collaboration. The agreement involved the development and production of small, entry-level

light commercial vehicles. The new models were to expand the product ranges of Peugeot, Citroën, and Fiat. They were to be manufactured at Tofas's plant in Bursa, Turkey, and were to be launched in 2008.

As of 2005, the PSA-Fiat partnership had jointly produced, since 1978, a total of 3.3 million light commercial vehicles and 400,000 multipurpose vehicles.

### Ford Motor Co.

PSA's cooperation with Ford began in September 1998. The two automakers announced a large-scale agreement to jointly develop four families of small diesel engines incorporating the latest technologies, including Common Rail Direct injection (CRDi).[16] The initial announcement put the development time for the new engines at two and a half years. In 1999, the initial agreement was expanded to include an extended range of small aluminum direct injection diesel engines for cars and light commercial vehicles. The new agreement also included technological upgrades of a midsized second generation engine and a range of V-diesel engines for the luxury vehicles of both companies. PSA and Ford shared the total cost of the project equally. The partnership with Ford developed in four phases.

In 2001, in the first phase, PSA and Ford unveiled the first direct injection diesel engine developed under the cooperation agreements, which replaced the TUD[17] range of engines. The 1,398 cc engines were sold as HDi 1.4 by PSA and Duratorq TDCi 1.4 by Ford. The engines were mounted on the Peugeot 206 and 307, the Citroën C2 and C3, and the Ford Fiesta and Fusion. Both companies identified 23 applications for the new engine family. The production of the engines at the Douvrin plant saw high productivity levels with daily production reaching 6,000 engines. As part of the first phase, a new 1.6-liter (1,590 cc) common rail diesel engine was also launched.

In early 2003, PSA and Ford introduced a 2-liter CRDi diesel engine (1,988 cc) developed in the second phase of their cooperative venture. These engines were manufactured at PSA's Trémery plant. The high-performance and low-noise engines were reportedly more fuel-efficient and cleaner than those available in the market. The aggregate investment for the development of the engines came to nearly €1 billion.

The first two phases of the cooperation were carried out under the leadership of PSA; the third and fourth phases were led by Ford. In June 2003, as part of the third phase, a new 2.7-liter V6 24-valve engine was unveiled. Production of the engine began in the following months. The engine was first mounted on the Jaguar S-Type. Subsequently, it was used in the Peugeot 607, the Land Rover Discovery, the Range Rover Sport, the Jaguar XJ, the Peugeot 407 Coupe, and the Citroën C6.

In October 2005, under the fourth phase of their cooperation, PSA and Ford started the production of a new series of 2.2-liter CRDi diesel engines for light and medium commercial vehicles. In addition, they introduced a new 2.2-liter HDi/TDCi diesel engine that was eventually mounted on several Peugeot, Citroën, and Ford upper/medium and executive passenger car platforms. The engines were produced at the Trémery plant. The HDi/TDCi engine showcased the companies' ability to work together in developing high-performance diesel engines (see Table 1.).

In all, PSA and Ford jointly produced four families of CRDi diesel engines, namely 1.4-liter/1.6-liter engines, a second-generation 2-liter engine, a 2.7-liter V6 engine, and a new family of engines for light commercial vehicles. The cooperation made PSA-Ford the world's leading diesel engine manufacturer. By 2005, they were jointly manufacturing more than 9,000 engines a day.

## Toyota Motor Corp.

In July 2001, PSA and Toyota signed a cooperation agreement in Brussels, Belgium, to establish a joint venture company. Toyota Peugeot Citroën Automobile (TPCA) Czech was established for the joint development and production of small cars designed mainly for the European market. The companies also announced that the small cars developed by the joint venture would be priced below the entry-level cars of the two partners, which meant that the factory for the production of these cars had to be established in a low-cost country and meet stringent requirements. After an extensive search, Kolin in the Czech Republic was identified as the location for the plant. The plant started production of Toyota, Peugeot, and Citroën branded cars in 2005. The capacity of the plant was 300,000 vehicles per year, with 100,000 cars for each of the brands – Peugeot, Citroën, and Toyota.

Toyota was in charge of development and production, while PSA was responsible for purchasing and logistics. The total investment, primarily for R&D and industrial expenditure, of about €1.5 billion, was shared between the two automakers.

## BMW AG

In 2002, PSA entered into a cooperation agreement with BMW to jointly develop and produce an all-new family of small 4-cylinder petrol engines incorporating the latest technologies. In June 2005, PSA and BMW presented the industrial plan for production of the engines. The engines

**TABLE 1**  A comparison of different manufacturers' diesel engines

| Manufacturer | Engine | Max. Power (PS) | Max. Torque (Nm) | Vehicles |
|---|---|---|---|---|
| PSA/Ford | 2.7-L V6 | 207@4000 rpm | 440@1900 rpm | Jaguar S-Type, Peugeot 607 |
| Isuzu | 3.0-L V6 | 180@4000 rpm | 370@1900 rpm | Saab: 9; Renault: Vel Satis; Opel: Vectra & Signum |
| Volkswagen | 2.5-L V6 | 180@6200 rpm | 370@1500 rpm | Audi A6 |
| DaimlerChrysler | 3.2-L I6 | 204@4200 rpm | 500@1800 rpm | Mercedes E- and S-class |

**Source:** http://www.autoreport.com.

were later used in Peugeot and Citroën cars and by Mini[18] (wholly owned by BMW). While the main engine was manufactured solely at PSA's Douvrin plant in Northern France, the engine assembly was done at Douvrin for PSA and Hams Hall in the United Kingdom for the Mini. PSA and BMW implemented a coordinated process to enable complete transparency between the two engine plants in order to deal effectively with any quality issues. PSA's Charleville and Mulhouse Metallurgy Division plants were assimilated into the industrial plan as suppliers of raw castings.

The design and development of the engine was done largely by BMW. PSA provided the logistics support for production of the engines. A complete production module was brought on line in late 2005 at the Francaise de Mecanique plant in Douvrin. The module was based on the development of a highly integrated, independent production unit that could easily be replicated on other sites. The plant was designed to produce 2,500 units a day. The first module, with an investment of €330 million, produced an engine every 26 seconds. At its maximum production capacity, overall annual production was expected to reach 1 million units. At full capacity, the module employed 1,120 employees, working in four shifts.

The cooperation resulted in a number of innovations.[19] The engines set new standards in performance, driving comfort, fuel economy, and $CO_2$ emissions.

## Mitsubishi Motor Corporation

In February 2005, PSA and Mitsubishi announced a cooperation agreement for a new SUV, with 30,000 vehicles to be produced every year in Japan and to be sold under the Peugeot and Citroën marques. The SUV model, which was expected to roll out by 2007, was to be styled differently for the Peugeot and the Citroën versions. However, the two versions were to be equipped with the latest HDi diesel engines. Initially, the SUVs were to be marketed only in Europe. However, the two companies were expected to enter other markets in the future.

## The rationale behind the alliances

In the 1990s and 2000s, intense competition in the auto industry led to a wave of consolidation. Several auto companies bought stakes in their competitors. For example, DaimlerChrysler bought a 37 percent stake in Mitsubishi, Ford bought a 33 percent stake in Mazda, GM held a 20 percent stake in Fiat Auto, and Renault acquired a 44 percent stake in Nissan. PSA did not make any effort to buy or acquire stakes in other auto companies. "We can definitely get by on our own,"[20] Folz said. PSA, however, concentrated on entering into strategic alliances to counter the challenges posed by its competitors. A major

advantage of such strategic alliances over a merger or acquisition was that PSA did not have to look for massive debt financing and experience years of inefficiencies due to duplications in manufacturing. PSA entered joint ventures mostly with strong players: Ford, Renault, Toyota, and BMW. And the purpose of these alliances was to share costs and investments and create synergies.

PSA believed that an important factor for success was the ability to bring out a variety of models with minimum costs. Folz said, "The key to succeeding in this car market is to rapidly produce cars as varied and attractive as possible and to do that at a competitive cost."[21] PSA's alliances with Toyota and Fiat helped it to expand its product range. At the same time, by sharing the costs and risks, it was able to provide more choice to its customers with minimum investment.

PSA's strategic alliances were also meant to achieve economies of scale, which in turn helped lower per unit costs and risks. The company brought out several models of cars based on a single platform using its superior styling and design skills to differentiate the models. Folz said, "The key to survival in the car industry today is not to produce three, four, or five million cars. The real challenge is one's ability to produce a maximum number of cars on a limited number of platforms. That's what we're trying to do."[22] The alliances with Toyota for small cars and with Fiat for light commercial vehicles served to create new platforms, which would be used to launch several future models.

PSA's alliances with Renault, Ford, and BMW helped it develop engines with the latest technology, something that it might have found it difficult to manage alone. The alliances were successful in creating synergies between PSA and its partners. Owing to its alliances with the major players, PSA managed to remain at the forefront of engine technology.

The shared costs and risks helped PSA not only to price its cars competitively but also enjoy higher margins. Even though Volkswagen, the market leader and PSA's rival in the European market, had a profit margin of less than 1 percent[23] in 2004, PSA enjoyed a margin as high as 4 percent in the same period.

Apart from sharing costs, risks, and investments, strategic alliances also helped PSA to acquire and develop new technologies. In the joint venture with Toyota, although the production was controlled by Toyota, 10 managers from PSA were stationed at the plant, providing them with the opportunity to learn about the world-renowned production system followed by Toyota. This experience was expected to improve the production system at PSA in the future.

PSA also seemed to be reaping unexpected rewards from its joint ventures. A case in point was again its joint

**TABLE 2**  2005 J.D. Power & Associates customer satisfaction index

| Rank | Brand | Score |
|------|-------|-------|
| 1 | Lexus | 84.8 |
| 4 | Toyota | 83.5 |
| | **Industry Average** | 78.6 |
| 26 | Citroën | 76.6 |
| 30 | Peugeot | 74.6 |

**Source:** http://www.motor.org.uk.

venture with Toyota for the Peugeot 107, Citroën C1, and Toyota Ayga city cars. Toyota is known the world over for the superior quality and dependability of its cars. The high quality was the direct result of the famed Toyota Production System (TPS). On the other hand, PSA cars didn't figure very high on dependability, as evidenced by their poor customer satisfaction scores and low resale values. (See Table 2 for the 2005 J.D. Power and Associates' customer satisfaction index.) Analysts however expected the 107 and C1 cars to have higher resale values owing to Toyota's involvement in their production.

The success of any alliance depends to a large degree on the partners having similar goals and common interests (refer Exhibit 6 for a short note on making alliances work). In the case of PSA's joint ventures, the alliances were as beneficial to the other partner as to PSA. For example, the former president of Toyota Motor Europe, Shuhei Toyoda, who was part of the negotiations with PSA, said, "We needed a partner to get the right volume for costs."[24] And the volumes were achieved by entering into a joint venture with PSA.

# Going it alone

PSA was well aware that in an increasingly competitive market, it could sell more only if its vehicles were superior, distinct and offered unique advantages. Therefore, in spite of its many alliances, PSA was investing in excess of €2 billion in exclusive Research & Development facilities and projects. Pascal Henault, vice president (Innovation and Quality) said, "Innovation is a way to differentiate our cars in terms of concepts, styling and features that deliver perceptible customer benefits at affordable cost."[25] At its R&D centers at Belchamp La Garenne-Colombes and Velizy, hundreds of engineers and scientists were working toward new and innovative solutions, with the result that PSA filed more than 300 patents every year. In October 2004, PSA unveiled a new design

**EXHIBIT 6**  Making alliances work

The success of an alliance depends on three main factors: partner selection, alliance structure, and the way in which the alliance is managed.

**Partner Selection:** The choice of partner can make or break the alliance. In other words, the strength and success of the alliance depends to a large extent on the partner's characteristics. A good partner helps an organization achieve its strategic goals, which could be to share costs, risks, and investment concerning new product development or to gain access to technology. Additionally, a good partner would have similar expectations for the alliance. And finally, a good partner would not exploit the alliance unfairly.

**Alliance Structure:** The structure of the alliance also has a bearing on the success and duration of the alliance. Issues such as percentage of ownership, mix of financing, technology, and machinery to be contributed by each partner figure prominently. The alliance should be designed in such a way that it is difficult to transfer technology that was not part of the agreement. Contractual safeguards should be included in the alliance to guard against risk of opportunism by a partner.

**Managing the Alliance:** The management of the alliance should be based on mutual trust. Such trust can be achieved by building interpersonal relationships between the managers/workforce of the partners. A major determinant of success of an alliance is the ability of partners to learn from each other. In most cases, learning takes place at the lower levels of the organizations. Therefore, the lower-level employees must be informed about the partner's strengths and weaknesses and taught the importance of learning particular skills from the partner so as to improve the competitiveness of the organization.

**Source:** Adapted from *Introduction to Business Strategy*, ICMR.

## EXHIBIT 7   PSA's worldwide production sites

| Country | Production Site | Output (2004) |
|---------|-----------------|---------------|
| Brazil | Rio de Janeiro | 50,000 |
| Argentina | Buenos Aires | 70,000 |
| United Kingdom | Ryton | 180,000 |
| France | Rennes | 292,000 |
| | Sevelnord | 162,300 |
| | Mulhouse | 379,100 |
| | Sochaux | 430,000 |
| | Poissy | 302,400 |
| | Aulnay | 418,380 |
| Portugal | Mangualde | 53,450 |
| Spain | Madrid | 138,100 |
| | Vigo | 458,550 |
| Italy | Val di Sangro | 183,195 |
| China | Wuhan | 141,000[#] |
| Iran^ | Tehran | 293,000 |
| Morocco^ | Casablanca | 8,000 |
| Indonesia^ | Jakarta | 500 |
| Turkey^ | Bursa | n.a |
| Nigeria^ | Kaduna | n.a |
| Egypt^ | Cairo | n.a |
| Czech Republic | Kolin | 105,000[+] |
| Slovakia* | Trnava | n.a |

Notes: ^ = assembly plant; * = will start operations in 2006; # = 2005 figure; n.a = not available.
**Source:** http://www.psa-peugeot-citroen.com.

center named Automobile Design Network near Paris to give a further thrust to its research initiatives.

PSA's research and development efforts were based on a "Research and Innovation Plan" that was an integrated and comprehensive system of research projects covering every area of automobile development. For example, PSA engaged scientists to improve the ergonomics, architecture, production process, and other aspects of its vehicles.

## EXHIBIT 8   Financial data of PSA Peugeot Citroën consolidated sales and revenue (in millions)

| | 2004 | 2005 |
|---|------|------|
| Automobile Division | 45,239 | 45,071 |
| Banque PSA Finance (car finance company) | 1,601 | 1,656 |
| Gefco (transportation and supply chain management company) | 2,894 | 3,000 |
| Faurecia (automotive equipment company) | 10,719 | 10,978 |
| Other Businesses | 899 | 709 |
| Intersegment Eliminations | (5,247) | (5,147) |
| Total | 56,105 | 56,267 |
| **Consolidated Financial Highlights** | **2004** | **2005** |
| Operating margin | 2,481 | 1,940 |
| Profit before tax and share in net earnings of companies at equity | 2,439 | 1,530 |
| Consolidated profit | 1,680 | 990 |
| Profit attributable to equity holders of the parent | 1,646 | 1,029 |
| **Financial Position** | **2004** | **2005** |
| Working capital | 4,561 | 4,133 |
| Gross capital expenditure | 2,804 | 2,873 |
| Equity | 13,703 | 14,406 |
| Net financial position of the manufacturing and sales companies | 1,347 | 381 |
| Number of employees | 207,600 | 208,500 |

**Source:** http://www.psa-peugeot-citroen.com.

At a strategic level, PSA adopted a product policy wherein it focused its research efforts particularly on three critical areas: safety, fuel economy, and comfort.

## EXHIBIT 9　Worldwide sales and production of PSA

|  | 2004 | 2005 |
|---|---|---|
| Worldwide unit sales | 3,375,300 | 3,389,900 |
| Worldwide production | 3,405,100 | 3,375,500 |

**Source:** http://www.psa-peugeot-citroen.com.

To improve the safety of its vehicles, the company conducted research on driver-support, anti-skid, and emergency braking systems. It was also working on energy-absorbing deformable mechanical structures. Fuel economy was another area on which the company focused its research efforts. Diesel and petrol engines with improved mileage, fuel cell technology, and hydrogen storage systems[26] were some of the research projects in which PSA was engaged. Driver-vehicle interface ergonomics was another area of focused research for PSA. The objective was to enhance driving pleasure and comfort.

## Challenges

Volkswagen was the undisputed leader (in terms of the number of cars sold) in the European car market in 2005. Even though PSA continued to retain its second position in Europe, the gap with Volkswagen was widening. Volkswagen managed to increase its market share from 18.6 percent in 2004 to 19.3 percent in 2005, while PSA's share fell from 13.8 percent to 13.5 percent. Although Toyota was a distant eighth in the rankings, it had improved its sales in a shrinking market.[27] Moving

toward its goal of capturing 15 percent of the world automobile market by 2010, Toyota was intensifying its efforts in Europe – an important market for the carmaker.

PSA's strength was in compact cars, which were hugely popular in most countries in Europe, its traditional market. However, the Japanese players (especially Toyota and Honda) were increasingly targeting the same segment. Even DaimlerChrysler and BMW were expanding their product ranges to include small cars.

PSA received a mere 15 percent of its revenues from outside Western Europe. In other markets where PSA had a presence, the company was not doing too well. In China, GM and Volkswagen were ruling the roost.[28] PSA's market share in China was stuck at about 5 percent over several years. And in India the company was not even present. However, its sales in Russia and Brazil were picking up (refer to Exhibit 7 for PSA's international presence).

Although PSA collaborated with its competitors, it was also sometimes critical of them. For example, PSA criticized some technologies introduced by Toyota. PSA was of the opinion that the Prius gasoline-electric hybrid car introduced by Toyota in the early 2000s was high-priced. The high price resulted in low sales, which it felt didn't do much to help the environment. "When you are not satisfying the mass market you are simply not doing the job," said Marc Boquet, a spokesman for PSA. "At PSA we produce advanced technology for everyone."[29]

Though PSA was considered a champion of alliances, analysts felt that competition from its partners in the

## EXHIBIT 11　World automobile market, 2005

| Region | Sales In 2005 (in million units) | Growth (% over previous year) |
|---|---|---|
| United States | 7.60 | 1.4 |
| Canada | 0.84 | 3 |
| Europe | 15.22 | –0.7 |
| China | 2.85 | 26.5 |

**Source:** Compiled from various sources.
Note: In 2005, the worldwide automobile market grew by 3.2 percent to 68.2 million passenger cars and light commercial vehicles. However, there was a marked difference in sales growth rates among different regions of the world. Owing to sluggish economic growth in several countries, the European automobile market shrank by about 3 percent. In the Central and East European market, after peaking in early 2004, a sharp decline occurred in 2005. Registrations in Poland slid 23.5 percent, and sales in Hungary slipped by 4.2 percent. The U.S. market showed growth with annual sales reaching 16.9 million units. The Canadian market grew by 3 percent to reach 1.58 million units. In Asia, the market expanded by 6.4 percent. The Latin American market rebounded with Brazil registering a healthy 9.5 percent. Argentina recorded a growth rate of 35.2 percent.

## EXHIBIT 10　Europe automobile market shares, 2005

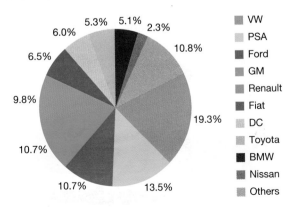

Legend: VW, PSA, Ford, GM, Renault, Fiat, DC, Toyota, BMW, Nissan, Others

Values: 5.3%, 5.1%, 2.3%, 6.0%, 10.8%, 6.5%, 9.8%, 19.3%, 10.7%, 13.5%, 10.7%

**Source:** Compiled from various sources, and based on volume.

## EXHIBIT 12 Estimated European passenger vehicle sales by company

| Manufacturer | 2005 Sales (in million units) | 2004 Sales (in million units) |
|---|---|---|
| Volkswagen | 2.944 | 2.853 |
| PSA | 2.061 | 2.122 |
| Ford | 1.628 | 1.686 |
| GM | 1.625 | 1.637 |
| Renault | 1.487 | 1.569 |
| Fiat | 0.988 | 1.129 |
| DaimlerChrysler | 0.914 | 0.922 |
| Toyota | 0.818 | 0.787 |
| BMW | 0.779 | 0.710 |
| Nissan | 0.357 | 0.381 |
| Hyundai | 0.317 | 0.313 |
| Honda | 0.259 | 0.236 |
| Kia | 0.242 | 0.173 |
| Suzuki | 0.234 | 0.204 |
| Mazda | 0.233 | 0.255 |
| Mitsubishi | 0.133 | 0.123 |
| Others | 0.195 | 0.225 |
| **Total** | **15.222** | **15.332** |

**Source:** Compiled from various sources.

future might affect its relationship with them. However, other analysts felt that the purpose of alliances was to lower costs and risks, and PSA was certainly reaping these benefits. Carlos Ghosn, chief executive for Renault talking about his company's alliances once said, "It [entering into alliances] doesn't mean that people will be complacent of each other. We're still competitors, and competing heavily. But at the same time we are business people. That means when an agreement makes sense it has to be done."[30]

In October 2005, PSA announced that its operating profits for the year 2005 would be less than 4 percent of sales (PSA traditionally enjoyed operating profits of

close to 4.4 percent of sales). In January 2006, the company announced a second profit warning that put the operating profits at 3.4 percent of sales (refer to Exhibit 8 for PSA's financials). PSA saw its sales in the European market slide by 2.7 percent in 2005 (refer to Exhibit 9 for PSA's worldwide sales and production).

The 2005 full-year report, which was released in February 2006, showed a 37 percent drop in net profits compared to 2004. Intense competition (refer to Exhibit 10 for estimated market shares in 2005, and Exhibits 11 and 12 for general information on the world automobile market), a gloomy European economy, rising prices of gasoline, and an unfavorable product range were cited as reasons.

## Outlook

The Peugeot 207 (refer to Exhibit 13 for a photograph of the Peugeot 207) was unveiled in early 2006, and was a successor to Peugeot 206 – the company's most popular car ever. In 2005, PSA launched several models including the Peugeot 407 (saloon), the 407 coupe, the 1007 (a small car with electric sliding doors), the 107, the Citroën C1 city car, and the Citroën C6 luxury limousine.

In January 2006, PSA launched a new fuel cell called Genepac. Genepac was considered a major step in fuel cell technology because it could power a car for a distance of up to 500 kilometers, which was much more than all other fuel cells available in the market. However, it suffered from most other drawbacks that made fuel cells unviable. The 80 KW cell was the size of a large suitcase which made it difficult to use in ordinary passenger cars. Moreover, the cost of manufacturing the cells was too high. PSA was conscious of the problems but felt that the technology had potential. Folz stated in a news

## EXHIBIT 13 The Peugeot 207

**Source:** http://www.peugeot.com.

conference, "This technology is still at its early stages but offers a real answer for the future."[31] The company promised that it would try and halve the price of the cells by 2010. It would also make efforts to make the cell more compact.

PSA's explicitly stated policy of cooperation and collaboration with independent auto companies was seen by the company as the best way to counter the challenges posed by globalization and its larger competitors. At the same time, the company was making sure that it secured competitive advantages by going solo on several vital research projects. This dual strategy demonstrated obvious advantages. At one level, PSA reaped benefits such as higher margins, lower development costs and less time to market new models. In Folz's words, "These 'win-win' agreements allow us to share development and production costs without renouncing our independence, and to pool skills and expertise. They also generate the economies of scale we need to be competitive, by speeding our development and increasing production capacity. In addition, such cooperations offer many opportunities to learn about each other's culture and processes."[32] At another level, the strategy allowed PSA to maintain its lead in technology and thus enhance its competitiveness.

## ADDITIONAL READINGS AND REFERENCES

2006, PSA Peugeot Citroen to sell diesel hybrids in 2010, http://www.planetark.com, February 1.

2006, PSA Peugeot Citroen "cautiously optimistic" about 2006, http://www.just-auto.com, January 18.

2006, Peugeot launches new 207 small car line, http://www.greencarcongress.com, January 12.

J. Marsden, 2006, Poor car sales lead PSA to cut outlook, http://www.icbirmingham.co.uk, January 12.

2006, PSA Peugeot Citroen unveils small fuel cell, http://www.fuelcelltoday.com, January 10.

J. Kanter, 2005, Toyota leads Asia drive in Europe, http://www.iht.com, July 23.

2005, Ford and PSA Peugeot Citroen strengthen diesel cooperation, http://www.media.ford.com, October 5.

2005, Peugeot deal boosts Mitsubishi, http://www.bbc.co.uk, February 4.

2005, Revved up for battle, http://www.businessweek.com, January 10.

D. Huq, 2004, Toyota and PSA Peugeot Citroën unveil jointly developed cars, http://www.jcnnetwork.com, December 2.

2003, Different brands, common strategy.

2002, BMW and PSA form joint engine project, http://www.all4engineers.com, October 18.

J. Madslien, 2002, French car maker takes on the world, http://www.bbc.co.uk, October 9.

2002, PSA Peugeot Citroën and Toyota announce the name of new joint-venture company, http://www.toyota.com, January 10.

2000, PSA Peugeot Citroen and Ford Motor Company announce cooperation in telematics in Europe, http://www.ford.com, September 27.

C. Tierney, 2007, Can Peugeot go it alone? http://www.businessweek.com, April 17.

1999, PSA aims to form joint venture with Japan's Koyo Seiko, http://www.bloomberg.com, November 25.

1999, J.-M. Lamy, Renault, Peugeot-Citroën, Michelin: Three flagships of the French motor industry, April.

1998, PSA launches mega depot joint venture, http://www.worldcargonews.com, July.

Mergers, takeovers and product differentiation, http://www.bized.ac.uk.

Engines: Peugeot (PSA Peugeot Citroën), http://www.grandprix.com.

http://www.psa-peugeot-citroen.com.

http://www.all4engineers.com.

http://www.media.ford.com.

## NOTES

1.  2003, Different brands, common strategy, http://www.zr.ru, April.

2.  Mitsubishi Motor Co. launched its first passenger cars in 1917. Until 1970, the company was part of Mitsubishi Heavy Industries (MHI), which was founded by Tsukomo Shokai in 1870. In the 2000s, Germany-based DaimlerChrysler acquired a 37 percent share in the company.

3.  Renault, the French automobile maker, was founded by Louis Renault in 1898. As of September 2005, the Renault group revenues touched €30.8 billion (nine-month period).

4.  FIAT or Fabbrica Italiana Automobili Torino, the Italian automaker, was founded in July 1899 by a group of investors. In the 2000s, the company faced a severe financial crisis with losses touching $1.2 billion, which necessitated a major restructuring exercise.

5. Ford was founded in 1903 by Henry Ford and a group of investors. In 2004, the company reported a loss of $155 million in its automotive business.

6. Toyota, the Japanese automaker, was established in 1937. The company has grown to become the second largest auto manufacturer in the world with net income crossing ¥1,171 billion in 2004–2005.

7. BMW or Bayerische Motoren Werke was founded in 1913 as Rapp Motoren Werke by an engineer Karl Friedrich Rapp. In 1917, the name was changed to BMW. The company caters to the premium segment and in 2004, its net profit had reached £2.2 billion.

8. The general shape of the "V" character, or a triangular shape pointing upwards/downwards, is referred to as chevron.

9. The black cruise, described as "a great route to a great isle," was a 28,000-kilometer trip undertaken by Georges-Marie Haardt and his team. The expedition, which started at Colomb-Bechar in Algeria, passed through Niger, Chad, Oubangui-Chari (Central African Republic), and the Belgian Congo (Democratic Republic of Congo). At Kampala, the team split into four groups and reached Tananarive in Madagascar, each taking a different route (Mombasa, Dar-es-salam, Mozambique, and the Cape).

10. The yellow cruise was meant to open up the old "Silk Route" (an ancient trade route that connected China, Persia, Arabia, and Europe) to cars. The 30,000-kilometer trip started in Beirut, Lebanon, and passed through the Pamir region (Central Asia). Another group, which started in Tien Tsin (Tianjin, China), joined the Pamir group at Aksu (Xinjiang Uygur, China) and together proceeded to Peking (Beijing).

11. Chrysler Motor Corporation was established in 1925 by Walter P. Chrysler. The company merged with Daimler Benz in 1998 to form DaimlerChrysler. In 2004, Daimler-Chrysler's revenues exceeded US$ 192 billion.

12. Societe Industrielle de Mecanique et Carrosserie Automobile or SIMCA was founded by Henri Pigozzi in Nanterre, France, in 1934. Initially, the company produced FIAT models under a license agreement. Subsequently, with the success of its Aronde models, the company's dependence on FIAT decreased. In the 1950s, the company acquired automobile companies such as Unic, Automobiles Talbot, and the French arm of Ford. In 1963, Chrysler bought a majority stake in Simca.

13. Sunbeam Motorcar Company Ltd. was established in 1905 by John Marston. In 1920, it merged with Darracq, a French automobile company. Darracq had earlier acquired Clement-Talbot Ltd, a London-based automobile company. STD Motors Ltd (where STD stood for Sunbeam-Talbot-Darracq) was created as the holding company. In 1935, due to financial problems, Clement-Talbot Ltd was sold to the Rootes Group. Soon, Rootes also purchased Sunbeam. In 1967, Chrysler took complete control of the Rootes Group.

14. Until 1998, Volvo Cars was part of AG Volvo. AG Volvo was founded in August 1926 in Gothenburg, Sweden. Volvo Cars was acquired by Ford in 1998.

15. V6 engine is a V engine with six cylinders. A V engine is a common configuration for an internal combustion engine wherein the pistons are aligned so that they appear to be in a V when viewed along the line of the crankshaft. (Source: http://www.wikipedia.org.)

16. CRDi is a modern variant of direct fuel injection system for diesel engines. It features a high-pressure (1000+ bar) fuel rail feeding individual solenoid valves as opposed to mechanical valves.

17. The PSA TU engines were a family of small four cylinder engines used in Peugeot and Citroen cars. The first TU engine was introduced in 1987. They came in petrol and diesel variants. The diesel variant was referred to as TUD.

18. Mini is a wholly owned subsidiary of BMW since 2001. It manufactures the MINI, a small car, which is a retro redesign of the classic Mini – a car made by British Motor Corporation from 1959 to 2000.

19. The innovations that came out of the alliance included the lost foam process for cylinder heads, pressurized aluminium casings with cast-iron jackets inserted into the casting, steel crankshafts with unmachined counterweights, connecting rods forged using the double impression method, and so on.

20. Radu Boghici, 1999, France's Peugeot on look-out for joint ventures, http://www.vectorbd.com, April 15.

21. C. Tierney, 2000, Can Peugeot go it alone? http://www.businessweek.com, April 17.

22. R. Boghici, 1999, France's Peugeot on look-out for joint ventures, http://www.vectorbd.com, April 15.

23. 2005, Volkswagen brakes for epic change, http://www.businessweek.com, July 25.

24. 2005, Revved up for battle, http://www.businessweek.com, January 10.

25. Strategy, 2004 Annual Report, http://www.psa-peugeot-citroen.com.

26. As part of its research on fuel cell technology, PSA designed two demonstrators powered by fuel cells – the TaxiPAC and $H_2O$. The TaxiPAC system uses hydrogen stored on board the vehicle. This system requires further refinement, and PSA was conducting research on making the hydrogen storage system safer and more efficient.

27. According to ACEA, the total light vehicle registrations in Europe (26 countries) in 2004 were 1.11 million. In 2005, the registrations dropped to 1.07 million.

28. In the first half of 2005, with 10.9 percent and 9.25 percent market shares, GM and Volkswagen (through their joint ventures) were the market leaders (in terms of sales) in the Chinese automobile industry.

29. J. Kanter, 2005, Toyota leads Asia drive in Europe, http://www.iht.com, July 23.

30. J. Madslien 2002, French car maker takes on the world, http://www.bbc.co.uk, October 9.

31. 2006, PSA Peugeot Citroën unveils small fuel cell, http://www.fuelcelltoday.com, January 10.

32. 2005, Citroën: Strength through cooperation, http://www.citroen.com, July 11.

# INTEGRATIVE CASE 13

# 13

# TESCO VERSUS SAINSBURY'S GROWTH STRATEGIES AND CORPORATE COMPETITIVENESS 1990–2007

Markus Kreutzer, and Professor Dr Christoph Lechner

*University of St Gallen*

## Introduction

In 2008, the UK-based international food and general merchandising retailer Tesco reached a market share of about 30% in the UK, roughly the same as its rivals Sainsbury's and ASDA combined. Tesco has greatly diversified, extending its business lines from food into non-food, clothing, financial services, and telecommunications. It ranks sixth in the international retail market behind Wal-Mart (US), Carrefour (France), Home Depot (US), Metro (Germany), and Royal Ahold (Netherlands).[1]

Tesco was not always the dominant player it is today. In 1990, it was a mid-sized food chain far behind its rival, Sainsbury's. Starting in the 1990s, it pursued a broad set of growth initiatives, steadily increasing its market share and gaining importance. In 1995, Tesco surpassed Sainsbury's to become the UK's market leader. Today, Tesco is the clear market leader. How did that happen? Why was Tesco so successful in growing sales and profits, while Sainsbury's could not keep pace? Where did the competitive actions of these firms differ? Let us start with a close look at their origins.

## Sainsbury's, Tesco, and the UK retail market in 1990

Sainsbury's was established in 1869 by John James and Mary Ann Sainsbury, making it the oldest food retailing chain in Britain. In 1922, J Sainsbury became a private company, with J Sainsbury plc acting as parent company of Sainsbury's Supermarkets Ltd, commonly known as Sainsbury's, a chain of supermarkets in the UK. In 1973, the company was floated as J Sainsbury plc in what was at the time the largest flotation on the London Stock Exchange. The family currently retains about 14% of its shares. The group is also engaged in property and banking, owning real estate worth about £8.6 billion. For much of the 20th century, Sainsbury's was the market leader in the UK supermarket sector, but in 1995 it lost its place to Tesco; in 2003, it was pushed into third place by ASDA.

Tesco was founded by Jack Cohen in London's East End. From a modest background, Cohen, the son of a Polish shopkeeper, began selling groceries in Well Street market, Hackney, in 1919, after World War I. At that time, food supplies were low, so he bought damaged goods from other stores and re-sold them at reasonable prices. The Tesco brand first appeared in 1924. The name originated after Cohen bought a shipment of tea from TE Stockwell. He made new labels using the first three letters of the supplier's name and the first two letters of his surname. The first Tesco store opened in 1929 in Burnt Oak, Edgware, Middlesex. Tesco was floated on the London Stock Exchange in 1947 as Tesco Stores (Holdings) Ltd. During the 1950s and 1960s, Tesco grew slowly, until it owned more than 800 stores. The company purchased 70 Williamsons stores (1957), 200 Harrow Stores outlets (1959), 212 Irwins stores (1960), 97 Charles Phillips stores (1964), and the Victor Value chain (1968) (sold to Bejam in 1986). In 1973, Jack Cohen resigned and was replaced as chairman by his son-in-law, Leslie Porter. Porter and managing director, Ian MacLaurin, abandoned the "pile it high and sell it cheap" philosophy of Cohen, which had left the company stagnating with a bad image. In 1977, Tesco launched "Operation Checkout," which included price reductions and centralized purchasing for all its stores. As a result, its market share rose by 4% within two months.

At the beginning of the 1990s, the UK retail market slowly increased its competitiveness. Three players dominated the food market: ASDA[2] (which became Wal-Mart's largest overseas subsidiary in 1999), Sainsbury's, and Tesco. ASDA positioned itself as the price leader and held this position for some time, closely followed by Tesco. Sainsbury's targeted the upper price segment, positioning itself in the middle between mass market and high-end.

In the mid-1990s, competition intensified as a price war among these players emerged, resulting in squeezed margins and cost cutting. It is not surprising that this also had an adverse impact on the service level these corporations could provide.

In general, prices of standard brands and private labels at both Sainsbury's and Tesco came closer, while the two firms differed slightly in their discounting policies. Tesco emphasized its low-price private label ("Value") and continued to cut prices, while Sainsbury's emphasized price reductions on the standard private labels. The price cuts were prompted by the increased price pressure from the market entry of discounters. For example, Aldi entered the market in 1990, followed by Lidl in 1994. In 2005, these two hard discounters had acquired a market share of 2.2% and 1.9%, respectively.

## Store formats

In 1975, Sainsbury's launched the "Sainsbury's SavaCentre" hypermarket format as a joint venture with British Home Stores. This was the first attempt in the UK to launch supermarkets with a large non-food range. SavaCentre became a wholly owned Sainsbury's subsidiary in 1989. As the hypermarket format became mainstream, with rivals such as ASDA and Tesco launching ever-larger stores, Sainsbury's decided that a separate brand was no longer needed. Over the following years, these stores were converted to the regular Sainsbury's superstore format and, subsequently, Sainsbury's retreated from hypermarkets and changed its store formats. Now, Sainsbury's operates three formats: regular Sainsbury's stores, Sainsbury's local stores (convenience stores), and Sainsbury's central stores (smaller supermarkets in urban locations). For an overview of Sainsbury's UK store portfolio at the end of fiscal year 2005–06, see Table 1 in the appendix.

While Sainsbury's retreated from hypermarkets, Tesco expanded Tesco Extra and strengthened its hypermarket formats.[3] Its overarching store strategy is reflected in its core marketing slogan adopted when Terry Leahy became CEO in 1997. "The Tesco Way" implies a shift from a focus on the corporation to a focus on people, both employees and customers. Tesco stores are divided into five formats, differentiated by size and range of products, and are customized to specific segments: Tesco Extra, Tesco Superstores, Tesco Metro, Tesco Express, and One Stop (see Table 2). The approximately 500 One Stop stores are the smallest units. They stay open in the late evening and feature a differentiated pricing and offer system. Tesco Extra, launched in 1997, is the largest format, consisting mainly of out-of-town hypermarkets that stock Tesco's entire product range and offer free parking. Their number has increased about 20% annually, mainly by conversions of other formats. Tesco Superstores are the standard large grocery supermarkets, with a much smaller range of non-food goods than Extra. They are referred to as "superstores" for convenience, but not as part of the name. It is the standard Tesco format. Most are located in suburbs of cities or on the edges of large- and medium-sized towns. Tesco Metro stores are sized between normal Tesco stores and Tesco Express stores. They are mostly located in city centers and on the high streets of small towns. The first Tesco Metro was opened in Covent Garden, London, in 1992. Tesco Express stores are neighborhood convenience stores, stocking mainly food, with an emphasis on high-margin products alongside everyday essentials. They are found in busy city centre districts, in small shopping precincts in residential areas, and in petrol station forecourts. As the CEO remarks:

*This obsession with our customers, their needs, and how these must be changing, means that you should not expect us to go on opening large edge-of-town superstores long after the need for new ones has passed. Expect ... continual evolution: expect us to provide a mix of formats in different locations ... to meet special needs of customers in each location.*

Terry Leahy, CEO Tesco
(Tesco Annual Report, 2000)

Much of Tesco's sales increases occurred through increases in total square footage with the opening of new stores, including new formats such as Metro and Express. From 1994 to 1996, selling areas increased by 22% for Tesco and 10% for Sainsbury's. At the same time, Tesco managed to increase sales per square foot by 14%, while Sainsbury's gained only 3%. In addition, acquisitions and alliances complemented the organic growth strategy. Tesco, for example, purchased Adminstore in 2004, owner of 45 Cullens, Europa, and Harts convenience stores, in and around London. In late 2005, it purchased the 21 remaining Safeway/BP stores after Morrison's dissolved the Safeway/BP partnership. In 1997, Tesco formed an alliance with Esso Petroleum Company Ltd (now part of ExxonMobil Corp.). The agreement included several petrol filling stations on lease from Esso, where Tesco would operate the store under the Express format. In turn, Esso would operate the forecourts and sell their fuel via the Tesco store. Ten years later, over 600 Tesco/Esso stores can be found across the UK.

Sainsbury's also expanded by acquisition. As part of the acquisition of Safeway Group by Morrison's, Morrison's was to dispose of 53 of the combined group's stores. In May 2004, Sainsbury's announced that it would acquire 14 of these stores, 13 Safeway stores, and one Morrison's outlet, all located primarily in the Midlands and the north of England. The first of these new stores opened in August 2004. In 2004, Sainsbury's also expanded its share of the convenience store market through other acquisitions. Bell's Stores, a 54-store chain based in northeast England, was acquired in February 2004. Jackson's Stores, a chain of 114 stores based in Yorkshire and the North Midlands, was purchased in August 2004. JB Beaumont, a chain of six stores in the East Midlands, was acquired in November 2004. SL Shaw Ltd, which owned six stores, was acquired in April 2005 for £6 million. On 29 September 2004, Sainsbury's established Sainsbury's Convenience Stores Ltd to manage its Sainsbury's local stores and the Bell's and Jackson's chains. The latter two were re-branded as Sainsbury's local stores in 2009.

# Service offerings and distribution systems

"An inclusive offer" is how Tesco describes its aspiration to appeal to upper-, medium-, and low-income customers in the same stores. According to Citigroup retail analyst David McCarthy, "They've pulled off a trick that I'm not aware of any other retailer achieving. That is to appeal to all segments of the market." One plank of this program has been Tesco's use of its private label products, including the upmarket "Finest" and low price "Value". Other examples include organic, kids, British specialty food, and "free from" brands. As one expert remarks:

*Tesco's winning formula is largely due to its ability to be all things to all people. According to TNS, over 60% of British households shop in Tesco every four weeks. That's 20% more than its nearest rival. The store appeals to wide reaching demographics across the country and has built up a heritage of reliability and trustworthiness, which keeps shoppers returning to its stores. These factors have enabled Tesco to gain close to a third of the British grocery market.*

Edward Garner, Communications Director of TNS Superpanel

Sainsbury's has also invested in private labels. A large Sainsbury's store typically stocks around 50,000 lines of which about 50% are private labels. These lines include, for example, "Basics" (an economy range similar to Tesco's "Values"), "Taste the Difference" (a premium range similar to Tesco's "Finest"), "Different by Design" (a smaller range of premium non-food lines), "Kids", "Be Good to Yourself" (products with reduced calorific and/or fat content), "Free from," "Sainsbury Organic," "Fair Trade," and "Super Naturals TM" (a range of ready-made meals with healthy ingredients). While service offerings today are quite similar, the rivals' distribution strategies differ significantly. In common with most other large retailers, Tesco decided to draw goods from suppliers into regional distribution centers for preparation and delivery to stores. Tesco is extending this logistic practice to cover collection from suppliers (factory gate pricing) and input to suppliers in a drive to reduce costs and improve reliability.

In contrast, Sainsbury's heavily invested in fully automated depots. On 14 January 2000, Sir Peter Davis was appointed Sainsbury's CEO. This decision was well received by investors and analysts, as in his first two years he raised profits above targets. By 2004, however, the group had suffered a decline in performance relative to its competitors and fell to third in the UK food market. Davis oversaw an almost £3 billion upgrade of stores, distribution, and IT equipment. Part of this investment included the construction of four fully automated depots, which, at £100 million each, cost four times more than standard depots.

# Loyalty programs

Retailers try to gain the loyalty of their customers in various ways. Tesco was the first to launch a clubcard system. It was introduced in 1995 and has become the most popular card in the UK, with around 13 million active Clubcard holders. Customers collect one Clubcard point for every £1 (€1 in Ireland) they spend in a Tesco store, Tesco Petrol, or Tesco.com. Customers also collect points by paying with a Tesco Credit Card or by using Tesco Mobile, Tesco Homephone, Tesco Broadband, selected Tesco Personal Finance products, or by using its Clubcard partners, Powergen or Avis. Each point is worth 1p in-store when redeemed or 4p when used with Clubcard deals (offers for holidays, day trips, etc). Every three months, holders receive a Clubcard statement offering discount coupons that can be spent in-store, online (if opted into eVouchers), or on various Clubcard deals. The program has numerous partners (e.g., hundreds of British pubs), but the Clubcard belongs to Tesco alone. Tesco implemented the Clubcard rewards program to gather customer information, which is then used to cater to specific potential customer needs and wants. When shoppers sign up for the card, they automatically submit their ages, genders, and incomes. Tesco segments their shoppers on the basis of these factors. As soon as the shopper uses the card online or in-store, product information is automatically uploaded into the Tesco database. Product information is used to cross-sell additional products and services, such as food delivery.

*Tesco is the most customer-focused business that I have ever worked for. They are absolutely obsessed with the customer.*

John Hoerner, Non-Food Director Tesco

Sainsbury's was "wrong-footed" in its original reaction to the Tesco Clubcard, showing "no immediate response apart from disdain."[4] It suffered from market share loss in subsequent years. In 2004, *The Times* quoted a former executive and others who viewed this event as the start of the company's downturn due to management failures by David Sainsbury and his successors, Dino Adriano and Peter Davis. David Sainsbury, who, in 1992, replaced his cousin, the long-time CEO John Sainsbury, first dismissed Tesco's Clubcard. After long internal debates, Sainsbury introduced the Sainsbury's reward card in 1996. A multiparty card program, "Nectar," was launched in the autumn of 2002. Nectar gives the customer a versatile and powerful point-gathering system to be used and redeemed at a variety of stores. In Nectar, Sainsbury's has strong partners such as Barclaycard, British Petroleum, and the department store chain Debenhams. The Nectar card was relaunched in summer 2007 to celebrate its fifth anniversary. The scheme was changed from a reward- to a treats-based

program. In its early days, the Nectar scheme was criticized as being among the worst card schemes offered. At the time, it was said that some consumers who spent £5,000 on Barclaycard received as little as £12.50 in points to redeem, while Sainsbury's customers had to spend as much as £1,000 just to get two tickets to the cinema. Today, points on spending in-store are earned at a rate of two points per £1 spent (except 1 point per liter of fuel); 500 points can subsequently be exchanged for a voucher worth £2.50 to spend in Sainsbury's. The card scheme is run by a third-party company, Loyalty Management UK (LMUK), which collects information on behalf of the partner sponsors.

# Online sales channels

Toward the end of the 1990s, both firms targeted online distribution channels that promised large growth potential. Non-store retailing growth rates were expected to be higher than store-based rates, as online usage gained popularity among British consumers (see Table 11.). Following these predictions, the UK has evolved today into a leader of Internet retailing in Europe, and growth is continuing.

Tesco[5] has operated on the Internet since 1994 and was the first retailer in the world to offer a robust home-shopping service in 1996. Tesco.com was formally launched in 2000. It also has online operations in the Republic of Ireland and in South Korea. Food sales are available within delivery range of selected stores, goods being hand-picked within each store, in contrast to the warehouse model followed by most competitors (e.g., Ocado[6]), which allows rapid expansion with limited investment. In 2003, Tesco.com's then CEO, John Browett, received the Wharton Infosys Business Transformation Award for the innovative processes he used to support this online food service. Today, Tesco operates the world's largest food home-shopping service, as well as providing consumer goods, telecommunications, and financial services online. As of November 2006, Tesco was the only food retailer to make online shopping profitable.

Sainsbury's has been involved in e-business and home-shopping development since 2000, when it launched Sainsbury's to You in April of that year. Although some employees transferred from the traditional side of the business, Sainsbury's also hired new staff with Web and marketing skills. Specific training was provided on e-business, as well as cross-functional training. Sainsbury's to You did not completely spin off but occupied a separate building, thereby combining entrepreneurial flexibility with the strength and security of a strong brand. Sainsbury's Online currently operates from 144 stores and uses two dedicated picking centers that are not open to the public. In addition to food, also available are flowers, wine, gifts, and electronics. In October 2007, Sainsbury was receiving around 80,000 online orders per week. This represents quite strong growth, but is far less than Tesco, which processes weekly orders of 250,000. Sainsbury's did not release any e-commerce sales figures, but said it was still on track to expand its Web service to 200 stores by March 2010. Tesco.com captured two-thirds of all online food orders in the first seven months of 2007, generating sales of approximately £2.5 million per day. Sainsburystoyou.com took third place with 14%, behind ASDA with 16%. Customers of Sainsbury's, however, spent the most per order, averaging almost £90 compared to £80 for both Tesco and ASDA. ASDA and Sainsbury's online shoppers also bought more items per order, with both averaging 69 units per order compared to 58 for Tesco. Sainsbury's online customers incurred the lowest average delivery charge during the period, at just over £3. Tesco online customers paid over £4 per delivery, and ASDA online customers paid nearly £5.50.

## Diversification into non-food

*A number of retailers have created such a sense of nearness with customers in terms of perception, safety and security that you can refer to them as brands.*
    Karel Vuursteen, Chairman & CEO, Heineken

Originally specializing in food, Tesco began early to diversify into areas such as discount clothes, consumer electronics, consumer financial services, DVD sales and rentals, compact discs and music downloads, Internet service, consumer telecoms, consumer health insurance, consumer dental plans, and budget software. In these new product segments, Tesco heavily built on its skills in private labels. For example, it introduced brands such as "Cherokke" and "F+F" in clothing, "Technika" and "Digilogic" in consumer electronics, and other labels ranging from DVD players to televisions and computers. Tesco used its food brands "Finest" and "Value" to expand into non-food items. In its Extra stores, Finest health and beauty, home, and clothing lines resulted.

In 1997, Tesco Personal Finance was launched as a fifty-fifty banking joint venture with the Royal Bank of Scotland. Products offered included credit cards, loans, mortgages, savings accounts, and several types of insurance, including car, home, life, pet, and travel. They are promoted by leaflets in Tesco stores and through its Web site. All of its offers are simple, providing customers few but clear options and choices. Profits were £130 million for the 52 weeks prior to 24 February 2007, of which

Tesco's share was £66 million. This move toward the financial sector has diversified the Tesco brand and provides opportunities for growth outside the retailing sector. For example, Tesco offers Clubcard points or free petrol when consumers purchase Tesco car insurance. The company is currently conducting trials at a finance centre in the Glasgow Silverburn Extra store, providing free financial advice and quotes for insurance and loans; this service is staffed by trained Royal Bank of Scotland employees. The centre also has a Euro cash machine providing commission-free Euros and a Bureau de Change run by Travelex. If successful, this service will be rolled out to more key and flagship stores.

Tesco also entered the telecommunications sector. Though it launched its Internet service provider in 1998, the company was not seriously active in telecommunications until 2003. Rather than purchasing or building its own telecom network, Tesco paired its marketing strength with the expertise of existing telecom operators. In autumn 2003, Tesco Mobile was launched as a joint venture with O2, and Tesco Home Phone was created in partnership with Cable & Wireless. In August 2004, Tesco Broadband, an ADSL-based service delivered via BT phone lines, was launched in partnership with NTL. In January 2006, Tesco Internet Phone, a Voice over Internet Protocol service, was launched in conjunction with Freshtel of Australia. Simple and clear offering logic is also evident in the strategic move into telecommunications. Tesco Mobile offers only four different pay-as-you-go tariffs: Value, Standard, Extra, and Staff (for employees). Tesco announced in December 2004 that it had signed up 500,000 customers to its mobile service in the 12 months since launch. By December 2005, one million customers were using its mobile service, and by April 2006, Tesco claimed over one and one-half million telecom accounts in total, including mobile, fixed line, and broadband. On 19 December 2006, Tesco Ireland announced that it would enter into a joint venture with O2 Ireland to offer mobile telecommunications services, also under the Tesco Mobile brand.

Recently, Tesco entered the housing market with a self-advertising Web site, Tesco Property Market. Other strategic initiatives into non-food items include, for example, following a successful trial in 2006, "Apple" zones in twelve outlets, where the iPod range is sold alongside Mac computers and other Apple products.

Sainsbury's was much more reluctant to move into non-food retailing. Inspired by the success of its main rivals (ASDA had also moved strongly into the non-food area) and the sheer size of the UK non-food retail market (in 2003, estimated at over £100 million), it launched 2,500 home and cookware products in September 2003. Copying Tesco, Sainsbury's also used its own food brands and transferred them to non-food items. For example, it extended its clothing range with an organic line. In addition to food and non-food items, Sainsbury's expanded into retail banking and property development. In 1997, Sainsbury's bank was established as a joint venture between J Sainsbury plc and the Bank of Scotland (now HBOS). Sainsbury's bank offers services similar to Tesco's, including travel (insurance and money), savings, and lending; it also offers a Sainsbury's credit card. By 2010, Sainsbury expects to achieve sales of £3.5 billion, with 33% of its total sales coming from non-food businesses.

# International diversification

*These results show that our new growth businesses – in international, in non-food and in services – have contributed as much profit as the entire business was making in 1997.*

Terry Leahy, CEO Tesco, 2005

Tesco's international expansion[7] began in the late 1970s with the purchase of a small company in the Republic of Ireland. The small-scale nature of this first foray was seen as a weakness, and the company was eventually sold in the mid-1980s. In 1994, Tesco acquired the Scottish supermarket chain William Low. Tesco successfully fought off Sainsbury's for control of the Dundee-based firm, which then operated 57 stores. This paved the way for Tesco to expand its presence in Scotland, where it was weaker than in England. Inverness was recently branded "Tescotown," because well over 50p in every £1 spent on food is believed to be spent in its three Tesco stores. On 21 March 1997, Tesco announced the purchase of the retail arm of Associated British Foods, which consisted of the Quinnsworth, Stewarts, and Crazy Prices chains in the Republic of Ireland and Northern Ireland, as well as associated businesses, for £640 million. This acquisition gave Tesco both a major presence in the Republic of Ireland and a larger presence in Northern Ireland than Sainsbury's, which had begun its move into the province in 1995.

In the 1990s, Tesco strongly expanded overseas by increasing investments into emerging markets such as Hungary, the Czech Republic, Thailand, and South Korea. Tesco was buying into successful companies, a strategy that resulted in strong positions in these markets. In 1997, the new CEO, Terry Leahy, enforced Tesco's international growth strategies beyond Great Britain. However, outside the UK the supermarket firm's position was far from dominant and remained in the shadow of larger, more high-profile international operators such as Wal-Mart and Carrefour. Tesco then analyzed countries for expansion, putting high emphasis on two dimensions: the market potential for growth and the

competitive situation in the market. Only if a market was characterized by relatively high growth potential and relatively low rivalry was it considered a real target market and approached in an orderly fashion.

In 2002, Tesco purchased 13 HIT hypermarkets in Poland. In June 2003, Tesco purchased the C Two-Network in Japan. It also acquired a majority stake in the Turkish supermarket chain Kipa. Another acquisition was the Lotus chain in Thailand. In mid-2006, Tesco purchased an 80% stake in Casino's Leader Price supermarkets in Poland, which were subsequently reconfigured as small Tesco stores.

Many British retailers attempting to build international businesses have failed. Tesco has responded to the need to be sensitive to local expectations in foreign countries by entering into joint ventures with local partners, such as Samsung Group in South Korea (Samsung-Tesco Homeplus), and Charoen Pokphand in Thailand (Tesco Lotus), and by appointing a high proportion of local personnel to management positions. In late 2004, the amount of floor space Tesco operated outside the UK surpassed its home market space for the first time, although the UK still accounted for more than 75% of group revenue due to lower sales per unit area outside the UK (for an overview of Tesco's international store portfolio, see Table 3). Tesco regularly continues to make small acquisitions to expand its international businesses. For example, in its 2005–06 fiscal year, acquisitions were made in South Korea, in Poland, and in Japan.

In September 2005, Tesco announced that it was selling its operations in Taiwan to Carrefour and purchasing Carrefour stores in the Czech Republic and Slovakia. Both companies stated that they were concentrating their efforts in countries where they had strong market positions. Tesco entered China by acquiring a 50% stake in the Hymall chain from Ting Hsin of Taiwan in September 2004. In December 2006, it raised its stake to 90% in a £180 million deal, which was just after Tesco lost out to Wal-Mart to partner with the Indian group, Bharti, to develop a national retail chain in India.

In February 2006, Tesco announced its intention to move into the US, opening a chain of convenience stores on the West Coast (Arizona and California), Fresh & Easy Neighborhood Market. The first store was opened in November 2007, with 100 more openings scheduled in the first year. By planning to open a new store every two-and-one-half days in the US, Tesco intends to mimic the successful expansion of US pharmacy chains, such as Walgreens. Tesco's strategy and unorthodox tactics have not been without controversy. In 2005 and 2006, the company covertly sent an advance team consisting of executives in disguise to conduct intelligence on potential competitors. Like a James Bond movie, the company's agents sought to keep their plans secret by posing as Hollywood film producers making a movie about supermarkets, according to *Business Week*. The bold operation collected intelligence on the US market and on competitors such as Wal-Mart, Kroger, Safeway, Albertson's, Whole Foods, and Trader Joe's. The covert operation was so unusual and unsettling that some potential rivals hired security teams to infiltrate Tesco and obtain information about executives involved in the operation. Yet, Tesco prevailed in obtaining the necessary information to proceed with its store openings.

> *For me, it is remarkable that in five years Tesco has moved from being a UK-based supermarket chain to become an international mixed retail and services business. This rapid transformation is based on clarity at the top and a tremendous creativity and energy in making it happen quickly.*
>
> Tesco senior manager

Sainsbury's international strategy can be described as that of fast follower, albeit with varying results and to a lesser extent. It expanded its operations into Scotland, opening a store in Darnley in January 1992. In June 1995, Sainsbury's announced its intention to move into the Northern Ireland market, which had until that point been dominated by local companies. Between December 1996 and December 1998, the company opened seven stores. Two others at Sprucefield, Lisburn, and Holywood Exchange, Belfast, would not open until 2003 due to protracted legal challenges. Sainsbury's move into Northern Ireland was undertaken in a very different way than that of Tesco. While Sainsbury's outlets were all new developments, Tesco (apart from one Tesco Metro) instead purchased existing chains from Associated British Foods (see Tesco Ireland). In 1999, Sainsbury's acquired an 80.1% share of the Egyptian Distribution Group SAE, a retailer in Egypt with 100 stores and 2,000 employees. However, poor profitability led to the sale of this share in 2001.

At the end of March 2004, Davis was promoted to chairman and was replaced as CEO of Sainsbury's by Justin King. Justin King joined Sainsbury's from Marks and Spencer plc, where he was a director with responsibility for its food division and Kings Super Markets, Inc, a subsidiary in the US. King was also previously a managing director at ASDA, with responsibility for hypermarkets. In June 2004, Davis was forced to resign as chairman in the face of an impending shareholder revolt over his salary and bonuses. Investors were angered by a bonus share award of over £2 million, despite poor company performance. In July 2004, Philip Hampton was appointed chairman. Hampton had previously worked for British Steel, British Gas, BT, and Lloyds TSB.

King perceived Sainsbury's to be not sufficiently focused on its customers or its main competitors. King ordered a direct mail campaign to one million Sainsbury's customers, asking what they wanted from the company and where the company could improve. Results reaffirmed the commentary of retail analysts; that is, the group was not ensuring that shelves were fully stocked, partly due to the failure of the IT systems introduced by Peter Davis. In October 2004, King unveiled the results of the business review and his plans to revive the company's fortunes. This was generally well received by both the stock market and the media. Immediate plans included terminating 750 headquarters staff and recruiting around 3,000 shop floor staff to improve the quality of service and the firm's main problem of stock availability. Another significant announcement was the decision to halve the dividend in order to increase funds available to offer price cuts and to improve quality. The company's fortunes have improved since the launch of this recovery program.

In 2004, King hired Lawrence Christensen, previously an expert in logistics at Safeway, as supply chain director. Immediate supply chain improvements included the reactivation of two distribution centers. In 2006, Christensen commented on the four automated depots introduced by Davis, saying, *"[N]ot a single day went by without one, if not all of them, breaking down ...; the systems were flawed. They have to stop for four hours every day for maintenance. But because they were constantly breaking down you would be playing catch up. It was a vicious circle."* Christensen felt that a fundamental mistake was to build four such depots at once, rather than building one and testing it thoroughly before building the others. In 2007, Sainsbury's announced an additional £12 million investment in its depots to keep pace with sales growth and to remove the failed automated systems from its depots.

## The competitive landscape today

The situation today is clear. Tesco has outpaced its closest rival in its local and international markets.

> *The results confirmed the undeniable success Tesco has had within the food market over the past years. TNS supermarket share information shows that the retailer's market share has grown consistently and strongly over the last decade and shows no sign of abating.*
>
> Edward Garner, Communications Director of
> TNS Superpanel

These events led to shifts in the competitive landscape. The UK retail industry has become highly concentrated. The top four store-based retailers – Tesco, Sainsbury, ASDA, and Morrison's Supermarkets – dominate the market; all are original food retailers.

This illustrates the status of food retailers in the market (see Table 12). All are British, except ASDA, which was acquired in 1999 by the US retail giant Wal-Mart. Discounters adapted to this less favorable environment by slightly improving their meager UK presence through expanding their number of outlets and moving upscale. This was helped by the trend of consumers to increasingly combine bargain shopping with purchases of luxury products or services. This "schizophrenic" shopping behavior blurs previously separate boundaries. The traditional structure of upper, middle, and mass market has been more or less abolished.

Since the launch of King's recovery program, Sainsbury's has reported nine consecutive quarters of sales growth, most recently in March 2007, even outpacing Tesco, making the company's performance the best since its glory days of the 1980s and early 1990s. Sales increases were credited to solving problems with the company's distribution system. More recent sales improvements have been attributed to significant price cuts and the company's focus on fresh and healthy food. On October 4 2007, Sainsbury's announced plans to relocate their Store Support Centre from Holborn to Kings Cross in 2011. This office, part of a new building complex, will allow both cost savings and energy efficiency.

Yet, according to the latest Taylor Nelson Sofres rankings published in March 2007, Sainsbury's market share in food retailing remains third in the UK at 16.37% compared to Tesco's 31.35%, ASDA's 16.83%, and Morrison's 11.08% (see Table 13.). Tesco remains the clear market leader. In the past, Tesco showed itself to be the quickest at seizing expansion opportunities. Furthermore, it has succeeded in building an image of providing good value at low prices.

> The recovery in the Sainsbury market share builds on the positive picture already established. This strong performance has been achieved in the face of relentless pressure from Tesco, which continues its recent run of double-digit turnover growth. ... Whilst Tesco remains dominant, there are signs that it is experiencing increased competition. It is still growing, but the year-on-year share increase is below the average we are seeing last year. Looking towards the future, Tesco will continue to face challenging competition from its nearest competitor Asda as well as the likes of Sainsbury's, which is showing positive growth trends and Morrisons once the Safeway store conversions are complete. Tesco will need to prove its ability to meet increasingly challenging consumer's demands and stay a step ahead of the competition. ... Future Internationalization: It has a long way to go before it overhauls Wal-Mart as the world's biggest groce –

> but analysts said the same about overhauling Sainsbury's in the UK market 15 years ago and now Tesco is almost double its size.
>
> Edward Garner, communications director of TNS Superpanel, 2007

## New challenges ahead

After a relatively long period of economic growth during the review period, conditions may well stagnate in the coming years, thus dampening the forecast performance of store-based retailing. Consumer debt levels have reached record highs and, with the UK's negative saving rate, there is less room for continued growth in consumption. As a result, discounters (both food and non-food) are well placed to gain importance. Euromonitor predicts food retailers to outperform non-food retailers with a value compound annual growth rate of 1%. Recent trends, such as health and wellness and ethical concerns, have opened opportunities, even in the saturated food category; however, most food retailers' growth is expected to stem from non-food items.

Consolidation is expected to continue (see the Safeway takeover), with independent shops either closing, being taken over, or joining larger chains. This is evident in the decline of the number of total outlets, particularly independent ones.

Sainsbury's might be the target of additional takeover bids, since family investment in the company is only 18%. A first private equity bid was considered by CVC Capital Partners, Kohlberg Kravis Roberts (which later left the consortium in order to focus on its bid for Alliance Boots), and Blackstone Group; in February 2007, this also included Goldman Sachs and Texas Pacific Group. The initial offer submitted in April 2007 of 562p a share was rejected after discussions between Sainsbury's top management and the two largest Sainsbury's family shareholders. The subsequent offer of 582p a share was also rejected. As a consequence, the CVC-led consortium abandoned its quest, stating "[I]t became clear the consortium would be unable to make a proposal that would result in a successful offer." In April 2007, Delta Two, a Qatari investment company, bought a 14% stake in Sainsbury's (causing its share price to rise 7.17%); this stake was increased to 25% in June 2007. On 18 July 2007, BBC News reported that Delta Two had tabled a conditional bid proposal. On 5 November 2007, it was announced that Delta Two had abandoned its takeover bid due to the "deterioration of credit markets" and concerns about funding the company's pension scheme. Following the withdrawal of the interest of Qatari investment, shares in Sainsbury's dropped about 20% (115p) to 440p on the day of this announcement.

# Appendix

**TABLE 1** Sainburys' store portfolio UK (at the end of 2006)

| Format | Number | Area (ft$^2$) | Area (m$^2$) | Percentage of space |
|---|---|---|---|---|
| **Supermarkets** | 455 | 15,916,000 | 1,467,000 | 95.1% |
| **Convenience stores** | 297 | 821,000 | 76,000 | 4.9% |
| **Total** | **752** | **16,737,000** | **1,543,000** | **100.0%** |

**TABLE 2** Tesco's store portfolio UK (at the end of 2007)

| Format | Number | Total area (m$^2$) | Total area (sq ft) | Mean area (m$^2$) | Mean area (sq ft) | Percentage of space |
|---|---|---|---|---|---|---|
| **Tesco Extra** | 147 | 952,441 | 10,252,000 | 6,479 | 69,741 | 36.89% |
| **Tesco** | 433 | 1,227,434 | 13,212,000 | 2,834 | 30,512 | 47.55% |
| **Tesco Metro** | 162 | 177,073 | 1,906,000 | 1,093 | 11,765 | 6.85% |
| **Tesco Express** | 735 | 145,114 | 1,562,000 | 197 | 2,125 | 5.62% |
| **One Stop** | 506 | 62,988 | 678,000 | 124 | 1,339 | 2.44% |
| **Tesco Homeplus** | 5 | 16,258 | 175,000 | 3,251 | 35,000 | 0.62% |
| **Total** | 1,988 | 2,581,310 | 27,785,000 | 1,298 | 13,976 | 100% |

**TABLE 3** Tesco's store portfolio "International"

| Country | Entered | Stores | Area (m²) | Area ( sq ft) | Turnover (£ million) |
|---------|---------|--------|-----------|---------------|----------------------|
| China | 2004 | 47 | 392,422 | 4,224,000 | 552 |
| Czech Republic | 1996 | 84 | 381,459 | 4,106,000 | 807 |
| France | 1992 | 1 | 1,400 | 16,000 | Note 2 |
| Hungary | 1994 | 101 | 448,164 | 4,824,000 | 1,180 |
| Republic of Ireland | 1997 | 95 | 205,780 | 2,215,000 | 1,683 |
| Japan | 2003 | 109 | 29,078 | 313,000 | 287 |
| Malaysia | 2002 | 19 | 174,750 | 1,881,000 | 247 |
| Poland | 1995 | 280 | 606,935 | 6,533,000 | 1,135 |
| Slovakia | 1996 | 48 | 225,475 | 2,427,000 | 498 |
| South Korea | 1999 | 81 | 473,340 | 5,095,000 | 2,557 |
| Thailand | 1998 | 370 | 698,166 | 7,515,000 | 1,326 |
| Turkey | 2003 | 30 | 102,936 | 1,108,000 | 256 |
| United States of America | 2007 | 6 | Unknown | 60,000 ( est.) | Unknown |

Note 1: the store numbers and floor area figures are as at 24 February 2007 but the turnover figures are for the year ended 31 December 2005, except for the Republic of Ireland data, which are at 24 February 2007, like the UK figures. This information is taken from the 2007 final broker pack.

Note 2: China: joint venture at February 2006; now a 90% owned subsidiary.

Note 3: France: Tesco owned a French chain called Catteau between 1992 and 1997. Its existing single store in France is a wine warehouse in Calais (opened in 1995 and targeted at British day trippers).

Note 4: Malaysia: Tesco Stores (Malaysia) Sdn Bhd was incepted on 29 November 2001, as a strategic alliance with local conglomerate, Sime Darby Bhd of which the latter holds 30% of total shares.

**TABLE 4** Retail: number of employees: 2001–2006 (in '000)

| | 2001 | 2002 | 2003 | 2004 | 2005 | 2006 |
|---|------|------|------|------|------|------|
| Retail employees | 3,048 | 3,077 | 3,136 | 3,308 | 3,329 | 3,316 |
| %growth | - | 1.0 | 1.9 | 5.5 | 0.6 | -0.4 |

**Source:** Official statistics, Trade associations, Trade press, Company research, Trade interviews, Euromonitor International estimates, Euromonitor, UK Retail Market: Market Overview (2007).

**TABLE 5** Number of employees of food retailers (full-time equivalents)

| Employees | 2006 | 2007 |
|-----------|------|------|
| Tesco | 380'000 | 318'283 |
| Asda | 150'000<br>90'000 part-time<br>60'000 full-time | 143'125 |
| Sainsbury | 96'200<br>104'100 part-time<br>49'200 full-time | 95'500<br>98'100 part-time<br>48'800 full-time |

**TABLE 6** Tesco's financial figures

| 52/3 weeks ended | Turnover (£m) | Profit before tax (£m) | Profit for year (£m) | Basic earnings per share (p) |
|------------------|---------------|------------------------|----------------------|------------------------------|
| **2007** | 46,600 | 2,653 | 1,899 | 22.36 |
| **2006** | 38,300 | 2,210 | 1,576 | 19.70 |
| **2005** | 33,974 | 1,962 | 1,366 | 17.44 |
| **2004** | 30,814 | 1,600 | 1,100 | 15.05 |
| **2003** | 26,337 | 1,361 | 946 | 13.54 |
| **2002** | 23,653 | 1,201 | 830 | 12.05 |
| **2001** | 20,988 | 1,054 | 767 | 11.29 |
| **2000** | 18,796 | 933 | 674 | 10.07 |
| **1999** | 17,158 | 842 | 606 | 9.14 |
| **1998** | 16,452 | 760 | 532 | 8.12 |

Note: The numbers include non-UK and Ireland results.

**TABLE 7** Growth rates (Tesco vs. Sainsbury) 1990–2007

| Growth Rates (%) | Sales | Operating Income | Net Income | Div Per Share | Equity | Total Assets |
|---|---|---|---|---|---|---|
| Sainsbury Y2007 | | | | 21,88 | | |
| Tesco Y2007 | 8,08 | 5,88 | 20,51 | 11,70 | 12,00 | 9,86 |
| Sainsbury Y2006 | 5,65 | 7,55 | −64,67 | 2,56 | −0,21 | 9,24 |
| Tesco Y2006 | 16,50 | 13,40 | 16,82 | 14,15 | 9,03 | 11,97 |
| Sainsbury Y2005 | −10,10 | −53,04 | −84,60 | −56,50 | −15,48 | −7,11 |
| Tesco Y2005 | 10,26 | 12,47 | 24,18 | 10,53 | 13,76 | 10,12 |
| Sainsbury Y2004 | −1,66 | −2,03 | −12,78 | 0,70 | 2,05 | 4,70 |
| Tesco Y2004 | 17,00 | 19,78 | 16,28 | 10,32 | 22,50 | 12,68 |
| Sainsbury Y2003 | 1,56 | 11,46 | 24,73 | 4,99 | 3,30 | 8,76 |
| Tesco Y2003 | 11,35 | 12,49 | 13,98 | 10,71 | 18,24 | 21,91 |
| Sainsbury Y2002 | 7,57 | 9,95 | 38,93 | 3,63 | −1,31 | 6,85 |
| Tesco Y2002 | 12,70 | 13,29 | 8,21 | 12,45 | 4,02 | 16,00 |
| Sainsbury Y2001 | −1,95 | −5,78 | −24,93 | – | 3,23 | −1,94 |
| Tesco Y2001 | 11,66 | 12,55 | 13,80 | 11,16 | 12,05 | 18,80 |
| Sainsbury Y2000 | −0,99 | −25,32 | −41,64 | – | 0,65 | 4,32 |
| Tesco Y2000 | 9,55 | 7,92 | 11,22 | 8,74 | 9,58 | 13,88 |
| Sainsbury Y1999 | 13,33 | 8,48 | 22,79 | 3,02 | 12,89 | 10,13 |
| Tesco Y1999 | 7,81 | 5,03 | 20,00 | 6,54 | 10,42 | 15,58 |
| Sainsbury Y1998 | 8,25 | 11,58 | 20,84 | 13,01 | 12,01 | 25,23 |
| Tesco Y1998 | 14,60 | 18,09 | −2,88 | 12,09 | −0,36 | 12,32 |
| Sainsbury Y1997 | 6,08 | −11,94 | −17.42 | 1,65 | 3,88 | 7,88 |
| Tesco Y1997 | 14,83 | 6,91 | 11,59 | 7,81 | 8,78 | 6,74 |
| Sainsbury Y1996 | 11,18 | −4,09 | −8,87 | 3,43 | 7,45 | 15,81 |
| Tesco Y1996 | 19,73 | 17,34 | 22,63 | 11,61 | 15,21 | 5,01 |
| Sainsbury Y1995 | 7,31 | 13,36 | 278,18 | 10,38 | 8,21 | 6,22 |
| Tesco Y1995 | 17,45 | 18,38 | 27,43 | 10,99 | 12,92 | 18,84 |
| Sainsbury Y1994 | 9,27 | 1,80 | −71,84 | 5,99 | 0,36 | 3,95 |
| Tesco Y1994 | 13,43 | −5,53 | −28,59 | 9,13 | −0,15 | 9,82 |
| Sainsbury Y1993 | 11,39 | 17,48 | 14,74 | 14,29 | 14,68 | 12,26 |

## TABLE 7 Continued

| Growth Rates (%) | Sales | Operating Income | Net Income | Div Per Share | Equity | Total Assets |
|---|---|---|---|---|---|---|
| Tesco Y1993 | 6,82 | 15,06 | 5,56 | 12,71 | 12,50 | 9,03 |
| Sainsbury Y1992 | 11,29 | 14,29 | 23,37 | 20,41 | 57,92 | 22,22 |
| Tesco Y1992 | 11,84 | 20,48 | 30,69 | 20,00 | 13,29 | 13,01 |
| Sainsbury Y1991 | 12,74 | 23,83 | 13,23 | 20,50 | 18,98 | 14,75 |
| Tesco Y1991 | 17,48 | 25,63 | 19,27 | 25,72 | 72,23 | 50,90 |
| Sainsbury Y1990 | 22,47 | 17,16 | 24,88 | 20,79 | 20,38 | 16,97 |
| Tesco Y1990 | 14,50 | 20,50 | 36,23 | 22,86 | 21,60 | 19,75 |

**Source:** Thompson Database 2007.

## TABLE 8 Financial leverage and return on equity/assets 1990–2007

| PROFITABILITY (%) | Financial Leverage TESCO | Financial Leverage SAINSBURY | Return on Equity TESCO | Return on Equity SAINSBURY | Return on Assets TESCO | Return on Assets SAINSBURY |
|---|---|---|---|---|---|---|
| Y2007 | 42,41 | 45,42 | 18,81 | | 8,62 | |
| Y2006 | 41,59 | 30,62 | 17,50 | 1,67 | 8,11 | 1,02 |
| Y2005 | 44,13 | 36,50 | 16,20 | −1,10 | 7,86 | 1,56 |
| Y2004 | 42,72 | 40,12 | 15,65 | 8,09 | 7,31 | 3,70 |
| Y2003 | 39,29 | 41,16 | 16,17 | 9,49 | 7,37 | 4,59 |
| Y2002 | 40,51 | 43,34 | 15,65 | 7,71 | 7,72 | 4,21 |
| Y2001 | 45,18 | 46,92 | 15,62 | 5,60 | 8,30 | 3,34 |
| Y2000 | 47,91 | 44,57 | 15,26 | 7,55 | 8,54 | 4,12 |
| Y1999 | 49,78 | 46,20 | 14,99 | 13,71 | 8,56 | 6,94 |
| Y1998 | 52,11 | 45,07 | 13,01 | 12,56 | 8,08 | 6,79 |
| Y1997 | 58,74 | 50,38 | 13,98 | 11,21 | 8,74 | 6,63 |
| Y1996 | 57,64 | 52,32 | 14,02 | 14,29 | 8,90 | 8,48 |
| Y1995 | 52,54 | 56,39 | 13,00 | 16,88 | 8,08 | 10,04 |
| Y1994 | 55,29 | 55,36 | 10,84 | 4,70 | 6,96 | 2,77 |
| Y1993 | 60,81 | 57,34 | 16,07 | 17,74 | 10,58 | 10,39 |

## TABLE 8   Continued

| PROFITABILITY (%) | Financial Leverage TESCO | Financial Leverage SAINSBURY | Return on Equity TESCO | Return on Equity SAINSBURY | Return on Assets TESCO | Return on Assets SAINSBURY |
|---|---|---|---|---|---|---|
| Y1992 | 58,93 | 56,13 | 17,17 | 19,88 | 11,18 | 11,96 |
| Y1991 | 58,79 | 43,44 | 19,36 | 23,11 | 11,12 | 12,05 |
| Y1990 | 51,51 | 41,90 | 21,05 | 24,40 | 12,82 | 12,20 |

**Source:** Thompson Database 2007.

## TABLE 9   Margins 1990–2007

| PROFITABILITY (%) | Gross Margin TESCO | Gross Margin SAINSBURY | Op Profit Margin TESCO | Op Profit Margin SAINSBURY | Pretax Prof Margin TESCO | Pretax Prof Margin SAINSBURY |
|---|---|---|---|---|---|---|
| Y2007 | 7,60 | 6,83 | 5,02 | 3,00 | 5,91 | 2,78 |
| Y2006 | 7,67 | 6,95 | 5,13 | 2,22 | 5,46 | 0,65 |
| Y2005 | 7,77 | 7,20 | 5,89 | 2,21 | 5,49 | 0,10 |
| Y2004 | 7,65 | 8,89 | 5,78 | 4,22 | 4,92 | 3,56 |
| Y2003 | 7,50 | 8,20 | 5,64 | 4,24 | 4,96 | 3,83 |
| Y2002 | 7,51 | 7,41 | 5,58 | 3,86 | 4,97 | 3,33 |
| Y2001 | 7,53 | 6,69 | 5,56 | 3,78 | 5,01 | 2,72 |
| Y2000 | 7,39 | 6,96 | 5,51 | 3,93 | 4,91 | 3,12 |
| Y1999 | 7,77 | 7,87 | 5,60 | 5,22 | 4,87 | 5,33 |
| Y1998 | 7,68 | 8,05 | 5,74 | 5,45 | 4,67 | 4,85 |
| Y1997 | 7,27 | 7,43 | 5,57 | 5,29 | 5,40 | 4,40 |
| Y1996 | 7,65 | 8,36 | 5,99 | 6,37 | 5,58 | 5,49 |
| Y1995 | 7,70 | 9,29 | 6,11 | 7,38 | 5,45 | 7,07 |
| Y1994 | 8,13 | 9,00 | 6,06 | 6,99 | 5,06 | 3,48 |
| Y1993 | 9,33 | 9,68 | 7,28 | 7,50 | 7,66 | 7,57 |
| Y1992 | 8,98 | 9,44 | 6,76 | 7,11 | 7,69 | 7,21 |
| Y1991 | 8,46 | 9,21 | 6,27 | 6,92 | 6,87 | 6,63 |
| Y1990 | 8,39 | 9,06 | 5,86 | 6,30 | 6,69 | 6,49 |

**Source:** Thompson Database 2007.

**TABLE 10** Sales per share, EPS and dividends 1990–2007

| PROFITABILITY (%) | Sales per share data TESCO | Sales per share data SAINSBURY | EPS TESCO | EPS SAINSBURY | Dividend TESCO | Dividend SAINSBURY |
|---|---|---|---|---|---|---|
| Y2007 | 5,37 | 10,14 | 0,24 | 0,19 | 0,10 | 0,10 |
| Y2006 | 5,04 | 9,57 | 0,20 | 0,04 | 0,09 | 0,08 |
| Y2005 | 4,41 | 8,81 | 0,18 | -0,03 | 0,08 | 0,08 |
| Y2004 | 4,22 | 10,24 | 0,15 | 0,24 | 0,07 | 0,18 |
| Y2003 | 3,77 | 10,42 | 0,14 | 0,27 | 0,06 | 0,18 |
| Y2002 | 3,43 | 10,28 | 0,12 | 0,22 | 0,06 | 0,17 |
| Y2001 | 3,09 | 9,59 | 0,11 | 0,16 | 0,05 | 0,16 |
| Y2000 | 2,81 | 9,72 | 0,10 | 0,21 | 0,04 | 0,16 |
| Y1999 | 2,59 | 9,84 | 0,09 | 0,36 | 0,04 | 0,16 |
| Y1998 | 2,43 | 8,87 | 0,08 | 0,30 | 0,04 | 0,16 |
| Y1997 | 2,14 | 8,34 | 0,08 | 0,25 | 0,03 | 0,14 |
| Y1996 | 1,92 | 7,94 | 0,07 | 0,31 | 0,03 | 0,14 |
| Y1995 | 1,68 | 7,22 | 0,06 | 0,34 | 0,03 | 0,13 |
| Y1994 | 1,46 | 6,79 | 0,05 | 0,09 | 0,03 | 0,12 |
| Y1993 | 1,30 | 6,27 | 0,07 | 0,33 | 0,02 | 0,11 |
| Y1992 | 1,22 | 5,83 | 0,07 | 0,29 | 0,02 | 0,10 |
| Y1991 | 1,28 | 5,81 | 0,06 | 0,26 | 0,02 | 0,08 |
| Y1990 | 1,13 | 5,19 | 0,05 | 0,24 | 0,01 | 0,07 |

**Source:** Thompson Database 2007.

**TABLE 11** Retailing: growth in value sales by broad sector/sector 2001–2006

| % current value growth | 2005/2006 | 2001-2006 CAGR | 2001/2006 TOTAL |
|---|---|---|---|
| **Non store retailing** | 13.3 | 13.8 | 91.2 |
| – Interest retailing | 24.8 | 32.9 | 313.9 |
| – Vending | 2.5 | 5.0 | 27.7 |
| – Homeshopping | 2.8 | 3.8 | 20.6 |
| – Direct Selling | –1.0 | –1.5 | –7.4 |
| **Store-based retailing** | 2.4 | 3.7 | 19.8 |
| – Food retailers | 3.0 | 4.0 | 21.7 |
| – Non-food retailers | 1.9 | 3.4 | 18.3 |
| **Retailing** | 3.1 | 4.2 | 23.1 |

**Source:** Official statistics, Trade associations, Trade press, Company research, Trade interviews, Euromonitor International estimates; Euromonitor, UK Retail Market: Market Overview (2007).

**TABLE 12** Retailing: company shares by value 2004–2006

| % retail value | 2004 | 2005 | 2006 |
|---|---|---|---|
| Tesco Plc | 10.2 | 11.0 | 11.4 |
| Sainsbury Plc | 5.4 | 5.8 | 5.9 |
| Asda Stores Ltd | 4.7 | 4.9 | 5.1 |
| Wm Morrison Supermarkets Plc | 3.7 | 3.7 | 3.5 |
| Marks and Spencer Plc | 2.7 | 2.7 | 2.7 |
| Alliance Boots Plc | – | – | 2.1 |
| Dixons Group Plc | 1.3 | 1.4 | 1.4 |
| Argos Plc | 1.3 | 1.4 | 1.4 |
| B&Q Plc | 1.5 | 1.5 | 1.4 |
| Somerfield Ltd | 1.7 | 1.7 | 1.3 |
| Waitrose Ltd | 1.0 | 1.0 | 1.2 |
| Co-operative Group (CWS) Ltd | 1.3 | 1.3 | 1.2 |
| Next Plc | 1.0 | 1.0 | 1.1 |
| Spar Ltd (UK) | 0.8 | 0.9 | 0.9 |
| Debenhams Retail Plc | 0.7 | 0.8 | 0.8 |
| … | | | |

**Source:** Official statistics, Trade associations, Trade press, Company research, Trade interviews, Euromonitor International estimates; Euromonitor, UK Retail Market: Market Overview (2007).

**TABLE 13** Food retailing: company shares by sales 1990–2007

| % retail value | 1990 | ... | 1994 | 1995 | .. | 2002 | ... | 2004 | 2005 | 2006 | 2007 |
|---|---|---|---|---|---|---|---|---|---|---|---|
| Tesco Pk | 9.7 | | 11.4 | 13.4 | | 16.7 | | 27.5 | 29.8 | 31.1 | 31.35 |
| Saiasbury Plc | 11.0 | | 12.3 | 12.2 | | 11.7 | | 15.5 | 15.9 | 16.0 | 16.37 |
| Asda Stores Ltd | 6.8 | | 6.7 | 7.2 | | 10.6 | | 16.6 | 16.5 | 16.4 | 16.83 |
| Wm Morrison Supermarkets Plc (Safeway included) | | | | | | 7.5 (only Safeway) | | 14.4 | 12.2 | 11.3 | 11.08 |

**Source:** TNS (Taylor Nelson Sofres) World Panel market-share data released 06/2007.

**TABLE 14** Food retailing: company shares by value 2004–2006

| % retail value | 2004 | 2005 | 2006 |
|---|---|---|---|
| Tesco Plc | 23.0 | 24.4 | 25.2 |
| J Sainsbury Plc | 12.5 | 13.1 | 13.3 |
| Asda Stores Ltd | 10.9 | 11.0 | 11.2 |
| Wm Morrison Supermarkets Plc | 8.7 | 8.5 | 8.1 |
| Sommerfield Ltd | 4.0 | 3.8 | 3.1 |
| Waitrose Ltd | 2.3 | 2.3 | 2.8 |
| Co-operative Group (CWS) Ltd | 2.7 | 2.6 | 2.5 |
| Spar Ltd (UK) | 2.0 | 2.0 | 2.0 |
| Musgrave Group Plc | 1.6 | 1.8 | 1.8 |
| Lidl Ltd | 1.0 | 1.1 | 1.1 |
| Aldi Stores Ltd | 0.9 | 1.0 | 1.1 |
| Iceland Frozen Foods Ltd. | 1.2 | 1.1 | 1.0 |
| ... | | | |
| Others | 26.6 | 24.8 | 23.6 |

**Source:** Official statistics, Trade associations, Trade press, Company research, Trade interviews, Euromonitor International estimates; Euromonitor, UK Retail Market: Market Overview (2007).

**TABLE 15** Food retailers: value sales by sector 2001–2006

| Million pounds, current rsp | 2001 | 2002 | 2003 | 2004 | 2005 | 2006 |
|---|---|---|---|---|---|---|
| Supermarkets | 40,502.8 | 42,591.0 | 43,106.1 | 44,356.0 | 45,198.8 | 46,284.0 |
| Hypermarkets | 22,766.5 | 24,677.2 | 27,569.9 | 31,698.9 | 35,521.1 | 38,175.9 |
| Convenience Stores | 10,514.3 | 11,895.7 | 13,729.7 | 14,306.0 | 14,577.8 | 14,875.2 |
| Food/Drink/Tobacco | | | | | | |
| Specialists | 12,074.0 | 11,460.6 | 11,100.0 | 10,700.0 | 10,144.0 | 9,667.0 |
| Independent grocers | 8,563.0 | 8,135.0 | 7,647.0 | 7,119.4 | 6,592.5 | 6,203.6 |
| Discounters | 2,395.0 | 2,582.6 | 2,672.2 | 2,725.4 | 2,980.2 | 3,375.5 |
| Other food retailers | 2,365.7 | 2,395.0 | 2,218.9 | 2,159.0 | 2,129.0 | 2,088.0 |
| FOOD RETAILERS | 99,181.2 | 102,737.0 | 108,043.9 | 113,064.6 | 117,143.4 | 120,669.1 |

**Source:** Official statistics, Trade associations, Trade press, Company research, Trade interviews, Euromonitor International estimates; Euromonitor, UK Retail Market: Market Overview (2007).

**TABLE 16** Food retailers: growth in value sales by sector 2001–2006

| % current value growth | 2005/2006 | 2001–2006 CAGR | 2001/2006 TOTAL |
|---|---|---|---|
| Hypermarkets | 7.5 | 10.9 | 67.7 |
| Convenience stores | 2.0 | 7.2 | 41.5 |
| Discounters | 13.3 | 7.1 | 40.9 |
| Supermarkets | 2.4 | 2.7 | 14.3 |
| Other food retailers | −1.9 | −2.5 | −11.7 |
| Food/Drink/Tobacco specialists | −4.7 | −4.3 | −19.9 |
| Independent grocers | −5.9 | −6.2 | −27.6 |
| FOOD RETAILERS | 3.0 | 4.0 | 21.7 |

**Source:** Official statistics, Trade associations, Trade press, Company research, Trade interviews, Euromonitor International estimates; Euromonitor, UK Retail Market: Market Overview (2007).

**FIGURE 1** Share price Tesco vs. Sainsbury (1990–2007)

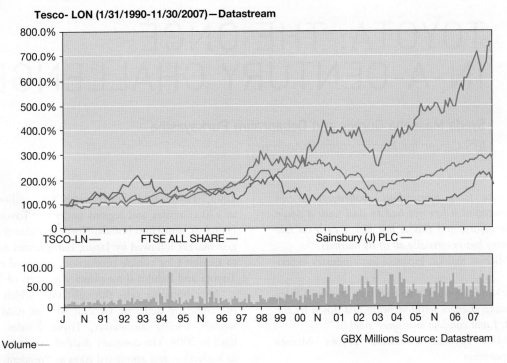

**Source:** Thompson Database 2007.

## NOTES

1. The largest retailers in the world ranked by sales in 2005, www.chainstoreage.com.

2. For more information on ASDA and how the purchase of Asda by Wal-Mart in 1999 changed the competitive scenario of the UK retail industry, see, for example, Dhar & Sushma (2005): Tesco vs Asda: UK's Retailing Battle, ECCH Case: 305-623-1.

3. For more detailed information on Tesco's store formats in 2003, see, for example, Padmini & Himansu, 2003, Tesco in 2003, ECCH Case: 304-173-1.

4. The article "Surpassing Sainsbury" describes Tesco's market-share dominance since the introduction of the Clubcard.

5. For Tesco's online sales strategy see also Pole (2007): Tesco's Online Sales Strategy, ECCH Case: 507-024-1 as well as Mukund (2003): Tesco.com: A rare profitable dot-com, ECCH Case: 903-034-1.

6. Ocado was launched in January 2002, in partnership with Waitrose and is today available to over 13.5 million house-holds in the UK.

7. For Tesco's global expansion strategies see also Bhavika & Phani Madhav (2005): Tesco: The British Supermarket Chain's Global Expansion Strategies and Challenges, ECCH Case: 305-350-1.

# 14

# INTEGRATIVE CASE 14

# TOYOTA: THE ONCE-IN-A-CENTURY CHALLENGE

Syeda Maseeha Qumer and Debapratim Purkayastha

*IBS Center for Management Research*

*"Toyota faces tremendous challenges. As an organization it has not had to deal with a down cycle before, and this is not just a cycle in one country but in virtually all of its markets."[1]*

Michael Smitka, Japanese auto industry expert

*"We're facing a once-in-a-century crisis... I'll try to make changes without being tied down by the past. I will consider measures quickly."[2]*

Akio Toyoda, President, Toyota Motors Corporation

## Introduction

On June 23, 2009, Akio Toyoda (Akio) took over as President of Japanese automaker Toyota Motor Corporation (Toyota). Akio's appointment came in the wake of the company reporting its first losses since 1963, the year it began reporting business data. Analysts felt that the global financial crisis had had its impact on the world's largest automaker and that the company was also trying to cope with a shift in the global automobile industry. The challenge before Akio, grandson of the founder of Toyota, was to bring the automaker back to profits.

The business segments of Toyota mainly include automotive operations, financial services operations, and other business operations.[3] Automotive operations accounted for 89% of Toyota's total revenues in 2008. The company manufactured vehicles at 53 production sites in 27 countries around the globe. In the fiscal year

2008,[4] Toyota sold approximately 8.91 million vehicles in 170 countries and regions under the Toyota, Lexus, Daihatsu, and Hino brands. North America was its biggest market followed by Japan, Europe, and Asia (Refer to Exhibit I for vehicle production, sales and exports of Toyota and Exhibit II for primary markets of Toyota).

After booming sales through 2007, which also saw the company dethrone General Motors (GM)[5] as the world's leading automaker, Toyota's sales were hit hard in 2008. The company decided to opt for a change in leadership and appointed Akio as President. Akio immediately announced a slew of measures in a bid to bring the company back to profits. "We are talking about a once-in-a-century transformation of the market. I believe the auto industry is now trying to face the challenges of presenting a solution to this once-in-a-century change. And what is clear to me is that what is going to happen will not just simply be an extension of the past. I believe it is an important time for Toyota to present some answers for the coming 100 years,"[6] he said.

Shortly after, Toyota announced that its net revenues for the first quarter ending June 30, 2009, totaled ¥3.836 trillion[7], a decrease of 38.3% compared to 2008.[8] The quarterly loss was estimated to be around ¥77.82 billion (US$819 million). It was the company's third quarterly loss in a row.[9] "Although we were able to make certain improvements in fixed cost and cost reduction efforts, the decline in vehicle sales and the appreciation of the Japanese yen had a severe impact on our earnings,"[10] said Takahiko Ijichi, Senior MD of Toyota.

While many analysts felt that Toyota would bounce back, some analysts expressed doubts over whether Akio would be able to manage a turnaround and pull the company out of the crisis. Some insiders were also worried that the selection of a member of the founding family as President might lead to disunity within the company. In this scenario, analysts felt that Akio had his task cut out for him. "It will be interesting to see whether Akio Toyoda will be able to bring about the change in mentality and imagination that the company seems to need,"[11] said Ian Fletcher, automotive analyst at IHS Global Insight.[12]

# The number one automaker

Over the years, Toyota had made a name for itself for its innovations, financial soundness, and global competitiveness (Refer to Exhibit III for world's most admired companies and Exhibit IV for Toyota's industry rank on key attributes). Toyota was founded by Kiichiro Toyoda in 1937. In its initial years, it focused on adapting the Ford Production System to suit the Japanese market. However, it later adopted its famed Toyota Production System[13] (TPS, also referred to as "lean

**EXHIBIT I** Vehicle production, sales and exports of Toyota:* 2008

|  | Toyota | Daihatsu | Hino | Total |
|---|---|---|---|---|
| Japanese Production | 4,012 | 793 | 106 | 4,912 |
| Overseas Production | 4,198 | 115 | — | 4,313 |
| Total Global Production | 8,211 | 908 | 106 | 9,225 |
| Sales in Japan | 1,470 | 642 | 41 | 2,153 |
| Overseas Sales | 6,526 | 224 | 69 | 6,819 |
| Total Global Sales | 7,996 | 866 | 110 | 8,972 |
| Exports | 2,586 | 130 | 67 | 2,783 |

*In units, 1 unit=1000 vehicles (figures rounded to the nearest hundred).
**Source:** Toyota in the world 2009.

**EXHIBIT II** Toyota's primary markets:* 2008

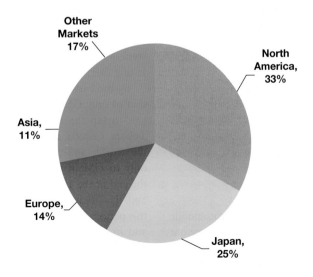

*Based on Vehicle Unit Sales for fiscal 2008.
**Source:** Toyota Motors 2008 Annual Report.

## EXHIBIT III   World's most admired companies

| 2009 Rank | Company name | 2008 Rank | Company name |
|---|---|---|---|
| 1 | Apple | 1 | Apple |
| 2 | Berkshire Hathaway | 2 | General Electric |
| 3 | **Toyota Motors** | 3 | **Toyota Motors** |
| 4 | Google | 4 | Berkshire Hathaway |
| 5 | Johnson & Johnson | 5 | Procter & Gamble |
| 6 | Procter & Gamble | 6 | FedEx |
| 7 | FedEx | 7 | Johnson & Johnson |
| 7 | Southwest Airlines | 8 | Target |
| 9 | General Electric | 9 | BMW |
| 10 | Microsoft | 10 | Microsoft |

**Source:** http://money.cnn.com.

## EXHIBIT IV   Toyota's industry rank on key attributes: 2009

| Attributes | Industry Rank |
|---|---|
| Innovation | 3 |
| People management | 3 |
| Use of corporate assets | 2 |
| Social responsibility | 1 |
| Quality of management | 2 |
| Financial soundness | 1 |
| Long-term investment | 2 |
| Quality of products/services | 2 |
| Global competitiveness | 2 |

**Source:** http://money.cnn.com.

manufacturing system"), which took the automobile industry by storm and enabled the company to come out with many innovative models in a cost-efficient way.

Following World War II, international manufacturers were concentrating on medium-sized and larger cars but Toyota kept its focus on small cars. Kiichiro resigned from Toyota in 1950 and the company saw a series of Presidents in subsequent years. The company started its globalization in the 1950s and entered the US market in 1957. It established its first overseas production unit in Brazil in 1959. It entered the European market in 1963. Besides manufacturing, the company started a global network of design and R&D facilities covering the three major car markets of Japan, North America, and Europe. The company underwent rapid expansion in the 1960s and 1970s and exported fuel-efficient small cars to many foreign markets. It focused on lowering its production costs and on developing more sophisticated cars. The Toyota Corolla, which went on sale in 1966, became Japan's most popular family car.

By the early 1970s, Toyota's production was behind that of only GM and Ford Motor Company. It also began to tap the markets in the Middle East. By 1974, Toyota Corolla had become the largest selling car in the world, and a decade later, Toyota ranked second only to GM in the total number of cars produced. By the end of the 1980s, Toyota began to build new brands and the luxury division, Lexus, was launched. During this period, Toyota continued to strive for improvements and its manufacturing processes served as a model for other companies.

After some setbacks in the early 1990s, the company began to grow further under the leadership of Hiroshi Okuda, who focused on international expansion and localization of production. He also developed a strong dealership network and increased advertising. This resulted in a significant increase in sales. One of Toyota's major innovations was the Prius, a gasoline-electric car and the world's first mass-produced hybrid car. The car was launched in 1997. Prius and all the subsequent models launched by Toyota were successful in the US and further consolidated the company's position in the country. The company's overseas production increased from 1.22 million units per year in 1994 to 1.54 million units per year in 1998.

In 1999, Fujio Cho became the President of Toyota. Besides increasing manufacturing centers and expanding sales networks worldwide, Cho focused on localizing design, development, and purchasing in every country. Toyota propagated the TPS and its unique corporate culture, 'The Toyota Way' throughout its global manufacturing units. Toyota employees the world over practiced philosophies such as *Kaizen* (continuous improvement), PDCA (plan, do, check, action), *Pokayoke* (mistake-proofing), and Just-in-Time (JIT).

During the 2000s, Toyota registered strong sales in the US and Japan. In 2000, for the first time ever, Toyota's total worldwide production exceeded five million vehicles. In 2001, Toyota started two new plants in Europe and in 2002 it established Toyota Motor Manufacturing Turkey to manufacture Corolla sedans for export markets. In April 2002, Toyota announced a new corporate strategy '2010 Global Vision' to achieve a 15% market share of the global automobile market by early 2010. By mid-2003, Toyota had a presence in almost all the major segments of the automobile market that included small cars, luxury sedans, full-sized pickup trucks, SUVs, small trucks, and crossover vehicles.

In 2005, Katsuaki Watanabe[14] (Watanabe) was appointed President of the company. In the first quarter of 2007, Toyota replaced GM as the world's leading automaker, breaking the latter's 77-year reign. The company sold about 2.35 million vehicles compared to GM's 2.26 million. Based on the market capitalization, Toyota was valued at almost 12 times GM's value.

## Problems

In the new millennium, automakers had to contend with many challenges including high gas prices. As the global financial crisis deepened in 2008, the consumer demand for cars and other goods plummeted, especially in the US and European markets. Because of the credit crunch, automobile sales dropped significantly as consumers stopped buying new cars. This led to a fall in vehicle sales of auto companies. Automakers reacted by cutting

back production and slashing jobs. In 2008, though Toyota's sales were down 4% from 2007, the company sold about 8.97 million vehicles compared to GM's 8.35 million.[15] Toyota's hybrid technology car Prius became popular due to the increase in gas prices. But eventually the company too was affected and its global sales fell 32.3% in October 2008.[16] In North America, which accounted for a third of Toyota's worldwide revenues, US sales fell 15.4% to 2,217,660 vehicles in 2008. The sales of large pickups were down about 25% and the sales of SUVs fell by 30%.[17] The company's sales were also affected in Europe and Japan.

In early 2009, Toyota projected a loss of ¥450 billion (US$5 billion) for the fiscal year 2009 in its vehicle-manufacturing operations. It also applied for an emergency loan of about US$2 billion funded by the Japanese government to make up for car loans in the US.[18] In April 2009, Toyota sold about 126,540 cars in the US, a 42% drop compared to the corresponding period of 2008. The company slipped behind Ford, which sold almost 130,000 cars during the same period. Unsold Toyotas lay piled up on storage lots. Toyota also witnessed a drop in sales in Japan and China, where it lost out to rivals who were coming up with a wider lineup of smaller cars at reasonable prices.

In May 2009, Toyota reported its first annual net loss in six decades as net revenues for the fiscal year 2009 totaled ¥20.53 trillion, a decrease of 21.9% compared to the previous year. Net income decreased from ¥1.72 trillion to a loss of ¥437 billion. Consolidated sales totaled 7.57 million units, a decrease of 1.34 million units compared to 2008[19] (Refer to Exhibit V, VI, and VII for balance sheet, income statement and five-year stock chart of Toyota respectively). Analysts felt that this was a dramatic turnabout for an automaker whose steady expansion and record profits had seemed unstoppable.

## What went wrong?

Analysts felt that Toyota's bad performance was due to the fact that it had expanded its global production facilities in the mid-2000s to meet brisk demand, particularly for its fuel-efficient cars, leaving it vulnerable to the current slump in worldwide sales. Toyota's drive into the American big truck market also contributed to its troubles. "The damage was great at Toyota because it was heading toward aggressive expansion with its foot slammed on the accelerator,"[20] said Tatsuo Yoshida auto analyst at UBS Securities Japan Ltd.[21]

Some analysts opined that Toyota's troubles had started in 2006. In November 2006, Toyota opened a

## EXHIBIT V  Toyota's balance sheet

| (All amounts in US$ millions except per share data) | 2009 | 2008 | 2007 |
|---|---|---|---|
| **Current Assets** | | | |
| Cash | 25,093.7 | 16,401.1 | 1,15.2 |
| Net Receivables | 56,618.1 | 63,864.0 | 55,513.1 |
| Inventories | 14,710.7 | 18,386.8 | 15,297.5 |
| Other Current Assets | 17,470.7 | 23,068.5 | 13,003.5 |
| Total Current Assets | 113,893.2 | 121,720.4 | 99,929.4 |
| Net Fixed Assets | 74,608.9 | 78,674.7 | 68,353.2 |
| Other Noncurrent Assets | 104,443.2 | 126,492.7 | 107,951.6 |
| Total Assets | 292,945.3 | 326,887.8 | 276,234.1 |
| **Current Liabilities** | | | |
| Accounts Payable | 13,098.5 | 22,284.8 | 18,754.3 |
| Short-Term Debt | 63,677.2 | 62,723.7 | 49,739.5 |
| Other Current Liabilities | 29,964.4 | 35,246.7 | 31,291.9 |
| Total Current Liabilities | 106,740.1 | 120,255.2 | 99,785.6 |
| Long-Term Debt | 63,518.8 | 60,244.0 | 53,115.2 |
| Other Noncurrent Liabilities | 21,269.5 | 26,850.5 | 22,963.3 |
| Total Liabilities | 191,528.4 | 207,349.7 | 175,864.1 |
| **Shareholder's Equity** | | | |
| Preferred Stock Equity | — | — | — |
| Common Stock Equity | 101,417.0 | 119,538.0 | 100,370.1 |
| Total Equity | 101,417.0 | 119,538.0 | 100,370.1 |
| Shares Outstanding (millions) | 1,567.9 | 1,567.9 | 1,567.9 |

*Toyota Motors financial year ends on March 31.
**Source:** www.hoovers.com.

new plant in San Antonio, Texas, to manufacture the largest pickup the company had ever built, the Tundra, just before cracks emerged in the US subprime-mortgage market. Usually Toyota designed each assembly line to accommodate many models, but in San Antonio, it broke the rule, dedicating a whole plant to the production of a single vehicle. Watanabe invested about US$3 billion in the plant and launched the Tundra in 2008. Analysts

pointed out that the pickup had been launched at a time when the global auto industry was witnessing a slump. The relatively high-priced Tundra failed to make a dent in the market and its inventory piled up. Subsequently with sales of pickups and SUVs tumbling, Toyota had to shut down truck production at its two US plants for about three months in 2008. "In many ways, Toyota's strategy hasn't been any different than

## EXHIBIT VI  Toyota's income statement

| (All amounts in US$ millions except per share data) | 2009 | 2008 | 2007 |
|---|---|---|---|
| Revenue | 206,938.1 | 264,758.9 | 203,079.8 |
| Cost of Goods Sold | 186,034.5 | 205,975.5 | 163,056.8 |
| Gross Profit | 20,903.6 | 58,783.4 | 40,023.0 |
| Gross Profit Margin | 10.1% | 22.2% | 19.7% |
| SG&A Expense | 25,550.6 | 25,162.5 | 21,039.0 |
| Depreciation & Amortization | 15,071.3 | 15,017.2 | 11,724.4 |
| Operating Income | (5,176.1) | 25,009.7 | 20,622.0 |
| Operating Margin | — | 9.4% | 10.2% |
| Nonoperating Income | (1,906.5) | 2,144.7 | 519.1 |
| Nonoperating Expenses | 923.2 | (464.4) | — |
| Income Before Taxes | (5,648.6) | 24,545.3 | 20,203.7 |
| Income Taxes | (568.9) | 9,179.7 | 7,617.7 |
| Net Income After Taxes | (5,079.7) | 15,365.6 | 12,586.1 |
| Continuing Operations | (4,404.3) | 17,300.8 | 13,941.4 |
| Discontinued Operations | — | — | — |
| Total Operations | (4,404.3) | 17,300.8 | 13,941.4 |
| Total Net Income | (4,404.3) | 17,300.8 | 13,941.4 |
| Net Profit Margin | — | 6.5% | 6.9% |
| Diluted EPS from Total Net Income (US$) | (2.80) | 10.89 | 8.68 |
| Dividends per Share | 2.07 | 2.84 | 1.91 |

\* Toyota Motors financial year ends on March 31.
**Source:** www.hoovers.com.

GM or Ford, which was to build bigger vehicles with bigger engines and bigger profits,"[22] said Maryann Keller, an industry consultant.

In February 2009, Toyota's Honorary Chairman Shoichiro Toyoda (son of Toyota's founder) summoned 400 company executives to the redbrick factory in Nagoya, Japan. During the meeting, he confronted Watanabe about the losses incurred by the company and the threat to everything his family had created over the years. Critics felt that Watanabe had failed miserably in predicting the loss in sales and also in taking quick decisive corrective action. Watanabe attributed the poor results to a fall in vehicle sales, particularly in the US and Europe, the strong appreciation of the yen against the dollar and the euro, and the rising cost of raw materials. Toyota manufactured about half of its vehicles in Japan and a stronger yen made exports from Japan more expensive. Experts were of the opinion that as Toyota exported about 40% of its American sales from Japan, the profit margins had been lowered. Talking about the problem, Nomura Securities Co., Ltd.[23] analyst Shinya Naruse said, "Automakers cannot profit from exported

**EXHIBIT VII**   Five-year stock chart of Toyota

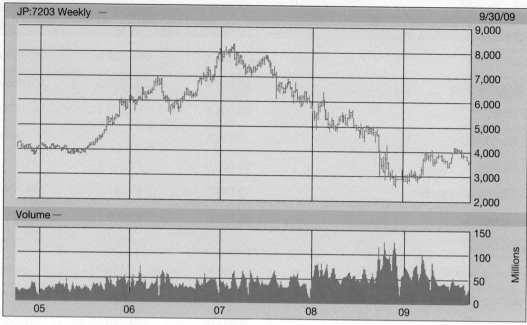

**Source:** http://bigcharts.marketwatch.com.

cars at current forex conditions. There is no way to recover without restructuring."[24]

Toyota announced that it would lose another ¥550 billion (US$5.5 billion) in 2009. Experts opined that the com-
pany, which was expected to lose US$5.7 billion more in the
fiscal year 2010, would not recover till 2012 even if sales
rebounded. According to Christian Takushi, a portfolio
manager for Swisscanto Asset Management AG,[25] "Toyota
has overdone itself with capital spending because they really
wanted to be No. 1. They're paying a high price."[26]

## Change in leadership

Toyota expected that the global vehicle demand would
eventually increase. However, for the fiscal year 2010,
the company expected its global unit sales to fall about
14% to 6.5 million vehicles.[27] The projected slip forced
Toyota to make changes at every level right from its
plants to its dealerships to the top management of the
company. The automaker made production cuts across
its 74 global assembly lines, laid off temporary workers
in Japan, and cut pay for its managers. It suspended production at some of its factories, implemented shorter
workweeks, and offered buyouts to American workers.
Toyota did not shut down any factories and retained its

production capacity of 10 million vehicles per year but
put construction of new plants on hold. Directors too
had to forego bonus pay and for the fiscal year 2009,
Toyota slashed its annual dividend by ¥40 to ¥100,
thereby ending a decade-long record in which the dividend had jumped six-fold.

The company began looking for a leader who would
steer the company back toward profits. In January 2009,
the company announced that it had selected Akio to
lead the company and manage a turnaround. In June
2009, the Toyota board replaced Watanabe with Akio,
heralding the return of a member of the founding family
as the head after 14 years. After a stint as an investment
banker, Akio had joined Toyota in 1994 as a junior
manager and had worked his way up. He had assumed
various domestic and international positions and was
also credited with spearheading some of Toyota's online
initiatives. He joined the Toyota board in 2000 and in
2001, he became the Chief Officer of the Asia and China
Operations Center. In 2002, he assumed the position of
MD and after a year he was made a senior MD. In 2005,
he became an Executive Vice-president (EVP) of the company and oversaw Toyota's China operations, Japan
sales, and the company's Internet business. At conservative Toyota, Akio was considered a bit of a radical and
was not averse to pushing through unpopular decisions.

Reactions to Akio's appointment were mixed among analysts as well as those in the company. Some welcomed the appointment as they felt that he had enough experience in the automobile market and was aware of all aspects of the company's operations. However, there were also murmurs in certain quarters that nepotism had played a role in Akio's accession to the top position. They felt that with less than a 2% stake in the company, the founding family could not make an automatic claim to this position. Chris Richter, a senior research analyst at CLSA,[28] said, "Good management requires good skill and good training and doesn't necessarily follow blood lines."[29] Many were surprised by the appointment as it was rare in Japan's conservative corporate culture that valued seniority, to appoint a person in his 50s as the President of the company. Some analysts were concerned that the company had been put in the hands of a relatively young member of the Toyoda family at such a turbulent time. James Womack, chairman, Lean Enterprise Institute, added, "I don't think anybody sees Akio as a highly original kind of guy, but he's really earnest. He's been in the Toyota system all his life. He doesn't know anything else but to go back to the basics."[30]

As part of the management reshuffle, five new EVPs and eight board members were appointed, while two key company members, Shoichiro and Senior Adviser Okuda, resigned from the board. Former Toyota executives Yoshimi Inaba and Yasumori Ihara were called back, while Watanabe was appointed Vice-chairman.

## Back to basics

Akio planned to adopt a "back to basics" approach to revive the company. "The global automobile industry has been facing extreme hardships since the latter half of last year … We expect our losses to deepen this fiscal year, and so all of us in the new management team at Toyota feel like we are setting sail during a storm. Unfortunately, we are currently losing money … So, we must start again from the very bottom up."[31] He planned to produce small, fuel-efficient and competitively priced cars that people could afford, cut costs, and establish a strong presence in emerging markets. Akio wanted to re-instill dedication to one of the pillars of TPS – genchi genbutsu[32] ("go and see for yourself"). "If I am going to be at the top of the car company, I want to be the owner-chef. I taste my car, and if it tastes good, I provide it to the customer,"[33] he said. He added that he would follow the corporate traditions of the company, embrace change, and at the same time, maintain his own individuality.

Akio intended to squeeze costs from the company's already lean operations so that the company would be profitable using just 70% of its production capacity and use the downtime to train workers. He had no plans to close plants or cut full-time jobs as he was banking on customers and the rank-and-file to steer the automaker out of its worst crisis. Akio volunteered to take a 30% pay cut for one year and other top managers too accepted pay cuts. The aim of the company was to save extra US$8.5 billion in costs in 2009.

According to Akio, the company's entire product lineup would be reviewed to ensure a better focus on its offerings to every region in the world. Toyota would concentrate on building more small cars and fewer large cars. "Rather than asking, "How many cars will we sell?" or, "How much money will we make by selling these cars?" we need to ask ourselves, "What kind of cars will make people happy?" as well as, "What pricing will attract them in each region?"[34] he said. Toyota was also to focus on "green" technology like hybrids and plug-in electric vehicles. Akio slashed the price of the third-generation Prius to a reasonable US$21,000, almost US$11,000 less than the fully equipped models. The company said that it would begin making its Prius gas-electric hybrids at a new plant in Mississippi by late 2010.

Toyota also planned to take advantage of government incentives around the world, such as the cash-for-clunkers[35] schemes, promoting more environmentally-friendly cars in Japan, Europe, and the US.

## Regional autonomy

The company's management was to place a priority on meeting the needs of regional markets by closely watching consumers and markets and noticing changes. In order to respond to consumer needs, each of the EVPs was to oversee a global region – North America, Europe, Japan, and emerging markets. Depending on the region, the company would then come out with an appropriate product strategy. Akio added that a more regionally-oriented management structure would help the company provide cars that met specific local tastes rather than offering a full lineup of vehicles in all markets. "Together, we will create clear 'Regional Vision' plans by determining what role Toyota should play and what we want to achieve in each region. We will also consider our capacity and the market situation in those regions, in order to identify areas where we want to advance, and areas where we need to take a step back. These decisions will allow us to better prioritize the allocation of our resources,"[36] he said. On July 31, 2009, Toyota announced that it was setting up two marketing companies, one to operate within Japan and one for the global market to handle marketing and focus on customer-centered activities. The companies would start operating on January 1, 2010.

In Japan, the size of the overall market was estimated at about 12 million vehicles. In 2009, the market size for new cars was expected to be less than 3 million units. In the Japanese market, Toyota's sales were stable mainly because of the incentives offered by the Japanese government such as the "eco-car tax deduction" and the "scrap incentive for buying eco-cars." Akio did not foresee any problems in sales but felt that its capacity in Japan was a problem area and the company needed to right-size.[37]

Though Toyota's sales in the North American market had dropped sharply because of the economic downturn, Akio was confident that the market would recover gradually. Toyota's US sales declined 38% in 2009.[38] As North America was one of the important markets for Toyota, Akio aimed to build more autonomous operations in this region and shift its focus to marketing a region-specific vehicle line-up. The company aimed to revamp its image in North America with the restructuring of the Lexus and the Scion. "Toyota had a strong desire to become a U.S. car company. I believe that decision was correct, and we will try to strengthen even more. Of course, looking at the current situation, I would say our production capacity may be a little bit too much,"[39] he said.

Akio said that the company would discontinue building pickups in Indiana and move all of its Tundra production to San Antonio and devote the new Mississippi facility to the Prius, which had earlier been built exclusively in Japan. As a cost-cutting measure, Toyota decided to suspend truck production at its plants in Princeton and San Antonio from August 2009 until November 2009. In July 2009, the company announced that it might end production at the NUMMI[40] plant in Fremont as its partner in the joint venture, GM, had decided to quit the facility.

Toyota also planned to bolster its presence in Europe by developing a distinctive Toyota business model in the region. Its presence had been rather weak in this region and the company wanted to change this by focusing on its hybrid technology. "[A]s stricter environmental regulations come into place, we are gradually shifting our focus to the hybrid segment. We are confident that this will create a stronger position for Toyota in Europe. Europe is also a place where Toyota can learn about "automotive culture." I have always admired the fact that cars play a major role in the lives of Europeans and that they love the experience of driving. Hopefully, we can find

ways to transfer that excitement to other regions around the world,"[41] said Akio. Toyota would start making hybrid cars in Europe from 2010 onwards.

Akio also gave more importance to emerging markets such as China, Asia, and South America as he felt that these regions had very good potential. "These markets have amazing growth potential, and I can see that China will someday stand alongside the United States as a giant single market. In order to meet customers' needs, we will – as always – take straightforward steps ... Expanding our reach in these markets will help increase our overall sales volume and profits, so I am determined to establish proactive business plans in these areas,"[42] he said.

## Challenges ahead

Akio expressed confidence that Toyota would bounce back but he added that it would take at least two more years for the company to turn a profit. Some analysts too echoed this view. According to CLSA's Richter, "Toyota has a history of rising to overcome crises. I think it will be quite a few years before anyone could challenge Toyota's No. 1 spot."[43] Despite the drop in sales by 26% in the first half of 2009, Toyota was still the world's top-selling automaker (Refer to Exhibit VIII for

**EXHIBIT VIII** World's top 10 auto groups by 2009 H1 sales

| Rank | Company | Sales (US$ million) |
|------|---------|---------------------|
| 1 | Toyota Motor Corp | 3.564 |
| 2 | General Motors Co | 3.553 |
| 3 | *Volkswagen AG | 3.265 |
| 4 | #Hyundai Motor Co | 2.153 |
| 5 | **Ford Motor Co | 2.145 |
| 6 | PSA Peugeot Citroen | 1.587 |
| 7 | Honda Motor Co | 1.586 |
| 8 | Nissan Motor Co | 1.546 |
| 9 | Suzuki Motor Corp | 1.15 |
| 10 | Renault SA | 1.107 |

* Excludes Scania, ** Ford publishes wholesale, not retail, figures, # Including Kia Motors Corp (000270.KS)
**Source:** www.reuters.com.

world's top 10 auto groups by 2009 H1 sales). Analysts also felt that the company's strong financial position would help it withstand even a situation in which sales continued to decline for another two years. They noted that Toyota was in a much better position than its major competitors whose very survival was at stake.

According to the company, Toyota was witnessing signs of recovery as its global production in June 2009 decreased by a modest 23.7% to 636,307 units from the same period in 2008.[44] The company forecast a smaller annual loss in 2009 due to deep cost reductions and predicted vehicle sales of 6.6 million units in 2009. The sales boost was expected from Japan where production had picked up due to incentives and tax breaks on environmentally-friendly vehicles. Toyota said that it expected a ¥450 billion (US$4.7 billion) loss for the fiscal 2010, less than the ¥550 billion loss that had been initially projected. Toyota might be able to boost its American market share to 21.3% by 2011 as GM and

Chrysler shut plants and dealerships, analysts said. According to James Hunt, an investor at Tocqueville Asset Management LP,[45] "Toyota should emerge from the downturn in an even stronger position relative to competitors."[46]

Toyota was optimistic that sales would improve gradually in all its major markets driven by the popularity of some of its models like the Prius. Commenting on how the company would respond to the challenges it faced, Akio said, "We may have to slightly change some of the ways of doing business, depending on the changes of the market. Some of the good things we did, and also not-so-good things we did, may not completely fit the situation. So while preserving our good DNA, I would like to have the courage to change some things if those things have to be changed."[47]

Economists warned that the economic situation would not bottom out until the second half of 2009 and that the sales trend in major markets such as the

## EXHIBIT IX  International car sales outlook (millions of units)

| | 1990–99 | 2000 | 2001–06 | 2007 | 2008 | 2009 |
|---|---|---|---|---|---|---|
| **Total Sales** | 39.20 | 46.64 | 48.63 | 54.92 | 52.17 | 48.19 |
| **North America*** | 16.36 | 19.77 | 19.45 | 18.83 | 15.85 | 12.44 |
| Canada | 1.27 | 1.55 | 1.60 | 1.65 | 1.64 | 1.42 |
| United States | 14.55 | 17.35 | 16.81 | 16.09 | 13.19 | 10.20 |
| Mexico | 0.54 | 0.87 | 1.04 | 1.09 | 1.02 | 0.82 |
| **Western Europe** | 13.11 | 14.75 | 14.54 | 14.75 | 13.54 | 12.93 |
| Germany | 3.57 | 3.38 | 3.32 | 3.15 | 3.09 | 3.71 |
| **Eastern Europe** | 1.18 | 2.38 | 2.36 | 3.58 | 4.01 | 3.41 |
| Russia | 0.78 | 1.03 | 1.25 | 2.31 | 2.73 | 2.18 |
| **Asia** | 6.91 | 7.85 | 10.23 | 14.42 | 15.07 | 15.78 |
| China | 0.33 | 0.61 | 2.26 | 5.15 | 5.04 | 6.30 |
| India | 0.31 | 0.60 | 0.75 | 1.18 | 1.20 | 1.32 |
| **South America** | 1.64 | 1.89 | 2.05 | 3.34 | 3.70 | 3.63 |
| Brazil | 0.94 | 1.17 | 1.30 | 1.98 | 2.19 | 2.30 |

*includes light trucks
**Source:** *Global Auto Report*, www.scotiacapital.com, July 31, 2009.

**EXHIBIT X** Car sales in developing nations remain in the fast lane

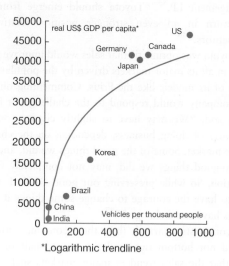

**Source:** *Global Auto Report*, www.scotiacapital.com, July 31, 2009.

US and Japan indicated that the demand for automobiles had not yet improved. Experts felt that Toyota would have to adjust to this new paradigm of lower sales growth and higher technology spending.[48] But some analysts felt that a cyclical recovery was underway in the industry. In June, purchases had started improving led

by China in the emerging markets and Germany in the developed markets (Refer to Exhibit IX for international car sales outlook and Exhibit X for car sales in developing nations).

Some analysts were, however, apprehensive about Toyota's future performance and said that the company faced an 'identity crisis' and might take time to adjust to the changes made by the new President. Some felt that Akio might not be able to take key decisions independently because at Toyota, major decisions were traditionally taken through consensus. In the US, its key market, the company would have to also closely analyze the changing political climate with President Barack Obama urging consumers to "buy an American car". Some analysts were also concerned that Toyota's focus on smaller vehicles might reduce its earnings.

Analysts felt that Akio had been handed over the reins of the company at a critical time and as such, every decision he took would be under scrutiny. In addition, there was pressure on him to prove his detractors wrong. According to Dirk Gibson of DCJAutoParts.com,[49] "The billion yen question is whether Akio Toyoda can pull it off? Can you imagine coming into a more difficult situation than the 2009 auto market? He seems ready for the task with his first step being to cut his own salary by 30 percent. While a good PR move, his decisions over the next two years will be far more telling when it comes to the restoration of the reputation of Toyota."[50]

## REFERENCES AND SUGGESTED READINGS

"Uncertainty Remains over NUMMI Plant's Fate," www.trading-markets.com, August 5, 2009.

"Toyota Announces First Quarter Financial Results," www.toyota.co.jp, August 4, 2009.

"Toyota Reports $819 million Quarterly Loss," http://news.moneycentral.msn.com, August 4, 2009.

Yuri Kageyama, "Toyota Reports $819 million Quarterly Loss," www.wtop.com, August 4, 2009.

Global Auto Report, www.scotiacapital.com, July 31, 2009.

"Toyota Clings to World Number-One Sales Spot Despite First-Half Decline, Sets Up New Marketing Companies," www.edmunds.com, July 29, 2009.

"Toyota's New President Switches Gears," www.miamiherald.com, July 20, 2009.

Ken Thomas, "Toyota Executive: Automaker Hoping to Make Quick Decision on California

Joint Venture Plant," http://gadgetophilia.com, July 20, 2009.

Alex Taylor III, "Toyota's New Man at the Wheel," http://money.cnn.com, June 26, 2009.

Robert Farago, "New Toyota CEO: "We Need Vehicles That Bring Joy to the Driving Experience," www.thetruthaboutcars.com, June 26, 2009.

Ian Rowley, "Japan: Toyota's New President Takes the Wheel," www.businessweek.com, June 25, 2009.

"New President at Toyota," http://english.ntdtv.com, June 25, 2009.

"Toyota's New Boss Vows Changes amid 'Stormy' Start," www.businessworld.in, June 25, 2009.

"Founder's Grandson to Lead Toyota," http://news.bbc.co.uk, June 23, 2009.

Jorn Madslien, "Toyota Scion to Revive Prudent Culture," http://news.bbc.co.uk, June 23, 2009.

Kae Inoue, "Toyota's President Toyoda Takes over Amid U.S. Slump," www.bloomberg.com, June 23, 2009.

"Toyota, Nissan Vow to do Better; Green Cars Key," www.reuters.com, June 23, 2009.

John Lippert, Alan Ohnsman and Kae Inoue, "Toyoda Asks How Many Times Toyota Errs Emulating GM Failures," www.bloomberg.com, June 22, 2009.

Micheline Maynard, "Toyota, Too, is Looking to Cut Costs," www.nytimes.com, May 12, 2009.

Hiroko Tabuchi, "Toyota Posts an Annual Loss," www.nytimes.com, May 8, 2009.

Todd Crowell, "Toyoda Takes Toyota Wheel," www.atimes.com, May 8, 2009.

"Toyota Announces Year-End Financial Results," www.toyota.co.jp, May 8, 2009.

"Toyota Motor Posts Annual Loss, Forecast Operating Loss of 850 Billion Yen for FY2010," www.domain-b.com, May 8, 2009.

Micheline Maynard, "Taking the Wheel as Toyota Skids," www.nytimes.com, February 14, 2009.

Martin Fackler, "Toyota Forecasts First Annual Net Loss since 1950," www.nytimes.com, February 6, 2009.

"Toyota Predicts Net Loss in Current Fiscal," www.thaindian.com, February 6, 2009.

Yuki Oda, "A Rough Road Ahead for Toyota's New Chief," www.time.com, January 22, 2009.

Martin Fackler and Bettina Wassener, "Grandson of Toyota Founder Will Lead," www.nytimes.com, January 20, 2009.

"Toyota Names Akio Toyoda as New President," www.telegraph.co.uk, January 20, 2009.

"Toyota Taps New President as Global Sales Slide 4%," www.usatoday.com, January 20, 2009.

"Toyota Taps Founder's Grandson as New President," www.chinadaily.com.cn, January 20, 2009.

Bill Vlasic and Nick Bunkley, "Toyota Scales Back Production of Big Vehicles," www.nytimes.com, July 11, 2008.

"Toyota 'World's Largest Carmaker'," http://news.bbc.co.uk, April 24, 2007.

Jeff Tyler, "Toyota's Number One," http://marketplace.publicradio.org, April 24, 2007.

www2.toyota.co.jp

Toyota Motors 2008 Annual Report

http://money.cnn.com

http://bigcharts.marketwatch.com

www.reuters.com

www.hoovers.com

# NOTES

1.  Todd Crowell, "Toyoda Takes Toyota Wheel," www.atimes.com, May 8, 2009.

2.  John Lippert, Alan Ohnsman and Kae Inoue, "Toyoda Asks How Many Times Toyota Errs Emulating GM Failures," www.bloomberg.com, June 22, 2009.

3.  Other business operations of Toyota include intelligent transport systems, IT and telecommunications, housing, motorboat manufacturing, and biotechnology and afforestation businesses.

4.  Toyota's financial year ends on March 31.

5.  General Motors Company, LLC (earlier General Motors Corporation) based in Detroit, is the second-largest automaker in the world. In June 2009, the company filed for Chapter 11 bankruptcy protection. The bankruptcy filing was a dramatic downfall for GM, which was founded in 1908 by William C. Durant. For the year ended 2008, the company reported revenues of US$148.979 billion.

6.  Alex Taylor III, "Toyota's New Man at the Wheel," http://money.cnn.com, June 26, 2009.

7.  As of September 2009, US$1 approximately equals ¥90.

8.  www.toyota.co.jp/en/news/09/0804_1.html.

9.  Hiroko Tabuchi, "Toyota Posts $819 Million Loss," www.nytimes.com, August 4, 2009.

10. "Toyota Reports $819 million Quarterly Loss," http://news.moneycentral.msn.com, August 4, 2009.

11. Jorn Madslien, "Toyota Scion to Revive Prudent Culture," http://news.bbc.co.uk, June 23, 2009.

12. Founded in 2001, IHS Global Insight provides economic, financial, and industry analysis, data and software solutions and consulting services.

13. The first principle of TPS was called "jidoka" which means that when a problem occurred, the equipment stopped immediately, thus preventing defective products from being produced. The second was the Just-in-Time (JIT) concept in which each process produced only what was required by the next process in a continuous flow.

14. Katsuaki Watnabe served as the president of Toyota from 2005 to mid 2009. He led Toyota on an aggressive and a largely successful growth track. He joined Toyota in 1964 and gained experience primarily in corporate planning and administrative affairs. In 1999, Watanabe was appointed as senior managing director, after which he assumed the position of executive vice-president in 2001. In June 2005 he was appointed as the president of Toyota.

15. Nick Bunkley, "Toyota Ahead of GM in 2008 Sales," www.nytimes.com, January 21, 2009.

16. http://topics.nytimes.com/top/news/business/companies/toyota_motor_corporation/index.html.

17. Bill Vlasic and Nick Bunkley, "Toyota Scales Back Production of Big Vehicles," www.nytimes.com, July 11, 2008.

18. Ian Rowley, "Auto Bailout: Et Tu, Toyota?" www.business-week.com, March 3, 2009.

19. www2.toyota.co.jp/en/news/09/0508_1.html.

20. "Toyota Reports $819 Million Loss," http://www.nytimes.com, August 4, 2009.

21. Based in Tokyo, UBS Securities Japan Ltd. is an investment-banking firm which provides financial advisory services.

22. Bill Vlasic and Nick Bunkley, "Toyota Scales Back Production of Big Vehicles," www.nytimes.com, July 11, 2008.

23. Nomura Securities Co., Ltd. is a brokerage firm in Japan.

24. Yuki Oda, "A Rough Road Ahead for Toyota's New Chief," www.time.com, January 22, 2009.

25. Swisscanto Asset Management AG is a Switzerland based asset management company which offers investment solutions to clients.

26. "Toyota's New President Switches Gears," www.miamiherald.com, July 20, 2009.

27. Hiroko Tabuchi, "Toyota Posts an Annual Loss," www.nytimes.com, May 8, 2009.

28. A Hong-Kong-based brokerage house.

29. Yuki Oda, "A Rough Road Ahead for Toyota's New Chief," www.time.com, January 22, 2009.

30. John Lippert, Alan Ohnsman and Kae Inoue, "Toyoda Asks How Many Times Toyota Errs Emulating GM Failures," www.bloomberg.com, June 22, 2009.

31. "Toyota Clings to World Number-One Sales Spot Despite First-Half Decline…," www.edmunds.com, July 30, 2009.

32. Genchi Genbutsu means "Go and see the problem first hand" The Company believed that practical experience is valued over theoretical knowledge.

33. Martin Fackler and Bettina Wassener, "Grandson of Toyota Founder Will Lead," www.nytimes.com, January 20, 2009.

34. www2.toyota.co.jp/en/about_toyota/message/index.html.

35. In April 2009, US officials introduced the cash-for-clunkers program under which car owners who upgraded to cleaner, fuel-efficient vehicles from cars that were at least 13 years old received government subsidies.

36. http://www2.toyota.co.jp/en/about_toyota/message/index.html.

37. http://www2.toyota.co.jp/en/about_toyota/message/index.html.

38. Ken Thomas, "Toyota Executive: Automaker Hoping to Make Quick Decision on California Joint Venture Plant," http://gadgetophilia.com, July 20, 2009.

39. Alex Taylor III, "Toyota's New Man at the Wheel," http://money.cnn.com, June 26, 2009.

40. GM and Toyota resurrected the plant after GM had closed it down in 1982. The NUMMI venture began production in 1984. In addition to the Vibe, the plant was making the Toyota Tacoma and Toyota Corolla in 2009.

41. www2.toyota.co.jp/en/about_toyota/message/index.html.

42. www2.toyota.co.jp/en/about_toyota/message/index.html.

43. Yuki Oda, "A Rough Road Ahead for Toyota's New Chief," www.time.com, January 22, 2009.

44. "Toyota Clings to World Number-One Sales Spot Despite First-Half Decline, Sets Up New Marketing Companies," www.edmunds.com, July 29, 2009.

45. Tocqueville Asset Management LP (TAM) is a US-based privately owned investment management firm.

46. John Lippert, Alan Ohnsman and Kae Inoue, "Toyoda Asks How Many Times Toyota Errs Emulating GM Failures," www.bloomberg.com, June 22, 2009.

47. Alex Taylor III, "Toyota's New Man at the Wheel," http://money.cnn.com, June 26, 2009.

48. "Toyota's New Boss Vows Changes amid 'Stormy' Start," www.businessworld.in, June 25, 2009.

49. DCJAutoParts.com is an online retailer of auto parts and accessories.

50. Dirk Gibson, "Toyota : A Look at the New CEO," www.articlealley.com, July 21, 2009.

# INTEGRATIVE CASE 15

15

# VODAFONE: OUT OF MANY, ONE[1]

Johannes Banzhaf, Ashok Som

*ESSEC Business School*

## Abstract

In 2006, Vodafone Group PLC was the world's largest cell phone provider by revenue. Since 1999, Vodafone had invested US$270 billion (€225 billion) mostly in stock, building an empire spanning 26 countries. It controlled cell phone operations in 16 countries and had minority stakes in companies in 10 other countries. This case traces the history of Vodafone's growth and its capability to transform and adapt itself to the dramatically changing market environment in the dynamic telecommunication sector. The case analyzes Vodafone's growth through acquisitions and the subsequent integration of acquired units with a key focus on how it manages to coordinate its businesses on a global scale.

Arun Sarin reclined in his seat in a first-class compartment en route to London. The CEO of Vodafone, the world's largest mobile telephone operator, began reflecting on the events of the last few days, in particular Vodafone's decision to exit the Japanese market by selling Vodafone's stake in Japan Telecom to Tokyo-based Softbank in a deal valued at $15.4 billion, confirming that after the sale the company would return $10.5 billion to its shareholders. Vodafone had trailed behind NTT DoCoMo and KDDI since its entry into Japan in 2001, thanks to fickle consumers, the lack of a low-end tier in the segment, and the challenge of coordinating terminals and technologies across borders. The time had come to make a hard decision, and Sarin had made it.

It was not the first time he had been faced with such a decision. Two years earlier Vodafone had made headlines in the financial press with its failed attempt to take over the U.S. mobile operator, AT&T Wireless. After a long takeover battle, Vodafone's American rival Cingular Wireless had offered $41 billion in cash for AT&T Wireless.[2] At the time, Sarin had not been sure whether to regret the failed takeover. He could have easily financed a larger sum for the bid, but major shareholders had been explicit that anything beyond an offer of $38 billion would be detrimental to their interests.[3] Vodafone's offer had forced Cingular to increase its bid from $30 billion to $41 billion, meaning that it might take Cingular many years to digest the merger (refer to Exhibit 1 for share prices of Vodafone since 1989). More promising and cheaper ways to enhance its presence in the world's largest economy with a huge growth potential might also come Vodafone's way.

Sarin knew he could not afford to alienate Vodafone's shareholders by pursuing growth at all costs. However, Vodafone's current hold in the U.S. market (the noncontrolling stake in Verizon Wireless but the only one in the United States) was not comforting either. The relationship with the other main shareholder, Verizon, was quite strained, management had refused to adopt the single Vodafone brand, and had insisted on using the outdated American CDMA network standard instead of the group-wide GSM/UMTS standard.[4]

Being the CEO was definitely not an easy job, with so many things to consider and the shadow of his larger-than-life predecessor Sir Chris Gent looming over him. But these reasons were exactly why he was being paid £1.2 million a year as base salary.[5]

# Company overview:
# Vodafone Group Plc

In 2005, Vodafone was the leading mobile phone operator in the world. It had more than 150 million customers worldwide in 26 different countries.[6] Vodafone employed approximately 67,000 people around the world and had its headquarters in Newbury, England. Being listed on the stock exchanges of New York (ticker: VOD), London, and Frankfurt, it boasted a market capitalization of US$165.7 billion[7] making it the eleventh most valuable company in the world. In financial year 2003 it suffered a loss of US$15.5 billion (on revenues of approximately US$48 billion). This figure was the result of large write-downs on the goodwill of acquired companies and huge amortization charges related to the acquisition of other mobile operators like Mannesmann D2. These charges amounted to US$18.8 billion.[8] In fact, if one excluded these extraordinary noncash charges, Vodafone was profitable, as indicated by its gross margins and its capacity to generate huge positive cash flows: The cash flow from operating activities (before capital expenditure and other outflows) amounted to £12.3 billion (approximately US$22.7 billion) in financial year 2004, while free cash flow exceeded an unbelievable £8 billion (US$15.7 billion – refer to Exhibit 2 for an overview of Vodafone Group's financials).[9] Vodafone had

been consistently paying dividends and had recently announced a £3 billion share repurchase program.[10]

# History of Vodafone[11]

The company was formed as Racal Telecom Limited in 1984 as a subsidiary of Racal Electronics Plc., a British electronics manufacturing company. It successfully bid for a private sector U.K. cellular license in 1982 and hosted the first-ever mobile phone call in the United Kingdom in 1985. The customer base stood at 19,000 on December 31, 1985.

In October 1988, Racal Telecom Ltd. went public by offering approximately 20 percent of the company's stock to the public. Three years later, it was fully demerged from Racal Electronics and became an independent company, with a different name – Vodafone Group Plc – which was listed on the London and New York stock exchanges. Corporate legend has it that the "founders had the foresight to realize that people would do more than talk over their phones and so created a future-proof name that would embrace both VOice and DAta mobile communication: Vodafone."[12] Due to its early start, it managed the largest mobile network in the world by 1987.

In 1992, Vodafone pioneered again when it signed the world's first international "roaming" agreement with Telecom Finland, allowing Vodafone's customers to use

**EXHIBIT 1** Vodafone share price since 2001 (in pence)

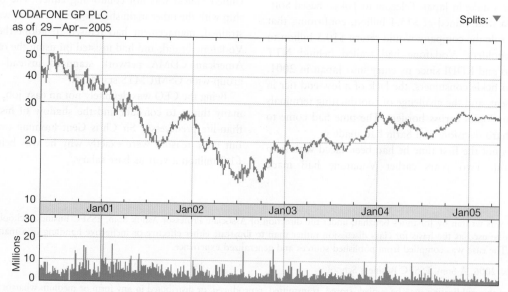

**Source:** http://finance.yahoo.com.

## EXHIBIT 2 Vodafone key financials, 1995–2004

| For the Financial Year Ended March 31 | Turnover (in £m) | Profit (loss) for the Financial Year (after taxation, in £m) | Net Cash Inflow From Operating Activities (in £m) | Dividends per Share (pence) | Registered Proportionate Customers (in thousands) |
|---|---|---|---|---|---|
| 1995 | 1,153 | 238 | 386 | 3.34p | 2,073 |
| 1996 | 1,402 | 311 | 615 | 4.01p | 3,035 |
| 1997 | 1,749 | 364 | 644 | 4.81p | 4,016 |
| 1998 | 2,408 | 419 | 886 | 5.53p | 5,844 |
| 1999 | 336 | 637 | 1,045 | 3.77p | 10,445 |
| 2000 | 7,873 | 487 | 2,510 | 1.34p | 39,139 |
| 2001 | 15,004 | (9,763) | 4,587 | 1.40p | 82,997 |
| 2002 | 22,845 | (16,155) | 8,102 | 1.47p | 101,136 |
| 2003 | 30,375* | (9,819) | 11,142 | 1.70p | 119,709 |
| 2004 | 33,559 | (9,015) | 12,317 | 2.03p | 133,421 |

*See following chart for group turnover by geographic region.

**Source:** Company annual reports.

| (in £ million) | 2003 | 2002 |
|---|---|---|
| **Mobile Telecommunications** | | |
| Northern Europe | 6,057 | |
| Central Europe | 4,775 | |
| Southern Europe | 8,051 | |
| Americas | 5 | |
| Asia Pacific | 8,364 | |
| Middle East and Africa | 290 | |
| = Total mobile operations | 27,542 | 20,742 |
| **Other Operations** | | |
| Europe | 854 | |
| Asia Pacific | 1,979 | |
| = Total Group Turnover | 30,375 | 22,845 |

Note: "Other operations" mainly include the results of the group's interests in fixed line telecommunications businesess in Germany (Arcor), France (Cegetel), and Japan (Japan Telecom). The turnover figure for the Americas does not include the 45% stake in Verizon Wireless (U.S.).

**Source:** Adapted from company annual report, 2003.

their phone on a different network while still being billed in their home country. Four years later, Vodafone became the first operator in the United Kingdom to offer so-called prepaid packages that do not require the customers to sign a long-term contract.

Christopher Gent succeeded Sir Gerald Whent at the helm of the company on January 1, 1997. Gent was responsible for shifting Vodafone's growth strategy from organic to aggressive external, orchestrating its move toward globalization. In the same year, Vodafone's 100th roaming agreement was signed.

In early 1999, Vodafone signed up its 10 millionth customer, 5 million of them in the United Kingdom. Vodafone's growth reached the next level when it successfully merged with AirTouch Communications Inc. of the United States – a $61 billion deal. Vodafone renamed itself briefly into Vodafone AirTouch and more than doubled its customer base to 31 million customers worldwide (September 1999), having operations in 24 countries across five continents.[13] In the late 1990s and the early new millennium, stock markets were steering toward a bubble, with "mobile" being the latest hype and insane sums being paid for mobile operators and the licenses to operate mobile networks. At the end of November 1999, the company had a market capitalization of approximately £90 billion. Vodafone's North American branch was integrated into a new entity branded Verizon Wireless together with Bell Atlantic's mobile business, with Vodafone retaining a 45 percent stake in the new venture. Verizon Wireless was the largest mobile phone operator in 2003 in a fragmented North American market (36 million customers, 24% market share as of September 30, 2003).[14]

In a move that sent shockwaves through corporate Germany in 1999, Vodafone launched a €100 billion takeover bid for Mannesmann in order to get hold of its D2 mobile phone business, the private market leader in Germany. A bitter struggle for Mannesmann's independence ensued, but finally the board of Mannesmann gave in and the deal was closed in 2000: €190 billion paid in stocks made it Germany's largest takeover ever.[15] The customer base was once again doubled and Vodafone found itself among the 10 largest companies in the world in terms of market capitalization. The mobile telephony boom reached its peak and former national providers (such as Deutsche Telekom, France Télécom, Telefonica) embarked on a buying binge that brought them on the verge of bankruptcy, when the bubble finally burst (Deutsche Telekom shares fell from more than €100 to €15).

The year 2001 saw a consolidation and restructuring within Vodafone, which reported 82.9 million customers for the financial year ending March 31, 2001. It grew at

a somewhat slower pace than in previous years, about half of it generated by internal growth and the other half by acquisitions (e.g., acquiring Ireland's Eircell and increasing its stake in Spanish AirTel Movil to 91.7%). However, slower growth still meant that Vodafone had added approximately 20 million customers by the end of the year 2002. At that time, the company board announced that the Indian-born American Arun Sarin would take over the CEO position on July 30, 2003.

No large scale acquisitions took place in 2002 and 2003, but instead a host of smaller deals and partnership agreements were made. In February 2004, Vodafone's bid for AT&T Wireless in the United States failed against a higher offer by Cingular, clearly indicating that Vodafone had all but renounced its growth ambitions.

## Growth at Vodafone

Traditionally growth at Vodafone was by acquisitions rather than organic. It had a track record in takeovers and their subsequent successful integration, Germany's Mannesmann being the most prominent example. Branded as "Vodafone Germany," Mannesmann was the group's most profitable venture (in terms of EBIT, which surpassed £2 billion in 2003) and its largest subsidiary. On the mobile telephony acquisition strategy, Alan Harper, Group Strategy and Business Integration Director, commented,

> In the past 10 years there had been a sea of change in the evolution of the telecommunication industry. The rule in this industry has been "Hunt or Be Hunted." The strategy of the global players had been mobile-centric, multi-market strategies. Most of the companies like Hutchison, Mannesmann, Airtouch started much smaller, like a startup, did not have any history as an operator and the parent company was usually a trading company. Vodafone acquired Mannesmann, Airtouch and the rest of the small players. FT acquired Orange. Docomo was restructured back into NTT.

Unlike many of its competitors, Vodafone used shares for its acquisitions. This practice might be one of the reasons why Vodafone emerged from the telecom crisis relatively early and could concentrate on growth again, while virtually all of its competitors were still occupied in trying to reduce their debt burden (Deutsche Telekom, France Télécom, MMO2, KPN, etc.).[16] However, Vodafone's shares had shown only lackluster performance in prior months, which meant that Vodafone increasingly had to use hard cash to increase its holdings in subsidiaries or for new acquisitions. Because Vodafone did not want to compromise its good credit ratings (by industry standards) under any circumstances, it slowed down on acquisitions and focused on internal growth for the preceding two years (refer to Exhibit 3 for Vodafone's strategic intent).

Vodafone had acquired other businesses along with the mobile phone business as in the case of Japan Telecom and Mannesmann, where it got ownership of fixed line operations. Vodafone had been always explicit in its concentration on its core business of mobile telecommunications. Usually it started looking for potential buyers for the other business. In the words of Alan Harper, Group Strategy and Business Integration Director,

> We had been always mobile focused. In 1995, when I joined Vodafone, it was mobile focused. It has a turnover of £8 billion, it was the third largest mobile operator in the UK and had 80% business in the UK. Today, in 2005, we are still mobile focused, with a turnover of £100 billion, biggest in the world and only 10% in the UK.

Vodafone balanced its investment options by taking its time to ensure a good investment and disinvestment option. For example, it sold Japan Telecom's fixed line operations in 2003 for ¥261.3 billion (£1.4 billion)[17] while it reinforced its long-term commitment to Japan in 2005 by making a further investment of up to £2.6 billion. Arun Sarin pointed out,

> Our transactions in Japan will simplify the structure, confirm our commitment to the Japanese marketplace, and enable us to deliver on the changes needed to improve our position.

Arcor was not divested and was still part of Vodafone Germany as of 2005. Arcor might even serve as a strategic weapon to cannibalize on incumbent Deutsche Telekom's profitable fixed line business.[18]

Since mid-2001, Vodafone had entered into arrangements with other network operators in countries where it did not hold any equity stake. Under the terms of so-called Partner Network Agreements, Vodafone cooperated with its counterparts in the development and marketing of global services under dual brand logos. By 2003, Vodafone had extended its reach into 11 other countries, thus establishing a first foothold in these markets.[19] Such an agreement was a classic win-win situation: Vodafone not only gained new market insight with little risk, but at the same time was able to assess the quality of the partner in order to identify possible takeover targets, while the partner benefited from Vodafone's unique marketing and technological capabilities.

Vodafone's acquisition strategy always followed a similar pattern: First, the number one or two player within a national market was identified, while it carefully avoided acquiring the incumbent mobile operator that was linked to the state-owned telecom monopoly (like T-Mobile, which was the mobile division of Deutsche Telekom, or Orange, a business unit of France Télécom). It seems that Vodafone feared a bureaucratic inertia of these organizations, and would rather focus on more flexible, entrepreneurially minded challengers (with Mannesmann's D2 once again being a good example, or France's SFR) that would challenge the incumbents in different local markets. Referring to this strategy Alan Harper explained,

## EXHIBIT 3 Strategic intent of Vodafone

The Company had maintained a strategy of focusing on global mobile telecommunications and providing network coverage to allow its customers to communicate using mobile products and services. The Company's strategy was increasingly focused on revenue growth and margin improvement from providing enhanced services to its customer base. This growth strategy had three principal components:

- to grow voice and data revenues through an increased marketing focus on our established high-quality customer base;

- to extend our operational leadership of the industry through maximizing the benefits of scale and scope, through the use of partner network agreements, by increasing equity interests in businesses where the Group had existing shareholdings and by promoting the Vodafone brand; and

- to extend service differentiation, investing in delivering Vodafone branded, easy to use, customer propositions for mobile voice and data.

Where appropriate, and if circumstances allow, the Company may also make further acquisitions or disposals of businesses.

**Source:** http://www.vodafone.com.

*Our vision has been to leverage scale and scope benefits, reduce response time in the market, and ensure effective delivery to customers. This we have achieved by collecting or acquiring national (operational) companies and gave them a mission of a "challenger company" in each of the national markets. For example, Vodafone with SFR is a challenger to France Telecom in France, Vodafone UK is a challenger to British Telecom in the UK, and Vodafone Germany a challenger to Deutsch Telecom in Germany. Together with this challenger mind-set, we nurture and instill an entrepreneurial spirit inside Vodafone Group companies, and in this respect we do not behave as a traditional telephone company. Since we differ from being a traditional company, the cultural alignment of people working for Vodafone is a key issue in sustaining this challenger and entrepreneurial mind-set. To focus on this cultural alignment, we give autonomy to the local entity and reiterate that the local entity did not join a global company like IBM or HP. The local entity has to work in a matrix structure and keep alive the "challenger mind-set" on fixed line telephony and other incumbents, challenge the status quo every day, and evolve by being local entrepreneurs.*

## Branding, identity, and pricing

After a successful bid for a takeover target, Vodafone followed a diverse strategy in terms of branding, creating its identity and its own pricing models. Alan Harper explained,

*We play different models of creating Vodafone's identity in the market. Which way we adapt depends on a number of factors and considerations, such as the strength of the local brand, the prevalent company culture and the general fit between Vodafone's processes and the acquired business' processes. But frankly, at the end of the day, it comes down to a question of management judgment. For example, in New Zealand when we acquired Bellsouth, we changed Bellsouth almost overnight to Vodafone New Zealand. Similarly in Portugal, we undertook an overnight integration of Telecel to Vodafone Portugal. Telecel transformed into Vodafone Portugal and became challenger to the traditional PTT. Whereas in Italy, when we*

*acquired Omnitel, it took us 2.5 years to change Omnitel to Omnitel Vodafone. Omnitel colours were Green and White and we could not change it to Vodafone Red immediately. It was because Omnitel had a strong brand image, very well known and we had to be very cautious during the transition. The market would never have accepted it. The same was the case with DT in Germany.*

The management judgment of fast or slow rebranding turned on the customer and organizational response of the acquired market and acquired company. Usually the national brand was kept alive for some time until the dust of the takeover battle had settled. Vodafone then carefully launched its phased rebranding campaign to bring the new subsidiary under the "Vodafone" umbrella. Usually, they added "Vodafone" to the original corporate brand. To better coordinate these branding efforts, Vodafone appointed David Haines, a former Coca-Cola manager, as global brand director.[20] Davin Haines explained,

*For example "D2" became "D2 Vodafone." Within a year, Vodafone modified the logo to its typical red color and changed the order of company name, for example "D2 Vodafone" to "Vodafone D2." During the last phase, the original "national" name was eliminated completely and only the global brand and logo remained. This process could take more than two years and usually passed almost unnoticed by the customers, who got accustomed to the new logo due to the extensive branding campaigns, often in conjunction with the launch of a new global product (like Vodafone's Mobile Connect Card, enabling e-mailing and Internet access via a laptop and the mobile network) or service (e.g., Vodafone live! mobile Internet portal). Following this pattern, Vodafone Omnitel in Italy and J-Phone Vodafone in Japan became a single brand in May 2003 and October 2003, respectively.[21]*

Vodafone launched its first truly global communications campaign in the beginning of August 2001 to reinforce its brand awareness and a global brand identity. Arun Sarin reiterated,

*Throughout the past few years, Vodafone has done a terrific job of building brand awareness as we have moved toward a single global brand. Beyond brand awareness, we want people to understand that the Vodafone name represents great service, great value and great innovation. When our name becomes synonymous with these attributes we will achieve brand preference and expect to see our market share climb as a result.*

Across all media, a homogenous corporate brand and identity was communicated including the slogan "How are you?" and introduced the inverted comma as logo. To keep in sync with Vodafone's global aspirations, the group selected two globally recognized brands: It sponsored the Manchester United Football Club and the Ferrari Formula 1 team to improve awareness and perception of the brand. In addition, it supported its brand by individual sponsorship contracts and other marketing communication programs at the local level. According to a Vodafone statement,

*An audit of the first year of sponsorship of Scuderia Ferrari reveals that the sponsorship had outperformed all of the annual targets set internally by Vodafone and helped establish exceptional global brand awareness.*[22]

Being number one or number two in most markets[23] it had entered, Vodafone never used "low prices" to attract new customers. Instead, it focused on creating and marketing new value-added services that enticed customers to sign up with Vodafone, even if it implied paying not the lowest rates available. According to Arun Sarin,

*We have rededicated ourselves to delighting our customers because we believe this is the foundation for our continued success. We recognise that every customer interaction provides another opportunity to win loyalty and that's why we continue to raise standards on the quality of customer care in our call centres and our stores and the quality of our networks. Key to delighting our customers is our ability to deliver superior voice and data services according to differing customer needs.*

Vodafone was not immune to the pricing policies of its competitors, which meant that it lowered its tariffs whenever the price differential became too great and the new subscriber market share dropped below a critical level. Given its size and healthy finances, it could usually weather price wars and simply waited until the aggressive player lost its thrust. Appendix I explores in some detail the role of fixed costs and their impact on pricing in the mobile telecommunication market.

## Integrating to One Vodafone

Vodafone realized that real business integration extends far beyond having a single brand. Critics had pointed out that establishing a global brand and logo is among the easier tasks of managing a multinational corporation. Alan Harper stressed,

*The careful re-branding policy not only targeted customers, but also tried to address the needs and concerns of the employees. The employees had to adjust to the fact that though they were "national challengers with an instilled entrepreneurial spirit," they were also part of the family of the global Vodafone Corporation based in Newbury, England. It was perceived that most employees were proud of having contributed to the success of challenging the incumbent operator and were reluctant to be incorporated into a larger corporation that they perceived as "distant."*

After the heady days of Chris Gent and the acquisitions by the dozen, Arun Sarin had to find innovative ways to integrate "a disparate group of national operations" into one company. Arun Sarin recognized that winning over the hearts of the employees and achieving cultural alignment was perhaps the "biggest challenge of all." An analyst of Merrill Lynch praised Arun Sarin as "smart" and "strategically as good as it gets."[24] Sarin seemed to be a good fit for this extraordinary task ahead, as he was described as "an operating man rather than a dealmaker" and "the archetypal international executive."[25] The portrait of Sarin went on like this:

*Born and brought up in India, but now an American citizen, Mr Sarin's background was an asset. There might seem to be a certain irony in putting an Indian-American in charge of the world's biggest mobile-phone operator, each of these countries had made a mess of introducing wireless telecoms. But Vodafone was a British company that aspired to be a true multinational. It had large operations in Germany, where it bought Mannesmann in 2000, in Italy and in Japan. To put another Brit into the top job might have bred resentment. [...] The son of a well-to-do Indian military officer, he went to a military boarding-school, but his mother encouraged him not to follow his father's career. Instead, he took an engineering degree at the Indian Institute of Technology, the country's equivalent of MIT. From there he went to the University of California at Berkeley on a scholarship, to earn a further degree in engineering and a MBA. He had lived in America ever since. The main remnants of his origins were an Indian wife (whom he met at Berkeley), a touch of an accent and a passion for cricket, which he shares with Sir Chris [Gent, his predecessor].*[26]

Sarin, however, was not the only director on Vodafone's board with a distinct international background. As a result of Vodafone's past acquisitions and their pragmatic integration into the group, many skilled foreign (non-British) managers had been retained and had since joined the board, including two Germans, one Italian, one South African, and one Swede (see Exhibit 4(a) and (b)).

At the annual general meeting in July 2003, Sarin emphasized the need to benefit from economies of scale and scope. In June 2004, Arun Sarin redefined,

> At Vodafone, everything we do furthers our desire to create mobile connections for individuals, businesses and communities. Our Vision is to be the world's mobile communications leader and we're delighted by the prospects for the future of our industry. Our commitment to this industry is underlined by our company values, which state that everything we do is driven by our passion for customers, our people, results and the world around us. ... Operating in 26 markets (together with Partner Networks in a further 14 countries, with approximately 151.8 million registered customers, and approximately 398.5 million total

venture customers) puts us in an enviable position to leverage our global scale and scope. ... Another competitive advantage is our leadership position on cost and time to market. From network services to sales, and marketing to customer care and billing, we have many varied systems in use across the business. With strong cooperation between our various operating companies we can achieve further savings.

To coordinate, restructure, and integrate its various systems across 26 countries, Vodafone launched its "One Vodafone" initiative that aimed to boost annual pretax operating profit by £2.5 billion by FY2008.[27] Alan Harper explained in detail:

> We are in a period when we are integrating our company. With acquisitions all over the world, one of our challenges is to integrate seamlessly not only technology (which by the way is more or less similar across the world) but people. And this is a key part of the Branding Evolution that we had witnessed. The challenge of this restructuring program is to balance the need of coordination and synergies while encouraging local initiatives.

## EXHIBIT 4(a)  Vodafone's executive and nonexecutive directors

As of July 30, 2005, Vodafone had six executive directors and eight nonexecutive directors, including the chairperson, Lord MacLaurin.

- **Lord MacLaurin of Knebworth,** *Chairperson*
- **Paul Hazen,** *Deputy Chairperson and Senior Independent Director*
- **Arun Sarin,** *Chief Executive* (Indian-born and raised, graduated from the Indian Institute of Technology, but now American citizen. Former chief executive officer for the United States and Asia Pacific region until April 15, 2000, when he became a nonexecutive director. Former director of AirTouch from July 1995 and president and chief operating officer from February 1997 to June 1999. Appointed chief executive on 30 July 2003.)
- **Peter R. Bamford,** *Chief Marketing Officer*
- **Thomas Geitner,** *Chief Technology Officer*
- **Julian M. Horn-Smith,** *Group Chief Operating Officer*
- **Kenneth J. Hydon,** *Financial Director*
- **Sir John Bond**
- **Dr. Michael J. Boskin**
- **Professor Sir Alec Broers**
- **Dr. John Buchanan**
- **Penelope L. Hughes**
- **Sir David Scholey, CBE**
- **Professor Jürgen Schrempp**
- **Luc Vandevelde**

## EXHIBIT 4(b)  Vodafone's executive and nonexecutive directors

- **Arun Sarin,** Chief Executive
- **Sir Julian Horn-Smith,** Deputy Chief Executive
- **Ken Hydon,** Financial Director
- **Peter Bamford,** Chief Marketing Officer
- **Thomas Geitner,** Chief Technology Officer
- **Jürgen von Kuczkowski,** Chief Executive Germany
- **Pietro Guindani,** Chief Executive Italy
- **Bill Morrow,** Chief Executive United Kingdom
- **Paul Donovan,** Regional Chief Executive
- **Brian Clark,** Chief Executive Asia Pacific and Group Human Resources Director Designate
- **Shiro Tsuda,** Chief Executive Japan
- **Alan Harper,** Group Strategy and Business Integration Director
- **Phil Williams,** Group Human Resources Director
- **Stephen Scott,** Group General Counsel and Company Secretary
- **Simon Lewis,** Group Corporate Affairs Director

**Source:** http://www.vodafone.com.

*The One Vodafone program is a business integration activity and we are in the process of "gradual integration of our business architecture." For example, we are running down a real-time billing system to an integrated system for 28mn customers. It is a very difficult task if one tries to understand the billing system of mobile telephones. Under the One Vodafone, there are currently 8 programs, Networks (design and supply procurement, coordination, and consolidation initiatives), IT (design, back office, billings, ERP/HR, operations – data centre processes), Service platforms, Roaming (mapping footprints), Customer (next practice services), Handset portfolio, MNC accounts, Retailing (one won't believe, we are the eighth largest retailer in the world taking together our stores that are owned or franchised). ... We are trying to integrate national operating units across footprints and trying to leverage scale and scope while trying to retain the local autonomy and responsiveness of our challenger national units.*

Alan Harper agreed that implementation of "One Vodafone" is a challenge. He explained,

*To implement One Vodafone, we have undertaken a change in organizational structure of the Group [refer to Exhibit 5]. We still operate in a matrix format. What One Vodafone tries to achieve is to simplify the integration issues in terms of brand strength and integrating local culture and processes. We centralize all our marketing efforts, branding and product development. Technology is standardized. Network design (switching, radio) are coordinated. Best practices are benchmarked by Advance Services such as service platforms and portals (Vodafone Live!). Knowledge is shared via the HQ, HR, strategy, and Marketing departments, through lateral processes, including our governance processes. We keep and encourage local initiatives such as customer services, sales, network billing, and IT systems. We are trying to incorporate the best of all the cultures to the maximum extent possible and in this way we tried to transform Vodafone UK into a new Vodafone.*

One Vodafone was clearly communicated across the company via the Internet, intranet, different training programs as well as a monthly employee magazine called "*Vodafone life! The global magazine for all Vodafone people.*" The HR department prepared special "initiation" training programs to acquaint new employees to the Vodafone way, labeled the "Vodafone footstep," which included its vision and values (see Exhibit 6) and the "Ten Business Principles."[28] On translating the vision and values alongside changes in structure and systems, Vodafone witnessed revamping of people processes

**EXHIBIT 5**  Board changes and new organizational structure as of January 2005

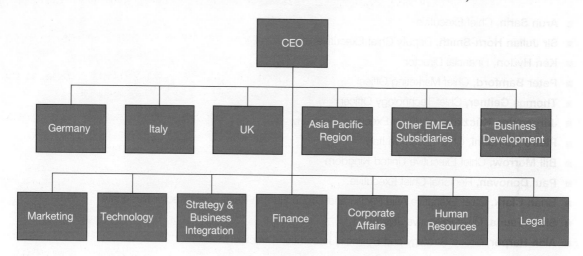

Vodafone Group Plc ("Vodafone") announces Board changes and a new organisational structure which will enable continued improvement in the delivery of the Group's strategic goals. This structure will become effective as of 1 January 2005.

The new organization is designed to:

- Focus more attention on customers in Vodafone's local markets;
- Enhance Vodafone's ability to deliver seamless services to corporations;
- Facilitate coordinated delivery of 3G across all markets;
- Function as an integrated company, delivering on One Vodafone; and
- Simplify decision-making, accountabilities and governance structures to speed up execution.

Vodafone will simplify its existing regional structure with major countries and business areas reporting to the Chief Executive. All first-line management functions in the Operating Companies will have a dual reporting line to the respective functions at Group level.

Arun Sarin, Chief Executive said: "We are creating an organisation that is better positioned to respond to the high expectations of our customers. Faster execution will enable us to extend our lead within the mobile industry and deliver the benefits to our customers, our employees and our shareholders."

## Main Board Appointments

Sir Julian Horn-Smith will be appointed Deputy Chief Executive with effect from 1 January 2005. Vodafone separately announces that Andy Halford has been appointed Financial Director Designate. Andy will succeed Ken Hydon when he retires on 26 July 2005.

## Operating Company Structure

Vodafone's operating company structure will be streamlined to ensure effective and fast decision making, enabling improved time to market across a number of business initiatives. Consequently, the following operating companies and business areas will report directly into the Chief Executive:

- European Affiliates (Belgium, France, Poland, Romania and Switzerland) and Non-European Affiliates (China, Fiji, Kenya, South Africa and United States), led by Sir Julian Horn-Smith;
- Germany, led by Jürgen von Kuczkowski;
- Italy, led by Pietro Guindani;
- United Kingdom, led by Bill Morrow;

- Other EMEA Subsidiaries (Albania, Egypt, Greece, Hungary, Ireland, Malta, Netherlands, Portugal, Spain and Sweden), led by Paul Donovan;

- Asia Pacific (Australia, Japan and New Zealand), led by Brian Clark who will also be appointed Group Human Resources Director Designate.

Vodafone's Group functions will be strengthened to support the delivery of seamless global propositions and Vodafone's continued integration. The following functions will also report directly to the Chief Executive:

- Marketing, led by Peter Bamford, the Chief Marketing Officer. This function will be reinforced by a newly created Multi National Corporate unit which will assume full accountability for serving Vodafone's global corporate customers. Group Marketing will also manage the global handset portfolio and procurement;

- Technology, led by Thomas Geitner, the Chief Technology Officer. In addition to standardized network design and global supply chain management, this function will introduce the concept of shared service operation for IT and service delivery;

- Business Development, a new function led by Sir Julian Horn-Smith. Sir Julian will be responsible for driving Vodafone's product and services portfolio into Vodafone's affiliates and the Partner Networks. In addition, this function will assume responsibility for expanding and consolidating Vodafone's footprint through the Partner Network programme and any Corporate Finance activities.

### New Governance Structure

Vodafone also announces changes to its governance process. The Group will have two management committees which will oversee the execution of the Main Board's strategy and policy.

- The Executive Committee
  Chaired by Arun Sarin, this committee will focus on the Group's strategy, financial structure and planning, succession planning, organizational development and group-wide policies.

- The Integration and Operations Committee
  Chaired by Arun Sarin, this committee will be responsible for setting operational plans, budgets and forecasts, product and service development, customer segmentation, managing delivery of multi-market propositions and managing shared resources.

**Source:** http://www.vodafone.com.

---

within the organization. Commenting on employees, Arun Sarin explained,

> As the business expands and the environment around us evolves, it is crucial for us to develop, recruit and retain the people that will lead us into this new world. We are working hard to make sure our employees have the right skills and knowledge to anticipate our customers' needs. We are identifying new ways to share the best of what we do on a global basis. We continue to reap the benefits of a motivated team with a strong customer service culture, which will help earn a reputation for Vodafone that is second to none.

The HR Department had set up a fast-track career path (the Global Leadership Programme, GLP) for high-potential managers, rotating them across business functions and countries and equipping them with crucial multicultural skills.

Despite the integration and standardization efforts, the corporate headquarters had to ensure a certain level of independence for individual country subsidiaries to take into account differing business models and customer expectations. For example, 48 percent of Vodafone's customers in Germany had a contract, while this kind of long-term commitment to an operator was almost unheard of in Italy (92 percent were prepaid customers).[29]

To orchestrate the move toward greater coordination as well as to identify and disseminate best practices, the group created two new central functions, Group Marketing (to drive revenue growth), and Group Technology and Business Integration (to drive cost and scale benefits).[30] Communicating Vodafone's new focus on integrating the bits and pieces resulting from past acquisitions was clearly a top management task. The Integration and Operations Committee was instituted, staffed with members of the executive board and chaired by Arun Sarin himself. This committee was responsible for "setting operational plans,

# EXHIBIT 6  Vodafone's vision and values

We have one vision and a set of values that underpins everything we do. Both our vision and our values were shared throughout the global organization.

## Our Vision

To be the world's mobile communications leader – enriching customers' lives, helping individuals, businesses and communities be more connected in a mobile world.

- Our customers use mobile communications to make their lives richer, more fulfilled, more connected. They will prefer Vodafone because the experience of using Vodafone will be the best they can find.
- We will lead in making the mobile the primary means of personal communications for every individual around the world.
- Through our leadership, our scale, our scope, and our partnerships, we will bring online mobile services to the world.

## Our Values

### Passion for customers

Our customers have chosen to trust us. In return, we must strive to anticipate and understand their needs and delight them with our service.

- We value our customers above everything else and aspire to make their lives richer, more fulfilled and more connected.
- We must always listen and respond to each of our customers.
- We will strive to delight our customers, anticipating their needs and delivering greater quality and more value, faster than anyone else.

### Passion for our people

Outstanding people working together make Vodafone exceptionally successful.

- We seek to attract, develop, reward, and retain outstanding individuals.
- We believe in empowerment and personal accountability.
- We enjoy what we do.
- We believe in the power of our teams.

### Passion for results

We are action-oriented and driven by a desire to be the best.

- We are committed to be the best in all we do.
- We all play our part in delivering results.
- We seek speed, flexibility, and efficiency in all we do.

### Passion for the world around us

We will help people of the world to have fuller lives – both through the services we provide and through the impact we have on the world around us.

- We recognize the responsibilities that accompany the growth we have achieved.
- We will be a force for good in the world.
- A spirit of partnership and mutual respect is critical in all our activities.

**Source:** http://www.vodafone.com.

budgets and forecasts, product and service development, customer segmentation, managing delivery of multi-market propositions and managing shared resources" across geographies.[31] Alan Harper, who had been heading the group strategy department at Vodafone since 2000, saw his job title changed to Group Strategy and Business Integration Director. Simultaneously, Vodafone restructured itself at the corporate level to include the two new functions, which directly reported to the group's COO, Julian Horn-Smith.

Thomas Geitner was appointed head of the new unit Group Technology & Business Integration as chief technology officer.

> *The purpose of Group Technology will be to lead the implementation of a standardized architecture for business processes, information technology and network systems. This will support the next generation of products and services and the critical role of introducing and operating 3G capacity.*[32]

A key focus of the Group Technology activities was the management and control of group-wide projects in relation to the ongoing rollout of "third generation" (3G) networks, the enhancement of Vodafone live! and the development of the Group's business offerings. This work included the continued development of technical specifications, creation and management of global contracts with suppliers as well as testing of terminals.[33]

It was committed to provide underlying terminal and platform technologies on a global basis. Within the mobile phone industry, a shift of power away from handset makers (Nokia, Siemens, Ericsson, etc.) could be observed. Global operators such as Vodafone had increasingly succeeded in forcing the producers to offer specially designed and branded products: the thriving Vodafone live! multimedia service was launched on Sharp GX-10 handsets, exclusively manufactured and branded for Vodafone.[34] If this trend persisted, Vodafone would be the first to benefit from its huge purchasing power and could even force Nokia (which had an almost 40 percent world market share) to cater more toward Vodafone's needs.[35] Vodafone could also use its unrivalled clout when negotiating with network equipment suppliers (such as Alcatel, Nokia, Siemens, etc.) to squeeze their margins.

Peter Bamford was appointed chief marketing officer and head of the Group Marketing department, which was in charge of

> *"providing leadership and coordination across the full range of marketing and commercial activities including brand, product development, content management, partner networks and global accounts."*[36]

For Vodafone, the question was how customers could derive a benefit from Vodafone's increasingly global reach, ultimately driving top-line growth. Alan Harper explains,

> *We are a technology and sales & distribution group focused on local companies winning market share against incumbents in respective countries. We do not develop technology but we are users of technology. Technology is developed by companies such as Nokia, Ericksson, Nortel. We buy their technology – and technology evolution in our sector is more or less standard, it evolves, grows without major differentiations and after a period of time it is standardized. Now the challenge is how best we can leverage using and integrating the technology across our companies. ... With the evolution and growth of our company we are today more of a company that prides itself in the differentiation of services that we bring to our customers. We are still 100 percent sales driven but we are much more customer centric and customer service oriented and take pride in understanding customer needs as we graduate to offering our customers the next best service and focusing on customer delight (e.g., Amazon). We now execute much better and it is because of the reason of the shift in our competencies.*

Vodafone started creating service offerings and product packages directly leveraging Vodafone's network and delivering tangible value to customers. For example, it created a tariff option that enabled customers to seamlessly roam the globe, on a special per minute rate, on the same network, without having to worry about high interconnection fees or differing technical standards. A new unit within Group Marketing was created to develop and market services specifically tailored to the needs of global coordination, such as seamless wireless access to corporate IT systems and special rates for international calls on the network. Such a global service offering could clearly serve as a differentiating factor to competitors that could not match Vodafone's global footprint.

## Woes in the United States and France

There were still two nagging issues for Arun Sarin: Vodafone's 45 percent stake in Verizon Wireless and the unresolved issues about control in France's SFR, for which Vodafone had been at loggerheads with Vivendi for several years now. Vodafone was far from happy about these minority stakes, because it did not fit with its single-brand, "One Vodafone" strategy.

In the United States, Vodafone customers still could not use their cell phones on the Verizon Wireless network, because it operated under a different standard. It was indicated that this situation was likely to continue well into the era of 3G, because Verizon planned to adopt an incompatible standard.[37] Without a single technological platform and a uniform brand, Vodafone could extract little value from its American venture (except the cash dividend of $1 billion a year it received from it).[38] After the failed bid for AT&T Wireless, Vodafone had several options at its disposal, all of them with their own pros and cons.

Probably the most obvious option would be to take over Verizon (the parent company of Verizon Wireless) completely, including its fixed line business, in order to force them to adopt Vodafone standards. It was deemed likely that such a bid could escalate to a US$150 billion hostile takeover battle, a figure that might be too large even for juggernaut Vodafone.[39] Verizon's management clearly was not willing to cede the wireless operations to Vodafone, but dreamed of becoming the single owner of Verizon Wireless itself.

Alternatively, Vodafone could buy another operator outright. But regulatory constraints would require it to sell its stake in Verizon Wireless first, because it was prohibited from owning more than a 20 percent stake in two competing operators at once. Under the current agreement with Verizon, Vodafone held a put option, which allowed it to sell some of the shareholding each year at a fixed price to Verizon. If Vodafone decided to exercise this option, it had to do so by July 2006 in order to realize a maximum value of US$20 billion. Verizon could choose to pay Vodafone either in cash or stock, although Vodafone had a right on a minimum cash sum of US$7.5 billion.[40]

Some observers questioned the idea of selling Verizon and buying another operator, because Verizon Wireless was the most successful and profitable one – why swap "a minority stake in a very good operator for a controlling stake in a less good one?"[41]

In France, Vodafone was in an equally uncomfortable position. It shared ownership of Cegetel, the parent company of France's number two mobile phone business SFR (35 percent market share with 13.3 million customers), with Vivendi having the majority stake in the venture. On March 31, 2003, Vodafone's ownership interest in SFR was approximately 43.9 percent, comprising a direct holding of 20 percent in SFR and an indirect holding through its stake in Cegetel.[42] Commenting on Vodafone's struggle with Vivendi about SFR, an analyst at

Global Equities SA joked: "We have a saying: small minority shareholdings for little idiots; big minority shareholdings for big idiots."[43]

Even though Vodafone managers had a certain say about the operations and strategy of SFR (SFR launched the co-branded multimedia services of Vodafone live!), Vivendi continued to refuse to sell SFR to Vodafone. Several talks between Sarin and Fourtou, the CEO of Vivendi, had not yielded any results, and Vivendi's true strategic intentions with SFR remained unclear.[44] The remaining 56 percent stake in SFR was valued at roughly £8 billion ($13 billion).[45] After Vivendi declined Vodafone's offer for SFR in 2002, Vodafone issued a statement claiming that it was "a long-term investor in Cegetel and SFR" and that it "looks forward to continuing its successful partnership with Vivendi."[46]

> *"France is a very simple market for us,"* noted Alan Harper in April 2005. *"We know the market, we know the business model and we know the management of SFR, which takes part in routine Vodafone management meetings."* Pugnaciously, he added, *"The natural home of SFR is Vodafone. We are a very patient company."*

It remains to be seen whether Vivendi wants to keep its cash cow or if it was simply trying to push the price in this cat-and-mouse game.

## Challenges ahead

Arun Sarin knew that his job would not become uninteresting anytime soon, as many challenges lay ahead! Certainly, Vodafone was the largest player in the industry, but being active in 26 countries out of 200 in the world left a lot of room to grow. As he closed his eyes and thought of Vodafone's global footprint, instantly he was reminded that Vodafone was not present in Latin America and in many African countries. Then there was the Middle East. Vast untapped markets lay ahead with today's mobile penetration of about 1.7 billion, of which Vodafone has about 3.5 million. In five years it shall be 2.5 billion, only half of world's population! And there was his native country, India, where he invested US$1.5 billion to buy a 10 percent stake in Bharti Tele-Ventures, the largest mobile operator in the country. Countries of Eastern Europe, many of which had recently entered the European Union (EU), should definitely become Vodafone's home turf: Vodafone had just announced that it would be willing to invest up to US $18 billion on acquisitions in Russia and other Eastern European countries.[47] The 2005 acquisition of the mobile operators MobiFon (Romania) and Oskar

(Czech Republic) was certainly just the first step in enlarging Vodafone's footprint.[48] Not to mention China. The sheer size of the market was awe-inspiring. Vodafone's strategic partner, China Mobile, alone had more than 150 million customers, but Vodafone only had a minuscule 3.27 percent stake in the company.[49] For Vodafone, according to Alan Harper, this stake served as a:

> strategic foothold in a very important market with a relatively small scale investment. China Mobile is the fastest growing mobile company in the world today, connecting about 2–3 million customers a month. It has 70% of the Chinese market share. Vodafone clearly understands that China Mobile can never become Vodafone China. That is a reality due to investment options and quasi-political situation of Chinese mobile telephony market. Knowing all this we still invested in China mobile because we feel that we learn everyday from China Mobile and our intention is to have regular knowledge flow between Vodafone and China Mobile. This is because our strategy is to make the technology standardized so that the learning between us is much faster. … Our investment in China mobile is through China Mobile HK. We have a clear exit strategy with liquid assets, if our investment does not do well in the future. If it does well, we might think of increasing our foothold but not to a sizeable extent. We are happy to have a foothold in one of the largest and fastest growing markets of the world, with our investment we have an insider position, we have a position of influence with the operator, with the Chinese government, we have seat on the board, we have regular dialogue and our interest is to make China use the same technology as ours so that we can benefit from the scale and scope.

At the same time, significant business risks lurked in all markets and Arun Sarin was well aware of them. In 2006, the merger of AT&T with Bellsouth Corp. put pressure on Verizon Wireless to buy off Vodafone and force it to exit the U.S. market. The introduction of 3G, which had a very promising start in Germany with good sales of mobile connect cards, might shift the focus of the whole industry away from networks to content. Revenue from voice traffic was flat or even declining due to competing technologies such as Internet calling that was fundamentally changing the telecom industry. Sarin knew that most of the growth would have to come from new data services. Competitors had also begun to get their feet on the ground again, with rumors about a merger between MMO2's German operations (O2 Germany) and KPN's E-Plus.

Nokia had just presented its first WiFi-powered phone that did not need the traditional mobile network but a wireless LAN hotspot. If this technology should ever become popular, it would undermine Vodafone's current business model and could turn billions of fixed assets into worthless electronic scrap.[50]

At the beginning of 2006, Arun Sarin made some tough decisions. He faced up to slowing growth in his core market by unveiling an impairment charge of £23 billion to £28 billion ($40 billion to $49 billion) and exited the Japanese market by selling its stake to Tokyo-based Softbank in a deal valued at $15.4 billion and confirmed that after the sale it would return $10.5 billion to its shareholders. Vodafone had trailed behind NTT DoCoMo and KDDI since its entry in 2001 in Japan, due to fickle consumers, the lack of a low-end tier in the segment, and the challenge of coordinating terminals and technologies across borders. He managed to tighten his grip on the company and put down a boardroom revolt that had questioned his leadership. He not only won a public expression of support from Lord Ian MacLaurin, the company's board chair, but he also forced out Sir Christopher Gent, the honorary life president and former chief executive.

Arun Sarin thought Vodafone could have the best of two worlds. Now was the time to combine Vodafone's superior skills in acquiring companies with best-of-breed business integration and operational capabilities. He could ensure Vodafone's exceptional profitability for many years to come by keeping Vodafone a wireless company to the core and also use innovations such as broadband wireless technology known as WiMAX, to offer new services. It was now up to him to shape Vodafone's future.

# Appendix 1 The economics of the mobile phone market: The role of fixed costs

The mobile phone market was characterized by extremely high fixed costs. The setting up of a nationwide network could require significant investments running into billions of euros.[51] Usually, an operator did not have the choice to offer network coverage limited to metropolitan areas (which would dramatically reduce the scale of initial investment required), either because of regulations prohibiting such a selective offer, or simply because national coverage was a key success factor for literally "mobile" customers.

In some countries, the licenses to operate using a certain bandwidth cost as much as €8 billion (the record price each operator in Germany paid for its UMTS license to the government), adding huge financing charges to the already existing fixed costs.[52] However, once capacity is installed, the cost of an additional customer using the network is virtually zero, and every euro of revenue adds to the companies' bottom line. An installed and running network provides a foundation for reaching very high operating margins. Vodafone, for example, estimates that once the initial investments had been made, less than 10 percent of revenues were needed to maintain the network.[53] Even the marketing campaigns benefited from the economies of scale: The larger an operator's customer base, the lower its per-user cost of such advertising efforts.

Much of the costs described here were not only fixed, but also sunk, further aggravating the problem of price pressure. The investment into network could hardly be sold to anybody else (because of differing technological standards) and hence the initial cost was "sunk." Companies realized that they could not undo their decision to invest, because the infrastructure was already there. Therefore, it is rational for companies to act as if their initial investment was zero.

The existence of high fixed costs explained the periodic price wars that had driven prices down ever since mobile telecommunications started. Some operators had begun offering free calls or flat rates during the weekend (when capacity utilization was at the lowest). Usually, it was the smaller operators and the new market entrants who offered lower prices to reach as quickly as possible a critical mass. In Germany, one of the largest markets for mobile telephony with more than 60 million customers and a high population density, the threshold for an acceptable return on investment was estimated to be about 20 percent of the total market share, which had neither been attained by O2 (a subsidiary of MMO2) nor by E-Plus (KPN).

The economics of the market necessitated no more than three or four operators in a country (refer to Exhibit 7). In Germany, Mobilcom and Quam never reached the critical size and had to exit the market in 2003 and 2002, respectively, writing off their individual investments of €8 billion each in 3G licenses.[54]

Growth for a mobile phone company had so far mainly come from increased penetration, which stood at about 80 percent (e.g., Germany: 74%) in most mature markets. With new customers becoming increasingly rare (refer to Exhibit 8 for customers by country of Vodafone), operators were constantly searching for new sources of revenues and had introduced text messaging and other basic value-added services, such as downloadable ringtones and logos.[55] The standard measure in the industry to gauge the quality of the customer base was the average revenue per user (ARPU).[56]

As the new 3G networks (third generation, enabling high-speed data transmission) go online, available capac-

**EXHIBIT 7** Customers by country, June 30, 2003

| Country | Customers |
|---------|-----------|
| United Kingdom | 13,313 |
| Ireland | 1,765 |
| Germany | 23,261 |
| Hungary | 952 |
| Netherlands | 3,312 |
| Sweden | 1,331 |
| Italy | 15,044 |
| Albania | 364 |
| Greece | 2,373 |
| Malta | 126 |
| Portugal | 3,129 |
| Spain | 9,184 |
| United States | 15,332 |
| Japan | 10,035 |
| Australia | 2,593 |
| New Zealand | 1,349 |
| Egypt | 1,609 |
| Others | 17,614 |
| Group Total | 122,686 |

**Source:** Adapted from Interim Report November 2003.

ity will take another quantum leap with unpredictable consequences for pricing. There seems to be promising opportunities to concentrate on the huge market for fixed line telephony. Not surprisingly, there was a clear relation between the per minute price of a call and the average amount of cell phone usage. Conversely, there was no relation between the ARPU and the average price per minute charged, which indicated that customers substituted their fixed line minutes with cell phone minutes whenever a price drop occurred. In other words, the increased quantity usually compensated the operator for the lower revenue per minute (refer to Exhibit 9).

Another key performance indicator that had attracted management attention in recent years was the so-called

**EXHIBIT 8** Vodafone's subsidiaries, partners, and investments around the globe

| Country | Service Name | Ownership (%) | Subsidiary (S), Associate (A), or Partner (P) | Proportionate Customers (1000s) | Number of Competitors |
|---|---|---|---|---|---|
| **Europe** | | | | | |
| Albania | Vodafone Albania | 83.0 | S | 472 (31 Dec 2003) | 1 |
| Austria | A1 | n/a | P | n/a | n/a |
| Belgium | Proximus | 25.0 | A | 1,067 (31 Mar 2003) | 2 |
| Croatia | VIP | n/a | P | n/a | n/a |
| Cyprus | Cytamobile | n/a | P | n/a | n/a |
| Denmark | TDC Mobil | n/a | P | n/a | n/a |
| Estonia | Radiolinja | n/a | P | n/a | n/a |
| Finland | Radiolinja | n/a | P | n/a | n/a |
| France | SFR | 43.9 | A | 5,931 (30 Jun 2003) | 2 |
| Germany | Vodafone Germany | 100.0 | S | 24,668 (31 Dec 2003) | 3 |
| Greece | Vodafone Greece | 98.2 | S | 2,373 (30 Jun 2003) | 2 |
| Hungary | Vodafone Hungary | 87.9 | S | 1,170 (31 Dec 2003) | 2 |
| Iceland | Og Vodafone | n/a | P | n/a | n/a |
| Ireland | Vodafone Ireland | 100 | S | 1,871 (31 Dec 2003) | 2 |
| Italy | Vodafone Italy | 76.8 | S | 15,852 (31 Dec 2003) | 3 |
| Lithuania | Bite GSM | n/a | P | n/a | n/a |
| Luxembourg | LUXGSM | n/a | P | n/a | n/a |
| Malta | Vodafone Malta | 100.0 | S | 162 (31 Dec 2003) | 1 |
| Netherlands | Vodafone Netherlands | 99.8 | S | 3,400 (31 Dec 2003) | 4 |
| Poland | Plus GSM | 19. Jun | A | 949 (31 Mar 2003) | 2 |
| Portugal | Vodafone Portugal | 100.0 | S | 3,332 (31 Dec 2003) | 2 |
| Romania | Connex | 20. Jan | A | 537 (31 Mar 2003) | 3 |
| Slovenia | Si.mobil | n/a | P | n/a | n/a |
| Spain | Vodafone Spain | 100.0 | S | 9,685 (31 Dec 2003) | 2 |
| Sweden | Vodafone Sweden | 99.1 | S | 1,409 (31 Dec 2003) | 3 |

**EXHIBIT 8** Continued

| Country | Service Name | Ownership (%) | Subsidiary (S), Associate (A), or Partner (P) | Proportionate Customers (1000s) | Number of Competitors |
|---------|--------------|---------------|-----------------------------------------------|----------------------------------|------------------------|
| Switzerland | Swisscom Mobile | 25.0 | A | 3,635 (31 Mar 2003) | 3 |
| United Kingdom | Vodafone Group | n/a | n/a | n/a | n/a |
| United Kingdom | Vodafone UK | 100.0 | S | 13,947 (31 Dec 2003) | 4 |
| **Americas** | | | | | |
| United States | Verizon Wireless | 44.3 | A | 16,638 (31 Dec 2003) | Various |
| **Africa and Middle East** | | | | | |
| Bahrain | MTC-Vodafone Bahrain | n/a | P | n/a | n/a |
| Egypt | Vodafone Egypt | 67.0 | S | 1,838 (31 Dec 2003) | 1 |
| Kenya | Safaricom | 35.0 | A | 303 (31 Mar 2003) | 1 |
| Kuwait | MTC-Vodafone | n/a | P | n/a | n/a |
| South Africa | Vodacom | 35.0 | A | 2,756 (31 Mar 2003) | 2 |
| **Asia Pacific** | | | | | |
| Australia | Vodafone Australia | 100.0 | S | 2,676 (31 Dec 2003) | 4 |
| China | China Mobile (Hong Kong) Ltd | 3.3 | Investment | 4,048 (31 Mar 2003) | 2 |
| Fiji | Vodafone Fiji | 49.0 | A | 44 (31 Mar 2003) | None |
| Japan | Vodafone K.K. (Japan) | 69.7 | S | 10,268 (31 Dec 2003) | 3 |
| New Zealand | Vodafone New Zealand | 100.0 | S | 1,527 (31 Dec 2003) | 1 |
| Singapore | M1 | n/a | P | n/a | n/a |

**Source:** Adapted from http://www.vodafone.com.

**EXHIBIT 9** Relationships between per-minute prices and ARPU in European countries

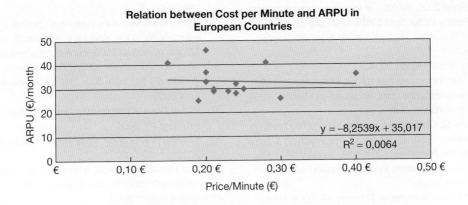

Note: Countries included in this sample are Belgium, Germany, Netherlands, Spain, Greece, Austria, Sweden, Italy, Denmark, France, Ireland, United Kingdom, Portugal, and Finland.

**Source:** Author's analysis based on data by Merrill Lynch, Diamond Cluster; published in the *Frankfurter Allgemeine Zeitung*, Octobre 27, 2003, 21.

"churn rate," a percentage of the customer base being lost to competitors each year. In competitive markets with high handset subsidies, churn rates of operators could be anywhere between 19 percent (Germany) and 30 percent (UK).[57] In other words, on average after three to five years, an operator had churned its entire customer base! These churn rates carried high costs for the operators, because they had to spend heavily mainly on marketing and handset subsidies to attract new customers and to retain the old ones. Customer acquisition costs easily exceeded €100 per new customer or made up to 12.4 percent of service revenue (figure for Vodafone Germany).[58] If an operator added low-value customers (i.e., those with a low monthly ARPU), it could take many months until the operator could break even on a customer.

## NOTES

1. Out of many, One comes from Latin *E Pluribus Unum,* signifying the harnessing of global scale and scope synergies of OneVodafone.

2. The scenario described herein was fictional. However, all data relating to the AT&T Wireless deal was factual. *Financial Times Deutschland*, February 17, 2004, http://www.ftd.de.

3. *Financial Times Deutschland*, February 12, 2004, http://www.ftd.de.

4. *Financial Times Deutschland*, February 17, 2004, http://www.ftd.de.

5. Equal to Christopher Gent's compensation as reported in the Company Annual Report 2003. This figure does not include stock options and performance-based pay.

6. Source: Corporate website http://www.vodafone.com/, data current as of December 31, 2003.

7. Source: Yahoo! Finance, http://finance.yahoo.com, March 13, 2004.

8. Annual Report 2003, available at http://www.vodafone.com.

9. Interim Results for the Six Months to 30 September 2003, published November 18, 2003; available at http://www.vodafone.com.

10. Company Annual Report 2004.

11. Source: This historic overview follows information provided at http://www.vodafone.com/, accessed on March 5, 2004.

12. http://www.vodafone.com.

13. Reportedly, Sir Gent closed the deal with AirTouch via his cell phone from Australia, where he was watching a game of cricket. *The Independent* (London), January 17, 1999: "Vodafone's boss realises longheld ambition with the acquisition of AirTouch."

14. *Financial Times Deutschland*, February 17, 2004, http://www.ftd.de.

15. A chronology of the takeover battle was provided at http://www.managermagazin.de/unternehmen/artikel/0,2828,242161-2,00.html.

16. A New Voice at Vodafone, *The Economist;* August 2, 2003, Vol. 368.

17. Interim Results for the Six Months to 30 September 2003, published November 18, 2003; available at http://www.vodafone.com.

18. Vodafone Starts Wireline Attack, First in Germany, *Dow Jones International* News; March 10, 2005.

19. Vodafone Starts Wireline Attack, First in Germany, *Dow Jones International News*; March 10, 2005.

20. Keeping pole position, *Total Telecom Magazine*, August 2003.

21. Keeping pole position, *Total Telecom Magazine*, August 2003.

22. www.vodafone.com.

23. With Australia and Japan being notable exceptions.

24. Quoted in "Vodafone dominance tipped to keep rolling," *Utility Week*, January 31, 2003.

25. A new Voice at Vodafone, *The Economist*; August 2, 2003, Vol. 368.

26. A new Voice at Vodafone, *The Economist;* August 2, 2003, Vol. 368.

27. Presentation to analysts and investors on September 27, 2004, available at http://www.vodafone.com.

28. http://www.vodafone.de and http://www.vodafone.com.

29. http://www.vodafone.de and http://www.vodafone.com.

30. Press release on June 23, 2003, available at http://www.vodafone.com.

31. http://www.vodafone.com.

32. http://www.vodafone.com.

33. Interim Results for the Six Months to 30 September 2003, p. 16.

34. According to the "Key Performance Indicators" for the quarter ended December 31, 2003; released on January 28, 2004; available at www.vodafone.com, Vodafone live! had over 4.5 million customers in 15 countries as of November 13, 2003.

35. Keeping pole position, *Total Telecom Magazine*, August 2003.

36. Keeping pole position, *Total Telecom Magazine*, August 2003.

37. A new Voice at Vodafone, *The Economist;* August 2, 2003, Vol. 368.

38. Where Does Vodafone Turn Now? *Business Week Online*; February 18, 2004. Keeping pole position, *Total Telecom Magazine*, August 2003, quoted £564 million as cash dividend in financial year 2002/2003, equivalent to 11% of Vodafone's free cash flow. This arrangement expired in April 2005.

39. Where Does Vodafone Turn Now? *Business Week Online*; February 18, 2004.

40. Keeping pole position, *Total Telecom Magazine*, August 2003.

41. Bob House of Adventis, a consultancy, quoted in: Vodafone's dilemma, *The Economist*, Feb 12, 2004.

42. Annual Report 2003.

43. Laurent Balcon quoted in: Keeping pole position, *Total Telecom Magazine*, August 2003.

44. Clear as mud: Vodafone versus Vivendi, *The Economist*; December 7, 2002.

45. *Euromoney*, Nov 2003, Vol. 34 Issue 415.

46. Clear as mud: Vodafone versus Vivendi, *The Economist*; December 7, 2002.

47. www.Vwd.de Vereinigte Wirtschaftsdienste GmbH, February 26, 2004.

48. According to a Vodafone press release on March 15, 2005, the Group paid approximately US$3.5bn in cash for the transaction and thus could add 6.7 mn customers.

49. Annual Report 2004, p. 8.

50. Nokia takes leap into Wi-Fi Phones, *Wall Street Journal Europe*, February 23, 2004.

51. Vodafone for example had £24.1 bn as gross fixed assets in its balance sheet, 83% of which were accounted for by network infrastructure. Annual Report 2003, p. 90.

52. Vodafone prescht im Rennen um UMTS-Einführung vor, Handelsblatt, February 13/14, 2004.

53. Annual Report 2003, p. 94.

54. Vodafone prescht im Rennen um UMTS-Einführung vor, Handelsblatt, February 13/14, 2004.

55. In some instances, these new services already generate up to 20% of revenues. Ibid.

56. For example, Vodafone's ARPU in the UK was £297 and €312 in Germany for the year, according to the Interim Results for the Six Months Ended September 30, 2003; available at http://www.vodafone.com.

57. Data for Vodafone, which can be considered as representative for the industry; For example, Vodafone's ARPU in the UK was £297 and €312 in Germany for the year, according to the Interim Results for the Six Months Ended September 30, 2003; available at http://www.vodafone.com.

58. Data for Vodafone, which can be considered as representative for the industry; For example, Vodafone's ARPU in the UK was £297 and €312 in Germany for the year, according to the Interim Results for the Six Months Ended September 30, 2003; available at http://www.vodafone.com.

# GLOSSARY

**Ability to learn** Ability to learn depends on the ability to value the new external knowledge, i.e. prior knowledge and experience.

**Ability** Ability relates to each firm's resources and the flexibility they provide in choosing to attack a competitor or to respond to an attack.

**Above-average returns** Above-average returns are returns in excess of what an investor expects to earn from other investments with a similar amount of risk.

**Absorptive capacity** Absorptive capacity is a firm's ability to value, assimilate and utilize new external knowledge.

**Acquisition** An acquisition is a strategy through which one firm buys a controlling, or 100 per cent, interest in another firm with the intention of making the acquired firm a subsidiary business within its portfolio.

**Acquisitions** Acquisitions are instances of corporate development where one corporate entity internalizes another entity, which subsequently ceases to exist independently.

**Adaptive resistance** Adaptive resistance (e.g. humour, anticipation) is related to habitual reluctance or the lack of incentives (e.g. political games), and it is constructive when compared to maladaptive (e.g. dissociation, denial, obstruction).

**Affiliation** Affiliation, of firms' relationships with customers, is concerned with facilitating useful interactions with customers.

**Agency costs** Agency costs are the sum of incentive costs, monitoring costs, enforcement costs and individual financial losses incurred by principals because governance mechanisms cannot guarantee total compliance by the agent.

**Agency relationship** An agency relationship exists when one or more persons (the principal or principals) hire another person or persons (the agent or agents) as decision-making specialists to perform a service.

**Alliances** Alliances are agreements between two or more parties to undertake activities to pursue shared goals or protect common interests.

**Ambidexterity** Ambidexterity is the ability to achieve high levels of exploration and exploitation.

**Assimilation** Assimilation means placing new knowledge within the existing frame of reference.

**Average returns** Average returns are returns equal to those an investor expects to earn from other investments with a similar amount of risk.

**Awareness** Awareness is a prerequisite to any competitive action or response taken by a firm and refers to the extent to which competitors recognize the degree of their mutual interdependence that results from market commonality and competitive rivalry.

**Balanced scorecard** The balanced scorecard is a framework firms can use to verify that they have established both strategic and financial controls to assess their performance.

**Board of directors** The board of directors is a group of elected individuals whose primary responsibility is to act in the owners' interests by formally monitoring and controlling the corporation's top-level managers.

**Business-level cooperative strategy** A firm uses a business-level cooperative strategy to grow and improve its performance in individual product markets.

**Business-level strategy** A business-level strategy is an integrated and coordinated set of commitments and actions the firm uses to gain a competitive advantage by exploiting core competencies in specific product markets.

**Capability** A capability is the capacity for a set of resources to perform a task or an activity in an integrative manner.

**Clusters** Clusters are regionally defined agglomerations of competing and cooperating firms and those with complementary products in the same or related industries.

**Combination structure** The combination structure is a structure drawing characteristics and mechanisms from both the worldwide geographic area structure and the worldwide product divisional structure.

**Competence trap** An overexploitation of existing competencies and specialized resources that is threatening firm's survival when environments change

**Competitive action** A competitive action is a strategic or tactical action the firm takes to build or defend its competitive advantages or improve its market position.

**Competitive advantage** A firm has a competitive advantage when it implements a strategy competitors are unable to duplicate or find too costly to try to imitate.

**Competitive behaviour** Competitive behaviour is the set of competitive actions and competitive responses the firm takes to build or defend its competitive advantages and to improve its market position.

**Competitive dynamics** Competitive dynamics refer to all competitive behaviours – that is, the total set of actions and responses taken by all firms competing within a market.

**Competitive form** The competitive form is a structure characterized by complete independence among the firm's divisions.

**Competitive response** A competitive response is a strategic or tactical action the firm takes to counter the effects of a competitor's competitive action.

**Competitive rivalry** Competitive rivalry is the ongoing set of competitive actions and competitive responses that occur among firms as they manoeuvre for an advantageous market position.

**Competitive scope** A narrow (broad) competitive scope means that the firm intends to serve the needs of a narrow (broad) target customer group.

**Competitor intelligence** Competitor intelligence is the set of data and information the firm gathers to better understand and better anticipate competitors' objectives, strategies, assumptions, and capabilities.

**Competitors** Competitors are firms operating in the same market, offering similar products, and targeting similar customers.

**Complementary strategic alliances** Complementary strategic alliances are business-level alliances in which firms share some of their resources and capabilities in complementary ways to develop competitive advantages.

**Complementors** Complementors are the network of companies that sell complementary goods or services or are compatible with the focal firm's own product or service.

**Consumer ethnography** Consumer ethnography is an approach that seeks to understand consumers and their behaviour by employing fieldwork and other ethnographic tools.

**Contextual ambidexterity** Simultaneous pursuit of exploitation and exploration within an organizational unit by creating an organizational context that stimulates individuals to do both.

**Cooperative form** The cooperative form is a structure in which horizontal integration is used to bring about interdivisional cooperation.

**Cooperative strategy** A cooperative strategy is a strategy in which firms work together to achieve a shared objective.

**Coopetition** Coopetition is the value creating constellation in which market players cooperate or develop complementary products and simultaneously compete, e.g. when it comes to value capture.

**Core competencies** Core competencies are capabilities that serve as a source of competitive advantage for a firm over its rivals.

**Core rigidities** Competences can turn into core rigidities when companies lose the ability to learn and end trapped with what mattered in the past.

**Corporate entrepreneurship** Corporate entrepreneurship is the use or application of entrepreneurship within an established firm.

**Corporate governance** Corporate governance is the set of mechanisms used to manage the relationship among stakeholders and to determine and control the strategic direction and performance of organizations.

**Corporate-level cooperative strategy** A firm uses a corporate-level cooperative strategy to help it diversify in terms of products offered or markets served, or both.

**Corporate-level core competencies** Corporate-level core competencies are complex sets of resources and capabilities that link different businesses, primarily through managerial and technological knowledge, experience and expertise.

**Corporate-level strategy** A corporate-level strategy specifies actions a firm takes to gain a competitive advantage by selecting and managing a group of different businesses competing in different product markets.

**Cost leadership strategy** The cost leadership strategy is an integrated set of actions taken to produce goods or services with features that are acceptable to customers at the lowest cost, relative to that of competitors.

**Costly-to-imitate capabilities** Costly-to-imitate capabilities are capabilities that other firms cannot easily develop.

**Cross-border acquisitions** Acquisitions made between companies with headquarters in different countries are called cross-border acquisitions.

**Cross-border strategic alliance** A cross-border strategic alliance is an international cooperative strategy in which firms with headquarters in different nations decide to combine some of their resources and capabilities to create a competitive advantage.

**Cyclical ambidexterity** Sequential pursuit of exploitation and exploration within an organizational unit over time.

**Demographic segment** The demographic segment is concerned with a population's size, age structure, geographic distribution, ethnic mix and income distribution.

**Design** Design is the pursuit of emotional, symbolic and functional performance of products.

**Determining the strategic direction** Determining the strategic direction involves specifying the image and character the firm seeks to develop over time.

**Differentiation strategy** The differentiation strategy is an integrated set of actions taken to produce goods or services (at an acceptable cost) that customers perceive as being different in ways that are important to them.

**Disruptive technologies** Disruptive technologies can destroy the value of an existing technology and create new markets.

**Diversifying strategic alliance** A diversifying strategic alliance is a corporate-level cooperative strategy in which firms share some of their resources and capabilities to diversify into new product or market areas.

**Downscoping** Downscoping refers to divestiture, spin-off, or some other means of eliminating businesses that are unrelated to a firm's core businesses.

**Downsizing** Downsizing is a reduction in the number of a firm's employees and sometimes in the number of its operating units.

**Due diligence** Due diligence is a process through which a potential acquirer evaluates a target firm for acquisition.

**Dynamic alliance networks** Dynamic alliance networks are used in industries characterized by frequent product innovations and short product life cycles.

**Dynamic capabilities** Dynamic capabilities are the firm's processes to integrate, reconfigure, gain and release resources to match and even create market change.

**Dynamic integration** Compared to stable and modular integration that result in more structural solutions, dynamic integration resembles a process.

**Dynamic strategic fit** Dynamic strategic fit refers to firm-specific fit over time between environmental factors and organizational contingencies.

**Economic environment**  The economic environment refers to the nature and direction of the economy in which a firm competes or may compete.

**Economies of scope**  Economies of scope are cost savings that the firm creates by successfully sharing some of its resources and capabilities or transferring one or more corporate-level core competencies that were developed in one of its businesses to another of its businesses.

**Entrepreneurial mindset**  The person with an entrepreneurial mindset values uncertainty in the marketplace and seeks to continuously identify opportunities with the potential to lead to important innovations.

**Entrepreneurial opportunities**  Entrepreneurial opportunities are conditions in which new goods or services can satisfy a need in the market.

**Entrepreneurs**  Entrepreneurs are individuals, acting independently or as part of an organization, who perceive an entrepreneurial opportunity and then take risks to develop an innovation to exploit it.

**Entrepreneurship**  Entrepreneurship is the process by which individuals, teams or organizations identify and pursue entrepreneurial opportunities without being immediately constrained by the resources they currently control.

**Equity strategic alliance**  An equity strategic alliance is an alliance in which two or more firms own different percentages of the company they have formed by combining some of their resources and capabilities to create a competitive advantage.

**Executive compensation**  Executive compensation is a governance mechanism that seeks to align the interests of managers and owners through salaries, bonuses and long-term incentive compensation, such as stock awards and options.

**Explicit collusion**  Explicit collusion is when two or more firms negotiate directly with the intention of jointly agreeing about the amount to produce and the price of the products that are produced.

**Exploitation**  Exploitation refers to refinement, choice, production, efficiency, selection, implementation and execution using existing knowledge.

**Exploitative learning**  Exploitative learning encompasses those actions that lie in line with the organization's current activities and competencies in existing domains.

**Exploration**  Exploration refers to search, variation, risk-taking, experimentation, play, flexibility, discovery and innovation using new learning.

**Exploratory learning**  Exploratory learning adds new attributes to the organization's current portfolio of activities and competencies.

**Exporting**  Exporting describes the international trade of goods or services shipped from an exporting company in one country to an importing company in another country or countries.

**External managerial labour market**  An external managerial labour market is the collection of managerial career opportunities and the qualified people who are external to the organization in which the opportunities exist.

**External resources**  External resources are assets, knowledge and skills that lie outside the boundary of corporations and are often owned by other market players.

**Fast-cycle markets**  Fast-cycle markets are markets in which the firm's capabilities that contribute to competitive advantages aren't shielded from imitation and where imitation is often rapid and inexpensive.

**Fieldwork**  Fieldwork is the methodological approach to generate data and insight in (consumer) ethnography.

**Financial controls**  Financial controls are largely objective criteria used to measure the firm's performance against previously established quantitative standards.

**Financial economies**  Financial economies are cost savings realized through improved allocations of financial resources based on investments inside or outside the firm.

**First mover**  A first mover is a firm that takes an initial competitive action in order to build or defend its competitive advantages or to improve its market position.

**Fitness**  Fitness is the organizational capacity to learn and change behavioural characteristics or capabilities to fit to new circumstances in organizational environments.

**Focus strategy**  The focus strategy is an integrated set of actions taken to produce goods or services that serve the needs of a particular competitive segment.

**Franchising**  Franchising is a corporate-level cooperative strategy in which a firm (the franchisor) uses a franchise as a contractual relationship to describe and control the sharing of its resources and capabilities with partners (the franchisees).

**Functional structure**  The functional structure consists of a chief executive officer and a limited corporate staff, with functional line managers in dominant organizational areas such as production, accounting, marketing, R&D, engineering and human resources.

**General environment**  The general environment is composed of dimensions in the broader society that influence an industry and the firms within it.

**Generic strategy**  Generic strategy is a strategy that can be used by any organization competing in any industry.

**Global economy**  A global economy is one in which goods, services, people, skills and ideas move freely across geographic borders.

**Global mindset**  A global mindset is the ability to analyse, understand and manage (if in a managerial position) an internal organization in ways that are not dependent on the assumptions of a single country, culture or context.

**Global segment**  The global segment includes relevant new global markets, existing markets that are changing, important international political events, and critical cultural and institutional characteristics of global markets.

**Global strategy**  A global strategy is an international strategy through which the firm offers standardized products across country markets, with competitive strategy being dictated by the home office.

**Globalization**  Globalization is the increasing economic interdependence among countries and their organizations as reflected in the flow of goods and services, financial capital and knowledge across country borders.

**Greenfield venture** The establishment of a new wholly-owned subsidiary is referred to as a greenfield venture.

**Heterogeneous top management team** A heterogeneous top management team is composed of individuals with different functional backgrounds, experience and education.

**Horizontal acquisition** Horizontal acquisition is the acquisition of a company competing in the same industry as the acquiring firm.

**Human capital** Human capital refers to the knowledge and skills of a firm's entire workforce.

**Hypercompetition** Hypercompetition is an environmental condition characterized by rapidly escalating competition, high uncertainty, heterogeneity of players, and constant disequilibrium and change.

**Imitation** Imitation is the adoption of a similar innovation by different firms.

**Industry** An industry is a group of firms producing products that are close substitutes.

**Industry environment** The industry environment is the set of factors that directly influences a firm and its competitive actions and competitive responses: the threat of new entrants, the power of suppliers, the power of buyers, the threat of product substitutes and the intensity of rivalry among competitors.

**Inertia** Inertia is a persistent resistance to changing organizational features.

**Innovation** Innovation is the process of creating a commercial product from an invention.

**Institutional owners** Institutional owners are financial institutions such as stock mutual funds and pension funds that control large-block shareholder positions.

**Intangible resources** Intangible resources include assets that are rooted deeply in the firm's history, accumulating over time, and are relatively difficult for competitors to analyse and imitate.

**Integrated cost leadership/differentiation strategy** The integrated cost leadership/differentiation strategy involves engaging in primary and support activities that allow a firm to simultaneously pursue low cost and differentiation.

**Internal managerial labour market** An internal managerial labour market consists of a firm's opportunities for managerial positions and the qualified employees within that firm.

**International diversification** International diversification is a strategy through which a firm expands the sales of its goods or services across the borders of global regions and countries into different geographic locations or markets.

**International strategy** An international strategy is a strategy through which the firm sells its goods or services outside its domestic market.

**Invention** Invention is the act of creating or developing a new product or process.

**Isomorphism** Isomorphism is similarity in strategy and behavioural characteristics between firms.

**Joint venture** A joint venture is a strategic alliance in which two or more firms create a legally independent company to share some of their resources and capabilities to develop a competitive advantage.

**Judgement** Judgement is the capability of making successful decisions when no obviously correct model or rule is available or when relevant data are unreliable or incomplete.

**Knowledge** Knowledge (information, intelligence, and expertise) is gained through experience, observation and inference.

**Knowledge processes** Knowledge processes are the ways organizations create, absorb, transfer and transform knowledge.

**Large-block shareholders** Large-block shareholders typically own at least 5per cent of a corporation's issued shares.

**Late mover** A late mover is a firm that responds to a competitive action a significant amount of time after the first mover's action and the second mover's response.

**Lead users** Lead users are often intrinsically motivated individuals or communities, who experiment to invent, improve and adapt existing products.

**Licensing** A licensing arrangement allows a foreign company to purchase the right to manufacture and sell the firm's products within a host country or set of countries.

**Managerial opportunism** Managerial opportunism is the seeking of self-interest with guile (i.e., cunning or deceit).

**Market commonality** Market commonality is concerned with the number of markets with which the firm and a competitor are jointly involved and the degree of importance of the individual markets to each.

**Market for corporate control** The market for corporate control is an external governance mechanism that becomes active when a firm's internal controls fail.

**Market power** Market power exists when a firm is able to sell its products above the existing competitive level or to reduce the costs of its primary and support activities below the competitive level, or both.

**Market segmentation** Market segmentation is a process used to cluster people with similar needs into individual and identifiable groups.

**Merger** A merger is a strategy through which two firms agree to integrate their operations on a relatively coequal basis.

**Mission** A mission specifies the business or businesses in which the firm intends to compete and the customers it intends to serve.

**Models of integration** Basic models of integration describe broad, alternative approaches to integrate internal and external knowledge.

**Modular integration** Modular integration is the purposeful selection of resources that are better sourced externally to substitute specific elements of the original value chain.

**Motivation** Motivation, which concerns the firm's incentive to take action or to respond to a competitor's attack, relates to perceived gains and losses.

**Multidivisional (M-form) structure** The multidivisional (M-form) structure consists of operating divisions, each representing a separate business or profit centre in which the top corporate officer delegates responsibilities for day-to-day operations and business unit strategy to division managers.

**Multidomestic strategy** A multidomestic strategy is an international strategy in which strategic and operating decisions are decentralized to the strategic business unit in each country so as to allow that unit to tailor products to the local market.

**Multimarket competition** Multimarket competition occurs when firms compete against each other in several product or geographic markets.

**Multipoint competition** Multipoint competition exists when two or more diversified firms simultaneously compete in the same product areas or geographical markets.

**Natural trajectory of routinization** A process of accumulation of specialized routines and fine-tuning of organizational conditions when firms age and competition decreases.

**Network cooperative strategy** A network cooperative strategy is a cooperative strategy wherein several firms agree to form multiple partnerships to achieve shared objectives.

**Nonequity strategic alliance** A nonequity strategic alliance is an alliance in which two or more firms develop a contractual-relationship to share some of their unique resources and capabilities to create a competitive advantage.

**Nonsubstitutable capabilities** Nonsubstitutable capabilities are capabilities that do not have strategic equivalents.

**Not invented here** Not invented here (NIH) refers to the closedness of organizations, or within organizations, to external ideas.

**Open innovation** Contrary to closed innovation, which relies primarily on internal resources, open innovation involves commercializing external ideas by deploying outside (as well as in-house) pathways to the market.

**Operational flexibility** Operational flexibility consists of routine capabilities based on present structures and goals of the organization, providing the firm with a capacity to respond to dynamic changes in the environment.

**Opportunity** An opportunity is a condition in the general environment that, if exploited, helps a company achieve strategic competitiveness.

**Organizational change** Strategy implementation is the necessary link between strategy formulation and performance that requires organizational change, which includes adapting structures, processes and methods, and cognition.

**Organizational controls** Organizational controls guide the use of strategy, indicate how to compare actual results with expected results, and suggest corrective actions to take when the difference is unacceptable.

**Organizational culture** An organizational culture consists of a complex set of ideologies, symbols and core values that are shared throughout the firm and influence the way business is conducted. It refers to the set of beliefs and assumptions held relatively commonly throughout the organization and taken for granted by its members.

**Organizational structure** Organizational structure specifies the firm's formal reporting relationships, procedures, controls, and authority and decision-making processes. It comprises the actual distribution of responsibilities and authority among the organization's personnel (basic

organizational form), the planning and control systems as well as the process regulations of decision-making, coordination, and execution.

**Organizational technology** Organizational technology refers to the hardware and the software used in the transformation of inputs into outputs, as well as the configuration of the hardware and software.

**Outsourcing** Outsourcing is the purchase of a value-creating activity from an external supplier.

**Ownership concentration** Both the number of large-block shareholders and the total percentage of shares they own define ownership concentration.

**Path dependence** Path dependence is the (constraining) influence of past stages in organizational development on future decisions and actions.

**Peripheral vision** Peripheral vision allows people to become aware of e.g. movement without visually focusing on what moves.

**Perpetual innovation** Perpetual innovation describes how rapidly and consistently new information-intensive technologies replace older ones.

**Physical environment segment** The physical environment segment refers to potential and actual changes in the physical environment and business practices that are intended to positively respond to and deal with those changes.

**Political/legal segment** The political/legal segment is the arena in which organizations and interest groups compete for attention, resources, and a voice in overseeing the body of laws and regulations guiding the interactions among nations as well as between firms and various local governmental agencies.

**Primary activities** Primary activities include inbound logistics, operations, outbound logistics, marketing, sales and services.

**Primary activities** Primary activities are involved with a product's physical creation, its sale and distribution to buyers and its service after the sale.

**Profit pool** A profit pool entails the total profits earned in an industry at all points along the value chain.

**Quality** Quality exists when the firm's goods or services meet or exceed customers' expectations.

**Rare capabilities** Rare capabilities are capabilities that few, if any, competitors possess.

**Reach** The reach dimension of relationships with customers is concerned with the firm's access and connection to customers.

**Reciprocal ambidexterity** Sequential pursuit of exploitation and exploration across domains, functions and hierarchical levels.

**Related acquisition** Related acquisition is the acquisition of a firm in a highly related industry.

**Relative inertia** Relative inertia is the notion that organizations' internal rate of change is too slow to respond to the rate of change in the external environment (e.g. threats and opportunities).

**Renewal trap** Overexploration of resources by overreaction and excessive search resulting in destroyed value.

852

GLOSSARY

**Resource integration** Resource integration is the mutually beneficial combination of external and internal resources.

**Resource similarity** Resource similarity is the extent to which the firm's tangible and intangible resources are comparable to a competitor's in terms of both type and amount.

**Resources** Resources are inputs into a firm's production process, such as capital equipment, the skills of individual employees, patents, finances, and talented managers.

**Restructuring** Restructuring is a strategy through which a firm changes its set of businesses or its financial structure.

**Richness** Richness, of firms' relationships with customers, is concerned with the depth and detail of the two-way flow of information between the firm and the customer.

**Risk** Risk is an investor's uncertainty about the economic gains or losses that will result from a particular investment.

**Routines** Routines are the regular and predictable behaviour patterns of firms with which day-to-day operations get done.

**Second mover** A second mover is a firm that responds to the first mover's competitive action, typically through imitation.

**Seizing** Seizing leads firms to act upon promising weak signals, opportunities or new knowledge.

**Sensing** Sensing leads to awareness of weak signals, opportunities or new knowledge.

**Simple structure** The simple structure is a structure in which the owner-manager makes all major decisions and monitors all activities while the staff serve as an extension of the manager's supervisory authority.

**Slow-cycle markets** Slow-cycle markets are those in which the firm's competitive advantages are shielded from imitation commonly for long periods of time and where imitation is costly.

**Social capital** Social capital involves relationships inside and outside the firm that help the firm accomplish tasks and create value for customers and shareholders.

**Socio-cultural segment** The sociocultural segment is concerned with a society's attitudes and cultural values.

**Stable alliance network** A stable alliance network is formed in mature industries where demand is relatively constant and predictable.

**Stable integration** For stable integration companies select and internalize resources without trying to change the new combination.

**Stakeholders** Stakeholders are the individuals and groups who can affect the firm's vision and mission, are affected by the strategic outcomes the firm achieves through its operations, and who have enforceable claims on the firm's performance.

**Standard-cycle markets** Standard-cycle markets are markets in which the firm's competitive advantages are moderately shielded from imitation and where imitation is moderately costly.

**Steady-state flexibility** Steady-state flexibility consists of static procedures to optimize the firm's performance when the level of throughput and the nature of throughput remain relatively stable over time.

**Strategic actions and strategic responses** A strategic action or a strategic response is a market-based move that involves a significant commitment of organizational resources and is difficult to implement and reverse.

**Strategic alliance** A strategic alliance is a cooperative strategy in which firms combine some of their resources and capabilities to create a competitive advantage.

**Strategic business unit (SBU) form** The strategic business unit (SBU) form consists of three levels: corporate headquarters, strategic business units (SBUs), and SBU divisions.

**Strategic competitiveness** Strategic competitiveness is achieved when a firm successfully formulates and implements a value-creating strategy.

**Strategic controls** Strategic controls are largely subjective criteria intended to verify that the firm is using appropriate strategies for the conditions in the external environment and the company's competitive advantages.

**Strategic drift** A process towards rigidity due to the fact that consciously managed incremental changes in the organization do not keep pace with more radical environmental changes.

**Strategic entrepreneurship** Strategic entrepreneurship is taking entrepreneurial actions using a strategic perspective.

**Strategic flexibility** Strategic flexibility consists of dynamic capabilities for adapting the goals of the organization, providing the firm with a capacity to respond to unpredictable changes in the environment.

**Strategic group** A strategic group is a set of firms emphasizing similar strategic dimensions to use a similar strategy.

**Strategic leaders** Strategic leaders are people located in different parts of the firm using the strategic management process to help the firm reach its vision and mission.

**Strategic leadership** Strategic leadership is the ability to anticipate, envision, maintain flexibility and empower others to create strategic change as necessary.

**Strategic management process** The strategic management process is the full set of commitments, decisions and actions required for a firm to achieve strategic competitiveness and earn above-average returns.

**Strategic neglect** A process towards chaos and reduction of decision-making capacity due to the deliberate tendency of management not to pay attention to a shared strategic orientation or a stable structure.

**Strategic renewal** Strategic renewal refers to the adaptive choices and actions a firm undertakes to alter its path dependence and maintain a dynamic strategic fit with changing environments over time.

**Strategy** A strategy is an integrated and coordinated set of commitments and actions designed to exploit core competencies and gain a competitive advantage.

**Structural ambidexterity** Simultaneous pursuit of exploitation and exploration across organizational units that each specialize in either exploitation or exploitation.

**Structural flexibility** Structural flexibility consists of managerial capabilities for adapting the organization structure and its decision and communication processes, providing the firm with a capacity to respond to complex changes in the environment.

**Stuck in the middle** Stuck in the middle means that the firm's cost structure is not low enough to allow it to attractively price its products and that its products are not sufficiently differentiated to create value for the target customer.

**Support activities** Support activities provide the assistance necessary for the primary activities to take place.

**Synergistic strategic alliance** A synergistic strategic alliance is a corporate-level cooperative strategy in which firms share some of their resources and capabilities to create economies of scope.

**Synergy** Synergy exists when the value created by business units working together exceeds the value that those same units create working independently.

**Tacit collusion** Tacit collusion is when several firms in an industry indirectly coordinate their production and pricing decisions by observing each other's competitive actions and responses.

**Tactical actions and tactical responses** A tactical action or a tactical response is a market-based move that is taken to fine-tune a strategy; it involves fewer resources and is relatively easy to implement and reverse.

**Takeover** A takeover is a special type of acquisition strategy wherein the target firm does not solicit the acquiring firm's bid.

**Tangible resources** Tangible resources are assets that can be observed and quantified.

**Technological segment** The technological segment includes the institutions and activities involved with creating new knowledge and translating that knowledge into new outputs, products, processes, and materials.

**Technology diffusion** Technology diffusion is the rate at which new technologies become available and are used.

**Threat** A threat is a condition in the general environment that may hinder a company's efforts to achieve strategic competitiveness.

**Top management team** The top management team is composed of the key individuals who are responsible for selecting and implementing the firm's strategies.

**Total quality management (TQM)** Total quality management (TQM) is a managerial innovation that emphasizes an organization's total commitment to the customer and to continuous improvement of every process through the use of data-driven, problem-solving approaches based on empowerment of employee groups and teams.

**Trajectories of revitalization** A process of developing dynamic capabilities and transforming organizational conditions to cope with increasing levels of competition.

**Transforming** Disruptive innovations make transforming the frame of reference, i.e. fundamental organizational change necessary.

**Transnational strategy** A transnational strategy is an international strategy through which the firm seeks to achieve both global efficiency and local responsiveness.

**Turnaround** Turnaround is the rare managerial accomplishment of organizational change that may follow dramatic performance decline.

**Valuable capabilities** Valuable capabilities allow the firm to exploit opportunities or neutralize threats in its external environment.

**Value** Value is measured by a product's performance characteristics and by its attributes for which customers are willing to pay.

**Vertical acquisition** Vertical acquisition is the acquisition of a supplier or distributor of one or more of the acquiring firm's goods or services.

**Vertical integration** Vertical integration exists when a company produces its own inputs (backward integration) or owns its own source of output distribution (forward integration).

**Vision** Vision is a picture of what the firm wants to be and, in broad terms, what it wants to ultimately achieve.

**Worldwide geographic area structure** The worldwide geographic area structure emphasizes national interests and facilitates the firm's efforts to satisfy local differences.

**Worldwide product divisional structure** In the worldwide product divisional structure, decision-making authority is centralized in the worldwide division headquarters to coordinate and integrate decisions and actions among divisional business units.

# NAME INDEX

Raisch, S.
    and Birkenshaw, J. 515
    *et al* 597
    and von Krogh, G. 124
Raj, T. *et al* 201
Rajagopalan, N. and Datta, D. 431
Rajan, R. *et al* 470
Rajand, M. and Forsyth, M. 313
Rajgopal, S. *et al* 469
Ralston, D.A. *et al* 354
Raman, A.P. 349
Ramaswamy, K. *et al* 469, 472
Ramseyer, J.M. *et al* 474
Ranson, L. 92
Rappaport, A.L. and Sirower, M.L. 310
Rauwald, C. 42, 353
    and Shirouzu, N. 392
Ravasi, D. and Schutz, M. 41
Ravenscraft, D.J. and Scherer, R.M. 273
Rawley, E. 261, 517
Ray, J. 764
Raynor, M.E. 270
    and Bower, J.L. 272
Ready, D.A.
    and Conger, J.A. 428
    *et al* 45
Rebeiz, K. 471
Redding, G. 434
Reed, J. 304, 357
Reed, R. *et al* 516
Rehbein, K. 472
Reid, G.C. and Smith, J.A. 544
Reinhardt, 431
Reinmoeller, P. 134, 154, 160, 515
    and Baaij, M. 159
    and van Baardwijk, N. 159
    and Yonekura, S. 41
Reitzig, M. and Puranam, P. 199
Ren, H. *et al* 394
Renneboog, L. 308
Reuer, J.J. 308
    and Arino, A. 389
    *et al* 390, 392, 396
    and Ragozzini, R. 312
Reynolds, S.J. *et al* 46
Rhoads, C. and Buckman, R. 723
Ribeiro, J. 459
Ricadela, A. 284
Ricart, J.E. *et al* 352
Richardson, J. 596
Ricker, T. 781
Rico, R. *et al* 429
Rigby, D. and Bilodeau, B. 158
Rigby, E. 199
Rindova, V.P. *et al* 200, 237
Ring, P.S. *et al* 359
Rivkin, J. and Siggelkow, N. 507, 515
Roberson, Q.M. and Colquitt, J.A. 544
Roberts, D. and Tschang, C.-C. 428
Roberts, J. *et al* 471
Roberts, P.W. and Dowling, G.R. 237–8
Robertson, J. 233
Robins, J. and Wiersema, M.E. 518

Robinson, W.T. and Min, S. 231, 236
Robson, M.J. *et al* 356
Rockoff, J.D. 393
Rod, M. 395
Rodrigues, S.B. and Child, J. 89
Rodriguez, E. 394
Rodriguez, G.C. *et al* 469
Rodriguez, P. *et al* 359
Rodriguez-Duarte, A. *et al* 271
Rodriguez-Pinto, J. and Gutierrez-Cillan,
    A.I. 234
Rohwedder, C. 190
Roll, M. 187
Roll, R. 311
Romanelli, E. and Tushman, M.L. 596
Rose, E.I. and Ito, K. 234
Ross, F. 709
Rostker, B.D. *et al* 434
Roth, A. 357
Roth, K. and O'Donnell, S. 472
Rothaermel, F.T. 395
    and Boeker, W. 127, 395, 543
    and Deeds, D.L. 391
    *et al* 200, 271, 309, 351, 392
    and Thursby, M. 392
Rottman, J.W. 396
Rowe, C. *et al* 516
Rowe, D. *et al* 101
Rowe, G. 434
    *et al* 100–1
Rowe, W.G. 275
    and Wright, P.M. 517
Rowley, I. 824, 826
Ruckman, K. 473
Rudberg, M. and Olhager, J. 395
Rugman, A.M. 499
    and Collison, 501, 519
    and Girod, S. 355, 519
    and Hodgetts, R. 519
    and Verbeke, A. 353, 355, 514
Rui, H. and Yip, G.S. 310
Ruigrok, W. *et al* 471
Rumelt, R.P. 270, 273
    *et al* 199, 272, 517
Rungtusanatham, M.J. and Salvador, F. 91
Rusch, R.D. 347
Rutherford, M.A. 468
    and Buchholtz, A.K. 430
    *et al* 467

Sabin, R. 154
Safizadeh, M.H. *et al* 130
Sage, P. *et al* 515
Saghieh, H. 347
Sahay, A. 234
Said, S. and Dvorak, P. 120
Saigol, L. 278
Sakkab, N. 150, 161
Salvador, F. and Forza, C. 91
Salvato, C. 90, 139
Sanchanta, M. 781
Sanchez, C.M. and Goldberg, S.R. 311,
    357

Sanchez, R. 126, 200, 238, 544, 595
    *et al* 539
    and Heene, A. 125, 126, 129, 159,
    160
Sanders, W.G.
    and Carpenter, M.A. 274, 473
    and Tuschke, A.C. 461, 474
Sanderson, M. 634
Sandle, P. and Prodhan, G. 431
Sandvig, J.C. and Coakley, L. 274
Sanna-Randaccio, F. and Veugelers, R. 89
Santala, M. and Parvinen, P. 516
Santalo, J. and Becerra, M. 311
Santiago-Castro, M. and Brown, C.J. 468
Santos, J. *et al* 542
Santos, V. and Garcia, T. 429
Saparito, P.A. *et al* 391
Sapienza, H.J. *et al* 351
Sarkar, M.B. *et al* 395, 544
Sawka, K.A. 92
Sawyer, K. 394
Saxton, T. and Dollinger, M. 311
Schäfer, D. 438
Schechner, S. and Holmes, E. 392
Scheck, J. and Wingfield, N. 401
Scheltzer, M.E. *et al* 434
Schendel, D.E. and Teece, D.J. 273
Scherer, R.M. and Ross, D. 273
Schiele, H. 235
Schildt, H.A. *et al* 541
Schilling, M.A. 389
    and Steensma, H.K. 515
Schmid, N.M. and Walter, I. 270, 518
Schmidt, A. 709
Schmidt, J.A. 310
Schminke, M. *et al* 434
Schnatterly, K. *et al* 470
Schneider, M. 431
Schodt, F.L. 154
Schoemaker, P.J.H. and Amit, R. 44
Schoorman, F.D. *et al* 396
Schrage, M. 233
Schultz, A. 46
Schultz, H. 228
Schumpeter, J. 215, 236, 541
Schwab, A. and Miner, A.S. 395
Schwartz, N.D. 484
Schwarz, J.O. 88
Schwarz, M.A. 682
Scott, W.R. 594
Searcey, D. 41
Selsky, J.W. *et al* 42, 233
Semadeni, M. 200
Senge, P.M. *et al* 389
Seppanen, R. *et al* 390
Serchuk, D. 451
Seth, A. and Easterwood, J. 313
Seward, J.K. and Walsh, J.P. 275
Seybold, P. 160
Shalley, C.E. and Perry-Smith, J.E. 542
Shamaguchi, M. *et al* 154
Shamsie, J. 44, 91, 124, 159
Shank, M. 236

# COMPANY INDEX

# SUBJECT INDEX